CONTINENTAL UNITED STATES 1853

PURCHASE

ORIGINAL
UNITED STATES
1783

1810-13   FLORIDA 1819

CROFTS AMERICAN HISTORY SERIES

Dixon Ryan Fox, General Editor

A *Diplomatic* HISTORY

OF THE AMERICAN PEOPLE

THOMAS A. BAILEY, *Stanford University*

FOURTH EDITION

APPLETON-CENTURY-CROFTS, INC.
NEW YORK

WHEN foreign affairs were ruled by autocracies or oligarchies the danger of war was in sinister purpose. When foreign affairs are ruled by democracies the danger of war will be in mistaken beliefs. The world will be the gainer by the change, for, while there is no human way to prevent a king from having a bad heart, there is a human way to prevent a people from having an erroneous opinion. That way is to furnish the whole people, as a part of their ordinary education, with correct information about their relations to other peoples, about the limitations upon their own rights, about their duties to respect the rights of others, about what has happened and is happening in international affairs, and about the effects upon national life of the things that are done or refused as between nations; so that the people themselves will have the means to test misinformation and appeals to prejudice and passion based upon error.

Ex-Secretary of State Elihu Root,
Foreign Affairs, I, 5 (September, 1922).

Diplomacy has been a favorite theme of history since the times of Thucydides, if not those of Homer. It has been the means of gaining benefits for the group without fighting for them or of securing benefits which fighting has already earned. As a contest of wits it has often been dramatic and nearly always momentous. History has usually treated it as a game, something like the game of chess, in which envoys cherishing the general objective of their country's good, as defined by their own fancy or by instructions from a royal master, sought to outplay other envoys similarly purposed and accredited.

So long as international relations were concerned, for the most part, with dynastic rivalries, with the safety and prestige of crowns, diplomacy was an esoteric matter arising and transacted wholly in the courts of kings and princes. But as soon as trade burst through the bounds of localism and, especially in the seventeenth century, developed into international exchange, merchants and producers pressed their needs too powerfully to be ignored. No longer could diplomatic history appropriately be written as though its subject were a game played out *in vacuo;* moves were made, it was realized, by the remote control of men in countinghouses and men on farm estates and trading vessels. It were better said that that is the way in which diplomatic history should have been written; too often it remained the story of technique.

But if such history was inadequate when dealing with the Stuarts and Louis XIV, it is intolerable when dealing with modern nations. In days of democratic governments, of citizen armies, and now of instantaneous communication, the mainspring is not the whim of a king or the calculation of merchants and manufacturers. It is public opinion, whatever facts or sentiments may lie behind it. Professor Bailey's analysis and narrative give us a clear and realistic understanding of the directing forces which shaped our diplomatic policies, especially as those forces expressed themselves in newspapers, magazines, and public addresses. It is hard to see how, within the compass of this volume, these factors could have been more fully and faithfully presented. With the evidence before us we could almost infer the whole history of the United States.

Our relations with governments across the sea went far toward dominating our thought and action at certain times during our colonial period and during a great part of the half century after 1765. The contention often involved the destiny of the great West beyond the Allegheny Mountains. By 1815 this seemed safely settled as far as the Rockies, and there was a growing confidence that the remaining territory out to the Pacific would be brought under the American flag as soon as it was necessary. Here was a theater vast enough for any people; we turned our energies to developing an empire of our own, and foreign policy dropped in relative importance. After Washington our Presidents for the next thirty-two years were men who had served as Secretaries of State or as diplomats at European courts. Excepting the experience abroad of Van Buren, William Henry Harrison, and Buchanan, totaling about seven years, our Presidents since have not found such service necessary in their rise to popular favor. Nevertheless, though we were at peace with Europe from 1815 to 1898, our diplomatic contacts with its governments, to say nothing of those with others in the Western Hemisphere and Asia, make fascinating, and sometimes amusing, reading as set forth by Professor Bailey.

When we come to the growing complications of the twentieth century, which many of us can personally remember, we can check more directly as to the author's fairness. In the light of the evidence which he adduces it is likely that even readers who have thought themselves particularly well informed will change their opinions on one point or another. Of course, the opinions that we hold on world affairs during the past four decades and on the part that the United States has played in them are the essential basis of our judgment as to what our government's policy ought now to be. Our inescapable position as a great trading and investing nation makes the knowledge of our recent foreign relations indispensable to constructive citizenship. Since history in the summer of 1939 saw fit to repeat itself as of 1914, the careful and deliberate, yet brilliantly written and vitally "human" chapters on American reactions—it is hard to speak of a foreign policy—during the ten years following Sarajevo will be deeply instructive to Americans in the nineteen forties.

In a sense nearly every work of scholarship is co-operative, since it has to build upon whatever has been done before by others, in addition to the foundations accumulated by the author's own researches in source material. Traces of this beneficent partnership with colleagues, living or dead, in the great enterprise of historical inquiry appear everywhere throughout this book, though the author has made his notes a natural supplement to his text, and not a pedantic exhibition. He has chosen to forgo an elaborate bibliography which might serve as a work of reference, but, rather, has appended appropriate brief reading suggestions directly to the chapters. More thoroughly and successfully than any other historian I know he has sought and secured a special corps of experts to give preliminary critical reading to each chapter. By this enterprise on his part, and generous co-operation on theirs, he can face his final public with an unusual assurance.

We should all like again to see the day (perhaps we shall never see it) when competent literary art might be assumed with respect to any work of history. When history was reckoned as a branch of literature, when a Macaulay or a Parkman fashioned an historical account, readers were in mind as well as facts. That whole generation of historians cherished a sense of responsibility as artists. The result was that they had readers. Some historians of our own day write in that way too, but, indulged by the lenient literary standards of university faculties, many do not. Professor Bailey would not rejoice in an editorial invitation to regard him as a stylist, with all the special expectations that that might imply, but I do think that this is a book for which American scholarship does not have to apologize in the matter of literary quality. He has given us a "reading book" as well as a "study book."

DIXON RYAN FOX

Union College

THIS BOOK is designed as a general introduction to American diplomatic history. I have therefore eliminated or subordinated much unessential detail so as to emphasize the main currents. I have also striven for simplicity and directness, and have introduced a considerable amount of interpretation. Since diplomatic affairs cannot be conducted in a vacuum, and since they cannot be isolated from political, economic, and social developments, I have made some attempt to present the subject in its proper setting. I have also endeavored to add color and vitality by stressing personalities and by introducing a large number of brief contemporary statements.

A great deal of American diplomatic history has been written by merely presenting digests of the official correspondence. Though important, this is but one side of the shield. In a democracy like the United States, where public opinion determines fundamental policies, it is necessary to consider what the people thought about what was happening, and to discover what pressure they brought to bear upon the government to change its course. The major emphasis of the present volume, as the title indicates, is upon public opinion, and the framework is chronological so that the reader may better follow the development of this phenomenon. If, at times, it seems as though the narrative were concerned with a series of unrelated incidents, it must be borne in mind that for considerable periods that is precisely what American diplomatic history has been.

The subject is so broad and the liability of error so great that I asked a number of specialists to read the manuscript or portions of it. The response was extraordinarily cordial and helpful. Without in any way reflecting upon the generosity of others, I must single out for special mention Professor Charles H. Hunter, of the University of Hawaii, who labored through the entire semifinal draft, and Professor Richard W. Van Alstyne, of Chico State College, who, except for two or three chapters, extended the same courtesy. President Dixon Ryan Fox, of Union College, read the completed manuscript and made a number of helpful suggestions. Others criticized individual chapters, or groups of chapters, generally covering periods relating to their special interests. Listed alphabetically these scholars are:

Paul S. Bachman, of the University of Hawaii; Eugene C. Barker, of the University of Texas; Charles A. Barker, of Stanford University; Samuel Flagg Bemis, of Yale University; Knight Biggerstaff, of Cornell University; Robert C. Binkley, of Western Reserve University; George Verne Blue, of the Department of State; Harold W. Bradley, of Stanford University; Philip C. Brooks, of the National Archives; Russell Buchanan, of Santa Barbara State College; James M. Callahan, of West Virginia University; Meribeth E. Cameron, of Western Reserve University; Lynn M. Case, of Louisiana State University; John W. Caughey, of the University of California at Los Angeles; Robert C. Clark, of the University of Oregon; Paul Hibbert Clyde, of Duke University; Albert B. Corey, of St. Lawrence University; Merle Curti, of Teachers College, Columbia University; Tyler Dennett, of Hague, New York; Clyde A. Duniway, professor emeritus of Carleton College; Brainerd Dyer, of the University of California at Los Angeles; Edward Mead Earle, of the Institute for Advanced Study, Princeton, New Jersey; Joseph W. Ellison, of Oregon State College; Amos A. Ettinger, of Lehigh University; Elliott Evans, of the University of Colorado; Victor J. Farrar, of the Department of State; Harold Henry Fisher, of Stanford University; Russell H. Fitzgibbon, of the University of California at Los Angeles; Denna Frank Fleming, of Vanderbilt University; Daniel J. Gage, of the Bucknell University Junior College; Mary Katherine Chase Geyer, formerly of the University of Hawaii; Cardinal Goodwin, of Mills College; Charles C. Griffin, of Vassar College; Luella J. Hall, of the Salinas Junior College; Osgood Hardy, of Occidental College; Fred Harvey Harrington, of the University of Wisconsin; W. Stull Holt, of the Johns Hopkins University; George F. Howe, of the University of Cincinnati; Yamato Ichihashi, of Stanford University; Ralph S. Kuykendall, of the University of Hawaii; E. Wilson Lyon, of Colgate University; Percy Alvin Martin, of Stanford University; Thomas P. Martin, of the Library of Congress; Bernard Mayo, University of Virginia; Frederick Merk, of Harvard University; Henry Miller Madden, of Stanford University; Hunter Miller, of the Department of State; Frank Monaghan, of Yale University; David Saville Muzzey, of Columbia University; Eugene I. McCormac, of the University of California; Allan Nevins, of Columbia University; Harley Notter, of the Department of State; Clarence G. Osborn, of San Diego State College; Frank L. Owsley, of Vanderbilt University; E. Taylor Parks, of Berea College; Dexter Perkins, of the University of Rochester; Robert T. Pollard, of the University of Washington; Julius W.

Pratt, of the University of Buffalo; Henry F. Pringle, of New York City; J. Fred Rippy, of the University of Chicago; Carl B. Robbins, of the Joint Preparatory Committee on Philippine Affairs; Edgar Eugene Robinson, of Stanford University; Charles Easton Rothwell, of Stanford University; Carlton Savage, of the Department of State; Maxwell H. Savelle, of Stanford University; Louis Martin Sears, of Purdue University; Lester B. Shippee, of the University of Minnesota; Charles Nelson Spinks, of the Tokyo University of Commerce; Graham H. Stuart, of Stanford University; Edward Howland Tatum, Jr., of the Huntington Library; Charles Callan Tansill, of Fordham University; William H. Taylor, of the University of Hawaii; Harold W. V. Temperley, of Cambridge University; Reginald G. Trotter, of Queen's University; Alice Felt Tyler, of the University of Minnesota; Glyndon G. Van Deusen, of the University of Rochester; Mary Wilhelmine Williams, of Goucher College; Joseph E. Wisan, of the College of the City of New York; Arthur Preston Whitaker, of the University of Pennsylvania.

Those whose names I have listed are not, of course, responsible for the errors I may have made, nor may it be assumed that they approve of what I have done. I merely acknowledge with gratitude the cooperation of a group of scholars whose friendly suggestions and criticisms have been of immeasurable benefit. I can only wish that it were possible within the conventional limits of a preface to give an adequate expression of my indebtedness. If, in any case, I have failed to make proper acknowledgment here, or have failed to express my thanks personally or by letter, I hope it will be understood that this is an oversight.

For valuable suggestions as to style and syntax I am grateful to the following members of the English faculty of Stanford University: John McClelland, Edith Ronald Mirrielees, and George Frank Sensabaugh. David N. Leff, a student at Stanford University, designed the maps, and I am under obligation to him for many original ideas.

Among those whom I have employed in various capacities, the following rendered service far beyond the maximum requirements: Thornton W. Mitchell, Mary L. Schofield, Marco G. Thorne, and Gordon J. Wright.

The following persons placed at my disposal useful information: Senator William E. Borah of Idaho; former Assistant Secretary of State Francis B. Loomis; the late Ambassador Hirosi Saito of Japan; Senator Charles L. McNary of Oregon; and various officials in the Department of State and in the Treasury Department.

The institutions mentioned in the Bibliographical Introduction extended the usual courtesies. In addition, I am indebted to the staffs of the Stanford University Library and the Library of the Carnegie Endowment for International Peace, Washington, D.C.

The following have graciously permitted me to quote from the copyrighted material indicated: D. Appleton-Century Company, from G. T. Curtis, *Life of Daniel Webster;* the *Christian Advocate,* from McKinley's statement of January 22, 1903; Doubleday, Doran and Company and Dr. Tyler Dennett, from the latter's *Roosevelt and the Russo-Japanese War;* Dodd, Mead and Company, from Bayard Tuckerman, ed., *The Diary of Philip Hone, 1828–1851,* from Allan Nevins, ed., *The Diary of Philip Hone, 1828–1851,* and from Philip C. Jessup, *Elihu Root; Foreign Affairs,* from Elihu Root's article quoted after the title page; Houghton Mifflin Company, from W. C. Ford, ed., *A Cycle of Adams Letters, 1861–1865,* from Charles Seymour, *The Intimate Papers of Colonel House,* from Bernard Mayo, *Henry Clay: Spokesman of the New West,* and from *The Poetical Works of Bret Harte;* the Johns Hopkins University Press and Professor Samuel Flagg Bemis, from the latter's *Pinckney's Treaty: A Study of America's Advantage from Europe's Distress, 1783–1800;* J. B. Lippincott Company and Mr. Albert E. Gallatin, from Henry Adams, *The Life of Albert Gallatin;* A. C. McClurg and Company, from M. M. Quaife, ed., *The Diary of James K. Polk;* John Jos. McVey, Publisher, from Gottlieb Mittelberger, *Journey to Pennsylvania;* the *New Republic,* from Professor W. R. Shepherd's article cited in the last chapter; Charles Scribner's Sons, from *A Great Peacemaker: The Diary of James Gallatin,* and from Henry Adams, *History of the United States during the Administrations of Jefferson and Madison.*

THOMAS A. BAILEY

Stanford University

So MUCH diplomatic history has been crowded into the past three years, and so many scholarly contributions have flowed from the press, that a revised edition has seemed desirable. My primary purpose has been to bring the volume up to date, both in chronology and in scholarship. In pursuance of the first objective, I have added two new chapters on America's entrance into the War of 1939; in pursuance of the second, I have indicated what new material has been published. Where recent scholarship has clearly invalidated my statements, I have changed them; where it has merely added supplementary information of interest, I have referred to these findings under Recent References at the end of each chapter, and in the Bibliographical Appendix. I have substantially changed or completely rewritten many paragraphs and some pages, although the pagination remains the same until Chapter XLV. Altogether—and this includes the second and third printings—I have made changes on about 175 of the plates.

I have purposely kept the original Bibliographical Notes intact, so that the reader may tell by glancing at the Recent References and the Bibliographical Appendix what new contributions of importance have been made. I have also attempted to indicate in a general way the comparative value of these recent works, and have developed rather fully their chief contributions to the general subject. I have gone to considerable pains to make these bibliographies complete (about 130 new titles are included), and they continue to serve in some measure as a supplement to the Bemis and Griffin *Guide*.

The index has been completely revised and reset, so as to cover the new chapters.

I am deeply indebted to many friends and correspondents for their suggestions as to correction and improvement, and I hope that they will continue to show the same helpful interest. I am particularly grateful to the following colleagues for reading and criticizing the new chapters on the war: Philip W. Buck, Henry M. Madden, John W. Masland, Jr., and Graham H. Stuart.

THOMAS A. BAILEY

Stanford University
July, 1942

THE GENERAL PLAN of revision follows rather closely that of the second edition. The most significant changes are two new chapters on the diplomacy of World War II, a partial rewriting of the last chapter, an expansion of the Bibliographical Appendix, the addition of New References to the end-chapter Bibliographical Notes, and an alteration of sentences and paragraphs where recent scholarship has necessitated change. The original Bibliographical Notes have been kept intact, so that the interested reader may note what new material has been made available. A few older titles which through inadvertence failed to appear in the earlier notes have been included in New References. The index has been completely revised and reset.

I am indebted to many friends for suggestions, particularly to Professor Walter B. Norris, of the United States Naval Academy, who not only read in galley proof the additional chapters of the second edition, but provided a list of criticisms growing out of his experience and that of his staff in using the book as a text. The two new chapters of the present edition were critically read by four colleagues: Georges E. Lemaitre, John W. Masland, Merrill Ten Broeck Spalding, and Graham H. Stuart. Their suggestions were more than ordinarily valuable, for each one of them was able to provide me with information, some of it growing out of official experiences, not readily available to the historian.

THOMAS A. BAILEY

Department of History
Stanford University
May, 1946

THIS REVISION, coming on the tenth anniversary of the book, follows the pattern set by the previous two revisions. Numerous plate changes have been made; the bibliographies have been brought up to date; two new chapters have been added on the events from 1945 to 1949; the index has been revised and reset; and a glossary of diplomatic terms has been added.

The glossary should prove to be of particular help to beginning students. I would suggest that at the outset they be required to familiarize themselves with these terms; if they do, their comprehension of the text, collateral readings, and classroom discussions should be increased. Some teachers have found it desirable to assign the last chapter before taking up the other chapters in sequence.

The emphasis in this book is still on the American people and their influence on the shaping of foreign policy. The two new chapters provide impressive confirmation of this process. The public opinion polls are used as evidence, despite their bad guesses in the election of 1948, primarily because, with all their faults, they are the most reliable means of assessing nationwide popular currents. Dr. George H. Gallup admits a four percentage point margin of error, and for this reason the pollsters invite disaster when they try to predict close elections. I have never assumed that public opinion could be measured with mathematical exactitude, and I have always employed the polls, here and elsewhere, in the belief that they are useful in determining broad trends of popular sentiment.

My list of benefactors continues to swell. Numerous scholars have sent me reprints of their articles, some of which I might have overlooked; and I hope that they will keep up this practice. Countless students, whether in theses or seminar reports, have broken ground and helped point the way to profitable paths of research. Mr. Stuart G. Cross, a graduate student, suggested the glossary; and the long-suffering members of my general course, History 130, gave me the student viewpoint in its formulation. In 1947 it was my good fortune to interview scores of officials, mostly Americans in the foreign service or the armed services in the various capitals of Europe, as well as in the American zones of Germany and Austria. Oral accounts of their experiences and observations, together with those of their colleagues in Washington, have proved most helpful. Associates and friends, without in all particulars approving the end result, have contributed valuable materials (some from first-hand observation) or have criticized the new chapters, or both. They are Claude A. Buss, David Harris, Anatole Mazour, Charles Easton Rothwell, and Wayne S. Vucinich, all of Stanford University; and Arthur P. Whitaker of the University of Pennsylvania and Gordon Wright of the University of Oregon. Charles Fairman and Graham H. Stuart, colleagues in political science, commented extensively on the glossary. I shall always be grateful for the generous assistance of all these friends.

THOMAS A. BAILEY

Department of History
Stanford University, California
November, 1949

THE SUBJECT of American diplomatic history—particularly of public opinion in relation to it—is so large that I would not have undertaken this task if many scholars had not already made important contributions to various phases of the problem. I have drawn freely upon their findings, and where they have already explored adequately, I have made little or no effort to go behind the returns. The works which I have found most useful are cited in the bibliographies and footnotes. If I have fallen into errors of fact or interpretation in using these contributions, I shall welcome corrections from the authors, or from any other readers of this book.

For certain periods, where special studies do not already exist, I have done considerable work with broadsides, newspapers, magazines, published documents, and the manuscript records of participants and of the Department of State. Many of these items are referred to specifically in the footnotes. Some of my conclusions, however, are based upon a large body of material, to which any precise reference is impossible. Certain observations on the years before the Civil War have been derived from an examination of the extensive broadside collections of the Library of Congress, the American Antiquarian Society (Worcester, Mass.), the Essex Institute (Salem, Mass.), the Massachusetts Historical Society (Boston, Mass.), the New York Public Library, and the Ridgway Branch of the Library Company of Philadelphia. A number of my conclusions regarding public opinion rest upon a study of substantially complete files of the following American weekly or monthly magazines: Niles' *Weekly Register* (Philadelphia), 1811–1849; *The North American Review* (Boston, New York), 1815 to date; *De Bow's Review* (New Orleans), 1846–1864, 1866–1870, 1879–1880; *The Democratic Review* (Washington, New York), 1837–1859; *The Nation* (New York), 1865 to date; *Harper's Weekly* (New York), 1857–1916; *Public Opinion* (Washington), 1886–1906; *Current Opinion* (New York), 1888–1925; *The Literary Digest* (New York), 1890–1938.

The observations as to British opinion have been based in part on an examination of virtually complete files of the following quarterlies: *Blackwood's Magazine* (Edinburgh, London), 1817 to date; *The*

Edinburgh Review (Edinburgh, London), 1802 to date; *The Quarterly Review* (London), 1809 to date; *The Westminster Review* (London), 1824–1914.

The relevant cartoons of the following magazines have been scrutinized, although it has been possible to reproduce only a few of them: *Fun* (London), 1861–1901; *Harper's Weekly; The Literary Digest; Public Opinion; Punch* (London), 1841 to date; *The American Review of Reviews* (New York), 1890–1936; *Vanity Fair* (New York), 1859–1863; *Yankee Doodle* (New York), 1846–1847. In addition, I have worked through the cartoon collections in the Library of Congress, the American Antiquarian Society, and the New York Public Library. William Murrell, *A History of American Graphic Humor* (2 vols., New York, 1933–1938), was indispensable.

The bibliographical notes at the end of each chapter are not exhaustive but are designed to give the beginning student some guidance to the best studies. The monumental work of Samuel Flagg Bemis and Grace Gardner Griffin, *Guide to the Diplomatic History of the United States, 1775–1921* (Washington, 1935), is so complete as to make fuller bibliographies unnecessary. I have endeavored to supplement this *Guide* by giving the significant works that have come out since it was published. With a few important exceptions, I have not listed documentary collections or works in foreign languages. These may be found in the Bemis and Griffin *Guide*, to which the interested student is strongly urged to turn. In general, I have made no reference to textbooks, though as a teacher of the subject I have derived many ideas and facts from the excellent treatises of Carl Russell Fish, John Bassett Moore, Randolph G. Adams, Louis Martin Sears, John Holladay Latané, and particularly of Samuel Flagg Bemis.

The footnotes of this book are designed to be used in connection with the bibliographical material listed at the end of each chapter. In general, they indicate the source of the longer quotations and support the more striking or challengeable statements. The complete bibliographical reference is given anew in the footnotes of each chapter, except for a few of the better-known works.

By far the most useful book on the maps of American diplomatic history is Charles O. Paullin, *Atlas of the Historical Geography of the United States* (Washington, 1932). There are also good maps in Hunter Miller, ed., *Treaties and other International Acts of the United States of America* (5 vols. to date, Washington, D.C., 1931–37), and in Samuel Flagg Bemis, *A Diplomatic History of the United States* (New York, 1936).

TABLE OF CONTENTS

TABLES AND APPENDICES

LIST OF MAPS

A DIPLOMATIC HISTORY

OF THE AMERICAN PEOPLE

CHAPTER I

Colonial Backgrounds

"America has been long enough involved in the wars of Europe. She has been a football between contending nations from the beginning. . . ." John Adams, 1782.

A PAWN ON THE EUROPEAN CHESSBOARD

A DIPLOMATIC history of the United States could properly begin with July, 1776, when Congress declared the thirteen colonies an independent nation. But to take this date as a starting point would be like writing a biography of George Washington and completely ignoring all the events of his life before he reached the age of twenty-one. The student of American history must never forget that a total of one hundred and sixty-nine years elapsed from the establishment of Jamestown, Virginia, to the Declaration of Independence—a period equal in length to that from 1776 to 1945. The impressions and experiences of the English colonists during this troubled century and a half not only determined the nature of the new republic but had an unmistakable influence upon its basic foreign policies.

It is not within the scope of this book to examine in detail the colonial backgrounds of American diplomatic history, interesting and significant though this subject may be. But a brief consideration of certain formative influences that were at work during these years will contribute to an understanding of American diplomacy during the national period.

At the outset we must bear in mind that the early English settlers in the New World were not Americans at all—at least from an international point of view—but Europeans planted on American soil. Their personal interests came second; those of England's empire first. In fact, several of the colonies were founded partially or primarily for purposes of imperial defense. The best example is Georgia, which was established as a buffer to protect the Carolinas from the Spaniards and the Indians. America, in brief, was but the farthest fringe of Europe—an offshoot from, an appendage to, the mother continent.

In no way was the subordinate status of the American settlers better exemplified than by the early intercolonial conflicts. Whenever trade rivalries, dynastic ambitions, or other causes plunged England and Spain into war, Spaniards would kill Englishmen along the southern frontier; whenever France and England clashed, the war whoop of French-led Indians would split the night air along the northern border. It was not the business of the colonials to reason why; they were but the vanguard of empire.

When war came in Europe the English colonists in America raised money and armies, and shouldered, albeit somewhat reluctantly, a share of the burden. But their achievements, though considerable, bore little relation to the terms of peace. In general, America was but the side show; the main tent was in Europe, and what happened there largely determined the final outcome. The classic example is the fate of the supposedly impregnable French fortress of Louisbourg, which, located on Cape Breton Island, had long been a thorn in the flesh of New England. By extraordinary good luck the English colonists managed to capture it in 1745. In Europe, however, the war ended in a virtual stalemate, and Louisbourg was restored to France. The English colonials naturally viewed with acute dissatisfaction the tossing away of the fruits of victory and the re-establishment of the old menace, but to no avail. Until the middle of the eighteenth century the colonies were in considerable measure but pawns on the European chessboard, and their interests were seldom considered, much less heeded.[1]

But what is true of the early intercolonial conflicts certainly is not true of the last one. When King William's War (the first of these struggles) broke out in 1689, a majority of the colonists in what is now the United States probably had no real desire to fight France. There were no acute friction centers vitally affecting the interests of large numbers of English settlers. The same is also true, though to a less extent, of Queen Anne's War (1702–1713). But following that struggle the advance guard of British empire in North America began to trickle over the mountain barrier into territory claimed by France. The subsequent rivalries of squatters, land speculators, and fur traders became increasingly intense;[2] and following King George's War (1744–1748) the English colonists apparently realized that the

---

[1] For a decade the Duke of Newcastle discussed Cape Breton without knowing that it was an island. George III was probably not the only Briton to confuse the Mississippi River with the Ganges, in India.

[2] By 1713, armed conflict had broken out or was about to break out in eight different places in the Western Hemisphere. M. H. Savelle, "Diplomatic Preliminaries of the Seven Years' War in America," *Canadian Hist. Rev.*, XX (1939), 17.

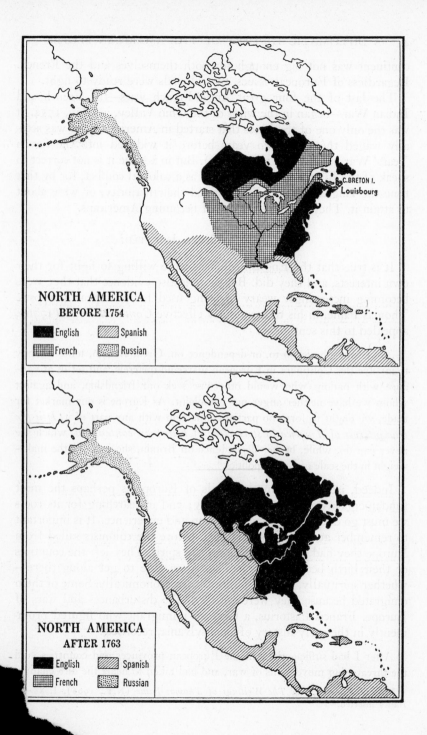

NORTH AMERICA
BEFORE 1754

English   Spanish
French   Russian

C.BRETON I.
Louisbourg

NORTH AMERICA
AFTER 1763

English   Spanish
French   Russian

continent was not big enough for both themselves and the French. Regardless of European issues, the colonials were ready to fight.

The last of the four great Anglo-French wars—the French and Indian War—began in the wilds of the Ohio Valley, in May, 1754. It was the only one of the series that started in America, and it was actually waged there for two years before it widened into the Seven Years' War in Europe (1756–1763). But in a sense it is not correct to speak of the French and Indian War as a colonial conflict, for by that time the English settlers had attained their majority, or were about to attain it. They were on the eve of becoming Americans.

WAS AMERICA EVER ISOLATED?

It is true that the English colonists were willing to fight for their own interests, and they did. But there is also evidence that they were becoming increasingly weary of being used for European purposes. Thomas Paine, in his tremendously effective *Common Sense* (1776), appealed to this sentiment:

> . . . Any submission to, or dependence on, Great Britain, tends directly to involve this Continent in European wars and quarrels, and set us at variance with nations who would otherwise seek our friendship, and against whom we have neither anger nor complaint. As Europe is our market for trade, we ought to form no partial connection with any part of it. *It is the true interest of America to steer clear of European contentions,* which she never can do, while, by her dependence on Britain, she is made the makeweight in the scale of British politics.[3]

Indeed, isolation from the broils of Europe is perhaps the most fundamental American foreign policy; and in searching for its roots we must go deep into colonial thinking and experience. It is important to remember at the outset that even before the colonists sailed from Europe they had become isolationists in spirit. They left the countries of their birth because they had not been able to get along there— whether spiritually, socially, politically, or economically. Some of them emigrated because they were weary of the disturbances and wars of Europe. Francis Pastorius, a German immigrant who figured prominently in the early history of Pennsylvania, recorded:

> After I had sufficiently seen the European provinces and countries, and the threatening movements of war, and had taken to heart the dire chang

---

[3] M. D. Conway, ed., *The Writings of Thomas Paine* (N.Y., 1906), I, 88–8
Italics inserted.

and disturbances of the Fatherland, I was impelled through a special guidance from the Almighty, to go to Pennsylvania.[4]

The voyage across the Atlantic usually lasted from one to three months, and involved such incredible hardships as normally to take a heavy toll of human life. One traveler testified:

. . . There is on board these ships terrible misery, stench, fumes, horror, vomiting, many kinds of sea-sickness, fever, dysentery, headache, heat, constipation, boils, scurvy, cancer, mouth-rot, and the like. . . . Add to this want of provisions, hunger, thirst, frost, heat, dampness, anxiety, want, afflictions and lamentations, together with other trouble, as *c. v.* the lice abound so frightfully, especially on sick people, that they can be scraped off the body. . . . We were compelled to eat the ship's biscuit which had been spoiled long ago; though in a whole biscuit there was scarcely a piece the size of a dollar that had not been full of red worms and spiders' nests.[5]

These prolonged nightmares had two inevitable results. The colonists realized keenly that they were isolated from Europe in space and time. And those who reached America alive did not go back except for very good reason. They began to develop a typically American way of living and thinking—a transformation that further widened the gulf between them and Europe. A distinguished Massachusetts clergyman, Increase Mather, declared in 1677 with obvious exaggeration: "There never was a generation that did so perfectly shake off the dust of Babylon, *both as to ecclesiastical* and *civil constitution*, as the first generation of Christians that came into this land for the gospel's sake." [6]

But only geographically, and in part spiritually, were the American colonists isolated from Europe. A thousand different ties—ties of race, kinship, language, literature, religion, custom, tradition, law, government, finance, trade—bound them to the mother country. However much they may have desired to carve out their own destiny without let or hindrance, they were repeatedly embroiled in wars of Europe's making. Between 1689 and 1815 England and France fought seven times—nearly sixty years of warfare in a period of one hundred and twenty-six years. Four of these wars, as we have seen, were waged while the Americans were still colonials. Even today the tourist may

---

[4] Quoted in J. F. Rippy and Angie Debo, "The Historical Background of the American Policy of Isolation," *Smith College Studies in History,* IX (1924), 71.

[5] Gottlieb Mittelberger, *Journey to Pennsylvania* (Phila., 1898), pp. 21–22, 24 (trans. from German by C. T. Eben).

[6] Quoted in J. W. Thornton, *The Pulpit of the American Revolution* (2nd ed., Boston, 1876), p. xviii.

visit the dungeons of the château at Nantes and find carved there the names of Gloucester and Nantucket fishermen who had been captured by the French during the intercolonial wars—visual evidence that America was then a part of Europe. Considering both the colonial and national periods, we find that between 1689 and 1945 there were nine general European wars.[7] And the American people were involved in every one of them, whether they wanted to be or not. Although one would not be justified in concluding that the United States must inevitably be drawn into every general war, it seems reasonably clear that America has never been, and probably can never be, completely separated from Europe.

As the Twig Is Bent

The policy of isolation—or rather the desire to be isolated—was not the only one to have its beginnings in the colonial period. The principle of the two hemispheres, which is the backbone of the Monroe Doctrine, may also be traced back to these troubled years. The Americans came to realize that the New World had a set of interests apart from those of the Old, and they sought to secure recognition of this fact. Why, indeed, should they dislocate profitable trade relationships, butcher their neighbors and be butchered by them, because of a European war in which they had no direct stake?

Similarly, there were faint foreshadowings of other fundamental policies in the colonial period: nonintervention in the wars of others, freedom of the seas, freedom of trade (the Open Door), and the pacific settlement of disputes. Some of the incidents exemplifying these principles are so scattered that it would be dangerous to hazard generalizations. But this much is clear: colonial experience convinced

[7]

In Europe	In America
1688–1697, War of League of Augsburg	King William's War
1701–1713, War of Spanish Succession	Queen Anne's War, 1702–1713
1740–1748, War of Austrian Succession	King George's War, 1744–1748
1756–1763, Seven Years' War	French and Indian War, 1754–1763
1778–1783, The War of the American Revolution	American Revolution, 1775–1783
1793–1802, Wars of the French Revolution	Undeclared French War, 1798–1800
1803–1815, Napoleonic Wars	War of 1812, 1812–1814
1914–1918, World War I	World War I, 1917–1918
1939–1945, World War II	World War II, 1941–1945

Note: The Crimean War (1854–1856), the Austro-Prussian War (1866), and the Franco-German War (1870–1871) are not included as general wars because they were localized and did not involve a contest for dominant sea power.

the leaders of the United States that it was decidedly to the advantage of the new nation to stay on its own side of the water and keep free from outside entanglements.[8] Geography led inexorably to the adoption of such a policy. And geography made possible its partial fulfillment during the national period.

BIBLIOGRAPHICAL NOTE

Suggestive outlines of the colonial backgrounds of American diplomatic history appear in S. F. Bemis, *The Diplomacy of the American Revolution* (N.Y., 1935), Ch. I; and in the same author's *A Diplomatic History of the United States* (N.Y., 1936), Ch. I. There is no comprehensive book on the subject. A very detailed contribution to one aspect of the problem is T. C. Pease, ed., *Anglo-French Boundary Disputes in the West, 1749–1763* (Springfield, Ill., 1936). M. H. Savelle has broken the ground in his "Colonial Origins of American Diplomatic Principles," *Pacific Hist. Rev.*, III (1934), 334–350; and has prepared the carefully documented *Diplomatic History of the Canadian Boundary, 1749–1763* (to be published by the Yale University Press), which complements and expands Pease. The notes of F. G. Davenport's monumental *European Treaties Bearing on the History of the United States and its Dependencies* (3 vols., Washington, 1917–1934) are helpful. The fourth volume, published in 1937, was edited by C. O. Paullin. An earlier sketch by F. G. Davenport, "America and European Diplomacy to 1648," appears in the Amer. Hist. Assn., *Annual Report, 1915,* 153–161. A classic account of British imperialism from 1763 to the outbreak of the Revolution is C. W. Alvord, *The Mississippi Valley in British Politics* (2 vols., Cleveland, 1917). For further references see footnotes of this chapter.

RECENT REFERENCES. Max Savelle's *Diplomatic History of the Canadian Boundary*, referred to above, was published in 1940. The same author also has a penetrating essay, "The American Balance of Power and European Diplomacy, 1713–78," in R. B. Morris, ed., *The Era of the American Revolution* (N.Y., 1939), pp. 140–169. He shows that the French were interested in the American Revolution from a desire to preserve a balance of power in the New World as well as in the Old. A. K. Weinberg categorizes eight concepts of isolation in "The Historical Meaning of the American Doctrine of Isolation," *Amer. Pol. Sci. Rev.*, XXXIV (1940), 539–547.

NEW REFERENCES. Felix Gilbert, "The English Background of American Isolationism in the Eighteenth Century," *William and Mary Quar.*, I (3d Ser.) [1944], 138–160, shows how English ideas of isolationism carried over to America. For an analysis of this article, see New References at the end of the next chapter.

4TH ED. REFS. See Max Savelle, "The Appearance of an American Attitude toward External Affairs, 1750–1775," *Amer. Hist. Rev.*, LII (1947), 655–666.

---

[8] See M. H. Savelle, "Colonial Origins of American Diplomatic Principles," *Pacific Hist. Rev.*, III (1934), 334–350. Alexander Hamilton pointed out in 1787 that England did not have to maintain a large standing army because the English Channel separated her from Europe. How much better situated, he noted, was the United States. E. M. Earle, ed., *The Federalist* (Washington, 1937), pp. 45–46 (No. 8).

CHAPTER II

The Diplomacy of the French Alliance, 1775–1778

*"Every nation in Europe wishes to see Britain humbled, having
all in their turns been offended by her insolence. . . ."*

Benjamin Franklin, 1777.

"Tyrant of the Seas"

GREAT BRITAIN emerged from the Seven Years' War (1756–1763)
the mightiest nation in the world. Her fleets whitened the seas and
her empire sprawled over two hemispheres. But with overweening
power went an arrogance that aroused hatred among the peoples of
Europe. Horace Walpole, the English author, described his contemporaries in England as "born with Roman insolence" and behaving
with "more haughtiness than an Asiatic monarch." He, himself, threatened to burn his Greek and Latin books—"those histories of little
people."

No nation felt the humiliation of defeat by the British more keenly
than France. Forsaken by allies and humbled on the battlefield, she
had been shorn of a vast empire, including all her possessions on the
mainland of North America. Formerly arbiter of the destinies of Europe, she now saw her ministers walk at the heels of those of Great
Britain in every chancellery on the Continent. Count de Vergennes,
French Minister of Foreign Affairs, wrote with bitterness: "England
is the natural enemy of France; and she is a greedy enemy, ambitious,
unjust and treacherous: the unalterable and cherished object of her
policy is, if not the destruction of France, at least her degradation and
ruin." [1]

To the dispirited French there was but one bright spot in the picture. The English colonists in America had huddled close to the wings
of the mother country while Canada was in the hands of France;
but now that the Gallic menace was removed the colonials might wan-
der afield—perhaps even slough off imperial control. Encouraged by
this possibility, the French government sent secret observers to

[1] Henri Doniol, *Histoire de la Participation de la France à l'Établissement des États-
Unis d'Amérique* (Paris, 1886), I, 244 (*Réflexions* of Vergennes, early in 1776).

America to report developments and, if possible, to foment trouble. When the British Parliament passed the ill-advised Stamp Act in 1765, and the English colonists cried out in protest, it seemed for a while as if the anticipated break would come. But the obnoxious measure was repealed the next year, and the French ministers began to lose hope.

The wound was reopened in 1773, when Parliament passed the famous Tea Act. This led to the Boston Tea Party, which in turn brought forth the so-called Intolerable Acts of 1774. The outraged colonials resisted; and blood was finally shed on the green at Lexington, Massachusetts, on April 19, 1775. But the great majority of Americans still hoped for reconciliation and for the reform of alleged abuses. France, however, was interested in the destruction, not the reformation, of the British Empire. Until the colonials were prepared to make the final break, she could offer no open aid.[2]

British bungling continued; and on July 2, 1776, the Continental Congress, responding to outraged public opinion, declared the colonies independent. Two days later it adopted Jefferson's immortal draft of the Declaration of Independence. This official severance of relations with the mother country was a diplomatic stroke of the greatest importance. It made possible foreign alliances, for which colonial sentiment was now ripe, and served notice on the European Powers that the easiest and most effective way to wreak vengeance upon Britain was to aid the struggling Americans in their attempt to break up a mighty empire. "The colonies," wrote Catherine II of Russia hopefully and prophetically, "have told England good-bye forever."

MILITIA DIPLOMATS AND MILITIA DIPLOMACY

During the American Revolution the foreign affairs of the United States were directed by Congress—not by a Department of State. As early as November, 1775, more than seven months before the Declaration of Independence, a secret committee of correspondence was appointed to maintain foreign contacts. It commissioned Arthur Lee, a Virginian then residing at London in the capacity of agent for Massachusetts, as its confidential correspondent. Then, on March 3, 1776, still four months before independence was declared, Congress decided

---

[2] The Boston *Gazette* (October 28, 1775) reported: "American sailors returning from France all declare that they are well received in the French ports and that the French are waiting only for an American declaration of independence to intervene." Quoted in Bernard Faÿ, *The Revolutionary Spirit in France and America* (N.Y., 1927), p. 75.

to send one of its members, Silas Deane, as a "commercial" agent to France.

Deane was instructed to secure military and financial assistance, and to sound out the French government on the possibilities of an alliance. Fearful of British spies, he adopted the name of Jones, wrote his letters in invisible ink, and vowed that in the presence of English-speaking people he would use only the French tongue. This led Foreign Minister Vergennes to remark: "He must be the most silent man in France, for I defy him to say six consecutive words in French." The well-meaning Deane, although not officially received, made naïve efforts to ingratiate himself with the French rulers.

The queen [he wrote home] is fond of parade, and I believe wishes a war, and is our friend. She loves riding on horseback. Could you send me a narrowhegansett horse or two; the present might be money exceedingly well laid out. Rittenhouse's orrery, or Arnold's collection of insects, a phaeton of American make and a pair of bay horses, a few barrels of apples, of walnuts, of butternuts, etc., would be great curiosities. . . .[3]

Nevertheless Deane did useful work in fitting out privateers, in securing military aid for the struggling colonies, and particularly in helping to create the machinery for later assistance.[4]

Silas Deane was but the first of a procession of envoys sent abroad by Congress. Uninvited and unwanted, these agents were generally rebuffed, except in France, where they were either secretly or informally welcomed.[5] This hesitancy is not difficult to explain. The official reception of diplomatic representatives is regarded as a recognition of the country from which they come; and the premature recognition of revolting colonies is generally considered just grounds for declaring war. The Powers of Europe all feared Britain's might, and none of them wanted to incur her wrath by receiving the American agents. Frederick the Great of Prussia, whose attitude was typical, instructed his ministers not to treat with the American envoy but

[3] Francis Wharton, ed., *The Revolutionary Diplomatic Correspondence of the United States* (Washington, 1889), II, 214 (Deane to Jay, Dec. 3, 1776).

[4] There is a controversy over Deane's honesty and loyalty during the Revolution. The most recent researches reveal that he used his official position to promote private speculations. T. P. Abernethy, *Western Lands and the American Revolution* (N.Y., 1937), Ch. XIV.

[5] Envoys are usually not sent to a foreign country until assurances are forthcoming that they will be received. Franklin objected to the course adopted, writing to Arthur Lee (March 21, 1777): "I have not yet changed the opinion I gave in Congress, that a virgin State should preserve its virgin character, and not go about suitering for alliances, but wait with decent dignity for the application of others." Wharton, *op. cit.*, I, 292.

"mit Complimenten abweisen" (put him off with compliments).[6]

These early American agents labored under other difficulties. Most of them, like Deane, were totally without experience in the wiles of European diplomacy. But John Adams did not feel that this was a serious handicap. "Wise men know," he wrote, "that militia sometimes gain victories over regular troops even by departing from the rules." Adams, however, was unduly optimistic. Most of the militia diplomats—that is, those without diplomatic experience—were as heavy a liability as the light-footed militiamen at home. Arthur Lee, for example, employed as clerks at least six British spies, who must have penetrated his *nom de plume*, "Mary Johnston." While he was in Prussia, and under circumstances that suggest the comic opera, his private papers were stolen and copied by the British minister, Hugh Elliott. Although Frederick the Great loudly cursed *"votre Gott Damme"* Elliott, there was nothing that could be done about the theft.

Yet these were not the only handicaps under which the militia diplomats worked. Under the most favorable circumstances it took two full months for instructions from Congress to reach Europe. Approximately one third of the American diplomatic correspondence failed to reach its destination. Some of it was seized by the swarming British cruisers; much of it was thrown overboard to avoid capture. At a time when the Continental Congress had twelve paid agents in Europe, eleven months once elapsed without a word from one of them. The secret codes, in which the correspondence was conducted, occasionally were lost or changed without notification; letters, when they did come through, arrived in formidable batches; and occasionally instructions dated, for example, December 30, would be received weeks before those dated November 30. John Adams, a militia diplomat himself, summarized these difficulties in a classic statement:

Ambassadors in Europe can send expresses to their courts and give and receive intelligence in a few days with the utmost certainty. In such cases there is no room for mistake, misunderstanding, or surprise, but in our case it is very different. We are at an immense distance. Despatches are liable to foul play and vessels are subject to accidents. New scenes open, the time presses, various nations are in suspense, and necessity forces us to act.[7]

[6] P. L. Haworth, "Frederick the Great and the American Revolution," *Amer. Hist. Rev.*, IX (1904), 468.

[7] Wharton, *op. cit.*, VI, 52 (Adams to Livingston, Nov. 18, 1782). On October 1, 1776, Deane complained to Congress, "For Heaven's sake, if you mean to have any connection with this kingdom [France], be more assiduous in getting your letters here." *Ibid.*, II, 153.

This complaint does much to explain some of the obstacles confronting American diplomacy before the Atlantic cable was successfully laid in 1866.

BEAUMARCHAIS' GREATEST PLOT

The story of Franco-American diplomacy from 1775 to 1778 would not be complete without reference to the work of Pierre Augustin Caron de Beaumarchais. The early years of this remarkable Frenchman were spent as an inventor and watchmaker, in which capacity he is best known for having constructed a watch small enough to be worn on the ring finger of Louis XV's mistress, Madame de Pompadour. Later, through audacity and brilliance, he distinguished himself as a courtier, a master of intrigue, and finally as a playwright-poet-politician. He is perhaps best remembered as the author of two of the most popular comedies of his day, *The Barber of Seville* and *The Marriage of Figaro*.

In 1775 Beaumarchais visited London and there met Arthur Lee, who discussed with him plans for assisting the rebellious Americans against Britain. The adventuresome Frenchman became enamored of the colonial cause, and threw himself into it with almost fanatical zeal. He stimulated the interest of Vergennes, who had already been watching developments in America with a calculating eye,[8] and through him—and even directly—bombarded the French king with his strikingly phrased arguments for assistance.

The inexperienced Louis XVI, although only twenty-one years of age and somewhat thick-headed, showed little enthusiasm for these impassioned importunities. He knew quite well that Britain would probably, and properly, declare war if France should lend open aid to the struggling colonies. But the king and his ministers finally decided that they could inflict the maximum damage on Great Britain with the minimum of risk and expense to themselves by encouraging the American rebels with secret shipments of sorely needed munitions, money, and supplies. This momentous decision was made on May 2, 1776, two months before Congress declared the colonies independent and before a single American agent had set foot on French soil. France could not afford to let the fire go out for want of fuel.[9]

[8] Recent scholarship reveals that Beaumarchais had a larger part in shaping Vergennes' policy of secret aid than had formerly been thought to be the case. J. J. Meng, "A Footnote to Secret Aid in the American Revolution," *Amer. Hist. Rev.*, XLIII (1938), 791–795.

[9] S. F. Bemis, *The Diplomacy of the American Revolution* (N.Y., 1935), p. 27.

So it was that a fictitious private concern, masquerading under the name of Roderique Hortalez et Compagnie, was organized in France to ship military supplies to America. With Beaumarchais as founder and guiding genius, and with the French and Spanish governments as the silent partners and financial backers, this bogus firm sent the colonials large quantities of all kinds of stores—many of them from the king's own arsenals and bearing his monogram. Agricultural America, with its serious lack of military equipment, could not have carried on without this aid. Ninety per cent of the powder used by the colonials during the first two and one half years of the war came from Europe [10]—most of it through Hortalez et Compagnie, which at one time was operating fourteen ships. Beaumarchais, prince of conspirators and imaginative playwright, never conceived a more successful plot.

Nor did secret aid end here. The French authorities, though officially issuing proclamations to the contrary, clandestinely permitted American privateers to fit out in their ports and prey upon England's commerce. The British diplomatic representative in France, Lord Stormont, was well aware of these activities; but his repeated protests were of no avail. When his representations became too pressing, Vergennes would order American privateers seized; later he would secretly compensate the owners for their losses and allow their vessels to escape. On one occasion Lord Stormont vehemently told Vergennes that even if the latter had the hundred eyes of the classical monster, Argus, he could not see all the violations of neutrality that were going on in French ports. "And if you had those eyes," Vergennes replied smoothly, "they would only show you our sincere desire of peace." [11] Had Britain not wished to avoid war with France at this time, she could have found abundant cause for hostilities in this flouting of neutrality.

A FUR CAP AMONG POWDERED HEADS

Not until September 26, 1776, nearly three months after the Declaration of Independence, did Congress appoint an official commission to France. It consisted of Arthur Lee and Silas Deane (who were already abroad), and, most important of all, Benjamin Franklin. The famous Philadelphian, then seventy years of age, had grave doubts as to his usefulness, remarking characteristically: "I am old and good

[10] O. W. Stephenson, "The Supply of Gunpowder in 1776," *Amer. Hist. Rev.*, XXX (1925), 277.

[11] C. H. Van Tyne, *The War of Independence* (Boston, 1929), p. 489.

for nothing; but as the store-keepers say of their remnants of cloth, I am but a fag end, and you may have me for what you please to give." [12] America, in truth, gave little for his services and received much; for few will deny that the next seven years were destined to be the most noteworthy of Franklin's remarkable career.

It is erroneous, however, to regard Franklin as a militia diplomat. America has never sent abroad a man better qualified by training, character, and temperament for the task at hand. For more than a decade Franklin had served in the quasi-diplomatic capacity of colonial agent in London, and he was regarded throughout Europe as the most distinguished man America had yet produced. His writings had been translated into Continental languages, and his spectacular experiments with electricity had captivated the imagination of the science-loving French.[13]

The venerable American, after braving a rebel's noose and a wintry sea, landed on French soil in December, 1776. Master psychologist and showman that he was, Franklin discarded his wig and substituted a fur cap.

Figure me in your mind [he reported] as jolly as formerly, and as strong and hearty, only a few years older; very plainly dressed, wearing my thin gray straight hair, that peeps out under my only *coiffure,* a fine fur cap, which comes down my forehead almost to my spectacles. Think how this must appear among the powdered heads of Paris! [14]

Lord Stormont warned Vergennes that he would leave Paris should the "chief of the American rebels" be allowed to enter the city. The French foreign minister replied that a special message had been sent warning Franklin not to come, but that if the American should fail to receive it he could not with propriety be expelled from Paris. It is unnecessary to add that the message did miscarry, and that Franklin was cordially, though of course unofficially, received.

Stripped of borrowed hair and attired in the simple costume of "an American agriculturist," Franklin took the blasé French society by storm. His patriarchal appearance, his unpretentious manner, his

---

[12] Wharton, *Revolutionary Diplomatic Correspondence,* I, 473 (Remark made to Dr. Rush, Sept. 27, 1776).

[13] In 1778 the French financier, Turgot, coined the most famous modern Latin epigram: *Eripuit caelo fulmen sceptrumque tyrannis* (He snatched the lightning from the sky and the scepter from tyrants). Carl Van Doren, *Benjamin Franklin* (N.Y., 1938), p. 606.

[14] John Bigelow, ed., *The Life of Benjamin Franklin* (3rd ed., Phila., 1893), II, 380 (Franklin to Mrs. Thompson, Feb. 8, 1777).

benevolent countenance, and his agreeable eccentricity all appealed to the Gallic mind. To the French he was the embodiment of the ideals of Rousseau and the personification of the American cause. Even Voltaire spoke quite unconsciously of Washington's army as "Franklin's troops." Unaffected by this adulation, the New World sage moved about unostentatiously and benignantly, phrasing piquant sayings that passed from mouth to mouth as *bons mots*. When asked, for example, if a statement of Lord Stormont about the American cause was true, he replied, "No, sir, it is not the truth, it is a—Stormont."

The adoring French compared Franklin with Phocion, Tell, Socrates, even Jesus; and he grew weary of sitting for his portrait. His face appeared everywhere on rings, medals, medallions, watches, bracelets, and snuff boxes. The French ladies, among whom Franklin was a great favorite, did him the honor to adopt the high *"coiffure à la Franklin"* in imitation of his cap. No social affair was a success without the famous American. So great were the crowds that followed and pressed about him that the curious even paid money for vantage points from which to see him pass by. "No man in Paris was more *à la mode*, more sought after, than Doctor Franklin," recorded Madame Lebrun; and the Duke de Lévis reminisced: "I was very young when I saw the illustrious Franklin, but his countenance, so full of candor and nobility . . . will never be forgotten by me." [15]

Without this background it is impossible to understand the remarkable success of Franklin's diplomacy. He took full advantage of his popularity to promote the American cause, and he published a number of newspaper articles and pamphlets to cast discredit upon the British. Most famous of his propaganda efforts was the forged letter which apparently proved that the British were buying bales of American scalps (including those of women and children) from the Indians.[16]

THE FRENCH DILEMMA

But Franklin's wiles alone were not sufficient to enlist France on the side of the collapsing colonies. The complexion of affairs was completely changed when, on October 17, 1777, the British commander, General Burgoyne, surrendered his entire force to the Americans at Saratoga, New York. In a diplomatic rather than in a military sense this disaster to Britain's arms must be regarded as one of the decisive

[15] D. J. Hill, "A Missing Chapter of Franco-American History," *Amer. Hist. Rev.*, XXI (1916), 712.

[16] Van Doren, *Benjamin Franklin*, pp. 671–673; see also pp. 574–575.

battles of the world. The American commissioners in Paris wrote home that the news had apparently caused as much joy in France "as if it had been a victory of their own troops over their own enemies." No one was more elated than Beaumarchais, who, in his haste to get to the king with the glad tidings (or perhaps to engage in private speculations), was injured in a carriage wreck.

The Saratoga disaster naturally turned the thoughts of the British ministry to the necessity of making concessions and ending the fruit-less war in America. At this point the astute Franklin played his cards with characteristic skill. He entered into negotiations with the princi-pal British agent, and let it appear that unless France could offer something better, the Americans might have to accept Great Britain's terms. Vergennes immediately bestirred himself. To him reconcilia-tion would be a catastrophe; for, as he pointed out, it would end the now-or-never opportunity to ruin Great Britain and restore French prestige on the Continent.[17]

But revenge was not the only argument that Vergennes used with his fellow ministers and with the king. He appealed to cupidity—the possibility of winning the lucrative American trade—and he appealed to fear. If Britain, he said, should reconcile her colonies, what was to prevent her from turning upon the profitable French sugar islands in the West Indies—France's most valuable colonial possessions—and there seeking compensation for the cost of the rebellion? In addition, the trend of events indicated that war between Great Britain and France was inevitable within a few years. Was it not far better to fight England when she had her hands full with the rebellious Ameri-cans than to wait until the reunited British Empire could marshal its entire strength against Louis XVI? This appeal to the instinct of fear, which Franklin also cleverly exploited, appears to have done more than anything else to bring the reluctant king and his ministers to the edge of the precipice.[18]

[17] Britain was not destroyed by the loss of her colonies. A second and greater em-pire arose on the ruins of the first, thus confuting the mercantilist philosophy. But Vergennes can hardly be blamed for subscribing to what the British themselves be-lieved. Lord Shelburne declared in Parliament that "the sun of Great-Britain is set, and we shall no longer be a powerful or respectable people, the moment that the independency of America is agreed to by our government!" *Parliamentary History of England*, XIX, 850–851 (March 5, 1778).

[18] Professor E. S. Corwin holds (contrary to C. H. Van Tyne) that Vergennes did not himself believe the validity of some of the arguments he used, particularly the West Indian danger. See E. S. Corwin, *French Policy and the American Alliance of 1778* (Princeton, 1916), Ch. VI.

BEYOND THE PYRENEES

But France was not entirely free to move as she chose. By the terms of the Family Compact of 1761 she was bound to act in close concert with Spain in matters of war. Besides, France needed the Spanish navy if she hoped to muster a fleet more formidable than England's. But, unfortunately for Vergennes' plans, Spain showed no great enthusiasm for the proposed war. It is true that she hated Britain with a consuming bitterness. No other nation had done more to reduce her from her former proud position to a secondary place in the family of nations. The rock of Gibraltar, which England had wrested from her in 1704, was a constant reminder of an implacable foe and of Spain's maddening impotence. Hatred, pride, and a desire for revenge and restitution alike cried aloud for war with Great Britain. But the Spanish Court recoiled from the thought of an independent and powerful American republic. Such a new state might reach over the Alleghenies into the Mississippi Valley and grasp territory that Spain wanted for herself; or, even worse, seize colonies that were already Spain's.

Yet the bogey that cast the longest shadow over the Spanish Court was rebellion. Charles III could not forget that he had the largest and most vulnerable colonial empire in the New World. If he openly assisted the American rebels in their uprising, the British might encourage his own subjects to revolt against the Spanish crown. Then, too, if rebellion and democracy were successful in the English colonies, these twin plagues might easily spread to the Spanish dominions, as indeed they did. The few secret contributions that Charles III made to the American cause were apparently given in the hope that both the colonies and the mother country would exhaust themselves, and thus render his own possessions and commercial monopoly more secure.

The procrastination of the Spanish Court drove Vergennes to the verge of distraction. He did his best to quiet Spain's fears, while dangling before her eyes the prospect of reconquering the Floridas, Gibraltar, and Minorca, and of securing a large slice of trans-Allegheny America. But still the Spanish Court wavered. Fearful that if he delayed longer Great Britain would conciliate her colonies, Vergennes decided to plunge into the war at once in the hope that Spain might be persuaded to join France later.[19]

[19] Bemis, *Diplomacy of the American Revolution*, p. 60.

THE RACE FOR EMPIRE

The Americans were at first reluctant to enter into a military alliance with France, for the memory of involvement in the conflicts of Europe was still painfully fresh.[20] But Congress, faced with the necessity of obtaining outside help, eventually modified its instructions to the commissioners so as to permit them to make binding engagements with the French government. The union between the two nations was cemented at Paris, on February 6, 1778, when Franklin, Deane, and Lee signed two epochal pacts. The first was an exceedingly liberal treaty of amity and commerce, which granted important privileges to American shipping.[21] This document constituted an official recognition of the United States, and as such meant that Great Britain would almost inevitably make war on France. When this happened, the second and more important treaty, that of alliance, would become effective. Its most significant provisions were: (1) Both nations agreed to fight until American independence was "formally or tacitly assured." (2) Neither France nor the United States would conclude a "truce or peace" with Great Britain without the "formal consent of the other first obtained." (3) Each of the two nations guaranteed the possessions of the other in America "mutually from the present time and forever against all other powers."

Meanwhile the British Prime Minister, Lord North, had been making plans to salvage the empire. On December 10, 1777, he announced to the startled Parliament that after the Christmas holidays he would move to consider concessions to the rebellious colonies. Early the next year he introduced his conciliation bills, which granted virtual home rule to the Americans; and on March 9, 1778, these measures were approved.

"The two greatest countries in Europe," remarked Edward Gib-

[20] In September, 1775, John Adams, then a member of Congress, opposed an alliance with France, declaring that "in any future war, we must become too subordinate and dependent on that nation, and should be involved in all European wars, as we had been hitherto; . . . in fine, we should be little better than puppets, danced on the wires of the cabinets of Europe." C. F. Adams, ed., *The Works of John Adams* (Boston, 1865), II, 505. For American isolationist sentiment during these years see J. F. Rippy and Angie Debo, "The Historical Background of the American Policy of Isolation," *Smith College Studies in History*, IX (1924), 71–165.

[21] The treaty followed closely the "Plan of 1776" drawn up by Congress and designed as a model for its negotiators in Europe. The plan reflected the views of the "small navy" neutral carrier powers, and contained such provisions as the liberalization of contraband lists and the immunity of noncontraband enemy goods from capture while being carried on neutral ships ("free ships, free goods"). See Bemis, *Diplomacy of the American Revolution*, pp. 45–48.

bon, then a member of Parliament, "were fairly running a race for the favor of America." The French terms were received with rejoicing in the United States, despite the growth of the isolationist tradition,[22] and they came just in time to stop the movement toward reconciliation that had followed the receipt of advance copies of Lord North's conciliation bills. Louis XVI held out to the Americans everything that the British were prepared to concede—and one thing more, independence. So the colonials, having tasted the sweets of freedom, cast in their lot with France. With the acceptance of the French treaties and the breakdown of conciliation, France and Great Britain drifted into war, June, 1778.

Incongruous Allies

In her haste to forestall Britain's conciliatory efforts, France promised much and received little. She dealt with the Americans on a plane of equality as if with a powerful and long-established nation. She even went so far as to bind herself by the treaty of alliance not to retain Canada or any of Britain's other mainland possessions in North America. She abandoned secret aid, which had proved so cheap and so effective, and gave the colonials, at a ruinous cost to herself, that open assistance without which they could scarcely have won their independence.

In their own minds Louis XVI and his ministers had compelling reasons for openly supporting the American cause. But with the wisdom of hindsight we can now see that nothing could have exceeded the folly of the French crown in plunging blindly into the struggle. We have here the anomalous spectacle of monarchy openly courting —and winning—both bankruptcy and revolution. Turgot, the great French minister of finance, had stated bluntly that war would mean ruin. But the heavy-witted Louis turned a deaf ear to these cold calculations—and dismissed him.[23]

The paradoxes, however, do not stop with France. Many observers were amazed at the eagerness with which the United States grasped the Gallic hand, drenched though it was with the blood of American settlers. In four successive wars, extending over three quarters of a century, Indians led by Frenchmen had ravaged the Anglo-American

[22] Rippy and Debo, "The Historical Background of the American Policy of Isolation," *loc. cit.*, p. 96.

[23] The king was told that his valets, clad in royal livery, were openly begging in the streets. "I believe it," he blandly replied, "they are paid nothing." C. H. Van Tyne, *England and America* (N.Y., 1927), p. 166.

frontier. Yet scarcely had the war whoop died away and the scalping knife become dry when the Americans found themselves arrayed beside their former archenemy against the country that had given them birth. As one commentator has well said, "when our house is burning, we do not inquire too curiously into the moral antecedents of those who hand the water-buckets." [24]

In America, British pamphleteers as well as the Loyalists ("Tories") did their best to undo the alliance by resurrecting the Gallic peril. They insisted that this was but the old story of the wooden horse over again, and that when the French came they would exact a heavy price for their help—perhaps American territory and sovereignty. In Protestant New England great stress was laid upon the hated Catholicism of the French, and the Loyalist newspapers made much of the expected arrival of ships laden with tons of holy water, crucifixes, hair shirts, and other "trappings of popery." The French representatives in America launched a counterattack of propaganda, and employed the magic pen of Thomas Paine at a salary of one thousand dollars a year to create sentiment favorable to France and the alliance.[25] But such efforts were probably unnecessary. Water buckets and water bucket carriers were too urgently needed.

SENTIMENT AND SELF-INTEREST

Now that the alliance was consummated, Louis XVI did the handsome thing by sending to his "very dear great friends and allies" a full-fledged minister plenipotentiary, Conrad Alexandre Gérard. Flattered by such attention, Congress engaged in a debate over the etiquette of receiving this Old World dignitary, and the discussion even embraced such subjects as the shape of shirt frills and the number of horses that should draw the carriages. The Loyalists hid their fear in derision:

> From Lewis [Louis XVI], Monsieur Gerard came,
> To Congress in this town, sir.
> They bowed to him, and he to them
> And then they all sat down, sir.[26]

[24] H. E. Egerton, *The Causes and Character of the American Revolution* (Oxford, 1923), p. 127.
[25] See J. J. Meng, "French Diplomacy in Philadelphia: 1778–1779," *Catholic Hist. Rev.*, XXIV (1938), 51, 56.
[26] *Rivington's Gazette*, Oct. 3, 1778, quoted in C. H. Van Tyne, *The Loyalists in the American Revolution* (N.Y., 1902), p. 153.

On the other hand, an ardent patriot journalist exulted:

Who would have thought that the American colonies, imperfectly known in Europe a few years ago and claimed by every pettifogging lawyer in the House of Commons, every cobbler in the beer-houses of London, as a part of their property, should to-day receive an ambassador from the most powerful monarchy in Europe.[27]

It was a red-letter day in the history of the United States.

The legend has persisted that France entered the war because she loved the United States, a legend that Vergennes deliberately encouraged. It is true that there was a considerable body of liberals and intellectuals in France, including Rousseau and Voltaire, who were fired with enthusiasm for the cause of liberty and for the American experiment in republicanism. It is also true that the struggle of the colonials touched the imagination of the more romantic and chivalrous elements in France, especially in the cities. Nor can it be denied that the American cause was popular at the French Court and in the inner circles of French society. The wily Franklin had done his work well. Even the frivolous queen, Marie Antoinette, inquired eagerly for "our good Americans," "our dear republicans." But it is not correct to say that the illiterate and ignorant French masses were on fire for America, and that they forced their government into the war. Such statements grossly exaggerate sentiment for the colonies and clothe the absolutist French monarchy with the responsiveness of a popular government. The documents do not reveal that the hard-headed Vergennes and his calculating fellow ministers were swayed to any appreciable extent by sentimental considerations. France came to the aid of the Americans because those in charge of her government concluded—whether wisely or not—that it was to her advantage to do so. Fear, cupidity, and a desire for revenge, restitution, and security dictated her course. France's distresses made possible America's success.[28]

BIBLIOGRAPHICAL NOTE

The best single book on the subject is S. F. Bemis' scholarly *The Diplomacy of the American Revolution* (N.Y., 1935), which has been followed in this chapter and the succeeding one. E. S. Corwin's *French Policy and the American Alliance of 1778* (Princeton, 1916), though older, is still useful. C. H. Van Tyne has a succinct account, less strictly diplomatic, in *The War of Independence*

[27] Quoted in Van Tyne, *England and America*, pp. 174–175.
[28] This phrase or a modification of it appears repeatedly in S. F. Bemis, *A Diplomatic History of the United States* (N.Y., 1936).

(Boston, 1929), pp. 441–501. Carl Van Doren's *Benjamin Franklin* (N.Y., 1938) is good on the diplomatic aspects of Franklin's career. Arthur Lee is rehabilitated in B. J. Hendrick, *The Lees of Virginia* (Boston, 1935). Two useful articles by C. H. Van Tyne are: "Influences which Determined the French Government to Make the Treaty with America, 1778," *Amer. Hist. Rev.*, XXI (1916), 528–541; and "French Aid before the Alliance of 1778," *ibid.*, XXXI (1925), 20–40. Further references: see footnotes of this chapter and S. F. Bemis and G. G. Griffin, eds., *Guide to the Diplomatic History of the United States, 1775–1921* (Washington, 1935), pp. 1–25. Hereafter cited as Bemis and Griffin, *Guide*.

RECENT REFERENCES. A. B. Darling, *Our Rising Empire, 1763–1803* (New Haven, 1940), Chs. I–II, is a rather detailed survey of early relations with France. An invaluable collection of documents, prefaced by an able introduction, is available in J. J. Meng, ed., *Despatches and Instructions of Conrad Alexandre Gérard, 1778–1780* (Baltimore, 1939). Both Darling and Meng, particularly Meng, throw into clear relief the extraordinary amount of French intrigue among the factions in Congress to influence American decisions in line with French interests. Specifically, the French representatives used various kinds of pressure, including outright bribery, to bring about a rejection of British conciliation; to change the personnel of the peace commission, as well as the instructions sent to it; to limit the territorial expansion of the United States; and to keep the Americans out of the fisheries.

NEW REFERENCES. See Felix Gilbert, "The English Background of American Isolationism in the Eighteenth Century," *William and Mary Quar.*, I (3d Ser.) [1944], 138–160. The debate that had been going on for more than fifty years as to whether England should eschew continental embroilments was brought to America by various agencies, including Benjamin Franklin and Thomas Paine. Paine in *Common Sense* stressed the idea that America's political connection with the mother country meant involvement in England's involvements. He recommended an independent course which Dr. Gilbert thinks influenced Washington's Farewell Address and Jefferson's foreign policy (p. 160).

4TH ED. REFS. Georges Lemaitre, *Beaumarchais* (N.Y., 1949), is the most recent life of the colorful Frenchman in English. Translations of the documents in the work by Meng, cited above, appear in J. A. Baisnée and J. J. Meng, "Philadelphia and the Revolution: French Diplomacy in the United States, 1778–1779," *Records of the Amer. Catholic Hist. Soc. of Philadelphia*, LVI (Dec. 1945), 307–328 and succeeding issues.

CHAPTER III

European Diplomacy and Peace with Britain, 1778–1783

"You will notice that the English buy the peace more than they make it."   Vergennes, 1782.

AN UNWILLING PARTNER

THE SPANISH Court was deeply offended by France's decision to enter the war against England without first securing the consent of Spain. Charles III, whose injured pride would not permit him to move hastily, knew that the French were in urgent need of his navy; and he was in an excellent position to drive a hard bargain. In the end, and only after costly delays, Vergennes succeeded in satisfying Castilian honor; and Spain and France came to terms at Aranjuez (April 12, 1779), more than a year after the signing of the Franco-American alliance.

The provisions of the secret convention of Aranjuez need not detain us, except for one startling article. Charles III, who desired above all else to attach Gibraltar once more to Spanish soil, forced France to agree to fight until Britain yielded the coveted citadel. Since the French had already bound the United States not to make a separate peace, the Aranjuez agreement "chained" the Americans, without their knowing it, to the rock of Gibraltar.[1]

Spain's belated entrance into the war as an ally of the French did not mean that she became an ally of the Americans. The Spanish government not only entertained unfriendly sentiments toward the new republic, but flatly refused to recognize its independence. Yet Congress, in the hope of persuading Spain to lend money and enter into an alliance, decided to send an envoy to the Spanish Court. The man selected was John Jay, thirty-four year old scion of a distinguished New York family, and one of the ablest statesmen of his day.

Jay's mission was one long purgatory. He was never officially received during the two and one half years of his sojourn in Spain, from January, 1780, to May, 1782. His mail was opened and read;

[1] S. F. Bemis, *The Diplomacy of the American Revolution* (N.Y., 1935), pp. 84–86.

his letters to the foreign minister, Conde de Floridablanca, lay unanswered; he was put off with the most transparent excuses. The frigidity of the Spanish Court was determined with almost barometric precision by the success or failure of American arms. Jay reported that the news of the loss of Charleston to the British had an effect "as visible the next day as that of a bad night's frost on young leaves." In desperation Congress instructed him, in spite of his better judgment, to offer an abandonment of American claims to navigate the Mississippi in return for recognition and an alliance. Fortunately for the United States, the Spanish government was unable or unwilling to come to terms on this basis.[2]

As if all this were not enough, Jay became involved in serious financial embarrassments. His salary failed; his meager funds gave out. His attempts to wring money from the unsympathetic Spanish Court met with scant success, and he wrote despondently that there was "little corn in Egypt." Floridablanca, disgusted with the American envoy's constant begging, wrote of him: "His two chief points were: Spain, recognize our independence; Spain, give us more money." Jay finally succeeded in borrowing a small sum, and he did encourage the Spaniards to keep up their half-hearted assistance to the colonials. Beyond this, his mission resulted in little but a profound distrust of European courts and European diplomacy.[3]

BRITAIN AT BAY

Before the end of 1779 Britain was fighting with her back to the wall. For the first time since 1690 her naval supremacy in the English Channel was jeopardized, and she was faced with the grim prospect of invasion. At last an opportunity had come for the smaller maritime nations of Europe to rise up and assert their rights—rights which, in their eyes, the mistress of the seas had for generations haughtily ignored or flagrantly abused. Catherine II of Russia, secretly encouraged by Vergennes,[4] took the lead in organizing the Baltic nations into the Armed Neutrality of 1780. This group of "small navy" Powers enunciated certain advanced principles of international law which were designed to improve the position of neutrals in time of war and

[2] E. S. Corwin, *French Policy and the American Alliance of 1778* (Princeton, 1916), pp. 324–325.

[3] For the Spanish mission see Frank Monaghan, *John Jay* (N.Y., 1935), pp. 125–183.

[4] J. J. Meng, *The Comte de Vergennes* (Washington, 1932), p. 110. Vergennes appears to very good advantage in this monograph.

weaken the preponderant sea power of England.[5] Almost all the neutral trading nations of Europe, eager to discomfit and shackle the "tyrant of the seas," openly or tacitly espoused the cause of the Armed Neutrality. Although they did not formally declare war, they assumed a hostile and menacing attitude, thus rendering Britain's position more precarious.

It would be easy, however, to overestimate the influence of the Armed Neutrality as a military or naval force. John Adams spoke disparagingly of the organization as a "sublime bubble"; and Catherine II herself contemptuously referred to it as the "Armed Nullity." Nevertheless it was a real beginning in the direction of clarifying and making more tolerable the position of neutral carriers. These principles eventually took root, and many of them were at last formally recognized by the Powers in the Declaration of Paris of 1856. But of more immediate importance was the fact that the Armed Neutrality discouraged the British and inspirited their enemies. It was now Great Britain against almost the entire trading world.

Meanwhile the Dutch had been taking advantage of England's preoccupation to win from their rival a lucrative carrying trade. They also developed profitable new markets, particularly with the American rebels by way of the hitherto little known Dutch island of St. Eustatius. This Caribbean rock, only six miles long and three miles wide, quickly became the halfway house for an enormous volume of European trade with the United States, much of it contraband. During one thirteen-month period of the Revolution 3182 ships touched at St. Eustatius, including many of those sent out by Hortalez et Compagnie.

This state of affairs in the Caribbean, as well as Dutch trade with France in naval supplies, finally became intolerable to Britain; and in December, 1780, she found a pretext for declaring war on the Netherlands.[6] Admiral Rodney, in command of a powerful British squadron, descended upon St. Eustatius and captured it, together with one hun-

---

[5] Such as "free ships, free goods" (*i.e.*, immunity of noncontraband enemy goods from capture while on neutral ships); no paper blockades (a blockade to be binding must be effectively enforced); and a liberal interpretation of contraband. See Bemis, *Diplomacy of the American Revolution*, pp. 149–163.

[6] In August, 1780, Henry Laurens, newly appointed minister to the Netherlands, was captured by a British cruiser. He threw his papers into the sea; but since he did not use enough iron shot they were "hooked up." Among them was a tentative plan of a commercial treaty which was in no way binding upon the Netherlands government. This was used as the excuse for goading the Dutch into war. Francis Wharton, ed., *The Revolutionary Diplomatic Correspondence of the United States* (Washington, 1889), I, 579–580.

dred and thirty ships. The spoils of war, so he boasted to his wife, were "rich beyond comprehension." But he dallied so long with the plunder of St. Eustatius that the French Admiral de Grasse was able to slip away from the West Indies to Yorktown, there to deal Britain a stunning blow by helping to force the surrender of the strong army under Cornwallis (October 19, 1781).

MILITIA DIPLOMACY IN THE NETHERLANDS

The embittered relations between the Netherlands and England led Congress to hope that the Dutch, who were the bankers of Europe, might be induced to make a commercial treaty and grant desperately needed loans. With these objects in view the American agent, John Adams, who had been lingering in Paris, was sent to the Netherlands in the summer of 1780. Although a man of great ability, Adams was pompous, egotistical, and conspicuously lacking in tact. His departure improved the atmosphere in Paris, for he was jealous of the aged Franklin (whose harmless goings on with the French ladies seemed time-consuming and disgraceful), and he quarreled with Vergennes. On one occasion Adams flatly informed the latter: "The United States of America are a great and powerful people, whatever European statesmen may think of them."[7]

Adams' mission to the Netherlands lasted nearly two years. Although he was coldly received at first, he applied himself to his task with patience, resourcefulness, and a surprising amount of tact. But he encountered the utmost difficulty in persuading the canny Dutch bankers to lend money to the colonials. On one occasion he reported: "I can represent my situation in this affair of a loan, by no other figure than that of a man in the midst of the ocean negotiating for his life among a school of sharks."[8] In spite of his personal shortcomings, Adams played his cards extremely well and, aided by the growing embarrassments of Britain, delivered what he not overmodestly described as "the greatest blow that has been struck in the American cause, and the most decisive." First of all, he secured from the Netherlands, in April, 1782, a formal recognition of the independ-

[7] Shortly after reaching France, Adams wrote: "I have been these twenty years too sanguine; constantly sanguine, yet eternally right." He admitted that he was vain, but added, "Thank God I am so!" Franklin wrote of him: "I am persuaded . . . that he means well for his country, is always an honest man, often a wise one, but sometimes and in some things absolutely out of his senses." *Ibid.*, VI, 582 (Franklin to Livingston, July 22, 1783).

[8] C. F. Adams, ed., *The Works of John Adams* (Boston, 1852), VII, 588 (Adams to Livingston, May 16, 1782).

ence of the United States. Soon afterward he made the final arrangements for a substantial loan, the beginning of financial assistance that averted complete bankruptcy in America. Finally, on October 8, 1782, he concluded a treaty of amity and commerce, the second that the young republic succeeded in negotiating. Adams returned to Paris in an exultant mood: "The compliment of 'Monsieur, vous êtes le Washington de la négociation' [you are the Washington of negotiation] was repeated to me by more than one person. . . . A few of these compliments would kill Franklin if they should come to his ears." [9]

BRITAIN OPENS NEGOTIATIONS

Meanwhile British arms had been faring badly. The disaster at Yorktown led to the resignation of Lord North, the Prime Minister, whose ministry was succeeded, on March 22, 1782, by that of the Whig Marquis of Rockingham. Public opinion in England, never enthusiastic about the war in America, was becoming increasingly vocal in demanding a cessation of hostilities with the colonies. In April, 1782, Lord Shelburne, who then had charge of colonial affairs, sent to France a retired Scotch trader, Richard Oswald, to enter into conversations with Franklin. From the standpoint of experience and temperament Oswald was fully as much a militia diplomat as Silas Deane. His chief qualifications for the task seem to have been an acquaintanceship with Franklin and some first-hand knowledge of the colonies, derived from an earlier residence in Virginia and from rather extensive commercial operations, including the slave trade. With remarkable candor Oswald admitted to Franklin that Britain had become "foolishly involved in four wars," and that her financial condition was such that peace was "absolutely necessary." The shrewd American at once perceived that here was a man after his own heart. Among other things Franklin suggested to Oswald that Britain cede Canada to the United States in order to salve the bitterness created by the war and to prevent future friction—a startling proposal when one considers the costly American failure to conquer Canada in 1775. Nevertheless, the British emissary was attracted by the idea, and he promised to present it to the Ministry upon his return to England. "We parted exceedingly good friends," wrote Franklin.

Oswald was as good as his word. He urged Franklin's proposal regarding Canada upon the Ministry with considerable warmth. Neither

[9] Wharton, *Revolutionary Diplomatic Correspondence*, I, 510 (a private journal of Adams).

Lord Rockingham nor Lord Shelburne, he reported, was "very averse to it," though Mr. Fox appeared to be "startled at the proposition." Fox, as Foreign Secretary, felt that negotiations with the Americans were within his province rather than within that of his rival, Lord Shelburne. The Cabinet finally decided to send an additional negotiator to Paris, and Fox appointed the young and ambitious Thomas Grenville, who was to represent him in all matters relating to a general peace. Oswald was to continue the negotiations for a settlement with the Americans. The upshot was that the two men, representing different and conflicting interests, worked at cross-purposes. The employment of such inexperienced and mediocre agents is in part explained by the fact that they were instructed to report their every movement to London. "We can consider ourselves," one of them wrote, "as little more than pens in the hands of the government at home. . . ."

JAY FIGHTS THE DEVIL WITH FIRE

Franklin now had the negotiations rather well in hand. But as he was suffering from various diseases of old age, he instructed Jay, who was still lingering impotently in Spain, to come on to Paris. When Jay shook the dust of Spain from his boots, he did not shake the violent prejudice he had developed against the Spaniards, and also against the French, who in his opinion were partly responsible for his misfortunes. After a long encounter with "bad roads, fleas, and bugs," he arrived in Paris (June, 1782) in a most suspicious frame of mind. There he found the situation exceedingly complex. The combined Spanish and French forces were making desperate but vain efforts to capture the rock of Gibraltar. And the longer the fortress resisted the more insistent Spain became. Vergennes, who was disturbed by his ill success in delivering Gibraltar, felt under strong obligations to support the demands of Spain for the area between the Alleghenies and the Mississippi—a region which the Americans regarded as peculiarly their own. Nevertheless he appears to have desired an independent, but not a powerful, America.[10] As John Adams aptly put it, Vergennes "means to keep us down if he can," to hold "his hand under our chin to prevent us from drowning but not to lift our heads out of water."

[10] As early as 1778 Vergennes had written: "We ask independence only for the thirteen states of America. . . . We do not desire that a new republic shall arise which shall become the exclusive mistress of this immense continent. . . ." Henri Doniol, *Histoire de la Participation de la France à l'Établissement des États-Unis d'Amérique* (Paris, 1888), III, 561 (Vergennes to Montmorin, Oct. 30, 1778).

Jay's distrust was further aroused when Vergennes' secretary, Rayneval, made the informal proposal that, primarily in the interests of Spain, the United States coop itself up east of the Alleghenies. The American envoy naturally concluded, and rightly so, that this was also the view of Vergennes. A short time later Jay learned that Rayneval had surreptitiously left Paris for London, the enemy's capital, after having taken elaborate precautions to keep his destination a secret. This incident, coming as the climax to a number of suspicious developments, convinced Jay that Vergennes was about to sacrifice American interests and, through clandestine negotiations with Britain, limit the United States to the area east of the Alleghenies.

Thoroughly aroused, Jay communicated these fears to the venerable Franklin, who was disposed to make light of them. Rather than sit supinely and see his country's interests betrayed, Jay decided, on his own responsibility and unknown to his colleague, to forestall the apparent treachery of the French by opening separate negotiations with Britain. On September 11, 1782, therefore, he sent a special emissary to London. Lord Shelburne, who had become Prime Minister on July 2, was delighted with the prospect of driving a wedge between the allies; and negotiations were soon opened with Jay.

Shortly after the Rayneval incident, the stiff-necked Adams arrived in Paris fresh from his triumphs in the Netherlands. He heartily approved of what Jay had done and was delighted to note that "no wrestler was ever so completely thrown upon his back as the Count de Vergennes." Franklin protested mildly against separate action, but finding himself outvoted by his younger and more energetic colleagues, and realizing that the best results could be obtained only through harmonious action, acquiesced in their course. His rather feeble protests, however, were probably largely for the sake of appearances; for there were earlier instances in the negotiations when Franklin had definitely foreshadowed Jay's independent course.[11] Finally, after protracted interchanges with Oswald, the American commissioners signed the preliminary treaty of peace with Great Britain, November 30, 1782.

THE ETHICS OF A SEPARATE PEACE

The separate negotiations of Jay and his colleagues did violence to the spirit, though not to the strict letter, of the treaty of alliance with France. Congress, moreover, had definitely instructed its envoys to

[11] Bemis, *Diplomacy of the American Revolution*, pp. 204, 208–209.

enter into the "most candid and confidential" relations with the French and to undertake no steps in the negotiations for peace without their "knowledge and concurrence." How can Jay's action be explained, much less justified?

It must be borne in mind, first of all, that this was before the laying of the Atlantic cable. The ambassador of today describes telegraphically the changing scene and receives new instructions to meet new exigencies. Jay could have written home; but months would have elapsed before a reply could have been received—and delay might have proved disastrous. Besides, Jay had no confidence in Congress. He knew that Vergennes, acting through the French minister in Philadelphia, had used his influence with that body to shape the personnel of the American peace commission, and to see that its members were specifically instructed to do nothing without the permission of their French allies. Adams shared Jay's feelings regarding these "tainted" instructions:

Congress surrendered their own sovereignty into the hands of a French minister. Blush! blush! ye guilty records! blush and perish! It is glory to have broken such infamous orders. Infamous, I say, for so they will be to all posterity. How can such a stain be washed out? Can we cast a veil over it and forget it? [12]

The documents now available reveal that Jay's suspicions of Vergennes, who himself was negotiating separately, were far from groundless. The French foreign minister may not have been seeking deliberately to betray the United States, but he certainly was trying to discharge his obligations to Spain at the expense of the Americans, and keep the young republic so weak that it would remain in French leading strings. Indeed, some have argued that Vergennes' double-dealing released the United States from any moral obligation to adhere strictly to the spirit of the alliance. Certainly, from the viewpoint of American interests, Jay would have been censurable if he had not acted as he did, for it seems clear that by an independent course he secured more advantageous terms than otherwise would have been possible.[13] As for the French alliance, Jay and his colleagues

[12] *Works of John Adams*, III, 359 (diary entry, Feb. 18, 1783). Some thirty years later Gouverneur Morris declared, "Jay, what a set of d——d scoundrels we had in that second Congress." "Yes," replied Jay, "that we had. . . ." George Pellew, *John Jay* (Boston, 1890), p. 157.

[13] See S. F. Bemis, "The Rayneval Memoranda of 1782," *Proceedings of the American Antiquarian Society*, XLVII (1937), 15–92.

did not, strictly speaking, make a separate peace. They merely negotiated and signed certain preliminary articles that were specifically
not to take effect until France had come to terms with England.

VERGENNES APPEARS ANNOYED

At this point the question naturally arises: What was the attitude
of Vergennes during these critical weeks? With a small army of spies
at his command, he must have known what the American commissioners were doing; yet he was silent. Indeed, the day before the
signing of the preliminary articles the Americans notified Vergennes
of their intention; and if he had been violently opposed to separate
action he could have lodged a strong protest at once. The explanation
of this riddle is that France, despite costly efforts, was finding it impossible to deliver Gibraltar to Spain, and Vergennes was faced with
the extremely disagreeable prospect of fighting indefinitely to discharge his obligations. The apparent defection of the United States,
with the consequent strengthening of Britain, was a strong argument
in favor of Spain's making peace and accepting something else in lieu
of Gibraltar. In brief, the independent action of Jay and his colleagues
actually helped Vergennes out of a serious predicament. Contrary to
a prevalent misconception, he seems to have been more pleased than
otherwise,[14] and he complimented the Americans on the excellence of
their terms.

It was only natural, however, that Vergennes should have felt
some resentment at the failure of the American envoys to consult
him. Two weeks after the separate articles had been signed (the delay
suggests that he could not have been greatly disturbed), he sent a
note of remonstrance to Franklin which was not nearly so strongly
worded as might have been expected. This would indicate that the
protest was lodged largely for the sake of form and probably with the
object of making the shamefaced Americans more subservient to
French influence. Vergennes' rebuke read in part:

I am at a loss, sir, to explain your conduct and that of your colleagues on
this occasion. You have concluded your preliminary articles without any
communication between us. . . . You are about to hold out a certain hope
of peace to America without even informing yourself on the state of the
negociation on our part.

You are wise and discreet, sir; you perfectly understand what is due to

[14] Bemis, *Diplomacy of the American Revolution*, pp. 239–241.

propriety; you have all your life performed your duties. I pray you to consider how you propose to fulfill those which are due to the King? [15]

Franklin, master diplomatist and facile penman, was called upon by his embarrassed colleagues to make the necessary explanations and apologies. The venerable philosopher truthfully pointed out in his reply that the Americans had not really made a separate peace at all but had merely agreed upon the preliminary articles of peace. He admitted, however, that in failing to consult with Vergennes they had been guilty of neglecting a point of *bienséance* (propriety), but not from "want of respect to the King, whom we all love and honor." Franklin hoped that this unhappy incident would cause no break in the ranks of the allies, for if this should happen all their common expenditure of blood and treasure would probably be for naught. Then came a touch, the cleverest of all, which must have caused Vergennes to smile at the craftsmanship of a fellow artist: "*The English, I just now learn, flatter themselves they have already divided us. I hope this little misunderstanding will therefore be kept a secret, and that they will find themselves totally mistaken.*" [16] With surprising self-assurance, and in the same letter, Franklin suggested the desirability of a further loan. Incredible though it may seem, the bankrupt French government, which the Americans had just offended, advanced another 6,000,000 livres. It could not afford, as Franklin slyly pointed out, to let the already costly fire die out for lack of fuel.

The American Birth Certificate

The terms of the final treaty, signed on September 3, 1783, with the full permission of France, were virtually the same as those of the preliminary articles. Britain recognized the complete independence of the United States and granted exceedingly liberal boundaries. The new republic was to stretch magnificently westward to the Mississippi, with the northern limits roughly what they are now. The southern boundary was to be the frontier of Spanish East and West Florida, though the Americans had made no real effort to conquer the vast area south of the Ohio. As for the region north of that river, it is true that the intrepid Virginian, George Rogers Clark, had seized the British posts in the southwestern part, and had established military control over a large portion of the entire area. But it is still disputed whether this

[15] Wharton, *Revolutionary Diplomatic Correspondence*, VI, 140 (Vergennes to Franklin, Dec. 15, 1782).

[16] *Ibid.*, 144 (Franklin to Vergennes, Dec. 17, 1782). Italics Franklin's.

situation was fully known to the negotiators, and whether it had any important bearing on the final disposition of the territory.[17]

The third article of the treaty related to the North Atlantic fisheries. The British contended that they should be reserved for the Canadians, since the United States was no longer a part of the empire. But these fisheries had for generations been "the gold mines of New England," and were not to be lightly yielded. Jay and Franklin might have given in; but John Adams, stanch New Englander, argued that the fisheries had been jointly acquired and that the Americans should retain their rights even after the partnership had been dissolved. At a critical point in the discussions, he brought his oratorical powers into full play:

When God Almighty made the banks of Newfoundland, at three hundred leagues distance from the people of America, and at six hundred leagues distance from those of France and England, did he not give as good a right to the former as to the latter? If Heaven in the creation gave a right, it is ours at least as much as yours. If occupation, use, and possession give a right, we have it as clearly as you. If war, and blood, and treasure give a right, ours is as good as yours.[18]

Adams carried the day and secured for his countrymen all the privileges of catching fish that were enjoyed by British subjects, though certain restrictions were placed on drying and curing.[19] But the British negotiators succeeded in inserting certain ambiguities in the treaty ("liberty" was substituted for "right" in two places) that helped lay the foundations for the most persistent international controversy in United States history.

The fourth article referred to the debts which a considerable number of Americans had owed British merchants when the Revolution broke out. Many of these colonials both hoped and believed that independence would result in a cancellation of prewar liabilities—an attitude that caused the Loyalists to sneer, "Liberty or debt." But the British creditors, not desiring to lose what they claimed was approximately £5,000,000, insisted upon writing certain safeguards into the treaty. After prolonged wrangling, during which Adams burst out

[17] Professor Bemis (*Diplomacy of the American Revolution*, p. 219 n.) finds no evidence that Clark's conquest played an important part in the negotiations. The opposite view is fully presented by J. A. James, *Oliver Pollock* (N.Y., 1937), pp. 242–248.

[18] *Works of John Adams*, III, 333–334 (Nov. 29, 1782).

[19] Americans were forbidden to dry fish on the coasts of Newfoundland, but they could use the unsettled parts of Nova Scotia, the Magdalen Islands, and Labrador.

that he had "no notion of cheating anybody," it was finally agreed that British merchants should "meet with no lawful impediment" in seeking to recover their bona fide debts. This article was of great importance in enlisting the support of the powerful British commercial class on the side of what was otherwise a very unpopular treaty.

The article that dealt with the Loyalists in America had proved to be a well-nigh insuperable stumbling block. Tens of thousands of these luckless persons, having remained loyal to their sovereign, had suffered confiscations, personal abuse, and finally exile. Perhaps as many as 80,000 of them had been driven from the United States. The British government naturally felt that it would be guilty of the basest ingratitude if it failed to secure restitution and compensation for those who had lost their all in support of the crown. But so ruthless had been the warfare between the Loyalists and their neighbors that the Americans would listen to no scheme for welcoming them back into their respective communities. Even the benign Franklin exclaimed: "Your ministers require that we should receive again into our bosom those who have been our bitterest enemies, and restore their properties who have destroyed ours; and this while the wounds they have given us are still bleeding!" [20]

At length, and only after a series of heated discussions, it was agreed that persecutions should cease, and that Congress would "earnestly recommend" to the states that they restore property taken from the Loyalists. But in view of the inflamed state of mind in America, the peace commissioners, British as well as American, must have foreseen that the recommendation would be ignored. Yet this empty formula was necessary to save the face of the British government. Without it peace probably could not have been made.

SHELBURNE LOOKS TO THE FUTURE

It is important to remember that the treaty with the United States was but a part of the general settlement that England made with her enemies. The preliminary articles of peace that had been drawn up with Spain, France, and the United States were all signed as definitive treaties on September 3, 1783. On the whole, and considering the odds against her, Britain emerged from these settlements remarkably well. The one exception was the American treaty, which was so extraordinarily generous that the preliminary articles evoked an out-

[20] Wharton, *Revolutionary Diplomatic Correspondence*, VI, 80 (Franklin to Oswald, Nov. 26, 1782).

burst of condemnation in England. There was, in fact, a widespread feeling that Britain's greatness was at an end. One Englishman wrote an open letter to Lord Shelburne urging him not to "submit to such a disgraceful ruin as American independence" until the "Tower of London be taken sword in hand." The articles concerning the Loyalists were denounced with great bitterness by those who regarded the arrangement as a base subterfuge. Lord North, now a member of the opposition, cried in Parliament: "Never was the honour of a nation so grossly abused as in the desertion of those men. . . . Nothing can excuse our not having insisted on a stipulation in their favour. . . ." [21] Under the storm of criticism the ministry of Lord Shelburne fell; and that of his successor concluded the definitive peace.

In America, public opinion was not altogether enthusiastic about the treaty. Considerable grumbling was heard about the liberal treatment of the Loyalists, the failure of the American negotiators to co-operate fully with the French, and the absence of an article guaranteeing a reopening of trade with the British West Indies. But the great majority of Americans seem to have been pleased with the settlement and with the success of their militia diplomats in dealing with the wiles of European diplomacy. And well they might have been; for judging by the terms of the treaty the United States had ground the mother country into the very dust. This, however, was far from being the case. Large and well-equipped British armies still held strategic points in America; and if England had not been war-weary and occupied elsewhere with her European foes, she might have crushed the disintegrating colonial armies. The highly advantageous terms of the treaty bore so little relation to the military situation in America as to lead to Vergennes' classic exclamation: "You will notice that the English buy the peace more than they make it. Their concessions, in fact, as much as to the boundaries as to the fisheries and the loyalists, exceed all that I should have thought possible." [22]

How can we account for this incongruous generosity? In the first place, Lord Shelburne had long been sympathetically disposed toward the colonials. He was eager to close the bloody chasm and avert future friction, particularly over the inevitable westward expansion of the American republic. He also desired to establish the basis for pleasant and profitable commercial relationships, and to wean the United States away from French postwar influence. Yet it should not be for-

[21] *Parliamentary History of England*, XXIII, 453 (Feb. 17, 1783).

[22] Wharton, *Revolutionary Diplomatic Correspondence*, VI, 107 (Vergennes to Rayneval, Dec. 4, 1782).

gotten that Lord Shelburne, despite his sympathy for America, was a Briton, stanchly upholding the interests of his country. The Americans had to fight with skill and persistence for every important concession they received.

This, however, is not the whole story. At the time when Jay opened separate negotiations, Great Britain was in desperate straits. Here was an opportunity for her to improve her position by enticing America from the ranks of the enemy. It is unthinkable that the colonials would have received such generous terms if Britain had not been at war with three European Powers. Again, Europe's distresses spelled America's successes. Without them the alliance would never have been made; without them independence could hardly have been won; without them the Americans would never have secured such highly advantageous terms of peace.

BIBLIOGRAPHICAL NOTE

The best book on this subject is S. F. Bemis, *The Diplomacy of the American Revolution* (N.Y., 1935), pp. 70–256. E. S. Corwin's older work, *French Policy and the American Alliance of 1778* (Princeton, 1916), Chs. VIII to XVI, is still valuable. A reasonably detailed sketch of the negotiations, by J. B. Scott, appears in S. F. Bemis, ed., *The American Secretaries of State and their Diplomacy* (N.Y., 1927), I, 24–111. Useful special studies are J. B. Scott, ed., *The Armed Neutralities of 1780 and 1800* (N.Y., 1918); P. C. Phillips, *The West in the Diplomacy of the American Revolution* (Urbana, Ill., 1913); T. P. Abernethy *Western Lands and the American Revolution* (N.Y., 1937), especially Ch. XXI; and Friedrich Edler, *The Dutch Republic and the American Revolution* (Baltimore, 1911). The standard biography of Jay is Frank Monaghan, *John Jay* (N.Y., 1935), which has revealing chapters on the Spanish mission and Paris negotiation. The best biographies of the other two leading American negotiators are Gilbert Chinard, *Honest John Adams* (Boston, 1933), and Carl Van Doren, *Benjamin Franklin* (N.Y., 1938). Articles of special significance are J. F. Jameson, "St. Eustatius in the American Revolution," *Amer. Hist. Rev.*, VIII (1903), 683–708; and Eunice Wead, "British Public Opinion of the Peace with America, 1782," *ibid.*, XXXIV (1929), 513–531. Further references: see footnotes of this chapter and Bemis and Griffin, *Guide*, pp. 3–48.

RECENT REFERENCES. The books by Meng and Darling (Chs. III–IV), cited under Recent References, p. 22, provide considerable justification for Jay's independent action. Territorial problems of the peace are discussed in N. V. Russell, *The British Régime in Michigan and the Old Northwest, 1760–1796* (Northfield, Minn., 1939), Ch. IX. The author accepts the theses that Clark "won" the Northwest and that Shelburne's generosity had much to do with the final terms.

CHAPTER IV

Foreign Affairs under the Articles of Confederation

"I am uneasy and apprehensive; more so than during the war."
John Jay, 1786.

THE WORLD'S UGLY DUCKLING

WHEN LINCOLN asserted at Gettysburg that the fathers had "brought forth a new nation" in 1776, his patriotic fervor outran his historical accuracy. He might better have said that those fathers had brought forth a litter of small nations. For during the six troubled years from the close of the Revolution to the establishment of the present government in 1789, the United States consisted of thirteen separate sovereignties each going its own way. "United" was merely a meaningless and ironical adjective. In fact, it was only with the most alarming difficulty that Congress was able to assemble a quorum to ratify the treaty ending the war. With apathy, bankruptcy, and anarchy threatening an impotent central government at home, the United States could not, and in fact did not, command respect abroad.

Most Europeans did not bother their heads about the new infant in the family of nations; or, if they did, their opinions were obscured by ignorance. Ministers representing the United States abroad had to go to considerable pains to explain that Americans were white and that they did not adorn themselves like savages. As Captain Snow testified in 1788: "I, sir, since the war, have had commerce with six different nations of the globe . . . and . . . I find this country held in the same light, by foreign nations, as a well-behaved negro is in a gentleman's family." [1]

Such indifference, however, was not shared by the monarchs of Europe. If the huge American experiment in democracy should be successful, the shortsighted sovereigns of France and Spain would have created a veritable Frankenstein monster. Groaning and oppressed subjects, pointing to the promised land of liberty and self-government, might well demand the same blessings for themselves.

[1] Jonathan Elliot, ed., *The Debates in the Several State Conventions on the Adoption of the Federal Constitution* (2nd ed., Phila., 1891), II, 34 (Jan. 17, 1788).

The ruling classes of the Old World were anxious, therefore, that the American experiment should fail. This attitude continued to be a basic factor in the relations between the United States and Europe far into the nineteenth century.

But jealousy was not the only motive present. The monarchs of Europe also cast greedy eyes upon the chaotic United States, and waited for the seemingly inevitable breakup. When that happened they would perhaps gather in the most desirable pieces. Or, failing a complete collapse, the Powers might use the helpless republic as a makeweight in their plans for aggrandizement.[2]

THE REBELLIOUS COLONIES ARE REBUFFED

Now that hostilities had ceased, many Americans expected "sweet reconciliation" with the motherland, and the restoration of commercial privileges and other advantages. But England was slow to forget that the Americans had raised the standard of rebellion; that they had called in foreign allies; that they had wrecked the British Empire; and that they had expelled thousands of His Majesty's most loyal subjects. Then, forsaking the role of rebels for that of suppliants, the Americans were expecting and even clamoring for the fatted calf. This was asking too much of human nature.

In 1785 John Adams was sent to England as the first minister of the United States. The London *Public Advertiser* was scandalized:

An Ambassador from America! Good heavens what a sound!—The Gazette surely never announced anything so extraordinary before. . . . This will be such a phenomenon in the Corps Diplomatique that 'tis hard to say which can excite indignation most, the insolence of those who appoint the Character, or the meanness of those who receive it.[3]

Adams soon discovered that the "popular pulse seems to beat high against America." Both he and Jefferson, who visited England about the same time, found ample evidence of a malicious campaign to poison public opinion against the United States.

---

[2] This is precisely what John Adams had feared at Paris, for his diary relates: " 'You are afraid,' says Mr. Oswald to-day, 'of being made the tools of the powers of Europe.' 'Indeed I am,' says I. 'What powers?' said he. 'All of them,' said I. 'It is obvious that all the powers of Europe will be continually manoeuvring with us, to work us into their real or imaginary balances of power. They will all wish to make of us a makeweight candle. . . . But I think it ought to be our rule not to meddle. . . .' " C. F. Adams, ed., *The Works of John Adams* (Boston, 1865), III, 316 (Nov. 18, 1782).

[3] Quoted in Gilbert Chinard, *Honest John Adams* (Boston, 1933), p. 195.

Adams, like other diplomats, was presented to George III, and made his three bows. The erstwhile rebel, who had been on the king's list of those to whom no mercy was to be shown, comported himself well and delivered a surprisingly gracious speech, to which His Majesty, not to be outdone, replied in kind. The noteworthy feature of this incident is not that both principals made felicitous remarks, but that any American minister should have been received so soon after the close of hostilities.

Despite this auspicious start, Adams' three years at the Court of St. James's were exceedingly trying. He was treated with a "dry decency and cold civility which appears to have been the premeditated plan from the beginning." He would be frozen out of conferences with dead silence, and he found it impossible to obtain an answer "from the ministry to any one demand, proposal, or inquiry." "In short, sir," he complained to John Jay late in 1785, "I am like to be as insignificant here as you can imagine." [4]

Even more vexatious was England's refusal to return the compliment and accredit a minister to the United States. The British Foreign Secretary rather cruelly suggested that if he sent one representative he would have to send thirteen. But America, though so weak as to be contemptible, was too important to be ignored; so Downing Street kept an eye on developments through unofficial observers and consuls.

The Bitter Fruits of Independence

One of the most exasperating controversies to embitter Anglo-American relations during these years arose over commerce. Before the war most of the colonial trade had naturally been with the mother country, and when hostilities came to a close American commerce just as naturally sought the old and familiar channels. But in the absence of a commercial treaty granting reciprocal privileges, the British government was at liberty to impose arbitrary and capricious regulations. Such a situation was highly unsettling to business; and the distressed American merchants talked of forcing a pact from England by resorting to retaliatory legislation. But the British laughed in their faces. It was perfectly clear, as the event proved, that the thirteen sovereign states could not unite on any such program. Lord Sheffield, whose famous pamphlet opposing commercial concessions to the United States profoundly influenced his countrymen, confidently asserted: "It will not be an easy matter to bring the American states to act as a nation.

[4] *Works of John Adams*, VIII, 355 (Adams to Jay, Dec. 3, 1785).

They are not to be feared as such by us. . . . We might as well dread the effects of combinations among the German as among the American states. . . ." [5]

England naturally had no desire to negotiate a commercial treaty with a government that was too weak to force the thirteen constituent states to observe it. And why should the British tie their hands with such an instrument when, without one, they were reaping all the advantages they desired? Americans were again buying English goods because of lifelong habits; because of a common heritage of race, language, custom, and law; and because British merchants were willing to extend long-term credits. By 1789 England's trade with America was actually greater than it had been before the war.

The Americans, on the other hand, were learning the disagreeable lesson that they could not have their cake and eat it too. Now that they had fulfilled their desire to shake off the duties and responsibilities of the British connection, they were confidently expecting to continue the privileges and profits that had formerly been theirs, particularly the once lucrative trade with the British West Indies. But the British naturally chose to treat the United States as the foreign nation it had so ardently desired to become, and they sought to strengthen the empire by reserving its benefits for those colonies, such as Canada, that had remained loyal. Certain English liberals, notably Lord Shelburne, felt that in the long run England would profit most by making concessions to the Americans and building up their good will; but powerful and selfish mercantile interests thwarted all effective moves in this direction.[6] Although the Americans succeeded in developing an illicit trade of considerable proportions with the British colonies, notably the West Indies, the whole situation was fruitful of ill will and misunderstanding.[7]

[5] Quoted in S. F. Bemis, "John Jay," in S. F. Bemis, ed., *The American Secretaries of State and their Diplomacy* (N.Y., 1927), I, 223–224. Washington confessed: ". . . It would be idle to think of making commercial regulations on our part. One State passes a prohibitory law respecting some article, another State opens wide the avenue for its admission. One Assembly makes a system, another Assembly unmakes it." W. C. Ford, ed., *Writings of George Washington* (N.Y., 1891), XI, 254 (Washington to Lafayette, April 28, 1788).

[6] On Anglo-American trade see S. F. Bemis, *Jay's Treaty* (N.Y., 1923), pp. 30–36.

[7] Symptomatic of embittered feeling was a broadside printed as an "extra" by the *Observer* and bearing the captions, "Great Britain is Endeavoring to Ruin and Impoverish the Country" and "Exertion or Ruin." Massachusetts Broadsides, File 42, Library of Congress (April 15, 1785). It was widely held in America that Great Britain and France had a secret agreement to throttle American trade. V. G. Setser, *The Commercial Reciprocity Policy of the United States, 1774–1829* (Phila., 1937), p. 54.

TREATY VIOLATIONS AND COUNTERVIOLATIONS

Another serious stumbling block in Anglo-American relations was the peace treaty of 1783. This instrument belied its name, for it was so far from being a peace pact that nearly every one of its major provisions led to years of bitter wrangling. One reason that British officials repeatedly gave for their unwillingness to make a commercial agreement was the failure of the United States to carry out the treaty that had ended the war. The peace of 1783 solemnly stipulated that British creditors should meet with "no lawful impediment" in attempting to collect what was owed them. The impotent Congress did what it could to execute this article; but the state legislatures and courts openly flouted the plain provisions of the treaty. Public opinion in Virginia was particularly strong against payment. Everywhere George Mason heard men say, "If we are now to pay the debts due to British merchants, what have we been fighting for all this while?" [8] Responding to such sentiment, the Virginia legislature enacted laws deliberately designed to prevent the collection of debts. One victim of such legislation disdainfully remarked, with more truth than tact, that some of the members were voting to retain the very shirts on their backs. He was brought before that august body and forced to kneel and apologize. As he arose he dusted off his knees and muttered with evident double meaning, "Upon my word, a domned dirty house it is indeed!"

More widely and flagrantly violated was the article in the treaty regarding the Loyalists. It provided that the persecution of these unfortunates was to cease, and that Congress was to *recommend* to the states the restoration of Loyalist property. The second part of this obligation was quickly discharged, for the recommendation to the states was duly made, though widely disregarded. But the first part of the obligation was deliberately violated. Seven years of Loyalist burning, killing, and inciting to Indian massacre had aroused an incredible amount of ill will. In May, 1783, the Massachusetts *Chronicle* reflected a common sentiment:

As Hannibal swore never to be at peace with the Romans, so let every Whig swear . . . by the shades of departed friends who have fallen in battle, by the ghosts of those of our brethren who have been destroyed on board of prison-ships and in loathsome dungeons, never to be at peace with

[8] Frank Monaghan, *John Jay* (N.Y., 1935), p. 253. These debts were estimated at from two to five million pounds.

those fiends . . . whose thefts, murders, and treasons have filled the cup of woe. . . .[9]

So, in plain violation of the treaty, proscriptions and even lynchings of the Loyalists continued during the months after the close of hostilities.

REASONS AND PRETEXTS

The Americans, for their part, had good reason to accuse the British of having violated the treaty. In spite of clear stipulations to the contrary, departing British armies had carried away some 3000 Negro slaves, whose owners clamored for indemnification. Far more serious

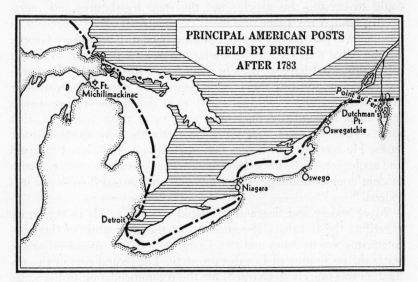

PRINCIPAL AMERICAN POSTS
HELD BY BRITISH
AFTER 1783

was the refusal of the British to turn over to the Americans a long chain of military and trading posts, stretching from Lake Champlain to Lake Superior within the river-and-lake boundary of the United States, despite the treaty provision for evacuation "with all convenient speed." The Canadians, who felt that their interests had been seriously neglected in the matter of the fisheries and boundaries, insisted that relinquishment of the posts would dislocate their immensely profitable fur trade and antagonize their Indian wards. They therefore sought to have the British occupation continued until such time as they could satisfactorily withdraw their property and reorganize their business.

[9] Quoted in J. B. McMaster, *A History of the People of the United States* (N.Y., 1893), I, 116.

On April 8, 1784, the Secretary of State for Home Affairs, responding to such pressure and seeking to prevent a bloody Indian uprising, ordered the posts to be held. Ironically enough, this order was issued the day before George III officially proclaimed ratification of the treaty of peace and solemnly enjoined his subjects to observe it.[10]

The saying goes that every man has two reasons for what he does—the real one and a good one. When the British decided to retain the posts in the interests of the Canadian fur traders and their red allies, they sought a plausible pretext to give to the world. They were not long in finding one. The Americans, as we have seen, were not faithfully carrying out the terms of the treaty regarding debts and Loyalists. So, alleging prior violations, the British announced that they would hold the posts until the debts were paid. Thus an impasse was reached. And it was not as a false prophet that John Jay, Secretary for Foreign Affairs of the Continental Congress, declared: "They may hold the posts, but they will hold them as pledges of enmity; and the time must and will come when the seeds of discontent, resentment, and hatred, which such measures always sow, will produce very bitter fruit." [11]

As time wore on Jay began to develop considerable sympathy for the British point of view regarding the posts. He was frank to confess that there had not been a single day since the ratification of the treaty on which it had "not been violated . . . by one or other of the states." With inexcusable indiscretion he revealed these opinions to the British consul at New York, Sir John Temple, with whom he was on terms of social intimacy, and the latter in turn hastened to relay this surprising information to the home government.[12] It is no small wonder that the British were adamant in their refusal to evacuate the posts when they knew that the American Secretary for Foreign Affairs believed that there was considerable justice in their contention.

There was also another serious problem on the northern frontier. Vermont, then an independent entity, had not been admitted to the Union because of boundary disputes with the neighboring states. The people of this area were vitally in need of the St. Lawrence outlet to the sea, and a considerable body of them, led by the slippery Allen

[10] S. F. Bemis, "John Jay," in Bemis, *American Secretaries of State*, I, 227.

[11] H. P. Johnston, ed., *The Correspondence and Public Papers of John Jay* (N.Y., 1891), III, 166 (Jay to Adams, Sept. 6, 1785). Until 1781, as has been noted, Congress directed foreign affairs through committees. In that year it established a Department of Foreign Affairs. Robert Livingston served as Secretary from 1781 to 1783, when he was succeeded by John Jay, whose office expired when the Department of State was created in 1789.

[12] Bemis, *Jay's Treaty*, p. 207.

brothers, was showing much interest in British overtures looking toward reunion with the mother country. No one could then tell whether Vermont would gravitate into the arms of Great Britain or the United States.

THE SPANISH DIKE

Relations with Spain were no less embittered than those with England. The Spanish Court had never been friendly to the rebel republic, and it felt even more ill-disposed when the United States snatched the great trans-Allegheny region from its grasp. The situation was further complicated by the development of a boundary dispute and, much more important, by friction over the navigation of the Mississippi River.

The definitive treaty of 1783 with Great Britain stipulated that the southwestern boundary of the United States should begin where the 31st parallel intersects the Mississippi River. Yet when West Florida had been in British hands (1763 to 1783) its northern boundary had not been the 31st parallel but the line cutting across the mouth of the Yazoo River, more than one hundred miles farther north.[13] Spain therefore refused to be bound by the line of the 31st parallel, and in addition claimed the area to the Ohio and Tennessee Rivers, by virtue of successful military operations against the British in the recent war. Thus a large and valuable part of the Old Southwest became involved in a twelve-year dispute between the Spaniards and the Americans. Within that region which the United States claimed as its own, the Spanish flag floated over Natchez and other posts, just as the British flag waved over American soil in the North. To strengthen her position Spain played a deep game of intrigue with the powerful Indian tribes of the Southwest, providing them with equipment for murderous forays against the American settlers, just as the British in the North were making more secure their hold on the posts by similar tactics. This common policy enabled Spain and England, through their posts and the influence which extended from them to the Indians, to exercise virtual control over more than one half of the territorial domain of the United States.[14]

---

[13] A separate article attached to the preliminary peace of 1782 (but not the final peace) stipulated that if England recovered West Florida at the end of the war, the northern boundary of that area would cut across the mouth of the Yazoo. This provision never became effective, primarily because Spain retained the Floridas.

[14] S. F. Bemis, "Thomas Jefferson," in Bemis, *American Secretaries of State*, II, 14.

Even more ominous was the dispute with Spain over the free navigation of the Mississippi. By 1785 some 50,000 adventuresome pioneers had trekked over the Alleghenies and had settled on the rich lands of what are now Tennessee and Kentucky. The cost of transporting their bulky agricultural produce over the mountains was prohibitively high. But nature had placed at their very

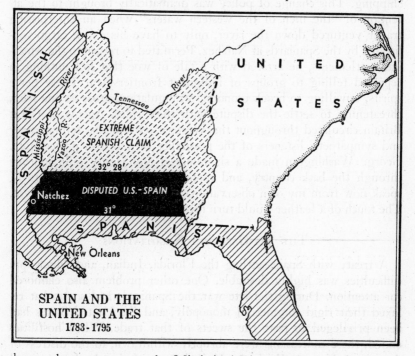

SPAIN AND THE
UNITED STATES
1783-1795

doors a huge waterway, the Mississippi River, which was capable of bearing their grain and tobacco inexpensively to ocean-going ships. Unfortunately for these settlers, the mouth of this stream was in the hands of the jealous and hostile Spaniard, who was determined to protect his own possessions from conquest by closing the river and damming up the American West. Such an eventuality the frontiersmen could not contemplate with equanimity. As John Jay had noted in 1780:

. . . The Americans, almost to a man, believed that God Almighty had made that river a highway for the people of the upper country to go to the sea by . . . [The] inhabitants would not readily be convinced of the justice of being obliged . . . to transport both over rugged mountains and through an immense wilderness, to and from the sea, when they daily saw a fine river flowing before their doors, and offering to save them all that trouble and expense, and that without injury to Spain.[15]

The controversy came to a head in 1784, when Spain announced that henceforth the Mississippi outlet would be closed to American shipping. This change of policy was dramatically brought to the attention of "the men of the western waters" when an enterprising trader ventured down the river, only to have his entire cargo confiscated by the Spaniards at Natchez. Permitted to return to the American settlements, he arrived with a tale of woe that lost nothing in repeated telling to groups of indignant frontiersmen. These fierce spirits, unwilling to brook economic strangulation, arose as one man, threatening to settle the dispute with their rifles. Agents of Great Britain circulated throughout the Western settlements, telling eager and sympathetic listeners of the possibility of a British protectorate. George Washington made a six hundred and eighty mile journey through the back country, and reported: "The western settlers (I speak now from my own observation) stand as it were upon a pivot. The touch of a feather would turn them any way." [16]

THE JAY-GARDOQUI NEGOTIATIONS

A treaty with Spain settling the Florida, Indian, and Mississippi difficulties was highly desirable. One other problem also clamored for attention. During the late war the Spaniards had somewhat relaxed their rigid commercial monopoly, and the United States had been privileged to taste the sweets of that trade. When hostilities ended, these concessions were abruptly withdrawn, to the distress of American shippers. With the United States facing bankruptcy and with the Spanish trade capable of providing a large quantity of gold and silver money, the negotiation of a treaty placing commercial relations on a more satisfactory footing seemed vitally necessary. Against this background we must consider the tortuous negotiations of 1785 and 1786 at New York, then the capital, between Secretary Jay and the Spanish diplomatic representative, Don Diego de Gardoqui.[17]

[15] *Jay Papers*, I, 395 (Conversations with Spanish officials, Sept. 3–15, 1780).
[16] *Washington's Writings* (Ford ed.), X, 408 (Washington to Harrison, Oct. 10, 1784).
[17] The Jay-Gardoqui negotiations are fully developed in S. F. Bemis, *Pinckney's Treaty* (Baltimore, 1926), pp. 78–123; the frontier aspects in A. P. Whitaker, *The Spanish-American Frontier: 1783–1795* (Boston, 1927), pp. 63–77.

Gardóqui, a smooth diplomat of the Old World school, had become acquainted with Jay during the latter's Spanish mission. The Spaniard had then taken the measure of his adversary, noting particularly the most vulnerable joint in his armor—vanity. Gardoqui's estimate of Jay, although not altogether fair, is revealing:

The American, Jay, who is generally considered to possess talent and capacity . . . appears . . . to be a very self-centered man, which passion his wife augments, because, in addition to considering herself meritoriously and being rather vain, she likes to be catered to . . . and even more to receive presents. This woman, whom he loves blindly, dominates him and nothing is done without her consent, so that her opinion prevails, though her husband at first may disagree. . . .[18]

Fortified with this knowledge, Gardoqui secured a liberal expense account from his government, rented a pretentious house in New York, and with lavish entertainment sought to ingratiate himself with the Jays and other prominent Americans. He "loaned" one member of Congress a total of $5000. When he learned that Washington desired some Spanish jackasses for breeding mules at Mount Vernon, he conveyed this information to his government, which had anticipated his request by sending a splendid animal to the General, who appreciatively named it "Royal Gift." Meanwhile Gardoqui continued his attentions to Mrs. Jay, whose extraordinary beauty and charm made the Spanish diplomat's self-imposed task by no means a disagreeable one. "Notwithstanding my age," he wrote, "I am acting the gallant and accompanying Madame to the official entertainments and dances, because she likes it and I will do everything which appeals to me for the King's best interest." [19] To judge from some of his official reports, Gardoqui danced his way through the negotiation—one of the few instances of terpsichorean diplomacy in American annals.

The light-footed envoy from Spain had received positive instructions that the free navigation of the Mississippi was not to be yielded under any circumstances. Jay had received equally positive instructions from Congress that no treaty should be concluded which did not secure this right. After months of wearisome negotiation, agreement seemed impossible. If, however, the Americans were willing to yield on the Mississippi issue, Spain was prepared to make important trade

---

[18] Quoted in Bemis, *Pinckney's Treaty*, p. 73.

[19] *Ibid.*, p. 84 (Gardoqui to Floridablanca, Feb. 1, 1786). For a favorable view of the proposed Jay Treaty, see Setser, *Commercial Reciprocity Policy of the United States*, pp. 94–98.

concessions. The Eastern merchants could see no valid reason whatever why such a prize should be denied them because of the interests of a crowd of uncouth backwoodsmen.

Jay had argued strongly for the American claims to the mouth of the Mississippi during his Spanish mission, but now, responding to the clamor of Eastern merchants, his views began to change. After all, the West was not populous, and it would work no great hardship on the entire country, as Washington himself admitted, if the right to navigate the Mississippi were yielded for a decade or two. With regard to the immediate future, it seemed as though a commercial agreement with Spain would offset by a considerable margin the economic loss resulting from a closure of the river. Besides, there was no other way to secure the treaty which languishing American commerce needed. On August 3, 1786, therefore, Jay urged Congress to change his instructions so as to permit the United States to "forbear" the right to navigation for twenty-five or thirty years in return for a treaty. After a bitter debate, in which the Southern states with Western interests violently protested, Jay's request was finally granted, on August 29, 1786, by a close vote of seven states to five. But since the approval of nine states would be necessary to ratify a treaty, it was evident that further negotiations were hopeless.

THE WEST IS HEARD FROM

When the turbulent men across the mountains learned that the Eastern merchants were proposing to sacrifice them for the sake of more trade, they arose in an outburst of anger. Patrick Henry, of Virginia, whose interests were identified with theirs, declared that he "would rather part with the confederation than relinquish the navigation of the Mississippi." There was wild talk in the West of an alliance with England, or even with Spain, or of making a descent upon New Orleans, rifle in hand. One of these inquiet spirits vented his indignation:

The [proposed] commercial treaty with Spain is considered to be cruel, oppressive and unjust. The prohibition of the navigation of the Mississippi has astonished the whole western country. To sell us and make us vassals to the merciless Spaniards is a grievance not to be borne. Should we tamely submit to such manacles we should be unworthy the name of Americans, and a scandal to the annals of its history.[20]

[20] *Secret Journals of Congress,* IV, 315 (Thomas Green to Georgia officials, Dec. 23, 1786).

In the face of this storm of protest the negotiations collapsed, leaving the problem exactly where it had been, except that it was complicated by a deep-seated distrust of the West for the East. Just a few months later, the ratification of the new federal constitution was almost defeated by Southerners with Western interests, who felt that the group which had backed the proposed Jay Treaty could not be trusted to draw up a framework of government. The constitutional provision that a two-thirds vote of the Senate be required for the ratification of treaties was a direct reflection of the suspicion engendered among the Southerners and Westerners by the Jay-Gardoqui negotiation. They felt that they needed at least a one-third veto voice to protect themselves against the selfishness of the East.[21]

But the United States could afford to be patient as long as the pressure of population in the West was not unendurable and as long as New Orleans and Florida were in the hands of the Spaniards. It was evident that America, with her multiplying millions, was growing stronger each year and that Spain, already having fallen upon evil days, was growing progressively weaker. A diplomatic crisis or a general war in Europe would enable the United States to press its claims with vigor. Thomas Jefferson, who with many American statesmen realized that Europe's distresses spelled America's success, advised from Paris:

I should think it proper for the western country to defer pushing their right to that navigation to extremity, as long as they can do without it tolerably. . . . A time of peace will not be the surest for obtaining this object. Those, therefore, who have influence in the new country, would act wisely to endeavor to keep things quiet till the western parts of Europe shall be engaged in war.[22]

For nearly ten years after the collapse of the Jay-Gardoqui negotiations, Spain made no serious effort to conclude a treaty with the United States. She found that the employment of Indian allies, as well as the use of gold among American leaders in the West, was affording her a reasonable degree of security. She was also able to mollify the West to some extent when, in 1788, she granted the right to navigate the Mississippi, subject to the payment of stipulated du-

---

[21] R. E. McClendon, "Origin of the Two-Thirds Rule in Senate Action upon Treaties," *Amer. Hist. Rev.*, XXXVI (1931), 768–772. New England also desired the safeguard of a two-thirds vote in order to protect its fishery interest.

[22] A. A. Lipscomb, ed., *The Writings of Thomas Jefferson* (Monticello ed., Washington, 1904), VII, 24 (Jefferson to John Brown, May 26, 1788).

ties. But on the whole the United States was content with the strategy of delay.

AMERICA'S BELOVED ALLY COOLS OFF

Throughout these turbulent years the Americans had reason to expect unfriendly treatment at the hands of both Great Britain and Spain. But what of their good ally, France? Following the tactics outlined by Vergennes, the French government continued its policy of trying to keep the United States weak. A feeble America would be much more dependent on the benevolent protection of France, and much less likely to embark on an ambitious foreign policy that would run counter to Gallic interests. It is not surprising, therefore, that the French looked with little satisfaction upon the movement to establish a stronger central government.

France did, however, grant the United States the right to trade with a few ports of her West Indies; but only in small ships and for a limited number of commodities. Although far from satisfactory, this was liberality itself when compared with the policy of Spain and Great Britain. France had so little confidence in American courts that she negotiated a consular convention in 1788 by the terms of which French consuls in the United States were empowered to try certain cases involving Frenchmen. Although similar privileges were extended to American consuls in France, this arrangement suggests the extraterritorial jurisdiction which the United States later insisted upon in its dealings with backward Asiatic countries.

During the most anxious years of the Confederation period Thomas Jefferson, *"connaisseur en révolutions,"* was the United States minister to France. He later remembered that the position "was an excellent school of humility":

On being presented to any one as the minister of America, the commonplace question used in such cases was *"c'est vous, Monsieur, qui remplace le Docteur Franklin?"* "it is you, Sir, who replace Doctor Franklin?" I generally answered, "no one can replace him, Sir: I am only his successor." [23]

Jefferson, however, was excessively modest. He developed a strong liking for the French, for whose revolution he acted as godfather, and they in turn found him a disciple after their own hearts. Nevertheless his position was an exceedingly uncomfortable one, largely by reason

[23] *Ibid.*, VIII, 130 (Jefferson to [illegible], Feb. 19, 1791).

of the American debt of 35,000,000 livres, for which he was "daily dunned." It was even rumored in diplomatic circles that France might take the Island of Rhode Island as payment. "We are," Jefferson wrote despairingly from Paris, "the lowest and most obscure of the whole diplomatic tribe." But Vergennes probably preferred a United States too weak to pay its debts to one that might take the bit in its teeth and break away from French influence.

BARBARY BAKSHEESH

The impotence of America under the Articles of Confederation was nowhere more strikingly revealed than in her dealings with the Barbary pirates. The rulers of the petty North African states of Morocco, Algiers, Tripoli, and Tunis loosed upon the commerce of the Mediterranean as ruffianly a lot of cutthroats as history can offer. These human harpies not only enslaved their captives for ransom but collected large sums of protection money from those nations that could afford to make payments. It was a profitable national industry.

Why should the Powers of Europe, with their great navies, have tolerated these piratical nests? Perhaps the basic reason was that in the long run the payment of blackmail seemed to be the cheapest, surest, and least troublesome method of dealing with the problem. Even Great Britain chose the easiest way out and paid tribute, as a result of which the American colonials had developed a thriving Mediterranean trade. But with the winning of independence the United States lost its British shield. The Barbary pirates fell upon the unprotected American ships, enslaved the crews, drove up insurance rates, and almost wiped the commerce of the United States from the Mediterranean Sea. It was America's misfortune to be too poor to pay blackmail, and too weak to offer effective resistance. England naturally rejoiced at the disappearance of a formidable shipping rival. Perhaps the chief reason why she did not use her navy to end these piratical depredations was that, under the existing system, the commerce of the Mediterranean was reserved for those nations which, like herself, were wealthy enough to pay protection money.[24]

---

[24] In 1783 the astute Franklin conjectured: "I think it not improbable that those rovers may be privately encouraged by the English to fall upon us, and to prevent our interference in the carrying trade; for I have in London heard it is a maxim among the merchants that if *there were no Algiers it would be worth England's while to build one.*" Francis Wharton, ed., *The Revolutionary Diplomatic Correspondence of the United States* (Washington, 1889), VI, 587 (Franklin to Livingston, July 25, 1783). Italics Franklin's.

In 1787, by a stroke of good fortune, the United States concluded a reasonably satisfactory treaty with Morocco, at the bargain price of less than $10,000. But there remained the swarm of pirates at Algiers, Tripoli, and Tunis. Secretary Jay viewed this degrading situation with a curious satisfaction. If the Barbary corsairs could only cause deep enough humiliation, the American people might be shamed into strengthening their national government to meet foreign peril. When Jay heard of a reported declaration of war upon the United States by Algiers, he was pleased. "This war," he wrote, "does not strike me as a great evil. The more we are ill-treated abroad the more we shall unite and consolidate at home."

Jay's hope was fulfilled in 1789 when the United States abandoned the inadequate Articles of Confederation and adopted the present federal constitution. Among the many forces that aroused public opinion in behalf of the change, humiliating impotence in foreign affairs must be given an important place. The mercantile interests that helped lead the movement for a stronger central government saw no other way of extorting treaties from the reluctant powers. In a very real sense the narrow commercial policy of Great Britain, as well as that of Spain and France, transformed the United States from thirteen squabbling states into one nation.

BIBLIOGRAPHICAL NOTE

The best reasonably detailed survey appears in the sketches of Robert Livingston (by M. L. Bonham, Jr.) and John Jay (by S. F. Bemis) in S. F. Bemis, ed., *The American Secretaries of State and their Diplomacy* (N.Y., 1927), I, 115–285. A brief but satisfactory chapter on Jay as Secretary for Foreign Affairs is Frank Monaghan, *John Jay* (N.Y., 1935), Ch. XIII. British-American difficulties are fully treated in S. F. Bemis' scholarly *Jay's Treaty* (N.Y., 1923). Spanish-American friction is discussed in two standard works: A. P. Whitaker, *The Spanish-American Frontier: 1783–1795* (Boston, 1927); and S. F. Bemis, *Pinckney's Treaty* (Baltimore, 1926). The most recent monograph on the Barbary powers is R. W. Irwin, *The Diplomatic Relations of the United States with the Barbary Powers, 1776–1816* (Chapel Hill, N.C., 1931). The development of machinery for handling foreign affairs during the Revolution and the Confederation is discussed in Gaillard Hunt, *The Department of State of the United States* (New Haven, 1914). A much more detailed study of these early years is G. C. Wood, *Congressional Control of Foreign Relations during the American Revolution, 1774–1789* (Allentown, Pa., 1919). Further references: see footnotes of this chapter and Bemis and Griffin, *Guide*, pp. 49–67, 156–161.

RECENT REFERENCES; 4TH ED. REFS. See Bibliographical Appendix, p. 922.

CHAPTER V

Embroilments with Britain, 1789–1795

"You cannot imagine what horror some persons are in, lest peace should continue." John Adams, April 19, 1794.

THE NEW ROOF

THE NEW Constitution, unlike the defunct Articles of Confederation, clothed the national government with sufficient authority to deal boldly and vigorously with both domestic and foreign affairs. But monarchical Europe, with its deep-seated distrust of democracy, was frankly skeptical. It remained to be seen whether General Washington, who was inaugurated President on April 30, 1789, would be able to infuse life into the parchment entrusted to his care.

Washington chose as his Secretary of the Treasury the brilliant young Alexander Hamilton, who, by a series of daring financial operations, resurrected the corpse of American credit. The new Department of State, which succeeded the old Department of Foreign Affairs under the Confederation, was put in charge of Thomas Jefferson, then United States minister to France. The appointment was an excellent one, for the distinguished Virginian was well qualified by intellectual background and practical experience for the duties of Secretary of State. His chief task, as it turned out, was to create precedent and to lay the substantial foundations upon which others were to achieve fame.

Unhappily, Jefferson was handicapped by friction with Hamilton, who regarded himself as a kind of prime minister and who repeatedly thrust his fingers into his colleague's business. Hamilton was a deep-dyed conservative and, although first of all an American, a devoted admirer of English institutions. Jefferson, his antithesis, was a pronounced liberal who, though passionately attached to his own country, admired the civilization of France. And he cherished little love for the English—those "rich, proud, hectoring, swearing, squibbling, carnivorous animals who lived on the other side of the Channel." [1]

[1] Gilbert Chinard, *Thomas Jefferson* (Boston, 1929), p. 217.

53

Partly as a result of such fundamental differences two political parties crystallized during Washington's first administration: the Federalists, led by Hamilton, and the Republicans, led by Jefferson.[2] Though both groups were fundamentally American, the Federalists believed that the interests of the United States would be best served by closer relations with England rather than with France; while the Republicans favored closer relations with France rather than with England. So anxious was Hamilton to preserve amicable intercourse with the motherland that he kept in close touch with the British officials in America, supplying them with highly confidential information. When, for example, Jefferson lodged a powerful 17,000-word protest against Great Britain's violation of the Treaty of 1783, Hamilton untruthfully informed His Majesty's minister in Philadelphia that the American note was not to be taken seriously because it did not represent the views of the Administration.[3] The force of Jefferson's note was consequently weakened.

NOOTKA AND NEUTRALITY

The first diplomatic crisis to confront the new government came from an unexpected and almost unheard-of quarter. In the summer of 1789 the Spanish seized several British trading ships that had ventured into Nootka Sound, a small inlet on the western coast of Vancouver Island over which Spain claimed jurisdiction. When the news reached England tremendous excitement prevailed, and the nation feverishly prepared for war. This was no mere question of the ownership of a few trading ships or squalid huts; the outposts of two great colonial empires had clashed in the Pacific Northwest.

It was generally assumed that in the event of war the British in Canada would strike at Spanish New Orleans, Florida, and Louisiana. If, as seemed probable, they asked permission to send troops across American soil to attain their objectives, the United States would be placed in an unenviable position. Acquiescence might mean war with Spain; refusal might mean war with Britain. Confronted with this fateful possibility, Washington sought the advice of his official family. As might be expected, opinions varied widely; but it was generally agreed that the United States should, if possible, keep out of the conflict. Washington's advisers saw clearly the folly of forsaking a policy

[2] Not to be confused with the present-day Republican party.
[3] S. F. Bemis, *Jay's Treaty* (N.Y., 1923), p. 106.

of neutrality and plunging blindly into the maelstrom of European wars.[4]

Fortunately for the United States, the anticipated request was never made. Spain turned desperately to her former ally, France, who was in the throes of the French Revolution and unable to lend assistance. War was hopeless; humiliation was the only alternative. Spain reluctantly accepted the British demands and, in the Convention of 1790, receded from her former position, leaving Nootka as the high-water mark of her magnificent empire.

From the standpoint of the United States, certain beneficial results flowed from the Nootka incident. The early discussion of a policy of neutrality—that is, aloofness from the wars of Europe—set America on a course from which statesmen of that generation made every effort not to deviate. Moreover, the prospect of hostilities following the Nootka difficulty opened British eyes to the importance of the United States—a revelation that elicited greater respect. It even dawned upon London officialdom that the Americans might go so far as to seize their own military and trading posts, which the British still occupied, when the mother country was at grips with an adversary elsewhere. Nor did the obvious strength of the new government under the Constitution fail to impress Great Britain. Congress was now in a position to enact retaliatory commercial legislation against England; indeed, such a measure had already made considerable headway in the House of Representatives.[5] The British were not slow to see that American tariff discrimination would deal their commerce a serious blow, for the United States was their best overseas customer. The Foreign Office now realized that it could no longer rely on the reports of consuls and unofficial observers. So, in 1791, seven years after the ratification of the peace treaty, England sent a full-fledged minister plenipotentiary to America in the person of George Hammond. The youthful envoy, who proceeded to fall in love with a Philadelphia belle, was not the ablest man who could have been chosen. But the significant fact is that Great Britain now considered the United States of sufficient importance to justify the presence of a diplomatic representative.

[4] For the discussion see W. R. Manning, "The Nootka Sound Controversy," *Amer. Hist. Assn., Annual Report, 1904*, pp. 412–423. Neutrality, as used in these chapters, means noninvolvement in the wars of others, rather than impartiality of thought or attitude. In the latter sense, the Americans were not neutral.

[5] Bemis, *Jay's Treaty*, p. 82.

GALLOMANIA AND GALLOMANIACS

Meanwhile, epochal events had been occurring on the continent of Europe. On July 14, 1789, a little more than ten weeks after Washington's inauguration, the maddened Parisian masses rose up and stormed the Bastille. The American people, many of whom felt that their own example had inspired the French to revolt against tyranny, greeted the news with a tidal wave of rejoicing that was called the "Bastille fever" and the "love-frenzy for France." [6] The names of streets in the United States that even suggested monarchy were quickly rechristened. In Boston, for example, Royal Exchange Alley became Equality Lane. Exclusive—consequently nondemocratic—societies fell into disrepute, including the infant scholarship fraternity, Phi Beta Kappa. Honorifics such as "Judge" or even "Mister" suggested social gradations; hence in American republican circles Mr. Smith became Citizen Smith, as in France. One scoffing critic, annoyed by such excesses, even suggested that "Biped" Smith, which included both men and women, was a much more generic and democratic form of address than "Citizen" Smith.

The French Revolution entered upon a new phase in 1792, when the monarchs of Europe, aided by the exiled nobles, began to invade France for the purpose of restoring the yoke to the necks of the peasants. Americans held their breath. If tyranny triumphed, perhaps the United States would be the next victim. When, therefore, the citizen army of France hurled back the foe, American enthusiasm knew no bounds. Frenzied crowds sang French songs and danced wildly in the streets. Through the haze of thirty years William Wirt could look back and write:

Even at this moment my blood runs cold, my breast swells, my temples throb, and I find myself catching my breath, when I recall the ecstasy with which I used to join in that glorious apostrophe to Liberty in the Marseilles Hymn. . . . And then the glorious, magnificent triumph of the arms of France. . . . O, how we used to . . . weep and to sing and pray over these more than human exertions and victories! [7]

[6] One New England orator declaimed: "It was a spark from the altar flame of liberty on this side of the Atlantic, which alighted on the pinnacle of despotism in France and reduced the immense fabric to ashes in the twinkling of an eye." C. D. Hazen, *Contemporary American Opinion of the French Revolution* (Baltimore, 1897), p. 244.

[7] J. P. Kennedy, *Memoirs of the Life of William Wirt* (Phila., 1856), II, 108 (Wirt to Judge Carr, May 14, 1821).

But centuries of pent-up emotion were not to be unloosed in France without frightful consequences. The revolution took an ugly turn when the guillotine was erected and aristocratic heads began to roll monotonously into executioners' baskets. In January, 1793, Louis XVI, who was well thought of in America for his assistance during the recent revolution, bowed his neck to the bloody knife. Several months later the frivolous queen, Marie Antoinette, was forced to do likewise. The Reign of Terror, with the ceaseless crash of the guillotine, was well under way.

In America, the archrepublicans rejoiced at the royal executions. The Pittsburgh *Gazette* gloated, "Louis Capet has lost his caput." William Cobbett, a prominent journalist, testified:

Never was the memory of any man so cruelly insulted as that of this mild and humane monarch. He was guillotined in effigy, in the capital of the Union [Philadelphia], twenty or thirty times every day, during one whole winter and part of the summer. Men, women and children flocked to the tragical exhibition, and not a single paragraph appeared in the papers to shame them from it.[8]

The bloody excesses of the French Revolution alienated the conservatives in America, especially the Hamiltonian Federalists. To them the new regime was merely the substitution of the tyranny of the unwashed masses for that of their legitimate rulers. It seemed to spell the end of religion, private property, and all that Americans held most dear. The fear was commonly expressed that this "moral influenza," more to be dreaded than a "thousand yellow fevers," might even spread to the United States.

Anglomen and Jacobins

On February 1, 1793, eleven days after the execution of Louis XVI, France declared war on Great Britain. This was the beginning of a titanic conflict that was destined to last almost uninterruptedly for twenty-two years and to suck the United States into its vortex. The

[8] William Cobbett, *History of the American Jacobins* (Phila., 1796), pp. 26–27. At a dinner in Philadelphia, upon the anniversary of the king's execution, the dead monarch was represented by a roasted pig. The animal was decapitated at the table, and each guest, donning the liberty cap, shouted "tyrant" as he chopped the severed head of the swine with a knife. The news of the beheading of Marie Antoinette was similarly greeted. Cobbett asserted: ". . . I have heard more than one young woman, under the age of twenty, declare that they would willingly have dipped their hands in the blood of the Queen of France." William Cobbett, *Porcupine's Works* (London, 1801), I, 113.

Federalists looked upon Great Britain as the world's last hope. But the pro-French faction, composed mostly of Jeffersonian Republicans, regarded the issue as that of 1776 over again. To them it seemed as though the tyrannical George III were once more using redcoats to suppress human liberties, this time at the expense of America's ally, France. Although French sympathizers in the United States were not altogether pleased with the gory by-products of the revolution, they felt that the sacrifice of a few thousand aristocratic necks was a cheap price to pay for the results to be achieved. Jefferson lapsed into characteristic extravagance:

> The liberty of the whole earth was depending on the issue of the contest, and was ever such a prize won with so little innocent blood? My own affections have been deeply wounded by some of the martyrs to this cause, but rather than it should have failed I would have seen half the earth desolated; were there but an Adam and an Eve left in every country, and left free, it would be better than as it now is.[9]

The Republicans, who were generally sympathetic with the French, thus found themselves arrayed in a hostile camp against the Federalists, whom they branded as "British bootlickers." Political passions, aroused by both domestic and foreign affairs, ran incredibly high. In every walk of life, including business and religion, men were divided into Federalist and Republican groups.

This was the age of personal journalism, and editors vied with one another in devising opprobrious epithets. The Republicans were called "filthy Jacobins," "a despicable mobocracy," "Gallic Jackals," "lying dogs," "stinking caitiffs," "tools of baboons," "frog-eating, man-eating, blood-drinking cannibals." The most venomous of the Federalist editors, William Cobbett, let fly the following blast at his Republican adversaries: "I say, beware, ye under-strapping cut-throats who walk in rags and sleep amidst filth and vermin; for if once the halter gets around your flea-bitten necks, howling and confessing will come too late."[10] The Republican editors were fully capable of replying in kind.

BRITAIN'S INDIAN ALLIES

With passions at fever heat many of the Federalists demanded intervention in the war on the side of Great Britain, while many of the

---

[9] A. A. Lipscomb, ed., *Writings of Thomas Jefferson* (Monticello ed., Washington, 1904), IX, 10 (Jefferson to Short, Jan. 3, 1793).

[10] *Porcupine's Gazette*, quoted in Charles Warren, *Jacobin and Junto* (Cambridge, Mass., 1931), p. 90.

Republicans clamored for intervention on the side of France. But the imperturbable Washington steered a sane middle course, and under circumstances which we shall consider in the next chapter, issued his famous Proclamation of Neutrality, April 22, 1793. This, however, by no means put an end to America's troubles, for a number of unfortunate developments brought Great Britain and the United States to the very brink of war.

The most rankling of American grievances was the British retention of the northern posts. The Union Jack still floated over these places—ten full years after England had solemnly promised to give them up. British fur traders were making off with rich profits that belonged to the Americans. And, what is more, the British authorities showed no intention whatsoever of relinquishing the highly profitable fur trade. Not only had they taken additional new steps to strengthen their hold on United States soil, but the commander of the fort at Niagara even refused to permit Americans to view the falls.[11] Apparently the British were there to stay.

A problem closely related to that of the posts, and perhaps even more inflammatory, was that of the Indians. The British perceived that they could maintain their hold on the fur trade more securely if they extended their influence to the surrounding Indian tribes. A primary object of England's frontier policy during these years was to unite the Indians and form a buffer state against the steadily advancing American frontiersman, thus protecting the source of the fur trade as well as the posts.[12] British agents encouraged the Indians to believe that the cession of the trans-Allegheny region to the Americans was but a temporary arrangement, and that in a few years the ascendancy of George III, the great white father with a red coat, would be restored. In pursuance of this policy England kept the Indians in a state of dependence, providing them with "firewater," blankets, muskets, ammunition, war paint, and even scalping knives.[13] As Professor A. P. Whitaker has well said, "the hand that sells the whiskey rules the tomahawk."

From 1783 to 1794 the butchering of American pioneers was a fre-

---

[11] J. M. Callahan, *American Foreign Policy in Canadian Relations* (N.Y., 1937), p. 25.

[12] For the development of this idea see Bemis, *Jay's Treaty*, pp. 109–133.

[13] One British officer wrote: "The Indians get this day from the King's stores the bread that they are to eat tomorrow, and from his magazines the clothing that covers their nakedness: in short they are not only our allies, but are a part of our family; and the Americans might as well . . . attempt to seduce our children from their duty and allegiance. . . ." *Ibid.*, p. 12 (Maclean to de Peyster, July 8, 1783).

quent occurrence on the Ohio frontier, as well as on the Spanish-controlled southern frontier. The very arms used by the red men bore fresh British trademarks; and it was the firm belief of the Westerners, as well as of many other Americans, that these murderous forays were deliberately incited and even directed by His Majesty's officers stationed at the unrelinquished American posts. There can, in fact, be little doubt that the liberal disbursement of arms to the Indians, together with assurances of a return of British authority, bore some relation to the numerous scalping expeditions.[14]

Anglo-American tension became worse in February, 1794, when Lord Dorchester, Governor-General of Canada, committed the serious indiscretion of making an incendiary speech to a delegation of Indians hostile to the United States. He openly encouraged them to believe that England and America would be at war within a year, thus affording them an opportunity to recover their lands from the "long knives." Two months later the British had the effrontery to penetrate American territory and establish a fort at the rapids of the Maumee, some sixty miles southwest of Detroit.

ON THE BRINK OF NATIONAL SUICIDE

As if difficulties over the posts and the Indians were not enough, England adopted a policy that struck heavily at the American merchant marine. An Order in Council, issued June 8, 1793, authorized the detention of all neutral vessels carrying certain foodstuffs to the ports of France, or to ports under French control, and the "purchase" of their cargoes. Far more serious from the point of view of the United States was a later Order in Council, that of November 6, 1793. It provided for the detention of all ships carrying the produce of a French colony, or supplies for the use of such a colony. This, of course, was an attempt to strike at the French West Indies, which had been heavily dependent upon American provisions since the outbreak of war between France and England.[15] The British naval commanders proceeded to carry out these orders with dispatch and ruthlessness.

---

[14] John Breckinridge wrote (Sept. 15, 1794): "Unassisted common sense & common honesty tell us, it is as criminal & treacherous in a British Subject to hire an Indian to murder our wives and children, as if he had committed the act himself. . . ." Washington informed Jay (Aug. 30, 1794) that there "does not remain a doubt" that the British agents were the source of "all the hostilities, the murders. . . ." Quoted in Bernard Mayo, *Henry Clay: Spokesman of the New West* (Boston, 1937), p. 48 n.

[15] The French had thrown open their West Indies (already partially open) to the Americans. The British ruled that this abnormal trade violated the Rule of 1756—commerce not permitted in time of peace could not be allowed in time of war.

Without adequate warning they seized scores of United States vessels, mostly in the West Indies, and threw many of their crews into foul dungeons. American shipping, which had experienced an exhilarating boom since the beginning of hostilities, was partially paralyzed.

The news of these confiscations, coming at the height of ill feeling over the Indians and the posts, produced an immediate outcry for war against George III, that "prince of land- and sea-robbers." Patriotic songs were on a thousand tongues; and citizens volunteered their services to erect fortifications. Even Hamilton was so far aroused as to refer to the British conduct as "atrocious"; and he advised President Washington to prepare for hostilities while continuing negotiations. An infuriated Charleston mob tore down the statue of Lord Chatham (William Pitt) which had been appreciatively erected a quarter of a century before. When John Hodgkinson, the popular actor, appeared on a New York stage in the uniform of a British officer, as the role required, he was greeted with a storm of derision which subsided only when he stepped forward and explained that he was playing the part of a coward and a bully. The governor of Upper Canada asserted on August 6, 1794: "I hold war to be inevitable. . . ." And three weeks later Washington declared: ". . . I will undertake, without the gift of prophecy, to predict, that it will be impossible to keep this country in a state of amity with Great Britain long, if the posts are not surrendered." [16]

Meanwhile, on March 26, 1794, Congress had struck back at the British Orders in Council by laying a thirty-day embargo, later extended one month, on all shipping in American harbors bound for foreign ports. This restriction, of course, was nominally nondiscriminatory, applying to France as well as to England. Shortly thereafter the Jeffersonian Republicans, riding on the crest of the wave of Anglophobia, threw their support behind a resolution to suspend all intercourse with Great Britain in British productions. Their object was to force a repeal of the odious Orders in Council. But the mother country, engaged in a desperate struggle, was in no mood to yield to the commercial hatchet. Many Federalists not unreasonably feared that discrimination would lead to war, and that war would spell disaster, perhaps suicide, for the defenseless and disorganized United States. Hamilton's elaborate financial structure, upon the successful operation of which the fate of the new government hinged, was based upon customs duties. Ninety per cent of America's imports came from Eng-

[16] W. C. Ford, ed., *Writings of George Washington* (N.Y., 1891), XII, 461 (Washington to Jay, Aug. 30, 1794).

land; and if they and the revenue from them should have been cut off by retaliation or war, the whole Hamiltonian edifice would probably have collapsed.[17] If this had happened American nationality might possibly have been extinguished, and Alexander Hamilton would have gone down in history not as the greatest Secretary of the Treasury but as the only one.

Hamilton and his Federalist following, who stalwartly opposed discriminatory legislation against England, held several strong cards. In the first place, the French, angered because the Washington administration was permitting the British to stop United States vessels laden with provisions for France, were retaliating by seizing American ships carrying supplies to England. These confiscations rapidly mounted into the hundreds, and incidentally involved the brutal treatment of crews. Secondly, the London government modified its Orders in Council early in 1794, thus allowing the Americans to enjoy for the time a thriving trade with the British West Indies. Finally, Great Britain arranged to pay for many of the confiscated American cargoes, which was more than the United States could expect from France. Technically, if the Americans were going to fight at all, they should have fought both England and France; and in some ways Britain's offenses on the high seas were less objectionable than those of France. Nevertheless, it was only after a bitter struggle in Congress that the Federalists were able to block the discriminatory legislation against the British, and temporarily quiet the Republicans by supporting a proposal to send a special envoy to England.

MR. JAY RISKS HIS REPUTATION

The name of Alexander Hamilton was at first proposed for the English mission; but he had made himself so offensive to the Jeffersonian following as to be unacceptable. John Jay, then Chief Justice, was selected instead. Like Hamilton, he was a stanch Federalist and a strong admirer of England—a circumstance that made him decidedly *persona grata* to the British government and aristocracy. Indeed, they knew both their man and the vulnerable joints in his armor, for they had been forewarned by one who had earlier known Jay:

[Jay] has good sense and much information; has great appearance of coolness; and is a patient hearer with a good memory. He argues closely, but is long-winded and self-opinioned. He can bear any opposition to what

17 Professor S. F. Bemis makes a strong point of this in his *Jay's Treaty*, p. 36.

he advocates provided regard is shown to his ability. He may be attached by good treatment but will be unforgiving if he thinks himself neglected. . . . He certainly has good sense and judgement. . . . But almost every man has a weak and assailable quarter, and Mr. Jay's weak side is *Mr. Jay*.[18]

The Anglophobe Republicans were outraged by the choice of so notorious an Anglophile. They professed to fear that the man who had tried to sell out the West to Gardoqui would probably sell the entire country to Great Britain. Jay's nomination was confirmed by the Senate on April 19, 1794, but only after a three-day debate in which partisan feelings ran high. John Adams, the Vice-President and presiding officer, noted that the "prospect of peace" threw some persons "into distress." Jay, who foresaw the possible consequences to his "personal popularity," reluctantly accepted. As he presciently remarked, "no man could frame a treaty with Great Britain without making himself unpopular and odious."

Upon arriving in London, Jay was most cordially received in English society. The Anglophobe following of Jefferson immediately raised the cry that the American envoy had sold out for British gold. In due season Jay was presented to the Queen. She graciously extended her hand to the American, who bowed and kissed it. When the news of this incident reached the United States, one rabid Republican exclaimed that Jay had "prostrated at the feet of her majesty the sovereignty of the people," and that "he richly deserved to have his lips blistered to the bone." Another jeered: "Hear the voice of truth, hear and believe! John Jay, ah! the arch traitor—seize him, drown him, hang him, burn him, flay him alive! Men of America, he betrayed you with a kiss!" [19] Even making due allowance for partisan exaggeration, it seems that the Jay who was wined, dined, and flattered by the British nobility, was not the vigilant, suspicious Jay of Paris days.

Hamilton Cuts the Ground from Under Jay

The American envoy was instructed to adjust the differences that had arisen out of the Treaty of 1783. He was also to secure compensation for seizures under the recent Orders in Council; to arrange for

---

[18] Frank Monaghan, *John Jay* (N.Y., 1935), p. 372 (Confidential report from one Elliot, who had known Jay in 1769).

[19] *Oracle of the Day*, Nov. 25, 1795 [1794?], quoted in J. B. McMaster, *A History of the People of the United States*, II, 213 n.

an opening of the British West Indian trade to American vessels; and, if possible, to negotiate a long-needed commercial treaty with England. Although Jay was allowed certain discretionary powers because of his distance from the United States, he was specifically instructed to sign no treaty contrary to American engagements with France.

It is true that Jay did not hold a strong hand, but he did have a few good cards. The British realized that the United States had been prodded to the verge of war; and they did not want war. It would disrupt their valuable commerce with America and divert strength from the real enemy, France. The London government therefore reprimanded Lord Dorchester for his indiscreet speech to the Indians,[20] and took further steps to ameliorate the objectionable Orders in Council. But rather than abandon entirely their offensive maritime practices and jeopardize their chances of beating France to her knees, the British would probably have accepted war. Under these circumstances it was difficult, if not impossible, to extort sweeping concessions.

Jay held but one ace—and a poor one at that. A new and weaker Armed Neutrality was being formed to resist England's arbitrary maritime practices, and the British officials did not want America to join it. Unknown to them, the Administration had already discussed the issue and adopted the policy of steering clear of European quarrels. Yet Hamilton, in his desperate efforts to keep peace and preserve his financial edifice, committed the serious indiscretion of informing the British minister in Philadelphia, George Hammond, that the United States would under no circumstances join the Armed Neutrality. Hammond promptly relayed this important information to London. Thus the only ace that Jay held was trumped with the card that Hamilton had furnished the British.[21] The unsatisfactory agreement that Jay finally signed on November 19, 1794, has therefore been called Hamilton's treaty, on the rather questionable assumption that the British could have been bluffed by the abortive Armed Neutrality.

The only immediate concession of any real value that Jay secured was a promise on the part of the British to surrender the posts that they had already promised to surrender in the Treaty of 1783. Other matters of controversy, including the Northeastern boundary, pre-Revolutionary debts, and compensation for the recent seizures, were referred to mixed arbitral commissions.[22] This arrangement was sig-

[20] Bemis, *Jay's Treaty*, p. 234.   [21] *Ibid.*, pp. 246–248.

[22] In 1798 the mixed commission appointed for that purpose established the identity of the St. Croix River, the principal issue in the Northeastern boundary dispute. But the problem was not finally settled until later. The arbitration of the debt question failed; and it was finally adjusted in the Treaty of 1802, by which Great Britain ac-

nificant for two reasons. In the first place, although international arbitration was not then unknown, the impetus it received from Jay's Treaty was so great that modern arbitration is generally dated from the ratification of this pact. Secondly, since the United States was then weak but growing rapidly, it was to the advantage of the Americans to postpone the final decision of pending questions.

But nothing was said in Jay's Treaty about the slaves who had been carried off; nothing about tampering with the Indians. The American envoy not only failed to wring concessions from the British in regard to such questions as seizures of ships, but he actually yielded ground. Contrary at least to the spirit of America's treaty engagements with France, he agreed that enemy property on neutral ships might be seized by the British, and that foodstuffs might be confiscated if paid for.

The commercial privileges that Jay secured were most illusory. Americans were permitted to trade between their own ports and the British West Indies if their vessels were limited to seventy tons carrying capacity. In return for this niggardly concession, Jay bound the United States not to export certain tropical staples, such as sugar and cotton, in American vessels. The year previous to the negotiation of the treaty, Eli Whitney had invented the cotton gin; and the restriction on tropical products, if adhered to, might have strangled the budding cotton industry of the South. Yet, unpalatable though these arrangements were to the United States, it is doubtful if anyone else under the circumstances could have secured substantially more.

THE DAMNATION OF JOHN JAY

So thoroughly unsatisfactory was the treaty that the Senate, fearful of a popular outcry, took steps to keep its provisions secret. Even the Federalist Senators hung their heads when they contemplated Jay's, or rather Hamilton's, handiwork. But in a short time the terms leaked out, and a prolonged chorus of condemnation reverberated throughout the land. "Mad Anthony" Wayne, the Revolutionary hero, had recently chastised the Indians at Fallen Timbers (August 20, 1794); and the Federal army had just finished crushing the Whisky Rebellion in Western Pennsylvania, thus demonstrating the might of the new national government. America was in no mood to yield to Britain.

---

cepted £600,000. In 1804 a mixed commission awarded the United States $11,650,000 for damages to American shipping resulting from the Orders in Council; on the other hand, the United States was assessed $143,428.14 for its derelictions as a neutral.

Scores of hamlets were lighted at night by the burning effigies of "that damned arch-traitor, Sir John Jay." Public meetings passed condemnatory resolutions, flags were lowered to half-mast, and hangmen officially burned copies of the treaty. In Charleston an effigy of Jay was hauled about in a dung cart and then hanged. The British minister at Philadelphia was openly insulted by jeering crowds; and when Hamilton attempted to speak in New York, he was stoned from the platform, bleeding at the mouth. One Irish orator shouted to an inflamed crowd: "What a damned treaty! I make a motion that every good citizen in this assembly kick this damned treaty to hell." [23] Jay was represented in effigy as holding a pair of scales, the document on one side and a bag of gold on the other, with the placard, "Come up to my price, and I will sell you my country." On the fence of Robert Treat Paine were chalked these words: "Damn John Jay! damn every one that won't damn John Jay!! damn every one that won't put lights in his windows and sit up all night damning John Jay!!!" [24] Those who were bold enough to defend the pact publicly did so at risk of life and limb.

A Devil's Choice

It was fortunate for America that in the midst of this crisis Washington stood at the helm. His heart must have sunk as he read the treaty; but at this point it would have been folly to send Jay back to London in the hope of negotiating a better one. The choice seemed to be either the pact or war. With the country disunited, Indians on the warpath, Spain on the Southwestern frontier, and Hamilton's intricate financial structure faced with ruin, hostilities would have spelled national disaster. Washington realized this full well. One of his cardinal policies was to avoid war at all costs while the United States was still weak and disunited. If the nation could only consolidate its strength and wait for the natural increase of population, it would one day become powerful enough to command respect. Time and pioneer fecundity were fighting America's battles.

As time wore on the Federalists, who had been badly demoralized by the fierce Republican uproar, recovered their composure. Hamilton entered the fray with his persuasive pen. An increasing number of persons came to the conclusion that the treaty could not be nearly so bad as partisan Republican sources represented. Washington threw his

---

[23] Monaghan, *John Jay*, pp. 393–394 (Blair McClenachan).
[24] John Jay, *Mr. Jay's Second Letter on Dawson's Introduction to the Federalist* (N.Y., 1864), p. 19.

powerful support behind the pact, and the Senate, by a close vote and with the West Indian article suspended, reluctantly consented to ratification (June 24, 1795). The President was bitterly condemned by the pro-French faction. Jefferson so far forgot himself as to exclaim, "Curse on his virtues; they have undone the country"; and to place Washington in the company of those "who have had their heads shorn by the harlot England." [25]

Washington's decision must be accounted one of the wisest and most courageous acts of his life. Jay's Treaty, unsatisfactory though it was, postponed war with Great Britain for eighteen years and enabled the young American republic to establish its footing. It was the price that the Hamiltonians were willing to pay for peace, financial stability, continuing prosperity, and the salvation of the new government. The significant thing about the agreement is not that the British drove a hard bargain, but that only eleven years after granting independence they deigned to meet the United States on terms of equality and sign a pact of any description. And even this might not have been conceded had not England needed all her resources for the exhausting war with France.

The pro-French group held one final card. If they could muster enough votes in the House of Representatives to defeat the appropriation necessary for carrying the treaty into effect, they would yet be able to undo Jay's work. Jefferson voiced a general Republican sentiment:

I join with you in thinking the treaty an execrable thing. . . . I trust the popular branch of our Legislature will disapprove of it, and thus rid us of this infamous act, which is really nothing more than a treaty of alliance between England and the Anglomen of this country, against the Legislature and people of the United States.[26]

Even the French minister tried to persuade individual members of the House to vote down the appropriation bill, while the British minister used his influence to secure its passage. Throughout a bitter, two-month debate the issue hung in doubt; and there was much wild talk that if the House failed to do its duty the Union would dissolve. At

[25] A Virginian toast ran: "A speedy death to General Washington." The speaker at a Lexington, Kentucky, dinner exclaimed: "May there be an universal *change* in the foederal [*sic*] Executive, from the highest officer, down to the lowest Maggot of Administration." A. P. Whitaker, *The Mississippi Question, 1795–1803* (N.Y., 1934), p. 24.

[26] *Writings of Thomas Jefferson* (Monticello ed.), IX, 314 (Jefferson to Edward Rutledge, Nov. 30, 1795).

a critical moment the ailing Fisher Ames, premier orator of the Federalist party, took the floor. He not untruthfully stigmatized the uproar of the Republicans as opposition not to the Jay Treaty but to any treaty with Britain. In solemn tones, which grew stronger as he summoned all his physical resources for this supreme effort, he insisted that the Union would collapse and that war would break out should the pact fail. Then "the wounds yet unhealed" would "be torn open again; the war whoop shall waken the sleep of the cradle." "I can fancy that I listen to the yells of savage vengeance and the shrieks of torture; already they seem to sigh in the western wind; already they mingle with every echo from the mountains." [27] Moved by this superlative oratorical effort, the House passed the necessary appropriation by a narrow margin, April 30, 1796.

The Redemption of American Nationality

One of the most important results of the Jay Treaty appeared in an unexpected quarter. In 1793, following the execution of Louis XVI, Spain had entered the war against France on the side of Great Britain and the other members of the First Coalition. In 1795, Spain withdrew from the war, and the next year allied herself with France, her former enemy, against England, her former ally. If this bold move should lead to war with Britain, as it eventually did, Spain would do well to placate the United States. She would thus lessen the number of her enemies, and at the same time protect her exposed flank against the Western frontiersmen. The full wisdom of such a policy dawned upon the Spanish ministers when they heard of the Jay Treaty, for it seemed to presage an alliance between England and America.

On October 27, 1795, therefore, the Madrid government concluded a highly important treaty with Thomas Pinckney, envoy extraordinary of the United States. It conceded to the American republic virtually everything that Spain had bitterly resisted for the past twelve years. Specifically, the United States secured free navigation of the Mississippi; the right to deposit goods at New Orleans for transshipment for a period of three years (the privilege to be renewed either there or at some equivalent place); the boundary of Florida at the 31st parallel; and a promise from Spain to restrain the Indians on the American frontier. [28] It is little wonder that this

---

[27] Seth Ames, ed., *Works of Fisher Ames* (Boston, 1854), II, 66 (Speech of April 28, 1796).

[28] Professor S. F. Bemis, in his *Pinckney's Treaty* (Baltimore, 1926), p. 307, stresses the influence of the European situation in bringing about the Spanish concessions.

agreement was as popular as that of Jay was unpopular, and that the Senate approved it unanimously, on March 3, 1796.

The Pinckney Treaty, although not removing all the sources of friction with Spain, was of great significance. It temporarily appeased frontier discontent by opening the Mississippi and by lessening the Indian menace. The national government thus struck a body blow at Spanish intrigue, removed the threat of disunion, and awakened a new sense of loyalty in the West. The concessions made by Spain marked a backward step in the policy of maintaining a buffer against the virile frontiersman, and did much to pave the way for the expansion of the United States into the Mississippi Valley. Finally, the treaty removed the necessity of America's becoming involved in European entanglements to secure those concessions that the Spaniards freely yielded.

Seven years earlier, when Washington had first taken office, Britain and Spain exercised control over the greater part of America's trans-Allegheny territory. Now, by virtue of the Jay and Pinckney Treaties, the United States had freed its own soil from foreign domination. The happy results were due in part to the growing pressure of the expansive Westerner on the Anglo-American and Spanish-American frontiers; in part to the "patient and persuasive" diplomacy of Washington, which so successfully employed the strategy of delay; and in part to Europe's distresses. If Britain had not been involved in a death struggle with France, it is unlikely that she would have concluded Jay's Treaty. If Spain had not been faced with war with Britain, she almost certainly would not have yielded Pinckney's Treaty in 1795. Europe's distress contributed to America's success not only in achieving independence but also in redeeming American nationality.

BIBLIOGRAPHICAL NOTE

The outstanding monograph covering this period is S. F. Bemis, *Jay's Treaty* (N.Y., 1923). Professor Bemis treats some of the same material more briefly in his sketch of Thomas Jefferson in S. F. Bemis, ed., *The American Secretaries of State and their Diplomacy* (N.Y., 1927), II, 3–93; see also the sketch of Edmund Randolph (by D. R. Anderson), *ibid.*, 97–159. The best book on the subject is C. D. Hazen, *Contemporary American Opinion of the French Revolution* (Baltimore, 1897). A good brief account of Jay's activities appears in Frank Monaghan, *John Jay* (N.Y., 1935), Chs. XVIII–XIX. W. R. Manning, "The

Professor A. P. Whitaker, in his *The Spanish-American Frontier: 1783–1795* (Boston, 1927), p. 209, lays strong emphasis on the threat from the American West. It is certainly true that the West was becoming increasingly exercised over the Mississippi issue. See the bellicose Kentucky broadsides, File 21, Library of Congress.

Nootka Sound Controversy," Amer. Hist. Assn., *Annual Report, 1904,* 279–478, is the best treatment of the affair. The relation of Jay's Treaty to Pinckney's Treaty is developed in detail in S. F. Bemis' *Pinckney's Treaty* (Baltimore, 1926), and in A. P. Whitaker's *The Spanish-American Frontier: 1783–1795* (Boston, 1927). For the organization of the State Department see the standard work of Gaillard Hunt, *The Department of State of the United States* (New Haven, 1914). Further references: see footnotes of this chapter, the bibliographical note at the end of next chapter, and Bemis and Griffin, *Guide,* Ch. IV.

RECENT REFERENCES. Henceforth Bemis' *Jay's Treaty* must be read in the light of A. L. Burt, *The United States, Great Britain, and British North America* (New Haven, 1940), Ch. VIII, which takes sharp issue with Bemis on several points. The abortive Armed Neutrality was so weak (including only Denmark and Sweden, not Prussia and Russia) that, according to Burt, if the United States had used it to force a showdown, there "probably" would have been "no treaty at all (p. 155 n.)." The author also concludes that the treaty not only is a real credit to Jay but that it appropriately bears his name, because he had long worked for the principle of arbitration which it strengthened. N. V. Russell, *The British Régime in Michigan and the Old Northwest, 1760–1796* (Northfield, Minn., 1939), deals with these problems (Ch. X), and suggests that the British gave up the posts in part because of the American movement west and the shift of the fur trade to Canada. A. B. Darling, *Our Rising Empire, 1763–1803* (New Haven, 1940), has a useful chapter (VIII) on Jay's treaty.

NEW REFERENCES. A valuable collection of diplomatic documents in Bernard Mayo, ed., *Instructions to the British Ministers to the United States, 1791–1812* (Washington, 1941). Among other things it appears that Foreign Secretary Grenville was genuinely concerned over the prospect that the United States might join the abortive Armed Neutrality (pp. 54, 67).

4TH. ED. REFS. Alice B. Keith, "Relaxations in the British Restrictions on the American Trade with the British West Indies, 1783–1802," *Jour. of Mod. Hist.,* XX (1948), 1–18, shows that American traders enjoyed great prosperity owing to relaxations brought about by British exigencies.

CHAPTER VI

Alliance and Misalliance with France, 1789–1800

"The nation which indulges toward another an habitual hatred or an habitual fondness is in some degree a slave."
Washington's Farewell Address, 1796.

THE ALLIANCE BECOMES LESS DESIRABLE

As LONG as the French Revolution and the wars growing out of it were confined to the continent of Europe, the United States was able to avoid serious international complications. But the picture was completely changed when, on February 1, 1793, France declared war on England. The news reached New York early in April; and a cry went up from thousands of Francophile throats that America should rush to the assistance of the nation that had helped her in the hour of need. The common foe—so it appeared—was Great Britain, that ancient enemy and oppressor of human liberty, that arrogant Power which seemed to be making every effort to strangle the United States in infancy. "Americans, be just!" proclaimed the New York *Journal.* "Remember . . . who stood between you and the clanking chains of British ministerial despotism."

President Washington now found himself in a serious predicament. His fixed policy was to avoid hostilities at all hazards while the nation was still feeble. Yet by the Treaty of 1778 the United States was bound "forever" to assist France in the defense of her West Indies. Unless America flagrantly disregarded her now onerous obligations, she could scarcely avoid the very calamity that the Hamiltonians were seeking desperately to avert—war with Great Britain.

At this critical juncture Washington characteristically turned to his Cabinet members for advice as to whether the treaties with France should now be considered binding. Hamilton, who had no love for the French or the French alliance, argued that the treaties were not in full force because they had been negotiated with the French monarchy under Louis XVI—and both the monarchy and Louis XVI were dead. Jefferson, though by no means desiring war with England

71

in behalf of France, insisted that simple honesty should govern the conduct of the American government:

> . . . The treaties between the United States and France, were not treaties between the United States and Louis Capet, but between the two nations of America and France; and the nations remaining in existence, though both of them have since changed their forms of government, the treaties are not annulled by these changes.[1]

As it turned out, France did not call upon the United States to defend her West Indies; hence the Washington administration was not compelled to take an official stand on the applicability of the Treaty of 1778. The course pursued by the French officials was not dictated by solicitude for the United States but by purely selfish motives. If the Americans had possessed a strong naval and military force, France would almost certainly have insisted that they live up to their treaty obligations. But since the United States had no considerable navy and since, as neutrals, the Americans were able to send food to both France and her starving West Indian colonies, the expected demand was never made. America could be more useful as a friendly neutral than as an ineffectual ally.

Washington also asked his advisers if, in their opinion, he should receive a diplomatic representative from the newly created French republic. This was an important point, for the reception of such an envoy would mean official recognition of his government. Jefferson, applying the "consent of the governed" philosophy of his own Declaration of Independence, had already outlined in classic form a recognition policy for the United States:

> We certainly cannot deny to other nations that principle whereon our government is founded, that every nation has a right to govern itself internally under what forms it pleases, and to change these forms at its own will; and externally to transact business with other nations through whatever organ it chooses, whether that be a King, Convention, Assembly, Committee, President, or whatever it be. The only thing essential is, the will of the nation.[2]

This policy—in effect a corollary of the Declaration of Independence—was adopted by Washington and was consistently followed by

---

[1] A. A. Lipscomb, ed., *Writings of Thomas Jefferson* (Monticello ed., Washington, 1904), III, 227–228 (April 28, 1793).
[2] *Ibid.*, IX, 7–8 (Jefferson to Pinckney, Dec. 30, 1792).

all his successors (with minor departures) until the time of Woodrow Wilson. Jefferson unquestionably did his most memorable work as Secretary of State in laying the bases for the American policies of recognition and neutrality. Although his personal sympathies were with France in her struggle with England, his official correspondence with the British and French ministers never betrayed the interests of the United States. As the French representative in America reported:

Mr. Jefferson likes us because he detests England; he seeks to draw near to us because he fears us less than Great Britain; but tomorrow he might change his opinion about us if Great Britain should cease to inspire his fear. Although Jefferson is the friend of liberty and science, although he is an admirer of the efforts we have made to cast off our shackles . . . Jefferson, I say, is an American, and as such, he cannot sincerely be our friend. An American is the born enemy of all the peoples of Europe.[3]

A DECLARATION OF DIPLOMATIC INDEPENDENCE

During these months of unbridled political passions, the danger was ever present that some irresponsible persons might plunge the country into war. Washington therefore considered with his advisers the desirability of issuing a pronouncement that would cool the ardor of the more bellicose spirits. Every member of the Cabinet strongly favored a policy of neutrality; but there was not unanimous agreement on the manner of announcing it. After considerable discussion the document that is known as Washington's Neutrality Proclamation was given to the world, April 22, 1793. Though its import was unmistakable, the declaration did not, curiously enough, contain the word "neutrality." It merely stated that the conduct of the United States should be "friendly and impartial toward the belligerent powers," and that American citizens found guilty of illegally assisting the warring nations would be prosecuted.[4] The Neutrality Proclamation was a notable document in that it further signalized the withdrawal of the United States from Old World embroilments. It was a manifesto of diplomatic independence and not, as erroneously believed, of isolation.

The proclamation came as a bitter disappointment to the great mass of Francophiles who were expecting active intervention in behalf of France. They denounced government "by proclamation" and offered such toasts as the following:

[3] Amer. Hist. Assn., *Annual Report, 1903*, II, 983 (Adet to Minister of Foreign Relations, Dec. 31, 1796).

[4] Congress added teeth to the proclamation by the Neutrality Act of 1794.

[Toast no.] 6. May the sister republics of France and America be as incorporate as light and heat; and the man who endeavors to disunite them, be viewed as the Arnold of his country. 7. May honour and probity be the principles by which the connexions of free nations shall be determined; and no Machiavelian [sic] commentaries explain the text of Treaties. 8. *The treaty of alliance with France;* May those who attempt to evade or violate the political obligations and faith of our country be considered as traitors & consigned to infamy! . . . 14. May all tories have a perpetual itching, and never the gratification of scratching.[5]

Upon Washington's head was loosed a storm of vituperation that sorely tried his spirit. But in the end saner counsels prevailed, and the rank and file of the American people accepted the proclamation as a wise and necessary measure.[6]

A Prince of Diplomatic Bunglers

The neutrality policy of Washington was given its severest test by the conduct of the first minister from the new French republic, Citizen Edmond Genêt. Although not yet thirty years of age, Genêt had behind him a remarkable record of intellectual achievement and diplomatic experience.[7] But unfortunately he lacked balance and sound judgment. Aflame with enthusiasm for the ideals of the French Revolution, ardent, impulsive, passionate, and hotheaded, he was all sail and no anchor.

Genêt reached Charleston early in 1793. There he was received with a wild enthusiasm that would have turned the head of an even less excitable man. Although he could not act in an official capacity until he had presented his credentials to the national government in Philadelphia, he was so carried away by the plaudits of the masses as to engage immediately in various activities. In disregard of American neutrality, he sent out French privateers from Charleston, which returned with British prizes, some of them taken within the three-mile limit. He also initiated negotiations with a number of American frontier leaders, notably the disgruntled George Rogers Clark, looking toward an attack upon the territory of Spain in Florida and

---

[5] *National Gazette* (Philadelphia), July 17, 1793, 3:2.
[6] C. M. Thomas, *American Neutrality in 1793* (N.Y., 1931), p. 48.
[7] Genêt spoke Greek at six; before reaching his teens he had translated two historical works from Swedish, ornamenting them with his own footnotes. He had already seen service at the most important European courts.

Louisiana.[8] It will be remembered that from 1793 to 1795 Spain was fighting against France on the side of England.

The enthusiastic French envoy might have proceeded to Philadelphia by any one of three routes: by sea, by land up the coast, or by land through the back country. Whether by accident or design, he chose the back country route, the one that best lent itself to his purposes. The people in this region were small farmers who favored the democratic, pro-French, Republican party and opposed the aristocratic, pro-British, Federalist party. It is no wonder, then, that Genêt's leisurely journey through the back country was one long ovation. The trip to Philadelphia, which might have been made in less than a week, was dragged out over twenty-eight days, to the accompaniment of salvos of artillery, fraternal embraces, and frantic cheering.[9]

The streets of the Quaker City throbbed with fanatical crowds as Genêt was welcomed to the nation's capital. At a banquet (four dollars a plate) the passionate diplomat thrilled the diners by singing a French fighting song. Throughout the city wild toasts were drunk to the guillotine, and showers of fiery poems descended upon the youthful minister. As one contemporary later exclaimed:

. . . Can it ever be forgotten, what a racket was made with the citizen Genet? The most enthusiastic homage was too cold to welcome his arrival; and his being the first minister of the infant republic . . . was dwelt upon, as a most endearing circumstance. What hugging and tugging! What addressing and caressing! What mountebanking and chanting! with liberty-caps, and the other wretched trumpery of *sans culotte* foolery! [10]

Whom the Gods Would Destroy

Shortly before arriving at Philadelphia, Genêt learned of the Neutrality Proclamation. He was profoundly shocked, though not disillusioned. His roaring reception had convinced him that American opinion overwhelmingly favored intervention on the side of France,

---

[8] See F. J. Turner, *The Significance of Sections in American History* (N.Y., 1932), Ch. III.

[9] One wag said that the Americans burned more powder celebrating French liberty than was used in achieving it. On the trip Genêt acted as godfather for a papoose who was named Genêt Republican Frenchman.

[10] A. Graydon, *Memoirs of a Life Chiefly Passed in Pennsylvania* (Harrisburgh, 1811), p. 335. Genêt's arrival and activities inspired numerous broadsides bearing such captions as "glorious news" and "great news." See particularly Files 4 (Conn.), 112 (N.Y.), 148 (Penn.), Library of Congress.

and he did not believe that the proclamation correctly represented the popular will. The Francophile editors agreed with the excitable Frenchman, one of them exulting:

Thanks to our God, the *sovereignty* still resides with THE PEOPLE, and that neither proclamations, nor *royal demeanor and state* can prevent them from exercising it. Of this the independent freemen of this metropolis [Philadelphia] gave a striking example in their reception of Mr. Genet.[11]

In due season the annoyed Genêt presented himself to Washington. He may possibly have expected the President to kiss him resoundingly on both cheeks, after the French fashion, and call him "Citizen." But Washington, always dignified and never effusive, was deeply displeased with Genêt's demagoguery and with the premature assumption of his ministerial functions. It is not surprising that the President's few remarks were severely formal—a reception that seemed all the more chilling when contrasted with the warmth of the populace. Genêt's displeasure was further heightened when he noticed medallions of the recently beheaded Louis XVI and his ill-starred family on the walls of the reception room. The impulsive plenipotentiary left in anger, convinced that "this old man" was not what history painted him and that he was an enemy of liberty. Genêt even attributed the President's frigidity to jealousy over his own popular reception, going so far as to report, "old Washington envies me my success."

The continued acclaim of the masses only strengthened the French envoy in his conviction that Washington was not faithfully interpreting the public will. Crowds of Francophiles damned the President for his coolness toward the French alliance, and accused him of seeking a crown and of trying to pass himself off as an honest man. Genêt admitted that one of these published attacks was the work of his own private secretary. Maddened Francophiles even went so far as to print woodcuts of the President being guillotined. In later years John Adams, Vice-President in 1793, reminisced to Thomas Jefferson:

You certainly never felt the terrorism excited by Genet, in 1793, when ten thousand people in the streets of Philadelphia, day after day, threatened to drag Washington out of his house, and effect a revolution in the govern-

---

[11] *National Gazette* (Philadelphia), May 22, 1793, 2:4. Genêt reported to the French Minister of Foreign Relations (May 18, 1793): ". . . You could appreciate the value of the declarations of neutrality . . . if you knew the enthusiasm and the entire devotion of our brothers in the United States." Amer. Hist. Assn., *Annual Report, 1903*, II, 214.

ment, or compel it to declare war in favor of the French revolution and
against England.[12]

Adams went on to say—probably with exaggeration—that he was informed by many of the "coolest" heads in Philadelphia that nothing
but the terrible epidemic of yellow fever which broke out at this time
"could have saved the United States from a fatal revolution of government." Yet in the midst of all this uproar, Washington remained
cool and unperturbed, determined not to be swayed from sound policy
by the clamor of a rabble aroused by foreign agents.

It is not surprising that Genêt was the storm center of American
politics from the time of his arrival in Philadelphia until his departure. He fitted out fourteen privateers, which swarmed from
American ports and brought back, under the very nose of the national
government, over eighty prizes, some of them taken within American
waters. John F. Watson later recorded his childhood memories:

> I remember with what joy we ran to the wharves at the report of cannon
> to see the arrivals of the Frenchmen's prizes,—we were so pleased to see
> the British union down! When we met French mariners or officers in the
> streets, we would cry "Vive la Republique." Although most of us under-
> stood no French, we had caught many national airs, and the streets, by day
> and night, resounded with the songs of boys, such as these: "Allons, enfans
> de la patrie, le jour de gloire est arrivé. . . ." It was a time, when, as it
> seems to me, that Philadelphia boys usurped the attributes of manhood;
> and the men, who should have chastened us, had themselves become very
> puerile! [13]

The privateering enterprises in which Genêt engaged appear to
have been flagrant violations of the neutrality of the United States.[14]
But offenders haled before the bar were freed by pro-French juries.
Public opinion was stronger than law. The British minister lodged
strongly worded protests against America's unneutral conduct, and
Secretary Jefferson made the appropriate representations to Genêt.
The latter indignantly accused the American Secretary of State of
hunting up excuses "in the dusty tomes of Vattel and Grotius." "I
thank God," the French emissary exulted, "I have forgot what these
hired jurisprudists have written."

The notes of the scatterbrained Genêt became more insistent, and

[12] C. F. Adams, ed., *Works of John Adams* (Boston, 1856), X, 47 (Adams to
Jefferson, June 30, 1813).

[13] J. F. Watson, *Annals of Philadelphia* (rev. ed., Phila., 1881), I, 180.

[14] Thomas, *American Neutrality*, pp. 130–131.

his conduct more indiscreet and arrogant. Jefferson obtained from him what appeared to be a promise that the British vessel, *Little Sarah*, which the French had recently captured, would not be sent to sea as a privateer. Yet a few hours later she slipped down the Delaware River to begin a career of destruction. Washington and Jefferson were both furious. Such defiance of the government was even turning the Francophiles against the French minister. Jefferson, who perceived that Genêt was proving to be a Jonah, wrote to Madison in alarm, "he will sink the Republican interest if they do not abandon him."

Genêt finally overreached himself. In a moment of fuming anger he threatened to appeal over the head of the cold and unresponsive government to the sovereign masses. Washington, oppressed by the heat of fetid, disease-ridden Philadelphia, exploded:

Is the minister of the French Republic to set the acts of this government at defiance *with impunity?* And then threaten the executive with an appeal to the people? What must the world think of such conduct, and of the government of the United States in submitting to it? [15]

Excited throngs of Francophiles might vilify Washington, but when it came to an issue between him and a foreign minister sanity returned with a rush. The Federalists gleefully spread broadcast the news of Genêt's indiscretion, and their most caustic spokesman, William Cobbett, branded the Republicans as "bastard offspring of Genêt, spawned in hell, to which they will presently return." Everywhere French sympathizers were hushed and shamed, except for a few who attempted to condone Genêt's offenses.

Washington's Cabinet met and unanimously agreed that the recall of Genêt should be demanded. A new faction had come into power in France, and they were eager to cut off the diplomatic career as well as the head of this *opéra bouffe* bungler, who, with all the cards in his favor, had stirred up an incalculable amount of ill will. But Washington, wisely declining to make a martyr of the fallen idol, refused to send Genêt back to France and almost certain death. The former minister (Hamilton called him a burned-out comet) retired to New York, where hand in hand with the daughter of Governor Clinton, he faced the altar instead of the guillotine.

[15] W. C. Ford, ed., *Writings of George Washington* (N.Y., 1891), XII, 302 (Washington to Jefferson, July 11, 1793).

Monroe's Pro-French Enthusiasms

While Genêt had been making himself *persona non grata*, the able United States minister to France, Gouverneur Morris, had been committing serious indiscretions. Morris was a conservative so openly hostile to the French Revolution that he had offered his house as an asylum to many a refugee from the guillotine. He even drafted and urged the carrying out of a plan to effect the escape of Louis XVI, who, in turn, made him the custodian of several hundred thousand livres to be used as bribe money.[16] When the United States demanded the recall of Genêt, the French government insisted that Morris be withdrawn.

Morris' successor, James Monroe, sympathized with the French Revolution so outspokenly that he should never have been chosen. He was officially received before the entire Convention, where, amid cries of "Vive la République," he made a flaming speech, and was most enthusiastically greeted by the President, who exclaimed:

I am impatient to give you the fraternal embrace, which I am ordered to give in the name of the French people. Come and receive it in the name of the American people, and let this spectacle complete the annihilation of an impious coalition of tyrants.[17]

Thereupon, amid frenzied cheering, Monroe received the fraternal kiss on both cheeks.

Such conduct was extraordinarily indiscreet. Washington had already proclaimed a policy of neutrality; yet here was the official representative of the nation, by word and deed, virtually ranging the United States on the side of France against Great Britain. With the delicate Jay negotiations then under way, the conduct of Monroe placed the United States in a most embarrassing, not to say perilous, position.

Monroe's pro-French excesses merely served to hasten his own undoing. The French officials were deeply concerned over Jay's mission, for they hoped that Great Britain would become involved in a war with the United States. Monroe, inadequately informed by the State Department as to Jay's instructions, gave assurances in good faith that there was nothing to be feared from the negotiations. When, there-

---

[16] Gouverneur Morris, *A Diary of the French Revolution* (ed. by B. C. Davenport, Boston, 1939), II, 475.

[17] S. M. Hamilton, ed., *The Writings of James Monroe* (N.Y., 1899), II, 34 n.

fore, the terms of the treaty were divulged, the anger of the French authorities was commensurate with the extent to which they had been unwittingly deceived by Monroe. The latter, after having achieved considerable temporary success in handling the matter of French seizures of American ships,[18] was thoroughly discredited. Although Jay's Treaty was not technically at variance with previous Franco-American commitments, it did violate the spirit of the Treaty of 1778 by conceding that provision ships sailing for France might be confiscated if the cargoes were paid for. To the French it seemed as if the Americans had turned against their benefactor and had virtually allied themselves with England.

The discomfited Monroe assured the French that Jay's Treaty would never be ratified. Again his predictions proved false. On July 2, 1796, some four months after the pact had been officially proclaimed, the government in Paris issued a decree announcing that it would treat neutrals as they permitted England to treat them. In other words, French seizures of American ships would be renewed. Desperate, Monroe promised that the Federalist administration would be overthrown by the people in the election of 1796, and that the shameful surrender to Britain would be annulled. His protestations were finally cut short by a peremptory recall (August 22, 1796).

WASHINGTON'S VALEDICTORY

Washington had wished to retire at the end of his first term, in 1793, but his friends persuaded him that the critical state of foreign affairs demanded a continuance of his strong hand at the helm. With the Jay and Pinckney Treaties now concluded, he felt that he could safely lay down his burdens. He therefore prepared his Farewell Address, and on September 19, 1796, published it in the newspapers. This memorable statement was written in collaboration with several of his intimate advisers, notably Hamilton, who contributed the literary grace. Washington's immediate object was to announce that he would not be a candidate for a third term; and to this declaration he thought it proper to add some sage advice, particularly with reference to involvement in the European situation.

It will be remembered that Vergennes and Genêt had both attempted to use the United States as a pawn in French schemes. The latter's successor, Fauchet, sought by every means at his command to

[18] B. W. Bond, Jr., *The Monroe Mission to France, 1794–1796* (Baltimore, 1907), p. 22.

block the ratification of Jay's Treaty. His successor, Adet, through subsidies to the press and through Republican societies, aroused the people against the treaty and labored with the House of Representatives to defeat the necessary appropriation. Failing in this, he attempted to bring about the defeat of Washington for re-election and the elevation of the presumably pro-French Jefferson to the presidency—a scheme that was blocked by Washington's withdrawal.[19]

It was with such foreign intermeddling specifically in mind that Washington issued his earnest warning to the American people. He particularly deplored the growth of a violent partisan spirit that inflamed the people with fierce likes or dislikes toward foreign countries.

Washington

. . . Nothing is more essential than that permanent, inveterate antipathies against particular nations and passionate attachments for others should be excluded, and that in place of them just and amicable feelings toward all should be cultivated. The nation which indulges toward another an habitual hatred or an habitual fondness is in some degree a slave. . . . Against the insidious wiles of foreign influence (I conjure you to believe me, fellow-citizens) the jealousy of a free people ought to be *constantly* awake. . . .[20]

Nor did Washington stop here. With the difficulties caused by the entangling treaty with France fresh in mind, he solemnly asserted: "It is our true policy to steer clear of *permanent* alliances with any portion of the foreign world. . . . [But] we may safely trust to temporary alliances for extraordinary emergencies."[21] Washington, in other words, was giving specific advice to a weak and disunited nation in the year 1796—advice that had been dictated by recent and painful experience. He was thinking of the existing situation, and probably had no intention of setting a specific course which the United States

[19] Adet continued to work for Jefferson against the presumably pro-British John Adams, the Federalist candidate, in the campaign of 1796. With an eye to influencing the election, he announced the suspension of his diplomatic functions, while at the same time addressing a rousing appeal to the American people (Nov. 15, 1796). S. F. Bemis, "Washington's Farewell Address: A Foreign Policy of Independence," *Amer. Hist. Rev.*, XXXIX (1934), 263–265.

[20] J. D. Richardson, ed., *Messages and Papers of the Presidents* (Washington, 1896), I, 221, 222. The French minister did not have to read this passage twice to conclude that it was directed at him. He wrote home in anger: "It would be useless to speak to you about it. You will have noticed the lies it contains, the insolent tone that governs it, the immorality which characterizes it." Amer. Hist. Assn., *Annual Report, 1903*, II, 954 (Adet to Minister of Foreign Relations, Oct. 12, 1796).

[21] Richardson, *Messages and Papers of the Presidents*, I, 223. Italics inserted.

would have to follow for all time.[22] The policy of isolation that he recommended was not so much aloofness from the affairs of Europe as the exclusion of European agents and influence from the affairs of the United States, so that the American people might enjoy the blessings of complete independence. This advice was based so clearly on geographic and economic realities, and was so definitely what American statesmen had been thinking since independence, that it was bound to be the keystone of the nation's foreign policy.

Talleyrand Overreaches Himself

Meanwhile French anger at the alleged duplicity of Jay's Treaty had continued to vent itself in the seizure of American ships and the mishandling of their crews. Secretary of State Pickering reported, June 21, 1797, that 316 vessels flying the Stars and Stripes had been captured by French cruisers since July, 1796. There was not, in fact, much to choose between British and French violations of American rights. The conduct of both nations would have justified war, had the United States been looking for war. In a final effort to patch up differences, Washington sent to France a distinguished South Carolina Federalist, Charles C. Pinckney, who could be counted on to avoid Monroe's pro-French excesses. The corrupt, five-headed French Directory, then in power, refused even to receive him; threatened him with arrest if he did not leave French soil; and gave point to its insolence by tendering a grand farewell reception to Monroe. The diplomatic rupture between the two governments was complete.

With affairs in this critical state John Adams, a Federalist, became President, March 4, 1797. In the hope of averting war he sent a commission of three men to France. It consisted of Charles C. Pinckney (then in the Netherlands), Elbridge Gerry, a prominent Massachusetts Republican, and John Marshall, a Virginia Federalist and future Chief Justice of the Supreme Court. The American envoys reached Paris on October 4, 1797, and after exasperating delay were approached by three mysterious personages who were obviously puppets of Talleyrand, the astute and unscrupulous French Minister of Foreign Relations. The three go-betweens were accompanied by the inevitable woman, without whom no European diplomatic intrigue was complete, and who, incidentally, made a very favorable impression on John Marshall.[23] The French agents announced that before actual

[22] Bemis, "Washington's Farewell Address," *loc. cit.*, p. 268.
[23] A. J. Beveridge, *The Life of John Marshall* (Boston, 1916), II, 290, 333.

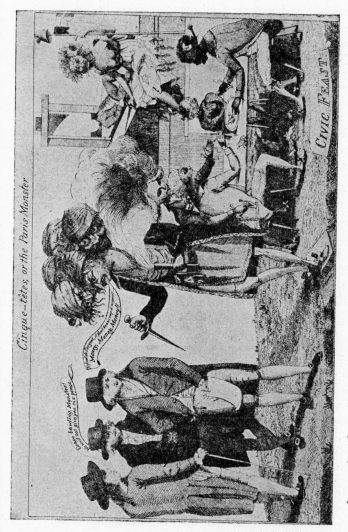

A rare American print (1799) showing the five-headed Directory demanding money of the Americans. The dagger and flaming torch, the Jacobin sitting at a "Civic Feast" of frogs with a Negro and the devil, and the terrible Goddess of Liberty guarding the guillotine, all reflect a Federalist bias. (Reproduced from Volume I of *A History of American Graphic Humor*, by William Murrell.)

negotiations could proceed, the Directory would have to receive an apology for certain allusions to France in President Adams' recent message to Congress. In addition, the Americans were to pay a bribe of 1,200,000 livres, and make a loan of 32,000,000 florins, which, under the circumstances, would be largely or wholly a gift. The American envoys, however, did not give a satisfactory answer. Their official report is revealing:

M. X. [a French agent] again returned to the subject of money: Said he, gentlemen, you do not speak to the point; it is money: it is expected that you will offer money. We said that we had spoken to that point very explicitly: We had given an answer. No, said he, you have not: what is your answer? We replied, it is no; no; not a sixpence.[24]

The three Americans could not have been greatly shocked at the mention of bribery, which was an accepted tool of eighteenth-century diplomacy.[25] But they rejected the French proposals because they had no instructions to pay such a large sum, and because a substantial loan at the time would have been a breach of neutrality and might have involved the United States in war with England. Even if otherwise unobjectionable, the terms demanded were excessive for mere recognition of the three Americans. Pinckney and Marshall, convinced that further negotiations were hopeless, left France in high dudgeon. The wily Talleyrand, who did not want war with the United States and who saw the wisdom of protracting negotiations, persuaded the pro-French Gerry to stay on. After some fruitless interchanges, the American envoy was summarily recalled.

FIGHTING FOR PEACE

When the news of Talleyrand's insolence reached America, early in 1798, the lusty young republic was aroused as probably never before. The excitement was increased when President Adams laid the dispatches from the American envoys before Congress, anonymously designating the French go-betweens as X, Y, and Z. Ten thousand copies of these documents were promptly distributed at public expense, and American sentiment was quickly lashed into a fury of indignation. War preparations were rushed, and even Quakers favored fighting. The slogan, "Millions for defense but not one cent

---

[24] *American State Papers, Foreign Relations*, II, 161 (Oct. 27, 1797).

[25] E. W. Lyon, "The Directory and the United States," *Amer. Hist. Rev.*, XLIII (1938), 521.

for tribute," was on every tongue.[26] Resolutions, addresses, public meetings, reams of patriotic poetry, songs, and banquets contributed to the crescendo of patriotic fervor. Popular among the toasts was: "May the American Eagle pluck out the Gills of the Gallic Cock." When John Marshall returned from France he received an ovation such as had been given to no other American save Washington. Countless thousands of husky throats bawled the words of "Adams and Liberty" and "Washington and the Constitution." The few bold Francophiles who tried to sing "Ça Ira" or the "Marseillaise" were quickly hissed down. Under the inspiration of the hour Joseph Hopkinson wrote his stirring "Hail Columbia," which was set to the tune of the popular "President's March." It was introduced to a Philadelphia audience by an actor in full sailor dress. William Cobbett's description is graphic:

Never was anything received with applause so hearty and so general. . . . At every repetition it was received with additional enthusiasm, 'till, towards the last, great part of the audience, pit, box, and gallery, actually joined in the chorus. . . . Every [stanza] . . . was closed with long and loud clappings and huzzas, but no sooner were the words, "Behold the *Chief who now commands*" pronounced, than the house shook to its very centre; the song and the whole were drowned in the enthusiastic peals of applause, and were obliged to stop and begin again and again, in order to gain a hearing.[27]

This patriotic song spread like a rushing torrent, and probably did more than anything else to express the new national consciousness of the United States. The citizens of the republic were for the most part no longer pro-French or pro-British—but Americans.

Responding to the popular clamor, Congress took a hand. In May and July of 1798 it authorized the capture of the armed ships of France, but not merchantmen, as would have been the case in a full-fledged war. On June 13, 1798, commercial intercourse with France was suspended; and eight days later President Adams informed Congress in a ringing message: "I will never send another minister to France without assurances that he will be received, respected, and honored as the representative of a great, free, powerful, and independent nation."[28] On July 7, 1798, Congress declared the treaties

---

[26] This slogan was erroneously attributed to Pinckney. Throughout his life he denied its authorship; yet when he died it was inscribed on a tablet to his memory in his native city, Charleston.

[27] *Porcupine's Gazette* (Philadelphia), April 28, 1798, 2:2.

[28] Richardson, *Messages and Papers of the Presidents*, I, 266 (June 21, 1798).

with France void on the grounds that they had already been violated by the French government.

As a result of Congressional authorization, the tiny but efficient American Navy, aided by privately owned vessels, began an undeclared naval war which lasted over two years and resulted in the capture of more than eighty armed French ships, principally privateers operating in West Indian waters. Washington was summoned from retirement to command the American army against the expected invader. These military preparations, together with a number of brilliant naval successes, further aroused patriotic enthusiasm. Seafaring men sang lustily:

> Now let each jolly tar, with one heart and one voice,
> Drink a can of good grog to the man of our choice;
> Under John, the State pilot, and George's command,
> There's a fig for the French and the sly Talleyrand.[29]

Second in command of the American army was the energetic Alexander Hamilton, who like many other Federalists wanted war with France so that he could despoil Spain of New Orleans and Florida. (It will be borne in mind that in 1796 Spain had forsaken England and allied herself with France.) Hamilton apparently dreamed of placing himself at the head of the victorious American troops, and returning a laurel-crowned conqueror.[30] Great Britain was delighted with the turn affairs had taken; and the presence of a common foe brought the two nations closer together than they were to be for many a year. There was, in fact, some talk of an alliance. The Duke of Gloucester actually proposed lending the Americans a number of warships. Although nothing came of this suggestion, the British did provide the United States with a considerable quantity of arms, and shared their naval signals so that American and British ships could recognize each other.[31] The pro-British party was everywhere in the ascendant; and the pro-French Republicans were disgraced. Many of them went so far as to join enthusiastically in the war preparations against France.[32]

[29] J. B. McMaster, *A History of the People of the United States* (N.Y., 1896), II, 406 n.

[30] A. P. Whitaker, *The Mississippi Question, 1795-1803* (N.Y., 1934), pp. 116-118.

[31] E. Channing, *A History of the United States* (N.Y., 1929), IV, 198-199.

[32] Louis-Guillaume Otto, former French *chargé d'affaires* in the United States, wrote in the summer of 1797: "Our agents wished to see only two political parties in the United States, the French party and the English party; but there is a middle party, much larger, composed of the most estimable men of the two other parties. This party, whose existence we have not even suspected, is the American party which loves

ADAMS PUTS COUNTRY ABOVE PARTY

President John Adams managed to keep a level head in spite of the dizzy heights of popularity to which his Administration had unexpectedly been elevated. Like Washington and other statesmen of his generation, he fully realized that war had to be avoided at all costs. Yet the Federalists, who had elected him to office, were making preparations for a conflict with France. In so doing they were discrediting their opponents and strengthening their hold on the national administration. Adams knew perfectly well that he would dig his political grave if he averted the war that his party so ardently desired. The inflated popularity of the Federalists would collapse, and he himself would probably not be re-elected in 1800. Yet it was obvious to him that France did not want war; for otherwise she would have replied to American reprisals with thoroughgoing offensive operations. Talleyrand feared that limited hostilities might spread into a genuine war, in which case his plans for resurrecting the French empire in Louisiana would be ruined, and France's commerce and colonies would be jeopardized. He therefore instructed the consul general in Philadelphia to issue propaganda that would counteract the anti-French agitation.[33] He also let it be known, particularly through the United States minister at The Hague, William Vans Murray, that he would respectfully receive an American diplomatic representative.

When Adams learned of the conciliatory attitude of the French Foreign Office, he decided upon a courageous course. Without consulting his Cabinet, he boldly sent to the Senate (February 18, 1799) the nomination of William Vans Murray as minister to France. The Federalist leaders were at first thunderstruck; then their fury was unbounded. If Murray went to France, there might be no war—no further discrediting of the Republican party, no conquest of New Orleans and Florida. The Federalists argued and pleaded with Adams, but to no avail. The only concession he would make was to expand the single nomination into a commission, adding William R. Davie of North Carolina and Oliver Ellsworth of Connecticut. The Federalists were forced to accept the compromise or incur the odium of deliberately rejecting peace. On this issue Adams had the country with him; and in spite of the vituperation of his opponents he saw to it that the envoys sailed.

its country above all and for whom preferences either for France or England are only accessory and often passing affections." Quoted in Lyon, "The Directory and the United States," *loc. cit.*, p. 520.

[33] *Ibid.*, p. 525.

This partisan obstruction cost the United States an opportunity to drive a hard bargain.[34] In the summer of 1799, when the negotiations should have begun, the allied coalition of Great Britain, Austria, and Russia was pressing hard upon France, and Napoleon was stranded in Egypt. By the time the American commission arrived, in March, 1800, the picture had changed. Napoleon was First Consul; and in June he crushed the Austrians at Marengo. But even with his improved position, Bonaparte had no desire to fight America, force her into an alliance with England, and at the same time ruin his plans for Louisiana. France's distress was still such as to contribute to an American diplomatic success.

The negotiations with Napoleon reached an impasse over claims. The envoys from the United States insisted that France pay approximately $20,000,000 for recent spoliations of American commerce. They also urged a mutual abrogation of the treaties that Congress had already denounced. After seven months of discussion the deadlock was broken by what amounted to a cancellation of both sets of demands. By the convention concluded on September 30, 1800, Napoleon agreed, as it was finally worked out, to forget about the treaties if the United States would forget about the claims—an arrangement which meant, of course, that the American government would have to reimburse its own citizens.[35]

But this was a small sum to pay for getting rid of the only formal treaty of alliance to which the United States has been a party. Nor did the benefits end here. The Convention of 1800 assured peace with France at a time when peace was imperative for the development of the United States. No less important is the fact that the agreement cleared the way for the incalculably significant purchase of Louisiana. If Adams had insisted on open hostilities with France in 1800, it is highly improbable that Napoleon, three years later, would have sold his enormous trans-Mississippi empire to the United States.

What Adams had foreseen came to pass. Although renominated by the Federalists in 1800, he was defeated by the Republicans. His party never regained control of the national administration, and he was never again elected to a federal office. But he had no regrets. In his declining years he wrote:

[34] *Ibid.*, p. 532.
[35] Article II of the convention provided for subsequent negotiations on claims and treaties. This was removed by the Senate. Talleyrand consented to the amendment with the understanding that it meant a "reciprocal renunciation" by both Powers of indemnities and treaties. E. Wilson Lyon, "The Franco-American Convention of 1800," *Jour. of Mod. Hist.*, XII (1940), 329–333.

. . . I will defend my missions to France, as long as I have an eye to direct my hand, or a finger to hold my pen. They were the most disinterested and meritorious actions of my life. I reflect upon them with so much satisfaction, that I desire no other inscription over my gravestone than: "Here lies John Adams, who took upon himself the responsibility of the peace with France in the year 1800." [36]

The Federalist party of Washington and Adams, whatever its shortcomings in dealing with domestic affairs, had done well in the field of foreign relations. When it laid down the reins of authority in 1801 there were no lowering clouds on the horizon. It had established as the polestar of American diplomacy the policies of peace, neutrality, noninterference, and nonintervention. Thanks to Europe's distresses it had persuaded Great Britain and Spain to make treaties adjusting existing grievances. Thanks also to Europe's distresses it had negotiated the Convention of 1800 with France, by which the United States honorably terminated its first and only entangling alliance, and by which it shook off the last diplomatic shackle binding it to Europe. Another chapter in American diplomatic history had come to a successful close.

BIBLIOGRAPHICAL NOTE

There is no single book that satisfactorily covers Franco-American relations from 1789 to 1800. Perhaps the most useful brief account is in E. Channing, *History of the United States* (N.Y., 1929), IV, Chs. V, VII. C. D. Hazen, *Contemporary American Opinion of the French Revolution* (Baltimore, 1897) is the best on the subject. C. M. Thomas, *American Neutrality in 1793* (N.Y., 1931) is a relatively recent doctoral dissertation. F. J. Turner, *The Significance of Sections in American History* (N.Y., 1932), has an important chapter (III) on Genêt's projected attack on Louisiana and another (V) on French policy toward the Mississippi Valley. A detailed and readable account of the XYZ mission may be found in A. J. Beveridge, *The Life of John Marshall* (Boston, 1916), II, 214–334. Old but still useful is B. W. Bond, Jr., *The Monroe Mission to France, 1794–1796* (Baltimore, 1907). B. Faÿ, *The Revolutionary Spirit in France and America* (N.Y., 1927), pp. 252–478, develops the cultural side of Franco-American relations for these years. The most satisfactory life of Adams is Gilbert Chinard, *Honest John Adams* (Boston, 1933). G. W. Allen, *Our Naval War with France* (Boston, 1909) is the best on the subject. J. A. James develops public opinion in two articles: "French Diplomacy and American Politics, 1794–1795," Amer. Hist. Assn., *Annual Report, 1911*, I, 153–163; and "French Opinion as a Factor in Preventing War between France and the United States, 1795–1800," *Amer. Hist. Rev.*, XXX (1924), 44–55. S. F. Bemis' "Washington's Farewell Address: A Foreign Policy of Independence,"

[36] *Works of John Adams*, X, 113 (Adams to Lloyd, Jan. 1815).

ibid., XXXIX (1934), 250–268, is significant. Talleyrand appears in a more favorable light than hitherto in E. W. Lyon, "The Directory and the United States," *ibid.*, XLIII (1938), 514–532. For further references see note at end of previous chapter, the footnotes of this chapter, and Bemis and Griffin, *Guide*, Ch. IV.

RECENT REFERENCES. The most valuable study of the Convention of 1800, based largely on French documents, is E. Wilson Lyon, "The Franco-American Convention of 1800," *Jour. of Mod. Hist.*, XII (1940), 305–333. The French negotiators, on the whole, appear to good advantage. A. K. Weinberg, "Washington's 'Great Rule' in Its Historical Evolution," in E. F. Goldman, ed., *Historiography and Urbanization: Essays in American History in Honor of W. Stull Holt* (Baltimore, 1941), pp. 109–138. The author discusses the ambiguity of Washington's (Hamilton's) phrases in the Farewell Address, and the subsequent disagreement among statesmen and publicists as to whether the prescription against alliances bound America for all time and in all parts of the world. Weinberg concludes that Washington's doctrine was essentially "freedom of action." Huntley Dupre's "The Kentucky Gazette Reports the French Revolution," *Miss. Valley Hist. Rev.*, XXVI (1939), 163–180, shows the great interest in and general sympathy for the Revolution on the Kentucky frontier.

NEW REFERENCES. Considerable light is shed on this period by Bernard Mayo, ed., *Instructions to the British Ministers to the United States, 1791–1812* (Washington, 1941). Suggestive of lend-lease operations in World War II was the lending by the British to the United States, during the XYZ crisis, of cannon and shot, which were to be returned upon demand (p. 168). Foreign Secretary Grenville also suggested, apparently without effect, that Britain would provide warships if America would supply needed seamen (pp. 155–160). Myrna Boyce, "The Diplomatic Career of William Short," *Jour. of Mod. Hist.*, XV (1943), 97–119, has considerable material on United States relations with Spain and France to 1795. Short, an able and long-suffering but ill-appreciated diplomat, laid the groundwork for the treaty of 1795 with Spain, but Pinckney got the credit.

4TH. ED. REFS. Margaret Woodbury, "Public Opinion in Philadelphia, 1789–1801," *Smith College Studies in History*, V, nos. 1–2 (1919–1920), has useful background material. Louis Guillaume Otto, *Considérations sur la conduite du gouvernement américain envers la France, depuis le commencement de la révolution jusqu'en 1797* (Gilbert Chinard, ed.) [Princeton, 1945]. G. W. Kyte, "Robert Liston and Anglo-American Cooperation, 1796–1800," Amer. Philosophical Soc. *Procs.*, XCIII (1949), 259–266, describes the close co-operation under the friendly new minister to the United States during the XYZ days. The British gave twenty-four heavy cannon and plans for manufacturing ordnance, made available some naval supplies and a few naval officers, exchanged military and naval intelligence, unsuccessfully sought an alliance, and promised (through Lord Cornwallis of Yorktown fame) thousands of muskets and a quantity of cannon in the event of full-dress hostilities with France.

CHAPTER VII

Jefferson and the Purchase of Louisiana, 1801–1803

"From this day [Louisiana purchase] the United States take their place among the powers of first rank. . . ."

Robert R. Livingston, 1803.

WAR BECOMES CHEAPER THAN PEACE

THE POLITICAL upheaval of 1800, which threw the Federalists out of power, brought Thomas Jefferson to the presidency in March, 1801. As if some evil genius were pursuing him, the exigencies of politics—particularly of foreign affairs—forced the distinguished Virginian to reverse virtually every policy that he had espoused while head of the opposition Republican party.

It will be remembered, first of all, that Jefferson, though fundamentally an American, warmly favored the French as against the British. Second, he was strongly opposed to European involvements; and in his inaugural address issued a solemn warning against "entangling alliances"—a phrase to which he, not Washington, gave currency. Third, he had pledged himself to a policy of economy and reduction of the national debt. Fourth, as leader of the agrarian party, he detested costly frigates, which he regarded as the tools of Federalist manufacturers and shippers; and he urged that these vessels be laid up on the Potomac. Fifth, he was a vigorous opponent of war, though not, strictly speaking, a pacifist. "Peace," he declared, "is our passion." Finally, he advocated a strict construction of the Constitution, and he had upbraided the Federalists for strengthening the central government at the expense of the states by broadly interpreting that instrument. These were the principal Jeffersonian tenets; and they soon clashed with practical necessities in dealing with the perennial problem of the Barbary pirates.

Washington and Adams had been forced to endure the humiliation of purchasing treaties with three of the North African states, and of sending them hundreds of thousands of dollars in protection money ("presents").[1] Ironically enough, at almost the very time when the citizens of the republic were shouting themselves hoarse with the slogan, "Millions for defense but not one cent for tribute," an American ship arrived at Algiers with twenty-six barrels of blackmail dollars. The depths of degradation were reached in October, 1800, when the Dey of Algiers forced a United States man-of-war, most inappropriately named the *George Washington*, to haul down the flag of the young republic, replace it with that of Algiers, and sail to Constantinople bearing an ambassador and presents to the Sultan. When Captain Bainbridge vainly protested, the Dey replied: "You pay me tribute, by which you become my slaves. I have, therefore, a right to order you as I may think proper."[2]

When Jefferson was minister to France, he had been charged with ransoming captive American sailors from the Barbary "hellhounds." Spurred on by the moans of his fellow citizens, he had then made the proposal that the Powers of Europe band together and wipe out these "pyrates." But nothing came of his suggestion. The heavy account was still unsettled when Jefferson, the so-called pacifist, became President. He had hardly taken office when the Pasha of Tripoli, feeling neglected in the apportionment of tribute, declared war on the United States by cutting down the flagstaff at the American consulate.

Three of Jefferson's most precious principles were immediately involved. He was pledged to economy (hostilities with Tripoli would be expensive); he disliked the navy; and he detested war. But concern for the honor of the flag and for the safety of American seamen, reinforced by a vivid memory of Barbary brutality, induced Jefferson to forsake consistency. He adopted the bold and in the long run the less expensive course of sending warships to Mediterranean waters. In 1805, after heroic exploits, the United States succeeded in extorting from Tripoli the most favorable treaty that any nation had yet secured from her. The War of 1812 delayed a thorough chastisement of the remaining North African states; but at the close of hostilities the United States dictated a satisfactory treaty with Algiers (1816) at the cannon's mouth.[3] Jefferson's courageous action inaugurated a policy

---

[1] These were Algiers (1795), Tripoli (1796), and Tunis (1797). The treaty of 1786 with Morocco had proved reasonably satisfactory. See R. W. Irwin, *The Diplomatic Relations of the United States with the Barbary Powers, 1776–1816* (Chapel Hill, N.C., 1931), pp. 82–91.

[2] G. W. Allen, *Our Navy and the Barbary Corsairs* (Boston, 1905), p. 77.

[3] The editor of the most influential weekly magazine in the United States expressed a not uncommon sentiment when he declared: "Oh! that it may fall to the lot of this

that freed American commerce, strengthened American nationality, and awakened a new respect for the United States.

THE SHADOW OF THE CORSICAN

Meanwhile, the attention of the American people had turned to a much more pressing and vital problem nearer home—the disposition of Louisiana. This magnificent expanse of territory had been ceded by France to Spain in 1762 to compensate the latter for her losses to Britain in the Seven Years' War. No true Frenchman could ever forget that this imperial wilderness, which immortalized the name of Louis XIV, had once belonged to France; and beginning about 1792 the French began to lay plans and enter into intrigues for regaining their lost colony. Napoleon Bonaparte, like Talleyrand and others, became fascinated by this vision; and, once in power, he proceeded to act with characteristic ruthlessness and energy.

The traditional story is that the masterful Napoleon put great pressure on the Spanish king and forced him to sell Louisiana. The fact is that the province was so heavy a liability to the Spaniards that they had been eager to dispose of it since 1795.[4] First, and most pressing, the administration and defense of the colony cost the Spanish treasury a heavy annual deficit. Second, the amorphous colony, defended by flimsy ramparts and a few rusty guns, was a standing invitation to an invader, and was likely to fall at the outbreak of hostilities with the United States, France, or Great Britain. Finally, Spain valued Louisiana chiefly as a buffer to protect her more valuable lands against the aggressive American frontiersmen. She was weary of holding them back, and nervous over the prospect of becoming involved in war. But if France could be persuaded to take over the province, she would have to shoulder the burden of keeping the purposeful Westerner in check—at no cost to Spain. As Talleyrand promised:

Let the Court of Madrid cede these districts to France, and from that moment the power of America is bounded by the limit which it may suit the interests and the tranquillity of France and Spain to assign her. The youthful republic to have the high honor of reducing this nest of pirates . . . and make the *civilized* nations of Europe blush for that vile jealousy, wicked policy, and dirty calculation of interest which induced them to permit or endure such depredations." Niles' *Weekly Register*, IX, 3 (Sept. 2, 1815). Several months earlier the same journal asserted: "The war against *Algiers* is among the most popular that one people ever declared against another. If we may judge the general feeling by what appears in the newspapers, it is almost universally approved." *Ibid.*, VIII, 105 (Apr. 15, 1815).

[4] A. P. Whitaker, *The Mississippi Question, 1795–1803* (N.Y., 1934), pp. 176–182.

French Republic . . . will be a wall of brass forever impenetrable to the combined efforts of England and America.[5]

Napoleon offered to give the son-in-law of the Spanish king the North Italian kingdom of Tuscany, or an equivalent, in exchange for Louisiana. Well might Charles IV of Spain think that he was getting a splendid bargain in trading his trans-Mississippi wilderness (with 50,000 inhabitants of various colors) for over one million civilized subjects on the banks of the Arno. The preliminary arrangements were concluded at San Ildefonso, on October 1, 1800, the day after the American envoys signed the Convention of 1800 with France. One year later to the day Napoleon concluded the preliminary Peace of Amiens with Great Britain. He was making sure that neither a war with the United States nor one with England would interfere with his adventure in empire building.

Over two years elapsed before Charles IV signed the order to deliver Louisiana to France. He had begun to suspect, with good reason, that Bonaparte was not going to carry through the exchange of Tuscany in good faith. To quiet his suspicions, the French minister to Spain was instructed to give a written pledge that under no circumstances would France ever transfer Louisiana to a third Power. Somewhat reassured by this promise, but still reluctant, Charles IV yielded to the peremptory demands of Napoleon and, on October 15, 1802, signed the fateful order.

THE RISING OF THE WEST

During 1801 and 1802 rumors of the Louisiana transaction drifted into the United States; but they do not appear to have caused undue alarm. Jefferson, however, was uneasy. At this time his friend, Pierre Samuel du Pont de Nemours, the distinguished French physiocrat, was about to return to France after a three-year sojourn in the United States, and Jefferson made unofficial use of him to lay before the French authorities the arguments against taking over Louisiana.[6] The

---

[5] Henry Adams, *History of the United States of America during the Administrations of Jefferson and Madison* (N.Y., 1889), I, 357.

[6] Du Pont de Nemours was one of the first, perhaps the first, to suggest the idea of purchase to Jefferson, though without effect at the time. His unofficial negotiations in France appear to have had some influence. Gilbert Chinard, *The Correspondence of Jefferson and Du Pont de Nemours* (Baltimore, 1931), pp. xxxiv–xliii. The two sons of Du Pont de Nemours became manufacturers of powder in Delaware, thus establishing the business for which the Du Pont family became famous in America.

full seriousness of the situation was not brought home to the American people until October 16, 1802, when the Spanish Intendant at New Orleans suspended the right of deposit without naming another place. This was a direct violation of the Pinckney Treaty of 1795; and although freedom of navigation was not affected, the Mississippi flatboatmen, who were now handling a large quantity of agricultural produce, would find it intolerably inconvenient not to land cargoes while waiting for ocean-going ships. "The Mississippi," wrote James Madison, "is to them every thing. It is the Hudson, the Delaware, the Potomac, and all the navigable rivers of the Atlantic States, formed into one stream." [7]

The ominous tidings from New Orleans traveled slowly up the great river and penetrated the valleys. The Westerners, whose wartime prosperity had recently been depressed by the Peace of Amiens (signed March 27, 1802, by England and France), gave vent to a prolonged cry of anger. The loss of the right of deposit was bad enough; but it was assumed that the order had been dictated by Napoleon and that the river would be completely closed when he took over Louisiana. The Frankfort (Kentucky) *Palladium* brought out an "extra"; there was wild talk of secession and of direct action. "The Kentuckymen," reported one American, "have often wished for an opportunity of sacking New Orleans, and the day may not be far distant." A bellicose Westerner wrote, "I am certain that I could raise 500 men in and have them Ready in one week if permesion [*sic*] was only gave." [8]

The demoralized Federalists, now the "outs," were overjoyed. Here was an excellent opportunity for them to pose as protectors of the West (whose interests they had hitherto opposed), and with the aid of Western votes ride once more into popularity and power. The Jefferson administration was confronted with a perplexing problem. Unless it took prompt and effective steps to quiet the restless Westerners, there might be a disruption of the Union. And if it did take strong measures, it probably would provoke a disastrous foreign war, which might bring the same result.

Fortunately, the Westerners, to whom the sudden conversion of the Federalists did not ring altogether true, showed an unexpected degree of moderation. They were preponderantly Jeffersonian Republicans; and as such were willing to give their President a fair

---

[7] *American State Papers, Foreign Relations*, II, 527 (Madison to Pinckney, Nov. 27, 1802).

[8] Whitaker, *The Mississippi Question*, p. 222.

chance to see what he could do by diplomacy.[9] In addition, even without the right of deposit the Spanish authorities were allowing produce to flow freely down the Mississippi. Spain had taken away enough to anger the Westerners; but had left enough to keep them from fighting. Finally, in spite of vainglorious boasting, "the men of the Western waters" perceived that a war with both France and Spain was not to be undertaken lightly. One Kentuckian faced realities:

. . . I am affraid the united States are too Weake to attempt any thing by force, therefore I Suppose some other means must be used. I fear we Shall be insulted by other nations and not have it in our Power even to make an attempt to Repell the Insult. No Army No Nevy and worst of all an Empty Treasury.[10]

PATCHING HOME FENCES

Jefferson, though outwardly maintaining a gentle optimism, was by this time genuinely alarmed, writing that the crisis was "the most important the United States have ever met since their independence." He was perfectly content to have the decrepit Spaniards as neighbors because he had long believed that the Americans could take what they wanted when they needed it. But if Louisiana fell into the clutches of France, the greatest military power in Europe, the future would be dark—and probably bloody.

Again the realist triumphed over the theorist. Faced with the necessities of the moment, Jefferson, the Francophile, the Anglophobe, and the isolationist, abandoned three of his most sacred principles. "We stand completely corrected of the error," he declared, "that either the Government or the nation of France has any remains of friendship for us." He added:

There is on the globe one single spot, the possessor of which is our natural and habitual enemy. It is New Orleans. . . . The day that France takes possession of New Orleans, fixes the sentence which is to restrain her [the United States] forever within her low-water mark. . . . From that moment, we must marry ourselves to the British fleet and nation.[11]

---

[9] In Kentucky a citizen who cried for direct action was jailed for disturbing the peace. Another who advocated an independent West or one allied with France was tried for sedition and burned in effigy, the crowd shouting, "Perpetuity to the Union! Confidence in Government! Free Navigation of the Mississippi!" Bernard Mayo, *Henry Clay: Spokesman of the New West* (Boston, 1937), p. 139.

[10] Whitaker, *The Mississippi Question*, p. 228.

[11] A. A. Lipscomb, ed., *Writings of Thomas Jefferson* (Monticello ed., Washington, 1904), X, 312–315 (Jefferson to Livingston, April 18, 1802).

It is astonishing to find Jefferson, whose phrase "entangling alliances" was still ringing in the ears of the American people, proposing an entanglement with his old enemy, England, to fight, if need be, his old friend, France. Nothing could better reveal his desperation.

Jefferson's most pressing problem was to take care of the home front. The Federalists might ride into power on the Louisiana issue; and Federalist control in Washington could scarcely have been less distasteful to the Republicans than French control in New Orleans. Moreover, if negotiations with France were to have any prospect of success, the Westerners had to be kept quiet, and above all restrained from making a rash descent upon New Orleans. Although Congress, reflecting the temper of the country, authorized the President to call upon the governors of the states for 80,000 militiamen, Jefferson went quietly about his business. He openly consorted with the British *chargé*, as if to announce that French policy was throwing the United States into the arms of Napoleon's enemy; and he cleverly used the outbursts of the Westerners to play upon the fears of the French and Spanish diplomatic representatives in Washington. Jefferson succeeded so well that the Spanish government proceeded with unaccustomed haste to restore the right of deposit. The United States was not officially informed of this about-face, however, until April 19, 1803. Meanwhile something spectacular had to be done to placate the West.

Fortunately, Jefferson hit upon the idea of sending James Monroe to France as a special envoy to assist Robert Livingston, the regular minister. The nomination was confirmed by the Senate on January 12, 1803. Livingston, however, needed no assistance. He had been presenting the disadvantages of Louisiana to the French authorities with such zeal that one of them offered to give him a certificate as the most importunate negotiator he had ever met. But Monroe possessed the confidence of the West to an unusual degree. He owned large holdings of land in that section; and of all the men then prominent in public life he had most conspicuously identified himself with the interests of the Westerners. The Monroe mission, in its primary object of quieting the West, was a success before Monroe even left the United States.[12]

The chances that a special envoy would accomplish anything by negotiation were exceedingly poor; only extraordinarily good luck would help Monroe. Nevertheless he and Livingston were instructed to offer as much as 50,000,000 livres (about $10,000,000) for New

[12] Whitaker, *The Mississippi Question*, pp. 207–208.

Orleans and West Florida. A few weeks later the two envoys received additional instructions authorizing them, should they fail to attain their objectives at Paris, to open negotiations looking toward an alliance with England. "On the event of this mission," Jefferson solemnly reminded them, "depend the future destinies of this Republic."

THE SANTO DOMINGO DEBACLE

Meanwhile Napoleon had been taking vigorous measures to occupy his newly acquired empire. The first task was to wrest the French colony of Santo Domingo from control of the revolted Negro slaves. This enormously productive sugar island, which had been by far the most profitable of France's overseas possessions, was largely dependent upon the United States for foodstuffs, lumber, and other necessities. One of Napoleon's principal reasons for securing Louisiana was to provide a granary within the French empire for the more important colony of Santo Domingo, which he intended to make both the capital and key of his New World domain.

Shortly after the preliminary Peace of Amiens (October 1, 1801), which removed the menace of the British navy, Napoleon sent to Santo Domingo a splendid army of veterans, under the command of his brother-in-law, the able Leclerc. The leadership of the maddened Dominican slaves had fallen to a gifted, full-blooded Negro, Toussaint L'Ouverture, whose career afforded a number of striking parallels to that of Napoleon.[13] Toussaint was aware of these similarities, and prided himself on being the "Bonaparte of the Antilles." The real Bonaparte, who feared that the apings of this "miserable negro" would make him the laughing stock of all Europe, ordered his men to make short work of these "gilded Africans."[14]

Napoleon planned to occupy Louisiana next. For this purpose a powerful army under General Victor was being organized in Holland with instructions to take up the strongest possible position and engage in intrigues with the Indians.[15] If the French empire had rolled into Louisiana, it probably could not have been dislodged by any force that the United States alone was then capable of raising.

[13] Toussaint's success was in considerable part due to the friendly co-operation of President Adams, whose policy harmonized with that of England. Jefferson pursued an opposite course, and at the outset was quite willing that France should regain Santo Domingo. C. C. Tansill, *The United States and Santo Domingo, 1798–1873* (Baltimore, 1938), pp. 79 ff.

[14] Adams, *History*, II, 387.

[15] E. W. Lyon, *Louisiana in French Diplomacy, 1759–1804* (Norman, Okla., 1934), pp. 135–136.

Toussaint's resistance collapsed in less than three months. He was treacherously seized, taken to France, and imprisoned in a chilly cell high in the Jura Mountains, there to cough his life away. But the fury of the former slaves swept away 17,000 Frenchmen, disrupted Napoleon's plans, and delayed complete conquest until the deadly scourge of yellow fever came to the assistance of the blacks. Five hundred thousand Negroes, heartened by this unexpected ally, and maddened by the news that Napoleon planned to rivet the shackles of slavery once more upon them, arose again with an almost unparalleled fanaticism. "These men may be killed," Leclerc reported, "but will not surrender. They laugh at death;—and it is the same with the women." [16] In one group of 176 Negro prisoners, 173 strangled themselves.

Decimated by bullets and disease, one French army after another melted away. "The rebellion grows," lamented Leclerc, "the disease continues." Over 4000 Frenchmen died of yellow fever in the month of September, 1802. Desperate, Leclerc begged for 12,000 more men at once, 600 more a month through the next hot season, and 15,000 more the following autumn. He reported that he could never subdue Santo Domingo without 12,000 acclimated troops, and he estimated that 70,000 Frenchmen would have to die before that many would be immune from the scourge. He recommended extreme methods:

We must destroy all the mountain negroes, men and women, sparing only children under twelve years of age. We must destroy half the negroes of the plains, and not allow in the colony a single man who has worn an epaulette. Without these measures the colony will never be at peace, and every year, especially deadly ones like this, you will have a civil war on your hands which will jeopardize the future.[17]

Less than a month after writing this letter Leclerc died of yellow fever.

NAPOLEON FORESTALLS THE BRITISH

Bonaparte, though outwardly calm, was inwardly frantic. Fifty thousand men had already been sacrificed in the fiery furnace of Santo Domingo. Fifty thousand more men and an enormous sum of money would have to be thrown into the pestilential island before it could be subdued. Even with such a force he might fail; but if he did succeed he would lose anyhow—for the island would be ruined. While

[16] T. L. Stoddard, *The French Revolution in San Domingo* (Boston, 1914), p. 335 (Leclerc to Bonaparte, Aug. 6, 1802).

[17] *Ibid.*, p. 342 (Oct. 7, 1802).

in this state of mind Napoleon received the news of Leclerc's death, a blow that staggered him. A few days later, during a private conversation on another subject, he suddenly burst out, "Damn sugar, damn coffee, damn colonies!" With his prestige suffering badly at home and abroad, he could not afford to go on with this mad venture and risk another setback. Since he had to abandon Santo Domingo, what need had he for the granary—Louisiana? [18]

The situation in America was intimately bound up with that in Europe. The Peace of Amiens with England was only a truce; the old sources of friction still remained and rankled; and there was bound to be a renewal of hostilities within a few months. Such an eventuality Napoleon now welcomed. He was tired of the role of beneficent shop-keeper; his destiny lay in war. A few glorious campaigns, and the people would forget all about his failure in Santo Domingo. Besides, he could not hold Louisiana against the naval power of England. But he would have to make haste, for word had come to him that the British were raising a large force to seize New Orleans. It would be far better to sell Louisiana to the Americans for a substantial sum than to let it fall into the maw of the British lion.

But money, although important to Napoleon, could hardly have been a paramount consideration, for Spain would almost certainly have been willing to outbid the United States in order to keep Louisiana out of American hands. Nor did Napoleon, as some have represented, dispose of the province because of the traditional French love for the United States. As far as his motives can be fathomed, he desired (1) to avert future wars with the expanding American republic; [19] (2) to avoid driving the United States into British arms; and (3) to raise up a powerful republic that would block the expansion of England, compete with her merchant marine, and, as he presciently put it, "sooner or later humble her pride."

Having made his decision, Bonaparte acted with Napoleonic unexpectedness and dispatch. On April 11, 1803, he summoned his finance minister, Barbé-Marbois, and, with a magnificent gesture, peremptorily announced:

Irresolution and deliberation are no longer in season. I renounce Louisiana. It is not only New Orleans that I will cede, it is the whole colony

---

[18] Lyon, *Louisiana in French Diplomacy*, pp. 194–199.

[19] A recent writer has marshaled some evidence to support this interesting thesis: Napoleon tried to secure the Floridas from Spain, so that he might use them to appease the Americans; failing in this, he decided to sell Louisiana. R. R. Stenberg, "Napoleon's Cession of Louisiana: A Suggestion," *Louisiana Hist. Quar.*, XXI (1938), 359.

without any reservation. I know the price of what I abandon. . . . I renounce it with the greatest regret. To attempt obstinately to retain it would be folly. I direct you to negotiate this affair. . . . Do not even await the arrival of Mr. Monroe: have an interview this very day with Mr. Livingston. . . .[20]

BUYING AN EMPIRE TO GET A CITY

Meanwhile Livingston had redoubled his efforts to persuade France to sell New Orleans and the Floridas. He was spurred on by the knowledge that Monroe was on his way, and by a desire to avoid sharing the possible glory of the negotiation with another man. On April 11, 1803, Talleyrand most unexpectedly asked Livingston what the United States would give for all Louisiana. Scarcely able to believe his ears (he was deaf anyway), Livingston replied that the wishes of the United States extended only to New Orleans and the area to the east.[21] But the negotiation had been opened.

Two days later, April 13, 1803, Monroe reached Paris and joined Livingston in the negotiations. For about a week the American envoys haggled—while an empire hung in the balance. At length the discussions ended; and the American representatives bound the United States to pay approximately $15,000,000 in cash and claims for all Louisiana. In so doing they knew perfectly well they were violating their instructions. Authorized to pay as much as $10,000,000 for New Orleans and as much *east* of the Mississippi as they could obtain, they had agreed to give $15,000,000 for New Orleans and a trackless expanse that lay entirely *west* of the river. But they were far from home; the situation demanded immediate action; Napoleon would sell all or none; and unless they took all they would not obtain the all-important window on the gulf for which they had come. They therefore felt justified in exceeding their instructions, counting on the good sense of the Administration and of the American people to uphold them. After setting his name to the treaty of cession and the two conventions effecting the financial arrangements, Livingston solemnly declared:

We have lived long, but this is the noblest work of our whole lives. . . . From this day the United States take their place among the powers of the

[20] Marquis de Barbé-Marbois, *History of Louisiana* (Phila., 1830), pp. 274–275.

[21] Livingston, as a matter of fact, had earlier and tentatively proposed that France cede all of Louisiana north of the Arkansas River. C. E. Hill, "James Madison," in S. F. Bemis, ed., *The American Secretaries of State and their Diplomacy* (N.Y., 1927), III, 24.

first rank. . . . The instruments which we have just signed will cause no tears to be shed: they prepare ages of happiness for innumerable generations of human creatures.[22]

What had the two American envoys bought? Did the purchase embrace Texas or either of the Floridas? Livingston approached the slippery Talleyrand, who knew perfectly well what Napoleon conceived the boundaries to be:

I [Livingston] asked the minister [Talleyrand] what were the east bounds of the territory ceded to us? He said he did not know; we must take it as they had received it. I asked him how Spain meant to give them possession? He said . . . I do not know. Then you mean that we shall construe it our own way? I can give you no direction; you have made a noble bargain for yourselves, and I suppose you will make the most of it.[23]

The United States did make the most of it—as the subsequent history of the Floridas and Texas will attest. Meanwhile the exact northern, western, and southeastern boundaries were undetermined. The only undisputed limits were the Mississippi on the east (which was constantly shifting its course), and the Gulf of Mexico on the south. But the American negotiators knew that they had bought the western half of perhaps the most valuable river valley on the face of the globe, stretching between the Rockies and the Mississippi, and bounded somewhere on the north by British North America.

Why all this evasiveness and downright mendacity on the part of Talleyrand? The answer is that Napoleon was pursuing a crafty course. He hoped that boundary disputes would embroil Spain and the United States, and that he could play one antagonist off against the other to his own advantage. "If an obscurity did not already exist," he cynically remarked, "it would perhaps be good policy to put one there." [24] His fondest dreams in this regard were abundantly realized.

METAPHYSICAL SUBTLETIES

The news of the purchase caused unrestrained joy in the West, where monster celebrations, speeches, and toasts were the order of the day. One heard little else but talk of "America's Extension of Em-

---

[22] Barbé-Marbois, *History of Louisiana*, pp. 310–311.

[23] *American State Papers, Foreign Relations*, II, 561 (Livingston to Madison, May 20, 1803).

[24] Adams, *History*, II, 43.

pire" and "The Immortal Jefferson." [25] The President, however, was not altogether happy over the turn affairs had taken. Having set out to buy a relatively small area at the mouth of the Mississippi, he now had well-nigh half a continent on his hands. Nor was this all. For over ten years he had been preaching strict construction and punctilious deference to constitutional niceties. But what article of his beloved Constitution stipulated that the federal government might buy and incorporate in the Union a partially inhabited wilderness as large as the Union itself?

With much anguish of spirit Jefferson turned over the problem in his mind. The only alternative seemed to be a constitutional amendment. But months, if not years, of precious time would be wasted by such a procedure. Meanwhile Livington and Monroe were urging Jefferson to make haste, for they well knew that Napoleon, with whom thought was action, might suddenly decide to sell the territory to a more appreciative buyer. Apparently, the only sensible solution was to accept the purchase and hope that a later constitutional amendment would legalize the transaction. Jefferson himself privately admitted that the transaction was "an act beyond the constitution," but hoped that Congress would overlook "metaphysical subtleties." He thus compromised with conscience:

It is the case of a guardian, investing the money of his ward in purchasing an important adjacent territory; and saying to him when of age, I did this for your good; I pretend to no right to bind you: you may disavow me, and I must get out of the scrape as I can: I thought it my duty to risk myself for you. [26]

The Federalists, in turn, found themselves in an awkward position. Just a few months before they had been advocating a seizure of New Orleans for the sake of the abused Westerner. This probably would have meant a disastrous war with both France and Spain. Now that Jefferson had succeeded in purchasing the coveted outlet at a bargain price and without the shedding of a single drop of blood, the Federalists raised a chorus of criticism. They argued that the Republicans were "tearing the constitution to tatters." They insisted that the title to Louisiana was illegal and immoral. They railed against paying such an enormous price for a worthless desert that was too vast to be governed. They condemned Jefferson, who had pledged the Administration to rigid economy, for having wasted a sum which, if piled in silver dollars, would make a stack three miles high or would fill 866 wagons.[27] Most of all they feared that in the course of time a group of agricultural states would be formed from the new territory, thus unhinging the political balance and causing the industrial and commercial East to be outvoted in Congress. There were even threats of secession; and Senator White of Delaware solemnly averred that Louisiana would be "the greatest curse that could at present befall us. . . ."

But the common sense of the American people ultimately prevailed. Hamilton could hardly object to Jefferson's sudden conversion to the Hamiltonian principle of broad interpretation of the Constitution; and he gave the purchase his blessing. On October 20, 1803, the Senate approved the three treaties effecting the transactions, by a vote of 24 to 7. The Senators, who could not fail to heed the public demand for Louisiana, particularly in the West, were capable of overlooking "metaphysical subtleties" when face to face with what was perhaps the greatest real-estate bargain in history—828,000 square miles of imperial domain at approximately three cents an acre.

ACCOMPLICES OF A HIGHWAYMAN

There was much truth in the Federalist charge that the title to Louisiana was cloudy. First of all, Napoleon had obtained the territory from Spain on the condition that he transfer Tuscany to the son-in-law of Charles IV. Bonaparte never completely fulfilled this promise, though solemnly bound to return Louisiana if he failed to carry out his agreement. Moreover, Charles IV had extorted from Napoleon a written pledge that Louisiana would never be handed over to a third nation. This obligation the Corsican flagrantly and cynically disregarded. Besides, Louisiana was not Napoleon's to sell. It was still occupied by Spanish troops; and not until seven months after the signing of the treaties did France take possession. In short, Bonaparte had sold the United States only a scrap of paper. No wonder he could gloat: "Sixty millions of francs for an occupation that will not perhaps last a day!" Finally, the French constitution, which was presumed to be in effect, provided that the Executive could not dispose of the nation's territory without the consent of the Chambers. But fortunately for the United States, Napoleon had decided to put

[27] J. B. McMaster, *A History of the People of the United States* (N.Y., 1896), II, 630.

himself above constitutional encumbrances and carry through what he called his "Louisianacide." [28]

All things considered, the title to Louisiana was not above question. Professor Edward Channing even went so far as to conclude that the United States had acted as "the accomplices of the greatest highwayman of modern history, and the goods which we received were those which he compelled his unwilling victim to disgorge." [29] Although this judgment is a bit harsh, there is much about the transfer that suggests the purchase of property known to have been stolen, or at least obtained under false pretenses. Why, then, should the Americans have been a party to the transaction, particularly in view of their repeated claims to moral superiority over Europe, and in view of the high value that they placed upon clear titles as a result of frontier experience? The answer is that the need for Louisiana was so pressing, and its acquisition by peaceful or bloody means so inevitable, that America would have been foolish to be finicky about the title. There was a "higher law" than mere titles,[30] and the United States was willing to take a chance when the stakes were so large. Besides, from time immemorial the Americans had regarded the Spaniard as grasping, bloody, perfidious; and they felt that if Napoleon had betrayed his confederate, the treacherous don had merely got what he deserved.[31]

The outraged Spanish government, as was to be expected, protested vigorously to both France and the United States against Napoleon's betrayal. The prospect of a refusal by Spain to carry out her part of the transaction caused another outburst in the West. One Kentuckian reported that "Nothing but war is the topick of the day"; while old General Russell exclaimed, "Our Western Country [is] all on fire!" [32] But Spain was not so foolhardy as to back up her protests with armed resistance, for that would have exposed her to the risk of war with both the United States and France over a liability she was well rid of.

On November 30, 1803, the Spanish governor of Louisiana handed to the French representative a silver platter containing the keys to the forts of New Orleans. This formal transfer of sovereignty occurred

---

[28] No real Frenchman ever forgave the Corsican, who never learned to speak French without an accent, for rudely shattering these visions of empire. Two of Napoleon's brothers rushed to him in his bath and argued so heatedly that Bonaparte terminated the quarrel by splashing water over them. Other acrimonious discussions followed while Livingston and Monroe were higgling over the price. Adams, *History*, II, 32–39.

[29] E. Channing, *The Jeffersonian System, 1801–1811* (N.Y., 1906), p. 79.

[30] On the use of the "higher law" by the Westerner see A. K. Weinberg, *Manifest Destiny* (Baltimore, 1935), pp. 82, et passim.

[31] Whitaker, *The Mississippi Question*, pp. 257–259.

[32] Mayo, *Henry Clay*, p. 141.

more than a year after it had been authorized by the Spanish king, and seven months after the signing of the purchase treaties with the United States. Leclerc's force had been wiped out in Santo Domingo; and Victor's fleet, which was to have sailed directly to Louisiana, was icebound in Holland during the crucial months of January and February, 1803, and then delayed by storms.[33] The French occupation of Louisiana actually lasted only twenty days. Then, on December 20, 1803, at New Orleans, the blue, white, and red of the descending French tricolor met the red, white and blue of the ascending Stars and Stripes. A cheer burst forth from the handful of Americans gathered in the square—and Louisiana belonged to the United States.

THE KEY TO A CONTINENT

The results of the Louisiana purchase were so far-reaching as almost to defy analysis. The acquisition of this vast area, dazzlingly rich in natural resources, meant that the American people had approximately doubled their original endowment and that they would have almost limitless room for expansion and development. Without Louisiana in their possession it would have been impossible to carry the flag of the republic on into Texas, California, Oregon, and the Pacific. The purchase also set the precedent for acquiring foreign territory and peoples by treaty. Nor should we fail to note that Jefferson's stroke gave a new vitality to the budding spirit of national unity and further reduced the Federalists to "sectional impotence." The Westerners, in particular, felt a new confidence in the central government. The removal of the mouth of the Mississippi from the reach of foreign faithlessness put an end to Western intrigue, and enabled the federal government to pursue its chosen policy of isolation without having to face wars with France or alliances with Britain.

America, indeed, was fortunate among the nations. Once more the rivalries and distresses of Europe had worked to her advantage. From them she won her independence; from them she acquired greatness. Maddened Negroes, yellow fever, personal jealousies, Napoleonic caprice, and even icebound ports and storms were all on her side. Perhaps the new republic did have a destiny to fulfill.

BIBLIOGRAPHICAL NOTE

The most useful special studies relating to the Louisiana purchase are A. P. Whitaker, *The Mississippi Question, 1795–1803* (N.Y., 1934), which is es-

[33] Lyon, *Louisiana in French Diplomacy*, pp. 139–140.

pecially valuable in developing the attitude of the West; and E. W. Lyon, *Louisiana in French Diplomacy, 1759–1804* (Norman, Okla., 1934), which presents the problem from the European side. Both monographs include findings earlier published in article form. The older classic work of Henry Adams, *History of the United States of America during the Administrations of Jefferson and Madison* (9 vols., N.Y., 1889–1891), has very readable and still-valuable chapters in vols. I and II. The most helpful brief accounts are C. E. Hill's "James Madison," in S. F. Bemis, ed., *The American Secretaries of State and their Diplomacy* (N.Y., 1927), III, 3–40 (Louisiana); 71–79 (Barbary Powers); and E. Channing, *A History of the United States* (N.Y., 1929), IV, Ch. XI. Both references, particularly the latter, should be read in the light of Lyon and Whitaker. The best account of American diplomacy in relation to Santo Domingo is C. C. Tansill, *The United States and Santo Domingo, 1798–1873* (Baltimore, 1938). R. W. Irwin, *The Diplomatic Relations of the United States with the Barbary Powers, 1776–1816* (Chapel Hill, N.C., 1931) is the most recent and detailed on the subject. Further references: see footnotes of this chapter and Bemis and Griffin, *Guide,* pp. 113–125; 156–161.

RECENT REFERENCES. Jefferson's relations with France, including the purchase of Louisiana, are treated in considerable detail in A. B. Darling, *Our Rising Empire, 1763–1803* (New Haven, 1940), Chs. XV–XIX. R. W. Logan, *The Diplomatic Relations of the United States with Haiti, 1776–1891* (Chapel Hill, N.C., 1941), is a sympathetic account with considerable detail on contacts with the Toussaint regime. Considerably briefer on this early period, but also quite adequate, is L. L. Montague, *Haiti and the United States, 1714–1938* (Durham, N.C., 1940). E. Wilson Lyon, *The Man Who Sold Louisiana* (Norman, Okla., 1942), is the first full-length biography of Barbé-Marbois. P. C. Brooks, in "Spain's Farewell to Louisiana, 1803–1821," *Miss. Valley Hist. Rev.,* XXVII (1940), 29–42, reveals Spain's bitterness over Napoleon's sale of Louisiana, and describes her extraordinarily persistent efforts, until as late as 1817, to win back Louisiana by securing the support of Britain and by intriguing among the Spaniards in New Orleans.

NEW REFERENCES. L. B. Wright and J. H. Macleod, *The First Americans in North Africa: William Eaton's Struggle for a Vigorous Policy against the Barbary Pirates, 1799–1805* (Princeton, 1945), deals with the incredible activities of Eaton in raising a motley army in Egypt and marching across the Libyan desert to attack the Tripolitan port of Derna. Ralph Korngold, *Citizen Toussaint* (Boston, 1944) is a popular life of the "Black Napoleon," drawn largely from French materials. It appears that Toussaint surrendered before being beaten in the expectation of using "Trojan horse" tactics (pp. 282–284). Napoleon at one time seems to have toyed with the idea of co-operating with Toussaint and of using the black army for an invasion of the United States (p. 233). The author feels that Napoleon's decision to attack Toussaint instead of joining with him ranks with the invasion of Spain and Russia as the Corsican's greatest military blunder (p. 232).

CHAPTER VIII

Jefferson and Neutrality, 1803–1809

> *"The winds and seas are Britain's wide domain,
> And not a sail, but by permission, spreads."*
> Motto of British *Naval Register.*

FEEDERS VERSUS FIGHTERS

ON MAY 18, 1803, scarcely two weeks after Bonaparte had cut loose from his Louisiana liability, France declared war on Great Britain. The titanic upheaval that followed did not subside until twelve years later, when Napoleon was safely marooned on the island rock of St. Helena. Thus the war that began in 1793 lasted (except for the breathing spell afforded by the Peace of Amiens) almost continuously for twenty-two years. The conflict kept Europe from casting greedy eyes on American possessions, and in the end left her so exhausted that the United States could face westward without fear. The American people owe a debt to Bonaparte for having shaken Europe so violently that Louisiana fell into their hands, and for having given them ten years in which to consolidate their gains. Although America was eventually sucked into the European maelstrom, every year of delay gave to the poorly defended yet rapidly growing republic the greatest of all boons—time.

From 1803 to 1812 the United States was the most important neutral carrier, particularly of foodstuffs. The preoccupation of warring Europe enabled American shippers to exploit markets hitherto closed to them, and to receive unprecedentedly high prices for their products. Such inducements led to a remarkable growth of shipping,[1] which the caustic John Randolph of Virginia referred to as "this mushroom, this fungus of war." What the people of the United States wanted was business as usual—unrestricted trade with all nations and interference from none.

Incredible though it may seem, for over two years after the re-

[1] See A. C. Clauder, *American Commerce as Affected by the Wars of the French Revolution and Napoleon, 1793–1812* (Phila., 1932), p. 25.

newal of hostilities the belligerents refrained from taking any drastic steps to interfere with American commerce. But this was merely the calm before the storm. British shippers watched with ill-concealed jealousy the growth of a competing merchant marine and the loss of their markets. And since much of America's newly won trade strengthened the enemy, England looked upon the United States as little better than an ally of Bonaparte.

THE NOOSE TIGHTENS

In normal times the French restricted the direct trade to and from their West Indian colonies to their own merchant marine. But when the British navy swept enemy shipping from the seas, France (as well as Spain) was forced to throw open her West Indies to the United States; otherwise her colonials would have starved. Great Britain, invoking the Rule of 1756,[2] prevented her American rivals from aiding Napoleon by engaging in direct trade between the enemy West Indies and Europe. But the British did permit the Yankees to enjoy the lucrative commerce between these West Indian islands and the mainland of the United States. The American shipper was clever enough to evade these restrictions by a subterfuge known as the broken voyage. He would, for example, carry his cargo of sugar from the French West Indies to an American port; pay duties on it; land it for a time (thus Americanizing the sugar); reload it (often on the same ship); receive back most or all of the money that he had paid in duties; and then carry the cargo to a European port under French control.

The English courts at first tolerated this circuitous trade. But the British shipping interests became increasingly vocal in their protests. Of what advantage was it, they complained, to sweep the enemy merchant marine from the seas and cut off competition with the West Indian islands if the grasping Yankee stepped in and took over this trade? The demands of interested Britons were finally heeded when, on July 23, 1805, the British Court of Appeals in Prize Causes handed down a celebrated decision in the case of the *Essex*. The tribunal, looking at the intent of the American shipper and the ultimate destination of his cargo, held that unless produce carried on a broken voyage between two enemy ports paid a bona fide duty, the shipper violated the Rule of 1756 and was engaged in a continuous voyage

[2] Trade not open in time of peace could not be permitted in time of war.

between those two ports.[3] Under this ruling British cruisers promptly seized scores of American merchantmen, chiefly those engaged in the roundabout West Indian trade. A storm of protest immediately arose from the commercial centers of the United States, mass meetings were held, and ringing memorials were addressed to Congress. "Never will neutrals be perfectly safe," insisted the Salem *Register*, "till free goods make free ships or till England loses two or three great naval battles." [4]

Nor did British measures stop here. In looking for evidence of continuous voyage, frigates flying the Union Jack hovered off American ports in such numbers as to establish a virtual blockade. Here they exercised the undoubted right of a belligerent to search neutral merchantmen in order to establish their identity and ascertain the nature of the cargo. Upon evidence, or even suspicion, of irregularity the American vessels were seized and sent to far-away Halifax, Nova Scotia, where, according to John Adams, the code of the Admiralty Court was "Rule, Britannia!" If the ships were not actually confiscated, they encountered inconvenience and delay that was frequently very costly.

At best, the practice of visit and search was annoying; but the British officers, who had nothing but contempt for their "money-grubbing" cousins, discharged their disagreeable duties in a manner offensive to the Americans. Basil Hall, then a young midshipman stationed off New York on His Majesty's ship, *Leander*, was not surprised to find the name of his ship held in execration by the people of that city twenty years later. The British were sometimes careless when they fired a solid shot across the bow of the American merchantmen as a signal to heave to. Hall described a distressing incident that happened in April, 1806:

A casual shot from the Leander hit an unfortunate sloop's main-boom; and the broken spar striking the mate, John Pierce by name, killed him instantly. The sloop sailed on to New York, where the mangled body, raised on a platform, was paraded through the streets, in order to augment the vehement indignation, already at a high pitch, against the English.[5]

---

[3] W. E. Lingelbach, "England and Neutral Trade," *Military Historian and Economist*, II (1917), 158–163. The author holds that the *Essex* decision was not "essentially unfair."

[4] Oct. 14, 1805, quoted in *ibid.*, p. 164.

[5] Basil Hall, *Fragments of Voyages and Travels* (First series, London, 1840), I, 47.

QUARTER-DECK JUSTICE

The most maddening of all American grievances against England was impressment. The United States had already suffered heavily from this offensive practice during the wars of the French Revolution (1793–1801); but with the renewal of hostilities the situation became well-nigh intolerable.

The British navy during these years was no place for weaklings, what with vile quarters, wretched food, and the savage cat-o'-nine-tails. It was difficult to induce men to volunteer, even in times of critical national need. The British therefore resorted to a form of conscription known as impressment. It consisted of sending out press gangs, on land or sea, to seize His Majesty's able-bodied subjects and forcibly enlist them in the service. Whatever its legal basis, this method had been employed by England for over four hundred years; and if long and undisputed usage is to be regarded as establishing a prescriptive right, impressment was legal.

The British naturally did not claim the right to exercise this harsh practice on foreign soil; and they did not claim the right to impress American citizens—only His Majesty's subjects. If a citizen of the United States was impressed, the government in London insisted that because of his similarity to an Englishman he had been seized by mistake. If his American birth could be established, his release might be obtained, though usually not until after several years of confinement in Britain's "floating hells."

The United States, which was largely a nation of immigrants, took strong exception to certain aspects of impressment. It was clear that an English press gang would not invade the streets of New York and there lay hold of either British or American sailors. That was American territory; and, besides, angry mobs would prevent such a practice. Similarly, the Department of State argued that the United States flag made the decks of the ship over which it waved virtually American territory; and that the crew, whatever its nationality, was not subject to impressment. But on the high seas the British navy made the law. As Lord Harrowby put it: "The pretension . . . that the American flag should protect every individual sailing under it on board of a merchant-ship is too extravagant to require any serious refutation." [6]

---

[6] Henry Adams, *History of the United States during the Administrations of Jefferson and Madison* (N.Y., 1889), II, 423 (Harrowby to Merry, Nov. 7, 1804). In 1797 a British commodore reported: "It is my duty to keep my Ship manned, and

Unfortunately, a wide gulf yawned between British theory and practice. The process of determining a seaman's nationality was always arbitrary, frequently capricious, and never judicial. His Majesty's boarding party, exercising the belligerent right of visit and search, would line up the crew of a neutral merchantman. If a sailor pronounced "peas" as "paise" he was an Irishman, hence a British subject. If he talked through his nose, he probably was a Yankee. If no one that even remotely resembled a British subject was found, and His Majesty's vessel was shorthanded, the boarding party would make convenient mistakes. The officer in command, performing the triple function of judge, jury, and jailer, would pick out a likely-looking hand and claim him as a fellow Englishman. The luckless seaman was forthwith dragged off; if so ill-advised as to resist, he was struck down and dragged off. In this way, Swedes, Danes, and Portuguese, who could not possibly be mistaken for Englishmen, were taken from American ships and condemned to nautical slavery.[7] Altogether, about ten thousand bona fide citizens of the United States fell victim to press gangs. Many of these men died in service or were killed in action. It is little wonder that the Americans regarded the British as scarcely any better than murderers.

Once an Englishman Always an Englishman

America, on the other hand, would have had a much better moral case if her own hands had been clean. Her grievance was impressment; England's was desertions. Lord Nelson reported that 42,000 British sailors had deserted during the war ending in 1801. With this terrific drain in man power, British warships were frequently left so short of hands that they could not sail; or, if they did, they occasionally foundered. If England was not to yield the trident to Napoleon, she had to find men by fair means or foul.

The same notoriously inhumane conditions in the British navy that made impressment necessary caused desertion to flourish. In addition, there was the allurement of the prospering American merchant marine, in which working conditions were much better and wages tempt-

---

I will do so wherever I find men that speak the same language with me." Quoted in Bernard Mayo, *Henry Clay: Spokesman of the New West* (Boston, 1937), p. 39.

[7] During the search American vessels were frequently delayed, thus losing wind, tide, and even markets. They were sometimes left so shorthanded that they sank in the next storm with all on board. The impressed seamen often left behind wives, children, and aged parents, all of whom sometimes suffered great hardship. See A. T. Mahan, *Sea Power in its Relations to the War of 1812* (Boston, 1905), I, 114-124.

ingly high. ("Dollars for shillings" was the current saying.) Virtually
every British frigate leaving New York during these years sailed
away shorthanded. In 1804 twelve of His Majesty's ships were detained at Norfolk at one time because of deserters, who not infrequently paraded the streets cursing their former officers and thumbing
their noses at them. This partially explains the arbitrariness of British
press gangs in dealing with American merchantmen.

Neither the United States government nor the local authorities
took any effective steps to discourage desertion; rather they encouraged it. Naturalization or "protection" papers could be legally
secured by a British deserter within a period of a few months. They
could be fraudulently obtained overnight from agencies that sold
them for as low as one dollar each.[8] When the deserter produced this
document, the press gang laughed in his face. Even if the certificate
had been secured in good faith, the British would have ignored it because then, and for many years after, they held to the doctrine of in-
delible allegiance; that is, if a man was born an Englishman he was
always an Englishman.

Great Britain needed men because she was fighting for her life;
America needed them because she wanted to make more money. The
British Ministry would have been swept from office if it had dared
to give up, at the behest of the Yankee, a practice already sanctified
by long usage. England would fight before she would yield.

The Abortive Monroe-Pinkney Treaty

In May, 1806, while the controversy over impressment and neutral trade was rapidly approaching the breaking point, President
Jefferson made an extraordinary effort to improve the situation by
associating William Pinkney, a distinguished Maryland lawyer, with
the American minister resident in England, James Monroe. The two
envoys were authorized to adjust all matters in dispute between the
United States and England, including a resumption of broken voyages and the payment of indemnity for recent seizures. Pinkney and
Monroe were also specifically instructed not to sign a treaty which
did not contain a renunciation of the alleged right to impress sailors
from American vessels on the high seas.

[8] The British minister in Washington recorded that one woman engaged in the
sale of "certificates" had a cradle large enough to accommodate a seaman. If haled
into court, she could swear that she had known the men "from their cradles." Mayo,
Henry Clay, p. 462. For frauds see also E. Channing, *A History of the United States*
(N.Y., 1929), IV, 366.-367.

The officials at Downing Street were aware of the rising American temper, which was strikingly reflected in a recent retaliatory act of Congress prohibiting the importation of certain English goods.[9] Great Britain was therefore persuaded to make certain concessions, particularly with regard to the West Indian trade. But the British public, angered because the Yankee had been "stealing" both commerce and seamen, would not permit a surrender to the demands on impressment. The Foreign Office did offer to give an informal pledge that every effort would be made to avoid molesting bona fide American seamen; but it refused to incorporate such a statement in a formal agreement. Monroe and Pinkney realized that they could obtain nothing more; so, disregarding their instructions, they signed a treaty on December 31, 1806.

President Jefferson was dissatisfied with the work of the negotiators, and, after painful deliberation, refused to submit the document to the Senate. Instead, he requested the envoys to reopen negotiations in conformity with their original instructions. It is possible that if Jefferson had been willing to accept a half loaf, some of his later difficulties might have been avoided.

THE LAW OF CLAW AND FANG

Meanwhile the world conflict had entered upon a new phase. Lord Nelson's crushing victory at Trafalgar over the combined French and Spanish fleets, on October 21, 1805, put to rest British fears of invasion. So complete was England's naval ascendancy that her frigates ceased gun practice. But scarcely more than a month later Napoleon overwhelmed the combined Russian and Austrian forces at Austerlitz. If Britain was the tyrant of the sea, Bonaparte was the despot of the land. Neither could get at the other; each was driven to indirect devices. England established a naval blockade against ports under French jurisdiction, and by a system of fees and licenses was able to curb neutral (including American) trade and at the same time derive a substantial revenue from it. Napoleon, in retaliation, proclaimed a "paper" blockade against the British Isles; and by closing the European ports under his domination to English goods, established his Continental System. He reasoned that this stoppage of trade would cause British factories to close, bread lines to form, riots to develop, revolution to break out. And once proud Albion would be forced to accept the conqueror's terms.

9 Signed April 18, 1806; but not put into effect until December, 1807.

Great Britain, in pursuance of her policy, announced a blockade (May, 1806) along the European coast between the River Elbe, in Germany, and the town of Brest, in France. This would have the incidental result of stifling that trade which the Yankee had wrested from English merchantmen. Some six months later Napoleon issued his Berlin decree, in which, although the remnants of his navy were bottled up, he declared the British Isles to be in a state of blockade. These were the opening guns in a retaliatory war of English Orders in Council and Napoleonic decrees during which one sweeping edict led to another.[10] When the system of mutual strangulation was well established, any ship of the United States that attempted to trade with England, or even allowed itself to be searched by the British, was subject to seizure by French privateers.[11] And any American vessel that attempted to trade with ports under French control without first having paid tribute to England and having received her permission, was liable to capture by British frigates. The United States was caught between the upper and nether millstones.

THE DREGS OF NATIONAL HUMILIATION

In America, public interest in the war of edicts was temporarily diverted by an extraordinarily distressing incident. In February, 1807, a boat's crew escaped to the Virginia shore from His Majesty's squadron, and four of the seamen enlisted on an American frigate, the *Chesapeake*. When the news reached Halifax, the hotheaded British commander, Vice-Admiral Berkeley, issued an order requiring his subordinates to retrieve the deserters from the American vessel. This action was taken on Berkeley's own responsibility, for Downing Street never claimed the right to impress seamen from the decks of a neutral man-of-war—only from merchantmen.[12]

[10] The principal orders and decrees of 1806 and 1807 were as follows: the British Order in Council of May 16, 1806; Napoleon's Berlin decree, Nov. 21, 1806; the British Orders in Council of Jan. 7, 1807, and Nov. 11, 1807; Napoleon's Milan decree of Dec. 17, 1807. For a complete list of restrictions on neutral trade from 1793 to 1810 see Clauder, *American Commerce*, pp. 9–14.

[11] Stephen Girard, a wealthy Philadelphia shipowner, at times carried a person of French extraction on his ships. If a French cruiser appeared, the latter assumed command and used his knowledge of the language to convince the boarding party of the French destination of the ship and the authenticity of its false papers. Lingelbach, "England and Neutral Trade," *loc. cit.*, p. 170.

[12] When Thomas Paine, a British subject, wished to return to America from France in 1801, he asked his friend, President Jefferson, for passage on an American warship, for he knew that there he should be safe from impressment. See W. D. Gould, "The Religious Opinions of Thomas Jefferson," *Miss. Valley Hist. Rev.*, XX (1933), 194.

On June 22, 1807, the *Chesapeake* left Norfolk for Mediterranean waters. When some ten miles off the Virginia coast, she was hailed by His Majesty's frigate, the *Leopard*. The American commander, Commodore Barron, thinking that the vessel was about to ask him to carry dispatches to Europe, allowed her to approach without calling his men to quarters and without having the loggerheads heated red-hot for firing guns. When the British commander requested permission to search the vessel, the astonished Barron quite properly refused. The *Leopard* thereupon fired three broadsides into the defenseless *Chesapeake*, killing three and wounding eighteen. After an American officer had brought up a live coal from the galley and had fired one gun in honor of the flag, the *Chesapeake* struck her colors. A searching party then boarded the vessel and removed the four deserters.

This disgraceful affair was not so much a case of impressment as the recovery of a specific group of deserters. Three of the four men seized (two Negroes and two whites) had allegedly been impressed into His Majesty's service but apparently had volunteered. The fourth seaman, who was dragged out of a coalhole, was indisputably a British subject and a deserter. He was tried by a court martial at Halifax and hanged from the yardarm of his own ship. The Americans were given less summary punishment.

When the bloody hulk that was the *Chesapeake* limped back to Norfolk with a tale of humiliation, an unparalleled wave of indignation swept over America. English officers on shore leave fled to their ships; infuriated mobs destroyed the water casks of the British fleet; the governor of Virginia was forced to call out the militia to maintain order. "But one feeling pervades the nation," wrote Joseph Nicholson. "All distinctions of federalism and democracy are vanished. The people are ready to submit to any deprivation. . . ."[13] The West, with its fighting breed and with its high ideals of national honor, vibrated with anger. "On my Conscience and Faith and Honor I hope that war will take place," wrote a friend of Andrew Jackson. Jackson himself, referring to the sensational Burr trial at Richmond, cried, "Millions to persecute an American; not a cent to resist England!"[14]

Not since the X Y Z days had the American people been more united on an issue. "Never since the battle of Lexington," wrote President Jefferson, "have I seen this country in such a state of exas-

[13] Henry Adams, *The Life of Albert Gallatin* (Phila., 1880), p. 360 (to Gallatin, July 14, 1807).
[14] Marquis James, *Andrew Jackson: The Border Captain* (Indianapolis, 1933), p. 139.

peration as at present, and even that did not produce such unanimity." [15] The Washington *Federalist* was similarly impressed:

We have never, on any occasion, witnessed the spirit of the people excited to so great a degree of indignation, or such a thirst for revenge, as on hearing of the late unexampled outrage on the *Chesapeake*. All parties, ranks, and professions were unanimous in their detestation of the dastardly deed, and all cried aloud for vengeance. The accounts which we receive from every quarter tend to show that these sentiments universally prevail. The Administration may implicitly rely on the cordial support of every American citizen, in whatever manly and dignified steps that they may take, to resent the insult and obtain reparation for the injury. [16]

BENDING THE BOW TOO FAR

Supported by an outraged public sentiment, Jefferson issued a proclamation ordering all British warships out of American waters. He summoned Congress in special session, although setting the date far enough ahead to permit the popular passions to cool. He knew perfectly well that he could lead the United States—a united United States —into war. But with peace his "passion" he was determined to avoid hostilities and, by capitalizing on the error of the British, wring concessions from them. He exulted because they had touched "a chord which vibrates in every heart. Now then is the time to settle the old and the new."

The chauvinistic press of England, angered by Jefferson's proclamation against British warships, applauded the *Leopard's* treatment of what it called the cowardly Yankees. But the Foreign Office, recognizing that Britain was clearly in the wrong, disavowed the act, and despite the protests of the merchant class, recalled Admiral Berkeley. He was further "punished" by being promoted to a new and more important command off the Portuguese coast. But Jefferson made the mistake of pushing the embattled British too far, of trying to settle both "the old and the new" at one stroke. He insisted on using the *Chesapeake* indignity as a lever, and on coupling a demand for reparation with one for a complete relinquishment of the practice of impressment. England was prepared to make amends for her attack on the American

[15] A. A. Lipscomb, ed., *Writings of Thomas Jefferson* (Monticello ed., Washington, 1904), XI, 274 (Jefferson to Du Pont de Nemours, July 14, 1807).

[16] Washington *Federalist*, July 3, 1807, quoted in Allan Nevins, ed., *American Press Opinion: Washington to Coolidge* (Boston, 1928), p. 37. Stirring broadsides attest to the popular excitement. See Files 151 (Penn.) and 182 (Va.), Library of Congress.

frigate; but she was convinced that impressment was essential for her national existence. Jefferson consequently drove the British from a defensive to an offensive position; [17] and the *Chesapeake* outrage, which could have been quickly atoned for, became so hopelessly entangled with other issues as to develop into a five-year running sore. So the war spirit was allowed to evaporate; America plumbed the depths of national degradation; and the disgusted French minister in Washington could report that America was "disposed to suffer every kind of humiliation, provided it can satisfy . . . its sordid avarice. . . ." [18]

THE "DAMBARGO"

The titanic conflict between "the tiger and the shark" increased in intensity and ferocity. The United States could have found ample reason to declare war upon both Britain and Bonaparte. But Jefferson, realizing full well the impotence of the country, was convinced that peace had to be maintained at almost any price. As clearly as any statesman of his generation, he saw the necessity of letting America's extraordinary birth rate fight her battles. [19] Time, he sagely remarked, was the "most precious of all things to us."

National honor, however, would no longer tolerate craven submission to the indignities of both belligerents. Yet war would be futile and disastrous. Jefferson had long toyed with the idea of economic coercion as a substitute for arms, and here seemed to be a splendid opportunity to carry out his pet scheme. The warring nations were drawing heavily upon the United States for foodstuffs and other commodities, and he reasoned that if America refused to ship anything to Europe both Great Britain and France would be forced to come to terms.

Despite Federalist opposition, Jefferson succeeded in forcing a sweeping embargo act through Congress in December, 1807. [20]

[17] The *Morning Post* (Oct. 24, 1807) revealed the temper of the British ruling class: "A few short months of war would convince these desperate [Yankee] politicians of the folly of measuring the strength of the rising, but still infant and puny, nation with the colossal power of the British empire." Quoted in Adams, *History*, IV, 54.

[18] *Ibid.*, p. 141 (Turreau to Talleyrand, Sept. 4, 1807).

[19] Several years later Jefferson wrote: "For twenty years to come we should consider peace as the *summum bonum* of our country. At the end of that period we shall be twenty millions in number, and forty in energy, when encountering the starved and rickety paupers and dwarfs of English workshops." *Writings of Thomas Jefferson* (Monticello ed.), XIV, 371 (Jefferson to Du Pont de Nemours, Dec. 31, 1815).

[20] The vote in the House, though widely scattered, shows that the embargo act received its strongest support in the South and West; its strongest opposition in the mercantile areas. See C. O. Paullin, *Atlas of the Historical Geography of the United States* (Washington, 1932), p. 108, and plate 112D.

Strengthened by supplementary legislation, it virtually prohibited the export of any goods from the United States, by sea or land. The withering hand of stagnation slowly but inexorably laid hold of American economic life. Ships rotted at the wharves; forests of bare masts were silhouetted in the harbors; grass grew on hitherto humming wharves; bankruptcies, suicides, and crimes increased; soup kitchens were established. From New England, where the Yankee had long wrested his livelihood from the sea, a cry arose against the "Virginia lordlings" in Washington who were sacrificing United States shipping to their own ends. What the American merchant wanted was to be let alone. In spite of spoliations, sequestrations, confiscations, and all this loose talk about national honor, he was making money. If one cargo out of three reached its destination safely he could still show a profit. And the greater the risk the greater the profit. But the embargo destroyed the very trade it was designed to protect. It was, so the New England Federalists insisted, like "cutting one's throat to cure the nosebleed."

Opposition to the embargo in New England breathed new life into the corpse of Federalism. The "Chinese" or "terrapin" policy of the Administration was savagely denounced. A New Hampshire poet vented his indignation in song:

> Our ships all in motion,
> Once whiten'd the ocean;
>   They sail'd and return'd with a Cargo;
> Now doom'd to decay
>   They are fallen a prey,
> To Jefferson, worms, and EMBARGO.[21]

The letters of the word "embargo" were transposed to read "o-grab-me," "go-bar-em," and "mob-rage," the last of which was declared to be the inevitable outcome of this outrageous policy. One irate New Englander wrote Jefferson a letter beginning, "You Infernal Villain": "How much longer are you going to keep this damned Embargo on to starve us poor people[.] one of my children has already starved to death of which I [am] ashamed and declared that it died of apoplexy. . . . I am a Federalist." [22]

---

[21] Song composed and sung at Dover, July 4, 1808, Mass. Hist. Society Broadsides. Federalist broadsides against the embargo were entitled "The Constitution Gone"; "Alarming State of Affairs"; and (with a heavy black border) "The Last Act of Slavery Arrived." Files 48 (Mass.) and 227 (U.S.), Library of Congress.

[22] L. M. Sears, *Jefferson and the Embargo* (Durham, N.C., 1927), p. 103 (Aug. 8, 1808).

New England was the most vocal section in condemning Jefferson's "Quaker-gun diplomacy." But the South and West, though probably even harder hit by losing the export market for their agricultural

OGRABME, or, *The American Snapping-turtle.*
(Courtesy of The New York Historical Society, New York City.)

produce, complained the least.[23] After all, this was an Administration measure; and Jefferson's stronghold was in the South. So loyal Republicans, in the South and elsewhere, made light of the country's sufferings. One Jerseyman defended the embargo in doggerel:

> Should Hessian fly our wheat destroy,
>   Or granaries crawl with weevil,
> *The Embargo's* curst in language worst,
>   As source of all the evil.
>
> . . . .
>
> Do vermin bold on trees lay hold,
>   And make their limbs quite bare go,

[23] The West, which attributed much of its economic depression to British blockade measures, supported the embargo in the hope of extorting redress. Two months after that measure was repealed the citizens of Vincennes (in what is now Indiana) were still drinking toasts to it. G. R. Taylor, "Agrarian Discontent in the Mississippi Valley preceding the War of 1812," *Jour. of Pol. Economy,* XXXIX (1931), 471 *ff.*

'Tis ten to one the mischief done
Is saddled on *the Embargo*.[24]

The inevitable happened. From the days of the colonial navigation acts respect for law has never been a conspicuous American virtue. The people of the United States demonstrated once again that when public opinion runs counter to law the law will be disregarded. The embargo was openly and flagrantly violated, in spite of tyrannical enforcing acts passed by Congress. An illicit trade of immense proportions immediately sprang up, particularly across the Canadian border. On Lake Champlain huge produce-laden rafts, manned by scores of armed men, openly defied the revenue officers and the state militia. It seemed as if law and order had completely broken down.

The Fruits of Economic Coercion

But what of the effect of the embargo on the warring Powers, against whom it was directed? Perhaps the first noticeable result was an aggravation of the bitter feeling that the British ruling class cherished for America.[25] In the summer of 1808, at a great dinner in London, Sir Francis Baring proposed as one of the regular toasts the health of the President of the United States. Instantly his voice was drowned in a chorus of hisses and protests. Britain was in a mood to endure much in the war of economic coercion before she would bend her knee to the Yankee.

Some of the other results of the embargo could hardly have been foreseen by Jefferson. The unfortunate American mariner was faced with the alternative of starving or finding employment elsewhere.[26] Hundreds of Yankee sailors, to say nothing of British subjects or deserters, were consequently driven into England's merchant marine and navy—a development that had the incidental result of easing the necessity for impressment. It should also be noted that the Canadian

---

[24] Boston *Independent Chronicle*, Oct. 27, 1808, 1:3.

[25] The *Edinburgh Review* confessed: "Neither the government nor the populace of this country have forgiven America for having made herself independent; and the lowest calumnies and grossest absurdities are daily employed by a court faction to keep alive the most vulgar prejudices." XII, 243 (April, 1808).

[26] One unemployed seaman met another on the streets of Hartford:
"Holla! messmate, where are you bound!
Bound to Halifax by the pipers, which way are you steering?
By the powers of Moll Kelly, I am steering the same course, for there's no standing this *dambargo* any longer."
Connecticut *Courant*, Jan. 13, 1808, 3:3.

smuggler prospered, and that the British shipper gladly took over the carrying trade relinquished by his Yankee rival.

On the other hand, as Jefferson had planned, the cutting off of American foodstuffs did cause intense distress in some parts of the British Empire, especially in the West Indies and Newfoundland. A number of English factories, dependent upon American cotton, were forced to close down. Their owners urgently petitioned the government for a repeal of the Orders in Council that had driven the Americans to the embargo. Thousands of unemployed operatives faced pauperism and starvation. The alarming shortage of grain even caused the authorities to curtail the manufacture of alcoholic liquor.[27]

Why, then, did not the American policy of boycott force Britain to make concessions? First of all, the classes hardest hit in England were unable to vote and could bring the least pressure to bear on the government. Moreover, the proud Briton, who resented the commercial restrictions of the United States, steeled himself to endure much before capitulating. Finally, the crops of 1808 were so unexpectedly good as to render the British Isles less dependent than usual upon American foodstuffs.[28]

As for Napoleon, the United States was playing his game. Since he was unable to blockade Great Britain, he was delighted to see the distress caused in England by the embargo, and he rejoiced over the widening rift between Britain and America. No wonder the French minister to Washington could say, "the Emperor applauds the embargo." Bonaparte even pretended to help the United States enforce it. By the Bayonne decree of April 17, 1808, he ordered the seizure of all American ships in French harbors on the pretext that, since the embargo was presumably effective, they must be disguised British. Within a year Napoleon confiscated American vessels and cargoes to the value of $10,000,000.

A Successful Failure

By the end of 1808 the patience of the country was fast approaching a breaking point. Threats of secession were heard on every hand. Even Dr. George Logan, the prominent Quaker, denounced the Administration for "dastardly attacking the humble cottage" instead "of meet-

---

[27] Sears, *Jefferson and the Embargo*, p. 293. The British also felt the loss of American naval stores. See Clauder, *American Trade*, p. 139.

[28] American commercial restrictions that followed the embargo were weakened by the outbreak of the Spanish American revolutions, in 1809–1810, which opened up substitute markets to British shippers.

ing in an open & honorable conflict the armed battalions of our enemy." The Washington *Federalist* demanded to know "how much longer we are to pant under the pestiferous breath of this poisonous dragon." And a Newburyport, Massachusetts, circular exhorted:

Let every man who holds the name of America dear to him, stretch forth his hands and put this accursed thing, this *Embargo* from him. Be resolute, act like sons of liberty, of God, and your country; nerve your arm with vengeance against the Despot who would wrest the inestimable germ of your independence from you—and you shall be *Conquerors* ! ! !— And all the People shall say Amen.[29]

Even Jefferson, who confessed privately that the experiment was three times more costly than war, declared in later years, "I felt the foundation of the government shaken under my feet by the New England townships." It seemed as if the only alternatives to repeal of the embargo were disunion and civil strife. On March 1, 1809, three days before Jefferson handed over the reins to Madison, a rebellious Congress repealed the unpopular measure. It substituted a nonintercourse law which legalized American commerce with all ports of the world except those under British and French control. America was still committed to economic coercion.

Why did the embargo fail? Why did what was perhaps Jefferson's most original and daring piece of statesmanship come to an inglorious end? Abroad, the bumper crops proved unfortunate. At home, conditions were such that the experiment was not given, and perhaps could not have been given, a thorough trial. Avarice and disloyalty weakened its force; and public opinion brought about its repeal before full advantage could be taken of the incomplete results.

But did the embargo fail? It drove capital and labor into manufacturing, thus establishing the real foundations of industrial America and lessening her dependence on Europe. This, however, was an unforeseen result. The embargo also relieved impressment and in other ways helped postpone war. And although the experiment was an economic boomerang, it gave the United States more of that greatest of boons—time. Finally, as we shall see, the cumulative effect of economic coercion did contribute to the repeal of the Orders in Council. In the end Jefferson's policy triumphed; but America was not patient enough to reap the benefits.

[29] Baltimore *Evening Post*, Dec. 1, 1808, quoted in W. W. Jennings, *The American Embargo, 1807–1809* (Iowa City, 1921), pp. 152–153.

BIBLIOGRAPHICAL NOTE

A helpful brief account of neutral difficulties under Jefferson is E. Channing, *A History of the United States* (N.Y., 1929), IV, Chs. XIII, XIV. Somewhat fuller on the diplomatic side is C. E. Hill's "James Madison," in S. F. Bemis, ed., *The American Secretaries of State and their Diplomacy* (N.Y., 1927), III, 80–148. The early chapters of A. T. Mahan's memorable *Sea Power in its Relations to the War of 1812* (Boston, 1905), are good on impressment and neutral difficulties. A very detailed and well-written treatment of the period may be found in Henry Adams' classic *History of the United States of America during the Administrations of Jefferson and Madison* (9 vols., N.Y., 1889–1891). J. F. Zimmerman, *Impressment of American Seamen* (N.Y., 1925), is the most complete study of the subject. A suggestive survey is W. E. Lingelbach's "England and Neutral Trade," *Military Historian and Economist*, II (1917), 153–178. A useful and detailed doctoral dissertation is A. C. Clauder, *American Commerce as Affected by the Wars of the French Revolution and Napoleon, 1793–1812* (Phila., 1932). The best study of the embargo is L. M. Sears, *Jefferson and the Embargo* (Durham, N.C., 1927), though W. W. Jennings, *The American Embargo: 1807–1809* (Iowa City, 1921) may still be consulted on the economic side. Two standard books on European orders and decrees are F. E. Melvin, *Napoleon's Navigation System* (N.Y., 1919) and E. F. Heckscher, *The Continental System* (Oxford, 1922). Further references: see footnotes of this chapter and Bemis and Griffin, *Guide*, pp. 137–147.

RECENT REFERENCES. A. L. Burt, *The United States, Great Britain, and British North America* (New Haven, 1940), has a penetrating analysis of the causes of the War of 1812 to 1809 in Chapter XII. Burt's principal contributions on this general subject of causes will be discussed at length in connection with the next chapter (see Bibliographical Appendix, pp. 823–824). It may here be noted that the author regards the *Chesapeake* affair as one of the major causes of the war (pp. 245 ff.). Fearing invasion, the British in Canada were forced to cultivate their neglected Indian allies, a course which led to more incursions on the American frontier, which in turn led to a Western demand for war. Herbert Heaton, "Non-Importation, 1806–1812," *Jour. of Economic Hist.*, I (1941), 178–198, stresses the fact that non-importation "paralleled, ran alongside, and outlived the Embargo." The author describes at considerable length the smuggling under these laws, and the inconveniences and losses to British shippers.

NEW REFERENCES. Considerable material, especially on impressment, may be found in Bernard Mayo, *Instructions to the British Ministers to the United States, 1791–1812* (Washington, 1941). I-Mien Tsiang, *The Question of Expatriation in America Prior to 1907* (Baltimore, 1942), shows that the English common law concept of indefeasible allegiance was widely adopted in America, particularly by Federalists, who resented the efforts of the Republicans to gain adherents by easy naturalization laws. For this reason many Federalists hotly denied that impressment was a just cause for war, and their conviction contributed to the unpopularity of the conflict in New England (p. 50).

CHAPTER IX

Drifting into War with Great Britain, 1809–1812

"May the Twelfth Congress no longer tamely submit to British outrages, but wrest from her every foot of possession she holds in North America."
    Toast reported in Pittsburgh *Mercury*, January 11, 1812.

The Erskine Agreement

On March 4, 1809, while the European conflagration was roaring with increased fury, the scholarly but somewhat irresolute James Madison took the presidential oath. "Little Jemmy," as he was rather contemptuously dubbed by his political opponents, inherited Jefferson's policy of economic coercion, which, upon the breakdown of the embargo, had taken the form of commercial nonintercourse with Great Britain and France.

The British minister in Washington at this time, David Erskine, had an American wife and, unlike most of his predecessors, cherished a sympathetic regard for the United States. The inflexible George Canning, then Foreign Secretary, instructed him to secure from the Madison administration a series of categorical avowals and disavowals in regard to the questions at issue. Erskine was extremely anxious to effect an understanding; and instead of reading these instructions to Secretary of State Robert Smith, as he was authorized to do, he outlined them in such a way as to gloss over their disagreeable features.[1] The subsequent negotiations proceeded smoothly; and in April, 1809, Erskine signed an important agreement. It bound Great Britain to withdraw her Orders in Council as regards the United States in return for a number of American concessions which yielded substantially all that Canning had demanded, although not in the explicit manner that he desired. The American government was even persuaded to ignore the burning subject of impressment.

At this point President Madison made the first of a series of disastrous blunders. He unwisely took it for granted that the Erskine

[1] C. C. Tansill, "Robert Smith," in S. F. Bemis, ed., *The American Secretaries of State and their Diplomacy* (N.Y., 1927), III, 159.

agreement would be promptly accepted by Canning, and issued a proclamation, effective June 10, 1809, withdrawing nonintercourse with Great Britain. "Great and glorious news," announced a broadside "extra" of the New Hampshire *Patriot*. "Our Differences with Great Britain Amicably Settled." [2] Hundreds of American vessels rushed to sea, heavily laden with those raw materials and foodstuffs which Britain sorely needed and which, incidentally, did much to wipe out the hard-won fruits of Jeffersonian coercion. For a few brief weeks Madison and his Administration lived in a fool's paradise.

Then came the news that Canning had disavowed the agreement and had abruptly recalled Erskine for having exceeded the strict letter of his instructions. America was deeply angered. "The late conduct of the British ministry," declared the Washington *National Intelligencer*, "has capped the climax of atrocity toward this country." Even pro-British Federalists were aroused, and one of them exclaimed that England could not expect to "crop off our noses and that we will remain content because our heads are spared." The crestfallen Madison, everywhere condemned as the dupe of Canning, was forced to restore nonintercourse with Great Britain, on August 9, 1809. Having thrown himself into the arms of England, he had been violently hurled back.[3]

The repudiation of the Erskine agreement marked the parting of the ways for the United States and Great Britain. With relations restored to their former instability, America tended more and more to gravitate toward the strangling embrace of Bonaparte, a course that led almost inexorably to hostilities.

"COPENHAGEN" JACKSON

Canning next decided to replace the conciliatory Erskine with a man of sterner stuff. He selected an overbearing ultra-Britisher, Francis James Jackson, who had presented the ultimatum which preceded the ruthless confiscation of the Danish fleet at Copenhagen in 1807. The choice of so offensive an emissary was regarded in the United States as nothing short of an insult. The American newspapers published nu-

[2] April 9, 1809, File 91, Library of Congress.
[3] A note written by the American Secretary of State regarding Admiral Berkeley was among the papers accompanying the agreement. When Canning read it he flared up in a scene that was vividly remembered by one of the Foreign Office underlings forty years later. This may have been an important factor in Canning's determination to deal harshly with the Yankee. Beckles Willson, *Friendly Relations* (Boston, 1934), p. 62.

merous invitations to tar and feather "Copenhagen" Jackson; and meetings were later held at which resolutions were passed "to resist all attempts to 'Copenhagen' us."

In September, 1809, Jackson reached America, and his first impressions added to his irritability. He regarded Madison as a "plain and rather mean-looking man," and his wife, the incomparable Dolly, as "fat and forty, but not fair." To him the Americans were "all alike," except that some few were "less knaves than others." The "mob" was "by many degrees more blackguard and ferocious than the mob in other countries." After Jackson had spent some time examining the correspondence in the British legation, he concluded that it was "charity" to call Erskine a "fool"; and that with respect to the American notes "Every third word was a declaration of war." [4]

With the British emissary in this mood, negotiations proceeded unsatisfactorily. They were brought to a climax when Jackson insisted on implying that the American government had known that Erskine was violating his instructions when the agreement was concluded. Following this charge of bad faith, which meant in effect that the United States government had lied, Secretary Smith refused to receive any further communications from him.[5] As Jackson became more and more insolent, he received a number of letters threatening personal violence, including horsewhipping. One irate Kentuckian ran afoul of the state profanity law when he shouted: "God damn Mr. Jackson;—the President ought to . . . have kicked him from town to town until he is kicked out of the country. God damn him!" [6]

Jackson was obviously doing more harm than good by his presence; yet he stayed on in America during the year for which he had been paid.[7] The Foreign Office, refusing to disapprove its representative's conduct, did not send a successor until nearly two years after his dismissal. Instead, the legation was left with a *chargé d'affaires*. The whole incident, coming so close upon the heels of the Erskine debacle, further widened the diplomatic breach.

Meanwhile relations with Napoleon had drifted from bad to worse. The conquering Corsican had naturally "applauded" the embargo,

[4] Henry Adams, *History of the United States during the Administrations of Jefferson and Madison* (N.Y., 1890), V, 119–120.

[5] Tansill, "Robert Smith," in Bemis, *American Secretaries of State*, III, 174.

[6] Bernard Mayo, *Henry Clay: Spokesman of the New West* (Boston, 1937), p. 325.

[7] Jackson tried "to correct the Public Mind" regarding Great Britain by engaging in numerous propaganda activities. His efforts in the press cost seven hundred pounds. See Josephine Fisher, "Francis James Jackson and Newspaper Propaganda in the United States, 1809–1810," *Maryland Hist. Mag.*, XXX (1935), 93–113.

which amounted to a partial blockade of Great Britain; yet he strongly objected to the nonintercourse act, which was aimed at France as well as England. In retaliation he issued the Rambouillet decree of March 23, 1810, as a result of which scores of American ships in French ports were confiscated.[8] The protests of the United States were so many wasted words.

NAPOLEON DUPES MADISON

The Jeffersonian act forbidding commercial intercourse with the two great belligerents was about to expire; and on May 1, 1810, Congress passed an ingenious if mischievous substitute, Macon's Bill No. 2. This measure reopened intercourse with both England and France. But it also provided that if France repealed her decrees, nonintercourse would be renewed against Great Britain; and that if Great Britain repealed her Orders in Council, nonintercourse would be renewed against France. This naïve experiment, which can be justified only by the desperate desire of the United States to keep out of war, created a situation made to order for Bonaparte. On August 5, 1810, he had his foreign minister, Duc de Cadore, send an ambiguous letter to the American minister in Paris. Although this communication ostensibly announced the repeal of the French decrees, there was a very important "string" attached. Either England would have to revoke her Orders in Council, or the Americans would have to "cause their rights to be respected" by establishing nonintercourse against her.[9] These, of course, were impossible conditions, for Britain was mistress of the seas, and the United States was but a third-rate power.

The fateful Cadore letter was worded so ingeniously as to commit France to nothing, and at the same time trick the distraught Madison into believing that a promise had been made. Eager to restore the tarnished prestige of his Administration, and not daring to look a gift horse in the mouth, the President issued a proclamation, on November 2, 1810, announcing that nonintercourse would be restored against Britain if the latter did not withdraw her Orders within three months. This was unduly precipitate; for Madison was bound by the terms of Macon's bill not to take such a step until he had convincing proof that the French decrees had been repealed. Napoleon, in fact, had accompanied his presumed pledge with no evidences whatsoever of good

---

[8] A. C. Clauder, *American Commerce as Affected by the Wars of the French Revolution and Napoleon, 1793–1812* (Phila., 1932), p. 180.
[9] *American State Papers, Foreign Relations*, III, 386–387.

faith. On the very date of the Cadore letter he secretly ordered the sale of a number of confiscated American ships. And every mail to the United States indicated that the French decrees were still in effect and that American vessels were being seized and scuttled.[10]

England naturally refused to repeal her Orders in Council because it was evident that Napoleon had not revoked his decrees. She felt a new bitterness against the United States for having been so willing to turn against her at the behest of Bonaparte. This feeling was not improved when Congress passed a new measure, on March 2, 1811, which officially renewed nonintercourse against Great Britain.

REDRESS AND RED MEN

In the summer of 1811, a new and more conciliatory British minister, Augustus Foster, landed in the United States. Although not authorized to make substantial concessions on any other important subject, he was instructed to offer formal reparation for the still-festering *Chesapeake* affair. To his astonishment he found interest in the four-year-old outrage almost completely eclipsed by enthusiasm for invading Canada and by excitement over the *Little Belt* incident.

On May 16, 1811, several weeks before Foster's arrival, a forty-four-gun American frigate, the *President*, had hailed in the gathering darkness the twenty-gun British corvette, *Little Belt*. Someone fired a shot; and in the ensuing engagement His Majesty's ship was almost knocked out of the water, suffering a loss of thirty-two killed and wounded. The *Little Belt* was about as severely handled as the *Chesapeake* had been, and suffered the loss of three killed for every one killed on the *Chesapeake*. In principle the two incidents were poles apart; yet undiscerning American opinion regarded the account with England as squared. Had not the *President* exacted three eyes and three teeth for every eye and tooth lost on the *Chesapeake?* A writer in the Philadelphia *Aurora* rejoiced that the proud Briton had got another taste of 1776, when with "our hay forks, pitch forks and grubbing hoes . . . we knocked down his teeth and scowered his blackhell throat." Although Minister Foster did make acceptable reparation for the *Chesapeake* affair, such medicine as he had to offer

---

[10] R. R. Stenberg advances the thesis that Madison, knowing the conditional nature of the Cadore letter, issued the proclamation "as a bribe to secure France's acquiescence in the American annexation of West Florida." "Louisiana and West Florida: a Few Notes," *Southwestern Soc. Sci. Quar.*, XVIII (1937), 249.

came too late to heal the wound. "Presented at *such a time*," scoffed the Baltimore *Whig*, "[it] is like restoring a hair after fracturing the skull." [11]

"The Americans grow warm very slowly," wrote the French minister in Washington, "but at last they are heated; and at any moment the least spark can light up a conflagration from the Gulf of Mexico to Canada." [12] An ominous spark was provided at this time by a dramatic incident on the frontier. For many years it had been a conviction among Americans, in the East as well as in the West, that the British were egging their red myrmidons upon the American pioneer, and paying a bounty (allegedly six dollars apiece) for the scalps of men, women, and children. The continual scalping forays were no doubt motivated primarily by the encroachments of the whites upon the red man's lands; but the general attitude of the British officers and their liberal distribution of arms unquestionably encouraged the Indians to resist. Whether true or not, the "hair-buying" charge was widely believed, and it had an incendiary effect on the American mind.

On November 7, 1811, a strong force of Americans, led by William Henry Harrison, engaged the Indians at Tippecanoe, near the Wabash River. Some doubt exists as to the decisiveness of the so-called victory; but the savages were beaten off, leaving newly marked British arms on the field of battle. The American casualties numbered several score killed and wounded; and from the frontier came the demand of Andrew Jackson, "The blood of our murdered heroes must be revenged." "*The War on the Wabash is purely British*," asserted the Lexington *Reporter*. "The British scalping knife has filled many habitations both in this state as well as in the Indiana Territory with widows and orphans." From the West to the East spread the cry, "Look to the Wabash, look to the impressed seamen!" [13]

---

[11] Quoted in Mayo, *Clay*, p. 388. Of the three Americans, one died in prison, and the other two, after five years of wrangling and delay, were returned with proper regrets to the decks of the *Chesapeake*, and the British government offered pecuniary reparation to the sufferers and their families. The case of the *Little Belt* involved a warm diplomatic exchange; but it was never satisfactorily determined who fired the first shot. The outraged London *Courier* cried: "The blood of our murdered countrymen must be revenged, and war must ensue. . . . We have behaved towards America with unexampled forbearance; but that forbearance has produced insolence, and that insolence must be punished." Quoted (with capitals, italics, and exclamation points) in Niles' *Weekly Register*, I, 39 (Sept. 21, 1811).

[12] Sept. 8, 1811, quoted in Mayo, *Clay*, p. 394.

[13] Quoted in *ibid.*, p. 398.

The Landlocked West Demands a Free Sea

On November 4, 1811, three days before Tippecanoe, the Twelfth Congress convened. As a result of the recent elections almost one half of the membership of the House had been swept out. The casualties were in the main senile "submission men." Conspicuous among the newcomers was a group of ultranationalists, called the War Hawks. Most of these "pepperpot politicians" were from the lower South and the West; from the new states, or from the frontier regions of the old ones. Their leaders were all comparatively young men, some in their late twenties and early thirties, who were determined to "pull John Bull by the nose" and end "putrescent peace." John Randolph contemptuously referred to these young "buckskin statesmen" as "the boys"; and Josiah Quincy called them "young Politicians, their pin-feathers not yet grown. . . ." Though lacking a majority, they succeeded in elevating to the Speakership their brilliant leader, the thirty-four year old Henry Clay of Kentucky, who proceeded to pack the important committees with War Hawks and make preparations for hostilities.

There can be no doubt that the driving impetus for a break with England came from the hot-blooded West, and that the movement was led by the ardent War Hawks. But the question of their motives is a complicated one that cannot be determined with such certainty.

The people of the West resented impressment as an intolerable outrage, though comparatively few from this section were actually impressed. The explanation seems to be that personal rights meant more to the Westerner than they did to the property-loving, conservative Easterner. The forcible seizure of an American and his "enslavement" in Britain's navy, with a very good chance of being killed, was, to the men beyond the mountains, an insult not to be tolerated. Their code called for a quick resort to arms to avenge an outrage against one's person. And to them an offense against an individual American was an offense against the entire nation.[14] The Westerners also felt that the patriotism of the East had become atrophied by money-making—what Clay branded as the "low groveling parsimony of the counting room." Although the Eastern seaboard, particularly New England, was still closely bound by cultural and commercial ties to

---

[14] Professor Mayo develops this point in his well-rounded discussion of American motives. *Ibid.*, p. 326.

Old England, the West was American to the core and eager to secure satisfaction for insults to the flag.[15]

The Westerner also resented Britain's restrictions on American commerce. But the Eastern shipper, who handled most of the nation's sea-borne trade, acquiesced in these restrictions, for if he sailed only one cargo in three between the Scylla of British orders and the Charybdis of French decrees, he would make a handsome profit. Then why should the Westerner have become aroused if he had no personal stake? The answer is that he did have a personal stake. If he had no ships to sail the seas, he had produce to put into those ships. Since 1808 he had been suffering from a serious depression; and he blamed his economic distress on the British regulations that ruined his market and dammed up his surplus.[16] He also believed that England was deliberately attempting to crush out American economic life so that her own would benefit. At first the West had supported the embargo and nonintercourse in the hope of forcing concessions; but such devices had proved unavailing. A Fourth of July toast at Frankfort, Kentucky, in 1811, reflected the new spirit: "Embargoes, nonintercourse, and negotiations, are but illy calculated to secure our rights. . . . Let us now try old Roman policy, and maintain them with the sword."[17]

"On to Canada!"

The West was determined to fight England in order to avenge the insults of the "haughty and imperious" mistress of the seas. But how could America attack her without a navy? The solution of the problem was Canada. Here was an eminently desirable, poorly defended territory, which could presumably be taken by the American frontiersmen with ridiculous ease. Clay boasted that the Kentucky militia could do it by themselves; just "a mere matter of marching," wrote Jefferson. But Western eyes were directed toward Canada for another burn-

[15] Clay exclaimed: "No man in the nation wants peace more than I; but I prefer the troubled ocean of war, demanded by the honor and independence of the country, with all its calamities and desolation, to the tranquil and putrescent pool of ignominious peace." *Annals of Congress*, 11 Cong., 1 sess., I, 579 (Feb. 22, 1810). The War Hawk House Committee on Foreign Affairs reported regarding impressment: ". . . while this practice is continued, it is impossible for the United States to consider themselves an independent nation. Every new case is a new proof of their degradation." *American State Papers, Foreign Relations*, III, 569 (June 3, 1812).

[16] This thesis is fully developed in G. R. Taylor, "Agrarian Discontent in the Mississippi Valley Preceding the War of 1812," *Jour. of Pol. Economy*, XXXIX (1931), 497.

[17] *American Republic* (Frankfort), July 5, 1811, quoted in *ibid*.

ing reason, perhaps the most important of all.[18] England was providing the murderous Indians with arms and other supplies; and it seemed that if the savages were ever to be removed, the United States would have to take over Canada and wipe out their base. As Representative Grundy of Tennessee, a leading War Hawk, three of whose brothers had been butchered by the red men, exclaimed in a fiery speech: "We shall drive the British from our Continent—they will no longer have an apportunity [sic] of intriguing with our Indian neighbors, and setting on the ruthless savage to tomahawk our women and children." [19]

Canada had still other attractions. With this vast territory under the Stars and Stripes, the United States could control the profitable fur trade with the Indians, as well as the coveted St. Lawrence outlet to the sea. Future generations of pioneers would have a marvelously fertile and richly wooded domain into which to expand. Moreover, the Americans would realize their dream of banishing the Union Jack and substituting for it the banner of freedom. The cynical John Randolph heard the War Hawks cry "On to Canada!" so frequently that he concluded the West was merely concealing its land lust behind the shield of American rights. Referring to all this talk about the Canadian "tit-bit," he asserted:

Agrarian cupidity, not maritime right, urges the war. Ever since the report of the Committee . . . we have heard but one word—like the whip-poor-will, but one eternal monotonous tone—Canada! Canada! Canada! Not a syllable about Halifax, which unquestionably should be our great object in a war for maritime security.[20]

A conflict with England would also make possible an attack on Florida, which still remained in the feeble grip of Spain, now Britain's ally. The acquisition of this area would end Indian forays, and round out the "natural boundary" of the United States. So, while the Northern War Hawks clamored for Canada, the Southern War Hawks demanded Florida. "Florida and Canada" ran a Kentucky toast— "A fee simple in the one, a mortgage upon the other." Josiah Quincy depre-

[18] J. W. Pratt, "Western Aims in the War of 1812," *Miss. Valley Hist. Rev.*, XII (1925), 36–50, holds that it was a desire to remove the Indian menace rather than a lust for land that actuated the Westerner, thus refuting the thesis of L. M. Hacker, "Western Land Hunger and the War of 1812," in *ibid.*, X (1924), 365–395.

[19] *Annals of Congress*, 12 Cong., 1 sess., I, 426 (Dec. 9, 1811). Clay had earlier cried: "The conquest of Canada is in your power. . . . Is it nothing to us to extinguish the torch that lights up savage warfare? Is it nothing to acquire the entire fur trade connected with that country . . . ?" *Ibid.*, 11 Cong., 1 sess., I, 580 (Feb. 22, 1810).

[20] *Ibid.*, 12 Cong., 1 sess., I, 533 (Dec. 16, 1811).

cated the clamor of the War Hawks when he summarized their argument: "We want West Florida. Our Western brethren will have West Florida. By G—— we will take West Florida. By G—— it is in the title deed." [21] The seizure of West Florida, late in 1810, under circumstances to be described in a later chapter, merely whetted Western appetites for all Florida.

The catchword "Manifest Destiny" had not come into use; yet America displayed all the symptoms of the spirit later associated with this phrase. The more men talked about the easy conquest of Canada— a mere "frontiersmen's frolic"—the more inflamed became their imaginations. Harper of New Hampshire declared on the floor of the House: "To me, sir, it appears that the Author of Nature has marked our limits in the south, by the Gulf of Mexico; and on the north by the regions of eternal frost." [22] And the editor of the Nashville *Clarion* posed a rhetorical question: "Where is it written in the book of fate that the American republic shall not stretch her limits from the Capes of the Chesapeake to Nootka sound, from the isthmus of Panama to Hudson bay?" [23]

The West Presents the East with a War

American bitterness against England was further aggravated by the publication, in March, 1812, of the Henry letters. John Henry, a British agent, had visited Boston and had reported the attachment of the Federalist leaders to England. He now offered to sell his correspondence regarding these matters to President Madison for $50,-000. The latter, thinking to discredit his political opponents and at the same time expose British machinations in New England, paid this exorbitant sum and laid the letters before Congress. When it was discovered that Henry had deleted the names of the Federalist leaders, and that in other respects the correspondence was rather commonplace, the exposé fell flat. Yet the unthinking found in it further evidence of England's perfidy. [24]

By the spring of 1812 the clamor for war, from the West and elsewhere, had become well-nigh irresistible. In April, Congress passed

21 Quincy to Sullivan, Dec. 21, 1810, quoted in Mayo, *Clay*, p. 365. The Florida aspect is fully developed in J. W. Pratt, *Expansionists of 1812* (N.Y., 1925), pp. 11 ff.

22 *Annals of Congress*, 12 Cong., 1 sess., I, 657 (Jan. 4, 1812).

23 Nashville *Clarion*, April 28, 1812, quoted in Pratt, *Expansionists of 1812*, p. 14.

24 Henry in turn was duped by a French swindler, who sold him for $50,000 a château that could not be located. J. W. Pratt, "James Monroe," in Bemis, *American Secretaries of State*, III, 229. The Henry affair is treated fully in E. A. Cruikshank, *The Political Adventures of John Henry* (Toronto, 1936).

an act establishing a ninety-day embargo, preparatory to hostilities. And on June 1 Madison sent his memorable war message to Congress.[25] In his review of accumulated grievances the President gave the first and most important place to impressment. After discussing at length other abridgments of American neutral rights, and after giving credence to the charges of British tampering with the Indians, he threw the whole question of hostilities into the lap of Congress. The bellicose House promptly passed a war resolution, on June 4, by the comfortable margin of 79 to 49. In the Senate, where the Federalist and conservative East was stronger, the debate was prolonged; [26] and not until June 17 did the resolution pass by the rather narrow margin of 19 to 13.[27] On the next day the amended resolution was concurred in by the House and signed by the President.

An analysis of the vote in Congress reveals that the alleged war for neutral rights was on the whole strongly opposed by maritime New England and the Middle States, and strongly supported by the agrarian states of the West and Southwest. The *Columbian Centinel* (Boston) complained bitterly:

We, whose soil was the hotbed and whose ships were the nursery of Sailors, are insulted with the hypocrisy of a devotedness to Sailors' rights, and the arrogance of a pretended skill in maritime jurisprudence, by those whose country furnishes no navigation beyond the size of a ferryboat or an Indian canoe.[28]

It has been repeatedly charged that the Westerner merely wrapped his selfish desire for Canada in the American flag, and prated loudly and insincerely for neutral rights. Yet, for reasons already indicated,

[25] The charge that Madison yielded to the War Hawks to purchase their support for his re-election is now discredited. The President and his Cabinet, especially Secretary of State Monroe, seemed hardly less desirous of hostilities than the War Hawks themselves. Mayo, *Clay*, pp. 511–513.

[26] War was by no means a foregone conclusion as far as the Senate and the Executive were concerned. During the two-week debate attempts were made to retreat from outright war, to substitute for it the issuance of letters of marque and reprisal against both France and England, and then against Britain alone. *Ibid.*, pp. 521–523.

[27] The sectional aspects of the war agitation and the vote in Congress are discussed in Pratt, *Expansionists of 1812*, pp. 26 ff. On Jan. 27, 1812, the Western members of Congress voted down a proposal to increase the navy, while the maritime states, though opposing war, went on record as favoring the measure. Harold and Margaret Sprout, *The Rise of American Naval Power, 1776–1918* (Princeton, 1939), pp. 64–65.

[28] Jan. 13, 1813, quoted in Allan Nevins, ed., *American Press Opinion* (Boston, 1928), p. 53. This same newspaper earlier described a Tennessee Representative as "a wild backwoodsman who perhaps never saw the ocean but on a map, or conceived the taste of it except from a salt-lick." Quoted in C. G. Bowers, *Jefferson in Power* (Boston, 1936), p. 465.

the men from the West appear to have been sincere. The presence of Canada, which was both a menace and a lure, not only added to the vigor of their cry but probably tipped the scales in favor of war.

BONAPARTE OR BRITAIN?

At this point the question may well be asked: Why did not the United States fight Napoleon rather than England? Certainly his conduct had been just as offensive—possibly more so. While the British had been highhanded, he had been treacherous and double-dealing. "His Majesty loves the Americans," declared the Cadore letter. Yet during five years prior to 1812 Bonaparte had confiscated 558 American vessels. In that same period the British had seized 389, though their record since 1803 totaled 917. In fact, Napoleon's ships had perpetrated about every outrage that the United States could lay at the door of England, although not on so large a scale or so close to home. French vessels even impressed a few American sailors; but because Bonaparte had little need for seamen this did not become a serious grievance. Even worse in some respects than the British practice of impressment was Napoleon's imprisonment of the crews of confiscated ships. The New York *Evening Post* reminded its readers that American sailors had been "robbed and manacled . . . and marched without shoes to their feet or clothing to their backs in the most inclement weather some hundreds of miles into the interior of France; lashed along the highway like slaves, treated with every possible indignity, and then immured in the infernal dungeons of Arras or Verdun." [29]

There was much truth in the Federalist accusation that the Madison administration, which carried on the Francophile tradition of the Jeffersonian Republicans, unprotestingly suffered insults from France that would not have been tolerated from Britain. One Massachusetts poet declared:

> If England look askance, we boil with rage;
> And blood, blood only, can the wound assuage;
> Yet, whipt, robbed, kicked, and spit upon, by France,
> We treat her with the greater complaisance. [30]

[29] New York *Evening Post*, July 12, 1809, 2:4.

[30] E. B. White, *American Opinion of France* (N.Y., 1927), p. 12. (Poem by Charles Prentiss.) Elijah Parish, a prominent Massachusetts clergyman, reflected a current Federalist view when he cried (Apr. 8, 1813): "Which sooty slave in all the ancient dominions, has more obsequiously watched the eyes of his master; or flew to the indulgence of his desires, more servilely, than they [at Washington] have waited and watched and obeyed the orders of the great Napoleon?" *Ibid.*

Just before the adjournment of Congress the Federalist members issued an address in which they proclaimed: "If honor demands a war with England, what opiate lulls that honor to sleep over the wrongs done us by France? On land, robberies, seizures, imprisonments . . . ; at sea, pillage, sinkings, burnings. . . ."[31]

There can be little doubt that the United States had ample reason to fight both France and Great Britain. "The Devil himself," asserted Nathaniel Macon, "could not tell which government, England or France, is the most wicked." Indeed, consistency would have dictated war with both antagonists. This was the thesis of the ever-logical Calhoun; but Jefferson properly regarded as quixotic the idea of choosing "to fight two enemies at a time rather than to take them in succession." Clay thought that after silencing "the insolence of British cannon . . . we can then speak to the hushed batteries of French aggression." President Madison, himself, gave serious thought to the advisability of declaring war on both belligerents, but in the end decided against such a course. A proposal to include France in the declaration of hostilities against Britain lost in the Senate by the narrow vote of 18 to 14.[32]

Beyond question, it would have been sheer folly for adolescent America to fight both powers. Why, then, did she choose as she did? First of all, England's offenses took place nearer home. An American sailor imprisoned by Bonaparte in faraway France excited much less popular indignation than one impressed by British frigates off New York.[33] And impressment, above all things, was humiliating and degrading to the American people. Secondly, England's conduct resulted in the actual killing of United States citizens, notably in the case of the *Chesapeake*. As the editor of Niles' *Weekly Register* reasoned:

[31] *Annals of Congress*, 12 Cong., 1 sess., II, 2219–2220 (1812). A number of broadsides, most of them issued in Massachusetts and filed in the Library of Congress, the American Antiquarian Society, and the Massachusetts Historical Society, register New England protest against French seizures as "piracy." One (c. 1811) is entitled "The Philometer or The Gauge of His Majesty's 'Love' towards the Americans," and gives a long list of French depredations. Mass. Hist. Society.

[32] Five days after the declaration of war the French minister in Washington reported: "I can assure Monseigneur the bitterness which has developed against France is really such that if the policy of the [American] Government had not arrested the movement in the Chambers, during the secret deliberations, war would have been declared against both Powers." R. B. Mowat, *The Diplomatic Relations of Great Britain and the United States* (London, 1925), p. 55.

[33] Jefferson wrote: "We resist the enterprises of England first, because they first come vitally home to us. . . . When the wrongs of France shall reach us with equal effect, we shall resist them also." A. A. Lipscomb, ed., *Writings of Thomas Jefferson* (Monticello ed., Washington, 1904), XIII, 147 (Jefferson to Maury, April 25, 1812).

The injuries received from *France* do not lessen the enormity of those heaped upon us by *England;* nor can the crimes of one nation palliate the offences of the other. In this "straight betwixt two" we had an unquestionable right to select our enemy. We have given the preference to *Great Britain* . . . on account of her more flagrant wrongs.[34]

Nor was this all. France had helped the United States win independence; England was the ancient foe. France was not tampering with the Indians of Canada; England was. Besides, it would do America no good to fight Napoleon. She had no navy and could not cross the seas to attack him. On the other hand, as Niles' *Weekly Register* pointed out, Great Britain was "tangible in her tenderest points." Rich English commerce would fall an easy prey to American privateers. And Canada, a tempting morsel indeed, would be quickly overrun by Kentucky militiamen. Can it be wondered that the United States overlooked French insults and declared war on England?

BLUNDERING INTO WAR

It is possible that hostilities would have been averted if a number of purely fortuitous occurrences had not helped defeat the work of diplomacy. In November, 1810, the aged George III went completely insane. A delay of several precious months was involved in establishing the regency, while American affairs received little attention. By May, 1812, increasing pressure from the British manufacturing and mercantile groups was foreshadowing a repeal of the odious Orders in Council.[35] Yet more confusion and delay were caused when Prime Minister Perceval was assassinated by a madman. It was not until June 16, 1812, that Lord Castlereagh, then Foreign Secretary, could announce in the House of Commons that the Orders in Council would be immediately suspended.[36] Joyfully confident that this concession would compose the existing differences, the British prepared to ship their surplus stocks to America. Yet two days after Castlereagh's announcement the United States declared war. If there had been a trans-

---

[34] Niles' *Weekly Register*, II, 284 (June 27, 1812).

[35] Petitions that poured in upon Parliament revealed the pathetic conditions produced by American nonintercourse. We read of closed factories, the high cost of living, the pawning of furniture, and diets consisting of oatmeal and water. A Parliamentary committee examined one hundred witnesses from thirty manufacturing districts, and elicited much information. See Clauder, *American Commerce*, pp. 213–216.

[36] *Parliamentary Debates*, XXIII, 542, 545–546. Formal repeal, June 23. Castlereagh reasoned that America would respond by repealing nonintercourse.

atlantic cable to convey this good news to America, Congress probably would not have voted for hostilities.

During these critical weeks the United States unfortunately had no first-class representative in England. The able William Pinkney, who had endured five years of evasion and delay, finally quit his post in February, 1811, leaving behind a *chargé d'affaires*. If he had been on the ground he would have been able to report that Britain, suffering from acute economic distress, did not want war; and he might have been able to foresee the imminent repeal of the Orders in Council.

By a curious coincidence, the United States plunged into the conflict at such a time as to be a virtual ally of the dreaded Bonaparte.[37] America's true interests pointed to the wisdom of fighting against the greatest despot of the age, Napoleon, on the side of England, the surviving champion of constitutional government. The British, in a sense, were fighting America's battle. This explains why New England Federalists could prayerfully drink Pickering's famous toast: "The world's last hope—Britain's fast-anchored isle." Yet at the very moment when the fate of democracy was trembling in the balance, when Napoleon was preparing to launch his mighty invasion of Russia, when England was nerving herself for the last desperate struggle, the United States proceeded to knife the mother country in the back and throw what strength it had on the side of despotism.

The War of 1812 was a rash departure from the true policy of Washington, Adams, and Jefferson—of playing for time and letting Europe's distresses fight America's battles. The grievances of the United States were perhaps less acute in 1812 than they had been at any time since 1807; and the discerning observer should have been able to see that the European cataclysm was coming to an end. And with the end of the war American grievances, including the intolerable practice of impressment, were bound to disappear, at least for some time. But the United States had suffered from such an accumulation of injuries that, when the War Hawks seized control, the issue was remitted to the sword.

---

[37] Madison counted on Napoleon's beating Britain to her knees and thus enabling the United States to secure advantageous terms. The Administration rejoiced at Bonaparte's triumphs. Following the news of Napoleon's victory at Lützen, in 1813, the French minister reported, "The Republicans of Congress . . . have received these news in triumph. All have come to congratulate me, and have told me that they, not less than we, had been victorious. . . ." Adams, *History*, VII, 391.

BIBLIOGRAPHICAL NOTE

The best survey of the diplomacy of the Madison administration may be found in the sketches of Robert Smith (by C. C. Tansill) and James Monroe (by J. W. Pratt) in S. F. Bemis, ed., *The American Secretaries of State and their Diplomacy* (N.Y., 1927), III, 151–265. An important monograph is J. W. Pratt's *Expansionists of 1812* (N.Y., 1925), which shows the influence of the West in bringing about a declaration of war. Bernard Mayo, *Henry Clay: Spokesman of the New West* (Boston, 1937), is excellent on the War Hawks and the growth of war spirit. Briefer is G. G. Van Deusen's *Life of Henry Clay* (Boston, 1937), which is the best one-volume treatment of the Kentuckian. Elizabeth White, *American Opinion of France* (N.Y., 1927), reveals American public hostility to France prior to the declaration of war against Great Britain. Consult the relevant pages in the older accounts of Henry Adams, Channing, and Mahan, all listed at the end of the previous chapter. See also G. R. Taylor, "Agrarian Discontent in the Mississippi Valley preceding the War of 1812," *Jour. of Pol. Economy*, XXXIX (1931), 471–505. Further references: see footnotes of this chapter and Bemis and Griffin, *Guide*, pp. 137–147.

RECENT REFERENCES. Two new studies are of indispensable value to the student of the causes of the War of 1812, and both of them either contradict or modify both the traditional and newer interpretations, notably those of Pratt. They are A. L. Burt, *The United States, Great Britain, and British North America*, and W. H. Goodman, "The Origins of the War of 1812: A Survey of Changing Interpretations," *Miss. Valley Hist. Rev.*, XXVIII (1941), 171–186. Both of these contributions are discussed at length in the Bibliographical Appendix, p. 923.

NEW REFERENCES. General backgrounds are treated in J. B. Brebner, *North Atlantic Triangle* (New Haven, 1945), and E. W. McInnis, *The Unguarded Frontier* (Garden City, N.Y., 1942). Consult Bernard Mayo, ed., *Instructions to the British Ministers to the United States, 1791–1812* (Washington, 1941). See also R. G. Albion and J. B. Pope, *Sea Lanes in Wartime* (N.Y., 1942) for a general discussion of the embargo, neutral commerce, and war traffic. Material on trade with Sweden may be found in H. Koht, "Bernadotte and Swedish-American Relations, 1810–1814," *Jour. of Mod. Hist.*, XVI (1944), 265–285. Abbot Smith, "Mr. Madison's War: An Unsuccessful Experiment in the Conduct of National Policy," *Pol. Sci. Quar.*, LVII (1942), 229–246, shows that Madison, although personally desiring war and having made up his mind for it prior to taking office in 1809, was betrayed by his strict regard for constitutional principles into a weak and compromising course.

CHAPTER X

The Peace of Ghent and After, 1812–1818

"Ghent, the city of Peace; may the gates of the temple of Janus, here closed, not be opened again for a century!"
Toast of John Quincy Adams, January 5, 1815.

Mr. Madison's War

AMERICA of 1812 was woefully unprepared for war. The army and navy were inadequate; the people were disunited. Federalist New England, which regarded Napoleon as anti-Christ and hostilities with Britain as immoral, almost solidly opposed what it called "Mr. Madison's war." "Is there a Federalist, a patriot, in America," exclaimed the Boston *Gazette*, "who conceives it his duty to shed his blood for Bonaparte, for Madison or Jefferson, and that Host of Ruffians in Congress who have set their faces against the United States for years . . . ?"[1] Such words were matched by deeds. New England defiantly withheld her troops from service, sold enormous quantities of provisions to the British invader, and in other ways hampered the American cause.

In view of all these circumstances the results of the war are not surprising. The Canadians, many of whom were descendants of the Loyalists who had been expelled from the United States, arose to defend their homes and firesides. The overconfident and bungling American armies were hurled back from their "mere marching" into Canada, and before long found themselves desperately defending their own territory. The British occupied considerable areas of the United States along the northern frontier; and when hostilities ended they held that part of Maine which lay east of the Penobscot River. The inhabitants of this region took the oath of allegiance to their old sovereign, George III, without undue protest.[2]

On the sea the heavier American frigates won a number of brilliant naval duels. These victories had no appreciable bearing on the outcome

[1] Boston *Gazette*, quoted in F. A. Updyke, *The Diplomacy of the War of 1812* (Baltimore, 1915), p. 134 (no date given). A number of broadsides protesting against the war were issued in New England. See Files 49, 50 (Mass.), Library of Congress.
[2] Henry Adams, *History of the United States during the Administrations of Jefferson and Madison* (N.Y., 1891), VIII, 96–97.

of the war; and the British, their pride stung, either destroyed or bottled up virtually every ship in the United States Navy. Much more important from a naval point of view were the American privateers, which even ventured boldly into the English Channel, where they brought the war home to the British shipper.

THE CZAR BEARS AN OLIVE BRANCH

Diplomatic machinery is ordinarily stilled when war breaks out. The armies clash on the field of battle; one of the antagonists is beaten to his knees; then the diplomats gather about the peace table to discuss terms. The War of 1812 was unusual in that negotiations for peace were initiated almost as soon as the conflict began, and they continued to, and even after, the signing of the treaty. In fact, the demands of the negotiators were strengthened or tempered by the news which was constantly arriving from the fighting front.

On June 26, 1812, a week after the declaration of war, Secretary Monroe instructed the American *chargé* in London to negotiate for a cessation of hostilities, provided England would renounce impressment. At the same time the British government made overtures to Washington. Both attempts at negotiation fell through because the Briton was unwilling to yield his ancient naval fetish. Whatever the causes of the hostilities, it seems clear that the United States government persisted in continuing them primarily on the grounds of impressment. The strength of American sentiment on this subject may be gauged by a statement appearing in Niles' *Weekly Register:* "*Accursed be the American government, and every individual of it, who . . . shall agree to make peace with Great Britain, until ample provision shall be made for our impressed seamen, and security shall be given for the prevention of such abominable outrages in future.*" [3]

In September, 1812, several months after these initial overtures, the Czar of Russia, Alexander I, proposed to mediate between the United States and his ally, Great Britain. Napoleon had marched into his territory at the head of a mighty host and had just captured Moscow. The Russian government naturally wished to see the American war come to an end, because it was diverting Britain's strength from the common effort against Bonaparte, and because it was cutting off much-desired trade with the United States. [4]

[3] Niles' *Weekly Register*, II, 119 (April 18, 1812).

[4] A. T. Mahan, *Sea Power in Its Relations to the War of 1812* (Boston, 1905), II, 411. For the suggestion that the Czar feared a Franco-American alliance see F. A. Golder, "The Russian Offer of Mediation in the War of 1812," *Pol. Sci. Quar.*, XXXI (1916), 380.

Bruin Become MEDIATOR or Negociation for PEACE

The Russian bear mediates between John Bull and America. Actually, Russia rather than England took the initiative. (Courtesy of The New York Historical Society, New York City.)

American fortunes were at low ebb when Secretary Monroe received the Russian proposal. The attempted invasion of Canada had
ended disastrously; and America would be lucky to escape from the
affair with a whole skin. By this time, too, the whole aspect of the
European situation had changed. Napoleon's army had been wiped
out during the memorable retreat from Moscow; and the crestfallen
Corsican was back in France feverishly attempting to raise a new force.
If Bonaparte's resistance collapsed, the United States would have to
face the wrath of Britain single-handed.

When, therefore, the Russian overture was officially presented at
Washington, on March 8, 1813, President Madison welcomed it.
Without even waiting to learn if England had accepted the proffered
mediation, he appointed two special envoys, Albert Gallatin and James
Bayard, who were instructed to join John Quincy Adams, United
States minister to Russia, in negotiations with Great Britain. Gallatin
and Bayard set sail for St. Petersburg in May, 1813. At almost the
same time the British Foreign Secretary, Lord Castlereagh, reluctantly informed the Czar that Britain could not accept mediation. His
chief excuse was that the questions in dispute with the United States
involved "principles of the internal government of the British nation
[impressment]." It is evident that the Foreign Office was not going to
permit the Czar to have a voice in the settlement, for the maritime
grievances of "small navy" Russia against Great Britain were strikingly similar to those of the United States.

Nevertheless the attempted Russian mediation did bring about one
important result. The British Foreign Office, wishing to mollify the
Czar and prevent the conflict in America from becoming entangled
with the general European settlement, proposed to the United States,
in November, 1813, that the two nations enter into direct negotiations looking toward peace.[5] President Madison accepted this proposition with alacrity; and promptly sent Henry Clay and Jonathan Russell to join the three envoys already selected. The ancient Flemish
town of Ghent, then garrisoned by British troops, was chosen as the
meeting place.

AN EMBARRASSMENT OF RICHES

The American peace commission, as finally constituted, consisted of
John Quincy Adams, Henry Clay, Albert Gallatin, James A. Bayard,
and Jonathan Russell. Although Russell was not a man of unusual

[5] *Cambridge History of British Foreign Policy* (Cambridge, Eng., 1922), I, 532–
533.

attainments, the other four were among the ablest Americans of their generation. In fact, the commission was too able for its own good. If there had been less ability, there would have been more harmony.

John Quincy Adams, already an experienced diplomat, was nominally head of the group; but no one deferred to him. In self-righteousness, chilling reserve, and strength of character he was a replica of his distinguished father. Like him, he found his colleagues frivolous, for he wrote:

> I dined again at the table-d'hôte, at one. The other gentlemen dined together, at four. They sit after dinner and drink bad wine and smoke cigars, which neither suits my habits nor my health, and absorbs time which I cannot spare. I find it impossible, even with the most rigorous economy of time, to do half the writing that I ought.[6]

Nevertheless Adams' unquestioned ability and industry were of great value to the commission.

Quite in contrast was the warm, impulsive, magnetic Henry Clay, who brought with him a reputation for dueling, horse racing, and gambling that was highly offensive to Adams. "Just before rising," the latter recorded (he rose habitually at five o'clock), "I heard Mr. Clay's company retiring from his chamber. I had left him . . . at cards. They parted as I was about to rise." [7] Despite such shortcomings, Clay's buoyancy and hopefulness shed a ray of light in the hour of darkest despair; his great shrewdness and persuasive powers proved invaluable; and his mastery of the Western game of brag (resembling poker) enabled him to sense when the British were bluffing.[8]

In happy combination of personality and ability, the tactful and urbane Albert Gallatin was the best qualified negotiator of the group. His Swiss birth and foreign training, while not dampening his patriotism, had endowed him with a breadth of view lacking in his somewhat provincial colleagues. Indeed, his most trying and useful work at Ghent was keeping the peace among the disputatious Americans rather than negotiating it with the British. Passages from his seventeen year old son's diary are revealing:

> This drafting still goes on—endless discussions and violent arguments which I can see father thinks futile, but he never loses patience. . . . It is a most difficult task, as both Mr. Adams and Mr. Clay object to every-

[6] C. F. Adams, ed., *Memoirs of John Quincy Adams* (Phila., 1874), II, 656 (July 8, 1814).

[7] *Ibid.*, III, 32 (Sept. 7, 1814).

[8] G. G. Van Deusen, *The Life of Henry Clay* (Boston, 1937), pp. 101–102.

thing except what they suggest themselves. Father remains calm but firm and does all he can to keep peace. . . . Clay uses strong language to Adams, and Adams returns the compliment. Father looks calmly on with a twinkle in his eye. To-day there was a severe storm, and father said, "Gentlemen, gentlemen, we must remain united or we will fail. . . ." [9]

James A. Bayard, a prominent Federalist from Delaware, was an able representative of one of the most distinguished families in American history. Like Gallatin, he brought to these heated deliberations a remarkably pacifying equanimity of temper. He was, in fact, the only member of the commission not cordially disliked by one or more of the others. Adams was *persona non grata* to all four.

BRITAIN PRESENTS THE BILL

It might almost seem as if an all-wise Providence had endowed the five Americans with a surplus of ability to compensate for the lack of it on the other side of the table. To Ghent the British Foreign Office sent a group of such inexperienced mediocrities as to cause Gallatin to suspect that England had no serious intention of making peace. The head of the British commission was Lord Gambier, whose elevation to the peerage had come as a result of his not altogether creditable part in the brutal bombardment of Copenhagen. Next was Henry Goulburn, an aggressive young under-secretary, of the "Copenhagen" Jackson type. Finally, there was one William Adams, doctor of civil law, a learned academician who was presumably appointed for his technical knowledge. As Henry Adams devastatingly remarks, he "was an unknown man, and remained one." [10] None of the three had ever had the slightest diplomatic experience.

Why were these three men chosen? First of all, the British envoys, like Oswald in 1782, were intended to be mere transmitting clerks for the Foreign Office.[11] Men of intelligence and spirit might have found it difficult to surrender all initiative to their superiors. Furthermore, from a military and naval point of view Britain held the high cards; and the Ministry may have concluded that able negotiators were un-

---

[9] James Gallatin, *A Great Peace Maker: The Diary of James Gallatin* (N.Y., 1915), pp. 33, 32, 28 (entries of Nov. 3, Oct. 29, Aug. 10, 1814, in that order).

[10] Adams, *History*, IX, 14.

[11] Young Gallatin recorded: "Father is not impressed with the British delegates. They are . . . men who have not made any mark and have no influence or weight. He attaches but little importance to them as they are but the puppets of Lords Castlereagh and Liverpool. Father feels he is quite capable of dealing with them. . . ." Gallatin, *Diary*, p. 28 (Aug. 8, 1814).

necessary. Finally, preparations were then being made for the great Congress at Vienna, where the map of Europe was to be unscrambled. This was the main tent; Ghent was a side show. And where the stakes were high Lord Castlereagh sent no underlings, able or mediocre. He went to Vienna himself and took the Duke of Wellington with him.

By early July, 1814, the five Americans had gathered at Ghent; but the British commissioners kept them waiting in suspense for a full month. Napoleon was now exiled on Elba, and two thirds of Wellington's crack veterans had been embarked for America or were about to be. It was obviously to the advantage of England to make no terms until she had learned of the confidently expected victories. The dilatory tactics of the British were exceedingly trying to the nerves of the Americans, as Gallatin's son reveals:

Still waiting to hear when the English Commission think of starting for Ghent. . . . Nothing to do. Mr. Adams in a very bad temper. Mr. Clay annoys him. Father pours oil on the troubled waters. . . . He will, I fear, have a very tough time of it in keeping his colleagues in unison. . . .[12]

The British commissioners finally arrived in Ghent, and on August 8, 1814, after the Americans had engaged in a quarrel about the building where the sessions should be held, negotiations got under way. The government in Washington had instructed its representatives to insist on the abandonment of impressment, the cessation of illegal blockades, and satisfaction with respect to other matters in dispute. But the British, assuming the offensive, presented demands that fairly took away the breath of the Americans. First of all, the United States was never thereafter to maintain either fortifications or armed naval vessels on the Great Lakes. The British felt that such a precaution was necessary to guard against another assault on Canada. The Canadians were to be further protected by the cession of American territory west of Lake Superior, an area in northern New York, and one in eastern Maine. Finally, and most stunning, an enormous expanse south of the Great Lakes was to be erected into a quasi-independent Indian buffer state, which would further safeguard the Canadians and their fur trade. The British commissioners, in accordance with their instructions, made this last demand a *sine qua non* (indispensable condition) of peace; but they went beyond their instructions when they declared that the territorial rectifications were "equally necessary."[13]

[12] *Ibid.*, pp. 20, 27 (entries of April 26, July 15, and April 26, 1814, in that order).
[13] *The Cambridge History of British Foreign Policy*, I, 537.

In short, the British were calmly asking the United States to surrender sovereignty over approximately one third of its domain—a
region larger than the combined areas of England, Scotland, Wales,
and Ireland. "Father mildly suggested," noted young Gallatin, "that
there were more than a hundred thousand American citizens settled
in these States and territories. The answer was: 'They must look after
themselves.' " [14] Goulburn cheerfully added that the 20,000 or so
savages there would treat their white wards well; he knew an Indian
who was very intelligent. So unthinkable were the British terms that
the five Americans rejected them out of hand without even referring
to their government for authorization.

This was the first crisis. The American commissioners (with the
possible exception of Clay, the brag expert) were convinced that England was unprepared to make a satisfactory peace, and they were so
sure their reply would end the discussions that they gave notice to
their landlord and began to pack their baggage.[15] Albert Gallatin reported:

> Our negotiations may be considered as at an end. Some official notes
> may yet pass, but the nature of the demands of the British . . . is such that
> there can be no doubt of a speedy rupture of our conferences, and that we
> will have no peace. Great Britain wants war in order to cripple us. . . .
> I do not expect to be longer than three weeks in Europe.[16]

But the Ministry in London was not prepared to break off negotiations. It realized that its commissioners had presented their demands
so forcibly as to enable the Americans to lay upon England the opprobrium of fighting merely for conquest and for the aggrandizement
of Canada, objectives that the groaning British taxpayer would not
tolerate. The results of employing such inferior instruments became
unpleasantly apparent to the Foreign Office, which rebuked Goulburn
for his clumsiness. The Ministry preferred to keep the discussions in
a state of suspense until the good news came from America. If the
British won their anticipated victories they would be in a position to
dictate, not negotiate. Meanwhile the American envoys would be kept
busy. Goulburn, who understood this game, observed that "as long
as we answer their notes, I believe that they will be ready to give us
replies."

[14] Gallatin, *Diary*, p. 28 (Aug. 8, 1814).
[15] Updyke, *Diplomacy of the War of 1812*, p. 234.
[16] Henry Adams, *The Life of Albert Gallatin* (Phila., 1880), p. 524 (Gallatin to
Dallas, Aug. 20, 1814).

Upon receiving the extravagant demands from Ghent, President Madison cleverly resorted to a bit of "shirt-sleeve" or "house top" diplomacy. He went so far as to make public the correspondence that had been interchanged, much to the annoyance of the British. But the stratagem worked. A wave of indignation swept over America—even up into the Federalist country. The *United States Gazette*, a Federalist newspaper published in Philadelphia, cried: "England now turns upon us in the fullness of her wrath and power. No alternative is left us but to resist with energy or submit with disgrace. As the latter is not possible to Americans, we must prepare our minds for an extremely long, arduous, and sanguinary war." [17] Legislative bodies vied with one another in passing defiant resolutions. In Newark, New Jersey, one thousand men volunteered for work on the city's defenses, marching forth with flags and music and wearing labels bearing the slogan, "DON'T GIVE UP THE SOIL!" [18]

The British were not slow to perceive the danger signal. Their success against the United States had in large measure been the result of disunion and apathy. Now the Americans might, if pushed far enough into the corner, unite and call forth their latent energies. Worse yet, the war might even become unpopular in England. The upshot was that the British Ministry decided to abandon its demands for exclusive control of the Great Lakes and for the establishment of an Indian buffer state. Instead, it consented to an innocuous provision regarding the Indians, to which the American commissioners consented. With the clearing away of these obstacles the first faint prospects of a treaty began to appear.[19]

THE "IRON DUKE" DEMURS

Early in October, 1814, the news reached Europe that the British forces had burned the government buildings in Washington; and word was momentarily expected of further victories by Wellington's veterans in northern New York and at New Orleans. The opportunity for which Downing Street had been delaying was now at hand. The British commissioners at Ghent were instructed to demand that peace be made on the basis of *uti possidetis* (actual occupation or possession of territory) subject to mutual accommodation. This would give Great Britain Fort Michilimackinac, Fort Niagara (with a surrounding strip

[17] *United States Gazette*, Oct. 19, 1814, quoted in Updyke, *Diplomacy of the War of 1812*, p. 280.

[18] Niles' *Weekly Register*, VII, 11 (Sept. 10, 1814).

[19] Updyke, *Diplomacy of the War of 1812*, p. 276.

of territory), and all of Maine north of the Aroostook River, thus insuring a practicable road between Quebec and Halifax. The American envoys, who regarded these terms as intolerable, again prepared to leave. But just at the critical moment came news of Macdonough's decisive victory on Lake Champlain, a stroke that frustrated the British invasion of New York. The five Americans at Ghent, greatly encouraged, declined to treat on any other basis than *status quo ante bellum* (mutual restoration of territory).

The British were now in an extremely embarrassing position. They either had to recede from their demands or redouble their efforts to conquer a peace. In desperation the Ministry turned to the Duke of Wellington, hero of the war against France in Spain, and offered him the command in Canada. To this chestnut-extricating invitation the "Iron Duke" replied that he could not promise much success without control of the Great Lakes. Since the British had little hope of gaining such superiority, this answer was equivalent to advising an abandonment of the projected invasion of the United States. Wellington went on to add:

> I confess that I think you have no right, from the state of the war, to demand any concession of territory from America. . . . You have not been able to carry it into the enemy's territory. . . . You can get no territory; indeed, the state of your military operations, however creditable, does not entitle you to demand any; and you only afford the Americans a popular and creditable ground . . . to avoid to make peace.[20]

With such an opinion from the foremost military authority in England, the British ministry had no choice but to abandon its demands for *uti possidetis*.

COMPROMISE AND CONCESSION

Meanwhile the United States had yielded ground. Secretary Monroe had originally instructed the American commissioners to insist upon an abandonment of impressment as a *sine qua non* of peace; otherwise, "the United States have appealed to arms in vain." But the obduracy of the British, and the cessation of impressment with the end of the Napoleonic wars, induced the Madison administration, in June, 1814, to modify these instructions. As a consequence the American commissioners consented to complete silence on the issue of impressment, as well as on other matters of neutral rights.

[20] Adams, *Gallatin*, pp. 538-539 (Wellington to Castlereagh, Nov. 9, 1814).

Then came a final stumbling block. The British unexpectedly insisted that the fishing privileges granted to the United States in the Treaty of 1783 should not be renewed without an equivalent. New England fortunately had on the ground, as in 1782, a stout champion in the person of an Adams.[21] In his fight for the fisheries John Quincy Adams was forced to contend not only with the British but with his own colleagues, notably Clay, who exploded when Adams proposed to concede the right to navigate the Mississippi in return for the fishing privilege. The dashing Kentuckian, after all his bombastic and unfulfilled promises to his constituents about Canada, could not afford to yield to the British a share in the West's great waterway. "The navigation principle," he declaimed, "is much too important to concede for the mere liberty of drying fish on a desert." Clay finally worked himself up to the point where he was in favor of continuing war for three years longer. "A dreadful day," wrote young Gallatin. "Angry disputes on the *contre-projet*. Father wishes the clause *re* the Mississippi accepted. Mr. Clay would not hear of it. Mr. Adams in opposition to Mr. Clay. Nothing arrived at. . . ." [22]

Months of close contact in stuffy lodgings had played havoc with the nerves of the American commissioners. It was all that the conciliatory Gallatin could do to prevent his colleagues from flying at one another's throats and thereby causing a complete collapse of the negotiations. To him goes the chief credit for persuading the British to omit all reference to the fisheries and the Mississippi, and to reserve these questions for future discussion. This final concession removed the last serious obstacle, and the formal signing of the pact took place on December 24, 1814.

Dishonors Even

The most significant thing that can be said about the Treaty of Ghent is that it restored peace. Ironically enough, no mention whatsoever was made of the neutral rights, especially impressment, for which the United States had presumably gone to war. The Napoleonic upheaval had subsided; and there seemed little point in continuing hostilities to force Britain to surrender in principle abuses which she had already abandoned in practice. In brief, the treaty was in the nature of an armistice or truce—a truce of exhaustion rather than of per-

[21] So vital was the Newfoundland fishery to Massachusetts (which then included Maine) that the governor of the state was prepared to cede a considerable amount of territory in return for a retention of the former privileges.

[22] Gallatin, *Diary*, p. 34 (Nov. 28, 1814).

suasion. Both sides simply agreed to stop fighting and restore the *status quo ante bellum*. Of great importance for the future, however, were those articles that provided for mixed arbitral commissions to make adjustments of the boundary disputes along the northern frontier.[23]

The question naturally arises why England, after having won a distinct though not an overwhelming advantage on land and sea, was willing to make a treaty granting such favorable terms to the United States. Aside from the factors already mentioned, the British Ministry, burdened with a heavy debt, was finding the American conflict more costly than anticipated. It had no stomach for continuing the onerous and highly unpopular property tax for a war of conquest in the interests of Canada. One Tory remarked that if the party in power "had not put an end to the war, the war would have put an end to their Ministry." Furthermore, agricultural distress in England had reached a serious state; and the powerful merchant class was complaining bitterly of the inroads of American privateers. But probably most persuasive of all was the European powder keg. France was seething with discontent, ready to rally to the banner of Napoleon should he return from Elba. The astute Talleyrand, now unwittingly helping America, had cleverly driven a wedge between the late allies over the division of spoils. In the face of the imminent explosion Britain realized the urgent necessity of being released from what Lord Castlereagh called "the millstone of an American war." [24] Once more Europe's necessities operated to America's advantage—perhaps to her salvation.

The Lion Licks His Wounds

The treaty was received with mixed emotions in England. The British had viewed the entrance of their seemingly treacherous offspring into the war on the side of Napoleon with an anger that was equalled only by their contempt. The Yankees, they felt, were degenerate Englishmen. "Despicable in the cabinet, ridiculous in the field!" growled one newspaper. ". . . Is Great Britain to be driven from the proud eminence," sneered the London *Evening Star*, ". . . by a piece of striped bunting flying at the mast-heads of a few

---

[23] The questions at issue were the ownership of certain islands in Passamaquoddy Bay and the Bay of Fundy; the boundary of the United States from the source of the River St. Croix to the St. Lawrence; and the boundary along the middle of the Great Lakes to the northwestern point of the Lake of the Woods.

[24] See Mahan, *Sea Power in Its Relations to the War of 1812*, II, 431, 434.

fir-built frigates, manned by *a handful of bastards and outlaws.*" [25]
Disillusionment on this score merely added to Britain's wrath. The
Globe expressed a general sentiment when it declared that the Yankee
should be "confoundedly well flogged." The London *Times* exploded:

They [the Americans] are struck to the heart with terror for their impending punishment,—and oh! may no false liberality, no mistaken lenity, no weak and cowardly policy interpose to save them from the blow! Strike, Chastise the savages; for such they are. . . . With Madison and his perjured set, no treaty can be made; for no oath can bind them. . . .[26]

When the Treaty of Ghent reached London the journals that had
expressed these sentiments were profoundly displeased. They felt, not
without reason, that Britain had thrown away at the peace table whatever she had gained on the battlefield. The London *Times* was sure
that the result would merely invite the scorn of other nations.

They will reflect that we have attempted to force our principles on America, and have failed. Nay, that we have retired from the combat with the stripes yet bleeding on our backs,—with the recent defeats, at Plattsburg, and on Lake Champlain, unavenged. To make peace at such a moment . . . betrays a deadness to the feelings of honour, and shows a timidity of disposition, inviting further insult. . . .[27]

Similar dissatisfaction was also expressed in Parliament, where the
British peace commissioners were roughly handled for their "gross
mismanagement."

Nevertheless the war-weary English masses, hungry and tax-burdened, welcomed the return of peace. They were joined by the merchants and manufacturers, who rejoiced at the end of privateering and
at the opportunity to dump the contents of their bulging warehouses
upon the American market. Within a few weeks even the diehards
were silenced. The news of Andrew Jackson's devastating victory at
New Orleans showed that there were worse things than peace; and
the Corn Riots and Napoleon's dramatic return from Elba diverted
public attention elsewhere. The ministers were left free, says Henry
Adams, "to redeem at Waterloo the failures they had experienced in
America."

[25] Niles' *Weekly Register*, III, 271 (Dec. 26, 1812).
[26] London *Times*, May 24, 1814, 3: 3–4.
[27] *Ibid.*, Dec. 30, 1814, 2: 2–3.

"From Gloom to Glory"

While the Treaty of Ghent was being slowly borne homeward, America plumbed the depths of despair. It was generally believed that the negotiations had collapsed. The British veterans were expected to rout General Andrew Jackson's motley collection of militiamen, creoles and pirates at New Orleans, and perhaps detach the entire Southwest. Disgruntled Federalists were talking of disunion in their convention at Hartford, Connecticut, and many people were confidently predicting the disruption of the United States.

Then, early in February, 1815, came the news of Jackson's astonishing victory over the British. The flagging American spirit bounded to extravagant heights of rejoicing. The streets were littered with broadsides bearing poems of praise. A week or so later came word of the peace of Ghent. Niles' *Weekly Register* rejoiced:

GLORIOUS NEWS!

Orleans saved and peace concluded.

'The star spangled banner in triumph shall wave
O'er the land of the free and the home of the brave!

. . . .

Who would not be an American? Long live the republic!
All hail! last asylum of oppressed humanity! [28]

The battle of New Orleans had actually been fought two weeks *after* the signing of the treaty; but the arrival of the news of both events at almost the same time led the unthinking to believe that the United States had beaten the British into submission and extorted a victor's terms. One contemporary rejoiced that "in the fullness of our glory we grant peace to a worsted enemy." The Administration was nothing loath to hide its blunders behind the smoke of Jackson's glorious victory.

Without even waiting to read the treaty the populace burst into the wildest demonstrations of joy.[29] It was enough to know that peace had come. Holidays were proclaimed; pupils were dismissed from school; militiamen paraded; bells were rung; guns were fired; and cheering, shouting, and drinking citizens embraced one another on the streets. The New York *Evening Post* recorded:

[28] Niles' *Weekly Register*, VII, 385 (Feb. 18, 1815).
[29] There were a few discordant notes from smugglers near the Canadian border, whose profitable game was at an end; from merchants who had on hand large stocks of high-priced manufactured goods; and from an occasional confirmed Federalist.

It has come, and the public expressions of tumultuous joy and gladness, that spontaneously burst forth from all ranks and degrees of people . . . evinced how really sick at heart they were of . . . war. . . . The public exhileration [*sic*] shewed itself in the illumination of most of the windows in the lower part of Broadway and the adjoining streets. . . . The street itself was illuminated by lighted candles, carried in the hands of a large concourse of the populace; the city resounded in all parts with the joyful cry of a peace! a peace! and it was for nearly two hours difficult to make one's way thro' unnumbered crowds of persons. . . .[30]

With the seas now open to commerce even the New Englanders rejoiced, although they had good reason to fear that they had lost both territory and the right to fish in Canadian waters. When they learned the actual terms of peace, their joy was naturally unbounded.[31] So confidently had they expected to lose something that a return to the *status quo ante bellum* was regarded as a victory. The slogan of the hour became "Not one inch of territory ceded or lost"—quite in contrast with "On to Canada!" The harassed Administration, to whom the pact had come as a "reprieve from doom," promptly submitted the document to the Senate, which approved it unanimously. It was certainly the most popular peace treaty with a major Power ever negotiated by the United States.

The Sequel to Ghent

The Canadians read the terms of peace with profound disappointment. They had fought bravely against great odds to repel the Yankee invader; and they felt that they should have been given exclusive control of their own fisheries, together with such territorial rectifications as would ensure maximum protection against future aggression. When the war came to an end both the recent belligerents had considerable naval forces on the Great Lakes; and the British either were building or were planning to build enough vessels to guarantee supremacy. John Quincy Adams, then United States minister at London, reported in 1816:

[30] New York *Evening Post*, Feb. 13, 1815, 2:1.
[31] See letter of Gouverneur Morris in *Amer. Hist. Rev.*, XLIII (1937), 74–75. For broadsides and poems proclaiming the "great," "happy," and "glorious" news of peace see File 50 (Mass.), Library of Congress. One Boston broadside declared, "This city is in a perfect uproar of joy, shouts, illuminations, &c. &c. &c." American Antiquarian Society.

In all the late debates in Parliament . . . the prospect of a new war with the United States has been distinctly held up by the ministers and admitted by the opposition as a solid reason for enormous and unparalleled expenditure and preparation in Canada and Nova Scotia. We hear nothing now about the five frigates and the bits of striped bunting. The strain is in a higher mood. Lord Castlereagh talks of the great and growing military power of the United States.[32]

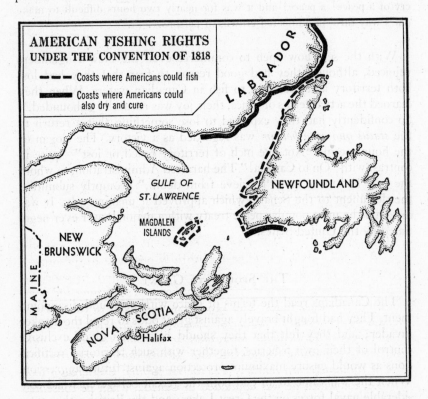

AMERICAN FISHING RIGHTS
UNDER THE CONVENTION OF 1818

- - - - Coasts where Americans could fish

▬▬▬ Coasts where Americans could also dry and cure

LABRADOR

GULF OF ST. LAWRENCE

NEWFOUNDLAND

MAGDALEN ISLANDS

NEW BRUNSWICK

MAINE

NOVA SCOTIA

Halifax

With the situation ripe for a frantic and disastrous naval race, the Washington government instructed Minister Adams to propose mutual disarmament on the Great Lakes to Lord Castlereagh. The suggestion was favorably received, though with some misgivings, and the negotiations were transferred to Washington, where the able Charles Bagot represented Great Britain. He disliked the Americans; but, spurred on by the prospect of a European promotion and acting under

[32] W. C. Ford, ed., *Writings of John Quincy Adams* (N.Y., 1915), V, 555 (Adams to Monroe, March 30, 1816).

explicit instructions from Castlereagh, he concealed his feelings and flattered the Yankees. At one of Madison's receptions he was heard to murmur—quite in contrast with "Copenhagen" Jackson—"Mrs. Madison looks every inch a Queen." It was not difficult for a man of his tact and ability to succeed where others had failed; and an exchange of notes between him and Acting Secretary of State Richard Rush, late in April, 1817, formed the basis of the Rush-Bagot executive agreement for mutual disarmament on the Lakes. This understanding was later approved by the Senate.

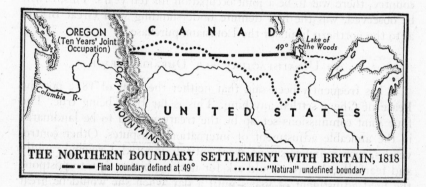

THE NORTHERN BOUNDARY SETTLEMENT WITH BRITAIN, 1818
— · — Final boundary defined at 49°   ········ "Natural" undefined boundary

Although the Rush-Bagot agreement has at times been severely strained, it has on the whole been faithfully observed to the present day.[33] The principle of demilitarization was ultimately extended to the land, resulting in an undefended frontier line stretching for more than three thousand miles. The agreement has given to the world a splendid object lesson in mutual disarmament. Certainly this understanding was of incalculable importance in clearing the fetid atmosphere and promoting Anglo-American accord during the troubled years of the nineteenth century. Yet the far-sighted Castlereagh took a chance, for which he was upbraided in Canada, when he consented to disarm in the face of the powerful and unrepentant Yankee.

The important Convention of 1818, which was concluded with Great Britain the next year, took care of several loose ends left by the negotiators at Ghent. It renewed the commercial treaty negotiated at London in 1815, and dealt with the problem of fisheries and

[33] In 1893, when it was proposed that an American warship be exhibited at the Chicago World's Fair, the United States government refused for fear of violating the Rush-Bagot agreement. A brick and mortar battleship was constructed and mounted with imitation guns. J. M. Mathews, *American Foreign Relations* (N.Y., 1928), p. 433.

boundaries. England maintained that the recent war had ended the fishing "liberties" granted to the United States by the Treaty of 1783, and His Majesty's cruisers had been causing much ill will by seizing American fishing craft. The Convention of 1818 narrowed the "liberties" of Americans within British jurisdiction, but granted enough privileges to permit a profitable continuance of fishing.[34] The agreement also ran the ill-defined northern boundary of the Louisiana purchase from the Lake of the Woods to the Stony (Rocky) Mountains along the forty-ninth parallel. Beyond that point, in the Oregon country, there was to be a joint occupation for ten years. This, it will be observed, was the first definite understanding with Great Britain as to the northern limits of the Louisiana purchase.

An Unsatisfactory but Durable Peace

It has frequently been said that neither the War of 1812 nor the Peace of Ghent settled anything. This is far from being true. The four joint commissions set up by the treaty proved to be landmarks in the amicable adjustment of international disputes. Other controversies, such as impressment, were entirely ignored. Growing rapidly and fearfully, America could ask for nothing better than to postpone the final adjustment of issues until a day when she would be great and powerful. A century later every unsettled dispute of 1814 had either faded into oblivion or had been amicably settled by mutual concessions.

Nor can we overlook the fact that the furnace of war brought forth a new nation. New England disloyalty hung its head when news came of the glorious victory at New Orleans. America's ignominious defeats slipped out of mind, while her glorious victories were celebrated in verse and song. The republic began to sense as never before its unlimited potentialities and its future greatness. Men began to see that America's destiny lay in the West—not on the ocean. Albert Gallatin concluded:

The war has been productive of evil and good, but I think the good preponderates. . . . The war has renewed and reinstated the national feelings and character which the Revolution had given, and which were daily lessened. The people have now more general objects of attachment. . . .

[34] Americans renounced all fishing "liberties" claimed under the Treaty of 1783, and were granted "forever" the "liberty" to fish along specified stretches of the coast of Newfoundland and Labrador, and to cure fish along less extensive parts of the same coasts, as long as they were unsettled. When they should become inhabited, other arrangements would have to be made.

They are more Americans; they feel and act more as a nation; and I hope that the permanency of the Union is thereby better secured.[35]

If America did not win an actual admission of her rights as a result of the war, she did gain a genuine respect from British statesmen and soldiers. Gone were the sneers about Yankee cowardice and degeneracy. American "fir-built frigates" had proved themselves. The words of Michael Scott, a young lieutenant in the British navy, are a remarkable tribute to what he called "those damned Yankees":

I don't like Americans; I never did, and never shall like them. . . . I have no wish to eat with them, drink with them, deal with, or consort with them in any way; but let me tell the whole truth, *nor fight* with them, were it not for the laurels to be acquired, by overcoming an enemy so brave, determined, and alert, and every way so worthy of one's steel, as they have always proved.[36]

Never again was the United States to be treated by Great Britain as other than a sovereign nation. In this sense the War of 1812 may properly be called the "second war for American independence."

But unhappily the conflict left bruised and bitter feelings on both sides of the Atlantic. The British might grudgingly entertain more respect for America's prowess; but they could not soon forget what they regarded as an attempt to hamstring them while they were fighting for their lives against Napoleon. Canadian distrust of the Yankee was increased many fold, a development which partially explains why subsequent agitation in the United States for the annexation of Canada was unsuccessful. And in America the embers of 1776 were stirred anew. When Congress was considering the appropriation of funds for reconstructing the buildings burned by the British troops in Washington, one member proposed to encircle the ruins of the Capitol with an iron balustrade and place thereon an inscription: "Americans! This is the effect of British barbarism! Let us swear eternal hatred to England!" The proposal was rejected; but the Anglophobia remained.[37]

Whatever its shortcomings, the Treaty of Ghent was not a victor's

[35] Henry Adams, ed., *The Writings of Albert Gallatin* (Phila., 1879), I, 700 (Gallatin to Lyon, May 7, 1816).

[36] *Blackwood's Magazine*, XXXII, 146 (Aug. 1832).

[37] Stratford Canning, British minister in Washington, wrote to his sister in 1822: ". . . I know two young ladies who can play 'God Save the King' on the harp, and who do occasionally play on the condition prescribed by their papa, of playing 'Yankee Doodle' immediately afterwards!" Beckles Willson, *Friendly Relations* (Boston, 1934), p. 121.

peace. It imposed no onerous conditions that made necessary another war. Yet, given the unsolved problems and the bitterness on both sides, few men of that generation could have believed that the two nations would celebrate in 1914 and 1915, as they did, the one hundredth anniversary of unbroken peace.

BIBLIOGRAPHICAL NOTE

The most comprehensive work on the subject is F. A. Updyke's detailed *The Diplomacy of the War of 1812* (Baltimore, 1915). Excellent brief accounts may be found in Henry Adams' classic *History of the United States during the Administrations of Jefferson and Madison* (N.Y., 1891), IX, Chs. I–III (particularly good on English backgrounds); and in A. T. Mahan's notable *Sea Power in Its Relations to the War of 1812* (Boston, 1905), II, Ch. XVIII (a good analysis of the diplomatic exchanges). Somewhat briefer is *The Cambridge History of British Foreign Policy* (Cambridge, 1922), I, 528–542. Clay's part in the negotiation is developed in G. G. Van Deusen's *The Life of Henry Clay* (Boston, 1937). Old but well worth reading is Henry Adams' *The Life of Albert Gallatin* (Phila., 1880). On the Rush-Bagot agreement see J. M. Callahan, *The Neutrality of the American Lakes and Anglo-American Relations* (Baltimore, 1898). Further references: see footnotes of this chapter and Bemis and Griffin, *Guide*, pp. 147–155, 277–280.

RECENT REFERENCES. The best brief accounts of Ghent, disarmament, and the Convention of 1818 are found in Chapters XV–XVII of A. L. Burt, *The United States, Great Britain, and British North America* (New Haven, 1940). H. A. Innis, *The Cod Fisheries: the History of an International Economy* (New Haven, 1940), is essentially an economic study. C. M. Gates, "The West in American Diplomacy, 1812–1815," *Miss. Valley Hist. Rev.*, XXVI (1940), 499–510, deals briefly with the formulation of British demands for American territory south of the Great Lakes, and the final withdrawal of those demands.

NEW REFERENCES. Background materials appear in J. B. Brebner, *North Atlantic Triangle* (New Haven, 1945), and in E. W. McInnis, *The Unguarded Frontier* (Garden City, N.Y., 1942). J. H. Powell, *Richard Rush, Republican Diplomat, 1780–1859* (Phila., 1942), Ch. V, deals with the Convention of 1818. Lord Castlereagh was most conciliatory in his negotiations with Rush. The two unsettled problems were the West Indian trade and impressment. The British were prepared to make certain concessions on impressment, and the author thinks that the United States was unwise not to accept them. R. W. Van Alstyne has some interesting interpretations in "New Viewpoints in the Relations of Canada and the United States," *Canadian Hist. Rev.*, XXV (1944), 109–130.

4TH ED. REFS. The standard biography is now S. F. Bemis' exhaustive *John Quincy Adams and the Foundations of American Foreign Policy* (N.Y., 1949). The role of Adams at Ghent is described.

CHAPTER XI

The United States and the Floridas, 1803–1821

"[Florida] will just as naturally come into our possession as the waters of the Mississippi seek the sea; and any thing done to obstruct the operation will be as useless, in the end, as an attempt to arrest and turn back the course of that mighty stream."

Niles' *Weekly Register,* May 29, 1819.

Geographic Predestination

THE PEACE of Ghent marked a turning point in the diplomatic history of the United States. Hitherto the fate of America had been intimately bound up with the course of hostilities on the other side of the Atlantic. But the general exhaustion of Europe following the Napoleonic nightmare gave the United States a splendid opportunity to work out its own destiny with a minimum of foreign meddling.[1] Responding to the robust new sense of nationalism growing out of the War of 1812, the American people turned their backs confidently on the Old World and addressed themselves to the task of filling out their natural boundaries.

From the earliest days of the republic American statesmen had been conscious of the great importance of Florida to the United States. President Jefferson, as we have seen, attempted to buy it; and the acquisition of Louisiana served to whet the American appetite. But land was by no means the sole attraction. The peninsula of Florida, thrust deeply into the Gulf of Mexico, possessed great strategic value, offering as it did a constant threat to the lines of communication and commerce between New Orleans and the Atlantic seaboard. In addition, most of the navigable rivers of the present states of Alabama and Mississippi flowed through East and West Florida while seeking the Gulf. Con-

---

[1] Relative indifference replaced the keenest interest in European affairs. The American people were so deeply concerned with material things, such as the price of cotton, that they paid little attention to Napoleon's return from Elba. In September, 1815, the Washington *National Intelligencer* complained that subscriptions had fallen off because of the belief that European affairs were no longer a concern of the United States. "They pay no more attention to us and our business," wrote the disgusted Russian *chargé* in Washington, "than if we were so many Chinamen." W. P. Cresson, *Diplomatic Portraits* (Boston, 1923), p. 334.

trol of the mouths of these streams by the Spanish officials created several New Orleans-Mississippi problems on a smaller but hardly less vexatious scale.

In 1803 both Monroe and Livingston had wanted to buy East and

THE ACQUISITION OF THE FLORIDAS
1810-1819

West Florida, as instructed. They knew perfectly well, however, that they were not doing so when they signed the Louisiana cession treaty. Yet Livingston, after wishfully studying the conditions under which France had ceded Louisiana to Spain in 1762, contended that Louisiana included that portion of Florida which lay between the Mississippi and the Perdido Rivers. President Jefferson adopted this view, and strikingly expressed his determination in 1803:

We have some claims . . . to go eastwardly. . . . These claims will be a subject of negotiation with Spain, and if, as soon as she is at war, we push them strongly with one hand, holding out a price in the other, we shall certainly obtain the Floridas, and all in good time.[2]

At first Jefferson tried the quiet ways of diplomacy; but they netted him nothing. His next move was to sound a surprising note in his annual message of December, 1805, when he referred in a bellicose tone to relations with Spain and hinted at the necessity of raising 300,000 soldiers for defense and offense. (His obvious purpose, of

[2] A. A. Lipscomb, ed., *Writings of Thomas Jefferson* (Monticello ed., Washington, 1904), X, 408 (Jefferson to Breckinridge, Aug. 12, 1803).

course, was to frighten the Spaniards into yielding West Florida.)
He then confidentially asked Congress for a secret appropriation of
$2,000,000, to be used in facilitating the negotiation. The fiery John
Randolph of Virginia denounced this as an attempt to bribe Napoleon into forcing Spain to cede Florida. Whatever the basis for such
a charge, Jefferson did enter into negotiations with Bonaparte, who
liked nothing better than to lure the American President on, with
Florida as the bait.

In the end Jefferson's rather questionable tactics brought him not
one whit nearer his goal. He exposed his gullibility to Napoleon; weakened his hand with the British, who distrusted his dealings with the
Corsican; and aroused the bitter hostility of Spain. Nevertheless Jefferson kept his eyes fixed steadfastly on the coveted prize. On the eve
of retiring from the presidency he was heard to say, "We must have
the Floridas and Cuba."

THE FIRST LONE STAR REPUBLIC

We have already noted that the clamor of the Southern War Hawks
for Florida played an important part in the preliminaries of the War
of 1812. As early as June, 1810, President Madison was prepared to
connive at a separatist movement in West Florida, where a group of
hardy American settlers had been chafing under Spanish rule. In September, 1810, these "inquiet spirits," encouraged if not actively assisted
by the Madison administration, arose in revolt and captured the Spanish fort at Baton Rouge. The Bourbon banner was torn down and
dragged through the village dust, later to be replaced with that of the
"Republic of West Florida"—a blue woolen flag with a lone silver
star. Having proclaimed its independence, the infant republic, like
Texas of a later day, knocked at the door of the United States. As
an officer at Baton Rouge observed:

Some may propose one thing and some another, but the Great Mass of
the People wants nothing more than to become American Citizens. But
they would prefer death Rather than again be subject to any of the dependencies of Spain. The United States certainly has it in their power to
obtain this Country and if they do not do so the people will accept of any
other protection that they can obtain.[3]

On October 27, 1810, almost exactly a month after the Baton
Rouge revolt, Madison issued a proclamation ordering the extension

[3] Quoted in I. J. Cox, *The West Florida Controversy, 1798–1813* (Baltimore, 1918),
p. 419 (Ballinger to Toulmin, Nov. 3, 1810).

of American authority over West Florida to the Perdido River. He based his action on the grounds that the territory in question had rightfully belonged to the United States since the purchase of Louisiana. But he could not have been altogether satisfied with this explanation, for he went so far as to falsify the dates of certain important documents, evidently in the hope of deceiving posterity.[4] The United States minister to Russia undertook to explain, apparently somewhat shamefacedly, how his country had acquired its neighbor's territory. The Czar bowed, and, obviously referring to Napoleon's reshaping of the map of Europe, remarked pleasantly, "Everybody is getting a little bigger, nowadays."

It is hardly necessary to say that Spain made heated but altogether fruitless protests to the United States against the strange doings in West Florida. Europe's distresses again operated to America's advantage, for Spain was too deeply involved in the war against Napoleon to consider hostilities with the United States. England was likewise displeased by this new evidence of Yankee aggression, and her minister in Washington protested against the occupation of West Florida as "contrary to every principle of public justice, faith, and national honor." Lord Liverpool, a prominent member of the Cabinet, solemnly asserted that the Florida business should be characterized as "one of the most immoral acts recorded in the history of any country." But Great Britain, like Spain, was too much embarrassed by the war with Napoleon to welcome hostilities with the United States over this issue. The British, however, did not forget. The London *Times*, while urging unrelenting war upon America in 1814, insisted that "Mr. Madison's dirty, swindling manoeuvres in respect to Louisiana and the Floridas remain to be punished."

NIBBLING AT EAST FLORIDA

Madison was not content to rest upon his West Florida laurels—if they may be called that. His direct if dubious methods had been so simple and at the same time so effective as to suggest the employment of a similar course in East Florida. The instrument that came to hand was one George Mathews, an almost illiterate former governor of Georgia, who, in spite of his seventy-two years, was more distinguished for energy and patriotism than for discretion. This colorful figure was secretly encouraged by the Madison administra-

---

[4] C. C. Tansill, "Robert Smith," in S. F. Bemis, ed., *The American Secretaries of State and their Diplomacy* (N.Y., 1927), III, 186.

tion to co-operate with American "insurgents" in an invasion of East Florida. Although he was supported by United States gunboats and regular troops, his offensive bogged down before St. Augustine in the spring of 1812. By this time the Madison administration had become thoroughly embarrassed. Mathews was tardily disavowed; but the captured territory was relinquished only after Congress had twice refused to sanction the occupation. Bitterly disappointed at his repudiation by the Washington authorities, Mathews swore that he would "be dam'd if he did not blow them all up." [5] But fortunately for the peace of mind of the Administration he suddenly died.

Although President Madison had extended the boundary of West Florida to the Perdido, within that area the Spaniards still retained control of the Mobile district. This eyesore was removed during the War of 1812, when, in April, 1813, the rascally General James Wilkinson effected a bloodless conquest of the town of Mobile. The Americans regarded the territory as their own; and the seizure seemed all the more justified because Mobile was being held by Spain, an ally of Great Britain. It is an ironical fact that, after all the boasting by the War Hawks about taking Canada, this was the only permanent territorial gain of the War of 1812. The United States again profited by Spain's distress at home and in her revolted colonies.

THE PROBLEM OF THE LATIN AMERICAN REPUBLICS

Following the Peace of Ghent, American interest in East Florida was stimulated by rumors that Spain had transferred the peninsula to Great Britain. Although such reports proved to be false, by 1816 both Madrid and Washington recognized that the cession of East Florida to the United States was inevitable. [6] The remaining question was one of terms—a problem that fell to the able and experienced Secretary of State, John Quincy Adams. Recognizing the importance of defining the western limits of the Louisiana purchase, he drew up, in January, 1818, a detailed proposal for including boundaries, claims, and the cession of Florida in one sweeping treaty. His task, however, was immensely complicated by the question of recognizing the newly born republics of Latin America.

When the South American revolutions broke out in 1809 and 1810,

[5] J. W. Pratt, *Expansionists of 1812* (N.Y., 1925), p. 115.

[6] P. C. Brooks, "The Pacific Coast's First International Boundary Delineation, 1816–1819," *Pacific Hist. Rev.*, III (1934), 64. For rumors of the transfer to Britain see E. H. Tatum, Jr., *The United States and Europe, 1815–1823* (Berkeley, Calif., 1936), pp. 158–159.

public opinion in the United States was somewhat confused; but by 1812 there was general sympathy with the rebels.[7] The people of the United States were flattered to think that Latin America was emulating their example; and they naturally favored the cause of democracy as against despotism. At a public dinner in Nashville the twenty-second toast was enthusiastically received: "*The patriots of South America:* palsied be the arm that would wrest from them the standard of liberty for which they have so nobly struggled. Six cheers." [8] Interest and prejudice were further stimulated by stories of Spanish atrocities, especially those describing the Inquisition.

Sympathy with the Spanish American insurgents was so strong in the United States that Congress, in 1818, passed a comprehensive neutrality act, which superseded all previous legislation on the subject. Nevertheless filibustering expeditions continued to be sent out with but scant restraint from the authorities. Several American ports, notably New Orleans and Baltimore, became the base of privateers supporting the Latin American cause. John Quincy Adams noted with much disgust that the federal officers in Baltimore, some of whom had become involved in privateering, were "all fanatics of the South American cause." Niles' *Weekly Register,* which had complained that the United States was "too neutral" and "so straight" that it "leaned the other way," was scandalized:

We yield to no one in our devotion to the cause of liberty in South America. The patriot cause has been as our own, since its beginning. But it is now disgraced by numerous vessels, bearing independent flags, whose *sole* purpose is plunder. The seas teem with sheer pirates. . . . The people of the United States are justly becoming disgusted with such conduct; and *public opinion* will soon support the laws enacted to restrain them.[9]

A demand for immediate recognition of the new Latin American republics arose from many sympathizers in the United States. These ardent spirits found an able spokesman in the impulsive and eloquent Henry Clay, who led a strenuous campaign in behalf of the new American states—a campaign that attracted a great deal of no-

[7] C. C. Griffin, *The United States and the Disruption of the Spanish Empire, 1810–1822* (N.Y., 1937), p. 68.

[8] James Parton, *Life of Andrew Jackson* (Boston, 1860), II, 575, quoting the Nashville *Whig.* Niles' *Weekly Register* customarily printed accounts of insurgent reverses under the caption "Bad News," and reported this as a popular toast: "*Spanish America;* let us pay to her the debt which we owe for the aid of others in our struggle for freedom." Niles' *Weekly Register,* IX, 316 (Dec. 30, 1815).

[9] *Ibid.,* XVI, 112 (Apr. 3, 1819).

tice in the press and undoubtedly influenced a considerable body of public opinion. The gallant Kentuckian warmly defended the practice of sheltering insurgent privateers, and roundly condemned the Monroe administration (partly if not primarily for political reasons) for its cautious if correct policy.[10] His enthusiasm led to some remarkable rhetorical flights on the floor of the House:

Within this vast region we behold the most sublime and interesting objects of creation; the loftiest mountains, the most majestic rivers in the world; the richest mines of the precious metals, and the choicest productions of the earth. We behold there a spectacle still more interesting and sublime —the glorious spectacle of eighteen millions of people, struggling to burst their chains and to be free.[11]

The problem that vexed Secretary Adams was one of the most delicate of his entire career. If the United States waited too long before recognizing the new republics, it would incur their lasting ill will—and probably a corresponding loss of trade to British rivals. If, on the other hand, the Washington government acted too soon, Spain would be justified in regarding such interference as a legitimate cause for war. And a conflict with Spain might mean that all the European monarchs unfriendly to democracy would rush to her assistance. Finally—and this was a matter of the greatest moment to Adams—premature recognition would so deeply offend the Madrid government as probably to ruin whatever chances there were of securing East Florida by amicable negotiation.

In these circumstances it was imperative that the Monroe administration should walk warily, and suppress whatever sympathy it may have cherished for the revolutionists. The hard-headed Secretary Adams was ideally equipped for the task at hand. Never one to let sentiment blind him to duty, he deprecated the popular enthusiasm for the revolutions and repelled the advances of the South American agents with a coldness that bordered on frigidity. He also made an important contribution to the policy of the United States when he framed a statement for the President in which he declared that recognition should be deferred until the chances of recovery by the mother country were "utterly desperate."[12] Since Spain's chances were by no

[10] G. G. Van Deusen, *The Life of Henry Clay* (Boston, 1937), p. 122.
[11] Calvin Colton, ed., *The Works of Henry Clay* (Federal ed., N.Y., 1904), VI, 140 (March 24, 1818). This speech, translated into Spanish, was read at the heads of the revolutionary regiments, which greeted it with applause.
[12] W. C. Ford, ed., *Writings of John Quincy Adams* (N.Y., 1916), VI, 442 (Aug. 24, 1818).

means hopeless, the Administration, supported by many of the most influential newspapers of the East, threw its weight against a recognition resolution then before the House. Amid great excitement, which caused some of the sick members to be carried into the chamber to vote, the resolution was defeated on March 30, 1818, by a count of 45 yeas to 115 nays.

GENERAL JACKSON'S FLORIDA JAUNT

For some little while Secretary Adams had been engaged in discussions with Luis de Onís, the Spanish minister in Washington, looking toward the acquisition of Florida and the settlement of other problems. The negotiations were proceeding rather favorably when an unexpected and dramatic incident threatened to disrupt completely all diplomatic relations.

Spain had greatly weakened her authority in East Florida by withdrawing troops to fight the South American insurgents. Amelia Island, an outpost near the Georgia border which had slipped away from Spanish control, became such an intolerable nest for buccaneers that an expedition authorized by the United States government seized the place in 1817. But far more offensive were the Seminole Indians of Florida, who, joined by runaway Negroes, white renegades and others, periodically sallied across the international line to pillage, burn, and murder. Although the Indians themselves had grievances against the Americans, the harboring of such a villainous lot of outcasts by the Spanish government was a violation of the good neighbor pledge embodied in the Pinckney Treaty of 1795. Spain, however, was admittedly powerless to control or restrain these lawless bands.

Late in 1817, Andrew Jackson, hero of New Orleans and idol of the Southwest, was commissioned by the Washington government to chastise the Seminoles. His general instructions were broad; and he was authorized to pursue the Indians across the Spanish boundary, if necessary. He was, however, to respect all posts under the Bourbon flag. Jackson later insisted that Monroe sent additional instructions through Congressman Rhea authorizing a seizure of the Spanish towns. This the President denied. In any event the hero of New Orleans apparently thought that he was proceeding with the blessing of the Administration.[13]

[13] The famous controversy over the so-called Rhea letter is discussed in Marquis James, *Andrew Jackson: the Border Captain* (Indianapolis, 1933), pp. 308–309, 408–411. The author concludes that the evidence supports Monroe on this specific point;

The tempestuous Jackson, who hated both the Spaniard and the red man with all the venom of a Westerner, burst into Florida and seized the military post of St. Marks, in April, 1818, replacing the Spanish flag with the Stars and Stripes. Two British subjects, Alexander Arbuthnot and Robert Ambrister, had the misfortune to fall into Jackson's clutches. Charged with inciting the Indians against the whites, they were tried by a court martial and executed. The zealous Jackson reported to the Secretary of War:

I hope the execution of these two unprincipled villains will prove an awful example to the world, and convince the Government of Great Britain, as well as her subjects, that certain, though slow retribution awaits those unchristian wretches who, by false promises, delude and excite an Indian tribe to all the horrid deeds of savage war.[14]

A short time later, learning that the Indians were being harbored at Pensacola, Jackson made a forced march and captured the town. Thus, in a few weeks' time, the energetic Tennessean had chastised the Indians, seized every important post in Florida save St. Augustine, confiscated the royal archives, deposed the Spanish governor and named an American in his place, executed two British subjects, and declared in force "the revenue laws of the United States." He later expressed regret that he did not hang the Spanish governor.

"OLD HICKORY" RESTS ON HIS LAURELS

The news that the "ruffian" Jackson had "murdered" two British subjects on Spanish territory led to an explosion of indignation in England. "We can hardly believe," one London journal remarked, "that any thing so offensive to public decorum could be admitted, *even in America!*" The press seethed with demands for disavowal, apology, and reparation. A foreign envoy in London told the United States minister, Richard Rush, that *"we have had nothing of late so exciting; it smacks of war."* Rush's own words are graphic:

Out-of-doors, excitement seemed to rise higher and higher. Stocks experienced a slight fall. The newspapers kept up their fire . . . [giving] vent to angry declamation. They fiercely denounced the Government of

---

but that the Administration understood Jackson's intentions, and, "by the absence of any restraining sign or syllable, gave its consent to them." R. R. Stenberg passes strong judgment against Jackson's honesty in "Jackson's 'Rhea Letter' Hoax," *Jour. of Southern Hist.*, II (1936), 480–496.

[14] *American State Papers, Military Affairs*, I, 702 (Jackson to Calhoun, May 5, 1818).

the United States. Tyrant, ruffian, murderer, were among the epithets applied to their commanding general. He was exhibited in placards through the streets. The journals, without distinction of party, united in these attacks.[15]

For a while it seemed as if the British government would be forced to demand redress—even at the risk of war. But Lord Castlereagh concluded, after a thorough examination of the evidence, that Ambrister and Arbuthnot had been involved in "practices of such a description as to have deprived them of any claim on their own government for interference." Accordingly, the London authorities neither demanded redress nor supported the energetic protests of Spain. Lord Castlereagh later told Minister Rush that war might have broken out "if the ministry had but held up a finger." This seems to have been an exaggeration; but the situation was certainly one to cause anxiety on both sides of the Atlantic.

Apparently unmoved by international repercussions, Jackson returned to Tennessee amid the plaudits of the masses—more than ever the hero of the West. No maudlin sympathy was wasted on Ambrister and Arbuthnot; in the eyes of the Westerner they were entitled to no more consideration than a sheep-killing dog. "Among the people of the west," observed Niles' *Weekly Register*," his [Jackson's] popularity is unbounded—old and young speak of him with rapture, and at his call, 50,000 of the most efficient warriors on this continent, would rise, armed, and ready for any enemy."[16] At public dinners given in honor of the unrepentant Jackson, patriotic toasts were received with tumultuous applause. In American eyes he had not only put the fear of God into the treacherous dons and Indians, but he had hurled his glove into the face of the hated Britons. Tammany Hall passed a rousing resolution:

. . . Resolved . . . That the conduct of General Jackson . . . was justified by the law of nations, and the laws of war, and the immutable principles of retaliation and self-defence; and we highly approve of the manly spirit of the American general, who promptly punished the offenders and culprits against humanity and the rights of his country, and taught foreign emissaries that the United States was not to be outraged by spies, traitors, and lawless adventurers.[17]

[15] Richard Rush, *A Residence at the Court of London* (London, 1833), p. 412 (Jan. 15, 1819).
[16] Niles' *Weekly Register*, XIV, 399 (Aug. 8, 1818).
[17] *Ibid.*, XVI, 30 (March 6, 1819).

But in Congress, where Jackson had powerful political enemies, including Henry Clay, the Florida raid was viewed more critically. A senatorial committee undertook an investigation, and its members began to carry arms after Jackson, raving "like a madman," allegedly threatened to cut off the ears of any who reported against him. After a twenty-seven day debate in Congress, during which the galleries were "crowded to suffocation" and cuspidors were overturned in the aisles, the four resolutions condemning Jackson's conduct were defeated by comfortable majorities. The news caused a slight fall of stocks in England, where the press renewed its denunciation of the "ruffian" Jackson. One British journal, at a loss to account for the unexpected result in the House, surmised that it was due to "the brutalizing influence of slavery." But Jackson was pleased, particularly when the people approved the judgment of Congress by tendering him rousing ovations in Philadelphia, New York, and Baltimore.[18]

ADAMS LAYS DOWN THE LAW

The entire Cabinet, with one exception, agreed with President Monroe that Jackson had committed an unauthorized and unjustifiable act of war against Spain. But "Old Hickory" (though he did not know it then) had an unexpected champion in Secretary Adams, who, in spite of strong personal antipathies for the Westerner, held out for a defiant course in dealing with Spain. His arguments prevailed, and caused the Administration to abandon any intention it may have had of disciplining Jackson. This decision was made less difficult by the obvious popularity of the Florida invasion among the unthinking masses. President Monroe was a wise enough politician to see the folly of tangling with the hot-tempered Jackson on an issue which could not fail to weaken the Administration politically. So the President steered a middle course. He mollified Spain by returning the captured posts, and at the same time he tactfully avoided a collision with Jackson, even offering to falsify the official documents so that the invasion of Florida would appear in a better light.[19]

The Spanish minister, de Onís, vigorously demanded indemnity for the losses inflicted and punishment for Jackson. Secretary Adams replied to his charges, and in a memorable instruction to the United States minister in Madrid, dated November 28, 1818, justified the

---

[18] That in Philadelphia lasted four days; that in New York five, and included the freedom of the city in a golden box. James, *Andrew Jackson*, pp. 324–325.

[19] *Ibid.*, p. 318.

foray on the grounds of self-defense. Spain, he declared, could not restrain her Indians; hence the United States would. Adams must have felt a bit uneasy when he enunciated this dictum, for he admitted that there were no citations in the treatises on international law to support him. "It is," he averred, "engraved in adamant on the common sense of mankind." Describing in lurid detail the butcheries of the Indians, he defended the execution of the British incendiaries. Jackson, he declared, would have been fully justified in hanging them both without the formality of a trial.

Adams then took the offensive. Far from apologizing, he charged the Spanish officials with having encouraged and sheltered the Indians. With surprising audacity he demanded the punishment of the culpable officers and an indemnity for the heavy expenses incurred in pursuing the Indians. If, ran Adams' thinly veiled threat, the situation was not remedied, the United States would have to do the same thing again, in which case "another unconditional restoration . . . must not be expected." In stressing the self-confessed impotence of the Spanish officials to control the Indians, Adams minced no words:

. . . Spain must immediately make her election, either to place a force in Florida adequate at once to the protection of her territory, and to the fulfilment of her engagements, or cede to the United States a province, of which she retains nothing but the nominal possession, but which is, in fact, a derelict, open to the occupancy of every enemy, civilized or savage, of the United States, and serving no other earthly purpose than as a post of annoyance to them.[20]

In short, control or cede. And since Spain had already admitted her inability to control, the only alternative was cession.

Adams' eloquent and devastating instruction, which comprises twenty-nine pages of his published works, was received with enthusiasm throughout the country. It voiced the rising spirit of American nationalism, and helped dispel lingering doubts in some parts of the United States as to the legality of the Florida invasion. But it must be confessed that there were passages in which Adams, who was writing largely for "home consumption," stood on untenable ground. His justification was not a judicial presentation of the facts; but as a brief for the defense it was magnificent.

[20] *American State Papers, Foreign Relations,* V, 542 (Adams to Erving, Nov. 28, 1818).

Spain Bows to the Inevitable

Adams' negotiations with de Onís for a definition of the western boundary of the United States and for the cession of Florida were temporarily suspended by the seizure of St. Marks and Pensacola. But, incredible though it may seem, Jackson's bull-in-the-china-shop tactics actually facilitated the work of diplomacy.[21] The procrastinating Castilian, distracted with domestic difficulties, faced with widespread revolution in his South American empire,[22] and lacking effective support from Great Britain, now saw that it would be difficult to prevent Florida from falling into American hands. It was obviously sound policy to dispose of the territory gracefully and for a consideration, while this could yet be done, rather than lose it after a bloody, expensive, and probably humiliating war. Spain's distresses again prepared the way for another American diplomatic success.

After prolonged negotiations the Adams-Onís treaty was finally signed at Washington, February 22, 1819. By its terms the United States received the Floridas, and secured a definition of the western boundary of the Louisiana Purchase. The new line began at the mouth of the Sabine River and zigzagged northwesterly to the forty-second parallel (the present northern limit of California), thence due west to the Pacific. This meant that Spain transferred to the United States all of its claims to the Oregon country. (See map on p. 181.)

In exchange for these substantial concessions America surrendered her shadowy title to Texas based on the Louisiana cession treaty. As an additional consideration, the United States assumed the claims of its own citizens against Spain amounting to $5,000,000. Thus it will be seen that America did not "purchase" Florida for $5,000,000, as it is customarily stated. In essence, Spain ceded Florida and her rights in Oregon for the American title to Texas, with the claims thrown in.[23]

The Senate approved the treaty unanimously only two days after the signing; and the country ratified its judgment. But the worries of

[21] Jackson's admiring fellow citizens in Nashville applauded the twelfth toast: "*The late treaty with Spain:* that which, long protracted, negotiations could not effect, was quickly accomplished by decision in the Cabinet and energy in the field. Six cheers." Quoted in Parton, *Andrew Jackson,* II, 574, from the Nashville *Whig.*

[22] The new Spanish foreign minister hoped to settle the Florida difficulty and free Spain's hands for a more energetic prosecution of the war against the South American rebels. Griffin, *Disruption of the Spanish Empire,* p. 177.

[23] See Brooks, "Pacific Coast's First International Boundary Delineation," *loc. cit.,* pp. 62–79. The author stresses the fact that the term "Florida purchase treaty" is a misnomer.

the Monroe administration were not ended, for the pact met with an unconscionable delay in Spain. As a consequence, the press of the United States became somewhat concerned over the rumor that Great Britain was attempting to thwart ratification.[24] The main reason for the delay in Madrid (personal intrigues were at first important) seems to have been Spain's fear that once Florida was safely in the possession of the United States, the Washington government would promptly recognize the revolted republics of Latin America. Adams, however, pursued the policy that he had followed earlier in the negotiation, and resisted all efforts to coerce the United States into a nonrecognition pledge. Yet the longer ratification was withheld, the more concerned the Administration became. President Monroe seriously discussed with his Cabinet the advisability of recommending to Congress a forcible occupation of the coveted territory.[25] Fortunately, however, a policy of patience was followed; and the Spanish government finally gave in.

It was necessary for the Senate to approve the treaty again, for the six-month time limit stipulated in the document had expired. Meanwhile considerable opposition had developed, particularly in the West, over the alleged surrender of Texas. Henry Clay, who was not unmindful of politics, denounced this as a base betrayal, while the Louisiana *Advertiser* declared that Texas was "worth ten Floridas." Nevertheless, on February 19, 1821, the Senate approved the treaty with only four dissenting votes.

In all fairness to Adams it must be said that he strongly favored retaining Texas; and we now know that he probably could have obtained the area to the Colorado River had he not felt obliged to yield to the President and his colleagues.[26] But practical politics, combined with the ominous slavery issue, pointed to the unwisdom of holding out for Texas. The South—even Andrew Jackson—had few qualms about sacrificing the West if, in so doing, it could acquire Florida. In fact, there probably would have been no treaty at all if the United States had not yielded its claims to at least a substantial portion of Texas. The Spanish minister had to have something to show for his concessions.

---

[24] Tatum, *United States and Europe*, pp. 160–163. For Britain's refusal to support Spain see J. F. Rippy, *Rivalry of the United States and Great Britain over Latin America, 1808–1830* (Baltimore, 1929), pp. 69–70.

[25] Dexter Perkins, "John Quincy Adams," in Bemis, *American Secretaries of State*, IV, 29–30, 33.

[26] Brooks, "Pacific Coast's First International Boundary Delineation," *loc. cit.*, p. 77.

FULFILLING A PHYSIOGRAPHIC DESTINY

On March 8, 1822, more than a year after the formal exchange of ratifications with Madrid, President Monroe sent a message to Congress advising recognition of the Latin American republics. He pointed out, in accordance with Adams' "utterly desperate" formula, that Spain's chances of reconquest were "most remote." Within two months the House and Senate approved the President's request by overwhelming votes, and the necessary steps were then taken to welcome the new republics into the family of nations.[27] Spain's protests were given scant consideration by the government in Washington.

The recognition of the South American republics, so soon after the United States had acquired Florida, has been branded as an act of "singular bad faith." But the Monroe administration had given no pledge, tacit or formal, not to recognize them; and it waited more than a year before taking action. Moreover, subsequent events conclusively supported Monroe's belief that Spain was incapable of winning back her colonies. It is perhaps unfortunate that all aspects of the Florida transaction are not so defensible as this one.

The ratification of the Adams-Onís Treaty was indeed an event of incalculable importance to the United States. In the West, the republic now had a corridor to the Pacific north of the forty-second parallel. It is true that Great Britain also claimed the Oregon country, to which she had admitted the United States to joint occupation by the Convention of 1818; but the problem was simplified by the elimination of all but two contestants. Although the United States inherited the Spanish claims, they were not emphasized in the diplomatic controversy with the British. Yet the westward-moving American pioneer tended to avoid California, which was a foreign land, and settle in Oregon, to which the United States had a good claim.[28] We shall later note that the presence of thousands of American pioneers in this region played an important part in the final diplomatic settlement.

But of more immediate importance was the acquisition of Florida. The hornet's nest of international renegades was removed; constant

[27] The Republic of Colombia (then embracing what became New Granada, Ecuador, and Venezuela) was formally recognized on June 17, 1822; "The Government of Buenos Ayres" (Argentina), on Jan. 27, 1823; Chile and Mexico on the same date; Brazil on May 26, 1824; the Federation of Central American States on August 4, 1824; Peru on May 2, 1826. See J. B. Moore, *A Digest of International Law* (Washington, 1906), I, 90–92.

[28] E. C. Semple, *American History and Its Geographic Conditions* (rev. ed., Boston, 1933), p. 204.

bickerings with Spain, in this region at least, ceased; the rivers of Mississippi and Alabama thenceforth ran freely to the Gulf; the southeastern corner of the United States was filled out and the rapid development of the Cotton Kingdom was made possible; and, finally, an area of enormous strategic value fell into the hands of the United States. "In a word," commented the *National Intelligencer*, "it is a treaty than which the most sanguine have not anticipated one much more favorable; it is one that fully comes up to the expectations of the great body of the American people." [29]

However much we may applaud the masterly diplomacy of Adams, there are features of the negotiation that are not altogether savory. Spain, to be sure, was shuffling, dilatory, and irresponsible; the United States was rough, highhanded, and arrogant. Some writers have called the acquisition of Florida a case of international bullying. Others have called it Manifest Destiny—the falling of ripe fruit. Perhaps it was the manifest determination of the American people to achieve their physiographic destiny coupled with the manifest weakness of Spain. As Niles' *Weekly Register* declared:

Every man, the least acquainted with the geography of our country, must have seen that the Floridas would certainly pass into the possession of the United States. They as naturally belong to us as the county of Cornwall does to England; and besides, the sovereignty of them was found by experience to be indispensable to the safety of our citizens—they had been to us as an enemy's country . . . and . . . ought to have been seized upon many years ago. [30]

The normal and inexorable push of the American pioneers was not to be denied. It was Spain's misfortune, as it was later that of Mexico, to be in their way.

BIBLIOGRAPHICAL NOTE

An excellent brief account of the period appears in Dexter Perkins' "John Quincy Adams," in S. F. Bemis, ed., *American Secretaries of State and their Diplomacy* (N.Y., 1928), IV, 1–35. I. J. Cox's *The West Florida Controversy, 1798–1813* (Baltimore, 1918) is exhaustive. Some of the author's more important conclusions are presented briefly in "The American Intervention in West Florida," *Amer. Hist. Rev.*, XVII (1917), 290–311. C. C. Griffin's *The United States and the Disruption of the Spanish Empire, 1810–1822* (N.Y., 1937), is useful on relations with the South American revolutionists. H. B. Fuller's *The Purchase of Florida* (Cleveland, 1906), though the most detailed account, is rather unsatis-

[29] Quoted in Niles' *Weekly Register*, XVI, 4 (Feb. 27, 1819).
[30] *Ibid.*, XVI, 161 (May 1, 1819).

factory. E. H. Tatum, Jr., presents a spirited background of the period in *The United States and Europe, 1815–1823* (Berkeley, Calif., 1936). An important article is P. C. Brooks, "The Pacific Coast's First International Boundary Delineation, 1816–1819," *Pacific Hist. Rev.*, III (1934), 62–79. This is based upon a monograph by the same author, *United States Diplomacy and the Spanish Borderlands: the Adams-Onís Treaty of 1819*, scheduled for publication by the University of California Press in the fall of 1939. Other worth-while articles are R. K. Wyllys, "The East Florida Revolution of 1812–1814," *Hispanic Amer. Hist. Rev.*, IX (1929), 415–445; W. S. Robertson, "The United States and Spain in 1822," *Amer. Hist. Rev.*, XX (1915), 781–800; and the same author's "Recognition of the Hispanic American Nations by the United States," *Hispanic Amer. Hist. Rev.*, I (1918), 239–269. Further references: see footnotes of this chapter and Bemis and Griffin, *Guide*, pp. 125–130; 162–189.

RECENT REFERENCES. The book by P. C. Brooks, listed above, which is by far the best on the subject, came out under the following title: *Diplomacy and the Borderlands: the Adams-Onís Treaty of 1819* (Berkeley, Calif., 1939). A. P. Whitaker, *The United States and the Independence of Latin America, 1800–1830* (Baltimore, 1941), discusses the Florida negotiations somewhat incidentally in conjunction with Latin American affairs. The author concludes that although other portions of the Adams-Onís treaty later took on great significance, contemporaries generally referred to the "Florida treaty" and regarded the settlement of the Florida question as its most important feature (p. 270 n.). He also concludes that the United States, contrary to a common allegation, did not purposely delay recognition of the Latin American states until after the Spanish treaty was ratified. Earlier action was withheld because of the inchoate nature of the governments concerned, and because the European situation was such that premature recognition might prove to be dangerously provocative (pp. 273–274). S. F. Bemis, in "Early Diplomatic Missions from Buenos Aires to the United States, 1811–1824," *Proceedings of the American Antiquarian Society*, XLIX (1939), 11–101, argues forcefully that American assistance to the revolting Latin American republics remained within the bounds of international law; that no other course was possible, because unneutrality might have provoked Spain to war; that a neutral America was more helpful to the republics than a harassed belligerent; and that the contributions of the United States to Latin American independence were more important than those of England (pp. 98–101).

NEW REFERENCES. For a discussion of S. F. Bemis, *The Latin American Policy of the United States*; Harry Bernstein, *Origins of Inter-American Interest, 1700–1812*; J. H. Powell, *Richard Rush, Republican Diplomat*; and an article by J. J. Johnson on early relations with Chile, see Bibliographical Appendix, p. 924.

4TH ED. REFS. W. L. Neumann, "United States Aid to the Chilean Wars of Independence," *Hispanic Amer. Hist. Rev.*, XXVII (1947), 204–219, shows that American contributions, especially in naval power, were by no means unimportant, even when compared with the British. S. F. Bemis, in his scholarly *John Quincy Adams and the Foundations of American Foreign Policy* (N.Y., 1949) discusses the Treaty of 1819 and concludes (p. 340) that it "was the greatest diplomatic victory won by any single individual in the history of the United States."

CHAPTER XII

Europe, America, and the Monroe Doctrine, 1815–1825

". . . The American continents . . . are henceforth not to be considered as subjects for future colonization by any European powers."
President Monroe, 1823.

MAKING THE WORLD SAFE FOR AUTOCRACY

THE POWERS of Europe, once they had disposed of Napoleon, banded together for the purpose of crystallizing the *status quo* and stamping out dangerous democratic tendencies. The Czar of Russia also devised a visionary and meaningless pact known as the Holy Alliance, which he persuaded most of the rulers of Continental Europe to accept. This organization was not, properly speaking, the instrument used by these monarchs to carry out their reactionary policies. But, to avoid confusion, the term Holy Alliance will be used here (as contemporaries used it) to refer to the concert of European Powers.

The fears of the despots were by no means groundless. In 1820 and 1821 a veritable epidemic of revolutions broke out in Spain, Portugal, Naples, and Greece. The alarmed monarchs hastened to plan repressive measures; and in 1821 Austria crushed the Italian uprisings with ferocity and dispatch. In the spring of 1823, a French army invaded Spain, and by October succeeded in restoring the vindictive Ferdinand VII to the throne of his fathers. The Powers then discussed plans for calling a congress at Paris, which, it was rumored, would send a powerful Franco-Spanish force to America for the purpose of mowing down the new crop of republics.

Great Britain, a lukewarm member of the European concert, viewed with ill-concealed dissatisfaction the ruthless suppression of the Italian and Spanish rebellions. For one thing, the British ministry was disturbed by the shift in the balance of power that would result from French influence in Spain. But vastly more important than either of these factors were the lucrative South American markets, which the recent revolutions had thrown open to England. A restoration of Spanish despotism would unquestionably mean an abrupt cessation of this trade; and the powerful British commercial classes, their appetites already whetted, would stop short of nothing to prevent such a misfortune.[1]

THE MOTHER OF REPUBLICS IS UNEASY

The United States was by no means an indifferent spectator of these portentous developments. At first the Holy Alliance seems to have caused little concern, though as early as 1816 the editor of a Baltimore newspaper declared that it was only a mask "to blind the misguided multitude." [2] But by mid-1821, after the Powers had determined the fate of Italy, America was thoroughly aroused. The Russian minister refused to attend a Fourth of July banquet because, as he reported, "some one would be sure to attack the Holy Alliance." "The Holy Alliance and the Devil," ran a contemporary toast: "May the friends of liberty check their career, and compel them to dissolve partnership." [3]

The course of events in Europe caused many people in the United States to fear that the forces of reaction, after having stamped out the last vestiges of liberty in Europe, might next turn to the Spanish American republics and do likewise. But would the despots be content to stop there? Why not, while they were engaged in such work, wipe out the real hotbed of democracy, which had propagated so many of their recent woes? Even if they did not attack the United States directly, they might secure enormous tracts of Spanish American territory and erect powerful monarchical establishments dangerously near by. In the spring of 1823 it was widely rumored that France would receive Cuba as her reward for assisting Spain to regain her ancient dominions.[4]

By the autumn of 1823, following the French invasion of Spain, the people of the United States seem to have been more disturbed by the designs of the Holy Alliance than by any other foreign problem. The

[1] The editor of Niles' *Weekly Register*, who recognized this situation, wrote with remarkable prescience that Great Britain "will not quietly suffer any other power than Spain, herself, to act against them [Spanish colonies]; and the strange event may take place, of Great Britain and the United States acting together in favor of the rights of man!" XIII, 297–298 (Jan. 3, 1818).

[2] In 1817 Niles published a report that Russia had engaged to help suppress the South American revolts with "a squadron of six ships of the line, and several smaller vessels, and with an army of 15 or 20,000 men, for which Spain cedes to Russia Old and New California, in America. . . ." *Ibid.*, XIII, 46 (Sept. 13, 1817).

[3] *National Intelligencer*, June 2, 1821, 3:1 (Toast at New Haven).

[4] See E. H. Tatum, Jr., *The United States and Europe, 1815–1823* (Berkeley, Calif., 1936), pp. 104 ff.

editor of Niles' *Weekly Register* remarked, "Though separated by a wide ocean from the old world, we are deeply interested in its concerns"; and he added as a warning, "In the perfection of the schemes of the 'holy alliance,' we must anticipate the extinction of civil and religious liberty. . . ."[5] Distrust of foreign despots was further reflected in a Maryland toast: "*The sovereigns of Europe*— In the words of Jacob Gruber's prayer—'convert them all—give them short lives, happy deaths—take them to heaven, and send us no more of them.'"[6]

Concern over the intentions of the Holy Alliance spread to the Administration in Washington. On November 13, 1823, following a gloomy Cabinet meeting, Secretary Adams wrote that Secretary of War Calhoun was "perfectly moonstruck" by the success of the French invasion of Spain; as for President Monroe:

I [Adams] find him . . . alarmed, far beyond anything that I could have conceived possible, with the fear that the Holy Alliance are about to restore immediately all South America to Spain. Calhoun stimulates the panic, and the news that Cadiz has surrendered to the French has so affected the President that he appeared entirely to despair of the cause of South America.[7]

Even Adams, who was less inclined to take an alarmist view than his colleagues, wrote, as late as November 25, 1823, that the challenge of the Alliance "is, and has been, to me a fearful question."

THE CZAR'S UKASE

Russia also entered the diplomatic picture on the northwest coast of North America. Annoyed by foreign contraband trade, the Czar issued an imperial edict or ukase, in September, 1821, forbidding foreign vessels to approach within one hundred Italian miles of the coast of Russian America (Alaska) north of the 51st parallel.[8] This was not only an indefensible assertion of sovereignty over the high seas, but it indicated that Russia was prepared to push the southern boundary of

---

[5] Niles' *Weekly Register*, XXV, 2 (Sept. 6, 1823).

[6] *Ibid.*, p. 19.

[7] C. F. Adams, ed., *Memoirs of John Quincy Adams* (Phila., 1875), VI, 185. On December 1, 1823, the British *chargé* in Washington reported considerable concern in the United States over the success of the French invasion of Spain. C. K. Webster, ed., *Britain and the Independence of Latin America, 1812–1830* (London, 1938), II, 499–501.

[8] The Italian mile is 6085.2 feet, as compared with 5280 feet in the English mile. The ukase also applied to the Siberian coast.

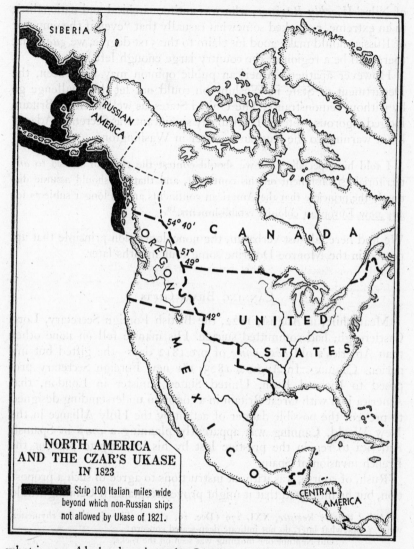

NORTH AMERICA
AND THE CZAR'S UKASE
IN 1823

Strip 100 Italian miles wide
beyond which non-Russian ships
not allowed by Ukase of 1821.

what is now Alaska deep into the Oregon country, which Great Britain
and the United States then claimed jointly.

Contrary to an erroneous conception, the Russian ukase did not
cause widespread alarm in the United States. The Pacific Northwest
was far away; there was plenty of land nearer home; the American
trading interests affected were not important; and what real menace
there was from Russia seemed to lie in the Holy Alliance. The editor

of Niles' *Weekly Register*, who was antimonarchical and nationalistic to an extreme, remarked somewhat casually that "even if the emperor of Russia should make good his claim to the 51st degree, we *guess* that there will be a region of the country large enough left for us." [9]

However apathetic American public opinion may have been, the Department of State in Washington could not let this challenge go by without remonstrance. The United States, as well as Great Britain, lodged vigorous protests. Particularly significant was Secretary Adams' blunt warning to the Russian minister in Washington:

I told him specially that we should contest the right of Russia to *any* territorial establishment on this continent, and that we should assume distinctly the principle that the American continents are no longer subjects for *any* new European colonial establishments. [10]

We find here, almost verbatim, the noncolonization principle that appeared in the Monroe Doctrine some four months later.

CANNING BEARS GIFTS

Meanwhile, in August, 1822, the British Foreign Secretary, Lord Castlereagh, had committed suicide. His mantle fell on none other than America's old *bête noire* of pre-1812 days—the gifted but imperious Canning. In August, 1823, the new Foreign Secretary proposed to Richard Rush, United States minister in London, that America join with Great Britain in a common understanding designed to prevent the possible danger of action by the Holy Alliance in the New World. Canning was apparently planning a *coup* in Spanish America to regain the prestige lost by his inability to prevent the French invasion of Spain.

Rush, of course, was without instructions to agree to such a proposition, but he intimated that it might prove acceptable if Canning would

[9] Niles' *Weekly Register*, XXI, 279 (Dec. 29, 1821). The views of a rhymester, writing somewhat later, do not indicate deep-seated concern:

> Old Neptune one morning was seen on the rocks,
> Shedding tears by the pailful, and tearing his locks;
> He cried, a *Land Lubber* has stole, on this day,
> Full four thousand miles of my ocean away;
> He swallows the *earth*, (he exclaimed with emotion),
> And then, to quench appetite, *slap* goes the *ocean;*
> Brother Jove must look out for his skies, let me tell ye,
> Or the Russian will bury them all in his belly.

Ibid., XXIV, 146 (May 10, 1823).

[10] Adams, *Memoirs*, VI, 163 (July 17, 1823).

consent to recognize the new American republics—a step that the conservative influences in England were delaying. Upon the Foreign Secretary's disinclination to take the hint, Rush referred the matter home.[11] President Monroe's first reaction was rather favorable; but before making so momentous a decision he decided to consult his two predecessors in office. Madison and the octogenarian Jefferson, both of whom had once been anti-British, counseled co-operation with England. Madison went so far as to urge a declaration in favor of Greek freedom, for which there was much enthusiasm in the United States.[12] But Secretary Adams, as in the Florida affair, held out for a course opposite to that most generally advised. Intensely nationalistic and individualistic, and having a high regard for the strength of the United States in the affairs of the New World, he was strongly opposed to associating with any other Power in this important enterprise. "It would be more candid," he insisted, "as well as more dignified, to avow our principles explicitly to Russia and France, than to come in as a cock-boat in the wake of the British man-of-war." [13]

But there were far more compelling considerations than these. Conspicuous in the Canning proposal was the proviso that neither the United States nor Great Britain would appropriate any part of Spanish America. Perhaps the American people would one day want Texas, California, or Cuba, in which case such a pledge would tie their hands. This, in fact, appears to have been the intention of Canning, who was particularly nervous about the fate of Cuba. But Adams feared that England was trying to inveigle the United States into a self-denying trap, and he forcibly expressed his views in a Cabinet meeting. He also suspected that the danger of interference by any one of the members of the so-called Holy Alliance was not great. Although there is

---

[11] Dexter Perkins, "John Quincy Adams," in S. F. Bemis, ed., *American Secretaries of State and their Diplomacy* (N.Y., 1928), IV, 64.

[12] In 1821 the Greeks revolted against Turkish rule. American interest in their cause was stimulated by a knowledge that Greece was the "classical creditor" of Western civilization; by the fact that the Greeks were Christians fighting against infidels; by a traditional devotion to liberty; and by a reaction to the despotic tendencies of the Holy Alliance. The so-called "Greek fever," stimulated by atrocity stories (the Turks reputedly collected bushels of ears), came to a head late in 1823. It took the form of sermons, orations, balls, mass meetings, poems (notably Halleck's "Marco Bozzaris"), the collection of funds (Yale students contributed $500), and the introduction of resolutions in Congress. Interest began to wane in 1824, and formal recognition was not accorded Greece until 1837. The "fever" did, however, stimulate the study of Greek and an appreciation of classical architecture. See M. A. Cline, *American Attitude toward the Greek War of Independence, 1821–1828* (Atlanta, 1930). For an analysis of recognition policy see E. M. Earle, "Early American Policy concerning Ottoman Minorities," *Pol. Sci. Quar.*, XLII (1927), 337–367.

[13] Adams, *Memoirs*, VI, 179 (Nov. 7, 1823).

some difference among historians as to the existence of any real peril,[14] it is certainly true that not a single one of the interested Powers had in mind a definite policy of intervention. Adams, to be sure, did not have all of the evidence before him; but that he could piece together isolated bits and make a shrewd deduction is a tribute to his statesmanship. Although the United States was not prepared to fight, neither, he suspected, was the Holy Alliance. The astute Secretary could therefore scoff at Calhoun's fears of intervention: ". . . I no more believe that the Holy Allies will restore the Spanish dominion upon the American continent than that the Chimborazo will sink beneath the ocean." [15]

Adams also surmised that even if the European Powers attempted to intervene, England, with her mastery of the seas, probably would not let them. Those Spanish American markets had to be kept open. So, whatever the Monroe administration did or failed to do, there would presumably be no intervention. Safely sheltered behind Britain's "stout wooden walls," America could blow a "republican blast" of defiance at all Europe. Again the discords of the European Powers—their diplomatic distresses—made possible an important achievement in American foreign policy.

Mr. Monroe Lectures the Powers

Adams did not encounter great difficulty in persuading his colleagues to acquiesce in a go-it-alone policy. But his suggestion that the Monroe Doctrine (as it was later known) be communicated to the foreign offices of the Powers through sharp diplomatic notes was not so favorably received. Instead, President Monroe hit upon the plan of giving his policy to the world in the form of a presidential message. He was warmly seconded by Calhoun, who felt that the Powers would be less likely to take offense at this more or less routine form of presentation.

On November 21, 1823, the President laid the first draft of his memorable message before the Cabinet for discussion. It was bold, even defiant, in tone. Adams immediately expressed alarm, particularly over

[14] Professor H. W. V. Temperley is much more inclined to credit the Powers, particularly France, with interventionist designs than is Professor Dexter Perkins. See H. W. V. Temperley, "French Designs on Spanish America in 1820–5," *Eng. Hist. Rev.*, XL (1925), 34 ff. Professor C. K. Webster (*Britain and Latin America*, I, 72–73) concludes that the French contemplated the use of force but never made any "concrete plans"; and that there was no possibility of interference before the Polignac memorandum or the Monroe Doctrine was composed.

[15] Adams, *Memoirs*, VI, 186 (Nov. 15, 1823).

the intention of the President to champion the cause of the Greek rebels. The next day Adams approached Monroe privately and expressed his views with characteristic vigor: "The ground that I wish to take is that of earnest remonstrance against the interference of the European powers by force with South America, but to disclaim all interference on our part with Europe; to make an American cause, and adhere inflexibly to that." [16] Monroe was at first a bit reluctant to accept Adams' clear-cut doctrine of the two hemispheres. But he was finally persuaded that anything savoring of gratuitous interference in the affairs of Europe would weaken his position. He therefore changed his ringing declaration in behalf of the Greeks to a pious wish for their success, and toned down his proposed reproof of France for invading Spain.

The now famous Monroe Doctrine was embedded in the President's annual message to Congress of December 2, 1823. It consisted of two widely separated passages, comprising about two printed pages out of a total of thirteen. After some preliminary remarks Monroe alluded to the negotiations with Russia over the Northwest coast.

In the discussions . . . the occasion has been judged proper for asserting . . . that the American continents, by the free and independent condition which they have assumed and maintain, are henceforth not to be considered as subjects for future colonization by any European powers.[17]

Thus was enunciated, rather incidentally, the significant noncolonization principle. Monroe's failure to make more of a point of it was probably a result of his knowledge that there was no serious Russian menace in the Northwest, and that negotiations were proceeding satisfactorily for an adjustment of the difficulty arising from the Czar's ukase.

There followed a seven-page intermission, devoted principally to domestic affairs. Then came the striking passages inspired by the rumored intervention of the Holy Alliance.

The political system of the allied powers is essentially different . . . from that of America. . . . We owe it, therefore, to candor and to the amicable relations existing between the United States and those powers to declare that we should consider any attempt on their part to extend their system to any portion of this hemisphere as dangerous to our peace and safety.

[16] *Ibid.*, VI, 197–198 (Nov. 22, 1823).
[17] J. D. Richardson, ed., *Messages and Papers of the Presidents* (Washington, 1896), II, 209 (Dec. 2, 1823).

Monroe continued:

With the existing colonies or dependencies of any European power we have not interfered [Florida?] and shall not interfere. But with the Governments who have declared their independence . . . we could not view any interposition for the purpose of oppressing them, or controlling in any other manner their destiny, by any European power in any other light than as the manifestation of an unfriendly disposition toward the United States.

Finally, Monroe completed his enunciation of the doctrine of the two hemispheres: "Our policy in regard to Europe, which was adopted at an early stage of the wars which have so long agitated that quarter of the globe, nevertheless remains the same, which is, not to interfere in the internal concerns of any of its powers. . . ." [18] In other words, the United States would refrain from intervention in such embroilments as the Greek war for independence. In return for this rather hollow act of self-denial Europe would be expected to keep her hands off the South American wars for independence.

The fundamental ideas of the Monroe Doctrine were neither new nor original. They go back to the colonial period, and they had been repeatedly foreshadowed if not definitely formulated by Washington, John Adams, Jefferson and others. Monroe, so to speak, merely codified such existing ideas as those of the two hemispheres, no transfer of territory, nonintervention, and nonentanglement. [19] The President was ably assisted by John Quincy Adams, who contributed so much to the formulation of the Doctrine that he has been frequently spoken of as the real author.

THE EAGLE SCREAMS

The people of the United States, on the whole, responded cordially if not enthusiastically to the President's pronouncement. The commercial world was gratified at this further assurance that the Spanish American markets would not be closed. More than that, the doctrine was exhilarating to the national spirit. The rising young republic, the strongest Power in America, had hurled defiance into the teeth of an effete and despotic Europe. Nothing could better illustrate the ris-

[18] *Ibid.*, pp. 218–219.
[19] For a convenient summary of incidents and statements foreshadowing the Monroe Doctrine see J. Reuben Clark, *Memorandum on the Monroe Doctrine* (Washington, 1930).

ing tide of nationalism than the confidence in the ability of the United States, without a formidable army or navy, to repulse the Holy Alliance should it make so bold as to challenge Monroe's pretensions. "If the Holy Alliance attempt to control the destinies of South America," remarked the Boston *Centinel,* "they will find not only a lion, but an eagle in the way." [20]

The press of the United States, which had expressed considerable fear of imminent European intervention, teemed with self-confident, exulting words of commendation. The *Eastern Argus* (Portland, Maine) observed that the message "has been received throughout the country with a warm and universal burst of applause." One Congressman remarked that the new doctrine was "as wise as it was magnanimous." At least two state legislatures passed commendatory resolutions. Perhaps the most trustworthy general observation was that of the British *chargé* in Washington:

The President's message . . . seems to have been received with acclamation throughout the United States. . . . The explicit and manly tone . . . has evidently found in every bosom a chord which vibrates in strict unison with the sentiments so conveyed. They have been echoed from one end of the Union to the other. It would, indeed, be difficult, in a country composed of elements so various . . . to find more perfect unanimity than has been displayed on every side. . . .[21]

But it seems unlikely that the United States, preoccupied with other problems, was quite so enthusiastic or unanimous as these words would suggest. Certain it is that here and there a dissenting voice was raised. One member of Congress found the pronouncement "rash and inconsiderate"; another "an unauthorized, unmeaning, and empty menace, well calculated to excite the angry passions and embroil us with foreign nations." The Richmond *Enquirer* wanted evidence of a real danger of intervention; and a writer for the Boston *Advertiser* demanded: "Is there anything in the Constitution which makes our Government the Guarantors of the Liberties of the World? of the Wahabees? the Peruvians? the Chilese? the Mexicans or Colombians?" [22] But such criticisms were generally overlooked in the widespread feeling of self-satisfaction.

[20] Quoted in E. B. White, *American Opinion of France* (N.Y., 1927), p. 76.

[21] Webster, *Britain and Latin America*, II, 508 (Addington to Canning, Jan. 5, 1824).

[22] Quoted in Dexter Perkins, *The Monroe Doctrine, 1823–1826* (Cambridge, Mass., 1927), p. 146.

Canning's Chagrin

Public opinion in England seems to have reacted favorably to the "bold" American message, for Englishmen were quite content to see the United States help pull their South American chestnuts out of the fire. An immediate rise in the value of Spanish American securities reflected British confidence in American support. The influential London *Times* applauded the "resolute policy" of the United States, and interpreted the doctrine as meaning that intervention in the Americas by the Holy Alliance would be "*a just cause of war*." "With what satisfaction," continued the *Times*, ". . . must we receive the tidings, when they announce the intended prosecution of a policy so directly British!" [23] Public opinion in England apparently did not realize at first that the noncolonization clause was no less applicable to Britain than to Russia. But the tone of the British press soon changed.

Canning, however, labored under no illusions. Annoyed because the United States had stolen his thunder in this "very extraordinary" pronouncement, he perceived that the noncolonization principle could be invoked against his own country as well as against the Powers of Continental Europe. Indeed, it is probable that the Monroe administration, looking some little distance into the future, may have had Great Britain, among others, specifically in mind. [24]

The attitude of Canning toward the Monroe Doctrine was to some extent based upon his positive knowledge that the Holy Alliance would make no hostile movement. After having waited briefly for something to come of his overtures to Rush, he had taken matters into his own hands. He was confident that if intervention should be attempted in America the French army would be used, as it had been in Spain, and that Russia would not embark upon such an enterprise alone. Accordingly, Canning brought strong pressure to bear upon Prince de Polignac, the French ambassador, as a result of which the

[23] London *Times*, Jan. 6, 1824, 2:4.

[24] During the months prior to December, 1823, there had been suspicious movements of British ships in the Caribbean, and the rumor had spread in America that England had designs on Cuba. This activity, which was not regarded very seriously by the Washington government, seems to have been undertaken to suppress piracy in that region. Webster, *Britain and Latin America*, II, 109–110. It is unlikely that the noncolonization clause was aimed directly at Britain, for the acquisition of thickly populated Cuba could hardly have been regarded as colonization; and the no-transfer corollary of the Monroe Doctrine was not developed until later. In the rest of his message, Monroe specifically referred to the "political system" of the "allied powers" [Holy Alliance], which would exclude England. The role of Great Britain is heavily stressed in Tatum, *The United States and Europe*, pp. 141 ff.

latter signed a memorandum, October 9, 1823, formally disclaiming any intention on the part of France to intervene in Spanish America.[25] Thus, nearly two months before Monroe's message to Congress, the British Foreign Office, without the President's knowledge, removed the most serious remaining threat to Latin American liberties.

Canning was not at all backward about advertising what he had done. Weeks before the Monroe message arrived in Europe, the substance of the Polignac memorandum was known in Austria, Russia, and France, and even by Minister Rush. In March, 1824, Canning published this document so that all the world would know that the might of Britain's fleet, and not the bombast of President Monroe, had given the death blow to any scheme that the Holy Alliance may have been contemplating.

An "Indecent" Declaration

Continental Europe viewed the Monroe Doctrine with mingled annoyance and contempt. The principle of America for the Americans came as a shock to Powers which for centuries had looked upon the Western Hemisphere as their own private preserves. If they had been willing and prepared to intervene, their first reaction probably would have been to do so just to put the Yankee in his place. Indeed, European interest in intervention seems to have been stimulated, if anything, by America's aggressive republicanism.[26]

In Austria, a ringleader of reaction, Chancellor Metternich denounced the "indecent declarations" of Monroe, while his colleague, the councilor of state, was startled by the presumption of "that new transatlantic colossus." The French minister of foreign affairs spoke jeeringly of the gulf between American pretensions and naval power, and *L'Etoile* (Paris) reflected a not uncommon viewpoint:

Mr. Monroe, who is not a sovereign has assumed in his message the tone of a powerful monarch, whose armies and fleets are ready to march at the first signal. . . . Mr. Monroe is the temporary President of a Republic situated on the east coast of North America. This republic is bounded on the south by the possessions of the King of Spain, and on the north by those

[25] On the Polignac memorandum, see Webster, *Britain and Latin America*, I, 19–20; II, 16, *et passim*.

[26] Temperley, "French Designs on Spanish America," *loc. cit.*, pp. 34 *ff*. This author (p. 52) reveals that France showed some disposition not to be bound by the Polignac memorandum. See also H. W. V. Temperley, "Documents Illustrating the Reception and Interpretation of the Monroe Doctrine in Europe, 1823–4," *Eng. Hist. Rev.*, XXXIX (1924), 591.

of the King of England. Its independence was only recognized forty years ago; by what right then would the two Americas today be under its immediate sway from Hudson's Bay to Cape Horn? [27]

Russia could not have been greatly surprised by the enunciation of the Monroe Doctrine. During the preceding weeks John Quincy Adams had given even sharper warning to the Russian minister than appeared in the published message. But the Czar was not frightened by the Yankee bombast. Of all the European monarchs he most warmly sympathized with Spain's aspirations for the recovery of her lost domain; and with France eliminated by the Polignac pledge, he was the ruler most likely to undertake intervention. Early in 1824 he appears to have given some thought to doing so.[28] But, lacking assistance from the other Powers, he soon abandoned any such plans that he may have had. The British navy could not be laughed aside.

In 1824, four and a half months after the enunciation of the Monroe Doctrine, Adams negotiated a treaty by which Russia agreed to retreat up the Northwest coast from 51° to 54° 40', the present southernmost tip of Alaska. This satisfactorily solved the problem raised by the ukase. Some writers have concluded that the Czar, alarmed by America's blunt warning, was forced to make this surrender. But it is now clear that even before Monroe proclaimed his remarkable dictum, the Russian government, preoccupied at home and possessing territory enough in Asia, had decided to make substantial concessions on the American coast. The terms that the Czar granted to the United States, despite the offensive message of Monroe, merely represented the execution of a predetermined policy.[29]

LATIN AMERICAN DISILLUSIONMENT

The people of the United States are prone to believe that the southern republics were duly grateful for their deliverance from the Holy Alliance by the chivalrous Uncle Sam.[30] Although our present knowledge of popular reactions in Spanish America is fragmentary, it is clear that in some quarters the message was greeted with rejoicing, in others with indifference, and in still others with dissatisfaction—on

[27] *L'Etoile*, Jan. 4, 1824, quoted in Perkins, *Monroe Doctrine, 1823–1826*, p. 30.
[28] Temperley, "French Designs on Spanish America," *loc. cit.*, p. 35.
[29] Perkins, "John Quincy Adams," in Bemis, *American Secretaries of State*, IV, 97.
[30] This view was not uncommon at the time. Senator Johnson of Louisiana declaimed: "The Powers of Europe paused. . . . The designs of the Holy Alliance were disconcerted. This memorable declaration has had its effect." *Register of Debates*, 19 Cong., 1 sess., p. 224 (March 14, 1826).

the whole with no more than moderate enthusiasm. Bolívar, the out-standing leader of the recent revolutions, apparently did not regard the pronouncement as of extraordinary importance.

Whatever doubts may exist as to the unanimity of Latin American enthusiasm, it is certain that the United States did not displace its great rival, Britain, as the moral and commercial leader of South America. Shortly after Monroe sent his message to Congress, the Polignac memorandum was published throughout Spanish America. The infant republics speedily recognized that they had been saved from the Holy Alliance not by the paper pronouncement of Monroe but by Britain's powerful fleet.[31] It was also evident that the new policy was essen-tially selfish. The United States, as was quite natural, had clearly been thinking first of its own safety, and only secondarily of that of its neighbors.

Two of the new South American states, Colombia and Brazil, inter-preted Monroe's message as an invitation to form an alliance with the United States against European aggression. But Adams, in accord-ance with the traditional policy of nonentanglement, did not respond to these overtures. He made it clear that his country would not act unless there were a general European intervention and unless Britain were on the American side.[32] The Monroe administration had, in short, created false hopes that it was forced to disappoint. All this did nothing to metamorphose the cautious Yankee into a dashing Sir Galahad.

The Monroe Doctrine: Fact and Fancy

What came to be known as the Monroe Doctrine was not law, na-tional or international. It was merely a simple, unilateral, presidential enunciation of foreign policy. Adams even spoke of it as a "lecture" to the Powers. It did not commit subsequent administrations to any definite course. As Lord Clarendon politely but pointedly remarked to the United States minister in London in the fifties, "The Monroe Doctrine is merely the dictum of its distinguished author." He might have added, no less pointedly, that it was no stronger than the power and influence of the United States.

The new dogma did not even need a distinguishing name. It might

---

[31] The English consul in Chile reported to Canning, "You, Sir, are styled, even in the Senate, by all the Officers of State, 'The Redeemer of Chile.'" H. W. V. Temperley, *The Foreign Policy of Canning, 1822–1827* (London, 1925), p. 165 (Nugent to Canning, July 30, 1824). See also Webster, *Britain and Latin America*, I, 74, 78, 79.

[32] Perkins, *Monroe Doctrine, 1823–1826*, pp. 186 ff.

just as well have been called the Self-Defense Doctrine—for that is essentially what it was. Monroe warned the members of the Holy Alliance to keep out of South America, and Russia to forego further colonization, primarily because he felt that their presence would be dangerous to the peace and safety of the United States. If, at a later date, the machinations of one of the great Powers should arouse the apprehensions of the Washington government, all it had to do was to base its protest on the grounds of self-defense, without having to mention the Monroe Doctrine. Nevertheless, President Monroe gave definite form, as well as considerable emphasis, to one of the nation's most fundamental foreign policies. And when in later years it became necessary to invoke the Doctrine, it carried greater weight with the American people because it had an "aura of antiquity."

One question remains unanswered. Did the Monroe Doctrine prevent the partition of Latin America? Granting that there was no immediate danger of intervention, were not the Powers checked in later years by the wide publicity that Monroe gave to the policy of the United States? One common answer is to point to the fact that there is much less European territory in the Americas now than in 1823; yet during the nineteenth and twentieth centuries European imperialism absorbed nearly all of Africa and huge areas elsewhere. But this analogy must be used with caution. Protected in large part by their remoteness, the larger states of South America were capable of putting up a stiff resistance; the European powers established profitable commercial and financial relationships with Latin America without the necessity of conquest; and during most of the nineteenth century Europe was too deeply preoccupied with difficulties elsewhere to give much thought to imperialism in America.[33]

When the Monroe Doctrine was first enunciated it commanded relatively little attention at home, and even less respect abroad. It was not even generally known as the *Monroe* Doctrine until the fifties. Yet by mid-century the Powers were aware that such a policy existed, and that it was backed by a sturdy and growing United States. It is possible—though by no means demonstrable—that there would be somewhat more European territory in the Americas today if the Monroe Doctrine, or some similar doctrine, had not been proclaimed.

[33] Dexter Perkins, *The Monroe Doctrine, 1867–1907* (Baltimore, 1937), pp. 134, 462.

BIBLIOGRAPHICAL NOTE

The standard monograph on the subject is Dexter Perkins' *The Monroe Doctrine, 1823–1826* (Cambridge, Mass., 1927). The same author has an excellent brief account of the origins of the Monroe Doctrine in his "John Quincy Adams," in S. F. Bemis, ed., *The American Secretaries of State and their Diplomacy* (N.Y., 1928), IV, 56–103. E. H. Tatum, Jr., *The United States and Europe, 1815–1823* (Berkeley, Calif., 1936), develops American opinion and background but disagrees with the other authorities in his contention that the Monroe Doctrine was aimed primarily at Britain. A valuable documentary collection, stressing the part played by England, is C. K. Webster, ed., *Britain and the Independence of Latin America, 1812–1830* (2 vols., London, 1938). The introduction, pp. 3–79, contains an excellent summary of the documents. The European background is also presented in H. W. V. Temperley, *The Foreign Policy of Canning, 1822–1827* (London, 1925). M. A. Cline, *American Attitude toward the Greek War of Independence, 1821–1828* (Atlanta, Ga., 1930) is the standard monograph. On the question of authorship of the Doctrine see W. C. Ford, "John Quincy Adams and the Monroe Doctrine," *Amer. Hist. Rev.*, VII (1902), 676–696, VIII (1902), 28–52; W. A. MacCorkle, *The Personal Genesis of the Monroe Doctrine* (N.Y., 1923), which presents the case for Monroe; and T. R. Schellenberg, "Jeffersonian Origins of the Monroe Doctrine," *Hispanic Amer. Hist. Rev.*, XIV (1934), 1–32. The Russian side is treated in J. C. Hildt, *Early Diplomatic Negotiations of the United States with Russia* (Baltimore, 1906); and B. P. Thomas, *Russo-American Relations, 1815–1867* (Baltimore, 1930). Useful additional articles are W. S. Robertson, "The Monroe Doctrine Abroad in 1823–24," *Amer. Pol. Sci. Rev.*, VI (1912), 546–563; and the same author's "South America and the Monroe Doctrine, 1824–28," *Pol. Sci. Quar.*, XXX (1915), 82–105. Further references: see footnotes of this chapter and Bemis and Griffin, *Guide*, pp. 189–198.

RECENT REFERENCES. A book of primary importance, which admirably supplements and in some particulars supersedes Perkins' *Monroe Doctrine, 1823–1826*, is A. P. Whitaker, *The United States and the Independence of Latin America, 1800–1830* (Baltimore, 1941), for an extended discussion of which, see Bibliographical Appendix, pp. 881–882. W. S. Robertson's scholarly *France and Latin-American Independence* (Baltimore, 1939), further supports Perkins' view that France had no immediate designs on Spanish America in 1823. Dexter Perkins, in *Hands Off: A History of the Monroe Doctrine* (Boston, 1941), Chs. I–II, presents in summary and highly readable form the principal findings of his earlier monograph on this period.

NEW REFERENCES. For S. F. Bemis, *The Latin American Policy of the United States*; J. H. Powell, *Richard Rush, Republican Diplomat*; two articles by Laura Bornholdt and T. B. Davis, Jr., respectively, on the origins of the Monroe Doctrine; and two articles, one by A. G. Mazour and the other by S. R. Tompkins, on the treaty of 1824 with Russia, see Bibliographical Appendix, p. 925.

4TH ED. REFS. S. F. Bemis, in his *John Quincy Adams and the Foundations of American Foreign Policy* (N.Y., 1949), concludes that the most important contribution of the Monroe Doctrine at the time was "in galvanizing the preponderant *republican character* of the new states at the outset" (p. 407).

CHAPTER XIII

Signs and Portents, 1825–1840

"There has, indeed, rarely been a period in the history of civilized man in which the general condition of the Christian nations has been marked so extensively by peace and prosperity."

President John Quincy Adams, 1825.

DIPLOMACY MARKS TIME

THE RECORD of American foreign affairs from 1825 to 1840 is not thickly dotted with sensational developments. During no other period of similar length prior to 1873 does the student of diplomacy find so little of a striking nature to chronicle. Of the numerous explanations that may be offered, two seem fundamental. First, the energy of the American people was absorbed by an amazing internal expansion; and second, the European theater was so quiet as to threaten no serious involvements.

The decreasing emphasis on foreign relations called for a different type of Chief Executive. With the exception of Washington, who nevertheless had successfully discharged a number of quasi-diplomatic duties, every one of the first six presidents had served as an envoy to a foreign court, or as a Secretary of State, or as both. But beginning with Andrew Jackson, in 1829, the American people summoned to their highest office—the one from which the foreign affairs of the nation are directed—a succession of men who were almost totally without diplomatic experience. (See Appendix B.)

John Quincy Adams, the last of the line of seasoned diplomats to become President, took office on March 4, 1825. Unhappily, he did not enjoy the success, either in foreign or domestic affairs, that his brilliant diplomatic record presaged. At home, he encountered serious political difficulties as a result of selecting Henry Clay as his Secretary of State—an office then regarded as the steppingstone to the presidency. Throughout four long years the noisy followers of Andrew Jackson cried that this appointment was but the fulfillment of a "corrupt bargain," by which Clay had thrown his support to Adams in the disputed election of 1824 and robbed Jackson of the presidency.

Abroad, Adams ran afoul of Foreign Secretary Canning, who could not forget the Monroe Doctrine and the American challenge to British influence in Latin America. Canning's hand was greatly strengthened when, late in 1824, he was able to win his government over to a policy of recognizing the Spanish American republics. "The deed is done," he gloated, "the nail is driven, Spanish America is free; and if we do not mismanage our affairs badly, *she is English.*" [1] Canning did not mismanage. Jealous of British markets and possible Yankee political domination, he thwarted Adams at nearly every turn.[2] It is not altogether surprising that when Canning died, in 1827, the American President noted the event in his diary with satisfaction.

THE PANAMA CONGRESS FIASCO

In 1825 the United States was invited to send delegates to the Panama Congress—a means devised by Simón Bolívar, South American revolutionary hero, to discuss problems common to the American republics. Secretary Clay, ever an enthusiast for Latin American cooperation, persuaded the President to accept. Adams then sought senatorial approval of his two appointees, and an appropriation from Congress for their expenses.

The immediate result was a lengthy and acrimonious debate. Much of the opposition, particularly that of the vociferous Jackson supporters, was due to a desire to embarrass the Administration. The vitriolic John Randolph of Virginia became involved in a bloodless duel with Henry Clay when he referred to the Adams-Clay combination as a "coalition between the Puritan and the blackleg." There were, however, bona fide objections to participation at Panama, prominent among which was the danger of foreign entanglements. In addition, the Southerners feared that Negro slavery would be discussed, and they vigorously objected to having anything to do with the scheme.

The press in the North was almost unanimous in favoring the Con-

---

[1] H. W. V. Temperley, "The Later American Policy of George Canning," *Amer. Hist. Rev.*, XI (1906), 796 (Canning to Granville, Dec. 17, 1824). Canning, probably with an eye to influencing Latin America, took credit for the Monroe Doctrine. Explaining why he had not halted the French invasion of Spain in 1823, he told the House of Commons: "I looked another way—I sought materials of compensation in another hemisphere. Contemplating Spain . . . I resolved that if France had Spain, it should not be Spain 'with the Indies' [Spanish colonies]. I called the New World into existence, to redress the balance of the Old." Hansard, *New Series*, XVI, 397 (Dec. 12, 1826).

[2] See J. F. Rippy, *Rivalry of the United States and Great Britain over Latin America, 1808–1830* (Baltimore, 1929), pp. 112 *ff.*

gress, for it was believed that co-operation was necessary to protect American commercial interests against British rivalry.[3] At length, and only after a four-month debate in the House, Congress gave its grudging consent. One of the delegates died en route; the other started so late that he finally abandoned his efforts to reach Panama.[4] Adams' numerous opponents rejoiced. The luckless President, after having aroused all this partisan rancor, had nothing to show for his pains.

Meanwhile, on June 22, 1826, the Panama Congress had convened with its wagon hitched to a star. One delegate rose to empyrean heights:

> An entire world is about to witness our labours. . . . Our names are about to be written either in immortal praise or in eternal opprobrium. Let us raise ourselves above a thousand millions of inhabitants, and may a noble pride inspire us, likening us to God himself on that day, when He gave the first laws to the Universe.[5]

Such gigantic pretensions were equaled only by the abysmal failure of the Congress. None of its recommendations was ever adopted; none of its projected meetings was ever held. Yet the germs of the Pan-American ideal, which was to assume considerable significance, were definitely planted.

Some commentators have seen in this serio-comic episode a lamentable failure on the part of the United States to assume the leadership of Latin America and alter the course of history. Such an interpretation seems unduly optimistic. Even if the delegates had arrived in time, they could have accomplished very little. And that little would have been thwarted by Canning, who saw to it that a British representative was at Panama, making the best of this excellent opportunity to put the United States in a bad light and strengthen Britain's influence in Latin America.[6]

One incidental development of some significance should be noted. During the debate in Congress there was a marked tendency to deny the binding nature of Monroe's recent pronouncement. Senator Berrien of Georgia insisted that it was "a mere gratuitous declaration to Congress, of one of the public functionaries of this Government."

[3] F. L. Reinhold, "New Research on the First Pan-American Congress Held at Panama in 1826," *Hispanic Amer. Hist. Rev.*, XVIII (1938), 348–350, 363.

[4] J. B. Lockey, *Pan-Americanism: Its Beginnings* (N.Y., 1920), p. 314.

[5] Temperley, "Later American Policy of Canning," *loc. cit.*, p. 786.

[6] Rippy, *Rivalry of United States and Great Britain*, pp. 227 ff.; C. K. Webster, *Britain and the Independence of Latin America, 1812–1830* (London, 1938), I, 51–52; 423.

Others felt that in any given case the principles laid down by Monroe might be invoked or ignored, depending upon the interests and policy of the United States at the moment. Certainly, there was no disposition to pay obeisance to the now-famous doctrine, or to wring from it the extravagant interpretations of a later day.[7]

ADAMS' WEST INDIAN REBUFF

The problem of reopening the lucrative trade with the British West Indies, which had been closed since the Americans decided to secede from the Empire, again became a burning diplomatic question during Adams' administration. It is true that the British had permitted a restricted trade during the Napoleonic wars, owing to a shortage of foodstuffs; but with the return of peace these concessions were withdrawn. Throughout the succeeding decade American diplomacy repeatedly tried to win these privileges. In 1817 the somewhat complaisant Lord Castlereagh did offer a limited trade with the British West Indies. But the United States, hoping to extort more, enacted countervailing or retaliatory legislation, beginning with the act of 1818. A writer in the Providence *Gazette* waxed poetical in his enthusiasm for strong measures:

> Tender handed press a nettle,
> And it stings you for your pains;
> Grasp it, like a man of mettle,
> And it soft as silk remains.[8]

Retaliatory laws, though hurting certain interests in the United States, did affect the British carrying trade and the West Indian plantations.[9] In 1822 Parliament went so far as to open certain ports in the West Indies, but on such unsatisfactory conditions that the diplomatic controversy was kept alive.

By the end of the first quarter of the nineteenth century the Providence *Patriot* could observe that the whole question presented "a Gordian knot, which will require an Alexander in diplomacy to untie if it ever is untied by negotiation." If America had a diplomatic Alexander at this time it was the able and experienced President Adams, who inherited the problem in March, 1825. Some four months later

---

[7] Dexter Perkins, *The Monroe Doctrine, 1823–1826* (Cambridge, 1927), p. 213.
[8] Quoted in F. L. Benns, *The American Struggle for the British West India Carrying-Trade, 1815–1830* (Bloomington, Indiana, 1923), p. 53.
[9] L. J. Ragatz, *The Fall of the Planter Class in the British Caribbean, 1763–1833* (N.Y., 1928), p. 359.

Parliament passed another act opening the West Indian trade—but still under restrictions that were somewhat distasteful to the United States. Instead of promptly accepting this half loaf, Adams dallied a year before taking active measures, and then sent the veteran Albert Gallatin to London in the hope of securing more favorable terms. The President's view was that access to the West Indian ports should be demanded as a right and not requested as a privilege. Meanwhile Great Britain, somewhat irked by the stiff attitude of Adams, had withdrawn her offer completely. *Bell's Weekly Messenger*, a British publication, hoped that the Cabinet would reply with "contemptuous defiance" to the threats of the Americans "to bully us out of a policy which has been one of the main pillars of the navigation system."

Canning, however, needed no urging. He had already told Minister Gallatin in blistering terms that what Britain did with the trade of her colonies was her own business. Adams was denounced in the United States for having bungled an opportunity to edge into the West Indian trade. The Richmond *Enquirer* employed caustic adjectives in describing "the clumsy and mischievous manner, in which the benefits of the Colonial Trade" had "been lost by the Administration." In fact, this failure of Adams' "diplomatised Administration" was one of the most vulnerable joints in the New Englander's armor during the presidential campaign of 1828.[10]

The Soldier Shames the Diplomat

The politically inept President Adams yielded the reins in 1829 to Andrew Jackson, hero of the recently enfranchised masses. Possibly because of his hatred of Adams and Clay, and a desire to succeed where they had failed, the fiery Tennessean curbed his violent anti-British prejudices, and his Administration took the position of requesting participation in the British West Indian trade as a privilege rather than demanding it as a right.[11] England was pleased by this unexpectedly moderate stand, and eventually consented to a compromise in 1830 by which direct commerce with her West Indies was thrown open to the United States, subject, however, to such duties as the

---

[10] See Benns, *The American Struggle*, p. 160.

[11] Secretary Van Buren, in his instructions to the minister in London, took the position that in 1828 the electorate had repudiated the false position taken by Adams with regard to the West Indian trade. These animadversions upon the conduct of a previous Administration in the field of foreign affairs were most unusual, and reacted violently upon Van Buren. J. S. Bassett, "Martin Van Buren," in S. F. Bemis, ed., *The American Secretaries of State and their Diplomacy* (N.Y., 1928), IV, 184–185.

London government chose to levy. But the trade was opened. American merchants and shippers rejoiced, while partisans of Jackson were elated. The *United States Telegraph* (Washington), a supporter of the colorful General, printed "extras" proclaiming "Honor to the President of the people's choice," and announcing that the trade which had been lost "by the blundering diplomacy of the coalition administration" had been restored "by the upright, able, and honest administration of Andrew Jackson." But more than one critic, pointing to the import duties which the United States would have to pay, complained that the alleged victory was more apparent than real. "A few more such *bargains*," growled a Baltimore editor, "and we may lay our shipping up in dry dock."

Admirers of "Old Hickory" have attributed his success to blunt and soldierly methods. However that may be, it is clear that the trend of international events played into Jackson's hands. The stiff-necked Canning had died in 1827, and Lord Aberdeen, who became Foreign Secretary the next year, was much more tractable. As a result of unforeseen economic changes, British faith in the time-hallowed navigation laws was definitely weakening, while demands of the West Indies themselves for American foodstuffs and lumber were not without influence.[12] It was Jackson's good fortune to inherit the West Indian problem just at the time when Britain's economic distresses made concessions possible.

THE FRENCH CLAIMS CONTROVERSY

The redoubtable hero of New Orleans ran much truer to form in his energetic handling of claims against France—claims that had grown out of the wholesale spoliations of American commerce during the wars following the outbreak of the French Revolution. For nearly two decades the United States had made repeated but unavailing efforts to secure pecuniary redress. This persistence was finally rewarded, in 1831, when the French signed a treaty agreeing to pay 25,000,000 francs in six annual installments. In March, 1833, when the first payment fell due, the Secretary of the Treasury drew a draft which the French finance minister refused to honor on the excellent grounds that the French Chambers had not appropriated the necessary funds.[13] The remissness of that body became more serious

---

[12] V. G. Setser, *The Commercial Reciprocity Policy of the United States, 1774–1829* (Phila., 1937), p. 230.

[13] The Bank of the United States assessed the Washington government nearly $170,000 for having presented a worthless instrument. Bearing in mind Jackson's

when, in April, 1834, it flatly refused to vote the first payment.

By this time Jackson was thoroughly aroused. "I know them French," he was reported to have shouted. "They won't pay unless they're made to." He decided to end all this shilly-shally (two payments had already been defaulted) by laying the whole matter before Congress in his annual message of December, 1834. The passage relating to French claims was couched in the most vigorous terms, and declared that if the payments were not voted at the next session of the Chambers a law should be passed authorizing the United States government to "seize" French property.[14]

The publication of this defiant pronouncement caused a surge of jingoistic excitement to sweep over the United States. Democrats acclaimed the fighting words of their fighting hero; but the Whigs, especially those who faced heavy commercial losses from war and rumors of war, condemned the message in such terms as "bad taste," "injudicious," "coarse and offensive," and "legalized piracy." Securities fell, and marine insurance companies refused to assume risks resulting from a war with France. Jackson's senatorial foes, led by the impassioned Henry Clay, pointed to this wild outburst as one more conspicuous example of the doughty general's unfitness for the presidency. Although Whig opposition in the Senate helped block defense measures, the country on the whole seems to have responded favorably to "Old Hickory's" sensational attempt to deal vigorously with the problem. Even the Whig *National Gazette*, an opposition newspaper, sided with the President, declaring, "We have negotiated enough,—more than enough: we are indisputably in the right . . . and the French government in the wrong. . . . The American people will, we doubt not, ratify this sentence of the Message." [15]

EXPLANATIONS WITHOUT APOLOGIES

However much young America may have applauded Jackson's smashing tactics, Gallic sensibilities were deeply hurt. The French

hatred for this institution, we must credit him with considerable restraint in not having exploded then and there. J. S. Bassett, *The Life of Andrew Jackson* (Garden City, N.Y., 1911), II, 667.

[14] Henry A. Wise records that when Jackson's advisers surreptitiously attempted to soften the wording the President shouted, "That, sir, is not my language; it has been changed, and I will have no other expression of my own meaning than my own words." The confidential proofreader reported that he did not know what sulphurous swearing was until this incident occurred. H. A. Wise, *Seven Decades of the Union* (Phila., 1881), p. 146.

[15] Quoted in E. B. White, *American Opinion of France* (N.Y., 1927), p. 99.

"A Hickory apology": "Old Hickory," egged on by Neptune, with warships in the background, threatens King Louis Philippe of France, whose crown is about to fall off, while a group of French frogs condemn the insulting American. (Courtesy of The New York Historical Society, New York City.)

minister in Washington demanded his passports and left the legation in the hands of a *chargé*. The French Chambers, stung to the quick, passed the belated appropriation, but with the proviso that the money was not to be paid until the language of the President's message was satisfactorily explained. This merely served to arouse Jackson further. He may not, as reported, have roared, "Apologize! I'd see the whole race roasting in hell first"; but it was quite evident that the hero of New Orleans was no man to eat his words. "France will get no apology," cried the powerful Washington *Globe*, "nothing bearing even the remotest resemblance to one." Throughout the United States popular excitement ran high. The slogans of the hour were: "Hurrah for Jackson!" "No explanations!" and "No apologies!"

The situation steadily drifted from bad to worse. The United States minister to France came home, and in November, 1835, the American *chargé* in Paris asked for his passports. Two months later, in January, 1836, the French *chargé* in Washington, Alphonse Pageot, returned to France with an infant son bearing the proud name of Andrew Jackson Pageot.[16] Diplomatic relations were completely suspended.

Both nations had now got themselves into a dangerous impasse. Neither could give way without an intolerable sacrifice of national pride. Vigorous naval preparations were undertaken in the United States; and the French government dispatched a special squadron for the protection of its West Indies. Faced with this ominous situation, and again exercising what was for him admirable self-restraint, Jackson attempted to make explanations without apologies in his annual message of December, 1835. The nearest that he came to an apology —and even this must have gone sorely against the grain—may be sought for in this passage: "The conception that it was my intention to menace or insult the Government of France is as unfounded as the attempt to extort from the fears of that nation what her sense of justice may deny would be vain and ridiculous." Lest this seem too much like obsequiousness, he hastened to add:

[16] Pageot had married the daughter of a bosom friend of Jackson. There is, indeed, much about this whole affair to suggest the *opéra bouffe*. The story is probably apocryphal that Jackson flared up when he saw "je demande" (meaning simply "I request") in a French note and shouted, "They demand, do they?" But it is true that the Washington government was irked because the French used the word *prétendu* in connection with American claims. The French foreign minister found it necessary to write a formal note solemnly explaining that the offensive word was not intended to mean "pretended" in the English sense. See Marquis James, *Andrew Jackson: Portrait of a President* (Indianapolis, 1937), pp. 386–405.

The honor of my country shall never be stained by an apology from me for the statement of truth and the performance of duty; nor can I give any explanation of my official acts except such as is due to integrity and justice and consistent with the principles on which our institutions have been framed.[17]

When 1836 dawned the passions of both the United States and France had perceptibly cooled. Both nations were now obviously willing to make concessions, provided they could do so without loss of face. The embarrassing deadlock was finally broken, in January, 1836, by the friendly mediation of the British. They did not want to see their ally, France, waste her strength in a fruitless war with the United States.[18] Again Europe's distresses operated to America's advantage. The French found that their wounded honor had been satisfied by Jackson's "explanatory" messages, and both disputants were now able gracefully to abandon their high ground. France arranged to pay the money; and Alphonse Pageot returned to Washington with little Andrew Jackson Pageot.

Probably at no time during the controversy was war really imminent. The dispute was too trivial; its cause was superficial rather than fundamental. Neither nation could gain from war; each stood to lose much. Nevertheless, where proud peoples are involved, offended national honor is a dangerous combustible. During the critical stage of the controversy John Quincy Adams expressed the opinion that "if the two countries be saved from war, it seems as if it could only be by a special interposition of Providence." [19] Similar fears were expressed in both London and Paris. But too much credence must not be given the excited observations of contemporaries.

In reviewing the whole serio-comedy it seems that, from a diplomatic viewpoint, the irascible old man in the White House was unnecessarily provocative. In part because he had never been abroad, Jackson did not fully realize that if the French ministry yielded too quickly on the unpopular American claims it would be thrown out of power. Nevertheless, his direct methods had the virtue of getting the money. By arousing the support of a public opinion that had

[17] J. D. Richardson, ed., *Messages and Papers of the Presidents* (Washington, 1896), III, 157, 160 (Dec. 7, 1835).

[18] See C. K. Webster, "British Mediation between France and the United States, 1834–36," *Eng. Hist. Rev.*, XLII (1927), 58–78.

[19] C. F. Adams, ed., *Memoirs of John Quincy Adams* (Phila., 1876), IX, 217 (March 7, 1835).

hitherto been apathetic, he patched up a difference that might ultimately have caused a violent rupture, and he created a new respect
in European chancelleries for the vigor of the hitherto underrated
United States.

ASSISTING IN THE ABOLITION OF MONARCHY

Jackson picked as his successor Martin Van Buren, the ingratiating
"Little Magician" from New York, who has not inaptly been described as a "first-class second-rate man." Before his first year in office
had ended, the new President was confronted with extremely grave
problems growing out of the unsuccessful Canadian insurrection of
1837.

Large numbers of people in the United States, particularly in the
northern states, enthusiastically applauded what they incorrectly regarded as the attempt of the Canadians to cast off the British yoke.
Hostile to monarchy anywhere, Americans were flattered to think of
this rebellion as the second chapter of their own glorious War of
Independence. Moreover, along the northern border there was a
strong New England Puritan element which felt a powerful missionary urge to carry the blessings of republicanism to its "benighted"
Canadian neighbor.[20] But enthusiasm in the United States was not
wholly unselfish. If, with the help of America's sturdy sons, the
Canadians should succeed in winning their independence, what would
be more logical than the union of the two English-speaking peoples
under "Old Glory"?

The British military forces and the Canadian militia were able to
cope with the insurrectionist forces, which represented a small minority, without much difficulty. But south of the border the still-
glowing embers of Anglophobia were fanned to a flame by sympathy for the underdog, by the failure of the rebels, and by exaggerated reports of the severity of their punishment. In addition, the
panic of 1837 had thrown a large number of Americans out of work,
particularly along the northern waterfront, and these hardy characters
were both irresponsible and desperate. Many of them, lured by prom-

---

[20] W. P. Shortridge, "The Canadian-American Frontier during the Rebellion of
1837–1838," *Canadian Hist. Rev.*, VII (1926), 16. The Montreal *Transcript* (Dec.
23, 1837) declared: "The . . . statements of the . . . American press . . . leave
no longer any doubt of a hostile feeling along, and within, the American frontier—a
cherished hope of perpetuating their own blind prejudices at the expense of the British Government, which, with all its noble characteristics, has in *their* eyes the damning
sin of being a monarchy." Quoted in *ibid.*, p. 16 n.

ises of land ranging from 160 to 320 acres, flocked noisily to the rebel banner.

On the American side of the border the Canadian sympathizers were so numerous, and federal officials so few, that the United States authorities, however zealous, found it impossible to preserve strict neutrality. American citizens, singing the "Marseillaise," openly enlisted in the rebel forces on United States soil, while mobs emptied several American arsenals and turned over their contents to the insurrectionists. The defeated William L. Mackenzie, leader of the rebellion in Upper Canada, found refuge in Buffalo, where, from his headquarters at the Eagle Tavern, the insurgent flag was flung to the breeze.

A COUNTERVIOLATION OF NEUTRALITY

With American help Mackenzie re-established himself on Navy Island, a small dot of land on the Canadian side of the Niagara River, a short distance above the great falls. A small American steamer, the *Caroline*, was engaged to carry supplies from the New York shore to the rebel rendezvous. The British were naturally annoyed by this unneutral assistance; and on the night of December 29, 1837, a volunteer party rowed across to the New York side, overpowered the men on board the *Caroline*, set fire to the vessel, and let it drift to destruction.[21] The Canadian loyalists and the British roundly applauded this bold act, and the officer responsible for it was knighted.

It is unquestionably true that the *Caroline* had been engaged in unneutral activity. But the seriousness of the offense was somewhat mitigated by the fact that the vessel had made only three trips to Navy Island, all on the afternoon of the day on which she was destroyed.[22] Yet the British took matters into their own hands without even protesting to the American authorities and without giving them an opportunity to act. Such hasty conduct would have been more defensible if the *Caroline* had been doing considerable damage to the British cause; but the rebellion had already been hopelessly crushed and the steamer had carried only a negligible amount of material to the insurgents.

---

[21] Contrary to the traditional accounts, the *Caroline* did not go over the falls but sank a mile or two above them. See Alastair Watt, "The Case of Alexander McLeod," *Canadian Hist. Rev.*, XII (1931), 146. Current American propaganda, pictorial and otherwise, had the vessel plunging to destruction with a number of trapped men on board.

[22] O. E. Tiffany, "The Relations of the United States to the Canadian Rebellion of 1837-1838," *Buffalo Hist. Soc. Pubs.*, VIII (1905), 33.

The destruction of an American vessel in American waters by a British force, with the killing of one American (Amos Durfee) and the wounding of others, set the border ablaze. Durfee's draped body was put on public display in Buffalo, and the funeral was widely advertised by coffin-shaped placards. "In recording this horrid tragedy," asserted the Rochester *Democrat*, "we dare not give utterance to our feelings; but we must say that if this outrage be not speedily avenged —not by simpering diplomacy—BUT BY BLOOD our national honor deserves the indignity it has received." [23] There can be no doubt that the British, in arousing a dangerously retaliatory spirit on the American side, harmed their own cause far more than a dozen *Carolines* could have done.

President Van Buren promptly issued a proclamation urging Americans to observe the neutrality laws, and summoning those who had enlisted under the Canadian banner (large numbers had done so in anger over the *Caroline* affair) to return home. He vigorously followed up the proclamation by sending General Winfield Scott to the border and requesting the governors of New York and Vermont to call their militia into service.

A number of the most influential Eastern newspapers, though greatly angered by the *Caroline* incident, advised caution. Indeed, the farther one traveled from the border, the less disposition one found to condemn the British invasion of American soil. The New York *Evening Star*, the New York *Commercial Advertiser*, and the Boston *Times* told their excited countrymen bluntly that the Americans themselves were largely to blame for the existing situation. As the Boston *Times* pointedly remarked, "It makes a vast deal of difference whose bull it was that gored the ox." [24]

Meanwhile the diplomats had not been idle. In Washington, the Secretary of State protested strongly against this "extraordinary outrage." The British minister refused to be drawn into the argument, and quite properly referred the matter to the London government. But his private observations to the home authorities reveal that the "international derelict" argument, which Adams had used to justify the Florida invasion, could be turned against the United States. Curiously enough, the news of the destruction of the *Caroline* did not arouse much interest in England, and there was only one brief reference to it in Parliament. The opinion was even expressed in certain

[23] Quoted in Watt, "Alexander McLeod," *loc. cit.*, p. 162.

[24] Shortridge, "The Canadian-American Frontier," *loc. cit.*, p. 18. As late as November, 1838, a broadside advertising a public meeting in behalf of "The Patriots of Canada" was issued in Washington, D.C. File 196, Library of Congress.

quarters that the mother country would do well to cut loose completely from Canada. The British government, however, continued to believe that it had acted in necessary self-defense, and it put off the demands of the United States for reparation and apology. But this delay was probably all for the best. It gave passions an opportunity to cool and enabled both nations to weather the *Caroline* crisis without resorting to arms.

RAIDS AND REPRISALS

Early in 1838 tension along the border was greatly eased by the almost complete stamping out of the Canadian rebellion. But throughout the ensuing months a number of provocative incidents occurred, notably the destruction of a Canadian vessel, the *Sir Robert Peel*, while plying within American jurisdiction on the St. Lawrence. Operating on the principle of "a steamboat for a steamboat," a party of disguised Americans boarded, looted, and burned the Canadian vessel, in May, 1838, yelling to the half-dressed passengers set ashore, "Remember the *Caroline*." [25]

Nervous excitement was further stimulated during the summer of 1838 by the organization of Hunters' Lodges along the American side of the border from Vermont to Michigan. Their membership embraced thousands of men (the estimates ran from 15,000 to 200,000), and their announced purpose was "to emancipate the British Colonies from British Thraldom." A part of the elaborate oath read: ". . . I promise, until death, that I will attack, combat, and help to destroy . . . every power, or authority, of Royal origin, upon this continent; and especially never to rest till all tyrants of Britain cease to have any dominion or footing whatever in North America. . . . So help me God." [26] Because of the increasing vigilance of the federal authorities, this organization was necessarily secret, with a fantastic hierarchy of degrees and an elaborate system of secret signs, grips, badges, and passwords. In September, 1838, it elected officers for the future Canadian Republic, consoling the former captain of the *Caroline* with the title of Admiral of Lake Erie.

[25] Several weeks later the well-known British novelist, Captain Marryat, who was then visiting Canada, gave a toast complimentary to the men who had destroyed the *Caroline*. The excited people of Lewistown, New York, held a town meeting, and resolved to burn all of Marryat's books that could be found. This was done with appropriate ceremony. Allan Nevins, ed., *The Diary of Philip Hone, 1828–1851* (N.Y., 1936), p. 323 (May 5, 1838).

[26] Charles Lindsey, *Life and Times of William Lyon Mackenzie* (Toronto, 1862), II, 199.

The Hunters, who confidently expected the Canadians to rise up and hail them as deliverers, projected a number of schemes for invasion. General Winfield Scott, an impressive figure of a man and a gifted pacificator, did yeoman's work in traveling up and down eight hundred miles of the frontier and using his great personal influence to soothe inflamed feelings.[27] Despite his generally successful efforts, several armed bands crossed the border in November ("Battle of the Windmill") and December of 1838. They were easily dispersed, and a number of them were shipped off to the penal colony in Van Diemen's Land, the present Tasmania.[28] From then on the influence of the Hunters, although still considerable, definitely waned; and by early 1839 the Administration in Washington could congratulate itself on having the situation well in hand.

THE WILL TO MAINTAIN PEACE

Van Buren has been severely criticized, particularly by Canadians, for having permitted such a great amount of unneutral activity. But when one considers the many miles of border, the inflammation of the popular mind, the small number of federal officials, and the inadequacy of the American neutrality laws, the Administration deserves credit for a sincere and vigorous attempt to maintain its international obligations. Aside from the precautions that we have already observed, Van Buren directed a vigorous prosecution of those Americans who had violated the neutrality laws. The highly popular "General" Rensselaer Van Rensselaer, one of the American ringleaders, was convicted by an American jury and sentenced to a year's imprisonment. Although Van Buren finally yielded to the pressure of 300,000 petitioners and issued a pardon, he waited until after the presidential election of 1840. There can be no doubt that the President's faithful discharge of the duties of his office hurt him politically. The influence of Canadian sympathizers, particularly of the Hunters, whose cry was "Woe to Martin Van Buren," undoubtedly contributed to his defeat in 1840.[29]

It is probably true that Great Britain and the United States were

[27] C. W. Elliott, *Winfield Scott* (N.Y., 1937), pp. 337-344.

[28] A public meeting in the city of Buffalo resolved "that Great Britain, in hanging, shooting or transporting American citizens who were assisting the Canadian revolutionists has infringed upon the rights of free men." H. L. Keenleyside, *Canada and the United States* (N.Y., 1929), p. 115.

[29] Tiffany, "Relations of the United States to the Canadian Rebellion," *loc. cit.*, pp. 105-106.

closer to hostilities during these years than is generally realized. Any one of a number of incidents might have been regarded as a legitimate cause of war—had the two nations been looking for war. But neither Power had a fundamental grievance; and neither wanted to fight. What is more, the British officials realized that the United States government was making a sincere attempt to restrain its overenthusiastic citizens. Probably a clash did not come because a will to keep the peace was present on both sides.

BIBLIOGRAPHICAL NOTE

A reasonably detailed treatment of the diplomacy of the period from 1825 to 1840 may be found in S. F. Bemis, ed., *The American Secretaries of State and their Diplomacy* (N.Y., 1928), IV, 115–343. On the Panama Congress see J. B. Lockey, *Pan-Americanism: Its Beginnings* (N.Y., 1920); and F. L. Reinhold, "New Research on the First Pan-American Congress Held at Panama in 1826," *Hispanic Amer. Hist. Rev.*, XVIII (1938), 342–363. For the relation of the Congress to the Monroe Doctrine see Dexter Perkins, *The Monroe Doctrine, 1823–26* (Cambridge, Mass., 1927), Ch. VI. On Canning's efforts to thwart the Americans consult H. W. V. Temperley, "The Later American Policy of George Canning," *Amer. Hist. Rev.*, XI (1906), 779–797; also J. F. Rippy, *Rivalry of the United States and Great Britain over Latin America, 1808–1830* (Baltimore, 1929). On the West Indies controversy the standard work is F. L. Benns, *The American Struggle for the British West India Carrying-Trade, 1815–1830* (Bloomington, Ind., 1923). On the French claims imbroglio see R. A. McLemore, *The French Spoliation Claims, 1816–1836; A Study in Jacksonian Diplomacy* (Nashville, Tenn., 1933). See also J. S. Bassett, *Life of Andrew Jackson* (N.Y., 1911), II, 663–673; and the racy chapter (XVIII) in Marquis James' *Andrew Jackson; Portrait of a President* (Indianapolis, 1937). For public opinion on the French imbroglio consult E. B. White, *American Opinion of France* (N.Y., 1927), Ch. IV. On the Canadian rebellion the most detailed study is O. E. Tiffany, "The Relations of the United States to the Canadian Rebellion of 1837–1838," *Buffalo Hist. Soc. Pubs.*, VIII (1905), 1–147. Briefer accounts appear in J. M. Callahan, *American Foreign Policy in Canadian Relations* (N.Y., 1937); and H. L. Keenleyside, *Canada and the United States* (N.Y., 1929). Further references: see footnotes of this chapter and Bemis and Griffin, *Guide*, pp. 238–240.

RECENT REFERENCES. Indispensable new works are A. P. Whitaker, *The United States and the Independence of Latin America* (on the Panama Congress); R. A. McLemore, *Franco-American Diplomatic Relations*; and A. B. Corey, *The Crisis of 1830–1842 in Canadian-American Relations*. For a detailed discussion of these and other references, see Bibliographical Appendix, p. 926.

NEW REFERENCES. General background material on this period appears in Ch. VIII of J. B. Brebner, *North Atlantic Triangle* (New Haven, 1945).

4TH ED. REFS. A full account of Adams' foreign policy as president appears in S. F. Bemis, *John Quincy Adams and the Foundations of American Foreign Policy* (N.Y., 1949).

CHAPTER XIV

Anglo-American Relations and the Webster–Ashburton Treaty

"The portraits of Webster and Ashburton that hang on the walls of the State Department at Washington commemorate two nego- tiators whose happy co-operation solved a problem the solution of which might, in the hands of lesser men, have been remitted to the sword."   James Bryce, 1914.

ANGLOPHOBIA COMES TO A HEAD

ILL FEELING between the United States and Great Britain neared the breaking point in the early forties. At bottom, there were the embers of 1776 and 1812, which Americans had assiduously kept alive. When Captain Hall, an Englishman, inspected a Boston school in 1827, a small boy was called upon to "speak" for the visitor's pleasure. The youth launched into a "furious philippic" against British tyranny. Three years later the distinguished French traveler, Alexis de Tocque- ville, observed that he could not conceive of a hatred more poisonous than that which the people of the United States felt for the mother country.

The atmosphere was in no wise improved when the Americans be- gan to borrow enormous sums of money from England to finance their ambitious schemes for internal improvements.[1] Rarely does the debtor cherish any love for the interest-exacting creditor; and it is not strange that during these years, and for a number of years to come, the contemptuously alliterative phrase, "bloated British bondholder," rolled from many an American tongue.

In England, there was no great love for a rebellious offspring whose most pronounced traits were regarded as swagger, arrogance, patriotic conceit, and a hemispheric appetite for neighboring territory. Often present was the jealous fear that a successful American democracy might prove an incendiary example to the inarticulate masses of

---

[1] By 1839 it was estimated that British subjects held between $110,000,000 and $165,000,000 in American securities. R. C. McGrane, *Foreign Bondholders and Amer- ican State Debts* (N.Y., 1935), p. 9.

England. Another prolific source of irritation was the absence of a copyright law in the United States to protect British writers against the flagrant pirating of their literary product. This situation became so intolerable that in 1836 fifty-six English authors petitioned Congress for copyright legislation, but in vain. It is not surprising that the members of this influential literary group should have dipped their pens in gall when writing of the United States.

During these troubled years tens of thousands of sturdy Britons were lured off to America by the promise of a more satisfying life— "three meat meals a day," they reported. The English upper classes, unwilling to lose their underpaid factory workers, naturally painted the United States in the blackest possible hues. These defamatory accounts were strengthened by the disastrous panic of 1837, which caused more than a half-dozen American states and one territory to default in their interest payments, or openly to repudiate their obligations. The British investing public, touched in the sensitive pocket nerve, poured the vials of its wrath upon this "nation of swindlers." The London *Punch* referred to the eagle as an "unclean bird" of "the vulture tribe" which was "extremely fatal to the large species of goose called the Creditor. . . ." [2] The Reverend Sydney Smith wrote to the London *Morning Chronicle:*

I never meet a Pennsylvanian [Pennsylvania had defaulted] at a London dinner without feeling a disposition to seize and divide him. . . . How such a man can set himself down at an English table without feeling that he owes two or three pounds to every man in the company, I am at a loss to concede; he has no more right to eat with honest men than a leper has to eat with clean men. . . . [3]

THE WAR OF THE QUARTERLIES

Fuel for the flames was supplied in abundance by a steady procession of British travelers who came to the United States. They viewed the rustic scene so unsympathetically as to raise the suspicion that they were hired lampooners sent over by the British government to discourage emigration. These transatlantic visitors were struck with the

[2] *Punch* (London), X, 238 (1846).

[3] Quoted in McGrane, *Foreign Bondholders,* p. 59. The London *Times* reported in October, 1844, that an American gentleman had been refused admission to a prominent London club on the sole grounds "that he belonged to a republic that did not fulfill its engagements." The poet Wordsworth, whose family had lost heavily in American bonds, expressed his views in two sonnets, "Men of the Western World" (1842) and "To the Pennsylvanians" (1845).

dirt, discomfort, and crudity of life in America (pigs ran wild in the streets of New York); with the general ignorance, shiftlessness, corrupt speech ("nasal jargon"), money grubbing, food bolting ("gobble, gulp and go is the order of the day"), quarrelsomeness, godlessness, and boastfulness ("lick all creation"). British observers were invariably struck with the prevalence of tobacco chewing ("the salivary propensity"), as well as the noisy, undiscriminating and none too accurate "cataract" of juice. They were scandalized by revival meetings, gambling, drunkenness, fisticuffs, dueling, cattle rustling, lynching, slave beating, and gouging (the gouging out of opponents' eyes in free-for-all fighting). The general theme of these self-appointed critics was that America had only to be seen to be despised.

The best known of the British travelers was the beloved Charles Dickens, whose host of American admirers tendered him a rousing welcome in 1842. But the author of *Pickwick Papers*, smarting from the absence of copyright laws and from heavy losses in his American investments, was not disposed to view the United States through rose-colored spectacles. Although he made some pleasant observations, he also described in detail a number of disagreeable things that he actually saw. When the Americans learned how the distinguished author had repaid their hospitality, they were immensely angered. "If the scamp," growled a New York merchant, Philip Hone, "had no regard for his own character, he ought to have had for ours, who made fools of ourselves to do him honor." [4] In England, the caustic Carlyle wrote gleefully that "all Yankee-doodle-dom blazed up like one universal soda bottle."

The influential British quarterlies gave a prominent place to notices of these travel books, and their omniscient reviewers improved upon the criticisms of eyewitnesses. Even when an occasional favorable feature of American life was discovered, it was treated with infuriating condescension. Sneering references were made to America's cultural advance, to the "miasma of democracy," to the "tyranny of the majority," and to the degenerate "bipeds" and "mammals" who inhabited the United States. To some of the reviewers these convict-descended Yankees were an "anarchic, godless, brutal crew," who spent their time cutting razor strops from the backs of still-living Indians. Particularly offensive to the South were the bitter criticisms of slavery and the slave trade; [5] and nothing short of maddening were the confident predic-

[4] Allan Nevins, ed., *The Diary of Philip Hone* (N.Y., 1936), p. 673 (Oct. 12, 1843).

[5] Jefferson was even accused of selling his own illegitimate black offspring under

tions that in time all Americans would be of a light chocolate hue.

The American journals, led by the *North American Review*, naturally took up the cudgels for their native land, and the wordy "war of the quarterlies" was on. Retort led to rejoinder in an ever-widening circle. The strongest American reply was to point to deficiencies in British society, including cockney English, political corruption, prize fighting, and class servility. A common language may draw nations together; but in this case it was a barrier because the people of each country were able to read the highly offensive descriptions written in the other. Ill feeling reached an extremely dangerous point.

One of the most potent factors working for peace—perhaps the most potent—was the economic interdependence of the two nations. Violent though the warmongers became on both sides, thinking men saw that hostilities would result in a disastrous commercial dislocation. The Americans were England's best customers, importing approximately fifteen per cent of her total exports. And Britain was heavily dependent upon the United States for raw materials, annually consuming about fifty per cent of its cotton crop, without which the whirling spindles of the textile centers would be stilled.[6] In short, each nation had given a hostage to the other. Even so, diplomacy could afford to make no false steps.

A Lumberjack War

As if the unfortunate incidents growing out of the Canadian rebellion of 1837 were not enough, the perennial Maine boundary dispute flared up again in 1838. Unable to reconcile the terminology of the Treaty of 1783 with realities, Great Britain and the United States had agreed in 1827 to submit the questions at issue to the King of the Netherlands. In 1831 the royal arbitrator, finding it impossible to hand down a judicial decision on the basis of the evidence then available, decided upon a compromise, which amounted roughly to splitting the difference. The people of Maine, who expected to get more than was awarded to them, protested vehemently against the proposed loss of

the hammer. A Southern magazine struck back at the *Edinburgh Review:* "Has this journal no pity upon its white slaves at home, that it should come across the ocean to shed its crocodile tears over the negro, whose dog is provided with more meat in a day than the British subject gets in a week?" *De Bow's Review*, X (1851), 513. As late as 1869 the *Fortnightly Review* accused Americans of cannibalism at the expense of the Indians.

[6] The textile industry had been vitally dependent upon Southern cotton since 1823. T. P. Martin, "Cotton and Wheat in Anglo-American Trade and Politics, 1846–1852," *Jour. of Southern Hist.*, I (1935), 293.

their territory.[7] On June 21, 1832, the United States Senate, responding to the outcry from Maine, declined by a vote of 21 to 20 to accept the recommendations of the King of the Netherlands. The principal objection raised was that he had made a political rather than a judicial decision. There the matter rested.

As the year 1838 approached, England betrayed increasing interest in the disputed area. During the recent Canadian insurrection, as well as during the War of 1812, British troop movements had been hampered by the freezing of the St. Lawrence in the winter. A military road from St. John and Halifax to Quebec and Montreal seemed to be imperatively necessary. The most practicable route ran through that part of the Maine salient, north of the St. John River, which was claimed by the Americans. A crisis was precipitated when, in February, 1839, a party of Canadian lumberjacks began operations on the Aroostook River, within the disputed area. Warned to depart, they seized the United States agent and stood their ground. Heavy-fisted American lumbermen moved into the no man's land singing lustily:

> Britannia shall not rule the Maine,
> Nor shall she rule the water;
> They've sung that song full long enough,
> Much longer than they oughter.[8]

Maine called out her militia; [9] New Brunswick did likewise. The Nova Scotia legislature, amid singing of "God Save the Queen," voted war credits. The fever spread to Washington, where Congress appropriated $10,000,000 and authorized the President to summon 50,000 volunteers. Even the mild-mannered Senator Buchanan of Pennsylvania exclaimed:

> . . . If war must come, it will find the country unanimous. On the part of Great Britain, it will be a war of pure aggression, waged, during the pendency of peaceful negotiations. . . . In such an event, the only alternative is war or national dishonor; and between these two, what American can hesitate? [10]

---

[7] H. S. Burrage, *Maine in the Northeastern Boundary Controversy* (Portland, Maine, 1919), pp. 167–168.

[8] J. T. Faris, *The Romance of the Boundaries* (N.Y., 1926), p. 4.

[9] One loyal Maine man asseverated: ". . . I had rather see our state *deluged in blood*, and every field bleached with the bones of our citizens, than that we should retrace our footsteps and submit to British arrogance." Niles' *Weekly Register*, LVI, 18 (March 9, 1839).

[10] *Cong. Globe*, 25 Cong., 3 sess., p. 239 (March 2, 1839).

Fortunately, the Aroostook "war" proved bloodless. President Van Buren sent to the danger zone his trusted pacificator, General Winfield Scott, who succeeded (March, 1839) in arranging a truce, during which neither side was to abandon its claims.[11] But this dispute was potentially too dangerous, as diplomats on both sides of the Atlantic now perceived, to be allowed to drift along indefinitely.

THE CASE OF ALEXANDER McLEOD

By the beginning of 1840 the tension in Anglo-American relations had been greatly eased. Popular excitement growing out of the Canadian insurrection had largely died down. But the fat was once more thrown into the fire when, in November, 1840, Alexander McLeod, a Canadian accused of participation in the *Caroline* raid, was arrested in New York state and imprisoned on charges of murder and arson.[12]

Great was the indignation of the British government (the spirited Palmerston was now Foreign Secretary) when it learned of the arrest. Downing Street made vigorous representations on the grounds that the party which had attacked the "pirates" on the *Caroline* was a regular military expedition, and that the participants, even assuming that the prisoner had been among them, could not properly be held for murder. The immediate release of McLeod was "formally demanded," and it was made clear that most serious consequences would follow should the United States refuse this request.

But Palmerston had reckoned without the peculiarities of the American federal system. The state of New York had sole jurisdiction over the prisoner; and Washington was powerless to intervene. The national government did, however, bring strong pressure to bear on New York to secure the release of McLeod, or the transfer of his case to a federal court. But feeling over the *Caroline* and other incidents was still too bitter to permit such a course. One member of the New York legislature insisted that "there was not power enough—there was not gold enough in Great Britain to take this man's body out of the county of Niagara, until he shall have gone through the form of a trial." [13] So the state of New York stood defiantly on its legal rights, and, ut-

[11] C. W. Elliott, *Winfield Scott* (N.Y., 1937), pp. 358–366.

[12] The traditional story that McLeod boasted of his exploit while under the influence of liquor is refuted by Alastair Watt, "The Case of Alexander McLeod," *Canadian Hist. Rev.*, XII (1931), 165–167.

[13] Albany *Argus*, April 19, 1841, quoted in Niles' *Weekly Register*, LX, 135 (May 1, 1841).

terly disregarding the consequences, went ahead with the trial.[14]

Feeling ran dangerously high in England. Public opinion found it difficult to believe that in a matter concerning foreign affairs the United States government was not sovereign. Widely echoed was the cry of the London *Times* that McLeod must be surrendered if alive, avenged if dead. The British dockyards became ominously active. The stock market fell. The swaggering Palmerston, greatly exercised over what he regarded as an impending "judicial murder," wrote plainly to the British minister in Washington: "McLeod's execution would produce war, war immediate and frightful in its character, because it would be a war of retaliation and vengeance." [15] And in Canada the Montreal *Courier* hurled defiance: ". . . If war must come, let it come at once, for it is very evident unless we settle all our disputes now, it will only be putting off the evil day to a period when we may not be so well prepared to deal with our wilful and headstrong neighbors." [16]

Meanwhile McLeod, with counsel provided by the government of Canada, went before a Utica jury. The town was full of strangers; there was some talk of lynching. Daniel Webster, now Secretary of State, took precautions to protect the prisoner, writing: ". . . It becomes us to take all possible care that no personal violence be used on McLeod. If a mob should kill him, War w'd be inevitable, in ten days. Of this there is no doubt." [17] Fortunately, the trial went ahead in an orderly fashion. Fortunately, also, the prosecution brought a weak and inconsistent case against McLeod, who stoutly maintained that he was five or six miles distant at the time of the raid. His alibi was convincing, for an American jury, obviously not prejudiced in his favor, took only twenty minutes to return a verdict of not guilty, October 12, 1841.[18]

We must not conclude that McLeod's conviction would necessarily have resulted in war. The British government was determined to take extreme measures only in the event of his execution.[19] Had the de-

---

[14] As a result of this experience Congress passed a law in 1842 providing that persons accused of crimes committed under the orders of a foreign state shall be tried in the federal courts. But there still remained many other opportunities for the states to embroil the federal government in their treatment of aliens.

[15] H. L. Bulwer and Evelyn Ashley, *The Life of Henry John Temple, Viscount Palmerston* (London, 1874), III, 49 (Palmerston to Fox, Feb. 9, 1841).

[16] Niles' *Weekly Register*, LX, 368 (Aug. 7, 1841).

[17] J. W. McIntyre, ed., *The Writings and Speeches of Daniel Webster* (National ed., Boston, 1903), XVI, 344 (Webster to Tyler, July, 1841).

[18] Watt, "Alexander McLeod," *loc. cit.*, p. 159.

[19] The British minister, Fox, was instructed to leave the United States should McLeod be executed. President Tyler took the extraordinary step of informing Fox

fendant been found guilty, his counsel could have tried the remaining legal expedients. And as a last resort, Governor Seward of New York probably would have pardoned the unhappy Canadian—at least, so he confidentially informed Webster.

LORD ASHBURTON AND THE "GODLIKE DANIEL"

Even with the removal of the Canadian insurrection and the Mc-Leod affair as active irritants, the outlook by the end of 1841 was still ominous. The smoldering Maine dispute was liable to flare up again at any time; the rankling *Caroline* raid remained unatoned for; and the call from the West for the occupation of Oregon (then jointly held with Britain) was becoming more insistent. Another problem also loomed large. The British, in an effort to stop the African slave trade, were attempting to establish a right to search American merchantmen in time of peace—an innovation that brought back memories of the pre-1812 days and deeply offended nationalistic Americans.[20] The people of the South, sensitive on the question of the slave trade, were further aroused by an incident that occurred in November, 1841. The officers on board the *Creole,* an American brig sailing from Hampton Roads to New Orleans, were overpowered by the cargo of slaves, and one white passenger was killed. The Negroes then put into the British Bahamas. Despite the demands of the owners and the strong protests of Southerners generally, the British officials refused to turn the blacks over to the United States authorities. The actual murderers were, however, held for their crime.

Fortunately, the conciliatory and peace-loving Lord Aberdeen succeeded the aggressive Palmerston in September, 1841. The new Foreign Secretary realized that the vexed American situation needed the attention of a special envoy, and he made the extremely happy choice of Lord Ashburton. This gracious and tactful Briton, though not a professional diplomat, was distinguished both in the political and financial world. He had visited extensively in America, where he had met his future wife, a wealthy Philadelphia woman; and his numerous social and commercial connections with the United States had caused him to perceive as clearly as any other man in British public life the desirability of cultivating cordial relations with the Americans—a

that in this case his passports would not be granted, and that he would be detained until the British government had time to reflect on its course. J. M. Callahan, *American Foreign Policy in Canadian Relations* (N.Y., 1937), p. 178.

[20] H. G. Soulsby, *The Right of Search and the Slave Trade in Anglo-American Relations, 1814–1862* (Baltimore, 1933), pp. 51 *ff.*

course which he had conspicuously championed for many years. It is not surprising that the United States, on the whole, was gratified by the appointment. The sending of a special mission was in itself proof of an earnest desire to settle outstanding disputes; and the choice of so distinguished and sympathetic an envoy gave promise of a lasting adjustment. As Philip Hone, a prominent New York Whig, remarked:

This is an unusual piece of condescension on the part of our haughty elder sister. It will make Brother Jonathan feel his importance, and the devil is in it if it does not put him in a good humor. Besides the gracious nature of the act itself, the choice of the messenger of peace may be considered highly complimentary.[21]

By a fortunate coincidence, the political overturn in England that brought Aberdeen to the Foreign Office was preceded by a Whig triumph in America that brought William H. Harrison to the presidency and, as we have seen, Daniel Webster to the State Department. The new President died a month after taking office; and Vice-President Tyler, a Democrat in Whig clothing, launched out on such an independent course on internal issues that he was read out of the Whig party and branded a Benedict Arnold.[22] The entire Cabinet, with the exception of Webster, resigned; but the Secretary of State, then in the midst of delicate negotiations with Great Britain, stayed on through two trying years of partisan perplexities.

Daniel Webster was admirably fitted for the task at hand through taste, talent, and sympathetic regard for the mother country. In 1839 he had visited England, where he met many of the leading British

---

[21] Bayard Tuckerman, ed., *The Diary of Philip Hone* (N.Y., 1910), II, 110 (Jan. 24, 1842). There were, however, a few discordant notes from the foes of big banks (Ashburton was a financier), from those who feared that concessions would be made to Maine in return for the payment of the defaulted debts, and from die-hard Anglophobes. Charles Dickens, then in America, was impressed by a Sandusky, Ohio, newspaper which, on the occasion of Lord Ashburton's arrival, asserted that "as America had 'whipped' England in her infancy, and whipped her again in her youth, so it was clearly necessary that she must whip her once again in her maturity; and . . . that if Mr. Webster did his duty in the approaching negotiations, and sent the English Lord home again in double quick time, they should, within two years, sing 'Yankee Doodle in Hyde Park, and Hail Columbia in the scarlet courts of Westminster!'" Charles Dickens, *American Notes* (N.Y., 1921), p. 196.

[22] An epidemic of influenza sweeping the country was named the "Tyler grippe." At a dinner given in New York City to Lord Ashburton, a toast to the President was announced. No one stood except the British guest and his suite. When the health of the Queen was proposed, the assemblage arose and gave three cheers. C. M. Fuess, *Daniel Webster* (Boston, 1930), II, 117–118.

statesmen, including Lord Ashburton. The American's obvious intellectual power, his leonine head, his masterful mien, and his distinguished bearing made a striking impression. Sydney Smith, a merciless critic of the United States, is credited with the witticism that Webster "was a living lie, because no man on earth could be so great as he looked." Everywhere the American visitor was lionized; and it is not strange that he should have returned home in a mood of sweet reasonableness toward Great Britain.

CARTOGRAPHICAL LEVERS

For some little while Webster had realized that it would be impossible to accomplish in a few weeks of negotiation what a small army of diplomats, historians, geographers, cartographers, and surveyors had failed to do in fifty-nine years. Lord Ashburton agreed with him; and the two decided at the outset to set aside the mass of accumulated data and attempt to agree upon a compromise line. Without this decision there would probably have been no treaty—at least not an acceptable one.

Lord Ashburton then proposed that the two negotiators step down out of the Olympian atmosphere which usually surrounds diplomatic negotiations, and arrive at a decision through informal discussions rather than through a formal interchange of notes. Webster acquiesced, with the result that no protocols or minutes were kept, and the few official documents that the diplomats did exchange were largely agreed upon in advance. This arrangement undoubtedly facilitated the negotiations, although it left little for the disappointed historian to examine in later years.

The boundary question was greatly complicated by a curious local problem. Maine had once been a part of Massachusetts, and both states had large vested interests in the disputed area. Both were vehemently opposed to any concessions until fortune placed in Webster's hand a timely and extraordinarily effective lever. The year before the negotiations began, Jared Sparks, a distinguished American scholar, had discovered a map in the French archives on which the northeastern boundary of the United States was marked with a red line. There was some reason to believe that it had been put there by Franklin in 1782 to indicate the frontier agreed upon by the peace commissioners. If this were true, then the map could be used to substantiate British claims to all of the Maine territory in dispute. Sparks made a copy of this map for Webster, who had himself picked up another of more dubious origin, which also strengthened the British case.[23] This evidence was made known to the proper authorities in Maine, who at once perceived that if the settlement should be further delayed, the British might learn of the maps and use them with damaging effect. After considerable difficulty, both Maine and Massachusetts consented to accept a compromise line, and their representatives, seven in all, arrived in Washington in June, 1842.

Splitting the Difference

As the negotiations wore on, the stubbornness of the state commissioners, to whom Webster was constantly forced to defer, rather unnerved Lord Ashburton. No longer young and almost prostrated by the heat of a cruel Washington summer, the distinguished Briton found it increasingly difficult to understand why he should be involved in a quadrilateral negotiation, or why a presumably sovereign government should have to get permission from two of its component parts before dealing with a matter concerning foreign affairs. As he perspiringly but good-naturedly complained to Webster:

I contrive to crawl about in these heats by day and pass my nights in a sleepless fever. In short, I shall positively not outlive this affair, if it is to be much prolonged. I had hoped that these gentlemen from the northeast would be equally averse to this roasting. Could you not press them to come to the point, and say whether we can or cannot agree? I do not see why I should be kept waiting while Maine and Massachusetts settle their accounts with the General Government. . . . Pray save me from these profound politicians, for my nerves will not stand so much cunning wisdom.[24]

Even Webster, usually optimistic, became somewhat discouraged.

At length the commissioners from Maine and Massachusetts protestingly consented to a compromise boundary line, but only after they had been offered a number of equivalents, including the payment of $150,000 to each of the two states by the United States government.

---

[23] On the question of the maps see Hunter Miller, *Treaties and other International Acts of the United States of America* (Washington, 1934), IV, 403–413. Two recent writers have concluded that when Jared Sparks informed Webster of his red-line map he ruined "a perfectly good title to five thousand square miles of territory abandoned by the compromise." Lawrence Martin and S. F. Bemis, "Franklin's Red-Line Map was a Mitchell," *New Eng. Quar.*, X (1937), 111. This, of course, assumes that the British would have been willing to give up their projected military road even in the face of overwhelming cartographical evidence.

[24] G. T. Curtis, *Life of Daniel Webster* (5th ed., N.Y., 1889), II, 113 n. (July 1, 1842).

The puzzled Ashburton objected to inserting such purely domestic stipulations into a treaty between two sovereign nations. Logic was on his side—but not practical politics. Webster eventually persuaded him to acquiesce by explaining that such a provision was necessary to

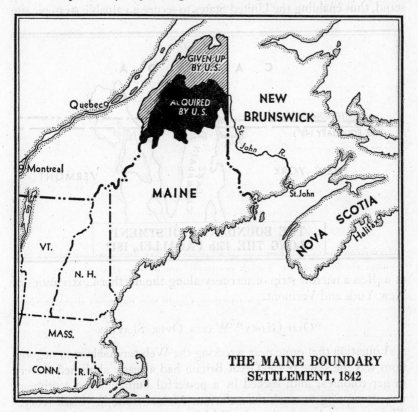

THE MAINE BOUNDARY
SETTLEMENT, 1842

secure the votes of the senators from Maine and Massachusetts when the treaty was submitted to the Senate.

The Maine boundary was finally settled by permitting Canada to have approximately 5000 of the 12,000 square miles of territory in dispute, thus insuring to the British their coveted military road.[25] To make this division more palatable, Lord Ashburton conceded the major portion of the American claim to approximately 200 square miles of land about the head of the Connecticut River, and arranged for a territorial adjustment along the 45th parallel. The latter controversy

[25] Maine would have received more than she finally obtained if the award of the King of the Netherlands (1831) had been accepted.

had arisen when a recent resurvey of the northern frontier revealed that a fort which the Americans were building at Rouses Point, at the head of Lake Champlain, was located on Canadian soil about half a mile north of the true line. Ashburton agreed to let the old boundary stand, thus enabling the United States to secure a valuable strategic site

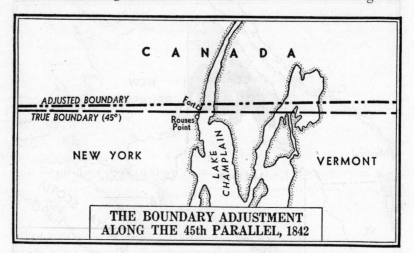

THE BOUNDARY ADJUSTMENT
ALONG THE 45th PARALLEL, 1842

as well as a narrow strip of territory along the northern extremities of New York and Vermont.

"OLD GLORY" WAVES OVER SLAVERS

A question that came near wrecking the Webster-Ashburton negotiations was the slave trade. Great Britain had already abolished slavery in her colonies; and, backed by a powerful humanitarian sentiment, was attempting to crush the nefarious African trade in "black ivory." The greatest obstacle that the British encountered was the American flag. A belligerent has a perfect right to search a neutral merchantman on the high seas in time of war; but in time of peace no such right exists unless specifically granted by treaty. A number of nations had already given Britain permission to search suspected slavers flying their flags.[26] But the United States, hypersensitive as to its maritime rights, refused to become a party to any such agreement. Thus it was that the American flag protected every slaver bold enough to raise it; and the Stars and Stripes waved from vessels so filthy that, in some cases, they could actually be smelled before they were sighted.

[26] *Cambridge History of British Foreign Policy* (Cambridge, Eng., 1923), II, 244.

The perpetuation of this scandalous traffic by the obduracy of the Americans was maddening to the British. They were forced to admit that there was no right of search in time of peace; but they attempted to establish the right to visit a suspected ship for the purpose of determining its true status. The United States insisted, however, that there was no essential difference between the two (Lord Aberdeen himself privately admitted this), and that the right of visit would inevitably become a wedge for asserting the odious right of search. If a British boarding officer could legally scrutinize the papers of a merchantman to determine its nationality, he would find it an easy step to examine the cargo, and perhaps impress a few American seamen. ". . . It is not African slavery, the United States wish to encourage," wrote Minister Cass, in France. "It is . . . American slavery, the slavery of American sailors, they seek to prevent." [27]

After prolonged discussions, Webster and Ashburton finally agreed upon a compromise. Each nation bound itself to keep a squadron with a total armament of no fewer than eighty guns on the African coast. Each would enforce its own laws on those merchantmen flying its flag, and both would act together when the necessity arose. Although the arrangement did not work out satisfactorily, owing in large part to the remissness of the United States in maintaining its naval force, it did relieve some of the tension caused by Britain's attempts to establish a right of visit in time of peace. [28]

ODDS AND ENDS

Webster and Ashburton also took up the subject of extradition, that is, the mutual return of fugitives from justice. The recent epidemic of disturbances along the northern border had been a painful reminder of the fact that the inadequate extradition provisions of the Jay Treaty had expired. It was finally agreed to include seven extraditable offenses of a nonpolitical nature in the Webster-Ashburton Treaty. Other crimes, including embezzlement, were not to be added until a number of years later, which explains why, during this period, "Gone to Canada" told the story of many an absconding bank clerk.

[27] Niles' *Weekly Register*, LXII, 54 (March 26, 1842). The fear was also expressed that Britain would use the right of visit to interrupt American trade. The South was afraid that Britain, flushed by a successful attack on slave trade, might next turn her guns upon American domestic slavery.

[28] Not until 1862, after the slaveholding South had seceded, was it possible for the United States to conclude a treaty with Great Britain arranging for a mutual right of search of suspected slavers in time of peace. Soulsby, *The Right of Search*, pp. 173–175.

In addition to the formal articles of the treaty, Webster and Ashburton made substantial progress on other matters through exchanges of notes. The question of the mutinous slaves who had been liberated when the _Creole_ reached the British Bahamas was so extraordinarily complicated as nearly to disrupt the entire negotiation. Although Ashburton had come without instructions to deal with the problem, Webster did persuade him to go so far as to promise that governors of the British colonies would be ordered to avoid "officious interference" with American vessels driven by accident or by violence into their ports. With these assurances, which did something to quiet dissatisfaction in the South growing out of the incident, Webster was content to let the matter drop.[29]

As for the _Caroline_ affair, Webster was unable to obtain complete satisfaction. The best he could do was to induce Ashburton, after lengthy discussions, to express "regret" that the event "should have disturbed the harmony" subsisting between Great Britain and America, and to add: "Looking back to what passed at this distance of time, what is, perhaps, most to be regretted is, that some explanation and apology for this occurrence was not immediately made. . . ."[30] A careful examination of this statement will reveal that Ashburton did not apologize. But he did use the word "apology"; and the resourceful Webster, in a reply obviously written primarily for home consumption, made it appear that the Briton had gone further than he really had.

While so many irritants were being disposed of, Webster attempted to wring from the British concessions on the long-dormant but vividly remembered practice of impressment. Lord Ashburton again revealed the willingness of the nonprofessional diplomat to discuss matters on which he had no instructions, and in his reply gave evidence of a desire to be conciliatory. But Foreign Secretary Aberdeen insisted upon upholding the full letter of British rights;[31] and nothing came of the interchange except, perhaps, to remind the British of American sensitiveness on this subject.

Lord Ashburton was authorized to bring up the matter of a fair division of the Oregon territory; but neither negotiator showed much enthusiasm for the subject. Webster was never deeply interested in

[29] The Anglo-American mixed claims commission ultimately awarded $110,330 to the United States for the slave property lost. See J. B. Moore, _Digest of International Law_ (Washington, 1906), II, 358–361.

[30] _Webster's Writings_ (National ed.), XI, 300 (Ashburton to Webster, July 28, 1842).

[31] E. D. Adams, "Lord Ashburton and the Treaty of Washington," _Amer. Hist. Rev._, XVII (1912), 777.

the Pacific Northwest; and Ashburton, who doubted whether the Americans would "for many years to come make any considerable lodgement on the Pacific," feared that an attempt to grapple with this knotty problem would endanger the other and more pressing negotiations. Each diplomat preferred to let well enough alone.[32]

A Solemn Bamboozlement?

Webster again made effective use of the magical Sparks map when he laid the treaty before the Senate. But several of the members refused to be browbeaten. James Buchanan of Pennsylvania lamented that on three sides Maine was now left "naked and exposed to the attacks of our domineering and insatiable neighbor." And Thomas Hart Benton of Missouri, who spoke for many Western expansionists, branded the treaty as a "solemn bamboozlement." Despite the intemperate criticism of the opposition, the treaty was approved on August 20, 1842, only eleven days after it was signed, by a vote of 39 to 9. Webster was pleasantly surprised, confessing that he did "not look for a majority quite so large." The news of the final ratification of the treaty by the British was greeted with salvos of artillery in New York, Brooklyn, and Jersey City; and the members of the New York Chamber of Commerce waited on Webster in a body to express their high appreciation.

The chief centers of dissatisfaction in the United States were naturally Massachusetts and Maine, particularly the eastern part of the latter state, where the treaty was regarded as a weak-kneed surrender.[33] Certain factors, however, combined to create an acquiescent sentiment. Among them may be mentioned the various equivalents (including the cash payments), a sense of obligation to the rest of the United States, and the clever employment by the State Department of special propaganda agents. In 1846 Webster could assert with some truth that there were not fifty respectable persons in Maine who wanted to see the treaty abrogated.[34]

[32] J. D. Richardson, ed., *Messages and Papers of the Presidents* (Washington, 1897), IV, 166. For Tyler's proposal to couple an Oregon settlement with California see p. 264 of the present volume.

[33] The Maine House of Representatives resolved: ". . . That the unquestionable right of the state to the whole of the territory embraced within her limits . . . ought never to have been submitted to arbitration; and, in the opinion of this house, to consent to another arbitration would be an abandonment of the rights and interests of Maine." Niles' *Weekly Register*, LXII, 374 (August 13, 1842).

[34] Fuess, *Daniel Webster*, II, 116.

THE BATTLE OF THE MAPS

As is inevitably true of compromises, the Webster-Ashburton Treaty was not completely satisfactory to either party. The Canadians assailed it, for they felt that, as in 1783 and 1814, they had been sacrificed on the altar of Anglo-American amity. In England, where the settlement was greeted with considerable relief, the opposition press was highly critical of concessions to the Yankee.[35] The London *Morning Chronicle* pointed out:

See the feeling with which the treaty has been received in America; mark the enthusiasm it has excited. What does this mean? Why, either that the Americans have gained a great diplomatic victory over us, or that they have escaped a great danger, as they have felt it, in having to maintain their claim by war.[36]

The belligerent Palmerston, now out of power, launched a sensational attack in the newspapers and in Parliament against what he branded the "Ashburton capitulation." In the heat of argument he went so far as to accuse the British negotiator of having fallen under the influence of his American wife. The opposition outburst rose to new heights when the existence of the Sparks map became known in England. Palmerston condemned Webster for his shyster-like duplicity in having withheld an important piece of evidence while professing a desire to arrive at a fair compromise.[37] At this point the confusion became worse confounded when another map turned up in England which strongly supported the American claim to the disputed area; and, what is more, its authenticity seemed more clearly established than that of Sparks. Thus, each party to the negotiation had secretly held its opponent's high card. The revealing of the British map had somewhat the same pacifying effect on the opposition as the Sparks map had produced on the two American states and the Senate.

It is unfair, however, to speak of the Treaty of 1842 as a "capitulation," whether referring to Webster or to Ashburton. Neither negotiator capitulated; both compromised. The territorial phases of the

[35] Adams, "Lord Ashburton and the Treaty of Washington," *loc. cit.*, p. 782.

[36] Quoted in Niles' *Weekly Register*, LXIII, 97 (Oct. 15, 1842).

[37] The two maps that Webster had were of doubtful authenticity, and their introduction would doubtless have made a settlement all the more difficult. Webster, as Ashburton agreed, was not ethically bound to hurt his client's case by presenting questionable evidence. As a matter of fact, it seems clear that Palmerston had learned of the British map as early as 1839, when he was Foreign Secretary. Miller, *Treaties*, IV, 409–410.

settlement represented a balancing of claims. It is true that the cartographical evidence now available proves that the United States was
entitled to the area north of Maine that the British received. Neither
negotiator knew this; and neither is to be blamed for not having acted
on the basis of yet undisclosed evidence. If America had insisted upon
her full claims, there probably would have been no treaty; and the
chances were excellent that there would have been war. The land
surrendered was of no vital value to a sprawling United States. If it
was the price of peace, as it may well have been, the republic obtained a
bargain.

The Webster-Ashburton Treaty had a wider significance than the
adjustment of a series of immediate problems. It resulted in a general
clearing away of the poisonous atmosphere that had enshrouded Anglo-
American relations, and it facilitated the amicable settlement of other
controversies that arose in the forties and fifties. And this happy result
was possible because the two diplomats approached their common
task in the spirit of judges seeking an equitable and lasting solution,
rather than as advocates attempting to overreach each other.

BIBLIOGRAPHICAL NOTE

The most detailed study of the Webster-Ashburton negotiations may be found
in Hunter Miller, ed., *Treaties and other International Acts of the United States
of America* (Washington, D.C., 1934), IV, 371–477. Briefer and more readable
is C. A. Duniway's "Daniel Webster," in S. F. Bemis, ed., *American Secretaries
of State and their Diplomacy* (N.Y., 1928), V, 3–53. A more popular account
appears in C. M. Fuess, *Daniel Webster* (Boston, 1930), II, Ch. XX. A careful
analysis of Lord Ashburton's instructions may be found in E. D. Adams, "Lord
Ashburton and the Treaty of Washington," *Amer. Hist. Rev.*, XVII (1912),
764–782. An excellent brief account of the "war of the quarterlies" appears in
J. B. McMaster, *A History of the People of the United States* (N.Y., 1900),
V, Ch. XLVIII. See also E. D. Adams, "The British Traveler in America,"
Pol. Sci. Quar., XXIX (1914), 244–264. A strong attack on British criticisms
is Gustavus Myers, *America Strikes Back* (N.Y., 1935). New light is thrown on
the McLeod trial by Alastair Watt, "The Case of Alexander McLeod," *Canadian
Hist. Rev.*, XII (1931), 145–167. On the aspect of slave trade herein discussed
the best study is H. G. Soulsby, *The Right of Search and the Slave Trade in
Anglo-American Relations, 1814–1862* (Baltimore, 1933). Further references:
see footnotes of this chapter and Bemis and Griffin, *Guide*, pp. 280–288.

RECENT REFERENCES. A. B. Corey's *The Crisis of 1830–1842 in Canadian-
American Relations* casts important new light on the Webster-Ashburton negotiations. For a detailed discussion of this work and of O. P. Chitwood's *John Tyler*,
see Bibliographical Appendix, p. 926.

NEW REFERENCES. See Bibliographical Appendix, p. 927.

4TH ED. REFS. See Bibliographical Appendix, p. 927.

CHAPTER XV

The Oregon Dispute and its Settlement

"The Rocky mountains are mere molehills. Our destiny is on-ward."

Congressman Robert Winthrop, 1845.

"WHERE ROLLS THE OREGON"

THE OREGON country was a magnificent expanse of territory embracing approximately a half million square miles. It lay west of the Rockies, north of the 42nd parallel (to which Spain had withdrawn following the Adams-Onís Treaty of 1819), and south of latitude 54° 40' (to which Russia had retreated as a result of the treaties of 1824 and 1825 with the United States and Great Britain respectively). Translated into present-day terms, Oregon included approximately half of British Columbia, all of the states of Washington, Oregon, and Idaho, and substantial portions of Montana and Wyoming.

With the elimination of Spain and Russia, the question of the ownership of Oregon narrowed down to the United States and Great Britain. The latter did not lay claim to the entire area, but looked forward to an equitable division with the United States. The British case was based primarily on the Nootka Convention signed with Spain in 1790; on the explorations of Cook, Vancouver, and Mackenzie; and on the establishment of fur-trading posts in the Oregon country. The American claims were supported by the Adams-Onís Treaty, which relinquished Spain's rights to the United States; by the explorations of Captain Gray, who in 1792 discovered the majestic river that bears the name of his ship, the *Columbia;* by the Lewis and Clark overland expedition of 1804–1806; by the establishment of the American fur-trading post at Astoria, in 1811; and by the principles of continuity and contiguity.[1]

---

[1] Hunter Miller, *Treaties and other International Acts of the United States of America* (Washington, 1937), V, 11–12. When the War of 1812 broke out the Americans at Astoria, learning that a British warship was on its way to seize the post, sold out to their British rivals of the Northwest Company. The Treaty of Ghent provided, however, for the *status quo ante bellum;* and Astoria was returned to the American flag.

Obviously, neither nation had a clear legal title to the whole region in dispute. With regard to discovery and exploration, as well as treaty rights, the claims of each nation more or less offset those of the other.

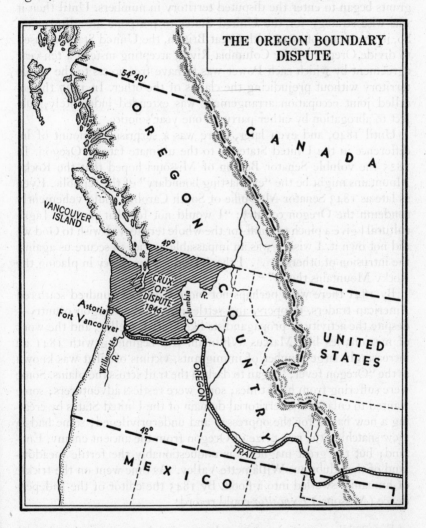

THE OREGON BOUNDARY DISPUTE

54°40'

C A N A D A

O R E G O N

VANCOUVER ISLAND

49°

O R E G O N   C O U N T R Y

CRUX OF DISPUTE 1846

Astoria
Fort Vancouver

Columbia R.

Willamette R.

UNITED STATES

OREGON TRAIL

42°

M E X I C O

But with regard to actual occupation there was little ground for dispute. By 1821 the powerful Hudson's Bay Company, a British organization, had become commercially and politically dominant in the entire Oregon country.

THE OREGON FEVER

The Oregon problem did not become acute until American immigrants began to enter the disputed territory in numbers. Until then it was wise strategy for the United States to postpone an adjustment. So, in the treaty of 1818 with Great Britain, the United States refused to divide Oregon by the Columbia River, accepting instead a ten-year agreement by which each Power was to have free access to the whole territory without prejudicing the claims of the other. In 1827 the so-called joint occupation arrangement was extended indefinitely, subject to abrogation by either party on one year's notice.

Until 1840, and even later, there was a surprising amount of indifference in the United States as to the ultimate fate of Oregon. In 1825 the voluble Senator Benton of Missouri hoped that the Rocky Mountains might be the "everlasting boundary" of the republic. Even as late as 1843 Senator McDuffie of South Carolina could vehemently condemn the Oregon country: "I would not for that purpose [agricultural] give a pinch of snuff for the whole territory. I wish to God we did not own it. I wish it was an impassable barrier to secure us against the intrusion of others. . . . I thank God for his mercy in placing the Rocky Mountains there." [2]

By 1841 there were perhaps not more than five hundred scattered American traders, trappers, and settlers in all the Oregon country—despite the activity of propagandists like Hall J. Kelley, and the work of missionaries like Marcus Whitman. But beginning with 1841 an increasingly large number of immigrants, victims of what was known as the "Oregon fever," began to darken the trail across the plains. Some were suffering from hard times; some were restless adventurers; some wanted to enlarge the territorial domain of the United States by creating a new haven for the oppressed and underprivileged; some had in view snatching the rich prize of Oregon from the ancient enemy, England; but the great magnet was unquestionably the fertile meadowland of the salubrious Willamette Valley. [3] As time went on the trickle of humanity swelled into a flood. By 1845 the editor of the Independence (Missouri) *Expositor* could record:

Even while we write, we see a long train of wagons coming through our busy streets; they are hailed with shouts of welcome by their fellow voyagers, and, to judged [*sic*] from the pleased expression on every face,

[2] *Cong. Globe*, 27 Cong., 3 sess., p. 200 (Jan. 25, 1843).
[3] See M. C. Jacobs, *Winning Oregon* (Caldwell, Idaho, 1938), pp. 34–65.

it "all goes merry as a marriage bell." . . . But they are past, and now comes team after team, each drawn by six or eight stout oxen, and such drivers! positively sons of Anak! not one of them less than six feet two in his stockings. Whoo ha! Go it boys! We're in a perfect *Oregon fever*.[4]

In this same year some 3000 immigrants, flushed with the "Oregon fever," made the long trek, bringing the total number of Americans south of the Columbia to approximately 5000, as compared with perhaps 700 British to the north of the river.

As early as 1841 it was evident that relations between the United States and Great Britain over Oregon were rapidly nearing a crisis. In that year a bill was introduced in Congress providing for the erection of forts along the route to Oregon and for the granting of land to American settlers there. The pugnacious Palmerston flared up in the House of Commons and declared that if the measure passed "it would be a declaration of war." But Senator John C. Calhoun was opposed to forcing the issue at that time, favoring instead a policy of "wise and masterly inactivity," while the footloose and fecund frontiersman solved the problem. This was also the view of Representative Kennedy of Indiana:

Our people are spreading out with the aid of the American multiplication table. Go to the West and see a young man with his mate of eighteen; after the lapse of thirty years, visit him again, and instead of two, you will find twenty-two. That is what I call the American multiplication table.[5]

The Oregon bill, though approved by the Senate and favored by rousing mass meetings in the Middle West, was fortunately allowed to die in the House, early in 1843.

In 1842, as we have seen, Webster and Ashburton decided to avoid the Oregon issue for fear of jeopardizing more pressing settlements. The alleged surrender of Maine's territory to the British elicited strong protests from the expansionist West; and when it was rumored during the ensuing months that Webster was going to settle the Oregon issue, many Westerners voiced their indignation in vituperative terms. In 1844 the Cincinnati *Enquirer* expostulated:

Webster aid in the Oregon question! We can imagine no greater insult to American feeling than this. Was it not enough that the purchased tool of British fund mongers should sell from us our own northern domain with-

<hr/>

[4] Niles' *Weekly Register*, LXVIII, 203 (May 31, 1845).
[5] *Cong. Globe*, 29 Cong., 1 sess., p. 180 (Jan. 10, 1846).

out suffering him to play a treasonable part in yielding up our exclusive rights to Oregon? [6]

Rather, insisted Senator Benton, should the issue be settled by the pioneers:

> Let the emigrants go on; and carry their rifles. We want thirty thousand rifles in the valley of the Oregon; they will make all quiet there. . . . Thirty thousand rifles on Oregon will annihilate the Hudson's Bay Company, drive them off our continent, quiet their Indians, and protect the American interests. . . .[7]

By 1844 the situation could be summarized in these words. Great Britain had repeatedly offered to compromise on the line of the Columbia. This meant that she tacitly conceded the claim of the United States to that part of Oregon which lay south of the river—the region of the fertile Willamette Valley, where nearly all the American immigrants had settled. Three times, and during two different administrations, the United States had offered to compromise on the 49th parallel, which is the present international boundary. This meant that the government in Washington virtually acknowledged the claim of Britain to the entire area north of that line. In short, by 1845 the only region in actual dispute was the rough triangle between the Columbia River and the 49th parallel, or approximately the northwest two thirds of the present state of Washington. Reduced to these terms, and left to the diplomats, the problem might have been quietly solved; but, unhappily, it was tossed into the noisy arena of partisan politics.

"Fifty-Four Forty or Fight"

In 1844 the Whigs nominated the popular Henry Clay as their standard bearer. The deadlocked Democrats compromised on James K. Polk, the first "dark horse" presidential candidate in American history. The Whig jeer, "Who is James K. Polk?" was unfair. Though a "dark horse," Polk lacked neither ability nor a program. Industrious, tenacious, and purposeful, he was an expansionist who knew what he wanted—and he got it.

The Democratic convention was remarkable not only for its candi-

[6] Quoted in Jacobs, *Winning Oregon*, p. 129 n. The Madison *Courier and Constitutional Advocate* added (March 16, 1844): "Let the whole west rouse up as one man, and her voice will not be unheeded except at the peril of those unheeding it." Cited in *ibid.*

[7] *Cong. Globe*, 28 Cong., 1 sess., p. 678 (June 3, 1844).

date but also for its platform, which screamed defiance at John Bull when it resolved:

That our title to the whole of the Territory of Oregon is clear and un-questionable; that no portion of the same ought to be ceded to England or any other power, and that the re-occupation of Oregon and the re-annexation of Texas at the earliest practicable period are great American measures, which this Convention recommends to the cordial support of the Democracy of the Union.[8]

In the light of this extravagant pronouncement it is worth recalling that few, if any, responsible Americans had ever maintained that the United States had a clear title to the "whole" of Oregon up to 54° 40'. It should further be observed that the Texas and the Oregon questions were tied together—Siamese twins as it were—in the same plank. The explanation is not difficult. The Southern wing of the Democratic party demanded Texas, which was a splendid field for slave expansion; while the Northern wing clamored for Oregon, which was a prospective free soil area. The platform represented a compromise.

Although the tariff was an important factor in the campaign, the issues of expansion gave free rein to the imagination of young America. Tens of thousands of lusty throats raised such cries as: "All of Oregon or none"; "Fifty-four forty or fight" (schoolboys chalked this alliter-ative bluster on fences); and "The re-annexation of Texas and the re-occupation of Oregon." The spirit of the times was reflected in a stump speech reproduced in a New Orleans newspaper:

Whar, I say *whar* is the individual who would give the first foot, the first outside shadow of a foot of the great Oregon? There aint no such individual. Talk about treaty occupations to a country over which the great American eagle has flown! . . . Some people talk as though they were affeerd of England. . . . Hav'nt we licked her twice, and can't we lick her again? Lick her! yes; jest as easy as a bar can slip down a fresh peeled saplin.[9]

These were the days when Manifest Destiny was a dynamic force—when it was widely believed that America's multiplying millions were manifestly destined to spread their republican institutions, though not necessarily by force, over at least the whole continent.[10] These were the days when men talked of "the universal Yankee nation" and "an

[8] K. H. Porter, ed., *National Party Platforms* (N.Y., 1924), p. 6.
[9] Quoted in Niles' *Weekly Register*, LXVI, 114 (April 20, 1844).
[10] See J. W. Pratt, "The Origin of 'Manifest Destiny,'" *Amer. Hist. Rev.*, XXXII (1927), 795–798.

ocean-bound republic"; when the eagle was made to scream and the buffalo to bellow. One impassioned spellbinder caught the spirit at the New Jersey Democratic State Convention of 1844:

Land enough—land enough! Make way, I say, for the young American Buffalo—he has not yet got land enough; he wants more land as his cool shelter in summer—he wants more land for his beautiful pasture grounds. I tell you, we will give him Oregon for his summer shade, and the region of Texas as his winter pasture. (Applause.) Like all of his race, he wants salt, too. Well, he shall have the use of two oceans—the mighty Pacific and turbulent Atlantic shall be his. . . . He shall not stop his career until he slakes his thirst in the frozen ocean. (Cheers.) [11]

On the burning Texas question, probably the most important one of the campaign, Henry Clay tried to carry water on both shoulders, and in this way placate both the slavery and antislavery elements. But these political acrobatics aroused widespread distrust and helped bring about his undoing. The election hinged on the state of New York, which gave its votes to Polk by a narrow margin and thus made possible his election. Yet in view of the closeness of the contest and the multitude of domestic issues, particularly the tariff, it is clear that the Democratic party did not receive a clear mandate to annex either Oregon or Texas. The British, however, were sufficiently disturbed by the rising temper of the United States to propose arbitration of the Oregon question; but this offer was declined by Secretary of State Calhoun, January 21, 1845.

BRITAIN ALSO HAS RIGHTS

Polk may not have received a mandate from the country to take Oregon, but he was certainly bound by the Democratic platform to assert the claims of the United States to the entire territory. Nor was he one to flinch from his responsibilities. In his forceful inaugural address, March 4, 1845, he declared that it was his

duty to assert and maintain by all constitutional means the right of the United States to that portion of our territory which lies beyond the Rocky Mountains. Our title to the country [not to the *whole* country] of the Oregon

[11] *Young Hickory Banner*, October 15, 1845, quoted in A. K. Weinberg, *Manifest Destiny* (Baltimore, 1935), p. 119.

"WHAT? YOU YOUNG YANKEE-NOODLE, STRIKE
YOUR OWN FATHER!"

A British conception of the Yankee at the time of the Oregon boundary
dispute. Note the belligerent attitude, unkempt hair, cigar, and slave driver's
whip. (From *Punch*.)

is "clear and unquestionable," and already are our people preparing to perfect that title by occupying it with their wives and children.[12]

The President then recommended that the protection of American laws be extended over American citizens who had ventured into this far country.

The inaugural address caused no great fluttering in an America which had been shouting "fifty-four forty" for several months past. But in England, where presidential messages were regarded as formal state papers rather than manifestoes of republicanism, Polk's declaration was regarded as a defiant challenge. It was one thing to proclaim extravagant and bellicose pretensions in a political platform; it was another to announce them to the world with the solemnity of an inaugural address. This latest "Yankee bluster" was looked upon as an attempt to bully Britain out of her rights; and the British press bristled up in instant resentment and denunciation. "It is the *manner*, not the matter in dispute, that is offensive," declared one journal.

Jingoism had its day on both sides of the Atlantic. There were ominous reports of British naval preparations. The powerful London *Times* asserted that "the territory of Oregon will never be wrested from the British Crown, to which it belongs, but by WAR." Foreign Secretary Aberdeen, though disposed to be conciliatory and to regard Polk's address as a declaration for political effect, solemnly asserted in the House of Lords: ". . . We possess rights which, in our opinion, are clear and unquestionable; and, by the blessing of God, and with your support, those rights we are fully prepared to maintain." [13] During the succeeding weeks the general tone of the British press was that Oregon possessed little value but that the "blustering attitude" of Polk should be resented. Only one important journal appears to have believed that war with the United States would be "productive of

[12] J. D. Richardson, *Messages and Papers of the Presidents* (Washington, 1897), IV, 381. The day before Polk's inauguration, Congress authorized the printing of 10,000 copies of Frémont's second report, which dispelled many horrors of the Oregon trail, and stressed the fertility and desirability of the Northwest. This document attracted wide attention and further stimulated interest in Oregon. See Allan Nevins, *Frémont: Pathmarker of the West* (N.Y., 1939), pp. 196–197.

[13] Hansard, LXXIX, 124 (April 4, 1845). The words of Prime Minister Peel in the House of Commons were no less positive. The enfeebled Andrew Jackson, with the grave yawning one month off, was so aroused by the British debates that he wrote Polk a fuming letter in which he spelled Oregon both "oragon" and "oragogon." "This," he declared, "is the rattling of British drums to alarm us. . . . The bold manner of peels [Peels] and Russells annunciation of the British right to oragogon . . . require a firm rebuke by you in your annual message. . . ." E. I. McCormac, *James K. Polk* (Berkeley, Calif., 1922), pp. 565–566 (Jackson to Polk, May 2, 1845).

good." The London *Times* opined that democracies found it necessary to resort to "grotesque exhibitions" of "overbearing recklessness toward foreign nations" in order to flatter the vanity of the masses, but that if Polk intended his tub thumping for more than home consumption, "he may rely on having before him a career of no ordinary toil, agitation, and peril."

In America, the attitude of the more extreme journals was no less determined. The Albany *Argus* insisted that "there is not the remotest possibility that our people will ever consent to surrender an acre." The Washington *Madisonian* declared:

We calmly, coolly, and dispassionately, say to Old England, that Oregon is our property; we own it, and we shall take possession of it. We ask not whether it is valueless or otherwise; be it a sterile rock, a barren desert of pathless sand, where no green spot blesses the aching eye, no bubbling fountain cools the parched lips,—*Oregon is ours*, and we will keep it, at the price, if need be, of every drop of the nation's blood.[14]

But from the ranks of the opposition Whig party, and from conservatives in general, came less bellicose expressions. The editor of Niles' *Weekly Register* asserted that war over Oregon would be one of "the most reckless and insane exhibitions that the civilized world has ever witnessed."

Looking John Bull in the Eye

President Polk, as we have seen, was to some extent committed by the offers of his predecessors; so before taking a more extreme position he decided to make one final effort at negotiation. On July 12, 1845, Secretary of State Buchanan informed the British minister in Washington, Richard Pakenham, that the United States was prepared to divide the Oregon country at the 49th parallel. This, it will be observed, was the fourth time that the American government had made such a proposition, although the three previous offers had also conceded free navigation of the Columbia to Great Britain. Pakenham should have referred this proposal, upon which hung peace or war, to the Foreign Office. Instead of doing so, however, he committed a major diplomatic blunder by flatly rejecting it on his own responsibility.

Polk now realized that tactically his position was strong. He had so

14 Niles' *Weekly Register*, LXVIII, 184 (May 24, 1845).

far retreated from his campaign pledges as to propose the 49th parallel—a compromise that had been peremptorily refused. He now felt justified in withdrawing the offer completely, reasserting America's claim to the entire area, and insisting that "if we do have war it will not be our fault." Although Pakenham's conduct was promptly disavowed by the Foreign Office, and although the chastened plenipotentiary made two offers of arbitration during the ensuing weeks, Polk obdurately maintained that it was Britain's turn to make some substantial concession. He recorded in his diary a conversation with a timid Congressman:

I remarked to him that the only way to treat John Bull was to look him straight in the eye; that I considered a bold & firm course on our part the pacific one; that if Congress faultered [sic] or hesitated in their course, John Bull would immediately become arrogant and more grasping in his demands. . . .[15]

Thoroughly in accord with this uncompromising attitude was Polk's annual message to Congress, December, 1845. The President reviewed the history of the Oregon dispute at some length and declared that the United States was now prepared to maintain its claim to the whole of Oregon. As an essential step in this direction he recommended giving Great Britain the year's notice necessary for ending joint occupation. Meanwhile such provision should be made for the protection of the "patriotic pioneers" who had ventured into Oregon as was consistent with existing treaty obligations. Then Polk proceeded to lay down a virtual ultimatum:

At the end of the year's notice, should Congress think it proper to make provision for giving that notice, we shall have reached a period when the national rights in Oregon must either be abandoned or firmly maintained. That they can not be abandoned without a sacrifice of both national honor and interest is too clear to admit of doubt.[16]

Nor did the President stop here. Leaving the question of Oregon, he proceeded directly to a strong reaffirmation of the dormant principles of the Monroe Doctrine. He declared unequivocally that "no future European colony or dominion shall with our consent be planted or established on any part of the North American continent." Although he did not refer specifically to Oregon, the inference was un-

[15] M. M. Quaife, ed., *The Diary of James K. Polk* (Chicago, 1910), I, 155 (Jan. 4, 1846).

[16] Richardson, *Messages and Papers of the Presidents*, IV, 397 (Dec. 2, 1845).

Monroe Doct revitalized

mistakable. He also had in mind checking what he suspected were British designs upon California.

The President's surprising reference to the Monroe Doctrine did not cause nearly so much excitement, either in the United States or in England, as his bolder assertions regarding America's title to Oregon. Nevertheless this resurrection of the well-nigh forgotten principles of 1823 remains the most significant development in the entire history of that great shibboleth, except, of course, its birth.[17] Since then it has been a vital force.

THE POLITICAL POT BOILS

Polk's resounding manifesto seems to have met with a generally favorable response, except for the opposition Whig party and sober men generally. It tickled the ego of sturdy young America to look John Bull unflinchingly in the eye. George D. Phillips reported from Georgia:

The President's Message has set all our mountain folks to thinking and talking. Every one understands, or thinks he understands, all about the Oregon question; and I heard a crowd on Christmas, not one of whom knew on which side of the Rocky Mountains Oregon was, swear they would support and fight for Polk *all over the world*, that he was right, and we would have Oregon and thrash the British into the bargain.[18]

One Maine Congressman praised the President for his firm stand, and added, with a slap at Webster, "We want no more half-English half-American secretaries to barter away any other portion of our territory." Senator Hannegan of Indiana, significantly of Irish extraction, proposed as a toast for a Philadelphia banquet: "Oregon—every foot or not an inch; 54 degrees and forty minutes or delenda est Britannia." Shortly thereafter he delivered a masterpiece of spread-eagleism against yielding fifty-four forty:

History, speaking from the sepulchre of the sainted dead, forbids it. The shades of Washington, of Adams, of Henry, and of their immortal compeers,

---

[17] This view is expressed by Professor Dexter Perkins in *The Monroe Doctrine, 1826–1867* (Baltimore, 1933), p. 62. Polk expanded the original doctrine, which was aimed at European colonization and armed intervention, when he forbade even diplomatic interposition. *Ibid.*, p. 90.

[18] Amer. Hist. Assn., *Annual Report, 1911*, II, 70 (Phillips to Cobb, Dec. 30, 1845). The French consul at Mobile reported in December, 1845, that opinion there was for war. G. V. Blue, "France and the Oregon Question," *Oregon Hist. Quar.*, XXXIV (1933), 144.

forbid it. The still small voice of Camden and Concord forbids it. The holy blood that fell in torrents in the parched fields of Monmouth, and Camden, and the Brandywine, forbids it. . . . In the name of the past, in the name of the unborn millions whose proud fortune it will be to direct the destinies of free America—I protest here, in the face of Heaven and all men, against any dismemberment of our territory—the surrender of our principle—the sacrifice of our honor! . . . Come weal or wo, come peace or war, here I hope to stand,[19]

The wordy debate in Congress over termination of joint occupation lasted throughout four months. Sectionalism and politics proved to be formidable obstacles to concerted action. The South had already acquired Texas, and its enthusiasm for America's claims to Oregon had largely evaporated. Representative Toombs of Georgia privately declared that "Mr. Polk never dreamed of any other war than a war upon the Whigs." [20] Continued attacks in the Senate and House led Polk to conclude, not illogically, that presidential aspirations were responsible for much of the furor. As he noted in his diary:

The truth is that in all this Oregon discussion in the Senate, too many Democratic Senators have been more concerned about the Presidential election in '48, than they have been about settling Oregon either at 49° or 54° 40'. 'Forty-eight' has been with them the Great question, and hence the divisions in the Democratic party.[21]

Finally, the resolution empowering the President to terminate joint occupation passed Congress, and was signed on April 27, 1846.

BRITISH INTEREST VERSUS BRITISH HONOR

The editor of Niles' *Weekly Register* concluded, after reading Polk's annual message, that "either England or the United States must back out of Oregon, or fight for it." This seems to have been the interpretation in Great Britain, for the war fever produced by the inaugural address was stimulated, and preparations for hostilities continued unabated. Even before the news of the second manifesto had reached London the amiable Aberdeen informed the United States minister in London that "with the sincerest desire to avoid it" the

---

[19] *Cong. Globe*, 29 Cong., 1 sess., p. 374 (Feb. 16, 1846).
[20] Amer. Hist. Assn., *Annual Report, 1911*, II, 73 (Toombs to Crawford, Feb. 6, 1846).
[21] Polk, *Diary*, I, 345 (April 22, 1846).

British found it necessary "to look to the possibility of a rupture with the United States."

Yet if Aberdeen had desired war, which he did not, he would have been restrained to some extent by certain domestic considerations. The nation had been rent asunder by the bitter agitation for and against the repeal of the corn laws—as the tariff on grain to protect British agriculture was called. The potato shortage in Ireland (a harbinger of the terrible famine of 1846 and 1847) was causing some distress.[22] Finally, British manufacturers were heavily dependent upon America for a consuming market, almost completely so for a supply of raw cotton.

In these circumstances public opinion in England was disposed to favor concessions, provided they could be made gracefully. A writer in the *Edinburgh Review* declared that Oregon was "a costly, unprofitable encumbrance." Even the crestfallen Pakenham confided to Secretary Buchanan with surprising frankness that "the British government would be glad to get clear of the question on almost any terms; that they did not care if the arbitrator should award the whole territory to us [United States]."[23]

Nonetheless Aberdeen found the path to concession blocked by an apparent need for consistency, by national honor, and by the bitterness of the opposition party. Palmerston, who had denounced the "Ashburton capitulation" in the Maine negotiation, was attacking the policy of the ministry as "resistance at home and . . . concession abroad." Obviously nothing could be done while the opposition was keeping up its furious verbal bombardment.

At this juncture there fortunately occurred a development of the greatest significance. In December, 1845, the Peel ministry resigned. Lord John Russell, leader of the opposition, was asked by the Queen to form a new ministry, but to his great humiliation found it impossible to do so. A major reason was that Palmerston's jingoistic utterances

---

[22] For the view that British policy in the Oregon crisis was affected in considerable measure by dependence upon the American food supply, see T. P. Martin, "Free Trade and the Oregon Question, 1842–1846," *Facts and Factors in Economic History: Articles by Former Students of Edwin Francis Gay* (Cambridge, Mass., 1932), 470–491; and the same author's "Cotton and Wheat in Anglo-American Trade and Politics, 1846–1852," *Jour. of Southern Hist.*, I (1935), 293–319. For a contrary view see Frederick Merk, "The British Corn Crisis of 1845–46 and the Oregon Treaty," *Agricultural Hist.*, VIII (1934), 95–123. Professor Merk holds that England was not vitally dependent upon the American corn supply. He does show, however, that the anti-corn law propagandists played upon this fear.

[23] J. S. Reeves, *American Diplomacy under Tyler and Polk* (Baltimore, 1907), p. 260.

had undermined confidence in the party. So, in February, 1846, Russell gave the Peel ministry definite assurances that his following would observe a truce while the Oregon question was being settled. With Palmerston, the *enfant terrible*, effectively muzzled, the Foreign Office could seriously contemplate concessions to the United States.[24]

Meanwhile Aberdeen had quietly but effectively begun a campaign of propaganda designed to prepare the British mind for a surrender of the Columbia. His chief instruments were leading journals and newspapers, notably the influential London *Times*. Through these he undertook to show that Oregon south of the 49th parallel was not of vital value to Great Britain. Fortunately the monopolistic Hudson's Bay Company had made itself unpopular in England by profiteering in furs. Fortunately, also, this was a period when the antiexpansionist "little Englanders" were strong. The recent bickerings and disorders in Canada were fresh in mind; and there was little disposition to wage a war for additional troublesome territory. Finally, British business was just recovering from the economic collapse of 1837–1841, and war with America would undoubtedly produce another serious setback.[25]

THE AMERICAN MULTIPLICATION TABLE WINS

It has often been said that the five thousand American immigrants in Oregon guided the hand that wrote the final settlement. This is an oversimplification. If possession had decided the issue the United States would have obtained no territory north of the Columbia because there were only eight Americans in that whole region in 1846.[26]

Nevertheless the American pioneers in the Willamette Valley did have considerable indirect influence upon the final settlement. First of all, the 5000 immigrants south of the Columbia could not be ignored. Some of these men were "border ruffians," skilled in the use of the bowie knife and "revolving pistol." Just across the Columbia was Fort Vancouver, a depository for the rich stores of that hated British monopoly, the Hudson's Bay Company. Perhaps the Americans would one day descend upon it and despoil it. Faced with this menace, and with the "trapping out" of its fur resources, the Hudson's Bay Com-

---

[24] Frederick Merk, "British Party Politics and the Oregon Treaty," *Amer. Hist. Rev.*, XXXVII (1932), 667–672.

[25] Frederick Merk, "British Government Propaganda and the Oregon Treaty," *ibid.*, XL (1934), 38–62.

[26] Frederick Merk, "The Oregon Pioneers and the Boundary," *Amer. Hist. Rev.*, XXIX (1924), 683. For a slightly higher estimate see Jacobs, *Winning Oregon*, pp. 218–219.

pany, in 1845, began to move its main depot from Fort Vancouver on the Columbia to Vancouver Island. Although this shift had been decided upon several years earlier, the presence of the aggressive American pioneers probably hastened the initial steps.[27]

The news of this transfer came as a godsend to the harassed Aberdeen. Until then members of his own Cabinet had steadfastly maintained that the Columbia was the St. Lawrence of the West—an indispensable artery for the western provinces. But if the Hudson's Bay Company, which knew the country best and had the most vital stake in it, could voluntarily withdraw, British public opinion could hardly regard a surrender of the area between the Columbia and the 49th parallel as a serious national loss.[28]

THE SENATE DECIDES

With the situation now highly favorable to compromise, Downing Street prepared to move. At this point the news came to England that the United States had given courteous notice of the termination of joint occupation. Aberdeen, choosing to regard this as a reopening of the negotiation by Polk, drew up a compromise offer of the 49th parallel. This was formally presented to Secretary Buchanan by Minister Pakenham on June 6, 1846.

Three days earlier Polk had received advance information of the British proposal, and he was "certain" that it ought to be rejected. Particularly offensive to his extreme nationalism was the guarantee of free navigation of the Columbia to the Hudson's Bay Company. But a majority of the Cabinet were strongly of the opinion that before the proposed treaty was either signed or rejected it ought to be referred to the Senate for *previous* advice—a most unusual procedure. If this should be done, the opprobrium for accepting or rejecting the compromise would fall squarely upon that body, and not upon the Administration. Polk, apparently with reluctance, consented.[29]

After two days of debate the Senate advised acceptance. On June 15, 1846, the treaty was formally signed without a single alteration. But this time fourteen "fifty-four forties" voted with the opposition, although the United States was then deep in the Mexican War. Most of the negative votes were from the states of what is now the Middle

[27] The possibility of a clash in Oregon seems to have expedited the final settlement of the crisis. *Ibid.*, pp. 220–221.
[28] Merk, "The Oregon Pioneers and the Boundary," *loc. cit.*, pp. 690–699.
[29] Polk, *Diary*, I, 445.

West, where the feeling was strong that Polk had cravenly betrayed their interests. Senator Hannegan of Indiana and Senator Allen of Ohio delivered memorable tirades against the Administration. The latter was so thoroughly outraged that he resigned in protest from his chairmanship of the Senate Committee on Foreign Relations.

These Western senators were merely reflecting the attitude of the large body of extremists in their section. On the very day that the treaty was signed the *Ohio Statesman* published an editorial under the title, "Shall the hated Cross of St. George, stream in triumph over the Soil purchased with Revolutionary Blood?" It continued:

> Withered be the hand that dismembers Oregon, and palsied the tongue that consents to an act so treasonable, foul and unnatural. Let Freedom's holy banner be planted upon the farthest ice-bound cliff, to which our title is clear and unquestionable, and our answer to our arrogant foe be given in the words of Vasa—"Here will we take our stand!" [30]

Except for the diehards in the West, the country approved the amicable settlement of the war-fraught question. The feeling of relief was particularly strong in the commercial East, and was shared by the South, which by this time had Texas safely annexed.

THE ABERDEEN CAPITULATION

Whatever advantage the British may have gained from the Maine settlement was more than offset by the concessions they yielded in the division of Oregon. On the basis of the terms that the Foreign Office had repeatedly insisted upon, and on the basis of actual occupation, the final settlement was a "capitulation" on the part of England. The great area north of the Columbia was the price that Aberdeen was willing to pay for peace, just as the Maine salient was the price Webster was willing to pay for peace. In acreage, at least, the United States got far the better of the exchange.

Polk has been branded a braggart who sounded his horn for fifty-four forty, and then beat a cowering retreat. Senator Benton scoffed: "And this is the end of that great line! all gone—vanished—evaporated into thin air—and the place where it was, not to be found. Oh!

---

[30] Columbus *Ohio Statesman*, June 15, 1846, quoted in Merk, "The British Corn Crisis of 1845-46 and the Oregon Treaty," *loc. cit.*, p. 117. Professor Merk states that the British repealed their corn laws in part to placate the United States, but that this move had no demonstrable effect in assuaging anti-British feeling, particularly in the West. *Ibid.*, p. 119.

mountain that was delivered of a mouse, thy name shall henceforth be fifty-four forty!" [31]

But Polk was not so inconsistent as the final result would indicate. Committed by his predecessors, he at first offered a compromise. When it was disdainfully rejected, he returned to fifty-four forty and stayed there to the end. The final settlement was not his, but the Senate's. Indeed, it is possible that he would not have given way to this extent if the Mexican War had not broken out at that time.[32]

It should also be noted that the nation had given Polk no clear mandate to fight for all of Oregon. The Whig party was certainly hostile to war for such an objective. Even within Polk's own Democratic following the Southern and moderate wings were content to accept the 49th parallel. If the President had gone to war over fifty-four forty, he would undoubtedly have had a disunited and mutinous nation on his hands. It would have been reprehensible for him to have persisted in his extreme demands at the cost of war when debate in the press and in Congress revealed clearly that not even a majority of his own party would support him in such a course. So Polk, though still consistent, did the expedient thing. The result was that he got neither fifty-four forty nor a fight, but something better: an advantageous settlement without spilling a drop of blood.

BIBLIOGRAPHICAL NOTE

The most detailed account of the diplomatic aspects of the Oregon dispute is Hunter Miller, ed., *Treaties and Other International Acts of the United States of America* (Washington, D.C., 1937), V, 5–101. The relation of the pioneers to the settlement is fully developed in M. C. Jacobs, *Winning Oregon* (Caldwell, Ida., 1938). A good brief treatment is St. George L. Sioussat, "James Buchanan," in S. F. Bemis, ed., *The American Secretaries of State and their Diplomacy* (N.Y., 1928), V, 245–264. A fuller account stressing Polk appears in E. I. McCormac, *James K. Polk* (Berkeley, Calif., 1922), pp. 555–611. Still useful is J. S. Reeves, *American Diplomacy under Tyler and Polk* (Baltimore, 1907). Frederick Merk has contributed a series of noteworthy articles on the subject, all of which are referred to in the footnotes of this chapter. See also Joseph Schafer, "The British Attitude toward the Oregon Question, 1815–1846," *Amer. Hist. Rev.*, XVI

[31] *Cong. Globe*, 29 Cong., 1 sess., pp. 852–853 (May 22, 1846). During these critical months Polk took no positive steps to prepare for war. The naval estimates sent to Congress in December, 1845, were only two-thirds those submitted the previous year by Tyler. This would indicate that Polk had no intention of fighting. H. and M. Sprout, *The Rise of American Naval Power, 1776–1918* (Princeton, 1939), pp. 129–130.

[32] Benton taunted Polk: ". . . Why not march up to 'Fifty-Four Forty' as courageously as we march upon the Rio Grande? Because Great Britain is powerful, and Mexico weak. . . ." T. H. Benton, *Thirty Years' View* (N.Y., 1856), II, 610.

(1911), 273–299. A. K. Weinberg's *Manifest Destiny* (Baltimore, 1935), is the fullest treatment of the subject. Additional articles that may be mentioned are: D. W. Howe, "The Mississippi Valley in the Movement for Fifty-Four Forty or Fight," Miss. Valley Hist. Assoc. *Procs.*, V (1912), 99–116; H. S. Commager, "England and the Oregon Treaty of 1846," *Oreg. Hist. Soc. Quarterly*, XXVIII (1927), 18–38; and R. C. Clark, "British and American Tariff Policies and their Influence on the Oregon Boundary Treaty," Pacific Coast Branch of Amer. Hist. Assn. *Procs., 1926,* pp. 32–50. Further references: see footnotes of this chapter and Bemis and Griffin, *Guide,* pp. 289–300.

NEW REFERENCES. F. W. Howay, W. N. Sage, and H. F. Angus, *British Columbia and the United States* (Toronto, 1942), outlines the Oregon problem with special reference to the contacts between the Americans and the Hudson's Bay Company (Chs. I–VI). The Company, headed by Dr. McLoughlin, was helpful to the American immigrants, a kindness which was ill requited (pp. 114–115). The British on the whole were indifferent to the fate of Oregon (pp. 126, 129). The transfer of goods from Ft. Vancouver on the Columbia, although begun in 1845, was not completed until about 1849 (p. 129). The Company fared badly in the post-treaty settlement of its legitimate claims (pp. 130–136). There is some popularized material on the Oregon settlement in Bernard DeVoto, *The Year of Decision, 1846* (Boston, 1943). J. W. Pratt, "James K. Polk and John Bull," *Canadian Hist. Rev.*, XXIV (1943), 341–349, produces evidence that Polk was much more compromising in private than in public, especially after word reached him, in February, 1846, that the British were not yielding but were making vigorous defensive-offensive preparations. As a result of laying responsibility at the door of the Senate, Polk—so the author concludes—should not be characterized as "Polk the mendacious" or "Polk the mediocre" but as "Polk the buck-passer" (p. 348). R. W. Van Alstyne, "International Rivalries in Pacific Northwest," *Oregon Hist. Quar.*, XLVI (1945), 185–218, is a review of the recent literature on the subject, especially as it relates to Oregon, with the author's own penetrating interpretations.

4TH ED. REFS. Brief but spirited is O. O. Winther, *The Great Northwest* (N.Y., 1947).

CHAPTER XVI

The Annexation of Texas, 1821–1845

"Man and woman were not more formed for union, by the hand of God, than Texas and the United States are formed for union by the hand of nature." Dollar Globe, August 29, 1844.

THE LURE OF THE RIO GRANDE

SECRETARY OF STATE John Quincy Adams, as we have seen, had been loath to surrender Texas in the Spanish Treaty of 1819, and he quite naturally resented the charge that he had been indifferent to the interests of the West. Upon becoming President in 1825, he instructed the State Department to open negotiations for purchasing the vast region beyond the Sabine River. Secretary Clay pointed out to the Mexicans, among other things, that if Texas were ceded to the United States, the capital of Mexico would then be situated nearer the center of the country.[1] But the Mexicans did not care to sell; and nothing came of these overtures or of those that were renewed in 1827.

President Jackson attempted to succeed where Adams had failed, and in August, 1829, reopened negotiations for Texas. Unfortunately for his plans, the United States minister to Mexico during these years was the unscrupulous Anthony Butler. Learning that $500,000 "judiciously applied" would secure Texas, the American envoy recommended to Jackson the employment of bribe money.[2] On the back of one of these surprising proposals the doughty general wrote, "A Butler. What a scamp." Yet the "scamp" was not recalled for over a year, by which time the Mexican government had become so seriously offended that it handed him his passports.

The somewhat tactless and blundering American offers to buy Texas were regarded in Mexico as studied insults; their repetition merely aroused deep suspicion. No Mexican government dared to sell. To do

[1] W. R. Manning, *Early Diplomatic Relations between the United States and Mexico* (Baltimore, 1916), pp. 287–288.
[2] "As the influence of money," Butler wrote, "is as well understood and as readily conceded by these people as any under Heaven, I have no doubt of its doing its office." E. C. Barker, "President Jackson and the Texas Revolution," *Amer. Hist. Rev.*, XII (1907), 791 (Butler to Jackson, June 23, 1831).

so would be to sign its own death warrant. So the rich and sparsely populated expanse of Texas remained in the hands of a people who were not able to develop or protect it, and who were too proud to dispose of it. The stage was set for trouble.

THE AMERICANIZATION OF TEXAS

In 1821, the Spanish administration in Mexico granted a huge tract of land in Texas to Moses Austin, an enterprising American, with the understanding that he would settle three hundred families on it. The work of actual colonization was begun the following year by Austin's son, Stephen; and in 1823 the new government of Mexico, which had recently won its independence, legalized the arrangement. This was but the beginning of a series of grants that were to divert the stream of the westward movement into Texas.

In later years antislavery agitators in the United States charged that the Americans who had pushed across the Sabine River were parties to a gigantic conspiracy designed to add new slave states to the Union. Color is lent to this charge by the fact that the great majority of these pioneers came from the Southwest. But historians have found no convincing evidence of a slave state conspiracy, and they have concluded that the exodus was but the normal and relentless course of the westward movement.[3] Since this was the case, it was only natural that the immigrants who entered Texas should have come from the states nearest that area. It was propinquity rather than conspiracy.[4]

The westward-movement theory is further strengthened by the motives that brought the frontiersmen to Texas. On the one hand, there was the propulsion of acute economic distress produced by the panic of 1819; on the other, the magnet of rich, cheap and easily accessible agricultural lands. There were, to be sure, vast unoccupied areas in the United States; but the soil was inferior and the price was $1.25 an acre cash, at a time when there was little cash. Across the southwestern frontier much better land could be had for about one tenth that price. The *Missouri Advocate* declared in 1825 that the emigration to Texas was explained by the difference between a republic that "gives first rate land gratis and a republic which will not sell inferior land for what it is worth." [5]

---

[3] C. S. Boucher, "*In Re* that Aggressive Slavocracy," *Miss. Valley Hist. Rev.*, VIII (1921), 21.

[4] E. C. Barker, *Mexico and Texas, 1821–1835* (Dallas, 1928), p. 15.

[5] Quoted in *ibid.*, p. 18.

By 1835, fourteen years after the Austin grant, there were about 30,-000 white settlers in Texas. Most of them were hard-working, God-fearing Americans, sincerely desirous of improving their lot. But a considerable sprinkling were those who had left their country for their country's good—frequently only a few moves ahead of the sheriff. (G.T.T. became current slang for "Gone to Texas.") One Savannah newspaper referred to Texas as the "Botany Bay" of the United States; and a Mexican journal branded the Texans as "a horde of infamous bandits." Notable among the aggressive type were Sam Houston, who settled down and developed remarkable powers of leadership; and James Bowie, reputed inventor of the murderous eighteen-inch knife that came to be known as a "genuine Arkansas toothpick." These were not men to bow their necks to a "greaser yoke." [6]

Given this situation, it is unnecessary to undertake a detailed study of the background of the Texas revolution. Its basic cause was a natural animosity between the energetic American and the easy-going Mexican, who too late attempted to slam shut the floodgates against the Yankee invasion. The immediate cause was the attempt of Mexico to establish a strongly centralized government at the expense of what the stalwart Texans regarded as their local rights. In 1835 the men of Texas arose in revolt.

"REMEMBER THE ALAMO!"

Led by General Santa Anna, the dictator of Mexico, an overwhelming Mexican force swarmed into Texas. At the Alamo, in San Antonio, approximately two hundred Texans held off some five thousand Mexicans for twelve days. Then, on March 6, 1836, the Americans perished to a man, surrounded by heaps of their dead foes. Three weeks later a Texan force under James Fannin, numbering about four hundred recent volunteers from the United States, surrendered at Goliad, and over three hundred of the men were massacred in cold blood.

The Mexican war cry was reported to be, "Exterminate to the Sabine!" Scores of panic-stricken Texan families were stampeding toward the American border. It seemed as if all that Santa Anna had to do was to reach out and crush Sam Houston's disorganized little force, and the rebellion would be over. But at San Jacinto, on April 21, 1836, the small Texan army turned furiously upon its overconfident pursuers, many of whom were enjoying their afternoon *siestas*, and with cries of

[6] J. H. Smith, *The Annexation of Texas* (N.Y., 1911), p. 34.

"Remember the Alamo," "Remember Goliad," and "Death to Santa Anna," routed the Mexican force.[7]

The cowering Santa Anna was found hiding in the tall grass near the battlefield. The feeling against him had run so high that it was only with great difficulty that Sam Houston, who realized that the Mexican

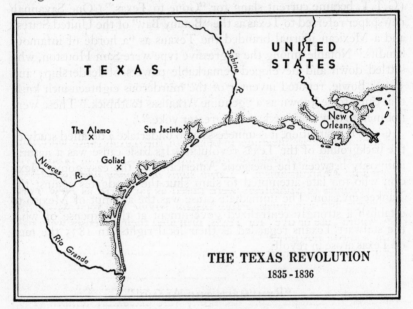

THE TEXAS REVOLUTION
1835-1836

leader was worth more alive than dead, dissuaded his followers from taking vengeance into their own hands. On May 14, 1836, the quaking dictator readily agreed to sign two treaties, by the terms of which the fighting was to cease, Mexican troops were to be withdrawn from Texas, preparations were to be made for a peace commission, and Texas was "not to extend beyond the Rio Grande." The provisions of the two treaties were vague and contradictory; and the slippery Santa Anna declared, when liberated, that he had not actually bound his nation to accept anything. He was naturally supported in this interpretation by the Mexican government.[8]

BLOOD IS STRONGER THAN LAW

It is not to be supposed that the people of the United States viewed with indifference the stirring events at the Alamo and at Goliad. Al-

---

[7] W. H. Callcott, *Santa Anna* (Norman, Okla., 1936), p. 136.
[8] *Ibid.*, p. 141.

ways quick to espouse the cause of freedom, they sympathized all the more keenly with the Texans because most of them were Americans: fathers, brothers, uncles, cousins, sweethearts of those left behind— "bone of our bone, and flesh of our flesh," as one Congressman put it. The widely repeated stories of Mexican atrocities, exaggerated of course in the telling, aroused bitter feeling in the United States. The Chief Justice of the Tennessee Supreme Court testified:

> The savage barbarities of murdering Fanning [sic] and his core [at Goliad], *after a Capitulation,* has so enraged the people of this Country, that they were raising men openly to fight St. Anna. . . . The men under 35, *and all the women,* are for having St. Anna shot, and the Texas *Eagle* planted on his capitol.[9]

Enthusiastic mass meetings in behalf of the Texan cause were held in the larger cities throughout the United States, even in Boston, the stronghold of abolitionism.[10] Large sums of money were subscribed and companies of volunteers were raised as far north as New York, Pittsburgh and Cincinnati. From distant Maine two men wrote that they would "fite or dye" for Texas, provided their expenses were paid to the scene of hostilities.

But American support was not prompted solely by love of liberty. The Texan government held out to volunteers the promise of handsome grants of land, which, in view of the mistaken belief that the "cowardly" Mexicans could not fight, were extremely tempting. On an occasion when a battalion of American volunteers was passing through an Alabama town under the banner, "Texas and Liberty," a local wit in the crowd cried out that the words ought to be changed to "Texas, Liberty, and Land." [11] The economic motive was unquestionably present.

Meanwhile, what was the United States government doing? It was attempting to enforce, albeit somewhat unenthusiastically, the inade-

---

[9] Smith, *Annexation of Texas,* p. 32 (Catron to Jackson, June 8, 1836). A broadside published in Georgia (1836) and announcing the massacre of a Georgia battalion by Santa Anna declared that Nero was "merciful" when "compared with this monster." File 14, Library of Congress.

[10] On the other hand, the Boston *Transcript* (October 30, 1835) reflected an abolitionist viewpoint when it scoffed: "What a capital chance for large cities to get rid of their *loafers.* What man in his senses would volunteer in a Texas Expedition, who could earn an honest living at home?" J. E. Winston, "The Attitude of the Newspapers of the United States towards Texas Independence," Miss. Valley Hist. Assn. Procs., VIII (1916), 173–174.

[11] G. P. Garrison, "The First Stage of the Movement for the Annexation of Texas," *Amer. Hist. Rev.,* X (1904), 80.

quate neutrality law of 1818. But public opinion was so overwhelmingly in favor of the Texans that if this statute had been perfectly drawn, it probably would have been ineffective. Some of the federal officials were, in fact, so sympathetic with the Texan cause as to connive at open violations of the law. And even if the Washington government had seized and brought to trial considerable numbers of offenders, no jury would have convicted them.[12] But this is not to say that the United States was absolved of all responsibility for what happened. It is the duty of governments to have adequate neutrality laws and to enforce them. Since the Texan revolution probably would not have succeeded without American support, Mexico had a very real grievance against the United States.

The Poor Relative is Snubbed

With independence achieved, although not recognized by Mexico, the Texans proposed to place their rich and unprotected country beneath the familiar folds of the Stars and Stripes. The chief stumbling block to annexation was the explosive slavery question in the United States. The abolitionists were already declaring with fanatical vehemence that the revolution had been a plot by the slave aristocracy, and that the Texans were a gang of land speculators, horse thieves, and desperadoes. The Salem *Observer* asserted in 1842 that the United States had territory enough, "bad morals enough, and public debt enough, and slavery enough, without adding thereunto by such a union." And in the same year William Lloyd Garrison, abolitionist editor of *The Liberator,* wrote with characteristic intemperance:

Texas is the rendezvous of absconding villainy, desperate adventure, and lawless ruffianism—the ark of safety to swindlers, gamblers, robbers, and rogues of every size and degree. Its distinguishing characteristic is unmitigated depravity. Nothing homogeneous is found among its population, except a disposition to extend and perpetuate the most frightful form of servitude the world has ever known, and to add crime to crime.[13]

It was clear to President Jackson that the annexation of Texas might split the Democratic party so badly as to make impossible the choice of

---

[12] Barker, "President Jackson and the Texas Revolution," *loc. cit.,* pp. 804–805. During the Texas revolt, a detachment of United States troops, under General Gaines, crossed the Texan border ostensibly to control the Indians. This movement was much criticized in Mexico as giving aid and comfort to the Texans. J. H. Smith, *The War with Mexico* (N.Y., 1919), I, 64–66; 420–422.

[13] *The Liberator,* Oct. 14, 1842, 3:2.

Martin Van Buren as his successor, to say nothing of disrupting the Union and goading Mexico into war. Although both houses of Congress passed resolutions favoring the recognition of Texas, the President advised caution. Not until the last day of his Administration, nearly a year after San Jacinto and several months after Van Buren had been safely elected, did Jackson recognize the independence of Texas. Whatever his motives, his course can hardly be described as unduly precipitate.[14]

Following recognition, the Lone Star Republic formally offered itself for annexation. But President Van Buren had as little desire as Jackson to espouse the quarrel of Texas or arouse the ominous question of slavery. So the proposal was somewhat frigidly rejected. For several years thereafter the United States showed little interest in Texas, and not a great deal was heard of it. The American people seemed to be proceeding with the comfortable assurance that they could pick up the infant republic whenever they wanted to.

THE BRITISH BOGEY

The Texans were now thoroughly weary of being kept waiting by the United States. In October, 1838, they formally withdrew their offer of annexation, and during the next six years launched out on an independent course beset with great uncertainty and danger. The anarchy-ridden Mexican government blindly refused to admit that the Texan ingrates had won their independence, and it continually threatened invasion. Twice in 1842 Mexican bands sallied across the Rio Grande and fled with their booty—an unpleasant foretaste of what were feared to be more formidable things to come. Texas had a population of perhaps 70,000; Mexico, 7,000,000. The threat of imminent chastisement from so large and vengeful a neighbor was demoralizing, both spiritually and economically; the cost of maintaining the semblance of an army was oppressive.[15]

Rebuffed by the United States in their offer of annexation, and unwilling to return to Mexican rule, the Texans were faced with the

[14] Although Jackson maintained a cold neutrality toward his friend Sam Houston during the dark days of the Texan revolution, after San Jacinto he privately subscribed some money to support the Texan cause. Marquis James, *Andrew Jackson: Portrait of a President* (Indianapolis, 1937), p. 412.

[15] In 1842 a resident of Galveston, Texas, lamented: "We have a bankrupt Treasury, a feeble and imbecile Executive, and disunion and confusion everywhere existing. A crisis seems to be approaching, and, unless *foreign aid* should interpose in our behalf, we cannot but anticipate the most disastrous consequences." *National Intelligencer*, Nov. 18, 1842, 3:5.

necessity of making their position more secure. With this end in view, they sent agents to Europe to work for a recognition of their independence, to negotiate treaties of commerce, and to borrow money for financing the government and developing the country.[16]

The Texan representative was welcomed with open arms by the British, who recognized many advantages in an independent Texas. The already powerful United States, whose expansion England had watched with jealousy, would be robbed of an imperial domain. Texas —stretching, as its leaders planned, to the Pacific—would interpose a barrier against the southward expansion of the Americans, safeguard Britain's interests in the Caribbean, and serve as a makeweight in the balance of power against the Yankee.[17] Moreover, the Lone Star Republic could relieve the important English textile industry of its dangerous dependence upon American cotton—a supply that might be cut off by war or other interruption. And an independent Texas would sell her cotton to England and in return buy British manufactured goods, which would enter duty-free. This arrangement would probably excite the jealousy of the tariff-burdened Southern states, which would demand free trade for themselves, thus making a breach in the American protective wall.

The English abolitionists, who were a force to be reckoned with, also favored an independent Texas. They cherished the hope that the Lone Star Republic might be persuaded, either through gold or through a guarantee of independence, to liberate its negro slaves. Having gained this citadel, the British abolitionists could then begin a flank attack on slavery in the United States—a prospect most unpalatable to the Southerners. The Washington *Madisonian* burst out:

If Great Britain . . . entertains a design . . . to interfere in any manner with the slaves of the Southern States, but a few weeks we fancy . . . will suffice to rouse the whole American People to arms like one vast nest of hornets. The great Western States . . . would pour their noble sons down the Mississippi Valley by MILLIONS.[18]

---

[16] For the work of these agents see Mary K. Chase, *Négociations de la République du Texas en Europe, 1837–1845* (Paris, 1932), pp. 17–182.

[17] *Cambridge History of British Foreign Policy* (Cambridge, Eng., 1923), II, 254–255.

[18] Washington *Madisonian*, June 24, 1843, quoted in Smith, *Annexation of Texas*, p. 115. John C. Calhoun wrote in alarm: "There is not a vacant spot left on the Globe, not excepting Cuba, to be seized by her [Great Britain], so well calculated to further the boundless schemes of her ambition and cupidity. If we should permit her to seize on it, we shall deserve the execration of posterity." Amer. Hist. Assn., *Annual Report, 1899*, II, 594 (Calhoun to Wharton, May 28, 1844).

The considerations that led England to favor the independence of Texas for the most part carried considerable weight with France also. Both nations recognized the new republic and concluded treaties of amity and commerce with it.

POLITICS AND SLAVERY

Both Jackson and Van Buren had shied away from the Texas question as one charged with too much political dynamite. But the unpopular President Tyler—a man without a party—was in a different position. He had everything to gain and nothing to lose by joining Texas to the Union. Perhaps this glorious achievement would enable him to carry the election of 1844. At least, this is what his enemies thought he had in mind.[19]

The Texans had no desire to receive another rebuff at the hands of the United States. But they were assured by the Administration in Washington that a two-thirds vote for an annexation treaty could undoubtedly be obtained in the Whig Senate. On the strength of these promises, the leaders of the young republic swallowed their pride and again knocked at the portals of the United States. President Sam Houston warned the aged Andrew Jackson:

Now, my venerated friend, you will perceive that Texas is presented to the United States as a bride adorned for her espousals; but if, in the confident hope of the Union, she should be rejected, her mortification would be indescribable. She has been sought by the United States, and this is the third time she has consented. Were she now to be spurned . . . she would seek some other friend. . . .[20]

Unfortunately for Tyler's plans, a tragic accident occurred on the warship *Princeton* during February, 1844. A giant wrought-iron cannon (the "Peacemaker"), which was being fired during a cruise on the Potomac for the entertainment of a group of visiting notables, burst and killed Secretary of State Upshur. This distressing incident not only interrupted the rather promising annexation negotiations that he had initiated but brought to the Secretaryship of State a leading Southerner, John C. Calhoun. Resentful of British abolitionist machinations in Texas, the fiery South Carolinian addressed to Her Majesty's minis-

[19] Representative Jarnagin of Tennessee proclaimed: "The truth is, this whole business is a fraud, a plan, with which John Tyler intends, if he can, to bamboozle the American people in the approaching presidential election." *Cong. Globe,* 28 Cong., 1 sess., appendix, p. 685 (June 6, 1844).

[20] *House Ex. Doc.,* 28 Cong., 1 sess., no. 271, p. 110 (Houston to Jackson, Feb. 16, 1844).

ter in Washington a vigorous defense of Negro slavery. Calhoun attempted to prove that bondage was beneficial to both master and slave by pointing to the alleged increase in deafness, blindness, and mental disorders among the free blacks. This indiscreet outburst merely served to hurt the cause of annexation by further antagonizing the abolitionists and free-soil advocates in the North.[21]

As a result of various delays the Texas treaty was not submitted to the Senate until late in April, 1844, just on the eve of the heated presidential campaign. Oregon and Texas, as we have noted, were the leading issues, and annexation, which was bitterly opposed by the antislavery forces,[22] became a political football. When the final vote was taken in the Senate on June 8, 1844, the treaty of the "renegade" President and his proslavery Secretary was overwhelmed by a vote of 35 to 16. Tyler was right when he predicted a two-thirds majority; but the majority was on the other side. Philip Hone reflected a common Northern Whig viewpoint when he rejoiced:

> Mr. Tyler's infamous treaty, by which he hoped to rob Mexico of her province of Texas, against the consent of the people of the United States, to promote his political ends with the Southern States, at the risk of plunging the country into an unjust and discreditable war, and to force the country to assume thereby the enormous debts of a set of vagabond adventurers, has received its quietus in the Senate. . . .[23]

During the ensuing presidential contest between the Democratic Polk and the Whig Clay, the Southerners whipped up tremendous enthusiasm for Texas. They were determined not to be robbed of this rich empire. "Texas or disunion" shouted the "fire-eaters," while the abolitionists threatened disunion if annexation were consummated. Andrew Jackson observed that one might just as well "attempt to turn the courrent [sic] of the Mississippi" as to keep the Democratic party from Texas. If other evidence were lacking as to the deadly earnestness of the South the words of Calhoun would be convincing:

[21] St. George L. Sioussat, "John Caldwell Calhoun," in S. F. Bemis, ed., *American Secretaries of State and their Diplomacy* (N.Y., 1928), V, 148–154.

[22] John Quincy Adams expressed a general antislavery point of view: "The treaty for the annexation of Texas to this Union was this day sent in to the Senate; and with it went the freedom of the human race." C. F. Adams, ed., *Memoirs of John Quincy Adams* (Phila., 1877), XII, 13–14 (April 12, 1844).

[23] Allan Nevins, ed., *The Diary of Philip Hone, 1828–1851* (N.Y., 1936), p. 706 (June 11, 1844). Some of the senators who were not averse to annexation voted against the treaty because of purely partisan motives. E. I. McCormac, *James K. Polk* (Berkeley, Calif., 1922), p. 262.

I regard annexation to be a vital question. If lost now, it will be forever lost; and, if that, the South will be lost. . . . It is the all absorbing question, stronger even than the presidential. It is, indeed, under circumstances, the most important question, both for the South and the Union, ever agitated since the adoption of the Constitution.[24]

At a critical moment Clay, as we have seen, attempted to straddle on the Texas issue. The purposeful Polk left no doubts as to his intention to take both Texas and Oregon. He was victorious; but the campaign was so confused and the margin of victory so narrow that he can hardly be said to have received a mandate on anything, much less the annexation of Texas.

ANNEXATION BY RESOLUTION

Polk was elected in November, 1844, but Tyler remained in office until March, 1845. The discredited, lame-duck President still desired the honor of bringing Texas into the Union, particularly since many regarded the recent election as a mandate from the American people to embrace the Lone Star Republic. But if he waited until Polk took office the British might succeed in snatching the rich prize from the grasp of the United States. The Texan leaders cleverly took advantage of this situation by alternately playing on the fears of England and America. To Great Britain they represented that annexation would be difficult to avoid; and to the Americans that acceptance of a British proposal of guaranteed independence was imminent. At one stage of the negotiations, Dr. Anson Jones, Texan Secretary of State, slyly remarked: "I will have to give them [the United States] another *scare*. One or two doses of *English* calomel and *French* quinine will have to be administered, and the case will be pretty well out of danger." [25]

It was obviously impossible to overcome the hostile two-thirds majority in the Senate and push through another treaty. But a joint resolution, although never used for this purpose before, would require only a simple majority in both houses of Congress. So an annexation resolution passed the House of Representatives (January 25, 1845) by a vote of 120 to 98, and the Senate (February 27, 1845) by a vote of 27

[24] Amer. Hist. Assn., *Annual Report, 1899*, II, 585–586 (Calhoun to Mrs. T. G. Clemson, May 10, 1844).

[25] Anson Jones, *Memoranda and Official Correspondence Relating to the Republic of Texas* (N.Y., 1859), pp. 335–336 (Jones' memorandum of April 4, 1844). Jones later remarked: "Texas was then a rich jewel lying *derelict* by the way."

to 25. On March 1, 1845, with the sands of his term fast running out, Tyler signed the fateful measure.

Those in the United States who denied the legality of acquiring territory by joint resolution—they were mostly Whigs and free-soilers —insisted that the Constitution was a "dead-letter." "The annexation of Texas," wrote John Jay, a descendant of the negotiator of Jay's Treaty, ". . . is a clear, deliberate, fraudulent, wished, and irremediable violation of the Constitution. The real object of the annexation is the protection of slavery." [26] Garrison's *Liberator* proclaimed "Diabolism Triumphant" and predicted the "Overthrow of the government and Dissolution of the Union."

THE LION'S PAW

Meanwhile Downing Street had been busy. In May, 1844, Lord Aberdeen made his first serious effort to establish a satellite republic in Texas when he proposed that England, France, Mexico, Texas, and the United States join in a "diplomatic act" guaranteeing both the independence and the boundaries of the Lone Star Republic. But the British minister in Washington, Richard Pakenham, supported by his French colleague, strongly advised the Foreign Office to move with the utmost caution. Should Clay triumph, as seemed likely, annexation by the United States would presumably be thwarted anyhow. On the other hand, if it became known that England was about to intervene in Texas, the American people would probably rise up in their wrath and elect Polk, the expansionist. The signers of an Illinois petition against Tyler's annexation project made it clear that they would rather take the Lone Star Republic than let Great Britain dominate it.[27] Her Majesty's minister in Washington, who was watching the situation carefully, warned the Foreign Office of the dangers of further arousing Anglophobia. As a consequence Lord Aberdeen, who was faced also with the unwillingness of the French government to guarantee the independence of Texas, decided to postpone action until after the election.

The results of the November balloting revealed that the British, in anticipating Clay's election, had been misled. The deadly earnestness

---

[26] Niles' *Weekly Register*, LXVIII, 89 (April 12, 1845).

[27] Chairman Ingersoll, of the House Committee on Foreign Affairs, asserted: ". . . I would give Great Britain to understand that that [Texas] is exclusively an American question . . . with which England has nothing to do, and with which we would not suffer her to have anything to do." *Cong. Globe*, 28 Cong., 1 sess., p. 410 (March 18, 1844).

of the American electorate demonstrated that to tamper with Texas was to play with fire. Aberdeen thereupon temporarily dropped his plans for guaranteed Texan independence.

Late in January, 1845, the London government began its second serious attempt to push matters to a conclusion. The chief theater of diplomatic activity now shifted to Mexico. In May, 1845, and only after much difficulty, a special British emissary succeeded in persuading the Mexican Cabinet to agree to recognize Texan independence. The Lone Star Republic, however, was to bind herself not to join any other Power. But in the meantime the United States Congress had passed its joint resolution of annexation, and the Texans were disposed to accept the American rather than the Mexican offer. Fortunately for the peace of the Americas, Aberdeen's house of cards lay in a flattened heap.[28]

Three snags proved the undoing of British plans. The first was France, which, though favoring an independent Texas, was unwilling to offend the United States by supporting any scheme of joint guarantee. The second snag was Mexico. Incapable of facing disagreeable facts, the Mexican government dallied with the British proposals until the time for decisive action had passed. The disgusted Aberdeen remarked to the Mexican minister in London, "You always do everything too late." The final snag, and in the last analysis the most important one, was Texas itself. If Mexico had been willing to recognize the Lone Star Republic earlier, it is quite possible that the Texans, cherishing transcontinental aspirations, would have spurned a union with the United States. But continuing Mexican hostility merely drove the Texans nearer the American fold. When the government of Mexico finally made its belated concession, Texas preferred to join the United States rather than continue as a weak republic bolstered up by the bayonets of foreign Powers.

In the summer of 1845 a convention was called in Texas to choose between annexation to the United States and the Mexican offer of guaranteed independence. The delegates voted practically unanimously to merge their Lone Star with "the constellation of the stars and stripes." Yet sentiment for an independent course was much stronger than this one-sided vote would indicate, particularly among

---

[28] Aberdeen did not appear so friendly to America in this matter as he did in the Maine and Oregon negotiations. A careful student of the British documents has concluded, however, that the "independence of Texas, in Aberdeen's eyes, was practically a negligible consideration when weighed against war with the United States." E. D. Adams, *British Interests and Activities in Texas, 1838–1846* (Baltimore, 1910), pp. 232–233.

the personally ambitious Texan officials. The President of Texas appeared to be lukewarm toward annexation, and his Secretary of State was twice burned in effigy for toying with the British proposal.

REMOVING AN INTERNATIONAL CANCER

The Texan revolution came about naturally, and largely as the result of Mexican blindness. The people of the United States rendered unneutral assistance, which their government technically should have prevented. But the annexation of Texas, as contrasted with the revolution, was a far different story. The United States put off the willing bride for nine long years—surely a decent wait between the beginning of the courtship and the consummation of the marriage. At the time of annexation Texas had been recognized not only by the United States but by such Powers as Great Britain, France, and the Kingdom of the Netherlands as well. Mexico, moreover, was clearly incapable of recovering her lost province. In spite of all her loud talk about crushing the revolt she had not made a single serious effort to do so; and the longer she waited the stronger the Lone Star Republic became. As early as 1840 Lord Palmerston remarked that any hope of recovery was "visionary"; and Lord Ashburton observed that Texas was more likely to overrun Mexico than the reverse.[29]

From the standpoint of the United States an independent Texas would be an international cancer. Serious border friction would inevitably arise over such problems as smuggled goods and fugitive slaves. An aggressive rival nation to the south, supported by British and French influence, would stand athwart the irresistible expansive energies of the United States—a situation that savored of gunpowder. Finally, it was feared that the Southern states would gravitate toward Texas and dismember the Union by forming a new confederacy of the South. "Let us take it [Texas] now," warned old General Jackson, "and lock the door against future danger."

Whatever may be said of the unneutral conduct of the United States during the Texan revolution, Tyler's course was perfectly honorable. He was faced with a condition, not a theory; and that condition was not of his making. Texas had pursued an independent course for nine years, and she was free to dispose of herself as she chose.

---

[29] As early as 1838 the British *chargé* in Mexico wrote home: "The re-conquest of that Country by the Mexican Government is highly problematical; its power to retain it, if re-conquered, scarcely within the bounds of possibility." Smith, *Annexation of Texas*, p. 77 (Ashburnham to Foreign Office, June 24, 1838).

Annexation would confer distinct benefits on both Texas and the United States. As President Tyler stated:

. . . There exists no civilized government on earth having a voluntary tender made it of a domain so rich and fertile, so replete with all that can add to national greatness and wealth, and so necessary to its peace and safety that would reject the offer.[30]

BIBLIOGRAPHICAL NOTE

The standard work on the subject is J. H. Smith, *The Annexation of Texas* (N.Y., 1911). A brief account appears in Edward Channing, *A History of the United States* (N.Y., 1921), V, 514–534; 541–547. J. M. Callahan, *American Foreign Policy in Mexican Relations* (N.Y., 1932), is a substantial survey. An older treatment is J. S. Reeves' *American Diplomacy under Tyler and Polk* (Baltimore, 1907). E. D. Adams has used the British documents in his *British Interests and Activities in Texas, 1838–1846* (Baltimore, 1910). The work of Texan agents in Europe is treated exhaustively in Mary K. Chase, *Négociations de la République du Texas en Europe, 1837–1845* (Paris, 1932). E. C. Barker's *Mexico and Texas, 1821–1835* (Dallas, 1928) contains suggestive lectures on the backgrounds of the Texan revolution. An important documentary collection is W. C. Binkley, ed., *Official Correspondence of the Texan Revolution, 1835–36* (2 vols., N.Y., 1936). Further references: see footnotes of this chapter and Bemis and Griffin, *Guide*, pp. 248–264.

RECENT REFERENCES. J. W. Schmitz, *Texan Statecraft, 1836–1845* (San Antonio, Tex., 1941), gives the best account of the years of independence, with particular attention to attempts at annexation, relations with Mexico, and negotiations for the support of the European Powers. Written from the point of view of Texas, it supplements, condenses, and in some particulars supersedes the works of Smith, Adams, and Chase listed above. The tribulations of the scantily populated republic, financial and otherwise, explain in large measure why annexation commanded strong support. O. P. Chitwood, *John Tyler, Champion of the Old South* (N.Y., 1939), Ch. XXII, emphasizes the President's part in annexing Texas. A valuable documentary collection is A. W. Williams and E. C. Barker, eds., *The Writings of Sam Houston, 1813–1863* (Austin, Tex., 1938–), the fifth volume of which, appearing in 1941, carries the material to March 14, 1854. W. C. Binkley, "The Activities of the Texas Revolutionary Army after San Jacinto," *Jour. of Southern Hist.*, VI (1940), 331–346, describes the difficulties of the Texan civil authorities when the army, swelled by American volunteers, clamored for action against Mexico.

NEW REFERENCES. See Bibliographical Appendix, p. 927.

4TH ED. REFS. H. P. Gambrell, *Anson Jones: The Last President of Texas* (Garden City, N.Y., 1948) ably portrays Jones as a proponent rather than an opponent of annexation.

[30] J. D. Richardson, ed., *Messages and Papers of the Presidents* (Washington, 1897), IV, 312 (April 22, 1844).

CHAPTER XVII

War and Peace with Mexico, 1846–1848

"There is not an American on earth but what loves land."
Sam Houston, 1848.

RIVERS AND CLAIMS

MEXICO had long threatened war if the United States should acquire Texas. Accordingly, on March 6, 1845, a few days after Congress passed the momentous annexation resolution, the Mexican minister in Washington lodged a formal protest and demanded his passports. Several months later the American representative in Mexico City was forced to return home, and all diplomatic intercourse between the two nations was severed.

Unfortunately, this rupture of relations made war more probable, because it made more difficult the adjustment of the pending boundary dispute. During the generations of Spanish and Mexican rule, the southern limits of Texas had generally been regarded as the Nueces River. Yet the Texans, relying upon the treaties extorted from Santa Anna under duress and upon an arbitrary act of their own Congress, insisted upon the Rio Grande. From the point of view of the Mexicans, however, there was no boundary dispute. It made no real difference to them whether the Nueces or the Rio Grande was the southern border of Texas because in their eyes the whole territory was still Mexican. But the Texans were now under the American flag, and President Polk felt obligated by a promise to protect them in the region that they claimed as their own.[1]

The boundary problem was complicated by claims for damages against the Mexican government. As a result of chronic anarchy in Mexico much American property had been destroyed and a number of Americans had been killed. In 1835, to cite a flagrant case, twenty-two citizens of the United States were accused of complicity in a revolution and executed without trial. President Jackson declared in a special message to Congress, on February 6, 1837, that the nature of these outrages and the unwillingness of the Mexican government to

---

[1] E. I. McCormac, *James K. Polk* (Berkeley, Calif., 1922), p. 382.

offer satisfactory redress "would justify in the eyes of all nations immediate war."

Faced with energetic action at the hands of the United States, the Mexican government finally agreed, in 1839, to submit the disputed claims to a mixed commission, which ultimately awarded $2,026,000

to American claimants. As might have been expected, the stipulated payments rapidly fell into arrears. But this, we should note, was not repudiation; Mexico merely confessed an inability to pay.

The United States, for that matter, was not being discriminated against in the matter of claims. The British and the French had also presented lengthy bills to the distraught Mexican government with similarly unsatisfactory results. In 1838 the French lost patience, and in the so-called "Pastry War" forced a settlement at the cannon's mouth—an incident that enabled Santa Anna heroically to lose a leg at Vera Cruz and regain the prestige that he had lost at San Jacinto.[2] The European Powers seemed to forget that Mexico had been plunged into independence without adequate preparation, and that confusion was inevitable before her house could be set in order. The Mexican government naturally felt that the other nations of the world were unfair in expecting too high a standard of accountability, and in demanding greater protection for their nationals than Mexicans themselves received.[3]

CALIFORNIA—ANOTHER DERELICT

But boundaries and claims were not all that puzzled Polk. With the division of Oregon apparently but a matter of time, the acquisition of California seemed essential to round out the southwestern corner of the United States. This vast and undeveloped region, with its sleepy settlements basking in the sun, was another potential Texas. Its nominal connection with the distant and chaotic Mexican government was tenuous in the extreme. Hundreds of intractable Americans, many of whom had "left their consciences at Cape Horn," were drifting into California and revealing their contempt for the regularly constituted authorities. A successful separatist movement seemed almost inevitable.

At an early date the roving eye of the Yankee had looked upon California and found it good. In 1835, President Jackson directed the Secretary of State to offer $500,000 for San Francisco Bay and the area to the north; but this overture was fruitless. In 1842, during the Webster-Ashburton negotiation, the expansionist President Tyler favored a project for settling the Oregon dispute on the line of the Columbia if Britain would bring pressure to bear on Mexico to sell northern California. The cash payment was to be used to reimburse British and American creditors. Nothing, however, came of the scheme.[4] The interest of both Tyler and Webster in California was certainly not dampened by the reports of Waddy Thompson, the able American representative in Mexico City, who looked upon the purchase of Cali-

---

[2] W. H. Callcott, *Santa Anna* (Norman, Okla., 1936), pp. 158–159. Santa Anna's amputated leg was interred with great ceremony in a monument. *Ibid.*, p. 186.

[3] It will be remembered that at this time several American states had repudiated or defaulted in much larger obligations to European investors.

[4] For the details of the proposal see M. C. Jacobs, *Winning Oregon* (Caldwell, Idaho, 1938), pp. 130–135.

fornia as a primary aim of his mission. One of his glowing descriptions would do justice to a present-day chamber of commerce:

. . . As to Texas, I regard it as of but little value compared with California—the richest, the most beautiful, the healthiest country in the world. . . . The harbor of St. [San] Francisco is capacious enough to receive the navies of all the world, and the neighborhood furnishes live oak enough to build all the ships of those navies.[5]

American interest in California was further betrayed by a surprising incident that occurred on October 20, 1842. A United States naval officer in Pacific waters, Commodore Thomas Ap Catesby Jones, received information which led him to believe that war had broken out with Mexico. Hoping to forestall what seemed to be the suspicious movements of British warships in the Pacific, he sailed into Monterey Bay, forced the Mexican authorities to surrender the fort, raised the Stars and Stripes, and issued a high-flown proclamation of annexation.[6] The next day he discovered, to his extreme embarrassment, that there was no war and that relations between the United States and Mexico were normal—that is, strained almost to the breaking point. Although Jones lowered the flag and made what amends he could for his precipitancy, he was temporarily relieved of his command.[7] The State Department forthwith tendered the necessary apologies to the Mexican government, which was deeply disturbed by this latest evidence of Yankee designs.

Commodore Jones' suspicions of Great Britain were not, however, without some foundation. Already there was a sprinkling of British subjects in California; and they were taking no great pains to conceal their preference for the Union Jack. The activities of zealous British agents, and to a lesser extent those of France, provided further grounds for American misgivings. There can be no doubt that these British representatives, both in Mexico and California, were enthusiastically involved in plans to further annexation to Great Britain, and with measures to defeat the ambitions of the United States.[8] But the

[5] R. G. Cleland, "Asiatic Trade and the American Occupation of the Pacific Coast," Amer. Hist. Assn., Annual Report, 1914, I, 287.

[6] J. S. Reeves, American Diplomacy under Tyler and Polk (Baltimore, 1907), pp. 105–106.

[7] J. M. Callahan, American Foreign Policy in Mexican Relations (N.Y., 1932), p. 139.

[8] Passing over the various rumors that British creditors had secured a mortgage on California, we should note that in May, 1846, a month after the outbreak of the Mexican War, the President of Mexico officially proposed to transfer California to Britain as security for a loan. Aberdeen might have been interested some months

British government, as distinguished from its agents, took a different view. For various reasons, including preoccupation with Texas, Downing Street was not actively interested in securing California. Lord Aberdeen therefore sent categorical instructions to his overzealous agents advising them to be "entirely passive" in their conduct.[9] Such progress as the British representatives in California were able to make was in part offset by the work of Thomas O. Larkin, an influential American residing at Monterey, who was made consul for the United States in 1844. On October 17, 1845, he was appointed confidential agent by Polk, and at the same time was instructed to counteract foreign influence and stimulate sentiment for annexation to the United States.[10]

It is not surprising, in view of all these circumstances, that considerable alarm should have been expressed in the United States over presumed British machinations. As the New York *Courier* put it, "This idea that England is desirous to possess herself of the Californias seems as great a bugbear with the American people as the designs of Russia on India are with the English." [11] Polk shared this alarm, for, as we have noted, his resurrection of the Monroe Doctrine in 1845 was aimed, in part, at Britain's designs on California.[12] Although we now know that his fears were exaggerated, he is not to be censured too severely for having drawn the obvious inference from the notorious activities of British agents. Perhaps he would not have been so eager to push matters to a conclusion with Mexico if it had not been for a situation in California that seemed to be fraught with peril for the United States. Again supposition proved to be stronger than the truth.[13]

THE CRUCIAL MISSION OF JOHN SLIDELL

Polk was determined to make one more serious effort to reopen diplomatic relations with Mexico before sending troops into the dis-

---

earlier, but he had no desire to provoke the Yankee by attempting to snatch the spoils from his grasp. E. D. Adams, "English Interest in the Annexation of California," *Amer. Hist. Rev.*, XIV (1909), 761.

[9] See *ibid.*, p. 762.

[10] R. W. Kelsey, "The United States Consulate in California," *Publications of the Academy of Pacific Coast History* (Berkeley, Calif., 1910), I, 59–60.

[11] Niles' *Weekly Register*, LXIII, 337 (Jan. 28, 1843).

[12] Conversing with Senator Benton, October 24, 1845, Polk referred to British designs on California, and added that "in reasserting Mr. Monroe's doctrine, I had California & the fine bay of San Francisco as much in view as Oregon." M. M. Quaife, ed., *The Diary of James K. Polk* (Chicago, 1910), I, 71 (Oct. 24, 1845).

[13] The concern of Frémont and other Americans in California over British designs is clearly brought out in Allan Nevins, *Frémont: Pathmarker of the West* (N.Y., 1939), pp. 247–249, 254, 272–273, 280, 282–283.

puted area between the Nueces and the Rio Grande. Through the American consul at Mexico City he inquired if an envoy would be received. The Mexican foreign minister replied (October 15, 1845) that "although the Mexican nation is deeply injured by the United States . . . my government is disposed to receive the *commissioner* of the United States who may come to this capital with full powers . . . to settle the present dispute in a peaceful, reasonable, and honorable manner. . . ." [14] Upon receipt of these assurances, Polk appointed John Slidell of Louisiana as the American emissary. Although the Mexican government had agreed to receive only a commissioner and to treat only on the Texas boundary difficulty, the United States disregarded these arrangements and made Slidell a full-fledged envoy extraordinary and minister plenipotentiary, empowered to discuss (1) claims, (2) California, and (3) the Texas boundary.

It was evident to Polk that the penniless Mexican government could not pay its obligations in cash; hence he was willing to accept land instead. The United States held that the claim of Texas to the Rio Grande from the mouth of that river to El Paso was incontestable. But Polk did acknowledge that there was a dispute as to the location of the western boundary of Texas. Slidell was therefore authorized to assume the claims of the United States against Mexico if the latter would consent to the Rio Grande as the western boundary of Texas, and he was instructed to secure, if possible, all New Mexico for an additional $5,000,000. Although the most pressing objectives of Slidell's mission were to adjust the claims and the boundary, the American plenipotentiary was to offer a maximum of $25,000,000 (in addition to assuming the American claims) for California and the intervening area. "Money would be no object," wrote Secretary Buchanan, in concluding the envoy's instructions, "when compared with the value of the acquisition." [15]

The news of Slidell's proposed mission soon leaked out, in spite of attempts to keep it secret. The articulate part of the Mexican populace was quickly aroused by the very suggestion of negotiating with the nation that had despoiled them of Texas. Even before Slidell was appointed, a Mexican newspaper had burst out:

This vile [Mexican] government has been and is in correspondence with the [American] usurpers. The Yankee [agent] . . . has departed for

[14] *Senate Doc.*, 29 Cong., 1 sess., no. 337, p. 12 (Peña y Peña to Black, Oct. 15, 1845). Italics inserted.

[15] *Sen. Ex. Doc.*, 30 Cong., 1 sess., no. 52, p. 79 (Buchanan to Slidell, Nov. 10, 1845).

the North to say to his government to send a commissioner to make with our government an ignominious treaty on the basis of the surrender of Texas and we know not what other part of the republic.[16]

No sooner had Slidell appeared in Mexico City, December 6, 1845, than printed material outlining the objects of his mission was scattered broadcast throughout the city, and the government was accused of a treasonable attempt to dismember the country. The tottering Herrera administration would obviously have been thrown out of power if it had attempted to treat with Slidell. It therefore refused to negotiate with the American envoy, primarily on the technically tenable grounds that it had agreed to receive a commissioner to discuss the Texas matter, not a minister plenipotentiary.

The rejection of Slidell did not suffice to save the fast-slipping Herrera government. It was overthrown by a military faction which charged it with "seeking to avoid a necessary and glorious war" and incurring an "ignominious loss of national dignity." Polk next instructed Slidell to open negotiations with the new government; but the American envoy met with no better success. His proposals were not even rejected; he simply was not given an opportunity to present them. "Be assured," he advised Polk, "that nothing is to be done with these people until they shall have been chastised." [17] So, on January 13, 1846, the day after learning of Slidell's rejection, the President issued the fateful order that sent General Taylor and his command from the Nueces to the Rio Grande.[18]

WAR "BY THE ACT OF MEXICO"

On May 9, 1846, the day after Slidell's return to Washington, Polk discussed the Mexican situation at length with his Cabinet. He asserted that there were ample grounds for sending a war message to Congress—referring, of course, to unpaid claims, the Slidell rejection, and other grievances.

I told them [Polk wrote] that I thought I ought to make such a message [to Congress] by tuesday next, that the country was excited and impatient on the subject, and if I failed to do so I would not be doing my duty. I then propounded the distinct question to the Cabinet and took their opinions

[16] *El Amigo del Pueblo*, Nov. 1, 1845, quoted in Reeves, *American Diplomacy under Tyler and Polk*, p. 273.

[17] Reeves, *American Diplomacy under Tyler and Polk*, p. 284.

[18] McCormac, *Polk*, p. 409. General Taylor, who realized that his presence would be provocative, moved to the Rio Grande with considerable reluctance.

individually, whether I should make a message to Congress on Tuesday, and whether in that message I should recommend a declaration of War against Mexico.[19]

Secretary of the Navy Bancroft demurred, but added that if the Mexicans were to commit an act of aggression he should favor immediate hostilities. Secretary of State Buchanan stated that he was prepared to vote for war, but that he should feel better satisfied if the Mexican forces attacked the Americans. It was finally agreed that a message should be prepared and submitted to the Cabinet for discussion at its next meeting.

Then occurred one of the strangest coincidences in history. That very evening dispatches arrived from General Taylor relating how the Mexicans had crossed the Rio Grande, on April 25, 1846, and had killed or wounded sixteen of his men. It was no longer necessary to declare war on the rather unsatisfactory basis of unpaid claims and the Slidell rejection. The misgivings of the more sensitive members of the Cabinet had been met; the public conscience would be salved; and the country would presumably be behind the President in the prosecution of the war.

Polk's war message of May 11, 1846, was an extraordinary document. It outlined at considerable length the twenty years of accumulated grievances against Mexico, stressing the events leading up to and following the rejection of Slidell "upon the most frivolous pretexts." Two passages near the end were striking:

The cup of forbearance had been exhausted even before the recent information from the frontier. . . . But now, after reiterated menaces, Mexico has passed the boundary of the United States, has invaded our territory and shed American blood upon the American soil. She has proclaimed that hostilities have commenced, and that the two nations are now at war.

Continuing, the President made this significant observation:

As war exists, and, notwithstanding all our efforts to avoid it, exists by the act of Mexico herself, we are called upon by every consideration of duty and patriotism to vindicate with decision the honor, the rights, and the interests of our country.[20]

[19] Polk, *Diary*, I, 384 (May 9, 1846).
[20] J. D. Richardson, *Messages and Papers of the Presidents* (Washington, 1897), IV, 442. Polk, a Scotch Presbyterian, regretted the necessity of having to work on his war message on Sunday, but salved his conscience (so his diary reveals) by interrupting his labors long enough to go to church.

Polk then urged Congress to recognize the existence of hostilities and to take steps for their vigorous prosecution. Two days later that body formally declared war, empowered the President to use the army and navy, and appropriated $10,000,000 for military purposes.

The promptness with which Congress responded to Polk's message is deceptive. Throughout the country there was strong sentiment against fighting, particularly among the opposition Whig party and the anti-slavery men. One abolitionist Congressman announced that the war was "unholy, unrighteous, and damnable." The distinguished Whig orator, Senator Corwin of Ohio, declared in a memorable speech that if he were a Mexican he would say to the Americans, "Have you not room in your own country to bury your dead men? If you come into mine, we will greet you with bloody hands; and welcome you to hospitable graves." [21] Abraham Lincoln entered the House as a Whig some ten months after the war began and, through his famous "spot resolutions," questioned the assertion of the President that hostilities had begun on American territory. [22] Certainly Polk would have been nearer the truth if he had said that "American blood has been shed on soil in dispute between the United States and Mexico."

Did Polk Want War?

The Whigs flatly challenged Polk's assertion that he had put forth "considerable efforts" to avoid war. If so, they asked, why had he sent troops into the disputed territory, within a provokingly short distance of a body of Mexican troops? And why, scholars have queried in later years, does the President's diary contain several references to the anticipated clash between Taylor's force and the Mexicans? War probably would have come in any event, since Polk was apparently determined to have it after Slidell's rejection. Yet it seems undeniable that if Taylor had not been sent to the Rio Grande, the conflict would not have broken out when it did or where it did.

The most convincing explanation of the President's course—assuming that he did not want to provoke war—is that he had obligated himself to protect the Texans, and that the occupation of the disputed area was a necessary defensive step. [23] But if the distracted Mexicans

---

[21] *Cong. Globe*, 29 Cong., 2 sess., appendix, p. 217 (Feb. 11, 1847).

[22] Lincoln pushed these resolutions with such assiduity that he was called "spotty Lincoln" by his political enemies, and "a second Benedict Arnold" by a Peoria newspaper. A. J. Beveridge, *Abraham Lincoln, 1809–1858* (Boston, 1928), I, 432.

[23] Before annexation was consummated, Polk appears to have urged the Texans to occupy the disputed area by force. If war had ensued, he would have been bound

had failed to make a serious effort to invade Texas during the nine years when the Lone Star Republic was weakly defended, it is improbable that they would have attempted to do so when the revolted province was under the formidable wing of the United States. As it turned out, the action of Polk gave the Mexicans a good excuse to start what they regarded as a defensive war.[24]

The Whigs also charged that Polk, having failed by every other method to win California, deliberately provoked war in order to conquer it. In this way, they alleged, he would be able to gratify his ambition and save the territory from the British. It seems clear, however, that Polk did not want war—provided he could get California without it.[25] But it is equally clear that he did not go out of his way to avoid hostilities when the news came to him that Slidell's attempts at purchase had failed. For him patience and forbearance had ceased to be virtues. Probably he welcomed war. He would have been a little less than human if, in the circumstances, he had not.

THE SPREAD OF WAR FEVER

Diplomacy broke down and war followed in 1846 because the will to preserve peace was not present on either side. In the summer and autumn of 1845, several months before Taylor's border skirmish, the United States was giving every evidence of a bellicose spirit. "Nine-tenths of our people," asserted the New York *Morning News*, "would rather have a little fighting than not." "LET US GO TO WAR," bluntly began an editorial in the New York *Journal of Commerce*. The Richmond *Enquirer* was confident that the American people favored "a full and thorough chastisement of Mexican arrogance and folly." On March 16, 1846, the New Orleans *Commercial Bulletin*

---

to protect them, and he would have been able to conquer the additional territory he desired from Mexico. The scheme failed because of the unwillingness of the Texan leaders to co-operate. R. R. Stenberg, "The Failure of Polk's Mexican War Intrigue of 1845," *Pacific Hist. Rev.*, IV (1935), 40.

[24] The Americans invaded territory to which Mexico had a better claim than they; they built a fort on the Rio Grande; their guns commanded the Mexican town of Matamoros on the other side; and their blockade of the Rio Grande, several days before the skirmish, is regarded by some authorities as the first overt act of war. To be sure, the Mexicans regarded the movement of American troops over the Sabine as an invasion of their territory; but it is doubtful if hostilities would have broken out on this score if the United States had been content to remain north of the Nueces.

[25] For an unfavorable view of Polk's machinations in California, particularly with John C. Frémont, see R. R. Stenberg, "Polk and Frémont, 1845–1846," *Pacific Hist. Rev.*, VII (1938), 211–227.

declared: "The United States have borne more insult, abuse, insolence and injury, from Mexico, than one nation ever before endured from another . . . [T]hey are now left no alternative but to extort by arms the respect and justice which Mexico refuses to any treatment less harsh." [26]

From all indications the Mexicans—at least those who made their views known—were more eager to fight the hated Yankees than the Yankees were to fight them. But it must be remembered that Mexico had been verbally reconquering Texas for nine years; and due allowance must be made for braggadocio. On paper the Mexican army (disproportionately overstaffed with generals) was nearly five times larger than that of the United States. One Mexican officer boasted that his cavalry could break the American infantry squares with the lasso. There was even wild talk of bursting into Louisiana, arming the slaves, and inciting the Indians. With the blundering attempt of the United States to invade Canada in mind, the Mexicans did not think the Americans either could or would fight—an impression that was confirmed by repeated attempts of Polk to buy a peace. To the Mexicans the United States was a nation of "money-grubbers" and dollar worshipers; the Yankee was an impossible braggart, and the Southern slaveholder a "degenerate portion of the English race." [27]

Mexico was counting to some extent, though apparently not heavily, on an outbreak of war between Great Britain and the United States over the Oregon dispute.[28] Although the government in London did what little it could to restrain the Mexicans, English public opinion encouraged them in their delusions. The London *Times* expressed a common view when it declared that "The invasion and conquest of a vast region by a State which is without an army and without credit, is a novelty in the history of nations. . . ." [29] And the weekly *Britannia* insisted that the United States as "an aggressive power is one of the weakest in the world . . . fit for nothing but to fight Indians."

THE STRANGE MISSION OF NICHOLAS TRIST

Despite the skirmish with Taylor on the frontier, there was still a chance that Polk would be able to buy what he wanted without having to prosecute a full-fledged war. Santa Anna was then exiled in Cuba;

[26] Quoted in J. H. Smith, *The War with Mexico* (N.Y., 1919), I, 121.
[27] *Ibid.*, I, 102 ff.
[28] Callahan, *American Foreign Policy in Mexican Relations*, pp. 154–155.
[29] London *Times*, April 15, 1845, 5:4.

and in February, 1846, it was made known to Polk, through an intermediary, that if the fallen dictator were allowed to return to Mexico, he would make peace with the United States and promptly sell the desired territory. Accordingly, on May 13, 1846, the day Congress declared war, orders were issued to let Santa Anna pass through the American blockade.[30] When the Mexican leader reached his native land, far from playing the "sell-out game" he used his remarkable talents to arouse his countrymen against the invader. The crestfallen Polk was farther than ever from a purchased peace.

There was nothing left now but to fight it out. Polk's plan was to seize what he wanted, hold it in pawn, and then force the Mexicans to come to terms—to "conquer a peace" was his own anomalous phrase. General Stephen W. Kearny marched overland from Fort Leavenworth, captured Santa Fé, and then pushed on to California. There American naval forces, acting in co-operation with the brilliant if enigmatic John C. Frémont, had already brought most of that area under control.[31] General Zachary Taylor pushed across the Rio Grande and won several brilliant victories; but this was lopping off the branches rather than striking at the trunk. The Administration then planned to bring the Mexicans to their knees by launching an attack on Mexico City. General Winfield Scott was placed in command of this expedition, and after capturing Vera Cruz, in March, 1847, he commenced the mountainous march toward Mexico City.

Then occurred one of the most curious incidents in American diplomatic annals. Polk decided to send along with the invading army an executive agent who was empowered to conclude peace whenever the moment seemed to be favorable to the Administration's aims.[32] The President preferred Secretary of State Buchanan; but since months might elapse before the Mexicans would consent to negotiate, so prominent a member of the Cabinet could not be spared.[33] At the suggestion of Buchanan, Polk appointed the chief clerk of the State Depart-

---

[30] Callcott, *Santa Anna*, pp. 230–238.

[31] Frémont entered California in December, 1845, with an official exploring party of several dozen men. It has been assumed that this force was to be used for the United States in the event of war with Mexico, but here Frémont contradicts himself. On this problem and Frémont's controversial part in the Bear Flag Revolt and the conquest of California, see Cardinal Goodwin, *John Charles Frémont* (Stanford University, 1930), Chs. VI–VII; also Nevins, *Frémont*, pp. 217–304.

[32] An executive agent does not require Senatorial approval; hence the President has more freedom in the negotiation. From 1789 to 1888, 483 such emissaries were appointed. Some of them played roles of great importance. See H. M. Wriston, *Executive Agents in American Foreign Relations* (Baltimore, 1929).

[33] Polk, *Diary*, II, 466–467.

ment, Nicholas Trist, a man of modest attainments and reputation. His selection would cause no jealousy among the leaders of the Democratic party; and if things did not go well he could be recalled—something that would be more awkward in the case of a prominent man.

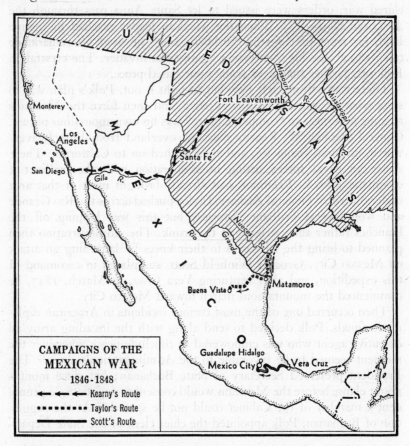

CAMPAIGNS OF THE
MEXICAN WAR
1846-1848

←— ←— ←— Kearny's Route

••••••••••• Taylor's Route

—————— Scott's Route

Meanwhile Scott had been fighting his way toward Mexico City in the face of great obstacles. His nerves were already frayed to the breaking point when Polk's plenipotentiary put in an appearance. Misunderstanding Trist's instructions and fearing that civilian interference with military operations would jeopardize his already perilous position, Scott sent a heated letter to the American envoy.[34] Trist, who was an exceedingly fluid penman, replied in a caustic thirty-page note.

[34] Hunter Miller, ed., *Treaties and other International Acts of the United States of America* (Washington, 1937), V, 271 *ff.*

After the quarrel had run its childish course, the two men patched up their differences and entered upon tortuous negotiations designed to bribe Santa Anna into a peace. The net result was an armistice which gave the Mexicans time to strengthen their defenses. But with the renewal of hostilities, Scott captured Mexico City, September 14, 1847.

Meanwhile the Administration in Washington was becoming increasingly dissatisfied with the fruits of Trist's mission. There seemed little prospect of his concluding a treaty, and his presence was thought to be causing the Mexicans to feel that the United States was unduly anxious to end hostilities. On October 6, 1847, therefore, Trist was summarily recalled. But shortly after receiving these instructions, the American envoy saw an opportunity to negotiate a treaty. He realized that if he did not take advantage of the opening, anarchy might result —with further bloodshed and uncertainty. Since communication with Washington was slow, and since the opportunity might be lost, he decided to stay on in spite of his recall. This was an exceedingly risky thing to do. If things went wrong he could expect little mercy from the determined Polk, whom he was now openly defying. But having made up his mind, Trist sent the President an extraordinary sixty-five page letter explaining why he was remaining. Polk was furious at the conduct of this "impudent and unqualified scoundrel." "I have never in my life," he noted in his diary, "felt so indignant. . . ." [35]

An Unauthorized Treaty by a Disavowed Agent

The way was paved for peace when Santa Anna abdicated. Yet two months elapsed before Trist could find a Mexican government that dared assume the responsibility of yielding territory. After prolonged negotiations the terms of peace were signed at Guadalupe Hidalgo, near Mexico City, on February 2, 1848.

The treaty ceded New Mexico and California outright to the United States, and confirmed the American title to Texas as far as the Rio Grande. This, including Texas, was approximately one half of Mexico. In return, the United States agreed to pay $15,000,000 and assume the claims of its own citizens to the extent of $3,250,000. Since Polk regarded the territory as an indemnity exacted from Mexico for having provoked the war, and since Slidell had been authorized to pay $25,000,000 for approximately the same area, it is somewhat surprising to find the victor granting so much money to the vanquished. Some have said that Polk's conscience troubled him; others, that this was "rather

[35] Polk, *Diary*, III, 301 (Jan. 15, 1848).

characteristic of American generosity and fair play." In any event the Mexican President was able to save his face by referring to the $15,-000,000 as an indemnity extorted from the Yankee.

Polk was greatly annoyed when the treaty negotiated by his disavowed agent arrived posthaste from Mexico. There were, however, several good reasons for accepting the instrument as it stood. First of all, Trist had in general conformed to his original instructions. If Polk should now repudiate a treaty made on the terms that he had authorized in April, 1847, the irate Whigs and antislavery agitators might get out of hand, and Congress might block further appropriations for the army in the field.[36] Should this happen the United States would probably not even acquire what the Trist treaty stipulated, and the party in power would probably be repudiated at the polls in the impending election.

Polk therefore submitted the treaty to the Senate, urging that it be approved despite "the exceptional conduct of Mr. Trist." The country wanted peace, and should there be further delay Mexico might fall into such anarchy as to make the negotiation of any peace an impossibility. So, on March 10, 1848, the treaty was approved, with minor amendments, by a vote of 38 to 14. The ardent Whig, Philip Hone, complained that the peace "negotiated by an unauthorized agent, with an unacknowledged government, submitted by an accidental President to a dissatisfied Senate, has, notwithstanding these objections in form, been confirmed. . . ."[37]

THE ALL-MEXICO MOVEMENT

The ratification of the Trist treaty must be read in the light of Manifest Destiny—"the great American disease"—which, as we have seen, was rampant in the forties. Early in 1846 William H. Seward testified that "The popular passion for territorial aggrandizement is irresistible." Under the spell of the Mexican War Senator Dickinson of New York offered this toast at a Jackson Day dinner: "A more perfect Union, embracing the Whole of the North American continent." Several years later one editor prophesied that before the end of

[36] Symptomatic of this feeling was the statement of the Boston *Atlas* (May, 1846): "It would be a sad and woeful joy, but a joy nevertheless, to hear that the hordes under Scott and Taylor were, *every man of them, swept into the next world.*" Quoted in Smith, *War with Mexico*, II, 281.

[37] Bayard Tuckerman, ed., *The Diary of Philip Hone, 1828–1851* (N.Y., 1910), II, 347 (March 13, 1848). Some of the opposition to the treaty was based on Trist's conduct. Miller, *Treaties*, V, 250.

PLUCKED:
or
THE MEXICAN EAGLE BEFORE THE WAR!   THE MEXICAN EAGLE AFTER THE WAR!

Yankee bumptiousness in the forties. (From *Yankee Doodle*, 1847.)

the century "every sea that laves the shores of North America will mirror the stars and stripes." [38]

The exhilarating victories of the United States over the Mexicans stimulated an already voracious appetite for territory and led to a growing demand for annexing all of Mexico. Sheer greed for land was curiously commingled with idealism. The idea took root that the "universal Yankee nation" had a mandate from Providence to embark upon a "civilizing mission" and rescue its neighbor from anarchy. The New York *Evening Post* declared:

Now we ask, whether any man can coolly contemplate the idea of recalling our troops from the territory we at present occupy . . . and . . .

[38] Even as late as 1859 the exuberant vision of Congressman Davis of Mississippi was not trammeled by the oceans: ". . . We may expand so as to include the whole world. Mexico, Central America, South America, Cuba, the West India Islands, and even England and France [we] might annex without inconvenience or prejudice, allowing them with their local Legislatures to regulate their local affairs in their own way. And this, Sir, is the mission of this Republic and its ultimate destiny." *Cong. Globe*, 35 Cong., 2 sess., p. 705 (Feb. 2, 1859). John Fiske records a toast allegedly proposed by an American during the Civil War at a Paris banquet: "I give you the United States,—bounded on the north by the Aurora Borealis, on the south by the precession of the equinoxes, on the east by the primeval chaos, and on the west by the Day of Judgement!" John Fiske, *American Political Ideas* (N.Y., 1885), p. 102.

resign this beautiful country to the custody of the ignorant cowards and profligate ruffians who have ruled it for the last twenty-five years? Why, humanity cries out against it. Civilization and christianity protests against this reflux of the tide of barbarism and anarchy.[39]

The movement for all Mexico, though poorly organized, was beginning to gather formidable momentum when the Trist treaty arrived. Polk did not favor this extreme demand because it would mean more fighting, with uncertain political and military results. One of the reasons why he accepted the treaty, in spite of his anger, was a desire to spike the guns of the extremists. He was supported by leading Southerners like Calhoun, who perceived that the Mexican territory was unlikely to prove fertile slave soil and that bending the bow too far would dangerously provoke the free-soil North. It now seems clear that the submission of the Trist treaty to the Senate before the extremists had time to organize effectively was the chief factor in stopping the all-Mexico boom.[40] The discredited Trist, by violating his instructions, probably saved the United States from the staggering problems that would have come from trying to absorb the more densely settled portions of Mexico—problems that the United States was to learn more about when it later took over the Philippines and Puerto Rico.[41]

THE FINAL NIBBLE

The Treaty of Guadalupe Hidalgo by no means ended the difficulties between the United States and Mexico. Serious disputes arose over Indian depredations and the exact location of the southwestern boundary. And with the remarkable growth of population in California, following the discovery of gold in 1848, the construction of a transcontinental railroad seemed increasingly necessary. The most feasible southern route lay through the area south of the Gila River, which was undeniably Mexican territory. On the recommendation of Jefferson Davis, Secretary of War in the expansionist Pierce adminis-

[39] Niles' *Weekly Register*, LXXIII, 334 (Jan. 22, 1848).

[40] J. D. P. Fuller, *The Movement for the Acquisition of All Mexico, 1846-1848* (Baltimore, 1936), p. 159.

[41] Dismissed from office, Trist sank into obscurity and poverty. The government refused to pay his salary and expenses for the period following his recall. Not until twenty-two years later did Congress vote Trist $13,647, and President Grant make him postmaster at Alexandria, Virginia. L. M. Sears, "Nicholas Trist, a Diplomat with Ideals," *Miss. Valley Hist. Rev.*, XI (1924), 98.

tration, a prominent Southern railroad man by the name of James Gadsden was chosen minister to Mexico in May, 1853. A primary object of his mission was to purchase the important right of way.

By another turn of the wheel of fortune Santa Anna was again in power, and as usual in need of money. On December 30, 1853, Gadsden signed a treaty by which Mexico agreed to sell the large area now comprising the southern portions of Arizona and New Mexico. This insured the coveted railroad route. An adjustment was also made of difficulties arising from marauding Indians. When the document reached the Senate it was roughly handled, becoming a football for the railroad speculators and also the antislavery agitators, who were aroused by recent Southern expansion.[42] The aged Senator Benton condemned the land included in the Gadsden purchase as so "desolate" and "God-forsaken" that "Kit" Carson, the famous scout, had reported that "a wolf could not make a living upon it." [43] But the treaty was finally approved after the boundary line had been changed and the purchase price reduced from $15,000,000 to $10,000,000.

From the standpoint of the future development of the southwestern part of the United States, it was unfortunate that Gadsden did not secure an outlet on the Gulf of California. It must be said to his credit, however, that he tried his best to do so. And although his treaty did not remove all the sources of friction between the Mexicans and their northern neighbors, it did settle several of the most pressing difficulties, and possibly averted another bloody war.

BIBLIOGRAPHICAL NOTE

The most important work on the subject is J. H. Smith, *The War with Mexico* (2 vols., N.Y., 1919). The author presents the American case in a favorable light. A good brief account of Polk's diplomacy is St. George L. Sioussat, "James Buchanan," in S. F. Bemis, ed., *The American Secretaries of State and their Diplomacy* (N.Y., 1928), V, 265–289. Somewhat more detailed treatments appear in E. I. McCormac, *James K. Polk: A Political Biography* (Berkeley, Calif., 1922); J. M. Callahan, *American Foreign Policy in Mexican Relations* (N.Y., 1932); and J. F. Rippy, *The United States and Mexico* (rev. ed., N.Y., 1931). The most detailed and erudite commentary on the negotiation of the Treaty of Guadalupe Hidalgo is Hunter Miller, ed., *Treaties and other International Acts of the United States of America* (Washington, 1937), V, 236–428. Two standard monographs are J. D. P. Fuller, *The Movement for the Acquisition of All Mexico, 1846–1848* (Baltimore, 1936); and P. N. Garber, *The Gadsden Treaty* (Phila., 1923). E. D. Adams' "English Interest in the Annexation of

[42] P. N. Garber, *The Gadsden Treaty* (Phila., 1923), pp. 182 *ff.*
[43] J. F. Rippy, *The United States and Mexico* (rev. ed., N.Y., 1931), p. 156.

California," *Amer. Hist. Rev.*, XIV (1909), 744–763, is significant. An interesting account of Trist is L. M. Sears, "Nicholas P. Trist, A Diplomat with Ideals," *Miss. Valley Hist. Rev.*, XI (1924), 85–98. Further references: see footnotes of this chapter and Bemis and Griffin, *Guide*, pp. 265–274.

RECENT REFERENCES. C. S. Ellsworth, in "The American Churches and the Mexican War," *Amer. Hist. Rev.*, XLV (1940), 301–326, finds that on the whole the churches favored the war, especially those in the Southwest, where expansionist sentiment was strong. The Congregationalist and Unitarian churches, which were powerful in anti-Administration New England, bitterly opposed hostilities. George Tays, "Frémont Had No Secret Instructions," *Pacific Hist. Rev.*, IX (1940), 157–171, argues the thesis that "Frémont acted on his own initiative in starting the revolt."

NEW REFERENCES. S. F. Bemis, *The Latin American Policy of the United States* (N.Y., 1943), Ch. VI, is a vigorous defense of Polk's policy leading to the Mexican War; the author thinks that in view of the anarchy and folly of the Mexicans, the President acted with patience and forbearance. A. P. Nasatir, *French Activities in California: An Archival Calendar-Guide* (Stanford University, 1945), is an important documentary collection which stresses French designs, particularly from 1841 to 1845. American opinion feared that France might act jointly with Britain to keep California in Mexican hands; the Franco-Mexican Pastry War aroused apprehensions as to a possible French descent on the coveted area (p. 19). British and American rivalry in California spurred the French, who in turn spurred the British and Americans (p. 19). France was doomed to lose out, for she had only some 80 nationals in California in 1842, and her naval strength was not adequate, although her ships showed considerable activity in Pacific waters. R. G. Cleland, *From Wilderness to Empire: A History of California, 1542–1900* (N.Y., 1944), covers familiar ground. Bernard DeVoto, *The Year of Decision: 1846* (Boston, 1943), although doing violence to chronology, overstressing the single year 1846, and indulging in injudicious judgments, presents a spirited and readable account of the Mexican War and the events leading up to it. Hunter Miller, ed., *Treaties and other International Acts of the United States of America* (Washington, 1942), VI, 293–437, has a scholarly commentary on the Gadsden Treaty, the main clauses of which were actually written by the Senate (p. 302). Gadsden did secure a small window on the Gulf, but this was lost when the Senate, perhaps through ignorance of geography, moved the boundary north (p. 332). The American envoy had been instructed to offer as much as $50,000,000 for all Lower California (p. 363), but among other things Walker's filibustering in Central America defeated his efforts (p. 317). Gadsden, who finally made himself extremely unpopular in Mexico, asked Washington for bribe money but was refused on the ground that there was no large sum available and a Congressional appropriation would air things too much (p. 390).

4TH ED. REFS. A. H. Bill, *Rehearsal for Conflict: The War with Mexico, 1846–1848* (N.Y., 1947), is a popularized and superficial defense of Polk and the American viewpoint.

CHAPTER XVIII

The Fitful Fifties

"These Yankees are most disagreeable Fellows to have to do with about any American Question; They are on the Spot, strong, deeply interested in the matter, totally unscrupulous and dishonest and determined somehow or other to carry their Point. . . ."

Lord Palmerston, 1857.

JONATHAN COMES OF AGE

TEXAS, Oregon, and the Mexican cession territory—an imperial domain—had fallen into the outstretched hands of the United States within the short space of three years. One would think that the American people, confronted with the task of settling such an enormous area, would be content. But this was far from being the case. Senator Mallory of Florida exclaimed that it was "no more possible for this country to pause in its career than it is for the free and untrammeled eagle to cease to soar." [1] The New York *Herald* shamed even Congressional bombast: "National glory—national greatness—the spread of political liberty on this continent, must be the thought and action by day, and the throbbing dream by night, of the whole American people, or they will sink into oblivion. . . ." [2] Had it not been for the widening chasm over the slavery issue the American people could hardly have failed to grasp more.

The swift and relatively easy victories of the Mexican War, operating as a heady intoxicant, caused the United States to rise to the full height of its "exulting manhood." [3] Although the rulers of Europe, particularly of Great Britain, were not pleased with the attitude of the

---

[1] *Cong. Globe*, 35 Cong., 2 sess., p. 1331.

[2] New York *Herald*, Oct. 11, 1852, 4:2.

[3] An Iowa newspaper ironically suggested that America repudiate her debts to Europe on the grounds that the latter had already been sufficiently rewarded by the spread of American civilization. A. K. Weinberg, *Manifest Destiny* (Baltimore, 1935), p. 127. The British *Literary Gazette* (June 7, 1851, p. 389) quoted an American as saying, "Your little isle, sir, would make a pretty addition to this fine country!"

Yankee or his latest exhibition of rapacity, they could not fail to be impressed with the uninterrupted triumph of American arms in the recent war. Early in 1847 the United States minister in London could report that "they do not love us; but they are compelled to respect us." In America, Philip Hone noted in his diary:

They [the British] may occasionally abuse us as an arrogant people. . . . But the language of contempt is heard no more . . . Brother Jonathan . . . is growing to be a "big boy," and must be treated with a little more respect. . . . The Yankees may be ignorant of the most approved method of using the knife and fork; but it cannot be denied that they are competent to make a good use of the sword and musket. They eat fast, but they go ahead wonderfully; they use some queer expressions, but in defence of their rights they are apt to talk much to the purpose.[4]

Nowhere was the heightened nationalism of the American people better illustrated than by their increased contempt for the "effete monarchies" of Europe and their "trappings." In 1853 Secretary of State Marcy, a New York spoilsman who had never set foot in Europe, issued his famous "Dress Circular," which carried the war into the enemy's camp. Convinced as he was that the gold braid, lace, and ostrich feathers of European diplomatic livery were out of harmony with American democracy, he issued an order requesting diplomats of the United States to appear "in the simple costume of an American citizen"—that is, the conventional black evening clothes.[5] With considerable misgivings Minister James Buchanan, in London, donned his black coat, and to avoid the embarrassment of being confused with the servants, who were similarly attired, fastened a dress sword to his side. The Queen was too well bred not to pass off the incident with amused tolerance, and Buchanan could report: "I must confess that I never felt more proud of being an American, than when I stood in that brilliant circle, 'in the simple dress of an American citizen.' "[6] But the London *Chronicle*, irked by this latest evidence of Yankee bumptiousness, printed an editorial on "American puppyism" which was directed at " 'the gentleman in the black coat' from

[4] Allan Nevins, ed., *The Diary of Philip Hone* (N.Y., 1936), pp. 869–870 (Feb. 5, 1848).

[5] Marcy also instructed American diplomats to employ only "the American language" in communicating with him. H. L. Mencken, *The American Language* (4th ed., N.Y., 1936), pp. 79–80.

[6] J. B. Moore, ed., *Works of James Buchanan* (Phila., 1909), IX, 159 (Buchanan to Miss Lane, Feb. 24, 1854).

THE LAND OF LIBERTY.

RECOMMENDED TO THE CONSIDERATION OF "BROTHER JONATHAN."

British satire: the leering, cigar-smoking, unprincipled Yankee, guarding his almighty dollar and his title to Oregon and Texas, with elevated feet, unkempt hair, slave driver's whip, repeating pistol, and liquor glass. Note slave trading, beating, and lynching; also references to repudiation, dueling, fighting with knives in Congress, and erecting gallows and pillaging churches in Mexico. (From *Punch*.)

Yankee-land." [7] It seems clear that this ostentatious unostentatiousness did nothing to increase respect for the United States or win converts to democracy.

STUMP-SPEECH DIPLOMACY

The revolutionary outbursts of 1848 in Europe acted as a powerful stimulus to the new spirit of American nationalism. The traditional friendliness of the United States to the cause of liberty in other lands was intensified by the presence of tens of thousands of recently arrived

GERMAN AND IRISH IMMIGRATION TO THE U.S.

BY DECADE

	Germany	Ireland	Total Immigration From All Other Countries	Total Continental U.S. Population
1821–30	6,761	50,724	85,954	1820:— 9,638,453 1830:— 12,866,020
1831–40	152,454	207,381	239,290	17,069,453
1841–50	434,626	780,719	497,906	23,191,876
1851–60	951,667	914,119	732,428	31,443,321
1861–70	787,468	435,778	1,091,578	38,558,371
1871–80	718,182	436,871	1,657,138	50,189,209
1881–90	1,452,970	655,482	3,138,161 *	63,069,756
1891–00	505,152	388,416	2,793,996	76,129,408
1900–10	341,498	339,065	8,114,823	92,267,080
1910–20	143,945	146,181	5,445,685	106,543,031
1920–30	412,202	220,591	3,474,416	123,091,000

* Note that in the eighties began the great influx from Southern and Central Europe.

[7] In Berlin the British ambassador accosted the American minister, George Bancroft, and asked in the presence of many listeners why the representatives of the United States appeared at court "all dressed in black, like so many undertakers." Bancroft retorted that "we could not be more appropriately dressed than we are—at European courts, where what we represent is the Burial of Monarchy." M. A. DeWolfe Howe, *The Life and Letters of George Bancroft* (N.Y., 1908), II, 174. Marcy's order, however, left some latitude to the minister. Simple costume was the rule for Americans throughout the remainder of the nineteenth century. Not until the 1920's did Ambassador George Harvey appear in England clad in knee breeches —a departure that aroused considerable criticism in the United States.

Irish and German immigrants, most of whom had poured in during the forties and many of whom had but recently cringed under the lash of despotism. A considerable group of enthusiasts in the United States inaugurated the "Young America" movement, which had as one of its goals active intervention in the affairs of Europe.[8] Americans were particularly stirred by the Hungarian revolution (led by Louis Kossuth), which was ruthlessly crushed by Austria, with the help of Russia. As Congressman Sweetster of Ohio cried out:

> If I was authorized to speak for the whole American people, and had the voice of ARTICULATE THUNDER, I would tell the despotic Governments of Europe that henceforth in contests for liberty . . . there must be no such interference as there has been in the past. . . . I will pledge that portion of the people of my State that I am authorized to represent, that they will, when the time comes, protest against the interference of Russia in another contest in Hungary for liberty.[9]

In June, 1849, while the Hungarian revolution was still running its course, the Whig administration of Zachary Taylor issued special instructions to A. Dudley Mann, an American diplomat then in Europe. He was authorized to proceed to Hungary and hold out to the revolutionary government assurances of recognition, if, in his judgment, such a step seemed warranted. Although the revolt quickly collapsed and Mann did not reach Hungary, the Austrian government instructed its *chargé* in Washington, Chevalier Hülsemann, to lodge a strong protest against this officious interference in the affairs of a friendly nation.

To Daniel Webster, again Secretary of State under the new Whig administration, the Hülsemann note presented both an opportunity and a challenge. The great orator, who was profoundly disturbed by the growing controversy over slavery and by increasing threats of secession, decided to "write a paper which should touch the national pride, and make a man feel *sheepish* and look *silly* who should speak of disunion." He also thought it desirable "to speak out, and tell the people of Europe who and what we are, and awaken them to a just sense of the unparalleled growth of this country." [10] It is not sur-

[8] See M. E. Curti, "Young America," *Amer. Hist. Rev.*, XXXII (1926), 34–55.
[9] *Cong. Globe*, 32 Cong., 1 sess., p. 177 (Jan. 3, 1852). The American people had also shown strong sympathy for the liberal revolutions of 1830 in Europe. E. N. Curtis, "American Opinion of the French Nineteenth-Century Revolutions," *Amer. Hist. Rev.*, XXIX (1924), 249 *ff.*
[10] G. T. Curtis, *Life of Daniel Webster* (5th ed., N.Y., 1889), II, 537 (Webster to Ticknor, Jan. 16, 1851).

prising, then, that Webster's reply to Hülsemann should have contained this bombastic passage:

> The power of this republic at the present moment is spread over a region one of the richest and most fertile on the globe, and of an extent in comparison with which the possessions of the house of Hapsburg [Austria] are but as a patch on the earth's surface.[11]

Webster did not mistake the public temper. His reply to Hülsemann aroused instant enthusiasm in the ranks of both parties. The New York *Herald* was led to declare: "We question if any document that ever emanated from the State Department gave more general satisfaction than the reply . . . to the insolent and supercilious letter of the Austrian Minister." [12]

THE KOSSUTH CRAZE

Scarcely had the excitement over the Hülsemann letter died down when Kossuth arrived in New York, on December 5, 1851. The health officer who boarded the vessel pitched his address of welcome in an appropriate key:

> Noble Magyar! Illustrious Kossuth! We greet you from the New World. Welcome to the land of free speech and action. Welcome to the American republic, which demonstrates successfully to the world man's capacity for self-government. Thrice welcome to our infant country, the hope and trust of the friends of liberty in every nation and clime.[13]

The "illustrious" Magyar, who was a gifted orator and a magnetic personality, was accorded a tumultuous welcome. In New York one burst of cheering, so it was reported, lasted without interruption for

[11] *Senate Ex. Docs.*, 31 Cong., 2 sess., no. 9, p. 7 (Webster to Hülsemann, Dec. 21, 1850). Another notable instance of stump-speech diplomacy developed out of the Koszta affair, in 1853. Koszta was a Hungarian refugee who had fled to the United States and had declared his intention of becoming an American citizen. He was later seized within Turkish jurisdiction by an Austrian naval officer, who was forced to release his captive by the commander of an American warship. To Hülsemann's protest Secretary Marcy, who desired the Democratic presidential nomination and who doubtless aimed at appealing to the large immigrant vote, returned a vigorous reply. The country applauded; and Marcy was the man of the hour. Although the note was used for political purposes, it appears that the American case rested on tenable ground. See J. B. Moore, *Digest of International Law* (Washington, 1906), III, 820–835.

[12] New York *Herald*, Jan. 3, 1851, quoted in J. G. Gazley, *American Opinion of German Unification, 1848–1871* (N.Y., 1926), p. 60.

[13] New York *Evening Post*, Dec. 5, 1851, 2:3.

fifteen minutes. Henry W. Longfellow, the well-known poet, remarked that the people had gone *"clean* daft." No foreign visitor since
Lafayette's triumphal tour had received such an ovation. With the
ghost of slavery temporarily laid by the Compromise of 1850, and
with the so-called second era of good feelings ushered in, America was
free to outdo herself.[14]

Diplomatically, the Kossuth incident was brought to a head when
Secretary Webster, speaking at a banquet in the Hungarian's honor,
and possibly overstimulated by champagne, asserted:

> We shall rejoice to see our American model upon the Lower Danube
> and on the mountains of Hungary. . . . I limit my aspirations for Hun-
> gary, for the present, to that single and simple point,—Hungarian inde-
> pendence, Hungarian self-government, Hungarian control of Hungarian
> destinies.[15]

Webster may have been motivated by a desire to repeat the success
of his Hülsemann note. Such, at least, was the interpretation of the
Austrian *chargé,* who regarded the new Websterian outburst as a thinly
disguised bid for the presidential nomination.[16] As the New York
Herald remarked, the Kossuth excitement was "a first-rate piece, as
good as a queen, in the political game of chess." The Austrian government was so deeply offended by the uproarious welcome extended to its
outstanding rebel, and by the indiscretion of the American Secretary
of State, that it instructed its representative to have no further dealings with Webster. Relations remained strained until the great orator
died in October, 1852.

Meanwhile the Kossuth infatuation was running its course. Hungarian history, music, dances, and wine became popular; Kossuth clubs
were organized; immense crowds turned out and shed tears while
the eloquent Magyar addressed them in flawless English; ladies im-
pulsively contributed rings and necklaces to the cause; and some money
was raised (much of which, to Kossuth's disgust, was frittered away on
parades and banquets). Nevertheless, traditional policy repelled the
United States from active intervention in Europe. When it became
evident that this was what Kossuth wanted, the enthusiasm evaporated
with a suddenness proportionate to its extravagance. The magnetic

[14] See J. W. Oliver, "Louis Kossuth's Appeal to the Middle West—1852," *Miss.
Valley Hist. Rev.,* XIV (1928), 481–495.

[15] J. W. McIntyre, ed., *The Writings and Speeches of Daniel Webster* (National ed.,
Boston, 1903), XIII, 461, 426 (Jan. 7, 1852).

[16] M. E. Curti, "Austria and the United States, 1848–1852," *Smith College Studies
in History,* XI (1926), no. 3, p. 185.

Hungarian sailed from America a sadder and wiser man, leaving behind him Kossuth beards, Kossuth hats, Kossuth overcoats, and even Kossuth County, Iowa.

ISTHMIAN INTERESTS

But there were more fundamental issues before the American people than the squabble growing out of the Hungarian revolution. Perhaps the most important of these in the field of foreign affairs was the question of an Isthmian canal route.

From the days of Balboa men's minds had toyed with the idea of severing North and South America by an artificial waterway. Although the American people had revealed some early interest in such a project, it was not until near the middle of the century that they began to show any vital concern about the Isthmus. The reasons are evident. In the forties the United States received its share of Oregon, and acquired from Mexico a vast frontage on the Pacific Ocean. Nine days before the signing of the Treaty of Guadalupe Hidalgo, gold was discovered in California, and there immediately began one of the great population movements of history. Control of water communication with American territory on the Pacific Coast rapidly became a question of vital importance to the United States.

In December, 1846, more than six months after the outbreak of the Mexican War, the United States minister in Bogotá had signed a treaty with New Granada (later Colombia) which greatly strengthened the Isthmian foothold of his country. The South American republic, fearing that Great Britain or some other power might seize the Isthmus of Panama,[17] agreed to grant the United States transit rights in that region. In return, the Washington government bound itself to maintain the "perfect neutrality" of the route to the end that "free transit of traffic might not be interrupted." Although this right of way was of incalculable value to American commerce, the Senate was suspicious of the entangling nature of the arrangement, and did not approve it until June 3, 1848.[18]

[17] J. B. Lockey, "A Neglected Aspect of Isthmian Diplomacy," *Amer. Hist. Rev.*, XLI (1936), 305. See also Hunter Miller, ed., *Treaties and other International Acts of the United States of America* (Washington, 1937), V, 115–160. The treaty with New Granada paved the way for the Panama railroad, which was completed by Americans in 1855.

[18] American interest in the Isthmus was shown in other ways. When, in 1848, it was rumored that the rulers of Yucatan were about to offer their peninsula to Great Britain or Spain, Polk announced in a special message (April 29, 1848) that the United States could not permit such a transfer, even with the consent of the inhabitants.

The British, who viewed both the recent territorial acquisitions of the United States and the treaty with New Granada with misgivings, were also vitally interested in the Caribbean region, where they had

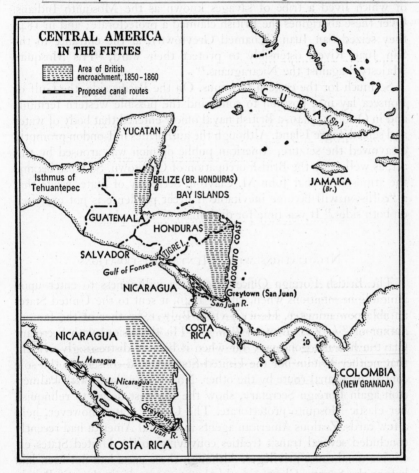

Jamaica, Belize (British Honduras), and other important colonies. As the commercially dominant Power, they would sacrifice much before permitting the Yankee to secure a monopoly over the Isthmus

This so-called Polk corollary to the Monroe Doctrine went a step further than the original dictum, which envisaged forcible intervention. Dexter Perkins, *The Monroe Doctrine, 1826–1867* (Baltimore, 1933), pp. 174 *ff.* It may also be noted, as indicative of Isthmian interest, that the Gadsden Treaty of 1853 assured the United States certain transit rights across the Mexican Isthmus of Tehuantepec. These were relinquished in 1937 by action of the United States Senate.

—one of the most important economic nerve centers of the world. The eastern terminus of the proposed Nicaragua canal, the route then regarded as the most feasible, was the San Juan River, near the mouth of which lived a tribe of savages known as the Mosquito Indians. Over these aborigines the British claimed a protectorate; and in 1848 they seized San Juan (renamed Greytown), at the entrance to the San Juan River, ostensibly to protect their ward, "His Mosquito Majesty," against the Nicaraguans.[19]

So much for the eastern terminus. On the Pacific side, the Gulf of Fonseca lay in a position to command the possible western termini; and in October, 1849, a British naval officer entered that body of water and seized Tigre Island. Although the authorities in London promptly disavowed the seizure, American public opinion was aroused by this act, as well as by the British occupation of Greytown. So tense became the atmosphere that John M. Clayton, Secretary of State, wrote that a "collision will become inevitable if great prudence is not exercised on both sides." It was time for diplomacy to take a hand.

NEGOTIATIONS WITH MENTAL RESERVATIONS

The British Foreign Office revealed a willingness to enter upon amicable negotiations when, late in 1849, it sent to the United States an able new minister, Henry Lytton Bulwer, brother of the famous author of *The Last Days of Pompeii*. His discussions with Secretary Clayton had not gone very far when it became distressingly evident that neither Britain nor the United States would consent to the sole control of a canal route by the other. Nor did England, with Palmerston again Foreign Secretary, show the slightest desire to relinquish her elastic Mosquito protectorate. The United States, however, held a few cards. Zealous American agents in Central America had recently concluded several transit treaties conveying to the United States exclusive canal-route privileges. Although these pacts had not been laid before the Senate, Clayton could threaten to submit them if Britain refused to come to terms. Moreover, several of the Central American states, including Nicaragua, had become so apprehensive of British aggression that they were looking to the United States for protection. As Clayton bluntly informed Bulwer:

[19] R. W. Van Alstyne, "The Central American Policy of Lord Palmerston, 1846–1848," *Hispanic Amer. Hist. Rev.*, XVI (1936), 352–357; see also Miller, *Treaties*, V, 705–706.

There is not one of these five Central American states that would not annex themselves to us tomorrow, if they could, and if it is any secret worth knowing you are welcome to it—*Some of them have offered and asked to be annexed to the United States already.*[20]

After protracted negotiations, the famous Clayton-Bulwer Treaty was signed, April 19, 1850. By its terms both parties agreed to cooperate in facilitating the construction of an Isthmian canal; both bound themselves never to fortify or exercise exclusive control over such a waterway. With reference to territorial ambitions in Central America, the stipulations were less clear. The British Foreign Office was adamant in the matter of relinquishing the Mosquito Coast, and had no intention whatever of abandoning British Honduras. Clayton knew this; yet he could not make specific concessions on these points for fear of arousing a partisan clamor from the Anglophobes in America. So both negotiators deliberately consented to the use of ambiguous language in order to conceal their official differences. Otherwise, a treaty probably could not have been made.[21] The famous Article I provided that neither party was to "occupy" or "colonize" or exercise "dominion" over "any part of Central America." When Bulwer consented not "to occupy" any part of Central America, he understood that Britain was not "to occupy" anything *further*. Clayton, on the other hand, hoped to make the provision retroactive. As the London *Times* not inaptly remarked, the negotiation was a struggle "for generalship in the use of terms." [22]

An Ignoble Surrender or a Diplomatic Victory?

Partly because the Senators had been consulted during the negotiation, and partly because they were able to read their own meaning into the ambiguous language of the document, the pact was approved after a brief debate by a vote of 42 to 11. Before the final ratification,

[20] M. W. Williams, "John Middleton Clayton," in S. F. Bemis, ed., *American Secretaries of State and their Diplomacy* (N.Y., 1928), VI, 57.

[21] This point is clearly brought out in Professor R. W. Van Alstyne's scholarly analysis of the problem, "British Diplomacy and the Clayton-Bulwer Treaty, 1850–60," *Jour. of Mod. Hist.*, XI (1939), 157, 161. Bulwer later gave as his aims in making the treaty: (1) To quiet angry feeling between the two Powers (2) To bind the United States against territorial acquisitions in Central America (3) To facilitate the construction of a canal (4) To open the way for a final settlement of the Mosquito controversy. *Ibid.*, p. 156.

[22] M. W. Williams, *Anglo-American Isthmian Diplomacy, 1815–1915* (Washington, 1916), p. 92.

however, Clayton and Bulwer exchanged confidential notes clarifying
—or attempting to clarify—their interpretation of what the treaty
was really intended to accomplish. Clayton resorted to this subterranean
device because he feared that the Senate would throw out the entire
pact if the reservations were made public—a rather disingenuous
method of short-circuiting the regularly constituted treaty-making
power.[23]

Whatever doubt there may be as to the negotiations, it is clear that
the Clayton-Bulwer Treaty was the most persistently unpopular pact
ever concluded by the United States. Former Secretary of State James
Buchanan, of the opposition party, wrote that Bulwer deserved a "British peerage"; and Senator Stephen Douglas, also a Democrat, condemned the agreement, to the accompaniment of Irish applause, as
"truckling to Great Britain." Specifically, opponents of the treaty declared that it was a self-denying pledge that would thwart the southward expansion of the American people. This it undoubtedly was; for
the United States formally bound itself not to acquire any of Central
America. Critics also charged that the treaty devitalized the Monroe
Doctrine by permitting Britain to keep what she had already illegally
seized in Central America. On this point there is some difference of
opinion, but it is clear that the Clayton-Bulwer Treaty, by placing an
obstacle in the path of British aggression in Central America, actually
strengthened the Monroe Doctrine. In a sense the pact marked the first
important acceptance by a foreign Power of the principles underlying
Monroe's noncolonization clause.[24]

On the credit side of the balance sheet it may be noted that the
United States, at no great cost to itself, averted serious difficulties—
possibly war—with Great Britain. It should also be pointed out that
the agreement marked the high tide of British expansion in Central
America. The treaty, to be sure, was unpopular; but this was largely
because it was a compromise. The United States abandoned its plans
for a canal under exclusive American control; Britain did likewise. But
without compromise and concession there would have been no agreement.

In later years, when the United States had become a world Power
and had outgrown the treaty, the talk of having been overreached by
slippery British diplomats was redoubled. So it seemed in 1900. But

[23] For a discussion of the question whether Clayton actually saw Bulwer's note
of July 4, 1850, after it had been filed with the State Department, see Miller,
Treaties, V, 691–703.

[24] Perkins, The Monroe Doctrine, 1826–1867, p. 210.

in 1850 the picture was different. America was still but a second-rate Power, torn by a violent slavery controversy. Yet she succeeded in stopping both British expansion in Central America and a formidable attempt to secure a strangle hold on the Isthmian route. Considering the times, the Clayton-Bulwer Treaty was not far short of a triumph for American diplomacy.[25]

The Central American Cockpit

The decade from 1850 to 1860 was one of misunderstanding and bickering over the terms of the Clayton-Bulwer Treaty, inflamed by serious difficulties arising elsewhere, particularly with reference to alleged designs of the United States on Hawaii, Santo Domingo, and Cuba. Whatever may have been American desires, the British showed little disposition to relinquish the Mosquito protectorate. They not only refused to abandon the Honduran Bay Islands (from which Clayton had hoped to force them by a strained interpretation of the pact), but they made these bits of territory a crown colony in 1852, thus serving notice that they intended to stay. From the point of view of the United States this "colony snatching" was both a deliberate evasion of a solemn treaty obligation and a provocative violation of the Monroe Doctrine.

The incendiary possibilities of the Mosquito controversy were dramatically illustrated in July, 1854. Disorders had flared up among the populace of Greytown, resulting in an attack upon a United States minister, whose face was cut by a broken bottle. An American naval officer demanded reparation, and when it was not forthcoming bombarded and destroyed the town. Though the property of foreigners, notably British and French, was damaged, fortunately no lives were lost.

President Pierce, in his annual message to Congress, defended the extraordinary act of the American commander. The London government, already disturbed by the aggressive policy of the United States toward Cuba, was greatly angered. Even the ordinarily unruffled Lord Clarendon, then Foreign Secretary, evinced extreme displeasure when

[25] *Ibid.*, 212–213. Professor R. W. Van Alstyne, after a careful examination of the gains and losses on both sides, points out that the British were pleased with the treaty; the Americans were not. This is a strong argument in support of the contention that England gained more. Professor Van Alstyne believes that the British "scored a victory over the Monroe Doctrine" when they secured recognition of the treaty and not the Doctrine as "the established rule of law in Central America." "British Diplomacy and the Clayton-Bulwer Treaty, 1850–60," *loc. cit.*, p. 182.

discussing the matter with the United States minister; and he informed the British representative in Washington that the bombardment was an outrage "without a parallel in the annals of modern times." The First Lord of the Admiralty declared, "We are fast 'drifting' into a war with the U. States. . . ." [26]

Downing Street naturally sought to secure a disavowal of the Greytown bombardment; but, finding the United States adamant, ceased to push the matter. For one thing, the bloody Crimean War had begun several months before, and England had her hands full without provoking the Yankee to hostilities over the somewhat ridiculous Mosquito protectorate. (Even at this date Europe's distresses were helping America.) Besides, the British were somewhat mollified when they observed that public opinion in the United States was far from unanimous in supporting the bombardment.

The already vexed situation in Central America was further complicated by the filibustering activities of an adventuresome Southerner, William Walker. This "grey-eyed man of destiny," a shy individual weighing scarcely one hundred pounds, led an unsuccessful foray into Lower California, in 1853, and followed it with three expeditions into Central America, in 1855, 1857, and 1860.

With the aid of a motley group of American adventurers and disaffected Central Americans, Walker finally established himself as dictator of Nicaragua, from 1855 to 1857. His complex plans seem to have embraced the formation of a Central American federation, with himself at the head.[27] But among Northerners in the United States he was generally, though mistakenly, regarded as being engaged primarily in an effort to secure more slave territory for the South—much as Texas had been acquired. Such an interpretation was strengthened when the Democrats, who were strong in the Southern states, put themselves on record in their platform of 1856 as approving Walker's efforts "to regenerate" Nicaragua. The British not unnaturally felt that this prince of filibusters was but "the advance guard of Manifest Destiny," and that he was engaged in a covert attempt to secure territory for the United States in Central America, in violation of both the letter and the spirit of the Clayton-Bulwer Treaty.[28] This

---

[26] R. W. Van Alstyne, ed., "Anglo-American Relations, 1853–1857," *Amer. Hist. Rev.*, XLII (1937), 497 (Graham to Clarendon, Oct. 24, 1854).

[27] W. O. Scroggs, *Filibusters and Financiers* (N.Y., 1916), p. 228.

[28] Representative Anderson of Missouri declaimed: ". . . Let no technical impediment be thrown in the way of our Americanizing Central America. Humanity, philanthropy, and Christianity, demand that it shall be done at no distant day. Such is our manifest destiny; and why should we be afraid to proclaim it to the world?

conclusion did not seem unreasonable in view of the lukewarm efforts being made by the government of the United States to enforce its antifilibustering laws. But fortunately for good feeling between the two English-speaking nations, Walker's plans were ruined by disease, bad liquor, treachery, the opposition of Cornelius Vanderbilt's transit company, and British and French hostility. The "grey-eyed man of destiny" fell before a Honduran firing squad on September 12, 1860.

Floating Through the Treaty of 1854

Bad feeling over the Central American situation was increased when Canada sought to circumscribe the limited privileges granted to American fishermen along the Newfoundland and Labrador coasts by the Convention of 1818.[29] As soon as the provincial authorities attempted to uphold these restrictions by seizing schooners from the United States, the hardy New Englanders flared up in instant resentment. They found an able advocate in Daniel Webster, a fellow New Englander, who publicly demanded that his countrymen be protected, " 'hook and line, and bob and sinker.' " [30] By July, 1853, American fishing craft were arming themselves for any possible contingency. President Pierce sent a fleet to the troubled waters with ominous orders to prevent, forcibly if necessary, interference with the rights of the United States. The possibilities of an armed clash were freely discussed on both sides. Senator Davis of Massachusetts asserted that "if Great Britain wants a war, undoubtedly she can have it." But across the Atlantic the London *Spectator* thought it nothing short of a "crime" that the "right of catching fishes in the Bay of Fundy" should have brought "two powerful nations linked by closest ties of kindred, sympathy and interest" to the verge of war. The London *Punch*, forsaking the usual role of lampooning its transatlantic kinsmen, observed:

Perish all the cod and mackerel in the Ocean—fine eating as they are— before we go to war with Brother JONATHAN for a cause as scaly as any fish can be that have no scales. We can't think of quarrelling with

---

Wave upon wave of immigration will roll in upon that country, until, ere long, its internal wars, ignorance, superstition, and anarchy, will be supplanted by peace, knowledge, Christianity, and our own Heaven-born institutions." *Cong. Globe,* 35 Cong., 2 sess., p. 299 (Jan. 10, 1859).

[29] Attempts were made to prevent Americans from "hovering" within three miles of the coast; from entering all bays and even all waters within lines drawn from headland to headland; from navigating the Gut of Canso; and from purchasing bait and supplies in British colonial ports.

[30] *Sen. Ex. Docs.,* 32 Cong., 2 sess., no. 22, pp. 444–445 (July 25, 1852).

JONATHAN about fish at a time when our general enemy is plotting everywhere to reduce us, in a greater measure than we like, to a fish diet. . . .[31]

Unfortunately, the controversy over the fisheries was intimately bound up with the internal situation in Canada. The repeal of the British corn laws in 1846, combined with the high American tariff and other factors, had brought much distress.[32] Because of economic pressure and political bitterness a considerable minority in Canada strongly agitated, particularly in 1849, for union with the great southern republic. If it had not been for Southern hostility to Northern expansion, the United States undoubtedly would have shown a much more lively interest in the possibilities of annexation.[33]

But Great Britain had her hands too full with the tangled European situation to permit the fisheries dispute to drift to a bloody conclusion. She finally decided to make an extraordinary effort to iron out the existing difficulties by sending a special mission to the United States, headed by the Governor General of Canada, Lord Elgin, a hard-headed but genial Scot who was famous for his racy anecdotes and brilliant repartee. The British delegation arrived in Washington a day or so before the passing of the fateful Kansas-Nebraska Bill of 1854. The South, which felt that it had made a substantial gain for slavery, was in a mood to placate the North by approving a treaty with Canada. The Americans wanted fishing privileges; the Canadian commercial interests wanted to batter down the Yankee tariff walls. Bargaining was in order.

Wise in the ways of men, Lord Elgin was well aware of the value of social amenities as a lubricant for diplomatic wheels. His brilliant young secretary, Laurence Oliphant, has left some vivid passages descriptive of the fortnight of wining and dining that accompanied the negotiations. One is impressed with his frequent mention of the champagne which "irrigated" the table.

It was the height of the season when we were at Washington, and our arrival imparted a new impetus to the festivities, and gave rise to the taunt,

[31] *Punch,* XXIII, 88 (Aug. 21, 1852).

[32] C. D. Allin and G. M. Jones, *Annexation, Preferential Trade and Reciprocity* (Toronto, 1912), pp. 13 *ff*. This book has an extended analysis of Canadian public opinion.

[33] D. C. Masters, *The Reciprocity Treaty of 1854* (London, 1937), pp. 54-55. The most recent treatment of the annexationist flurry of 1849 in Canada, which was the work of a small but vocal minority, is L. B. Shippee, *Canadian-American Relations, 1849-1874* (New Haven, 1939), pp. 1-20.

after the treaty was concluded . . . that "it had been floated through on champagne." Without altogether admitting this, there can be no doubt that, in the hands of a skilful diplomatist, that beverage is not without its value.[34]

The kind of diplomacy that the British employed was cynically described by Oliphant as "chaffing Yankees and slapping them on the back." "If you have got to deal with hogs," he queried, "what are you to do?"

The Reciprocity Treaty of 1854, the first of its kind entered into by the United States government, was signed in Washington on June 5th of that year. By its terms the Americans were given greatly extended privileges as compared with the Convention of 1818. Specifically, they were permitted to engage in the sea fishery virtually without restriction along the shores of Canada, New Brunswick, Nova Scotia, Prince Edward's Island, and a number of smaller islands. In return, and of less importance, British subjects were to be permitted to fish along the shores of the United States as far as the 36th parallel, which is some little distance south of Chesapeake Bay. Of much greater significance to the Canadians were the reciprocity provisions. The treaty stipulated that a long list of commodities, largely agricultural produce, should be admitted to both Canada and the United States without duty.

The North approved the agreement because it was looked upon as a step toward annexation. The South was favorable because it believed that reciprocity would relieve Canada's economic distress and quiet such demands as were being made for annexation. With the two sections supporting the treaty for opposite reasons, it was approved by the Senate with little opposition. Lest there be any slip, the State Department employed a very able lobbyist, Israel D. Andrews, who later claimed that he spent $118,000 with members of Congress and others.[35]

It was necessary for the provincial legislatures to pass the needed legislation before the treaty could become effective. The State Department had anticipated trouble in this quarter, and during the winter of 1853–1854 had employed Andrews to smooth the way in the Canadian Maritime Provinces. This clever agent spent over $90,000 for news-

[34] Laurence Oliphant, *Episodes in a Life of Adventure* (4th ed., Edinburgh, 1887), pp. 46–47. The reports of Minister Crampton do not reveal that champagne was served at the British legation, but that Congressmen consumed numerous "segars" and twenty-four bottles of pure brandy in a room set aside for that purpose. Van Alstyne, "British Diplomacy and the Clayton-Bulwer Treaty, 1850–60," *loc. cit.*, p. 183.
[35] Masters, *Reciprocity Treaty of 1854*, p. 84 n.

paper articles, entertainment, and various kinds of bribery.[36] He paid $840 to one New Brunswick legislator who had been "adverse to a surrender of the fisheries," but who, after the "disbursement," became an ardent supporter of the treaty.[37] But perhaps the end justified the means. The reciprocity treaty temporarily removed the more serious sources of friction between the United States and her neighbor, and inaugurated a new era of commercial prosperity, particularly for Canada.

DIPLOMACY YIELDS TO POLITICS

When the British declared war on Russia, in 1854, they were surprised and mortified by the lack of sympathy shown in the United States. Congenital American Anglophobes, reinforced by tens of thousands of Irish expatriates, naturally concluded that in any war between Great Britain and a foreign Power Great Britain could not be right. There was also much sympathy in the United States for Russia because of the traditionally but anomalously friendly relations between the two nations. The Russian minister in Washington actually received a communication from three hundred Kentucky riflemen who asked to be sent to the Crimea.[38] The sentiment of the American people, however, was probably more anti-British than pro-Russian.

British bungling and stubborn Russian resistance caused an alarming drain on the man power of the United Kingdom. The brilliant but futile charge of the light brigade at Balaklava, which was soon immortalized by the British poet laureate, Tennyson, brought home with crushing force the seriousness of the problem. To fill decimated ranks Her Majesty's government turned to foreign lands. The British minister in the United States, John Crampton, was instructed to take discreet steps looking toward the enlistment of volunteers. Ere long a trickle of prospective recruits was being directed to Halifax, in conformity, so Crampton insisted, with the strict letter of the inadequate American neutrality law of 1818.[39] But public opinion in the United States reacted so violently against this recruiting activity that Secretary Marcy

---

[36] Of the $90,000, $40,000 was provided by the Canadian government; the rest by the State Department and by Andrews himself. The American became involved in serious financial embarrassments as a result of his personal commitments. Shippee, *Canadian-American Relations*, pp. 74–77.

[37] C. C. Tansill, *The Canadian Reciprocity Treaty of 1854* (Baltimore, 1922), p. 73.

[38] F. A. Golder, "Russian-American Relations during the Crimean War," *Amer. Hist. Rev.*, XXXI (1926), 471.

[39] R. W. Van Alstyne, "John F. Crampton, Conspirator or Dupe?" *Amer. Hist. Rev.*, XLI (1936), 495.

found it expedient to protest to Crampton against his unneutral conduct. When remonstrances proved ineffective, Marcy demanded his recall. The Foreign Office refused to consent to such summary action; whereupon Crampton was abruptly dismissed, on May 28, 1856, together with three British consuls implicated with him.

On May 14, 1856, two weeks before sending Crampton home, President Pierce had shamelessly extended recognition to the bayonet-supported government of Walker in Nicaragua. Both incidents should be interpreted in the light of current politics. The Democratic national nominating convention assembled in Cincinnati only four days after Crampton's dismissal, and the news of his fate was promptly telegraphed to the assembled delegates.[40] This move becomes more understandable when we remember that Pierce was an active candidate for renomination, that the great body of politically potent Irish-Americans was enrolled in the ranks of the Democratic party, and that these rabid expatriates enjoyed the protesting roars of the British lion when his tail was given a twist. It should also be noted that the Democrats, whose militant slavery policy was under fire, were not unwilling to divert attention to Crampton and Central America on the eve of an election.

The British were intensely angered by the treatment of their representatives. Nor was the atmosphere improved by Pierce's recognition of the Walker government and by the apparent disposition of the United States to violate the Clayton-Bulwer Treaty by annexing Nicaragua. English newspapers bristled with war talk. The American minister in London, George M. Dallas, confidently expected the axe to fall on his neck in retaliation for the Crampton dismissal:

If *The Times* and the *Post* are reliable *organs*, I shall probably quit England soon, *never* to return. . . . It will not surprise me if I should turn out to be the last Minister from the United States to the British Court, and that will certainly be fame if it be not honour.[41]

Fortunately, the saner counsels of the British shipping and manufacturing interests, as well as of other moderates, prevailed.[42] The London *Morning Star* attacked the *Times* for its recklessness of tone and for "hurling insults across the Atlantic with as little thought as a schoolboy." Moreover, the Crampton controversy involved nothing fundamental; and, as the American minister in London observed,

[40] R. F. Nichols, *Franklin Pierce* (Phila., 1931), p. 463.
[41] Beckles Willson, *America's Ambassadors to England* (London, 1928), p. 298.
[42] *Cambridge History of British Foreign Policy* (Cambridge, Eng., 1923), II, 276. Crampton was knighted and promoted; and no minister was sent to take his place until Pierce went out of office some ten months later.

Southern cotton, upon which English spindles were dependent, was "pretty good bail for the peaceful behavior of this country." Enough blood had been let during the recent war with Russia.

JOHN AND JONATHAN

The possibilities of a fratricidal conflict over such matters as the Mosquito protectorate and the enlistment controversy opened the eyes of the British public to a situation that had been allowed to drift from bad to worse. Opposition to the Yankee had merely stimulated his aggressiveness and endangered the peace. Was it wise to risk a war with the United States, whose trade amounted to more than that with all of the other republics of the Americas combined? Besides, if the Yankee should absorb all of North America to the Isthmus, would not that bring stability to this revolution-torn region and make for the improvement of British trade? In June, 1856, the powerful London *Times* could "look with great resignation and even pleasure" to the day when the United States would extend to the Isthmus of Panama. That same month the London *Economist* came out flatly:

We could not hinder the ultimate absorption by the Anglo-Saxon republicans of the whole of Central America if we would;—and we are by no means certain that we would if we could. . . . Central America peopled and *exploité* by Anglo-Saxons will be worth to us tenfold its present value.[43]

In February, 1856, Minister Buchanan could report from London that there "has been a marked and favourable change of feeling here within the last month towards the United States. I am now made something of a lion wherever I go. . . ."[44]

The improvement of relations between England and America during the later fifties, though set back by the effect of the panic of 1857 on British investments, was facilitated by a number of developments. Among them should be mentioned a literary *rapprochement* which resulted from the acceptance of the work of hitherto scorned American

---

[43] *Economist*, XIV, 641–642 (June 14, 1856).

[44] G. T. Curtis, *Life of James Buchanan* (N.Y., 1883), II, 167 (Buchanan to his niece, Feb. 29, 1856). Pleading that the strictures of British travelers be bygones, *Punch* wrote:

> Say is it your intent to wallop
> Us on account of Mrs. TROLLOPE?
> Or are we by you to be smitten
> By something DICKENS may have written?
> *Punch*, XXX, 258 (June 28, 1856).

writers, like Longfellow; [45] the temporarily successful laying of the Atlantic cable, in 1858, which resulted in an exchange of felicitations between Queen Victoria and President Buchanan; and the relative decline of the American merchant marine, whose remarkable rise and challenge for ascendancy had greatly disturbed British shippers.[46]

The End of an Era

An alarming development occurred in 1858, the happy solution of which illustrates strikingly the new cordiality between England and the United States. Early in that year some zealous British officers stationed in West Indian waters began a systematic search of American merchantmen suspected of being slavers, even going so far as to fire upon several that refused to show their colors.[47] This resurrection of the right of search caused American indignation to mount dangerously; and warships were rushed to the Gulf of Mexico with orders to resist illegal practices. But when Secretary of State Cass lodged a ringing protest, the British Foreign Secretary, Lord Malmesbury, wrote a memorable reply, dated June 8, 1858, in which he formally disclaimed any pretension to a right of search in time of peace.

Under the therapeutic influence of the new Anglo-American accord the Central American snarl was untangled. British public opinion seems to have favored a settlement, provided it could be accomplished honorably. But, as a writer in *Blackwood's* put it, Britain "cannot consent to be bullied out of her rights." The Foreign Office revealed its willingness to abandon the Bay Islands and the Mosquito protectorate when Lord Clarendon signed a convention with George M. Dallas, the American minister in London, on October 17, 1856. The Senate approved the agreement with amendments, but when these proved unacceptable to Downing Street, the so-called Dallas-Clarendon Convention was dropped. Henceforth Britain bided her time while waiting for a favorable opening. As Lord Clarendon confided to President Buchanan:

. . . Pray bear in mind that beyond the point of honor respecting the Mosquito Indians we possess no interest in Central America, & that, so far

[45] A. H. Quinn, *The Soul of America* (Phila., 1932), p. 68.
[46] See H. J. Carman and Samuel McKee, Jr., *A History of the United States* (Boston, 1931), I, 621–623.
[47] R. W. Van Alstyne, "The British Right of Search and the African Slave Trade," *Jour. of Mod. Hist.*, II (1930), 39.

from wishing to create one, we would not accept such a "damnosa possessio" as Central America if it could be offered to England as a gift.[48]

The immediate problems in dispute between England and America in the Isthmian region were finally settled when Great Britain made separate treaties with the interested Central American republics. By the pact of 1859 with Honduras the British recognized that the Bay Islands belonged to that republic; and by the treaty of 1860 with Nicaragua they relinquished their claims to the Mosquito territory.[49]   In his annual message of December, 1860, on the eve of civil war, President Buchanan could report that these two treaties had resulted "in a final settlement entirely satisfactory to this Government." Time, patient diplomacy, and fortuitous developments had won a diplomatic victory for the United States.

BIBLIOGRAPHICAL NOTE

The diplomacy of the fifties is covered with reasonable detail, though from a biographical point of view, in S. F. Bemis, ed., *The American Secretaries of State and their Diplomacy* (N.Y., 1928), V. On the diplomacy of the Hülsemann and Kossuth affairs see M. E. Curti, "Austria and the United States, 1848–1852," *Smith College Studies in History*, XI (1926), no. 3; on public opinion consult J. G. Gazley, *American Opinion of German Unification, 1848–1871* (N.Y., 1926). The most detailed discussion of the Clayton-Bulwer Treaty and its aftermath appears in Hunter Miller, ed., *Treaties and Other International Acts of the United States of America* (Washington, 1937), V, 675–802. The standard monograph is M. W. Williams, *Anglo-American Isthmian Diplomacy, 1815–1915* (Washington, 1916). See also Dexter Perkins, *The Monroe Doctrine, 1826–1867* (Baltimore, 1933), for the bearing of the Monroe Doctrine on the Isthmian problem. The standard work on Walker is W. O. Scroggs, *Filibusters and Financiers* (N.Y., 1916). The most recent study of the Reciprocity Treaty of 1854 may be found in L. B. Shippee, *Canadian-American Relations, 1849–1874* (New Haven, 1939). Professor R. W. Van Alstyne, the most active student of Anglo-American relations during the fifties, has contributed a number of revealing articles, all of which are mentioned in the footnotes of this chapter. A valuable synthesis of these earlier studies appears in his "British Diplomacy and the Clayton-Bulwer Treaty, 1850–60," *Jour. of Mod. Hist.*, XI (1939), 149–183. Further references: see footnotes of this chapter and Bemis and Griffin, *Guide*, pp. 203 ff.

RECENT REFERENCES. For articles by W. H. Gray on United States diplomacy in Venezuela, 1835–1865, and by G. A. Nuermberger on a South American attempt at union in 1856, see Bibliographical Appendix, p. 928.

NEW REFERENCES. See Bibliographical Appendix, p. 928.

[48] *Works of James Buchanan*, X, 115 (Clarendon to Buchanan, March 13, 1857).
[49] Miller, *Treaties*, V, 801–802.

CHAPTER XIX

The United States and Cuba to 1860

"[America is bounded on the] East by sunrise, West by sunset,
North by the Arctic Expedition, and South *as far as we darn
please."* Philadelphia *Public Ledger,* July 8, 1853.

THE KEY TO THE GULF

SPAIN was banished completely from the continents of North and South
America by the upheaval of the Spanish American revolutions. From
the wreckage she was able to salvage only two insular remnants,
Puerto Rico and Cuba. The latter was by far the more valuable, so
valuable in fact as to cause the government in Madrid many anxious
moments. Flowing with sugar and molasses, this fertile island fully
justifies such appellations as "The Pearl of the Antilles" and "The
World's Sugar Bowl."

Cuba, moreover, enjoys a unique strategic position. Located at the
crossroads of the Caribbean and the Gulf trade routes, it is wedged
into the mouth of the Gulf of Mexico in such a way as to dominate
the only two entrances to that body of water. A powerful and unfriendly nation could have transformed Havana into a veritable
Gibraltar, thus jeopardizing the Caribbean communications of the
United States, threatening its control of an Isthmian route, bottling
up its Gulf ports, and virtually closing the mouth of the Mississippi.

When, in addition to these facts, we note that Cuba is geographically
almost a part of the United States, and remember that during the
forties and fifties of the last century the American people were expanding with seemingly irresistible energy, it will be interesting to
discover why the island did not fall safely into the basket of Manifest
Destiny.

A RIPENING APPLE

At an early date American statesmen, notably Jefferson, were fully
aware of the importance of Cuba to the United States. Their solicitude was definitely stimulated by the Louisiana Purchase and by the

threatened break-up of Spain's colonial empire. Late in 1808, follow-ing overtures by Cuban delegates, Jefferson's Cabinet put itself on record as strongly opposing the acquisition of the island by Great Britain or France—thus foreshadowing the no-transfer principle of the Monroe Doctrine.

In 1817 considerable concern was caused in the United States by newspaper reports to the effect that Britain was about to acquire Cuba from Spain as payment for large monetary claims. These rumors appear to have been without substantial foundation, and interest died down. In 1819, however, when the negotiations for Florida were in progress, the English press loudly demanded the acquisition of Cuba as an offset to Yankee penetration southward.[1] The American public was again aroused; but the British government failed to take any ag-gressive action.

New rumors that Great Britain was about to take over Cuba were stimulated in 1823 by the activity of a British fleet in Caribbean waters, and, as we have seen, these reports may have had some bearing on the enunciation of the Monroe Doctrine.[2] In April of that year Secretary of State Adams sent a memorable instruction to the United States minister in Spain in which he asserted that "the annexation of Cuba to our federal republic will be indispensable to the continuance and integrity of the Union itself." He concluded:

. . . There are laws of political, as well as of physical gravitation; and if an apple, severed by the tempest from its native tree, cannot choose but fall to the ground, Cuba, forcibly disjoined from its own unnatural connexion with Spain, and incapable of self-support, can gravitate only towards the North American Union, which, by the same law of nature, cannot cast her off from its bosom.[3]

In 1825 the unexplained presence of a powerful French squadron in Cuban waters elicited strong protests from both Foreign Secretary Canning and Secretary of State Clay. The latter declared that the United States could not consent to the acquisition of Cuba "by any other European power than Spain under any contingency whatever." Fearful of both French and Yankee aggression, Canning proposed in 1825 that America, France, and Britain enter into a tripartite guaran-

---

[1] E. H. Tatum, Jr., *The United States and Europe, 1815–1823* (Berkeley, Calif., 1936), pp. 164–168.

[2] See Niles' *Weekly Register*, XXIV, 72 (April 5, 1823) for a discussion of this problem and of the desirability of constructing a Florida canal.

[3] *House Ex. Docs.*, 32 Cong., 1 sess., no. 121, p. 7 (Adams to Nelson, April 28, 1823).

tee of the island to Spain. But both France and the United States refused to be drawn into such an agreement.[4] By 1840 the Washington government had become so keenly conscious of the problem that Secretary Forsyth sent extraordinary instructions to the American minister in Spain:

. . . You are authorized to assure the Spanish government, that in case of any attempt, from whatever quarter, to wrest from her this portion of her territory, she may securely depend upon the military and naval resources of the United States to aid her in preserving or recovering it.[5]

Three years later Secretary Webster put the Administration on record in almost identical terms.

Perhaps the basic reason why the United States, France, or Great Britain did not acquire Cuba during the decades before the Civil War is that each of these powers was so jealous of the others that no two of them would permit the third to despoil decadent Spain. The London *Courier*, referring to a similar situation in Europe, pointedly remarked in 1825 that Cuba was a transatlantic Turkey "kept from falling only by the struggles of those who contend for the right of catching her in her descent." [6] Spain was indeed the "sick man" of America, and this very weakness proved to be a source of strength.

We may summarize the attitude of the American government up to this point by saying that, even before the Monroe Doctrine was enunciated, the United States had developed a definite policy toward Cuba. First and foremost, the island should never pass into the hands of a powerful foreign nation. Secondly, it was rather generally taken for granted, if not baldly stated, that Cuba would ultimately be gathered beneath the pinions of the American eagle. As a determined American told the British consul at Philadelphia in 1851: "When we Yankees have once set our *souls* upon a thing, we always have it. Not England, France, and Spain, united, can prevent Cuba from one day becoming ours." [7]

---

[4] J. F. Rippy, *Rivalry of the United States and Great Britain over Latin America, 1808–1830* (Baltimore, 1929), p. 87. For documents relating to Cuba see C. K. Webster, ed., *Britain and the Independence of Latin America, 1812–1830* (London, 1938), II, 518 ff.

[5] *House Ex. Docs.*, 32 Cong., 1 sess., no. 121, p. 37 (Forsyth to Vail, July 15, 1840).

[6] Quoted in J. M. Callahan, *Cuba and International Relations* (Baltimore, 1899), p. 140.

[7] Quoted in L. A. White, "The United States in the 1850's as Seen by British Consuls," *Miss. Valley Hist. Rev.*, XIX (1933), 528 (Peter to Foreign Office, Oct. 7, 1851).

Too Proud to Sell

Until the Mexican War the attitude of the United States toward Cuba had been defensive and protective. Following that conflict the well-established negative policy was abandoned in favor of an acquisitive one. *De Bow's Review* (New Orleans) trumpeted the spirit of the times:

The North Americans *will* spread out far beyond their present bounds. They *will* encroach again and again upon their neighbors. New territories *will* be planted, declare their independence, and be annexed! We have New Mexico and California! We *will* have old Mexico and Cuba! The isthmus cannot arrest—nor even the Saint Lawrence! ! Time has all of this in her womb.[8]

There were, however, more definite reasons for the covetous interest of the United States at this time. Havana was a natural port of call for ships engaged in trade with newly acquired California and Oregon; and with that harbor in the hands of an unfriendly nation, American commerce would be seriously hampered by annoying regulations. Cuba was also in a position to command the vital Isthmian routes, in which great interest had been aroused since the acquisition of California.

But probably the most important factor in developing an appetite for Cuba was the slavery issue. As a result of the Mexican War the South had secured disappointingly little territory into which its "peculiar institution" could expand. If Northern preponderance in Congress were to be checked, the Southerners would have to find land from which new slave states could be carved. Cuba was by far the most desirable territory for such a purpose, and presumably the most available. But if Spain should retain the rich island and free the slaves, an incendiary example to the Negroes of the South would be created at the very doors of the United States. Perhaps there would be a repetition of the Negro butcheries in Haiti, the establishment of a black government, the "Africanization" of Cuba. In the eyes of many Southerners annexation would solve these problems and avert these disasters.

In 1848 the purposeful Polk, ever-willing servant of Manifest Destiny, confidentially authorized the United States minister to Spain, Romulus M. Saunders, to open negotiations for the purchase of Cuba

[8] *De Bow's Review*, VI, 9 (July, 1848).

and, if necessary, to offer as much as $100,000,000. The news of the scheme leaked out, and Spanish public opinion reacted so violently that the Ministry dared not dispose of the island, even if it had been willing to do so. Saunders' blundering overtures were unhesitatingly rebuffed, the Spanish minister declaring that "sooner than see the island transferred to any power, they would prefer seeing it sunk in the ocean." This untimely maneuver served only to increase the distrust of the Spaniards, and strengthen them in their determination not to sell at any price.[9]

THE FILIBUSTER REPLACES THE DIPLOMAT

With Cuba so desirable, and with Spain so obdurate, the thoughts of adventuresome Americans turned naturally to filibustering expeditions as a means of shaking the tree of Manifest Destiny. A leader appeared in the person of General Narciso López, a daring Venezuelan adventurer who had recently been involved in an uprising in Cuba and who believed that the various disaffected elements there would welcome a deliverer. He apparently planned to land in Cuba with a considerable force, summon the Cubans to raise the banner of freedom, wrest the island from Spanish dominion, and then offer it to the Americans. Fortunately for his plans the spirit of expansion was abroad in the land, particularly in the South. As John A. Quitman, one of the most ardent Southern expansionists, insisted: "Our destiny is intertwined with that of Cuba. If slave institutions perish there they will perish here. Thus interested, we must act. Our government, already distracted with the slavery question, can not or will not act. We must do it as individuals." [10]

Other circumstances favored López. Hundreds of restless Mexican War veterans were eager to help carry out the dictates of Manifest Destiny, and at the same time thwart what were presumed to be the designs of Britain on the "Pearl of the Antilles." Some of these adventurers doubtless looked upon themselves as bearers of the torch of liberty, which had been snuffed out in the recent European revolu-

[9] Saunders' laziness and ineptitude were severely criticized in the press of the United States. James Buchanan, then Secretary of State, later confessed: "It must be admitted that a more skilful agent might have been selected to conduct the negotiation in Spain, as our present minister speaks no language but English, & even this he sometimes murders. . . ." J. B. Moore, *Works of James Buchanan*, VIII, 360 (Buchanan to Clayton, Apr. 17, 1849).

[10] J. F. H. Claiborne, *Life and Correspondence of John A. Quitman* (N.Y., 1860), II, 208 (Quitman to Reed, Aug. 24, 1854).

tions. But probably many more of them were attracted by promises of lavish rewards, such as confiscated sugar plantations. And American speculators, who had bought up Cuban bonds at from three to twenty cents on the dollar, could scarcely restrain their enthusiasm for Cuban liberty.

López's first expedition, that of 1849, was prevented from leaving port by the vigilance of the United States authorities. Nothing daunted, the venturesome Venezuelan organized another expedition, slipped out of New Orleans with several hundred men, and landed in Cuba, May, 1850.[11] But when the inhabitants, who were represented as panting for liberty, failed to rise up and greet their deliverer, López was forced to flee to the United States, arriving in Key West just a few minutes ahead of a pursuing Spanish warship. Arrested at Savannah on a charge of having violated the neutrality laws, he was released for want of sufficient evidence, and was greeted as a conquering hero. López and other leaders were indicted at New Orleans, but public opinion was so sympathetic toward the filibusters that three successive juries disagreed. Prosecutions in New York and Ohio met with similar failures.

Still undaunted, López laid plans for his third and last descent upon Cuba.[12] He offered the command of the expedition successively to Jefferson Davis and Robert E. Lee, both of whom were interested but not sufficiently so to risk their necks. In August, 1851, López stole out of New Orleans (with the connivance of the collector of the port) at the head of about five hundred men, mostly Americans. After landing in Cuba, the tiny army was defeated by Spanish troops, López and fifty of his followers were speedily executed, and more than one hundred of the remaining prisoners were condemned to penal servitude. The severity of the punishment was doubtless designed to discourage these annual descents upon the island. In fact, a large number of Americans in New Orleans were awaiting only the news of López's success before pushing on to his assistance.[13]

When the news of the mass execution of "the gallant fifty-one"

[11] Doubtless as a reflection of the zeal for liberty aroused in America by the European revolutions of 1848, a number of the participants in this enterprise stupidly wore red shirts, thus increasing the risk of detection from passing steamers. R. G. Caldwell, *The López Expeditions to Cuba, 1848–1851* (Princeton, 1915), pp. 65–66 n.

[12] A poster was issued in Washington, D.C. (Sept. 1, 1851) bearing such captions as "Ho for Cuba"; "Grand Mass Meeting"; "Huzzah for Lopez." File 200, Broadsides, Library of Congress.

[13] Caldwell, *López Expeditions*, p. 114.

reached New Orleans, hotbed of filibusterism, the indignation of the populace rose to fever heat. Many of the ill-fated adventurers were representatives of the "best families" of the South, and their kinsfolk and friends were inexpressibly shocked. When, in these circumstances, a Spanish newspaper in New Orleans was so ill-advised as to gloat over the outcome of the expedition, a mob rose up and wrecked the establishment, destroyed other property belonging to Spaniards, sacked the Spanish consulate, defaced portraits of the Queen and of the Captain-General of Cuba, and tore to bits a Spanish flag.

Violence also flared up in Key West, Florida, where sympathy for the filibusters was strong. Mass meetings were held in cities as far north as Cincinnati and Pittsburgh. Even in Philadelphia, where there had been strong opposition to the activities of López, the reports of Spanish ruthlessness produced a revulsion of sentiment.[14]

In Spain, where a mob was with difficulty restrained from sacking the American legation by way of retaliation, there was much talk of dismissing the American envoy and of declaring war. The Spanish minister in Washington, Calderón de la Barca, demanded redress and reparation. It was perhaps fortunate that the Whigs, less aggressively expansionist than the Democrats, were in power; and Secretary Webster did not see fit to employ the same rabble-rousing tactics that he had used against Hülsemann. Although pointing out certain mitigating circumstances, the American Secretary wholeheartedly acknowledged the wrong and promised the necessary apologies.

Webster's unexpectedly soft answer helped turn away the wrath of the Spaniards. Early in 1852 the Spanish minister in Washington, Calderón, announced that the Queen, as an act of grace, had pardoned the American survivors of the López expedition. Gratified by this act of magnanimity, Congress in turn voted $25,000 as compensation for the damage done to Spanish property by the New Orleans mob.

America Declines to Tie Her Hands

In 1849, when López attempted his first expedition, difficulties with Great Britain in Central America were, as we have seen, drawing to a head; and Cuban filibusterism aggravated an already dangerous situation. The London *Times,* fearing for Canada, prophesied:

If the Southern States are allowed to incorporate Cuba . . . the North will turn in self-defence upon the nearest territory which it may seize to restore the balance of power, and that territory is our own. One act of violence

[14] *Ibid.,* p. 115.

and rapine will follow another, until the popular cry will be for the expulsion of European authority from the North American continent and the West Indian Islands.[15]

The London *Spectator* referred with disgust to the "arrogance" of the "Model Republic" and to the motives of the "loafers" and "vagabonds" who made up the filibustering expeditions. A British fleet was ordered to Cuban waters to co-operate with the French in protecting the island. The British minister in Washington was instructed to explain that this was being done in the most friendly spirit, which, of course, the American people did not believe. Fortunately, López's failure prevented serious international complications.

Apprehensions aroused by this outburst of filibusterism prompted the British and French governments, at Spain's instigation, to propose (April 23, 1852) a tripartite convention with the United States by which Cuba would be guaranteed to Spain. Secretary Webster favored the scheme; but after he had died and after the American people had shown themselves favorable to expansion in the November election, President Fillmore balked. To Edward Everett, Webster's successor, fell the task of explaining to Madrid why the United States could not tie its hands by such an agreement. Among other things, Everett adverted to the time-honored policy of no entanglements, declared that no American government "could stand a day" if it bound itself in no circumstances to acquire the island, and suggested that if Cuba lay off the mouth of the Thames River, Britain would propose no such arrangement. In one memorable passage the American Secretary, who was a distinguished orator, rose to heights of eloquence:

> The island of Cuba lies at our doors. It commands the approach to the Gulf of Mexico, which washes the shores of five of our States. It bars the entrance of that great river which drains half the North American continent, and with its tributaries forms the largest system of internal water-communication in the world. It keeps watch at the door-way of our intercourse with California by the Isthmus route. . . . Under certain contingencies it might be almost essential to our safety.[16]

PIERRE SOULÉ—EXTRAORDINARY ENVOY

Following a four-year Whig interlude, from 1849 to 1853, the expansionist Democratic party returned to power with the amiable

[15] London *Times*, Sept. 9, 1851, 5:1.
[16] *Senate Ex. Docs.*, 32 Cong., 2 sess., no. 13, pp. 17–18 (Everett to Sartiges, Dec. 1, 1852).

Franklin Pierce as President. It was to be expected that the new Administration, strongly under Southern influence, would take active steps to acquire Cuba. But the South was by no means alone in its enthusiasm for the "Pearl of the Antilles." In New York City the Democratic victory of 1852 was celebrated by a night parade, in which one of the transparencies read: "The Acquisition of Cuba by Purchase." At a Democratic gathering in Albany popular toasts were: "Cuba and the Sandwich Isles—may they soon be added to the galaxy of States"; "The fruits of the late Democratic victory—Pierce and Cuba"; and "May the Queen of the Antilles be added to our glorious Confederacy under the prosperous administration of Pierce." The new President, responding to such enthusiasm, and nothing loath to divert attention from the burning slavery issue by a spirited foreign policy, left no doubts as to his attitude on expansion in general and on Cuba in particular when he asserted in his inaugural address:

. . . The policy of my Administration will not be controlled by any timid forebodings of evil from expansion. Indeed . . . our attitude as a nation and our position on the globe render the acquisition of *certain possessions not within our jurisdiction* eminently important for our protection, if not in the future essential for preservation of the rights of commerce and the peace of the world.[17]

With Cuba the focal point of the Administration's foreign policy, the post of United States minister to Spain took on more than ordinary importance. For this critical position Pierce chose the hotheaded Pierre Soulé, United States Senator from Louisiana, a naturalized American who had been exiled from France for his unrestrained republicanism. He had commended himself to the Pierce administration as a result of his notorious enthusiasm for seizing Cuba; and for this reason, if for no other, his appointment was little short of an insult to the Spanish government.

The beginnings of Soulé's mission were singularly inauspicious. On the eve of sailing he made an indiscreet proannexationist speech to a group of Cuban sympathizers in New York, and after various vicissitudes arrived in Spain, only to get into difficulties over an offensively worded address to the Queen. The attitude of Soulé's diplomatic colleagues was unfriendly. Several of them, notably the French ambassador, the Marquis de Turgot, had allegedly sought to have the middle-class French expatriate rejected. During a ball given by Tur-

[17] J. D. Richardson, *Messages and Papers of the Presidents* (Washington, 1897), V, 198–199 (March 4, 1853). Italics inserted.

got, one of the guests made an offensive remark about Madame Soulé's low-cut gown. The upshot of the affair was that the American envoy challenged the French ambassador to a duel on the grounds that the alleged insult had occurred at the latter's home. In the resulting encounter Soulé had the satisfaction of shooting his adversary in the thigh and laming him for life. The unpleasant notoriety attaching to these incidents caused the American minister to be ostracized socially; and his usefulness was so definitely circumscribed that he should have been peremptorily recalled. Although the antics of the "damned little Frenchman" met with considerable censure in the press of the United States, the nationalistic journals were disposed to condone his conduct. The Boston *Post* hoped that "the exhibition of a little American grit may do these lacqueys [*sic*] of despotism some good." The Detroit *Free Press* exulted that "they are beginning to find out on the other side that Americans are considerable pumpkins, all right." [18]

THE BLACK WARRIOR AFFAIR

As a result of the López expeditions the Spanish officials in Cuba developed a bitterness toward the United States that was reflected in the offensive enforcement of shipping regulations.[19] A long series of vexatious incidents culminated in the seizure, on February 28, 1854, of the *Black Warrior*, an American steamer engaged in coastwise trade between Mobile and New York. This drastic action was based on a technicality that had been ignored during the thirty-odd times the vessel had previously touched at Havana.[20]

A wave of indignation, fed by smoldering resentment over the outcome of the López expeditions, swept the United States. Although the country was convulsed over the Kansas-Nebraska affair, the tone of the press was unmistakably bellicose. The Washington *Union*, organ of the Pierce administration, declared that the time had come when Spain must be met in Cuba with "the purse in one hand and the sword in the other." The New York *Herald* was no less belligerent:

[18] A. A. Ettinger, *The Mission to Spain of Pierre Soulé, 1853–1855* (New Haven, 1932), pp. 237–238.

[19] At best the laws had been capriciously and arbitrarily enforced. Nicholas Trist, then consul in Havana, wrote in 1835: "God help the man who once gets the clutches of Spanish judges upon him, and has nothing to depend upon but the 'courts established by law.'" H. B. Learned, "William Learned Marcy," in S. F. Bemis, ed., *The American Secretaries of State and their Diplomacy* (N.Y., 1928), VI, 188.

[20] H. L. Janes, "The Black Warrior Affair," *Amer. Hist. Rev.*, XII (1907), 281.

If the administration have any heart left, if there be among them one spark of American spirit, let them take up this matter in the tone which befits the gravity of the case, and the chronic character of the Cuban disease. No ambassadors, or diplomatic notes are needed. Let them simply fit out, in a week at farthest, three or four war steamers, and despatch them to Cuba, with peremptory orders to obtain satisfaction for the injury done to the Black Warrior.[21]

President Pierce, doubtless influenced by the strong Southern element in his Cabinet, submitted a special message to Congress, March 15, 1854, in which he announced that satisfaction proportionate to the magnitude of the offense would be demanded.

Meanwhile the theatrical Soulé had been champing at the bit in Spain, specifically forbidden by his instructions to attempt to purchase Cuba and thus provoke the antislavery elements at home. Then came the news of the *Black Warrior* affair. Soulé was overjoyed, for here was a splendid opportunity to lay down the law to the high-spirited Spaniard, goad him into war, and then rob him of his Caribbean pearl.

Soulé's note to the Spanish Foreign Office, dated April 8, 1854, employed strong, not to say offensive, language in demanding redress for what was described as a premeditated and highhanded outrage. The next day was Palm Sunday, which was observed with great solemnity in Spain; and on Monday began Passion Week. Although the Spanish Foreign Office, normally dilatory, could not be expected to labor feverishly during this period, and although time was necessary to prepare a reply, in three days Soulé's scanty store of patience evaporated. He delivered an ultimatum in which he demanded a $300,000 indemnity, the dismissal of all persons responsible for the *Black Warrior* seizure, and a reply within forty-eight hours. The bearer of the note pointed to the clock in the Spanish Foreign Office and dramatically announced that an answer was due in precisely two days by the selfsame timepiece.

Soulé's ultimatum was a violation of instructions—ordinarily a serious offense for a diplomat. Although Secretary Marcy had specified that the American envoy should demand an indemnity of $300,000, and that he was to secure "as early a reply as practicable," nothing whatever was said about demanding an immediate answer or about dismissing the responsible Spanish officials.[22] But Soulé apparently regarded himself as a colleague of Secretary Marcy, not as a subordinate.

[21] New York *Herald*, March 9, 1854, 4:4.
[22] Ettinger, *Mission to Spain of Pierre Soulé*, p. 261.

As the New York *Herald* pointedly asserted, "We wanted an ambassador there, we have sent a matador."

The Spanish foreign minister, Calderón, who had recently been minister in Washington, shrewdly suspected that the impetuous Frenchman had exceeded his instructions, and he skillfully parried Soulé's thrusts. Through the Spanish representative in America the Madrid government presented to Secretary Marcy such an able and tactful defense of the Spanish position as to make a deep impression on the Cabinet. Rather than bicker with the overbearing Soulé, Calderón dealt directly with the American owners of the *Black Warrior*; and months before the affair had ceased to be a diplomatic problem the vessel was plying its usual course in the usual way, except that it was receiving unusual deference from the Spanish officials at Havana. The owners were fully satisfied even if Soulé was not.[23]

THE AIX-LA-CHAPELLE DISPATCH

The British and French governments sympathized with Spain in the *Black Warrior* crisis; but they had their own hands full with the Crimean War, which broke out twelve days before Soulé delivered his ultimatum. Although Europe's distresses strengthened the United States diplomatically, Spain had one powerful and unexpected ally in America—slavery. The Pierce administration had aroused so much resentment in the North by its efforts to jam the Kansas-Nebraska bill through Congress that it simply did not dare take a second forward step in behalf of the "peculiar institution" by provoking a war for Cuba. The New York *Courier and Enquirer* asserted:

Does the sane man live who believes that if Cuba was tendered us tomorrow . . . that this people would consent to receive and annex her? . . . There was a time when the North would have consented to annex Cuba, but the Nebraska wrong has forever rendered annexation impossible.[24]

The Pierce administration could not have failed to perceive that war with Spain for Cuba would alienate the northern wing of the party

[23] The vessel was released on March 16, 1854, two weeks after its seizure. A fine of $6000 was then exacted but later remitted. Before the next year had ended Spain had voluntarily paid the owners $53,000 damages, on the grounds that the port authorities had erred in not allowing the *Black Warrior* the customary twelve hours to present a corrected manifest. Janes, "The Black Warrior Affair," *loc. cit.*, pp. 288–289.

[24] June 1, 1854, quoted in J. F. Rhodes, *History of the United States* (N.Y., 1896), II, 33 n.

and hopelessly disunite the entire country. One wonders if the South did not make a colossal blunder when it traded the dubious advantages (they later proved to be liabilities) of the Kansas-Nebraska bill for the undeniable advantages of Cuba.[25]

Though unprepared to go to war with Spain over the *Black Warrior*, the Pierce administration thought the time opportune to reopen negotiations for the purchase of Cuba. In his remarkable instruction of April 3, 1854, Secretary Marcy directed Soulé to make a determined effort in this direction. If Spain should prove unwilling to accept a reasonable sum, even a maximum of $130,000,000, "you will then direct your efforts to the next most desirable object which is *to detach* that island from the Spanish dominion and from all dependence on any European power." [26] The succeeding passage indicates that what Marcy had in mind by "detach" was to assist Cuba to become independent, whereupon she would doubtless fling herself into the outstretched arms of the United States.

On August 16, 1854, Marcy sent additional instructions, which apparently were prompted in part by the ever-present fear that the blacks might seize control of Cuba, and in part by the preoccupation of the Powers with the Crimean War. He suggested that Soulé arrange a conference with James Buchanan, United States minister to England, and John Y. Mason, minister to France.[27] The three envoys were to exchange opinions and report their conclusions in a dispatch to the Department of State.

The ministerial trio finally met at Ostend, Belgium, in October, 1854. The European press, suspecting that the secret conference boded no good, indulged in wild speculation as to the fate of the "Pearl of the Antilles." The London *Morning Advertiser*, which feared for both Cuba and Hawaii, remarked, "Jonathan's legs are getting so long that he requires more room." The three ministers, apparently desiring greater privacy, left Ostend after three days for Aix-la-Chapelle, in Rhenish Prussia, where they concluded their work six days later, October 18, 1854.

The recommendations of the three ministers were embodied in a memorable diplomatic dispatch to Marcy subsequently known as the

[25] Secretary Marcy wrote (July, 1854) that "the Nebraska question has sadly shattered our party in all the free states and deprived it of that strength which was needed and would have been much more profitably used for the acquisition of Cuba." R. F. Nichols, *Franklin Pierce* (Phila., 1931), p. 343.

[26] Learned, "Marcy," in Bemis, *American Secretaries of State*, VI, 193 (Marcy to Soulé, April 3, 1854). Italics inserted.

[27] Ettinger, *Mission to Spain of Pierre Soulé*, pp. 341–342.

Ostend Manifesto. It was really the work of Soulé, though Buchanan tempered and wrote it. After recommending that an immediate effort be made to purchase Cuba for a price not to exceed $120,000,000, the American representatives then discussed what should be done if Spain refused to sell. If this happened, and if her continued presence in Cuba should be regarded as dangerous for the United States:

. . . Then, by every law, human and divine, we shall be justified in wresting it from Spain if we possess the power; and this upon the very same principle [referring to "Africanization"] that would justify an individual in tearing down the burning house of his neighbor if there were no other means of preventing the flames from destroying his own home.

Under such circumstances we ought neither to count the cost nor regard the odds which Spain might enlist against us.[28]

In short, first undertake peaceful negotiations with Spain; then, *if the danger seemed great enough*, direct action.

It should be noted at this point that the term Ostend Manifesto is a misnomer. In the first place the document was not signed at Ostend but at Aix-la-Chapelle; and in the second place it was not a manifesto. A manifesto is a public declaration of policy; and the misuse of the word in this connection has given rise to the mistaken conception that the document was presented to Spain in the form of an ultimatum. On the contrary, the so-called Ostend Manifesto was a confidential dispatch, drawn up in secrecy and sent by a special messenger to the State Department. Neither the American nor the Spanish government took official cognizance of it.

SOULÉ IS MADE THE SCAPEGOAT

The semitransparent machinations of the three ministers at Ostend and Aix-la-Chapelle excited much hostile comment in European circles. Observing that the naïve Americans did not even bother to hatch their mischief in secret, the London *Times* pointedly remarked: "The diplomacy of the United States is certainly a very singular profession." In October, 1854, before the official copy of the dispatch had reached Secretary Marcy, the American press was publishing garbled versions of the Manifesto, and the antislavery and anti-Democratic newspapers were attacking the Administration and its "Democratic minions." Marcy was probably startled when, on November 4, 1854, he received

[28] *House Ex. Docs.*, 33 Cong., 2 sess., no. 93, pp. 129, 131 (American ministers to Marcy, Oct. 18, 1854).

the report of the three ministers. After prolonged Cabinet discussions, he framed a reply to Soulé, dated November 13, 1854, in which he politely but firmly refused to accept the suggestions of his agents. This repudiation becomes more understandable when we note that the Democratic party had suffered severe losses in the recent Congressional elections, partly, it appears, as a result of the Administration's Cuban policy.

Buchanan and Mason were disturbed by Marcy's answer; but Soulé, who was directed to continue his negotiations for a peaceful purchase, was "stunned." Repudiated and humiliated, he saw that there was no prospect whatsoever of being able to buy Cuba, particularly since his participation in the notorious Ostend conference was well known in Spain.[29] Unable to linger on "in languid impotence," the dynamic Soulé resigned on December 17, 1854.

The outburst of criticism against the Administration continued in the United States, much of it directed at "that French fop, Soulé." So confirmed a Democrat as Senator Cass of Michigan condemned the attempt to "steal" Cuba, and asserted: "Such a case of rapacity will, I trust, never stain our annals." The public demand for an authentic copy of the Manifesto became so great that Congress published the relevant papers in March, 1855. Immediately the opposition press renewed its uproar. The New York *Evening Post*, referring to "The Three Wise Men of Ostend," branded the dispatch as "weak in its reasonings and atrocious in its recommendations." The New York *Tribune* condemned this "manifesto of brigands," which could be paraphrased: "If Spain will not sell us Cuba, we must steal it in order to preserve our national existence."

For many years historians assumed that nothing essential had been omitted from the published documents. But in 1928 it was revealed that several important passages had been deleted, notably the one containing the famous "to detach" clause.[30] When these missing links are supplied, a flood of light illuminates the formerly incomprehensible aspects of the Ostend affair.

It will be remembered that on April 3, 1854, Secretary Marcy directed Soulé to offer as much as $130,000,000 for Cuba, and then, if unsuccessful, to take steps "to detach" the island from Spain. Surprising though it may seem, the essential portions of the Ostend Manifesto

---

[29] Soulé's secretary wrote: "He is isolated in Spain. . . . He is in many respects a superior man, but as a diplomatist he has missed his career. . . ." Learned, "Marcy," in Bemis, *American Secretaries of State*, VI, 203 (Perry to Marcy, Sept. 6, 1854).

[30] This discovery was published by H. B. Learned in *ibid.*, p. 214.

are not altogether out of harmony with these instructions. The three ministers had suggested that the United States offer $120,000,000 for the island, and then "wrest" it from Spain. It is certainly not a far cry from the ambiguous "detach" to the more direct "wrest." Soulé was merely acting in conformity with both the spirit and, in large measure, with the exact letter of his instructions. But the Ostend Manifesto excited so much partisan opposition in the United States that Marcy could not afford to blacken both himself and the Administration by revealing that he was in considerable measure responsible for the damaging document. Soulé was made to suffer for the sins of his superior.[31]

So Near and Yet So Far

Even before the distracted Pierce administration came to a close, its blundering domestic and foreign policy had ruined whatever chance there may have been of acquiring Cuba. But the Southern annexationists, not realizing that they had slain their prospects of acquiring the island on the altar of the Kansas-Nebraska Act, refused to give up hope. They elevated to the presidency the complaisant James Buchanan, who had commended himself to the favorable attention of the Southern Democrats by his part in framing the Ostend Manifesto.[32] Two days after he took office the Supreme Court handed down its momentous Dred Scott decision, which intensified the bitterness of the struggle over slavery and further foreshadowed the impending breach. Yet Buchanan, blind to the fact that Cuba was lost, still cherished a lively hope of securing the island. In three of his four annual messages he urged upon Congress the desirability of taking steps to purchase this Antillean jewel—pronouncements which did nothing to allay the distrust of Spain.

But Buchanan's appeals fell upon deaf ears. Cuba became less important as an increasing amount of commerce that formerly had gone through the Gulf was now carried by railroads and canals. The Republicans in Congress wanted to pass the Homestead Act in order to open up Western lands to white settlers; the Southern Democrats desired Cuba in order to open up slave lands to slave owners. Neither would gratify the aspirations of the other. As the outspoken "Bluff Ben" Wade cried in the Senate, "Shall we give niggers to the niggerless

---

[31] Ettinger, *Mission to Spain of Pierre Soulé,* p. 412.

[32] On the other hand, Buchanan was pilloried by his political foes for his part in the Ostend Manifesto. See particularly cartoons numbered 3 and 4 in *American Caricatures Pertaining to the Civil War* (N.Y., 1918).

or land to the landless?" And the galleries burst into applause. With passions as inflamed as they were, it is doubtful whether the North would have permitted the acceptance of Cuba if it had come as a voluntary gift from Spain. Nevertheless, as late as 1860 the platforms of the divided Democratic party declared for Cuba.[33]

Then came the Civil War, knotty reconstruction problems, and amazing internal expansion. Slave territory was no longer needed; the United States already had enough territory, and a very large number of Negroes. The long-projected transcontinental railroad was completed in 1869, binding California to the rest of the Union. The pressure for an Isthmian canal decreased, and the agitation for annexing Cuba declined. But the island had yet to play its most important role in American diplomacy.

BIBLIOGRAPHICAL NOTE

An excellent brief account of the Cuban diplomacy of the Pierce administration is H. B. Learned, "William Learned Marcy," in S. F. Bemis, ed., *The American Secretaries of State and their Diplomacy* (N.Y., 1928), VI, 183–216. Stronger on the political backgrounds are the chapters (XLII–XLVIII) in R. F. Nichols, *Franklin Pierce* (Phila., 1931). An excellent detailed treatment of the subject is A. A. Ettinger, *The Mission to Spain of Pierre Soulé, 1853–1855* (New Haven, 1932). Older but still useful on the earlier years are J. M. Callahan, *Cuba and International Relations* (Baltimore, 1899); and J. H. Latané, "The Diplomacy of the United States in Regard to Cuba," Amer. Hist. Assn., *Annual Report, 1897,* pp. 217–278. The most satisfactory account in English of the subject is R. G. Caldwell, *The López Expeditions to Cuba, 1848–1851* (Princeton, 1915). A useful article is H. L. Janes, "The Black Warrior Affair," *Amer. Hist. Rev.,* XII (1907), 280–298. Further references: see footnotes of this chapter and Bemis and Griffin, *Guide,* pp. 302–308.

RECENT REFERENCES. G. B. Henderson, "Southern Designs on Cuba, 1854–1857, and Some European Opinions," *Jour. of Southern Hist.,* V (1939), 371–385, presents documents which show clearly British solicitude for Cuba. The editor suggests that if the Southerners had not made themselves so offensive to Britain by their outspoken designs on the island, British sympathy for them during the Civil War might have taken on more tangible form.

NEW REFERENCES. Hunter Miller, ed., *Treaties and other International Acts of the United States of America* (Washington, 1942), VII, 31–111, has the most detailed documentary discussion of the *Black Warrior* affair.

4TH ED. REFS. Basil Rauch, *American Interest in Cuba: 1848–1855* (N.Y., 1948), is broader in treatment than Ettinger's. Polk's administration betrayed López in 1848 hoping to win Spain's good will for a sale of Cuba (77–80).

[33] *Vanity Fair* (New York), in its issues of May 12, 1860 (I, 312) and June 2, 1860 (I, 360), printed cartoons showing the United States about to take Cuba.

CHAPTER XX

The Dawn of Asiatic Interests

"Who does not see, then, that . . . the Pacific Ocean, its shores, its islands, and the vast regions beyond, will become the chief theatre of events in the world's great hereafter?"

Senator Seward, 1852.

THE TRADER PRECEDES THE DIPLOMAT

WHILE America was absorbed with the dramatic happenings of the "roaring forties" and the "fitful fifties," quieter but hardly less significant events were taking place on the other side of the globe. Although the United States, to be sure, was only secondarily interested in the Orient, it was nevertheless interested. How did this all come about?

On February 22, 1784, a month after the proclamation of peace with Great Britain, a small merchantman, the *Empress of China*, slipped quietly out of New York harbor with a cargo of products for China. More than a year later the vessel created something of a sensation when it returned with a cargo of strange-smelling products. Though the reported profits of twenty-five per cent were not extraordinarily high in view of the investment and the risk,[1] other merchants were tempted to follow suit, and a new avenue of commerce was opened.

The Old China trade grew so rapidly that in the year 1801 thirty-four American vessels reached Canton—some of them so tiny as to astonish foreign observers. Though crippled by the embargo and the War of 1812, this newly found Oriental commerce expanded during the thirties and forties, and from 1850 to 1855—the heyday of the stately clipper ship—American carrying trade reached its peak.[2] Only two aspects of this fascinating story need be mentioned here. The demand at Canton for sea-otter pelts lured venturesome "Boston men" to the Pacific Northwest and did something to build up a demand for

---

[1] *The Journals of Major Samuel Shaw* (Boston, 1847), p. 218.
[2] For the figures through 1844 see F. R. Dulles, *The Old China Trade* (Boston, 1930), pp. 210–211.

the retention of Oregon. The use of the Sandwich (Hawaiian) Islands as a halfway station for the fur trade, and also as a source for
the sandalwood so highly prized by the Chinese, gave to Americans
an early foothold on the shores of the glamorous Hawaiian archipelago.[3]

Unfortunately for Occidental trade, the Chinese had long held that
China was *the* great nation, and that all other states were inferior.
Accordingly, when "foreign devils" ventured into the presence of the
Emperor (Son of Heaven), they were forced, as were the Chinese
themselves, to prostrate themselves before him in the kowtow. Although China was economically self-sufficient, and although the government was not eager to engage in outside trade, foreigners were
permitted to carry on commerce at the single port of Canton, in
South China. Here a group of Occidental traders lived rather pre-
cariously, suffering various indignities, which included occasional ston-
ings.[4] This is not altogether surprising when we remember that Chinese merchants themselves were looked down upon, and that foreign
"barbarians" who forsook the tombs of their ancestors for mere profit
were regarded as particularly despicable.

It was not, however, until the early 1830's, when the murder of an
American crew in Sumatra aroused public interest, that the United
States attempted to establish formal diplomatic relations with a Far
Eastern nation.[5] Edmund Roberts, a sea captain of considerable mercantile experience, was sent out as a special agent in 1832, with instructions to draw up commercial treaties with Cochin China, Siam,
Muscat, and later with Japan. China was not included on the list apparently because the American merchants at Canton were willing to
let well enough alone. The mission was not considered to be of primary importance, for Roberts was entered on the rolls as "secretary
to the commander" at a salary of $1500 a year, and was forced to sleep
on the gun deck with the crew a part of the way.

In Cochin China the American envoy was unsuccessful because he

---

[3] K. S. Latourette, *The History of Early Relations between the United States and
China, 1784-1844* (New Haven, 1917), pp. 43–44. The fur seals of the South
Pacific also figured prominently in this early trade. *Ibid.*, pp. 38–40. See also H. W.
Bradley, "The Hawaiian Islands and the Pacific Fur Trade, 1785–1813," *Pacific
Northwest Quar.*, XXX (1939), 275–299.

[4] In an official Chinese customs report we find this entry: "The barbarian Marks,
[a merchant] residing in the English devil factory; . . . the barbarian Just, residing in the French devil factory." J. W. Foster, *American Diplomacy in the Orient*
(Boston, 1903), p. 44.

[5] It is significant that not until 1831 was the word China mentioned in a public
presidential message or paper; and not until 1852 was Japan referred to.

refused to submit to the kowtow, which foreigners regarded as degrading.[6] But in Siam and Muscat he did succeed in negotiating treaties (1833) that were designed to free American trade from onerous restrictions. Roberts thought it inadvisable to go on to Japan and attempt to open negotiations because he was without funds to buy presents, and because he felt that his expedition was too small to impress the Japanese. He thereupon came back to the United States with his two treaties, which were approved by the Senate; then he returned to the Orient to exchange ratifications and open negotiations with Japan. While in China he died of the plague, June 12, 1836—the pioneer, and a not unworthy one, in the Far Eastern diplomacy of the United States.

GROWING AMERICAN INTEREST IN CHINA

Three years later, in 1839, Great Britain and China went to war. To the Chinese the one cause was the determination of the British to force the opium trade upon the Celestial Empire; to foreigners in general the real issue was the struggle for international equality.[7] The British were victorious, and in the treaty of Nanking (1842) forced China to cede Hongkong outright, and throw open five Chinese ports to unrestricted foreign residence and trade.

This Anglo-Chinese war (generally referred to as the Opium War) seems to have aroused the first widespread American interest in China. These were the years when Anglophobia was rampant (the Ashburton and Nanking treaties were signed during the same year), and the American people were angered by what they regarded as Britain's bullying attempt to force opium on the poor heathen Chinese. But John Quincy Adams braved "the strong current of popular opinion" and delivered a lengthy lecture before the Massachusetts Historical Society, in which he justified Great Britain's course. The doughty New Englander recorded: "The excitement of public opinion and feeling by the delivery of this lecture far exceeds any expectation that I had formed. . . ."[8]

The sympathy for China evoked by the Opium War served to bring

[6] Discovering that here he had to have titles, the resourceful Roberts reeled off the names of the counties of New Hampshire, his native state, and was just beginning with the towns, rivers, and lakes when a halt was called. Foster, *American Diplomacy in the Orient*, p. 49.

[7] H. B. Morse and H. F. MacNair, *Far Eastern International Relations* (Boston, 1931), p. 114.

[8] C. F. Adams, ed., *Memoirs of John Quincy Adams* (Phila., 1876), XI, 31 (Dec. 3, 1841).

to a head a quiet educative process that had been going on in the United States over a period of years. The interest of American com-

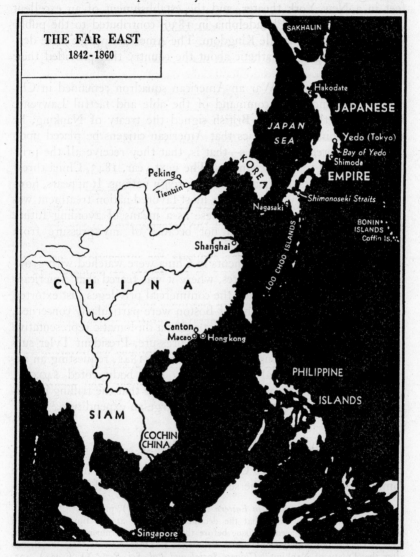

THE FAR EAST
1842-1860

SAKHALIN

Hakodate

JAPANESE

JAPAN
SEA

Yedo (Tokyo)
Bay of Yedo
Shimoda

KOREA

Peking

Tientsin

EMPIRE

Nagasaki

Shimonoseki Straits

BONIN
ISLANDS
Coffin Is.

Shanghai

LOO CHOO ISLANDS

CHINA

Canton
Macao   Hongkong

PHILIPPINE

ISLANDS

SIAM

COCHIN
CHINA

Singapore

mercial groups, particularly those in the shipping centers of New England and the Middle Atlantic states, has already been noted. Farther south, cotton growers were beginning to speculate on "China's illimitable markets." In 1830 the first American missionaries had arrived in

China, and reports from them, together with financial support of their work, attracted attention.[9] The exhibition of a Chinese girl with bound feet in a New York theater, and the establishment of an excellent Chinese museum in Philadelphia in 1839, contributed to the public knowledge of the Middle Kingdom. The American people were definitely becoming less apathetic about the country that provided their tea.

During the Opium War an American squadron remained in Chinese waters under the command of the able and tactful Lawrence Kearny. Shortly after the British signed the treaty of Nanking, he asked the Chinese authorities that American citizens be placed upon the most-favored-nation basis—that is, that they receive all the privileges extended to other countries. The next year, 1843, China threw open the new ports on equal terms to foreign nations. It appears, however, that this policy of extending most-favored-nation treatment was deliberately adopted by the Chinese as a means of avoiding future difficulty with foreigners, and not because of any pressure from Kearny.[10]

These portentous developments in China were watched with growing interest in the United States, where it was feared that Americans might not be allowed to enjoy the commercial privileges just extorted by the British. The merchants of Boston were particularly concerned, and they urged with increasing vigor that a diplomatic representative be sent to China. Responding to such pressure, President Tyler submitted a message to Congress, December 30, 1842, requesting an appropriation for a special commissioner. That body voted $40,000, though some objection was raised on the score that the trifling importance of the mission did not warrant so large an expenditure.[11]

THE CUSHING MISSION

On May 8, 1843, Caleb Cushing was appointed the first American commissioner to China. The selection, though dictated in part by po-

---

[9] Tyler Dennett, *Americans in Eastern Asia* (N.Y., 1922), p. 102.

[10] It is probable, however, that the decision was made at this time rather than later because Kearny placed the issue before the Chinese government. T. F. Tsiang, "The Extension of Equal Commercial Privileges to other Nations than the British after the Treaty of Nanking," *Chinese Social and Pol. Sci. Rev.*, XV (1931), 435. The entire article is important on the subject. For the controversy about it, see *ibid.*, XVI (1932), 75–109.

[11] One Representative from South Carolina suggested that great quantities of American tobacco would be consumed if the Chinese could be persuaded to chew it instead of opium. *Cong. Globe*, 27 Cong., 3 sess., p. 325 (Feb. 21, 1843).

litical considerations, was an exceedingly happy one, for the pages of American history reveal no more brilliant and versatile man than this handsome scholar-politician.[12] Cushing had, in fact, already become interested in the China trade, and had acquired a considerable store of information about the Celestial Empire.

In July, 1843, the Cushing mission left the United States. It consisted of four warships laden with specimens of Western scientific wonders and other gifts—a more imposing array than American diplomats were accustomed to. Cushing carried instructions which stated that his primary object was to secure for the United States those privileges that had recently been gained by the British. The somewhat childish letter that he bore from President Tyler to the Son of Heaven reflected the "lick-all-creation spirit" of the "roaring forties":

I hope your health is good. China is a Great Empire, extending over a great part of the World. The Chinese are numerous. You have millions and millions of subjects. The Twenty-six United States are as large as China, though our People are not so numerous. The rising Sun looks upon the great mountains and great rivers of China. When he sets, he looks upon rivers and mountains equally large, in the United States. Our territories extend from one great ocean to the other. . . .[13]

The arrival of the Cushing expedition at Macao, southern China, February 27, 1844, created something of a sensation. Although the Chinese had already granted most-favored-nation privileges to foreign countries, they were not particularly eager to make another treaty, and Cushing decided upon a policy combining force with suavity. Backed by the obvious power of the fleet, he declared that not to receive envoys was, among Western nations, considered as "an act of national insult and a just cause for war"—and the recently defeated Chinese wanted no war. As a club for getting favorable action, he threatened to take the extraordinary step of going to Peking and there dealing directly with the Emperor. To the Chinese such a course would have been highly undesirable, and to them the chief concern was preventing it, rather than extending by treaty the commercial

[12] Cushing was a remarkable linguist and a profound student. When the publishers sent him a well-known dictionary he found over five thousand errors in the vocabulary of modern geographical names alone. A State Department tradition has it that when he had nothing else to do he would memorize groups of figures in the cipher code. J. B. Moore, *The Principles of American Diplomacy* (N.Y., 1918), pp. 176–177.

[13] Hunter Miller, ed., *Treaties and other International Acts of the United States of America* (Washington, 1934), IV, 661.

privileges that had already been less formally granted.[14] After weeks of delay, the Son of Heaven finally condescended to dispatch an imperial commissioner to southern China for the purpose of treating with Cushing. The negotiations, once formally opened, were speedily concluded within a fortnight, and the famous Treaty of Wanghia was signed near Macao, July 3, 1844.[15]

It is now clear that Cushing's success in obtaining commercial privileges has been much overemphasized, and that his most serious initial difficulties were of his own creation. Nevertheless he succeeded in putting the recently granted concessions on a treaty basis and in gaining a most-favored-nation clause. Taking advantage of Chinese inexperience and ignorance of Western ways, he inserted a clear statement of extraterritoriality—that is, the right of Americans accused of crimes in China to be tried before an American official rather than to be left to the caprice of Chinese justice.[16] Altogether, Cushing's treaty was so far superior to that negotiated by the British in 1842 that until 1858 it served as a model of its kind.[17]

After Wanghia

In the decade following the Cushing treaty the commerce between the United States and China boomed.[18] The American clipper ship showed its rivals "a streak of foam," and carried the new tea crop so swiftly as to wrest shipments to the London market from British vessels. Missionaries from the United States, assured of a foothold under the Cushing treaty, came to China in increasing numbers, and ex-

[14] P. C. Kuo, "Caleb Cushing and the Treaty of Wanghia, 1844," *Jour. of Mod. Hist.*, V (1933), 52.

[15] During the negotiations several alarming incidents occurred, including a mob demonstration against a weather vane which Cushing had brought and which was allegedly causing an epidemic of sickness. In the ensuing disturbances a Chinese was killed by an American, thus complicating Cushing's problem. See C. M. Fuess, *The Life of Caleb Cushing* (N.Y., 1923), I, 432.

[16] The issue of extraterritoriality had been dramatically brought to the fore in 1821. An Italian on an American ship accidentally, it appears, killed a Chinese woman. After farcical judicial procedure he was strangled to death by the Chinese authorities. The Cushing treaty did not, as sometimes asserted, introduce the principle of extraterritoriality into China. The British and Portuguese already enjoyed to a limited extent what amounted to the same thing. C. G. Osborn, "American Extraterritorial Jurisdiction in China to 1906" (ms. doctoral dissertation, Stanford University, 1935), pp. 23 ff.

[17] Morse and MacNair, *Far Eastern International Relations*, p. 136.

[18] On this subject see the exhaustive monograph of Eldon Griffin, *Clippers and Consuls: American Consular and Commercial Relations with Eastern Asia, 1845–1860* (Ann Arbor, Mich., 1938).

tended their activities into the interior. These earnest soul savers, though a source of disturbance to the Chinese, were of some assistance in facilitating the work of diplomacy,[19] and of great service in awakening American interest in the Celestial Empire. Throughout the forty years after 1847 books written by missionaries, though reflecting a Christian bias, were the most reliable sources of information about the Far East generally circulated in the United States.

Unhappily for American interests, the Chinese government did not carry out all the stipulations of the Cushing treaty, and citizens of the United States, as well as other "foreign devils," suffered repeated indignities. The empire was so sprawling that the central government, even if it had earnestly desired to do so, could not have fully guaranteed foreign treaty rights in the semiautonomous provinces. Internal disorder was further aggravated by the most bloody civil war in history, the Taiping Rebellion, which lasted from 1850 to 1864 and took an estimated toll of 20,000,000 lives.

During the tumultuous years from 1842 to 1860 America was on the whole ill-represented in China. The commissioners and ministers were so poorly paid that their positions frequently went begging. One of the better men was Humphrey Marshall (a distant kinsman of the famous Chief Justice), who strongly urged that it was to the interest of the United States to support the Chinese Empire against foreign aggression and internal disorder.[20]

After the Crimean War (1854–1856) France and Britain demanded enforcement of their treaties with China, reparations for losses, and greater trade concessions. The United States was invited to join in coercive measures, but declined. America was then torn by the slavery controversy; joint action with other Powers ran counter to her traditional policy; and she was quite willing to let Great Britain and France pull her chestnuts out of the fire. The Department of State declared, however, that it believed the objects of the allies to be "just and expedient." Thus the United States found itself in the pusillanimous but profitable position of avoiding the expense and ill will of warfare, while holding the coats of the aggressors and preparing to demand all the advantages extorted by force of arms.

Joint British and French armies administered a chastisement to the ill-prepared Chinese, and exacted new treaties at Tientsin, in June,

[19] Dr. Peter Parker, a well-known American medical missionary familiar with the Chinese language and customs, ably assisted Cushing during the latter's negotiations, as did S. Wells Williams, who later accompanied Perry to Japan as an interpreter. Dennett, *Americans in Eastern Asia*, p. 142.

[20] *Ibid.*, p. 215.

1858. The victors won the right to diplomatic representation at Peking as well as additional trade privileges, including the opening of a number of new treaty ports. A few days before the French and British pacts were signed, the American minister, William B. Reed, negotiated a new treaty at Tientsin. One of its chief features was a most-favored-nation clause, which gave the United States substantially all the advantages that France and Britain had wrested after costly naval operations.[21]

Fresh hostilities broke out in June, 1859, when the British attempted to force their way up the Pei-ho River to exchange ratifications of their treaties at Peking. In the engagement the British were badly worsted, and an American naval officer, Josiah Tattnall, ignoring the requirements of neutrality and allegedly muttering "blood is thicker than water," went to their rescue.[22] The discomfited allies collected a powerful force, captured Peking, destroyed the priceless summer palace of the Emperor, and extorted new concessions in the Convention of Peking (1860). These additional commercial advantages also accrued to the United States under the beneficent operation of the most-favored-nation clause.

PERRY AND HIS BLACK SHIPS

Meanwhile no less significant developments had been taking place off the mainland of China, where lay the Japanese archipelago. The inhabitants of these islands, like the Chinese, wanted little traffic with the Occidentals. It is true that from 1550 to 1620 the Japanese had welcomed the Western world; but the excesses of religious zealots and the sharp practices of traders caused them to slam their gates and pursue a rigid policy of both exclusion and seclusion. The Dutch had been the least offensive of the Europeans; so for over two centuries they, together with the Chinese, were allowed a severely restricted trade at the single port of Nagasaki. Through this tiny wicket in the

[21] *Ibid.*, p. 314.

[22] It may be noted that Tattnall did not mention in any of his dispatches having used the words "blood is thicker than water." Secretary of the Navy Hunt to J. H. Morris, Feb. 13, 1882, Navy Department, Washington, D.C. Mr. Thornton Mitchell, of Stanford University, directed the present writer's attention to this letter. Interesting enough, the British commander, Admiral Hope, did not even mention Tattnall in his official report (July 5, 1859) to the Admiralty, though Lord Lyons, British minister in Washington, did convey the official thanks of Her Majesty's government for the assistance rendered. President Buchanan, so Lyons reported (Oct. 19, 1859), declared that Tattnall's conduct had "met with the hearty approbation of the great majority of the People of the United States." Transcripts from British Admiralty.

gate filtered virtually all of Japan's intercourse with the outside world.

During the first half of the nineteenth century both the United States and the European Powers made repeated but unavailing attempts to persuade Japan to emerge from her chrysalis. The problem, hitherto approached with only half-hearted determination, took on a new importance in the fifties. Shipwrecked mariners, chiefly from America's large North Pacific whaling fleet, were treated by the Japanese as felons. Some alleged that they had been required to trample and spit upon the Christian cross, and that their companions had died as a result of having been shut up in small cages and exposed to the elements in stocks.[23] Moreover, uncharted Japanese waters lay in the path of the most direct route from rapidly expanding San Francisco to Shanghai, and the requirements of steam navigation made imperative the establishment of coaling stations in the Land of the Rising Sun. In addition, far-sighted American business men were already looking hungrily upon Japan as a prospective market. As early as 1852, *De Bow's Review*, an influential Southern journal, prophesied a $200,000,000 annual trade with Japan.

Aroused by petitions to Congress and other evidences of public interest, Fillmore's administration decided to make a determined effort to open Japan. In January, 1852, the command of an expedition was entrusted to Commodore Matthew C. Perry, a younger brother of the hero of Lake Erie and a distinguished naval officer in his own right. The ensuing preparations excited considerable comment both in America and Europe, and though many expressed hope for success, there was a general note of skepticism. The London *Sun* looked forward to the result with as much interest as if a balloon were "to soar off to one of the planets under the direction of some experienced aëronaut." The Washington correspondent of the Philadelphia *Public Ledger* dismissed the expedition as a "romantic notion"; while his colleague on the Baltimore *Sun* scoffed that "it will sail about the same time with Rufus Porter's aërial ship." Even after the fleet had departed, the Baltimore journalist insisted on "abandoning this humbug, for it has become a *matter of ridicule abroad and at home.*"[24]

After various vicissitudes Perry entered the beautiful Bay of Yedo (later called Tokyo) with four men-of-war, July 8, 1853. The Japa-

[23] In 1852 *De Bow's Review* (New Orleans) declared: "It is stated by writers that there are numerous European and American captives now in the hands of the Japanese, and that they are 'exhibited in iron cages in various parts of the Japanese territory.'" XIII, 562 (Dec. 1852).

[24] Inazo Nitobe, *The Intercourse between the United States and Japan* (Baltimore, 1891), pp. 43–44.

nese had never before seen steamers of this type; and as the American flagship, belching black smoke, steadily moved up the bay in the face of a strong head wind the people were struck with consternation. A curiously prophetic folk song returned to their minds as they made haste to defend themselves:

> Thro' a black night of cloud and rain,
> The Black Ship plies her way—
> An alien thing of evil mien—
> Across the waters gray.[25]

But the American expedition, in spite of its warlike appearance, was under strict orders not to resort to force except in self-defense or to resent an insult.[26] Deciding to outdo the Orientals in the matter of ceremony, Perry secluded himself and refused to have dealings with any but the highest officials. When he was requested to repair to Nagasaki, he refused to do so on the grounds that he was charged with delivering a friendly letter from the President of the United States to the Emperor of Japan. He significantly added that if rebuffed he should consider his country insulted and would not "hold himself accountable for the consequences." This mixture of firmness, dignity, and tact finally induced the Japanese to receive his documents. Perry realized that the answer would require mature deliberation; so he sailed away at the end of ten days, pointedly indicating that he would return in the spring with a much more powerful squadron.

Internal conditions in Japan were such that Perry could hardly have come at a more opportune time. The country was ripe for change, since the feudal system of Japan was breaking down, and a new commercial and urban class, eager for power, was rapidly rising. Since the early seventeenth century the shogunate, which represented the military, had exercised *de facto* sovereignty in Japan, though in theory subordinate to the Emperor. Faced with the momentous issue resulting from Perry's visit, the Shogun took the unprecedented step of not only referring the matter to the feudal barons but also to the Emperor himself. The more progressive leaders of Japan, who were reasonably

[25] *Ibid.*, p. 1.

[26] P. J. Treat, *Diplomatic Relations between the United States and Japan, 1853–1895* (Stanford University, 1932), I, 17. In 1846, while trying to open relations with the Japanese, Commodore Biddle, U.S.N., had either been struck or pushed by a Japanese soldier. Biddle's magnanimous course following this humiliating incident appears to have been misinterpreted by the Japanese as weakness or lack of dignity. See C. O. Paullin, *Diplomatic Negotiations of American Naval Officers, 1778–1883* (Baltimore, 1912), pp. 228–229.

well informed as to what was going on in the outside world, favored opening negotiations with Perry. They knew of the power of Western arms, and with the object lesson of China before them they perceived the wisdom of adopting modern weapons to combat aggressive foreigners, particularly Russians.[27] After a prolonged debate the views of these far-visioned statesmen prevailed.

REOPENING THE GATES OF JAPAN

In February, 1854, Perry again sailed into the Bay of Yedo, this time with seven black ships. The negotiations proceeded smoothly, and were facilitated by a number of curious and costly presents that the Americans had brought, including various kinds of liquors, which were fully appreciated, and a miniature telegraph and steam locomotive, the operation of which delighted the ingenious Japanese and doubtless impressed them with the power of Western nations.[28] A high point in the ceremonies was a sumptuous banquet on board the American flagship, at which the Japanese consumed great heaps of food and imbibed large quantities of alcoholic beverages. Perry's official chronicler recorded:

It was now sunset, and the Japanese prepared to depart with quite as much wine in them as they could well bear. The jovial Matsusaki threw his arms about the Commodore's neck, crushing, in his tipsy embrace, a pair of new epaulettes, and repeating, in Japanese, with maudlin affection, these words, as interpreted into English: "Nippon and America, all the same heart."[29]

Amid such festivities the famous treaty between Japan and the United States was signed, March 31, 1854.

The Perry pact was in many ways a disappointment—particularly when one considers the display of force that accompanied it. It was in

---

[27] Treat, *United States and Japan*, I, 22. Europe's wars probably proved Japan's salvation during the eighteenth and nineteenth centuries. Morse and MacNair, *Far Eastern International Relations*, p. 294.

[28] One slightly tipsy visitor asked for a cake and a bottle of hock that took his fancy. Perry promised to send them ashore in the morning, by which time the cake had been stolen by an American sailor. Perry thereupon delivered the liquor together with a message that in America cake was presented only in the evening. By that time a new cake was baked, and everyone was happy. J. S. Sewall, "With Perry in Japan: Personal Recollections of the Expedition of 1853–54," *Century Magazine*, LXX, 358 (July, 1905).

[29] F. L. Hawks, *Narrative of the Expedition of an American Squadron to the China Seas and Japan* (N.Y., 1856), I, 438.

fact little more than a convention for shipwrecked sailors—a "wood and water treaty." Only two ports, Shimoda and Hakodate, which were relatively inaccessible, were thrown open to American trade, and no adequate provisions were made for coaling stations. Commercially, Perry had just got his foot in the door—he had not opened it. There was, to be sure, a most-favored-nation clause, but no extraterritorial provision. Superficially, it looked as if Perry had won no great diplomatic triumph, and that the Japanese negotiators had done very well.

But it is not fair to judge the treaty too narrowly. The seemingly meager concessions were revolutionary when one considers the former Japanese policy. Perry was pursuing a far-sighted course. He was looking to the future and preparing the ground for the sweeping commercial treaty later negotiated by Townsend Harris. It was enough for him to drive the entering wedge and to make the next step relatively easy for the Japanese. In accomplishing his purpose, he fired no shot, as he might well have done, and left no rancor. His statesmanlike diplomacy won the respect of the Japanese, and laid the foundations of the famous "historic friendship." [30]

Viewed from any angle the reopening of Japan was a red-letter day in the history of the world. If the Land of the Rising Sun had continued its exclusion-seclusion policy it might soon have been dismembered by Russia, for the scattered islands were far more vulnerable to naval attack than the continental Chinese Empire. Japan was opened not because Perry forced it open but because the Shogun's advisers were convinced of the wisdom of taking this step. As an American humorist of a later generation, Finley Peter Dunne (Mr. Dooley) put it, "Whin we rapped on the dure, we didn't go in, they come out." [31]

Few, if any, Americans grasped the significance of what had been accomplished. Certainly the event attracted little attention. Though New York presented Perry with a set of silver plate, and the merchants of Boston had a medal struck off in his honor, President Pierce

---

[30] Perry is better known in Japan than in the United States. The Japanese erected an imposing monument in his honor on the shores of the Bay of Yedo, and dedicated it with appropriate ceremony on July 14, 1901, the forty-eighth anniversary of Perry's first landing.

[31] In 1871 an American naval officer, John Rodgers, tried to blow Korea open, and although he demolished the Korean forts he accomplished nothing. In 1882 Commodore Shufeldt, U.S.N., succeeded in concluding the first treaty that the Hermit Kingdom made with a Western Power, the Japanese having signed one in 1876. Although this event had only relatively minor direct implications from the standpoint of American diplomacy, it was of importance in projecting Korea into the international arena. See Dennett, *Americans in Eastern Asia*, p. 450.

gave the opening of Japan (undertaken by a rival Whig administration) but two sentences in his twenty-one page annual message to Congress. The *North American Review* wondered why "the funeral of Bill Poole, or the [Walker] filibustering operations in the Gulf of Mexico, should have awakened more display of interest among the people" than "one of the most honorable triumphs of our age." [32]

KEEPING THE GATES AJAR

The Washington government, in accordance with its understanding of the Perry treaty, appointed a consul general at Shimoda, August 4, 1855. The man chosen, Townsend Harris, was a merchant with considerable experience in the Far East, and he had suffered such heavy financial reverses as to be an active candidate for the position. [33] The Japanese, however, interpreted the Perry treaty to mean that a consul was to be appointed only by mutual consent; and since they did not want one at that time, they put Harris off with obstruction, evasion, and prevarication. The only Occidental with whom he came in contact was his secretary. He did not see an American naval vessel for fourteen months, and he was without communication from the State Department for eighteen months. [34] As if unfamiliar Japanese food and the annoyances of rats and cockroaches were not enough, the natives regarded the earthquakes, typhoons, and cholera which followed his coming as evidences of divine disapproval of the Perry treaty. Yet Harris, working quietly, tactfully, and above all patiently, gradually won the respect and even the admiration of the Japanese.

The Perry agreement, it will be remembered, had opened scarcely more than a crack in the door; and it was the chief task of the newly appointed American consul to negotiate a comprehensive commercial treaty. [35] Harris finally succeeded in obtaining an audience with the Shogun, and the Japanese were astonished to see him, as he wrote home, "look the awful 'Tycoon' in the face, speak plainly to him, hear his reply—and all this without any trepidation, or any 'quivering of

---

[32] *North American Review*, LXXXIII, 236 (July, 1856).

[33] See Carl Crow, *He Opened the Door of Japan* (N.Y., 1939), pp. 28–34.

[34] Such pathetic entries appear in his diary as "Where, oh! where is Commodore Armstrong?" He referred to Shimoda as "a prison—a large one it is true—but still a prison." See M. E. Cosenza, ed., *The Complete Journal of Townsend Harris* (N.Y., 1930), p. 377.

[35] In June, 1857, Harris concluded a convention which secured additional concessions, especially as regards trade, residence, extraterritoriality, and currency. *Ibid.*, pp. 373–374. (June 8, 1857).

the muscles of the side.' " [36] During the following months Harris emphasized the disinterestedness of the United States, made a strong point of the rapacity and strength of the European Powers, and pointed out how much better it would be if Japan could only voluntarily make to the United States those concessions that the nations of the world would ultimately force her to yield.[37]

Such persuasive diplomacy, combined with friendliness and helpfulness, bore fruit in an epochal commercial treaty, signed July 29, 1858. Other ports were thrown open, greater trade and residential rights were granted, reciprocal diplomatic representation was provided for, and a species of extraterritoriality for Americans was established. Indeed, the treaty of 1858 was so well drawn that it became a foundation stone of Japan's foreign relations to near the end of the century. Harris recorded:

> The pleasure I feel in having made the treaty is enhanced by the reflection that there has been no show of coercion, nor was menace in the least used by me to obtain it. There was no American man-of-war within one thousand miles of me for months before and after the negotiations. I told the Japanese at the outset that my mission was a friendly one; that I was not authorized to use any threats; that all I wished was that they would listen to the truth that I would lay before them.[38]

EAST BECOMES WEST

The Harris treaty of 1858 provided that a Japanese mission should journey to the United States and exchange ratifications. A party of envoys and their retinue, totaling more than seventy persons, was accordingly brought to the United States on an American man-of-war early in 1860. Congress appropriated $50,000 for the entertainment of the wide-eyed little visitors, who for seven weeks were whirled past the wonders, mechanical and natural, of America. They were feted by the cities of the Atlantic seaboard, and honored by a great parade up Broadway. The American people were fascinated by the gentlemanly behavior and quick intelligence of the Japanese, and another barrier of ignorance was partially beaten down.[39]

The overnight transformation of Japan from an isolated feudal

---

[36] *Living Age*, LX, 570 (Feb. 26, 1859). Harris to a friend, July 3, 1858.

[37] See Treat, *United States and Japan*, I, 54.

[38] *Living Age*, LX, 572–573 (Feb. 26, 1859). Harris to a friend, July 6, 1858.

[39] Another Japanese mission came in 1872, was given a somewhat similar reception, and attracted wide attention.

state to a member of the family of nations was inevitably accompanied by severe dislocations. The numerous and powerful opponents of the new policy united in opposition to the Shogun, who had been responsible for forsaking isolation. During the ensuing disorders a number of foreigners, including the secretary of the American legation, were killed. But Harris, who had been elevated to the rank of minister resident, stuck to his post until 1862 and, though shattered in health, labored manfully to preserve the gains already made. Certainly no American diplomat has ever done better work in the face of great personal hardship.[40] Perry, the opener, has received the plaudits; Harris, the pioneer, is well-nigh forgotten, except by the Japanese, who, in 1927, erected a monument to his memory near Shimoda.

Harris' successor, Robert H. Pruyn, was fortunately an able man. His conciliatory work during the tempestuous years from 1862 to 1865 entitles him to a high place in American diplomatic annals. If Perry unlocked the gates, and Harris opened them, Pruyn was in large measure responsible for keeping them from being slammed.[41] It is interesting to note that during this period the United States embarked upon a curious departure from its traditional policy of avoiding entanglements with other Powers. One of the intractable Japanese feudal lords, whose cannon commanded the straits of Shimonoseki, began to fire upon "barbarian" (foreign) ships. Since the Shogun was not powerful enough to stop him, the offended Powers organized a joint punitive expedition in 1864. The United States was invited to join, but because of involvement in the Civil War was able to send only one hastily improvised warship. The obstreperous feudal lord was severely handled, and the Japanese government, in the Convention of 1864, agreed to pay an idemnity of $3,000,000.[42]

Unforgettable lessons at Shimonoseki and elsewhere convinced the antiforeign element in Japan that the only way to combat the West was to adopt Western ways—fight the devil with fire, so to speak— and unite under the Emperor. The subsequent centralization of authority contributed powerfully to the amazing transformation of Japan. In 1894, on the eve of their surprising victory over China, the Japa-

[40] See Treat, *United States and Japan*, I, 126–127. At the beginning of his mission Harris recorded: "I hope I may so conduct myself that I may have honorable mention in the histories which will be written on Japan and its future destiny." *Journal of Townsend Harris*, p. 196 (Aug. 19, 1856).

[41] Treat, *United States and Japan*, I, 131.

[42] The share of the United States, $785,000, was grossly disproportionate to the loss sustained, and in 1883 Congress voted to return this sum to Japan. This gesture paid ample dividends in good will, and the Japanese expended the money on the breakwater in Yokohama harbor. *Ibid.*, II, 545–559.

nese secured a general revision of treaties, thus freeing their nation from a number of inequities that had been imposed upon it.[43] Without ignoring the work of other foreign nations, notably that of Great Britain, it may be concluded that Japan at the turn of the century was in considerable measure the child of American diplomacy.

THE CRUMBLING WALL OF CHINA

Returning to the mainland of Asia, we find that the most noteworthy feature of Chinese-American relations during the decade after 1858 was the work of Anson Burlingame, United States minister at Peking for six years. Burlingame was a Massachusetts Congressman of great personal charm who, in 1861, was rewarded for his oratorical contributions in the recent presidential campaign by being appointed minister to China. Here he encountered a perplexing situation. The Chinese government, ever the despair of its friends, found itself powerless to carry out the recent treaties because of the semiautonomous status of the provinces; yet the foreign merchants were belligerently clamoring for rights which in some cases went beyond treaty stipulations. Burlingame, though a newcomer among the diplomats, quickly assumed the leadership of the foreign envoys at Peking, and persuaded them to co-operate in withstanding the extreme demands of the foreign merchants and in adopting a more tolerant attitude toward the vexed Chinese government.[44] This conciliatory course may have forestalled a situation that would have led to the partition of China by the European Powers. Burlingame's conduct naturally won the confidence of the Chinese government, which showed its appreciation in one way by giving orders not to succor the Confederate cruiser *Alabama*. On a return visit to the United States (1865–1866), the energetic minister did yeoman's work, through speech and conference, in enlisting sympathy for the Chinese among influential Americans.

Burlingame had long urged upon the Chinese the wisdom of sending diplomatic representatives abroad. When, therefore, it became known in 1867 that he was about to resign as minister, the Peking government asked him to represent China on a mission to the principal Powers. The object was to correct misapprehensions abroad, and

---

[43] In 1866 the United States had entered into a tariff convention jointly with the other Powers. This, together with the Shimonoseki Convention of 1864, was one of the few instances in the nineteenth century of a joint treaty to which the United States was a party. See *ibid.*, I, 273–274.

[44] Dennett, *Americans in Eastern Asia*, pp. 372–378.

to persuade the interested nations not to demand more than China could reasonably be expected to concede when the time should come for treaty revision. The selection of Burlingame to head the mission was a great compliment to him, particularly since he did not know the Chinese language.[45] In 1868 a picturesque party, numbering more than thirty, came to the United States and attracted wide attention. Everywhere the mission was wined, dined, and greeted by cheering crowds, thus giving Burlingame, who was a superb showman, an opportunity to burst into oratory and paint China's condition in somewhat more roseate colors than strict truth would permit.

The tangible result of the mission's work in the United States was the Convention of 1868, known generally as the Burlingame Treaty. It could more properly be called the Seward Treaty, for Secretary of State Seward, who showed more interest in the Far East than any other Secretary since Webster, seems to have desired it more than Burlingame. At that time Chinese coolies were much in demand for Western railroad construction, and Seward, who was a "cheap labor" man, wrote into the convention a guarantee to the Chinese of unrestricted immigration to the United States.[46] Interestingly enough, the West—particularly California—applauded the arrangement at the time,[47] although this section was soon to change its views.

Burlingame went on to Europe, where he achieved considerable success, and died of pneumonia in Russia. He was the ablest American representative in China since Cushing, and one of the most notable products of American amateur diplomacy.[48]

THE AMERICAN DOUBLE STANDARD

The taproot of American policy in the Far East during the nineteenth century was the most-favored-nation treatment—a precursor, as we shall see, of the Open Door. A logical corollary was that the Far Eastern nations, notably China, should be made strong enough not only to keep the door open but to be their own doorkeepers. The United

[45] Though heading the mission, Burlingame did not have a higher rank and title than his two coenvoys, as he represented to the State Department. Knight Biggerstaff, "The Official Chinese Attitude toward the Burlingame Mission," *Amer. Hist. Rev.*, XLI (1936), 694.

[46] Seward later told Dr. W. A. P. Martin, "with no little satisfaction, that he, and not Burlingame, had drafted the treaty." W. A. P. Martin, *A Cycle of Cathay* (N.Y., 1897), p. 376.

[47] F. W. Williams, *Anson Burlingame and the First Chinese Mission to Foreign Powers* (N.Y., 1912), pp. 153-155.

[48] Dennett, *Americans in Eastern Asia*, p. 368.

States also worked for peace in the Orient, since war and land-grabbing were disturbing to both commerce and soul-saving. It must be constantly borne in mind that the American missionaries, and those contributing to their work, were numerous enough and influential enough to make their wants known at Washington.

During this period the United States steadfastly refused to acquire naval stations in Asiatic waters, and secured no territory until it most unexpectedly obtained the Philippines in 1898.[49] Inasmuch as America had a weak navy at home and no naval bases in the Far East, the Washington government was of necessity forced to rely upon treaty commitments and international law for the protection of its interests. This general avoidance of a "gunboat policy" (in part because America had few gunboats) placed the United States in a more favorable position than the aggressive Powers. Although the Americans generally refrained from co-operative military or naval demonstrations, they were not slow to claim, under their most-favored-nation clauses, whatever advantages the others might secure. It should be noted, however, that foreign nations also benefited, under similar most-favored-nation guarantees, from the treaties concluded by the United States.

Throughout the mid-century years, and somewhat later under Secretary Seward, the United States generally pursued a policy of co-operation with the European Powers in the maintenance of trade privileges. It is curious that during this period America held to a double standard: isolation and nonentanglement with regard to Europe, co-operation and entanglement in the Far East. But in the last quarter of the century, when interest in foreign affairs was at low ebb, the United States lapsed back into a policy of isolation in the Far East—a position which, as we shall see, enabled John Hay to play a dramatic if somewhat ineffective lone hand.

BIBLIOGRAPHICAL NOTE

The most satisfactory general work on the diplomacy of the United States in the Far East during the nineteenth century is Tyler Dennett, *Americans in Eastern Asia* (N.Y., 1922). The most exhaustive account of Japanese-American relations is P. J. Treat, *Diplomatic Relations between the United States and Japan, 1853–*

---

[49] Perry had urged the necessity of establishing coaling stations along the Chinese coast. On his famous mission he made the Loo Choo Islands a temporary base, raised the flag and purchased a coaling depot at Port Lloyd (Bonin Islands), took possession of the Coffin Islands, and suggested a protectorate over Formosa. All this was too far advanced for his superiors, who reversed his policy. See F. R. Dulles, *America in the Pacific* (Boston, 1932), pp. 68 ff.

1895 (2 vols., Stanford University, 1932). K. S. Latourette, *The History of Early Relations between the United States and China, 1784–1844* (New Haven, 1917), is the best on the subject. F. R. Dulles' popularly written *The Old China Trade* (Boston, 1930) is useful. A monumental work, in which the United States appears somewhat incidentally, is H. B. Morse, *The International Relations of the Chinese Empire* (3 vols., London, 1910–1918). This has been abridged and brought up to date by H. B. Morse and H. F. MacNair, *Far Eastern International Relations* (Boston, 1931). The most erudite commentary on the Cushing treaty is Hunter Miller, ed., *Treaties and other International Acts of the United States of America* (Washington, 1934), IV, 626–662. P. C. Kuo, "Caleb Cushing and the Treaty of Wanghia, 1844," *Jour. of Mod. Hist.*, V (1933), 34–54, emphasizes the Chinese side. See also the popular account of C. M. Fuess, *The Life of Caleb Cushing* (N.Y., 1923), I, Ch. X. For the Perry negotiations consult Treat, *op. cit.* There is also a brief narrative in C. O. Paullin, *Diplomatic Negotiations of American Naval Officers, 1778–1883* (Baltimore, 1912), Ch. IX. F. W. Williams, *Anson Burlingame and the First Chinese Mission to Foreign Powers* (N.Y., 1912), is a full account; it should be read in the light of Knight Biggerstaff, "The Official Chinese Attitude toward the Burlingame Mission," *Amer. Hist. Rev.*, XLI (1936), 682–701. Further references: see footnotes of this chapter and Bemis and Griffin, *Guide*, pp. 469–489.

RECENT REFERENCES. The present writer has been in receipt of several letters from a kinsman of Lawrence Kearny arguing that the latter was the real founder of the Open Door policy. It is to be noted that Kearny's biographer, C. S. Alden, *Lawrence Kearny: Sailor Diplomat* (Princeton, 1936), makes no such extravagant claims, but states that the American officer "promoted friendly feeling during an extremely critical period," "urged equal rights for America," and by his "timely representations" prompted the sending of Cushing (pp. 184–185). P. H. Clyde, ed., *United States Policy toward China: Diplomatic and Public Documents, 1838–1939* (Durham, N.C., 1940), is a convenient and discriminating compilation. An early commercial contact is described in C. C. Stelle, "American Trade in Opium to China, Prior to 1820," *Pacific Hist. Rev.*, IX (1940), 425–444. A. B. Cole, ed., "Captain David Porter's Proposed Expedition to the Pacific and Japan, 1815," *ibid.*, pp. 61–65, definitely establishes that this distinguished officer suggested the opening of Japan to President Madison as early as 1815. Chitoshi Yanaga, "The First Japanese Embassy to the United States" [1860], *ibid.*, pp. 113–138, is a colorful and competent account.

NEW REFERENCES. A. B. Cole, ed., *With Perry in Japan* (Princeton, 1942), is a diary that adds some details to the well-known story. T. E. La Fargue, *China's First Hundred* (Pullman, Wash., 1942), a chapter in the Westernization of China, deals with the careers of 120 Chinese boys sent to the United States (1872–1874) to learn American technology. Hunter Miller, ed., *Treaties and other International Acts of the United States of America* (Washington, 1942), VI, VII, gives the Perry and Harris treaties, with much documentation. Perry was suspicious of the Dutch, who in 1852 had fruitlessly proposed a treaty to Japan, a step which apparently had some influence on the later American negotiations (VI, 541).

4TH ED. REFS. See Bibliographical Appendix, p. 928.

CHAPTER XXI

Civil War Diplomacy: First Phase, 1861

*"The Confederates . . . are fighting for independence. . . .
But with the Northerners all is different. They are not content
with their own. They are fighting to coerce others. . . ."*

London *Times*, September 13, 1862.

AMATEUR DIPLOMATS

DURING the heated presidential election of 1860 the Southerners made it clear that if the antislavery Republican party of the North elected its candidate, Abraham Lincoln, the Union would be dissolved. The Republicans triumphed in November. The next month South Carolina seceded, and by February 1, 1861, six states of the lower South had followed her example. This was the critical situation that confronted the untried prairie politician, Abraham Lincoln, on March 4, 1861. Fortunately for the foreign affairs of the United States, he had an abundance of common sense, a willingness and capacity to learn, and an uncanny instinct for not interfering when he could do no good.

The outstanding man in the Republican party was not Lincoln, but William H. Seward. The latter, however, had made too many enemies, and had been passed by in favor of a less well-known candidate. In the circumstances Lincoln was compelled by custom and courtesy to offer his defeated rival the Secretaryship of State, the highest office at the President's disposal. Seward accepted the consolation prize after some hesitation, confiding to his wife that his "distracted country" could not spare him in the hour of crisis. He felt that his mission was to grasp the helm while the inept Lincoln, a yokel whom the wheel of chance had placed over him, occupied the role of figurehead.[1]

Like a number of otherwise sensible Americans, Seward believed that a rousing foreign war would bring the South back into the Union. On All Fool's Day, 1861, he submitted to Lincoln a memorandum in which he recommended a "wrap-the-world-in-fire" policy:

[1] H. W. Temple, "William H. Seward," in S. F. Bemis, ed., *American Secretaries of State and their Diplomacy* (N.Y., 1928), VII, 22–23.

I would demand explanations from Spain and France, categorically, at once.
I would seek explanations from Great Britain and Russia, and send agents
    into Canada, Mexico, and Central America, to rouse a vigorous conti-
    nental spirit of independence on this continent against European inter-
    vention.
And, if satisfactory explanations are not received from Spain and France,
Would convene Congress and declare war against them.[2]

Lincoln firmly but tactfully refused to accept Seward's insane suggestions, and magnanimously forgave him his temporary aberration.
    It was unfortunate for the cause of the North that Seward was dis-
trusted by the British government. In 1860 he had told the Duke of
Newcastle, who was visiting America, that if he became Secretary of
State it would be his "duty to insult England" and that he intended
"to do so." The story went the rounds in Great Britain, where it was
believed, whether correctly or not, that Seward had not been jesting.[3]
Nor did Seward's inexperience in foreign affairs and his known attachment to the "foreign war panacea" inspire confidence at Downing
Street. Several of his early instructions to the American minister in
London were so belligerently worded that if they had not been toned
down in delivery grave consequences might easily have followed.[4] Yet
Seward settled down after these first months of service, and finally
came to be regarded as one of America's most distinguished Secretaries
of State. Like Lincoln, he grew with experience.
    Seward's early vagaries were to a considerable degree offset by the
presence in London of one of the ablest diplomats in American history,
Charles Francis Adams. Lacking none of the ability of his father and
grandfather, John Quincy Adams and John Adams, Charles Francis
Adams possessed two gifts in which they had been painfully deficient:
balance of mind and ability to get along pleasantly with his fellow
men. Educated in an English boarding school,[5] cultured, intelligent,

[2] J. G. Nicolay and John Hay, *Abraham Lincoln: a History* (N.Y., 1890), III, 446.
[3] C. F. Adams, *Charles Francis Adams* (Boston, 1900), p. 165. Minister Adams wrote to his son (Dec. 20, 1861): "The impression is general that Mr. Seward is resolved to insult England until she makes a war. He is the bête noir, that frightens them out of all their proprieties . . . . an ogre fully resolved to eat all Englishmen raw." W. C. Ford, ed., *A Cycle of Adams Letters, 1861–1865* (Boston, 1920), I, 88.
[4] Henry Adams, secretary at the United States legation in London, referred to Seward's "crazy dispatch" of May 21, 1861, adding that if it had been obeyed "literally," war would have resulted "in five minutes." *Ibid.*, I, 17 (Adams to C. F. Adams, Jr., July 2, 1861).
[5] This was just after the War of 1812, when John Quincy Adams was minister in London. Adams' playmates tauntingly asked him if he had ever been in the

well bred, and reserved, he had much in common with the English ruling class, intellectually and socially. And, unlike Seward, he enjoyed the respect and confidence of the British government.

INDEPENDENCE OR EMPIRE?

On April 12, 1861, the Southerners opened fire on Fort Sumter, in Charleston harbor, and two days later forced its surrender. Lincoln promptly called for 75,000 militiamen; and four additional Southern states seceded from the Union. The long-threatened war had definitely begun.

At the outset it was evident that England would be the focal point of American diplomacy during the conflict. France, of course, was important; but Napoleon III, though sympathetic with the Southern Confederacy, was unwilling to interfere without backing from the British fleet. If England had intervened in behalf of the Southern states, the North in all probability would have declared war on her. Powerful British ironclads would unquestionably have broken the blockade and perhaps have bombarded Northern cities; and in the general conflict the South would doubtless have made good its independence. In brief, the great diplomatic problem confronting Lincoln was to keep England neutral.

When the Civil War broke out, relations between Great Britain and the United States were probably more friendly than they had been at any time since the turn of the century. The Isthmian controversy had just been settled; and no serious dispute divided the two peoples. As a special mark of friendship the Prince of Wales had made a twenty-nine day tour of America in 1860, and had escaped from crushing crowds, balls, and torchlight processions long enough to sleep in the White House and plant a tree at the tomb of Washington.[6]

When secession first began, press opinion in England was rather favorable to the cause of the North. It was generally assumed, whether correctly or not, that the struggle was one for the freedom of the slaves—an objective for which the British had long been agitating. But during the first year and a half of the war the Washington government was powerless to capitalize on this strong moral issue. The

recently burned Washington. The young Yankee retorted with more resourcefulness than truth, "No, but I have been in New Orleans." J. T. Adams, *The Adams Family* (N.Y., 1930), p. 164.

[6] See Lord Newton, *Lord Lyons* (London, 1913), I, 24–28.

important border states of Maryland, Kentucky, and Missouri, in all of which slavery still existed, would be driven into the arms of the Confederacy if the Administration should proclaim that this was a war to free the Negroes. Lincoln categorically stated in his inaugural address, and repeatedly insisted on other occasions, that the North was not fighting to unshackle the slaves but to preserve the Union. It is not remarkable that the British came to take his word at its face value.

In these circumstances, the moral cause of the underdog South was definitely the stronger, and enlisted much British abolitionist sentiment that otherwise would have gone to the North. A number of English liberals, failing to see that Lincoln's hands were tied on the slavery issue, regarded the attempt of the Washington government to pin one section to the other with bayonets as positively immoral. A comparison of particular relish to Englishmen suggested itself to the London *Times:*

> . . . The contest is really for empire on the side of the North, and for independence on that of the South, and in this respect we recognize an exact analogy between the North and the Government of George III., and the South and the Thirteen Revolted Provinces. These opinions may be wrong, but they are the general opinions of the English nation. . . .[7]

It is not surprising, then, that the great majority of English newspapers and journals were unfriendly to the North, particularly during the first half of the war. Consistently unsympathetic were the magisterial London *Times* and the caustic London *Punch.* Both journals mirrored the prejudices of the privileged classes and exercised great influence not only in England but on the Continent as well. *Punch* persistently caricatured Lincoln as a boor, a churl, a sharper, a braggart, a poltroon, and even as the devil. Aroused by these attacks, the American press (notably the New York *Herald*) replied in kind, and once more ill feeling began to mount dangerously.

Understandable though the British attitude may be today, the Northerners were deeply angered by the failure of their kinsmen to look beneath the surface and perceive what they regarded as the real, if unannounced, issue of the conflict, particularly after years of criticizing America's "peculiar institution." What the North wanted was sympathy—not cold neutrality. There was much aggrieved feeling in James Russell Lowell's lament:

[7] London *Times,* Nov. 7, 1861, 6:3.

> We know we've got a cause, John,
> Thet's honest, just, an' true;
> We thought 't would win applause, John,
> Ef nowheres else, from you.[8]

A SMOKING CHIMNEY TAKES FIRE

The bulwark of British unfriendliness toward the North during these years was to be found in the upper classes. Socially, there was a strikingly close affinity between the landed aristocracy of Great Britain and the plantation aristocracy of the South. To the cultured English-man the Southerner was more a "gentleman" than the noisy, boastful, and vulgar Yankee. When, for example, the American correspondent of the London *Times* saw Jefferson Davis, President of the Con-federacy, he recorded, "Wonderful to relate, he does not chew [to-bacco], and is neat and 'clean looking, with hair trimmed, and boots brushed." [9]

Then, too, the British aristocrats detested "demon democracy." They had long expected the collapse of the ungainly American gov-ernment, supported, so they believed, by a "gibbering mob" derived largely from the "scum of Europe." Now their expectations were being realized.[10] The caustic Carlyle wrote that America was but a "smoky chimney which had taken fire." Another British commentator remarked: "The republic had rotted into Empire and the gangrene had burst." *Blackwood's* was especially savage in castigating "the ob-scure and commonplace man" who was now the "imbecile executive" of America. It sneered:

Every four years the constitution is in travail . . . and the latest result is—Mr. Abraham Lincoln. The great achievement in self-government of this vaunted democracy, which we have been so loudly and arrogantly called on to admire, is, to drag from his proper obscurity an ex-rail-splitter and country attorney, and to place what it calls its liberties at his august dis-posal. . . . It would have been impossible for him, or any of his Cabinet, to have emerged, under British institutions, from the mediocrity to which

---

[8] James Russell Lowell, *Poems* (Boston, 1891), II, 296.

[9] W. H. Russell, *My Diary North and South* (London, 1863), I, 250 (May 9, 1861). The Duke in Disraeli's novel, *Lothair*, remarked that the Southern Colonel Campian "is a gentleman; he is not a Yankee."

[10] The distinguished English historian, Edward A. Freeman, published in 1863 the first volume of a work entitled: *History of Federal Government, from the Foundation of the Achaian League to the Disruption of the United States*. The sec-ond volume never appeared.

nature had condemned them, and from which pure democracy alone was capable of rescuing them.[11]

There seems little doubt that British contempt for American institutions was to a considerable extent a cloak for fear. Should the North triumph, the disfranchised masses of England would clamor louder than ever for democracy. (In fact, the success of the Union was a strong argument advanced in behalf of the great Reform Bill of 1867.) To discredit democracy abroad was to discredit it at home; and it is not surprising that the British aristocrats should have felt some satisfaction at the apparent disruption of the United States.[12]

DIVIDE AND CONQUER

But there were additional reasons for the attitude of the English ruling classes. In their eyes the United States was an ominously growing power, a formidable commercial competitor, and a potential menace to Canada and other British possessions in the Western Hemisphere. The London *Morning Post* felt that if the North triumphed "Democracy will be more arrogant, more aggressive, more levelling and vulgarizing, if that be possible, than . . . ever . . . before." After a series of Northern defeats the London *Times* reported that "people are breathing more freely, and talking more lightly of the United States, than they have done any time these thirty years." [13]

The British aristocrats would certainly have been less than human if they had failed to rejoice at the discomfiture of a rival nation, whatever its form of government. If the South should succeed, there would be at least two snarling republics where only one had grown before; and England would no longer have to fear a unified and aggressive democracy.[14] Europe could extend the principle of the balance of power to a "Balkanized" Western Hemisphere and play the hoary game of divide and conquer. This, indeed, was the best opportunity that had presented itself since the pre-Monrovian period for the Old World to reassert its influence in America.

[11] *Blackwood's Magazine*, XCI, 121 (Jan. 1862).

[12] Donaldson Jordan and E. J. Pratt, *Europe and the American Civil War* (Boston, 1931), pp. 55 ff.

[13] London *Times*, Aug. 15, 1862, 6:2.

[14] The London *Economist* observed that instead of one nation "showing an encroaching and somewhat bullying front to the rest of the world, we shall have *two*, showing something of the same front to each other. Each will be more occupied with its immediate neighbour, and therefore less inclined to pick quarrels with more distant nations." *Economist*, XIX, 58 (Jan. 19, 1861).

Economic considerations also colored the thinking of the British ruling classes. Early in 1861 Congress enacted the highly protective Morrill tariff. England was a free-trade nation; and she regarded this measure as aimed directly at herself.[15] But the Confederacy, which was primarily an agricultural area, would presumably establish a tariff for revenue only—thus enabling the British manufacturer to compete on a much more satisfactory basis with his Yankee rival.

There was another aspect of the tariff problem. Great Britain's vitally important textile industry drew approximately eighty per cent of its cotton from the South. An independent Confederacy would send its fiber to England and receive in exchange British manufactured goods. Aside from an expanded free-trade market and an enlarged carrying trade, Great Britain would secure the additional advantage of having a cotton supply free from the control of the aggressive Yankee. The grizzled Palmerston, now Prime Minister, could scarcely have compressed more into fewer words when he said, "We do not like slavery, but we want cotton, and we dislike very much your Morrill tariff."

THE NORTH FIGHTS DEMOCRACY'S BATTLE

There were, on the other hand, powerful forces in England pulling in the direction of nonintervention. Lincoln was upholding law, order, and legitimate rule; and Great Britain, with her sprawling empire, would be ill-advised to give open encouragement to rebellion. In addition, there were many educated Englishmen who were indifferent to the struggle and genuinely desirous of remaining neutral. A more positive force was an influential group of liberals, including Richard Cobden and John Bright, who early concluded that this was a war involving slavery and perhaps the fate of democracy. These men labored valiantly to keep Great Britain out of the quarrel.[16]

The British economic interests were also opposed to intervention. Shippers realized that their business would be ruined by Yankee privateers if England and America clashed. But the longer the civil conflict lasted in the United States the greater the inroads the Confederate commerce destroyers would make on the American merchant

[15] The American historian, J. L. Motley, wrote from England that "there has been a change, a very great change, in English sympathy since the passing of the Morrill Tariff Bill." G. W. Curtis, ed., *The Correspondence of John Lothrop Motley* (N.Y., 1889), I, 364 (Motley to his mother, March 15, 1861).
[16] E. D. Adams, *Great Britain and the American Civil War* (London, 1925), I, 232 ff.

marine—Britain's most formidable competitor. In addition, there were the merchants in England who were reaping extraordinary wartime profits by supplying the needs of the North, and to some extent those of the South. Neutrality was obviously to their advantage.[17]

Possibly the most powerful single force in keeping the London government neutral was the English laboring class. Upon this group Harriet Beecher Stowe's *Uncle Tom's Cabin* had made a profound impression; and the British workingman concluded that the war in America was one in which he had a genuine stake. If the North won and the slaves were liberated, free labor would be exalted; if the South triumphed, free labor would be debased. The dead hand of Uncle Tom undoubtedly exercised a powerful restraining influence on the British government.[18]

The English masses also regarded the North, to which hundreds of thousands of their countrymen had emigrated, as the haven of free labor and democracy. They realized that if the Union triumphed their own chances of securing the ballot would be greatly improved. On the other hand, as John Bright put it, "There would be a wild shriek of Freedom to startle the world if that republic was overthrown." The battle for democracy in England was indeed being fought in America. The British government probably knew that the English workingmen would never willingly consent to intervention in behalf of slavery. Though the upper classes, with their powerful press, generally favored the South, the attitude of the masses could not be ignored.

NEUTRAL ROLES REVERSED

On April 19, 1861, a week after the firing on Fort Sumter, Lincoln proclaimed a blockade of the Southern ports, thus elevating the struggle from a domestic insurrection to a full-fledged war. The patrol of some 3500 miles of coastline was never completely effective, but, as finally established, it was sufficiently close to make ingress and egress hazardous for ordinary shipping. Whatever the degree of effectiveness, the great powers recognized the blockade as binding, and recognition was the acid test.[19]

Great Britain, moreover, did not insist that the Union maintain

---

[17] F. L. Owsley, *King Cotton Diplomacy* (Chicago, 1931), pp. 569 ff.

[18] E. Channing, *A History of the United States* (N.Y., 1925), VI, 114–115.

[19] Professor F. L. Owsley (*King Cotton Diplomacy*, pp. 250–291) marshals considerable evidence against the effectiveness of the blockade.

impossibly high blockade standards; and the Admiralty carefully instructed British naval officers in American waters to observe a punctilious neutrality.[20] Such solicitude, however, did not spring from a regard for the North, but from a desire to establish a precedent that might later be used to good advantage. As the London *Times* asserted, "a blockade is by far the most formidable weapon of offence we possess. Surely we ought not to be overready to blunt its edge or injure its temper?" [21] There can be no doubt that Britain's acquiescence in the Union's belligerent practices conferred a great advantage upon the Washington government.

In maintaining the blockade the North employed the doctrine of continuous voyage. For example, the port of Nassau, in the British Bahamas, suddenly began to receive enormous quantities of munitions and other contraband of war from England. Since the islanders themselves obviously could not use all these stores, it was clear that they were destined for transfer to Southern blockade runners. Union cruisers, operating on the high seas, captured contraband-laden British merchantmen bound for Nassau, on the ground that their cargoes were ultimately destined for the South. The United States also seized ships carrying noncontraband if it seemed that the cargoes were to be run by water into the Confederacy. The London government acquiesced in this interpretation, though objecting strongly to some of the methods employed in carrying it out.[22] And when the World War came, in 1914, England used a greatly expanded form of the doctrine of continuous voyage against America in the economic strangulation of Germany. The British, in playing the unusual role of neutral carrier during the Civil War while the Union played the unaccustomed role of dominant sea power, were taking a long view.[23]

[20] J. P. Baxter, 3rd, "The British Government and Neutral Rights, 1861–1865," *Amer. Hist. Rev.*, XXXIV (1928), 11.

[21] London *Times*, Feb. 24, 1862, quoted in *ibid.*, p. 12.

[22] See F. L. Owsley, "America and the Freedom of the Seas, 1861–65," in Avery Craven, ed., *Essays in Honor of William E. Dodd* (Chicago, 1935), pp. 196 *ff.* With particular reference to the town of Matamoros, Mexico, which received an enormous amount of contraband to be run across the border into the Confederacy, the United States held that contraband which was destined for the South by land might be seized on the high seas, but not noncontraband. The three most important Civil War cases decided by the Supreme Court involved the *Bermuda*, the *Springbok*, and the *Peterhoff*. See Carlton Savage, *Policy of the United States toward Maritime Commerce in War* (Washington, 1934), I, 94–97, 454–476. During the World War the British invoked the doctrine of ultimate destination against noncontraband consigned to cross land frontiers.

[23] See Baxter, "The British Government and Neutral Rights," *loc. cit.*, pp. 9 *ff.*

BRITAIN'S WELL-MEANING BLUNDER

Whatever the sympathies of the various classes, Downing Street had no desire to become involved in the internal difficulties of the United States. The problem before the Foreign Office became more complicated, when, on May 4, 1861, unofficial news of Lincoln's blockade proclamation reached England. Two days later it was announced in Parliament that the government would issue a proclamation of neutrality, that is, recognize the belligerent status of the Confederacy. This was done on May 13, 1861. There can be little doubt that from a purely technical point of view such action, sooner or later, was necessary. A blockade had been instituted, and it was desirable to warn British shippers of its existence, lest they become involved in serious difficulties with Union cruisers.[24]

From the outset Lincoln had attempted to maintain the legal fiction that the conflict was merely a domestic disturbance that would soon be brought under control. But the recognition of the Confederates as belligerents upset his plans. He failed to realize, however, that he had already recognized the belligerency of the Confederacy, for proclamations of blockade are not issued unless a state of war exists. In any event, the British declaration of neutrality placed the infant and partially organized Confederacy on the same plane with the long-established United States. It gave the Southerners license to send forth privateers and commerce destroyers, and to float loans abroad. It raised their morale and stiffened their resistance; it encouraged them to believe that recognition of independence would soon follow; and it set an example which was followed by the other Powers of the world. Although Downing Street knew that Minister Adams was en route to England, the proclamation was issued on the very day that he arrived—thus giving rise to the impression that it had been promulgated hastily in order to forestall his protests. In view of these circumstances it is not surprising that the North was immensely angered, and regarded the recognition of belligerency as the first conspicuously hostile act on the part of Great Britain.

It seems probable, however, that the British proclamation operated more to the advantage than to the disadvantage of the North. First, it recognized and consequently strengthened the blockade. Secondly,

---

[24] The proclamation of neutrality was such an obvious step that it received little editorial attention in England. Jordan and Pratt, *Europe and the American Civil War*, p. 9.

the time of its enunciation proved to be highly favorable to the Union. If the British had waited until two months later, when the disgraceful rout at Bull Run tarnished Northern arms, they probably would have recognized the independence rather than the mere belligerency of the Confederacy—a step that would have been much worse from the standpoint of the North. It was also probably a blessing for the Union that the proclamation was issued before the arrival of Adams in England. The newly-appointed minister had delayed his departure from America for six weeks, in order to be present at the wedding of his son. Adams later lamented that these nuptials cost the United States dear; but if he had been on the ground earlier he probably would have known that the proclamation was about to be issued, and he would have been obliged to protest in the strongest terms. As it turned out, he was faced with an accomplished fact, which he had to meet with the best possible grace.[25]

The British, thinking that they had done the right thing, were astonished at the bitterness expressed in the North. During the subsequent months they moved with the greatest circumspection, at times leaning over backward in an effort to avoid further offense. The twenty-three year old Henry Adams, who was then serving as his father's secretary at the Court of St. James's, noted:

The English . . . thought that . . . their Proclamation was just the thing to keep them straight with both sides, and when it turned out otherwise they did their best to correct their mistake. . . . Now that England has eaten her humble-pie for what was, I must say, a natural mistake from her point of view, I cannot imagine why we should keep on sarsing her.[26]

Whether consciously or not, the London government made partial amends for its recognition of Confederate belligerency. On June 1, 1861, it issued a proclamation forbidding the armed ships of either combatant to bring their prizes to British ports. Since the South had no merchant marine upon which the North could prey, and since the Confederacy could not send its prizes through the Northern blockade,[27] this was the death blow to Confederate privateering.

[25] E. D. Adams, *Great Britain and the American Civil War*, I, 111–112.

[26] Ford, *Cycle of Adams Letters*, I, 16–17 (Henry Adams to C. F. Adams, Jr., July 2, 1861).

[27] The United States had refused to subscribe to the Declaration of Paris of 1856, which prohibited privateering. Early in the war Seward made a belated effort to correct this mistake in the hope of interdicting Confederate privateering. The effort came to naught and further aroused British suspicion of Seward's slipperiness. E. D. Adams, *Great Britain and the American Civil War*, I, 141 ff.

As time wore on the Northern tempers cooled, though bitterness lingered; and by July 18, 1861, Adams, who until then had not dared engage quarters for more than a month at a time, took a house for a year.

THE TRENT AFFAIR

During the hundred days after the firing on Fort Sumter, British opinion, on the whole, was not conspicuously unfriendly to the Union. Then, on July 21, 1861, came that disgraceful and disillusioning encounter at Bull Run, where the "uniformed civilians" of the North revealed astonishing celerity in departing from the scene of battle.[28]

Unquestionably, Bull Run produced a great revulsion of feeling in England. The aristocratic press chortled over the "wretched" and "gibbering" mobs of "Irish and German mercenaries"—"scum" who had been "drugged with whiskey" and then enlisted. But even among the more reasonable and temperate Englishmen the conviction took root that the Confederacy could not be overthrown. The pro-Union Cobden did not believe that the North and the South would "ever lie in the same bed again." Since it seemed reasonably certain that the South could never be conquered, and since the prolongation of the conflict would merely result in senseless slaughter, a considerable body of opinion in England veered around to the view that an uncontested divorce should be granted.

This was the situation late in 1861, when the Confederate government, dissatisfied with the earlier efforts of its commissioners in Europe to secure recognition, decided to send abroad two of its best known statesmen, James M. Mason and John Slidell.[29] After running the blockade the two men arrived at Havana, where they boarded a British mail steamer, the *Trent*. Meanwhile the overzealous Captain Wilkes, of the Union sloop *San Jacinto*, learning of the plans of the Confederate commissioners, and acting wholly without orders from Washington, waylaid the *Trent*, on November 8, 1861, fired two shots across her bow, and sent a party of men on board. Mason, Slidell, and their two secretaries were removed after a show of force; but the *Trent* was allowed to continue on her way. This was a strik-

---

[28] Young Henry Adams, in spite of his mortification, could not "help howling with laughter" as he read in the London *Times* how the swift-footed Yankees saved their "precious carcasses" by precipitate flight. Ford, *Cycle of Adams Letters*, I, 26 (Henry Adams to C. F. Adams, Jr., Aug. 26, 1861).

[29] John Slidell had gone on the unsuccessful mission to Mexico in 1846. James Mason was not the John Y. Mason of Ostend Manifesto notoriety.

ing case of search and seizure, in many respects similar to what America had suffered at the hands of England during the Napoleonic wars.

The news of the *Trent* affair caused the North to break into delirious rejoicing. Charles Francis Adams, Jr., then a young law student in Boston, later recorded:

> . . . I do not remember in the whole course of the half-century's retrospect . . . any occurrence in which the American people were so completely swept off their feet, for the moment losing possession of their senses, as during the weeks which immediately followed the seizure of Mason and Slidell.[30]

This wild outburst can be understood only in the light of the existing atmosphere.

For months the North had been on edge, confidently awaiting news of victory but repeatedly receiving only disheartening reports of defeat. Captain Wilkes' bold stroke was the first considerable Northern success of the war; and it produced an hysterical reaction. With only two or three possible exceptions no men in the South were more cordially hated in the North than Mason and Slidell.[31] The latter, in particular, enjoyed an almost superhuman reputation for diplomatic prowess; and it was widely believed that if he reached Europe, intervention and the breaking of the blockade were virtually assured. The Northerners also felt that by giving Britain a dose of her own quarter-deck medicine they were getting sweet revenge for old wrongs as well as for the recognition of Confederate belligerency. The governor of Massachusetts publicly expressed satisfaction that the captain of the *San Jacinto* had "fired his shot across the bows of the ship that bore the British lion at its head."

Captain Wilkes became the hero of the hour. He was wined, dined, serenaded, and promoted. The Secretary of the Navy wrote him a letter expressing his "emphatic approval"; the House of Representatives passed an official vote of thanks. The New York *Times* asserted:

> There is, consequently, no drawback whatever to our jubilations. The universal Yankee Nation is getting decidedly awake. . . . As for Commodore Wilkes and his command, let the handsome thing be done. Consecrate another *Fourth* of July to him. Load him down with services of plate

[30] C. F. Adams, Jr., "The Trent Affair," *Mass. Hist. Soc. Procs.*, XLV, 37 (Nov. 1911).

[31] J. F. Rhodes, *History of the United States* (N.Y., 1896), III, 521.

LOOK OUT FOR SQUALLS.

Jack Bull. "YOU DO WHAT'S RIGHT, MY SON, OR I'LL BLOW YOU OUT OF THE WATER."

Britain's strong stand on the *Trent* against the swaggering, sharp-nosed, cigar-smoking Yankee.

and swords of the cunningest and costliest art. Let us encourage the happy inspiration that achieved such a victory.[32]

But Lincoln was uneasy, remarking prophetically that Mason and Slidell might yet "prove to be white elephants."

When the news of the seizure reached England a veritable "typhoon of fury" swept the country, though at first even the ponderous London *Times* counseled moderation. The "Rule Britannia" group, assuming that the seizure had been authorized, rose up in arms over the "ruffianly outrage" offered the flag by the "impudent pirate" Wilkes, whose "swagger and ferocity" made him, said the London *Mercury*, "an ideal Yankee." [33] It was widely assumed that Seward was trying to provoke his foreign war, and feverish military and naval preparations were begun in England and Canada. Henry Adams wrote from London, "This nation means to make war. Do not doubt it." Eleven thousand crack troops embarked for Canada. Two of the departing transports were serenaded by a volunteer band playing, "I Wish I Was in Dixie." [34]

SATAN REPROVES A SINNER

Three days after the news of the *Trent* affair reached England, Earl Russell, Foreign Secretary, dispatched an ultimatum to Washington. Several days later the news of the mad outburst of rejoicing in America reached London, and aroused the popular indignation to an even higher pitch. Fortunately for the Union there was no Atlantic cable; [35] for if the British had known of Northern jubilation, Earl Russell's demands would probably have been presented in such terms as to make war the only honorable alternative. Even so, the original ultimatum was couched in language so peremptory that Prince Albert, though suffering from the illness that was to take his life three weeks later, wrote a memorandum (December 1, 1861) in which he pointed

[32] New York *Times*, Nov. 17, 1861, 4:3.

[33] A story was widely related in England to the effect that the British captain of the *Trent* had stepped between the Yankee bayonets and the undefended breast of Slidell's daughter, crying, "Back, you damned cowardly poltroons!" Jordan and Pratt, *Europe and the American Civil War*, pp. 34–35.

[34] An amusing anticlimax developed when a British troopship, unable to enter the ice-bound St. Lawrence, put into Portland, Maine. Seward graciously granted permission for the troops to cross Maine. Frederic Bancroft, *The Life of William H. Seward* (N.Y., 1900) II, 245.

[35] A cable had been laid in 1858, but a short time later had ceased to operate. A successful cable was not put into operation until 1866.

out how the statement could well be toned down.[36] The sick man's wishes were respected. In its final form Russell's note demanded the release of the prisoners and a suitable apology for the affront to the British flag. Lord Lyons, Her Majesty's minister in Washington, was ordered to wait seven days for a reply, and if a satisfactory one was not forthcoming, to return home immediately.

Again the absence of a cable played a vital part. The conciliatory Lord Lyons, who had maintained a most discreet silence, did not receive the British ultimatum until more than a month after the news of the *Trent* affair had reached the United States. Meanwhile the North had cooled down; and the Lincoln administration was left in a distressing position.[37] If it released the prisoners, public rage might result in the overthrow of the government. If it did not, war would undoubtedly ensue, and this would mean the independence of the South. The North, moreover, was so clearly in the wrong that France and several of the other Powers supported Britain's position. To be sure, a case could have been made out for Captain Wilkes if he had brought the entire ship before a prize court for adjudication.[38] But this he did not do. So the United States found itself in the position of denying the very principles for which it had presumably fought Great Britain in 1812. Young Henry Adams expostulated to his brother: "Good God, what's got into you all? What do you mean by deserting now the great principles of our fathers, by returning to the vomit of that dog Great Britain? What do you mean by asserting now principles against which every Adams yet has protested and resisted?"[39]

After a prolonged debate in the Lincoln Cabinet, it was finally decided that the prisoners should be released; and upon Seward fell the task of making official explanations to Lord Lyons. In his memorable note of December 26, 1861, the American Secretary asserted that

---

[36] See Theodore Martin, *The Life of His Royal Highness the Prince Consort* (London, 1880), V, 421–423.

[37] C. F. Adams (the minister's son) suggests that the Administration missed a stroke of Bismarckian brilliance when it did not free the men in advance of the British ultimatum, and thus leave Downing Street in a ridiculous position. "The Trent Affair," *Amer. Hist. Rev.*, XVII (1912), 558–560.

[38] C. C. Hyde, *International Law Chiefly as Interpreted and Applied by the United States* (Boston, 1922), II, 639. Apparently the British law officers concluded in advance of the *Trent* affair that such a seizure would be justified; the next day (Nov. 12, 1861) they held that the entire ship would have to be seized. In any event, the latter opinion was written before the news of the incident reached England. Baxter, "The British Government and Neutral Rights," *loc. cit.*, pp. 15–16.

[39] Ford, *Cycle of Adams Letters*, I, 83 (Henry Adams to Charles Francis Adams, Jr., Dec. 13, 1861).

Captain Wilkes' mistake had been not to seize the entire ship; but since he had erred the Confederate commissioners would be released. With an eye to placating public opinion, Seward expressed satisfaction that Britain had finally accepted the principles for which the United States had fought in 1812.[40] This adroit sweetening of the pill, which ignored the points at issue, seemingly put England on the defensive and caused the release of the men to be more palatable to the Northerners. But Seward's stump-speech reply to Lyons revealed that his familiarity with American psychology was sounder than his knowledge of international law.

The Trent Aftertaste

From the standpoint of the North the *Trent* affair left a most unfortunate legacy. Many Americans were angered because Britain had adopted so strong a tone with regard to a practice that she herself had long exercised. Many more resented what appeared to be a bullying attempt to take advantage of Northern internal misfortunes. As James Russell Lowell protested:

> It don't seem hardly right, John,
> When both my hands was full,
> To stump me to a fight, John—
> Your cousin, tu, John Bull! [41]

Representative Lovejoy of Illinois, who "literally wept tears of vexation" at the outcome, expressed a not uncommon sentiment when he announced:

> . . . I hate the British government. I have never shared in the traditional hostility of many of my countrymen against England. But I now here publicly avow and record my inextinguishable hatred of that Government. I mean to cherish it while I live, and to bequeath it as a legacy to my children when I die. And if I am alive when war with England comes, as sooner or later it must, for we shall never forget this humiliation, and if I can carry a musket in that war I will carry it.[42]

[40] "We are asked to do to the British nation," wrote Seward, "just what we have always insisted all nations ought to do to us." J. B. Moore, *Digest of International Law*, VII, 629 (Seward to Lyons, Dec. 26, 1861).

[41] Lowell, *Poems*, II, 266.

[42] *Cong. Globe*, 37 Cong., 2 sess., p. 333 (Jan. 14, 1862). One of Minister Adams' sons wrote to his father: "I at least would care to impress but one thing on a son of mine, and that should be inveterate, undying, immortal hatred of Great Britain." C. F. Adams, Jr., "The Trent Affair," *Mass. Hist. Soc. Procs.*, XLV (Nov., 1911), p. 68 (Dec. 30, 1861).

On the other hand, British public opinion (except, perhaps, in certain aristocratic quarters) was relieved by the amicable solution of the controversy, particularly when the news came that the seizure was unauthorized.[43] The Queen was deeply appreciative of the work of Lord Lyons, who had discharged his disagreeable duties with a consummate blend of firmness and tact; and she awarded him the Grand Cross of the Order of the Bath. As sober afterthoughts the British realized that Ireland was restive; that the prosecution of an overseas war would be immensely difficult; that Canada was vulnerable to the swarming Northern armies; and that Great Britain's merchant marine would probably be swept off the ocean by Yankee privateers. Moreover, the English laboring classes had no real desire to fight their kinsmen as the allies of slave power.

All things considered, the *Trent* affair, which served as an emotional outlet, probably improved feeling for the North in England. Seward's specious note did not instill confidence among British statesmen; but, on the other hand, he had had his opportunity to fight and had passed it by. Minister Adams in London observed:

The Trent affair has proved . . . somewhat in the nature of a sharp thunderstorm which has burst without doing any harm, and the consequence has been a decided improvement of the state of the atmosphere. Our English friends are pleased with themselves and pleased with us for having given them the opportunity to be so.[44]

So passed the first great diplomatic crisis of the war; and Minister Adams confided to his diary: "I am to remain in this purgatory a while longer."

BIBLIOGRAPHICAL NOTE

For brief accounts of Civil War diplomacy during 1861 consult E. Channing, *A History of the United States* (N.Y., 1925), VI, 332–359; and H. W. Temple, "William H. Seward," in S. F. Bemis, ed., *The American Secretaries of State and their Diplomacy* (N.Y., 1928), VII, 3–70. Two indispensable works are E. D. Adams, *Great Britain and the American Civil War* (2 vols., London, 1925), which is full on the British side; and F. L. Owsley, *King Cotton Diplomacy*

[43] Thomas Harris, *The Trent Affair* (Indianapolis, 1896), pp. 234–238. See also Karl Marx and Frederick Engels, *The Civil War in the United States* (N.Y., 1937), p. 47. Marx, who was then living in England as a newspaper correspondent, has an excellent analysis of public reaction to the incident.

[44] Ford, *Cycle of Adams Letters*, I, 114 (C. F. Adams to his son, Feb. 21, 1862). The British humor magazine, *Fun*, published a cartoon in which John Bull declared to Jonathan, "I accept your hand ten times more willingly than I would have taken up your glove." *Fun*, I, 177 (Jan. 18, 1862).

(Chicago, 1931), which is the most satisfactory treatment of the attempts of the Confederates to secure foreign support. A useful book on public opinion abroad is Donaldson Jordan and E. J. Pratt, *Europe and the American Civil War* (Boston, 1931). On the blockade and maritime rights see J. P. Baxter, 3rd, "The British Government and Neutral Rights, 1861–1865," *Amer. Hist. Rev.*, XXXIV (1928), 9–29, and the accompanying documents, pp. 77–91; also the same author's "Some British Opinions as to Neutral Rights, 1861 to 1865," *Amer. Jour. Internat. Law*, XXIII (1929), 517–537. On the same general subject consult also Carlton Savage, *Policy of the United States toward Maritime Commerce in War* (Washington, 1934), I, 87–97, 415–476; and F. L. Owsley, "America and the Freedom of the Seas, 1861–65," in Avery Craven, ed., *Essays in Honor of William E. Dodd* (Chicago, 1935), pp. 194–256. Frederic Bancroft, *The Life of William H. Seward* (2 vols., N.Y., 1900), is still standard. A detailed account of the subject is Thomas Harris, *The Trent Affair* (Indianapolis, 1896). See also the analysis of C. F. Adams, Jr., "The Trent Affair," *Amer. Hist. Rev.*, XVII (1912), 540–562. Further references: see footnotes of this chapter and Bemis and Griffin, *Guide*, Ch. XIII.

RECENT REFERENCES. Carl Sandburg, *Abraham Lincoln: The War Years* (N.Y., 1939), I, 358–369, tells of Lincoln's conciliatory part in the *Trent* crisis. After counseling "One war at a time," the President reluctantly allowed the men to be surrendered. *The History of The Times: The Tradition Established, 1841–1884* (London, 1939), Ch. XVIII, is a most revealing account of how the *Times*, despite the pro-Southern bias of its owners and editors, consistently stood for neutrality during the war. The ostracism of this journal's able American correspondent, W. H. Russell ("Bull Run" Russell), following his truthful account of the disgraceful affair at Bull Run, led to his resignation in disgust (not recall, as some writers have it), and paved the way for his violently anti-Northern successor, Charles Mackay, who presented a distorted picture to his superiors on which to base their editorials. A. M. McDiarmid, "American Civil War Precedents: Their Nature, Application, and Extension," *Amer. Jour. of Internat. Law*, XXXIV (1940), 220–237, emphasizes the relation of these precedents to belligerent practices in 1914–1918. The author makes a strong point of the fact that the initial proclamation of blockade "was merely a notice of intention and remained without effect at any particular port until a blockading force was stationed there (p. 231)."

NEW REFERENCES. Jay Monaghan, *Diplomat in Carpet Slippers: Abraham Lincoln Deals with Foreign Affairs* (Indianapolis, 1945), rather overstresses the role of Lincoln and contributes color rather than significant new material. Most noteworthy perhaps is the treatment (Ch. XIV) of Lincoln's efforts to influence British opinion through propaganda agents. J. G. Randall, *Lincoln the President* (2 vols., N.Y., 1945), Ch. XVI, stresses the skill of Lincoln and the mediation of Senator Sumner in dealing with the *Trent* affair. W. W. Jeffries, "The Civil War Career of Charles Wilkes," *Jour. of Southern Hist.*, XI (1945), 324–348, shows how the overzealous "hero" of the *Trent* affair aroused the foreign Powers and drove Britain to the verge of war by his high-handed blockade operations in the West Indies.

CHAPTER XXII

Civil War Diplomacy, 1862–1865

*"No, sir, you dare not make war on cotton. No power on earth
dares make war upon it. Cotton is king."*

Senator Hammond of South Carolina, 1858.

A MAGNIFICENT OBSESSION

WHEN the Civil War broke out, one fifth of the population of England drew its livelihood, directly or indirectly, from the manufacture of cotton products. Approximately eighty per cent of the fiber that supported this huge industry came from the South. It was obvious that if the American supply should suddenly be cut off, the most important single manufacturing industry in England would be paralyzed, and the economic life of the British Isles would suffer a stunning blow. In March, 1861, before the war had actually begun, *Punch* confessed:

> Though with the North we sympathise,
> It must not be forgotten
> That with the South we've stronger ties,
> Which are composed of cotton,
> Whereof our imports mount unto
> A sum of many figures
> And where would be our calico
> Without the toil of niggers? [1]

The potential coercive power of "King Cotton" fascinated the imagination of many Southerners. They confidently believed that if the North should establish a strangling blockade, the English cotton operatives would be thrown out of work, and starving mobs would literally force the British government to intervene. "The cards are in our hands!" gloated the Charleston *Mercury* seven weeks after the firing on Fort Sumter; "and we intend to play them out to the bankruptcy of every cotton factory in Great Britain and France or

[1] *Punch*, XL, 134 (March 30, 1861).

the acknowledgment of our independence." [2] When William H. Russell, the London *Times* correspondent, was visiting Charleston, in April, 1861, one of his hosts exclaimed:

Why, sir, we have only to shut off your supply of cotton for a few weeks, and we can create a revolution in Great Britain. There are four millions of your people depending on us for their bread, not to speak of the many millions of dollars. No, sir, we know that England must recognize us. . . . [3]

Indeed, the Southerners perceived that the tighter the blockade, the greater the pinch in England; and they themselves restricted cotton production and burned some 2,500,000 bales in order to cause a more acute shortage abroad. [4]

WHY KING COTTON LOST HIS SCEPTER

On paper the case made out for "King Cotton" seemed flawless. Why, then, did he fail? The basic answer seems to be that when Fort Sumter fell there was a fifty per cent oversupply of raw cotton in England, largely because the South had already shipped most of its bumper crop of 1860. The surplus also extended to the manufactured product, and when the war came the factory owners were being forced to shut down completely, or work on a part-time basis. Indeed, the Union blockade of the South came as a godsend to the British cotton manufacturers. It increased the value of their huge stocks of raw material, in some cases five- or sixfold. And it gave them an opportunity eventually to dispose of their manufactured goods, then a glut on the market, at three or four times their normal price.

Other unforeseen developments combined to dethrone "King Cotton." During the course of the war approximately 1,500,000 bales of cotton were run through the blockade—about three fourths of a normal year's export to England. New sources of supply were developed in India and particularly in Egypt. As the war progressed and the Northern armies penetrated the South, the Lincoln administration made strenuous efforts to secure cotton and ship it to England. When the pinch came in 1863, the North was committed to an

---

[2] Charleston *Mercury*, June 4, 1861, quoted in F. L. Owsley, *King Cotton Diplomacy* (Chicago, 1931), pp. 25–26.

[3] W. H. Russell, *My Diary North and South* (London, 1863), I, 170–171 (April 18, 1861).

[4] Owsley, *King Cotton Diplomacy*, pp. 44–51.

antislavery crusade and any real danger of British intervention had passed.[5]

"King Cotton" also met an unexpected adversary in "King Corn." During the years of the Civil War serious crop shortages at home forced the British to turn elsewhere for a grain supply. They found it convenient and profitable to exchange large quantities of munitions for "corn," as they denominated American cereals in general, the most important of which was wheat. Seward and other Northern propagandists harped on the theme that if England went to war on behalf of the Southern states, she would be deprived of her grain supply and faced with starvation. As a versifier in the American *Continental Monthly* exulted:

> Wave the stars and stripes high o'er us,
> Let every freeman sing,
>
> . . . .
>
> Old King Cotton's dead and buried: brave young Corn is King.[6]

Recent students have cast serious doubt on the "King Wheat" theory by pointing out that although England needed grain, she could, if necessary, have secured it in Europe at a somewhat higher price. But many uninformed Englishmen *thought* that they were fatally dependent upon American foodstuffs; and this impression, though erroneous, probably did something to strengthen the Ministry's policy of neutrality.[7]

"King Cotton" encountered another powerful rival in war profiteering. In England, the steel, munitions, and shipbuilding industries were booming; shippers were wresting trade from their Yankee rivals; cotton speculators, who had cornered all available fiber, hoped that the war would go on for years; and the languishing linen and woolen industries, with competition in cotton lessened, were experiencing unprecedented activity. So great was the general prosperity that, even with several hundred thousand cotton operatives thrown out of work, the total number of unemployed in England during the war was ap-

[5] E. Channing, *A History of the United States* (N.Y., 1925), VI, 338–339; Owsley, *King Cotton Diplomacy*, pp. 568 ff.

[6] August, 1862, quoted in Channing, *History of the United States*, VI, 340.

[7] A full exposition of the "King Wheat" theory is L. B. Schmidt, "The Influence of Wheat and Cotton on Anglo-American Relations during the Civil War," *Iowa Jour. of Hist. and Pols.*, XVI (1918), 400–439. See the criticisms of it in Owsley's *King Cotton Diplomacy*, p. 568; E. D. Adams, *Great Britain and the American Civil War* (London, 1925), II, 13–14; and Eli Ginzberg, "The Economics of British Neutrality during the American Civil War," *Agricultural Hist.*, X (1936), 147–156.

proximately normal.[8] As the London *Times* complacently observed: "We are as busy, as rich, and as fortunate in our trade as if the American war had never broken out, and our trade with the States had never been disturbed. Cotton was no King, notwithstanding the prerogatives which had been loudly claimed for him."[9]

IDEALS AND FOOD

Although the general economic picture in the British Isles was good, a vast amount of misery was concentrated in the cotton manufacturing industry. By December, 1862, over 400,000 operatives were unemployed, or working only part time. Slender stores of savings had disappeared; virtuous daughters were being driven into prostitution. The question immediately arises why these unfortunates did not get out of hand and force the government to break the blockade.

First of all, the submerged classes of England had no vote and very little voice. They were docile and uncomplaining, used to having little. There was, moreover, a general impression that they were suffering in the interests of democracy and free white labor, an impression which Northern propagandists assiduously cultivated and which undoubtedly had some influence.

But one finds it difficult to believe that the English workers would have quietly starved to death simply because they sympathized with the abstract ideals of the North—that conscience was stronger than the need for cotton. The famishing operatives appear to have been held in line because private and public benefactions relieved the worst of their suffering.[10]

Public opinion in the North was keenly aware of the necessity of keeping the British workingmen from rioting. Farsighted and philanthropically-minded citizens collected money and sent several shiploads

---

[8] Owsley, *King Cotton Diplomacy*, p. 577.

[9] London *Times*, Jan. 7, 1864, 8:6. The spectacle of Britain waxing fat at the expense of the United States aroused much jealousy. An anonymous Northerner wrote a bitter parody on "God Save the King."

> God save me, great John Bull!
> Long keep my pockets full!
> God save John Bull.
> Ever victorious,
> Haughty, vainglorious,
> Snobbish, censorious,
> God save John Bull!

Harper's Weekly, V, 723 (Nov. 16, 1861).

[10] Owsley, *King Cotton Diplomacy*, p. 162.

of food to England.[11] These donations, as well as the larger ones dispensed at home, were received with gratitude. The unfortunate cotton workers sang in awkward verse:

> Our mules and looms have now ceased work, the Yankees are the cause.
> But we will let them fight it out and stand by English laws;
> No recognizing shall take place, until the war is o'er;
> Our wants are now attended to, we cannot ask for more.[12]

THE CRISIS OF THE CONFEDERACY

During the first half of 1862 the Northern armies were generally successful; and in March, 1862, the ironclad Union *Monitor* halted the destructive career of the Confederate *Merrimac*. Although the British had made considerable progress in building armored ships, they were not so sure as before of their ability to cope with the Yankees on the sea. Then came a staggering setback to Confederate hopes when, in April, 1862, the Union forces captured New Orleans, the largest city and chief seaport of the South—an achievement that sobered Southern sympathizers abroad.[13]

The North confidently expected additional successes of General George B. McClellan, who was fashioning and polishing the formidable Army of the Potomac. But the utter failure of his Peninsular campaign completely changed the outlook. "There is an all but unanimous belief," wrote the friendly Cobden from England to Charles Sumner, "that you *cannot* subject the South to the Union."

In September and October, 1862, following a crushing Northern defeat at the Second Battle of Bull Run, there came what was probably the most critical period of the war for the Union. An increasing number of Englishmen felt that this bloody and fratricidal strife would probably be inconclusive anyhow, and that in the interests of

[11] Among the Pennsylvania broadsides (File 157) in the Library of Congress is one (Dec. 1862) requesting relief for the starving thousands of England. *Vanity Fair* (N.Y.) published an interesting cartoon entitled "Columbia Brings Substantial Blessings to Her Poor Relations over the Sea." VI, 295 (Dec. 20, 1862).

[12] E. D. Adams, *Great Britain and the American Civil War*, II, 17 n.

[13] Benjamin F. Butler, a "political" general with an unsavory reputation, was placed in command of the Northern troops occupying New Orleans. The women of the city evinced great contempt for the Yankee invader; and Butler issued an order (May 15, 1862) declaring that any "female" insulting his officers and men should be locked up as a prostitute. Public opinion in Europe, particularly in England, was outraged. But Minister Adams handled the impulsive Palmerston with skill; and the sensation quickly passed. See Henry Adams, *The Education of Henry Adams* (N.Y., 1931), p. 136.

humanity it should be made to cease. Accordingly, on September 14, 1862, Prime Minister Palmerston, noting that the Northerners "had got a very complete smashing," wrote to Earl Russell at the Foreign Office suggesting that Great Britain and France join in proposing to the Washington government an arrangement "on the basis of a separation." In his reply three days later, Russell favored such a plan of mediation and suggested that "in case of failure, we ought ourselves to recognize the Southern States as an independent State." But on September 23, 1862, Palmerston, having learned of the Confederate drive into Maryland under General Robert E. Lee, wrote to Russell in a more cautious vein:

It is evident that a great conflict is taking place to the northwest of Washington, and its issue must have a great effect on the state of affairs. If the Federals sustain a great defeat, they may be at once ready for mediation, and the iron should be struck while it is hot. If, on the other hand, they should have the best of it, we may wait awhile and see what may follow. . . .[14]

By the end of September, 1862, the news came from America that Lee's invasion had been halted at Antietam Creek, Maryland. The battle revealed that the North was stronger than had been supposed; and, as a result, interest in intervention waned so rapidly that by late October, 1862, only two members of the British Cabinet supported it. Though hardly more than a draw, Antietam was, diplomatically speaking, one of the decisive battles of the world. The South was probably never so near success as on the eve of that engagement.

Other developments contributed to the thwarting of the intervention movement. Notable among them was the conduct of William E. Gladstone, Chancellor of the Exchequer, the third member of the Cabinet in importance and the most strongly pro-Southern member of the group. On October 7, 1862, Gladstone delivered an important speech at Newcastle, and he went so far as to assert, amid loud cheers and cries of "Hear, hear!":

. . . There is no doubt that Jefferson Davis [President of the Confederacy] and other leaders of the South have made an army; they are making, it appears, a navy; and they have made what is more than either—they have made a nation. (Loud cheers.) . . . We may anticipate with certainty the success of the Southern States so far as regards their separation from the North. (Hear, hear.) [15]

[14] Spencer Walpole, *Life of Lord John Russell* (London, 1891), II, 362.
[15] London *Times*, Oct. 9, 1862, 7:6; 8:1.

The Cabinet, as we have seen, was not prepared to move following the recent news of Antietam.[16] But for Gladstone publicly to recognize the Confederate "nation" left the impression that he was speaking for the government, and that recognition and intervention were to follow. The prospect of breaking the blockade caused the price of cotton in England to fall; and panic prevailed in the business world. Gladstone's indiscretion also caused the pro-Northern group in England to cry out in protest, thus revealing to the Cabinet that intervention would encounter formidable opposition. In the end the speech appears to have worked to the advantage of the North.

Probably the basic reason why Britain did not officially propose mediation was the conviction that such a step, vigorously pushed, would mean war.[17] And war with the North, particularly after the show of strength at Antietam, was even less inviting than at the time of the *Trent* affair. Russell and Palmerston were both old enough to have vivid memories of Yankee privateering. Neutrality had on the whole proved highly profitable to the British; and since it seemed probable that the war would result in Southern independence anyhow, why become embroiled with the United States?

NAPOLEON: THE PEACEMAKER

Palmerston and Russell, in their discussions of mediation, had taken it for granted that Napoleon III of France would co-operate with them. From first to last the French Emperor had been willing to join with Great Britain. As early as October, 1861, after previous hints of mediation, he had made a proposal to England looking toward a joint breaking of the blockade; and periodically he had renewed this suggestion. Britain was the bulwark that stood between the South and success.

The reasons for Napoleon's attitude are not far to seek. Both jealousy of the growing might of the United States and the desirability of establishing an American balance of power seem to have loomed large in his Machiavellian calculations. But more important was the fact that he had just launched his mad enterprise of establishing a

[16] It appears that Gladstone, who had been absent from London for some time, was unaware of this change of opinion. E. D. Adams, *Great Britain and the American Civil War*, II, 48.

[17] Seward had made it abundantly clear to Minister Adams that intervention would mean war. Seward to Adams, Aug. 2, 1862, Department of State, *Instructions, Great Britain*, XVIII, no. 314. The import of this instruction was conveyed to W. E. Forster, who probably informed the British government.

French puppet empire in Mexico. A division of the United States into two nations, with possible Southern support in return for his intervention, would make the success of his Mexican scheme more probable. On the other hand, a victory for the North would seriously jeopardize his position.

Nor was Napoleon far in advance of French public opinion in his unfriendliness to the North. The French cotton textile factories suffered acutely from the blockade, as did many other industries that depended on Southern patronage. Except for the first months of the war, French public opinion seems to have favored mediation either alone or in the company of other Powers, provided actual hostilities could be avoided.[18]

Late in October, 1862, a short time after the complete collapse of the intervention movement in the British Cabinet, the French Foreign Office proposed joint action with Great Britain and Russia to secure a six-month armistice in America. This proposition was all the more plausible because it was cloaked in a humanitarian guise. After a two-day debate the British Cabinet rejected the offer. It was evident that intervention by France alone would mean war; and though Napoleon had a powerful fleet of ironclads, he was not willing to try conclusions with the North single-handed.[19]

In January, 1863, following the bloody Northern defeat at Fredericksburg, Napoleon returned to the charge and offered mediation directly to the Lincoln government. This overture was firmly but politely declined. Congress registered its disapproval of such meddling by overwhelmingly passing a resolution which declared that a proposition from a foreign Power for mediation or any other form of intervention would be regarded as an unfriendly act. Although Napoleon continued to play a deep game, this was the last noteworthy attempt on his part to intervene.[20]

A PROCLAMATION THAT DID NOT EMANCIPATE

As the war dragged on President Lincoln became increasingly aware of the incongruity of smiting the South with his right hand while upholding slavery in the loyal areas with his left, and he longed

[18] L. M. Case, ed., *French Opinion on the United States and Mexico, 1860–1867* (N.Y., 1936), pp. 257–258.

[19] Owsley, *King Cotton Diplomacy*, pp. 563–564.

[20] Napoleon's dealings with Roebuck, who introduced a resolution in Parliament looking toward intervention, fell flat in July, 1863. See E. D. Adams, *Great Britain and the American Civil War*, II, 176–177.

for the day when the domestic front would permit some decisive action regarding slavery. On July 22, 1862, following an apathetic reception in the border states of his plans for compensated emancipation, the President called a memorable Cabinet meeting, and read the draft of an emancipation proclamation that he proposed to issue. The idea met with general favor, but Secretary Seward questioned the wisdom of publishing the document at precisely that moment. The North had just suffered a succession of defeats, and such action, Seward pointed out, would look very much like an attempt to incite a servile war as a last desperate expedient—"our last shriek, on the retreat." Lincoln was struck with the force of this observation and pigeonholed the statement until such time as a victory should crown Northern arms. As he quaintly remarked several weeks later: "I do not want to issue a document that the whole world will see must necessarily be inoperative, like the Pope's bull against the comet." [21]

On September 17, 1862, came the battle of Antietam; and Lincoln seized upon this indecisive success as the victory upon which to launch his preliminary emancipation proclamation, which was published on September 23, 1862. It announced that on January 1, 1863, all slaves held in areas in rebellion against the United States government would be "forever free." But slaves in the loyal border states were not to be affected.

The immediate results of this announcement were disappointing to Lincoln. The South regarded it as an inhuman attempt to stir up the "hellish passions of servile insurrection," and regirded its loins for the battle. The Northern abolitionists demanded a more thoroughgoing measure; and the border states feared that they were reading the ultimate doom of their own valuable slave property. The Congressional elections of October and November, 1862, went heavily against the Administration, partly, it appears, because of dissatisfaction with Lincoln's new policy.

In Europe the preliminary proclamation did little to strengthen the cause of the Union. The pro-Southern sympathizers cried that this was a public confession that the North had come to the end of its tether. It was, they declared, a desperate and diabolical attempt to conquer the South by a stroke of the pen, now that arms had failed. Pointing to the fact that the proclamation was a war measure and that it was designed to free only the slaves of the Confederacy, the London *Spectator* scoffed:

[21] J. G. Nicolay and John Hay, *Abraham Lincoln: a History* (N.Y., 1890), VI, 155.

The Government liberates the enemy's slaves as it would the enemy's cattle, simply to weaken them in the coming conflict. . . . The principle asserted is not that a human being cannot justly own another, but that he cannot own him unless he is loyal to the United States.[22]

Blackwood's Magazine spoke of the document as a "monstrous, reckless, devilish" "project," and declared that rather than lose the South "the North would league itself with Beelzebub, and seek to make a hell of half a continent." [23]

Undeterred by criticisms at home and abroad, Lincoln issued the final proclamation, January 1, 1863. It required courage to take this step, in the face of a reverse at the ballot box and a crushing defeat at Fredericksburg. But it was well for the cause of the North that the preliminary announcement had been made following Antietam, for no signal success crowned Union arms until Gettysburg, nearly ten months later. Even so, the final edict did suggest what Lincoln had wanted to avoid: a papal bull against a comet. Since it applied to only those areas over which the North had no control, the so-called Emancipation Proclamation did not strike the shackles from a single slave. It was merely a presidential pronouncement of doubtful constitutionality, designed chiefly as a war measure.

The news of the final proclamation caused a fresh outburst of indignation among the pro-Southern group in England. They had inveighed against the Lincoln administration because it would not at the outset proclaim a crusade against slavery; now they were irked because it did. But the evident determination of the North to wipe out the black curse greatly encouraged the antislavery elements in England. They had at first doubted the sincerity of the preliminary edict, or had been slow to grasp its implications; but now they vented their delight in various ways, including rousing mass meetings. Referring to one of these demonstrations, Henry Adams related:

As for enthusiasm, my friend Tom Brown of Rugby school-days, who was one of the speakers, had to stop repeatedly and beg the people not to cheer so much. Every allusion to the South was followed by groaning, hisses and howls, and the enthusiasm for Lincoln and for everything connected with the North was immense. The effect of such a display will be very great. . . .[24]

[22] *Spectator*, XXXV, 1125 (Oct. 11, 1862).
[23] *Blackwood's Magazine*, XCII, 636 (Nov., 1862).
[24] W. C. Ford, ed., *A Cycle of Adams Letters, 1861–1865* (Boston, 1920), I, 251 (Henry Adams to C. F. Adams, Jr., Jan. 30, 1863).

ABE LINCOLN'S LAST CARD ; OR, ROUGE-ET-NOIR.

A British view of Lincoln's Emancipation Proclamation. Note the satisfied expression of Jefferson Davis and the Negro face on the ace of spades.

The great English clergyman, C. H. Spurgeon, prayed before a congregation of many thousands: "*God bless and strengthen the North! give victory to their arms. . . .*" The audience responded with a mighty "amen."

Unquestionably the Emancipation Proclamation was a cardinal stroke in Northern diplomacy. It robbed the South of its moral cause and elevated the conflict into a holy crusade against human bondage. It helped nerve the British workingman to withstand the famine; it demonstrated that the masses in England would be loath to stand behind the government in intervention. As Henry Adams reported from London: "The Emancipation Proclamation has done more for us here than all our former victories and all our diplomacy. It is creating an almost convulsive reaction in our favor all over this country." [25]

JEFFERSON DAVIS MAKES A NAVY—IN ENGLAND

The next crisis in the foreign relations of the United States grew out of Confederate commerce destroyers. Southern privateering had proved unsuccessful because, under the peculiar conditions of the war, it could not be pursued with profit. But government owned and operated commerce destroyers could be used with devastating effect; and the Confederacy, lacking shipbuilding facilities, turned to the shipyards of England. Although the British Foreign Enlistment Act of 1819 was presumably designed to prevent the building of warships for belligerents, the strict letter of the law could be circumvented by not arming the vessels in Great Britain. The *Florida* and *Alabama*, for example, sailed from England unarmed, and received their equipment elsewhere. This meant that as far as the shipbuilders and the strict letter of the law were concerned they were not warships at all. But the construction of such vessels appears to have been inconsistent both with true neutrality and with the spirit of Britain's own statutes. [26]

Altogether, Confederate commerce destroyers constructed in England burned, sank, or otherwise incapacitated more than two hundred and fifty Yankee ships, thus virtually driving the American merchant marine from the high seas. Most of this damage was done by three raiders, the *Florida*, the *Shenandoah*, and the *Alabama*, particularly the *Alabama*.

The "290" (as the *Alabama* was then known) was built by the

[25] *Ibid.*, I, 243 (Henry Adams to C. F. Adams, Jr., Jan. 23, 1863).
[26] Professor F. L. Owsley argues (*King Cotton Diplomacy*, pp. 426–428, 449) that the construction of such ships was not contrary to international law.

Lairds at Birkenhead, and launched in May, 1862. It was common knowledge among the workingmen and others that she was being constructed for the Confederacy; in fact, her sides were actually pierced for guns. Minister Adams collected a mass of affidavits as to her true character and presented them to the proper authorities. But the British officials, who were not conspicuously friendly to the North anyhow, feared an outcry in Parliament if the vessel should be seized without full warrant. Although the moral evidence was strong, the courts would probably decide against the government on technical grounds, and it would be liable for heavy damages. As the sequel proved, however, the British would have been far better off if they had seized the vessel and paid a large fine.

Adams continued to keep his secretarial son, Henry, busy copying affidavits and other documents regarding the character of the *Alabama*. This evidence was finally sent to the desk of the Queen's Advocate, who meanwhile had gone insane. Throughout a critical five-day period the papers lay untouched.[27]

Those who were constructing the *Alabama* suspected that detention was imminent, and made ready for her escape. On July 29, 1862, the vessel slipped down the Mersey, ostensibly on a trial spin, with a party of sight-seers on board, including builder Laird and his little daughter. When the vessel had put to sea the visitors were sent ashore on a tug and the *Alabama* continued to the Azores, under Portuguese jurisdiction, where she received her equipment and crew from two other vessels that arrived from England. She then proceeded to light the skies from Europe to the Far East with the burning hulks of Yankee merchantmen.

The *Alabama* had escaped scarcely a moment too soon. The papers were finally retrieved from the desk of the demented Queen's Advocate, London officials sprang to life, and orders were telegraphed to hold the *Alabama*—but the ship had left. Many Northerners felt that Her Majesty's government was culpable in not making determined efforts to pursue the vessel, which did not leave British waters till some thirty-one hours later. Nevertheless, no credible evidence has come to light proving that the Ministry connived at her escape.

Adams continued to harass Downing Street with a monotonous list of sinkings and burnings, and with rapidly mounting bills for damages. Under such tutelage the British began to see that they had created a precedent that might one day be used against them with terrible effect by a foe without a navy or without even a coast. An-

[27] J. F. Rhodes, *History of the United States* (N.Y., 1899), IV, 88–89.

other significant development also contributed to the uneasiness of the London government. In March, 1863, Congress passed a bill authorizing the President to commission Northern privateers. Since there were no Southern merchantmen upon which such raiders might prey, could it be possible that the North was preparing this weapon for use against Britain? The next month Lord Lyons reported from Washington:

I think the state of things here, as far as peace with us is concerned, more alarming than it has been since the *Trent* affair. . . . I would rather the quarrel came, if come it must, upon some better ground for us than the question of the ships fitted out for the Confederates.[28]

Assailed by doubts, the British government decided to cast caution to the winds. In April, 1863, it issued orders for the seizure of the *Alexandra,* another warship being built for the Confederates. In the subsequent litigation the government was unable to produce convincing evidence to support its action, and, to the accompaniment of applause from the crowded courtroom, was assessed costs and damages. Yet the proceedings involved such long delays that the vessel, when finally released, arrived in American waters too late to be of use to the Confederacy. The North at last had the satisfaction of knowing that the British government was actively supporting the spirit as well as the letter of its neutrality policy.

THE LAIRD RAMS CRISIS

The *Alabama* and her sister ships were designed primarily as commerce destroyers, and their activities, though highly destructive, had no vital bearing on the actual prosecution of the war. But the so-called Laird rams were different. They were powerful ironclad steam warships which the Confederacy had arranged to have built by the same firm that had constructed the *Alabama*. They were notoriously designed to break the blockade. Equipped with powerful wrought-iron "piercers" or rams, these floating fortresses could have smashed the wooden ships of the Union blockading squadron like egg shells; and then, with their powerful nine-inch rifled guns, they could have laid

[28] Lord Newton, *Lord Lyons* (London, 1913), I, 101 (Lyons to Russell, April 23, 1863). The American Secretary of the Navy recorded: "We shall, however, have a day of reckoning with Great Britain for these wrongs, and I sometimes think I care not how soon nor in what manner that reckoning comes." *Diary of Gideon Welles* (Boston, 1911), I, 207 (Dec. 29, 1862).

the Northern seaport cities under tribute and caused the North to cry for mercy. In short, if the rams had put to sea, the South would probably have won its independence, and the North, already angry over the *Alabama* affair, would almost certainly have declared war on Britain. The imminent departure of these vessels precipitated the final great diplomatic crisis of the war.

At first it was given out that the rams were intended for the French Emperor; then the Pasha of Egypt was named as the purchaser. But both of these allegations were denied by official sources. The Confederate agents, fearing seizure, transferred ownership of the rams to a private French company, with the understanding that the vessels would be resold to the Confederacy at a handsome profit after they had escaped to sea.[29] Even the London *Times* admitted that ninety-nine people out of a hundred believed that these rams were "intended to carry on hostilities sooner or later against the Federals [Northerners]." Nevertheless, the papers were in perfect order and legally unassailable.

Earl Russell had no desire to provoke the United States into a declaration of war—a United States that had just triumphed at Gettysburg and Vicksburg. On the other hand, he was advised by the crown counsel that the government could not legally seize the rams; and he feared the consequences of a heavy damage suit. But time was short; and in a few days the first of the vessels would be ready for sea. So as a matter of expediency rather than of strict conformity to the law, Russell privately issued an order, on September 3, 1863, that the rams be held. When the news was finally made public, Confederate bonds sank fourteen points, and Confederate hopes even lower. The problem was finally adjusted when the British government bought the rams for Her Majesty's navy at a figure considerably in excess of the contract price.[30]

Meanwhile Minister Adams had been making persistent and insistent representations. Fearing that the rams would not be detained, he sent his memorable note of September 5, 1863: "I trust I need not express how profound is my regret at the conclusion to which her Majesty's Government have arrived. . . . It would be superfluous

---

[29] Rhodes, *History of the United States*, IV, 378.

[30] In 1867 Adams attended the great naval review at Portsmouth, where one of the two Laird rams, already obsolete, was pointed out to him. He wrote that "as I looked on the little mean thing, I could not help a doubt whether she was really worthy of all the anxiety she had cost us." C. F. Adams, *Charles Francis Adams* (Boston, 1900) p. 316.

in me to point out to your Lordship that this is war. . . ." [31] Adams' famous "superfluous" note was really superfluous; for he did not know that two days earlier Russell had issued the order to detain the rams. When, shortly thereafter, the correspondence was published in the United States, it gave the unfortunate impression that Adams had bullied the British into yielding.

The last hope of the Confederates for vessels with which to break the blockade was France. Napoleon III, quite in contrast with the British government, actively connived with the Confederate agents. In April and June, 1863, contracts were signed for four ships of the *Alabama* type (allegedly for service in China waters) and two powerful rams. Napoleon, not wishing to be publicly involved, gave his approval to the transaction on the condition that the real destination of the vessels be kept confidential. But the secret finally leaked out, and in June, 1864, the builders received official orders to sell all these ships and provide proof of a genuine transaction. One of the rams, though sold to Denmark, finally reached American waters, but too late in the war to be of service.

THE SANDS OF THE CONFEDERACY RUN OUT

As if the detention of the rams and the ill success of the Confederates in the field were not enough to blight Southern hopes of intervention, unexpected developments in Italy, and particularly the Polish and Schleswig-Holstein crises, caused Europe to become much less interested in the transatlantic conflagration. Henry Adams wrote gleefully in November, 1863:

. . . Nothing has caused us more gentle slumbers since the seizure of the iron-clads than the delicious state of tangle Europe has now arrived at. Nothing but panic in every direction and the strongest combination of cross-purposes you can conceive. The King of Denmark has just died with a clearly perverse purpose of increasing the confusion, and any day may see a Danish war. Russia expects war and France acts as though it were un-

[31] The note is susceptible of a double interpretation. Adams possibly did not mean, as is generally supposed, that the North would declare war on Great Britain if the rams escaped, but that the British, by their unneutral course, were actually making war on the United States. In April of the same year the British government had given a pledge not to permit the rams to escape; yet in September, 1863, Minister Adams evidently feared that the pledge would be broken. See E. D. Adams, *Great Britain and the American Civil War*, II, 141–144.

avoidable. Meanwhile England hulks about and makes faces at all the other nations. Our affairs are quite in the back-ground, thank the Lord.[32]

Europe's distresses continued to help the Union, for six months later Minister Adams could write, "America is not much talked of here. Never so little since I first came."

But the South died hard. In November, 1864, the Northern commander, General Sherman, began his devastating march to the sea, which the London *Times* described as "the wild and desperate effort of an out-manoeuvred General" to extricate himself from an untenable situation. Lincoln's triumphant re-election that same month, combined with General Grant's elephantine progress toward the Confederate capital and Sherman's swath east and northward, further opened British eyes.

The South played its final card when it made desperate, last-minute efforts to secure assistance from Great Britain and France by promising abolition of slavery; but these overtures came to naught. Rumors of the end drifted across the Atlantic to England, only to cause panic among cotton and other speculators. With delicate irony Charles Francis Adams described the effect of one of these false reports:

The consternation was extraordinary. The public funds fell. . . . You would have thought that a great calamity had befallen the good people of England. . . . Happily for the distressed nerves of our friends, the next day brought them a little relief. A steamer had come with . . . later news. It was not so bad as they had feared. . . . There would be no peace. Hurrah. The papers of this morning are all congratulating the public that the war will go on indefinitely.[33]

Then came the news of Lee's surrender, closely followed by that of Lincoln's assassination. As if conscience-stricken for its years of defamation, even the pro-Southern press of England outdid itself in writing tributes to the fallen President, who was now proudly claimed as a fellow Anglo-Saxon. The most remarkable recantation of all came from the vitriolic pen of Tom Taylor and was published in *Punch*. which had distinguished itself for coarse caricatures of Lincoln:

> Yes, he had lived to shame me from my sneer,
> To lame my pencil, and confute my pen—

[32] Ford, *Cycle of Adams Letters*, II, 103 (Henry Adams to C. F. Adams, Jr., November 20, 1863).

[33] *Ibid.*, II, 256–257 (C. F. Adams to his son, Feb. 17, 1865).

> To make me own this hind of princes peer,
> This rail-splitter a true-born king of men.[34]

Charles Francis Adams' great work was now done. No other diplomatic representative of the United States had ever had to endure, at least for so protracted a period, critical official responsibility combined with tense excitement and a hostile atmosphere. And his foot did not slip once. As James Russell Lowell, one of his successors, well put it: "None of our generals in the field, nor Grant himself, did us better or more trying service than he in his forlorn outpost of London." [35]

BIBLIOGRAPHICAL NOTE

Brief accounts of Civil War diplomacy from 1862 to 1865 may be found in E. Channing, *A History of the United States* (N.Y., 1925), VI, 357–370; and H. W. Temple, "William H. Seward," in S. F. Bemis, ed., *The American Secretaries of State and their Diplomacy* (N.Y., 1928), VII, 71–105. Standard accounts of indispensable value are E. D. Adams, *Great Britain and the American Civil War* (2 vols., London, 1925); and F. L. Owsley, *King Cotton Diplomacy* (Chicago, 1931). For European opinion in general consult Donaldson Jordan and E. J. Pratt, *Europe and the American Civil War* (Boston, 1931). For France see W. Reed West, *Contemporary French Opinion on the American Civil War* (Baltimore, 1924). Though still useful this book must be read in the light of L. M. Case, ed., *French Opinion on the United States and Mexico, 1860–1867* (N.Y., 1936), an important work that utilizes materials unavailable to West. Significant articles are J. H. Park, "The English Workingmen and the American Civil War," *Pol. Sci. Quar.*, XXXIX (1924), 432–457; and L. M. Sears, "A Confederate Diplomat [Slidell] at the Court of Napoleon III," *Amer. Hist. Rev.*, XXVI (1921), 255–281. Further references: see note at end of previous chapter, the footnotes of this chapter, and Bemis and Griffin, *Guide*, pp. 340–349.

RECENT REFERENCES. M. P. Claussen, "Peace Factors in Anglo-American Relations, 1861–1865," *Miss. Valley Hist. Rev.*, XXVI (1940), 511–522, stresses the North's dependence on the British money market, and Britain's concern for her commerce, markets, merchant marine, and American investments. The author believes that British labor had little direct influence on the government (p. 522), and that the noninterventionist attitude of the working classes "was based on sympathies larger than antislavery, particularly on the hope of greater political democracy and wider economic opportunity in the United States (p. 521)."

NEW REFERENCES. See works at end of preceding chapter. The effects of the Confederate commerce destroyers are described in R. G. Albion and J. B. Pope, *Sea Lanes in Wartime* (N.Y., 1942), Ch. VI. See also E. S. Pomeroy, "French Substitutes for American Cotton, 1861–1865," *Jour. of Southern Hist.*, IX (1943), 555–560.

4TH ED. REFS. See Bibliographical Appendix, p. 929.

[34] *Punch*, XLVIII, 182 (May 6, 1865).
[35] C. F. Adams, *Charles Francis Adams*, p. 345.

CHAPTER XXIII

France and Maximilian's Mexican Empire, 1861–1867

"What a lot of cannon-shots it will take to set up an emperor in Mexico, and what a lot to maintain him there."
Prince Metternich, Austrian Minister to France, 1861.

MR. MONROE'S DOCTRINE IS SNUBBED

BEHIND the smoke screen of the American battlefields two European nations, Spain and France, undertook to challenge the vitality and validity of the Monroe Doctrine. The first important case developed in the revolution-rent Dominican Republic, which, officially at least, asked for reannexation to Spain. The mother country accepted this unique invitation, and in May, 1861, incorporated the prodigal daughter in the Spanish empire.

A month earlier, on April 2, 1861, Secretary Seward had addressed a menacing note to the Spanish minister at Washington in which he challenged Spain's right to take back Santo Domingo. The Spanish Foreign Office did not bother to reply. The American minister at Madrid next made strong representations to the effect that the course of Spain was directly at variance with the principles of the Monroe Doctrine. (Monroe, however, had made no reference to the reincorporation of colonies with the consent of the colonials.) In reply, the Spanish foreign minister stood his ground, and did not even deign to allude to the Monroe Doctrine. Seward emerged from this verbal duel with his fingers burned, doubtless realizing that the magic memory of Monroe commanded less respect in the chancelleries of Europe than on the public platforms of America.[1]

The oppressive measures of the purblind Spanish officials soon drove the Dominicans to a bloody and costly revolt, to which were added the ravages of yellow fever, Toussaint L'Ouverture's ancient ally. Disease and the desperate courage of the islanders ultimately succeeded where Seward's bluster and the dead hand of Monroe had failed. In 1865, with victorious Northern armies on the march, the Spaniards voluntarily withdrew, thus removing the necessity of Ameri-

[1] Dexter Perkins, *The Monroe Doctrine, 1826–1867* (Baltimore, 1933), p. 302.

ca's vindicating the principles of 1823. There remained, however, a second and far more serious challenge to the Monroe Doctrine—that from the French in Mexico.

THE BEGINNINGS OF A PUPPET EMPIRE

Relations between the United States and its southern neighbor had continued to be unsatisfactory during the fifties. Chronic disorder had resulted in heavy loss of both American and European life and property. Conditions finally became so intolerable that in December, 1859, President Buchanan urged Congress to pass a law authorizing him to send a military force into Mexico for the purpose "of obtaining indemnity for the past and security for the future." The Buchanan administration also made several unsuccessful proposals to the Mexican government looking toward the purchase of generous areas in northern Mexico, particularly Lower California. In 1859 the United States did negotiate a treaty securing a perpetual right of way across the Isthmus of Tehuantepec; but the Senate voted down the pact during the internal excitement preceding the outbreak of the Civil War.[2] The aggressive policy of Buchanan unquestionably aroused fear in Europe that the Yankees were bent upon absorbing all Mexico, and helped crystallize the schemes of those who were planning armed intervention.[3]

The crisis finally came in bankrupt Mexico when the Congress passed a law, on July 17, 1861, providing that payments on the government's foreign obligations were to be suspended for two years. An outcry immediately arose from British investors, whose stake in Mexico was the largest, as well as from those of Spain and France. The legitimate demands of creditors must not be confused, however, with the notorious Jecker claim, which Napoleon III backed.[4] At length, in October, 1861, representatives of Great Britain, France, and Spain signed the Convention of London, which provided for a joint military expedition to collect the debts in default.[5] The tripartite agreement

[2] H. L. Wilson, "President Buchanan's Proposed Intervention in Mexico," *Amer. Hist. Rev.*, V (1900), 696.

[3] Perkins, *The Monroe Doctrine, 1826–1867*, p. 343.

[4] Jecker was a Swiss banker who, in 1859, lent a nominal 75,000,000 francs to the Mexican government, which actually received only 3,750,000 francs. When Jecker failed in 1860, the half brother of Napoleon entered into a deal by which he was to receive 30 per cent of the profits from collection. *Ibid.*, p. 382 n.

[5] The Powers invited the United States to join the expedition; but Seward declined. The latter's idea of an American loan to Mexico to enable her to pay off her creditors did not meet with much favor in the United States. See J. M. Callahan, *American Foreign Policy in Mexican Relations* (N.Y., 1932), p. 285.

incorporated the important proviso that none of the signatory nations would attempt to secure for itself any "peculiar advantage."

In December, 1861, a Spanish force captured Vera Cruz; but a rift soon developed in the ranks of the allies. The British and the Spanish withdrew from the enterprise, leaving a clear field to the scheming Napoleon III. It soon became evident that the French Emperor was planning to establish a satellite government in Mexico with a European puppet prince at its head. Napoleon had, in fact, made overtures to the Archduke Maximilian of Austria some three weeks *before* the solemn signing of the Convention of London. Although it is difficult to fathom with certainty the mind of "the great Imperial Sphinx," the French Emperor seems to have desired to relieve his country of her dangerous dependence upon the cotton supply of the South, and at the same time curry favor with the strong Catholic element at home by rescuing the Church in Mexico from the attacks of the anticlericals. He appears also to have desired to erect a Latin, Catholic monarchy in Mexico as a dike against the expansionist waves of the Anglo-Saxon, Protestant republic to the north.[6] And he doubtless felt that the resurrection of France's colonial empire would strengthen his prestige with the French masses.

The time for starting the venture could hardly have been better chosen, for the embattled Yankees were in no position to defend the Monroe Doctrine. Napoleon also recognized that it was to his advantage to have the United States permanently sundered. This in large part explains his sympathy for the South, and why he toyed with the idea of exchanging recognition of the Confederacy for permission to work his will in Mexico.[7]

The Man Who Would Be King

The conquest of Mexico proceeded with vigor. Although President Juárez, a remarkable full-blooded Indian, led the Mexican patriots in a stubborn resistance, the opposition was ultimately reduced to guerrilla bands; and the French forces occupied Mexico City on June 7, 1863. A hand-picked Assembly of Notables, consisting almost entirely of clericals and Mexican reactionaries, then met and voted to offer the throne to the Archduke Ferdinand Maximilian of Austria.

Maximilian had been willing for some little time. He was a handsome, fair-haired, and extremely likable man of thirty-one, with

[6] Perkins, *The Monroe Doctrine, 1826–1867*, pp. 364–365.
[7] See F. L. Owsley, *King Cotton Diplomacy* (Chicago, 1931), pp. 527–528.

artistic tastes and a somewhat modest intellectual endowment. Unhappily, he was without serious occupation, and his aimless existence —even in a beautiful palace overlooking the blue Adriatic—palled on the young archduke. His bride, the young, beautiful, and extravagant Carlotta, daughter of the King of the Belgians, was inordinately ambitious for her Hapsburg husband and extremely eager to be an empress—a desire which had little chance of being satisfactorily gratified except in Mexico.

A delegation of Mexican monarchists formally offered the new crown to Maximilian in October, 1863. The invitation presumably was based upon the vote of the people, although, as a prominent British diplomat contemptuously remarked, the plebiscite had been held in places that "were possibly inhabited by two Indians and a monkey." The Archduke knew that the French armies had pacified little more than the area from the sea to the capital, and he replied that he would not accept the invitation unless it was confirmed by the will of the entire nation. If the ill-starred young Hapsburg had adhered to this wise decision his career, in all probability, would not have had such an abrupt and dramatic termination. But like many another wishful thinker under the influence of an ambitious wife, Maximilian listened to the false assurances of sycophants, flouted the advice of influential members of the royal family, and even ignored the words of Carlotta's exiled and worldly-wise grandmother, former Queen of the French, who reputedly said, "They will murder you." [8] On April 10, 1864, six months after receiving the original invitation, and without any convincing plebiscite having been taken in the meantime, Maximilian permitted himself to believe what he wanted to believe and accepted the call. On the same day he signed the Convention of Miramar, by which France bound herself to lend him military support until 1867, in return for heavy financial guarantees.

SEWARD'S SOFT ANSWERS

Meanwhile the United States had not been an indifferent spectator of the events in Mexico. Napoleon had not been a popular figure in America since 1852, when he had broken faith with the French Republic and established himself as Emperor. At that time the three epithets most commonly used to describe him were "murderer," "perjurer," and "traitor." The New York *Tribune* called him a "perjured

[8] Count E. C. Corti, *Maximilian and Charlotte of Mexico* (trans. from the German, N.Y., 1928) I, 332.

villain," a "knave," and a "bankrupt profligate living in open adultery." But the press at length settled down to the employment of milder adjectives, such as "unscrupulous," "faithless," "insincere," "crafty," "treacherous," and "selfish." [9]

Preoccupation with the Civil War, and ignorance of the true designs of Napoleon, caused the American public to show surprisingly little concern during the early months of the Mexican venture. Several newspapers went so far as to suggest that a sound chastisement might do unruly Mexico some good. During 1861 and 1862 little was said in Congress about the French invasion, and the Mexican minister in Washington experienced great difficulty in keeping alive an interest in his country's misfortune. [10]

But as the cause of the North grew brighter, and as the objectives of France became clearer, public opinion in the United States showed increasing dissatisfaction. Shortly before the crown was formally offered to Maximilian, the influential Senator Sumner delivered a powerful speech in New York in which he paid his respects to Napoleon: "Trampler upon the Republic in France, trampler upon the Republic in Mexico, it remains to be seen if the French Emperor can prevail as trampler upon this Republic." [11] And the New York *Herald* sounded a bold note:

As for Mexico, we will, at the close of the rebellion, if the French have not left there before, send fifty thousand Northern and fifty thousand Southern troops, forming together a grand army to drive the invaders into the Gulf. That is the way we shall tolerate a French monarchy in Mexico. [12]

In the midst of the rising tide of public opinion Seward kept his counsel. He fully realized that his hands were tied with the Civil War, and that if he pushed France too strongly he might easily force her

[9] See J. G. Gazley, *American Opinion of German Unification, 1848–1871* (N.Y., 1926), pp. 265–267. The American newspapers delighted in stories like this: During a triumphal tour through France, Napoleon was to pass under an arch from which hung a crown with the placard, "He well deserves it!" Before his arrival the wind blew away the crown, leaving only the dangling rope and "He well deserves it." E. B. White, *American Opinion of France* (N.Y., 1927), p. 132.

[10] Perkins, *The Monroe Doctrine, 1826–1867*, pp. 437–438.

[11] *The Works of Charles Sumner* (Boston, 1880), VII, 373 (Sept. 10, 1863).

[12] New York *Herald*, Jan. 21, 1864, 4:4. H. L. Higginson expressed a sentiment that was probably not uncommon in the Union army when he wrote: ". . . I mean to go to Mexico and fight the French after this war is done. It . . . would certainly be good fun to cut off those little red-legged sinners, who have been swelling about their fighting and victory." Bliss Perry, *Life and Letters of Henry Lee Higginson* (Boston, 1921), I, 177 (Higginson to sister, Jan. 4, 1863).

into an alliance with the South. He therefore adopted the strategy of reasserting America's traditional policy with firmness but not aggressiveness, and of reserving to the future the right to act. Throughout the war the State Department wisely did little more than put its position on record, so that the Monroe Doctrine would not be allowed to go by default. In response to a plea from the United States consul general at Paris for more vigorous action, Seward answered:

I think . . . that, with our land and naval forces in Louisiana retreating before the rebels instead of marching toward Mexico, this is not the most suitable time we could choose for offering idle menaces to the Emperor of France. We have compromised nothing, surrendered nothing, and I do not propose to surrender anything. But why should we gasconade about Mexico when we are in a struggle for our own life? [13]

Early in 1864 Congress, traditional weathercock of public opinion, began to get out of hand. On April 4, a week before Maximilian accepted his synthetic throne, the House of Representatives passed a ringing resolution, 109 to 0:

. . . The Congress of the United States are unwilling by silence to leave the nations of the world under the impression that they are indifferent spectators of the deplorable events now transpiring in the republic of Mexico, and that they therefore think fit to declare that it does not accord with the policy of the United States to acknowledge any monarchial Government erected on the ruins of any republican Government in America under the auspices of any European Power.[14]

The House resolution was naturally rasping to Gallic sensibilities; and when the United States minister in Paris, William L. Dayton, hastened to the French Foreign Office, he was greeted with these words, "Do you bring us peace or bring us war?" The difficulty was finally patched up by pointing out that a resolution passed by one branch of the Congress could not properly be regarded as an expression of the attitude of the Administration, and that no departure from existing policy regarding Mexico was contemplated. When this explanation, described by the opposition press as "Seward's apology,"

[13] Frederic Bancroft, *The Life of William H. Seward* (N.Y., 1900), II, 430 (Seward to Bigelow, May 21, 1864).

[14] *Cong. Globe*, 38 Cong., 1 sess., p. 1408. In May and June of 1864, the Radical Republican Convention and the Republican National Convention respectively put themselves strongly on record against the invasion of Mexico. The Democratic platform was silent. See Callahan, *American Policy in Mexican Relations*, pp. 297–298.

was published, it caused a strong reaction in the United States.[15] The tide of American sentiment against France was plainly rising.

SEWARD TURNS ON THE PRESSURE

As the North pushed the war to a victorious conclusion, public opinion began to demand in increasingly strident tones that the French be expelled. Napoleon had definitely bet on the wrong horse in sympathizing with the Confederacy; and matters were not helped when Maximilian gave support to the South during the closing months of the war. Andrew Johnson, whom the Republicans had just nominated as their candidate for the vice-presidency, declared in a speech at Nashville:

The day of reckoning is approaching. It will not be long before the Rebellion is put down. . . . And then we will attend to this Mexican affair, and say to Louis Napoleon, "You cannot found a monarchy on this Continent." (Great applause.) An expedition into Mexico would be a sort of recreation to the brave soldiers who are now fighting the battles of the Union, and the French concern would be quickly wiped out.[16]

After Lee's surrender at Appomattox the victorious North had over 900,000 men under arms, and some of their officers could scarcely be restrained from attempting to throw Maximilian, bag and baggage, out of Mexico. Notable among these was General Grant, who ordered General Sheridan with about 50,000 men to the Texas border, and took steps to send General Schofield to Mexico, there to organize an army of unemployed Confederate and Union veterans. But Secretary Seward removed the danger in this quarter by persuading Schofield to undertake a mission to France instead. According to the recollections of the General, "Mr. Seward's explanation and instructions to me, after several long conversations on this subject, were summed up in the words: 'I want you to get your legs under Napoleon's mahogany, and tell him he must get out of Mexico.' " [17] Although this may have been just a ruse to divert Schofield elsewhere,[18] there

---

[15] White, *American Opinion of France*, p. 159. In New Orleans a group of young men formed a society known as the Defenders of the Monroe Doctrine. On April 26, 1864, the French minister in Washington protested against its activities. *House Ex. Doc.*, 39 Cong., 1 sess., pt. 2, no. 73, p. 308.

[16] Perkins, *The Monroe Doctrine, 1826–1867*, p. 471 n. (June 10, 1864).

[17] J. M. Schofield, *Forty-Six Years in the Army* (N.Y., 1897), p. 385.

[18] H. M. Wriston concludes that Schofield was probably sent by Seward in all seriousness. *Executive Agents in American Foreign Relations* (Baltimore, 1929), pp. 780–788.

can be no doubt that the secrecy-enshrouded presence of a leading Northern general in France caused much disquietude, and probably further impressed upon the French people the wisdom of withdrawing from Mexico.

By this time Seward held most of the high cards, and it was possible for him to speak with a plainness that hitherto would have been impolitic. "It is clear," declared the New York *Herald*, "that our foreign relations need to be taken up in a new and vigorous spirit, and our despatches to France to be written in quite another than the sweetened water style that now flavors them through and through." [19] The New York *Evening Post* feared that "trifling will drift us into war." "Let Mr. Seward," it insisted, "tell Napoleon to get out of Mexico. That is all we need." In commenting on this statement the Washington correspondent of the London *Times* reported:

That these words express the feeling of the American people is absolutely certain. . . . The people, I repeat, would rather go to war with France than see her remain in Mexico. . . . They would, of course, much prefer that France withdraw peaceably; but if she will not do that they mean to make her go. That is their own language, used at every public meeting, and at every dinner table, and in every paper, from Maine to California. [20]

But Seward realized that the French were a proud and sensitive people, and that unless he played his hand with the utmost caution he might drive them into a corner where the only honorable alternative would be war. His policy was to push Napoleon gently with one hand while courteously showing him the door with the other. It was not, therefore, until well into 1865 that anything suggesting a threat crept into Seward's communications to Paris. In September, 1865, they revealed an unmistakable note of "veiled hostility." Two months later his tone was "positively shrill"; and when John Bigelow, the new American minister in Paris, read this instruction to the French Foreign Minister the latter replied that "he derived neither pleasure nor satisfaction from its contents." Then came Seward's demand of February 12, 1866: ". . . We shall be gratified when the Emperor shall give to us . . . definitive information of the time when French military operations may be expected to cease in Mexico." [21] Stripped of diplomatic verbiage, these were strong words. On April 5, 1866,

[19] New York *Herald*, Jan. 28, 1866, 4:4.
[20] London *Times*, Nov. 18, 1865, 9:5.
[21] *House Ex. Doc.*, 39 Cong., 1 sess., no. 93, p. 34 (Seward to Montholon, Feb. 12, 1866).

the official organ of the French government announced publicly (this had been decided upon privately several months before) that the Emperor had decided to withdraw the French troops from Mexico over a period of nineteen months.

This, of course, was pleasing to the United States. But when it was reported that 4000 Austrian volunteers might come to Mexico to bolster up the tinsel throne of their compatriot, Seward took even more vigorous action. He instructed the United States minister in Vienna to protest, and then to demand his passports if the men were sent. Austria, faced with serious complications in Europe, was forced to adopt a humble tone. Seward promptly communicated the relevant correspondence to Congress, possibly with a view to strengthening the foundering Johnson administration.[22]

One other opportunity presented itself to Seward for a dramatic gesture. Napoleon had originally agreed to withdraw his troops from Mexico in three installments; but for military reasons he announced that they would all be removed in a body in the spring of 1867. Seward recognized here another opportunity to strengthen the Johnson administration, which had lost heavily in the late Congressional elections. On November 23, 1866, he sent a lengthy cabled instruction to Minister Bigelow, in Paris, insisting upon strict compliance with the terms of the agreement. He then gave the text of this demand to the press. Bigelow recognized that the cablegram "was written more for the edification of Congress than for mine"; so he merely presented a mild paraphrase, and accepted an equivocal reply. Seward was satisfied; the home fences had been properly cared for. And the cable company, which had begun operations only the year before, pocketed $13,000.

Napoleon Takes French Leave

Historians are by no means agreed as to what motives caused Napoleon to cut loose from Maximilian, or precisely how much weight ought to be attached to the motives that were indisputably present. Nevertheless, certain facts stand out.

First of all, it is clearly established that French public opinion, which was opposed to the mad enterprise from the beginning, became increasingly hostile as time went on.[23] Exactly what influence this factor had on Napoleon, who was not immediately responsive to pub-

[22] Perkins, *The Monroe Doctrine, 1826–1867*, pp. 521–532.
[23] L. M. Case, ed., *French Opinion on the United States and Mexico, 1860–1867* (N.Y., 1936), pp. 310–311, 349, 402–403.

lic sentiment, is difficult to ascertain.[24] But it is certain that he was constantly apprised of the growing opposition; and, as a usurper of a throne, he must have seen that he could not defy the wishes of the people indefinitely.

The second indisputable fact is that the Mexican venture was appallingly expensive. By the end of 1865 the armed expedition to collect a nominal 40,000,000 francs had cost 274,698,000 francs—a burden profoundly disturbing to the traditionally thrifty French taxpayer. Napoleon could not have been altogether unconcerned about this aspect of the problem.

A third factor that the French could not ignore was the guerrilla war that Juárez doggedly sustained. This resistance added enormously to the cost of the expedition, raised serious doubts as to the possibility of ever completely subduing the Mexicans, and probably did more than any other one thing to bring Napoleon to his senses. It is altogether likely that if the United States had refrained from bringing any kind of pressure to bear upon France, the Maximilian house of cards would have collapsed of its own weight.[25]

We come now to two probable motives that are not so clearly established. It used to be taken for granted that a major factor in the French withdrawal was the increasingly ominous attitude of Prussia, and a desire on the part of Napoleon to withdraw his armies from Mexico and free his hands. If true, this would be another excellent example of Europe's distress contributing to America's advantage. But recent scholarship indicates that the French Emperor was not particularly concerned about the European situation when he made the decision to withdraw the troops from Mexico.[26] It is quite possible, however, that his solicitude was greater than the rather fragmentary contemporary documents reveal.[27]

[24] F. E. Lally, *French Opposition to the Mexican Policy of the Second Empire* (Baltimore, 1931), p. 147, concludes that French domestic opposition had no important bearing on the withdrawal policy.

[25] Perkins, *The Monroe Doctrine, 1826–1867*, p. 521. Great Britain, France, and other powers recognized Maximilian, though the United States persisted in regarding the fugitive Juárez government as that of Mexico. See S. A. MacCorkle, *American Policy of Recognition towards Mexico* (Baltimore, 1933), pp. 61–66.

[26] See Perkins, *The Monroe Doctrine, 1826–1867*, pp. 515–518. The author takes exception to the earlier findings of C. A. Duniway, "Reasons for the Withdrawal of the French from Mexico," Amer. Hist. Assn., *Annual Report, 1902*, I, 323.

[27] For evidence that the presence of the French force in America materially weakened the French army, that France could not take a strong tone in dealing with Prussia as long as there was danger of a Franco-American war, and that these facts entered into the calculations of the Prussians, see Count Otto zu Stolberg-Wernigerode, *Germany and the United States of America during the Era of Bismarck* (trans. from

FUN.—September 22, 1866.

LETTING HIM SLIDE.

Nap. (to Max. of Mexico):—"I AM REALLY VERY SORRY, BUT I MUST LET GO, OR YOU MIGHT
PULL ME OVER!"

Much has also been made of the assumption that Napoleon feared
the enormous armies of the United States. But the exhausted republic was hardly in a position to undertake a conflict with a first-class
Power, at least, this is what the Secretary of the Navy and the Secre-

the German, Reading, Pa., 1937), pp. 77–85. This evidence supports certain of
Professor Duniway's conclusions.

tary of the Treasury testified in Cabinet meeting.[28] Nevertheless, the obvious military power of the United States, combined with the great difficulty of prosecuting a war overseas, could scarcely have failed to make some impression on the French Emperor.

THE LAST OF THE CONQUISTADORES

With the withdrawal of Napoleon's steel and gold in the spring of 1867, the deluded Austrian "archdupe" was left to shift for himself, and his flimsy empire tottered to its fall. The beautiful Carlotta returned to France to plead with the Emperor that he fulfill his solemn written pledge of military support. But the dissolute and calloused Napoleon was not one to be turned from his course by the tears of a woman, albeit a physically attractive one. Carlotta then took her case to the Pope, who could do nothing. The unfortunate woman's reason fled; and she lived on in insane impotence until 1927, when she died at the age of eighty-seven—a tragic reminder of a shattered dream.

Maximilian was urged by his well-wishers to desert the sinking ship while there was yet time. But the fatuous young man, torn by pride, duty, and love, insisted that every drop of his blood was now Mexican and that he would stay. He soon fell into the hands of the Juaristas, who condemned him to death. The European governments made strong efforts to save him, and they were joined by Seward. But Juárez was determined to make an object lesson of this prince for the benefit of other ambitious noblemen; so the Archduke fell gallantly if stupidly before a firing squad on June 19, 1867. The Portland *Transcript* not inaptly observed, "If anybody deserves to be shot it is Louis Napoleon. He is the chief criminal in this great national crime." [29]

THE MONROE DOCTRINE COMES OF AGE

Maximilian's Empire was at once the most serious and the most insolent challenge ever offered to the Monroe Doctrine. It involved not only the forcible subjection of a neighboring republic by a hostile European Power but the substitution of a monarchial form of government as a barrier against the United States. Maximilian even dreamed of extending his control as far south as Brazil. Yet in this

---

[28] *Diary of Gideon Welles* (Boston, 1911), II, 333 (July 14, 1865).
[29] Portland *Transcript*, June 8, 1867, quoted in Gazley, *American Opinion of German Unification*, p. 308.

first real test of the Monroe Doctrine Secretary Seward never once referred to the dictum by name.[30] His disillusioning Santo Domingo experience had demonstrated that the Doctrine was unpopular in Europe, and he may have concluded that strong insistence upon it might so provoke the Powers that they would recognize the Confederacy and possibly intervene.

But probably the basic reason why Seward did not invoke the Monroe Doctrine was that he did not need to. The French invasion of Mexico threatened America's national security, and on the basis of self-defense the United States was fully justified in asking the French to leave. Although the Monroe Doctrine was not once officially mentioned by name, its principles were implicit in the diplomatic discussion; and not for a single moment did Seward surrender them. In Europe, as newspaper and parliamentary discussion reveals, it was perfectly well understood that the Maximilian affair was a direct challenge to the doctrine of Monroe. In the American Congress and in the American press the now sacred shibboleth was repeatedly invoked by name with reference to the Mexican invasion.[31] When the Civil War came to an end, and a new and mightier United States arose from its ashes and demanded the evacuation of Mexico, European respect for the Yankee and his pretentious doctrine was immeasurably increased. *Harper's Weekly* gave expression to a not uncommon feeling:

The United States Government has now furnished Europe with an argument which every government understands. It has proved itself, by the most tremendous test, to be practically invincible. We are not surprised, therefore, to hear of the sudden and amazed respect for us which has suddenly arisen in the most hostile foreign circles.[32]

With the Civil War, therefore, the Monroe Doctrine came of age. In the thirties it had been ignored if not forgotten; in the forties it had been reasserted without commanding much respect; in the fifties it had come to be rather generally accepted by the Democratic party;

[30] Prior to this time the Monroe Doctrine had been appealed to, in diplomatic controversy, only by Buchanan in 1854 and Seward in 1861. Dexter Perkins, *The Monroe Doctrine, 1867–1907* (Baltimore, 1937), p. 31.

[31] On January 6, 1866, a giant mass meeting was held in New York City to protest against recent violations of the Monroe Doctrine. A resolution was passed expressing confidence in the willingness of the President to uphold American principles, "among which the Monroe doctrine is one of the most vital, and, at this moment, of first and practical importance." New York *Herald*, Jan. 7, 1866, 1:3.

[32] *Harper's Weekly*, IX, 418 (July 8, 1865).

but in the sixties, acknowledged and respected both at home and abroad, it attained the dignity of a national heritage.[33]

THE MAXIMILIAN AFTERMATH

The Mexicans were naturally pleased by Seward's vigorous handling of Napoleon III. It was evident, however, that the United States had been thinking primarily of itself, and only secondarily of its neighbor. Nevertheless the affair did something to wipe out the bitterness resulting from the Mexican War; and when Seward visited Mexico in 1869 he was hospitably received.[34]

With France the situation was reversed. The Maximilian affair produced a definite rift in the somewhat illusory traditional Franco-American friendship—illusory because from 1798 to 1867 the Paris government was probably as unfriendly to the United States as that of any other Power. For a number of years after the withdrawal of the last bayonets from Mexico, the press in France expressed much hostility toward the United States. Although the Americans lost none of their hatred for the slippery Napoleon, they were more favorably disposed toward the French people, whom they felt the Emperor did not properly represent.

When the Franco-Prussian War broke out in 1870 Napoleon had relatively few well-wishers in America, especially in the North. The Germans were fighting for national unity, just as the United States had been. Nor could the Northerners forget that while the French had been lending money to the Confederates and intervening in Mexico, the Germans had bought large numbers of United States bonds.[35] Moreover tens of thousands of German-born soldiers, mostly volunteers, had served in the armies of the North. "I side with the Prussians," wrote Louisa M. Alcott, the well known American writer, "for they sympathized with us in our war. Hooray for old Pruss!"[36]

When the Franco-Prussian War ended with the overthrow of Na-

---

[33] Perkins, *The Monroe Doctrine, 1826–1867*, pp. 547–548. European governments were, however, reluctant to give official recognition to the Doctrine. As late as April 24, 1914, the French Foreign Minister declared that in addressing the Washington government it would be "preferable not to mention the Monroe Doctrine, for we should appear to recognize its legitimacy, which is impossible." Sir Edward Grey, who was present, agreed with him. *Documents Diplomatiques Français*, 3e Série, X, 265.

[34] There were, however, evidences of suspicion. Callahan, *American Foreign Policy in Mexican Relations*, p. 333.

[35] Stolberg-Wernigerode, *Germany and the United States of America*, p. 58.

[36] Gazley, *American Opinion of German Unification*, p. 332. See the entire chapter.

poleon, and the erection of a republic on the ruins of empire, much of the old sentiment for France returned. The period closed with the semimythical Franco-American friendship still a factor to be reckoned with.

BIBLIOGRAPHICAL NOTE

Brief accounts treating the United States and the Maximilian venture appear in J. F. Rippy, *The United States and Mexico* (rev. ed., N.Y., 1931), Ch. XIV; J. M. Callahan, *American Foreign Policy in Mexican Relations* (N.Y., 1932), Ch. IX (Ch. VIII relates to Buchanan's Mexican policy); and E. P. Oberholtzer, *A History of the United States since the Civil War* (N.Y., 1917), I, 495–523. The most useful detailed work is Dexter Perkins, *The Monroe Doctrine, 1826–1867* (Baltimore, 1933), pp. 318–548. For American opinion regarding the French venture see J. G. Gazley, *American Opinion of German Unification, 1848–1871* (N.Y., 1926), Chs. VII–VIII; and E. B. White, *American Opinion of France* (N.Y., 1927), Ch. V. On the downfall of Napoleon III consult C. E. Schieber, *The Transformation of American Sentiment toward Germany, 1870–1914* (Boston, 1923), Ch. I. For French opinion see W. R. West, *Contemporary French Opinion on the American Civil War* (Baltimore, 1924), which must be read in the light of L. M. Case, ed., *French Opinion on the United States and Mexico, 1860–1867* (N.Y., 1936). The best work on Maximilian is Count E. C. Corti, *Maximilian and Charlotte of Mexico* (trans. from German, 2 vols., N.Y., 1928). An old but stimulating article is C. A. Duniway, "Reasons for the withdrawal of the French from Mexico," Amer. Hist. Assn., *Annual Report, 1902*, I, 315–328. Further references: see footnotes of this chapter and Bemis and Griffin, *Guide*, pp. 349–359.

RECENT REFERENCES. Ollinger Crenshaw, "The Knights of the Golden Circle," *Amer. Hist. Rev.*, XLVII (1941), 23–50, reveals how one George Bickley won much popular support in the South during 1860–61 for his filibustering organization designed to annex Mexico and add as many as twenty-five slave states to the Union. He was perhaps the last of the line of important filibusters who flourished in the fifties. W. S. Robertson, "The Tripartite Treaty of London," *Hispanic Amer. Hist. Rev.*, XX (1940), 167–189, shows that the treaty broke down because the Allies did not agree in advance on a specific mode of coercing Mexico, because there was no definite plan for securing reparations, and because the French signed the agreement with mental reservations. For an extended discussion of N. L. Ferris' article on United States relations with South America during the Civil War, see Bibliographical Appendix, p. 929.

NEW REFERENCES. Sister Claire Lynch, *Diplomatic Mission of John Lothrop Motley to Austria, 1861–1867* (Washington, 1944), touches on Motley's minor relationship with Maximilian backgrounds. R. W. Frazer, "Maximilian's Propaganda Activities in the United States, 1865–1866," *Hispanic Amer. Hist. Rev.*, XXIV (1944), 4–29, describes a belated effort to work up popular support by lobbying, articles, speeches, and the purchase of press support. Although foredoomed to failure, the campaign was conducted on too small a scale by agents who were disorganized and working at cross-purposes.

4TH ED. REFS. See Bibliographical Appendix, p. 929.

CHAPTER XXIV

Postwar Expansion, 1865–1867

"Our population is destined to roll its resistless waves to the icy barriers of the north, and to encounter oriental civilization on the shores of the Pacific."

William H. Seward, 1846.

THE SEARCH FOR ISLAND BARGAINS

THE great Civil War, and the events leading up to it, brought an end to the heyday of American expansion. Yet, as fate would have it, William H. Seward, who served as Secretary of State from 1861 to 1869, had repeatedly and emphatically put himself on record as an expansionist of hemispheric voracity. The war broke out the month after he took office, and he reluctantly came to the conclusion that an America fighting for its existence could not expand. But with the close of the conflict the old dreams returned. On June 24, 1867, Seward declared in a Boston speech:

> Give me only this assurance, that there never be an unlawful resistance by an armed force to the . . . United States, and give me fifty, forty, thirty more years of life, and I will engage to give you the possession of the American continent and the control of the world.[1]

But the revival of Seward's expansionist urge was perhaps not solely the result of a fevered imagination. President Johnson, who had become Chief Executive upon Lincoln's death, had made himself extremely unpopular with the vindictive members of his own Republican party by not reconstructing the South with lash and rope. Secretary Seward, who was being roundly condemned for remaining in the Cabinet, doubtless felt that he could improve his own political standing and strengthen the Administration by a sensational program of annexation.[2]

Recent experiences with Confederate blockade runners pointed to

[1] V. J. Farrar, *The Annexation of Russian America to the United States* (Washington, 1937), p. 113.
[2] See *Diary of Gideon Welles* (Boston, 1911), III, 125 (July 2, 1867).

the necessity of having a naval and coaling station in the Caribbean; and Seward began to cast about for such a spot. As soon as the Maximilian affair seemed to be nearing a satisfactory solution, he suddenly left for the Antilles on a cruise "for his health." After studying the situation at first hand he entered into negotiations for a base, or seriously contemplated doing so, with Spain, Sweden, Haiti, the Dominican Republic, and Denmark. Only two of these overtures were of any real importance.

The spacious Bay of Samaná, in the Dominican Republic, early became an object of Seward's covetous concern. The rulers of the Republic, harassed by revolution and bankruptcy, successively tried to transfer the harbor and then the entire island to the United States.[3] But Congress did not look favorably upon the proposal, and early in 1869 the House twice overwhelmed resolutions looking for a closer relationship with the Dominican Republic. "It may be convenient to have a naval station in the West Indies," declared *Harper's Weekly;* "but is it wise to buy it by adding to our population nearly a million of creoles and West Indian negroes, and by the assumption of nobody knows what debts and liabilities?" [4]

Denmark Keeps Her West Indies

More noteworthy was Seward's attempt to purchase the Danish West Indies (Virgin Islands), which boasted an excellent harbor on St. Thomas. Early in 1865 Seward approached the Danish minister in Washington, General Raasloff, and the ensuing negotiations continued for more than two years. When the news leaked out that the United States was proposing to offer several million dollars for these insular crumbs, a storm of ridicule burst upon the Administration. The hostile New York *Herald* ran a facetious advertisement:

> A FEW WEST INDIA ISLANDS WANTED.—Any distressed persons having a few islands to dispose of in the Spanish Main can find a purchaser by applying to Washington, D. C. . . . References exchanged.[5]

The Danish Treaty, which was formally signed on October 24, 1867, provided that the United States would obtain the Virgin Islands

[3] C. C. Tansill, *The United States and Santo Domingo, 1798–1873* (Baltimore, 1938), pp. 213 ff.

[4] *Harper's Weekly,* XIII, 130 (Feb. 27, 1869).

[5] New York *Herald,* April 12, 1867, 6:4.

(except Santa Cruz) for $7,500,000, subject to a favorable plebiscite among the inhabitants. But hardly was the ink dry when the islands were ravaged by an earthquake, a hurricane, and a tidal wave. A good many Americans heartily agreed with the New York *Tribune* that "our proposed foothold in the West Indies is likely to be a shaky one." Bret Harte laughed:

> Till one morn, when Mr. Seward
> Cast his weather eye to leeward,
> There was not an inch of dry land
> Left to mark his recent island.[6]

These natural cataclysms did not help the Danish Treaty. But there were more fundamental reasons, aside from the unpopularity of the Johnson administration, for opposition to the proposed transaction. First of all, the task of reconstruction was so overpowering as to preclude the shouldering of new burdens in the Caribbean. Moreover, the United States had a vast undeveloped hinterland; and expansion begins at home. Finally, the navy was rapidly being reduced to a normal footing; and in time of peace the needs of war become less apparent. On November 25, 1867, the House of Representatives resolved, by a vote of 93 to 43, that it was "under no obligation to vote money to pay for any such purchase unless there is greater present necessity for the same than now exists."[7] The New York *Nation* agreed that "If the national future be in peril at all, it is not for want of territory but from excess of it. . . ."[8]

In spite of these rumblings, the Danish government formally ratified the treaty. The inhabitants of the islands overwhelmingly voted to come under the powerful and prosperous wing of the United States. But the treaty languished in the Senate. The Danish minister, General Raasloff, was disturbed by the turn affairs had taken. He realized that these defenseless islands were of little use to his country, and that he had secured the promise of a handsome price for them. In desperation he went so far as to employ lobbyists and publicists to create favorable sentiment.[9] His efforts, however, were unavailing; the United States was not in an expansive mood.

The treaty was still gathering dust in a Senatorial pigeonhole when

---

[6] *The Poetical Works of Bret Harte* (Boston, 1912), p. 44.

[7] *Cong. Globe*, 40 Cong., 1 sess., p. 792.

[8] New York *Nation*, VI, 5 (Jan. 2, 1868).

[9] This group included Robert J. Walker, the well-known ex-Senator, and James Parton, the prolific biographer. See C. C. Tansill, *The Purchase of the Danish West Indies* (Baltimore, 1932), pp. 126–127.

Grant became President, on March 4, 1869. The hero of Appomattox, who had quarreled with the previous Administration, contemptuously waved aside the Danish Treaty as a "scheme of Seward's"; and it was allowed to die in the Senate. The government of Denmark, to which the first overtures had been made, was gravely affronted; and there was a good deal of criticism at home and abroad of America's breach of faith. But it is well to bear in mind that the Senate shares the treaty-making power, and that no pact can be concluded until that body consents to ratification. Ironically enough, the only semitropical outposts of any importance acquired during Seward's term as Secretary of State were the Midway Islands, tiny dots of land one thousand miles west of Hawaii, which were occupied by an American naval officer in August, 1867.[10]

STRANGE BEDFELLOWS

While Seward was eagerly reaching down into the tropics for a Caribbean coaling station, he suddenly became interested in the enormous Arctic expanse of Russian America, now known as Alaska. This story must be projected against the international background.

Russian-American relations had on the whole been quite friendly from the beginning.[11] This is puzzling; for what kinship could the most advanced democracy of the New World find with what was perhaps the most illiberal monarchy of the Old—"an absolutism tempered by assassination"? At the outset, certain points of similarity suggest themselves. Both countries were huge, self-sufficing areas; both were energetic and expanding nations; both had the task of fusing many different peoples; both were faced with the problem of suppressing insurrection;[12] and both had almost simultaneously freed millions of subject peoples—slaves in America, serfs in Russia. In

[10] Seward also had designs on Hawaii, Cuba, Puerto Rico, Canada, Sweden's St. Bartholomew's Island (West Indies), Greenland, Iceland, and, if we may believe his enemies, a part of China.

[11] There had, however, been some temporary ill feeling over the ukase of 1821, and the ruthless suppression of the Polish insurrections of 1830 and 1863. See B. P. Thomas, *Russo-American Relations, 1815–1867* (Baltimore, 1930), pp. 41 ff.

[12] During the year of the Polish insurrection, *Punch* had Lincoln say to Czar Alexander:

> "Imperial son of Nicholas the Great,
> We air in the same fix, I calculate,
> You with your Poles, with Southern rebels I,
> Who spurn my rule and my revenge defy."
>
> *Punch*, XLV, 169 (Oct. 24, 1863).

1866 Oliver Wendell Holmes reflected this fraternal spirit in his "America to Russia."

> Though watery deserts hold apart
> The worlds of East and West,
> Still beats the selfsame human heart
> In each proud Nation's breast.[13]

But these parallels, interesting though they are, do not provide the real explanation of this anomalous friendship. More important is the fact that there was an almost complete absence of friction between Russia and the United States. "The two peoples," the Czar remarked pleasantly in 1866, "have no injuries to remember." Both nations, moreover, had been repeatedly harassed and thwarted by the predominant sea power of Great Britain. Misery and common enemies sometimes make strange bedfellows.

In the autumn of 1863, when the outcome of the Civil War was still undecided and both Great Britain and France seemed hostile to the Union, two Russian fleets dropped anchor in American waters, one at New York, the other at San Francisco. The people of the North immediately leaped to the conclusion that the Russian naval force had been sent to strengthen the United States in its efforts to prevent British and French interference. It mattered not that all real danger of intervention had passed; or that the Russian ships were antiquated and not very seaworthy. The visiting Russians were overwhelmed with entertainment; the name of the Czar was extolled; and new life was infused into the cause of the North. The entire nation echoed Secretary of the Navy Welles' fervent "God bless the Russians." [14]

A year following the close of the Civil War, the Czar narrowly escaped assassination at the hands of a fanatic. Congress passed a resolution of felicitation, which the distinguished Assistant Secretary of the Navy carried to Russia on a United States warship. In 1871, the Grand Duke Alexis visited America. He was received with great rejoicing, and was even taken to Nebraska to shoot buffalo. Oliver Wendell Holmes wrote his memorable "Welcome to the Grand Duke Alexis," which was sung to the Russian national air by the children of the public schools:

> Bleak are our shores with the blasts of December,
> Fettered and chill is the rivulet's flow;

---

[13] The Complete Poetical Works of Oliver Wendell Holmes (Boston, 1923), p. 198.

[14] Thomas, Russo-American Relations, pp. 137–138.

Throbbing and warm are the hearts that remember
Who was our friend when the world was our foe.[15]

Carried away as they were by enthusiasm, the American people
failed to heed Washington's farewell warning against expecting "real
favors from nation to nation." Although a few of the more clear-
headed or cynical guessed that there was something ulterior behind
the visit of the fleets, it was not until 1915 that the Russian archives
gave up their secret. In 1863 war was imminent between Russia on the
one side and England and France on the other. In the event of hostilities the decrepit Russian fleet would probably be bottled up in the
Baltic by the British navy. But each Russian ship might become a
veritable *Alabama* if the vessels could be transferred to strategically
located neutral ports before the outbreak of war. The United States
happened to be ideally situated for this purpose; so the fleets came
here.[16] The American assumption that this was primarily a gesture of
friendship was based upon a misapprehension; but whatever its foundation the illusion existed and played an important part in paving the
way for the purchase of Alaska. Myths are often more potent than
facts in the making of history.

UNLOADING A FROZEN ASSET

By 1867 Russia had come to regard Alaska as potentially valuable
but immediately worthless. The Russian American Company, which
administered the region, had ravaged its fur resources and was facing
bankruptcy. Unwilling to take over the burdens of the Company, the
Czar's advisers remembered that several years earlier certain American
officials had shown a mild interest in purchasing Alaska.[17] Perhaps it
would be possible to capitalize on the friendliness created by the recent
visit of the fleets and sell this bothersome liability for a substantial
sum. The Russians fully realized that in the probable event of another
war with England, their archenemy, nothing could prevent all Alaska
from falling an easy prey to the ubiquitous British navy. A transfer of
the territory to the Americans would forestall this loss and at the same
time strike a blow at Britain's ambitions in the Pacific. Nor did the
Russians overlook the fact that Alaska was breeding trouble with the

[15] Holmes, *Works*, p. 199.
[16] F. A. Golder, "The Russian Fleet and the Civil War," *Amer. Hist. Rev.*, XX
(1915), 802-803. Professor Golder, who secured access to the Russian documents,
was the first American scholar to demolish the fleet legend.
[17] Farrar, *Annexation of Russian America*, pp. 1-14.

United States. The monopolistic tactics of the Russian American Company were causing increasing friction and thus jeopardizing a valuable friendship. Besides, the inscrutable operations of Manifest Destiny, together with a momentarily expected gold rush (the Russians knew that rich ores were here), might enable the Americans to acquire Alaska anyhow, by methods unpleasantly reminiscent of those employed in West Florida and Texas. A momentary scare had already been caused by a rumor that the prolific Mormon following of Brigham Young was planning to settle in and overrun Alaska. It was obviously the part of wisdom to sell while the selling was good, and pocket the money, even though the price obtained did not, in Russian eyes, come anywhere near the potential value of the territory.

The Russian minister to the United States, Édouard de Stoeckl, was much too clever to approach Seward directly with his proposal. He let it be known through one of the Secretary's friends that Russia might be coaxed into selling Alaska. Seward, who had long dreamed of extending American hegemony to the Arctic, immediately became interested and made the first overtures, in March, 1867.[18] He was much too eager a purchaser to be a good bargainer; and the wily Muscovite minister took full advantage of him. After considerable haggling the price finally agreed upon was $7,200,000, or $2,200,000 more than the minimum price set by the Russian minister's superiors. Congress was about to adjourn; and Seward, anxious to secure immediate action, had Stoeckl send an outline of the proposed treaty to St. Petersburg over the newly laid and expensive Atlantic cable.

On the evening of March 29, 1867, Stoeckl called at Seward's home with the welcome news that the Czar had given his consent to the transaction, and suggested that the treaty be concluded the next day at the State Department. The eager Seward pushed away the whist table:

"Why wait till tomorrow, Mr. Stoeckl? Let us make the treaty tonight!"

"But your Department is closed. You have no clerks, and my secretaries are scattered about the town."

"Never mind that," responded Seward. "If you can muster your legation together, before midnight you will find me awaiting you at the Department, which will be open and ready for business." [19]

[18] F. A. Golder, "The Purchase of Alaska," *Amer. Hist. Rev.*, XXV (1920), 419.
[19] F. W. Seward, *Reminiscences of a War-Time Statesman and Diplomat, 1830–1915* (N.Y., 1916), p. 362. F. W. Seward was Seward's son, and at the time Assistant Secretary of State.

So, at four o'clock on the morning of March 30, 1867, the treaty was put into final form and signed.

A National Icehouse

Only an expansionist of Seward's undiscriminating voracity could have seriously entertained the thought of buying Alaska. The people of the United States today probably know more about Antarctica than their countrymen knew about Russian America in 1867. Senator Sumner, later a stalwart champion of the treaty, admitted that only Greenland and Central Africa were less well known.

It is not surprising, therefore, that when the American people heard of the transaction—"a dark deed done in the night"—they could scarcely believe their senses. Surprise and ignorance immediately manifested themselves in an outburst of derision and scorn; and for a time the treaty was in danger of being hooted out of court. It was "an egregious blunder," a "bad bargain," palmed off on "the silly administration" by the "shrewd Russians." Alaska, the land "of short rations and long twilights," was "a barren, worthless, God-forsaken region," "a hyperborean solitude" consisting of nothing but "walrus-covered icebergs." It was "Walrussia," "Seward's Folly," "Johnson's Polar Bear Garden," "Polario," "a national icehouse," "Seward's Icebox." [20] The New York *Herald* ran this filler: "HOW TO MAKE BOTH ENDS MEET—Buy Patagonia, Mr. Seward." The same newspaper published a fictitious advertisement:

> CASH! CASH! CASH!—Cash paid for cast off territory. Best price given for old colonies, North or South. Any impoverished monarchs retiring from the colonization business may find a good purchaser by addressing W. H. S. [Seward], Post Office, Washington, D. C.[21]

The prospects of ratification appeared so hopeless that Senator Sumner advised Stoeckl to withdraw the treaty and avoid the inevitable rebuff to America's good friend, Russia.[22] But Seward did not lose heart. He realized that the most vociferous opposition came from those who were most ignorant of the resources of Alaska, and he perceived that a vigorous campaign of education might save the treaty.

[20] For a convenient summary of press reactions see E. P. Oberholtzer, *A History of the United States since the Civil War* (N.Y., 1917), I, 540–542.

[21] New York *Herald*, April 12, 1867, 6:5.

[22] Golder, "The Purchase of Alaska," *loc. cit.*, p. 421.

He therefore handed over to the press a number of letters that had come to his office from influential men who favored the transaction; and when he discovered that the opposition was voicing the same objections that had been used against the acquisition of Louisiana, he sent a clerk to New York to copy material from the newspapers of 1803, which in turn the daily press of 1867 published.[23] So successful were Seward's efforts in marshaling public opinion for the treaty that charges of bribery were brought against him. He later testified, however, that he had spent only $500 in his "campaign of education." The truth appears to be that the people were eager for information about their new acquisition, and that the press was willing to publish without charge much of what Seward gave out.

THE SENATORIAL GAUNTLET

But the Senate was yet to be heard from; and there Seward was cordially hated for his unswerving loyalty to President Johnson. Some of the members even went to Stoeckl and explained that they were going to vote against the treaty simply because Seward was behind it.[24] But the resourceful Secretary of State called certain Senators to his office one by one, and there made confidants of them. Senator Cole of California later confessed that Seward did "a good deal of hustling" in behalf of the treaty. The Washington correspondent of the New York *Herald* graphically described what was happening:

Secretary Seward has another diplomatic symposium at his elegant establishment to-night, at which Mr. Sumner is present, with numerous other Senatorial luminaries. Madame Rumor again associates Russian-American icebergs and refrigerated champagne; and, putting this and that together, makes Mr. Seward's dinner bear in some way on the proposed slice of hyperborean territory.[25]

All these devices would probably have proved unavailing, however, if Seward had not had the foresight to secure the support of Charles Sumner. As chairman of the important Senate Committee on Foreign Relations, and as one of the most powerful orators in the United States, he was in a position to make or break the treaty. At first he showed little enthusiasm for Alaska; but, once enlisted, he

[23] T. A. Bailey, "Why the United States Purchased Alaska," *Pacific Hist. Rev.*, III (1934), 43–44.
[24] Golder, "The Purchase of Alaska," *loc. cit.*, p. 421.
[25] New York *Herald*, April 9, 1867, 3:1.

threw himself into the cause with tremendous vigor. After a short period of intensive study, and with only one sheet of notes before him, he made an impressive three-hour speech in support of the treaty. Sumner particularly emphasized the great natural resources of Alaska, and the commercial advantages that would accrue to the Pacific Coast from its acquisition. He also pointed to the gain for republican institutions that would come from the complete banishment of the Russian monarchy from North America, and he noted that in acquiring Alaska the United States would steal a march on Britain and put the seal upon its friendship with Russia.[26] Influenced, it appears, by Sumner's great effort, the Senate approved the treaty on that same day, April 9, 1867, by a vote of 37 to 2.

THE HOUSE HURDLE

But the other branch of Congress was yet to be heard from. Many of its members were indignant because Seward had bound them to pay the sum of $7,200,000 without so much as saying "by your leave." The question again arose as to whether, in such instances, the House of Representatives was a part of the treaty-making power. The members delayed coming to grips with the problem until after the United States had formally taken possession of Alaska. Then they were confronted with an accomplished fact. If they refused to vote the money they would affront Russia and at the same time humiliate the United States by making it necessary to haul down "Old Glory." [27]

Most of the Congressional opponents of the purchase seemed to be more concerned about their injured dignity than anything else; but they dwelt at considerable length on the worthlessness of Alaska. Representative Washburn of Wisconsin suggested that Seward could have purchased a much superior white elephant in Siam or Bombay "for one hundredth part of the money" and "with not a ten thousandth part of the expense incurred in keeping the animal in proper condition." Others objected that there was no point in provoking Britain unnecessarily because in due time the United States would get Alaska for nothing when it annexed Canada. Representative Cul-

[26] For the speech see *The Works of Charles Sumner* (Boston, 1883), XI, 186–349 (April 9, 1867). With Seward obviously in mind Sumner warned: "There is one other point on which I file my *caveat*. This treaty must not be a precedent for a system of indiscriminate and costly annexion." *Ibid.*, 232.

[27] This was a powerful argument in the House debates. Representative Orth of Indiana shouted: "Shall that flag which waves so proudly there now be taken down? Palsied be the hand that would dare to remove it! Our flag is there, and there it will remain." *Cong. Globe*, 40 Cong., 2 sess., appendix, p. 432 (July 10, 1868).

lom of Illinois introduced the ever-recurring fruit metaphor: "I believe that we are destined to own and control the whole western continent from Baffin's bay to the Caribbean sea. But, sir, we need not be in a hurry. When the fruit is ripe it will fall into our hands." [28]

The opponents of Alaska in the House also made much of the argument that America was establishing the dangerous precedent of acquiring great areas of noncontiguous territory. One of the Representatives spoke feelingly and perhaps facetiously in behalf of a compact country, opposing one so large that he could love only "half of it at a time." Others feared that this purchase would pave the way for further indiscriminate annexation. There was no telling what Seward would do next if he were able to acquire Alaska.[29]

In spite of this barrage of criticism, supporters of the purchase in the House stood their ground. They stressed particularly Russian friendship, and the economic, commercial, and strategic potentialities of Alaska. They also argued that if the United States did not take the territory Great Britain would; and that it was sound policy to snatch this choice morsel from the lion's jaws. Other Congressmen asserted that with Alaska on the north and the United States on the south, British Columbia (and with it all Canada) would be caught in the jaws of a vice and forced into a union with America. "Canada will fall into our lap like a ripe apple," declared Representative Mungen.[30]

Some of the Representatives, in spite of the general apathy toward expansion at the time, insisted that the acquisition of Alaska was but the simple and inevitable workings of Manifest Destiny. Outside of Congress the press echoed these sentiments, and the New York *Herald* spoke of carrying out "the fiat of inevitable destiny, which, in time, must give us the whole of the North American continent." The Sacramento *Union* reflected the prevailing spirit in an editorial entitled, "We Approach the Pole":

There once floated about the world of humor a definition of the boundaries of the United States, which ran as follows: On the north by the aurora borealis, on the east by the Atlantic, on the west by the Pacific, and

---

[28] *Ibid.*, p. 474 (July 10, 1868).

[29] The New York *Herald* emphasized this possibility in fictitious advertisements. "THE MILK IN THE COCOANUT.—We can get it with the Feejee Islands. Having commenced the purchase of outside countries, we can go on. We have icebergs, but we want cocoanuts." April 12, 1867, 6:2.

[30] The New York *World* expressed the same thought somewhat more delicately: ". . . A gap in our possessions on the Pacific Coast will always be an eyesore to the nation, whose sense of symmetry will be offended by the ragged look of the map." April 1, 1867, 4:2.

on the south by manifest destiny. Despite the smack of Yankee exaggeration in this, we are getting along. Our flag has advanced to the northern verge of the continent—the auroral land fringed by the ice of the Arctic Sea.[31]

THE ACCEPTANCE OF "WALRUSSIA"

The prolonged debates in the House drove Stoeckl almost to distraction. His heavy subsidies to the press and his highly paid lobbyists apparently were accomplishing nothing.[32] In profound discouragement he suggested to his superiors that they offer Alaska to the United States as a gift, and thus shame the Americans into paying the money. The Czar promptly vetoed this suggestion: he feared that the Yankees might accept it. As a last resort bribery appears to have been employed. We do not know specifically which Congressmen accepted Stoeckl's gold; but the Russian documents indicate that some of them did.[33] Finally, on July 14, 1868, the debate ended and the appropriation carried, 113 to 43. Stoeckl then requested that he be allowed to go somewhere where he might "breathe for a while a purer atmosphere than that of Washington."

But Russian gold apparently had little to do with the result. Much more important was Russian friendship. It was generally stated, in Congress and out, that since America had solicited Alaska from Russia, the great territory could not honorably be thrown back into her face. Many felt with Senator Cameron of Pennsylvania that the purchase was "an act of recompense to a tried friend."

The influence of Russian friendship, powerful though it was, probably would not have sufficed to carry the treaty and the appropriation had not the American people come to realize that the territory was potentially valuable. Seward's campaign of education was effectively conducted, and an examination of contemporary newspapers reveals that as knowledge regarding the resources of the new territory spread, enthusiasm for it increased correspondingly. The members of the House could not mistake or fail to heed the ground swell of approval.

[31] Sacramento *Union*, April 1, 1867, 2:2.

[32] Much of the opposition in the House came from a group which was backing a malodorous private claim against Russia. At Seward's suggestion, Stoeckl employed ex-Senator Robert J. Walker, at an honorarium approaching $30,000, to lobby for the appropriation. See R. H. Luthin, "The Sale of Alaska," *Slavonic Review*, XVI (1937), 171.

[33] Golder, "The Purchase of Alaska," *loc. cit.*, p. 424. For less satisfactory evidence that one Congressman accepted $10,000 and another $8000, see W. A. Dunning, "Paying for Alaska," *Pol. Sci. Quar.*, XXVII (1912), 386.

Fundamentally, the American people appear to have accepted Seward's treaty because it was demonstrated to them that Alaska was worth the money.[34] Yankee love for a bargain and a highly developed speculative instinct were not to be denied. Bret Harte caught the spirit:

> 'T ain't so very mean a trade,
> When the land is all surveyed.
> There's a right smart chance for fur-chase
> All along this recent purchase,
> And, unless the stories fail,
> Every fish from cod to whale;
> Rocks, too; mebbe quartz; let's see,—
> 'T would be strange if there should be,—
> Seems I've heered such stories told:
> Eh!—why, bless us,—yes, it's gold! [35]

Harte was right. There are few today who, on economic grounds at least, will accuse Seward of folly in having bought this princely domain for one and nineteen-twentieth cents an acre. The almost unscratched natural resources of Alaska, including rich deposits of gold, have paid for the territory many times over. Nor has the last chapter been written, for the Aleutian archipelago, with its strategically located harbors and potential air bases almost in Japan's back yard, beckons, for weal or woe, to the Far East.

BIBLIOGRAPHICAL NOTE

Two brief accounts of postwar expansion, though old, are still useful: Frederic Bancroft, *The Life of William H. Seward* (N.Y., 1900), II, 470–491; and T. C. Smith, "Expansion after the Civil War, 1865–1871," *Pol. Sci. Quar.*, XVI (1901), 412–436. Seward's attempts to purchase the Danish West Indies and Santo Domingo are fully treated in C. C. Tansill's standard monographs, *The Purchase of the Danish West Indies* (Baltimore, 1932); and *The United States and Santo Domingo, 1798–1873* (Baltimore, 1938). The Russian background of the Alaska purchase, as well as the purchase itself, is adequately covered in B. P. Thomas, *Russo-American Relations, 1815–1867* (Baltimore, 1930). An article of prime importance is F. A. Golder, "The Russian Fleet and the Civil War," *Amer. Hist. Rev.*, XX (1915), 801–812. The most comprehensive monograph on the Alaska purchase is V. J. Farrar, *The Annexation of Russian America to the United States* (Washington, 1937). F. A. Golder, "The Purchase of

[34] Bailey, "Why the United States Purchased Alaska," *loc. cit.*, p. 49.
[35] Harte, *Poetical Works*, p. 42. In 1907, when Taft visited Moscow, the Czar remarked that there were people in Russia who criticized their government for having disposed of this rich province. H. F. Pringle, *The Life and Times of William Howard Taft* (N.Y., 1939), I, 332–333.

Alaska," *Amer. Hist. Rev.*, XXV (1920), 411–425 is still valuable. The debates
in the House are summarized in J. M. Callahan, *The Alaska Purchase and
Americo-Canadian Relations* (Morgantown, W. Va., 1908); somewhat more
briefly in F. R. Dulles, *America in the Pacific* (Boston, 1932), Ch. VI. American
public opinion is analyzed in T. A. Bailey, "Why the United States Purchased
Alaska," *Pacific Hist. Rev.*, III (1934), 39–49. On the irregularities attending
the House appropriation see R. H. Luthin, "The Sale of Alaska," *Slavonic Rev.*,
XVI (1937), 168–182; and W. A. Dunning, "Paying for Alaska," *Pol. Sci. Quar.*,
XXVII (1912), 385–398. Further references: see footnotes of this chapter and
Bemis and Griffin, *Guide*, pp. 360–369.

RECENT REFERENCES. A. G. Mazour, "The Prelude to Russia's Departure
from America," *Pacific Hist. Rev.*, X (1941), 311–319, explodes the old thesis
that the Czar stupidly sold Alaska, not knowing its wealth. Russia wished to
withdraw because (1) she knew of rich gold and other deposits, and hoped to
avoid an inrush of Americans; (2) she was so deeply involved in Europe and
Asia that she wanted her hands free; (3) she wished to cultivate friendly relations with America as a makeweight against Britain. Virginia H. Reid, *The Purchase of Alaska: Contemporary Opinion* (Long Beach, Calif., 1940), supports the
conclusion of the present writer that on the whole the press favored the purchase,
notably in the West. Some attention is given to foreign opinion; and there is a
useful if sophomoric bibliography. H. E. Blinn, "Seward and the Polish Rebellion
of 1863," *Amer. Hist. Rev.*, XLV (1940), 828–833, reveals that Seward won
Russia's gratitude by declining to intervene with the other Powers; also, that
by so doing he strengthened America's hand in opposing British intervention in
the Confederate States, and French intervention in Mexico. Brainerd Dyer, "Robert J. Walker on Acquiring Greenland and Iceland," *Miss. Valley Hist. Rev.*,
XXVII (1940), 263–266, shows that Walker, at Seward's suggestion, drew up
a report in 1867 on the desirability of securing these two areas from Denmark;
but the project was dropped following the defeat of the Danish West Indies treaty
and the Alaska debate over "hyperborean liabilities." R. W. Logan, *The Diplomatic Relations of the United States with Haiti, 1776–1891* (Chapel Hill, N.C.,
1941), Ch. XI; and L. L. Montague, *Haiti and the United States, 1714–1938*
(Durham, N.C., 1940), Ch. VI, have interesting accounts of Seward's alleged designs on a naval base in Haiti.

NEW REFERENCES. F. R. Dulles, *The Road to Teheran* (Princeton, 1944),
is general. J. A. James, *The First Scientific Exploration of Russian America and
the Purchase of Alaska* (Evanston, Ill., 1942), gives some climatological data which
Senator Sumner used. Hunter Miller, "Russian Opinion on the Cession of Alaska,"
Amer. Hist. Rev., XLVIII (1943), 521–531, shows that there was some Russian
press opposition to the sale; and presents official documents giving reasons for
and against the transfer. D. M. Dozer, "Anti-Expansionism during the Johnson
Administration," *Pacific Hist. Rev.*, XII (1943), 253–275, concludes that anti-
expansionism was a forerunner of later anti-imperialism. H. Koht, "The Origin
of Seward's Plan to Purchase the Danish West Indies," *Amer. Hist. Rev.*, L
(1945), 762–767, suggests that Seward may have been partly motivated by fear
of a possible transfer to Austria. See A. J. May, "Crete and the United States,
1866–1869," *Jour. of Mod. Hist.*, XVI (1944), 286–293, for a latter-day public
interest in Greek rebels.

4TH ED. REFS. See Bibliographical Appendix, p. 930.

CHAPTER XXV

Anglo-American Relations and the Grant Administration

"If the Americans don't embroil us [England] in war before long it will not be their fault. What with their swagger and bombast, what with their claims for indemnification, what with Ireland and Fenianism, and what with Canada, I have strong apprehensions."

Charles Dickens, 1865.

ANOTHER UNION EMERGES FROM THE CIVIL WAR

WHEN the Civil War broke out, Canada was strongly sympathetic with the antislavery North. Even the children who played North and South with wooden guns found it difficult to persuade enough of their fellows to represent the Confederates. But the rancor aroused in the United States by Britain's conduct was in large measure directed at nearby but unoffending Canada. Violent American accusations led to bitter Canadian recriminations; and the fat was once more in the fire.[1]

Ill feeling reached a high point when Confederate agents, in spite of the vigilance of the Canadian authorities, began to use Canada as a base for annoying raids against the United States. The most serious of these was the one against St. Albans, Vermont, on October 19, 1864. Nervous tension on the American side of the frontier caused Secretary Seward to inform the British government of his intention to terminate the Rush-Bagot disarmament agreement. Fortunately, however, the border quieted down, and Seward rescinded his action in March, 1865.[2] But the Canadian Reciprocity Treaty of 1854 fared less well. Partly as a result of the animosity engendered by the war, and partly as a result of jealousy over Canadian prosperity under the arrange-

[1] H. G. MacDonald, *Canadian Public Opinion on the American Civil War* (N.Y., 1926), pp. 79 ff.
[2] See J. M. Callahan, *The Neutrality of the American Lakes and Anglo-American Relations* (Baltimore, 1898), pp. 136–167.

406

ment, the United States gave formal notice of abrogation, in March, 1865, effective twelve months later.[3]

All these developments did nothing to quiet Canadian fears. Moreover, the Americans, who were flushed with victory, talked casually and confidently of pouring into Canada and taking it over as part payment for the wrongs suffered at the hands of Great Britain. A Northern marching song, set to the tune of "Yankee Doodle" during the war, ran:

> Secession first he would put down
> Wholly and forever,
> And afterwards from Britain's crown
> He Canada would sever.[4]

American spread-eagle orators spoke grandiloquently of the boundaries that "God Almighty had established, reaching to the Aurora Borealis on the north." A bill was introduced in the House, in July, 1866, making provision for the admission of Canada into the Union.

Indeed, it seemed as though the object of America's desires might fall into her arms without the necessity of a forcible embrace. The spirit of disunion was widespread in Canada, especially in faraway British Columbia, where, in 1869–1870, over one hundred residents petitioned the United States for annexation.[5] The British minister in Washington and other influential Englishmen were declaring that if Canada chose to join the United States peaceably the mother country would raise no serious objections.[6] But Great Britain would fight to the last man before she would permit the colony to be wrested from her.

Though sentiment for annexation was strong in certain parts of Canada, it was never that of a majority. The necessity of unifying in the face of the powerful and vengeful Yankee was a potent factor in bringing about the passage of the British North America Act, effective July 1, 1867, by which the Dominion of Canada came into being.[7] But unity was not what the United States wanted. In disunity lay annexation. On March 27, 1867, the House of Representatives actually

---

[3] L. B. Shippee, *Canadian-American Relations, 1849–1874* (New Haven, 1939), pp. 159 *ff*. See Chs. VI and VII of this scholarly work for Canadian-American relations during the Civil War.

[4] Quoted in H. L. Keenleyside, *Canada and the United States* (N.Y., 1929), p. 139.

[5] Allan Nevins, *Hamilton Fish* (N.Y., 1936), p. 390.

[6] Shippee, *Canadian-American Relations*, pp. 189, 205–206.

[7] J. M. Callahan, *American Foreign Policy in Canadian Relations* (N.Y., 1937), pp. 303–304.

passed a resolution in which it deplored the formation of the Dominion of Canada as a step in the direction of strengthening monarchy.

FENIAN FORAYS

Anglo-American relations were further embittered during these
postwar years by the activities of the Fenians—a secret Irish brother-
hood, organized in the fifties, whose objective was the independence
of Ireland.[8] Using the United States as a base, they planned first to
conquer Canada, and perhaps involve America and Great Britain in a
war that would result in the freeing of the Emerald Isle.

During the Civil War many Irishmen had served in the Northern
armies, and one of their marching songs read:

> We are the Fenian Brotherhood, skilled in the art of war,
> And we're going to fight for Ireland, the land that we adore.
> Many battles we have won along with the boys in blue,
> And we'll go and capture Canada, for we've nothing else to do.[9]

Following the close of the war, numerous Fenian balls, picnics, and
conventions were held in the United States, and an Irish "Republic"
was formally organized. After much drill and parade, and much excitement and alarm, the Celtic "armies" were finally mobilized on the
Northern frontier.[10] The first serious effort was made in May and
June of 1866, when a few hundred Irishmen crossed the Niagara
River, only to flee after a lucky initial success known as "the
battle of Limestone Ridge." But the faithful kept up the agitation,
and did not despair of success. The next Fenian invasion of any consequence came four years later, in May, 1870, when the nondescript
force of "General" John O'Neill was completely dispersed after a

[8] Some of the Fenians returned to Ireland, and there were arrested for inciting revolt. The news aroused great indignation in America. The difficulties in which the
British government became involved as a result of trying to distinguish between
naturalized Americans born in Ireland and Americans of Irish descent born in the
United States led in part to the conclusion of the Treaty of 1870, by which the
mutual right of naturalization was recognized. It was an epochal abandonment of
the hoary shibboleth, "Once an Englishman, always an Englishman." See R. L.
Morrow, "The Negotiation of the Anglo-American Treaty of 1870," *Amer. Hist.
Rev.*, XXXIX (1934), 663–681.

[9] Keenleyside, *Canada and the United States*, pp. 146–147.

[10] A handbill issued to discharged Union soldiers read: "Volunteers for Canada.
One Hundred Pounds Bounty! 200 Acres of Land." The British consul general at
New York reported (May 13, 1865) that an advertisement had appeared in the
Brooklyn *Eagle* for filibusters against Canada. J. P. Smith, *The Republican Expan-
sionists of the Early Reconstruction Era* (Chicago, 1933), pp. 31–32, 78.

United States marshal had arrested the leader. The belatedly energetic action of the American officials, who won the commendation of the British minister in Washington and the execration of "professional" Irishmen everywhere, stamped out the remaining areas of infection.

The Canadians, who had been put to considerable expense to repel these invasions, were more angered than alarmed. They did not fully appreciate the difficulties confronting the United States authorities; and they were outraged that Irish armies should be openly raised and that the American press should egg the Fenians on. Altogether, these flurries probably did more than anything else to dampen annexation sentiment in Canada; certainly they further developed a national feeling.[11]

JUNKETING REVERDY JOHNSON

When the Civil War came to an end, England viewed the reunited United States with apprehension. She was particularly worried about the unfortunate precedents she had recently created. ". . . The sunken *Alabama*," noted a writer in the *Fortnightly Review*, "leaves a brood of her kind to be hatched out by the heat of the next English war. . . ."[12] The nightmare began to take on reality when, in the summer of 1866, the House of Representatives unanimously modified the Neutrality Act of 1818 so as to permit Americans to sell vessels to belligerents. This was an unmistakable invitation to the nations of the world to wipe out Britain's rich and vulnerable merchant marine in time of war. Indeed, many Irishmen hoped to see American-built *Alabamas* ravaging the seas under the flag of the Irish republic. Though the bill slept in the Senate, Britain began to see a new light.

The prospect of settling the *Alabama* claims brightened in June, 1866, when a change of ministry retired Earl Russell from the Foreign Office and ushered in a series of more tractable successors. Secretary Seward, who was eager to revitalize the discredited Johnson administration, hastened to take advantage of the opening. Unfortunately, he could no longer work through the able Charles Francis Adams, who had resigned. His successor, the garrulous and convivial Reverdy Johnson of Maryland, attempted to woo the British with speeches that were so effusive as to elicit amused comments even in

[11] C. P. Stacey, "Fenianism and the Rise of National Feeling in Canada at the Time of Confederation," *Canadian Hist. Rev.*, XII (1931), 261. There is an excellent brief account of the Fenians in Shippee, *Canadian-American Relations*, Ch. X.

[12] *Fortnightly Review* (London), III, 459 (Jan. 1, 1866).

England. His worst *faux pas* was cordially shaking the hand of Laird, the unrepentant builder of the *Alabama*. When the news reached America, "Junketing Reverdy Johnson," as he was called, was undone. The Irish and other Anglophobes demanded his instant recall. *Harper's Weekly* published a cartoon with these words:

> And here's a hand my trusty Laird,
> And gie's a hand o' thine,
> And we'll tak a right gude willie-waught
> For auld lang syne.[13]

The negotiations that followed these unfortunate preliminaries resulted in the Johnson-Clarendon Convention, which was signed on January 14, 1869. It made provision for the adjustment of individual claims *on both sides* since 1853—"both batches on an equality." There was not a word of regret about the *Alabama;* there was nothing said about the indirect damages caused by British-built, British-manned, and British-succored commerce destroyers.

It seems clear that American public opinion was overwhelmingly opposed to the treaty. The document might have been accepted, with amendments, in 1865, when the nation was war-weary—but not in 1869. Americans were entertaining extravagant ideas; sane men were talking seriously of taking Canada in part payment for the *Alabama* claims. The Senate, moreover, did not appreciate the hasty efforts of the unpopular Johnson administration to adjust the matter. On April 13, 1869, as everyone expected, the treaty was struck down by a vote of 54 to 1.

THE SPEECH THAT SHOOK TWO HEMISPHERES

The action of the Senate was such a foregone conclusion that there was no need for speech making. But Senator Charles Sumner, humorless, intolerant, and egotistical, attached an exaggerated value to his oratory; and, on April 13, 1869, he delivered a tremendous indictment against Great Britain. He first of all declared that England owed the United States $15,000,000 for the actual damages to American ships caused by the *Alabamas.* But there were also "national" losses connected with the destruction of the American merchant marine, such as the transfer of registry to neutral flags and the increase of insurance rates. This item alone would total $110,000,000. In addition, Brit-

---

[13] *Harper's Weekly*, XII, 816 (Dec. 19, 1868). For a defense of Johnson see B. C. Steiner, *The Life of Reverdy Johnson* (Baltimore, 1914), pp. 236 ff.

ain's moral and material support to the Confederacy had prolonged the war by two years, a four year conflict that had cost $4,000,000,000. After this Sumner closed moderately—for him. He did not say that Great Britain owed the United States, for direct and indirect damages, a total of $2,125,000,000. He merely remarked, "Everybody can make the calculation." Nor did he say that since England could not pay this enormous sum in cash America would accept Canada instead. But this idea was so prevalent in the United States that the inference was unmistakable.[14]

Sumner's sensational speech was widely reproduced and read, and James Russell Lowell probably was not far from the mark when he said that it "expressed the feeling of the country very truly." The New York *Nation* found that it "set about all Americans swinging their hats for eight or nine days. . . ." But thoughtful men feared that this intemperate outburst would put another obstacle in the way of settlement. Henry Adams, then in Washington, entertained grave doubts as to Sumner's sanity.[15]

In England, disgust was mingled with indignation. The British had extended what they regarded as a friendly hand in the Johnson-Clarendon Convention. It had been rudely rebuffed. Then, as if to turn the knife in the wound, the most influential member of the Senate had made these preposterous demands, apparently with the approval of his colleagues. A British correspondent of the New York *Tribune* wrote that "England will fight rather than even negotiate on any such basis"; and the London *Spectator* declared that "it is war that speeches like those of Mr. Sumner would force on us." United States bonds dropped five per cent. It was evident that many months would have to elapse before Great Britain would again consent to negotiate on the *Alabama* claims.

A General in the White House

Five weeks before the rejection of the Johnson-Clarendon Convention, General Ulysses S. Grant became President. This narrow and bewildered military hero, suddenly elevated from a seat in the saddle to one in the White House, was a pathetic and gullible misfit. By a happy accident he chose Hamilton Fish, a wealthy and socially prominent New Yorker, as his Secretary of State. Though Fish was without

[14] See C. F. Adams, *Lee at Appomattox and Other Papers* (Boston, 1902), pp. 152–153.

[15] Henry Adams, *The Education of Henry Adams* (N.Y., 1931), p. 275.

diplomatic experience and though he had retired after an undistin guished career as a one-term Congressman, Governor of New York, and United States Senator, he was a student of international affairs and had the breadth which comes from social background and extensive travel. Even though he lacked the brilliance of Seward, he nevertheless brought to the bewildered Grant administration a soundness of judgment that may have saved it from complete disaster.[16]

The important position of minister to England was awarded to the brilliant but high-spirited historian, John Lothrop Motley, whose candidacy had been vigorously championed by his close friend, Senator Sumner. Grant made the appointment with reluctance, for he had nothing in common with the intellectual Motley, and he did not like men who parted their hair in the middle.[17] With both Grant and Fish inexperienced in foreign affairs, Sumner, veteran chairman of the Senate Committee on Foreign Relations, looked upon himself as the director—perhaps the dictator—of the Administration's foreign policy. Motley shared this view. The retired Charles Francis Adams acidly but correctly observed that the historian evidently expected to represent two powers abroad: Mr. Sumner and the United States government.

Tension reached a climax when Motley, in flat violation of Fish's instructions, represented Sumner's views on claims to the British government. Grant, whose military mind regarded disobedience of orders as an unpardonable sin, declared, "Motley must be dismissed at once." Perhaps he should have been. But Fish remonstrated, for he feared that a quarrel with Sumner at this point would further discredit the already discredited Administration, and make more difficult a settlement with Great Britain. The upshot was that Fish sent Motley a tactful reprimand, and transferred the negotiations from his hands to Washington.[18]

---

[16] Grant was indebted to E. B. Washburne for personal favors and made him Secretary of State for a few days (March 5–16, 1869) so that he would have greater prestige when he arrived in France as United States minister. It was alleged that Washburne preferred France to England because he could not speak good enough English to avoid embarrassment in London, whereas he could use an interpreter in France. Grant's practice of rewarding friends or getting enemies out of the country by appointing them to diplomatic posts brought new disrepute to the service. A nephew of Congressman "Beast" Butler was made consul general in Egypt, where he caused a minor scandal by drunkenness, brawling, a shooting affray, and the purchase of dancing girls. See New York *Nation*, XV, 342 (Nov. 28, 1872).

[17] W. B. Hesseltine, *Ulysses S. Grant: Politician* (N.Y., 1935), p. 141.

[18] Nevins, *Hamilton Fish*, pp. 205–207.

GRANT LEARNS SOME INTERNATIONAL LAW

Meanwhile smoking Cuba claimed attention. The rebellion against Spain which had broken out in October, 1868, was being prosecuted with cruelty on both sides. The American people, ever sympathetic toward liberty and hostile to monarchy, were deeply interested in the revolt. Cuban exiles in the United States formed *juntas* which disseminated propaganda, held mass meetings, offered bribes of bonds to the press and to Congressmen, and organized filibustering expeditions. Such activity naturally aroused the Spanish government to wrath. The situation became worse when American property was destroyed in Cuba, and American citizens (mostly naturalized and of Cuban birth) were summarily shot or imprisoned. Press, pulpit, and platform demanded intervention—at least recognition of belligerency. Dana's New York *Sun* and Bennett's *Herald* beat the tom-toms of war. Ominous movements of fleets took place on both sides.

But war with Spain was not to be undertaken lightly, what with overpowering problems of reconstruction, a colossal debt, a worm-eaten navy, and a tiny army. Secretary Fish further realized that hostilities would weaken his hand with Great Britain and postpone, if not prevent, a final settlement of outstanding difficulties. Yet many Americans, including President Grant, favored recognizing the belligerency of the insurgents. War would probably have followed such a step, because the Cuban government was but a shadow, and Spain was already in a resentful mood. Nevertheless, on August 14, 1869, Grant wrote Fish a letter instructing him to issue a proclamation recognizing the belligerency of the Cubans, a document which had already received the presidential signature.[19] Fortunately, Fish quietly pigeonholed the pronouncement, while the President, momentarily distracted by pressing financial difficulties, forgot about his blunder.

In the early summer of 1870 the Cuban belligerency agitation came to a head in Congress. Secretary Fish, under threats of resignation, persuaded the reluctant Grant to send a special appeal to Congress, on June 13, 1870, urging strict neutrality. The message was strongly applauded by the more conservative newspapers, and made a strong impression on the House. Yet the belligerency resolution was reported favorably and, after a bitter debate, was voted down, on June 16, 1870, by the not too comfortable margin of 101 to 88 votes. It is probable that the timely Grant-Fish message spiked the resolution and averted war.

[19] *Ibid.*, pp. 239 *ff.*

The Santo Domingo Smoke Screen

The Cuban and British crises were inextricably bound up with the agitation to annex the Dominican Republic. The President of this bankrupt and war-torn nation was willing to merge his domain with that of the United States if the latter would assume the public debt. The plan was enthusiastically supported by an unscrupulous group of American speculators and promoters, and by the Navy men, who were particularly eager to secure the magnificent Bay of Samaná. The gullible Grant soon swung into line and embraced the annexation project; or, better, the idea embraced him. It became an obsession.

Secretary Fish was not enthusiastic about the Santo Domingo scheme, but he perceived that if Grant became wrapped up in it he would be more likely to keep his clumsy hands out of the delicate Cuban and British negotiations.[20] So, late in 1869, the Dominican annexation treaty was finally completed in due form. Public opinion, however, did not respond favorably to the idea. The nation, vexed as it was with reconstruction and other problems, was not yet ready to annex insular possessions that were thickly populated by alien peoples.

Grant, in his enthusiasm for the project, went to see Charles Sumner, chairman of the Senate Foreign Relations Committee. After a conversation in which the President several times addressed the Senator as chairman of the Judiciary Committee, Grant went away thinking, apparently with some justification, that Sumner had pledged his support to the project.[21] But the latter, after careful study, turned his influence against it. In spite of the President's personal and political power, the final vote, taken on June 30, 1870, was 28 to 28, far short of the necessary two thirds.

Deeply angered by Sumner's apparent treachery, Grant promptly demanded the bifurcated scalp of the Senator's friend, Motley, who was summarily removed from his post.[22] The dogged hero of Ap-

[20] See C. C. Tansill, *The United States and Santo Domingo, 1798–1873* (Baltimore, 1938), p. 412. In this important monograph the author shows that, contrary to the traditional accounts, Fish was well aware of the negotiations; that he himself prepared the necessary instructions; that he did not threaten to resign because Grant went over his head in the matter; and that Grant did not urge him to remain in the Cabinet because he needed him as the Administration's "social guide." See *Ibid.*, pp. 366 ff.

[21] *Ibid.*, pp. 384 ff.

[22] Motley's successor, General Schenck, reputedly wormed his way into Grant's good graces by bringing Mrs. Grant a stylish hat from Paris. The new minister became the lion of the hour when he introduced draw poker into London society, and established himself as the leading authority on the game. His downfall came when

pomattox kept up the fight for Santo Domingo with all the weapons at his command, while the embittered Sumner attacked the President's methods in lengthy and spectacular speeches on the floor of the Senate. In private the Senator would roar "like the bull of Bashan" and condemn Grant as "a colossus of ignorance"; while the latter, when told that Sumner did not believe in the Bible, snapped, "No, he did not write it." Grant even shook his fist as he passed the Senator's residence; and hinted that if he were not President there would be a challenge to a duel.

When Congress met again in March, 1871, Grant used his influence to have Sumner shorn of his chairmanship of the Foreign Relations Committee. Fish acquiesced in this move in the interests of the Administration's foreign policy. Whether rightly or not, he feared that Sumner, with his fantastic ideas as to indirect damages and the annexation of Canada, might use his post to ruin the delicate negotiations with Great Britain.[23]

The fruitless Santo Domingo scheme, judged by itself, was of secondary importance. But it had wide ramifications. Grant became so deeply engrossed in the project that he turned against the dangerous Cuban belligerency proposal. The disgraceful quarrel over the annexation treaty cleared the way for a pact with England, because Sumner and Motley were removed, and because Grant, who had formerly favored the Senator's extravagant claims for indirect damages, changed his views and became more friendly to a settlement on a reasonable basis. Altogether, the Santo Domingo imbroglio was a godsend to the prudent policies of the long-suffering Secretary Fish.

John Bull Goes the Whole Way

Meanwhile Anglo-American negotiations had been making headway. An adjustment of the *Alabama* claims was complicated, however, by two other problems that clamored for attention. First, there was the dangerous North Atlantic fisheries question. With the Treaty of 1854 at an end, the Canadian authorities were causing great dissatisfaction among American fishermen by an illiberal interpretation of the old Convention of 1818. Secondly, there were periodic flare-ups over the

---

he permitted his name to be used to influence wealthy Britons to invest in unprofitable mining stock. Beckles Willson, *America's Ambassadors to England* (N.Y., 1929), pp. 358–367.

[23] Nevins, *Hamilton Fish*, p. 463. For a view more favorable to Sumner see Tansill, *The United States and Santo Domingo*, pp. 453 ff.

Northwest water boundary, which involved ownership of the small but strategically located San Juan Islands.[24]

Informal conversations were begun in Washington, in July, 1869, when the Canadian Minister of Finance, Sir John Rose, a canny Scot who had made both reputation and fortune in Canada, arrived on a confidential mission. Secretary Fish advised the postponement of negotiations until the unfortunate effects of the Johnson-Clarendon treaty

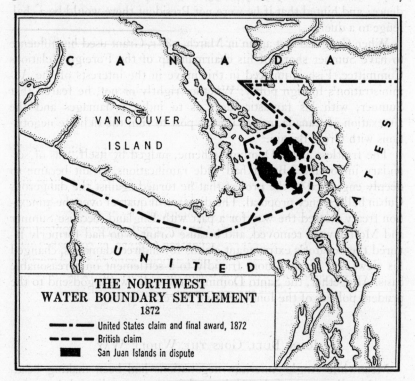

THE NORTHWEST
WATER BOUNDARY SETTLEMENT
1872
———·——— United States claim and final award, 1872
——————— British claim
▮▮▮ San Juan Islands in dispute

rejection and the Sumner speech were less keenly felt. Rose, still in an unofficial capacity, then went to England, where he discussed the problem with leading men. He found the atmosphere rather favorable to a general settlement, for the ticklish international situation was threatening to involve Britain in a war in which her enemies might unleash dozens of *Alabamas* upon her.

In January, 1871, a year and a half after the initial conversations, Rose returned to Washington. He was authorized to inform Fish that

---

[24] For a detailed discussion of this problem see Shippee, *Canadian-American Relations*, pp. 240–261.

Downing Street was ready to settle the outstanding disputes. Although not willing to admit liability for damage done by the *Alabama*, Great Britain was prepared to submit the question to arbitration.[25] After a good deal of informal negotiation, preliminary arrangements were made for a joint commission which would meet in Washington to draw up a treaty. Rose then bowed himself out of the picture, and the British minister in Washington concluded the final agreement.

The first meeting of the Joint High Commission was held in Washington on February 27, 1871; the last on May 8. The five Americans, on the whole able men, were headed by Secretary Fish. The five British representatives, a truly distinguished group, included the Canadian Prime Minister, Sir John A. MacDonald, who championed Dominion interests. Fish declined the honor of being named chairman, preferring that the discussions be kept informal. The best spirit prevailed on both sides, particularly in view of the recent bitterness of feeling. Nor were the social amenities neglected. Diversions included a spring fox hunt in Virginia, and a round of balls and receptions, during which both sides entertained lavishly.[26]

The final treaty, a lengthy document consisting of forty-three articles, was comprehensive in scope.[27] The San Juan boundary dispute, which had threatened to disrupt the negotiations, was referred to the German Emperor as arbitrator. The perennial fisheries controversy took more time than any other—seventeen sessions, as compared with ten for the *Alabama* claims. The final articles gave to the Americans much more extensive privileges than the Treaty of 1818, and permitted them to engage in the sea fishery, virtually without restriction, along the shores of the provinces of Quebec, Nova Scotia, and New Brunswick, the colony of Prince Edward's Island, and numerous small islands. In return, British subjects were permitted to fish along the coast of the United States as far south as the 39th parallel, approximately the latitude of Delaware Bay. Since the Canadians insisted that this was not a fair exchange, provision was made for a commission to

[25] At dinner tables and elsewhere Rose did much to moderate the views of the leading New York editors, as well as those of some in the West. See R. C. Clark, "The Diplomatic Mission of Sir John Rose, 1871," *Pacific Northwest Quar.*, XXVII (1936), 227–242.

[26] At one of Fish's dinners a newspaper reporter concealed himself under the table and took notes on the conversation. Nevins, *Hamilton Fish*, p. 473.

[27] Articles of secondary importance provided for the settlement of such disputes as claims for damages growing out of the war (except commerce destroyers), the navigation of the St. Lawrence, the use of canals, the navigation of Lake Michigan, duty on lumber cut in Maine, and the conveyance of merchandise in bond through the United States.

award an appropriate cash equivalent to that nation which had made the greater sacrifice. Even this concession, which Sir John A. MacDonald agreed to under protest, caused great dissatisfaction in Canada.[28]

THE JOINT HIGH COMMISSION.

Reconciliation of JOHN and JONATHAN. — Felicitations over the great Anglo-Saxon Victory.

John Bull and Uncle Sam felicitate each other on the Treaty of Washington, while the Irishman in the background, with a whisky bottle in his pocket, looks disgusted. (From *Harper's Weekly.*)

More spectacular was the disposition of the *Alabama* claims. The treaty provided for an arbitral commission of five members, to be ap-

[28] MacDonald was in a difficult position, for he had to uphold the claims of Canada against both the United States and his British colleagues. For the reception of the treaty in Canada, and MacDonald's successful fight to secure enactment of the legislation to carry it into effect, see Shippee, *Canadian-American Relations,* pp. 381-425.

pointed by the rulers of Great Britain, the United States, Italy, the Swiss Confederation, and Brazil. The British inserted in the treaty a frank expression of regret for the escape of the *Alabama*—an unusual if not unique international apology. They further agreed to a set of rules, defining neutral obligations, which were to guide the arbitrators in their decision. These stipulations went beyond generally accepted international law, and amounted to a virtual surrender of the British case, leaving the arbitral body a mere fact-finding commission. Unfortunately, it proved impolitic to insert in the treaty a categorical statement ruling out all claims for indirect damages. Such a renunciation would have antagonized the Senate.

In general, the press of the United States was enthusiastic about the settlement. The New York *World* was but one of a number of newspapers to discover that "nearly all of the concessions were made on the British side." There was, however, some dissatisfaction among fishermen and among those ardently in favor of the annexation of Canada.[29] The Senate spent several days wrangling over the treaty, while petitions favoring ratification showered upon it. The Democrats, for partisan reasons, voted against the settlement, though some of them secretly favored it. On May 24, 1871, the Senate consented to ratification by a vote of 50 to 12.

THE CRISIS AT GENEVA

The arbitral tribunal that gathered by the quiet waters of Lake Geneva, in Switzerland, as provided by the treaty, was on the whole an able body. President Grant chose the judicious and able Charles Francis Adams. Queen Victoria unfortunately selected the Lord Chief Justice of England, Sir Alexander Cockburn, an excitable Briton of French ancestry who antagonized his colleagues by his supercilious manner, and who, when angry, pounded the table so hard as to knock stationery onto the floor. The Swiss, Brazilian, and Italian members were men of varying legal ability.

The tribunal met on December 15, 1871, to receive the printed arguments. The lengthy American case most unexpectedly revived indirect damages, including the entire cost of the war since the battle of Gettysburg (a period of about two years) *with seven per cent interest.* The ordinarily cautious Fish apparently authorized the inclusion of indirect damages because he feared that if they were ignored Congress might refuse to execute the treaty. It also seemed wise to

[29] *Ibid.*, pp. 377–381.

dispose of the issue once and for all, since it would almost certainly bob up through the ensuing years to embroil Anglo-American relations.

It will be remembered that nothing whatever was said in the treaty about indirect damages. The British assumed, therefore, that the question had been dropped by tacit agreement. The unexpected reaffirmation of these "monstrous" claims led to a tremendous outcry in England, and to widespread charges that the British had been made the victims of a dishonorable Yankee trick.[30] It was conceivable that Great Britain, according to the calculations of Prime Minister Gladstone, might be assessed a sum totaling the enormous figure of $8,000,000,-000, as compared with the $1,000,000,000 that Germany had recently exacted from conquered France. *Punch* expressed a not uncommon sentiment:

> Very likely 'twere cheaper at once to risk fight
> Than to venture a ruinous payment,
> Which would serve but to arm the unquenchable spite
> Of the cunning, unscrupulous claimant.
> For we fools having paid those 'cute Yankees in full
> An indemnity heavy as France's,
> A fresh quarrel they'd pick, and to war with *John Bull,*
> Go supplied by himself with finances.[31]

The demand from angered Britons that arbitration be abandoned grew to such proportions that the Ministry was in danger of being overthrown—and with it the treaty.

An ominous undertone of war talk on both sides spurred friends of peace to exert themselves. Prayers were offered in English churches beseeching divine interposition. The influential editor of the New York *Nation* wrote: "We might find ourselves in war with England to-morrow without more than a dozen men among us being able to say exactly what caused it, or whether it might not have been avoided." [32] The prospect of hostilities caused panicky European investors to unload their American securities on a cascading market. The crisis was costing the United States each day far more in dollars and cents than

---

[30] The English humor magazine *Fun* had John Bull tell Jonathan, "Look here my young friend! If you don't stop that howling about indirect damages, I'll give you some direct damages to howl for!" XV (n.s.), 132 (March 30, 1872).

[31] *Punch*, LXII, 55 (Feb. 10, 1872).

[32] New York *Nation*, XIV, 181 (March 21, 1872).

it could reasonably expect from the Geneva Tribunal. In the face of such pressure, the American press began to veer around and urge the Administration to exert itself in the direction of moderation. Desperate attempts by both sides to effect a compromise ended in failure, primarily because neither was willing to concede enough. During the late spring of 1872 the treaty hung by a hair.[33]

BRITAIN PAYS THE PIPER

The Geneva Tribunal was saved—and with it perhaps the Treaty of Washington and peace as well—by a somewhat irregular proceeding. Acting in close accord with the American representatives, Charles Francis Adams induced his colleagues on the Tribunal to rule out the indirect claims, although that question was not then before it for adjudication.[34] So, on June 19, 1872, the arbitrators took matters into their own hands and rendered an "extrajudicial" decision to the effect that if they were competent to decide on the indirect claims they would find them insupportable in law. The American government acquiesced—Fish had made his gesture to public opinion and precedent—and the deliberations continued.[35]

The final decision was handed down on September 14, 1872. The Tribunal found that Britain had violated the rules of "due diligence" agreed upon in the Treaty of Washington in the case of the *Alabama* and two other cruisers, and awarded to the United States the sum of $15,500,000. Applause burst forth from the hushed audience, and outside the hall salvos of artillery heralded the victory for peace. The choleric Cockburn filed a violent and voluminous dissenting opinion, and departed unceremoniously from the room. Fortunately, the British public showed a greater degree of sportsmanship, though it cannot be said that they were overjoyed by the decision. The general feeling

[33] On May 3, 1872, Minister Schenck, in England, came home and threw his hat down. "It is all over. This is the end of the treaty." "Very well, sir," replied his young secretary, Woodhull, "we shall fight Great Britain, and, thank God, we are ready for it!" F. W. Hackett, *Reminiscences of the Geneva Tribunal of Arbitration, 1872* (Boston, 1911), p. 202 n.

[34] Brainerd Dyer, *The Public Career of William M. Evarts* (Berkeley, Calif., 1933), pp. 123–126.

[35] J. C. B. Davis, in charge of the American case, dipped liberally into his $250,-000 expense account in order to create a backfire of sentiment, through the press and other agencies in Continental Europe, favorable to the American position. The Tribunal may not have been impervious to this influence. Nevins, *Hamilton Fish*, pp. 554–556.

seems to have been that England was lucky to come out of the affair as well as she did. ". . . We simply wanted," declared the London *Times*, "the judgment of five men of sense and honor; we have obtained it, and we cheerfully abide by it." [36]

THE SEQUEL TO GENEVA

But what of the other three arbitrations provided for by the Treaty of Washington? On October 21, 1872, the German Emperor upheld the contention of the United States regarding the San Juan Islands. Thus Grant could proudly declare, on the eve of the election of 1872, that not only had the *Alabama* claims been settled but that for the first time in the history of the republic there was no boundary dispute with Great Britain.

The commission established to consider the general claims of both sides met in Washington from September, 1871, to September, 1873. The sum of $1,929,819 was awarded to Great Britain, while the American claims were all disallowed.

After considerable delay the fisheries commission met at Halifax, June, 1877, and in November awarded $5,500,000 to Great Britain. Many Americans felt that the sum was excessive and unfair, and the United States commissioner, like Cockburn, refused to sign the award.[37] The amount assessed was belatedly and reluctantly paid.

The final result of the awards under the Treaty of Washington was that the United States received $15,500,000 from Great Britain, and paid to her $7,429,819, netting only about $8,000,000. There was considerable resentment in America that the *Alabama* award should have been thus whittled down. But few today will deny that on the whole the settlements were advantageous to both parties.

In assessing the Treaty of Washington, we may conclude that it was the greatest triumph for arbitral methods that the world had yet witnessed. It provided for four significant arbitrations, three of them of major importance. It was one of those periodic purgations that dispelled every serious cloud in Anglo-American relations. It was not only Fish's greatest diplomatic success, but it was also the most substantial accomplishment of eight long years of Grantism—an oasis of achievement in a desert of scandal.

[36] London *Times*, Sept. 18, 1872, 7:2. "Cheap at the Price," ran a caption in the London *Fun* (n.s.), XVI, 123 (Sept. 21, 1872).
[37] Dyer, *The Public Career of William M. Evarts*, pp. 207-208.

American Blood on Spanish Soil

Meanwhile the Cuban insurrection had been running its destructive course. A series of disagreeable incidents involving American citizens and property culminated in the *Virginius* affair. This vessel was owned by Cubans, and for several years had notoriously been running arms and supplies into the gore-soaked island. While sailing under papers obtained by perjury and fraud, illegally flying the American flag, and carrying a party of revolutionists and some munitions, she was captured on the high seas (October 31, 1873) by a Spanish warship.

The passengers and crew were brought to Santiago, Cuba, where, after hasty and secret courts-martial, fifty-three of them were summarily shot as pirates, among them a number of Americans and Englishmen. Probably more would have been executed had not Captain Lorraine, of the British warship *Niobe*, arrived in haste and trained his guns on the city.[38]

This insult to the American flag caused an outburst of righteous anger that had no parallel since the firing on Fort Sumter. Indignation meetings were held from Boston to New Orleans. The Cuban *juntas* in the United States, now hopeful of intervention and liberation, capitalized on the incident. Dana's sensational New York *Sun* rang the tocsin of war. The excitement was reciprocated in Spain, where a mob was with difficulty restrained from sacking the American legation.

Fortunately, certain factors in America made for peace. The horrors of the Civil War were still fresh; the United States had no pressing desire to annex Cuba; internal problems absorbed American energy (the panic of 1873 had struck with devastating force the month before); the decrepit navy was in a pitiable condition;[39] and the dubious character of the *Virginius* gave men pause. Though a false step might easily have precipitated war, the country was not in the dangerous mood that existed when the *Maine* went down in 1898.

Secretary Fish dispatched a virtual ultimatum demanding an apology and redress within twelve days. The United States was then close

[38] Lorraine was later feted and presented with a service of plate by the grateful citizenry of New York. Nevada miners sent him a fourteen-pound silver brick. The affair was one of those blood-is-thicker-than-water incidents that helped pave the way for the Anglo-American *rapprochement* at the end of the century.

[39] The *Nation* reported that a naval officer had seriously declared, in speaking of one of the ironclads, that "he had no doubt she could be got to Cuba in calm weather." New York *Nation*, XVII, 364 (Dec. 4, 1873). See also Harold and Margaret Sprout, *The Rise of American Naval Power, 1776–1918* (Princeton, 1939), p. 175.

to war, and naval and military preparations were frantically rushed. But when Fish learned of the questionable character of the *Virginius*, and realized that the wobbling Spanish government could not be pushed too fast or too far, he moderated his demands. After anxious days, Fish worked out an amicable adjustment with the able Spanish minister in Washington, and Spain eventually paid an indemnity of $80,000 to the families of the executed Americans. Less satisfactory was the treatment of the officer responsible for the massacre. He was removed from his command and further "punished" by being promoted to a higher rank.

THE END OF GRANTISM

From 1874 to 1877 diplomacy was largely routine. The energy of the country was absorbed by such occupations as Indian fighting, railroad building, westward expansion, and the tremendous acceleration of the Industrial Revolution. The interest of the people was occupied with inflation agitation, race riots, centennial celebrations, the Beecher adultery scandal, and the Belknap impeachment proceedings —to mention only a few headlines.

There were, however, certain diplomatic problems of at least secondary importance. Border difficulties with Mexico resulted in the usual demands for intervention, which the Administration successfully resisted. Bickerings arose with Britain over the execution of the Treaty of Washington. And the Cuban insurrection, dragging to its sanguinary close, was always a potential combustible. In the latter part of 1875 the interventionists renewed their pressure on Grant. But Secretary Fish succeeded in preserving a hands-off policy and in persuading the President to take another strong stand against interference in his annual message to Congress.

Fish took an important step when, on November 5, 1875, he proposed that the six principal European Powers bring diplomatic pressure upon Spain to end the war in Cuba. But this famous dispatch (No. 266), which was criticized in the United States as an unfortunate departure from the Monroe Doctrine,[40] came to nothing. Europe gave it a chilly reception, and Spain countered with enough concessions to take the edge off the American proposal.

Hamilton Fish could lay down the Secretaryship of State in 1877

---

[40] The historian of the Monroe Doctrine concludes that this view was incorrect because Fish envisaged diplomatic rather than forcible intervention. Dexter Perkins, *The Monroe Doctrine, 1867–1907* (Baltimore, 1937), p. 110.

knowing that, even with old-man-of-the-sea Grant on his back, he had made no irreparable blunders; that he had avoided some which the President had seemed bent on making; that he had averted possible war with Great Britain and Spain; and that he had either settled or arranged for the settlement of every pressing diplomatic problem. If by their fruits Secretaries of State are known, the long-suffering and prudent Fish deserves a high place among them.

BIBLIOGRAPHICAL NOTE

By far the most important book on the diplomacy of the Grant administration is Allan Nevins' lengthy and revealing *Hamilton Fish* (N.Y., 1936), upon which this chapter has drawn heavily. Briefer, and written without benefit of Fish's diary, is J. V. Fuller, "Hamilton Fish," in S. F. Bemis, ed., *The American Secretaries of State and their Diplomacy* (N.Y., 1928), VII, 125–214. C. F. Adams, "The Treaty of Washington: Before and After," in his *Lee at Appomattox and Other Papers* (Boston, 1902), pp. 31–255, is an older, though still valuable, account based in part on the Fish papers. C. C. Tansill, *The United States and Santo Domingo, 1798–1873* (Baltimore, 1938), treats Grant's relation to Santo Domingo, and corrects a number of errors given currency by older works like Rhodes and Oberholtzer. The most recent scholarly account of Canadian-American affairs during these years is L. B. Shippee, *Canadian-American Relations, 1849– 1874* (New Haven, 1939). Brainerd Dyer, *The Public Career of William M. Evarts* (Berkeley, Calif., 1933), Ch. VIII, throws some new light on the Geneva Tribunal. F. E. Chadwick, *The Relations of the United States and Spain: Diplomacy* (N.Y., 1909), Ch. XVII, has a full treatment of the *Virginius* affair. Further references: see footnotes of this chapter and Bemis and Griffin, *Guide*, pp. 397–415.

RECENT REFERENCES. Goldwin Smith, *The Treaty of Washington, 1871: A Study in Imperial History* (Ithaca, N.Y., 1941), is a compact monograph written from the point of view of Canada's relations with the Empire. It does not supplant Nevins' *Fish* and Shippee's *Canadian-American Relations*, but is a useful supplement to them, particularly on Canadian public opinion. J. P. Baxter, 3rd, "The British High Commissioners at Washington in 1871," Mass. Hist. Soc. *Procs.*, LXV (1940), 334–357, is a useful sketch, especially strong on personalities.

NEW REFERENCES. I-Mien Tsiang, *The Question of Expatriation in America Prior to 1907* (Baltimore, 1942), relates the Anglo-American convention of 1870 to the *Alabama* and San Juan problems. F. W. Howay, W. N. Sage, and H. F. Angus, *British Columbia and the United States* (Toronto, 1942), shows that although annexation was a distinct possibility, the petition of 1869–1870 to Grant contained only 104 names out of some 10,000 white inhabitants, and more than half of the 104 were Germans or Jews (p. 207). Two works by Hunter Miller are definitive: *San Juan Archipelago: Study of the Joint Occupation of San Juan Island* (Bellows Falls, Vt., 1943); and *Northwest Water Boundary: Report of the Experts Summoned by the German Emperor* ... (Seattle, Wash., 1942).

4TH ED. REFS. A monographic treatment is William D'Arcy, *The Fenian Movement in the United States: 1858–1886* (Washington, 1947).

CHAPTER XXVI

The Nadir of Diplomacy, 1877–1889

"We have separated ourselves so completely from the affairs of other people that it is difficult to realize how large a place they occupied when the government was founded."

Henry Cabot Lodge, 1889.

DIPLOMACY IN THE DOLDRUMS

THE American people are normally far more interested in their own domestic affairs than in their relations with foreign nations. This was strikingly evident during the two decades following the *Virginius* crisis of 1873. So little concerned were the rank and file of the American people with diplomacy that the New York *Sun* could declare in 1889: ". . . The diplomatic service has outgrown its usefulness. . . . It is a costly humbug and sham. It is a nurse of snobs. It spoils a few Americans every year, and does no good to anybody. Instead of making ambassadors, Congress should wipe out the whole service." [1]

How can this indifference be explained? First of all, the sore spots in Anglo-American relations had been salved by the Treaty of Washington. The remaining source of danger, Cuba, was temporarily removed when the Spanish government, by sheer force and seductive promises, stamped out the insurrection. Elsewhere in the world there were no great wars threatening to embroil the American people. The one possible exception was troubled Ireland, where disorders reached a high point in the eighties. The outraged Irish voter in the United States demanded cavalier treatment of the mother country—and frequently his desires were gratified. [2]

During the years after the Civil War the energies of the American people were absorbed by an amazing industrial transformation. The

---

[1] Quoted in *Public Opinion*, VI, 367 (Feb. 9, 1889). In 1892 the New York *Herald* conducted a campaign in which it insisted that with the invention of the cable foreign ministers were no longer necessary. *"Abolish our foreign Ministers!"* it cried. "Recall our farcical diplomats!" See issue of Nov. 14, 1892, 3:1–5.

[2] In 1886, the Senate refused to include dynamiters in the extradition treaty with England because a considerable number of Irishmen had been involved in efforts to blow up British buildings. See New York *Nation*, XLIII, 130 (Aug. 12, 1886).

consequent economic maladjustments brought about a number of crusades for popular panaceas, notably greenbacks and free silver. At the same time the enormous task of conquering the continent involved railroad building, Indian fighting, buffalo shooting, homesteading, and other pursuits. These were the years, also, of close and colorful presidential elections; and politics was the great national game. In brief, Americans were so busy with their own affairs that, in the absence of compelling issues of foreign policy, they had little time to give to their relations with other Powers. This preoccupation explains, in part, why the navy was allowed to fall into a dangerous state of decay. Indeed, it was only with great difficulty, and in the face of strong apathy, that Congress appropriated money in 1883 for four modern steel ships, which were to form the nucleus of the new navy.[3]

The five Secretaries of State from 1877 to 1893, with one exception, were without previous diplomatic experience (see Appendix C), and they were appointed primarily for political reasons. There were reversals of policy when Democratic administrations succeeded Republican, and even reversals within the same administration. Whatever continuity existed in the State Department was provided in large measure by two extraordinarily useful public servants, William Hunter and A. A. Adee.[4] Hunter entered the Department in 1829, and served for fifty-seven years, eventually becoming Second Assistant Secretary of State. Adee came in 1878, rose to the rank of Second Assistant Secretary, and remained altogether for forty-seven years, dying in 1924, at the age of eighty-two.[5] From 1829 to 1924, a period of nearly one hundred years, either Hunter or Adee was behind the front lines with his remarkable knowledge of precedent, international law, and diplomatic procedure. This partially explains why the inexperienced Secretaries of State made so few serious mistakes.

[3] An able account of the development of the new Navy is Harold and Margaret Sprout, *The Rise of American Naval Power* (Princeton, 1939), pp. 165–201.

[4] John Bassett Moore, the distinguished authority on international law, served the Department at various times and in various capacities from 1885 to 1914.

[5] When, in 1882, Adee was made Third Assistant Secretary of State, his friend John Hay telegraphed, "God bless you, my boy; the country is safe." Tyler Dennett, *John Hay* (N.Y., 1933), p. 197. This was more than a witticism. Deaf, retiring, unmarried, Adee would install a cot in his office when the pressure of work became great. For thirty years scarcely a written communication went out until he had passed on it. Thousands of them he drafted himself with his extraordinarily facile pen. See *Dictionary of American Biography*, I, 105–107.

"THE CHINESE MUST GO!"

Like President Grant, whom he succeeded in March, 1877, Rutherford B. Hayes was a war hero and a Republican. Two persistently vexatious problems in the field of foreign affairs continued to harass his Administration.

Disorders along the Mexican border during these years were so destructive of American life and property that the Secretary of War, on June 1, 1877, issued an order authorizing American troops to pursue marauders across the border.[6] The government of Mexico resented this move as an invasion of the nation's sovereignty, and orders were issued to repel any such incursions by force. The Mexican press clamored for war, and in the United States enemies of the Administration castigated Hayes for having taken so belligerent a course. But outrages along the border were such a hackneyed story that it was difficult to sustain public interest in them. As the situation in Mexico straightened out under the iron hand of Porfirio Díaz, the objectionable order was withdrawn, February 24, 1880.

Much more unusual was the diplomatic problem aroused by the influx of Chinese coolies from the seemingly inexhaustible "hives" of the Orient. Although the docile and industrious "John Chinaman" had at first been welcomed as a laborer, he and his brothers continued to come in such numbers—they totaled 75,000 in California in 1880, or nine per cent of the population—as to cause increasing alarm. Perhaps the most serious objection voiced against the Chinese was an economic one. Able to live in a hovel and subsist on "the smell of a greasy rag," they could undercut the white man and sabotage his standard of living. The fundamental objection to the Orientals was not that they were inefficient but that they were too efficient.[7] In a catch-as-catch-can contest, the beefeater had no chance against the rice eater. The present thousands were regarded as a menace; the prospective millions as a calamity. Alarmed Californians sang:

> Oust the pagans, far and near,
> From your fields and homes so dear,

[6] R. D. Gregg, *The Influence of Border Troubles on Relations between the United States and Mexico, 1876–1910* (Baltimore, 1937), pp. 50 ff. At one time feeling was so strong in Mexico City that the United States minister fled from the theater he was attending and sought refuge in the American legation. Brainerd Dyer, *The Public Career of William M. Evarts* (Berkeley, Calif., 1933), p. 198.

[7] The New York *Nation* ironically noted that the Chinese had caused much alarm on the Pacific Coast by perpetuating "those disgusting habits of thrift, industry, and self-denial. . . ." XXXVII, 152 (Aug. 23, 1883).

Falter not, your duty's clear;
They or you must go.[8]

Almost from the first the Orientals were subjected to discrimination
and some physical abuse, as white "foreign devils" had been in China.[9]
Conditions became much worse in the early seventies, when hard times
drove to the Golden State large numbers of economic derelicts, including many Irishmen, who showed the usual contempt of the older
immigrant for the newer. San Francisco overflowed with malcontents
and thugs, who vented their wrath on the defenseless and thrifty
Chinese. Hoodlums, young and old, dumped his freshly ironed laun-
dry into the mire; set dogs upon him; stoned and kicked him; fired
his house; put his priceless queue "under the scissors" ("chasing pig-
tails" was a favorite sport of adolescent rowdies); and even murdered him.[10] In the courts he did not have "a Chinaman's chance."
He invariably came out on the short end—not infrequently the rope's
end.

The king of the San Francisco hoodlums was Denis Kearney, an
Irish-born and recently naturalized agitator of great power and volu-
bility. Exhibiting four feet of noosed hemp, he yelled to his wild
"sand lot" following, "The Chinese must go!" Or, as some of his
unnaturalized Irish adherents shouted, "Immeriky fur Immerikans,
bejabers." An enterprising saloonkeeper caught the spirit when he
solicited trade with verse:

His drinks are A 1 and his prices are low,
His motto is always, "The Chinese Must Go!"
So call on your friends, workingmen, if you please,
Take a good solid drink and drive out the Chinese.[11]

This agitation, which came to a head in the summer of 1877, resulted
in boycotts against Oriental labor, and the open murdering of some
of the Chinese.

[8] Quoted in E. P. Oberholtzer, *A History of the United States* (N.Y., 1931), IV,
278.
[9] See R. W. Paul, "The Origin of the Chinese Issue in California," *Miss. Valley
Hist. Rev.*, XXV (1938), 185 *ff.*
[10] Bret Harte's obituary to Wan Lee is a classic: "Dead, my reverend friends,
dead. Stoned to death in the streets of San Francisco, in the year of grace 1869
by a mob of half grown boys and Christian school children." L. L. Hazard, *The
Frontier in American Literature* (N.Y., 1927), p. 197.
[11] Quoted in R. G. Cleland, *A History of California: the American Period* (N.Y.,
1922), p. 419.

The Closed Door for China

Members of Congress from the Pacific Coast were not slow to take up the cry of their constituents for legislation excluding Orientals. On this issue the West was supported by the Irish (there was no "Chinese vote"), and by labor in general. Opposition to Oriental exclusion came from employers, steamship companies, railroad lines, and missionaries. Throughout the East, however, there was considerable indifference to the problem, and in some quarters a "holier than thou attitude" infuriating to the Californians. The San Francisco *Argonaut* painted an unfair, though typically Western, picture of the Chinese when it remonstrated:

Let a colony of these Asiatic brethren, with souls to save, camp down beside Boston Common, with their filthy habits, their criminal practices, and their nasty vices, and how long would it be before Beacon Hill would sniff the polluted atmosphere, and all the overgodly of New England would send up their prayers for relief.[12]

The big stumbling block to Chinese exclusion was the Burlingame Treaty of 1868, which solemnly guaranteed to Chinese the right of unrestricted immigration to the United States. Despite this compact, Congress took the bit in its teeth and passed a law in 1879 forbidding any ship to bring more than fifteen Chinese to the United States on one trip. President Hayes, a man of sterling honesty, found that the law amounted to virtual exclusion, and vetoed it (March 1, 1879) as contravening the Burlingame Treaty. His action was greeted with execration in the West, where flags were hung at half-staff and "Missey" Hayes was burned in effigy.[13] But the Eastern newspapers found the message "wise and manly." It had, said the New York *Tribune*, "saved the character of the country from humiliation among the family of nations."

The only honorable way to bring about Chinese exclusion was to revise the Burlingame pact. A special commission of three Americans journeyed to Peking and there negotiated the Treaty of 1880, which gave the United States the right to "regulate, limit or suspend" but not "absolutely prohibit" the immigration of Chinese laborers. After another heated battle in Congress a bill was passed suspending immi-

[12] San Francisco *Argonaut*, II, 5 (Jan. 19, 1878).
[13] C. R. Williams, ed., *Diary and Letters of Rutherford Birchard Hayes* (Columbus, Ohio, 1924), III, 525–526 (Feb. 28, 1879).

gration from China for twenty years. President Arthur, now Chief Executive, vetoed it, on April 4, 1882, as an "unreasonable" restriction rather than a suspension as provided for by the treaty. Many Eastern journals praised the President, but the West again burst into a blaze of indignation. Flags were hung at half-mast in San Francisco, and merchants draped their stores in black, while labor organizations in the larger Eastern cities upheld the demands of their Western brethren by parades and mass meetings.

Congress reconsidered its action and passed the law of 1882, which suspended Chinese immigration for only ten years. President Arthur approved the bill, and the West rejoiced over this temporary relief. The Act of 1882, which was later renewed and strengthened,[14] constituted a radical departure from America's policy of maintaining a haven for the oppressed and underprivileged of every race and clime. American missionaries found it embarrassingly difficult to explain why a Chinaman could go to the white man's heaven but not to the white man's country.[15]

The exclusion law of 1882 did not, however, stop anti-Chinese outbursts in America. Continued agitation was much too profitable for the demagogue and the salaried labor organizer. Ill feeling came to a head at Rock Springs, Wyoming, in the late summer of 1885, when the whites arose and attacked some five hundred docile Chinese miners, massacring twenty-eight in cold blood and wounding fifteen others. Riots hardly less serious occurred elsewhere in the West. There was, however, no danger of war with the weak Celestial Empire, though there was some talk in China of a boycott and other reprisals. The Peking government, which was accustomed to receive prompt and onerous demands for indemnity from the Occidental powers following anti-"foreign devil" disorders, made vigorous representations at Washington. But here it encountered the gap in federal jurisdiction: the United States government had no authority over purely state disorders. In 1887 Congress, braving the displeasure of labor and the Pacific Coast, voted an indemnity of $147,000 as a matter of comity and not of right.

[14] The Act of 1882, as amended in 1884, did not expire until 1894; but in 1892, on the eve of a presidential election, Congress enacted an even more stringent Chinese exclusion law. Subsequent legislation kept the bars firmly in place. M. R. Coolidge, *Chinese Immigration* (N.Y., 1909), pp. 168 ff.

[15] *Puck* gibed: "'But why is it,' asked the thoughtful Chinese, 'that I may go to your heaven while I may not go to your country?' The American missionary shrugged his shoulders. 'There's no labor vote in heaven!' said he." Quoted in *Literary Digest*, XXI, 796 (Dec. 29, 1900).

Extending the American Coast Line

While Denis Kearney was busy exhorting his hoodlums, another foreign-born promoter was causing the American people considerable concern. In 1879 a French company, headed by the dynamic Ferdinand de Lesseps, builder of the Suez Canal, began to push its plan for separating the two continents at Panama. The American people, who had long dreamed of constructing the waterway themselves, became somewhat alarmed, for they could not tolerate foreign control of this commercial nerve center.[16] Even though the company was a private one, the French government might find it necessary to intervene for the protection of so enormous an investment of capital.

On March 8, 1880, President Hayes sent a vigorous message to Congress in which he declared that the proposed canal would be "virtually a part of the coast line of the United States" and that "the policy of this country is a canal under American control." The press responded most cordially to Hayes' stirring sentiments, which resurrected Monroeism and jolted the French. Within the year both houses of Congress protested against a canal built by foreign capital or controlled by foreign regulations.

Two weeks before Hayes' surprising message, de Lesseps, still enthusiastic in spite of his seventy-five years, arrived in the United States. He was primarily a promoter, and his chief purposes were to propitiate American public opinion and raise funds.[17] He toured the country as far west as San Francisco, and his magnetic personality and great reputation attracted much favorable attention. In New York he gave a grand banquet at Delmonico's to six hundred of the "right people." He also created an American advisory board, and made Secretary of the Navy Thompson its head at a salary of $25,000. Although Thompson was forced to resign after accepting this position, the connection of so prominent a figure with the enterprise tended to give it an American character, which is exactly what the far-sighted de Lesseps intended. The sum of $1,500,000 was judiciously spent on editors, politicians, bankers, lobbyists (and allegedly on Congressmen) in an effort to create a favorable or at least an acquiescent sentiment. So much money was poured out that when de Lesseps' enterprise finally crashed, the New York *Nation* queried:

---

[16] See Dexter Perkins, *The Monroe Doctrine, 1867–1907* (Baltimore, 1937), pp. 71 *ff*. The author concludes that the principles of the Monroe Doctrine were not at variance with an internationalized canal.

[17] E. B. White, *American Opinion of France* (N.Y., 1927), pp. 221 *ff*.

Are we never to know how much it cost to draw the fangs of the Monroe Doctrine during those critical years, or who were the men superintending the operation? Such dentistry not only comes high, but also requires great skill, and the public is entitled to know who the expert operators were.[18]

But one should not overestimate the influence of de Lesseps' money and propaganda. The American people refused to become unduly concerned because many of them believed that the task was too formidable for the French company, and because most of them were busy with other things.

"Jingo Jim" Blaine

The Republican party was continued in office when, in 1881, the amiable James A. Garfield succeeded Hayes as President. The outstanding figure in the party was James G. Blaine, the brilliant "Plumed Knight" from Maine, who, like Seward in 1860, had been passed over in favor of a more available candidate. His appointment to the position of Secretary of State was a foregone conclusion, particularly in view of his close friendship with President Garfield. Under these circumstances Blaine could hardly avoid regarding himself as the "premier" of the Administration.

Although the new Secretary had great personal magnetism, a quick mind, and a lively imagination, he was totally without diplomatic experience and without formal training in the law, whether domestic or international.[19] His profession, aside from politics, had been journalism; and the terse style and dogmatic assertiveness of the editor were poor training for diplomatic correspondence. Long years of service in Congress had developed oratorical brilliance and unbending partisanship rather than appreciation of an adversary's point of view—a prime essential in diplomacy. He was accustomed to bask in the limelight and curry popular favor, perhaps not realizing that the best diplomats are those who work the most quietly. His energy, thwarted ambition, and devoted following presaged an aggressive or "spirited" policy, rather than an opportunistic handling of problems as they arose.

One of the earliest difficulties to confront Blaine grew out of the ill-starred de Lesseps enterprise. The American people were beginning to see with increasing clearness the wisdom of constructing the Isth-

[18] New York *Nation*, LVI, 170 (March 9, 1893).
[19] See J. B. Lockey, "James Gillespie Blaine," in S. F. Bemis, ed., *American Secretaries of State and their Diplomacy* (N.Y., 1928), VII, 263 ff.

mian waterway themselves. But it would be folly for them to sink an enormous sum of money into the enterprise unless they could own the canal outright and fortify it against an enemy. This, however, could not be done so long as the Clayton-Bulwer Treaty remained on the books. In the closing days of the Hayes administration, therefore, the House of Representatives formally resolved that the President take immediate steps to abrogate the objectionable pact.

Conscious of the growing public demand, Secretary Blaine entered upon a diplomatic interchange in an effort to induce the British Foreign Office to modify the treaty. He argued that it had been negotiated thirty years earlier under exceptional circumstances which no longer existed; that it offended the spirit of the Monroe Doctrine; and that it impeached "our rightful and long established claim to priority on the American continent." [20] It was therefore desirable, asserted Blaine, that the United States should build and fortify the canal itself.

The "Plumed Knight's" vigorous contentions were not difficult to answer. The British Foreign Secretary, Lord Granville, riddled his arguments, and stood squarely on the treaty. Critics of "Jingo Jim" Blaine accused him of having made a play to the gallery, and contrasted his uncompromising tone with his obvious rebuff at the hands of the British. Though it is true that Blaine advanced some rather extravagant Americanisms, and revealed a certain amount of naïveté, his position was honest and aboveboard. He did not suggest abrogation of the treaty without the consent of Britain, as he might have done. He merely expressed, rather eloquently, the views of a large body of Americans, and even evoked praise from some of his most unfriendly critics. [21]

It is now clear that mere notes, no matter how or by whom drafted, would not have extorted the necessary concessions from England at that time. But Blaine undoubtedly caused the British to think about the problem, and helped prepare their minds for the inevitable. In 1884, three years later, the London *Daily Telegraph* declared that a wise England would not oppose the United States "over the long-forgotten Clayton-Bulwer Treaty, to which few Englishmen attach very great importance." [22] And in 1901, Great Britain surrendered her case when she negotiated the Hay-Pauncefote Treaty, which embodied essentially what Blaine had contended for.

---

[20] *Foreign Relations, 1881*, p. 555 (Nov. 19, 1881).
[21] Alice F. Tyler, *The Foreign Policy of James G. Blaine* (Minneapolis, 1927), p. 40; D. S. Muzzey, *James G. Blaine* (N.Y., 1935), p. 200.
[22] Quoted in New York *Nation*, XL, 5 (Jan. 1, 1885).

Latin America

MEDDLING AND MUDDLING IN SOUTH AMERICA

Like Henry Clay, whom he much admired, Blaine had a deep interest in Latin America. His ideal was to persuade the neighboring republics to accept a kind of "elder sister" relationship. Fundamentally, however, his policy seems to have been influenced by economic rather than altruistic motives. As a "big business" Republican, Blaine was grieved to note that his country's adverse balance of trade with Latin America amounted to something over $100,000,000. This huge disparity was largely due to the fact that the southern republics, though sending enormous quantities of raw materials to the United States, bought the great bulk of their manufactured goods from Europe. Blaine's idea was to dislodge competitors of the United States by forming closer commercial ties with Latin America. And since profitable economic relationships could not exist amid the clash of arms, the United States would use its good offices to terminate wars in Latin America.

Blaine's vigorous ventures as a peacemaker were not altogether appreciated. Finding that a boundary dispute between Mexico and Guatemala might eventuate in war, he pressed arbitration upon the larger republic, revealing at the same time considerable sympathy for the underdog. Mexico politely declined these good offices, and then indignantly rejected them. The upshot was that Blaine neither protected Guatemala nor earned the good will of Mexico. Two other republics, Costa Rica and Colombia, arranged to lay their boundary dispute before European arbiters. Blaine's strong objections to referring so purely an American matter to Europeans, without consulting the United States, resulted in a further harvest of ill will.[23]

A far more serious problem grew out of the War of the Pacific (1879–1884) between Chile on the one hand and Peru and Bolivia on the other. Chile had been overwhelmingly victorious and was demanding the valuable nitrate beds of Peru as her share of the spoils. Blaine opposed territorial cessions in the Americas; but he ran into an impossible situation because Chile had the upper hand and because the American people were patently unwilling to back his policy with force. Nor can it be said that Blaine handled the situation with great skill. His quick, nervous temperament was out of tune with the slower tempo of the Latin. Then, too, the ministers through whom he had to work were unfortunate selections. Hugh J. Kilpatrick, in Chile, strongly espoused the cause of the Chileans, and quarreled bitterly with Stephen

[23] Tyler, *Foreign Policy of James G. Blaine*, pp. 64 ff.

A. Hurlbut, in Peru, who as vigorously championed the Peruvians. The net result of Blaine's well-meaning intermeddling was that he incurred the lasting ill will of Chile, and provided his political enemies with more ammunition.[24]

In pursuance of his policy of promoting peace (and commerce) in Latin America, Blaine also favored the idea of calling an International American Conference to consider methods of preventing war. The general idea, of course, dated back at least to Henry Clay and Bolivar, and since then had received considerable support in Latin America itself. Blaine secured the rather unenthusiastic consent of President Arthur, who had succeeded the assassinated Garfield late in 1881, and promptly issued invitations to the Latin American republics. Three weeks later, finding himself increasingly out of harmony with the new President's faction of the Republican party, Blaine felt obliged to resign. The abrupt reduction of his "premiership" from a prospective eight years to ten months was one of the bitterest disappointments of a life filled with frustration.

REPUBLICAN REVERSALS OF POLICY

Blaine's successor—and in many ways his antithesis—was Frederick Frelinghuysen, a conservative corporation lawyer of phlegmatic Dutch extraction. His policy was in general the traditional one of opportunistic drifting and negativism—of not going out to look for trouble but settling troubles when they arose.[25] It was said, a bit unkindly, that he regarded the American eagle as a mere hen—past middle age.

Frelinghuysen promptly cancelled Blaine's invitations to the International American Conference, a number of which had been cordially accepted. The reasons advanced for this peremptory and embarrassing step were not altogether satisfying to those who were working for closer co-operation with Latin America. Both Blaine and Arthur were leading contenders for the presidential nomination in 1884; and it is entirely possible that Arthur did not want his rival to appear before

[24] It must be remembered, in assessing Blaine, that during these years he was a leading presidential prospect, and consequently was under bitter attack by enemies in both parties. Shortly after he left office, a House committee investigated charges that his intermeddling in Chile had been motivated by an improper financial interest in the guano and nitrate beds of Peru. Although nothing was proved against Blaine personally, the charge was repeated that he had tried "to put the guano beds in his pocket." Cartoonists featured "guano statesmanship"; and one vicious campaign pamphlet against him was entitled "Meddling and Muddling: Mr. Blaine's Foreign Policy." Muzzey, *Blaine*, p. 213 n.

[25] See P. M. Brown, "Frederick T. Frelinghuysen," in Bemis, *American Secretaries of State*, VIII, 3–6.

the national convention wreathed with Pan-American laurels. Though Blaine and his friends bitterly protested against this unmannerly reversal, and though a considerable body of opinion in the United States continued to agitate for the conference, the average American was apparently content to let matters drift.

But the cautious Secretary Frelinghuysen was not altogether consistent in his stay-at-home policy. A perceptible beginning was made in the direction of co-operation with other nations when the United States became a member of the International Red Cross and participated in the Berlin Conference of 1884 regarding the International Association of the Congo.[26] Although the press emitted the usual groans about forsaking traditions and becoming involved in dangerous entanglements, it had legitimate cause for concern over developments in the Isthmian region.

Blaine, as we have noted, made a spirited but unsuccessful effort to persuade Great Britain to modify the Clayton-Bulwer Treaty. But the ordinarily prudent Frelinghuysen, without even attempting to secure a release from this commitment, negotiated an extraordinary pact with Nicaragua. This instrument made provision for joint ownership of an Isthmian canal, and further stipulated that the United States was to protect the territory of Nicaragua against outside aggression. The publication of the Frelinghuysen-Zavala Treaty naturally caused a sensation. America was not only abrogating her treaty with Great Britain in what many regarded as a dishonorable fashion, but was committing herself to inevitable difficulties in Central America over Nicaragua's boundaries. The pact was still before the Senate, lacking five votes of approval, when a change of administration occurred in March, 1885.

CLEVELAND AND BICKERINGS WITH BRITAIN

Grover Cleveland, the first Democratic President since the Civil War, had risen from the mayoralty of Buffalo to the presidency of the United States in four years. His interests were narrow and his mental visibility low; in fact, he had never been to Washington before he went there to be inaugurated President. He did, however, bring to the administration of foreign affairs a rugged honesty and a determined opposition to imperialism, protectorates, and other foreign entanglements. It did not take him long to decide that the unratified treaty with Nica-

[26] By 1884 the United States had officially participated in only two international conferences. In the next three decades the figure rose to twenty-eight; and in the nineteen thirties the number was sometimes forty or fifty each year. B. H. Williams, *American Diplomacy: Policies and Practice* (N.Y., 1936), p. 19.

Cleveland

ragua was inconsonant with America's obligation to England, and fraught with peril. On March 13, 1885, therefore, he resorted to the rather unusual step of withdrawing the treaty from the Senate.

While the death of the pact made possible the avoidance of grave difficulties with Great Britain in Central America, others of a serious nature arose elsewhere. The United States had found the fisheries provisions of the Treaty of Washington unsatisfactory, and notice had been given of their termination, effective July 1, 1885. The Canadians, irked by this action, fell back upon an illiberal interpretation of the Treaty of 1818, and their cruisers began to arrest American schooners for alleged violations of the regulations. Much ill feeling was aroused by these disagreeable incidents, especially in New England. Henry Cabot Lodge, a young Congressman from the fishing state of Massachusetts, declared, ". . . Whenever the American flag on an American fishing smack is touched by a foreigner, the great American heart is touched." [27]

Popular excitement mounted high early in 1887, when the House passed a bill authorizing the President to retaliate against the Canadians by debarring their ships and their goods from American ports. There was, in fact, considerable talk of an armed clash. The Detroit *News* boasted:

When the next war closes, there should be but one flag floating from the Rio Grande to the pole. The Canadian provinces will make elegant States in the Union. It will be better for them and better for us.

We do not want to fight,
But, by jingo, if we do,
We'll scoop in all the fishing grounds
And the whole Dominion, too. [28]

But the Nashville *American* (Democrat) viewed the problem from a more southerly latitude: ". . . We are very certain that the people of this part of the country are not impatient to undergo the miseries and privations of another war all for the sake of a few hundred Yankee fishermen and a few stinking codfish." [29] Though Cleveland signed the retaliation bill in March, 1887, he had no intention of putting it into execution. He merely planned to use it as a club for extorting concessions.

Continued agitation over the fisheries led to the meeting of a joint

[27] New York *Nation*, XLIV, 417 (May 19, 1887).
[28] *Public Opinion*, II, 346 (Feb. 5, 1887).
[29] *Ibid.*, p. 345 (Feb. 5, 1887).

commission in Washington, on November 22, 1887. The three British representatives were headed by the distinguished Joseph Chamberlain; the three Americans by Secretary of State Bayard. For a time it seemed as if the negotiations would terminate in failure, but timely concessions from Ottawa, together with the personal charm of Chamberlain and the brilliant entertainments at the British legation, contributed to a meeting of minds. The Bayard-Chamberlain pact, signed February 15, 1888, was a compromise yielding substantial advantages to each party and giving promise of ending, for a time at least, the squabble over the fisheries.[30]

But the treaty encountered hopeless odds in the Senate. The Republicans, who controlled that body by a small margin, were acutely conscious of the imminence of the presidential election of 1888. One of them let the cat out of the bag when he said, "We cannot allow the Democrats to take credit for settling so important a dispute." Other members, with the Irish vote in view, wanted to make the President appear to be yielding American interests to the British. Accordingly, the Senate voted to remove the then customary injunction of secrecy so that the Republican speeches against the treaty might go forth to the Irish voters of the country.[31] Senator Hoar of Massachusetts declared that when Grant was in the White House "no petty British officer hauled it [Old Glory] down from an American masthead." Senator Riddleberger of Virginia cried that the Administration "is pro-English from the President to the last Cabinet officer." The Republican press, no less conscious of the Hibernian vote, insisted that Bayard and Cleveland had been "duped"; and the New York *Tribune* was sure that "It was the most barren and dishonorable compact ever made by an American Secretary of State with a foreign power."[32] On August 21, 1888, the Republican Senators killed the treaty by a vote of 27 yeas to 30 nays.

The rejection did not prove disastrous because a working arrangement, already in effect, was continued.[33] But Cleveland felt that since the Republican Senate was not willing to accept a treaty of mutual

[30] The treaty delimited more specifically the waters in which Americans were forbidden to fish; all bays not more than ten miles wide at the mouth were to be treated as territorial waters; and all restrictions were to be removed from the purchase of bait, supplies, and outfits, as well as from the transshipment of the catch and the shipping of crews, whenever the United States removed its duties on the fishery products of Canada and Newfoundland.

[31] W. S. Holt, *Treaties Defeated by the Senate* (Baltimore, 1933), pp. 144 ff.

[32] *Public Opinion*, V, 428 (Aug. 25, 1888).

[33] Americans were entitled to privileges in the ports of British North America upon the payment of a tonnage fee.

concessions, the next logical step was to adopt a strong policy. Accordingly, on August 23, 1888, he sent a sensational message to Congress, nominally aimed at Canada, but really at the Senate. It recommended in no uncertain terms that Congress clothe the Executive with retaliatory power to suspend the transportation of all bonded goods across the Canadian border.

Cleveland was immediately deluged with a snowstorm of telegrams from a host of Rileys, Murphys, and Ryans, who applauded this slap at Britain. "God bless you for your devotion to old Erin," telegraphed one. The Democratic New York *World* was pleased to note that "The Republican fishers for votes were hard hit by the President's unexpected message." [34] So the event proved. For the Republicans, fearing business losses and unwilling to face the logic of their partisan rejection of the treaty, refused to heed Cleveland's recommendation, and there the matter stood.

TRUCKLING TO THE SHAMROCK

The presidential campaign of 1888, in which the Democratic Cleveland ran against the Republican Benjamin Harrison, aroused an extraordinary amount of Anglophobia. Cleveland had courageously made tariff reduction—not free trade—the paramount issue. Great Britain was then the great free trade nation; and the Republicans, who had waxed fat on the high protective tariff, cried that Cleveland had been bribed by English gold. Republican campaign literature portrayed Cleveland under the British flag, Harrison under the American. Slogans used during the campaign were:

"Protection to American Labor, No Free Trade for us."
"America for the Americans—No Free Trade."
"American Wages for American Workingmen."
"Cleveland Runs Well in England." [35]

So delicate was the political situation that when the visiting British statesman, Joseph Chamberlain, became engaged to the daughter of Cleveland's Secretary of War, the secret was carefully guarded until after the election.[36]

[34] *Public Opinion*, V, 445 (Sept. 1, 1888).

[35] Oberholtzer, *History of the United States*, V, 47. A popular Republican campaign document printed the statement, falsely attributed to the London *Times*, "The only time England can use an Irishman is when he emigrates to America and votes for free trade."

[36] Allan Nevins, *Grover Cleveland* (N.Y., 1934), p. 412.

Cleveland's retaliation message had been so pleasing to the Anglophobes as to suggest that it was a bid for Irish support. A Californian by the name of George Osgoodby, who represented himself as a naturalized citizen of English birth and who signed his name Murchison, wrote to the British minister in Washington, Sir Lionel Sackville-West, asking confidentially where Cleveland really stood concerning England. Disregarding the time-honored dictum that diplomats must not interfere in domestic matters, Sackville-West answered the letter and declared that Cleveland, in spite of his retaliation message, was at heart friendly to the mother country. In short, a vote for Cleveland was a vote for England.

Osgoodby turned the letter over to the Republican managers, whose agent he may originally have been. They cleverly held it back until just before the election, and then unloosed it.[37] The Republicans were jubilant; the Irish apoplectic. Van loads of the letter were scattered broadcast. One New York newspaper published a full page facsimile with the significant headlines: "THE BRITISH LION'S PAW THRUST INTO AMERICAN POLITICS TO HELP CLEVELAND." "Bounce him," cried the New York *World*.

Cleveland waited a day; but Sackville-West's excuses were weak, and he made matters worse by talking to reporters. The Democratic National Committee telegraphed that the Irish vote "is slipping out of our hands because of diplomatic shilly-shallying." The British Foreign Secretary, Lord Salisbury, who was greatly annoyed by this low electioneering trick, refused to throw his minister to the Irish without a dignified investigation of the affair. But the election was just a few days off; so Cleveland peremptorily dismissed Sackville-West. The Republican New York *Tribune* published a jingle in which Cleveland addressed John Bull:

> Believe me that I made him go
> For nothing that he wrote,
> But just because, as well you know,
> I feared the Irish vote! [38]

It is possible, though not demonstrable, that the Sackville-West incident cost Cleveland the close election of 1888. Certainly the affair further embittered Anglo-American relations. The British press, as

---

[37] *Ibid.*, p. 430.

[38] New York *Tribune*, Nov. 4, 1888, 7:2. Sackville-West declined to accept the offer of a New York "Hippodrome" and "Wild West" show to appear on exhibition for $2,000 a week. Beckles Willson, *Friendly Relations* (Boston, 1934), p. 259.

well as the Foreign Office, was greatly displeased by the indecent haste with which Sackville-West had been bundled out of the United States. Lord Salisbury indicated his displeasure by refusing to fill the vacancy until Cleveland had left office several months later. This unfortunate incident strikingly indicates that during these years foreign affairs were of secondary importance, and that friendly relations with a great foreign Power were a minor consideration when compared with possible political advantage.

BIBLIOGRAPHICAL NOTE

The diplomacy of the years from 1877 to 1889 is covered with reasonable detail, though from a biographical point of view, in S. F. Bemis, ed., *The American Secretaries of State and their Diplomacy* (N.Y., 1928), VII, VIII. Secretary Evarts is more fully treated in Brainerd Dyer, *The Public Career of William M. Evarts* (Berkeley, Calif., 1933), Chs. XII, XIII. For a discussion of the canal issue see Dexter Perkins, *The Monroe Doctrine, 1867–1907* (Baltimore, 1937), Ch. II. Alice F. Tyler's *The Foreign Policy of James G. Blaine* (Minneapolis, 1927), is the best work on the subject. D. S. Muzzey, *James G. Blaine* (N.Y., 1935), though much briefer, is helpful. Other useful biographical studies are G. F. Howe, *Chester A. Arthur* (N.Y., 1934); and Allan Nevins, *Grover Cleveland* (N.Y., 1934). M. R. Coolidge, *Chinese Immigration* (N.Y., 1909), is the most detailed study of the problem. E. P. Oberholtzer, *A History of the United States since the Civil War* (5 vols., N.Y., 1917–1937), projects a study of diplomatic problems against the political background. Volume IV, 213–308, has a detailed discussion of the Chinese problem. Further references: see footnotes of this chapter and Bemis and Griffin, *Guide*, pp. 384 *ff.*

RECENT REFERENCES. By far the most exhaustive account of the diplomacy of Cleveland's first administration appears in C. C. Tansill, *The Foreign Policy of Thomas F. Bayard, 1885–1897* (N.Y., 1940). One or more chapters are devoted to the Chinese problem, Corea, the fisheries, the seals, Canadian annexation, the Mexican tangle, and the Sackville-West incident (Ch. XI: "Lord Sackville Gains Immortality by Merely Being Stupid"). It is clear that the British minister increased the enormity of his blunder by impugning the good faith of Cleveland's retaliation message, and in assuming a jaunty attitude toward the reporters. C. L. Barrows, *William M. Evarts* (Chapel Hill, N.C., 1941), has the fullest and most recent account of the diplomacy of Hayes' Secretary of State, with particular attention to the Mexican, Latin American, and Chinese difficulties. For E. C. Sandmeyer's *Anti-Chinese Movement in California*, Perry Belmont's *Recollections*, an article by J. F. Rippy on Barrios and the Nicaraguan Canal, and an article by L. F. Sensabaugh on the United States and the Colombia-Costa Rica arbitration, see Bibliographical Appendix, p. 930.

NEW REFERENCES. For additional works, particularly on the De Lesseps enterprise, the fisheries dispute, Anglo-American relations, and the foreign policy of Cleveland, see Bibliographical Appendix. p. 930.

CHAPTER XXVII

Blaine and Spirited Diplomacy, 1889–1893

"[We view] with alarm the tendency to a policy of irritation and bluster which is liable at any time to confront us with the alternative of humiliation or war."

Democratic Platform, 1892.

THE FIRST INTERNATIONAL AMERICAN CONFERENCE

WHEN Benjamin Harrison came to the White House in 1889 he, like Garfield, was obliged to make a place for Blaine, who was still the outstanding figure in the Republican party. The new President, who did not relish the thought of being overshadowed by his subordinate, reluctantly appointed Blaine as Secretary of State. This step, though considered inevitable, aroused some misgivings, for it was feared that Blaine's thwarted ambition, together with a proneness to take "the hated foreigner by the beard," would inevitably involve the country in war.[1] The Chileans were disturbed, and the Spanish government showed some concern about its Cuban defenses.

By a remarkable coincidence Blaine returned to the Department of State just in time to play host to the First International American Conference (Pan-American Conference), for which he had issued the invitations eight years before. During this intervening period the idea had met with some slight increase in popular approval, and in May, 1888, Congress had authorized President Cleveland to take steps to call a conference. On July 13th Secretary Bayard formally invited the nations of Latin America to send delegates to Washington, for the purpose of discussing problems of mutual interest, principally questions of peace, trade, and communication.[2]

---

[1] Such charges were used effectively against Blaine in 1884, when he ran for the presidency. A convention of the Irish Land League at Boston declared that if Blaine were elected "Ireland would be free in thirty days." D. S. Muzzey, *James G. Blaine* (N.Y., 1935), p. 309.

[2] Specifically, the subjects to be discussed were: (1) measures to preserve peace and promote prosperity; (2) the formation of a customs union; (3) improvement of communication; (4) uniform customs regulations; (5) uniform system of weights and measures; (6) laws to protect patents, copyrights, and trade marks; (7) extradition; (8) adoption of a common silver coin; (9) erection of adequate machinery for arbitrating disputes.

On the appointed day, October 2, 1889, representatives of the Latin American states (seventeen ultimately sent delegates) assembled in Washington. They listened to an eloquent, if somewhat high-flown, address of welcome by Blaine, who concluded by extending to them a cordial invitation to tour the industrial areas of the United States as guests of the nation. The object of the trip was to impress upon the visitors the size and wealth of the United States, presumably as a step in weaning them away from their European commercial connections.[3] The bewildered delegates traveled some 6000 miles on a special train through forty-one cities, viewed giant factories and other mechanical marvels, listened to speeches and brass bands, and witnessed various displays, including the firing of a natural gas well. It is doubtful if the sight-seers, a number of whom knew the United States already, got much out of the trip except fatigue, and possibly, as the London *Spectator* suggested, a wholesome respect for a people "so fearfully energetic that it considers a journey of six thousand miles by rail an entertainment."[4] At all events, the junket did serve to popularize the Pan-American idea in the United States.

The Conference reassembled on November 18, 1889, and settled down to serious work. Blaine, though not officially representing the United States, presided with his customary brilliance and tact, and used his influence to support two objectives which concerned him deeply. First, he planned to draw the United States and Latin America into a customs union, in which tariff barriers would be beaten down and the flow of trade to Europe curtailed. This scheme met with many expressions of sympathy but was finally voted down as impracticable. Secondly, Blaine advocated the erection of machinery for the arbitration of disputes. Although he took the floor and spoke passionately for this proposal, it likewise lost by a wide margin. Mutual jealousies, and particularly distrust of a dominating United States, entered into the final decisions. Nor were the nations of Europe, who feared for their trade, indifferent to the Conference. They took steps, particularly in those Latin American countries where their stake was large, to create a backfire of opposition to the better understanding that was being attempted in Washington.

[3] At the large department store of Postmaster General Wanamaker, in Philadelphia, the delegates received an ornate "souvenir volume" descanting upon the glories of the establishment and expressing the hope "that it contains information sufficient to warrant its submission to your Government as a portion of your report. . . ." H. T. Peck, *Twenty Years of the Republic, 1885–1905* (N.Y., 1929), pp. 175–176. Comments in the press ran the gamut from mirth to disgust.

[4] *Spectator*, LXIII, 664 (Nov. 16, 1889).

THE FIRST FRUITS OF PAN-AMERICANISM

In spite of fanfare and high hopes, the Conference could point to only one tangible achievement: the creation of what came to be known as the Pan American Union—an organization designed as a clearing house for disseminating information and encouraging co-operation among the constituent nations.[5] The press of the United States, particularly the anti-Administration Democratic sheets, sneered at the scanty results accomplished by the high tariff Republican party, which, they charged, was hypocritically posing as the foe of trade barriers. The Philadelphia *Record* declared that the Conference would leave little of value "unless it be the brass tablet which is to commemorate the event." [6]

Yet it must be conceded that the First International American Conference was the entering wedge for the succeeding gatherings.[7] Moreover, the friendly reception given to the Latin American delegates probably did something to dispel their suspicion and fear of the United States. Finally, reciprocal tariff reductions by treaty, which the Conference found to be more practicable than a customs union, received considerable impetus.

Blaine foresaw the difficulty of negotiating individual reciprocity treaties with each of the Latin American countries, and he sought to secure from Congress blanket authorization to make the necessary arrangements. The "standpatters" in the protectionist Harrison administration were suspicious of attempts to lower trade barriers, and the McKinley tariff bill of 1890 was so foreign to Blaine's wishes that he appeared before the Senate Committee on Finance to plead for reciprocity. Carried away by the vehemence of his argument, he brought his fist down upon the table, so the story went, only to crush the hat he had carelessly laid there.[8]

The dynamic Secretary of State, in an important speech delivered in Maine, next appealed to the great court of public opinion. He received a gratifying response, especially in the West, which wanted

[5] In 1907 Andrew Carnegie, who had been a delegate of the United States at the First International American Conference, donated the money for constructing the beautiful Pan American Union building in Washington.

[6] For press reactions in the United States see A. C. Wilgus, "James G. Blaine and the Pan-American Movement," *Hispanic Amer. Hist. Rev.*, V (1922), 700-701.

[7] Mexico City (1901-1902); Rio de Janeiro (1906); Buenos Aires (1910); Santiago (1923); Havana (1928); Montevideo (1933); Lima (1938).

[8] Muzzey, *Blaine*, p. 445. The headlines ran, "Blaine Smashes His Hat On the McKinley Bill."

more markets. But the "old guard" Republican phalanx was adamant, and the best that Blaine could secure was a minatory type of reciprocity. For example, important raw materials from Latin America, notably sugar, were placed on the free list; but the President was authorized to proclaim punitive duties against those Latin American nations that did not reciprocate this generosity. With such a club held over them, several of the Latin American republics entered into executive reciprocity agreements.[9] But after Cleveland returned to power in 1893 this policy was reversed, and it is not possible to say what the results would have been had these pacts continued in effect over a long period.

Britain Upholds Freedom of the Seas

The widespread agitation for reciprocity with Latin America revived the hopes of the Canadians, who regretted the termination of the Reciprocity Treaty of 1854. During the late eighties and early nineties there was much discussion, in both Canada and the United States, of trade, tariffs, commercial unions, and even outright annexation. But the diplomatic problem that threatened to become acute involved the fur seals of the North Pacific.

With the purchase of Alaska the United States had acquired the Pribilof Islands, in the Bering Sea, on which a magnificent herd of some four million seals had their rookeries. These interesting animals are polygamous; and since most of the males are not necessary for the propagation of the herd, the government leased the privilege of killing "bachelors" to a private company. All went reasonably well until the caprice of feminine fashion brought about such a demand for sealskin coats and muffs as to increase the value of the skins many fold. The new price scale made profitable pelagic sealing, that is, the killing of the animal while it was swimming or floating.

The United States could exercise complete jurisdiction over the seal herd on the Pribilof Islands and within national waters, but no farther. Pelagic sealers—most of them Canadians—stationed their schooners outside the three-mile limit and slaughtered the animals as they came to and from the breeding grounds. Swimming females cannot be distinguished from males, and the death of a female ordinarily meant the loss of a nursing pup on land, and an unborn pup in the seal. Since about half of the animals shot in the water were not recovered, every skin obtained in the open sea represented the death of approximately

[9] Alice F. Tyler, *The Foreign Policy of James G. Blaine* (Minneapolis, 1927), pp. 188–189.

four seals.[10] As the value of the fur was enhanced, the number of pelagic schooners multiplied; and as they increased the herd decreased, with a consequent further rise in prices. The whole wasteful process threatened the seals with extermination.

In 1886, United States revenue cutters began to seize Canadian pelagic schooners outside the three-mile limit.[11] This was justifiable only on the grounds that the Bering Sea was a *mare clausum* (a closed sea), as much under American jurisdiction as Chesapeake Bay. The Canadians not unjustifiably flared up at this unlawful interference with their lawful though disagreeable business, and the British minister in Washington lodged protests. Nevertheless Congress, under the lash of the Alaskan seal lobby, formally authorized the President (March 2, 1889) to seize vessels encroaching upon American rights in the "waters of Bering Sea." It is curious that the United States, traditional defender of the freedom of the seas, even in the interests of slavers, should have appeared in this anomalous role.

When, in 1889, Blaine became Secretary of State for the second time, the seizures had already been made, and the issue was squarely drawn. Feeling bound to uphold both the law of Congress and public sentiment, he entered upon a lengthy diplomatic duel with the British Foreign Office, beginning January 22, 1890. In his first note Blaine argued forcefully that the United States was not contending that the Bering Sea was a *mare clausum*, but that pelagic sealing was so destructive as to be *contra bonos mores* (against good public morals). "The law of the sea," he insisted, "is not lawlessness." He also declared that the United States had acquired a prescriptive right to fence off that part of the Bering Sea which contained the seals because not until recent years had the Canadians attempted to poach there. In this passage we see Blaine the journalist and orator:

Whence did the ships of Canada derive the right to do in 1886 that which they had refrained from doing for more than ninety years? Upon what grounds did Her Majesty's Government defend in the year 1886 a course of conduct in the Behring Sea which she had carefully avoided ever since the discovery of that sea? By what reasoning did Her Majesty's Government conclude that an act may be committed with impunity against the rights of the United States which had never been attempted against the same rights when held by the Russian Empire? [12]

[10] T. A. Bailey, "The North Pacific Sealing Convention of 1911," *Pacific Hist. Rev.*, IV (1935), 2.

[11] Tyler, *Foreign Policy of Blaine*, pp. 305 ff.

[12] *Foreign Relations, 1890*, p. 368 (Blaine to Pauncefote, Jan. 22, 1890).

"One step beyond that which Her Majesty's Government has taken in this controversy," Blaine declared with startling directness, "and piracy finds its justification."

Unhurriedly and urbanely, Lord Salisbury, British Foreign Secretary, answered Blaine's nervous notes, raking the American arguments fore and aft. The noble Briton stood squarely on the unassailable ground that, except for piracy or under mutual agreement, no nation in time of peace can seize the ships of another nation on the high seas. The Canadians were engaged in a legitimate if unpleasant industry, and they had to be protected until it was made illegal. In his next note Salisbury delivered a virtual ultimatum: ". . . Her Britannic Majesty's Government must hold the Government of the United States responsible for the consequences that may ensue from acts which are contrary to the established principles of international law." [13]

The whole affair gave rise to the inevitable war talk, particularly after it had been reported that British warships were gathering in the North Pacific. The Sioux City *Journal* insisted that "the thing to do" was to "shoot *any* British ship which is in those waters." The Detroit *News* concluded that "British dominion on the North American continent should be given an end at as early a date as possible." But such jingoistic utterances were the exception rather than the rule. The New York *Sun* sneered at the attempt to police the "open ocean in the interests of good morals and pup seals"; while the Spokane Falls *Review* was confident that "The United States and Great Britain are not going to fight over a few greasy, ill-smelling sealskins." [14]

The lengthy diplomatic interchange culminated in the signing of an arbitration treaty at Washington, February 29, 1892. A mixed tribunal of seven members met at Paris, in 1893, and rendered a decision adverse to the American contention on every one of the five major counts. The United States was ultimately assessed $473,151 damages for the unwarranted seizures of Canadian schooners. The Tribunal also made an effort to protect the seals by certain illusory regulations which may have slowed up the process of depletion.[15] About the best that can be said of the Paris Award is that it was a victory for arbitration and the pacific settlement of disputes—not for the seals.

[13] *Ibid.*, p. 436 (Pauncefote to Blaine, June 14, 1890).

[14] *Public Opinion*, IX, 383 (Aug. 2, 1890).

[15] The most important regulations were: (1) the nationals of neither country were to engage in pelagic sealing within a zone extending sixty miles around the Pribilof Islands; (2) pelagic sealing was forbidden during certain specified months. W. M. Malloy, ed., *Treaties . . . between the United States of America and Other Powers* (Washington, 1910), I, 754–755. The zone was not wide enough, and the months for the close season were unwisely chosen.

The complete overthrow of the American case caused Blaine's numerous enemies to brand him a bombastic bungler. The New York *Nation* rejoiced that the Tribunal had declared Blaine's history "to be fiction, his geography pure fancy, and his international law a mere whim. . . ." [16] But this is hardly fair. Blaine did not start the con-

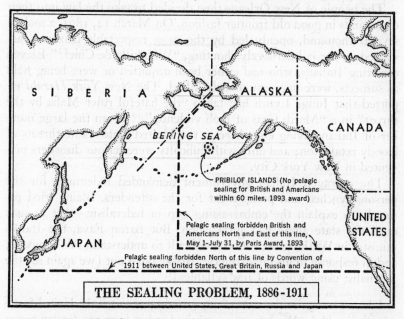

PRIBILOF ISLANDS (No pelagic sealing for British and Americans within 60 miles, 1893 award)

Pelagic sealing forbidden British and Americans North and East of this line, May 1-July 31, by Paris Award, 1893

Pelagic sealing forbidden North of this line by Convention of 1911 between United States, Great Britain, Russia and Japan

THE SEALING PROBLEM, 1886-1911

troversy—the Cleveland administration did. He did not pass the law directing the seizures—Congress did. He did not desire to become involved with Britain on this issue—American public opinion did.[17] Like a prosecuting attorney charged with making the best of an impossible case, he advanced what were inevitably weak arguments in behalf of a good moral cause.

THE MAFIA AFFAIR

While the question of the seals was still under discussion, the United States became involved in its first major diplomatic controversy with Italy. Large numbers of Italian subjects from Sicily, some with a criminal background and many of them allegedly members of the Mafia Black Hand society, had congregated in New Orleans, where

[16] New York *Nation*, LVII, 113 (Aug. 17, 1893).
[17] Muzzey, *Blaine*, p. 410.

they carried on their vendettas, chiefly against fellow Sicilians. An enterprising chief of police, who was ferreting out the wrongdoers, was himself foully murdered. A number of Italian suspects were brought to trial, but none was convicted. It seemed as though bribery were clogging the wheels of justice.[18]

The people of New Orleans then decided to take the law into their own hands in good old frontier fashion. On March 14, 1891, a mob of several thousand, openly led by the most respectable citizenry, advanced on the jail derisively shouting, "Who killa de Chief?" Eleven cowering Italians, who had either been acquitted or were being held as suspects, were unceremoniously killed. The New York *Herald* reported that Judge Lynch had taken "the hateful ruler Mafia by the throat" in a "Mardi Gras of mob violence."[19] From the large number of Italians living elsewhere in the United States came threats of bloody retaliation; and only with difficulty were serious disorders prevented in New York City.

The outraged Italian government demanded indemnity for the persons lynched and punishment for the offenders. Blaine tried patiently to explain the embarrassing gap in federalism—that in such cases the state alone had jurisdiction. But Baron Fava, the Italian minister in Washington, found it difficult to understand this anomaly; and in response to his importunities Blaine burst out (we again see the journalist using words of few syllables):

I do not recognize the right of any government to tell the United States what it should do. We have never received orders from any foreign power and we will not begin now. . . . It is a matter of total indifference to me what persons in Italy may think of our institutions. I cannot change them, still less violate them.[20]

The Chicago *Tribune*, which was sympathetic with Blaine, rejoiced that this "vigorous assertion of American rights" took away "the breath from the monkey and hand-organ man and he at once changed his tune."

In Italy the masses vented their wrath in heated meetings and in

[18] J. E. Coxe, "The New Orleans Mafia Incident," *Louisiana Hist. Quar.*, XX (1937), 1084.

[19] New York *Herald*, March 15, 1891, 17:1.

[20] *Ibid.*, May 22, 1891, 3:3. This version is what Baron Fava reported to his government, which published it in a Green Book, together with other relevant documents. See also Porter to Blaine, May 4, 1891, Department of State, *Despatches*, *Italy*, XXIV. The conclusions here expressed are based upon an examination of the State Department records.

indignities to Americans. The shaky Italian ministry found it necessary to make some face-saving gesture; and, finding Blaine powerless
to do anything, abruptly withdrew Baron Fava from Washington,
March 31, 1891. The United States instructed its minister in Rome to
come home on leave of absence. But this did not mean a severance of
diplomatic relations; each nation left its legation in the hands of a
chargé.

Inflamed feelings, particularly in Italy, led to some little discussion
of the possibility of war. In armored ships the Italians outnumbered
the Americans nineteen to one, and these vessels could probably have
devastated America's large coastal cities. But Italy was financially unable to sustain a prolonged war with the United States; she had everything to lose and nothing to gain by hostilities; and the New Orleans
incident did not involve a fundamental grievance.

In the United States, where mob violence was an ancient heritage,
the flare-up over a lynching caused little real alarm. *Harper's Weekly*
declared that if Italians did not like the protection extended by American laws they were at liberty to go home. The Atlanta *Journal* jokingly
hoped that Italy was sending a warship to New Orleans, as rumored.
"We are," it said, "too much in need of a navy to let a thing like that
escape." The Salt Lake *Herald* was contemptuous:

> The Italian press may rage and fume, and Italian officials may threaten,
> but they can do nothing. They are absolutely powerless. The nation is weak
> in every respect, and financially is almost bankrupt. It has a magnificent
> navy for which it owes, and has a large army for which it has absolutely
> no use. The idea of making war upon the United States, the greatest power
> on earth, is so ridiculous as to be laughable.[21]

Nor was the United States government greatly perturbed. While the
crisis was supposedly acute, President Harrison left Washington on
a six weeks tour; and in 1892, before either minister had returned to
his post, the American *chargé* in Rome requested and received permission to come home to be married.[22]

Fortunately, tempers on both sides of the Atlantic cooled with the
passage of time; and the government in Rome felt somewhat better
about the affair when it was discovered that only three of the eleven
lynched were bona fide Italian subjects. The incident was officially

[21] *Public Opinion*, X, 588 (March 28, 1891).
[22] Wharton (acting) to Whitehouse (*chargé*), March 14, 1892 (telegram), Department of State, *Instructions, Italy*, II.

closed when the United States government, as a friendly act, paid $25,000 to Italy.

THE BALTIMORE BRAWL

While the Mafia affair was causing the diplomats some concern, public attention suddenly shifted to relations with Chile. This elongated republic had not welcomed the return of Blaine, for it could not forget his apparent efforts to snatch away the fruits of victory in 1881. Matters were not improved when Blaine selected Patrick Egan as minister at Santiago. Egan was a refugee Irish agitator, who had but recently been naturalized; [23] and his presence proved highly offensive to the influential British colony in Chile.

In 1891 civil war broke out in Chile when the Congressionalists raised the standard of revolt against the president, who was attempting to assume dictatorial power. A rebel steamer, the *Itata*, made its way to California for the purpose of obtaining arms. The United States authorities, fearing possible complications, detained the ship at San Diego. On May 6, 1891, the crew overpowered the guard, and shortly thereafter the vessel started for Chile.[24] A United States cruiser took up the chase; a Congressionalist cruiser prepared to defend the *Itata*; and word was momentarily expected of a clash. But the fugitive ship reached Chile, where it was reluctantly surrendered by the rebels to the United States, and then freed by the American courts as improperly detained. By that time the Congressionalists had triumphed, and they were naturally slow to forget the *Itata* affair, as well as other incidents which seemed to reveal hostility by the United States to their cause.[25]

While feeling in Chile was still extremely bitter, Captain Schley, of the U.S.S. *Baltimore*, then in Valparaiso harbor, ill-advisedly gave shore leave to about one hundred and twenty unarmed men. That afternoon, October 16, 1891, a riot started in the True Blue saloon

---

[23] The Democrats criticized Egan as a "Blaine Irishman" and "an escaped jailbird" of the Irish "dynamite school." Though the appointment was made for political purposes, it must be said, legend to the contrary, that Egan was a man of ability. See Osgood Hardy, "Was Patrick Egan a 'Blundering Minister'?" *Hispanic Amer. Hist. Rev.*, VIII (1928), 65–81.

[24] See Osgood Hardy, "The Itata Incident," *Hispanic Amer. Hist. Rev.*, V (1922), 195–226.

[25] Minister Egan, with commendable humanitarian impulses but with arguable legality, gave asylum in his legation to a number of prominent Chileans who fled the vengeance of the victorious Congressionalists. J. B. Moore, *Digest of International Law* (Washington, 1906), II, 791 *ff.*

when a Chilean allegedly spat in the face of an American. In the brawl that resulted two United States sailors were killed (one receiving eighteen bayonet and knife wounds), seventeen were injured, and some of the remainder were beaten and imprisoned. The local police were said to have helped the mob of Chilean rioters against the American sailors.[26]

Public sentiment in the United States was outraged. Many felt that the affair was no mere lynching of Italians or Chinese but an insult to the uniform and flag of the United States Navy. Captain Schley declared that the men were well behaved and not drunk—at least not when he had last seen them. But Captain "Fighting Bob" Evans, who arrived in Valparaiso harbor on the U.S.S. *Yorktown* eager, as he put it, "to fill hell with garlic," thought Schley's argument irrelevant:

His men were probably drunk on shore, properly drunk; they went ashore, many of them, for the purpose of getting drunk; which they did on Chilean rum paid for with good United States money. When in this condition they were more entitled to protection than if they had been sober.[27]

Chile Eats Humble Pie

Days dragged by without an apology or even an expression of regret from the Chilean government. The Acting Secretary of State (Blaine was then ill) sent a sharp note complaining of the delay in acknowledging responsibility. The Chilean Foreign Minister procrastinated, failed to make what the United States regarded as a proper apology, and asserted that though the law of Chile might be "slow in its processes" it was "exact in its conclusions."

President Harrison, in his annual message to Congress of December 9, 1891, strongly expressed the hope that the current investigation would bring full satisfaction to the United States. He ended on this ominous note: "If these just expectations should be disappointed or further needless delay intervene, I will by a special message bring this matter again to the attention of Congress for such action as may be necessary." [28] The Chilean Foreign Minister, who was angered

[26] These facts have been taken from the report (October 19, 1891) to Captain Schley by the officers who investigated the riot. *Foreign Relations, 1891*, pp. 206–207.

[27] R. D. Evans, *A Sailor's Log* (N.Y., 1901), pp. 259–260.

[28] J. D. Richardson, ed., *Messages and Papers of the Presidents* (Washington, 1898), IX, 186.

by the President's statement and by the documents that accompanied it, committed the extraordinary indiscretion of scattering broadcast a note of rebuttal in which he impugned Harrison's good faith and veracity.

The fat was now in the fire. War feeling ran dangerously high in both countries, particularly in the United States, which had experienced no jingoistic outburst since the *Virginius* affair nearly twenty years earlier. Young Theodore Roosevelt was on fire to lead a cavalry charge against the Chileans.[29] A Kentucky Congressman declared that a million men would respond to a call to arms. The navy yards worked overtime. The body of one of the murdered seamen lay for a time in state in Independence Hall, Philadelphia—an honor previously accorded only to Abraham Lincoln and Henry Clay.[30] The warlike Chileans, rendered over-confident by their victories over their weak neighbors, boasted of what their navy would do. There can be no doubt that it was definitely superior in certain types of ships; and for a time panic struck the vulnerable Pacific Coast of the United States.[31] But Chile had a population of only three million; and the ultimate advantage was so certain to lie with the United States, with its population of sixty-three million, that war would have been suicidal for the South American republic, and not altogether honorable for its powerful adversary.

Meanwhile the Department of State had been busy. On January 21, 1892, Blaine sent an ultimatum to Chile written by Harrison:

I am now, however, directed by the President to say that if the offensive parts of the dispatch of the 11th of December are not at once withdrawn, and a suitable apology offered, with the same publicity that was given to the offensive expressions, he will have no other course open to him except to terminate diplomatic relations with the Government of Chile.[32]

The new Chilean Foreign Minister bowed to the inevitable and wrote an apology which left nothing to be desired. But while the note was being decoded, Harrison sent a special message to Congress, January 25, 1892, in which he outlined the affair at great length and submitted the relevant papers for "the grave and patriotic considera-

[29] H. F. Pringle, *Theodore Roosevelt* (N.Y., 1931), p. 167.
[30] New York *Nation*, LV, 121 (August 18, 1892).
[31] See T. A. Brassey, ed., *The Naval Annual, 1892* (Portsmouth, Eng., 1892), *passim*. The Navy Department in Washington made more energetic preparations for war at this time than the public generally realized. W. D. Puleston, *Mahan* (New Haven, 1939), p. 114.
[32] *House Ex. Docs.*, 52 Cong., 1 sess., I, 308.

tion" of Congress "and for such action as may be deemed appropriate." This virtual invitation to declare war, at a time when Chile's
capitulation was hourly expected, brought down a storm of criticism
on Harrison's head. The Democratic press openly accused the President of angling for re-election, and of planning to precipitate hostilities so that he could sweep to victory with the slogan, "don't swap
horses in the middle of the stream." [33]

It is a grave charge to say that Harrison deliberately attempted
to provoke war for political purposes; but he probably realized that
a strong tone would commend him to the electorate. Whatever his
purposes, the apology ended the crisis; and the government of Chile
ultimately paid $75,000 to the injured men and to the families of
the deceased.

Blaine has been accused of excessive severity in his demands upon
a weak sister republic—of having broken a butterfly on the wheel. A
New York *Herald* correspondent declared that he was trying to be
the "John L. Sullivan of diplomacy." But we now know that it was
Blaine who restrained Harrison's bellicosity, not vice versa.[34] The
Secretary of State was too thoroughly wrapped up in the ideal of
American friendliness to go much beyond what seemed to be the
plain requirements of the case. Nevertheless, the Chileans could not
forgive the United States for having demanded what seemed to them
a humiliating degree of abasement. This imbroglio, which was not of
Blaine's making, unfortunately did much to offset the few happy results of the First Pan-American Conference.

THE PASSING OF THE PLUMED KNIGHT

Three other diplomatic problems claimed Blaine's attention. The
Samoan controversy with Germany, which was of major importance,
will be discussed at some length in the next chapter. Related to it was
the growing interest of the United States in Hawaii. During his first
administration as Secretary of State, Blaine had espoused a policy
looking toward the ultimate annexation of the archipelago.[35] In his

---

[33] See W. R. Sherman, *The Diplomatic and Commercial Relations of the United
States and Chile, 1820–1914* (Boston, 1926), pp. 187–188.

[34] Muzzey, *Blaine*, pp. 422–423; Tyler, *Foreign Policy of Blaine*, pp. 159 *ff*.

[35] Blaine wrote to the United States minister in Honolulu (Dec. 1, 1881) that the
government could not permit either Cuba or Hawaii to be cut "adrift from the American system, whereto they both indispensably belong." *Foreign Relations, 1881–1882*,
p. 638. Some writers have seen in this an extension of the Monroe Doctrine to Hawaii,
but Professor Perkins thinks otherwise. Dexter Perkins, *The Monroe Doctrine, 1867–
1907* (Baltimore, 1937), p. 278.

second he arranged for the appointment of the annexationist John L. Stevens, a journalist friend, as minister to the island kingdom. Of the machinations of this individual we shall hear more later.

Blaine also had to cope with problems resulting from the changing relationship between the United States and Germany during the eighties and nineties. Despite memories of sympathy during the Civil War, and despite the bond of hundreds of thousands of German immigrants, the two nations were drifting apart. The basic explanation is that both countries became highly industrialized at about the same time, and each took steps to protect itself against an inundation of commodities from the other. America employed highly protective tariffs, which caused the Germans much hardship; Germany, as well as other western European countries, placed restrictions upon American fruit, meat, and other exports.

Embargoes upon pork products, which the Germans and other Europeans alleged were infected,[36] caused much dissatisfaction among American farmers. The outraged hog producers brought great pressure to bear on Congress and the Department of State, and after ten years of wrangling the dispute was adjusted by the establishment of adequate export inspection in the United States. Blaine, who handled the final negotiations in 1891, received some credit for the satisfactory outcome, though his participation called for no spectacular work.[37]

In June, 1892, on the eve of the Republican National Convention, Blaine abruptly resigned from the Department of State. This strange move gave added currency to the rather improbable rumor that he was again a candidate for the Presidency. Whatever the truth, Harrison received the Republican nomination, Cleveland the Democratic. Indicative of the distrust abroad of the Administration's aggressive foreign policy is the fact that Cleveland's victory, in November, 1892, called forth loud rejoicing in Latin America.[38]

Blaine's second term as Secretary of State was less spirited than his first—the obvious reason being that he had less spirit. Older, disappointed, ill, and working under a jealous chief, he did not take the diplomatic offensive, as before, but dealt almost solely with inherited problems or isolated incidents as they arose. And in handling the

---

[36] Count Otto zu Stolberg-Wernigerode, *Germany and the United States of America during the Era of Bismarck* (trans. from German, Reading, Pa., 1937), pp. 150 ff. See also Alfred Vagts, *Deutschland und die Vereinigten Staaten in der Weltpolitik* (N.Y., 1935), I, 41 ff.

[37] Tyler, *Foreign Policy of Blaine*, p. 301.

[38] Wilgus, "James G. Blaine and the Pan-American Movement," *loc. cit.*, pp. 705–706.

Mafia and *Baltimore* crises, as well as the Samoan affair, he displayed far less vigor than might have been expected.

Whatever may be said of Blaine, it is clear that he had energy and imagination, and that he was more actively interested in a constructive and far-visioned foreign policy than any other Secretary of State between Seward and John Hay. More than any other statesman of his generation he focused attention on foreign affairs at a time when interest was at low ebb, and in so doing may have contributed substantially to the imperialistic urge at the end of the century.

It is remarkable that Blaine, despite the commotion he caused, could point to few immediate achievements. This is largely because he laid the foundations upon which others built. His Hawaiian and Isthmian policies found fruition under McKinley, Hay, and Theodore Roosevelt; his seal preservation policy under Taft; his reciprocal trade policy, in part, under Franklin D. Roosevelt and Secretary of State Cordell Hull. By common consent Blaine's chief claim to fame lies in his espousal of closer commercial and cultural contacts with Latin America, and his encouragement of the pacific settlement of disputes. Every succeeding Pan-American Conference has been a tribute to his foresight and zeal.

BIBLIOGRAPHICAL NOTE

For a sketch of Blaine's second administration as Secretary of State see J. B. Lockey, "James Gillespie Blaine," in S. F. Bemis, ed., *The American Secretaries of State and their Diplomacy* (N.Y., 1928), VIII, 109–184. Another good brief account is D. S. Muzzey, *James G. Blaine* (N.Y., 1935), Ch. XV, which is excellent on the political background. The standard monograph. is Alice F. Tyler, *The Foreign Policy of James G. Blaine* (Minneapolis, 1927). A useful article is A. C. Wilgus, "James G. Blaine and the Pan-American Movement," *Hispanic Amer. Hist. Rev.*, V (1922), 662–708. Rather sketchy accounts of the Chilean crisis appear in H. C. Evans, Jr., *Chile and Its Relations with the United States* (Durham, N.C., 1927), Ch. X; and W. R. Sherman, *The Diplomatic and Commercial Relations of the United States and Chile, 1820–1914* (Boston, 1926), Ch. VI (stronger on press of United States). Two revealing articles by Osgood Hardy are "The Itata Incident," *Hispanic Amer. Hist. Rev.*, V (1922), 195–226; and "Was Patrick Egan a 'Blundering Minister'?", *ibid.*, VIII (1928), 65–81. On the pork controversy and other economic disputes with Germany see Count Otto zu Stolberg-Wernigerode, *Germany and the United States of America during the Era of Bismarck* (trans. from German, Reading, Pa., 1937), Ch. I, Pt. II. The same subjects are exhaustively treated in Alfred Vagts' monumental *Deutschland und die Vereinigten Staaten in der Weltpolitik* (N.Y., 1935), I, Chs. I–VII. Further references: see footnotes of this chapter and Bemis and Griffin, *Guide*, pp. 453 *ff.*

RECENT REFERENCES. See Bibliographical Appendix, p. 931.

NEW REFERENCES. See Bibliographical Appendix, p. 932.

CHAPTER XXVIII

Samoa and Hawaii: Imperialistic Beginnings

*". . . I think we should accept the issue like a great Nation,
and not act the part of pigmies nor cowards."*

John L. Stevens, United States Minister
to Hawaii, March 25, 1892.

THE REBIRTH OF MANIFEST DESTINY

WHILE the Department of State was engaged with purely American problems during the late eighties and early nineties, the United States became involved in serious international friction over the ownership of two tiny archipelagoes lost in the vastnesses of the Pacific. Why should the American people, with their pressing domestic problems and their undeveloped continental domain, have become so deeply aroused over these distant insular outposts? Where were their traditional policies of staying at home and keeping out of foreign entanglements? The story cannot be understood unless it is remembered that during these years there occurred the birth of a spirit of imperialism.

Whence came the urge for overseas empire? Its roots are to be sought for in a number of developments. The Darwinian theory, as popularly interpreted by men like John Fiske in the eighties, helped to prepare the American mind for the comfortable belief that the world belonged to the nations that were strong and fit—like the United States.[1] The spirited foreign policy of Blaine caused many a red-corpuscled American to experience a pleasant titillation that may have been the quickening sap of imperialism. During these years the distinguished American writer, Captain A. T. Mahan, began to preach the gospel that naval power and world power are Siamese twins.[2] The American people glimpsed faintly the destiny they were to fulfill; and the new navy was rushed to completion. The demand

[1] J. W. Pratt, *Expansionists of 1898* (Baltimore, 1936), pp. 3 ff. This whole chapter on the "New Manifest Destiny" is well worth reading.

[2] It is interesting to note that Mahan had at first been an anti-imperialist, and that his writings were more enthusiastically received in Europe, particularly in England and Germany, than at home. See W. D. Puleston, *Mahan* (New Haven, 1939), pp. 110, 129.

for more and bigger battleships had its counterpart in the growing agitation for an Isthmian canal to increase the mobility of the navy in protecting both coasts. This also meant that outlying islands, like Cuba, the Danish West Indies, and Hawaii, would have to be secured to guard the approaches to the proposed waterway.

By 1890 post-Civil War reconstruction had virtually been completed, and the last desirable free land was fast disappearing. During these years the country experienced a marvelous increase in its industrial production, and American manufacturers were looking for

FOREIGN TRADE OF THE UNITED STATES

FOR THE GIVEN YEARS

Year	Total Exports	Total Imports
1800	$ 70,972,000	$ 91,253,000
1810	66,758,000	85,400,000
1820	69,692,000	74,450,000
1830	71,671,000	62,721,000
1840	123,669,000	98,259,000
1850	144,376,000	173,510,000
1860	333,576,000	353,616,000
1870	392,772,000	435,958,000
1880	835,639,000	667,955,000
1890	857,829,000	789,310,000
1900	1,394,483,000	829,150,000
1910	1,744,985,000	1,562,904,000
1920	8,108,989,000	5,278,481,000
1930	3,843,181,000	3,060,908,000

foreign markets to absorb their growing surpluses. It was clear to discerning observers that outlets would have to be found for the Vesuvian energy and expansive power of an America that needed "elbow room." [3]

Everywhere in the United States there were evidences of a growing national consciousness. American history was introduced into the

[3] The Overland *Monthly* observed: "The subjugation of a continent was sufficient to keep the American people busy at home for a century. . . . But now that the continent is subdued, we are looking for fresh worlds to conquer. . . ." XXXI (1898), 177–178.

lower schools; scores of patriotic societies sprouted up; genealogists pored over musty documents; respect for the flag was taught in the classrooms; and the propriety of displaying the national colors in comic opera aroused serious debate. In 1893 Congress created the rank of ambassador: that of minister would no longer do. All signs indicated that America was turning her eyes outward. She was restless, tired of a drab and colorless life, bored by such prosaic issues as the tariff and currency, eager for new thrills—and a stage commensurate with her bursting power.

Coconuts and Coaling Stations

The Samoan archipelago, with its fine harbor of Pago Pago on the island of Tutuila, commands a number of the important ocean lanes of the South Pacific. As early as 1838 the United States government, responding to pressure from the whaling interests, sent a scientific expedition to the Pacific under Lieutenant Charles Wilkes, who visited Samoa.[4] But it was not until after the Civil War that the American people began to show a real interest in the island paradise. For one thing, pursuit of the Confederate commerce destroyer *Shenandoah* had demonstrated the wisdom of having a coaling station in these waters. In addition, the completion of the transcontinental railroad in 1869 stimulated trade with the Antipodes and directed attention to the Samoan way station.

In 1872 an American naval officer, Commander Meade, drew up a treaty with the Great Chief at Pago Pago. It provided that the United States was to have the exclusive privilege of establishing a naval station there in return for extending "friendship and protection." President Grant submitted the document to the Senate, which, in its nonexpansive postwar mood, took no action.

But American interest did not die with the treaty. In 1873 the Department of State sent Colonel A. B. Steinberger to Samoa as a special observer. The American representative won the confidence of the natives by his fair dealing, and ultimately became premier. His humanitarian policies aroused the distrust of the English and German merchants, and in the end he was unceremoniously arrested and deported on a British man-of-war.[5] American public opinion was not

[4] G. H. Ryden, *The Foreign Policy of the United States in Relation to Samoa* (New Haven, 1933), pp. 13 *ff*. This was the Wilkes of *Trent* affair fame.

[5] For a favorable picture of Steinberger's activities see J. W. Ellison, "Opening and Penetration of Foreign Influence in Samoa to 1880," *Oregon State Studies in History* (Corvallis, Oregon), No. 1 (March, 1938), pp. 46 *ff*.

at all friendly to Grant's intermeddling on these distant islands, and journals like the New York *Herald* and the New York *Times* criticized the whole affair, while the House of Representatives adopted a resolution, on March 15, 1876, instructing the Committee on Foreign Affairs to inquire into Steinberger's conduct.

In 1878 a six-foot-four, highborn Samoan, Le Mamea, came to Washington, where he made a striking impression. Negotiations with the "tattooed Prince" resulted in the treaty of January 17, 1878, a cornerstone of America's Samoan policy.[6] It provided that in return for the rights to a naval station at Pago Pago, the United States would employ its good offices to adjust any differences that should arise between Samoa and a foreign Power. This, however, was not a protectorate; and the consent of the Senate was secured without serious difficulty. The New York *Times* rejoiced at obtaining these advantages without an equivalent entanglement. But the United States was now formally bound to support the weak native government against foreign Powers—a course fraught with difficulties.

Furor Consularis

The year following the negotiation of the treaty of 1878 both Great Britain and Germany secured treaty rights in Samoa. The Germans, who were late-comers in the scramble for colonies and who found most of the desirable areas already staked out, were obviously eager to pick up these insular crumbs. The consular representatives of Germany, Great Britain, and the United States were, in these circumstances, highly suspicious of the annexationist designs of each other. Since the nearest cable was in distant New Zealand, each consul was forced to act on his own responsibility—and the resulting tension wrought havoc with frayed nerves. It was the period, wrote Robert Louis Stevenson, who arrived in Samoa in 1889, of *furor consularis* (consular fury).[7]

The tiny islands fairly seethed with the intrigues of land-grabbers, concessionaires, naval officers, commercial agents, and consuls. The natives were bullied and browbeaten, and brother was set upon brother in the blood and turmoil of civil war. Nervous consuls hoisted the

---

[6] Ryden, *Foreign Policy of United States in Samoa*, pp. 196 ff.

[7] The phrase appears to have been coined by Bismarck. "I never saw so good a place as this Apia," Stevenson reported one politician as saying; "you can be in a new conspiracy every day!" R. L. Stevenson, *A Footnote to History* (N.Y., 1895), p. 26. Stevenson's account is a classic.

flags of their governments, only to be disavowed. By the summer of 1887 the situation had become so unendurable that Secretary of State Bayard called the British and German ministers in Washington into a conference, which met during June and July of 1887.[8] The German representative urged that the Power commercially dominant in Samoa be allowed to control the islands—which, of course, meant the Fatherland. He was supported by his British colleague, for Great Britain had secured equivalents elsewhere from Germany. But the United States stood firm for the preservation of Samoan autonomy, and the conference broke up without agreement.

The unseemly scramble now became worse, if possible. The Germans brought demands upon the Samoan king for alleged wrongs, and solemnly declared war upon him. The unhappy Polynesian potentate was deported; but the natives took to the bush in revolt against the German-manipulated puppet king. In December, 1888, a party of German sailors was ambushed with humiliating losses; whereupon the Germans shelled the native villages and declared martial law. A fleet of one British, three German, and three American warships gathered in crowded Apia harbor, and the tense seamen glared at one another over shotted guns.

Nature Intervenes

By this time American public opinion had become genuinely aroused over the events in distant Samoa. Reports of the trampling on "Old Glory," of the destruction of American property, and of the general jeopardizing of American interests gave the jingoes their inning. There was a serious discussion of war with Germany. The New York *World* rattled the saber:

The American hog has been discriminated against in Germany and the German hog in Samoa must not be permitted to uproot the rights of Americans there. Our Government has wisely ordered two more war vessels to reinforce the . . . cruisers now in Samoan waters. Perhaps the presence of this small fleet will have the effect of cooling the hostile officers of the German gunboats. . . .[9]

[8] See Alfred Vagts, *Deutschland und die Vereinigten Staaten in der Weltpolitik* (N.Y., 1935), I, 638 ff.

[9] Quoted in *Public Opinion*, VI, 322 (Jan. 26, 1889). On the other hand, journals like the New York *Nation* condemned this "wild goose chase" as "sheer Jingoism and meddlesomeness in other people's affairs." XLVIII, 84 (Jan. 31, 1889).

Congress promptly passed an appropriation of $500,000 for the protection of American lives and property in Samoa, and another $100,-000 for the development of Pago Pago.

With opinion in the United States already aroused by the pork controversy and other German restrictions, the Samoan crisis took on a decidedly unpleasant aspect. But Prince Bismarck, the Iron Chancellor, had no desire to antagonize the United States, whose friendship he valued.[10] He therefore suggested a renewal of the fruitless Washington negotiations, and the proposal was favorably received. On March 14, 1889, President Harrison appointed three delegates to attend a conference in Berlin, where representatives of the three great Powers were to assemble in an attempt to adjust the Samoan imbroglio.

Meanwhile the American and German ships lay in Apia harbor. Although the tension was somewhat relieved by the approaching Berlin Conference, the situation was still dangerous. Then, on March 16, 1889, a terrific hurricane descended upon the poorly protected harbor. All three American and all three German warships were wrecked, sunk, or driven upon the beach with heavy loss of life. With straining boilers, the British *Calliope* headed out to sea, and as she crept to safety a cheer arose from the Americans on the doomed *Trenton*—and it was returned with a will. This dramatic instance of good sportsmanship was probably not without influence in ushering in the new era of Anglo-American friendship that was approaching. As a Canadian poet, Charles Roberts, wrote:

> The memory of those cheers
> Shall thrill in English ears
> Where'er this English blood and speech extend.[11]

A TRICEPHALOUS PROTECTORATE

The Berlin Conference convened on April 29, 1889, with the atmosphere definitely improved by the Apia disaster. Contrary to ex-

---

[10] Count Otto zu Stolberg-Wernigerode, *Germany and the United States of America during the Era of Bismarck* (trans. from German, Reading, Pa., 1937), p. 258.

[11] B. E. Stevenson, ed., *Poems of American History* (Boston, 1908), p. 598. Although the tale was not mentioned in any of the official American reports, and although garbled versions of it appeared later in the press, Captain Kane of the *Calliope* reported to the British Admiralty (March 24, 1889): "As we passed the 'Trenton' all the officers and men who were on deck gave us a ringing cheer, which was heartily returned by us. We were much affected by that proof of goodwill from another ship at a time when they might well have been thinking about themselves alone." Unpublished Admiralty Records.

pectations, and certainly contrary to a persistent legend, the imperious Prince Bismarck was in a conciliatory mood. Even American jingoes were sobered. The New York *World* adopted a solemn tone:

> Men and nations must bow before the decrees of nature. . . . Surely the awful devastation wrought in the harbor of Apia makes our recent quarrel with Germany appear petty and unnatural. Can it not be confidently predicted that the bonds which now join us to Germany as together we mourn the fate of those who perished in their duty will make the coming diplomatic conference at Berlin a council of friends, not a quarrel of restless rivals.[12]

It was expected that Secretary Blaine, advocate of a "spirited" foreign policy, would take a strong tone in dealing with Bismarck. The unfriendly New York *Nation* predicted that his dispatches would be like the rumble "of distant but fast approaching thunder." But such was not the case. Blaine revealed a conciliatory disposition and, despite a widely repeated tale, did not lay down the law to the allegedly irritable Bismarck.[13]

Much difficulty probably would have been avoided if the final partition of the islands had taken place then and there instead of in 1899. But the United States was not ripe for tropical annexations; and Blaine's insistence upon the preservation of native Samoan autonomy blocked any division. The only feasible solution seemed to be a condominium or three-Power protectorate over Samoa, with the restored native dynasty nominally ruling. Germany and Great Britain were not altogether pleased with this arrangement, but, on June 14, 1889, their representatives formally agreed to it.

In the United States the pro-Administration Republican press was sure that Blaine had won a signal triumph; the Democrats were confident that he had surrendered to Bismarck.[14] A number of American newspapers, notably the influential New York *Herald* and the New York *Evening Post*, were much concerned over this apparent

---

[12] New York *World*, March 31, 1889, quoted in Public Opinion, VI, 571–572 (April 6, 1889).

[13] The story is that the American commissioners found Bismarck overbearing and cabled home in perturbation about his irritability. Blaine promptly replied, "The extent of the Chancellor's irritability is not the measure of American rights." Whereupon Bismarck gave in, and the American Secretary won a victory. What Blaine actually sent was a reproof to the American delegates; it came at the close of the negotiations; and probably never was brought to the attention of Bismarck at all. Alice F. Tyler, *The Foreign Policy of James G. Blaine* (Minneapolis, 1927), pp. 247–249.

[14] See *Public Opinion*, VIII, 403–404 (Feb. 1, 1890). The St. Paul *Globe* (Democratic) said: "It is the squarest back-down in the history of diplomacy. . . ."

reversal of the historic policy of nonentanglement. Though many people, including Blaine, regarded the Samoan condominium as merely a temporary departure, there was something remarkable about the determination of the United States, ten years before Dewey's guns boomed at Manila, to go to the very brink of war rather than yield negligible commercial and questionable strategic advantages in this distant archipelago.

DIVIDING THE BOOTY

The tripartite protectorate proved inherently unworkable. It was the old story of too many cooks—jealous ones at that. Nevertheless, the arrangement did produce, temporarily at least, a somewhat better

Honest Friendship with All Nations, Entangling Alliances with None.—THOMAS JEFFERSON.

(From the New York *World*, 1899.)

feeling among the three nations involved. The well-being of the natives was throughout a secondary consideration. But inevitable rivalries among the Powers and the Samoans again turned the verdant islands into a battlefield. Jealousy, intrigue, and murder once more became the order of the day. Disagreeable incidents involving the United States and Germany again agitated the American press. The Pittsburgh *Dispatch*, for example, emphatically declared that "If there should ever be a popular vote whether the money of the people of the United States should be expended in bulldozing the Samoans . . . the people would record a very emphatic negative." [15]

In 1893 Grover Cleveland, archfoe of expansion, again became President. In successive messages to Congress he used the Samoan entanglement as an illustration of the folly of departing from the policy of the Fathers. He even invited Congress to take steps to terminate the existing arrangement. His Secretary of State, Walter Q. Gresham, who was no less hostile, drew up a strong arraignment:

> Soberly surveying the history of our relations with Samoa, we well may inquire what we have gained by our departure from our established policy beyond the expenses, the responsibilities, and the entanglements that have so far been its only fruits. . . . The general act of Berlin . . . has utterly failed to correct, if indeed it has not aggravated, the very evils which it was designed to prevent.[16]

But the Spanish War wrought a change in the American mind. With the Philippines, Hawaii, Guam, and Puerto Rico recently acquired, Samoa seemed but a logical complement to the far-flung American empire. Late in 1899, therefore, the Samoan group was divided between Germany and the United States. Germany made off with the two largest islands, which pleased her; [17] but America secured the remainder, including Tutuila, with the harbor of Pago Pago, on which she had kept an unwavering eye since Grant's day. The embarrassing protectorate was terminated, and decades of squabbling were ended. The arrangement was approved by the Senate without serious difficulty, although the bitter anti-imperialist, Senator Pettigrew of South Dakota, shouted: "We blot out, then, a sovereign nation, a

---

[15] *Literary Digest*, IX, 95 (May 26, 1894). For an interesting analysis of American opinion see Vagts, *Deutschland und die Vereinigten Staaten in der Weltpolitik*, I, 745.
[16] *Foreign Relations, 1894*, appendix, I, 513 (May 9, 1894).
[17] Stolberg-Wernigerode, *Germany and the United States*, pp. 269–270. Great Britain received compensations elsewhere. See the full treatment of J. W. Ellison, "The Partition of Samoa: A Study in Imperialism and Diplomacy," *Pacific Hist. Rev.*, VIII (1939), 259–288.

people with whom we have treaty obligations, and divide the spoils."
But the American public, surfeited already with troublesome island
populations, paid little attention to these minor pickings.

THE BIBLE PRECEDES THE FLAG

Much more understandable and natural than the involvement in
Samoa was the increasingly close connection between the United
States and Hawaii. The first Americans to reach this tiny kingdom
were Pacific traders, and they found the idyllic islands an indispensable halfway house for refreshment and supplies. They were followed
in 1820 by the first band of New England missionaries, who established a remarkable influence over the natives. After these fishers
of men came American fishers of whales, who, throughout the four
decades preceding the Civil War, made the archipelago both a base
and a rendezvous.[18] During the heyday of whaling, hundreds of
rollicking seamen could be found ashore enjoying the languorous de-
lights of living and loving in Hawaii. By 1842 five-sixths of all ships
calling at this mid-Pacific paradise flew the Stars and Stripes; and
American cultural influence had become so widespread that there was
much about Honolulu to suggest a typical New England town.[19]

But other nations were not indifferent to the great strategic advantages of Hawaii, and British influence, in particular, was also
strong in the islands. In 1842, following evidences of British designs,
both Secretary Webster and President Tyler declared that while the
United States had no intention of acquiring Hawaii, it could not view
with equanimity the annexation of the archipelago by a foreign Power.
This policy was reiterated on several other occasions by succeeding
Secretaries of State. In 1843 an overzealous British naval officer
took over Hawaii, but he was promptly disavowed and restitution
was made. Nevertheless American public opinion was disturbed by
this incident.[20] Hugh S. Legaré, Secretary of State *ad interim,* wrote
that "we might even feel justified, consistently with our own princi-

[18] See R. S. Kuykendall, *The Hawaiian Kingdom, 1778–1854* (Honolulu, 1938),
pp. 304–313. This multiple-archive work is exhaustive.

[19] Professor H. W. Bradley regards Hawaii during these years as "the farthest extension of the American frontier." "The American Frontier in Hawaii," Pacific Coast
Branch of Amer. Hist. Assn., *Proceedings,* 1930, p. 150.

[20] The British minister in Washington wrote that "the American newspapers, with
very few exceptions, are filled in relation thereto with vehemently abusive articles
against Great Britain." Fox to Aberdeen, June 13, 1843, quoted in Kuykendall, *The
Hawaiian Kingdom,* p. 200. For a full discussion of the British occupancy, see Ch. XIII
of *ibid.*

ples, in interfering by force to prevent its [Hawaiian kingdom] falling into the hands of one of the great powers of Europe." [21]

That same year, 1843, the British and French signed an agreement by which they bound themselves not to annex the Hawaiian islands. Though applauding this step, the Washington government, true to its policy of nonentanglement, declined to join Great Britain and France.[22]

In the fifties, after America had acquired a Pacific frontage, and after the French had temporarily seized Honolulu in 1849, a genuine flurry for annexing Hawaii developed in the United States. In 1851 a San Francisco newspaper declared:

The native population are fast fading away, the foreign fast increasing. The inevitable destiny of the islands is to pass into the possession of another power. That power is just as inevitably our own. . . . The pear is nearly ripe; we have scarcely to shake the tree in order to bring the luscious fruit readily into our lap.[23]

During the next three years there were wild rumors of filibusters about to descend upon Hawaii; and annexation proposals were debated in Congress and in the press. In 1854 the expansionist Pierce administration, with Marcy as Secretary of State, negotiated a treaty of annexation with the Hawaiian kingdom. But the pact proved to be unsatisfactory to the United States, largely because of the article making provision for immediate statehood. This stipulation apparently had been inserted through the influence of those in Hawaii who were anxious to defeat annexation.

Secretary Marcy next attempted to salvage something by concluding, in 1855, a commercial reciprocity treaty. The Senate failed to approve it, in part because of opposition from the sugar producing state of Louisiana.[24] Another reciprocity treaty, negotiated in 1867, was defeated primarily, it appears, because certain Senators feared that acceptance might block ultimate annexation.[25]

The advocates of reciprocity finally triumphed in 1875, when a

[21] *Sen. Ex. Docs.*, 52 Cong., 2 sess., no. 77, p. 109 (Legaré to Everett, June 13, 1843).

[22] R. W. Van Alstyne, "Great Britain, the United States, and Hawaiian Independence, 1850-1855," *Pacific Hist. Rev.*, IV (1935), 15-16.

[23] *Alta California* (San Francisco), April 22, 1851, quoted in Kuykendall, *The Hawaiian Kingdom*, p. 408.

[24] O. E. Hooley, "Hawaiian Negotiation for Reciprocity, 1855-1857," *Pacific Hist. Rev.*, VII (1938), 144.

[25] John Patterson, "The United States and Hawaiian Reciprocity, 1867-1870," *ibid.*, VII (1938), 25.

sweeping treaty was concluded. The miniature kingdom bound it-self to make no territorial concessions to foreign Powers, and in re-turn was permitted to export sugar to the United States duty free. So favorable was this arrangement that the languishing sugar in-dustry of Hawaii experienced an unprecedented boom, and the eco-nomic life of the islands became so inextricably bound up with the United States as to make political union practically inevitable. This, in fact, is what many supporters of the treaty intended.

The reciprocity treaty, though opposed by American sugar and rice interests, was renewed in 1884, but it was not approved until 1887, when the Senate amended it so as to secure an exclusive right to use the invaluable Pearl Harbor as a naval station. Slowly and inexorably Hawaii was being drawn into the American orbit.

ANOTHER TEXAS

As the century neared its end a small group of Americans, some of them the sons of missionaries, had come to control about two thirds of the total taxable real estate of the Hawaiian Islands. They had prospered remarkably until 1890, when the Congress of the United States put sugar on the free list and provided a bounty of two cents a pound for American producers. Hawaiian sugar, no longer benefit-ing from the same privileges as the American-grown product, suf-fered a damaging blow. Annexation was clearly the only sure safe-guard against such discrimination.

This obvious economic motive led to "sugar conspiracy" charges, and to the allegation in the United States that the revolution of 1893 was "of sugar, by sugar, and for sugar." The New York *Herald* re-peatedly used as an editorial filler the italicized inquiry: "*Is Sprec-kels & Co.* [a leading Hawaiian producer] *the little nigger in the fence of the sugar islands?*" But a number of Hawaiian cane planters, in-cluding Spreckels himself, were opposed to annexation because they feared that the contract labor laws of the United States would cut off the Oriental labor supply and reduce the islands to "a cow pas-ture." [26] There can be no doubt, however, that a larger economic motive was present. The decadent native dynasty was extravagant, corrupt, capricious; and the whites would be much more certain to retain their valuable property, as well as their lives and liberties, if the islands were annexed and white supremacy was guaranteed.

In 1891, Queen Liliuokalani came to the tottering Hawaiian

[26] Pratt, *Expansionists of 1898*, pp. 156–157.

throne. She bitterly resented the liberal constitution of 1887, which the whites, though outnumbered, had imposed upon her weak-kneed brother and through which they had strengthened their power. Adopting the rallying cry of "Hawaii for the Hawaiians," Liliuokalani attempted, on January 14, 1893, to promulgate a new and autocratic constitution by royal edict.

The white leaders of Hawaii, fearing for their position and property, had already taken steps to organize a revolution. Since the great majority of them were Americans or of American ancestry, they besought the notoriously proannexationist United States minister in Honolulu, John L. Stevens, to support them. On January 16, 1893, Stevens responded to their entreaties when he ordered more than one hundred and fifty armed men to be landed from the U.S.S. *Boston*, then in Honolulu harbor, for the presumed purpose of protecting American life and property. It is remarkable, however, that most of these troops were not stationed near the American property, but where their presence would intimidate the Queen. The next day, January 17, 1893, Stevens precipitantly accorded recognition to that revolutionary government which, a few hours before, had been so helpless as to cry for assistance. The Queen, overawed by the American troops and the obvious hostility of the United States, yielded her authority under protest. Less than two weeks later, February 1, 1893, the enthusiastic Stevens proclaimed Hawaii a protectorate, hoisted the American flag, and advised the State Department: "The Hawaiian pear is now fully ripe, and this is the golden hour for the United States to pluck it. If annexation does not take place promptly . . . these people, by their necessities, might be forced towards becoming a British colony. . . ." [27]

RUSH-ORDER ANNEXATION

Three days after the landing of the American troops a Hawaiian commission (four Americans and one Englishman) was hurrying to Washington to lay the islands at the feet of the United States. Their arrival came as no surprise to the Harrison administration. Secretary of State Foster had not only allowed Stevens' proannexationist ardor to go unrebuked, but, expecting a blowup, had been quietly preparing American public opinion for annexation. [28] On February 15, 1893, less than one month after Queen Liliuokalani's downfall, a hastily

[27] *Foreign Relations, 1894*, appendix II, p. 402 (Stevens to Foster, Feb. 1, 1893).
[28] Pratt, *Expansionists of 1898*, p. 70.

drawn, hastily signed, and hastily submitted treaty of annexation was before the Senate.

The American public forthwith found itself involved in its first major debate on the portentous issue of imperialism. A popular jingle swept the country:

> . . . Liliuokalani
> Give us your little brown hannie! [29]

From a large section of the press, chiefly big-navy, expansionist, and Republican, there came a cry of welcome. Strategic, commercial, and humanitarian considerations, it was alleged, pointed to the desirability of annexation. Besides, if the United States did not annex the islands, the British or Japanese, who were both actively interested, might take them and use them to America's disadvantage. The New York *Independent* changed Stevens' fruit but not his figure of speech: "The ripe apple falls into our hands, and we would be very foolish if we should throw it away." "The popular verdict is clear, unequivocal, and practically unanimous," declared the expansionist New York *Tribune*. "Hawaii is welcome."

But the voices of doubting Thomases, chiefly Democrats, spoiled the harmonic symphony. There was much about this business, they said, especially the "sugar baron" angle, that required a thorough airing. Why not give the Queen her day in court? Why all the haste to depart from the traditional policy of isolation, which had served America so well, and embark upon the uncharted sea of imperialistic difficulties? Could Hawaii, with its polyglot population, ever become a state? There was food for thought in Roger Camerden's "Warily Brothers":

> "Shall we take Hawaii in, sirs?" that's the question of the day.
> Would the speedy annexation of that dusky country pay?
> Would the revenues from sugar and from smuggled opium
> Counteract the heavy burdens that with them are sure to come? [30]

A little more than two weeks of Harrison's Republican administration remained when the treaty was rushed to the Senate. Not geared to the speed of the Hawaiian commissioners and the State Department, the Senators had failed to dispose of the issue when the anti-imperialistic Grover Cleveland returned to the presidency, March 4, 1893.

---

[29] Allan Nevins, *Grover Cleveland* (N.Y., 1934), p. 552.
[30] *Harper's Weekly*, XXXVII, 299 (Apr. 1, 1893).

CLEVELAND BLOCKS MANIFEST DESTINY

A man of lesser mettle than Cleveland would have closed his eyes to the unsavory features of the Hawaii business and would not have attempted the impossible task of sweeping back the tide of expansionist sentiment. But the new President was "a slave to conscience"; and his exacting standards of public as well as of private honor led him to suspect that Queen Liliuokalani had been wronged.[31] He wanted particularly to discover whether the dwindling native element, to whom the islands had originally belonged, favored annexation.

On March 9, 1893, Cleveland sent a curt, five-line message to the Senate in which he resorted to the unusual step of withdrawing the treaty for examination. He next appointed a special commissioner, ex-Congressman James H. Blount, to make a thorough investigation. Upon arriving in Hawaii, Blount hustled the American troops back to their ship and ordered the flag to be hauled down. The New York *Commercial Advertiser* could endure no more:

In ordering "Old Glory" pulled down at Honolulu President Cleveland turned back the hands on the dial of civilization. Native rule, ignorant, naked, heathen, is re-established; and the dream of an American republic at the cross-roads of the Pacific—a dream which Seward and Marcy and Blaine indulged, and the fulfillment of which the more enlightened of our 65,000,000 people awaited with glad anticipation, has been shattered by Grover Cleveland, the Buffalo lilliputian! [32]

During his stay in Hawaii Blount conducted an investigation of acknowledged thoroughness but disputed impartiality.[33] He finally reported to Cleveland that Stevens had improperly interfered with the revolution, and that a strong majority of the voters, including the disease-decimated natives, were opposed to annexation. One did not have to deny the right of the whites to revolt, or challenge the justice of their cause, to gather from Blount's facts that the uprising would not have succeeded without American assistance, and that it probably would not have been undertaken without Stevens' assur-

[31] Nevins, *Grover Cleveland*, p. 553.

[32] New York *Commercial Advertiser*, April 14, 1893, 4:3.

[33] Blount was a Georgian; and the Royal Hawaiian Band, led by a German not familiar with American Civil War history, thought to do him honor by playing "Marching Through Georgia." S. B. Dole, *Memoirs of the Hawaiian Revolution* (Honolulu, 1936), p. 97. It is unlikely, however, that Blount's observations were materially affected by this occurrence.

ances of support. In fact, the evidence was so damning as measurably to dampen the annexation craze in America. The New York *Times* found that a conspiracy had been exposed, which, "if not repudiated by this nation, would sully the honor and blacken the fair name of the United States."

To Cleveland the only possible course was to make honorable amends for the grave wrong that had been done Queen Liliuokalani, and put the fallen pear back on the tree. He instructed the new American minister in Honolulu to secure pledges from the deposed Queen that, if restored to her throne, she would deal leniently with the white conspirators. The dusky monarch, with the calm fury of a woman scorned, at first replied that she would have both their heads and their property. But the white oligarchy, whose tiny army was in complete control of the situation, steadfastly refused to bow itself out. The storm of criticism in America redoubled its fury, greatly augmented by the church-missionary element. The Massachusetts Republican platform of 1894 proclaimed: "No barbarous Queen beheading men in Hawaii." Mutterings rose even from the Democratic camp, where the Atlanta *Constitution*, which opposed reinstatement of the Queen, reminded the President that the "Democratic party has not been in the habit of restoring monarchies anywhere."

Cleveland's motives, in a day of international land grabbing, were honorable both to himself and his country.[34] But he could enthrone the deposed Polynesian potentate only by using superior force—and American public opinion would never have sanctioned the slaying of fellow Americans in Hawaii for such a purpose. Cleveland thereupon dumped the whole problem on the doorstep of Congress in a lengthy message in which he reviewed the whole affair and excoriated the policy of his predecessor. Congress passed two resolutions of noninterference; and there the matter rested until the advent of a President less troubled by conscience and better able to read the signs of the times.

CONSUMMATION—NOT CHANGE

From 1894 to 1898 the partially Americanized republic of Hawaii, though recognized by Cleveland in the summer of 1894, waited outside the gate. The Honolulu government, stressing "Mongolization" of the islands by the Japanese, propagandized [35] actively in the United

[34] Nevins, *Grover Cleveland*, p. 561.
[35] This conclusion is based upon an examination of the correspondence relative to the propaganda which is filed in the Archives of Hawaii, Honolulu.

States for annexation. But nothing could be accomplished until Cleveland went out of power in March, 1897. The new Republican administration of William McKinley was more favorable to the importunities of the Hawaiian government, and a new treaty of annexation was signed, June 16, 1897.

Unexpected opposition came from Japan, which, having recently defeated China, was beginning to feel her strength and glimpse her role. On June 19, 1897, the Japanese minister lodged a strong protest against annexation on the grounds that it would disturb the *status quo* in the Pacific and jeopardize the interests of some 25,000 remarkably reproductive Japanese in Hawaii.[36] Secretary of State Sherman parried these arguments, and replied that annexation was but the logical culmination of seventy years' association and of progressively closer contacts. But in spite of the Japanese bogey, which was pressed into overtime service, the treaty was blocked in the Senate by determined Democrats. Cleveland's former Secretary of State, Richard Olney, wrote exultingly that the annexation project was "in the soup," while the New York *Nation* declared that it was "dead beyond the hope of resurrection."

Then, as if Providence were on the side of Manifest Destiny, came Dewey's breathtaking victory over the Spaniards at Manila, May 1, 1898. It seemed that Hawaii would be useful, not to say indispensable, in the expeditious sending of supplies and reinforcements to the Americans in the Philippines. "Bridge the Pacific," cried the Philadelphia *Press*. The need for haste seemed so obvious that the slumbering treaty was shelved and a joint resolution of annexation, which would require only a simple majority vote, was hastily drawn and submitted to Congress.

During the subsequent debates it was warmly argued that America needed to acquire the islands in order to succor Dewey. This was not true because the Hawaiian government, hoping to create sentiment in the United States favorable to annexation, was openly violating its neutrality and giving the Americans every kind of assistance pos-

---

[36] T. A. Bailey, "Japan's Protest against the Annexation of Hawaii," *Jour. of Mod. Hist.*, III (1931), 51 ff. The strong tone of the Japanese protest may have been due to an affront to the Japanese representative growing out of the forgetfulness of the aged Secretary Sherman. The latter informed the Japanese minister that no annexation treaty was being negotiated; a short time thereafter its signature was announced. Apparently Sherman had forgotten all about the matter. J. W. Foster, *Diplomatic Memoirs* (Boston, 1909), II, 173. For additional explanations of the strong tone of the Japanese protest see P. J. Treat, *Diplomatic Relations between the United States and Japan, 1895–1905* (Stanford University, 1938), p. 45.

sible.[37] There was, nevertheless, a general feeling that Dewey should not be "let down." It was also argued, in Congress and out, that since the United States had allowed the Hawaiian government to compromise its neutrality, there was no honorable alternative but to bind the islands to America in the bonds of annexation.

Advocates of a powerful navy also took a leading part in the discussion. Men like Captain Mahan refurbished the old argument—and a strong one—that the United States needed Hawaii as a first line of defense to ward off attacks on the mainland. It was also repeatedly pointed out that if the islands should fall into the hands of a hostile foreign Power, say Japan, they could be used as a base to menace the security of the United States. This argument had been used before, but the fear recently aroused by the operations of the Spanish fleet gave it a new validity.

Finally, there were the advocates of expansion, in Congress and out. As Representative Gibson cried: "Manifest Destiny says, 'Take them in.' The American people say, 'Take them.' Obedient to the voice of the people, I shall cast my vote to take them in; and tomorrow this House of Representatives will by a good round majority say, 'Take them in.' [Applause.]" [38]

War hysteria and the new imperialism were not to be denied. "The jingo bacillus," declared Representative Champ Clark of Missouri, "is indefatigable in its work." The joint resolution passed Congress by large majorities and was signed, on July 7, 1898, by President McKinley, who remarked, "Annexation is not change; it is consummation." [39] It was indeed a consummation of the work of American missionaries, traders, whalers, sugar planters, big-navyites, and imperialists. The time had finally come when it seemed to the American people that an independent Hawaii was both an anachronism and a danger.

BIBLIOGRAPHICAL NOTE

REFERENCES ON SAMOA. The most detailed account in English is G. H. Ryden, *The Foreign Policy of the United States in Relation to Samoa* (New Haven, 1933), which somewhat neglects the German side, a deficiency supplied by Alfred

[37] T. A. Bailey, "The United States and Hawaii during the Spanish-American War," *Amer. Hist. Rev.*, XXXVI (1931), 554–555.

[38] *Cong. Record*, 55 Cong., 2 sess., appendix, p. 549 (June 14, 1898).

[39] To his private secretary McKinley remarked: "We need Hawaii just as much and a good deal more than we did California. It is manifest destiny." C. S. Olcott, *The Life of William McKinley* (Boston, 1916), I, 379.

Vagts' exhaustive *Deutschland und die Vereinigten Staaten in der Weltpolitik* (N.Y., 1935), I, Ch. X. A briefer treatment (from the German point of view) is Count Otto zu Stolberg-Wernigerode, *Germany and the United States of America during the Era of Bismarck* (trans. from German, Reading, Pa., 1937), pp. 196–270. Sylvia Masterman, *The Origins of International Rivalry in Samoa, 1845–1884* (Stanford University, 1934), is useful for the British side. Blaine's policy is most fully developed in Alice F. Tyler, *The Foreign Policy of James G. Blaine* (Minneapolis, 1927), Ch. IX. American public opinion regarding Germany with reference to Samoa is developed in Clara E. Schieber, *The Transformation of American Sentiment toward Germany, 1870–1914* (Boston, 1923), Ch. II. REFERENCES ON HAWAII. The best study of the movement culminating in the annexation of Hawaii is J. W. Pratt, *Expansionists of 1898* (Baltimore, 1936). A good brief account is Allan Nevins, *Grover Cleveland* (N.Y., 1934), Ch. XXX. For a very readable survey on both Samoa and Hawaii see F. R. Dulles, *America in the Pacific* (Boston, 1932), pp. 98–198. An exhaustive study by a recognized authority is R. S. Kuykendall, *The Hawaiian Kingdom, 1778–1854* (Honolulu, 1938). On Japan's protest see P. J. Treat, *Diplomatic Relations between the United States and Japan, 1895–1905* (Stanford University, 1938), Ch. III; also T. A. Bailey, "Japan's Protest against the Annexation of Hawaii," *Jour. of Mod. Hist.*, III (1931), 46–61. Further references: see footnotes of this chapter and Bemis and Griffin, *Guide*, pp. 372–383.

RECENT REFERENCES. C. C. Tansill, *The Foreign Policy of Thomas F. Bayard, 1885–1897* (N.Y., 1940), pp. 3–119, has an exhaustive account of relations with Samoa until 1889. It is clear that affairs were in a serious posture before the Apia crisis, and that Bayard's policies regarding Samoa were taken over by Blaine and embodied in the Berlin agreement (p. 119). Particularly useful is the treatment of the Washington conference in 1887. There is also a full chapter on relations with Hawaii during Cleveland's first administration. Bayard was unfavorable to the Pearl Harbor amendment to the treaty of 1884. Early American interest in Hawaii and Samoa is treated in the larger setting by Jean I. Brookes, *International Rivalry in the Pacific Islands, 1800–1875* (Berkeley, Calif., 1941). How the United States picked up the lesser bits, like Wake and Baker, is told briefly in D. N. Leff, *Uncle Sam's Pacific Islets* (Stanford University, 1940). A. T. Volwiler, "Harrison, Blaine, and American Foreign Policy, 1889–1893," Amer. Philosophical Soc. *Procs.*, LXXIX (1938), 637–648, concludes that the "Empire Days" of the United States dawned in the Harrison administration. Harrison, Blaine, and the active Secretary of the Navy Tracy sought the Danish West Indies, a lease of Samaná Bay (Santo Domingo), a concession at Môle St. Nicholas (Haiti), a naval base at Chimbote (Peru), all of Canada, and a naval base in Samoa (p. 639). When Harrison left office the Navy ranked seventh instead of twelfth.

NEW REFERENCES. For a general monograph on Cleveland's foreign policy, for one on Americans in Hawaii (1789–1843), and for articles on Hawaiian sugar, Hawaiian reciprocity, Hawaiian immigration, and on Hawaii as an American frontier, see Bibliographical Appendix, p. 933.

4TH ED. REFS. See Bibliographical Appendix, p. 933.

CHAPTER XXIX

Cleveland and the Venezuela Crisis with Great Britain

". . . In English eyes the United States was then [1895] so completely a negligible quantity that it was believed only words the equivalent of blows would be really effective."

Richard Olney, 1912.

Twisting the Lion's Tail

DURING the late eighties and early nineties Anglophobia was still a force to be reckoned with in American political life. The old embers were being constantly stirred by anti-British textbooks, patriotic juvenile fiction, and the ubiquitous Fourth of July "orator of the day," who annually and perspiringly berated George III. Hundreds of thousands of Americans firmly believed that England was an arrogant and antidemocratic land-grabber; that she was a hard-fisted creditor who held the republic's financial destinies in her grasp; that she flooded America with gold in an effort to bribe the United States into forsaking protection—a theme constantly used by high-tariff Republicans against the tariff-for-revenue Democrats.[1]

Whatever the validity of such charges, it is undeniable that during these years Great Britain was the leading sponsor of the gold standard. This was also the period when millions of the despairing masses of America were turning to free silver as a cure for all their ills, and they bitterly resented the attitude of the British. Senator Chandler of New Hampshire was reported as advocating "a war with England, with or without cause, in the interests of silver." William H. Harvey's "Coin's Financial School," the most effective free-silver pamphlet of the

---

[1] Thomas Marshall, the Indianian who served as Vice-President from 1913 to 1921, remembered how small boys chanted on the Fourth of July:

> Fee, fi, fo, fum,
> I smell the blood of an Englishman;
> Dead or alive, I'll have some.
> Fee, fi, fo, fum.

Recollections of Thomas R. Marshall (Indianapolis, 1925), p. 125.

period, declared that war with England would be the most "popular" and "just war ever waged by man." [2]

Hate-ridden immigrants from the land of Erin also contributed powerfully to the growth of ill will. From 1876 to the close of the century the presidential elections were all relatively close; and the Irish, who were congested in pivotal Eastern cities, could not be ignored.[3] Legislative bodies, as well as the national conventions of both parties, repeatedly declared in favor of Irish independence—as if that were legitimate business of the United States. Even the State Department was not above giving the lion's tail a vigorous twist on the eve of presidential elections. Fortunately, the British statesmen were not wholly ignorant of this state of affairs, and they made due allowances for it.

Fortunately, also, certain influences were operating to draw the two peoples closer together. The increasing democratization of England probably brought about a stronger feeling of kinship. The assassination of President Garfield, in 1881, shocked the British and elicited from them expressions of good will pleasing to America.[4] In the same year the centennial of the battle of Yorktown was celebrated with a display of good sportsmanship on both sides. The long and respectable reign of Queen Victoria, who had many admirers in the United States, together with several blood-is-thicker-than-water incidents, also made for a happier feeling. Educated Americans held the writers of Victorian England in high esteem; and when in 1888 James Bryce published his penetrating classic, *The American Commonwealth*, the people of the United States were gratified that a Britisher could actually understand their good qualities. For their part, the English authors were much pleased when, in 1891, Congress belatedly passed a law making possible the obtaining of an international copyright. The defeat in 1896 of the Democratic candidate for the presidency, William Jennings Bryan, whose unorthodox financial views had caused much uneasiness among British investors, also contributed substantially to Anglo-American amity.[5] The great increase in transatlantic travel, in part a result of the improvement in steam navigation, led to the formation of important Anglo-American friendships (largely among

---

[2] J. F. Rhodes, *The McKinley and Roosevelt Administrations, 1897–1909* (N.Y., 1922), p. 23.

[3] In the campaign of 1896 the Republicans sought Irish support for their candidate, William McKinley, by a pamphlet entitled, "How McKinley is hated in England."

[4] See the striking cartoon in *Punch*, LXXXI, 151 (Oct. 1, 1881).

[5] See the cartoon in *ibid.*, CXI, 223 (Nov. 7, 1896), indicating satisfaction over McKinley's election.

what Artemus Ward called the "Atlantic Monthly fellers"), with a consequent warming of the handclasp across the sea. Nor should we fail to note that another strong bond was the great respect which members of the American bar had for British legal principles.

GOLD AND BOUNDARIES

Such was the general atmosphere in 1893, when Grover Cleveland, the well-known foe of sensationalism in foreign affairs, became President for the second time. The attention of the Department of State had already been drawn to a boundary dispute between British Guiana and Venezuela. The area in question had considerable strategic value, particularly to the Venezuelans, for it commanded the mouth of the Orinoco, their most important river. As far back as 1840 the British government had commissioned Sir Robert Schomburgk to ascertain the true boundary. Although he made a careful survey, the Venezuelans refused to accept his line, and the dispute dragged on and on without prospect of settlement.[6] With true horse-trading instinct, both sides advanced extreme pretensions, particularly the Venezuelans, who claimed approximately one half of British Guiana.

THE
VENEZUELA-BRITISH GUIANA
BOUNDARY DISPUTE
•••••• Schomburgk Line
——— Final Settlement
▨▨▨ Extreme British claim
▧▧▧ Extreme Venezuelan claim

But the British were not greatly concerned about the dispute. They had territory the world over; the area meant much less to them than to Venezuela; and they were powerful enough to adjust the matter satisfactorily in their own good time. On several different occasions, however, they did offer to settle on the Schomburgk line, with one extremely important exception: they would yield Point Barima, which commanded the Orinoco. The Venezuelans, who hoped for much more,

---

[6] P. R. Fossum, "The Anglo-Venezuelan Boundary Controversy," *Hispanic Amer. Hist. Rev.*, VIII (1928), 299–329.

refused this overture; whereupon the British withdrew their offer. The Foreign Office in London seems to have been much less interested in further concessions after the discovery of new gold deposits in the disputed area.

Throughout these years the South American republic repeatedly insisted on arbitration. Since the Venezuelan claims were extravagant, and since arbiters have a tendency to split the difference, Downing Street declined the offer. The London government did not think it fair to expose some 40,000 subjects, who were enjoying the stability of Anglo-Saxon institutions, to the hazard of Venezuelan misrule. Besides, if the British consented to arbitrate in this instance, claims against their undarkened empire would sprout forth all over the world. So England, though unwilling to yield any of the area she had long held (roughly, east of the Schomburgk line), was prepared to arbitrate her claims, which were considerable, west of that line. In 1887 the disgruntled Venezuelans abruptly suspended diplomatic relations with London—a rash act that made amicable adjustment all the more difficult.

It is probable that the Venezuelans adopted a defiant attitude because they could be sure of the sympathetic support of the United States in any clash with Great Britain. The Venezuelan minister in Washington repeatedly presented his case to the American authorities in such a way as to leave the impression that England was the wanton aggressor and that his nation was wholly without guile.[7] He invoked the name of the "immortal Monroe," and strongly urged the United States to use its good offices to bring about arbitration. The British, on the other hand, failed to present their case so actively to the Department of State. This would have been undignified; besides, to them the dispute was relatively unimportant.

Responding to the importunities of the Venezuelan minister, the Department of State repeatedly brought to Britain's attention the desirability of an amicable settlement, and in 1887 formally suggested arbitration. But the London government, for reasons that seemed sufficient to it, declined America's good offices. There the matter rested.

[7] Dexter Perkins, *The Monroe Doctrine, 1867–1907* (Baltimore, 1937), pp. 50 ff. Thomas Bayard, United States ambassador in London, who, as Secretary of State, had earlier investigated the problem, wrote of the "wholly unreliable character of the Venezuelan Rulers and people. . . ." He also found that "Speculators in the U.S. have thrust their soiled hands into the business—and sought to embroil the U.S. in sustaining their corrupt contracts." Bayard to Cleveland, Dec. 4, 1895, Feb. 12, 1896, Cleveland Papers, Library of Congress. The facts and conclusions of the present chapter have been drawn in part from an examination of the Olney and Cleveland papers, and the records of the Department of State.

Olney Takes a Twist

President Cleveland gradually began to develop a keen interest in the Venezuela boundary dispute. He had no particular reason to love Great Britain, particularly after the Sackville-West incident, which may have cost him the election of 1888. Superficially, the Venezuela matter looked like just another case of land-grabbing at the expense of a weak nation; and Cleveland was further disturbed when, in April 1895, British troops undertook to collect claims for damages by temporarily seizing the customs house at Corinto, Nicaragua.[8] Cleveland's sympathies naturally went out to the underdog, as Liliuokalani could attest; and he was annoyed because Downing Street refused to respond with cordiality to America's overtures regarding Venezuela.

The boundary dispute entered upon a new phase when the Venezuelan government employed as its propagandist William L. Scruggs, a former minister to Venezuela under the Harrison regime. Scruggs prepared a clever pamphlet, entitled "British Aggressions in Venezuela, or the Monroe Doctrine on Trial," which he began to distribute in the fall of 1894. This booklet quickly ran through four editions, was sold on newsstands, and fell into the hands of editors, governors, Congressmen and other leaders of opinion.[9] Scruggs also sought out his Congressman, who introduced a resolution urging arbitration of the dispute. Early in 1895 this declaration was speedily adopted by both houses of Congress.

The Cleveland administration could hardly fail to note the ground swell of protest against Britain's course. Editorials and articles were clamoring for action. Young Senator Henry Cabot Lodge of Massachusetts, a Republican and a leading Anglophobe, was writing for the *North American Review:*

If Great Britain is to be permitted to occupy the ports of Nicaragua and, still worse, take the territory of Venezuela, there is nothing to prevent her taking the whole of Venezuela or any other South American state. If Great Britain can do this with impunity, France and Germany will do it also. . . . The supremacy of the Monroe Doctrine should be established and at once—peaceably if we can, forcibly if we must.[10]

It was evident that if the Democratic administration did not give the lion's tail a good old-fashioned twist, and get credit for it, the jingoes

[8] Allan Nevins, *Grover Cleveland* (N.Y., 1934), p. 632.
[9] Perkins, *The Monroe Doctrine, 1867–1907*, pp. 143–144.
[10] *North American Review*, CLX, 658 (June, 1895).

(Republicans and others) might take things in hand themselves. So Secretary of State Olney undertook to prepare a note to Great Britain.

The obstinate and unbending Olney, who had come down from a stern line of New England Puritans, had made his mark as an aggressive railroad attorney—certainly not the best training for delicate diplomatic correspondence. The defiant note that he drafted regarding Venezuela impressed Cleveland favorably, though the latter "softened" the "verbiage" here and there. The main theme of Olney's declaration, which went to England under date of July 20, 1895, was that Great Britain was violating the Monroe Doctrine. This venerable dictum, Olney held, meant that any European (British) interference in the affairs of the New World (Venezuela) would be regarded by the United States as an unfriendly act. The American people were vitally concerned in the Venezuela boundary dispute because they could not permit any flouting or weakening of the doctrine that had served them so well. Downing Street was therefore asked to declare categorically whether it would or would not submit the dispute to arbitration.

This was certainly a strained interpretation of the Monroe Doctrine. Olney would have been on firmer—but not too firm—ground if he had regarded the alleged attempt of the British to push their boundary into Venezuela as a violation of Monroe's noncolonization dictum.[11] Yet it must be remembered that sovereign nations enjoy the privilege of interpreting their own policies—and the Monroe Doctrine was a policy peculiarly American. If Olney had stated his case concisely and temperately in language appropriate for diplomatic intercourse, the British could hardly have taken serious offense.

But the note was neither temperate nor concise. The tone was swaggering, even belligerent. Though Olney denied that he was passing judgment upon the merits of the case, he had obviously drawn his review of the controversy from Venezuelan sources. There were, indeed, glaring inaccuracies in his impeachment of Britain's conduct. Even his exposition of the Monroe Doctrine bristled with serious historical errors. One passage in the note shamed Webster's memorable reply to Hülsemann. Olney stated that as a result of the beneficent operations of the Monroe Doctrine:

To-day the United States is practically sovereign on this continent, and its fiat is law upon the subjects to which it confines its interposition. Why? It is not . . . because wisdom and justice and equity are the invariable

[11] Perkins, *The Monroe Doctrine, 1867–1907*, p. 44.

characteristics of the dealings of the United States. It is because, in addition to all other grounds, its infinite resources combined with its isolated position render it master of the situation and practically invulnerable as against any or all other powers.[12]

Hereafter, thought Olney, Great Britain will sit up and listen respectfully when the United States suggests arbitration.[13]

SALISBURY CONDESCENDS TO ANSWER

Cleveland, who later dubbed his Secretary's effort a "twenty inch gun" note, was confident that the British would be startled into a prompt reply. In fact, Olney had concluded by expressing the hope that an answer would be forthcoming before Congress met in December. But Downing Street was maddeningly deliberate. The American press seethed with rumors, and the New York *Herald* ran big headlines (for that time) about a ninety-day ultimatum to Britain. There was still no answer when Congress met; and the Chaplain of the House, reflecting the belligerent mood of the members, prayed: "Heavenly Father, let peace reign throughout our borders. Yet may we be quick to resent anything like an insult to this our nation." [14] When the British reply was at length forthcoming, after an interval of four months, Cleveland's patience had worn thin, and neither he nor Olney was in a genial mood.

Why the delay? First of all the American note was extremely long (about 10,000 words) and raised issues that required careful study. Lord Salisbury, whose ministry had come into power only a few weeks before, was carrying a double burden as Prime Minister and Foreign Secretary. Not only was the government fully occupied at home, but there were pressing problems abroad, notably in the Near East. The amiable and somewhat pro-British Thomas Bayard, United States ambassador in London, failed to impress upon Lord Salisbury the seriousness of the situation.[15] This remissness not only left the London

[12] *Foreign Relations, 1895*, I, 558 (Olney to Bayard, July 20, 1895).

[13] See Henry James, *Richard Olney and His Public Service* (Boston, 1923), p. 140 (Olney to Knox, Jan. 29, 1912).

[14] *Cong. Record*, 54 Cong., 1 sess., p. 26 (Dec. 3, 1895).

[15] Bayard was regarded in America as an Anglophile, chiefly because of two speeches in which he had reflected unfavorably upon the Americans. These earned him the execration of Irish-Americans, and a vote of censure in the House of Representatives. The Buffalo *Express* declared, "Thomas Francis Bayard is the most popular Englishman ever born in the United States." Olney wrote of his disgust at the "constant stream of taffy played by Mr. Bayard upon the English people," while John Hay objected to his "slobbering over the British."

government in the dark but added to Cleveland's anger. Finally, the British had come to expect a "tail-twister" on the eve of a presidential election, and they probably thought that they were dealing with another "Jingo Jim" Blaine, who would indulge in bombast for home consumption and then beat a quiet retreat when his pretensions were challenged. As if this were not enough, the Foreign Office, which had planned to have its answer ready by the time Congress met, made a mistake about the date of convening.

Lord Salisbury, one of the most experienced diplomats and distinguished statesmen of the century, was fully as inflexible as Olney and Cleveland, whom he doubtless regarded as rank amateurs. The essence of his reply, embodied in two notes dated November 26, 1895, was that the seventy-two year old Monroe Doctrine was not applicable to existing conditions, that it was not recognized as international law, and that it was not relevant to a boundary controversy. Salisbury declared:

> The disputed frontier of Venezuela has nothing to do with any of the questions dealt with by President Monroe. It is not a question of the colonization by a European Power of any portion of America. It is not a question of the imposition upon the communities of South America of any system of government devised in Europe. It is simply the determination of the frontier of a British possession which belonged to the Throne of England long before the Republic of Venezuela came into existence.[16]

Great Britain could not, therefore, accept the suggestion of the United States that the matter be referred to arbitration. In short, it was none of America's affair.

Whatever the legal merits of Salisbury's argument—on the whole he had a strong case [17]—there can be no doubt that he erred in underestimating the attachment of the American people for the Monroe Doctrine. It is also clear that the tone of his reply was not such as to pour oil on the waters. There was about it a note of "civil indifference with just a touch of boredom"—what Andrew D. White referred to as a "rather cynical, 'Saturday Review,' high-Tory way." The noble lord corrected the obvious historical errors in Olney's composition much as a learned professor would pick to pieces a college freshman's composition. Besides, the British answer had a disquieting tone of finality. Olney had asked England if she would arbitrate. She had replied, flatly, "No." Salisbury seems to have committed a serious diplomatic

---

[16] *Foreign Relations, 1895*, I, 564–565 (Salisbury to Pauncefote, Nov. 26, 1895).
[17] See Perkins, *The Monroe Doctrine, 1867–1907*, pp. 178–180.

error when he failed to keep the negotiations open by making some kind of counterproposal or even by inviting further discussion. As it was, Olney and Cleveland were left in a most embarrassing position. They either had to admit that they had thrust their noses into somebody else's business or else plunge straight ahead.

Jingoism Has Its Day

When Cleveland read the Salisbury notes he felt, according to an intimate friend, "mad clear through." He sat up all night redrafting a message which had already been outlined by the ruffled Olney.[18] On December 17, 1895, the President sent this famous pronouncement to Congress.

Cleveland took sharp issue with Salisbury's interpretation of the Monroe Doctrine, and deplored the rebuff to the Administration's friendly attempt to end this dispute—a dispute that might eventuate in war and jeopardize the peace and safety of the people of the United States.[19] Thus far, he added, the Washington government had not undertaken to pass upon the merits of the controversy; but the time had come when it must determine where the line should be drawn. Cleveland therefore recommended that Congress pass an appropriation for the expenses of an investigating commission. When the report was completed, the United States "must resist by every means in its power" any attempt by Britain to exercise jurisdiction over territory that "we have determined of right belongs to Venezuela." In conclusion, Cleveland ominously declared that he was "fully alive to the responsibility incurred, and keenly realize[d] all the consequences that may follow." [20] In brief, the President was soberly recommending that the United States run the boundary line itself, and, if necessary, fight to maintain it.[21]

Cleveland's ringing message swept Congress off its feet. The House cheered these fighting words to the echo, while the ordinarily sedate Senate burst out in applause. Members of both parties, including such

[18] Nevins, *Grover Cleveland,* p. 639. Professor Nevins believes that Olney lost his temper in this affair, and that Cleveland did not. Nevins to writer, March 22, 1939.

[19] This was perhaps the strongest argument for American interference; yet it seems unlikely that weak Venezuela would have precipitated hostilities. Professor Perkins concludes that "no real national interest" justified Cleveland's message. *The Monroe Doctrine, 1867–1907,* p. 463.

[20] *Foreign Relations, 1895,* I, 545 (Dec. 17, 1895).

[21] The London *Punch* caused Cleveland to drawl: "Waal, Salisbury, Sir, whether you like it or not, We propose to arbitrate this matter Ourselves, and, in that event. We shall abide by Our Own decision." CIX, 302 (Dec. 28, 1895).

a bitter critic of Cleveland as Senator Lodge, were unstinting in their praise. Congress promptly, enthusiastically (there was "loud applause" in the House), and unanimously appropriated $100,000 for the expenses of the boundary commission. War seemed possible, even probable. Many thought it desirable. Senator Stewart of Nevada (a silver state) insisted that "war would be a good thing," even if the United States lost, "for it would rid the country of the English bank rule"; while other members of Congress thought it would submerge the economic and social discontent of the country.[22] Yet few Congressmen—or others—stopped to realize that the nation had negligible coast defenses, and that Britain had fifty battleships of the battleship class to three for the United States.

A wave of jingoism swept over the entire country with the speed of a prairie fire. Public men in all walks of life applauded. Twenty-six of twenty-eight governors who were approached pledged their support. Civil War veterans offered their services. The Irish National Alliance pledged 100,000 volunteers. The virile Theodore Roosevelt hoped that if there was a "muss," he might "have a hand in it myself." "Personally," he wrote, "I rather hope that the fight will come soon. The clamor of the peace faction has convinced me that this country needs a war." [23] The New York *Sun* carried the headline, "WAR IF NECESSARY."

THE RETURN OF SANITY

Fortunately, the voices of moderation were not completely drowned out in the wild outburst, which began to subside after about three days. The clergy, in particular, exercised a strong influence for a pacific settlement. Bishop Potter condemned the jingoes as "pinchbeck patriots," and a convocation of Baptist ministers declared that the United States might better go to war to save the Armenians from the Turks. Peace societies on both sides of the Atlantic also labored manfully.[24] Students of international law, like John Bassett Moore, found America's position untenable, while intellectuals like Carl Schurz, Edwin L.

[22] See Alfred Vagts, *Deutschland und die Vereinigten Staaten in der Weltpolitik* (N.Y., 1935), I, 511.

[23] *Selections from the Correspondence of Theodore Roosevelt and Henry Cabot Lodge, 1884–1918* (N.Y., 1925), I, 204–205 (Roosevelt to Lodge, Dec. 27, 1895). Roosevelt also wrote: "Let the fight come if it must; I don't care whether our sea coast cities are bombarded or not; we would take Canada." *Ibid.*, I, 200 (Roosevelt to Lodge, Dec. 20, 1895).

[24] Merle Curti, *Peace or War: The American Struggle, 1636–1936* (N.Y., 1936), pp. 159–160.

Godkin, editor of the New York *Nation,* and President Charles W. Eliot of Harvard University, condemned Cleveland's stand.

Financial interests also acted as a powerful brake on jingoism. The tremendous shock produced by Cleveland's message caused American securities to tumble in value approximately a half billion dollars. The New York Chamber of Commerce passed resolutions deploring the "war craze." Other financial leaders, whom the red-blooded Theodore Roosevelt condemned as "patriots of the ticker," voiced similar views.[25]

Perhaps the individual who did the most to quiet the uproar was Joseph Pulitzer, enterprising editor of the New York *World.* His journal insisted:

There is no menace in the boundary line, it is not our frontier, it is none of our business. To make it such without cause, and to raise the spectre of war over a false sentiment and a false conception is something more than a grave blunder. If persisted in, it will be a colossal crime.[26]

Pulitzer cabled to a number of prominent Englishmen, including the Prince of Wales, the Duke of York, and William E. Gladstone, asking their views on the crisis. Since the replies were uniformly conciliatory and expressive of warm friendship for America, their publication had a steadying effect on public opinion.

The average Englishman had never heard of the Venezuelan boundary dispute prior to Cleveland's message to Congress.[27] It is not surprising, therefore, that many Britons were at first disposed to dismiss the President's declaration as the kind of Yankee bluster that was to be expected on the eve of elections.[28] But the British government quickly perceived that it was face to face with a serious problem. If it yielded to the stinging ultimatum of the United States, it would humiliate itself; if it did not, there would be war. And why should it yield? British military and naval forces were incomparably stronger than those of the challenger. It would be mere child's play to lay waste the great coastal cities of the United States. The jingoes, the fire-eaters,

[25] Olney wrote later that "the press of the country, except so far as it was under the influence of Wall Street and speculators in the Stock Market, very generally supported the President." Vagts, *Deutschland und die Vereinigten Staaten,* I, 513 (Olney to Dana, Sept. 19, 1910).

[26] New York *World,* Dec. 21, 1895, quoted in J. E. Wisan, *The Cuban Crisis as Reflected in the New York Press, 1895–1898* (N.Y., 1934), p. 23 n.

[27] London *Times,* Jan. 1, 1896, 10:5. James Bryce wrote that not "one man out of ten in the House of Commons even knew there was such a thing as a Venezuelan question pending." H. A. L. Fisher, *James Bryce* (N.Y., 1927), I, 319 (Bryce to Roosevelt, Jan. 1, 1896).

[28] Mann to Cutting, Dec. 25, 1895 (copy), Cleveland Papers, Library of Congress.

and the "Rule Britannia" class—who fortunately did not constitute a majority—were all for administering a sound chastisement to the insolent Yankee. One irate Tory declared that "no dog of a Republican can open its mouth to bark without our good leave. . . ."

It takes two to make a quarrel; and perhaps the major reason why war did not result was that the great majority of the British people, who showed remarkable forbearance in the face of great provocation, did not want to fight. They regarded as "unthinkable" a war with the United States over a few thousand square miles of mosquito-infested jungle land.[29] Protestations of esteem for America were heard at every hand. A total of 354 members of the House of Commons signed a memorial asking for arbitration of all future disputes—a document which they forwarded to Cleveland and Congress. Thirteen hundred British authors sent an appeal to America urging an amicable settlement. Eight hundred English workingmen adopted a resolution urging their government to arbitrate the matter, for "a war between England and the United States of America would be a crime against the laws of God and man; and would cause unspeakable misery to the peoples of both countries." [30] From London, Ambassador Bayard reported: ". . . I have heard nothing but sorrow, alarm, and, indeed, horror, expressed at the suggestion of a conflict of force . . . not only over this case . . . but in relation to any other question of difference." [31]

THE KAISER LENDS A HAND

A number of considerations gave Her Majesty's government pause, among which two may be mentioned. First, Canada and the British merchant marine were vulnerable to American attack. Secondly, Great Britain's flank, in the event of war with the United States, would be turned to Europe. And there she had no allies and few friends. In particular, the rapid rise of a united and powerful Germany had already begun to cause some disquietude.

By a striking coincidence, British attention was diverted to Germany at this very time. Great Britain was having serious trouble with the Dutch-descended Boers of South Africa, and an impulsive Englishman

---

[29] Jennie A. Sloan, "Anglo-American Relations and the Venezuelan Boundary Dispute," *Hispanic Amer. Hist. Rev.*, XVIII (1938), 495–496.

[30] Bayard to Olney, Dec. 31, 1895 (enclosure), Department of State, *Despatches, Great Britain*, CLXXXI.

[31] Bayard to Olney, Dec. 24, 1895, *ibid.*

by the name of Jameson led an unauthorized raiding party against them. The Boers forced the expedition to surrender, and on January 3, 1896, the Kaiser, not to be outdone by Cleveland, sent a telegram to President Kruger (the Boer leader) congratulating him on having repelled the invader "without appealing to the help of friendly powers [*i. e.*, Germany]. . . ."[32]

This gratuitous insult to England caused the British to rise as one man in furious resentment. "Yankee Doodle" was cheered in London music halls, while "Die Wacht am Rhein" was hissed. Although the Anglo-American crisis appears to have passed its peak when the Kaiser blundered in,[33] the telegram to Kruger blunted British anger toward America, reminded Great Britain that Germany lay on her flank, and made surrender to the United States more palatable.[34] Europe's discords were still operating to America's advantage.

Months of wearisome negotiation between London and Washington followed the sending of the Kruger telegram. The British revealed a conciliatory disposition, and cheerfully co-operated in providing the American boundary commission with data. Finally, as the result of the good offices of the United States, representatives of Venezuela and Great Britain signed a treaty on February 2, 1897. It provided for the submission of the dispute to an arbitral board, but significantly exempted from arbitration those areas that had been held by either party over a fifty-year period.[35] From the very first Britain had steadfastly refused to expose her subjects east of the Schomburgk line to an arbitral body, and even in apparent defeat she had won her main contention.

The final decision was not handed down until October 3, 1899, when public interest in the matter had largely flickered out. The settlement was substantially in accord with the Schomburgk line, with two important exceptions. First, Venezuela secured a considerable area at the southern end; secondly, and much more significant, she obtained control of the mouth of the Orinoco. This whole arrangement, however, was essentially what Britain had several times offered the Venezuelans. (See map on page 479.) Such was the victory that Cleveland won after skating perilously close to the edge of war.

[32] W. L. Langer, *The Diplomacy of Imperialism, 1890–1902* (N.Y., 1935), I, 237.
[33] Professor Allan Nevins (*Grover Cleveland*, p. 646) makes a strong point of this.
[34] J. L. Garvin, *The Life of Joseph Chamberlain* (London, 1934), III, 95–96. For evidence that Olney did not think Britain would fight because of the possibility that Russia would attack India from Afghanistan see the note that appears on p. 648 of the later printings of Nevins' *Grover Cleveland*.
[35] A. L. P. Dennis, *Adventures in American Diplomacy, 1896–1906* (N.Y., 1928), p. 43.

All's Well that Ends Well

Conventional diplomacy finds little to commend in the Cleveland-Olney technique. It was crude, blustering, bellicose. It involved an extreme interpretation of the Monroe Doctrine, and seemed far afield from any direct concern of the United States. It gave a costly shock to a none too stable financial structure. It further accelerated a rising jingoistic spirit. (Strangely enough, the anti-imperialistic Cleveland may have been one of the real fathers of American imperialism.) Finally, the extreme pretensions of the United States aroused a vast amount of ill will in Continental Europe, especially Germany,[36] and did much to determine the hostile attitude of these Powers during the Spanish-American War.

On the other hand, the Venezuelan danger spot, which might have involved the United States if the two disputants had gone to war, was finally removed. The prestige of the United States was enormously enhanced when the British lion slunk away with "his much-twisted tail between his legs." Perhaps this incident—not the Spanish-American War—should date the emergence of America as a world Power. Nor can it be denied that the outcome immeasurably strengthened the Monroe Doctrine. "Never again," enthusiastically declared the Chicago Journal, "will a European nation put forth claims to American territory without consulting the government of the United States."[37]

In Latin America, there were both profit and loss. The weaker nations generally applauded the protective position of the United States; the stronger ones resented the pretensions of Cleveland and Olney to hemispheric overlordship.[38] Venezuela, at first pleased, resented the final treaty, and Olney had to coerce her into signing.

[36] See Vagts, *Deutschland und die Vereinigten Staaten*, I, 617. Professor Dexter Perkins concludes (*op. cit.*, p. 205) that the Cleveland message was more "harshly judged" in Continental Europe than in England.

[37] *Public Opinion*, XXI, 647 (Nov. 19, 1896). It was perhaps more than coincidental that, on April 11, 1897, France signed a treaty with Brazil by which the French Guiana-Brazil boundary dispute was to be submitted to arbitration by the Swiss government. Thompson to Sherman, May 31, 1897, Department of State, *Despatches, Brazil*, LX. Another case is of some significance. In February, 1895, the British occupied the uninhabited island of Trinidad, some 650 miles off the coast of Brazil, presumably for a cable station. The Brazilians, who claimed ownership, complained bitterly, and late in July, 1895, there was much agitation in the United States in behalf of invoking the Monroe Doctrine. Possibly because of the attitude of Olney and Cleveland, the British accepted mediation by the Portuguese government and withdrew in August, 1896. Observations based on the State Department records, and on the Olney Papers in the Library of Congress.

[38] Perkins, *The Monroe Doctrine, 1867-1907*, pp. 210 ff.

The most significant result of the Venezuela flare-up was the vast improvement in Anglo-American relations. Americans were pleased with the surrender to Cleveland's ultimatum; while the British, astonished by the outburst of Anglophobia, were impressed with the necessity of cultivating friendly relations. The Kaiser's telegram gave further point to the inadequacy of England's policy of "splendid isolation," and to the desirability of seeking friends if not allies. So the period of "twisting the lion's tail" was followed by one of "patting the eagle's head," [39] during which British statesmen went out of their way to cultivate America. Thus the path was smoothed for the highly important *rapprochement* between Great Britain and the United States at the end of the century.

The Senate and the Arbitration Treaty

One important by-product of the Venezuela crisis was the impetus given to the erection of machinery for the amicable adjustment of disputes. Many people on both sides of the Atlantic perceived that if such machinery had existed the two great nations would not have come so close to war. Secretary Olney and Sir Julian Pauncefote, the British ambassador in Washington, entered upon negotiations, and on January 11, 1897, signed a general arbitration treaty.[40] The document was laid before the Senate, but, largely as a result of partisan bitterness against Cleveland, was talked over into the next Administration.

President McKinley threw his strong support behind the pact; and public opinion throughout the country was mightily aroused in its behalf.[41] Most of the enthusiasm was spontaneous, but some of it was deliberately cultivated by peace and arbitration propagandists. Senatorial desks groaned with hundreds of petitions, letters, and telegrams from church congresses, bar associations, universities, women's groups, and business men's organizations—all the "best people." The Omaha *World-Herald* waxed ecstatic when it declared that the treaty was "one of the grandest triumphs of humanity." Only a few newspapers, notably Dana's New York *Sun*, had the temerity to oppose the agreement; and a few dissentient voices arose here and there from Irish clubs and societies.

But the Senate, unperturbed by this great upsurge of popular feel-

[39] See cartoon in *Punch*, CX, 247 (May 23, 1896). On this whole subject see L. M. Gelber, *The Rise of Anglo-American Friendship* (London, 1938), pp. 7 *ff.*

[40] R. B. Mowat, *The Life of Lord Pauncefote* (Boston, 1929), p. 167.

[41] On the treaty see W. S. Holt, *Treaties Defeated by the Senate* (Baltimore, 1933), pp. 154–162.

ing, and ordinarily critical of arbitration pacts, went quietly about its business. First, it methodically emasculated the treaty by attaching a series of amendments that would exempt certain questions from arbitration and would require a two-thirds vote of the Senate before submitting any other. Then, after having taken so much of the life out of the document that it was scarcely an arbitration treaty at all, the Senate showed its mettle by rejecting the "miserable remnant" (so the New York *Times* called it) on May 5, 1897, by a vote of 43 to 26. A change of three votes would have reversed the result.

A mixture of motives entered into the final decision. Important among them was a desire on the part of the Senate not to allow important questions affecting foreign policy to slip out of its hands into those of an arbitral board. Virulent Anglophobia, which had resisted the advances of the British, played a conspicuous part. The campaign of 1896 over free silver had aroused bitter animosities, and Britain had been condemned by the silverites as the bulwark of the gold standard. Significantly, a considerable body of Senators who voted against the treaty were silverites. Then, of course, there were the other Anglophobes, notably sons of the shamrock. The Hibernian-tinged Boston *Pilot* boasted:

Had Irish-Americanism anything to do with the failure of the English arbitration treaty? We trust so, and believe so. We should be very much ashamed of our fellow citizens of Irish blood if they had not done their utmost to baffle the attempt to place this republic before the world as a mere colony of Great Britain.[42]

Although the debate over the treaty did much to popularize the principle of arbitration, the result was a blow to the lovers of peace. The action of the Senate revealed again how a strongly entrenched minority can defy a very articulate public opinion. Yet the outcome did not materially dampen the newly found British friendliness for America. The United States was potentially too useful to let a little thing like the Senate stand in the way. So, on the eve of the Spanish-American War, Britain, alone of the European Powers, was ready to cheer America along the path of imperialism.

BIBLIOGRAPHICAL NOTE

The best brief accounts of the Venezuela crisis are: Allan Nevins, *Grover Cleveland* (N.Y., 1934), Ch. XXIV; and A. L. P. Dennis, *Adventures in American Diplomacy, 1896–1906* (N.Y., 1928), Ch. II. The latter stresses the diplomatic

[42] *Literary Digest*, XV, 140 (May 29, 1897).

side. The best detailed treatment, with emphasis on the Monroe Doctrine, is Dexter Perkins, *The Monroe Doctrine, 1867–1907* (Baltimore, 1937). There is some valuable material in Allan Nevins, ed., *Letters of Grover Cleveland, 1850–1908* (Boston, 1933), Ch. XIII. An older but still useful account is J. F. Rhodes, *History of the United States from Hayes to McKinley, 1877–1896* (N.Y., 1919), Ch. XX. Henry James, *Richard Olney and His Public Service* (Boston, 1923), is the standard life. See also Montgomery Schuyler, "Richard Olney," in S. F. Bemis, ed., *The American Secretaries of State and their Diplomacy* (N.Y., 1928), VIII, 273–325. On the arbitration treaty of 1897 consult W. S. Holt, *Treaties Defeated by the Senate* (Baltimore, 1933), pp. 154–162. Useful articles are W. S. Robertson, "Hispanic American Appreciations of the Monroe Doctrine," *Hispanic Amer. Hist. Rev.*, III (1920), 1–16; and J. F. Rippy, "Some Contemporary Mexican Reactions to Cleveland's Venezuelan Message," *Pol. Sci. Quar.*, XXXIX (1924), 280–292. Further references: see footnotes of this chapter and Bemis and Griffin, *Guide*, pp. 429–436.

RECENT REFERENCES. As the most exhaustive treatment of the Venezuela dispute in English, C. C. Tansill's *The Foreign Policy of Thomas F. Bayard, 1885–1897* (N.Y., 1940), pp. 621–781, must be bracketed with Perkins' somewhat less detailed account. The author is highly critical of Cleveland and Olney, especially Olney, and sympathetic toward Bayard's Anglophilism and distrust of the Venezuelans. The treatment of public opinion on both sides of the Atlantic is particularly good. N. M. Blake, "Background of Cleveland's Venezuelan Policy," *Amer. Hist. Rev.*, XLVII (1942), 259–277, holds that the steadily rising clamor of Republicans and jingo Democrats for a more assertive foreign policy and a more vigorous enunciation of the Monroe Doctrine (especially after British intervention in Nicaragua), created a climate of opinion which probably infected both Cleveland and Olney. The author thinks that if Cleveland had acted otherwise, the explosion of 1898 might have been directed against Britain rather than Spain. T. C. Smith, "Secretary Olney's Real Credit in the Venezuela Affair," *Mass. Hist. Soc. Procs.*, LXV (1940), 112–147, argues strongly, on the basis of published materials, that Olney, far from being "a blustering, ill-mannered attorney," showed genuine diplomatic ability, after the British had consented to mediation, in bringing about the final adjustment. He contends that the Venezuelans won a greater victory than is generally recognized, in that the area near the southern end of the Schomburgk line was the entire British "grab" of 1886 and the cause of American intervention. W. H. Gray, "American Diplomacy in Venezuela, 1835–1865," *Hispanic Amer. Hist. Rev.*, XX (1940), 551–574, shows that the United States declined to invoke the Monroe Doctrine during five different collisions between Venezuela and the European Powers from 1850 to 1865.

NEW REFERENCES. For a monograph on Cleveland's foreign policy, for a book dealing with the Anglo-American literary *rapprochement*, and for two noteworthy articles—one on Olney and the Venezuela crisis and another on the abortive arbitration treaty of 1897—see Bibliographical Appendix, p. 934.

4TH ED. REFS. For evidence that Venezuela lost out in the final arbitration because the two British arbitrators made a deal with the Russian arbitrator, see Otto Schoenrich, "The Venezuela-British Guiana Boundary Dispute," *Amer. Jour. of Internat. Law*, LXIII (1949), 523–530.

CHAPTER XXX

The Coming of the War with Spain, 1895–1898

"We are all jingoes now; and the head jingo is the Hon. William McKinley, the trusted and honored Chief Executive of the nation's will."

New York *Sun*, April 20, 1898.

"CUBA LIBRE!"

As THE nineteenth century neared its close, the American people were revealing unmistakable evidences of a desire for a larger stage. The Samoan and Hawaiian adventures have already been considered as aspects of the nascent spirit of imperialism; and the Venezuela outburst did nothing to quiet the urge. The United States had had no real war since 1865, no foreign war since 1848. A younger generation was coming on—a generation wearied with hearing about the deeds of its sires and uninitiated to the horrors of Mars. By 1897 the American people were definitely recovering from the panic of 1893 and from the effects of the Venezuela scare, and prosperity was going to their heads. Expand or explode is a fundamental law—and America, bursting with power, was prepared to follow its dictates.

Cuba proved to be the spark that set off the American powder magazine. The "Ever-Faithful Isle," long restive under Spanish misrule, was already ripe for revolt when the American tariff of 1894 wiped out the reciprocity agreement of 1891 with Spain, and, by placing relatively high duties on sugar, visited the island with economic prostration.[1] On February 24, 1895, the Cubans unfurled the standard of rebellion.

The *insurrectos*, whose methods were no less cruel than those of the Spaniards, adopted the deliberate policy of devastating the island so completely that Spain would be willing to withdraw.[2] The Cubans

[1] R. H. Fitzgibbon, *Cuba and the United States, 1900–1935* (Menasha, Wis., 1935), p. 14.

[2] The United States consul general in Havana, General Fitzhugh Lee, reported that innocent women and children were being murdered by both sides. Admitting that many reports were exaggerated, he concluded that the "number of unwarranted atrocities is much greater than the average general record." See particularly Lee to Olney, June 27, July 13, 1896, Department of State, *Consular Letters*, CXXV, CXXVI.

either destroyed American property (American citizens had invested about $50,000,000 in Cuba) with the intention of forcing the United States to intervene, or spared it when the owners paid the necessary protection money.[3] This, in fact, was one of the principal methods of financing the uprising. Hornet bands of *insurrectos* also resorted to such desperate expedients as dynamiting passenger trains. But Cuban propaganda, disseminated by expatriates in New York and elsewhere, glossed over the seamy side of the rebel cause and painted the Spanish "butchers" in the blackest possible hues.[4] Horrified America, traditionally friendly to the ideals of liberty, democracy, and the banishment of monarchy from the Americas, naturally thrilled to the cry, *Cuba Libre!*

The Cuban revolutionists capitalized on American sympathy by using the shores of the United States as a base for filibustering expeditions. The vigilance of the United States authorities prevented about two thirds of these enterprises from reaching their destinations—an excellent record in view of the 5470 miles of coastline that had to be patrolled.[5] The Spaniards were bitterly unappreciative of these efforts, and repeatedly charged (with considerable measure of truth) that assistance from the United States alone kept the revolt alive.[6]

CLEVELAND AND THE BELLIGERENCY CRAZE

Meanwhile clouds of smoke from charred cane fields continued to roll over the island. In desperation the Spanish government decided to take more energetic measures, and it sent the ruthless General Valeriano Weyler to Cuba. "Butcher" Weyler, as he was called by the American press, arrived in February, 1896. After surveying the situation, he concluded that the uprising could never be suppressed while the countryside teemed with civilians who clandestinely gave aid and comfort to the rebels. He therefore ordered the populace to be kenneled in reconcentration camps. In the absence of proper hygienic precautions, the unfortunate victims, chiefly women and children, died by the cartload. The American people, who were outraged by the gross

[3] Mr. James Truslow Adams remembers that a large sugar estate in which he was interested paid New York representatives of the Cuban "patriots" bribes running as high as ten thousand dollars. J. T. Adams, *The Epic of America* (Boston, 1931), p. 335.

[4] Walter Millis, *The Martial Spirit* (Boston, 1931), pp. 44 *ff.*

[5] F. E. Chadwick, *The Relations of the United States and Spain: Diplomacy* (N.Y., 1909), pp. 411 *ff.*

[6] The notable Spanish memorandum of July, 1896, which was intended for presentation to the Powers, stressed this point. Orestes Ferrara, *The Last Spanish War* (N.Y., 1937), p. 36.

inhumanity of reconcentration, began to demand with increasing vigor that this nuisance at their very doors be abated. As a first step it was widely urged that the shadowy Cuban government be accorded recognition as a belligerent.

President Cleveland, who referred privately to the "rascally Cubans," set his face against the mounting clamor. But Congress refused to respond to pressure from the White House, and in February and April of 1896 the Senate and House of Representatives overwhelmingly passed a concurrent resolution favoring recognition of Cuban belligerency. The accompanying debates were so intemperate that anti-American riots broke out in Spain. In Barcelona a mob of 15,000, shouting "down with the American pig killers," stoned the United States consulate and tore up the American flag. There were counterdemonstrations in America by Princeton University students and Leadville miners; and the Youngstown Chamber of Commerce voted to boycott the Spanish onion.[7]

The passing of the belligerency resolution was in part dictated by partisan politics—a move to embarrass the Democratic administration on the eve of the presidential election. Cleveland, however, ignored the action of Congress, for he regarded it as unwarranted interference with the Executive's conduct of foreign affairs. To one group of Congressmen he said that there would be no war with Spain, even if Congress should declare it, because "I will not mobilize the army." [8] There the matter rested, despite an outburst of criticism from the jingo journals.

In April, 1896, Secretary Olney attempted to mediate between Spain and her rebellious colony. But the Spanish government declined to accept America's good offices; and during the summer of 1896 the Madrid Foreign Office worked out an extraordinary plan for joint European action to prevent the United States from intervening in Cuba. But the American minister to Spain got wind of the scheme, and, following his strong representations, the Spanish Foreign Minister decided to drop it.[9]

Meanwhile the interest of the American people had shifted from free Cuba to the free coinage of silver, which was the leading issue of the heated presidential campaign of 1896. The month after the election Cleveland bluntly hinted to Spain, in his annual message to Congress,

---

[7] J. E. Wisan, *The Cuban Crisis as Reflected in the New York Press, 1895–1898* (N.Y., 1934), p. 132.

[8] Robert McElroy, *Grover Cleveland* (N.Y., 1923), II, 250.

[9] This dramatic story is told in Ferrara, *The Last Spanish War*, pp. 21 ff.

that intervention was inevitable if the struggle should continue to degenerate into "senseless slaughter." Three months later he left office, and though the jingo press branded him an "ally of Spain" and as one who would deserve the "damnation of history," few today will deny that he showed courage in withstanding the clamor of the crowd.

THE BATTLE OF THE YELLOWS

While the revolution in Cuba was running its course, a hardly less significant revolution was taking place in American journalism. In September, 1895, a wealthy young man by the name of William Randolph Hearst purchased a staid but fast-failing newspaper, the New York *Journal*, and straightway entered upon a race for circulation with Joseph Pulitzer's New York *World*, which hitherto had been regarded as the high point in sensationalism. By lurid style, reckless liberties with the truth, imaginative illustrations, screeching headlines, and other innovations, Hearst was completely successful in his efforts to out-Pulitzer Pulitzer.[10]

The Cuban conflagration was a godsend to the yellow sheets. They burst out in "typographical paroxysms" when disagreeable incidents arose from the attempts of the Spanish authorities to suppress filibustering. The searching of three Cuban women on a ship flying American colors was reported in Hearst's *Journal* under the headlines, "Does Our Flag Protect Women?" [11] The yellow press made much of the destruction of American property in Cuba, while glossing over the fact that most of this was done by the *insurrectos*. It also sprang to the defense of imprisoned or reconcentrated American citizens, most of whom were naturalized Cubans with embarrassing Spanish names.[12]

[10] Hearst spent money lavishly in employing journalists and illustrators. Notable among the latter was Frederic Remington, whom Hearst sent to Cuba to draw pictures. Upon arriving the artist allegedly telegraphed: "Everything is quiet. There is no trouble here. There will be no war." Hearst, so the story goes, replied, "You furnish the pictures and I'll furnish the war." J. K. Winkler, *W. R. Hearst* (N.Y., 1928), p. 144.

[11] Frederic Remington illustrated the story with a picture of several brutal Spanish officials completely disrobing a comely and defenseless female in her cabin. A prompt attack on this scoop by the jealous Pulitzer (who was now accusing Hearst of sensationalism) revealed that the searching had been quite properly done by matrons. M. M. Wilkerson, *Public Opinion and the Spanish-American War* (Baton Rouge, La., 1932), p. 44. Consul General Lee did, however, report that ladies on an American steamer were twice searched by men before women were employed. Lee to Rockhill (telegram), Feb. 18, 1897, Department of State, *Consular Letters*, CXXVIII.

[12] Dr. Ricardo Ruiz, a Cuban dentist who had been naturalized in 1880, died in prison, in February, 1897, after extraordinarily brutal treatment. The case caused a great uproar in the United States, and Consul General Lee was reprimanded by the

But the *Journal* was not content to get "scoops"; it proceeded to manufacture them. Hearst aroused enormous interest, chiefly among American women, in an imprisoned Cuban girl, Evangelina Cisneros. Though the young woman had apparently been implicated in the revolt, the *Journal* declared that her only sin had been to defend her virtue against the lust of a brutal Spanish officer. With interest in the case at fever heat, a Hearst reporter, acting under orders, spirited Señorita Cisneros from her cell and smuggled her into the United States. It was a nine days' wonder. The *Journal* not overmodestly admitted, in banner headlines, "AN AMERICAN NEWSPAPER ACCOMPLISHES AT A SINGLE STROKE WHAT THE RED TAPE OF DIPLOMACY FAILED UTTERLY TO BRING ABOUT IN MANY MONTHS." [13] The Bishop of London cabled congratulations and the Governor of Missouri suggested that the *Journal* send five hundred of its reporters down and free the entire island.[14]

The yellow press displayed its greatest inventive genius, however, in reporting atrocity stories. "Butcher" Weyler was called "Wolf" Weyler, a "human hyena," a "mad dog." His men, it was alleged, massacred prisoners or threw them to the sharks, dragged the sick from their cots, shot them, and fed their bodies to the dogs. The *Journal* solemnly asserted:

It is not only Weyler the soldier . . . but Weyler the brute, the devastator of haciendas, the destroyer of families, and the outrager of women. . . . Pitiless, cold, an exterminator of men. . . . There is nothing to prevent his carnal, animal brain from running riot with itself in inventing tortures and infamies of bloody debauchery.[15]

A *World* correspondent reported:

Blood on the roadsides, blood in the fields, blood on the doorsteps, blood, blood, blood! The old, the young, the weak, the crippled—all are butchered without mercy. . . . Is there no nation wise enough, brave enough, and strong enough to restore peace in this bloodsmitten land? [16]

State Department for not acting more energetically. See Olney to Lee, Feb. 21, 1897 (telegram), Department of State, *Consular Letters*, CXXVIII.

[13] New York *Journal*, Oct. 10, 1897, p. 1. Consul General Lee reported that the young woman was about to be pardoned when the press agitation in the United States caused the Spanish officials to change their minds. Lee to Day, Aug. 27, 1897, Department of State, *Consular Letters*, vol. 130½.

[14] Wisan, *The Cuban Crisis in the New York Press*, p. 330.

[15] New York *Journal*, Feb. 23, 1896, 27: 1, 2, 3.

[16] New York *World*, May 17, 1896, 1: 8, 2: 1.

Though no one will deny that conditions in Cuba were bad, these atrocity stories, as is almost invariably the case, were greatly exaggerated. Yet, judging from subscription figures, the American people were avid for such things. By 1898 each of the rival "Czars of sensation" was selling over 800,000 newspapers a day; and after Dewey's victory at Manila Hearst's *Journal* reached the 1,500,000 mark. Nor was the influence of the yellow press felt only in New York. A crop of lesser imitators sprang up over the country, using the methods and buying the stories of Hearst and Pulitzer.[17]

THE MAINE GOES DOWN TO HAVANA

The stirring free silver campaign of the summer and fall of 1896, together with the Armenian massacre of that year, did much to divert public attention from the fiery furnace of Cuba. The Republicans returned to power in March, 1897, when the amiable William McKinley took the presidential oath. In Cuba, the energetic measures of General Weyler were producing results, and as 1897 wore on it became increasingly evident that the insurrectionist cause was losing ground. News from the war-torn island was fast fading from the front page.

In October, 1897, a liberal Spanish ministry came into power, recalled Weyler, modified the reconcentration methods, released all American citizens from prison, and granted the Cubans a species of autonomy. But the islanders, having glimpsed the sweets of independence, spurned the new concession, while the Spanish sympathizers (loyalists) in Havana flared up in a riot of protest on January 12, 1898, shouting "Death to Autonomy" and "Viva Weyler!" The American press was greatly disturbed by the danger to American lives, and the *Journal* cried, "NEXT TO WAR WITH SPAIN."

The United States consul general in Havana, Fitzhugh Lee, had earlier suggested to the State Department that a naval force be stationed at Key West, from which warships could speedily be sent to protect American life and property, as well as the consulate, should the need arise. On January 13, 1898, the day after the outburst of rioting, Lee telegraphed that "ships may be necessary later but not now."[18] Despite this advice and despite the quieting down of the

---

[17] Wisan, *The Cuban Crisis in the New York Press*, p. 33.

[18] As early as July 8, 1896, Lee had suggested to the Department that a man-of-war be stationed at Key West, subject to his call should the mob get out of control and the Spanish government refuse protection. On December 11, five months later, Secretary Olney instructed Lee, in certain circumstances, to pursue such a course. On June 9, 1897, in response to Lee's inquiry, the new Administration renewed this au-

mob, the second-class battleship *Maine* was ordered to Havana, January 24. The obvious purpose was to protect American life and property, and impress the Spaniards in Cuba with the willingness of the Washington government to take energetic action. But the official statement announced that this was merely an act of "friendly" courtesy—an assertion belied by the critical situation in Havana and by the cessation of such visits during the previous three years. Neither the Spanish government nor the loyalists in Cuba were pleased by this gesture.[19]

THE DE LÔME INDISCRETION

While the *Maine* lay at anchor in Havana harbor, a sensational revelation occurred in the United States. Dupuy de Lôme, Spanish minister in Washington, had written an indiscreet private letter to a friend. It had been purloined by a Cuban sympathizer, and had fallen into the hands of Hearst, who, on February 9, 1898, emblazoned a facsimile of it in his *Journal*. The letter not only revealed bad faith in de Lôme's dealings with the United States on pending commercial matters but, worst of all, it included a most unflattering commentary on McKinley's recent annual message to Congress:

Besides the ingrained and inevitable bluntness (*groseria*) with which is repeated all that the press and public opinion in Spain have said about Weyler, it once more shows what McKinley is, weak and a bidder for the admiration of the crowd, besides being a would-be politician (*politicastro*) who tries to leave a door open behind himself while keeping on good terms with the jingoes of his party.[20]

Hearst's "scoop" of the de Lôme letter was the most sensational of the year. For five days the press made high carnival; and even conservative newspapers agreed that the minister's usefulness was at an

---

thority. See particularly Lee to Olney, July 8, 1896; Lee to Day, June 3, 1897, Department of State, *Consular Letters*, CXXVI, CXXX. The present writer has examined the material in the Navy Department and State Department records relating to the dispatch of the *Maine* to Havana.

[19] Although Captain Sigsbee had repeatedly reported a strong undercurrent of hostility among the Spanish element in Cuba, he nevertheless concluded that the arrival of the *Maine* had had a tranquilizing influence by producing a "paralyzing effect on the Spaniards and their adherents." See particularly Sigsbee to Secretary of Navy, Jan. 29, 1898, Navy Department, Washington, D.C.

[20] J. B. Moore, *Digest of International Law*, VI, 176. De Lôme to Canalejas, undated, but probably written about the middle of December, 1897. For a circumstantial if not too trustworthy account of how the Cubans used the letter see H. S. Rubens, *Liberty: The Story of Cuba* (N.Y., 1932), pp. 287–292.

end. A *Journal* cartoon showed an angry Uncle Sam pointing to the door of the White House with a single word to the Spanish envoy, "git!" The New York *Mail and Express* declared: "The necessary preliminaries to his departure cannot be too speedy to satisfy public opinion. . . . Señor de Lôme—the door stands open!" [21]

The Spanish government made what amends it could by accepting the unhappy minister's resignation before the demand for his recall could be presented. Although many Americans thought he had not been punished severely enough, the matter soon became, diplomatically at least, a closed incident. But the public mind, already inflamed to an extraordinary degree by what would ordinarily have been a more or less routine affair, was slow to forget.

"Remember the Maine!"

The de Lôme indiscretion had hardly ceased furnishing headlines when a supersensation broke—the greatest news story since the assassination of President Garfield. On February 15, 1898, a terrific explosion sank the *Maine* in Havana harbor with a loss of over 250 officers and men.

The captain of the vessel, who realized that many of his unthinking countrymen would leap to the conclusion that Spain had deliberately blown up the ship, promptly sent a telegram to Washington urging a suspension of judgment pending an official investigation. It must be said to the credit of the American people that this injunction was rather generally heeded.[22] "A great nation," insisted the Kansas City *Star*, "can afford to take time to be perfectly just."

Nevertheless, the yellow journals flooded the country with "war extras." Hearst's headlines blared: "THE WARSHIP MAINE WAS SPLIT IN TWO BY AN ENEMY'S SECRET INFERNAL MACHINE"; "THE WHOLE COUNTRY THRILLS WITH WAR FEVER"; "THE MAINE WAS DESTROYED BY TREACHERY." The *World* published a cartoon showing Uncle Sam drawing his sword to liberate a shackled Cuba. The caption read, "The Only Atonement—Free Cuba." Three days after the disaster the *Journal* insisted, "Intervention is a plain and imperative duty."

The exhortations of the sensational press gave additional stimulus to the outburst of jingoism. In Buffalo, three mass meetings urged McKinley to declare war on Spain. Lehigh University students held

---

[21] Feb. 9, 1898, quoted in Wisan, *The Cuban Crisis in the New York Press*, p. 383.
[22] See New York *Nation*, LXVI, 139 (Feb. 24, 1898).

daily drills and paraded under the banner, "To Hell With Spain." The Reverend Thomas Dixon elicited cheers when he sermonized against "hesitation, delay, diplomacy and idle talk." The jingoistic Assistant Secretary of the Navy, Theodore Roosevelt, wrote: ". . . I would give anything if President McKinley would order the fleet to Havana tomorrow. . . . The *Maine* was sunk by an act of dirty treachery on the part of the Spaniards. . . ."[23]

Responding to the wave of hysteria sweeping the country, Congress, on March 9, 1898, unanimously voted $50,000,000 for war preparations. This gesture, together with other military and naval activities, strengthened the determination of the Cubans to hold on and aroused doubts in the Spanish mind as to the sincerity of American professions of peace. Spain, reported Stewart L. Woodford, United States minister at Madrid, was "simply stunned."[24]

Then, on March 17, 1898, Senator Proctor of Vermont delivered one of the most striking speeches ever heard on the floor of Congress. He had gone to Cuba on a private tour of inspection, and had returned to make his report. His description of the several hundred thousand *reconcentrados* was appalling:

> Torn from their homes, with foul earth, foul air, foul water, and foul food or none, what wonder that one-half have died and that one-quarter of the living are so diseased that they can not be saved? . . . Little children are still walking about with arms and chest terribly emaciated, eyes swollen, and abdomen bloated to three times the natural size. . . . I was told by one of our consuls that they have been found dead about the markets in the morning, where they had crawled, hoping to get some stray bits of food from the early hucksters. . . .[25]

Here was the firsthand report of a respectable Senator; and it had a profound effect upon many sober citizens who hitherto had discounted the lurid tales of the yellow journals.

On March 28, 1898, the roaring flames received additional fuel when the *Maine* report was published. The American Court of Inquiry, which consisted entirely of United States naval officers, found that the vessel had been blown up by a submarine mine. This body did not, however, attempt to fix responsibility. Even assuming that the investigators were infallible in declaring that the explosion was external (they were not a disinterested group and they worked under

[23] Roosevelt to Diblee, Feb. 16, 1898, Roosevelt Papers, Library of Congress.
[24] Chadwick, *Relations of the United States and Spain: Diplomacy*, p. 545.
[25] *Cong. Record*, 55 Cong., 2 sess., p. 2917.

severe handicaps), it is unthinkable that the Spanish government, which was desperately trying to avert war with the United States, deliberately destroyed the vessel.[26] A mine may have been discharged accidentally; the Cuban insurgents may have perpetrated the deed to bring the United States to their aid; and irresponsible Spanish subalterns or loyalists, acting without orders, may have taken things into their own hands. Nor can the possibility of an accidental internal explosion be entirely ruled out.

But the lid was now off. To the unthinking masses an external explosion meant that Spain had deliberately blown up the ship. Restraint and suspended judgment were thrown to the winds. The slogan of the hour became:

> Remember the Maine!
> To hell with Spain!

The New York *World* branded the explosion as "an act of war" and demanded, "Are we waiting to be smitten on the other cheek?"

Regardless of the question of Cuban independence . . . the DE-STRUCTION OF THE MAINE BY FOUL PLAY should be the occasion of ordering our fleet to Havana and *demanding proper amends within forty-eight hours under threat of bombardment.* If Spain will not punish her miscreants, we must punish Spain.[27]

The *Journal* reported the hanging of McKinley in effigy in Durango, Colorado, together with the burning of the Spanish flag by students in Omaha and by a mob in Chicago. "Give Congress a chance to know what the people think," cried Hearst's mouthpiece.

The destruction of the *Maine* was unquestionably the most important single precipitant of war with Spain. Nothing could have more convincingly brought home to the American people the unsavory conditions in Cuba and the conviction that the island ought to be free. The irony of it is that to this day no credible evidence has been forthcoming that a Spaniard, official or unofficial, authorized or unauthorized, blew up the ship. But America no longer thought; she merely felt.

[26] It should be noted that Captain Sigsbee seems never to have entertained any doubts as to the sincerity of the grief of the Spanish officials in Cuba, and that both he and Consul General Lee referred to the explosion as an accident. See Sigsbee to Secretary of Navy, Feb. 18, 1898, Navy Department, Washington, D.C.

[27] New York *World*, April 1, 1898, 6:2. Ill feeling in the United States had its counterpart among the Spanish masses, who were ignorant of the odds they were facing. The press in Spain bristled with insults aimed at the "Yankee pigs."

DIPLOMACY POINTS THE WAY OUT

During these hectic months perhaps the most important single restraint on the jingoistic spirit was big business. Except for a relatively small group who had investments in Cuba or a stake in the Cuban trade (it amounted to about $100,000,000 annually), the financial and commercial interests of the United States were almost solidly opposed to war.[28] They particularly feared that hostilities would retard returning prosperity and dislocate the economic structure. The calculating attitude of the financiers was infuriating to the warmongers. "We will have this war for the freedom of Cuba," shouted Theodore Roosevelt, as he shook his fist at Senator Mark Hanna of Ohio, the prototype of big business in politics, "in spite of the timidity of the commercial interests." [29]

The McKinley administration was essentially a businessman's administration, and the President, who owed his election largely to Mark Hanna, was naturally opposed to war. He therefore made strong efforts to adjust the Cuban problem through the quiet channels of diplomacy.

On March 27, 1898, after weeks of wearisome negotiation, the State Department instructed Minister Woodford, in Madrid, to ascertain if Spain would consent to the following: (1) the granting of an armistice to the insurgents until October 1; (2) immediate revocation of the *reconcentrado* order. This was not an ultimatum; but it represented what the United States apparently regarded as indispensable concessions for keeping the peace.[30]

The Spanish ministry was in a precarious position. If it yielded too much it would face revolution at home; if too little, war with the United States abroad. As usual, it vacillated. It proposed submission of the *Maine* question to arbitration and it agreed to grant an armistice to the Cubans only if they would ask for it—which they patently would not. Though Woodford was discouraged, he cabled home:

---

[28] This subject is fully developed by J. W. Pratt, *Expansionists of 1898* (Baltimore, 1936), pp. 230 *ff.* Contrary to a prevalent misconception, Professor Pratt finds no evidence that pressure for markets had an appreciable bearing on the Cuban intervention. He also points out that some of the American investors in Cuba opposed intervention.

[29] H. F. Pringle, *Theodore Roosevelt* (N.Y., 1931), p. 179.

[30] In the same instruction Woodford was asked to obtain a third concession, "if possible"; namely, if Spain could not make peace with the Cubans by October 1, the President of the United States was "to be final arbiter between Spain and insurgents." This, in effect, meant that Cuba was to become independent. But the third concession was not put in the same imperative category with the first two. *Foreign Relations, 1898*, p. 712.

I am told confidentially that the offer of armistice by the Spanish Government would cause revolution here. . . . The ministry have gone as far as they dare go to-day. I believe the ministry are ready to go as far and as fast as they can and still save the dynasty here in Spain. They know that Cuba is lost. Public opinion in Spain has moved steadily toward peace. No Spanish ministry would have dared to do one month ago what this ministry has proposed to-day.[31]

On April 3, 1898, a rift appeared in the clouds. Woodford learned that the Spanish ministry, responding to the intercession of the Pope, was preparing to grant an armistice. He promptly cabled to McKinley:

I know that the Queen and her present ministry sincerely desire peace and that the Spanish people desire peace, and if you can still give me time and reasonable liberty of action I will get for you the peace you desire so much and for which you have labored so hard.[32]

Two days later, April 5, a striking concession came from Spain, meeting fully the second American demand. The new Spanish minister in Washington informed the Secretary of State that the Governor General of Cuba had issued an order completely revoking reconcentration throughout Cuba.

On April 9, 1898, Spain capitulated to the first of the two American conditions. The Spanish Foreign Minister notified Woodford that on that day the Spanish government "directs the general-in-chief of the army in Cuba to grant immediately a suspension of hostilities *for such length of time as he may think prudent* to prepare and facilitate the peace earnestly desired by all." [33] The words here italicized constitute a "string," which Spain might have found convenient to pull. Nevertheless, this represented substantially a yielding to the two essential demands of the United States—certainly as great a concession as Spanish public opinion would have permitted. Woodford cabled optimistically to McKinley the next day:

I hope that nothing will now be done to humiliate Spain, as I am satisfied that the present Government is going, and is loyally ready to go, as fast and as far as it can. With your power of action sufficiently free you will win the fight on your own lines.[34]

Diplomacy had won a substantial victory—but would this be enough?

[31] *Ibid.*, p. 727 (Woodford to McKinley, March 31, 1898).
[32] *Ibid.*, p. 732 (April 3, 1898).
[33] *Ibid.*, p. 746 (Woodford to Day, April 9, 1898). Italics inserted.
[34] *Ibid.*, p. 747 (Woodford to McKinley, April 10, 1898).

THE VOICE OF THE PEOPLE

The issue was now in the hands of the President. There can be no doubt that the kindly McKinley abhorred the thought of war; but he was deeply moved by the gross inhumanity of the Cuban struggle and desired to have it end. Not until after his death was it learned that he had anonymously contributed $5000 to the sufferers. Spain, moreover, had pursued such a tortuous course that McKinley had little faith in her promises, or in her ability to carry them out even if they were sincerely made. It takes two to make an armistice as well as a quarrel; and since the insurgents had flatly announced that they would not accept the Spanish terms, the war would still go its bloody way.[35]

Even so, the result would probably have been different if diplomacy could have been conducted in a vacuum.[36] The Spanish ministry was obviously attempting to cut loose from Cuba just as fast as public opinion in Spain would permit. But the tidal wave of sentiment in America, especially after the *Maine* report, would not wait. Within the President's own party a group of young jingoes was making a commotion out of all proportion to its numbers. "McKinley," the bellicose Theodore Roosevelt is reported to have shouted, "has no more backbone than a chocolate eclair!"[37]

But the cry for blood was not confined to only a few small groups. There can be no doubt that following the report on the *Maine* the masses were on fire for war. Ex-Confederates, ex-bandits, and Sioux Indians were among those who volunteered their services. Even the Church prayed for hostilities. One Presbyterian journal declared: "And if it be the will of Almighty God, that by war the last trace of this inhumanity of man to man shall be swept away from this Western hemisphere, let it come!"[38]

McKinley was an able politician, and by no means blind to political considerations. He could not have failed to see that if he tried to thwart the popular will he would undoubtedly jeopardize, perhaps

---

[35] Wisan, *The Cuban Crisis in the New York Press,* p. 437.

[36] See L. B. Shippee, "Germany and the Spanish-American War," *Amer. Hist. Rev.,* XXX (1925), 759.

[37] The story is that a friend met Roosevelt coming away from the White House in a state of great anger: "Do you know what that white-livered cur up there has done? He has prepared *two* messages, one for war and one for peace, and doesn't know which one to send in!" Millis, *The Martial Spirit,* p. 130.

[38] *Evangelist* (New York), March 31, 1898, quoted in J. W. Pratt, *Expansionists of 1898* (Baltimore, 1936), p. 285.

ruin, his chances of re-election in 1900. Bryan, his prospective opponent, was arousing tremendous enthusiasm by his speeches for an independent Cuba. To a stanch party man and sound money advocate like McKinley, few things could have been more calamitous than to have the Democratic party, as Senator Platt pointed out, sweep to

ANOTHER OLD WOMAN TRIES TO SWEEP BACK THE SEA.

Public opinion in favor of war overwhelms McKinley. (From the New York *Journal*, 1898.)

victory in 1900 with "Free Cuba" and "Free Silver" emblazoned on its banners.[39]

Lashed by the yellow press, Congress responded to the clamor of the masses, and in some respects was in advance of them. One Maine Representative declared that every Congressman "had two or three newspapers in his district—most of them printed in red ink . . . and shouting for blood." [40] The Republicans feared that if they did not give the country the war it wanted they would be unseated by the Democrats in the approaching fall elections. If the pressure became too great Congress—Republicans as well as Democrats—might pass

[39] New York *Nation*, LXVI, 293 (April 21, 1898); see also letter of Elihu Root (April 2, 1898) in P. C. Jessup, *Elihu Root* (N.Y., 1938), I, 196–197.

[40] J. F. Rhodes *The McKinley and Roosevelt Administrations, 1897–1909* (N.Y., 1922), p. 55.

a war resolution over the head of the President, which would be ruinous to his prestige and leadership.[41] A belligerent Senator shouted to the Assistant Secretary of State, "Day, by ——, don't your President know where the war-declaring power is lodged? Tell him by ——, that if he doesn't do something, Congress will exercise the power." [42]

CONGRESS TAKES HOLD

Overborne by this tremendous pressure, McKinley made a momentous decision. On April 11, 1898, two days *after* the Spanish capitulation, he sent his famous war message to Congress in which he asked for authority to use the army and navy to end hostilities in Cuba. He emphasized, first of all, the urgent need of abating a nuisance which cried to heaven off America's very doors; second, he stressed the obligation to protect American property and trade; and third, he pointed to the necessity of ending a disturbance which was a constant menace to the peace of the United States. Convincing though these arguments may have been to the American people, it should be noted that many, if not most, of the authorities on international law agree that each one of the reasons given for intervention was legally inadequate.[43]

This memorable message had been prepared several days before the eleventh-hour Spanish capitulation arrived.[44] So, near the end of a formidable document written on the assumption that conditions were unchanged, the President added one sentence in which he stated that Spain had made concessions. He hoped that Congress—a war-

[41] Congressman Boutelle of Maine later asserted that forty or fifty Republican members of Congress threatened "to turn upon their own Administration if it did not go to war." New York *Nation*, LXVII, 379 (Nov. 24, 1898). Senator Spooner wrote to C. W. Porter (May 2, 1898): "I think . . . possibly the President could have worked out the business without war, but the current was too strong, the demagogues too numerous, the fall elections too near." Spooner Papers, Library of Congress.

[42] C. S. Olcott, *The Life of William McKinley* (Boston, 1916), II, 28.

[43] Humanitarian grounds were perhaps the strongest; but for one nation to set itself up as a judge of what is humane or inhumane on the part of others is a grave responsibility. The Spanish were not slow to point to America's treatment of the Indians, and to the ravages of General Sheridan and General Sherman (the Secretary of State's brother) during the Civil War. Intervention on moral or humanitarian grounds would have been much more defensible if undertaken in co-operation with other Powers. See E. J. Benton, *International Law and Diplomacy of the Spanish-American War* (Baltimore, 1908), pp. 101–108; H. E. Flack, *Spanish-American Diplomatic Relations Preceding the War of 1898* (Baltimore, 1906), pp. 81–82.

[44] It was to have been sent in on April 4, but McKinley delayed in order to permit Americans to evacuate Cuba. Olcott, *McKinley*, II, 26–29.

mad Congress—would give them "just and careful attention. . . ."

McKinley has been severely criticized for not having laid more emphasis upon the belated Spanish concessions. But even assuming that they would have brought a speedy end to the conflict in Cuba, we should note that the press knew of the offer of an armistice and spurned it as just another attempt at procrastination. On the day the President submitted his war message the New York *World* cried:

Action, Action, Action! Jackson, Jackson, Jackson!
Stop the nonsense! Stop the trifling, let us have peace even at the muzzle of our guns.
Negociate afterward if negociation is necessary.[45]

With the hysterical Congress clamoring for war, McKinley's request for authority to use warlike measures needed no urging. During the debates passions ran incredibly high. The London *Times* correspondent thus reported the scene on the floor of the House:

Men fought; "Liar," "Scoundrel," and other epithets were bandied to and fro; there were half-a-dozen personal collisions; books were thrown; members rushed up and down the aisles like madmen, exchanging hot words, with clenched fists and set teeth; excitement was at fever heat. Not for years has such a scene occurred.[46]

Knots of Congressmen in the lobbies sang "The Battle Hymn of the Republic," "Dixie," and "Hang General Weyler to a Sour Apple Tree As We Go Marching On." Finally, on April 19, 1898, Congress passed a fateful joint resolution (in four parts) that was tantamount to a declaration of war. It (1) declared Cuba free; (2) demanded the withdrawal of Spain; (3) directed the President to use armed force to secure these ends; and (4) disclaimed any intention on the part of the United States to annex Cuba. This last stipulation, the so-called Teller Amendment, was approved without dissent and was symptomatic of the spirit with which America embarked upon the crusade.[47] On April 20, 1898, the President signed the joint reso-

[45] New York *World*, April 11, 1898, 6:2.
[46] London *Times*, April 14, 1898, 3:1.
[47] The New York *Sun* asserted (March 25, 1898, 6:2):

"No annexation talk, so far as Cuba is concerned! If the United States government undertakes this high enterprise, there must be no taint of ulterior self-interest in its motives.

"For human lives and the liberty of human beings, for Cuba Libre; not for an extension of United States territory!" The Teller Amendment was not entirely altruistic. The American sugar interests, who wanted Cuba to remain outside the tariff wall, opposed annexation; but precisely what influence they had is not known.

lution of intervention; and by an act of Congress, approved April 25, war was declared to have existed since April 21.

Although the genial McKinley was an ear-to-the-ground type rather than a dynamic leader, he was a much stronger man than Roosevelt gave him credit for being. He had labored long and earnestly for peace. So frayed were his nerves at the critical period that he was forced to resort to sleeping powders. Even today there is no adequate appreciation of the tremendous pressure to which he was being subjected by Congress and the public.[48] And why, he doubtless reasoned, should he have continued his resistance to that pressure when further negotiation would merely prolong the bloodshed in Cuba? Perhaps McKinley was right in concluding that the Gordian knot could be cut only with the sword.

It is bootless to say that Grover Cleveland or John Adams would have kept the nation out of war. We simply do not know. But it does seem clear that the tide of public opinion had become so overwhelming that it could not have been stemmed by any ordinary mortal. The American people, whipped to a frenzy by the yellow press, were determined to have their war to free Cuba—and they got it.

BIBLIOGRAPHICAL NOTE

A brief account of the diplomacy leading up to the war appears in L. B. Shippee and R. B. Way, "William Rufus Day," in S. F. Bemis, ed., *The American Secretaries of State and their Diplomacy* (N.Y., 1929), IX, 41–95; and in A. L. P. Dennis, *Adventures in American Diplomacy, 1896–1906* (N.Y., 1928), Ch. III. A somewhat fuller and older account is F. E. Chadwick, *The Relations of the United States and Spain: Diplomacy* (N.Y., 1909), pp. 411–587. Valuable new material from the Spanish archives appears in Orestes Ferrara, *The Last Spanish War* (N.Y., 1937). There are three useful studies of public opinion: M. M. Wilkerson, *Public Opinion and the Spanish–American War* (Baton Rouge, La., 1932), is a general study, documented but brief; J. E. Wisan, *The Cuban Crisis as Reflected in the New York Press, 1895–1898* (N.Y., 1934), is a very detailed documented work; Walter Millis, *The Martial Spirit* (Boston, 1931), is undocumented and less sound, but brilliantly written. J. W. Pratt, *Expansionists of 1898* (Baltimore, 1936), has a revealing chapter (VI) on the rise of an expansionist spirit, and one (VII) on the attitude of business. See also the same author's "The 'Large Policy' of 1898," *Miss. Valley Hist. Rev.*, XIX (1932), 219–242. On aspects of international law see E. J. Benton, *International Law and Diplomacy of the Spanish-American War* (Baltimore, 1908). Further references: see footnotes of this chapter and Bemis and Griffin, *Guide*, pp. 510–523.

RECENT REFERENCES; NEW REFERENCES; 4TH ED. REFS. See Bibliographical Appendix, pp. 934–935.

[48] Professor Allan Nevins, after reading the diary of McKinley's private secretary, concludes that the President showed "real backbone" and that history will effect a reversal of opinion regarding him. Nevins to author, March 22, 1939.

CHAPTER XXXI

The United States as a World Power, 1898–1900

> "My countrymen, the currents of destiny flow through the
> hearts of the people. Who will check them? Who will divert
> them? Who will stop them?"
>
> President McKinley, 1898.

A New Day in Anglo-American Relations

GREAT BRITAIN, alone among the Powers of Europe, was conspicuously friendly to the United States during the crisis with Spain. There was, of course, a reason. The might of an ominously rising Germany, to say nothing of other European complications, had awakened British statesmen to the necessity of finding allies. And powerful young America, formerly a poor relation, was decidedly worth cultivating.[1] In March, 1898, Alfred Austin, the poet laureate of England, addressed the people of the United States in behalf of his own:

> Yes, this is the Voice on the bluff March gale,
> "We severed have been too long:
> But now we have done with a worn-out tale,
> The tale of an ancient wrong,
> And our friendship shall last long as Love doth last,
> and be stronger than Death is strong." [2]

The news of the declaration of war was greeted in England with a great display of the Stars and Stripes, and an enormous crowd assembled before the American embassy to cheer the United States. Although Great Britain adhered to the strict letter of her neutral obligations throughout the war, there could be no doubt as to where her sympathies lay.

British bidding for American support reached a high point when, early in the conflict, Colonial Secretary Joseph Chamberlain declared

---

[1] L. M. Gelber, *The Rise of Anglo-American Friendship* (London, 1938), pp. 17 *ff*. See also B. A. Reuter, *Anglo-American Relations during the Spanish-American War* (N.Y., 1924), pp. 1–60.

[2] London *Times*, March 29, 1898, 8:3.

in a public speech: ". . . I even go so far as to say that, terrible as war may be, even war itself would be cheaply purchased if in a great and noble cause the Stars and Stripes and the Union Jack should wave together [loud and prolonged cheers] over an Anglo-Saxon alliance." [3] Though an Anglo-American League was founded in London, and an Anglo-American Committee was organized in New York, the idea of an alliance never got beyond mere talk. The United States was pleased with British sympathy and applause, but saw no need of a foreign entanglement. Even if there had been such a need, the dead hand of George Washington, to say nothing of the live hands of the Irish and other groups, would have raised insuperable obstacles.

EUROPEAN SYMPATHY FOR SPAIN

Quite in contrast with Britain, the Continental European Powers were virtually unanimous in viewing with various shades of disapproval what seemed to them a war of unprovoked aggression against Spain. They were motivated in large part by dynastic sympathies, concern for investments in Spain and Cuba, distrust of American democracy, and solicitude for the monarchial principle. [4]

At the forefront of the unfriendly European Powers—at least in the American mind—stood Germany. Relations with her had not been good since the pork and Samoan controversies; and public opinion in the United States had been considerably disturbed by the German seizure of Kiao-Chau, China, in November, 1897. On the other hand, there was much resentment in Germany against the Monroe Doctrine (what Bismarck called "a species of arrogance peculiarly American"), for it stood in the way of Europe's colonizing poorly defended South America. Moreover, the Germans did not relish the prospect of America's strengthening both herself and the Monroe Doctrine by elbowing Spain out of the Western Hemisphere and appropriating the latter's possessions.

[3] *Ibid.*, May 14, 1898, 12:3.

[4] All the Powers were of course officially neutral, but in some countries the press was quite outspoken in its anti-American sentiments. This was true of Russia and Italy, and particularly of France and Germany. At the request of the American ambassador in Paris, the Department of State authorized the expenditure (June 22, 1898) of $2500 to bring about a more favorable French opinion. The ambassador reported on December 19 that $500 had been spent. On July 18 the Department authorized the American ambassador in Berlin to spend $2000 to improve German-American press relations. Ambassador White declined to use the money, in part because the news of such activity might leak out. The conclusions herein expressed are based upon an examination of all the State Department records relative to the attitude of the Powers toward the United States during the war.

Germany, France, and Austria-Hungary appear to have favored effective mediation or intervention to prevent Spanish-American hostilities. But none of these three Powers was willing to assume the responsibility of leading such a movement.[5] The United States was now too powerful to be lightly offended; and the British navy, as in the days of President Monroe, could not be laughed aside.

So the European nations could proceed only clandestinely or falteringly. The climax of their interventionist efforts came on April 7, 1898. Spain had requested the European Powers to employ their good offices in her behalf; so Austria-Hungary, acting under pressure from her ally, Germany, led in preparing a joint remonstrance which was signed by representatives of the six great Powers and presented to President McKinley. The British ambassador, Sir Julian Pauncefote, had been instructed from London to make sure that the presentation of the note would be inoffensive to the United States, and that its precise terms would be tactful. There is, in fact, some reason to believe that Pauncefote submitted an advance draft of the statement to Secretary Day, who suggested alterations that were finally adopted.[6] It is not surprising, then, that both the joint note and McKinley's reply were models of propriety. The affair was aptly summarized by one newspaper:

Said the Six Ambassadors: "We hope for humanity's sake you will not go to war."

Said Mr. McKinley in reply: "We hope if we do go to war, you will understand that it is for humanity's sake."

And the incident was closed.[7]

Thus ended the most serious effort at intervention.

A WORLD POWER IS BORN

The Spanish-American War, though short, provided more than its measure of thrills. Assistant Secretary of the Navy Theodore Roosevelt was one of the relatively few politicians in Washington who knew that there were Philippine Islands, and that Spain owned them. He

[5] L. B. Shippee, "Germany and the Spanish-American War," *Amer. Hist. Rev.*, XXX (1925), 756.

[6] R. B. Mowat, *The Life of Lord Pauncefote* (Boston, 1929), p. 214. See also Alfred Vagts, *Deutschland und die Vereinigten Staaten in der Weltpolitik* (N.Y., 1935), II, 1299.

[7] New York *World*, April 8, 1898, 6:3. For the abortive attempt at joint intervention of April 14, 1898, see Orestes Ferrara, *The Last Spanish War* (N.Y., 1937), Ch. IX.

therefore used his influence to have a fighting man of the Farragut school, George Dewey, placed in command of the American Asiatic squadron. And then, when the Secretary of the Navy was away, the bellicose Roosevelt cabled Dewey orders to hold himself in instant readiness to attack the Spaniards in the Philippines. America, of course, was fighting to free Cuba, not the Philippines; but an elementary rule of warfare is to beat the enemy to his knees by striking him wherever he is vulnerable.

Dewey moved energetically as soon as war was declared. Undeterred by reports of mines, he sailed boldly into Manila harbor and blew out of the water the collection of marine antiquities that passed for the Spanish fleet. Europe was impressed; America was electrified. Hearst's *Journal* gloated as it heralded the victory, "How Do You Like the *Journal's* War?"

A tiny and ill-equipped American army blundered into Cuba. Lieutenant-Colonel Theodore Roosevelt, who had resigned from the Navy Department, won a disproportionate amount of publicity by his spectacular antics as second in command of the volunteer "Rough Riders." The Spanish fleet, which had scurried into the harbor of Santiago, Cuba, ran out to save the honor of Spain, and was completely destroyed. In the closing days of the war American troops hastily occupied the island of Puerto Rico.

Meanwhile queer things had been happening in Manila Bay. Although Dewey had destroyed the Spanish fleet, he was forced to wait for troop reinforcements from the United States before he could capture the city. During these anxious weeks several of the Powers dispatched warships to the Philippines for the purpose of protecting the interests of their nationals. Although the financial stake of Germany in the islands ranked far below that of Great Britain, the Germans gradually assembled five men-of-war at Manila, as compared with two for the British. The German squadron was not only the most powerful neutral force there, but it was considerably stronger than Dewey's fleet.

This unusual situation aroused grave suspicions in the United States that the German warships were there to support the Kaiser's designs on the Philippines. The documents now available reveal that this surmise was correct. Germany had no desire to provoke a war with the United States or challenge its pretensions; but having entered the colonial scramble late, she was eager to pick up whatever crumbs might fall from the world's banquet table. The Berlin government believed that if America chose to abandon the Philippines, in whole or in part, the presence of a strong fleet at Manila would buttress German claims to the archipelago.[8]

Dewey was vastly annoyed by the presence of the German fleet. Its commander, Vice-Admiral von Diederichs, disagreed with his interpretation of international law, and failed to observe punctiliously the American blockade regulations. Following a series of unpleasant incidents, Dewey heatedly informed von Diederichs that "if Germany wants war, all right, we are ready." The tension was finally relieved; but the yellow journals in the United States further inflamed German-American relations with their lurid reports. The New York *Times* declared:

We may not care particularly about taking the Philippines, but we can assure our European friends that we are not going to be dictated to as to the manner in which we shall dispose of them or any part of them. Expansion is a new idea with us. The defense of our rights is an old habit.[9]

In marked contrast with the Germans, the British commander at Manila, Captain Chichester, was conspicuously friendly to the Americans. On August 13, 1898, the day of the fall of Manila, he quietly moved his ships so as better to observe the effect of the American bombardment. This chanced to bring him between the German fleet and that of the United States; and the wholly groundless legend took root that Chichester had saved the American squadron by thus serving notice on the Germans, who allegedly were about to attack Dewey, that in the event of a showdown the two Anglo-Saxon fleets would "shoot the same language."[10]

Duty, Dollars, or Destiny?

By this time Spain had had more than enough. After preliminary peace feelers had been sent out by the Spanish government, the French ambassador in Washington, acting on behalf of Spain, signed a protocol (August 12, 1898) which brought hostilities to an end and roughly outlined the terms of peace. Spain agreed to relinquish Cuba; to cede Puerto Rico and an island in the Ladrones (ultimately Guam) to the United States; to permit the Americans to occupy and hold "the city, bay, and harbor of Manila, pending the conclusion of a treaty of peace which shall determine the control, disposition and government of the

---

[8] See Shippee, "Germany and the Spanish-American War," *loc. cit.*, pp. 767, 774.

[9] *Literary Digest*, XVII, 92 (July 23, 1898).

[10] See T. A. Bailey, "Dewey and the Germans at Manila Bay," *Amer. Hist. Rev.* XLV (1939), 59–81.

Philippines." [11] This last clause was left purposely vague because the McKinley administration did not then know what it wanted to do with the islands. During the ensuing weeks preparations were made for the final peace negotiations at Paris, as provided for by the protocol.

Ever the astute politician, McKinley chose the five American commissioners with an eye to placating the Senate. Three of them were members of that body. William P. Frye of Maine held the position of president pro tempore of the Senate; while Cushman K. Davis of Minnesota was chairman of the Senate Committee on Foreign Relations. The third Senator, George Gray of Delaware, was the sole Democrat on the commission, the rest being Republicans. He was also the only one of the group definitely opposed to overseas expansion. The chairman of the commission was Secretary of State William R. Day, and the fifth member was Whitelaw Reid, a prominent Republican journalist and an ardent expansionist.[12]

The negotiations opened in Paris on October 1, 1898. Nearly a month was consumed in a discussion of the Cuban question. The Spaniards proposed that the island be transferred to the United States, and with it a debt of some $400,000,000 that had been incurred by the Spanish authorities there, largely in attempting to suppress the insurrections. The United States rejected this proposal.

On October 31, 1898, the commission took up the Philippine question. The platitudinous instructions from McKinley on this subject read:

The march of events rules and overrules human action. . . . We can not be unmindful that, without any desire or design on our part, the war has brought us new duties and responsibilities which we must meet and discharge as becomes a great nation on whose growth and career from the beginning the Ruler of Nations has plainly written the high command and pledge of civilization.[13]

The President's instructions also alluded to the commercial advantages that possession of the Philippines would bring, and stated that the United States could not accept less than Luzon, the largest island in the group, on which was located Manila, the principal seaport in the archipelago.

Meanwhile American public opinion regarding the Philippines had

[11] *Foreign Relations, 1898*, p. 829. Guam had already been captured on June 20, 1898, by an American expedition en route to the Philippines.

[12] McKinley was criticized for having "packed" the commission with Republicans, expansionists, and Senators. Much discussion took place as to the propriety of appointing members of the Senate, who would in turn have to vote on their handiwork.

[13] *Foreign Relations, 1898;* p. 907 (Sept. 16, 1898).

been crystallizing. At first there had been considerable ignorance of the very existence of the islands. McKinley himself confessed: "When we received the cable from Admiral Dewey telling of the taking of the Philippines I looked up their location on the globe. I could not have told where those darned islands were within 2000 miles!" [14] During the period when public opinion was most ill-informed, there was much sentiment for giving the Filipinos their immediate independence. Dewey reported that the natives were more intelligent and more capable of self-government than the Cubans. But as evidence began to pile up from competent observers as to the great economic and strategic value of the archipelago, less was said about the capacity of the natives for governing themselves.

Business men, hitherto partially blind to commercial opportunities in the Far East, now came to life.[15] The European Powers were carving up China, and American merchants were beginning to fear that they might be excluded from this great market. As an offset, it seemed desirable to have Manila, which would provide a vestibule for the trade of Eastern Asia. Besides, a naval base in the Philippines would serve to protect American interests and increase American prestige. The distinguished financier, Frank Vanderlip, published a telling article in the *Century Magazine* for August, 1898, in which he declared that half the people of the earth lived in countries that might easily be reached from the Philippines. Senator Mark Hanna, the "mentor" of McKinley, asserted, "If it is commercialism to want the possession of a strategic point giving the American people an opportunity to maintain a foothold in the markets of that great Eastern country [China], for God's sake let us have commercialism." [16]

The United States might, of course, have given the Filipinos their immediate independence. But the natives were untrained for self-government, and anarchy would probably have resulted. In this case the Powers would almost certainly have intervened, and in the general scramble Germany (against whom American opinion had been strongly aroused) might have made off with the lion's share. Indeed, the imperialistic nations might easily have come to blows over the Philippines, thus precipitating a world war into which the United States could

[14] H. H. Kohlsaat, *From McKinley to Harding* (N.Y., 1923), p. 68. Popular ignorance of the Philippines was not, however, so complete as generally pictured. The press had shown some little interest in the revolt that broke out in 1896 against Spanish authority.

[15] J. W. Pratt, *Expansionists of 1898* (Baltimore, 1936), p. 266. This entire chapter is most revealing.

[16] Quoted in F. R. Dulles, *America in the Pacific* (Boston, 1932), pp. 227–228. This view was expressed in October, 1900.

quite conceivably have been drawn. It is well worth noting that opinion in Japan, both public and official, much preferred American ownership of the Philippines to any other possible alternative, short of cession to the Japanese.[17] And Japan was much more vitally concerned about the peace of the Far East than the other Powers.

There were also moral considerations. The United States could withdraw and let the islands revert to the Spaniards, whose misrule, now that their power had been shattered, would be worse than before.[18] This prospect was intolerable to the American people—a people who had recently thrown themselves into a great humanitarian crusade to free Cuba. Many of them concluded that the problem was of their own making, and that they had a moral obligation not to wash their hands of all responsibility for the backward Filipinos, particularly after having destroyed their guardians. Finally, the church element in the United States welcomed the "little brown brother" as one to whom the gospel should be carried.[19] A White House visitor found Mrs. McKinley, who presumably had considerable influence with her husband, deeply concerned about "converting the Igorrotes."

Meeting Destiny Halfway

At first McKinley seems to have been thinking of a coaling station only; then, as we have seen, he reached the point where he instructed the commissioners to take at least Luzon. But if the United States annexed only one island, the other Powers (Germany, Japan, and Britain had all shown a lively interest) [20] might seize upon the rest,

[17] A conclusion based upon an examination of the State Department records. Significant excerpts are published in P. J. Treat, *Diplomatic Relations between the United States and Japan, 1895–1905* (Stanford University, 1938), pp. 56–58.

[18] The unpublished reports of Consul General Williams at Manila indicate that the foreign colony, and even wealthy Spaniards and Filipinos, favored American control. Department of State, *Consular Letters, Manila*, XIII. It was believed in the United States that the Filipino insurrection would be renewed against Spanish authority. Williams' lurid reports of Spanish atrocities were copied for the peace commission, and may have had some influence.

[19] This subject is well treated in Pratt, *Expansionists of 1898*, Ch. VIII. One clergyman declared: "Manila stretches out her torn and bleeding hands, and we must clasp them and accept our work of redemption, not as a piece of political ambition, but as a mission we have from God." New York *Herald*, Aug. 22, 1898, 6:3.

[20] German interest was quite obvious. On July 26, 1898, Ambassador Hay cabled from London that Britain insisted upon an option in case of a future sale of the Philippines. Department of State, *Despatches, Great Britain*, CXCII. On July 6 and September 6, Minister Buck, in Tokyo, informed the Secretary of State of Japan's interest in the Philippines, should the United States decide not to take them over. Department of State, *Despatches, Japan*, LXXVI, LXXVII.

thus menacing and weakening the strategic value of America's holding. It was not possible, as the New York *World* pithily put it, to take "the juice of the orange without the rind and pulp." Of course, some kind of joint protectorate might be devised; but such a scheme had only sown dragons' teeth in Samoa. To McKinley there seemed to be no acceptable middle ground between taking all and taking none—and either alternative was a devil's choice.

UNCLE SAM—By gum, I rather like your looks.

Uncle Sam feels the imperialist urge. (From the *Rocky Mountain News*, Denver, 1898.)

In these circumstances, and in response to an old habit, McKinley's ear sought the ground. While on his way to and from the Omaha Exposition, in October, 1898, he let fall a number of orotund generalities at convenient rail stops. References to "duty," "destiny," and "Dewey" brought such enthusiastic responses that he could hardly escape the conclusion that the sovereign people welcomed the idea of far-flung dependencies.

Nor did McKinley lack other means of plumbing public opinion. Senator Lodge had noted as early as June 24, 1898, that "The Republican Conventions are all declaring that where the flag once goes up it must never come down." The *Literary Digest* had, during September, 1898, published the results of a poll of 192 newspaper editors, the overwhelming majority of whom favored outright annexation or naval bases.[21] As a last resort, McKinley prayed. As he himself later confessed to a group of his Methodist brethren:

The truth is I didn't want the Philippines and when they came to us as a gift from the gods, I did not know what to do about them. . . . I sought counsel from all sides—Democrats as well as Republicans—but got little help. I thought first we would take only Manila; then Luzon; then other islands, perhaps, also. I walked the floor of the White House night after night until midnight; and I am not ashamed to tell you, gentlemen, that I went down on my knees and prayed Almighty God for light and guidance more than one night.

The President's patience was finally rewarded.

And one night late it came to me this way—I don't know how it was, but it came: (1) that we could not give them back to Spain—that would be cowardly and dishonorable; (2) that we could not turn them over to France or Germany—our commercial rivals in the Orient—that would be bad business and discreditable; (3) that we could not leave them to themselves—they were unfit for self-government—and they would soon have anarchy and misrule over there worse than Spain's was; and (4) that there was nothing left for us to do but to take them all, and to educate the Filipinos, and uplift and civilize and Christianize them, and by God's grace do the very best we could by them, as our fellow-men for whom Christ also died. And then I went to bed, and went to sleep and slept soundly. . . .[22]

So when the peace commissioners cabled for specific instructions, on October 25, 1898, McKinley replied that since the only alternatives were all or none, the United States would have to take all.

The Spanish commissioners fought strenuously to salvage the Philippines; and their position was not so weak as it might seem. By a quirk of fate, the American troops had captured Manila a few hours *after* the signing of the protocol that officially brought hostilities to an end.[23] The United States could hardly claim the islands by right of conquest,

[21] Of 192 replies, 84 favored possession of the entire group, and 63 only naval bases. A total of 45 desired some other settlement. *Literary Digest*, XVII, 307–308 (Sept. 10, 1898). None favored returning the islands to Spain.

[22] *Christian Advocate* (N.Y.), Jan. 22, 1903. It seems probable that McKinley confused the voice of the people with the voice of God, for he touched upon "almost every string in the familiar harmony of imperialism." P. T. Moon, *Imperialism and World Politics* (N.Y., 1929), p. 394.

[23] The protocol was signed on August 12; the city fell on August 13. Because of the difference in time it was 6 A.M. on August 13 in Manila when the protocol was signed in Washington.

though under the terms of the protocol the American commissioners could negotiate for them. The McKinley administration was anxious to avoid further delay; and, recognizing that its case was not perfect, finally offered $20,000,000 to resolve the difficulty. The Spanish representatives reluctantly accepted this solution.

The terms of the treaty, signed December 10, 1898, provided that Spain was to relinquish sovereignty over Cuba, and to cede the Philippines, Puerto Rico, and Guam outright to the United States. McKinley, remembering past troubles, believed that complete banishment of Spain from the Americas was necessary for permanent peace.

TRADITIONALISM VERSUS IMPERIALISM

The debate over the Spanish treaty, in Congress and out, was one of the most heated and momentous in all American history. The anti-imperialists, who were opposed to overseas expansion, pointed out that hitherto the United States had acquired no territory that could not be Americanized and erected into states. Yet the Philippine archipelago, to say nothing of Puerto Rico, was remote and populated by seven million people of alien race and language. There was much truth in the assertion of Senator Pettigrew of South Dakota that bananas and self-government could not grow on the same piece of land.

Opponents of expansion further argued that the forcible annexation of millions of people against their will violated the spirit of the Constitution, and the very terms of the Declaration of Independence; [24] and tyranny abroad, it was charged, would beget tyranny at home. Moreover, the United States did not need land, least of all expensive colonial dependencies; and by projecting itself into the Far East, the republic would become involved in European entanglements and lose the strong moral position it had formerly occupied under the Monroe Doctrine. [25]

[24] The abstract ideals of the Declaration of Independence and of Washington's Farewell Address were stressed more frequently by the anti-imperialists than any other issue. F. H. Harrington, "The Anti-Imperialist Movement in the United States, 1898–1900," *Miss. Valley Hist. Rev.*, XXII (1935), 211. See also the same author's "Literary Aspects of American Anti-Imperialism, 1898–1902," *New England Quar.*, X (1937), 650–667.

[25] *Punch* had Dame Europa say to Uncle Sam, who was entering the Far East, "To whom do I owe the pleasure of this intrusion?" Uncle Sam: "Ma'am—my name is Uncle Sam!" Dame Europa: "Any relation of the late Colonel Monroe?" CXV, 55 (Aug. 6, 1898). Contrary to the anti-imperialists, Professor Perkins holds that the Doctrine relates to European intermeddling, not American. Dexter Perkins, *The Monroe Doctrine, 1867–1907* (Baltimore, 1937), p. 130; see also pp. 282 ff.

The anti-imperialists also made much of America's inconsistency in entering the war to free the Cubans, and then finding herself some eight thousand miles away in the Philippine Islands attempting to subject millions of protesting people to her will. Finally, the foes of overseas expansion pointed to the indisputable fact that the time-honored policy of the Fathers had served well. As long as America stayed at home and minded her own business, she could easily protect her shores without an enormous military establishment. But if the republic were to plunge into the Far Eastern vortex, it would have to maintain a powerful navy to protect its colonies. This would be expensive and, in addition, would expose the United States to foreign wars. The Philippines would be, as Theodore Roosevelt himself came to admit, a veritable heel of Achilles.[26]

The Mirage of Empire

The expansionists, on the other hand, advanced the familiar arguments about economic and strategic advantages; about national honor and responsibility; about destiny and the cowardice of "hauling down the flag." The fiery young imperialist orator, Albert J. Beveridge, cried that only those should have self-government "who are capable of self-government!" He passionately met the argument of noncontiguity:

The ocean does not separate us from the lands of our duty and desire—the ocean joins us, a river never to be dredged, a canal never to be repaired. [Applause.] Steam joins us, electricity joins us—the very elements are in league with our destiny. [Continued applause and cheers.] Cuba not contiguous? Porto Rico not contiguous? The Philippines not contiguous? Our navy will make them contiguous! [he thundered, as the thousands shouted their delight].[27]

Some of the imperialists wrapped their selfish motives in humanitarian phrases; others sincerely believed that it was America's duty to extend an uplifting hand to the benighted "brown brother." Great Britain naturally cheered the Americans on. She had investments in the Philippines, as well as an enormous economic stake in the Far East, and she desired support for a policy of equal commercial opportunity. And of course the Americans could not disappoint the nation that had stood by them so nobly when Continental Europe seemed unfriendly.

[26] Roosevelt to Taft, Aug. 21, 1907, Roosevelt Papers, Library of Congress.
[27] C. G. Bowers, *Beveridge and the Progressive Era* (N.Y., 1932), pp. 75–76 (Speech delivered in Indiana, Sept. 1898).

Rudyard Kipling, a minor prophet and major poet of British imperialism, appealed to the United States with his "White Man's Burden":

> Take up the White Man's burden—
> Ye dare not stoop to less—
> Nor call too loud on Freedom
> To cloke your weariness.[28]

The poem caught the mood of the hour in America, and "became hackneyed in a day." But the Omaha *World-Herald* kept its head better than most of its contemporaries when it remarked, "In other words, Mr. Kipling would have Uncle Sam take up John Bull's burden." [29]

THE SENATE VOTES FOR PEACE

The Spanish treaty encountered bitter opposition in the Senate. The Democrats, though expansionists under Jefferson and Polk, were opposed to imperialism, if for no better reason than that a Republican administration was in power. But William Jennings Bryan, titular leader of the Democratic party, came to Washington and urged his followers in the Senate to support the treaty so that the United States could end the war, take over the Philippines, and then grant the Filipinos independence.[30] Bryan's influence apparently turned the tide.[31] Enough Democrats voted for the treaty to secure its approval, on February 6, 1899, by a count of 57 to 27. It was one of the bitterest and closest fights on record, the nays failing by two votes to block ratification.

But the action of the Senate was not a fair test of sentiment in that body or throughout the country as to the Philippines. In order to reject

---

[28] *McClure's Magazine*, XII, 291 (Feb., 1899). This was the first appearance of the poem in America. It was published in the London *Times*, Feb. 4, 1899, under the caption, "An Address to the United States." Apparently the poem came out in America a few days before this date.

[29] Lord Salisbury privately encouraged the Americans to take the Philippines. Henry White to Hay, Nov. 2, 1898, Hay Papers, Library of Congress.

[30] M. E. Curti, "Bryan and World Peace," *Smith College Studies in History*, XVI, nos. 3–4 (1931), p. 122.

[31] W. S. Holt, *Treaties Defeated by the Senate* (Baltimore, 1933), p. 174. The outbreak of the Filipino insurrection, two days before the final vote, may have tipped two waverers into the affirmative camp. See *ibid.*, pp. 170–171. Lodge, who led the fight, thought that the revolt had no appreciable effect; Senator Hoar, a leading opponent, thought it "probable" that it did. Hoar to Schurz, Feb. 9, 1899, Schurz Papers, Library of Congress. In any event, enough Republican Senators had been elected in the November elections to assure ratification in March, 1899. Hoar to Schurz, Jan. 17, 1899, Schurz Papers.

the islands it was necessary to reject the treaty. This would have resulted in repudiating the President, unsettling business, and adding to the international uncertainties. On the clear-cut issue of retaining the archipelago the imperialists would almost certainly have failed to obtain a two-thirds majority.[32]

It has been fashionable to condemn the annexation of the Philippines as a grievous diplomatic error. But it must be remembered that McKinley was finally forced to choose among several possible courses, all of which presented momentous problems. He chose—perhaps wisely—the one that he and his advisers, and possibly a majority of the American people, thought the least undesirable. It would probably be fair to say that, from the standpoint of the United States, the misfortune was not the decision to annex the Philippines, but the fortuitous set of circumstances that seemed to make annexation necessary.[33]

DESTINY DESCENDS TO BUSHWHACKING

Perhaps the most serious avoidable mistake made by the United States during this period was the failure to quiet the fears of the Filipinos. They had been encouraged to believe—whether with proper authority or not—that they would be given their independence, and they had assisted materially in the capture of Manila. But when it dawned on them that they were merely going to exchange Spanish for American overlords, they arose in revolt, February 4, 1899.

This unfortunate outbreak might have been avoided if Congress had unequivocally declared, in January, 1899, that it would give the Filipinos their independence as soon as order was restored. A resolution looking to this end was postponed until after the insurrection began; then, in the form of an amendment, it was defeated (February 14, 1899) by the casting vote of the Vice-President.[34] Whatever its motives, Congress was unwilling to make a self-denying pledge, as it had done for Cuba during the enthusiasm of a humanitarian crusade.

---

[32] At least two Senators who voted for the treaty had no enthusiasm for the Philippines, but believed that ratification was the only practicable alternative. Hawley to Croffut, June 5, 1899, Croffut Papers, Library of Congress; Spooner to Bigelow, Feb. 20, 1899, Spooner Papers, *ibid.*

[33] This conclusion is based in part on an examination of all the relevant State Department records for the period of the war and the peace negotiations, and upon a number of private collections in the Library of Congress.

[34] Instead, the Senate adopted the McEnery resolution, which declared that the United States would not annex the Philippines permanently, but would "in due time" "make such disposition of said islands as will best promote the interests of the citizens of the United States and the inhabitants of said islands." *Cong. Record*, 55 Cong., 3 sess., p. 1830.

"Old Glory" had now been fired on, and it was necessary to crush the insurrection. The United States sent some 70,000 men to the Philippines, an army about four times as large as that which had invaded Cuba. The semicivilized little Filipino brothers used primitive methods of warfare, and inevitably dragged the American soldiers down to their level. The republic was shaken by scandalous reports that United States troops were torturing and butchering prisoners. The exasperating guerrilla tactics of the natives caused the Americans to feel some measure of sympathy for "Butcher" Weyler, and to do him the honor of adopting a form of reconcentration. It was not until after over two years of inglorious bushwhacking that the heart was taken out of the insurrection by the capture of its leader, Emilio Aguinaldo.

Some eight months after the Filipino outbreak the British encountered an even more formidable problem with the Boers in South Africa. There was a great deal of agitation in the United States, much of it in a rich Irish brogue, in behalf of aiding the Boers; but the Washington government preserved a strict neutrality.[35] It seems obvious that if the same uprising had come five years earlier there would have been much more pro-Boer feeling in the United States. But Americans could overlook neither British sympathy during the Spanish War, nor the fact that the United States had a not dissimilar problem in the Philippines.

While both the Filipino insurrection and the Boer War were still dragging to a dreary conclusion, the American people were plunged into the presidential campaign of 1900. The Democrats nominated Bryan for the second time and declared in their platform that imperialism was both the "burning" and the "paramount" issue. The Republicans renominated McKinley for the presidency, and drafted Theodore Roosevelt, the popular war hero, for the vice-presidency. Roosevelt protestingly consented to run for an office that had hitherto been regarded as the graveyard of political hopes. The Republicans vigorously denied that imperialism was the "paramount" issue, and charged that the threat to prosperity from the financial heresies of Bryan was the burning question.

There can be no doubt that many voters regarded the choice as one between two evils: the platitudinous McKinley and the financially heretical Bryan. One voter wrote to Grover Cleveland, "It is a choice between evils, and I am going to shut my eyes, hold my nose,

---

[35] The pro-British Hay pursued such a rigidly hands-off policy as materially to help the British and harm the Boers. A less friendly Administration would doubtless have supported American rights with much more vigor. See J. H. Ferguson, *American Diplomacy and the Boer War* (Phila., 1939).

vote, go home and disinfect myself." [36] Many refused to become alarmed about imperialism because they felt that the United States was already committed to retaining the Philippines. Others who disliked the Administration's policy of expansion believed that the menace of Bryanism was more immediate and should be disposed of first.

The Republicans won a sweeping victory in the election of 1900, and straightway announced that McKinley's Philippine policy had been vindicated. But the issues were so numerous and so confused that if the results were a mandate on anything they were not a mandate on imperialism. Prosperity rather than McKinley won. If the out-and-out question of approving the annexation of the Philippines had been presented to the electorate, as it never was, it is possible that the Administration would have been repudiated. [37]

THE HIPPISLEY-ROCKHILL OPEN DOOR NOTES

Meanwhile other significant developments had been taking place in the Far Eastern policy of the United States. After China had betrayed her weakness in the war with the Japanese (1894-1895), the European Powers descended upon her "living carcass" and extorted great leaseholds and spheres of influence. American merchants, whose commerce with China was about two per cent of the total foreign trade of the United States, viewed this process with alarm, for they feared that the predatory nations would erect prohibitively high tariff barriers and other restrictions within the areas under their control. The British, who had by far the largest foreign trade stake in China, were even more concerned. As early as March 8, 1898, the British ambassador in Washington, Sir Julian Pauncefote, suggested to Secretary of State Sherman that the two nations join in co-operative efforts to insure equal commercial opportunity in China—that is, the Open Door. The proposal was renewed on January 8, 1899, but was both times refused as inconsistent with the traditional policy of the United States. [38]

Outside the British Foreign Office a number of Englishmen were vigorously championing the Open Door. Notable among them was Lord Charles Beresford, a recent visitor to the Far East, whose book, *The Breakup of China*, had attracted considerable attention. He fur-

[36] J. S. Morton to Cleveland, Nov. 2, 1900, Cleveland Papers, Library of Congress.
[37] See T. A. Bailey, "Was the Election of 1900 a Mandate on Imperialism?" *Miss. Valley Hist. Rev.*, XXIV (1937), 43-52.
[38] This section on the Far East has drawn heavily from A. W. Griswold, *The Far Eastern Policy of the United States* (N.Y., 1938), Ch. II, which reproduces important Hippisley and Rockhill papers.

ther popularized the concept of the Open Door by a series of speeches in the United States. The idea of equal commercial opportunity in China began to meet with increasing favor; and pressure from American economic and missionary interests finally became so strong that the Department of State found it desirable to do something.

Behind the scenes two private individuals were actively at work. The first was A. E. Hippisley, a British subject employed in China, and a persistent advocate of the Open Door. While in the United States on leave of absence, he had a number of conversations with his old American friend, W. W. Rockhill, who had seen diplomatic service in China, and who was then the valued private adviser of Secretary of State John Hay on matters of Far Eastern policy. Hippisley, like other Britishers, was eager to have the United States rather than Great Britain take the lead in espousing the Open Door, for the Irish and other Anglophobes in America would have protested bitterly against subscribing to any such proposal from the mother country. Accordingly, on August 17, 1899, Hippisley drew up a memorandum embracing his ideas on the subject of equal commercial opportunity in China. On August 28th Rockhill revised this memorandum for presentation to President McKinley, who was apparently convinced by it. On September 5, 1899, Rockhill put the substance of his memorandum in the form of diplomatic notes which, with minor changes, were adopted by Secretary John Hay. Thus the British succeeded in committing the United States to a policy favorable to their Chinese interests.

On September 6, 1899, the day after Rockhill completed the drafts, Secretary Hay sent essentially identical instructions to the United States representatives in Berlin, London, and St. Petersburg (later to Tokyo, Rome, and Paris), asking them to request the foreign offices concerned for assurances regarding the points summarized below:

1. *Within its sphere of interest or leasehold in China,* no Power would interfere with any treaty port or any vested interest.
2. The Chinese treaty tariff would be applicable within such spheres of interest, and the duties were to be collected by the Chinese government.
3. *Within its sphere* no Power would discriminate in favor of its own nationals in the matter of harbor dues and railroad charges.

Each nation was urged not only to subscribe to these principles but to use its influence to secure acceptance by the others.[39]

Secretary Hay's summons at once placed the Powers in a most awkward position. It was like asking all persons in a room who were not

[39] The correspondence appears in *Foreign Relations, 1899,* pp. 128–142.

thieves to stand up. Replies were at length forthcoming from all of the nations addressed, but each statement (except that of Italy, which had no spheres of influence) contained some evasion or qualification. Each government, except the Italian, declared that its acceptance was contingent upon that of the others. Russia's response was in effect a polite declination, which meant that technically the other Powers giving qualified answers were released from their commitment. But Hay, rather than press Russia for a less equivocal reply and run the risk of a blunt refusal, resorted to Yankee bluff. On March 20, 1900, he declared that the assent of all the Powers was "final and definitive." In these circumstances Russia could hardly come forward and loudly insist that she had not consented. Apparently Japan was the only Power to challenge Hay's unwarranted assumption.[40]

There has been, and still is, much misunderstanding of the Open Door. In popular phrase it means equal commercial opportunity in China—a policy as old as America's Far Eastern trade. But the concept, as defined by Hay in 1899, was actually much narrower. The United States did not insist upon the territorial integrity of China. Indeed, Hay assumed that the "sphering out" of the helpless empire would continue, and he omitted all reference to mining and railroad concessions, and to capital investment. Hay's Open Door applied to only the relatively small leaseholds and spheres of influence, and even within them it did not guarantee equality of treatment. Vested interests were to be undisturbed, which meant that within the German sphere, for example, the Germans would have an advantage. The Open Door declaration was merely a dramatic statement of Hay's policy, based upon commercial rather than altruistic motives, which did not become binding upon the Powers because they did not accept it. As far as the United States was concerned, it was a hope rather than a reality.

THE OPEN DOOR IN PERIL

The Hay notes of 1899 were but academic discussions as compared with the dramatic happenings of 1900, when a group of fanatical Chinese, called "Boxers" in the Western world, rose up against the "foreign devils." After widespread murder and pillaging had occurred, a group of whites, including members of the foreign legations, were besieged in Peking and cut off from the rest of the world. Hay refused to give up hope for their safety, and at length succeeded in establishing telegraphic contact with the American minister, who pleaded for quick

[40] Treat, *United States and Japan, 1895–1905*, p. 87.

relief. The certain knowledge that the legations were still holding out caused the international rescue expedition of some 20,000 men to hasten its efforts; and the beleaguered legations were rescued on August 14, 1900. It is significant that the United States, contrary to the nonentanglement precepts of the Fathers, contributed 2500 soldiers to the enterprise.

Meanwhile Hay strongly suspected that the Powers would take advantage of the situation to do violence to the Open Door. He therefore undertook by skillful diplomacy to localize the uprising so that there would be less excuse for attacking and perhaps dismembering the rest of China. His most notable effort in this direction was a circular note to the Powers, dated July 3, 1900. It significantly declared that the "policy of the Government of the United States is to seek a solution" which may "preserve Chinese territorial and administrative entity" and "safeguard for the world the principle of equal and impartial trade with all parts of the Chinese Empire." [41]

This, it will be observed, was an important corollary to the original notes of September 6, 1899. Hay had then applied the Open Door only to commercial activity, and only within foreign leaseholds and spheres of interest. Now he went much further and declared that the United States stood for the *territorial integrity* of all China, and for commercial equality in *"all parts"* of the Chinese Empire. Unlike the original notes, the circular of July 3, 1900, did not call for an answer; it was merely a statement of American policy. Nevertheless the Powers found it to their advantage to give some heed to the principles enunciated by Hay.

The victorious and vindictive Powers levied an indemnity of a third of a billion dollars upon the Chinese government. It is possible that the sum would have been much larger, and that territorial cessions would have been demanded, if Hay had not used his influence on the side of moderation. The share of the United States—nearly $25,000,-000—was found to be unnecessarily large, and the unexpended balance was later remitted to China." [42]

Although John Hay won great acclaim for his spectacular strokes,[43]

---

[41] *Foreign Relations, 1900*, p. 299.

[42] The first remission was authorized in 1908, the second in 1924. Altogether the United States returned $18,098,674.66 of the $24,440,778.81 assessed. The Chinese government used this money to educate selected students in the United States.

[43] The New York *Nation* spoke of "a splendid instance of American sagacity winning a peaceful victory"; the Chicago *Times-Herald* declared that "there has never been a more brilliant and important achievement in diplomacy." " . . . Splendid work, splendid diplomacy," commented the Philadelphia *Inquirer*. See particularly *Public Opinion,* XXVIII, 420 (Apr. 5, 1900).

it became increasingly evident that the Open Door was little more than an empty phrase. John Hay, as well as the European Powers, realized perfectly well that the American people did not have a vital enough stake in the Far East to fight for commercial equality in China—to go to war for about two per cent of their foreign trade. Nor did they have sufficient strength to do so effectively, even if they had wanted to. If China was saved at this time it was not by John Hay's pen, but by the international difficulties which involved the European Powers in a political stalemate and which made it desirable, from their point of view, to pay some deference to the Open Door—at least temporarily.[44]

It has often been said that if the British and the Americans had formed an alliance at this time to uphold equality of commercial opportunity in Eastern Asia, the principle might have been made effective. But American tradition made such a course impossible. Hay himself must have realized that the Open Door was futile, for in November, 1900, at the instance of the Navy Department, he secretly attempted to enter the territorial scramble when he instructed the United States minister in Peking to take steps in the direction of obtaining a naval base and territorial concessions at Samsah Bay, southern China. The Japanese, who had prior rights there, thwarted the American move and gently, if somewhat ironically, reminded Hay of his recently announced guardianship of Chinese territorial integrity.[45]

FORSAKING OLD TRADITIONS

The Spanish-American War is usually taken as the date for the emergence of the United States as a world Power. In a little over two years the republic annexed Hawaii, secured a definitive title to American Samoa, acquired Puerto Rico, the Philippines, Guam, and Wake,[46] and undertook to establish a protectorate over Cuba. With the acquisition of the Philippines the United States became a Far Eastern Power, and ere long was taking extraordinary steps to thwart the other nations in their designs on China.[47]

[44] Griswold, *Far Eastern Policy of the United States*, p. 82; Treat, *United States and Japan*, p. 88.

[45] This surprising development was kept secret until 1924, when the documents were published in *Foreign Relations, 1915*, pp. 114–115. For fuller excerpts from the diplomatic correspondence see Treat, *United States and Japan*, pp. 109–112. Later American interest in the project is discussed in Vagts, *Deutschland und die Vereinigten Staaten*, II, 1134–1135.

[46] The U.S.S. *Bennington* took possession of this place, on January 17, 1899.

[47] The United States also showed its willingness to forsake tradition and participate in world affairs when it sent delegates to the First International Peace Conference at

It was perhaps fortunate for the United States that during these transitional years a man of John Hay's stature served as Secretary of State. He boldly assumed leadership of the United States as a world Power; he revealed qualities of courage and imagination; and he probably accomplished as much in the Far East as was possible without either an entangling alliance or a show of force. Although he did not succeed in committing the Powers to the principles of commercial equality and territorial integrity in China, he mobilized public opinion behind this concept, and helped formulate and publicize a new Open Door policy which his successors—for weal or for woe—felt obliged to uphold. Finally, he brought a moral flavor to the conduct of America's foreign affairs, and aroused new interest in diplomacy, hitherto regarded as a "foreign luxury" or the "deleterious appendage" of effete monarchies. As Hay himself put it, "The United States of today can not go back to what the country was fifty or a hundred years ago. Whether we will or not, whether for better or for worse, we must go forward." [48]

BIBLIOGRAPHICAL NOTE

A survey of the period appears in S. F. Bemis, ed., *The American Secretaries of State and their Diplomacy* (N.Y., 1929), IX, 89–151. (Sketch of Secretary Day by L. B. Shippee and R. B. Way, of Secretary Hay by A. L. P. Dennis). A detailed study is B. A. Reuter, *Anglo-American Relations during the Spanish-American War* (N.Y., 1924). On German-American relations see L. B. Shippee, "Germany and the Spanish-American War," *Amer. Hist. Rev.*, XXX (1925), 754–777; J. F. Rippy, *Latin America in World Politics* (3rd ed., N.Y., 1938), Ch. X. On German-American relations for the period from 1898 to 1900 see the detailed work of Alfred Vagts, *Deutschland und die Vereinigten Staaten in der Weltpolitik* (2 vols., N.Y., 1935), II, Chs. XI, XII. On public opinion consult C. E. Schieber, *The Transformation of American Sentiment toward Germany, 1870–1914* (Boston, 1923), Ch. III. The peace negotiations are treated in F. E. Chadwick, *The Relations of the United States and Spain: The Spanish-American War* (N.Y., 1911), II, Chs. XX–XXI. For the movement that culminated in the annexation of the Philippines see J. W. Pratt, *Expansionists of 1898* (Baltimore, 1936), Chs. VII–IX. A thoughtful analysis of the same movement appears in J. F. Rippy, *America and the Strife of Europe* (Chicago, 1938),

---

The Hague in 1899. No agreement regarding disarmament proved possible, and the most important achievement was the establishment of the Permanent Court of Arbitration at The Hague. The American delegates took a leading part in sponsoring this proposal. See F. W. Holls, *The Peace Conference at The Hague* (N.Y., 1900), p. 231. To the innocuous convention providing for the Court the Americans attached a reservation in behalf of the Monroe Doctrine. Thus was created the precedent for emasculating later proposals for peace and arbitration by bringing in the Doctrine. See Perkins, *The Monroe Doctrine, 1867–1907*, p. 292.

[48] *Public Opinion*, XXIX, 553 (Nov. 1, 1900).

Ch. V. A useful survey is F. H. Harrington, "The Anti-Imperialist Movement in the United States, 1898–1900," *Miss. Valley Hist. Rev.*, XXII (1935), 211–230. An excellent account of the fight in the Senate for ratification may be found in W. S. Holt, *Treaties Defeated by the Senate* (Baltimore, 1933), Ch. VIII. The best treatment of the Open Door notes is A. W. Griswold, *The Far Eastern Policy of the United States* (N.Y., 1938), Ch. II. On the same subject and the Boxer difficulty see Tyler Dennett, *John Hay* (N.Y., 1933), Chs. XXIV–XXVI; see also the same author's *Americans in Eastern Asia* (N.Y., 1922), Chs. XXXI–XXXIII; Vagts, *Deutschland und die Vereinigten Staaten*, II, Ch. XI; A. L. P. Dennis, *Adventures in American Diplomacy, 1896–1906* (N.Y., 1928), Chs. VIII, IX. Further references: see footnotes of this chapter and Bemis and Griffin, *Guide*, pp. 489–491, 523–530.

RECENT REFERENCES. R. H. Heindel, *The American Impact on Great Britain, 1898–1914* (Phila., 1940), though concerned primarily with economic and cultural "impacts," nevertheless contains much information bearing upon the political *rapprochement*, and thus complements L. M. Gelber's *Rise of Anglo-American Friendship*. R. B. Mowat, *The American Entente* (London, 1939), is a sketchy account of the drawing together of the two Anglo-Saxon nations. It contributes little to our knowledge of American diplomacy but is useful as reflecting the British point of view. J. K. Eyre, Jr., "Japan and the American Annexation of the Philippines," *Pacific Hist. Rev.*, XI (1942), 55–71, shows that, as stated in the present book, the Japanese preferred American occupancy to that of any other Power, aside from themselves. Nevertheless, a considerable body of minority opinion opposed lodgment of a strong nation so close to Formosa. As a matter of expediency, Japan needed to co-operate with America and Britain to offset Germany, Russia, and France in China. The Japanese "could afford to wait for a more opportune moment" to raise their voices "against American sovereignty in the Islands (p. 70)." The same author, in "Russia and the American Acquisition of the Philippines," *Miss. Valley Hist. Rev.*, XXVIII (1942), 539–562, concludes that while the Russian government was friendly to American acquisition, it would "undoubtedly" have taken a more active interest had the islands been in danger of falling to some European Power. These two articles provide substantial justification for McKinley's fear that, should the United States withdraw, the resulting scramble might touch off a world war.

NEW REFERENCES. Merze Tate, in *The Disarmament Illusion: The Movement for a Limitation of Armaments to 1907* (N.Y., 1942), deals with the First Hague conference, and shows that the United States, stimulated by the recent war with Spain, was not primarily interested in peace and disarmament (pp. 211–215). L. W. Walker, "Guam's Seizure by the United States in 1898," *Pacific Hist. Rev.*, XIV (1945), 1–12, explains why Captain Glass made the mistake of asking for the surrender of Guam rather than all the Marianas. P. E. Quinn, "The Diplomatic Struggle for the Carolines, 1898," *ibid.*, XIV (1945), 290–302, shows how German assiduity (including pressure on American representatives in Washington and Paris), together with lukewarmness in the United States, won the Carolines. S. W. Livermore, "American Naval-Base Policy in the Far East, 1850–1914," *ibid.*, XIII (1944), 113–135, describes the designs of the Navy (chiefly 1900–1903) on possible bases along the China coast, including Samsah and particularly the Chusan Islands.

4TH ED. REFS. See Bibliographical Appendix, p. 935.

CHAPTER XXXII

Acquiring the Panama Canal Zone, 1900–1903

". . . I took the Canal Zone and let Congress debate. . . ."
Theodore Roosevelt, 1911.

CANAL CONSCIOUSNESS

THE UNITED STATES emerged from the Spanish-American War a Caribbean as well as a Pacific Power. This changed status brought about a remarkable resurgence of interest in an Isthmian canal. Such a waterway now seemed imperatively necessary if the American people were to take full advantage of their new trade opportunities in the Pacific, and at the same time unfetter their fleet. The recent hostilities had, in fact, provided a dramatic object lesson in naval needs. The United States battleship *Oregon*, ordered from Puget Sound to Cuban waters, had been forced to make a breakneck voyage around South America—three times the distance that would have been necessary had there been a canal—while all America breathlessly watched her progress.

The chief initial obstacle in the path of building the canal was diplomatic rather than physical. As long as the Clayton-Bulwer Treaty stood, the United States could not honorably construct an Isthmian waterway and maintain exclusive control over it. Knowing the desires of the American people, Downing Street at first attempted to wring concessions from the Washington government in the matter of the Alaska-Canada boundary dispute; but nothing came of these negotiations.[1] In January, 1900, a bill was introduced in Congress providing for the construction of a Nicaraguan Canal in defiance of the Clayton-Bulwer Treaty. There was a good chance that it would be passed, for, as Secretary of State Hay reported, some of the Senators were saying, "dishonor be damned." The London government, already involved in the Boer War and faced with an unfriendly Europe, decided that rather than risk the new Anglo-American friendship it would make concessions without insisting upon an equivalent. Accordingly, on February 5, 1900, Lord Pauncefote, the British ambassador in Washington,

---

[1] L. M. Gelber, *The Rise of Anglo-American Friendship* (London, 1938), p. 45.

concluded a treaty with John Hay. This pact provided that the United States could construct, own, and neutralize an Isthmian waterway, but under no circumstances fortify it.

At first the treaty was rather favorably received in America, for it was a definite improvement on the Clayton-Bulwer encumbrance, and it was consonant with the traditional policy of a neutralized canal. But this was the year of a presidential election, and the Democratic platform inveighed against the pact as a base surrender to Britain. The Irish, who deprecated the recent friendliness with the mother country, added their voices to the outcry, and they were joined by the German-Americans, who had been greatly aroused by the killing of their fellow Teutons in the Boer War. These were the "idiots," wrote John Hay, who yelled that he was not an American because he did not say, " 'To Hell with the Queen,' at every breath."

The most serious objection to the Hay-Pauncefote Treaty was the nonfortification clause. This meant that America's enemies could use the proposed canal against her or, if they possessed a superior force, seize it for their own. The New York *Journal* and the New York *Sun*, leading jingo newspapers, whipped up a loud outcry against the treaty, and they were joined by many others. "Another of the administration's 'great diplomatic victories,'" asserted the Detroit *News*, "has been won—by the British government." [2]

Britain Bows to the Inevitable

When the Senators heard the rumblings of protest against the Hay-Pauncefote Treaty, they undertook to make provision for fortification of the proposed canal. Their amendments were so sweeping and so definitely to America's advantage that the British government, supported by a robust sentiment in the English press, refused to accept them. The entire negotiation collapsed in March, 1901.

Hay was so crestfallen that he promptly tendered his resignation as Secretary of State, but was finally persuaded to remain. Though conceding that the treaty was not perfect, the disgusted Secretary felt that on a give and take basis the arrangement was a fair one. He asserted:

I long ago made up my mind that no treaty . . . that gave room for a difference of opinion could ever pass the Senate. When I sent in the Canal Convention I felt sure that no one out of a mad house could fail

[2] *Public Opinion*, XXVIII, 199 (Feb. 15, 1900).

to see that the advantages were all on our side. But I underrated the power of ignorance and spite, acting upon cowardice.[3]

He added that "there will always be 34% of the Senate on the blackguard side of every question." [4] But whatever excuses may be offered, the fact remains that, considering American interests and the final arrangements, the Senate was right and Hay was wrong. The first Hay-Pauncefote Treaty is the example most frequently cited in support of the much criticized two-thirds rule.

Throughout the months that followed the failure of the Hay-Pauncefote negotiations, there was much talk in the United States of abrogating the Clayton-Bulwer Treaty outright, or of going to war to end England's thwarting of American aspirations. All this, of course, was profoundly disturbing to the British. America was powerful; her friendship was valuable; the Boer War was exhausting; and relations with Germany were growing worse. Why not, concluded Downing Street, permit the United States to build the canal—a canal that would double the power of its navy and enable it to guarantee the *status quo* in America against England's rivals, notably Germany? [5] Once more the distresses of Europe were operating to America's advantage.

On November 18, 1901, the London government went the whole way when the second Hay-Pauncefote Treaty was concluded. By its terms the Clayton-Bulwer agreement was expressly superseded, and the United States was given a free hand to build, control, and *fortify* (this was tacitly conceded) an Isthmian canal. Not content with relinquishing to America the key to a maritime empire—without exacting an equivalent—England reduced her West Indian fleet and garrison during the next few years, thus recognizing the supremacy of the United States in the Caribbean.[6]

---

[3] A. L. P. Dennis, *Adventures in American Diplomacy, 1896–1906* (N.Y., 1928), p. 168 (Hay to McCook, Apr. 22, 1900). Hay later wrote: "A treaty entering the Senate is like a bull going into the arena: no one can say just how or when the final blow will fall—but one thing is certain—it will never leave the arena alive." W. R. Thayer, *The Life and Letters of John Hay* (Boston, 1915), II, 393.

[4] Born to ease and endowed with brilliant gifts, Hay did not accept disappointments with good grace, particularly since chronic ill health was adding to his irritability. He made little effort to conceal his contempt for the Senate, and he leads all other Secretaries in the number of treaties rejected, in the number amended, and in the delay encountered. R. J. Dangerfield, *In Defense of the Senate* (Norman, Okla., 1933), pp. 175 ff.

[5] Gelber, *Rise of Anglo-American Friendship*, p. 91. There seems to be no basis for the hypothesis that Hay co-operated with Britain in the Open Door negotiations in return for the Hay-Pauncefote Treaty. A. W. Griswold, *The Far Eastern Policy of the United States* (N.Y., 1938), p. 85.

[6] Gelber, *Rise of Anglo-American Friendship*, p. 103, *et passim*.

ENGINEERS AND POSTAGE STAMPS

On September 14, 1901, two months before the signing of the second Hay-Pauncefote Treaty, William McKinley died from an assassin's bullet, and Theodore Roosevelt assumed the presidency. The colorful "Rough Rider," who did not relish being dubbed "His Accidency," set out to prove that he was entitled to be elected President "in his own right." Nothing, he believed, would more impress the American people than starting the much-talked-about canal—"making the dirt fly."

The second Hay-Pauncefote Treaty cleared away the diplomatic obstacles. The next question was that of a choice between the Panama and the Nicaraguan routes. The New Panama Canal Company, successor to the defunct de Lesseps organization, was asking the exorbitant sum of $109,000,000 for its holdings. On November 16, 1901, two days before the signing of the second Hay-Pauncefote Treaty, the Walker Commission (a group of engineers appointed by McKinley in 1899) reported in favor of the Nicaraguan route, primarily on the grounds of lower cost. Panicky, the directors of the French canal company dropped their price to $40,000,000, a saving of $69,000,000 that tipped the scales in favor of Panama. Up to this point President Roosevelt seems to have favored the Nicaraguan route; but he now persuaded the Commission to change its recommendation and support the Panama Canal, which it did on January 18, 1902.[7]

On January 9, 1902, nine days before this reversal, the House of Representatives voted in favor of a Nicaraguan waterway, 308 to 2. Thoroughly alarmed, the French company swung into action with its resourceful lobbyists. Conspicuous among these was a prominent New York attorney, William N. Cromwell, who had recently contributed $60,000 to the Republican campaign chest in order to prevent the party from going on record in 1900 as favoring the Nicaraguan route.[8]

The company was also well served by a remarkable Frenchman, Philippe Bunau-Varilla, former chief engineer of the original organization and a large stockholder of the new concern. In the interests of his fellow investors he came to America and made contacts with the "right people," including John Hay, Mark Hanna, and Theodore Roosevelt. Bunau-Varilla attempted to disparage the Nicaraguan route by raising the bogey of volcanic activity, but his efforts did not meet

---

[7] See H. C. Hill, *Roosevelt and the Caribbean* (Chicago, 1927), p. 36.

[8] H. F. Pringle, *Theodore Roosevelt* (N.Y., 1931), p. 304. Cromwell charged his contribution to the French company, and later presented a bill for $800,000 as compensation for his services. *Ibid.*

with much success until May, 1902, when Mont Pelée, on the West Indian island of Martinique, suddenly erupted and wiped out a town of 40,000 people. A few days later a Nicaraguan volcano became active —the very mountain that was engraved on the postage stamps of the republic. Bunau-Varilla hastened to the stamp dealers of Washington.

I was lucky enough [he later wrote] to find there ninety stamps, that is, one for every Senator, showing a beautiful volcano belching forth in magnificent eruption. . . .

I hastened to paste my precious postage stamps on sheets of paper. . . . Below the stamps were written the following words, which told the whole story: "An official witness of the volcanic activity of Nicaragua." [9]

Bunau-Varilla then took steps to place one of these stamps in the hands of each Senator.

Such astute lobbying was not without its influence on the Senate, and there the Panama adherents rallied in force. They were led by Mark Hanna, who, as chairman of the Republican National Committee, was doubtless grateful for Cromwell's $60,000 contribution. After extended debate the Senate amended the original Nicaraguan bill so as to provide for a *Panama* canal. The measure stipulated, however, that the President was to secure a right of way across the Isthmus of Panama from Colombia, but that if he could not do so "within a reasonable time and upon reasonable terms" he was to turn to Nicaragua. The amended bill became law on June 28, 1902.

Colombia's Congress Also Blocks Treaties

The way was now clear for an agreement with Colombia to obtain the Panama route. Secretary Hay, by threatening to turn to Nicaragua and by using other methods of suasion, finally succeeded in extorting a treaty from the Colombian *chargé* in Washington, Tomás Herrán, who signed with misgivings on January 22, 1903. Three days later a telegram came from Bogotá instructing him not to sign and to await new instructions, an eventuality which Hay and Cromwell had foreseen and forestalled.[10] On March 17, 1903, after a brief but bitter flare-up from the Nicaragua supporters, the Senate approved the treaty.

So far so good—for the Roosevelt administration. The United States was to obtain a canal zone six miles wide for a cash payment of $10,-

[9] Philippe Bunau-Varilla, *Panama: the Creation, Destruction, and Resurrection* (N.Y., 1914), p. 247.
[10] Tyler Dennett, *John Hay* (N.Y., 1933), p. 373.

000,000 and an annuity of $250,000. But the treaty struck a snag in Colombia. There the financial arrangements were not regarded as satisfactory; and, as Bunau-Varilla himself admitted, the instrument seriously impinged upon Colombian sovereignty in Panama. The United States minister in Bogotá had no doubt that public opinion in the South American republic was violently opposed to the treaty.[11]

The dictator of Colombia was the weakening octogenarian, José Marroquín. He presumably could have brought about ratification by decree, even though such action was unconstitutional. But so strong was popular opposition that he decided to summon Congress (which he had dispensed with for several years) to pass upon the pact. On August 12, 1903, the Senate, while favoring a renewal of negotiations, voted unanimously against ratification.[12]

The primary motive for Colombia's opposition to the treaty appears to have been a not unnatural desire for more money. Indeed, the government at Bogotá expressed a willingness to accept an additional $15,000,000.[13] Displeasing though this was to the United States, the simple facts are that the Colombians owned the canal strip, that it was one of their most valuable resources, and that they were at liberty to demand the price they wanted. The best chance for more money lay in securing a substantial slice of the $40,000,000 that the United States was prepared to pay the French stockholders for their rights. But by the terms of the treaty Colombia was forbidden to deal with the company. That privilege, thanks in large part to the foresight of Cromwell and Bunau-Varilla, was specifically reserved to the United States. There was, however, another possible approach for Colombia. The French concession would expire in October, 1904.[14] When this happened Colombia would take over the physical assets of the company and dispose of them to the United States for the tempting $40,000,000. It was obviously to the advantage of Colombia to delay action for a little over a year.

As time marched on, the impatient Roosevelt, who ardently desired the Republican nomination in 1904, became well-nigh apoplectic. In various utterances, chiefly private, he denounced the "corrupt pithecoid community" of Colombians as "inefficient bandits," "foolish

---

[11] See Foreign Relations, 1903, pp. 142–143.

[12] E. T. Parks, Colombia and the United States, 1765–1934 (Durham, N.C., 1935), p. 396.

[13] See Sen. Doc., 58 Cong., 2 sess., no. 51, pp. 22, 35.

[14] It is true that President Marroquín had extended the concession to 1910 (without the approval of Congress); but the Colombian government could doubtless have persuaded the courts to declare the extension invalid. Dennett, Hay, p. 376.

and homicidal corruptionists," "contemptible little creatures," "jack rabbits," and "cat rabbits." [15] He asserted that the situation was "exactly as if a road agent had tried to hold up a man," and he insisted that the "cut throats" and "blackmailers of Bogotá" should not be permitted "permanently to bar one of the future highways of civilization." He went so far as to draft a message—he did not send it to Congress—suggesting that the canal strip be taken over by force.[16]

But the savage strictures of Roosevelt were not altogether fair. Even assuming that the Congress at Bogotá was wholly corrupt, it is clear that the motives which cause a sovereign state to reject a treaty are no proper concern of any other state. Hay's assertion that the Colombians were honor bound to ratify a treaty that had been approved under protest by Herrán would be more convincing if the Department of State had not brought such great pressure on Herrán to sign. No one knew better than Hay, whose recent experiences with the Pauncefote Treaty were fresh in mind, that the United States Senate frequently delayed or rejected treaties signed by American representatives. And no one knew better than Hay that such action had often been prompted by partisan or other questionable motives.

A Republic is Born

Like Roosevelt and Hay, the press of the United States was sorely displeased by Colombia's conduct. The newspapers teemed with such expressions as the "thieves of Bogotá," "brigand Senators," and "organized rapacity." Some journals favored turning to the Nicaraguan route; others advocated seizure of the Panama canal strip under the "right" of international eminent domain; still others urged that Panama be encouraged to secede so that the United States could make terms with her. "What other world Power," queried the New York *Commercial Advertiser*, "has ever hesitated to use force under similar circumstances?" But the *Literary Digest* found that more newspapers favored the Nicaraguan route than advocated connivance at revolt.[17]

Meanwhile the pot had been boiling in Panama. This department had once been independent but had voluntarily joined Colombia, only to have its rights usurped by a Colombian dictator in the 1880's. The Panamanians had evidenced their discontent with the rule of Bogotá

[15] Pringle, *Roosevelt*, p. 311.

[16] *Theodore Roosevelt: an Autobiography* (N.Y., 1922), pp. 530–531. Hay cabled a virtual ultimatum to Colombia, hinting at the use of force. This was regarded as a threat by the Colombians. See Hill, *Roosevelt and the Caribbean*, p. 53.

[17] *Literary Digest*, XXVII, 416 (Oct. 3, 1903).

by numerous uprisings—fifty-three in fifty-three years, according to Roosevelt's count.[18] Now came the rejection of the Hay-Herrán Treaty, from which the people of Panama had expected great commercial benefits. Disappointment rapidly gave way to anxiety when the Panamanians realized that the United States might next turn to Nicaragua. Plainly the situation was ripe for revolt—another revolt.

The conspirators carried on their work both in Panama and in the United States. A center of revolutionary activity was Room 1162 of the Hotel Waldorf-Astoria, in New York City, and here the energetic Bunau-Varilla worked out many of the necessary details and raised funds for bribery.[19] The revolutionists were finally able to muster a "patriot" army at Panama City consisting of 500 "bought" Colombian troops (cost about $100,000), in addition to 441 members of the local fire department.[20] Obviously, it would be suicidal to raise the standard of revolt with this tiny force unless assurances could be obtained as to the attitude of the Roosevelt administration toward the Treaty of 1846 with Colombia (New Granada).

By the terms of this ancient document the United States had bound itself to maintain the "perfect neutrality" of the Isthmus so that "free transit" might not be interrupted. At the time the treaty was drawn up it was designed to prevent some outside power, particularly Britain, from seizing Panama; and Colombia certainly would never have approved it if she had suspected that it would some day be invoked against herself.[21] During the numerous revolutionary outbursts in Panama prior to 1903, the United States on seven different occasions had landed troops to protect "free transit." In each instance these forces had been used only with the approval or consent of the Colombian authorities. Only once had such an intervention interfered with the movements of the Colombian troops, and then the Washington government had expressed regret for the occurrence.[22]

But would the United States, if another insurrection should break out, fly in the face of its own precedents and, by a strained interpretation of the treaty of 1846, keep the Isthmus open by refusing to permit Colombian troops to land and crush the revolt? Bunau-Varilla con-

[18] *Roosevelt's Autobiography*, p. 516.

[19] Francis B. Loomis, then Assistant Secretary of State and in close touch with the Panama affair, told the present writer (Feb. 17, 1939) that the revolution was financed by a personal loan from J. P. Morgan to Bunau-Varilla.

[20] See J. F. Rippy, *The Capitalists and Colombia* (N.Y., 1931), pp. 97–101.

[21] It is true that a strictly legalistic case could be made out (as John Bassett Moore, the distinguished international lawyer, did for Roosevelt) in support of the course taken by the United States. Pringle, *Roosevelt*, p. 316.

[22] Hill, *Roosevelt and the Caribbean*, p. 45.

ferred with Roosevelt, Hay, Assistant Secretary of State Loomis, and others in Washington, and came to the conclusion that the United States would not allow a Panama revolution to fail. Apparently acting on "inside information," the astute Frenchman cabled his fellow conspirators that the U.S.S. *Nashville* would reach Colón, Panama, on November 2, 1903. It arrived on schedule. The faint-hearted revolutionists, encouraged by this visual evidence that the United States would support them, went ahead with their plans. Bunau-Varilla later asserted that he was able to predict the movements of the American ships by reading notices of their sailing in the newspapers. Roosevelt, who denied with vehemence that he had conspired with the scheming Frenchman, declared:

He is a very able fellow, and it was his business to find out what he thought our Government would do. I have no doubt that he was able to make a very accurate guess, and to advise his people accordingly. In fact, he would have been a very dull man had he been unable to make such a guess.[23]

On November 3, 1903, the day after the arrival of the U.S.S. *Nashville*, the patriot "army" of Panama revolted. The American naval forces, acting under orders, kept the Isthmus clear by preventing the Colombian troops from landing, and thus insured the success of the uprising. The next day, November 4, the infant republic proclaimed itself a member of the family of nations. A little more than an hour after receiving the news, Roosevelt authorized recognition, which was granted on November 6, only three days after the revolution. This was so precipitate as to lend additional color to the charge that the Administration in Washington had connived at the outbreak.

Whatever the validity of such an accusation, several facts stand out. In the first place, Roosevelt was glad that the revolution succeeded, and he made little effort to conceal his joy. Moreover, he and his advisers knew a good deal about the situation in Panama, more, in fact, than they were willing to admit.[24] Finally, there can be no doubt that

[23] J. B. Bishop, *Theodore Roosevelt and His Time* (N.Y., 1920), I, 296 (Roosevelt to Bigelow, Jan. 6, 1904). Bunau-Varilla told Elihu Root that Roosevelt gave him no specific assurances, but that the vehemence of the President's conversation made it clear that the United States would not permit the Colombians to crush a revolution in Panama. P. C. Jessup, *Elihu Root* (N.Y., 1938), I, 403–404. The then Assistant Secretary of State, Francis B. Loomis, told the present writer substantially the same thing, Feb. 17, 1939.
[24] See W. D. McCain, *The United States and the Republic of Panama* (Durham, N.C., 1937), p. 15.

the general attitude of the Administration gave that encouragement without which the conspirators probably would not have gone ahead.

THE END JUSTIFIES THE MEANS

The bustling Bunau-Varilla now managed to have himself, though a French citizen, represent the Republic of Panama in Washington. On November 13, 1903, the new envoy was officially received; and on November 18, only fifteen days after the revolution, he signed a pact which he had induced his superiors to approve unseen.

The Hay-Bunau-Varilla Treaty conveyed to the United States in perpetuity a zone ten miles wide in return for a payment of $10,000,-000 down and $250,000 a year. The terms were so extraordinarily advantageous as to make Panama virtually a military outpost of the great northern Republic—to the increasing discontent of the Panamanians.[25] On February 23, 1904, the United States Senate approved the treaty, 66 to 14, after another bitter flurry of opposition.

Roosevelt's "cowboy diplomacy" aroused a vast amount of criticism in his own country, particularly among liberals and partisan Democrats. The press heatedly referred to a "cooked-up republic," "piracy," "scandal, disgrace, and dishonor," and "indecent haste." The Springfield *Republican* branded the incident as one of the "most discreditable in our history." The New York *American* would "rather forego forever the advantage of an interocean waterway than gain one by such means as this." "Even the buccaneers who sailed the Spanish Main," lamented the New York *Nation*, "would have found it too much for them."

In Europe, where the seizure of territory from weak neighbors was an old story, there was much condemnation of Roosevelt's course. One English journal declared that "the United States has shaken the confidence of the civilized world in her honesty." The Glasgow *Herald* found that "Expediency has been stronger than morality." In Latin America, there was no universal outburst of indignation, partly because Roosevelt's role was not fully appreciated; but important elements, who grew in strength with the passage of time, deplored and feared America's buccaneering tactics.

[25] This document, though following the general outlines of the Hay-Herrán Treaty, was considerably more favorable to the United States, particularly in regard to sovereignty over the Canal Zone. As Hay rushed the agreement to ratification he knew that two bona fide Panamanians were coming to help Bunau-Varilla. (They arrived in Washington six hours late.) Hay's conscience probably troubled him, for he suggested to the Frenchman that an indemnity be paid Colombia. This Bunau-Varilla brushed aside as "blackmail." *Ibid.,* p. 17.

Nevertheless, Roosevelt's tactics commanded considerable support at home, particularly among Republicans. Such direct methods at least had the virtue of getting results. The *Literary Digest* analyzed the views of some seventy American newspapers and found that fifty-three favored the *coup* and seventeen criticized it. The Hartford *Times* ex-

Theodore Roosevelt in action. (From the New York *World*, 1903.)

pressed a rather common sentiment when it remarked that Colombia's plight was "entirely her own fault," while the Atlanta *Journal* found that she was "needlessly obstructing the world's commerce." *Public Opinion* thus summarized sentiment:

. . . No one can deny that the majority opinion of the country approves the course of the administration, little as this course can be justified on moral grounds. . . . The sum of public opinion in this matter being simply that we want an isthmian canal above all things, and that the government has taken the surest means of attaining this object.[26]

[26] *Public Opinion*, XXXV, 643 (Nov. 19, 1903).

A Mandate From Civilization

The brunt of the defense was borne by Roosevelt himself. He declared that "every action" of his Administration in the affair had been "carried out in accordance with the highest, finest, and nicest standards of public and governmental ethics." He insisted that intervention had been necessary for a proper discharge of the treaty obligation to guard the Isthmus, as well as to protect American lives and property. In his annual message to Congress he put his action on a much broader basis:

> . . . I confidently maintain that the recognition of the Republic of Panama was an act justified by the interests of collective civilization. If ever a Government could be said to have received a mandate from civilization . . . the United States holds that position with regard to the interoceanic canal.[27]

Let us assume for the moment that Roosevelt did have a "mandate from civilization." Would not the interests of "civilization" have been about as well served by a Nicaraguan waterway? Nicaragua was already an independent state: no revolution was needed. Nicaragua was eager to come to an agreement with the United States, and had already revealed a willingness to do so on more advantageous terms than were obtainable from Colombia. The Isthmian Canal Commission had twice endorsed the feasibility of the Nicaraguan route, which, though longer, was nearer the United States. Its estimated cost was greater; but the ultimate expenditures on the Panama Canal far exceeded estimates. Whatever the expense of construction, a Nicaraguan waterway would cost little or nothing in ill will. Indeed, as we have seen, the President was required by law to adopt this route after a "reasonable time"; and he himself was beginning to have misgivings as to whether or not a "reasonable time" had elapsed.

Roosevelt's desperate determination to "make the dirt fly" was a fundamental factor in this affair. But what, aside from politics and the President's stubborn desire not to be thwarted when he had once set his heart on Panama, was the pressing need for haste? The canal had remained uncut for many centuries. In the long view, a few years one way or another would have made little difference. By the very terms of the Hay-Herrán Treaty provision was made for delays totaling thirty-six years. It is conceivable that Roosevelt could have waited one year, whereupon the concession of the canal company could have been made

[27] *Foreign Relations, 1903*, p. 275.

to expire; Colombia would then have obtained the $40,000,000; and the United States would have secured the canal. But the impetuous Rough Rider could brook no postponement. Congress would meet in December; and the press had already begun to clamor for the Nicaraguan alternative. If the President wanted a canal at Panama he would be wise to present Congress with an accomplished fact—which is exactly what he did.

As time wore on Roosevelt became more belligerent and less discreet in defending his course. Speaking at Berkeley, California, in 1911, he made this unfortunate but characteristic boast:

> I am interested in the Panama Canal because I started it. If I had followed traditional, conservative methods I would have submitted a dignified State paper of probably 200 pages to Congress and the debates on it would have been going on yet; but I took the Canal Zone and let Congress debate; and while the debate goes on the Canal does also.[28]

It seems probable that Roosevelt's direct methods hastened the construction of the canal by at least a few months. And for that slight gain in time he gave a definite setback to the pacific settlement of international disputes, created a damaging precedent, grievously offended a weaker sister republic, and aroused the suspicion and distrust of all Latin America.

OLEAGINOUS DIPLOMACY

The Colombians repeatedly proposed that their grievance be submitted to arbitration. But the United States, though traditionally a stalwart champion of such methods, refused. Roosevelt would consent to no such confession of wrongdoing while he was President. Under Taft, his political creature and successor, attempts were made to placate Colombia. They all ended in failure. But the Democratic administration of Woodrow Wilson did not find it difficult to do penance for what it regarded as the sins of the Republican Roosevelt. In 1914 a treaty was signed with Colombia in which the United States expressed "sincere regret" for the unfortunate Panama business and agreed to pay $25,000,000 as pecuniary balm. But Roosevelt was still very much

[28] New York *Times*, March 25, 1911, 10:3. See also Roosevelt's speech in Washington in 1918. Bishop, *Roosevelt*, I, 308–309. Roosevelt could make out a legal case for his conduct under the Treaty of 1846, and he did, but he had now got to the point where he could not be bothered. This was the view of Elihu Root, Roosevelt's Secretary of War. Jessup, *Root*, I, 403. Root, who was a distinguished lawyer, supported his chief on legalistic grounds.

alive, and he was determined that no such acknowledgment of guilt should be made. His view now was that Colombia had wronged the United States by not allowing "herself to be benefited." Roosevelt's friends in the Senate, notably Henry Cabot Lodge, sprang to his defense, and the treaty was shelved.

In 1921 there was a revival of the agitation to indemnify mutilated Colombia. Harding, a Republican, was President; Roosevelt was in his grave. The seven-year-old treaty was amended so as to eliminate "sincere regret"; but it still provided for a payment of $25,000,000, which in itself was an eloquent apology.[29] Lodge now vigorously supported the pact on the grounds that it would improve commercial relations and that Roosevelt would favor it if he were alive. But, as critics pointed out, there lurked a "colored gentleman in the Colombian cordwood." Oil, an increasingly essential element in world leadership, had been discovered in great quantities in the South American republic. The government at Bogotá, naturally unfriendly to the United States, was disposed to deny concessions to Americans while granting them to British and other rivals. The payment of $25,000,-000 would presumably pave the way for a treaty of amity and commerce under which the United States could secure its share of the "black gold" and other privileges.

Some of the Senators taunted the Republican majority on having reversed itself. Johnson of California, himself a nominal Republican, was unable to understand how "blackmail for 17 years had ripened now into honest obligation." Senator Watson of Georgia suspected that "an oil proposition" had been "pipe-lined into this treaty," and that the United States was going to pay "an indirect subsidy to the oil interests." Other Senators stoutly maintained that the payment of "conscience money" was an admission of guilt. But such arguments proved unavailing in the face of a Senatorial machine well lubricated with Colombian oil; and the treaty was approved on April 20, 1921, by a vote of 69 to 19.[30] One of the most striking aspects of this whole unfortunate affair is that if the $25,000,000 finally paid to Colombia had been offered in 1903, a vast amount of unpleasantness would almost certainly have been avoided.

[29] See Watt Stewart, "The Ratification of the Thomson-Urrutia Treaty," Southwestern Pol. and Soc. Sci. Quar., X (1930), 427–428. Roosevelt had never differentiated between the payment of $25,000,000 with an apology and the payment of a like sum without an apology. "Either there is or there is not warrant for paying this enormous sum or for making the apology. . . . The payment can only be justified on the ground that this nation has played the part of a thief, or of a receiver of stolen goods." Works of Theodore Roosevelt (National ed., N.Y., 1926), XVIII, 436.

[30] See Parks, Colombia and the United States, Ch. XXVII ("Oil and Ideals").

BIBLIOGRAPHICAL NOTE

There is a good summary discussion of the Hay-Pauncefote negotiations in Tyler Dennett, *John Hay* (N.Y., 1933), Ch. XXI. Also brief is A. L. P. Dennis, *Adventures in American Diplomacy, 1896–1906* (N.Y., 1928), Ch. VII. An excellent account of the "taking" of Panama is H. F. Pringle, *Theodore Roosevelt* (N.Y., 1931), pp. 301–338. The author is highly critical, quite in contrast with the "official" biography, J. B. Bishop *Theodore Roosevelt and His Time* (2 vols., N.Y., 1920), I, Ch. XXIV, which presents Roosevelt's case. See also *Theodore Roosevelt: an Autobiography* (N.Y., 1922). A good critical survey of the problem is H. C. Hill, *Roosevelt and the Caribbean* (Chicago, 1927), Ch. III. A valuable detailed account, projected against a background of Colombia–Panama–United States relations, is E. T. Parks, *Colombia and the United States, 1765–1934* (Durham, N.C., 1935), particularly Chs. XX–XXVII. There is a useful summary of the Panama revolution in J. F. Rippy, *The Capitalists and Colombia* (N.Y., 1931), Ch. V. The best work on relations with Panama since 1903 is W. D. McCain, *The United States and the Republic of Panama* (Durham, N.C., 1937). Further references: see footnotes of this chapter and Bemis and Griffin, *Guide*, pp. 423–428; 554–564.

RECENT REFERENCES. The best book on the phases of the subject it emphasizes is D. C. Miner, *The Fight for the Panama Route: The Story of the Spooner Act and the Hay-Herrán Treaty* (N.Y., 1940). Cromwell emerges as the real savior of the Company's interests, at least in the earlier stages. He had a large hand in persuading Congress to accept the Panama route (even providing data for Senator Hanna's speeches); worked closely with Hay and Herrán in drafting the treaty; and prepared memoranda from which Hay drafted pressure notes to Colombia. More general in scope is M. P. DuVal, *Cadiz to Cathay* (Stanford University, 1940), which, unlike Miner, employs the papers of Herrán, who repeatedly warned his "imbecilic" government of what would befall it (pp. 215–218). Of particular interest is Chapter XV, which describes the military and naval precautions taken by the United States to repel a threatened Colombian attack on Panama. Philippe Bunau-Varilla, *From Panama to Verdun* (Phila., 1940), adds little to what the author has already written in his apologia. He repeats, without proof, the story that Bogotá was under German influence. It is true that the German bogey was abroad at the time, but it apparently had little effect in the United States. E. T. Parks and J. F. Rippy, in "The Galápagos Islands: A Neglected Phase of American Strategy Diplomacy," *Pacific Hist. Rev.*, IX (1940), 37–45, reveal that in 1899 Secretary Hay, in order to protect the Pacific approaches of the Canal and forestall other Powers, took steps to secure a coaling station on Ecuador's Galápagos group but lost interest when he found the price too high. The authors also treat of rumored European occupation and America's interest in preventing such a violation of the Monroe Doctrine.

NEW REFERENCES. For a book on the Caribbean policy of the United States, for one on the Panama incident, and one on legal aspects of administering the Canal; and for an important revisionist article on Latin American reactions to the "rape" of Panama, see Bibliographical Appendix, p. 935.

CHAPTER XXXIII

Theodore Roosevelt and Big Stick Diplomacy, 1901–1906

"I have always been fond of the West African proverb: 'Speak softly and carry a big stick, you will go far.' "

Theodore Roosevelt, 1900.

FROM LIBERATOR TO STEPFATHER

THE canal problem was not the only one that Roosevelt inherited from his amiable predecessor. The prostrate island of Cuba presented difficulties hardly less knotty than those that had existed before the war. To many expansionists in the United States the obvious solution was to annex the Pearl of the Antilles outright, and fulfill the long-deferred mandate of Manifest Destiny. But the Teller Amendment stood in the way—that solemn and embarrassing pledge by which America had denied herself the prize. Even so, some prominent citizens, like Joseph H. Choate, were arguing that the promise had been made in ignorance of actual conditions, and that the unexpected results of the war released the United States from its obligation.

Whatever desire the McKinley administration may have had to retain Cuba was dampened by the unfortunate Philippine insurrection, and by the constant nagging of the Democrats that the Teller Amendment be carried out in good faith. But obviously the anarchic island could not be turned loose without some kind of leading strings. A first-class power—Germany was particularly feared in these years—might secure a foothold there and jeopardize not only the Isthmian life line but the very shores of the United States.[1]

The problem was solved by making Cuba a quasi protectorate of the United States under the Platt Amendment to the army appropriation bill which was approved on March 2, 1901. The Cubans, responding to strong pressure from the United States, reluctantly incorporated this restriction in their constitution, June 12, 1901. In summary form the principal provisions of the Platt Amendment stipulated:

[1] P. C. Jessup, *Elihu Root* (N.Y., 1938), I, 314. Root wrote in 1934: "You cannot understand the Platt amendment unless you know something about the character of Kaiser Wilhelm the Second."

1. Cuba was not to permit a foreign power to secure partial or complete control of the island.
2. Cuba pledged herself not to incur too large an indebtedness. [It might result in foreign intervention.]
3. The United States was at liberty to intervene for the purpose of preserving order and maintaining Cuban independence.
4. Cuba agreed to sell or lease to the United States sites for naval and coaling stations.[2]

The temptation to remain in Cuba was great, but in May, 1902, the Roosevelt administration surprised the imperialistic world by withdrawing. During the following years disorders broke out, thus reviving annexationist sentiment in the United States. "It is manifest destiny," declared the Indianapolis *News*, "for a nation to own the islands which border its shores." But Roosevelt, who for once did not welcome an opportunity to brandish the Big Stick, was profoundly disgusted:

Just at the moment I am so angry with that infernal little Cuban republic that I would like to wipe its people off the face of the earth. All that we wanted from them was that they would behave themselves and be prosperous and happy so that we would not have to interfere. And now, lo and behold, they have started an utterly unjustifiable and pointless revolution and may get things into such a snarl that we have no alternative save to intervene—which will at once convince the suspicious idiots in South America that we do wish to interfere after all, and perhaps have some land-hunger! [3]

The situation finally became so bad that in 1906 United States troops were landed to restore order. "Necessity," as one New York journal remarked, "is the mother of in(ter)vention."

The events of 1906 reawakened the die-hard annexationists in the United States. "What a pity," said a Southern paper, "we did not keep Cuba and let the Philippines find another owner." But public opinion in the United States reacted favorably when, after order had been restored, the American troops were withdrawn in 1909—again to the surprise of the outside world. As before, the Cubans were left with

---

[2] W. M. Malloy, *Treaties*, I, 362–363. Upon American withdrawal from the island, the Platt Amendment was incorporated in the treaty of 1903. The real author of the Platt Amendment was Secretary of War Elihu Root. Jessup, *Elihu Root*, I, 310–312; see also R. H. Fitzgibbon, *Cuba and the United States, 1900–1935* (Menasha, Wis., 1935), p. 81.

[3] Roosevelt to White, Sept. 13, 1906, Roosevelt Papers, Library of Congress.

only a limited sovereignty; but under these circumstances the alternative was no sovereignty at all.

The Mailed Fist in Venezuela

The Platt Amendment was but one evidence of the suspicious attitude of the United States toward Germany. During these years it was widely rumored that the Kaiser was scheming to pick up naval bases in American waters, and in other ways to challenge the Monroe Doctrine. Fear that Germany might acquire the Danish West Indies led to a revival of interest in those islands; and in 1902 Secretary Hay concluded a treaty of annexation with Denmark, only to have it rejected by the Danish Parliament. It was generally believed in American quarters, both official and unofficial, that German pressure upon Copenhagen thwarted ratification. The documents do not reveal, however, that this view is well founded.[4]

Much of America's distrust of Germany was focused on the Kaiser, whom the press of the United States regarded as an ambitious and theatrical blunderer. His "me und Gott" attitude and his fierce mustaches made him a favorite with cartoonists and doggerel writers. The Emperor was keenly aware of the disfavor into which he and his country had fallen, and he took extraordinary steps to ingratiate himself with the American people.[5] He caused a medal to be conferred on Roosevelt (John Hay said it was worth about thirty-five cents and of questionable artistic merit); he sent Prince Henry to the United States in 1902 on a good will mission; he ordered a yacht to be built in America; and he presented a bronze statue of Frederick the Great to the United States. The Washington *Star* suggested as a countercompliment that the Kaiser be given a statue of James Monroe.[6]

Whatever ground the German Emperor may have gained by his clumsy courtship was thrown away in Venezuela. This unhappy country was then under the domination of an unscrupulous dictator, Cipri-

[4] C. C. Tansill, *The Purchase of the Danish West Indies* (Baltimore, 1932), pp. 452–453. On this subject and alleged German plans for American naval bases, consult Alfred Vagts, *Deutschland und die Vereinigten Staaten in der Weltpolitik* (N.Y., 1935), II, 1411–1524.

[5] For an account of how the German ambassador attempted to bribe the New York *Evening Post* into supporting the German viewpoint, see O. G. Villard, *Fighting Years* (N.Y., 1939), p. 243.

[6] See C. E. Schieber, *The Transformation of American Sentiment toward Germany, 1870–1914* (Boston, 1923), pp. 251–256. The Kaiser asked Roosevelt's daughter, Alice, to christen the yacht. The President suggested that her christening speech be, "Damn the Dutch." H. F. Pringle, *Theodore Roosevelt* (N.Y., 1931), p. 282.

ano Castro. Almost perpetual civil war had been ruinous to foreign investments, particularly British and German. The Powers of Europe were tempted to intervene but they were very reluctant to challenge the now powerful Monroe Doctrine. Roosevelt, however, did not regard mere intervention without territorial designs as a violation of Monroe's principles, and he felt that irresponsible Latin American nations should not attempt to hide behind the skirts of the United States. "If any South American country misbehaves toward any European country," he wrote in 1901, "let the European country spank it." There can be no doubt that the official attitude of Washington offered no deterrent to those Powers that wished to "spank" Castro.[7]

In 1901 Germany proposed arbitration of her Venezuelan claims by the Hague Court; but Castro would have none of it. Then the British, whose financial stake was five times larger than that of the Germans, took the initiative in proposing joint collection at the cannon's mouth. Reassured by the acquiescent attitude of the Roosevelt administration, Berlin consented to co-operate.

Germany and Great Britain (later joined by Italy) instituted a blockade of Venezuela early in December, 1902. The allies seized several gunboats, and the Germans sank two. These determined measures brought the contumacious Castro to his knees, and he hastened to accept the arbitration he had once spurned. On December 12 the United States transmitted his proposal to the Powers concerned, without comment, and within a week both London and Berlin had accepted limited arbitration in principle. But the blockade continued until February 17, 1903, pending the signing of a protocol by Venezuela.[8] Contrary to a general misconception, there was no diplomatic crisis as far as the United States was concerned.

Fourteen years later, when Roosevelt was profoundly stirred by Germany's part in the World War, he made public a dramatic account of the Venezuela affair. He related how he called in the German ambassador, laid down an ultimatum, backed it up with a threat to send Admiral Dewey's entire fleet to Venezuela, and forced the Kaiser to

[7] Dexter Perkins, *The Monroe Doctrine, 1867–1907* (Baltimore, 1937), p. 333. This account and that of Vagts, *Deutschland und die Vereinigten Staaten*, Ch. XV, have been most heavily relied upon for the Venezuela incident.

[8] The Venezuela claims were settled by the Hague Court in 1904. It is surprising how little official interest there was in Latin America about the matter. (See Perkins, *The Monroe Doctrine*, p. 350.) A significant exception was the statement of Luis M. Drago, Argentine Minister for Foreign Affairs, that armed intervention to collect public debts was inadmissible. Although the Washington government responded coldly to this overture, a modified form of the Drago Doctrine (supported by the United States) was embodied in a convention by the Second Hague Conference in 1907.

arbitrate. Although it is possible that Roosevelt did bring some kind of informal pressure to bear on Germany, scholars have recently discredited the sensational account published in 1916.[9]

But Roosevelt did not need the Big Stick to bring an end to the Venezuela intervention. Other forces, even more potent, were at work. First of all, public opinion in the United States was far less tolerant of the Venezuelan blockade than the State Department. Germany was suspected anyhow, and her mailed fist tactics, necessary though they may have been from a military standpoint, aroused much distrust. "There is a tendency under this administration," declared William Jennings Bryan, "to allow the Monroe Doctrine to acquire a mothballish flavor." A writer in the Minneapolis *Tribune* expressed a not uncommon sentiment in verse:

> Yankee Dewey's near La Guayra,
> Yankee Dewey Dandy.
> Maybe just as well to have our
> Yankee Dewey Handy.[10]

In January, 1903, the Germans bombarded Fort San Carlos, in Venezuela, and incidentally destroyed the village. American public opinion was strongly aroused by this incident, and the press generally referred to it as an "outrageous" and "wantonly reckless act"—"a tactless exhibition of vindictiveness and brutality." The New York *Times* stated bluntly: "Worse international manners than Germany has exhibited from the beginning of this wretched Venezuela business have rarely come under the observation of civilized men." [11] In the face of this outburst it is not surprising that the German Emperor, who still had illusions of winning American friendship, revealed a willingness to liquidate the intervention as quickly as possible.

The British government was not unaware of the flare-up in the American press, or impervious to the even more potent criticisms in the English journals. The latter were demanding to know why the Foreign Office had ever become involved in this stupid business. Perhaps it was a plot on the part of the Kaiser to destroy the newly

[9] Some of these writers have gone too far in declaring that Roosevelt fabricated the entire incident under the influence of anti-German World War hate. The main outlines of a story involving an ultimatum to the Kaiser were in his mind, as several of his private letters show, before he left the presidency. Conclusion based upon an examination of Roosevelt's private correspondence. See particularly the letter to Whitelaw Reid, Dec. 4, 1908, Library of Congress.

[10] *Review of Reviews*, XXVII, 15 (Jan., 1903); see also Perkins, *The Monroe Doctrine*, pp. 387 *ff*.

[11] New York *Times*, Jan. 23, 1903, 8:1.

achieved Anglo-American accord. The poet Kipling, referring to "the Goth and the shameless Hun," wrote:

> 'Neath all the flags of all mankind
>   That use upon the seas,
> Was there no other fleet to find
>   That ye strike hands with these? [12]

UNCLE SAM—THAT'S A LIVE WIRE, GENTLEMEN!

(From the New York *Herald*, by permission of the New York *Sun*.)

In the face of the swelling protest at home, to say nothing of that in the United States, it is not surprising that the British ministry welcomed a peaceful escape from the impasse.

There can be no doubt that the Monroe Doctrine emerged from the Venezuela imbroglio with new laurels. Although the United States did not invoke the principles of 1823, it is noteworthy that the Powers took extraordinary steps, before they intervened, to make sure that their action would not be objectionable to Washington.[13] Such deference to the United States and its Monroe Doctrine had not been customary during the latter half of the preceding century.

[12] London *Times*, Dec. 22, 1902, 9:5; see also Perkins, *The Monroe Doctrine*, p. 343.
[13] *Ibid.*, p. 394.

THE ALASKA BOUNDARY DISPUTE

At almost the same time the Panama and Venezuelan problems were coming to a head, the United States was taking steps to settle a smoldering boundary dispute in northern latitudes. Upon the dis-

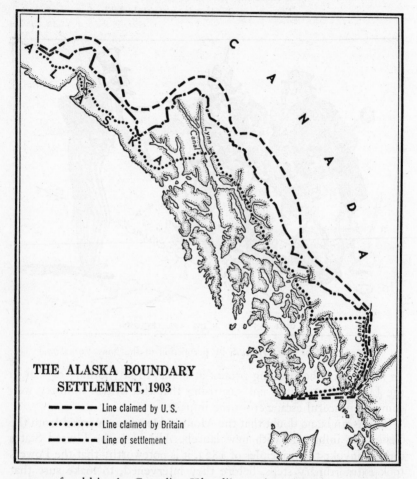

THE ALASKA BOUNDARY
SETTLEMENT, 1903

━ ━ ━ ━ Line claimed by U. S.
•••••••••• Line claimed by Britain
━ ━ ━ ·━ Line of settlement

covery of gold in the Canadian Klondike region, August, 1896, it was found that the best practicable water approaches to the goldfields lay through the Alaska panhandle, which belonged to the United States. The Canadians thereupon scrutinized the rather ambiguous Anglo-Russian Treaty of 1825, and presently advanced the claim that the boundary, which roughly extended thirty miles inland from the ocean, should run in a straight line and not follow the sinuosities of the coast-line. This meant that the heads of the deep inlets, including the important Lynn Canal, would remain in the hands of the Canadians, who would then possess a deep-sea corridor cutting off the panhandle from the rest of Alaska. Whatever the technicalities of the argument, it is clear that the negotiators of the Treaty of 1825 had intended that the entire area should be contiguous.

The Canadians evinced a willingness to arbitrate their claim, at the same time reminding the United States of Cleveland's belligerent action in dealing with the Venezuela boundary dispute. But Secretary Hay, who realized that arbitrators sometimes split the difference, resolutely refused such an alternative. In 1899 he succeeded in arranging a *modus vivendi* or temporary settlement, without prejudice to the claims of either party. This agreement, though viewed with considerable dissatisfaction in the United States, fortunately permitted passions to cool.[14]

Referring to the Alaska boundary dispute shortly after becoming President, Roosevelt remarked, "Let sleeping dogs lie." But the more he looked into the controversy the more convinced he became that the Canadian case was a trumped-up one, and the more determined he was not to yield one inch of good American territory. He unbosomed himself to Hay:

I think that the Canadian contention is an outrage pure and simple. I do not regard the Canadians as having any more right to the land in question than they have to Maine or than we have to New Brunswick. The fact that they have set up such an outrageous and indefensible claim and in consequence are likely to be in hot water with their constituents when they back down, does not seem to me to give us any excuse for paying them in money or territory. To pay them anything where they are entitled to nothing would in a case like this come dangerously near blackmail.[15]

By the middle of 1902 grave apprehensions were felt that the unruly mining element might get out of hand, particularly if gold deposits were discovered in the disputed area.[16] High Canadian officials, regretful that the issue had ever been raised, were revealing a willingness to make concessions. They were backed by certain British officials

---

[14] Tyler Dennett, *John Hay* (N.Y., 1933), p. 233.

[15] Roosevelt to Hay, July 10, 1902. Roosevelt Papers, Library of Congress.

[16] Roosevelt ordered Secretary of War Root to send more troops to Alaska, not to threaten the British (as is generally assumed) but to prevent a serious disturbance. Jessup, *Root*, I, 390–392.

who feared that the dispute might alienate hard-won American friendship.

The situation had now so shaped itself that Secretary Hay succeeded in negotiating the Convention of 1903 with Great Britain. It provided that "six impartial jurists of repute" (three chosen by the President of the United States and three by His Britannic Majesty) were to meet in London and by a majority vote decide the issues in dispute relating to the Alaska boundary. The treaty encountered considerable opposition in the Senate, particularly among representatives of the Northwestern states. They feared that if the "right men" were not selected the United States might lose; but if "right men" were chosen the United States could get no worse than a tie. Senator Lodge (according to his own story) went to Roosevelt and obtained in advance the names of the jurists who were to be appointed. The Senate then gave its approval.[17]

BIG-STICKING THE BRITISH

The three jurists chosen by Roosevelt were Secretary of War Elihu Root (who accepted under protest), ex-Senator George Turner, and Senator Lodge. Although Root was a leader of the American bar, his connection with the Administration raised grave doubts as to his impartiality. George Turner, whose term as United States Senator from Washington expired in March, 1903, had no wide repute as a jurist, and in view of the financial interest of his state in the decision was not regarded as impartial. Lodge had no standing as a jurist; what repute he enjoyed had come from writing and politics; and he was certainly not impartial. Not only had he publicly scoffed at the Canadian claims, but he was probably the leading professional Anglophobe of his generation. Amid the general outburst of derisive laughter that greeted the appointments, the Brooklyn *Eagle* suggested that the chances of the Canadians were about equal to the possibility of a blizzard "in Hades."

His Britannic Majesty chose Lord Alverstone, Lord Chief Justice of England, and two prominent Canadians, one of whom had had judicial experience. The people of Canada were outraged by Roosevelt's selections, for they had assumed that the three American jurists would be taken from such a body as the Supreme Court.[18] The British were

[17] C. G. Washburn, "Memoir of Henry Cabot Lodge," Mass. Hist. Soc. *Procs.*, LVIII (1925), 340.

[18] Roosevelt did make a half-hearted attempt to secure the services of a Supreme Court justice, but failed. See T. A. Bailey, "Theodore Roosevelt and the Alaska Boundary Settlement," *Canadian Hist. Rev.*, XVIII (1937), 125–128.

embarrassed, but rather than bring about a crisis in Anglo-American relations, they decided to carry out the treaty.

The Alaska Boundary Tribunal met in London on September 3, 1903, and continued deliberations to October 20th. It soon became evident that the two Dominion jurists would uphold the Canadian claims, and that the avoidance of a deadlock rested squarely on Lord Alverstone. Aware of this situation, Roosevelt privately made use of his Big Stick. In letters and conversations he let it be known that if the tribunal should fail to decide properly, he would occupy the disputed area with troops and run the line the way he thought it should go. This, of course, would mean war. Roosevelt's views, as he intended, were relayed to high British officials, who undoubtedly communicated them to Lord Alverstone.[19]

The American contention regarding the sinuosities of the coast line was strong, and the tribunal sustained it by a vote of four to two, Lord Alverstone siding with the Americans. The United States, however, received a somewhat narrower strip than it had claimed. The Canadians received a consolation prize of two rather inconsequential islands in the Portland Canal—a solution that seems to have been a compromise rather than a purely legal settlement.[20] The people of Canada angrily charged that Lord Alverstone had been swayed by political considerations; but the distinguished Briton insisted that his decision was purely "judicial." Whether he was influenced, consciously or unconsciously, by Roosevelt's threats, it is clear that his course was judicious if not judicial.[21]

The newspapers of the United States naturally greeted the sweeping American victory with jubilation. Some of them thought that it portended the ultimate annexation of Canada; others rejoiced that a "dynamite charge" in Anglo-American relations had been removed. The Canadians, on the other hand, were acutely unhappy. Their anger was directed in part against the Yankee, and in part against the mother country, which they felt had again sacrificed them on the altar of Anglo-American amity.[22] Unfortunate though this reaction was, the

[19] Ibid., pp. 127–129; also Jessup, Root, pp. 396–397.

[20] Hay wrote jubilantly: "We agree that the Boundary shall be by the North Channel instead of the South, which gives them those two little Islands—worth nothing to us. That is all poor Canada gets by the decision, and I do not wonder they are furious but as Will Thomson used to say 'Serves 'em right, if they can't take a joke.'" Dennett, John Hay, p. 362 (Hay to Mrs. Hay, Oct. 23, 1903).

[21] L. M. Gelber, The Rise of Anglo-American Friendship (London, 1938), pp. 153 ff., makes out a strong case against Alverstone's purely judicial conduct.

[22] See H. L. Keenleyside, Canada and the United States (N.Y., 1929), pp. 227–228.

peaceful acceptance of the award removed a serious source of international discord.

NONINTERVENTION BECOMES INTERVENTION [23]

Lesser peoples than the British also felt the impact of Roosevelt's Big Stick. By 1904 the Dominican Republic, after an orgy of civil war and murder, was confessedly bankrupt. Rumors repeatedly came to the State Department that the European nations which had investments there—Germany was particularly mentioned—might find it necessary to collect their debts by arms, in a manner unpleasantly reminiscent of the recent Venezuelan imbroglio.[24] If foreign forces came, they might succumb to the temptation to stay. In this event the Monroe Doctrine would be violated, America's Isthmian life line would be threatened, and the United States might have a full-fledged war on its hands.

Roosevelt realized that the "insurrectionary habit" of these "wretched republics" imposed certain obligations on the United States —as the European nations themselves had for some time pointed out. He also concluded that since the Monroe Doctrine would not permit outside Powers to keep order south of the Rio Grande, the United States itself had a "moral mandate" to intervene and force the recalcitrant republics to pay their bills. Accordingly, the President proclaimed, on December 6, 1904, what has since then been known as the Roosevelt corollary to the Monroe Doctrine:

Chronic wrongdoing . . . may in America, as elsewhere, ultimately require intervention by some civilized nation, and in the Western Hemisphere the adherence of the United States to the Monroe Doctrine may force the United States, however reluctantly, in flagrant cases of such wrongdoing or impotence, to the exercise of an international police power.[25]

In short, the Monroe Doctrine, originally designed to prevent intervention by the European Powers, would be used to justify intervention by the United States.

The next step was customs house control in the Dominican Republic.

[23] The phrase is Professor Dexter Perkins'.
[24] See J. F. Rippy, "The Initiation of the Customs Receivership in the Dominican Republic," *Hispanic Amer. Hist. Rev.*, XVII (1937), 429 *ff.*
[25] *Cong. Record*, 58 Cong., 3 sess., p. 19. The same policy was announced with less definiteness in a letter from Roosevelt which Root read at a banquet in New York, May 20, 1904. Professor Perkins, in *The Monroe Doctrine, 1867–1907*, p. 401, sees in the Platt Amendment a definite foreshadowing of the policy of protective intervention.

This idea was first suggested by officials in the State Department; and, after a show of force by the United States, the island government was persuaded to invite Washington to step in.[26] On January 21, 1905, a protocol was drawn up stipulating that the United States would take over the customs collecting, retain forty-five per cent of the receipts for Dominican expenses, and allocate fifty-five per cent for the outstanding indebtedness.

After a partisan debate the United States Senate adjourned without approving the protocol. President Roosevelt, who had scant respect for the "angleworm" Senators, went ahead and drew up a temporary executive agreement which accomplished the same ends. Although the Democrats denounced the arrangement as illegal, unconstitutional, and tyrannical, it was continued in operation for twenty-eight months. Finally, on February 25, 1907, the Senate approved a new treaty which incorporated, with some modifications, the substance of the unratified protocol. With the customs houses in the hands of Americans, revolution was no longer profitable, and the Dominican Republic settled down to the enjoyment of an era of peace and prosperity.

Public opinion in the United States generally approved the Roosevelt corollary, although there were some angry protests from the Democratic camp. Continental Europe, though welcoming the prospect of debt repayment, revealed the customary hostility to the pretensions of the Yankee. The British, on the other hand, applauded Roosevelt's course, and even regretted that he did not go further.[27] The republics of Latin America, contrary to the assumption generally made, showed remarkably little concern over this extraordinary development.[28] It was not until later years, when the Roosevelt corollary was used to justify wholesale landings of marines in the Central American and Caribbean republics, that Latin America expressed violent dissatisfaction.

[26] Rippy, "Customs Receivership in the Dominican Republic," *loc. cit.*, pp. 441 *ff*. Professor Rippy concludes that the idea of customs control originated with Assistant Secretary of State Loomis or his subordinates. Mr. Loomis informed the present writer (Feb. 17, 1939) that this is correct.

[27] British bondholders approved Roosevelt's action, and appear to have had something to do with it. See J. F. Rippy, "The British Bondholders and the Roosevelt Corollary of the Monroe Doctrine," *Pol. Sci. Quar.*, XLIX (1934), 198.

[28] Perkins, *The Monroe Doctrine*, p. 453. The other conclusions regarding public opinion are drawn from this revealing chapter. Root, then Secretary of State, made a memorable tour of Latin America while on his way to and from the Third Pan-American Conference at Rio de Janeiro, which opened July 31, 1906. His speeches, in which he paid deference to the rights of smaller states, were well received. Outwardly, at least, the trip was successful in improving relations with Latin America. See Jessup, *Root*, I, Ch. XXIII.

MEDDLING IN MOROCCO

Not content with the American theater, Roosevelt also cast the shadow of his Big Stick into far-away Morocco. On May 18, 1904, Ion Perdicaris, presumably a naturalized American citizen, was seized by one of the native Moroccan chieftains, Raisuli. The Mediterranean and South Atlantic squadrons of the United States were promptly rushed to Tangier. The Republican National Convention was then meeting in Chicago, and Roosevelt, who was about to be nominated, was displeased with the lethargy of that body. Although arrangements had already been made for the release of the captive, the President consulted Secretary Hay, who, on June 22, 1904, drafted and sent a famous telegram to the American consul general at Tangier, insisting that the United States must have "Perdicaris alive or Raisuli dead." [29] When the message was read to the Republican Convention it elicited the expected cheers for the President, its presumed author. "It is curious," wrote Secretary Hay, "how a concise impropriety hits the public." [30]

The most "curious" part of this "impropriety" has only recently been revealed. Two weeks before the stirring cablegram was dispatched, evidence came to the State Department indicating that Perdicaris might be a Greek subject rather than an American citizen.[31] When the relevant papers were sent to Roosevelt he waved them aside. After the great display of force at Tangier his prestige as a world leader would be damaged by such an admission.

The Perdicaris excitement had hardly died down when friction between Germany and France over Morocco came to a head. By 1905 it was evident that the French were attempting to close the Open Door

[29] Two facts are generally overlooked. First, Hay's message came after a cabled appeal from the American consul general at Tangier that some kind of ultimatum be sent. Second, the latter was instructed in Hay's telegram not to land marines or take over the customs house without specific instructions. This part was not made public at the time. *Foreign Relations, 1904*, pp. 502–503; New York *Times*, June 23, 1904, 1:5.

[30] The Roosevelt administration also used diplomacy as the handmaiden of politics in connection with the Jewish problem in Europe. In 1902 the State Department, heeding the cry of Jewish citizens in the United States, protested against Rumanian persecutions of Jews, although the matter was so largely a domestic one as to make American intervention questionable. But the protest seems to have helped the Republicans in the Congressional election of 1902. Hay wrote: ". . . The Hebrews—poor dears! all over the country think we are bully boys. . . ." Dennett, *Hay*, p. 397. Roosevelt also took vigorous, if futile, action in protesting against Russian massacres of the Jews in 1903. In 1911 the United States terminated its commercial treaty with Russia in protest against a refusal to honor passports issued to American Jews.

[31] *Ibid.*, pp. 401–402; Vagts, *Deutschland und die Vereinigten Staaten*, II, 1822.

in this rich North African area. With France's ally, Russia, "mired down" in the Russo-Japanese War, the Kaiser was persuaded by his alarmed advisers to go to Tangier. There, on March 31, 1905, he made a defiant, saber-rattling speech, which was profoundly disturbing to the newly born Anglo-French Entente.

The tension became so acute that the Kaiser sought the support of Roosevelt in bringing about an international conference. The President was loath to do this, for he privately admitted that the United States had no direct concern of any significance in Morocco. But he saw that unless prompt and vigorous steps were taken the crisis would probably eventuate in a general European war. Such a development would ruin his plans for acting as peacemaker between Russia and Japan in the Far Eastern conflict.[32] So he finally consented to bring pressure to bear on Great Britain and France. The latter, faced with the splendid German army, was nervous; and after the French Foreign Minister had been forced out of office and replaced by a more conciliatory successor, the government in Paris responded to Roosevelt's good offices and on June 30, 1905, agreed to attend a conference at Algeciras, in southern Spain.

When the delegates assembled, on January 16, 1906, the United States had two official representatives present. Such intermeddling in the affairs of Europe and Africa could be justified, however, by treaty relations with Morocco; by the desirability of keeping the door open for a negligible American trade (and also strengthening the Open Door principle in the Orient); and, most important, by the danger that if the crisis widened into a general war, the peace and general interests of the United States would be gravely jeopardized.

Germany had won something of a diplomatic victory in forcing the calling of the conference. But at Algeciras the majority of the votes were against her, and she was confronted by the determined Anglo-French Entente. The only alternatives were to yield or fight—and since the German military machine was not quite ready, Germany was forced to beat a retreat. Although Roosevelt, who was warmly pro-French,[33] did exercise some influence upon the final settlement, it was the international situation rather than the Big Stick (contrary to the President's own heroic version) that seems to have played the decisive part. Nevertheless, the tactful and conciliatory Henry White, senior

---

[32] J. B. Bishop, *Theodore Roosevelt and His Time* (N.Y., 1920), I, 477.

[33] Pringle, *Roosevelt*, p. 393; Vagts, *op. cit.*, II, 1869. Roosevelt wrote: ". . . You will notice that while I was most suave and pleasant with the Emperor [Kaiser], yet when it became necessary at the end I stood him on his head with great decision. . . ." Royal Cortissoz, *The Life of Whitelaw Reid* (N.Y., 1921), II, 332.

American delegate, did useful work in composing the differences of the two conflicting groups. The General Act of Algeciras, which was signed by the Powers on April 7, 1906, represented a greater defeat for both Germany and the Open Door than was apparent at the time.

The United States Senate was not altogether happy over the Algeciras Convention. After considerable debate, during which the Democrats put up a strong fight, the necessary approval was reluctantly given, with the reservation that this step was taken "without purpose to depart from the traditional American foreign policy. . . ." [34]

In general the American press rejoiced at the Kaiser's discomfiture. Yet numerous critics of Roosevelt, pointing to the remoteness of Morocco and the small American commercial stake there, condemned the Administration for departing from the time-honored policy of nonentanglement and for weakening the position of the United States under the Monroe Doctrine. But in a sense Roosevelt added a second corollary to the Doctrine when he took the position that the United States would be justified in intervening in outside affairs if it seemed necessary to maintain world peace. [35]

Perhaps the fairest estimate of Roosevelt's role in the Moroccan crisis is that he played an important, if not a decisive, part in putting into motion the machinery by which the European statesmen were able to save face and extricate themselves from an untenable situation. Probably his work in connection with the Algeciras Conference was more important from the standpoint of world peace than his more highly publicized part in terminating the Russo-Japanese War. It is indeed one of the prettiest ironies of history that the Rough Riding President, whose earlier years had been more distinguished by bellicosity than temperate judgment, was awarded the Nobel Peace Prize in 1906.

BIBLIOGRAPHICAL NOTE

The best brief account of Roosevelt's Big Stick Diplomacy is H. F. Pringle, *Theodore Roosevelt* (N.Y., 1931), pp. 279–300, 372–397. CUBAN RELATIONS. See R. H. Fitzgibbon, *Cuba and the United States, 1900–1935* (Menasha, Wis., 1935); and D. A. Lockmiller's detailed *Magoon in Cuba* (Chapel Hill, N.C., 1938). VENEZUELA DEBTS. The best account in English is Dexter Perkins, *The Monroe Doctrine, 1867–1907* (Baltimore, 1937), Ch. V, which may be supplemented by Alfred Vagts' exhaustive Ch. XV in *Deutschland und die Vereinigten Staaten in der Weltpolitik* (N.Y., 1935), II. Other useful treat-

[34] W. M. Malloy, *Treaties*, II, 2183.

[35] A strong point is made of this in L. J. Hall, "The United States and the Moroccan Problem" (ms. doctoral dissertation, Stanford University, 1937), p. 425. This is the most exhaustive study of the American aspects of the Algeciras Conference.

ments are: J. F. Rippy, *Latin America in World Politics* (rev. ed., N.Y., 1938), Ch. XI; H. C. Hill, *Roosevelt and the Caribbean* (Chicago, 1927), Ch. V; and A. L. P. Dennis, *Adventures in American Diplomacy, 1896–1906* (N.Y., 1928), Ch. XI. ALASKA BOUNDARY. Helpful discussions appear in Tyler Dennett, *John Hay* (N.Y., 1933), Chs. XIX, XXIX; Allan Nevins, *Henry White* (N.Y., 1930), Ch. XII; and Dennis, *Adventures*, Ch. VI. The Canadian viewpoint is fully presented in L. M. Gelber, *The Rise of Anglo-American Friendship* (London, 1938), Ch. VII. See also T. A. Bailey, "Theodore Roosevelt and the Alaska Boundary Settlement," *Canadian Hist. Rev.*, XVIII (1937), 123–130. DOMINICAN RECEIVERSHIP. An excellent general account is Perkins, *Monroe Doctrine*, Ch. VI, which should be supplemented by J. F. Rippy, "The Initiation of the Customs Receivership in the Dominican Republic," *Hispanic Amer. Hist. Rev.*, XVII (1937), 419–457. See also Hill, *Roosevelt and the Caribbean*, Ch. VI. ALGECIRAS CONFERENCE. The best published account is Vagts, *op. cit.*, II, Ch. XVII. See also Dennis, *Adventures*, Ch. XIX. The work of the senior American delegate is stressed in Nevins' *Henry White*, Ch. XVI. Further references: see footnotes of this chapter and Bemis and Griffin, *Guide*, pp. 577–581 (Cuba); 436–440 (Venezuela); 415–420 (Alaska); 581–583 (Dominican Republic); 389 (Algeciras).

RECENT REFERENCES. J. F. Rippy, "Antecedents of the Roosevelt Corollary of the Monroe Doctrine," *Pacific Hist. Rev.*, IX (1940), 267–279, shows that the policy of preventive intervention was foreshadowed by the Mexican disorders of the fifties and sixties, by the situation in Venezuela in the late sixties and seventies, and particularly by the Venezuela incidents of 1895–96 and 1902–03. In the latter two instances the British pointed out to the United States its moral responsibility to maintain order. Professor Rippy develops this subject somewhat more briefly in *The Caribbean Danger Zone* (N.Y., 1940), Ch. III. According to H. E. Davis, in "The Citizenship of Jon Perdicaris," *Jour. of Mod. Hist.*, XIII (1941), 517–526, the State Department later ruled that Perdicaris had always been an American citizen, although Roosevelt and Hay knew at the time that his citizenship was "questionable." The author concludes that the President had "no practical alternative" in view of the fact that the kidnapping had been undertaken "to create an international incident." Alfred Vagts, "Hopes and Fears of an American-German War, 1870–1915," *Pol. Sci. Quar.*, LIV (1939), 514–535; LV (1940), 53–76, has some illuminating material on the Venezuela incident, the Monroe Doctrine, and naval rivalry. The latter was soon eclipsed early in the century by the building race between Germany and Britain.

NEW REFERENCES. For two books dealing with the Venezuela affair, for three on the Alaska boundary, for two on the Roosevelt corollary and Santo Domingo, for one on the Jewish problem, and for two articles (one on the Kaiser's relations with Roosevelt in peacemaking and another on Root's reform of the consular service), see Bibliographical Appendix, p. 936.

4TH ED. REFS. S. W. Livermore, "Theodore Roosevelt, the American Navy, and the Venezuelan Crisis of 1902–1903," *Amer. Hist. Rev.*, LI (1946), 452–471, confirms rather than refutes Roosevelt's version of big-sticking the Kaiser.

CHAPTER XXXIV

Theodore Roosevelt and Japanese-American Relations

*". . . I never take a step in foreign policy unless I am assured
that I shall be able eventually to carry out my will by force."*
                                                Theodore Roosevelt, 1905.

JAPAN PLAYS AMERICA'S GAME

IN 1898 the United States refused Great Britain's overtures for close
co-operation in the Far East, and, as we have seen, played a lone hand
with the Open Door notes. Rebuffed by America, and determined to
check Russia's penetration into Asia, the British succeeded in concluding an alliance with the Japanese, January 30, 1902. This agreement
proved to be a tower of strength to both.

Meanwhile Secretary Hay had been making valiant efforts to preserve the territorial integrity of China and thus uphold the Open Door.
In an attempt to prevent the Russians from securing exclusive industrial privileges in Manchuria, then under Chinese sovereignty, he sent
another circular note to the Powers, dated February 1, 1902. This
communication, which was perhaps the most conspicuous of several
steps that Hay took during these months in support of his policy, expanded the original Open Door concept to include industrial as well as
commercial development.[1]

The Japanese were much more vitally concerned than the British or
the Americans over the attempts of the Russians to absorb Manchuria
and the nominally independent kingdom of Korea. Strategically, these
areas were a pistol pointed at the heart of Japan. Economically, they
were regarded by the Japanese as natural and legitimate areas for commercial expansion. Friction between Russia and Japan became increasingly serious, and culminated in an outbreak of war, February 8, 1904.

Although both combatants were traditional friends of the United
States, the sympathies of the American people immediately went out
to the little yellow men. By this time Russia had definitely lost favor

[1] P. J. Treat, *Diplomatic Relations between the United States and Japan, 1895–1905*
(Stanford University, 1938), pp. 158–159.

in America as a result of Siberian dungeons, naked imperialism in the Far East, and the merciless persecutions of Jews. It appeared, moreover, that tiny Japan, though having struck the first blow without warning, was being bullied by the mighty Russian bear—a concept encouraged by Japanese propaganda.[2]

President Roosevelt strongly shared the sympathies of the American people for underdog Japan. He thought the Czar "a preposterous little creature," and he feared that the Russians were scheming to shut the Open Door against American commercial enterprise in Manchuria. If the Nipponese could stop them, he concluded, the United States would benefit. "Japan," he wrote, "is playing our game." [3]

Accordingly, the President took (or said he took) an audacious step. "As soon as this war broke out," he wrote privately, "I notified Germany and France in the most polite and discreet fashion that in the event of a combination against Japan . . . I should promptly side with Japan and proceed to whatever length was necessary on her behalf." [4] Like Roosevelt's own version of the Venezuela blockade and the Algeciras Conference, this account has been discredited by recent scholarship. No record of such an ultimatum has been found in the relevant archives or private papers.[5] Moreover, a warning of this kind was unnecessary, since Germany and France obviously had no intention of intervening.

It is clear, however, that the State Department sent a note to Russia, Japan, and China, on February 10, 1904, shortly after the outbreak of the Russo-Japanese War. This communication was strikingly like Hay's "integrity of China" notes of 1900. It urged the belligerents to respect the "neutrality" and "administrative entity" of China during the war; and a copy was sent to the interested neutral Powers urging them to co-operate to this end. The reply of neither Russia nor Japan was completely satisfactory, but Secretary Hay, resorting to his original Open Door technique of bluff, announced that assurances had been given.[6] On January 13, 1905, Hay circularized the interested neutral Powers in similar terms, and though they gave prompt and favorable responses, the Russian government declined to heed their action, and

---

[2] Tyler Dennett, *Roosevelt and the Russo-Japanese War* (Garden City, N.Y., 1925), pp. 238–239.

[3] Many of the most influential American newspapers shared Roosevelt's views. See E. Tupper and G. E. McReynolds, *Japan in American Public Opinion* (N.Y., 1937), pp. 6–11.

[4] Dennett, *op. cit.*, p. 2 (Roosevelt to Spring-Rice, July 24, 1905).

[5] Alfred Vagts, *Deutschland und die Vereinigten Staaten in der Weltpolitik* (N.Y., 1935), II, 1178–1179.

[6] *Foreign Relations, 1904*, pp. 2–3.

declared that it would consider Chinese neutrality "from the stand-point of its own interest." [7]

ROOSEVELT: THE HONEST BROKER

Left to themselves, the Japanese succeeded in winning an astonishing succession of triumphs on land and sea. Yet they drew so heavily on their man power and financial resources that, even in victory, they were near collapse. We now know that Japanese military and naval leaders actually returned home in the spring and summer of 1905 to insist that the Cabinet make peace.[8] If the Russians had been able to prolong their resistance, they might have worn down their enemy and won a final victory. But by the summer of 1905 they had lost the will to fight. Revolution was spreading in Russia; the Moroccan crisis was coming to a head; and France was urging her Russian ally to stop the struggle before she fruitlessly wasted all her strength.

On May 31, 1905, the exhausted but victorious Japanese secretly asked Roosevelt to act as mediator. The dynamic Rough Rider was not at all enthusiastic about assuming this responsibility; but he finally concluded that it was to the best interests of the United States to bring the bloody conflict to an end. He was especially anxious to preserve the balance of power in the Far East between Russia and Japan, for if either should become dominant—he particularly distrusted Russia—there was reason to believe that the Open Door would be closed.

Before definitely consenting to serve as peacemaker, Roosevelt sought assurances from Tokyo as to the disposition of the territory in dispute. On April 25, 1905, the Foreign Office assured him that "Japan adheres to [t]he position of maintaining [the] Open Door in Manchuria and of restoring that province to China." [9] This was the nearest thing to a pledge of support for the Open Door that Roosevelt was able to win from either Japan or Russia, despite numerous attempts.

After considerable difficulty, Russia was persuaded to discuss peace terms, and under Roosevelt's auspices delegates from the warring Powers met near Portsmouth, New Hampshire, on August 9, 1905. The Japanese demanded, among other things, the Russian island of Sakhalin, and, above all, a huge monetary indemnity. But the Russian government, suspecting the desperate financial straits of its adversary, stubbornly refused to consent to either. Roosevelt thereupon

[7] *Ibid.*, *1905*, pp. 1–4; A. W. Griswold, *The Far Eastern Policy of the United States* (N.Y., 1938), pp. 93–94, 102–103.

[8] *Ibid.*, p. 118.

[9] Dennett, *Roosevelt and the Russo-Japanese War*, p. 180.

appealed to the Czar through the American ambassador in Russia, and urged the Kaiser to bring pressure to bear on his fellow monarch. At the same time the President warned the Japanese delegates against persisting in their demand for money.[10]

Meanwhile American opinion had been turning to some extent against Japan, partly because of Japanese bumptiousness and Russian propaganda, which played up the grasping and imperialistic ambitions of the bloodthirsty Nipponese.[11] Although American sentiment never became pro-Russian, Tokyo finally responded to Roosevelt's warnings when it suddenly abandoned the claim for indemnity and settled for the southern half of Sakhalin.

There can be no doubt, however, that Japan was the victor. She emerged with considerable territorial gains, and established herself as the dominant power in the Far East. In Korea she strengthened her position; in Manchuria she secured from Russia the Liaotung leasehold, the South Manchuria Railway, and the economic privileges attaching to them.

Japan might not have won all these advantages without the friendly mediation of Roosevelt; yet the tax-burdened Japanese masses, who had been counting heavily on an indemnity, turned bitterly against both the United States and their own statesmen. Riots against the government resulted in incidental damage to several American churches.[12] Although Roosevelt's reputation as a world leader was tremendously enhanced both at home and in Europe by his efforts at peacemaking, there can be no doubt that the results of the Portsmouth Conference did much to cloud the friendly relationship between America and Japan, and further becloud Russian-American affairs.

Was Roosevelt's mediation a serious mistake, as some have charged? Would not Japan have collapsed if he had not stepped in? And would not a dominant Russia have been a better guardian of the Open Door than Japan has since then been? These questions cannot, of course, be answered with finality. But as one viewed the problem in the year 1905, there was much to be said for the balance of power idea.

THE DOOR IS CLOSED IN KOREA

The smashing Japanese victories over Russia had aroused considerable uneasiness in the United States as to the security of the Philip-

[10] *Ibid.*, pp. 249 *ff*.
[11] *Ibid.*, pp. 238 *ff*.
[12] Treat, *United States and Japan*, p. 249; Griswold, *Far Eastern Policy*, p. 121.

pines. On July 29, 1905, Secretary of War Taft, then on a mission to Manila, negotiated in Tokyo an "agreed memorandum" with Prime Minister Katsura. By its terms the Japanese disavowed any aggressive designs on the Philippines, and in return the United States approved Japan's "suzerainty over" Korea.[13] This executive agreement—it was not a treaty and it bound only the Roosevelt administration—was enthusiastically approved by the President. He had concluded that since America could not prevent Japanese absorption of Korea, the next best thing was to recognize the inevitable and secure something in return.

The United States carried out its part of the bargain regarding Korea to the letter. On November 23, 1905, the Japanese ambassador in Washington advised Secretary of State Root that henceforth Tokyo would control the foreign affairs of the Hermit Kingdom. The next day Root informed him that the American mission had been withdrawn, and that henceforth the United States would deal with Japan in matters relating to Korea.[14]

The Japanese were profoundly grateful for the prompt and generous recognition of their position in Korea, and the resulting good feeling did something to assuage the recent bitterness of Portsmouth.[15] Nevertheless, Roosevelt's realistic course was a backward step in upholding the Open Door in the Orient.

JAPANOPHOBIA ON THE PACIFIC COAST

Unfortunately, the Russo-Japanese War marked a sharp turning point in the traditionally friendly relations between America and Japan. Not only were the people of the island kingdom displeased with the results of Portsmouth, but considerable friction began to develop between the two nations in Manchuria. There the Japanese were attempting to consolidate their improved economic position at the expense—so American traders loudly claimed—of the Open Door. Moreover, the recently displayed prowess of Japan caused many Americans to experience a fear that sooner or later the very formidable military power of the Nipponese might be directed against them. As Mr. Dooley put it:

[13] For text, see Dennett, *Roosevelt and Russo-Japanese War*, pp. 112–114.

[14] Treat, *United States and Japan*, p. 255. Twenty-five years later Root was convinced that his course had been the proper one: "Many people are still angry because we did not keep Japan from taking Korea. There was nothing we could do except fight Japan; Congress wouldn't have declared war and the people would have turned out the Congress that had. All we might have done was to make threats which we could not carry out." P. C. Jessup, *Elihu Root* (N.Y., 1938), II, 62 (Root to Jessup, Sept. 5, 1930).

[15] Treat, *United States and Japan*, pp. 256, 271.

A few years ago I didn't think anny more about a Jap thin about anny other man that'd been kept in th' oven too long. They were all alike to me. But to-day, whiniver I see wan I turn pale an' take off me hat an' make a low bow.[16]

A more immediately alarming by-product of the conflict was a rapidly rising tide of emigration from Japan to the United States. This was entirely natural, for war begets a restless and adventuresome spirit, and many of the discharged Japanese veterans had no desire to return to their former humdrum life and shoulder heavy tax burdens.[17] To them California was the Promised Land. But the people of the Golden State, who could not forget their earlier experience with the Chinese problem, were determined not to be overrun by a race whose standard of living was so low as to jeopardize that of the white laborer. Their natural anxiety was increased by the recent Japanese victories and by the exhortations of the yellow press. Congress was lethargic; so the Californians, whose political power was not negligible, took things into their own hands.

In October, 1906, the San Francisco Board of Education passed a memorable order requiring all Oriental pupils to attend a public school specially set aside for them. The principal excuse given for this action was that the Japanese children (ninety-three in number) were crowding the whites out of the schools; the basic reason was a desire to express dissatisfaction with the influx of so much cheap coolie labor.[18]

In ordinary circumstances the Japanese are particularly sensitive to any suggestion of racial inferiority. But having recently demonstrated in a convincing fashion their military superiority over the most populous white nation, they were in no mood to brook what they regarded as a studied insult. When the news of the school order reached Japan there was a tremendous flare-up of public opinion. One reputable newspaper expressed an extreme view:

Stand up, Japanese nation! Our countrymen have been HUMILIATED on the other side of the Pacific. Our poor boys and girls have been expelled from the public schools by the rascals of the United States, cruel and merciless like demons. . . . Why do we not insist on sending [war] ships?[19]

[16] F. P. Dunne, *Mr. Dooley Says* (N.Y., 1910), p. 200.

[17] R. L. Buell, "The Development of the Anti-Japanese Agitation in the United States," *Pol. Sci. Quar.*, XXXVII (1922), 615.

[18] T. A. Bailey, *Theodore Roosevelt and the Japanese-American Crises* (Stanford University, 1934), p. 44.

[19] *Mainichi Shimbun*, Oct. 22, 1906, cited in *ibid.*, p. 50.

But most of the press, particularly after the first shock had passed, showed considerable moderation.

This, it will be noted, was another spectacular case of the embarrassing gap in federalism. The authorities in Washington had no jurisdiction whatsoever over the public schools of San Francisco. All that the federal government could legally do was to bring a test case into the courts with the object of reinstating the Japanese children; but that would take time—and public opinion in Japan had to be mollified. The situation might have become dangerous if Roosevelt had not stepped into the breach and in various ways shown that the United States government was not responsible for the action of the school board and did not approve of it. His most conspicuous gesture was to send Secretary of Commerce and Labor Metcalf to San Francisco to make a personal investigation—a step that did much to soothe the inflamed Japanese mind. But Roosevelt was plainly worried, writing privately: "I am being horribly bothered about the Japanese business. The infernal fools in California . . . insult the Japanese recklessly and in the event of war it will be the Nation as a whole which will pay the consequences." [20]

Unable to budge the San Franciscans from their position, Roosevelt assailed them in his annual message of 1906. Not only did he brand their action as a "wicked absurdity" but he hinted at strong measures. This was naturally gratifying to the Japanese; but Roosevelt's intemperate words stirred up a veritable hornet's nest in California and elsewhere on the Pacific Coast. "Our feeling is not against Japan," snarled the San Francisco *Chronicle*, "but against an unpatriotic President who unites with aliens to break down the civilization of his own countrymen." [21]

The Eastern press, fearing that Californian bullheadedness would precipitate war, generally supported Roosevelt. The Cleveland *Plain Dealer* was but one of a number of journals which regretted that "California is beyond reach of the paternal slipper of the national administration." The San Francisco *Chronicle* was disgusted at this lack of support:

There is an astonishing disposition shown by Eastern editors to crawl on their bellies when discussing the Japanese question. Is it really a fact that the prowess displayed by the little brown men in their recent war with Russia has so frightened them that they feel compelled to ask whether

[20] Roosevelt to Kermit Roosevelt, Oct. 27, 1906, Roosevelt Papers, Library of Congress.
[21] San Francisco *Chronicle*, Dec. 10, 1906, 5:2.

American polity must be governed by fear of the consequences of the wrath of foreigners? [22]

BLUDGEONING THE BOARD OF EDUCATION

At the outset of the immigration trouble in California, Roosevelt declared that the race feeling on the Pacific coast was "as foolish as if conceived by the mind of a Hottentot." But he at length perceived that no amount of browbeating was going to remove Western fear of an Oriental inundation. He finally swung around to the view that the attitude of the Californians was basically proper—"but its manifestations are often exceedingly improper." And he realized that if he were going to unsnarl the school tangle he would have to change his methods and resort to finesse. This he did when he invited the entire San Francisco school board to junket across the continent at government expense to discuss the problem with him.

A party of eight men left San Francisco for Washington early in February, 1907. They were headed by Mayor Schmitz, a former bassoon player then under indictment for graft. When this little group of politicians fell under the shadow of the Big Stick, surrender was inevitable. The San Francisco delegation finally agreed to permit Japanese children of a proper age and preparation to attend school with the whites. In return, Roosevelt promised the Californians what they most desired—an end to the Japanese influx.

The President carried out his part of the bargain, chiefly through the Gentlemen's Agreement of 1907–08. This arrangement was not embodied in any one document, but in a series of diplomatic notes by which the Japanese government bound itself to issue no more passports to coolies coming directly to the mainland of the United States.[23] The San Francisco Board of Education rescinded the objectionable school order, and the difficulty was finally settled.

BRANDISHING THE BIG STICK AT JAPAN

Roosevelt somehow got the impression that the Japanese interpreted his sympathetic attitude as evidence that he was afraid of them. He confided to a friend:

---

[22] *Ibid.*, Nov. 7, 1906, 6:1.

[23] By statute Congress regulated the immigration of Japanese from Hawaii and other areas outside the mainland of the United States. Bailey, *Theodore Roosevelt*, p. 146.

I am exceedingly anxious to impress upon the Japanese that I have nothing but the friendliest possible intentions toward them, but I am none the less anxious that they should realize that I am not afraid of them and that the United States will no more submit to bullying than it will bully.[24]

To remind the Japanese that the United States had the second largest navy (theirs was fifth), and to convince them that it was prepared for any contingency, Roosevelt adopted the spectacular plan of sending the entire American battleship fleet around the world. This gesture was not so much a threat at Japan as a demonstration for the benefit of Japan.[25]

The original announcement (July 9, 1907) was that the fleet would move only from Atlantic waters to San Francisco on a "practice cruise." But there were few intelligent observers who failed to discern that this audacious flourish was intimately associated with the Administration's Japanese policy. A cry of protest immediately arose from the Eastern states, which objected to stripping the Atlantic of its defenses and which feared that the fleet might be destroyed by the elements or by a Japanese surprise attack. The chairman of the Senate Committee on Naval Affairs informed the President that the money would not be appropriated for this harebrained venture. Roosevelt, his fighting blood aroused, replied that he had sufficient funds on hand to send the fleet to the Pacific coast, and that it could stay there if Congress did not want to bring it back. That ended the argument.

The announcement of the fleet cruise had the unfortunate effect of causing the jingo journals of the United States, including the Hearst sheets, to whip up a first-class war scare. The real yellow peril of this period was not from the Japanese but from the yellow newspapers, which the dispassionate Secretary of State Root branded as "leprous vampires." But in spite of all this agitation Roosevelt managed to keep a remarkably even keel. He wrote to Lodge:

I shall continue to do everything I can by politeness and consideration to the Japs to offset the worse than criminal stupidity of the San Francisco mob, the San Francisco press, and such papers as the New York *Herald*. I do not believe we shall have war; but it is no fault of the yellow press if we do not have it. The Japanese seem to have about the same proportion of prize jingo fools that we have.[26]

[24] Allan Nevins, *Henry White* (N.Y., 1930), pp. 292–293 (Roosevelt to White, July 30, 1907).

[25] Bailey, *Theodore Roosevelt*, p. 224.

[26] *Selections from the Correspondence of Theodore Roosevelt and Henry Cabot Lodge* (N.Y., 1925), II, 275 (Roosevelt to Lodge, July 10, 1907.)

In December, 1907, the fleet left Hampton Roads for what its commander thought might be a "feast, a frolic, or a fight." The sixteen armored battleships aroused frenzied rejoicing in the South American ports at which they stopped, and left behind an unmistakable trail of good will. The entire fleet arrived without a mishap at Magdalena Bay, Lower California, two days ahead of schedule and in fighting trim.

It was now possible to announce that the battleships would continue around the world, and the Australians and Japanese (among others) invited the Americans to visit their lands. The fleet was greeted with overwhelming enthusiasm in Australia, and then steamed on to Japan, where the people, as if to spike rumors of their unfriendliness, welcomed the Americans with an unparalleled exuberance which effectively dispelled all war clouds. So painstaking had been the preparations that thousands of Japanese children lined the roads singing the American national anthem in English. The press of the United States was gratified by this reception, though Hearst's New York *American* sneered that "the size of the fleet affected the cordiality."

After continuing on through the Mediterranean, the battleships finally arrived home on February 22, 1909, just in time to usher out the Roosevelt administration in a blaze of glory. The American people were naturally delighted with the success of this unprecedented achievement, and even former critics of Roosevelt were loud in their praise. The voyage contributed markedly to the prestige of America, and proved to be a spectacular step in her coming of age. Roosevelt himself later concluded, presumably not overlooking the Algeciras and Portsmouth Conferences, that sending the battleships around the world was "the most important service that I rendered to peace. . . ."[27]

THE ROOT-TAKAHIRA AGREEMENT

One striking evidence of the better feeling that followed the cruise of the fleet was the conclusion of an important agreement with Japan. More than a year earlier Ambassador Aoki, the Japanese representa-

---

[27] Roosevelt confessed that he was too much disturbed by the Japanese situation to give proper attention to the Second Hague Peace Conference, which convened on June 15, 1907. On the whole the results were even more disappointing than those of the First Hague Conference. Of the fourteen conventions drawn up, twelve had to do with the regulation of war rather than its prevention. Nevertheless, the Conference was an important step in co-operative effort toward peace. The American delegates and the United States Senate attached to the convention for the pacific settlement of international disputes the customary reservation designed to protect traditional policies. See J. B. Scott, *The Hague Peace Conferences of 1899 and 1907* (Baltimore, 1909), I, 88 ff.

tive in Washington, alarmed by the growing tension between the two countries, had approached Roosevelt. He proposed that Japan and the United States agree mutually to respect (1) the *status quo* in the Pacific and (2) the territorial integrity of China and the Open Door there. But Aoki had made his overture without instructions; so he was reproved by the Japanese Foreign Minister, and shortly thereafter recalled.[28]

A year later, in 1908, there was a new Foreign Minister in Tokyo, and the Japanese ambassador in Washington, Takahira, was instructed to enter into negotiations with Secretary Root on the same general basis as that proposed by Aoki. During the subsequent conversations Root suggested that some reference be made to the "territorial integrity" of China. The Japanese, though regarding this as unnecessary and as liable to offend the Chinese, agreed to do so, but in the final draft of the agreement the word "territorial" was dropped.[29] The unpublished records in the State Department do not reveal that the Japanese insisted on this change. In fact, the statement is actually stronger without the qualifying "territorial." [30]

The Root-Takahira Agreement was concluded by an exchange of notes on November 30, 1908. It was not a treaty (though Root deferentially communicated its terms to the Senate), but merely an executive agreement binding the Roosevelt administration. Briefly it provided that both Powers agreed:

1. To subscribe to the policy of maintaining the *status quo* in the Pacific area.
2. To respect each other's territorial possessions in that region [*e.g.*, Philippines, Hawaii, Formosa].
3. To uphold the Open Door in China.
4. To support by pacific means the "independence and integrity of China. . . ." [31]

The notes were received with marked favor in Europe, for they were consonant with treaties that several of the Powers had recently concluded with Japan. The Chinese, however, were displeased that the

---

[28] See O'Brien (ambassador in Tokyo) to Root (telegram), Nov. 3, 1907, file 1797, Department of State. The present writer has examined all the unpublished correspondence in the Department of State relevant to the Root-Takahira Agreement.

[29] Root to Takahira, Nov. 11, 1908; Takahira to Root, Nov. 14, 1908, file 16533, Department of State.

[30] See S. C. Y. Pan, *American Diplomacy concerning Manchuria* (Providence, R.I., 1938), pp. 119 n; Jessup, *Elihu Root*, II, 37.

[31] *Foreign Relations, 1908*, pp. 511–512.

Root-Takahira Agreement should have been made without deference to them. It was, in fact, concluded shortly before a special Chinese mission arrived in Washington for the ostensible purpose of tendering thanks for a remission of the Boxer indemnity, but probably also for concluding a similar understanding with the United States in the hope of thwarting Japan's aspirations in China and breaking through the encirclement of the Powers.[32] In certain quarters it was felt that the agreement would tend to isolate the Chinese diplomatically and weaken them in their efforts to prevent foreign encroachments.[33]

The American press reacted quite favorably to the exchange of notes, because the United States, which had no designs on the Open Door or on Japanese territory, secured from Japan a pledge to respect the Open Door and the Philippines, on both of which the Japanese were suspected of malign intentions. The apparent one-sidedness of the arrangement has led commentators to conclude that Roosevelt tacitly gave the Japanese a free hand in Manchuria for the advantages secured.[34] It is not clear, however, that a secret bargain was necessary, for if, as the State Department has ruled, the Pacific area included Manchuria, then a recognition of the *status quo* there was equivalent to recognizing the economic ascendancy of the Japanese.

THE END OF A GOLDEN AGE

It is evident that by the close of his Administration Roosevelt had retreated substantially from his earlier championship of the original Open Door. Ever a believer in military might as the right arm of diplomacy, he was enough of a realist to conclude that there was no advantage in fighting to stop what one could not prevent. Rather, it was wise statesmanship to exchange the inevitable for concessions.

In retrospect it also becomes clear that the Roosevelt era marked a transition in the relations between the United States and Japan. The days when America could manifest a parental pride in her Far Eastern protégé had passed. Within the space of seven years both nations had stepped onto the world stage. The United States left its continent to become an insular Power in the Far East; Japan left her islands to become a continental Power in Asia. The interests of both nations came increasingly into conflict; and suspicion and jealousy, not unmingled

---

[32] Rockhill (U.S. minister to China) to Root, Dec. 3, 1908, file 16533, Department of State.

[33] See Herbert Croly, *Willard Straight* (N.Y., 1924), pp. 270–276.

[34] This view is fully developed in Griswold, *Far Eastern Policy of the United States*, op. 129–130.

with fear, were bound to be the unhappy results of this changed status. It was the price that both Japan and America had to pay for becoming world Powers.

BIBLIOGRAPHICAL NOTE

The best summary account is A. W. Griswold, *The Far Eastern Policy of the United States* (N.Y., 1938), Chs. III, IX. An excellent biographical treatment is H. F. Pringle, *Theodore Roosevelt* (N.Y., 1931), pp. 372–412. The standard monograph on the subject is Tyler Dennett, *Roosevelt and the Russo-Japanese War* (Garden City, N.Y., 1925). This should be supplemented by A. L. P. Dennis, *Adventures in American Diplomacy, 1896–1906* (N.Y., 1928), Ch. XIV; by P. J. Treat's *Diplomatic Relations between the United States and Japan, 1895–1905* (Stanford University, 1938), Chs. IX to XII; and by the exhaustive chapter in Alfred Vagts, *Deutschland und die Vereinigten Staaten in der Weltpolitik* (N.Y., 1935), II, 1122–1256. The immigration issue and the cruise of the fleet are most fully treated in T. A. Bailey, *Theodore Roosevelt and the Japanese-American Crises* (Stanford University, 1934). Valuable new material on the negotiation of the Gentlemen's Agreement and the Root-Takahira Agreement appears in P. C. Jessup, *Elihu Root* (N.Y., 1938), II, Chs. XXVII, XXVIII. The best study of public opinion is Eleanor Tupper and G. E. McReynolds, *Japan in American Public Opinion* (N.Y., 1937), Chs. I, II. See also R. L. Buell, "The Development of the Anti-Japanese Agitation in the United States," *Pol. Sci. Quar.,* XXXVII (1922), 605–638; XXXVIII (1923), 57–81. Further references: see footnotes of this chapter and Bemis and Griffin, *Guide*, pp. 491–494; 500–506.

RECENT REFERENCES. T. A. Bailey, "The Root-Takahira Agreement of 1908," *Pacific Hist. Rev.*, IX (1940), 19–35, is a detailed account of the negotiations, based upon unpublished State Department records, with particular attention to the place of the agreement in the network of treaties relating to East Asia. The essential documents constituting the administrative measures of the Gentlemen's Agreement of 1907–08 (effective 1908), have now been published in *Foreign Relations, 1924*, II, 339–369.

NEW REFERENCES. F. H. Harrington's able and interesting *God, Mammon, and the Japanese: Dr. Horace N. Allen and Korean-American Relations, 1884–1905* (Madison, Wis., 1944), centers around the machinations of an almost incredible missionary-doctor-diplomat, who was at first anti-Russian but later anti-Japanese, and who unsuccessfully sought to block Roosevelt's pro-Japanese policy in Korea (see pp. 317–318). Merze Tate, *The Disarmament Illusion* (N.Y., 1942), shows that American opinion became more friendly to disarmament after the Russo-Japanese war and other developments. E. E. Morison, *Admiral Sims and the Modern American Navy* (Boston, 1942), indicates that Sims' Anglophilism did something to improve British-American relations, 1898–1914. There is much on Roosevelt and the Navy. W. B. Thorson, "Pacific Northwest Opinion on the Russo-Japanese War of 1904–1905," *Pacific Northwest Quar.*, XXXV (1944), 305–322, reveals strong anti-Russian and pro-Japanese sentiment, and naive faith that Japan was fighting America's battle for the Open Door.

4TH ED. REFS. See Bibliographical Appendix, p. 937.

CHAPTER XXXV

Taft and Dollar Diplomacy

"The diplomacy of the present administration has sought to respond to modern ideas of commercial intercourse. This policy has been characterized as substituting dollars for bullets. It is one that appeals alike to idealistic humanitarian sentiments, to the dictates of sound policy and strategy, and to legitimate commercial aims."

President Taft, December 3, 1912.

THE DOLLAR BECOMES A DIPLOMAT

THE amiable William H. Taft, upon whose portly frame Roosevelt cast his mantle, possessed a strong judicial temperament. He wanted to be, as he ultimately became, a justice of the Supreme Court; but the force of circumstances brought him first to the highest executive office. Temperamentally unfitted to be a dynamic leader like Roosevelt, he knew that he would be unable to thump the tub, herd emperors, and settle the destinies of continents with one grand flourish.[1] "Our ways," he remarked, "are different." So the Big Stick gathered cobwebs; and the American people, having perhaps mistaken noise and fury for statesmanship, doubted if they had inherited a President of Rooseveltian proportions.

Taft, unlike Roosevelt, did not attempt to be his own Secretary of State. For that post he chose Philander C. Knox, an able corporation lawyer thoroughly sympathetic with the point of view of big business. The new Secretary was a forceful figure who dominated the Cabinet and regarded himself as a kind of prime minister. As befitted his corporation background, he favored a "spirited foreign commercial policy," and reorganized the State Department so as to further this objective.[2]

[1] In contrast with Roosevelt, Taft pursued a strict hands-off policy toward the Moroccan crisis of 1911, which followed the sending of the German *Panther* to Agadir to protect the interests of Germany. While desiring mediation, he did not interfere in the Italo-Turkish War of 1911, and the First Balkan War of 1912.

[2] H. F. Wright, "Philander Chase Knox," in S. F. Bemis, ed., *American Secretaries of State and their Diplomacy* (N.Y., 1929), IX, 325 ff.

Taft had ambitious plans for the diplomacy of his country. He realized that the republic was experiencing a great boom in its export trade, that the Panama Canal was about to be completed, and that the United States should take its proper place as a world Power. He felt that the time had come when domestic affairs should no longer overshadow foreign affairs; that the nation was now "too mature" to use diplomacy as "a mere assertion of the right to international existence"; and that the "outworn dogmas of the past," which had been designed for "colonial times and conditions," had to be adjusted to the "conditions of to-day." [3]

In an attempt to carry out these ideas, Taft inaugurated a policy that has been popularly and somewhat opprobriously referred to as Dollar Diplomacy. Unlike his predecessors he was not content with merely protecting American property and investments abroad. On the contrary, his Administration announced that it would actively encourage and support American bankers and industrialists in securing opportunities for profit in foreign lands. [4]

The best illustration of the workings of Dollar Diplomacy may be found in China. The Taft administration coincided with one of the greatest expansions of foreign investment in the history of the United States. But for various reasons American capital showed little interest in China. This was a source of deep regret to the dynamic and far-visioned Willard Straight, who, though only in his twenties, served as United States consul general at Mukden, Manchuria, from 1906 to 1908. Straight viewed with apprehension the economic penetration of the Japanese into Manchuria and China proper, and concluded that the United States lacked power and influence in the Far East because of the small amount of capital invested there. He firmly believed that if his country was to have a decisive voice in preserving the territorial integrity of China (and the Open Door), American bankers would have to be persuaded to invest large sums there, particularly in the construction of railroads. [5]

[3] *Foreign Relations, 1912*, p. xxvii (Dec. 3, 1912). The entire message to Congress is a revealing summation of Taft's foreign policy.

[4] Knox was able to clothe his policy with a humanitarian garb. "If," he said, "the American dollar can aid suffering humanity and lift the burden of financial difficulty from States with which we live on terms of intimate intercourse and earnest friendship, and replace insecurity and devastation by stability and peaceful self-development, all I can say is that it would be hard to find better employment." Wright, "Knox," *loc. cit.*, pp. 327-328.

[5] A. W. Griswold, *The Far Eastern Policy of the United States* (N.Y., 1938), pp. 136 *ff*. Professor Griswold thinks that the "imprint of Willard Straight's personality is no less vivid than Hay's or Rockhill's" in the development of America's Far Eastern policy.

Straight returned to the United States as Acting Chief of the Division of Far Eastern Affairs (1908–1909), and in that capacity exercised a strong influence upon the policy of the new Taft administration. His views were accurately reflected in a departmental memorandum signed by Secretary Knox:

The nations that finance the great Chinese railways and other enterprises will be foremost in the affairs of China and the participation of American capital in these investments will give the voice of the U.S. more authority in political controversies in that country which will go far toward guaranteeing the preservation of the administrative entity of China.[6]

In short, Taft and Knox embarked upon an attempt "to force American capital by diplomatic pressure into a region of the world where it would not go of its own accord."[7]

Battling for the Dollar in China

Taft's first sally into eastern Asia involved the Hukuang railway project, which a consortium of British, French, and German bankers was proposing to build in central and southern China. At the instance of the Department of State an American banking group was formed, headed by J. P. Morgan, and the Taft administration insisted that this organization be allowed to join the consortium. When the British objected, the Washington government sought to prevent the Chinese authorities from signing the contract until American terms were met. President Taft went so far as to send an extraordinary personal appeal to the Chinese Prince Regent:

I have resorted to this somewhat unusually direct communication with Your Imperial Highness, because of the high importance that I attach to the successful result of our present negotiations. I have an intense personal interest in making the use of American capital in the development of China an instrument for the promotion of the welfare of China. . . .[8]

After further difficulties and delay, the American banking group was reluctantly admitted to the consortium, the final arrangements for which were signed on May 20, 1911. The American capitalists, however, showed only a fitful interest in their responsibilities. Little, if anything, was done to preserve the integrity of China; and the intrusion of the United States deeply embittered the foreign Powers. Willard Straight, who had resigned from the State Department to

[6] *Ibid.*, p. 144.
[7] *Ibid.*, p. 146.
[8] *Foreign Relations, 1909*, p. 178 (July 15, 1909).

act as agent for the American group, privately confessed that "the mere mention of Hukuang is like a red rag to a bull to these European Foreign Offices!" [9]

During the years of Taft's presidency the Russians had a strong position in northern Manchuria with their Chinese Eastern Railway, while the Japanese were firmly entrenched in South Manchuria with their South Manchuria Railway. Knox felt that the increasingly dominant influence of Japan and Russia in this area boded ill for the sovereignty of China and for the Open Door. So he cast about for some scheme that would block foreign penetration, and at the same time provide a place for American dollars. He finally worked out an extraordinary proposal, which he communicated to Great Britain, on November 6, 1909, and to the other interested Powers, on December 14, 1909. Its most important feature was that banking groups from the various Powers would advance China a large sum of money. This would enable her to buy the Manchuria railroads, which in turn would be controlled by an international board pending the repayment of the loan.[10] Secretary Knox privately confessed that he was attempting to "smoke Japan out" from her dominant position.

The Japanese, who had established themselves in Manchuria by the bloody sacrifices of the Russo-Japanese War, were deeply offended by this thinly veiled attempt to jockey them out of their sphere of influence. Russia saw eye to eye with Japan, and these two Powers, whose relations had become seriously embittered, were driven into each others' arms. Both returned an unequivocal refusal which was couched in such similar terms as to suggest collaboration.[11]

If Knox had taken the precaution to sound out Russia and Japan in advance, he probably would not have made his blundering proposal.

[9] Herbert Croly, *Willard Straight* (N.Y., 1924), p. 392 (Straight to Dorothy Whitney, Feb. 19, 1911).

[10] The great American railroad promoter, E. H. Harriman, had laid plans for establishing a round-the-world transportation system. One vital link was the Chinese Eastern Railway through Manchuria, which the Russians would not sell. Harriman (with Straight's enthusiastic co-operation and the help of British capital) planned to build another line from Chinchow to Aigun, a project that alarmed the Japanese because it would take business from their South Manchurian line. In his famous proposal, Knox suggested that, if neutralization were not practicable, the Powers support British and American capital in the building of the Chinchow-Aigun railroad. This scheme was also spurned. For text of the Knox note see *Foreign Relations, 1910*, pp. 234–235.

[11] Rockhill (U.S. ambassador to Russia) to Knox, Jan. 20, 1910, file 5315, Department of State. The Russian Foreign Office was resentful because it was the last to be informed. Rockhill to Knox, Jan. 24, 1910, *ibid*. The present writer has examined all the manuscript material in the Department of State relevant to the Knox Manchurian proposal.

As it was, he weakened the integrity of China by driving Japan and Russia together.[12] He also offended the Japanese, who not only had a vital stake in Manchuria but who believed that their special position had already been recognized by the United States. He angered the American banking group, which felt that the Department of State had been unduly precipitate. In fact, Knox had to plead with these capitalists to continue to support their government—a striking commentary on the alleged wickedness of Wall Street.[13] Finally, much ill feeling was aroused in the United States by what were presumed to be the ulterior designs of Japan. American jingoes were spurred to renewed activity, and a war scare developed, one feature of which was strong agitation for the construction of bigger and better battleships. But the clergy, the peace organizations, and the conservative newspapers threw their influence on the side of moderation, and the outburst died out.[14]

Knox's naïve, lone-hand policy was foredoomed to failure from the start. The United States, acting alone, did not have the naval or military force to halt either Japan or Russia in the Far East. And regardless of the relative size of armaments, American public opinion would not have tolerated a war over interests that were of such small importance.[15] Roosevelt had followed a policy of recognizing (for a consideration) what he could not prevent, and he was sorely displeased by the Administration's tactics. In a strong letter to Taft he minced no words:

I utterly disbelieve in the policy of bluff, in national and international no less than in private affairs, or in any violation of the old frontier maxim, "Never draw unless you mean to shoot." I do not believe in our taking any position anywhere unless we can make good; and as regards Manchuria, if the Japanese choose to follow a course of conduct to which we are adverse, we cannot stop it unless we are prepared to go to war, and a successful war about Manchuria would require a fleet as good as that of England, plus an army as good as that of Germany.[16]

[12] Knox to Peking Legation (telegram), Feb. 8, 1910, file 5315, Department of State.

[13] Griswold, *Far Eastern Policy of the United States*, p. 157.

[14] E. Tupper and G. E. McReynolds, *Japan in American Public Opinion* (N.Y., 1937), pp. 86–91.

[15] Elihu Root wrote in 1931: "It never entered the head of any President or Secretary of State or Chairman of the Committee on Foreign Relations of the Senate or Chairman of the Committee on Foreign Affairs of the House that we *would* ever send forces to China to maintain the open door." P. C. Jessup, *Elihu Root* (N.Y., 1938), II, 452.

[16] Tyler Dennett, *Roosevelt and the Russo-Japanese War* (Garden City, N.Y., 1925), p. 320 (letter of Dec. 22, 1910).

Dollar Diplomacy Becomes Life Line Diplomacy

The Dollar Diplomacy of the Taft administration is generally associated with Latin America, and there it proved more successful—superficially at least—than in the Far East. But in neither area was the dollar supported for its own sake. In the Far East, as we have seen, the objective was to bolster up Chinese territorial integrity; in Latin America it was to safeguard the Panama life line of the United States.

The approaching completion of the Panama Canal, the jugular vein of American sea power, caused the American people to become more and more sensitive to conditions in the nations fronting the Caribbean. Disorders in the "banana republics" of Central America which had formerly been ignored could no longer be tolerated, for they might invite foreign intervention and a consequent threat against the Panama waterway. Secretary Knox put it baldly in a speech before the New York State Bar Association:

The logic of political geography and of strategy, and now our tremendous national interest created by the Panama Canal, make the safety, the peace, and the prosperity of Central America and the zone of the Caribbean of paramount interest to the Government of the United States. Thus the malady of revolutions and financial collapse is most acute precisely in the region where it is most dangerous to us. It is here that we seek to apply a remedy.[17]

Faced with these dangers, Taft cheerfully accepted the wider implications of the Roosevelt corollary to the Monroe Doctrine. Since the Washington government would not permit foreign nations to intervene for the purpose of protecting the investments of their nationals, the United States was morally obligated to keep order. Moreover, European investments could be squeezed out of these strategic areas by putting pressure on the Latin American governments; and American capital could be pumped in by holding out inducements and assurances of protection to Wall Street.

Taft's endeavors to "encourage and support American bankers" resulted in pushing the financial empire of the United States into the Caribbean. In 1909, for example, the Department of State became much concerned over the difficulties that Honduras was having with

[17] *Foreign Relations, 1912,* p. 1092 (Jan. 19, 1912). Huntington Wilson, Assistant Secretary of State under Taft, complained of the "great pertinacity" with which certain European Powers have "poached upon our preserves in the Caribbean and even on the Isthmus itself."

British bondholders, and the Washington government made strong efforts to interest American bankers in taking over the Honduran debt.[18] The next year, when Knox was anxious to force United States capital into the National Bank of the Republic of Haiti, he requested that several New York bankers meet with him in Washington to discuss the project.[19] The upshot was that four American houses invested heavily in the Haitian institution. Taft felt that American capital used in this way not only helped protect the Canal Zone, but benefited the Latin American countries by bringing them peace and stability. At the same time the investor in the United States derived a profit.[20]

The Dollar Diplomacy of Taft and Knox in Latin America was perhaps most conspicuous in Nicaragua. American investments in that country were small as compared with those in the other Caribbean republics, but here lay the alternate canal route, which the Washington government could not permit to fall under foreign control. Unfortunately, Nicaragua was under the iron rule of an international troublemaker of the first water, José Zelaya, whose general attitude is admirably summed up in a statement attributed to him, "I ridicule the United States, laugh at Germany, spit on England." The inevitable revolution against him broke out in 1909, and during the course of hostilities two Americans serving with the insurgents were summarily executed. Knox drafted a peremptory note in which he condemned the Zelaya regime, expressed sympathy for the revolutionists, and notified the Nicaraguan *chargé* that he was dismissed. The drastic nature of this communication excited much adverse comment, both abroad and at home. The New York *Nation* remarked that Knox "attacks diplomatic problems of the first rank as easily as he would discharge a refractory window-cleaner in the State Department." [21]

The Knox plan for dealing with the Nicaragua and the other storm centers of the Caribbean was simple. First, the government was to be stabilized by reorganizing the finances. This would prevent foreign intervention. Second, the customs houses were to be removed from

[18] *Ibid.*, pp. 549–554 (State Department memorandum, *circa* Sept. 1909).

[19] B. H. Williams, *American Diplomacy* (N.Y., 1936), pp. 194, 199. In 1912 a concession by Panama to British and German investors was cancelled after strong objections had been made by Washington. *Foreign Relations, 1912*, pp. 1167 ff.

[20] *Ibid.*, p. xii (Message of Dec. 3, 1912).

[21] New York *Nation*, XC, 27 (Jan. 13, 1910). In later years Elihu Root wrote: "Knox was a peppery sort of fellow. He got mad very easily. He did mix into things too much. . . . He was . . . absolutely antipathetic to all Spanish-American modes of thought and feeling and action, and pretty much everything he did with them was like mixing a Seidlitz powder." Jessup, *Elihu Root*, pp. 250–251.

the reach of the revolutionists. This would eliminate a major incentive to armed uprisings. In pursuance of its general policy, the Taft administration refused to recognize the new Nicaraguan government until the latter had secured a large loan from American bankers with which to refund the debt that it owed the British. When the United States minister found that a strong majority of the Nicaraguan voters were opposed to such a step, he urged upon the State Department "the advisability of stationing permanently, at least until the loan has been put through, a war vessel at Corinto." [22] A warship soon appeared, and the proper ratification of the transaction was secured.

Secretary Knox continued to push ahead with his plan of customs supervision. In November, 1911, an American citizen was selected as collector general of the customs, with the approval of the Nicaraguan government. And during outbreaks in subsequent years the marines repeatedly landed and engaged in fighting to protect American interests.

Knox realized that his policy of forcibly enlarging the economic orbit of the United States was highly unpopular in Latin America. Early in 1912 he made a good will tour of most of the republics touching on the Caribbean. "I beg to assure you," he proclaimed in one speech, "and I am sure that what I say meets with the approval of the people and President of the United States, that my Government does not covet an inch of territory south of the Rio Grande." [23] But these fine words were strangely inconsistent with economic imperialism, financial receiverships, and forcible intervention.

THE SOLUTION OF THE SEAL PROBLEM

While Taft was being severely criticized at home and abroad for his Dollar Diplomacy, he could point with pride to the happy solution of two extraordinarily complicated and persistent problems: those involving seals in the North Pacific and fish in the North Atlantic.

Secretary Blaine's efforts to put an end to pelagic sealing had met with failure because the Powers concerned would not consent to an international agreement abridging their rights on the high seas. From that time on the destruction of the seals went forward so rapidly that they were threatened with extermination. By 1910 the magnificent herd that had once numbered some 4,000,000 had dwindled to about 100,000.

[22] *Foreign Relations, 1911*, pp. 661–662 (Northcott to Secretary of State, May 25, 1911).
[23] Wright, "Knox," *loc. cit.*, p. 339.

The problem was complicated by the fact that the Japanese and Canadian pelagic sealers, who owned a considerable fleet of schooners, did not want to be deprived of their business. It was evident, however, that if pelagic sealing continued there would soon be no business to be deprived of. After months of patient diplomacy, representatives of the four great Powers bordering the North Pacific (Russia, Japan, Great Britain, and the United States) were brought together in Washington in the summer of 1911. When the conference became deadlocked, Taft took the extraordinary step of making an appeal directly to the Mikado. The result was a moderation of Japanese demands and the signing of the North Pacific Sealing Convention of 1911. By its terms the signatory powers bound their nationals not to engage in pelagic sealing. But to compensate them for having to abandon their business, it was provided that the United States would annually pay Japan and Great Britain a stipulated percentage of the proceeds from the strictly regulated land kill. (See map on page 449.)

Under the new dispensation the herd on the Pribilof Islands increased to well over a million by 1932. But the Japanese found that the seals were making heavy inroads on their vital fisheries, and in 1940 gave notice of the termination of the agreement, effective the next year (see p. 792). During the thirty years that it lasted the pact not only removed a serious source of friction but provided an outstanding example of international co-operation.

The Settlement of the Fisheries Question

At the turn of the century the perennial fisheries problem bobbed up again. With the passage of time the shores of Newfoundland had been settled by local fishermen, who resented the incursions of ships from New England. The Newfoundland Parliament therefore passed regulations (such as forbidding fishing on Sunday) which placed the American fishermen at a great disadvantage, and which evoked a loud protest from the "sea-going voters" of Massachusetts.

Before taking over his duties as Secretary of State in 1905, Elihu Root journeyed to Newfoundland, where he gained a sympathetic appreciation of the problem at first hand. A clash between the two groups of fishermen was averted by temporary arrangements; and after painstaking negotiations a convention was concluded between Great Britain and the United States, on January 27, 1909, by the terms of which the questions at issue were to be submitted to the Hague Court. The signing of this instrument was one of Root's last acts before leaving the Cabinet, and, according to his biographer, it was "perhaps his greatest diplomatic triumph as Secretary of State." [24]

Root next journeyed to the Netherlands, where he served as American counsel before the tribunal. The decision, which was handed down on September 7, 1910, was in the nature of a compromise. Although it provided safeguards for New England fishermen, it sustained the Newfoundland claim to local jurisdiction, and was consequently hailed as a British victory. Root, however, was satisfied that the United States had obtained about all it could reasonably have expected.

The Hague award, with certain modifications, was confirmed by the Anglo-American Convention of July 20, 1912. The most important feature of this settlement was the establishment of a permanent body to adjust disputes as they arose; hence there would no longer be the danger of a festering accumulation of grievances. Although Root was largely responsible for this settlement, the final steps were carried through in the Taft administration and redounded to its credit. Thus ended the most persistently vexatious dispute in the diplomatic history of the United States.[25]

THE UNION JACK VERSUS OLD GLORY

Although Canadian-American relations were definitely improved by the settlement of the fisheries and sealing problems, Taft was much less fortunate in another quarter. The Canadians had prospered so greatly under the Reciprocity Treaty of 1854 that they continued to agitate for another such arrangement. The matter came to a head when the highly protectionist American tariff law of 1909 caused the Canadians seriously to consider retaliation. This possibility was disconcerting to the Washington government, which was being severely criticized at home for its high tariff policy. In January, 1911, therefore, the Administration signed a sweeping agreement with Canada.[26] It provided that a long list of commodities, principally foodstuffs, would be reciprocally admitted free or with reduced duties.

The agreement was not a treaty but was subject to approval by a simple majority of both branches of Congress. The House of Representatives passed the measure without undue delay; but the Senate, responding to the outcry of the American lumber, grain, and fish interests,

[24] Jessup, *Elihu Root*, II, 83.

[25] Also important was the Boundary Waters Treaty of 1909, which set up a permanent commission to adjust disputes between Canada and the United States.

[26] See W. G. Swartz, "The Proposed Canadian-American Reciprocity Agreement of 1911," *Jour. Econ. and Business Hist.*, III (1930), 120 ff.

proved far less tractable and adjourned without taking action. Taft's fighting blood was now aroused. Desperately eager to crown his rather unpopular Administration with a substantial achievement in the field of

THE STRAW MAN.

(From the New York *World*.)

foreign affairs, he called a special session of Congress in April, 1911. The sizzling heat of Washington, combined with the votes of the low-tariff Democrats, finally forced the measure through in July, 1911.[27]

But enthusiastic supporters of reciprocity left the impression that this was but an insidious step toward the annexation of Canada. Several

27 For a map and illuminating figures on the sectional aspects of the fight in Congress see C. O. Paullin, *Atlas of the Historical Geography of the United States* (Washington, D.C., 1932), p. 121 and Plate 120 B. See also L. E. Ellis, "The Northwest and the Reciprocity Agreement of 1911," *Miss. Valley Hist. Rev.*, XXVI (1939), 55–66.

of the Congressmen made speeches in this vein, notably Speaker Champ Clark, who asserted: "I am for it, because I hope to see the day when the American flag will float over every square foot of the British-North American possessions clear to the North Pole." [28] President Taft himself was so indiscreet as to tell Congress that the Canadian people were coming "to the parting of the ways."

William Randolph Hearst, who was eager to secure cheap wood pulp for his newspapers, vigorously supported reciprocity. He even shipped large numbers of his sensational journals into Canada, where they made many votes—for the other side. Taft was so ill-advised as to express his "high appreciation" to the unpopular Mr. Hearst in helping "spread the gospel of reciprocity."

The issue was finally thrown into the dusty arena of the Canadian general election of 1911. The embattled vested interests insisted that Canada would become "the backyard and lumber camp of New England," and they used all their resources, including the indiscreet statements of Americans, to arouse Canadian nationalism and a lurking distrust of the United States. "I do not understand," announced Rudyard Kipling, "how nine million people can enter into such arrangements with ninety million strangers . . . and at the same time preserve their national integrity. It is her own soul that Canada risks today." [29] Thousands of Canadians thronged to the polls convinced that the choice lay between "the Union Jack or Old Glory," and that the fate of the empire hung on their ballots.

The result of the election was a victory for the Conservative or antireciprocity party. The newly elected majority in Parliament voted down reciprocity, and the friendly hand which Taft had extended at the solicitation of the Canadians was soundly rebuffed. The whole incident further discredited the Taft administration, rasped Canadian-American relations, and gave the death blow to whatever lingering sentiments for annexation may have persisted in Canada.

STRETCHING MR. MONROE'S DOCTRINE

The unwillingness of the Republican Senate to follow Taft's leadership in the reciprocity struggle was also revealed in two other questions that arose in 1911. The first had to do with Magdalena Bay, in Lower California. This magnificent body of landlocked water had long been

---

[28] *Cong. Record*, 61 Cong., 3 sess., p. 2520 (Feb. 14, 1911).

[29] H. L. Keenleyside, *Canada and the United States* (N.Y., 1929), p. 319. The Canadian campaign is fully presented in L. E. Ellis, *Reciprocity 1911* (New Haven, 1939), pp. 141 ff.

an object of concern to the United States because of its potentialities as a naval base. In the hands of a powerful foreign nation it would seriously menace the Panama Canal and California, as well as the line of communications between these two points. In 1911 the news leaked out that a Japanese company was negotiating with a syndicate in the United States for a huge tract of land in the vicinity of Magdalena Bay. A momentary flurry of excitement, led by the vociferously anti-Japanese Hearst sheets, swept over the country.[30] But when the Department of State frowned upon the transaction the Japanese concern dropped the project.

Henry Cabot Lodge of Massachusetts took advantage of this situation to introduce a resolution in the Senate. It declared that the United States disapproved of the transfer of strategic spots in the Americas to non-American private companies which might be acting as agents for a foreign Power. Though both President Taft and the Department of State regarded the resolution as unnecessary and provocative, it was approved on August 2, 1912, by a vote of 51 to 4. The declaration was regarded as a corollary to the Monroe Doctrine because it extended the principles of 1823 to an Asiatic Power and to a foreign company, as distinguished from a government. Japan, of course, was not mentioned by name, but the intent was perfectly clear.

The Lodge corollary has been generally dismissed as unimportant because it was not signed by Taft (as a matter of fact, the President never signs Senate resolutions), and because it was simply a pronouncement of the Senate. Yet the record shows that the Department of State has accepted the corollary and has invoked it at least four times since 1912, in each case to discourage Americans from disposing of their holdings in Mexico to Japanese.[31] Although not in itself of great importance, the Lodge resolution remains a warning to foreign nations and illustrates strikingly the expansive powers of the Monroe Doctrine.

The Taft-Knox Arbitration Treaties

Taft encountered much more serious difficulties with the Senate over another issue. In 1905 that body had objected to a series of arbitration treaties negotiated by Hay, and had finally amended them so as to make necessary its consent to every specific arbitration. Roosevelt thereupon withdrew the pacts. Secretary Root took up the general problem of arbitration and persuaded Roosevelt to meet in some meas-

---

[30] Tupper and McReynolds, *Japan in American Public Opinion*, pp. 105–106.

[31] T. A. Bailey, "The Lodge Corollary to the Monroe Doctrine," *Pol. Sci. Quar.*, XLVIII (1933), 235–236.

ure the demands of the Senate. In the pacts that he drew up all disputes affecting the "vital interests, the independence, or the honor of the two contracting states" were excepted, and a special treaty was required for each arbitration. Twenty-five of these Root agreements were signed in 1908 and 1909.

The legalistic and conservative Taft favored law and order throughout the world, and he was eager to secure much more sweeping arbitration pacts than those obtained by Root. It was widely feared that if Japan and America went to war, Great Britain would be bound by the terms of the Anglo-Japanese Alliance to fight the United States. The British were conscious of this feeling, and when the Alliance was renewed, July 13, 1911, succeeded in having a new clause inserted. This provided that neither Japan nor Great Britain would fight a nation with which it had a treaty of general arbitration.[32]

Taking the cue, the Taft administration signed sweeping treaties with both Great Britain and France, on August 3, 1911. These were designed as models for others, and provided for the arbitration of all "justiciable" questions, not even excepting "vital interests" and "national honor." If there should be a dispute as to whether a particular case was covered by the treaty, the question was to be decided by a joint high commission of inquiry. This stipulation seemed to place a restriction upon the veto power of the Senate, although this body was privileged to concur in each arbitration agreement. The Senators sprang to arms, led by Henry Cabot Lodge, who had little sympathy with the "mushy philanthropists." Partisanship, wounded dignity, and jealousy of senatorial prerogative all entered into the picture.

President Taft, now thoroughly aroused, went before the country in a vigorous defense of his pacts. There can be little doubt that public opinion was strongly behind him. The Baltimore *Sun* was but one of the many newspapers to say that rejection of the agreements would be "an international misfortune." [33] Nevertheless, the Senate stubbornly settled down to the task of amending the treaties. It exempted from arbitration about every question of importance that any other nation would want to arbitrate, including state debts, the Monroe Doctrine, and Oriental immigration. Then, on March 7, 1912, it consented to ratification of what was left by a vote of 76 to 3.[34]

The treaties were so thoroughly mutilated that the President did not

[32] Griswold, *Far Eastern Policy of the United States*, p. 168.

[33] *Current Literature*, LI, 354 (Oct. 1911); also W. S. Holt, *Treaties Defeated by the Senate* (Baltimore, 1933), pp. 230–231.

[34] Secretary Knox probably erred in not deferring more to the Senate during the course of the negotiations. Jessup, *Elihu Root*, II, 271.

go through with ratification, remarking resignedly, "We shall have to begin all over again." He hoped, to use his own words, that "the Senators might change their minds, or that the people might change the Senate; instead of which they changed me."

So Taft's foreign policy ended on a note of futility. The canal tolls problem, the Nicaragua treaty, and the Mexican tangle were, as we shall see, all left on the doorstep of the Wilson administration. The arbitration treaties were amended to death; reciprocity was spurned; Dollar Diplomacy was at least nominally repudiated by President Wilson; the Manchurian proposal was rejected by Japan and Russia; and the Lodge corollary was passed in the face of Administration disapproval. The only solid major achievements in the field of foreign affairs to which Taft could point were the preservation of the seal herd and the final settlement of the North Atlantic fisheries controversy.

BIBLIOGRAPHICAL NOTE

The best sketch of the Taft-Knox policies is H. F. Wright, "Philander Chase Knox," in S. F. Bemis, ed., *The American Secretaries of State and their Diplomacy* (N.Y., 1929), IX, 303–357. H. F. Pringle's *The Life and Times of William Howard Taft* (2 vols., N.Y., 1939) is a definitive biography. DOLLAR DIPLOMACY: FAR EAST. The best account is A. W. Griswold, *The Far Eastern Policy of the United States* (N.Y., 1938), Ch. IV. Consult also the carefully documented work of J. G. Reid, *The Manchu Abdication and the Powers, 1908–1912* (Berkeley, Calif., 1935); also Herbert Croly's *Willard Straight* (N.Y., 1924). DOLLAR DIPLOMACY: LATIN AMERICA. See the very critical work of Scott Nearing and Joseph Freeman, *Dollar Diplomacy* (N.Y., 1925); also B. H. Williams, *Economic Foreign Policy of the United States* (N.Y., 1929); D. G. Munro, *The Five Republics of Central America* (N.Y., 1918); C. L. Jones, *The Caribbean Since 1900* (N.Y., 1936). SEALING CONVENTION. The fullest account, based on unpublished State Department records, is T. A. Bailey, "The North Pacific Sealing Convention of 1911," *Pacific Hist. Rev.*, IV (1935), 1–14. FISHERIES. See Robert Lansing, "The North Atlantic Coast Fisheries Arbitration," *Amer. Jour. of Internat. Law*, V (1911), 1–31; and the revealing account in P. C. Jessup, *Elihu Root* (N.Y., 1938), II, Ch. XXX. CANADIAN RECIPROCITY. The most recent and authoritative treatment is L. E. Ellis, *Reciprocity 1911* (New Haven, 1939). LODGE COROLLARY. The fullest analysis is T. A. Bailey, "The Lodge Corollary to the Monroe Doctrine," *Pol. Sci. Quar.*, XLVIII (1933), 220–239. ARBITRATION TREATIES. An excellent brief account is W. S. Holt, *Treaties Defeated by the Senate* (Baltimore, 1933), pp. 230–235. Further references: see footnotes of this chapter and Bemis and Griffin, *Guide*, pp. 494–498 (China); 531 ff. (Latin America); 453–458 (seals); 445–453 (fisheries); 460–465 (Canadian reciprocity); 620–632 (arbitration).

RECENT REFERENCES; NEW REFERENCES; 4TH ED. REFS. See Bibliographical Appendix, pp. 937–939.

CHAPTER XXXVI

Wilson and the New Diplomacy, 1913–1917

*"It is a very perilous thing to determine the foreign policy of a
nation in the terms of material interest."*

Woodrow Wilson, 1913.

"Grape Juice Diplomacy"

THE Republican dynasty, which had been in power uninterruptedly
since 1897, was broken in 1913, after Theodore Roosevelt had split the
party wide open in the election of 1912. The new Chief Executive,
Woodrow Wilson of New Jersey, a Democrat, was a relatively new
figure in politics. Three years earlier he had resigned from the presidency of Princeton University under fire; now, as if by a miracle, he
was President of the United States. Although this "professor in politics"
was well equipped to handle the pressing domestic problems, he had
given much less thought to foreign policy.[1] Yet, as fate would have it,
diplomatic difficulties were destined to overshadow all others during
much of his Administration.

William Jennings Bryan, like Seward in 1861, was the uncrowned
king of his party, and Wilson, though profoundly distrustful of
Bryan's intellectual vagaries, was forced to offer him the Secretaryship
of State.[2] The President probably felt, as Mr. Dooley expressed it,
that the silver-voiced orator would cause less trouble "in his bosom than
on his back." But in all fairness it must be said that Bryan proved to
be loyal, co-operative, and self-effacing. The most recent researches
indicate not only that Bryan was a competent Secretary of State, but
that he kept his head, particularly during the European crisis, when
his more highly esteemed colleagues were losing theirs.[3]

The appointment of Bryan, whose name had long been connected

---

[1] See Harley Notter, *The Origins of the Foreign Policy of Woodrow Wilson* (Baltimore, 1937). The author concludes (p. v) that "all the essential elements of thought
governing Woodrow Wilson's foreign policy were determined, and in several instances specific policies were formulated, before he took the oath of office. . . ."

[2] R. S. Baker, *Woodrow Wilson: Life and Letters* (Garden City, N.Y., 1931), III,
438–442.

[3] C. C. Tansill, *America Goes to War* (Boston, 1938), pp. 165–166.

with monetary inflation, aroused bitter criticism, particularly from Republicans. The atmosphere was not improved when the new Secretary, a lifelong teetotaler, announced that he would not serve alcoholic beverages, thus inaugurating an era of aridity which caused some of the diplomatic dignitaries to fortify themselves in advance—in some cases too well.[4] The opposition press indulged in loud laughter at the expense of "grape juice diplomacy."

The Republican newspapers were provoked to further criticism when it was learned that Bryan would be obliged to supplement his salary by continuing his Chautauqua lectures on peace, prohibition, and kindred subjects—"grape juice guff" and "peace piffle."[5] But the real storm broke when news leaked out of the new Secretary's unabashed spoilsmongering. Bryan had run for the presidency three times, and he now felt that he could discharge some of his political debts by parceling out diplomatic offices. In a communication to the American receiver general of Dominican customs he asked for information as to "what positions you have at your disposal with which to reward deserving Democrats?"[6] The publication of this indiscretion naturally elicited a pharisaical outburst from the "resolute Republicans."

The "Cooling Off" Treaties

In all diplomatic problems of major importance Wilson acted as his own Secretary of State. But Bryan was given a free rein in drawing up his much-discussed peace treaties, a task into which he threw himself with all the enthusiasm of an ardent pacifist. The thirty pacts that he negotiated during 1913 and 1914 were conciliation rather than arbitration treaties.[7] In general, they provided that every otherwise insoluble dispute, not even excepting questions of national honor, should be submitted to permanent commissions for investigation. There was to be no resort to arms until a recommendation was forthcoming, ordinarily within a year. The disputants could then accept or reject the findings. But by that time they presumably would have cooled off, and

[4] Mark Sullivan, *Our Times* (N.Y., 1933), V, 150.

[5] It was felt that the dignity of the government was lowered when published notices showed Bryan's address sandwiched between acts by Tyrolese yodlers and Neapolitan troubadours. One cartoon had Bryan being congratulated after a performance by the strong man: ". . . Old pal, youse got a swell act. Youse is killin' 'em dead out in front." *Literary Digest*, XLVII, 514 (Sept. 27, 1913).

[6] Baker, *Woodrow Wilson*, IV, 40 (Bryan to Vick, Aug. 20, 1913).

[7] Twenty-two of the thirty treaties finally became effective. On October 29, 1938, nineteen were still in force. Information provided by the Treaty Division, Department of State.

world opinion would have been marshaled on the side of peace. The Brooklyn *Eagle* saw in the plan a diplomatic adaptation of the juvenile adjuration, "when angry count fifty, when very angry count a hundred."

Bryan showed genuine skill in dealing with the somewhat refractory Senate. But the taint of cheap money, grape juice, and Chautauqua lectures caused the "wait-a-year" pacts to be greeted less favorably in the United States than they otherwise would have been. A large portion of the press believed that the treaties could do no harm and might do some good, an attitude which accounts for a certain amount of amused contempt.[8] A few newspapers thought the treaties positively vicious because they lacked teeth. It is improbable, however, that a stronger kind of pact would have met with Senatorial approval.

These efforts at peacemaking have been generally underrated, partly because of Bryan's connection with them and partly because the outbreak of the World War converted treaties into "scraps of paper." There can be little doubt that the existence of one of the pacts with Great Britain, together with the absence of one with Germany, had some bearing on the chain of events that brought the United States into the war on the side of the Allies.[9] It is also true that Secretary Bryan's work was reflected in the peace machinery set up at the close of the World War. To the end of his days Bryan regarded the "cooling off" pacts as his most notable contribution to the nation; and his official portrait in the Department of State shows him with a copy of one of them in his hand.

The Dollar Is Rebuffed

Among the half dozen or so vexatious diplomatic problems that confronted the new Administration, Latin America seemed to require first attention. On March 11, 1913, therefore, Wilson made public a strong statement of policy. After vigorously condemning disorder in Latin America, he struck out at Dollar Diplomacy by announcing that the Administration was not interested in supporting any "special group or interests." Instead of communicating his declaration to the em-

---

[8] The Memphis *Commercial-Appeal*, for example, gibed: "Secretary Bryan's completed arbitration treaties with Switzerland, Denmark, and Uruguay take a great load off our minds. The thought of war with them was terrible." *Literary Digest*, XLVIII, 96 (Jan. 17, 1914).

[9] M. E. Curti, "Bryan and World Peace," *Smith College Studies in History*, XVI, nos. 3-4 (1931), 160-164. A recent writer concludes that it would have been "impossible" for the United States to declare war in April, 1917, if Germany had adhered to a "cooling off" treaty. Tansill, *America Goes To War*, p. 442.

bassies through the conventional channels of the State Department, Wilson resorted to the irregular procedure of giving it directly to the newspapers. This hasty move, though suggestive of "shirt sleeves," appears to have met with generally favorable comment in the press. The friendly New York *World* rejoiced:

There is not a word of encouragement here for the big exploiters, not a word to hearten a murderous uprising, not a word to stir the greed of a dictator disguised as a deliverer, and not a word to expedite the sales of stocks and bonds in the United States by marauding corporations.[10]

A week later, on March 18, 1913, Wilson apparently dealt Dollar Diplomacy an even more decisive blow. A group of Wall Street bankers, who had been actively encouraged by the Taft administration, was preparing to participate in a $125,000,000 six-Power loan to the Chinese government. Already experiencing strong misgivings, the American financiers declared that they would have to have more than mere approval by the State Department; they would have to be asked by the Washington government to go ahead.[11] To this request Wilson provided the answer—also in the press. He declared that because the terms of the loan compromised the sovereignty of China and might possibly involve intervention on the part of the United States, American investors could expect no support from the Administration. The next day the bankers announced their withdrawal from the enterprise. Wall Street, in the language of its enemies, had received a "knockout."

It must be noted, however, that Wall Street had no great enthusiasm for the project, and was probably not greatly displeased by the turn of events. Nor was Wilson's action, strictly speaking, a reversal. His predecessor had reversed traditional American policy; Wilson was returning to the old course. Moreover, the new President was an idealist who had long distrusted powerful vested interests, and he doubtless derived satisfaction from rebuking them. Yet in doing so he did not even consult the experts in the State Department, but plunged ahead in a manner that suggested both precipitancy and amateurishness. His outburst of idealism did not meet with universal approbation, especially among diplomats and bureaucrats.[12] As the *Wall Street Journal*

[10] New York *World*, March 13, 1913, 10:3.

[11] A. W. Griswold, *The Far Eastern Policy of the United States* (N.Y., 1938), 172–173. The action of Wilson was not so hasty as is generally believed. He had advices from men in the field as to the inadvisability of participation. D. J. Gage, "Paul S. Reinsch and Sino-American Relations" (ms. doctoral dissertation, Stanford University, 1939), p. 20.

[12] Assistant Secretary of State Huntington Wilson, a holdover from the Taft administration, wrote a scorching letter of resignation. Baker, *Woodrow Wilson*, IV, 72.

caustically remarked, "Dollar diplomacy was at least better than none at all." Yet on the whole the country seems to have applauded Wilson's course, in part because of the current attack on trusts, and in part because of the popular prejudice against Dollar Diplomacy.

THE DOLLAR IS REVIVED

President Wilson, like another distinguished idealist, Thomas Jefferson, found it difficult to square his theories with stern realities. This was particularly true of Central America and the Caribbean.

In 1913 the expiring Taft administration had drawn up a treaty with Nicaragua which, in the form as ratified, gave the United States a renewable ninety-nine year lease of the Great and Little Corn Islands, the privilege for a like period of establishing a naval base on the Gulf of Fonseca, and, most important of all, an option in perpetuity on the canal route. For these privileges the United States was to pay $3,000,000, a sum which would enable the Nicaraguan government to meet its obligations to American bankers. The pact was another embarrassing legacy for Wilson and Bryan. Although they disliked Dollar Diplomacy, they could not ignore the advantages of the treaty, particularly the removal of a rival canal route from possible foreign control. So Wilson not only supported the proposed agreement, but endeavored to strengthen it by adding an article suggestive of the Platt Amendment. This unexpected development led the New York *Times* to remark that the new Administration was making the "dollar diplomacy" of Taft and Knox "more nearly resemble ten-cent diplomacy." But the Senate refused to accept the protectorate feature; and a pact, without the objectionable article, was finally approved in 1916. A number of Republicans voted for the new Bryan-Chamorro Treaty on the grounds that it was a logical continuation of Taft's Dollar Diplomacy.[13]

Nor did Wilson's embarrassments cease with the Nicaragua Treaty. It is an ironical fact that his Administration carried out more armed interventions in Latin America than that of any of its predecessors.[14] The first of the Caribbean republics to require attention was the Franco-African republic of Haiti. A kaleidoscopic procession of presidents had held office, most of them being elected for the term ending with the next revolution—provided they were not shot, poisoned, or blown up

[13] T. A. Bailey, "Interest in a Nicaragua Canal, 1903–1931," *Hispanic Amer. Hist. Rev.*, XVI (1936), 6. See the remainder of the article for the diplomatic controversy with the Central American states arising out of the treaty.

[14] C. E. Chapman, *Republican Hispanic America* (N.Y., 1937), p. 150.

in the meantime. Matters came to a head in 1915, when President Sam engineered a wholesale butchering of about one hundred and sixty imprisoned political foes. A frenzied mob dragged him from behind a dresser in the French legation and literally tore him limb from limb. The government in Washington found this situation intolerable, for it was feared that Germany, or some other Power, would step in and jeopardize the Panama life line. So American troops landed and restored order, finally forcing the Haitians to accept a treaty, in 1915, which made the republic a virtual protectorate of the United States.[15] The nature of the intervention is clearly indicated in a telegram sent by Admiral Caperton to the Secretary of the Navy: "Next Thursday . . . unless otherwise directed, I will permit Congress to elect a president." [16]

Many of the Haitians resented foreign control; and the American marines shot more than 2000 of them while pacifying the country. Although these drastic measures provoked much criticism among liberals in the United States, there can be no doubt that the American occupation brought order and unprecedented prosperity. But the professional revolutionists in Haiti, and the more ardent defenders of sovereignty, loudly cried that their republic was a "territory of the National City Bank" of New York.

Haiti's neighbor, the Dominican Republic, presented a parallel if somewhat less dramatic problem. Though this country had been blessed with material well-being since Roosevelt's customhouse intervention, political development had lagged. In 1914 the "insurrectionary habit" brought a United States warship, and in 1916 the marines. American naval officers bodily took over the government and established a dictatorship altogether foreign to the principles of the Declaration of Independence. It was even found necessary to dispose of some nonconformists. Roads, schools, improved sanitation, and prosperity followed the intervention, as they usually have under such conditions. But disappointed politicians and genuine patriots alike were unhappy.

Although intervention in Haiti and in the Dominican Republic was motivated by solicitude for the Panama Canal as well as for American

[15] The constitution of Haiti was written, it appears, by Franklin D. Roosevelt, then Assistant Secretary of the Navy. In a campaign speech (1920) he declared: "You know I have had something to do with the running of a couple of little republics. The facts are that I wrote Haiti's Constitution myself, and, if I do say it, I think it a pretty good Constitution." New York *Times*, Aug. 19, 1920, 15:3.

[16] *Foreign Relations*, *1915*, p. 431 (Aug. 7, 1915). For pressure by the State Department on Haiti to contract a loan in New York with which to liquidate certain French obligations, see B. H. Williams, *American Diplomacy* (N.Y., 1936), pp. 191–192.

life and property, a revival of interest in the Danish West Indies (Virgin Islands) was prompted almost solely by strategic considerations. Upon the outbreak of the World War in 1914 it was feared that the islands might fall into the hands of some great European Power, perhaps Germany, and be used as a base against the United States and the canal defenses.[17] On August 4, 1916, therefore, the State Department concluded a treaty for the purchase of the islands. The wartime value of the group was so great that the price was set at $25,000,000, as compared with the $7,500,000 that Denmark had been willing to accept in 1867. The acquisition of the archipelago further strengthened the position of the United States in the Caribbean.

CALIFORNIA VERSUS THE UNITED STATES

The Japanese problem on the Pacific Coast again became acute at the very outset of the Wilson administration. The Californians were particularly disturbed by the remarkable fecundity and acquisitiveness of the Japanese. Although the figures both as to population and land-holding cause such fears to appear ridiculous, alarmists with slide rules could prove that at the current rate of reproduction the Japanese would elbow all of the whites into the ocean within a century or so.

During the Roosevelt and Taft administrations the California legislature almost precipitated an international crisis when it considered legislation that was designed to debar the Japanese from owning land in the state. But vigorous protests from Washington postponed the evil day until Wilson came into power. The new President was handicapped at the outset, for the California legislature was predominantly Republican. It is now clear that the determination of the Californians to take drastic action against the Japanese was motivated in part by a desire to embarrass the Wilson administration.[18]

Wilson became genuinely alarmed by reports of giant protest meetings in Japan, and he sent earnest but ineffective telegraphic appeals to the California authorities, urging them to go slowly. This is another notable instance of the gap in federalism. California seemed bent on provoking a war which the other forty-seven states did not want but would have to fight—and the government in Washington was power-

[17] C. C. Tansill, *The Purchase of the Danish West Indies* (Baltimore, 1932), pp. 467 ff. Secretary Lansing went so far as to inform the Danish minister that if German control of the islands should seem imminent, the United States would have to seize them. A. K. Weinberg, *Manifest Destiny* (Baltimore, 1935), p. 402.

[18] T. A. Bailey, "California, Japan, and the Alien Land Legislation of 1913," *Pacific Hist. Rev.*, I (1932), 42.

less to intervene. The Hartford *Times* expressed a not uncommon Eastern view when it remarked, "Of the two it might be cheaper to go to war with California than with Japan." [19]

As a last resort Wilson sent Bryan to California, late in April, 1913, to plead with the governor and the legislature. Although the Secretary was unable to stop the passage of the alien land law, his mission did much to mollify feeling in Japan by demonstrating that the federal government was sympathetic.[20] The act, as finally passed by the California legislature, was so ingeniously worded as to debar Japanese from owning land without conveying a direct affront to Japan or violating the strict letter of the existing treaty obligations.

The Tokyo government deeply resented this thinly veiled discrimination against its people, and lodged several vigorous protests at Washington, one of which was couched in such strong terms that the State Department returned it to Ambassador Chinda to be toned down. The possibility of an armed conflict was seriously discussed in Wilson's Cabinet. But Bryan confided to the Secretary of Agriculture, "There will be no war. I have seen the Japanese Ambassador, and I am letting the old man down easy." [21] Thanks in large measure to the conciliatory attitude of the Washington government, the crisis was safely passed.

NATIONAL HONOR OR SELF-INTEREST?

Another troublesome offspring of the Taft administration lay on Wilson's doorstep. In 1912 Congress had passed an act providing for the operation of the Panama Canal, which was then nearing completion. The most significant provision was that which specifically exempted American coastwise shipping from paying any tolls, in spite of a plain stipulation in the Hay-Pauncefote Treaty that "all nations" observing the rules would be required to pay the same rates. The legalists argued that "all nations" meant "all other nations," and pro-

---

[19] Though sentiment on the Pacific Coast seems to have supported California, a poll conducted by the Japan Society of New York among leading newspapers found 207 condemning and only 25 supporting the state. New York *Times*, May 10, 1913, 1:6.

[20] Bailey, "California, Japan, and the Alien Land Legislation of 1913," *loc. cit.*, p. 56.

[21] D. F. Houston, *Eight Years with Wilson's Cabinet* (Garden City, N.Y., 1926), I, 67. On another occasion the ambassador asked Bryan if the reply of the United States to his protest would be final, and the Secretary answered, "There is nothing final between friends." Not long after this Bryan obtained some old swords from the War Department, had them beaten into miniature ploughshare paperweights, with the inscription, "Nothing is final between friends," and distributed them among a selected few. Stephen Gwynn, ed., *The Letters and Friendships of Sir Cecil Spring-Rice* (Boston, 1929), II, 274 n.

ceeded to spin out a lengthy case justifying America's position.[22] But with the rank and file of the people the assertion of the Progressive Republican platform of 1912 needed no legal support: "The Panama Canal, built and paid for by the American people, must be used primarily for their benefit."

The British were profoundly disturbed by what they regarded as an act of bad faith. They were also concerned over the possible loss to their commerce through discrimination. On November 14, 1912, the Foreign Office sent a strong protest to Washington, and suggested arbitration as a possible solution. In reply, Secretary Knox vigorously upheld the American view, and declined to consider arbitration until the canal had begun to operate and the British could claim actual damages to their shipping. Although Taft and Knox were both outstanding lawyers, and although the technicality of the law may have been on their side, liberals throughout the United States were disgusted. The New York *Nation* insisted that the canal act was "a greater disgrace to this country than would have been a naval defeat in the waters off Colón." The British, who remembered Cleveland's insistence upon arbitration in the Venezuela dispute, were thoroughly aroused. Walter Hines Page, whom Wilson had appointed as ambassador in London, reported:

And everywhere—in circles the most friendly to us, and the best informed—I receive commiseration because of the dishonorable attitude of our Government about the Panama Canal tolls. This, I confess, is hard to meet. We made a bargain—a solemn compact—and we have broken it. Whether it were a good bargain or a bad one, a silly one or a wise one; that's far from the point.[23]

The problem was extraordinarily embarrassing to Wilson. He had been elected on a platform which had declared in favor of the canal act—a twist to the lion's tail which had been extremely popular with the large Irish element in the Democratic party.[24] But after mature reflection he concluded that this was basically a question involving national honor, and that if reasonable doubts existed they should be resolved in favor of an honest course.

[22] Although four members of Taft's Cabinet thought discrimination proper, Root was opposed. He insisted that he knew the intent of the treaty, for he had participated with Hay in the discussions at the time it was negotiated. P. C. Jessup, *Elihu Root* (N.Y., 1938), II, 263–264, 266.

[23] B. J. Hendrick, *The Life and Letters of Walter H. Page* (Garden City, N.Y., 1922), I, 249 (Page to Wilson, Sept. 10, 1913).

[24] See Baker, *Woodrow Wilson*, IV, 396 ff.

First of all some pressing domestic legislation had to be disposed of. Then, on March 5, 1914, Wilson made one of his precedent-shattering personal appearances before Congress, and in a brief but dramatic message urged repeal of the discriminatory clause.

Whatever may be our own differences of opinion concerning this much debated measure, its meaning is not debated outside the United States. . . . We . . . are too big, too powerful, too self-respecting a Nation to interpret with too strained or refined a reading the words of our own promises just because we have power enough to give us leave to read them as we please.

Then he closed with these cryptic and much-debated words:

I ask this of you in support of the foreign policy of the administration. I shall not know how to deal with other matters of even greater delicacy and nearer consequence if you do not grant it to me in ungrudging measure.[25]

Wilson apparently wanted to make the United States a moral leader in the world; and these words suggested that he would be unable to do so without repeal.[26] Moreover, he was encountering difficulties in dealing with Mexico because the British were pursuing a policy counter to his. But Great Britain was more interested in the Panama Canal than in Mexican oil, and there appears to have been an informal understanding that if the tolls exemption was repealed the British would support America's policy in Mexico.[27]

The British press warmly praised Wilson's honest message to Congress. But in America the Anglophobes, aided and abetted by the Hearst press, emitted a loud outcry, and cartoons showed "the angular professor-president" cringing before the British throne. After a heated debate the House finally passed repeal by a comfortable margin; but the real battle took place in the Senate. The President was particularly embarrassed by the fact that a number of Democratic Senators (notably the Irish-supported O'Gorman of New York) opposed the Administration's cause, while a number of prominent Republicans favored

[25] *Cong. Record*, 63 Cong., 2 sess., p. 4313.

[26] Notter, *Origins of the Foreign Policy of Woodrow Wilson*, pp. 286-287.

[27] See Charles Seymour, *The Intimate Papers of Colonel House* (Boston, 1926), I, 202. The evidence as to the existence of this informal understanding, however, is not altogether satisfying. At the time, Wilson denied that the phrase "nearer consequence" had any particular significance. E. E. Robinson and V. J. West, *The Foreign Policy of Woodrow Wilson, 1913-1917* (N.Y., 1917), p. 29.

it. Finally, on June 11, 1914, amid oratorical fireworks and near fist fights, repeal passed the Senate, 50 to 35.

Wilson's insistence upon honorable conduct increased the prestige of the United States abroad, and removed the last major dispute in Anglo-American relations. With the World War about to break out, and the controversy with Great Britain over neutral rights again to become acute, the settlement of the canal tolls problem proved to be an achievement of primary importance.

HUMAN RIGHTS AND PROPERTY RIGHTS

The Mexican tangle, another holdover from Taft, was the most persistently vexatious non-European problem to confront Wilson. Since 1877, when Porfirio Díaz began his three-decade dictatorship, the normally troubled relations of the United States with Mexico had been comparatively good. Strong-arm rule had brought order—and order made the "Mexican cornucopia" safe for foreign concessionaires. In the scramble for natural resources, particularly the rich oil fields, the Americans were able to outdistance their closest competitors, the British.[28] By 1913 there were over 50,000 Americans in Mexico, and their investments totaled about one billion dollars, more than those of all of the other foreign nations combined.

One commentator has said that "Mexico was rich, but the Mexicans were poor." Despite order and outward evidences of prosperity, the masses were landless and poverty-stricken, reduced to a state of peonage. They finally found an able champion in Francisco Madero, an idealist and reformer, who, in May, 1911, succeeded in driving Díaz into exile. Revolutionary disturbances continued; and President Taft, under authority granted by Congress in March, 1912, placed an embargo on munitions for the rebels, while permitting such shipments to the government in Mexico City. The situation became more complicated when, in February, 1913, Victoriano Huerta deposed Madero. Several days later the latter was killed in cold blood under circumstances that pointed the finger of suspicion unwaveringly at Huerta.[29]

During these disturbances, which resulted in heavy losses to Amer-

---

[28] J. M. Callahan, *American Foreign Policy in Mexican Relations* (N.Y., 1932), pp. 516 ff.

[29] The United States ambassador in Mexico City, Henry Lane Wilson, adopted a most unfriendly attitude toward the idealistic Madero; made no effort to save him (he may have even abetted the conspirators); and he urged a prompt recognition of Huerta. See J. F. Rippy, *The United States and Mexico* (rev. ed., N.Y., 1931), pp. 345–346.

ican life and property, Taft pursued a consistent policy of nonintervention. His passive course elicited loud condemnation from many newspapers, including those of William Randolph Hearst, who had inherited immense landholdings in Mexico. And when Huerta came into power early in 1913, Taft forbore to recognize his regime or take any step that would embarrass President Wilson.

Woodrow Wilson was unwilling to be a party to saddling the bloody-handed Huerta on the Mexican masses, and steadfastly refused to recognize what he regarded as another Díaz. "My ideal," he declared, "is an orderly and righteous government in Mexico; but my passion is for the submerged eighty-five per cent of the people of that Republic who are now struggling toward liberty." [30] Wilson officially based his nonrecognition policy on the grounds that Huerta had come into office as the result of murder and that he did not truly represent the people. He summed up his views to a visiting Briton, "I am going to teach the South American republics to elect good men!" [31]

The President's attitude toward Mexico represented a sharp clash between idealism and legalism. From the days of Thomas Jefferson it had generally been the policy of the United States to recognize established governments, no matter under what circumstances or how often they came into power. A long list of powers applied this simple test to Mexico and accorded recognition. Among them was Great Britain, which saw in Huerta another "strong man" who would keep order and permit British concessionaires to exploit Mexican oil, a supply important to the British navy.

If Wilson had followed the path of least resistance, he would have closed his eyes to conditions in Mexico and recognized "government by murder." Such a course would have avoided a vast amount of criticism, such as that of the prominent journalist, George Harvey, who demanded: "What legal or moral right has a President of the United States to say who shall or shall not be President of Mexico?" [32] But Wilson, who was troubled by a Calvinistic conscience, could not get the struggling Mexican masses out of his mind. He also suspected that the British oil interests were backing the "unspeakable Huerta"; and he hated the abuses of the power of wealth in foreign as well as in domestic relations. Wilson therefore pursued a policy of nonrecognition and noninterference (which, under the circumstances, was really

[30] Interview with Samuel G. Blythe, *Saturday Evening Post*, May 23, 1914, p. 3.
[31] Baker, *Woodrow Wilson*, IV, 289. (Wilson to Sir William Tyrrell, Nov. 13, 1913.)
[32] *North American Review*, CXCVIII, 740 (Dec., 1913).

interference); and the State Department repeatedly warned Americans to leave Mexico.

The President further clarified his Latin American policy in general and his Mexican policy in particular in a memorable address at Mobile, Alabama, October 27, 1913. In ringing tones he asserted:

We dare not turn from the principle that morality and not expediency is the thing that must guide us and that we will never condone iniquity because it is most convenient to do so. . . . It is a very perilous thing to determine the foreign policy of a nation in the terms of material interest. It not only is unfair to those with whom you are dealing, but it is degrading as regards your own actions.

Then, for good measure, he threw in a striking pledge:

I want to take this occasion to say that the United States will never again seek one additional foot of territory by conquest. She will devote herself to showing that she knows how to make honorable and fruitful use of the territory she has. . . .[33]

This last statement was reassuring to the Latin Americans, who detected in it a self-denying application of the Monroe Doctrine.

"Wrathful Waiting"

What Wilson called his policy of "watchful waiting" took on a more aggressive character when, in November, 1913, he formally insisted upon the resignation of that "desperate brute," Huerta. In this demand he was supported by the British, who appear to have swung behind the Washington administration as a result of the "deal" on the tolls question. Then, in February, 1914, the United States lifted the arms embargo so as to permit the materials of war to reach Huerta's two leading opponents, Carranza and Villa.

The President was savagely criticized at home and abroad for thus prolonging anarchy in Mexico. A recognition of Huerta would presumably bring peace and order; and order, not the welfare of the Mexican masses, was the paramount consideration in the eyes of foreign investors. In Europe, Wilson's policy was regarded as "impractical" and "idealistic"; and one Berlin newspaper branded it as "colossal arrogance." The Kaiser reflected the spirit of the times when he queried, "morality [is] all right, but what about dividends?" [34]

[33] *Cong. Record*, 63 Cong., 1 sess., pp. 5846, 5845 in that order.
[34] Remark reported by Ambassador Gerard, in Berlin, to Secretary Bryan, Dec. 20, 1913. Baker, *Woodrow Wilson*, IV, 300.

In the United States, particularly among Republicans, there was a vociferous condemnation of "deadly drifting" and a demand for "robust representations." [35] Advocates of a "strong" policy insisted that Wilson's blood was lacking in red corpuscles. One critic wrote, "He's a damned vegetarian, I believe." The virile Theodore Roosevelt cried, "He kissed the blood stained hand that slapped his face."

American investors added their voices to the chorus of criticism. Every day of nonrecognition was costing tens of thousands of dollars, to say nothing of lives. Altogether, from 1913 to 1915 more than seventy Americans were slain in Mexico. Even Ambassador Page wrote from London of the necessity of intervening and shooting Mexicans until order could be restored— "shooting men into self-government" as he phrased it. But more dangerous was the increasingly strident demand in Congress for intervention. In the Senate a leading advocate of armed action was Senator Fall of New Mexico, mouthpiece of the oil interests. And in the House such men as Wingo of Arkansas were shouting, "I think those hearing me will live to see the Mexican border pushed to the Panama Canal." But Wilson, steeling himself against pressure from the "favored few," remarked to his secretary: "I have to pause and remind myself that I am President of the United States and not of a small group of Americans with vested interests in Mexico." [36]

EVENTUALLY!—WHY NOT NOW?

(Plaschke in the Louisville *Times*.)

Meanwhile Huerta, more stubborn than ever, continued to stand by his guns. He seemed to thrive on opposition, for the hostility of the "Colossus of the North" strengthened him with Mexican Yankeephobes. The long-expected explosion came at Tampico, April 9, 1914, where a boat of the United States navy, with colors plainly displayed, was engaged in loading supplies. The crew was arrested by a Mexican force and then marched through the streets for having allegedly vio-

[35] A dance step then popular was called the Wilson tango. It consisted of one step forward, two backwards, a side step, and then a moment of hesitation. Sullivan, *Our Times*, IV, 137.

[36] J. P. Tumulty, *Woodrow Wilson as I Know Him* (Garden City, N.Y., 1921), p. 146.

lated martial law. Shortly thereafter the Americans were released, and the commanding officer verbally expressed regret that the ignorance of a subordinate had caused the misunderstanding. But Admiral Mayo, commanding the American fleet, felt that there should be a more formal apology, and he precipitately and totally without authority delivered an ultimatum to the Mexican general in Tampico, to be complied with in twenty-four hours:

. . . I must require that you send me, by suitable members of your staff, formal disavowal of and apology for the act, together with your assurance that the officer responsible for it will receive severe punishment. Also that you publicly hoist the American flag in a prominent position on shore and salute it with twenty-one guns, which salute will be duly returned by this ship.[37]

The commanding Mexican officer expressed regret in writing, and Huerta announced that the Mexican government "deplores" the unfortunate incident. He added that disciplinary punishment had been meted out to the offending subordinate. But Huerta balked at saluting the flag without the guarantee of a gun-for-gun return salute, which the United States refused to give. There were many who felt that sufficient apology had already been forthcoming without insistence on this latter point.[38] Yet once Admiral Mayo's ultimatum was issued, even the pacifist Secretary Bryan was convinced that the dignity and honor of the nation demanded that it be supported.

Huerta proved to be infinitely resourceful in evasion and excuse-making. Meanwhile the war spirit in the United States rapidly rose. "I'd make them salute the flag," insisted Senator Chilton of West Virginia, "if we had to blow up the whole place." On April 20, 1914, Wilson went before Congress and in a solemn address asked for authority to intervene by force of arms in Mexico. He made it clear that the Tampico incident was but the culmination of a series of grievances, and that America's quarrel was with Huerta and his supporters, not with the Mexican people. After a two-day debate Congress gave its consent.

[37] *Foreign Relations, 1914*, p. 448. George Harvey and other critics of the Administration insisted that Germany's disregard of America's rights was largely inspired by Wilson's "spinelessness." W. F. Johnson, *George Harvey* (Boston, 1929), p. 243. In any event, Admiral Mayo took a strong stand at this time.

[38] Ex-Secretary of State Root did not think that the salute incident provided sufficient grounds for war. Jessup, *Elihu Root*, II, 260.

The End of Watchful Waiting

On April 21, 1914, the day after the House had voted to authorize intervention but the day before the Senate did so, the crisis came. A German merchantman was about to land a cargo of arms at Vera Cruz, arms which might be used by Huerta against the United States. At two thirty in the morning of April 21, Secretary Bryan and Secretary of the Navy Daniels telephoned the White House about this development. The President, aroused from a deep sleep, gave the necessary consent for armed intervention; and later that day American forces bombarded and captured Vera Cruz, with considerable loss of life. But the dogged Huerta stuck fast; and even Carranza, his chief opponent, protested against this invasion of Mexican sovereignty. Diplomatic relations were completely severed. War hysteria, the like of which had not been seen in the United States since 1898, swept the country. Wilson now found himself in an impossible situation: he could not risk the humiliation of withdrawal without atonement from Huerta; and a full-fledged war with Mexico, which seemed to be the only other alternative, would be costly, bloody, and entirely at variance with the policy to which he had steadfastly adhered.

At this critical juncture, the ABC powers (Argentina, Brazil, and Chile), fearful of the consequences of another Mexican War, most opportunely stepped forward with an offer of mediation. Wilson promptly and gratefully accepted this unexpected way out. His evident determination to redeem the Mobile pledge of nonaggression caused feeling in Latin America to rebound strongly, even hysterically, in favor of the United States.[39]

Late in May, 1914, representatives of the ABC Powers met with those of the United States and Mexico at Niagara Falls, Canada. After much discussion, a plan was agreed upon, on June 24; but it proved completely ineffectual because Carranza refused to accept it. The conference, however, enabled the United States to avoid war, and it relieved the suspicions of the rest of the world as to Yankee designs on a weak neighbor. Unable to resist Wilson's pressure further, Huerta went into voluntary exile in July, 1914. He was succeeded by Carranza, whom Wilson had reluctantly championed.[40] The sympathetic New York *Times* was enthusiastic: "The result of the Niagara Falls con-

[39] Baker, *Woodrow Wilson*, IV, 337.

[40] In the summer of 1913, Wilson appointed John Lind of Minnesota his personal representative in Mexico. Lind recommended support of Carranza. G. M. Stephenson, *John Lind of Minnesota* (Minneapolis, 1935), pp. 247 ff.

ference, so far as it has gone, is such a triumph for President Wilson's much-misunderstood policy as to astonish even the stanchest supporters of the President." [41]

AMERICAN BLOOD ON AMERICAN SOIL

The elimination of Huerta from the picture and the subsequent elevation of Carranza to the presidency by no means brought peace to troubled Mexico. Francisco Villa, a picturesque combination of bloodthirsty bandit and Robin Hood, raised the standard of revolt against Carranza, who now showed no great enthusiasm for the reforms to which he had previously paid lip service. The revolution of 1910 entered upon an even bloodier phase. In January, 1916, the followers of Villa showed their contempt for the "gringo" by massacring eighteen American citizens at Santa Ysabel in cold blood. The temper of the American people rose to the boiling point and a number of the more sober newspapers swung over to intervention.[42] On the floor of Congress the clamor for "cleaning up" Mexico rose to a crescendo. Representative Humphrey served notice:

When the shrieks and groans of murdered and tortured men, the sobs and cries of starving women and children in Cuba reached us the American people demanded that these atrocities should end, and when that demand was disregarded our answer was not "watchful waiting" . . . but the American people arose as one man, drove the yellow flag of Spain from the Western Hemisphere. . . . And the day is not far off when the people of this country, regardless of the attitude of the administration, will see that peace is brought to unhappy Mexico.[43]

Flesh and blood could endure no more when, on March 9, 1916, a band of *Villistas* sacked Columbus, New Mexico, leaving behind seventeen slain Americans. Senator Ashurst of Arizona cried for more "grape shot" and less "grape juice"; and the swashbuckling Senator Fall of New Mexico demanded the complete occupation of all Mexico by an army of half a million men. To chastise Villa and to end the border raids, Wilson ordered General Pershing with several thousand cavalry to pursue the bandit leader into Mexico and capture him dead or alive.

[41] New York *Times*, June 26, 1914, 12:1. The Catholics in the United States, who regarded Carranza as hostile to their faith, opposed Wilson's recognition of the new government, on October 19, 1915. Stephenson, *John Lind of Minnesota*, p. 238.

[42] Rippy, *The United States and Mexico*, pp. 345 *ff.*

[43] *Cong. Record*, 64 Cong., 1 sess., p. 1638 (Jan. 27, 1916).

Carranza rather grudgingly and ambiguously consented to a reciprocal agreement by which the invasion was permitted.

The Pershing punitive expedition penetrated deep into Mexico with astonishing celerity, and in spite of the difficulty of the task narrowly missed capturing Villa.[44] But as the fruitlessness of the search became more apparent, as the hostility of the *Carranzistas* to the pollution of Mexican soil became more ominous, and as the imminence of America's entrance into the World War became more apparent, Wilson withdrew the troops in February, 1917. They left behind a snarling Carranza, a defiant and unrepentant Villa, and a revolution that had yet to run its course.

Whatever may be said of Wilson's policy it is clear that he adhered consistently to the ideal of encouraging the Mexican masses to work out their own destiny. "We can afford," he told Congress, "to exercise the self-restraint of a really great nation which realizes its own strength and scorns to misuse it." [45]

BIBLIOGRAPHICAL NOTE

The most useful works for this period are Harley Notter, *The Origins of the Foreign Policy of Woodrow Wilson* (Baltimore, 1937), which discusses critically the diplomatic problems of the Administration; and the relevant chapters of R. S. Baker's *Woodrow Wilson: Life and Letters* (8 vols., Garden City, N.Y., and N.Y., 1927–1939), particularly vols. IV to VI. This is the sympathetic official biography. Older but still useful is E. E. Robinson and V. J. West, *The Foreign Policy of Woodrow Wilson* (N.Y., 1917). A brief sketch of Bryan by J. V. Fuller (then anonymous) appears in S. F. Bemis, ed., *The American Secretaries of State and their Diplomacy* (N.Y., 1929), X, 3–44. A significant study is M. E. Curti, "Bryan and World Peace," *Smith College Studies in History*, XVI, nos. 3–4 (1931). For Japanese-American relations see T. A. Bailey, "California, Japan, and the Alien Land Legislation of 1913," *Pacific Hist. Rev.*, I (1932), 36–59. On Caribbean problems consult Carl Kelsey, *The American Intervention in Haiti and the Dominican Republic* (Phila., 1922); and D. G. Munro, *The United States and the Caribbean Area* (Boston, 1934). For briefer accounts of the Mexican problem see J. F. Rippy, *The United States and Mexico* (rev. ed., N.Y. 1931), Chs. XX, XXI, and J. M. Callahan, *American Foreign Policy in Mexican Relations* (N.Y., 1932), Ch. XIV. Further references: see footnotes of this chapter and Bemis and Griffin, *Guide*, pp. 500–506 and Ch. XIX.

RECENT REFERENCES; NEW REFERENCES; 4TH ED. REFS. See Bibliographical Appendix, pp. 939–940.

[44] Frank Tompkins, *Chasing Villa* (Harrisburg, Pa., 1934), p. 87.
[45] *Cong. Record*, 63 Cong., 1 sess., p. 3803 (Aug. 27, 1913).

CHAPTER XXXVII

World War Neutrality: First Phase, 1914–1915

"It is difficult for people to think logically when their sympathies are aroused."

Woodrow Wilson, 1915.

UNNEUTRALITY IN THOUGHT

THE SHOT that felled the Archduke Francis Ferdinand at Serajevo, June 28, 1914, created only a flurry of excitement in the United States.[1] Americans had heard the cry of "wolf" too often to believe that the pack was loose at last. But when it finally became evident that Europe was being sucked into war, the first reaction of the United States was to keep out of the senseless conflict. "Peace-loving citizens of this country," declared the Chicago *Herald*, "will now rise up and tender a hearty vote of thanks to Columbus for having discovered America." [2] The Wabash *Plain Dealer* chimed in, "We never appreciated so keenly as now the foresight exercised by our forefathers in emigrating from Europe." The *Literary Digest* thus summed up newspaper reaction: "Our isolated position and freedom from entangling alliances inspire our press with the cheering assurance that we are in no peril of being drawn into the European quarrel." [3] America felt strong, smug, secure.

As one nation after another slipped into the abyss, President Wilson issued the routine proclamations of neutrality. But from the very outset it was clear that the American people would find it more than ordinarily difficult to avoid taking sides. This was a *world* war; and the United States, the historic asylum of the oppressed, contained a "menagerie of nationalities." However much orators might descant on the magic of the melting pot, millions of "hyphenated Americans" could not completely forget the land of their birth and cultural heritage—German-Americans, Irish-Americans, Jewish-Americans, and other "hyphenates." "America," wrote the British ambassador, "is no nation, just a collection of people who neutralize one another."

---

[1] C. C. Tansill, *America Goes to War* (Boston, 1938), p. 17.

[2] *Literary Digest*, XLIX, 260 (Aug. 15, 1914).

[3] *Ibid.*, p. 215 (Aug. 8, 1914).

In the United States feeling became exceedingly bitter between the pro-Ally sympathizers on the one hand and the pro-German sympathizers on the other. The caustic Briton, George Bernard Shaw, observed, "America, to judge by some of its papers, is mad with

PRINCIPAL EUROPEAN ELEMENTS IN U.S. AT THE OUTBREAK OF THE WORLD WAR *

WITH REFERENCE TO THEIR ORIGIN IN THE WARRING NATIONS

(Total population of Continental U.S.: 91,972,266)

Country of Origin	Foreign-born	Both parents foreign-born	One parent foreign-born; one U.S.	Total
Germany (Central Power)	2,501,181	3,911,847	1,869,590	8,282,618
Ireland (Allies)	1,352,155	2,141,577	1,010,628	4,504,360
England, Scotland & Wales (Allies)	1,219,968	852,610	1,158,474	3,231,052
Russia & Finland (Allies)	1,732,421	949,316	70,938	2,752,675
Austria & Hungary (Central Power)	1,670,524	900,129	131,133	2,701,786
Italy (Allies)	1,343,070	695,187	60,103	2,098,360
Total for all countries (including those not listed)	13,345,545	12,916,311	5,981,526	32,243,382

* These figures (1910 census) do not take into account the influence of foreign-born grandparents.

British patriotism, Polish nationality, and Belgian freedom." A rhymester for the New York *Sun* described a harrowing experience in a barber shop:

> The barber to the right of me was hoching for the Kaiser.
> The barber to the left of me was hacking for the Czar.
> A gentleman from Greece was shearing off my fleece,
> While very near a swart Italian stropped his scimitar.
> And when presently discussion, polyglot and fervid,
> On political conditions burst about my chair,
> I left the place unshaven—I hope I'm not a craven,
> But I sort of like to wear a head beneath my hair! [4]

President Wilson favored a strict neutrality. And when he foresaw that outbursts of sympathy for the belligerents would create

[4] Mark Sullivan, *Our Times* (N.Y., 1933), V, 140–141.

difficulties, he issued an appeal to the American people, August 18, 1914, urging them to be "impartial in thought as well as in action." But this was an admonition impossible of fulfillment. As one editor insisted, "Only persons mentally unsexed or paralyzed" could be neutral in thought—"moral eunuchs," as W. R. Thayer described them.

The great majority of Americans wanted no part of the war; but on the whole their sympathies lay on the side of Great Britain, France and the other Allies, and against Germany, Austria, and their allies (the Central Powers). Despite a century of Anglophobia and tail-twisting, the people of the United States, particularly the wealthy and well-educated groups, could not forget their Anglo-Saxon blood and cultural heritage. Moreover, relations with Great Britain had on the whole been friendly since the Venezuela blowup of 1895–1896; very friendly since the recent repeal of the canal tolls exemption. But important though these influences were, it is doubtful if America could have developed any great sentimental enthusiasm for the Allies if France had not been among them; and the United States seemingly owed her an unrepayable debt of gratitude. From the pen of Robert Underwood Johnson came:

> Forget us, God, if we forget
> The sacred sword of Lafayette! [5]

German-American relations, on the other hand, had not been particularly friendly since the eighties. And by 1914 the people of the United States had come to regard German militarism and navalism as an international menace. The ruthless invasion of Belgium, despite a solemn treaty obligation to respect her neutrality, merely confirmed the deepest American suspicions. Matters were made infinitely worse when the German chancellor blunderingly explained that the Belgian neutrality treaty was but a "scrap of paper." Americans deeply sympathized with "poor little Belgium" in her heroic but vain resistance, and they were outraged by the destruction of the priceless library at Louvain and the savage suppression of civilian resistance. The editor of *Life* declared:

[5] Quoted in E. B. White, *American Opinion of France* (N.Y., 1927), p. 278. The Chicago *Herald* (Apr. 16, 1915) commented on the large number of Americans who were enlisting under French colors, while avoiding those of Great Britain, Russia, or the Central Powers. See *ibid.*, pp. 276 ff. On the other hand, "to the average church-goer, the French seemed a trifle wicked." H. C. Peterson, *Propaganda for War* (Norman, Okla., 1939), p. 5.

For us the great, clear issue of this war is Belgium. If we see anything right at all in all this matter, Belgium is a martyr to civilization, sister to all who love liberty or law; assailed, polluted, trampled in the mire, heelmarked in her breast, tattered, homeless. . . . The great unconquerable fact of the great war is Belgium.[6]

But this did not mean that the American people wanted to get into the fight. Nor did it mean that they now loved Great Britain. Although the great majority of those who took sides favored the Allies, this feeling was probably more anti-German than pro-British.[7]

FACT PLUS PROPAGANDA

In recent years much has been written about British propaganda having seduced America into the war. There can be no doubt that there was much Allied propaganda; but there is considerable doubt as to its effect. It seems reasonably clear that American opinion was anti-German before the war began; it also seems clear that American opinion was outraged by the acts of Germany. Belgium was a fact; the *Lusitania* was a fact. And although British propaganda unquestionably embellished these facts, its effect would have been incomparably weaker without them.

British attempts to sway the mind of America were made through two major instruments. The first was censorship of all cables to the United States. American newsmen soon learned that if they wanted their stories to get through they had better write them as an Englishman would write them.[8] The net result was that the Americans came to view the war largely through Allied glasses.

The second British instrument was a well-developed propaganda organization in the United States. Understanding Anglo-Saxon psychology better than the Germans, and enjoying the advantage of a common language, the British were quiet, discreet, and effective. Their great success was to enlist a number of influential Americans—preachers, teachers, politicians, and journalists—to espouse the Allied cause,

[6] *Life*, LXV, 20 (Jan. 7, 1915).

[7] Of the 367 editors who replied to a *Literary Digest* poll, 20 favored the Germans, 105 the Allies, and 242 neutrality. XLIX, 939 (Nov. 14, 1914).

[8] W. G. Shepherd, *Confessions of a War Correspondent* (N.Y., 1917), p. 37. At one time a correspondent estimated that nearly three fourths of the dispatches "written by American correspondents in Central Europe were perishing under the shears of the British censors." Peterson, *Propaganda for War*, p. 14.

and these volunteer propagandists did much to persuade their countrymen that England was fighting their fight.[9] But the Germans, thrown on the defensive by the invasion of Belgium, began a desperate and clumsy courtship of American opinion. A self-appointed guardian of Germany's honor, one Julius Meyer, poured out his soul to a New York editor:

Down with England! Down with the boot-licking, kowtowing British hirelings in our press and in our Administration. . . . Up and at them! Enough of truckling to their good graces, enough of asking for fair play. . . . Up and at them! Up you Americans, who have not forgotten 1776! Up you Poles, Hungarians, Austrians, Czechs, Germans, Irish, Swiss, Scandinavians, up everybody, who stands for Old Glory first and all the time, for his fatherland next and the rest of the time. . . .[10]

The American people, while writing down German protestations as lies, firmly believed the tales of Hunnish diabolism which came out of Belgium, including such palpable inventions as the crucified Canadian, the corpse factory, and Belgian babies with their hands cut off.[11] On the other hand, the American people heard few atrocity stories about the Allies, of which there were inevitably some.

The facts of German aggression, together with various distortions and interpretations, had a profound effect on public opinion. Before long it became an article of faith with the man in the street that the Kaiser (known as "the Beast of Berlin") had wantonly provoked the war; that when he had won it he would come over with millions of spiked helmets and make short work of the United States and the Monroe Doctrine; [12] and that the Allies, including autocratic Russia, were fighting a purely defensive war to make the world "safe for democracy." The American people finally reached the point where they did not think that a man was a "one hundred per cent American" if he did not believe all these things.

Nor was the Wilson administration itself immune from Allied influence. Every member of the Cabinet, except one, had pro-Ally leanings. Secretary Bryan, who apparently was more genuinely neutral

---

[9] See *ibid.*, pp. 32–35; also J. D. Squires, *British Propaganda at Home and in the United States from 1914–1917* (Cambridge, Mass., 1935), pp. 16 ff.

[10] New York *Evening Post*, Jan. 15, 1915, 8:6. See also Carl Wittke, *German-Americans and the World War* (Columbus, Ohio, 1936), pp. 8 ff.; Peterson, *Propaganda for War*, p. 142.

[11] Arthur Ponsonby, *Falsehood in War-Time* (London, 1928), pp. 78 ff.

[12] This argument was strongly emphasized by the violently pro-Ally but still influential Theodore Roosevelt. Russell Buchanan, "Theodore Roosevelt and American Neutrality, 1914–1917," *Amer. Hist. Rev.*, XLIII (1938), 777, 779.

than the others, was regarded by his colleagues as pro-German. Wilson himself was of British ancestry, and a strong admirer of English culture.[13] He made a genuine effort to pursue a strictly neutral course, but as the war progressed he found his sympathies gravitating more and more to the side of the Allies, and occasionally in private he would betray himself. Once he burst out, "England is fighting our fight." [14]

INTERNATIONAL ANARCHY

It was no easy task for the United States government to keep out of war and at the same time maintain its rights. America was not only the wealthiest neutral state, but also the most important neutral carrier. And it was inevitable that her shipping would run afoul of belligerent restrictions, just as it had during the Napoleonic era.

The Powers had anticipated such difficulties, and in 1909 had drawn up the Declaration **of London, a document that was in** general a codification of existing international law. This, however, proved unacceptable to "big navy" Britain, and as a result was never ratified. When the World War broke out, the United States attempted to protect itself against capricious interpretations of international law by inviting the powers to accept the Declaration of London.[15] Germany and Austria, faced with a naval blockade, promptly expressed their willingness to do so. But the British, who were naturally unwilling to place trammels on their dominant sea power, proved to be the stumbling block. In the end the United States withdrew its proposal, and fell back upon the uncertain and ill-defined rules of the pre-1914 period.[16]

Two nations locked in armed combat usually make genuine efforts to avoid flagrant violations of international law. They are restrained

[13] Harley Notter, *The Origins of the Foreign Policy of Woodrow Wilson* (Baltimore, 1937), pp. 15–16, 29, 77–78.

[14] In December, 1915, the United States minister to Belgium saw Wilson in Washington, and the former said (if we may trust his recollection in 1924), " 'Mr. President . . . I ought to tell you that in my heart there is no such thing as neutrality. I am heart and soul for the Allies.' Wilson responded at once: 'So am I. No decent man, knowing the situation and Germany, could be anything else.' " Charles Seymour, *Intimate Papers of Colonel House* (Boston, 1926), II, 50. See also Peterson, *Propaganda for War*, pp. 10–11, 181.

[15] See R. W. Van Alstyne, "The Policy of the United States regarding the Declaration of London, at the Outbreak of the Great War," *Jour. of Mod. Hist.*, VII (1935), 435 ff. Colonel House, Wilson's personal adviser, acting in concert with the British ambassador, emasculated the efforts of the State Department.

[16] A recent writer concludes that "the handling of the first phase of the Anglo-American dispute can hardly be criticized too severely," and that the Americans "gave away a good legal case without any compensation." Alice M. Morrissey, *The American Defense of Neutral Rights, 1914–1917* (Cambridge, Mass., 1939), pp. 30, 199.

in large part by a desire to enlist the moral if not the physical support of the rest of the world, or at least not to alienate it. But during the years from 1914 to 1917 every great Power was involved except the United States. And the United States, though possessing a strong navy, had a contemptibly small army. So, in general, no nation scrupulously observed any rule of international law if it felt that there was more to be gained than lost by ignoring or modifying it.

In this war, as in other world wars, the rules were interpreted, modified, or rewritten by the dominant sea power. There was no higher law; there was no other arbiter. If Britain had punctiliously observed the strict letter of international law, she would have partially shackled her navy, and probably would have lost the war. She therefore proceeded to take liberties with the traditional rules, justifying her "exceptional measures" by the age-old argument that this conflict had brought about "new," "peculiar," or "unusual" conditions, and by invoking "reprisal," "retaliation," and "military necessity." All this was offensive to neutrals, as well as to the enemy; but it was probably what any other Power would have done in similar circumstances.

MODIFYING INTERNATIONAL LAW

One of America's earliest and most serious disputes with Britain arose over contraband. The mistress of the seas ultimately took the position that in this highly mechanized and nationalized conflict practically no important article (including foodstuffs) could fail to be of direct or indirect aid to the belligerent forces. Beginning with the Order in Council of August 20, 1914, the British arbitrarily redefined contraband, and intercepted American ships carrying proscribed items to the enemy. But Great Britain was careful not to add cotton to the list at first, because the South, which was suffering acutely from the depression of 1913–1914, might have forced the Wilson administration to take strong measures. Even so, the governor of Texas demanded, in November, 1914, that "American ironclads" be sent "to England's door" to enforce American rights. The Department of State was deluged with protests from all over the United States; but the ensuing representations were unavailing.

The British also took unprecedented liberties with the traditional right of visit and search.[17] From time immemorial it had been permis-

[17] German reservists were also seized on board American merchantmen in a manner reminiscent of pre-1812 impressment. See T. A. Bailey, "World War Analogues of the *Trent* Affair," *Amer. Hist. Rev.*, XXXVIII (1933), 286–290.

sible for a belligerent warship to visit a neutral merchantman and inspect it for evidence of contraband. If none was found, the ship was allowed to go on its way; otherwise it was sent to a prize court for adjudication. But the British, again alleging "exceptional" conditions, altered this practice. Modern ships, they insisted, were so large that it was impracticable to make a thorough examination without bringing the vessel to port, where it was even possible to X-ray bales of cotton. Besides, a cruiser engaged in searching a merchantman was a perfect target for a lurking submarine. So, frequently on the basis of mere suspicion, a neutral vessel was forced to change its course and tie up for months in a port. All this caused loss to American owners, and not infrequently operated to the advantage of British competitors. In May, 1915, the British-born Secretary of the Interior, Franklin K. Lane, exploded:

> There isn't a man in the Cabinet who has a drop of German blood in his veins, I guess. Two of us were born under the British flag. I have two cousins in the British army, and Mrs. Lane has three. . . . Yet each day that we meet we boil over somewhat, at the foolish manner in which England acts. Can it be that she is trying to take advantage of the war to hamper our trade . . . ? [18]

It is true that the British did pay for many of the cargoes that they confiscated; and as a rule the American shipper realized a good profit, though perhaps not so much as he would have made if he had not been interfered with. It is also true that many of the claims for damages that he brought against Great Britain were later found to be legally unsupportable.[19] But law or no law, the British would not relax their hold upon neutral commerce. They were fighting for their very lives; and to them American profits were a minor consideration.

Another grievance of the United States was the so-called British blockade. The generally accepted practice was to station a cordon of vessels just off the ports of the blockaded country. But Great Britain, again alleging the "exceptional" conditions of a war that involved submarines and long range guns, early decided that this would be hazard-

[18] Seymour, *House Papers*, I, 459 (Lane to House, May 5, 1915).

[19] By an executive agreement concluded May 19, 1927, the United States agreed reciprocally not to press any claims for damages on behalf of its citizens against Great Britain. Individual Americans might bring action in the British prize courts. This decision was apparently due in part to the fact that the United States had weakened its position by participating in the war on the side of Britain. See E. M. Borchard, "The Neutrality Claims against Great Britain," *Amer. Jour. of Internat. Law*, XXI (1927), 764–768.

ous and impracticable. Instead, His Majesty's warships were stationed on the high seas in such a way as to intercept neutral commerce going to Germany. The British not only invoked against the United States its own Civil War doctrine of continuous voyage, but they improved upon it and went so far as to stop American merchantmen sailing to neutral countries that were near enough to Germany to act as "conduit pipes." [20] There was much justification for such a course, since, to take only one example, American lard exports to Denmark increased from nothing to 22,000,000 pounds during the first few months of the war. Obviously, the great bulk of this was being transshipped to Germany. Great Britain finally adopted a system of rationing neutral countries accessible to Germany and forbade them to import substantially more than the prewar figure.

U.S. FOREIGN TRADE DURING THE WORLD WAR *

	Dollars	Index (1914=100)
A. To Allied Countries, England, France, Italy, Russia:		
1914	$ 824,860,237	100.0
1915	1,991,747,493	241.0
1916	3,214,480,547	389.7
B. Central Powers, Austria-Hungary, Germany:		
1914	169,289,775	100.0
1915	11,878,153	7.0
1916	1,159,653	0.68
C. Neutrals (Northern), Denmark, Holland, Norway, Sweden:		
1914	187,667,040	100.0
1915	330,100,646	175.8
1916	279,786,219	149.0

* Note the tremendous growth of Allied war trade; the almost complete cessation of commerce with the Central Powers; the shifting of some of that trade to the neutral "feeders"; and the curtailment of neutral commerce under British rationing.

The British took a momentous step in the direction of perfecting their blockade of Germany when, on November 3, 1914, they declared the North Sea a military area. Then they proceeded to mine it so thoroughly that no neutral dared sail through without first stop-

[20] Although the Americans used the doctrine of continuous voyage during their Civil War, they did not invoke it against noncontraband being shipped to a neutral country (Mexico) for overland transportation to the Confederacy. The British made this extension. Tansill, *America Goes to War*, pp. 142, 196.

ping at an English port for sailing directions. Since such instructions were not provided if the cargo was objectionable, all commerce passing through these waters was squeezed through the neck of the British bottle. This was so radical a departure from international usage as to constitute a serious grievance to neutrals.[21]

DIPLOMATIC DEMORALIZATION

It is not to be supposed, however, that the United States supinely consented to the wiping out of its trade with Germany. British restrictions hurt both American pockets and American pride. The Department of State sent a number of strongly worded protests to Great Britain, some of them masterly expositions of international law as of July, 1914.[22] The British countered, and most effectively, with delay— a synonym for their diplomacy during this period. Britain's policy was to take ample time in answering protests; to submerge the real issues in verbosity; to concede little or nothing; and to hope that the next passing sensation in America, or an offense at the hands of Germany, would blunt the edge of American resentment. The strategy was perfect; and, what is more, the United States played the British game. The longer the State Department deferred pushing matters to a showdown, the more perfect the British strangulation of Germany became, the more closely the United States was bound by economic ties to the Allies, and the greater the chance that the German submarines would drive the country to war. The British problem was later lucidly explained by Sir Edward Grey, then Foreign Secretary: "The Navy acted and the Foreign Office had to find the argument to support the action; it was anxious work. . . . British action preceded British argument; the risk was that action might follow American argument." [23]

[21] Morrissey, *American Defense of Neutral Rights*, p. 16.

[22] One day, when Ambassador Page was presenting a protest, his eye fell on the *Alabama* claims voucher in the sum of $15,500,000, which hung on the wall of the Foreign Office. Turning to Foreign Secretary Grey he jokingly said, "If you don't stop these seizures, Sir Edward, some day you'll have your entire room papered with things like that!" B. J. Hendrick, *The Life and Letters of Walter H. Page* (Garden City, N.Y., 1922), I, 391.

[23] Viscount Grey, *Twenty-Five Years, 1892–1916* (N.Y., 1925), II, 110. Vastly annoyed by the acquiescence of the Washington government, one German-American newspaper published a satirical British version of the "Star-Spangled Banner":

> "Then conquer we must, for the Yankee we trust
> To kindly forget we are ever unjust;
> And the star-spangled banner we earnestly crave
> May enable Britannia to still rule the wave."

Cincinnati *Volksblatt*, Feb. 13, 1915, quoted in Wittke, *German-Americans and the World War*, p. 69 n.

But why did the Washington government not enforce what it so stalwartly asserted were its rights? America had a powerful navy; and if she had seen fit to convoy her ships, the British in all probability would have had to yield to her demands. They simply could not afford to quarrel with their munitions depot—as Sir Edward Grey himself confessed in later years.[24]

There were several basic reasons why the United States failed to take advantage of its strong position. We have already noted that the Wilson administration sympathized with the Allies almost from the beginning. In addition, the President's most trusted adviser, Colonel Edward M. House, was strongly pro-Ally. The well-intentioned but inexperienced House, who held no official position but preferred to be a "power behind the throne," influenced a number of Wilson's most critical decisions, generally in the interests of the Allies.

The most important of the diplomats abroad was the American ambassador in London, Walter Hines Page, likewise totally inexperienced, who, with his literary background, soon became captivated by British society and culture. Before long he was thanking "Heaven I'm of their race and blood," and praising the English race as the one that had "guts." The British statesmen, particularly the charming Sir Edward Grey, easily led Page to believe that the Allies were fighting America's battle for democracy, and that the United States should join them. In this frame of mind Ambassador Page had the utmost contempt for the protests framed by the "library lawyers" in the State Department, and he either watered down his instructions or presented them in such a way that the British were not convinced of America's seriousness. Sir Edward Grey reminisced:

> Page came to see me at the Foreign Office one day and produced a long despatch from Washington contesting our claim to act as we were doing in stopping contraband going to neutral ports. "I am instructed," he said, "to read this despatch to you." He read, and I listened. He then said: "I have now read the despatch, but I do not agree with it; let us consider how it should be answered!"[25]

Thus, instead of representing the United States in England, Page represented the British cause to the government in Washington.[26]

---

[24] Grey, *Twenty-Five Years*, II, 107.

[25] *Ibid.*, II, 110.

[26] In 1915 the *Dacia*, a German ship transferred to the American flag, left the United States with a cargo of cotton for Germany. The British felt bound to intercept her, but feared American public opinion. The alarmed Page hastened to Sir Edward Grey and suggested, "Why not let the French fleet seize it and get some advertising?"

Perhaps more useful to the Allies was Robert Lansing, who was first Counselor of the State Department, and then Secretary of State (June, 1915, to February, 1920). He was a strong partisan of the Allies, and he not only drafted many of the protests to London but exercised strong influence on Wilson's judgment in a number of critical matters.[27] He also co-operated whole-heartedly with the British in their diplomatic methods. As he records in his *Memoirs:*

. . . I saw with apprehension the tide of resentment against Great Britain rising higher and higher in this country. . . . I did all that I could to prolong the disputes by preparing . . . long and detailed replies, and introducing technical and controversial matters in the hope that before the extended interchange of arguments came to an end something would happen to change the current of American public opinion or to make the American people perceive that German absolutism was a menace to their liberties and to democratic institutions everywhere.[28]

It is not surprising that, between Page and Lansing, the British did not become more disturbed by American protests.

NURSING THE ECONOMIC "WAR BABIES"

Another situation played into the hands of the British. Early in the war the House of Morgan asked the State Department if there would be any objection to making a private loan to the French government. In a memorable letter to the President, dated August 10, 1914, Secretary Bryan sagely observed that "money is the worst of all contrabands because it commands everything else." He further pointed out that the bankers would probably use their influence with the press to support the cause to which they had lent money, thus making neutrality more difficult.[29] Accordingly, on August 15, 1914, Bryan telegraphed to J. P. Morgan that loans to belligerents, though legal, were not consistent with the true spirit of neutrality.[30] The bankers, who had not regarded the French loan with great enthusiasm, decided not to go ahead without the blessing of the State Department.

Grey gratefully accepted the suggestion, and when a cruiser from the land of Lafayette stopped the *Dacia* the American people were only mildly aroused. Hendrick, *Page*, I, 395. Roosevelt made the same suggestion to the British ambassador in Washington. Buchanan, "Theodore Roosevelt and American Neutrality," *loc. cit.*, p. 789.

[27] Tansill, *America Goes to War*, p. 77, *et passim.*

[28] *War Memoirs of Robert Lansing* (Indianapolis, 1935), p. 112.

[29] Carlton Savage, *Policy of the United States toward Maritime Commerce in War* (Washington, 1936), II, 186–187.

[30] *Foreign Relations, 1914 Supplement*, p. 580.

The inexorable force of circumstances brought about a changed viewpoint in Washington. At the outbreak of the war the United States had been wallowing in a depression more serious than the panic of 1907; [31] but the phenomenal development of war trade ushered in an era of feverish prosperity. At first it was not necessary for the Allies to borrow money with which to make purchases in the United States; they could use the large American debits in Europe. But as the months slipped by these were rapidly exhausted. It soon became apparent that if loans or credits could not be obtained in the United States, the mushroom traffic in war supplies would abruptly cease, and the nation would be plunged back into the dreary depression. In short, the trade was perhaps as essential to the economic life of America as it was to the military life of the Allies.

Faced with this situation, the President reversed the State Department's original ruling, and in October, 1914, privately and orally informed certain interested bankers that the Administration would sanction the advancing of credits. In the same clandestine manner permission was later extended, in August, 1916, to lend money outright. Several of the most important loans handled by the New York bankers were floated by popular subscription, notably the $500,000,000 Anglo-French issue of 1915. The anti-British Hearst press and the pro-German element voiced violent opposition, while sandwich men paraded up and down Wall Street proclaiming, "Billions for King George." A total of 1567 individuals and concerns, located in the financial centers of the country, subscribed to the loan. When the United States finally entered the war, American private bankers had advanced approximately $2,300,000,000 to the Allies in cash and credit, and only $27,000,000 to Germany.[32] Speaking for the House of Morgan, Thomas W. Lamont later declared:

Those were the days when American citizens were being urged to remain neutral in action, in word, and even in thought. But our firm had never for one moment been neutral: we didn't know how to be. From the very start we did everything that we could to contribute to the cause of the Allies.[33]

It has frequently been alleged that the United States could have forced the Allies to respect its rights by instituting an embargo on

---

[31] Morrissey, *American Defense of Neutral Rights*, p. 6.

[32] R. W. Van Alstyne, "Private American Loans to the Allies, 1914–1916," *Pacific Hist. Rev.*, II (1933), 180, 189.

[33] Manchester *Guardian*, Jan. 27, 1920, p. 68.

war materials. Such a course was repeatedly proposed, particularly during the early stages of the war by the pro-German elements; [34] but it met with considerable apathy. As the weeks passed by, the American economic structure gradually became so inextricably interlaced with the cause of the Allies that public opinion would not have tolerated an embargo.[35]

BLOOD MONEY

During the first six months of the war the United States was involved in virtually no serious difficulties with Germany. It is an anomalous fact that these two nations were then contending with Great Britain for the freedom of the seas. But the mounting trade in war materials brought about a change. The Americans were not only shipping enormous quantities of munitions to the Allies with which to kill Germans, but were soon to advance the necessary money from their own pockets. The chief German propaganda newspaper in the United States cried: "We [Americans] prattle about humanity, while we manufacture poisoned shrapnel and picric acid for profit. Ten thousand German widows, ten thousand orphans, ten thousand graves bear the legend 'Made in America.' " [36]

The German and Austrian governments naturally lodged strong protests against the traffic in war materials. The State Department correctly replied that it was not unlawful for an individual or firm in a neutral country to sell military supplies to a belligerent; the Germans themselves had done so during previous wars. Furthermore, the Secretary of State added, an embargo on munitions would operate so definitely to the advantage of the Germans, who were much better supplied with munitions factories than their enemies, as to constitute an unneutral act. The United States had no objection to selling arms and ammunition to Germany; but if she could not import them be-

---

[34] C. J. Child, "German-American Attempts to Prevent the Exportation of Munitions of War, 1914–1915," *Miss. Valley Hist. Rev.*, XXV (1938), 351–368.

[35] Colonel House declared (July 22, 1915) that "our whole industrial and agricultural machinery would cry out against it [an embargo]." The then German ambassador testified in 1919: ". . . American commerce was so completely tied up with the interests of the Entente that it was impossible for Wilson to disturb these commercial relations without calling forth such a storm of protest on the part of the public that he would not be able to carry out his intention." *Official German Documents Relating to the World War* (N.Y., 1923), I, 234. A *Literary Digest* poll published as early as January, 1915, indicated that even then public opinion, especially in the industrial centers, opposed an embargo. *Literary Digest*, L, 225–226 (Feb. 6, 1915).

[36] *The Fatherland*, June 9, 1915, 5:1; see also Tansill, *America Goes to War*, pp. 60–62.

624 A DIPLOMATIC HISTORY OF THE AMERICAN PEOPLE

cause of the British navy, that was one of the misfortunes of war. In short, an embargo on munitions would favor Germany; the absence of one would favor the Allies. So the United States followed the profitable path of least resistance.

It is undeniable, however, that the Washington government had a perfect legal right to embargo military supplies—just as a number of the other neutrals did for the purposes of conservation.[37] But this could be done only by act of Congress; and by the time the American people came seriously to grips with the problem, the traffic had assumed such proportions as to be able to defy its enemies. The government therefore continued to pursue a policy that violated the true spirit though not the strict letter of neutrality; bound the nation even tighter to the wheels of the Allied economic chariot; and so inflamed the German mind as to provide a partial justification—to the Germans at least—for unrestricted submarine warfare.

THE PERISCOPE EMERGES

Relations with Germany entered upon a new phase, on February 4, 1915, when the German government announced that it would establish a war area around the British Isles and attempt to destroy all enemy ships found within that zone. The official announcement declared that this drastic step had been made necessary as a result of Allied attempts to starve out Germany by illegal practices, and that these practices had been acquiesced in by the neutral Powers (including the United States).

This startling declaration brought inescapably to the fore the problem of using the submarine as a commerce destroyer. It had long been an established rule of international law that no belligerent warship should destroy an enemy merchantman without first stopping it, ascertaining its identity, and making adequate provision for the safety of passengers and crew. This practice had grown up during the days of the sailing ship, when no merchantman dared to engage in battle with a well-armed warship. But the submarine was fragile; and a single shot or a well-directed prow could easily send it to the bottom. And since many British merchantmen were armed, the Germans insisted that it would be foolhardy to give the conventional warning.[38]

[37] Spain, Italy, Denmark, Sweden, Norway and the Netherlands. *Ibid.*, p. 57.

[38] It has been rather dubiously held that if the United States had forbidden British armed merchantmen to enter its ports (as the Dutch did), these ships would have had to discard their armament, and the U-boat commanders might have been more willing to warn them before firing. *Ibid.*, pp. 410 ff. For an account of how

Great Britain, as we have seen, repeatedly took liberties with international law because of the "peculiar" nature of the conflict. But when the Germans argued that because of the "unusual" conditions of this war they too were justified in departing from the rules, they were

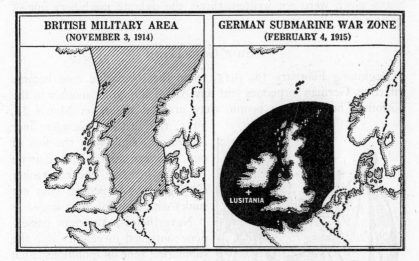

met with the Allied argument that torpedoing vessels without warning was so inhumane as to be unjustifiable. The Germans replied that the slow starvation of a vast civilian population by means of an illegal blockade was far more inhumane than sinking passenger ships without warning.[39]

The published German announcement of the war area pointed out that neutrals on board enemy merchantmen, or even neutral ships themselves, might incidentally be destroyed. On February 10, 1915, the State Department strongly protested against these "unprecedented" methods, and solemnly declared that if American lives or vessels were lost as a result of them the German government would be held to "strict accountability." Diplomatic language could hardly be any stronger. Yet when in November, 1914, the British had proclaimed the North Sea a military area—a liberty with the freedom of the seas comparable with the German war zone—not a word of protest

Colonel House blocked a promising move on the part of the State Department, in February, 1916, to debar armed merchantmen from American ports, see *ibid.*, 427-429.

[39] The then German ambassador to the United States later wrote, "In any case, the melancholy fact remains that the blockade killed more women and children than the U-Boat war." *Memoirs of Count Bernstorff* (trans. from German, N.Y., 1936), p. 129.

was lodged, although more than two years later Washington formally reserved its rights. As Bryan later observed: ". . . I submit the thought that the administration was lacking in neutrality—not in commission, but in omission; not the notes which were written, but the notes which were not written, threw the delicate machinery out of balance. . . ." [40]

A Ship Goes Down

Beginning February 18, 1915, when the submarine zone became effective, German torpedoes sent one Allied ship after another to the bottom. The American people were aroused when, on March 28, 1915, the British passenger liner *Falaba* was sunk with the loss of one American citizen; and again on May 1, when the American tanker *Gulflight* was torpedoed (but not sunk) with a loss of three lives.

"BUT WHY DID YOU KILL US?"

Children of the *Lusitania* condemn the Kaiser. (From the New York *World*.)

Nevertheless, American passengers continued to venture into the submarine zone on munitions-laden British liners. Secretary Bryan repeatedly urged the President to take steps to stop this practice, lest some tragedy occur; but Wilson steadfastly upheld the undoubted right of Americans to travel on belligerent merchantmen. The German representatives in the United States shared Bryan's fear (one of them said "there will be hell to pay"), and they took the extraordinary step of publishing an advertisement in the New York newspapers, May 1, 1915, warning Americans that they sailed on Allied vessels at their own risk.

Later that same day 197 Americans, undeterred by the German notice and by the daily loss of life in the submarine zone, sailed from New York on an unarmed British liner, the *Lusitania*. On May 7, 1915, when off the Irish coast, the vessel chanced to meet a German submarine, which, without any warning, launched a fatal torpedo. [41]

[40] W. J. Bryan and M. B. Bryan, *The Memoirs of William Jennings Bryan* (Chicago, 1925), p. 404.

[41] T. A. Bailey, "German Documents relating to the 'Lusitania,'" *Jour. of Mod. Hist.*, VIII (1936), 320–321, 334.

The ship sank in eighteen minutes with a loss of 1198 persons, 128 of whom were United States citizens.

It is undeniable that the *Lusitania* was carrying 4200 cases of rifle cartridges, as well as other contraband; but the nature of the cargo had no legal bearing on the old rule that an enemy merchantman must be warned before destroyed. German apologists and some legalists have proved to their own satisfaction that the sinking was justified on technical grounds. But whatever the legal or ethical arguments, there can be no doubt that the terrible inhumanity of the act—the indiscriminate killing of women, children, and babes in arms—turned world opinion against Germany.[42]

For perhaps the first time the war was really brought home to the American people. The press rang with denunciation of what it regarded as "mass murder." The New York *Times* insisted upon a demand that "the Germans shall no longer make war like savages drunk with blood." The New York *Nation* voiced its indignation:

> It is a deed for which a Hun would blush, a Turk be ashamed, and a Barbary pirate apologize. To speak of technicalities and the rules of war, in the face of such wholesale murder on the high seas, is a waste of time. The law of nations and the law of God have been alike trampled upon. . . . The torpedo that sank the *Lusitania* also sank Germany in the opinion of mankind. . . . It is at once a crime and a monumental folly. . . . She has affronted the moral sense of the world and sacrificed her standing among the nations.[43]

A prominent clergyman declared, "It is a colossal sin against God and it is premeditated murder," while the well-known evangelist, Billy Sunday, cried, "Damnable! Damnable! Absolutely hellish!"[44]

On May 12, 1915, just five days after the *Lusitania* tragedy, the British made public their Bryce Report on alleged German atrocities in Belgium. The document was designed for propaganda purposes, and the horrible evidence it presented seems flimsy today. But America,

---

[42] T. A. Bailey, "The Sinking of the Lusitania," *Amer. Hist. Rev.*, XLI (1935), 73. Recent commentators to the contrary, the present writer stands on his original statement (*ibid.*, p. 71) that no credible evidence has been forthcoming to indict the British government of having deliberately exposed the ship. It is true that on the morning the vessel sank, King George said to Colonel House, "Suppose they [the Germans] should sink the *Lusitania*. . . ." This does not mean, however, that the King was betraying a secret of state, for the warning published six days before was a matter of common knowledge in England.

[43] New York *Nation*, C, 527, 528 (May 13, 1915).

[44] Russell Buchanan, "European Propaganda and American Public Opinion, 1914–1917" (ms. doctoral dissertation, Stanford University, 1935), pp. 264 ff.

stunned by the *Lusitania* holocaust and reposing great confidence in the beloved Lord Bryce (author of *The American Commonwealth*), found it easy to believe the worst about Germany.[45] The New York *World* expressed a common thought when it declared that a government that would murder 1198 innocent noncombatants "would shrink at nothing done in Belgium."

"Too Proud to Fight"

Stirred though they were, the American people showed a remarkable willingness to suspend judgment. In fact, very few newspapers advocated hostilities with Germany.[46] There was, however, some little talk of war in the industrial East, which had become bound to the Allied cause by the golden chains of trade. But the Middle West, the stronghold of German-American influence, and the far-away West, seemed bent on maintaining peace.[47] In brief, American opinion demanded strong words but shrank from deeds. General Leonard Wood noted in his diary, "Rotten spirit in the *Lusitania* matter. Yellow spirit everywhere in spots."

Wilson was profoundly shocked by the tragedy, but he steeled himself against letting the cries of women and children draw his attention from the legal aspects of the problem. He was, moreover, too careful a student of American history to repeat Madison's mistake of leading a disunited country into war. Three days after the *Lusitania* disaster, the President addressed a large gathering in Philadelphia. Envisaging America's great moral mission, and emphasizing an ideal that had guided him during the Mexican difficulties, he asserted: "There is such a thing as a man being too proud to fight. There is such a thing as a nation being so right that it does not need to convince others by force that it is right."[48]

---

[45] Peterson, *Propaganda for War*, p. 58. The Bryce Report was rushed to completion so that the British could take advantage of the inflamed state of mind in America.

[46] British propaganda agents found that fewer than six editors out of a thousand wanted war at the time of the *Lusitania* tragedy. For the attitude of the Middle West and West see *ibid.*, pp. 163, 170, 175.

[47] Secretary of Agriculture Houston, then in California, found the people much more interested in citrus fruits and road improvements than in the *Lusitania*. D. F. Houston, *Eight Years with Wilson's Cabinet* (Garden City, N.Y., 1926), I, 132. In June, 1915, Bryan congratulated the inhabitants of Lincoln, Nebraska, on living thirty-six hours from New York. He said that the Allegheny Mountains were the salvation of the rest of the country because "they serve as a dike to keep the prejudice, the venom, the insolence, and the ignorance of the New York press from inundating the Mississippi Valley." Bryan, *Memoirs*, p. 425.

[48] New York *Times*, May 11, 1915, 1:8. For an analysis of Wilson's intended mean-

The much-misunderstood phrase, "too proud to fight," was quickly wrenched from its context and used tellingly against Wilson by his enemies. Theodore Roosevelt inveighed against "Professor Wilson," "that Byzantine logothete," who was supported by all the "flubdubs," "mollycoddles," and "flapdoodle pacifists." The Allies were bitterly disappointed. They had hoped that the United States would join the bath of blood and help them fight their fight.

The first American note to Germany regarding the *Lusitania*, dated May 13, 1915, vigorously upheld the "indisputable" right of American citizens to sail the high seas, and demanded disavowal of the act and reparation for the damage done. In reply, the German Foreign Office adopted a strong tone. It argued at length that the *Lusitania*, because of its cargo of munitions and because of other circumstances, was not "an ordinary unarmed merchant vessel." Though regretting the loss of American lives, the Foreign Office asserted that the destruction of the liner was an act of "just self-defense." The United States ambassador to Germany reported pessimistically: "I am afraid that we are in for grave consequences. It is the German hope to keep the *Lusitania* matter 'jollied along' until the American people get excited about baseball or a new scandal and forget. Meantime the hate of America grows daily." [49]

The second *Lusitania* note, that of June 9, 1915, was so resolute in tone as to alarm Bryan, who feared that it would bring war. When he found that he was unable to make his views prevail, he resigned. His departure at this critical time, though presumably motivated by conscience, created the unfortunate impression that the government was badly divided on the *Lusitania* issue, and consequently weakened Wilson's hand. An avalanche of abuse descended upon Bryan, the New York *World* insisting that his action was "unspeakable treachery not only to the President but to the nation." [50]

Further diplomatic interchanges with Germany failed to settle the *Lusitania* matter, and American interest began to flag. The Columbia (South Carolina) *State* paraphrased John Paul Jones, "We have not yet begun to write." And the bellicose Roosevelt muttered something about Wilson's last note having been "No. 11,765, Series B" on the

---

ing see Notter, *Origins of the Foreign Policy of Woodrow Wilson*, pp. 404–405. O. G. Villard, in his *Fighting Years* (N.Y., 1939), pp. 257–258, declares that he gave the phrase to Wilson's secretary, who in turn passed it on to the President.

[49] Seymour, *House Papers*, I, 454–455 (Gerard to House, June 1, 1915).

[50] The Louisville *Courier-Journal* referred to Bryan (June 12, 1915) in these words: "Men have been shot and beheaded, even hanged, drawn and quartered for treason less serious!" Quoted in Villard, *Fighting Years*, p. 276.

subject. Not until February, 1916, did Germany agree to assume liability for the loss of American lives and to pay a suitable indemnity. This, however, was not regarded as satisfactory by the Washington government; and the dispute was still unsettled when the United States went to war.

THE ARABIC CRISIS

The German government recognized the danger of provoking America further, and on June 6, 1915, issued an order requiring submarine commanders to spare large passenger liners, even those of the enemy. This safeguard worked reasonably well until August 19, 1915, when the commander of a German submarine, in violation of his instructions, sank the British passenger ship, *Arabic*, with a loss of two American citizens. Secretary Lansing seriously considered the severance of diplomatic relations, but feared that the country would not sustain the government. Even so, the German ambassador in Washington, Count Bernstorff, was alarmed by the inflamed state of public sentiment; and on September 1, 1915, he gave the following reassuring statement to the State Department: "Liners will not be sunk by our submarines without warning and without safety of the lives of noncombatants, provided that the liners do not try to escape or offer resistance." [51] Bernstorff was not authorized to make public these instructions; and their publication, though quieting to American public opinion, drew a reprimand from Berlin.[52]

The German government responded to the vigorous representations of the United States when it announced, October 5, 1915, that the orders issued to the submarine commanders "have been made so stringent that a recurrence of incidents similar to the *Arabic* case is considered out of the question." Regret was also expressed that American lives should have been lost on the *Arabic*, and assurances were given that an indemnity would be paid.[53]

The outcome of the *Arabic* case was a triumph for Wilson's methods. Chief Justice White acclaimed it as "the greatest victory for American diplomacy in a generation." Even Theodore Roosevelt was forced to concede that the result was "most gratifying"; while a feeling of relief swept over the United States. Wilson himself was pleased,

[51] *War Memoirs of Lansing*, p. 48.

[52] Bernstorff was twice reprimanded during this crisis for exceeding his instructions; but his vigorous methods undoubtedly contributed to an amicable settlement. Tansill. *America Goes to War*, pp. 359–376.

[53] *Foreign Relations, 1915 Supp.*, p. 560 (Bernstorff to Lansing, Oct. 5, 1915).

remarking to Colonel House: "The country is undoubtedly back of me in the whole matter, and I feel myself under bonds to it to show patience to the utmost. My chief puzzle is to determine where patience ceases to be a virtue." [54]

War might yet be avoided if the submarine could be kept leashed.

BIBLIOGRAPHICAL NOTE.

The most critical work on the subject is C. C. Tansill's detailed but isolationist *America Goes to War* (Boston, 1938). Briefer and more conservative in judgment is Charles Seymour, *American Diplomacy during the World War* (Baltimore, 1934). Harley Notter has a critical analysis of the problem in *The Origins of the Foreign Policy of Woodrow Wilson* (Baltimore, 1937). R. S. Baker's *Woodrow Wilson: Life and Letters*, vols. V and VI (Garden City, N.Y., 1935, 1937), contains valuable material presented by Wilson's sympathetic official biographer. Walter Millis, *Road to War: America, 1914–1917* (Boston, 1935), is a brilliantly written, but not altogether sound, journalistic account, which does something with public opinion and leans heavily on the documented work of C. H. Grattan, *Why We Fought* (N.Y., 1929), a pioneer effort of the "disillusionist" school. F. L. Paxson, *American Democracy and the World War: Pre-War Years, 1913–1917* (Boston, 1936), weaves together both domestic and foreign affairs. The problems of international law are fully presented in Alice M. Morrissey, *The American Defense of Neutral Rights, 1914–1917* (Cambridge, Mass., 1939). Edwin Borchard and W. P. Lage, in their *Neutrality for the United States* (New Haven, 1937), argue with much force that unneutrality brought the nation into war. The *War Memoirs of Robert Lansing* (Indianapolis, 1935) is a valuable record left by a leading participant. On propaganda and public opinion two works are significant: H. C. Peterson, *Propaganda for War* (Norman, Okla., 1939), which is the fullest treatment of British propaganda in the United States; and Carl Wittke, *German-Americans and the World War* (Columbus, Ohio, 1936). Two articles may be noted: J. V. Fuller, "The Genesis of the Munitions Traffic," *Jour. of Mod. Hist.*, VI (1934), 280–293; and T. A. Bailey, "The Sinking of the Lusitania," *Amer. Hist. Rev.*, XLI (1935), 54–73. Further references: see footnotes of this chapter, note at the end of next chapter, and Bemis and Griffin, *Guide*, pp. 655–672.

RECENT REFERENCES. The best book on the subject, though not directly relevant to the United States, is J. M. Read, *Atrocity Propaganda, 1914–1919* (New Haven, 1941). An able discussion of a famous case, involving the seizure by the British of American food shipments to Germany, is J. C. Crighton, *"The Wilhelmina:* An Adventure in the Assertion and Exercise of American Trading Rights during the World War," *Amer. Jour. of Internat. Law*, XXXIV (1940), 74–88.

NEW REFERENCES. See Bibliographical Appendix, p. 940.

4TH ED. REFS. See Bibliographical Appendix, p. 941.

[54] Charles Seymour, *American Diplomacy during the World War* (Baltimore, 1934) pp. 103–104 (Sept. 20, 1915).

CHAPTER XXXVIII

World War Neutrality: Second Phase, 1915–1917

"If there is an alternative [to war], for God's sake, let's take it!"

President Wilson, April, 1917.

SPIES AND RUMORS OF SPIES

DURING the seven months after the sinking of the *Arabic*, the German submarines refrained from killing American citizens. But a vast amount of suspicion and ill feeling was created in the United States by the alleged machinations of German secret agents, particularly by their attempts to sabotage the munitions trade. The Allies, of course, did not become involved in such objectionable activity because they had every reason to encourage the traffic. The most startling revelations were made when an American secret-service operative purloined a brief case from a German espionage agent, Dr. Heinrich Albert, who absent-mindedly let it out of his sight for an instant in a New York streetcar. Secretary of the Treasury McAdoo turned over some of the documents to the New York *World;* and their publication, on August 15, 1915, created a sensation out of proportion to their significance.[1]

Hardly less dramatic was the downfall of the Austrian ambassador to the United States, Dr. Constantin Dumba. Some of his papers relating to the fomenting of strikes in American munitions factories fell into the hands of the British, who revealed them to Ambassador Page. On September 8, 1915, Secretary Lansing requested Dumba's recall, and the hapless diplomat, whose name suggested the current slang for stupidity, was jeered out of the country. The Boston *Post* gibed:

> O Constantin Theodor Dumba,
> You've roused Uncle Sam from his slumba:
> That letter you wrote,
> Got the old fellow's goat—
> Now his path you'll no longer encumba.[2]

Evidence also fell into the hands of the State Department proving that Captain von Papen and Captain Boy-Ed, German attachés sta-

[1] C. C. Tansill, *America Goes to War* (Boston, 1938), p. 357.
[2] Boston *Post*, Sept. 23, 1915, 12:3.

tioned in the United States, were implicated in plots. Adding insult to injury, von Papen had written to his wife, "I always say to these idiotic Yankees that they should shut their mouths. . . ." [3] On December 1, 1915, Secretary Lansing requested the withdrawal of these two officials.

These were but the most conspicuous figures among those involved in objectionable activity in behalf of Germany and Austria. Others, less well known, were accused of bombing American ships and factories, and engaging in less serious forms of obstruction. Although many of the alleged German plots were figments of fevered imaginations,[4] the "witch-hunting" hysteria that swept the country deepened distrust of Germany, and further prejudiced the American mind against the Central Powers.

A PLEDGE THAT WAS NOT A PLEDGE

Early in 1916 Congress threatened to get out of hand and destroy the President's leadership. There was a strong fear on Capitol Hill that Wilson was determined to plunge the country into war if Americans were killed on armed belligerent merchantmen; [5] and many Congressmen threw their support behind two resolutions designed to prohibit American travel on belligerent ships passing through the war zone. According to the testimony of the Speaker, the House at one time was prepared to approve the McLemore resolution by a two to one vote. But Wilson, resenting this challenge to his authority, sent a strong letter to the chairman of the Senate Committee on Foreign Relations:

For my own part, I cannot consent to any abridgement of the rights of American citizens in any respect. . . . Once accept a single abatement of right, and many other humiliations would certainly follow, and the whole fine fabric of international law might crumble under our hands piece by piece. What we are contending for in this matter is of the very essence of the things that have made America a sovereign nation. She cannot yield them without conceding her own impotency as a nation, and making virtual surrender of her independent position among the nations of the world.[6]

---

[3] *Foreign Relations, 1915 Supp.*, p. 941.

[4] See *War Memoirs of Robert Lansing* (Indianapolis, 1935), p. 84.

[5] For Wilson's alleged belligerent utterances at the "Sunrise Conference" with three Congressional leaders, see A. M. Arnett, *Claude Kitchin and the Wilson War Policies* (Boston, 1937), pp. 183–192; Tansill, *America Goes to War*, pp. 465–486.

[6] *Foreign Relations, 1916 Supp.*, pp. 177–178 (Wilson to Stone, Feb. 24, 1916).

As a result of strong political pressure from the White House upon the Democratic majorities, to say nothing of parliamentary legerde-main,[7] the two "scuttle resolutions" were sidetracked, March, 1916. The New York *Herald* rejoiced: "Pro-Germans Are Swept to Defeat as the House Votes to Sustain American Rights." Yet American men, women, and children continued to embark on contraband-laden British liners for submarine-infested waters. There seemed little doubt as to their technical right to do so; but when they were killed they were just as dead as if they had been wrong. And the consequences for the United States were momentous.

Meanwhile the shadow of the periscope continued to fall across America. On November 7, 1915, the Italian passenger liner, *Ancona*, was sunk by a submarine under particularly brutal circumstances. Among those killed or injured were several American citizens. The State Department promptly made vigorous representations; and the Austrian government acknowledged responsibility for the deed and agreed to pay indemnity.

On March 24, 1916, an unarmed French passenger ship, the *Sussex*, was torpedoed (but not sunk) by a German submarine, with heavy loss of life and with serious injury to several Americans. The attack was unquestionably a direct violation of the German pledge not to sink unresisting passenger liners without warning. America was in-stantly aroused, and the resulting diplomatic crisis was the most serious yet to confront the United States.[8] The already bad situation was made worse when the German Foreign Office, misinformed by the Admiralty,[9] attempted to evade responsibility for the attack. Secretary Lansing favored an immediate rupture; but Wilson, faced with the Mexican crisis and divided public opinion, shrank from strong meas-ures. The note that Lansing finally sent to Berlin, on April 18, 1916, unequivocally asserted:

Unless the Imperial Government should now immediately declare and effect an abandonment of its present methods of submarine warfare against passenger and freight-carrying vessels, the Government of the United States can have no choice but to sever diplomatic relations. . . .[10]

The German reply, dated May 4, 1916, acceded to the American demands, and declared that orders had been issued that no more unre-

[7] Arnett, *Claude Kitchin*, p. 181.
[8] Charles Seymour, *American Diplomacy during the World War* (Baltimore, 1934), p. 120.
[9] Tansill, *America Goes to War*, pp. 490 *ff.*
[10] *Foreign Relations, 1916 Supp.*, p. 234.

sisting merchantmen were to be sunk without warning and without humanitarian precautions. But a long "string" was attached to this assurance. If the United States did not persuade the other belligerents to respect the "laws of humanity" (that is, force Britain to relax the starvation blockade), "the German government would then be facing a new situation in which it must reserve [to] itself complete liberty of decision." [11] Wilson accepted these assurances—without the "string."

Technically, the so-called *Sussex* pledge was not a pledge at all, because Germany qualified it by insisting that the United States fulfill an impossible condition. Yet Wilson won, temporarily at least, a diplomatic victory. He averted hostilities, maintained American prestige, and forced the Germans to emasculate their most effective sea weapon. But, ominously, he took such a strong position that it would be virtually impossible honorably to avoid war if the Germans should open an unrestricted submarine campaign.

COLONEL HOUSE: AMATEUR DIPLOMAT

As the passage of time brought no cessation in the hostilities, Wilson became convinced that the only sure way to keep the American people out of the World War was to bring it to an end. He had already taken a step in this direction when, in January, 1915, he sent his intimate personal adviser, the strongly pro-Ally Colonel Edward M. House, on a peace mission to Europe. For a number of weeks the earnest Colonel was "jollied along" by the British, the French, and the Germans. The simple truth is that both sides had already poured so much blood and treasure into the bottomless pit that they did not have the courage to face their people without some fruits of victory. After an interview in England with George V, House reported: "His idea seemed to be that the best way to obtain permanent peace was to knock all the fight out of the Germans, and stamp on them for a while until they wanted peace and more of it than any other nation." [12]

Early in 1916 Colonel House again arrived in Europe on another peace mission. Acting as Wilson's personal plenipotentiary, he came to an agreement with Sir Edward Grey. The latter recorded the conversation in a memorandum dated February 22, 1916:

Colonel House told me that President Wilson was ready, on hearing from France and England that the moment was opportune, to propose that

[11] *Ibid.*, pp. 259–260.
[12] Charles Seymour, *The Intimate Papers of Colonel House* (Boston, 1926), I, 385 (House to Wilson, March 1, 1915).

a Conference should be summoned to put an end to the war. Should the Allies accept this proposal, and should Germany refuse it, the United States would *probably* enter the war against Germany.[13]

Grey's memorandum of his understanding with House went on to say that even if such a conference met and failed to secure peace, "the United States would [probably] leave the Conference as a belligerent on the side of the Allies. . . ." In short, House virtually pledged the United States to become a member of the Allied coalition.

But the quiet Colonel, it now appears, exceeded his instructions.[14] Wilson had authorized him to urge peace negotiations, and to promise that America would throw her "*moral* force" against Germany and her allies if they should refuse to co-operate. There were already two safeguarding "probablys" in the House-Grey memorandum, a copy of which was sent to the President. Wilson, who could not completely ignore Congress, promptly added a third "probably" when he changed the statement to read, "the United States would *probably* leave the Conference as a belligerent on the side of the Allies. . . ."

This, of course, was not a hard and fast pledge by the Washington government. The upshot was that nothing came of the negotiations. Neither side wanted a peace conference. Germany had the military advantage; and the Allies, confident of ultimately landing a "knock-out" blow, did not want to be handicapped at the peace table by Wilson's embarrassing idealism. With the House-Grey memorandum drawn up they could go ahead with the comfortable assurance that the United States government, though outwardly professing neutrality, was morally committed to their side. This also meant that there was no pressing necessity of deferring too punctiliously to American rights.[15]

Approaching a Break with Britain

During the nine months following the so-called *Sussex* pledge, the German submarines were on their good behavior as far as the United States was concerned. American public opinion was therefore left free

[13] *Ibid.*, II, 201–202. Italics inserted. House told the British: "The United States would like Great Britain to do those things which would enable the United States to help Great Britain win the war." *Ibid.*, II, 124.

[14] Harley Notter, *The Origins of the Foreign Policy of Woodrow Wilson* (Baltimore, 1937), p. 467.

[15] The question of whether or not the British made a great mistake in not accepting the American proposition to enter the war at this time is discussed in Seymour, *American Diplomacy during the World War*, pp. 161 *ff*.

to concentrate on the accumulation of grievances, old and new, at the hands of Britain. Particularly galling was the British practice of opening United States mail, ostensibly in search of contraband being sent to Germany. The resentment of the American people was further increased when it was alleged that trade secrets were being filched from these letters and turned over to British commercial rivals.

The State Department protested against this "vexatiously inquisitorial" procedure; but the British again invoked the customary plea of "unusual conditions." Then, late in April, 1916, after an unconscionable delay of more than six months, the Foreign Office finally answered Secretary Lansing's masterly summation of America's grievances—a protest which Ambassador Page sorrowfully described as an "uncourteous monster of 35 heads and 3 appendices. . . ." The fifty-one-headed British reply, which conceded essentially nothing, further taxed American patience.

On July 18, 1916, came the British blacklist—a list of eighty-five persons or firms in the United States who were suspected of giving aid to Germany and with whom, as a consequence, His Majesty's subjects were forbidden to trade.[16] This latest move caused the anti-British Hearst press and the pro-German elements in the United States to rend the heavens. The strongly pro-Ally New York *Times* described the blacklist as "the most tactless, foolish, and unnecessary act of the British Government during the war." Even Ambassador Page was disgusted. Wilson declared that the "poor boobs" on the other side of the Atlantic had "got on his nerves." To Colonel House he confessed:

I am, I must admit, about at the end of my patience with Great Britain and the Allies. This blacklist business is the last straw. I have told Spring-Rice [British ambassador] so, and he sees the reasons very clearly. Both he and Jusserand [French ambassador] think it is a stupid blunder. . . . Can we any longer endure their intolerable course? [17]

The protest of the Washington government against the blacklist was based on international morals rather than on international law, for Britain had an undeniable legal right to forbid her subjects to trade with firms in the United States. Both the strong tone of the American note and its prompt publication suggest that the Administration, which

---

[16] T. A. Bailey, "The United States and the Blacklist during the Great War," *Jour. of Mod. Hist.*, VI (1934), 21.

[17] Seymour, *American Diplomacy during the World War*, pp. 76–77 (July 23, 1916). See also Alice M. Morrissey, *The American Defense of Neutral Rights, 1914–1917* (Cambridge, Mass., 1939), p. 143.

was then in the midst of a campaign for re-election, was not overlooking the Irish and German vote.[18] The British stood their ground; but, recognizing their tactical error, gradually "whittled down" the blacklist.

The possibility of a rupture with Britain was squarely faced when

THE SAME FROM BOTH SIDES.

(From the Tacoma *Daily Ledger*.)

Congress clothed the President with retaliatory powers (which were never used) against nations that blacklisted Americans. At almost the same time that body passed the largest peacetime naval appropriation then on record. "Let us," insisted Wilson, "build a navy bigger than hers [Great Britain's] and do what we please." In later years Colonel House stated, doubtless with exaggeration, that if it had not been for the more serious offenses of Germany in her submarine warfare it would have been well-nigh impossible to avoid hostilities with Great Britain.[19]

"He Kept Us Out of War"

Meanwhile interest in foreign affairs had become partially submerged by the heated presidential campaign of 1916. The Republicans passed by the vehemently outspoken Theodore Roosevelt and picked their candidate, Charles Evans Hughes, from the cloistered Supreme Court. The Democrats renominated Wilson by acclamation in a convention best remembered for the keynote speech of Martin H. Glynn, a former governor of New York. The orator defended Wilson's record by citing precedent after precedent to show that the traditional policy of the United States had not been to fight every time its rights were violated. After each case (including the *Chesapeake*), the crowd broke into a chant, "What did we do?" From Glynn came the stirring response, "We didn't go to war." [20] In this wildly shouting convention was born the slogan, "He kept us out of war."

Early in the campaign it seemed as though the hyphenate vote would prove decisive. The Republicans made a determined effort to

[18] Bailey, "The United States and the Blacklist," *loc. cit.*, p. 25.
[19] Seymour, *House Papers*, II, 311.
[20] Walter Millis, *Road to War: America, 1914–1917* (Boston, 1935), p. 318.

woo the pro-German element; but they found themselves in the awkward position of condemning the Administration for not having dealt with Berlin in a more forceful fashion. In reply, the Democrats attempted to pin the mantle of pro-Germanism on the Republicans. The Democratic New York *World* challenged, "Can the Kaiser Defeat the President?" and defended Wilson for "the crime of being an American President instead of a German President." Hughes, who condemned Wilson's "leisurely discussions" of the nation's rights, tried to "straddle" on the pro-German issue, announcing that he was for "America first and America efficient." Such vague phrases led to his being renamed Charles "Evasive" Hughes, and to the quip that he had left the bench for the fence. On the other hand, Wilson was accused of being "the best President England ever had." When an Irish agitator telegraphed Wilson denouncing him for his "pro-British policies," the Chief Executive promptly and devastatingly replied: "Your telegram received. I should feel deeply mortified to have you or anybody like you vote for me. Since you have access to many disloyal Americans and I have not, I will ask you to convey this message to them." [21]

There were many issues in the campaign—Mexico, the railroads, the tariff—but there can be no doubt that a leading one, if not the leading one, was the tacit promise of the Democrats to maintain neutrality. The country was plastered with placards bearing the slogan, "He Kept Us out of War." A Democratic appeal to workingmen read:

> You Are Working;
> —*Not Fighting!*
> Alive and Happy:
> —*Not Cannon Fodder!*
> Wilson and Peace with Honor?
> or
> *Hughes with Roosevelt and War?* [22]

On election night, when the first returns poured in, it seemed clear that Hughes had won by a landslide. But the voters of the Middle and Far West, who were farther removed from the war and strongly set against participation, turned the tide for Wilson, who won by the

---

[21] New York *World*, October 1, 1916, 1:7. Bryan did yeoman's work in campaigning for Wilson, while Roosevelt's ranting speeches (he compared the President to Pontius Pilate, with apologies to the latter) and his bellicose utterances probably alienated many pro-German and peace-loving Republican voters. See Carl Wittke, *German-Americans and the World War* (Columbus, Ohio, 1936), p. 106.

[22] New York *Times*, Nov. 4, 1916, 6:4–8 (Paid advertisement).

narrowest of margins. It seems evident that although the President may not have received a clear mandate to keep the country out of war, his re-election was made possible by those people who believed that he would do so.[23] Wilson, of course, had promised nothing. "He Kept Us out of War" referred only to the past, and was historically true. But there were those who felt that the slogan was a tacit pledge which Wilson was morally bound to observe.

"PEACE WITHOUT VICTORY"

Shortly after the election Wilson entered upon a final desperate attempt to secure peace. He drafted an identical note appealing to the belligerents to state specifically what they were fighting for. But before he could present it the Germans, either wittingly or unwittingly, stole his thunder by publishing, on December 12, 1916, a statement in which they indicated their willingness to discuss peace. This left Wilson in a most embarrassing predicament. If he went ahead the Allies would infer that the United States and Germany were acting together.[24] If he delayed, an opportunity to stop hostilities would pass, and the United States probably would be dragged into the war. So Wilson sent the note, December 18, 1916.

The Allies were displeased with this presumed evidence of German-American collusion, and were mortally offended by Wilson's blunt statement that "the objects which the statesmen of the belligerents on both sides have in mind in this war are virtually the same. . . ." The British and French particularly resented Wilson's attempt "to smoke them out" and force them to confess their war aims. If the Allies did so their people might stop fighting. The outspoken British militarist, Sir Henry Wilson, fumed, "That ass President Wilson has barged in and asked all belligerents for their terms." Lord Northcliffe told Ambassador Page, "Everybody is mad as hell." The King broke down and wept.

On January 22, 1917, Wilson gave his reactions to the belligerent replies in a memorable address to the Senate—or, rather, to the world. He suggested his proposed League of Nations for establishing world accord, and bluntly warned the embattled Powers that only "peace

[23] This was the conclusion of the British propaganda agents in America. H. C. Peterson, *Propaganda for War* (Norman, Okla., 1939), p. 282. The hyphenate vote does not appear to have played an important part in the election. It seems that the "He Kept Us out of War" issue split the pro-Germans in such a way as to neutralize their influence. See Wittke, *German-Americans and the World War*, pp. 110–111.

[24] Notter, *Origins of the Foreign Policy of Woodrow Wilson*, p. 588.

without victory" could bring a permanent settlement. In general, the people of the United States welcomed the speech with enthusiasm. Senator Tillman of South Carolina, a Democrat, remarked that it was the "noblest utterance since the Declaration of Independence." But the frank phrase, "peace without victory," was a bucket of cold water to the Allies, who could not afford to accept a stalemate. As far as immediate objectives were concerned, the speech accomplished nothing. But it further strengthened Wilson's moral leadership of the world.

THE BREAK WITH BERLIN

With the echoes of Wilson's "peace without victory" pronouncement still reverberating, the German government announced, on January 31, 1917, its unrestricted submarine campaign. Henceforth U-boat commanders would attempt to sink all ships—neutral or belligerent, passenger or merchant—in the specified zone. The war had reached a deadlock; the British blockade (in which the United States protestingly acquiesced) was pinching tighter; and unless Germany staked everything on this last desperate throw it seemed inevitable that superior Allied resources would prevail. The Germans knew perfectly well that an unrestricted submarine campaign would force the United States into the war; but they not unreasonably concluded that England would be starved out before America could raise an effective fighting force. They also believed that in the meantime the United States could scarcely give the Allies much more assistance as a belligerent than it was then doing as a neutral. But Germany did make one meager concession—a concession that was nothing short of insulting to a great sovereign nation. The Americans might send one ship a week through a specified part of the war zone, provided it arrived at Falmouth on Sunday, carried no contraband, was painted with wide red and white stripes, and flew a checkered flag. Such a ship might sail back to America from the same port on Wednesday.[25] The Brooklyn *Eagle* not inaptly remarked that the "freedom of the seas will now be enjoyed by icebergs and fish."

To Wilson the German announcement came as a body blow. At that time, as had been the case for many months, diplomatic relations with Germany were more amicable than with the Allies. But Wilson had so irrevocably committed himself as to what he would do if the Germans should violate their *Sussex* pledge, that both consistency and national honor pointed to a severance of relations. After much travail of spirit

[25] *Foreign Relations, 1917, Supp. I*, p. 102.

he appeared before Congress, on February 3, 1917, and in a dramatic speech announced that the necessary steps had been taken to end all diplomatic intercourse with Germany.

Congress greeted the announcement with frenzied applause, and the country responded "with a near approach to unanimity. . . ." [26] Wilson's bitterest critics applauded; and Wall Street, fearing that the sinking Allies would carry down its billions, raised the American flag. Messages of support poured in on the President from J. P. Morgan and Company, the United States Steel Corporation, the Bethlehem Steel Company, and the Remington Arms Company.[27] Even the West was falling in line. The Denver *Post* conceded that there was no other choice but to break. In Iowa, by February 8, 1917, long lines of young men were waiting to enlist.

After the rupture of relations with Germany, war was virtually inevitable. Yet Wilson hoped against hope that the Germans might avoid an overt act against the United States. But if their submarines destroyed American ships and lives he would come before Congress again and recommend extreme measures. This was a wise decision, for public opinion in the United States was far from unanimous on the desirability of war. "I could not move faster," Wilson remarked to his secretary, "than the mass of our people would permit."

Then came an astounding surprise. On January 16, 1917, the German Foreign Secretary, Zimmermann, had cabled the German minister in Mexico, instructing him that in the event of war with the United States he should attempt to effect a German-Mexican alliance, holding out to Mexico the inducement of recovering New Mexico, Texas, and Arizona. He was also to ask the President of Mexico to invite Japanese adherence to this plan.

The fantastic Zimmermann note was intercepted and deciphered by the British authorities, who turned it over to the United States government. On March 1, 1917, the news was emblazoned in the press, and created, Lansing thought, a greater sensation than the submarine announcement itself. It came as something of a shock to Americans to realize that Germany, if struck by the United States, would strike

---

[26] Notter, *Foreign Policy of Woodrow Wilson*, p. 617.

[27] R. S. Baker, *Woodrow Wilson* (Garden City, N.Y., 1937), VI, 460–461. The *Wall Street Digest* noted that the "upward movement in the price of stocks dates from the day the German Ambassador was handed his passports." Throughout 1916 the news of German victories or peace offers had a most depressing effect on the stock market. These facts, together with the rejoicing in financial circles over the break with Germany, indicate the closeness of the economic relationship between the United States and the Allies. Peterson, *Propaganda for War*, p. 267.

back in the New World. Immediately a tremendous wave of anti-German sentiment swept over the country, particularly in the hitherto apathetic South and Southwest, where there was alarm over the threat of being conquered by Mexico. Nor was the immigration-conscious Pacific Coast pleased by the proposed overtures to Japan. A more nearly united America was now one step nearer the brink.[28]

The Pen Yields to the Sword

Meanwhile American shipping, paralyzed with the fear of submarine attack, clung tenaciously to port. Great quantities of wheat and cotton were piling up and threatening to dislocate American economic life. On February 26, 1917, Wilson went before Congress and asked for authority to provide arms for American merchantmen. The House approved the request by an overwhelming majority. But a group of eleven "peace-at-any-price" Senators filibustered the bill to death. The increasingly vocal "war hawks" branded the recusant Senators as "Iscariots" and "traitors," and demanded that they be hanged, while enthusiastic audiences roared approval. Wilson himself declared publicly in an ill-considered outburst that a "little group of wilful men had rendered the great government of the United States helpless and contemptible." Then, after assurances that he had the authority to do so, he proceeded to arm American vessels anyhow. In March, 1917, the first American armed merchantmen put to sea, provided with navy gunners and with orders to shoot submarines at sight in the war zone.

The country waited breathlessly for the "overt act." It was not long in coming. On March 12, 1917, approximately six weeks after the German announcement, the unarmed American merchantman *Algonquin* was sunk without warning. On March 19 the United States learned that three unarmed American ships had been destroyed within twenty-four hours, one of them losing fifteen members of its crew. A few days earlier the news had come that the Czar had been overthrown, and that the Allies were now apparently fighting foursquare for democracy. The period of "armed expectancy" was over.

[28] *Ibid.*, pp. 314–315. Few stopped to realize that the instructions were not to be acted upon *until* the United States entered the war, when they would be proper strategy. Zimmermann made a bad blunder when he naïvely admitted the genuineness of the note. The charge that it was a British forgery was making considerable headway; and the note had been received from the British on such terms of secrecy that the State Department could not reveal the facts behind it. Wilson was vastly annoyed because the Germans had abused a courtesy extended by the State Department in sending the note. *War Memoirs of Robert Lansing* (Indianapolis, 1935), pp. 225–232.

Wilson, however, did not want to go to war. But he felt that Germany's flagrant disregard of American rights left no other honorable alternative. Recent allegations to the contrary, no convincing evidence has yet been forthcoming to show that Wilson's decision was influenced by big business and the munitions makers. But it is clear that he would not have asked Congress to declare war if he had not known that the country would support such a move.[29] And it is undeniably true that the strongest clamor for war came from the industrial East, which had an enormous trade and investment stake in the cause of the tottering Allies. Thomas W. Lamont, of Morgan and Company, later estimated that 500,000 Americans had invested in loans to the Allies —and this group consisted of the more substantial and influential citizens.[30]

After an agonizing debate with himself, Wilson appeared before Congress on April 2, 1917, and in solemn tones asked that body to recognize the fact that Germany was now waging war upon the United States. ". . . The right," he asserted, "is more precious than peace. . . ." When he had finished, there was a moment of eloquent silence; then deafening applause. Even political foes rushed forward to congratulate him. But Wilson, pale and silent, later remarked to his secretary, "My message to-day was a message of death for our young men. How strange it seems to applaud that."[31]

Two days later, on April 4, 1917, the Senate passed the fateful war resolution by a vote of 82 to 6. Among the dissentients were members of the "wilful" group. On April 6 the House gave its approval by a vote of 373 to 50. The fifty who opposed the resolution showed courage, for the country as a whole seemed overwhelmingly in favor of a war to defend American rights and honor, even though there was no clear idea of raising a huge army to do so.[32] It is true that only one of the negative votes represented the industrial East, which had a huge investment stake in Allied victory and which was nearer geographically to the German menace. But it is no less true that the

---

[29] See Notter, *Foreign Policy of Woodrow Wilson*, pp. 636–637.

[30] Tansill, *America Goes to War*, p. 657 n.

[31] J. P. Tumulty, *Woodrow Wilson as I Know Him* (Garden City, N.Y., 1921), p. 256.

[32] It is probably true that if the ballot had been a secret one, and if it had been known that America was to send a conscript army overseas, the vote would have been closer. Although it seems clear that a majority of the people were resigned to war, British propaganda agents were distressed by the lack of enthusiasm. Peterson, *Propaganda for War*, pp. 322–323. See also Baker, *Woodrow Wilson*, VII, 235. For evidence that Congress was not so favorable to war as the vote would indicate, see O. G. Villard, *Fighting Years* (N.Y., 1939), pp. 322–323; Morrissey, *American Defense of Neutral Rights*, pp. 190–191.

great impulse for hostilities came from the vast body of common citizens who recognized that Germany was already waging war on the United States.[33]

THE WAGES OF UNNEUTRALITY

There are two sharply divergent points of view on America's entrance into the war. If, as many think, German militarism was a menace to the world, and if the self-interest of the United States demanded an early alignment with the Allies, then the traditional neutrality policy of Wilson was shortsighted, and he should have tried to lead the nation into war sooner.

But if we assume, as some do, that the United States should have stayed out of the conflict, and that in the long run Europe could have best set its own house in order without American intervention, it is not purely academic to inquire whether the nation could have kept out.

It seems reasonably certain that if the Germans had not begun their unrestricted submarine campaign, the United States would not have been dragged into the war—at least not at that time.[34] But this, certain critics insist, is not the whole story. The large-scale assistance of the Americans to the Allies, coupled with American acquiescence in the British blockade, drove the Germans to desperate measures which ultimately involved the United States. If this is true, then it may be argued that a more rigid observance of neutrality by America might have averted war.[35]

There can be no doubt that both sets of belligerents had flagrantly violated American rights—or what the State Department declared were American rights. Throughout the entire period of neutrality the Allies did so more consistently and persistently than Germany. Why, then, did America not fight them? Why did she not declare war

[33] According to the editorials of sixty-eight contemporary American newspapers, America went to war primarily because she was forced into it by the submarine. Other reasons for action were German intrigue and fear of attack by a victorious Germany. Only one of the editors opposed war after its declaration, the general conviction being that the nation had been attacked. Russell Buchanan, "American Editors Examine American War Aims and Plans in April, 1917," *Pacific Hist. Rev.*, IX (1940), 254.

[34] Charles Seymour, *American Neutrality, 1914–1917* (New Haven, 1935), p. 56.

[35] Charles Seymour (*ibid.*) stresses the submarine; Edwin Borchard and W. P. Lage, *Neutrality for the United States* (New Haven, 1937), emphasize the results of American unneutrality; also Peterson, *Propaganda for War*, particularly pp. 270–272. Professor Alice M. Morrissey concludes (*American Defense of Neutral Rights*, p. 197): "Since the United States had become a base of supplies for the Allies, it had laid itself open to German attack, for it could not expect the Germans to buy American neutrality at the price of victory."

against both groups of belligerents, just as it had been proposed that she fight both Great Britain and France in 1812?

The basic reason appears to have been that Allied practices hurt only American property rights. The United States could lodge protests, and perhaps collect damages when the war was over. The German submarine took American lives. And there seemed to be no proper recompense for lives. So the United States fought Germany. As the Boston *Globe* remarked: one was "a gang of thieves"; the other was "a gang of murderers. On the whole, we prefer the thieves, but only as the lesser of two evils."

In retrospect it seems as though there were two ways by which America could have avoided war. First, she could have kept her citizens and ships out of the combat zones, as was later done under the neutrality legislation of the 1930's. But to Wilson and others such a course was dishonorable and a base surrender of historic rights. Second, the nation could have lowered its standards of national honor. Norway, Sweden, and Denmark all stayed out of the war, although losing more nationals from submarine attacks than did the United States while neutral. But it was unthinkable that a great and proud nation would consent to be an international doormat.

Wilson was thoroughly in accord with American policy and tradition when he insisted upon upholding historic rights. Perhaps his basic error was not to take an early lead in building up adequate military and naval strength, so that Germany would respect those rights when the pinch came.

One thing is clear. The United States was not dragged into the war by the propagandists, by the bankers, by the munitions manufacturers, or by other interested groups, even though such groups may have influenced American policies that were distasteful to Germany. America fought because she was attacked.[36] Sympathy with the Allies and distrust of Germany made easier an acceptance of the challenge when it finally came. But in the final analysis the decision that the nation should fight was made in Germany, not in the United States.

[36] During World War II, and partly because of a projection of current happenings back into the past, it became fashionable to believe that the United States rushed into World War I to save the collapsing Allies and thus protect America from future German attack. Yet it was not known when Wilson severed relations that the Allies were collapsing; in fact they were then thought to be winning. Disillusionment came after actual entrance into the war. Moreover, the nation did not "rush" into the conflict; and there was considerable sentiment for a limited-liability participation. On these points, and particularly on the role of the submarine, see T. A. Bailey, *Woodrow Wilson and the Lost Peace* (N.Y., 1944), Ch. I and Bibliographical Notes.

BIBLIOGRAPHICAL NOTE

See the note at the end of the preceding chapter, especially the books by Tansill, Seymour, Notter, Baker, Morrissey, Borchard and Lage, Peterson, and Millis. Certain additional references relate more particularly to the period following the *Arabic* crisis. J. W. Pratt, "Robert Lansing," in S. F. Bemis, ed., *The American Secretaries of State and their Diplomacy* (N.Y., 1929), X, 47–98, is a useful survey of the diplomacy of the period. Charles Seymour has several informative essays on the problems of neutrality in *American Neutrality, 1914–1917* (New Haven, 1935). A. M. Arnett, *Claude Kitchin and the Wilson War Policies* (Boston, 1937), is a sympathetic biography of a Democratic Congressional leader who opposed the Wilson policies as leading to war. See also T. A. Bailey, "The United States and the Blacklist during the Great War," *Jour. of Mod. Hist.*, VI (1934), 14–35. Further references: see footnotes of this chapter and Bemis and Griffin, *Guide*, pp. 655–672.

RECENT REFERENCES. *Papers Relating to the Foreign Relations of the United States: The Lansing Papers, 1914–1920* (2 vols., Washington, 1939–1940), is a documentary collection of primary importance. In his *Memoirs*, which were published eighteen years after the event in a different climate of opinion, Lansing appears as a strong Anglophile scheming to get his country into the war. In these contemporary papers, which are more reliable, he emerges as a champion of neutrality who opposed hostilities with Germany until after the resumption of unrestricted submarine warfare. It is probable that the truth lies somewhere between these two extremes. C. J. Child, *The German-Americans in Politics, 1914–1917* (Madison, Wis., 1939), complements Carl Wittke's *German-Americans and the World War*, and stresses pressure for an arms embargo and hostility to Wilson. The author discounts the anti-Wilson influence of the German vote in 1916, in part because the German-Americans were traditionally Republican, and in part because the violent language of the hyphenates drove voters into the Wilson camp (pp. 150–151). A. D. H. Smith, *Mr. House of Texas* (N.Y., 1940), is an undocumented and somewhat uncritical biography. Strong evidence as to the primacy of the submarine issue appears in Russell Buchanan, "American Editors Examine American War Aims and Plans in April, 1917," *Pacific Hist. Rev.*, IX (1940), 253–265. *Foreign Relations, 1926*, II, 214–308, has some valuable data on the exaggerated nature of American claims against Britain growing out of seizures and detentions from 1914 to 1917. In 1926 an official of the State Department examined 2658 unsettled cases, and concluded that only 11 were worthy of serious consideration (p. 286).

NEW REFERENCES. See works by Perkins, Daniels, and Bell, cited on p. 940. See also the book discussed in the last footnote of the present chapter. Wilson's efforts for a negotiated peace are considered briefly in Kent Forster, *The Failures of Peace* (Washington, 1941), Ch. IV. H. C. Syrett, "The Business Press and American Neutrality, 1914–1917," *Miss. Valley Hist. Rev.*, XXXII (1945), 215–230, shows that these papers were pro-profit and pro-Ally but, after January 31, 1917, not more interventionist than other journals. Most editors agreed that war would cut profits. (Failure to mention loans may indicate that patriotism was being used to cover up solicitude for investments with the Allies.)

4TH ED. REFS. O. J. Clinard, *Japan's Influence on American Naval Power, 1897–1917* (Berkeley, Calif., 1947), concludes (p. 171) that the great "Naval Construction Act of 1916 was directed against Japan. . . ."

CHAPTER XXXIX

The Peace of Versailles, 1918–1919

"Only a peace between equals can last."

Woodrow Wilson, 1917.

LINKING SHIELDS WITH THE ALLIES

BELLIGERENT status brought with it a new viewpoint. Formerly the United States had been the leading champion of neutral rights. Now it became a silent or active partner of the Allies in "modifying" international law. The Washington government refused, however, to support some of the Allied practices to which it had strongly objected during the neutrality period. Others that it had protested against only mildly were accepted and even improved upon. Notable in this category were the blacklist and the economic control of the neutrals near Germany.[1] But the United States was able to make out some kind of legal case for virtually everything it did—just as the Allies had been able to do before America entered the war.

The transition from a neutral to an "Associate"[2] of the Allies was not accomplished without some difficulty. The anti-British textbooks had been poisonously pervasive; the Irish were acutely unhappy; and the recent controversies with the London government over neutral rights had left an unpleasant aftertaste. The situation called for a new propaganda campaign, and, as before, the British were conspicuously successful.[3] The King practiced baseball throwing and ate an American buckwheat cake, which he pronounced "good." On July 4, 1917—of all days—the Union Jack and the Stars and Stripes floated side by side over Westminster Abbey and the Houses of Parliament. The Americans suddenly discovered that the anti-British textbooks were hurtful

[1] See A. M. Morrissey, "The United States and the Rights of Neutrals, 1917–1918," *Amer. Jour. of Internat. Law*, XXXI (1937), 17–30.

[2] True to her traditions, America never became an Ally. Officially she was an "Associated Power," and the Allies were her "Associates." See Wilson's insistence upon this point in R. S. Baker, *Woodrow Wilson* (N.Y., 1939), VII, 403.

[3] C. H. Hunter, "Anglo-American Relations during the Period of American Belligerency, 1917–1918" (ms. doctoral dissertation, Stanford University, 1935), pp. 602 ff.

to Allied morale; and a rewriting program was launched, as a result of which liberties were taken with the truth.

In pursuance of the campaign for better feeling and closer co-operation, commissions of distinguished statesmen from the principal Allied powers hastened to America to concert plans for a speedy victory. Their efforts were directed largely, and successfully, toward a much-needed co-ordination of effort.[4] But money and supplies, though lavishly provided, were not enough. The Allies were in desperate need of man power; and the United States agreed to send a large body of men to France, ultimately two million—something that the American people had hardly foreseen when they were pushed into the struggle.

The Pen is Mightier

Wilson's moral leadership was enormously strengthened as a result of America's entrance into the conflict. One factor that made his decision in favor of war possible was a realization that the United States, as a participant rather than as an onlooker, would be able to exert greater influence in behalf of Wilsonian ideals for a new order and a just peace. In numerous addresses the President held aloft with passionate conviction the principles for which America was fighting—or thought she was fighting. But these speeches from the "presidential pulpit" were too long to lend themselves effectively to pamphleteering propaganda. This deficiency was remedied when, on January 8, 1918, Wilson appeared before Congress and delivered his famous Fourteen Points address.

The Fourteen Points were designed as a statement of war aims and as an instrument of propaganda, both at home and abroad.[5] It was hoped that they would nerve the Allied peoples to fight harder, and that they would weaken the resistance of the enemy nations by holding out to them the seductive hope of a just peace—not one of vengeance. In summary form Wilson's program follows:

1. Abolition of secret diplomacy.

   [The liberals in all countries would approve.]
2. Freedom to navigate the high seas in peace and war.

   [Pleasing to the Germans, who distrusted British sea power.]
3. Removal of economic barriers among the nations.

[4] Charles Seymour, *American Diplomacy during the World War* (Baltimore, 1934), pp. 212 *ff.*

[5] For reactions abroad see Baker, *Woodrow Wilson*, VII, 456.

[Reassuring to the Germans, who feared economic reprisals at the end of the war.]

4. Reduction of armaments.

[Gratifying to taxpayers in all countries.]

5. Adjustment of colonial claims in the interest of both the inhabitants and the Powers concerned.

6. Restoration of Russia and a welcome for her in the society of nations.

7. The return of Belgium to her people.

8. Evacuation and restoration of French territory; and righting of Alsace-Lorraine wrong.

[It was understood that France would receive Alsace-Lorraine.]

9. Readjustment of Italian frontiers "along clearly recognizable lines of nationality."

10. Free opportunity for "autonomous development" for people of Austria-Hungary.

[An appeal to the submerged minorities of the ramshackle empire.]

11. Restoration of the Balkan nations and free access to the sea for Serbia.

12. Protection for minorities in Turkey.

13. An independent Poland.

[Seductive to the Poles of Austria-Hungary and Germany.]

14. "A general association [League] of nations" to secure "mutual guarantees of political independence and territorial integrity to great and small states alike."

The League of Nations, the basic idea of which had been strongly espoused since 1914 by numerous peace, religious, and business organizations,[6] was regarded by the President as the capstone point.

In subsequent addresses Wilson elaborated, clarified, and supplemented the original Fourteen Points. He declared for a just, permanent, open peace, and emphasized the necessity of consulting the wishes of the people concerned in the prospective settlements. This last point —Secretary Lansing called it self-determination "dynamite"—raised up unrealizable hopes all over the world. All the points and principles, totaling more than twenty, will be here referred to as the Fourteen Points.

Wilson's fascinating phrases proved to be a mighty propagandist engine. George Creel, head of the American Committee on Public Information, scattered over the world a grand total of some sixty million pamphlets, booklets and leaflets containing Wilsonisms. In

[6] C. A. Berdahl, *The Policy of the United States with Respect to the League of Nations* (Geneva, 1932), pp. 26 *ff.*

China, a translated volume of the President's speeches became a "best seller." In Poland, university men clasped hands when they met and soulfully uttered one word, "Wilson." In a lonely Italian mountaineer's cabin Creel found a wax figure of a local patron saint on one side of the chimney and a likeness of the American President on the other. Innumerable leaflets containing the Fourteen Points were rained upon Germany and Austria from the sky. It is not surprising that these penetrating appeals spread unrest among submerged minorities within enemy territory, and weakened the morale of the troops at the front.[7]

THE FOURTEEN POINTS DISARM GERMANY

Fresh man power from the aroused Western giant tipped the scales in favor of the Allies, and the German military leaders saw the beginning of the end. In October, 1918, they induced the Berlin government to propose to Wilson the calling of a conference which would make peace on the basis of the Fourteen Points. They chose Wilson, rather than the Allies, because they expected that the somewhat visionary President would be less difficult to deal with, and because they feared that the embittered Allies would return a point-blank refusal, thus making inevitable a bloody invasion of the Fatherland. The German generals also hoped to trap Wilson into a cessation of hostilities, which would enable them to re-form their lines and recuperate their strength.

But Germany picked the wrong man. Few chapters of American diplomatic history reveal greater skill than Wilson's series of interchanges with the German officials during October, 1918.[8] The President had consistently preached that America had no quarrel with the German people but with their "military masters." He now made it clear that the Kaiser and his following would have to be thrown overboard before the terms of an armistice could be agreed upon. The war-wearied German people were not slow in responding to this appeal; and the pressure quickly became so great that the Kaiser was forced to abdicate and flee the country, November 9, 1918.

The American President expressed his willingness to come to terms with Germany on the basis of the Fourteen Points. But the Allies,

---

[7] George Creel, *How We Advertised America* (N.Y., 1920), pp. 283 *ff.*; see also G. G. Bruntz, *Allied Propaganda and the Collapse of the German Empire in 1918* (Stanford University, 1938), pp. 212 *ff.*

[8] Seymour, *American Diplomacy during the World War*, pp. 324–325.

who had enthusiastically preached the gospel according to Wilson for war purposes, were far less enthusiastic about these principles for peace purposes. Before America entered the war these Powers had made a number of secret treaties among themselves, whereby they had agreed to carve up some of the choicest of the enemy's possessions. A strict application of the Fourteen Points would deprive them of the spoils of war. Besides, Britain balked at accepting Point II, the freedom of the seas. She would not throw away the blockade, her chief offensive weapon, at the behest of the idealistic Wilson. Moreover, the thrifty French peasants were determined to have monetary payments for the damage caused by the German invader; and the Fourteen Points were not sufficiently clear on this issue.

These objections were serious; but Colonel House, who represented Wilson in Europe, held high cards. The Allies were economically no less dependent upon American support for reconstruction than they had been for war. If the United States should break loose from them, and make a separate peace, the consequences might be disastrous.[9] The Germans probably would be heartened to take up arms again, and without the assistance of the United States it might prove impossible to extort satisfactory terms. After House had intimated that America might have to make a separate peace,[10] the Allies consented to accept the Fourteen Points as the basis of negotiations—with one important modification and one important elucidation. The reservation was that the Allies should retain complete liberty in the matter of the freedom of the seas; the elucidation was that restoration of evacuated territory by Germany should include compensation for damages to the civilian population, that is, reparations.

Though Wilson would have preferred an unreserved acceptance of the Fourteen Points as the basis for the peace, it was a triumph, considering the secret aims of the Allies, to have secured as much as he did.[11] The Armistice was finally signed on November 11, 1918. Contrary to a common misconception, Wilson was not responsible for its terms. The instrument was drawn up and approved by the Allied

[9] Wilson recognized the advantage that America held in this regard. See Baker, *Woodrow Wilson*, VII, 180.

[10] Seymour, *American Diplomacy during the World War*, pp. 324–325.

[11] Lloyd George, then British Prime Minister, has since insisted that except for the two reservations mentioned, the Allied war aims were in essential agreement with the Fourteen Points. David Lloyd George, *Memoirs of the Peace Conference* (New Haven, 1939), I, 46, 47, 49, 50, 88. The British, he says, were determined to continue the war without Wilson rather than give in on the freedom of the seas. *Ibid.* p. 44. For Wilson's bitter fight on this point and his contemplated public appeal for support, see Baker, *Woodrow Wilson*, VIII, 529, 533, 537–538.

High Command, which made sure of the fruits of victory without the necessity of a bloody invasion of Germany.[12]

There was, nevertheless, much dissatisfaction in the United States over the outcome. All America had been keyed up to a march on Berlin, and to leave the enemy soil untouched seemed to many a base betrayal. "Our answer to the Hun's twaddle," exclaimed the Cleveland *Plain Dealer*, "shall be more war." The Charleston *News and Courier* would have no bargaining "with the blood-stained gang of thugs and pirates . . . who deliberately . . . plunged the world into war." It would "smash them utterly and completely." Prominent Republicans, like Senator Lodge, feared a "soft peace." "Let us," cried Roosevelt, "dictate peace by the hammering guns and not chat about peace to the accompaniment of the clicking of typewriters." [13]

GERMAN "REPENTANCE."

American dissatisfaction with non-punitive victory. (Knott in the Dallas *News*.)

WILSON'S OCTOBER APPEAL

The President realized that he was faced with a desperate fight to persuade the Allies that they should accept a peace on the basis of the Fourteen Points. He knew that his hand would be greatly weakened if his leadership should be repudiated by a defeat in the November Congressional elections. On October 25, 1918, therefore, he issued his famous appeal to the voters, beginning:

If you have approved of my leadership and wish me to continue to be your unembarrassed spokesman in affairs at home and abroad, I earnestly beg that you will express yourselves unmistakably to that effect by returning a Democratic majority to both the Senate and the House of Representatives.[14]

During the war the popular slogan, sponsored by Wilson, had been: "Politics is adjourned." In fact, the Republicans in Congress

[12] Frederick Palmer, *Bliss, Peacemaker* (N.Y., 1934), p. 350.
[13] D. F. Fleming, *The United States and the League of Nations, 1918–1920* (N.Y., 1932), pp. 30–31.
[14] New York *Times*, Oct. 26, 1918, 1:6–7.

had supported parts of Wilson's war program more whole-heartedly than the Democrats. Now the Republican leaders rent the air with a cry that Wilson had broken the truce.[15] After a heated campaign, the voters marched to the polls in November, 1918, and returned Republican majorities to both houses of Congress. The victory, however, was by no means of landslide proportions; and Republican control of the Senate rested on the slender margin of two votes.

It is futile to argue what would have happened if Wilson had not made the appeal. He might conceivably have lost even more support if he had not taken this action. There is normally a swing against the Administration in the mid-term Congressional elections, and this was to be expected in 1918, particularly since the end of the war was in sight. It is well worth noting that a number of Democratic Representatives were delighted with the assistance that the President's appeal would presumably give them. Perhaps Wilson's greatest mistake was wording the statement so bluntly and so narrowly. He might better have followed the advice of several of his Cabinet members and asked for a Congress, both Democrats and Republicans, which would support him.[16]

JOVE STEPS DOWN FROM OLYMPUS

On November 18, 1918, two weeks after the election, Wilson startled the nation by the announcement that he was going to Paris as the head (it later developed) of the American peace delegation. He seems to have felt that only by appearing in person, and using the weight of his enormous prestige, could he secure the just and lasting peace which he had been advocating.

A cry of protest went up from Wilson's critics, chiefly partisan Republicans. They insisted that no President had ever gone to Europe before; that Wilson was needed at home to grapple with the pressing problems of domestic reconstruction; that his going was merely an

[15] Politics, in fact, was not adjourned. For some while Theodore Roosevelt, dominant leader of the reunited Republican party, had been carrying on a vigorous partisan campaign against the President, perhaps with the purpose of goading him into a public declaration. Fleming, *The United States and the League*, pp. 30–31. In 1898, McKinley had made a similar, though less spectacular, appeal for support in making peace with Spain. Roosevelt, also a Republican, had then applauded.

[16] Baker, *Woodrow Wilson*, VIII, 513–514; see also Selig Adler, "The Congressional Election of 1918," *South Atlantic Quar.*, XXXVI (1937), 457–458. This writer concludes that the result of the election was anti-Democratic rather than anti-Wilson, and that domestic and sectional issues were more important than peacemaking.

exhibition of his Messiah complex; and that he would be the only head of a delegation who had recently been repudiated by the electorate. Theodore Roosevelt loudly proclaimed that ". . . Mr. Wilson has no authority whatever to speak for the American people at this time." [17] It was also alleged that the President, who was already in poor health, could use his enormous influence to much better advantage by acting through instructed representatives, as McKinley had done in 1898. In America, at one end of the cable, Wilson could make his decisions calmly and unhurriedly, removed from enormous personal pressure, and in touch with American opinion. But this is all pure conjecture. The fact is that he decided to go.

The country—at least the Republicans—received another shock on November 29, 1918, when the personnel of the American peace commission was announced. In addition to Wilson, the membership consisted of Secretary Lansing, Colonel House, General Tasker Bliss, and Henry White, an outstanding career diplomat.

The foes of the Administration were far from satisfied. The Republicans complained bitterly because there was only one member of their party, Henry White, on the commission; and he was not an outstanding figure like Ex-President Taft or Elihu Root. The Senators were offended on two counts. First, Wilson had not consulted them in advance; and second, unlike McKinley, he had not selected a single member from their ranks. It was unfortunate for Wilson's program that he did not find it desirable or possible to defer to the Senate.[18]

Yet it seems reasonably clear, with politics reconvened, that whatever Wilson did would have been subjected to strong criticism from the Republicans. He was the only Democrat since Andrew Jackson to serve two consecutive terms, and he had pushed through Congress an extensive program of domestic reform. This had proved exceedingly distasteful to the big business interests, which were chiefly Republican, and they were determined to bring about a return of the good old days of *laissez faire*. If the President were triumphantly

---

[17] Kansas City *Star*, Nov. 25, 1918, 1:2.

[18] There were serious objections, from Wilson's point of view, to both Root and Taft. See P. C. Jessup, *Elihu Root* (N.Y., 1938), II, 379-380. The outstanding Republican in the Senate for such a purpose was Henry Cabot Lodge, who was conspicuously unfriendly to Wilson. To have chosen any other Senate Republican would have affronted the Massachusetts Senator. Wilson canvassed all of these possibilities, and he had good reasons, in his own mind at least, for what he did. See Allan Nevins, *Henry White* (N.Y., 1930), pp. 347-348.

to dictate a liberal peace to the world, his prestige would be so great that he might accept a third term, or possibly name his successor. Wilson and his work had to be defeated at all costs.[19]

A Prophet Is Not Without Honor

On December 4, 1918, five days after the names of the commission were announced, Wilson sailed from New York on the *George Washington*, with a small army of experts who were to assist him.[20] The great prophet arisen in the West—and apparently repudiated by his own people—received a tumultuous reception in Paris. *L'Europe Nouvelle* declared, "Never has a king, never has an emperor received such a welcome." One woman wrote:

Wilson, you have given back the father to his home, the ploughman to his field. . . . You have saved our fiancés; love blooms again. Wilson, you have saved our children. Through you evil is punished. Wilson! Wilson! Glory to you, who, like Jesus, have said: Peace on Earth and Good Will to Men! [21]

Delirious throngs turned out to cheer this American savior who had helped defeat the Germans, and who seemed to promise an immediate millennium. And he would draw up a just peace—which, of course, meant grinding Germany down to the very dust.

While waiting for the Conference to convene, the President journeyed to England, where he was warmly greeted, and to Italy, where the demonstration of blind devotion to "Voovro Veelson" was indescribable. One workingman declared:

They say he thinks of us—the poor people; that he wants us all to have a fair chance; that he is going to do something when he gets here that will make it impossible for our government to send us to war again. If he

---

[19] W. E. Dodd, *Woodrow Wilson and His Work* (N.Y., 1920), pp. 268–269. Sir John Simon told O. G. Villard, who was then in England, that an American lawyer had drawn up a careful statement of Wilson's weaknesses, and that this was being circulated among the members of the British delegation to the Conference. Villard, *Fighting Years* (N.Y., 1939), p. 374.

[20] In September, 1917, Colonel House, at the request of President Wilson, began to assemble a body of experts in New York, many of whom were college professors, for the purpose of collecting and studying data that might be useful to the Peace Conference. This organization was known as "The Inquiry," and it was the group of advisers who accompanied Wilson to Europe. For a valuable account by one of the members see J. T. Shotwell, *At the Paris Peace Conference* (N.Y., 1937), pp. 1–19.

[21] *L'Oeuvre*, Dec. 15, 1918, quoted in G. B. Noble, *Policies and Opinions at Paris, 1919* (N.Y., 1935), p. 73.

had only come sooner! I have already lost my two sons. Do you believe he is strong enough to stop all wars? [22]

OPEN COVENANTS SECRETLY ARRIVED AT

The first formal meeting of the Conference was held on January 12, 1919. From Wilson's point of view the start was inauspicious. The first of his Fourteen Points declared for "Open Covenants of peace, openly arrived at." Wilson did not mean by this that there was to be house-top diplomacy—that all the "birth pangs of the peace" were to be exposed to the public gaze. But he felt that the texts of treaties should be published so that the people concerned would know what obligations had been assumed by their governments.

American newspapers alone had sent about one hundred and fifty of their ablest correspondents to report in great detail how the peace was made. The door was barred against these eager reporters; and at the end of the first day a secretary slipped out and read to them a dry, five-line summary. The correspondents thereupon made a tremendous outcry.[23] Wilson fought vigorously for more publicity, since the United States was the one great nation whose aims could bear the full light of day. But the other Powers blocked any such course. In the end, the scanty official statements were supplemented with "careful leakages," "grapevine" rumors, and other "drippings" from the Conference.[24] One result of this secrecy was a most unfortunate atmosphere of suspicion and distrust.

The Peace Conference had not been at work very long when it was discovered that the hundreds of delegates of the twenty-seven Allied and Associated Powers gathered in plenary session made too unwieldy a group for effective work. The confusion was described by Harold Nicolson, a British observer, as "that sense of riot in a par-

[22] Norval Richardson, *My Diplomatic Education* (N.Y., 1929), pp. 182–183. Life-sized portraits of Wilson were everywhere in evidence. Mrs. Wilson tells of the extraordinary efforts that were made to keep the President from speaking to the Italian and French masses, presumably because he might be able to turn them against their governments in a demand for the pristine Fourteen Points. Edith Bolling Wilson, *My Memoir* (Indianapolis, 1939), pp. 217, 235. To Wilson's annoyance, the Allied statesmen did not want him to come to Paris. Baker, *Woodrow Wilson*, VIII, 585–586.

[23] R. S. Baker, *Woodrow Wilson and World Settlement* (Garden City, N.Y., 1922), I, 138 ff.

[24] The French fed information to their carefully controlled press calculated to prejudice the public mind against Wilson and his ideals. At one time the French newspapers became so abusive that the President threatened to move the whole Conference to Geneva; whereupon the tone of the press changed. See Noble, *Policies and Opinions at Paris, 1919*, pp. 82 ff.

rot house." The Supreme Council or the Council of Ten was therefore designated to do the most important work. It was composed of the two ranking delegates from each of the five great Powers: Great Britain, France, Italy, Japan, and the United States. Its decisions, arrived at with the help of numerous experts, were reported from time to time to the plenary conference for final action.

The Council of Ten itself proved to be too cumbersome and too leaky a body, and in March, 1919, it gave way to the Council of Four, or the "Big Four." This consisted of President Wilson; David Lloyd George, Prime Minister of Great Britain, alert, magnetic, shifting, master politician; Georges Clemenceau ("The Tiger"), President of the Council of France, grizzled, fiery, cynical, dogged champion of French interests; and Vittorio Orlando, Premier of Italy, a genial and cultured gentleman. Some of the time it was the Council of Three, for Orlando was not infrequently absent. Three lone men in a room determining the destiny of the world!

There was urgent need for haste. Europe was exhausted and hungry. "The wolf," said Herbert Hoover, "is at the door of the world." The red cloud of Bolshevism was spreading over Western Europe. Perhaps there would not even be a responsible government in Germany when the time came to offer the treaty.

Whatever the course adopted, it was evidently the part of wisdom to grapple with the most urgent problems first. Yet in the early days of the Conference the victors proposed dividing the booty, Germany's colonies—perhaps the least pressing major problem. Australia, New Zealand, and the Union of South Africa were insistent on this point, for they had not only played an important part in conquering them, but were anxious to remove future German naval and military bases. After a bitter fight, and in conformity with Point V, Wilson successfully resisted a division along old imperialistic lines. Instead, he was able to secure acceptance of the principle upon which the mandate system of the League of Nations was ultimately based.[25]

In Wilson's eyes the drawing up of the Covenant of the League of Nations, which would ensure a just and lasting peace, was the most important work of the Conference. But the Allied spokesmen, as well as many Republicans at home, insisted that the more pressing problem of the peace settlement be disposed of first, and that the League of Nations be organized afterward. Wilson feared, however, that if he did not get his views adopted at the outset, they would be shelved in the scramble for spoils. He was able to carry the day by the sheer

[25] Lloyd George, *Memoirs of the Peace Conference,* I, 121, 342–343, 359–360.

weight of his prestige, by diplomatic skill, and by logrolling.[26] It was nothing less than a triumph for him when the Conference voted, on January 25, 1919, that the League of Nations should be made an integral part of the treaty.

Wilson, himself, was appointed chairman of the commission to draft the Covenant of the League of Nations. Although the basic ideas of the scheme were not original with him, and although a number of Europeans had already done much work on such a plan, Wilson made the idea peculiarly his own. By laboring under great pressure, the commission was able to draw up a draft in ten days. On February 14, 1919, Wilson appeared before the Conference in plenary session and triumphantly read the completed League Covenant. "A living thing is born," he solemnly declared.[27]

By this time Wilson had been at the Conference for a month, from January 12 to February 15, 1919. It was now necessary for him to return to America for the purpose of signing necessary bills and of explaining the League Covenant to the American people. Thus far he had done well. He had successfully resisted a snarling division of the booty, and he had committed the Conference to his capstone point, the League of Nations. And his prestige, though waning, was high. Perhaps, as some have suggested, he would have been well advised if he had directed the subsequent negotiations by wire from the United States.

The Republican Round Robin

Before leaving Paris for home Wilson sent a cabled invitation to the House and Senate committees concerned with foreign affairs, asking them to dine with him at the White House and discuss the League of Nations. He also requested that Congress refrain from debating the subject until his arrival. But while Wilson was on the high seas

[26] Wilson won the support of the Italians by promising them the Brenner frontier in the Tyrol, with about 200,000 Germans. This was a glaring violation of the principle of self-determination, and was profoundly disillusioning to minority groups. At the time Wilson was apparently in ignorance of the facts, and having committed himself he felt unable to withdraw. Baker, *Wilson and World Settlement*, II, 146.

[27] D. H. Miller, *The Drafting of the Covenant* (N.Y., 1928), II, 563. Lloyd George challenges the assumption that the Americans forced the League on an unwilling Europe. He insists that the Allies were not only prepared to adopt some such scheme, but that they had made much greater progress in working out the details than Wilson had when he reached France. Lloyd George, *Memoirs of the Peace Conference*, I, 50, 153, 180–182, 403–425. House, however, reported at the time that Lloyd George and Clemenceau regarded the League as "an after consideration. . . ." Baker, *Woodrow Wilson*, VIII, 554.

the Senate swung into action. Senator Borah of Idaho attacked the League Covenant bitterly as "the greatest triumph for English diplomacy in three centuries of English diplomatic life," while Senator Reed of Missouri castigated the League of Nations as "a sort of international smelling committee."

The historic gathering of the Senate and House committees took place at the White House on the evening of February 26, 1919. The President, who agreed to answer all questions regarding the League, was closely cross-examined by his Congressional inquisitors. His friends thought that he appeared to good advantage; his critics otherwise. Republican Senator Brandegee of Connecticut remarked, "I feel as if I had been wandering with Alice in Wonderland and had had tea with the Mad Hatter." [28]

On the eve of Wilson's return to Europe, the opposition in the Senate flared up ominously. As the Sixty-fifth Congress expired, opponents of the President filibustered to death important appropriation bills. This made inevitable the calling of an extraordinary session, during which the Senate would be in a more advantageous position to attack Wilson and his treaty. On the last day of the Congress, March 4, 1919, the Senatorial foes of the League showed their teeth when Henry Cabot Lodge introduced the Republican Round Robin. It was signed by thirty-nine Senators or Senators-elect, more than the one third plus one necessary to defeat the treaty. The most striking passage of the ultimatum read:

Resolved . . . That it is the sense of the Senate that while it is their sincere desire that the nations of the world should unite to promote peace and general disarmament, the constitution of the league of nations *in the form now proposed* to the peace conference should not be accepted by the United States. . . .[29]

The Round Robin then went on to say that the proposal of a league of nations should be considered only after peace had been made. Obviously, this startling manifesto was designed to serve notice on the world, and particularly on the representatives of the Powers at Paris, that the United States Senate would approve no treaty embodying the League Covenant.

The Round Robin was warmly praised by Republican foes of the President. "Woodrow Wilson's League of Nations died in the Senate tonight," reported the New York *Sun*. George Harvey's *Har-*

[28] Fleming, *The United States and the League of Nations*, p. 134.
[29] *Cong. Record*, 65 Cong., 3 sess., p. 4974. Italics inserted.

vey's Weekly, which had been jeering at "the President's League of Nations Claptrap" and the "League of Denationalized Nations," cried "Honor and Praise" to Lodge, who had "fathered" the Round Robin, and to those who had co-operated in promulgating it.

Smarting from these attacks, Wilson addressed an enthusiastic crowd in New York, on the evening of March 4, 1919. He defiantly revealed his strategy in an unfortunate combination of boast and threat:

. . . When that treaty comes back, gentlemen on this side will find the covenant not only in it, but so many threads of the treaty tied to the covenant that you cannot dissect the covenant from the treaty without destroying the whole vital structure. The structure of peace will not be vital without the League of Nations, and no man is going to bring back a cadaver with him.[30]

Wilson apparently did not think that the Senate would dare incur the odium of rejecting the entire treaty.

THE BLUNTING OF THE FOURTEEN POINTS

The Round Robin and the other attacks on Wilson were widely heralded in Europe, where the foes of the President, thinking that he had been repudiated at home and that the League was dead, took heart. When Wilson returned, March 14, 1919, he was alarmed to discover that Lansing and House had, in his opinion, been too willing to make concessions during his absence.[31] He halted what he regarded as a movement to "sidetrack" the League when he dramatically declared that he would stand squarely on the action of the Conference in making the League an integral part of the treaty of peace.

The original draft of the League Covenant had been so hastily thrown together that it bristled with defects. Critics in America, many of them sincere and constructive, pointed to the desirability of amendment. They stressed particularly the necessity of safeguarding the Monroe Doctrine, of exempting domestic issues, and of providing a

[30] New York *Times*, March 5, 1919, 1:4.

[31] Those who do not believe that Wilson would have done better if he had stayed at home point to the fact that while he was absent from Paris, and while the negotiations were in the hands of instructed subordinates, the situation, from Wilson's point of view, began to get out of hand. For this episode see Baker, *Wilson and World Settlement*, I, 307 ff. Mrs. Wilson portrays the incident in dramatic terms, and takes House to task for his alleged treachery. Secretary Lansing, who was out of sympathy with Wilson's ideals, added to the jealousy among the American delegates. At one time Wilson seriously considered asking for his resignation. Edith Bolling Wilson, *My Memoir*, pp. 236, 245–246, 251, 252.

method for withdrawing from the League. Wilson finally succeeded in forcing the more reasonable of the American demands into the Covenant; but in so doing he weakened his hand with the other Powers, which insisted upon equivalent concessions.

The chief battle was with France. The grizzled Clemenceau, who remembered that the invader had been turned back by bayonets and bullets, not by idealism, was skeptical of the Fourteen Points. "God gave us his Ten Commandments," he said, "and we broke them. Wilson gave us his Fourteen Points—we shall see." [32]

Clemenceau's first demand was reparation for the damages caused by the Teuton invader. To determine how much Germany should pay, and how much she could pay, would take too much time and cause too much embarrassment. So the exact sum was left to the future. This, in effect, was a blank check against Germany's resources. Nevertheless, when one considers the current war hatreds, postponement probably was a gain for sanity.

Clemenceau's second demand was for security against a repetition of the horror of 1914, when the German host had thundered toward Paris. The French desired either to occupy Germany to the Rhine, or to create a buffer state there. But the placing of millions of Germans under the French flag would be a gross violation of the principle of self-determination. Against such an arrangement Wilson fought Clemenceau with all his soul, while the French press showered the American idealist with abuse. Ray Stannard Baker went to see the President in the evenings and he would find him "utterly beaten, worn out, his face quite haggard and one side of it and the eye twitching painfully; but the next morning he would appear refreshed and eager to go on with the fight." [33]

On April 3, 1919, at the peak of the crisis, Wilson was stricken with influenza. His temperature mounted to 103°, and he was seized with "violent paroxysms of coughing." Outside his bedroom, in the study, sat the other members of the "Big Four." To their every demand the sick man replied, "No!" On April 7, his patience exhausted, Wilson inquired when the *George Washington* could be made ready to take him back to the United States. Although a representative of the French Foreign Office sneered that the Americans "were going home to mother," this dramatic gesture may have played some part

---

[32] W. A. White, *Woodrow Wilson* (Boston, 1929), p. 384. "I can get on with you," said Clemenceau to House. "You are practical. I understand you, but talking to Wilson is something like talking to Jesus Christ!" *Lord Riddell's Intimate Diary of the Peace Conference and After, 1918–1923* (N.Y., 1934), p. 78.

[33] Baker, *Wilson and the World Settlement*, II, 43.

in effecting a compromise. France was to occupy the Rhineland for a maximum of fifteen years, and the Saar Valley for a like period, with a plebiscite in the Saar at the end of that time. In return, Britain and the United States were to sign a treaty with France promising her armed assistance in the event of an "unprovoked" attack by Germany. Although both Clemenceau and Wilson must have feared that the United States Senate would spurn such an entangling alliance—as it did—this proposal, fortified by indefinite French occupancy of the Rhineland, was too attractive for Clemenceau to refuse.[34]

The next crisis of the Conference was precipitated by Italy. She had entered the war on the side of the Allies only after she had been promised various parts of the enemy's territory by the secret Treaty of London. She now put forth an additional demand for Fiume, the only desirable ocean corridor of the newly created state of Yugo-slavia—a claim that was difficult to support on a self-determination basis. When Wilson found the Italian delegates obdurate, he appealed over their heads to their people, April 23, 1919.[35] The delegation heads temporarily left the Conference in anger; the Italian people rallied enthusiastically to their support; and Wilson was anathematized where he had shortly before been idolized. But he did win a hollow victory for self-determination.

The Japanese, who had been quietly biding their time, now took advantage of the Italian crisis to press their demands for German economic rights in China's province of Shantung, which they had recently wrested from Germany. On the basis of treaties and actual occupation, they had a far better case than Italy had in Fiume. Moreover, by the secret pact of February 16, 1917, Britain had agreed to support Japanese claims in Shantung and to the German Pacific islands north of the equator, in return for Japanese support of British claims to the German islands south of the equator. But since Shantung was Chinese, and contained some 30,000,000 people, Wilson feared a violation of self-determination if Japan were given so strong a foothold. If, however, the Japanese as well as the Italians were to withdraw from the Conference, it might collapse, and the precious

[34] The treaty was signed by President Wilson on June 28, 1919, and was sent to the Senate on July 29. It was referred to the Senate Foreign Relations Committee, from which it was never reported. H. C. Lodge, *The Senate and the League of Nations* (N.Y., 1925), p. 156.

[35] Lloyd George, *Memoirs of the Peace Conference*, II, 546–548. The British and French held Wilson's views regarding Fiume but, much to his anger, did not support him publicly, apparently preferring that he should receive the condemnation of the Italians. Edith Bolling Wilson, *My Memoir*, p. 255.

League of Nations might be lost.[36] So Wilson reluctantly consented to a compromise by which the Japanese were to retain the economic holdings of Germany and ultimately return the peninsula to China. Japan also received, under a mandate, the German Pacific islands north of the equator. This whole arrangement was expediency rather than justice —a disastrous blow to Wilson's prestige as the champion of self-determination. The surrender of Shantung lent point to Clemenceau's alleged remark that Wilson "talked like Jesus Christ but acted like Lloyd George."

VICTORY WITHOUT PEACE

On May 7, 1919, the fourth anniversary of the sinking of the *Lusitania*, the German delegates assembled at Versailles to receive the treaty. In one of the most dramatic moments in history, admirably staged by the French in the Trianon palace, Clemenceau bitingly addressed the fallen foe:

It is neither the time nor the place for superfluous words. . . . You have before you the accredited plenipotentiaries of all the small and great Powers united to fight together in the war that has been so cruelly imposed upon them. The time has come when we must settle our accounts. You have asked for peace. We are ready to give you peace.[37]

The Germans were given an opportunity to study the bulky two hundred page treaty thus presented to them on the point of a bayonet. They made bitter but generally futile protests. In particular, they resented having been disarmed by a promise of the Fourteen Points, and then having this peace of imperialism rammed down their throats. But to no avail. Marshal Foch, at the head of the French armies, was ready to march. At the Hall of Mirrors, Versailles, where forty-eight years earlier the German empire had been born, the German delegates reluctantly signed the treaty, June 28, 1919.

Why was not the peace a better one? Why was it that so many of the Fourteen Points were ignored, violated, or compromised away? Why was it that Wilson departed from Europe a fallen Messiah?

---

[36] T. E. La Fargue, *China and the World War* (Stanford University, 1937), Chs. VII and VIII, has a full discussion of the Shantung question.

[37] Baker, *Wilson and World Settlement*, II, 501. It will be noted that the Conference was not a conference in the ordinary sense. The Allies conferred only among themselves, not with the fallen foe. Wilson had favored a negotiated peace with Germany after the Allies had worked out their preliminary program; but he was unable to carry his plan through. Shotwell, *At the Paris Peace Conference*, p. 31.

The answer is not far to seek. Wilson essayed an impossible task. Each nation had its own selfish aims, many of them recognized in the vexatious secret treaties, some of them mutually conflicting, and others at variance with the principle of self-determination. Clemenceau fought bitterly for the objectives of France. He has been criticized for having been obdurate and selfish. But he was immediately responsible to the electorate, and if he had not vigorously supported the interests of the French people, he would have been replaced by some one who would do so. This, in fact, was true of all the Big Four, except Wilson. Nor was the United States willing to sacrifice any of its traditional policies or vital interests to insure a more satisfactory settlement.[38]

In essence, the problem was this. There had to be a peace, and a speedy peace, or Europe would fall into complete chaos. And since there were many conflicting aims, there would have to be compromise or no treaty. So there was compromise—and some injustice. Even so, there was much to be said in behalf of the treaty, particularly the liberation of millions of oppressed minorities. And even more could now be said in its behalf if the Allies had proceeded to carry it out in fairness and good faith, especially the pledge to reduce arms.[39] Nor is it reasonable to suppose that a victorious Germany would have dictated a better one. Given a Europe seething with war hatreds, and given all other factors and conditions, it is remarkable that the Treaty of Versailles was not more imperfect. Wilson, of course, was deeply distressed by the outcome, but he hoped that the League of Nations would be able to iron out the more serious injustices, and that American participation would soften the treaty's terms. The next task was to induce the United States to accept the pact.

BIBLIOGRAPHICAL NOTE

The best summary treatment of the period from April, 1917, to November, 1918, is Charles Seymour, *American Diplomacy during the World War* (Baltimore, 1934), pp. 212–403. There is a wealth of documentary material for the same years in R. S. Baker, *Woodrow Wilson: Life and Letters*, vols. VII and VIII (N.Y., 1939). The most important work on Wilson and the Paris Conference,

---

[38] The United States refused to accept the French security treaty, declined a mandate for Armenia and Constantinople, and, by failing to ratify the Treaty of Versailles, was not represented on the Reparations Commission. The absence of an American representative enabled France to dominate that body, and saddle an enormous reparations burden on Germany. See Lloyd George, *Memoirs of the Peace Conference*, I, 117, 189, 340–341.

[39] Lloyd George argues strongly that many of the ills attributed to the treaty were not the fault of that document but of the men who executed it. *Ibid.*, II, 906–915.

based on the President's papers and favorable to him, is R. S. Baker, *Woodrow Wilson and World Settlement* (2 vols., Garden City, N.Y., 1922). Also important is Lloyd George's apologia, *Memoirs of the Peace Conference* (2 vols., New Haven, 1939), which must be used with caution. Robert Lansing, *The Peace Negotiations* (Boston, 1921), is strongly biased against Wilson. Edith Bolling Wilson (Mrs. Woodrow Wilson), *My Memoir* (Indianapolis, 1939) is favorable.. Accounts by American advisers of the commission appear in E. M. House and Charles Seymour, eds., *What Really Happened at Paris* (N.Y., 1921); C. H. Haskins and R. H. Lord, *Some Problems of the Peace Conference* (Cambridge, 1920); and J. T. Shotwell, *At the Paris Peace Conference* (N.Y., 1937). The last-named contains valuable contemporary observations. Important biographies of two of the commissioners are Allan Nevins' *Henry White* (N.Y., 1930) and Frederick Palmer's *Bliss, Peacemaker* (N.Y., 1934). D. H. Miller, *The Drafting of the Covenant* (2 vols., N.Y., 1928), is an important work by a leading participant. For a briefer secondary account see D. F. Fleming, *The United States and the League of Nations, 1918–1920* (N.Y., 1932). On French public opinion consult G. B. Noble, *Policies and Opinions at Paris, 1919* (N.Y., 1935). Significant articles are: R. C. Binkley, "New Light on the Paris Peace Conference, *Pol. Sci. Quar.*, XLVI (1931), 335–361; 509–547; and a bibliographical study by the same author, "Ten Years of Peace Conference History," *Jour. of Mod. Hist.*, I (1929), 607–629. Further references: see footnotes of this chapter and Bemis and Griffin, *Guide*, pp. 673–684.

RECENT REFERENCES. All of the above general works must now be read in the light of Paul Birdsall, *Versailles Twenty Years After* (N.Y., 1941), which, in addition to presenting new materials, is a critical summation of recent scholarship. The author concludes that Wilson was consistent and "the only man of real stature at Paris (p. 295)"; House was the compromiser who seriously weakened the President's position; Lloyd George was a slippery double-dealer. In order to block French and British demands that Germany pay the entire cost of the war, Wilson was forced, against his better judgment and against the specific terms of the pre-Armistice contract with Germany, to allow pension and other charges in addition to civilian damages. This, writes Birdsall, was an "egregious breach of faith" in dealing with Germany (p. 6), which in the end reacted disastrously upon the Allies. But at the time of the reparations surrender, Wilson was ill and Colonel House played an unfortunate role in the solution (pp. 258–259). The author believes that on every major question, except reparations, Versailles "would have been a worse treaty had Wilson remained in Washington (p. 295)." The settlement, Birdsall concludes, was not so bad as painted; its failure was largely due to American unwillingness to co-operate and to French intransigence, especially in regard to the Ruhr. For a discussion of other important works on Versailles, see Bibliographical Appendix, p. 941.

NEW REFERENCES. T. A. Bailey, *Woodrow Wilson and the Lost Peace* (N.Y., 1944), the most recent critical survey of the subject, elaborates many of the points which the same author outlines in the present chapter. The bibliographies supplement those herein given. For numerous other new contributions, see Bibliographical Appendix, p. 942.

4TH ED. REFS. See Bibliographical Appendix, p. 943.

CHAPTER XL

The Fight for the Treaty in America, 1919–1920

"The League was defeated in the United States, not because it was a League of Nations, but because it was a Woodrow Wilson league, and because the great leader had fallen and there was no one who could wield his mighty sword."

T. W. Gregory (Wilson's Attorney General), 1925.

THE PARADE OF PREJUDICE

THE lengthy Treaty of Versailles, with the League firmly "riveted in," faced a formidable gauntlet of opponents in America. Partisan Republicans, humiliated and hurt by six years of Democratic rule, had their knives sharpened for Wilson—that "drum-major of civilization." In addition, there was a considerable body of liberals who were profoundly disappointed by what they regarded as the bartering away of the Fourteen Points and the imposition of a victor's peace. "The treaty," said the Springfield *Republican*, "was dictated in a paroxysm of hate."

The "hyphenates" were also a force to be reckoned with. Tens of thousands of German-Americans felt that the treaty was a base betrayal of the Fatherland. Hundreds of thousands of Italian-Americans, a great body of whom lived in Senator Lodge's Massachusetts, were bitterly dissatisfied with Wilson's course regarding Fiume.[1] Millions of Hibernian-Americans were indignant because the President had not affronted Great Britain by pressing the cause of Irish independence at Paris. They were alarmed by a League in which the component parts of the British Empire would have six votes to one for the United States. They were angered by Article X of the Covenant, which suggested the use of force to maintain the *status quo* and which, they felt, would hinder the realization of their aspirations. Dr. F. P. Mc-

---

[1] Senator Lodge insisted that Fiume was as essential to the well-being of Italy as the mouth of the Mississippi was to the United States. In vain did Henry White point out that this was true of Yugoslavia, not Italy. But there were not enough Yugoslav voters in Massachusetts to make it politically profitable for the Senator to admit his error. Allan Nevins, *Henry White* (N.Y., 1930), p. 431.

Carthy declared that as a result of it "Ireland is to be in perpetual slavery." Senator Johnson of California insisted that under Article X "The British Empire can demand American blood to subdue Ireland." The name of Wilson was repeatedly hissed by huge Irish crowds, who wildly cheered their own leaders. Two "prominent Republicans" went to the British ambassador in Washington and explained to him that in using the Irish question to defeat Wilson and the League they would flay England without mercy; but they wanted it understood in official British circles that they meant nothing by it.[2]

Perhaps the most formidable opponents of the League were dead men: Washington, Jefferson, Monroe, and Theodore Roosevelt.[3] America was strong and self-sufficient, and her traditional policy of isolation had served her well. Why should she become involved in a "League of Denationalized Nations" which might conceivably order American soldiers to Hejaz to protect King Hussein against the Bedouins? Why should the Stars and Stripes fly below the flag of some superstate? "One-hundred per cent Americanism," with William Randolph Hearst a leading trumpeter, became the slogan of the hour. The advertisement of an anti-League meeting in Boston read:

AMERICANS, AWAKE!

Shall We Bind Ourselves to the War Breeding Covenant?
It Impairs American Sovereignty!
Surrenders the Monroe Doctrine!
Flouts Washington's Warning!
Entangles us in European and Asiatic Intrigues!
Sends Our Boys to Fight Throughout the World by Order of a League!
"The evil thing with a holy name!"[4]

The United States had, to be sure, forsaken Washington's warning when it sent two million men to France to fight "a war to end wars" and to "make the world safe for democracy." Wilson's inspiring leadership had keyed the American people up to a spirit of self-sacrifice that even brought prohibition of alcoholic beverages. But all that was now ended. Victory had brought an emotional letdown—"the slump in idealism." America had got little or nothing at the peace table but opposition and ill will. She was weary of war. Hundreds of thousands of boys were returning from France, homesick, irritated,

[2] *Ibid.*, p. 456.
[3] On his deathbed, late in 1918, Roosevelt had conspired with Lodge to defeat the yet unborn League of Nations. *Ibid.*, p. 351.
[4] Boston *Herald*, July 8, 1919, 1: 1–2.

disgusted. As R. L. Duffus wrote in the New York *Globe,* they were "only too glad to shut the front gate and stay at home for a while." Would Wilson be able to arouse the American people again—this time to a self-sacrificing adherence to the League?

THE SENATE PLAYS FOR TIME

The great debate over the League of Nations centered in the Senate. This body was Republican; and it would be poor politics to assist a Democratic President in a great personal triumph. Nor had Wilson shown much respect for what he called the "pigmy-minded" gentlemen on Capitol Hill. He had also assumed much legislative prerogative during his wartime dictatorship; and Congress was in a mood to reassert itself.

The leader of the Republican opposition in the Senate was Henry Cabot Lodge, "ambassador from Massachusetts to the United States." He was a man of considerable intellectual force, a skillful political leader, and a partisan Republican who hated Wilson with consuming bitterness.[5] Lodge had at first openly espoused a league of nations; but when the President began to champion such an organization, the Massachusetts Senator turned against it. His entire record of inconsistencies and partisanship indicates that he attacked the Treaty of Versailles largely, if not primarily, because of his antipathy for Wilson.

When the pact finally came to America, Lodge found the tide of public opinion running so strongly for the League that he despaired of defeating it outright.[6] The best he could hope for was "to Americanize" it by adding a number of amendments or reservations for which the Republicans could take credit. Perhaps the stubborn Wilson

[5] Senator Depew likened Lodge's mind to the New England landscape—"naturally barren, but highly cultivated." Prior to Wilson's advent Lodge had been known as "the scholar in politics," and he may have resented the loss of that distinction to the President.

[6] After Borah's first major speech against the League, early in 1919, Lodge congratulated him, but added despairingly: "What are you going to do? It's hopeless. All the newspapers in my state are for it." According to Borah, Lodge was a League man at heart, but opposed Wilson's League for partisan reasons. Interview with Senator Borah, Washington, D.C., April 21, 1937. For further evidence of Lodge's basic sympathy with the League see P. C. Jessup, *Elihu Root* (N.Y., 1938), II, 402–403. Other Republican Senators told Borah after his speech of February 21, 1919: "That was great; that was fine; we agree with you; but we have got to have some sort of league; everybody is for it." Senator Harding told Borah: "Bill, I'd like to get in the fight against this League of Nations, but the people of my state are all for it I'm afraid." C. O. Johnson, *Borah of Idaho* (N.Y., 1936), pp. 232, 233.

would refuse to accept such an emasculated treaty, in which case the President and his party would receive the blame.[7]

When Congress met in extraordinary session, on May 19, 1919, the Senate consisted of 49 Republicans and 47 Democrats.[8] The Republicans were able to place a majority on the Senate Committee on Foreign Relations, of which Lodge was chairman, and pack it with men unfriendly to the League. This was a great advantage to the opponents of the treaty, for they could delay it in committee until a hostile public opinion could be aroused. Several years later Senator Moses of New Hampshire declared that if the rules of the Senate had permitted quick action "the Versailles treaty would have been ratified without reservations."

An unofficial copy of the document was laid before the Senate on June 9, 1919. At this time a clear majority of the American people apparently favored ratification, if not *in toto*, at least with some reservations. Thirty-two state legislatures had endorsed the League in concurrent resolutions, and two others conditionally; thirty-three governors had gone on record as favoring a League of Nations; and a *Literary Digest* poll of newspaper editors indicated the same trend. By May 1, 1919, Lodge himself admitted:

. . . What I may call the vocal classes of the community, most of the clergymen, the preachers of sermons, a large element in the teaching force of the universities, a large proportion of the newspaper editors, and finally the men and women who were in the habit of writing and speaking for publication, although by no means thoroughly informed, were friendly to the League as it stood and were advocating it.[9]

But Lodge was by no means daunted. Time and money might yet save the country from the League. Time he had, because he could tie the treaty up in the committee. Money he secured by tapping the reserves of Henry Clay Frick and Andrew Mellon, two Republican

[7] H. C. Lodge, *The Senate and the League of Nations* (N.Y., 1925), p. 164.

[8] The Republicans were able to control the Senate by virtue of the victory of Newberry in Michigan over his Democratic opponent, Henry Ford, by the narrow margin of 220,054 to 212,487. Newberry was subsequently convicted of having incurred excessive campaign expenditures, freed on a technicality, and finally forced from the Senate by public opinion. But by that time the treaty had been defeated. If Ford had won, there would have been 48 Republicans and 48 Democrats. The Vice-President, a Democrat, would have cast his vote with the Democrats, the Foreign Relations Committee would have contained a majority of Democrats and would have had a Democratic chairman. By such small margins is the course of history changed. D. F. Fleming, *The United States and the League of Nations, 1918–1920* (N.Y., 1932), p. 401 n.

[9] Lodge, *Senate and the League*, p. 147.

millionaires who had been heavy beneficiaries of the Republican tariff.[10] The campaign of anti-League propaganda could now be undertaken with full force.

In due season the printed treaty was sent to the Senate Committee on Foreign Relations. There Senator Lodge read aloud the entire document of 264 quarto pages, a process that consumed two weeks. During some of the time not even the clerk of the committee was present. This unedifying and totally unnecessary procedure can be rationally explained only on the ground that the Republicans wanted time to organize their opposition and to wait for public opinion to turn against the League.

Another means of consuming time was provided by hearings before the Senate Committee on Foreign Relations. These took an additional six weeks. Though ostensibly conducted for the information of the Senate, the hearings were obviously held to embarrass the President. Some sixty witnesses were summoned, and their remarks filled over twelve hundred pages of printed material. Some of those who testified, including Secretary Lansing and the American experts who had advised Wilson at Paris, were able to throw real light on the subject.[11] Less defensible was the hearing given to representatives of racial minorities. Self-appointed spokesmen appeared in behalf of the disappointed and frequently conflicting aspirations of a score of different groups, ranging from Ireland to Korea. The Senators solemnly listened to arguments for the breaking up of the British Empire, as if that were germane to the business at hand. The ultimate was reached when a woman with an Irish name argued the claim of Italy to Yugoslavia's Fiume.

Not content with these proceedings, Lodge arranged for a public conference between his committee and the President at the White House, August 19, 1919. Although Wilson answered questions for three hours, he apparently did not succeed in changing the views of the Senators. In commenting on the affair afterwards, he remarked "that Senator [later President] Harding had a disturbingly dull mind, and that it seemed impossible to get any explanation to lodge in it." [12]

---

[10] Fleming, *The United States and the League of Nations*, pp. 209–210.

[11] *Ibid.*, pp. 298 ff.

[12] D. F. Houston, *Eight Years with Wilson's Cabinet* (Garden City, N.Y., 1926), II, 17. On this occasion Wilson declared that it was not until he had reached Paris that the secret treaties were revealed to him for the first time. Whether he was weary and confused in mind, or whether he deliberately misled his inquisitors, the evidence is incontrovertible that he had learned of the agreements earlier. See R. S. Baker, *Woodrow Wilson* (N.Y., 1939), VII, 44 n., 74–75, 80, 162, 180, 346, 350–351, 380, 387, 407, 512.

TAKING THE LEAGUE TO THE COUNTRY

By the first of September, 1919, the treaty was plainly losing ground. It was still tied up in committee nearly two months after it had been presented; and the hearings were stirring up an incalculable amount of prejudice. Lodge and his colleagues were attacking the League with great vigor on the floor of the Senate. It seemed as if the pact might be emasculated or even defeated unless heroic measures were taken.

Wilson then decided upon an audacious step. During the war he had repeatedly and, on the whole, successfully appealed to the people to support him. He was convinced that if he should take his case to the country, the masses would rally once more, and an organized and overwhelming public opinion would force the Senate to act promptly and favorably.

The fighting President, now sixty-three years of age, undertook this arduous journey against the advice of physicians and friends.[13] His health had never been robust, and he was now weak, trembling, exhausted. Six years as Chief Executive, with the inferno of a World War and the madhouse of a Peace Conference thrown in, had taken their toll. The Republican opposition at home, to say nothing of oppressing domestic problems and the heat of Washington, had further sapped his strength. And now he insisted on a "barnstorming" campaign that would have taxed the endurance of William Jennings Bryan in his prime.[14] The President knew that he was taking a grave chance; but he said that he would be glad to give his life for the cause.[15]

Wilson left Washington on September 3, 1919. After speaking in Ohio and Indiana, he passed on to the trans-Mississippi Middle West, where there was a strong German-American element. His receptions here, though enthusiastic, were not all that his friends might have

[13] Edith Bolling Wilson, *My Memoir* (Indianapolis, 1939), p. 274. This book contains a colorful account of Wilson's tour West, and stresses the tremendous strain on the President.

[14] Over a period of twenty-two days Wilson delivered thirty-seven speeches which averaged an hour in length. During this time he traveled more than 8000 miles and participated in about a dozen parades, throughout which he was forced to stand in a swaying automobile for an hour at a time. It is interesting to speculate what might have been the result if Wilson, who was a persuasive speaker, could have sat before a radio and explained the League of Nations in several "fireside chats." Whereas his successors can reach millions effortlessly, Wilson found it necessary to dissipate his energy in speaking to only a few thousand at a time.

[15] J. P. Tumulty, *Woodrow Wilson as I Know Him* (Garden City, N.Y., 1921), p. 435.

desired.[16] The President, of course, was not at his best. Already exhausted, he did not have time to prepare his speeches properly. He made some palpable errors of fact, and he so far lost his customary

GOING TO TALK TO THE BOSS

Wilson appeals to public opinion. (From the Chicago *News*.)

dignity as to brand his adversaries as "contemptible quitters if they do not see the game through," and to challenge them to "put up or shut up." He was also under the handicap of placing the best possible interpretation on what he knew was an imperfect treaty. But when Wilson reached Montana and Idaho, he was welcomed with demonstrations of enthusiasm that were well-nigh unbelievable. Washington, Oregon, and California warmed the President's heart. The West had elected him in 1916, and it was still with him.

Disturbed by the reception that Wilson was receiving, several of the "irreconcilable" Senators, notably Borah of Idaho and Johnson of California, carried through plans to "trail" the President, speaking in some of the same cities a little later on the other side of the subject. These orators, who were better able to play on the emotions of the masses than Wilson, attracted enthusiastic, hat-throwing crowds. When the President's name was mentioned on one occasion, cries came back, "Impeach him, impeach him!"

Wilson's ovations reached a high point in Pueblo, Colorado, on September 25, 1919. The *Rocky Mountain News* reported that when he appeared "the entire audience arose and cheered for fully ten

[16] See Fleming, *The United States and the League of Nations*, pp. 337 ff., for an account of the tour.

minutes." With tears in his eyes, the President pleaded for his League of Nations to end war, while the crowd roared its approval "time and time again." But this was the end for Wilson. Although he had planned to carry the fight into Lodge's New England, his frail body now refused to go on. The remaining speeches were canceled; and he was whisked back to Washington, where he lay a shell of his former self—as much a victim of the war, said his Attorney General, as the unknown soldier at Arlington.[17]

For weeks the President lay helpless. During a period of seven and one half months he did not meet his Cabinet. No outsiders were permitted to see him while he was most seriously ill. His coolness toward House and Lansing, both of whom had not seen eye to eye with him at the Conference, developed into an open break. He failed to answer House's letters; he dismissed Lansing from the Cabinet. Who ran the government during this interregnum is still something of a mystery.[18] People noted the bars on the White House windows (put there to keep the ball-playing Roosevelt children from smashing them), and whispered about the insane man inside. But the President's mind remained clear throughout;[19] and gradually some of his strength came back to him.

At the time Wilson was stricken the League seems to have been gaining momentum. The President's illness left public opinion confused and drifting, and deprived the Democrats in the Senate of their only effective leader. As the event proved, Wilson would have been well-advised to remain in the White House, conserving his strength, conciliating the Senate opposition, and compromising enough to make possible the acceptance of a treaty that was already a "bundle of compromises."

Wilson Spurns the Senate Reservations

Two weeks before the President's collapse at Pueblo, the Senate Committee on Foreign Relations acted. The report of the Republican majority—a bitterly partisan document—proposed forty-five amend-

---

[17] New York *Times*, Jan. 29, 1925, 18:8. (T. W. Gregory).

[18] Mrs. Wilson studied the various state papers and permitted only the most pressing matters to go to the President. "I, myself," she writes, "never made a single decision regarding the disposition of public affairs. The only decision that was mine was what was important and what was not, and the *very* important decision of when to present matters to my husband." Edith Bolling Wilson, *My Memoir*, p. 289.

[19] The Republicans in the Senate arranged to have a committee visit Wilson to determine whether or not he was mentally sound. Senator Fall entered and remarked, "Well, Mr. President, we have all been praying for you." "Which way, Senator?" inquired the President with a chuckle. *Ibid.*, p. 299.

ments and four reservations. After prolonged debate, the amendments were all rejected on the ground that the entire Peace Conference would have to be reconvened to make them valid. Instead, the Senate, by an almost solid Republican vote, added fourteen so-called Lodge reservations. These were ostensibly designed to release the United States from certain entanglements, and to safeguard American institutions and historic policies, including the Monroe Doctrine.

Wilson had repeatedly expressed a willingness to accept mild reservations, but he balked at those of Senator Lodge, particularly the one that struck at Article X, "the heart of the Covenant." The President felt, not without reason, that if he should consent to the Senate reservations, the opposition would add others that he could not accept. He also believed that the Senate would eventually be forced into line because "the alternative of going back to Germany to negotiate a new treaty is too absurd." At this critical moment Wilson wrote a letter to his loyal Democratic following:

. . . In my opinion . . . [the Lodge resolution] does not provide for ratification but, rather, for the nullification of the treaty. I sincerely hope that the friends and supporters of the treaty will vote against the Lodge resolution of ratification.

I understand that the door will probably then be open for a genuine resolution of ratification.

I trust that all true friends of the treaty will refuse to support the Lodge resolution.[20]

The crucial vote was taken on the next day, November 19, 1919. The treaty, with the fourteen reservations, was defeated by a vote of 39 yeas to 55 nays. The yeas consisted of thirty-five "reservationist" Republicans and four Democrats; the nays consisted of thirteen "irreconcilable" Republicans, together with the overwhelming majority of the Democrats, forty-two altogether, who loyally followed their fallen leader's request. Since these Democratic votes defeated the treaty with reservations, there is much truth in the assertion that Wilson himself kept the United States out of the League of Nations.[21]

Jubilation reigned in many Republican quarters. Senator Borah proclaimed the result as "the greatest victory since Appomattox."

[20] *Cong. Record*, 66 Cong., 1 sess., p. 8768. Letter dated Nov. 18, 1919.
[21] The treaty without reservations was defeated by a vote of 38 yeas to 53 nays. The majority of the Democrats voted yea; the Republicans voted nay. For an analysis of the votes in the Senate see W. S. Holt, *Treaties Defeated by the Senate* (Baltimore, 1933), pp. 294–298.

"Thanks be to God which giveth us the victory," declared the Boston *Transcript*. The defeat of the treaty was, said the Republican Cleveland *News*, a "twin-victory of independence and democracy." [22] On the other hand, critics of the Republican opposition regretted the "low political intrigue" and partisan obstruction of the Senate. One friend of the League bemoaned "the greatest tragedy since the crucifixion of the Saviour of Mankind."

THE TRIUMPH OF PARTISANSHIP

But the treaty was not yet dead. A war-weary public simply would not tolerate the quiet interment of the pact just because the Senate, an overwhelming majority of whose members professed to favor the League, could not come to an agreement over a few reservations. Senator Lodge was visited by representatives of twenty-six great national organizations whose combined membership totaled 20,000,000 voters, and they urged immediate approval of the treaty.[23] A poll was taken in several hundred colleges and universities after rejection, and it revealed strong sentiment for ratification. There can be little doubt, judging from petitions and other appeals, that the intellectual leadership of America supported the League of Nations. It also seems probable that the eighty per cent of the Senate membership which favored the treaty in some form represented a like proportion of public opinion throughout the country.[24] Both Democrats and Republicans refused to accept the decision as final.

Under the lash of a strong public reaction the Senate voted to reconsider its decision, and on February 16, 1920, the debate was resumed. The treaty came to a vote on March 19, 1920. There were fifteen reservations this time—one had been added in favor of Irish independence. As before, Wilson wrote a letter to the rudderless

[22] *Literary Digest*, LXIII, 11 (Nov. 29, 1919).

[23] Responsive to the public demand, Lodge attempted to work out with Senator Simmons, a Democratic leader, a reservation to Article X. Borah got wind of this on January 23, 1919, mustered his "irreconcilable" following, haled Lodge into his office, and threatened to disrupt the party and depose Lodge as majority leader if he did not stand his ground. Lodge thereupon abandoned his separate negotiation, and America's entrance into the League was perhaps prevented. Interview with Senator Borah, Washington, D.C., April 21, 1937. A similar version is given by Borah's authorized biographer. See Johnson, *Borah of Idaho*, pp. 246–247. Senator McNary, who was then a "mild reservationist," told the present writer (May 7, 1937) that this story is substantially correct and that he has in his possession the original of the Simmons compromise resolution, on which appear changes in the handwriting of Lodge.

[24] Holt, *Treaties Defeated by the Senate*, p. 290.

Democrats in the Senate expressing his desire that the treaty with reservations be rejected. He insisted:

Either we should enter the league fearlessly, accepting the responsibility and not fearing the rôle of leadership which we now enjoy, contributing our efforts towards establishing a just and permanent peace, or we should retire as gracefully as possible from the great concert of powers by which the world was saved.[25]

The treaty failed to receive the necessary two-thirds majority by a vote of 49 yeas to 35 nays. The nays consisted of twelve "irreconcilable" Republicans (the "Battalion of Death"), plus twenty-three Democrats who remained loyal to Wilson. Since it was obvious that the treaty would not be ratified without reservations, twenty-one Democrats forsook their leader and voted for approval. If only seven of the faithful twenty-three had transferred their votes, the decision would have been reversed. It seems highly probable that if the President had kept silent this would have happened. He asked for all or nothing— and got nothing.

Various elements combined to bring about the result. Ignorance of the treaty, confusion of thought, jealousy of Senatorial prerogative, personal hatred of Wilson, and a devotion to the traditional policy of isolation were all important factors. Friends of the League thought it strange, however, that Washington, Jefferson, and Monroe could not keep America out of the war, but they could keep her out of the peace and a League of Nations designed to end war. Yet in the final analysis it seems that partisan politics pure and simple contributed more than anything else to the defeat of Wilson in the Senate. Reservations killed the treaty. And the Lodge reservations were added by an almost solid Republican vote and opposed by an almost solid Democratic vote. All of which suggests that if the President had been a Republican the decision would have been reversed.

Wilson's physical collapse was a vital factor in the outcome. He might have seen the wisdom of accepting a compromise if he had been well and had been more closely in touch with the drift of public opinion. But he probably was not fully cognizant of the true state of affairs. Stubborn and of a single-track mind, he was permitted to see only a few people, and these were loath to shock the sick man with disagreeable realities. Whether properly informed or not, Wilson rejected the Lodge reservations outright, apparently hoping that in 1920 the voters would rise up and demand an unemasculated League.

[25] *Cong. Record*, 66 Cong., 2 sess., p. 4052 (March 8, 1920, Wilson's letter).

A League—But not This One

A year and a half after the Armistice the United States was still technically at war with Germany—an anomalous situation disturbing to trade and other relationships. In May, 1920, therefore, Congress passed a joint resolution declaring hostilities at an end. Wilson vetoed this measure, confidently expecting the people to return a mandate for the treaty in the approaching presidential election.

The Republican National Convention found it difficult to frame an acceptable plank on the League. Within the party there were "irreconcilables," reservationists, and advocates of the League. The platform as finally drawn up was a masterpiece of ambiguity. It was so artfully worded as to enable all shades of Republicans to support the party in the confident belief that their views would be sustained.

Deadlocked over a nominee, the Republican Convention turned, as a compromise choice, to the handsome and affable Senator Warren G. Harding of Ohio.[26] He was easily manageable, and a regular Republican. He had been a somewhat mechanical opponent of the League during the fight, and had commended himself to the attention of the party bosses months before the convention met. His prospects improved when he declared that "America's present need is not heroics but healing; not nostrums but normalcy; not revolution but restoration. . . ." "Normalcy" may not have been in common usage, but it was what the people wanted. Suffering from "moral overstrain," they were tired of being asked to exert themselves nobly in behalf of idealism. Harding, the antithesis of Wilson, was the man for the times. Unlike the somewhat unapproachable President, he was a hail-fellow-well-met. In other words, he was "just folks"—"folksy" as one word-coiner put it. To be sure he was not an intellectual heavyweight. Wilson spoke of his "bungalow mind." But, as one Republican Senator said, the times did not demand "first raters."

The Democratic Convention, though not opposing mild reservations, endorsed the League. Governor Cox of Ohio, the nominee, declared himself four-square for the Covenant. The resulting campaign was a listless affair, in spite of Wilson's request that it be "a great and solemn referendum." There can be no doubt that by this time the electorate was thoroughly weary of the treaty issue, now nearly two years old. The New York *Call* declared that politically the League

[26] George Harvey said afterward, "He was nominated because there was nothing against him, and because the delegates wanted to go home." W. F. Johnson, *George Harvey* (Boston, 1929), p. 278.

was "as vital as a dead cat in a gutter." The somewhat confused Harding took, so claimed his opponent, fourteen different stands on the League question. Perhaps his most consistent note was that after the election he would consult with the "best minds" "to the end that we shall have an association of nations for the promotion of international peace." In short, not a Democratic "League" but a Republican "Association." Mr. Chester Rowell, a well-informed Republican journalist, wrote:

One half of the speeches were for the League of Nations if you read them hastily, but if you read them with care every word of them could have been read critically as against the League of Nations. The other half were violent speeches against the League of Nations if you read them carelessly, but if you read them critically every one of them could be interpreted as in favor of the League of Nations.[27]

But all this did not disturb the electorate very much. "Back to Normalcy" was the winning slogan.

The result was a foregone conclusion. On the eve of the election odds were ten to one against Cox. Hundreds of thousands of eligible voters stayed away from the polls. Wearied of Wilsonism, the rest rose up and cast a tremendous vote for Harding. "It was not a landslide," said Joseph P. Tumulty, Wilson's secretary, "it was an earthquake."

Was the Republican triumph a repudiation of the League, as Lodge gloatingly asserted? As a matter of fact, there were dozens of issues, ranging from prohibition of alcoholic beverages to self-determination for Ireland, and it would be absurd to say that the results were a mandate on any one of them. The Republican platform was so ambiguous and the candidate so platitudinous that "irreconcilables" like Senators Borah and Johnson supported Harding as the surest way of keeping the country out of the League, while thirty-one prominent Republicans, including Root, Hughes, and Hoover, signed a manifesto announcing that they were voting for Harding as the surest way of getting the country into the League.[28] Perhaps the Democratic New York *World* was not far from the mark when it observed: "The American people wanted a change, and they have voted for a change. They did not know what kind of change they wanted, and they do not

---

[27] Quoted in Fleming, *The United States and the League of Nations*, p. 460.

[28] New York *Times*, Oct. 15, 1920, 1:7. It now appears that the manifesto was designed by Republicans who did not want to bolt the party but who wished to commit Harding more definitely to the League. Jessup, *Elihu Root*, II, 414.

know today what kind of change they have voted for." If the results were a mandate on anything they were a mandate from the people to relax—to get away from Wilsonism and to return to "normalcy."

Should the United States have entered the League? Would the subsequent history of the League have been more happy if the great American republic had not abandoned it? Did the United States give civilization a setback by not assuming its responsibilities?

Whatever the final answer to these questions, it is clear that the forces that kept America out of the League were not altogether creditable. As if to mock her, there stands a tablet at Geneva, inscribed:

A LA MEMOIRE DE
WOODROW WILSON
PRESIDENT DES ETATS UNIS
FONDATEUR DE LA SOCIETE DES NATIONS

BIBLIOGRAPHICAL NOTE

The most detailed general work is D. F. Fleming, *The United States and the League of Nations, 1918–1920* (N.Y., 1932), which is favorable to Wilson. The best brief study is H. B. Learned, "The Attitude of the United States Senate towards the Versailles Treaty: 1918–1920," in H. W. V. Temperley, ed., *A History of the Peace Conference of Paris* (London, 1924), VI, Ch. V. H. C. Lodge, *The Senate and the League of Nations* (N.Y., 1925), reveals the Senator's bitter partisanship. For a sympathetic account of Wilson's fight for the League, and particularly his Western tour, see Edith Bolling Wilson, *My Memoir* (Indianapolis, 1939). The best analysis of the action of the Senate is W. Stull Holt, *Treaties Defeated by the Senate* (Baltimore, 1933), Ch. X. A colorful account by a contemporary journalist is Mark Sullivan, *Our Times* (N.Y., 1933), V, 547–574. Useful articles are: G. A. Finch, "The Treaty of Peace with Germany in the United States Senate," *Amer. Jour. of Internat. Law*, XIV (1920), 155–206 (a factual account); and H. M. Darling, "Who Kept the United States out of the League of Nations?" *Canadian Hist. Rev.*, X (1929), 196–211 (the blame is placed on Lodge). Further references: see footnotes of this chapter and Bemis and Griffin, *Guide*, pp. 673–684.

RECENT REFERENCES. Dexter Perkins, *Hands Off: A History of the Monroe Doctrine* (Boston, 1941), Ch. VIII, has an excellent discussion of the successful struggle to insert a reference to the Doctrine ("regional understanding") in the Covenant, and the attempts of the Senate to secure safeguarding reservations concerning it. The basic difficulty was that "the Covenant was conceived in the spirit of internationalism. The Doctrine was a manifestation of the spirit of nationalism (p. 305)." H. F. Pringle, *The Life and Times of William Howard Taft* (N.Y., 1939), has a revealing chapter (XLIX) on Taft's support for the League of Nations, despite a personal distaste for Wilson.

NEW REFERENCES; 4TH ED. REFS. See Bibliographical Appendix, pp. 943–944.

CHAPTER XLI

Harding and the Washington Conference

". . . The problems of the Pacific are to my mind the world problems of the next fifty years or more."

General Jan Smuts, 1921.

ADVANTAGES WITHOUT OBLIGATIONS

PRESIDENT HARDING, the apostle of "normalcy," partially redeemed his promise to enlist the "best minds" when he named the able Charles Evans Hughes as Secretary of State. Although it was rather generally assumed that the new Administration would discard all the policies of the recently repudiated Wilson, this was not to be the case. Secretary Hughes, like his predecessor, adopted a strong tone in dealing with Mexico, where recent disorders were jeopardizing American life, and where the provisions of the Constitution of 1917 were threatening foreign property rights. He also refused to recognize the Russian government, which was regarded as faithless to its obligations and inimical to American institutions.

Oil was also an object of major concern to the diplomats. The British, who fully recognized the value of fuel for their navy, were revealing a disposition to monopolize the "black gold" of Mesopotamia, which had been assigned to them as a mandate. The Greenville (South Carolina) *Piedmont* was not far from the mark when it observed, "Unto the victors belong the oils." The expiring Wilson administration had vigorously declared that since America had contributed materially to the Allied victory, she should not be without a voice in the disposition of the spoils. Secretary Hughes stalwartly upheld this view, and was ultimately able to effect an arrangement acceptable to the American oil companies.

Perhaps the most pressing problem confronting the new Administration was to bring to an official end the war that had actually ended in November, 1918. Congress passed a joint resolution, on July 2, 1921, declaring that hostilities had ceased, and reserving to the United States the rights and privileges of the victorious Powers. In this man-

681

ner America claimed the fruits without shouldering the responsibilities. Late in August, 1921, nearly three years after the Armistice, separate treaties were signed with Germany, Austria, and Hungary, and were promptly approved by the Senate.[1] Thus the United States made peace with Europe—a peace of advantages without obligations.

In one important particular Harding reversed the policy of his predecessor. His Administration retreated into what ex-President Wilson described as "sullen and selfish isolation," and turned its back on Europe. It not only declined to have anything to do with the League of Nations, but even refused to support the League's health program, which suffered without American co-operation.[2] Communication after communication was sent by the League to the government at Washington, but none was answered. It was not until September, 1921, that the Department of State, responding to a popular outcry, replied to all fourteen of the unanswered communications in one batch. It is hardly necessary to add that these answers did not commit the United States to anything.

In his first message to Congress, Harding announced that America would have nothing to do with the League; in one of his last speeches he declared that the issue was "as dead as slavery."[3] The United States might deny any communion with the League, but it could not, as a world Power, be totally indifferent to its existence. Distinguished Americans, like Elihu Root and John Bassett Moore, served on the World Court, the judicial arm of the League. "Unofficial observers" hung around Geneva, somewhat like detectives shadowing a criminal, and made their reports. As the witty Clemenceau remarked in another connection, the United States was represented by "an ear but not by a mouth."

What of the "Association of Nations," about which so much had been heard during the recent campaign? It was generally forgotten, while the American people turned to pressing problems of reconstruction. Like Mexico, Ecuador, Hejaz, and the others which did not enter the League, America was content to till her garden alone.

[1] The United States did not go to war with Turkey and Bulgaria, the other two Central Powers. Not until December 7, 1917, as compared with April 6, 1917, for Germany, was war declared on Austria-Hungary.

[2] D. F. Fleming, *The United States and World Organization, 1920–1933* (N.Y., 1938), pp. 64–65.

[3] New York *Times*, June 22, 1923, 2:4. Harding also declared in a speech that the United States "does not propose to enter now [Applause] by the side door, or the back door or the cellar door [Applause]." *Ibid.*, April 25, 1923, 2:3.

GUARDIANS OF THE OPEN DOOR

While the United States might feign indifference to developments on the other side of the Atlantic, it made no effort to conceal a growing apprehension over the course of events in the Far East. A series of untoward incidents had, in fact, caused Japanese-American relations to take on an ominous aspect.

Early in the war Japan had joined the Allies and had seized the German holdings in Shantung, China. Then, taking advantage of the death grapple of the Occidental Powers, she had presented her notorious Twenty-one Demands to the Chinese government, January 18, 1915. The terms of this startling ultimatum were so inimical to China's sovereignty as to create a strong presumption that Japan was preparing to lock the Open Door. Public opinion in the United States was profoundly shocked; [4] and Secretary Bryan sent an identic note to both Japan and China, dated May 11, 1915, in which he declared that the United States "cannot recognize any agreement or undertaking . . . impairing the treaty rights of the United States and its citizens in China, the political or territorial integrity of the Republic of China, or the international policy . . . commonly known as the open door policy." [5] Thus was the later Hoover-Stimson doctrine significantly foreshadowed.

In the summer of 1917, Viscount Kikujiro Ishii, a distinguished Japanese diplomat, arrived in the United States on a special mission. His object was to come to grips with the whole problem of Japanese-American relations in China, and to quiet American suspicions of Japan. He was warmly received; and his felicitous speeches helped prepare the public mind for the ensuing negotiations with Secretary Lansing.[6] Ishii hoped to have the United States recognize the "paramount interests" of Japan in China; Lansing desired to have Japan reaffirm the

[4] E. Tupper and G. E. McReynolds, *Japan in American Public Opinion* (N.Y., 1937), pp. 114–118.

[5] *Foreign Relations, 1915*, p. 146.

[6] "In the United States," Ishii records, "where state policies are determined by the drift of public opinion, it is frequently necessary for a foreign envoy, at the same time as he is carrying on discussions with the authorities at Washington, to win the understanding of the people, so that the authorities, influenced by the wishes of the people, might more readily come around to his way of thinking." Viscount Kikujiro Ishii, *Diplomatic Commentaries* (ed. and trans. by W. R. Langdon, Baltimore, 1936), p. 118. Secretary Lansing privately urged the press not to comment on or speculate about his negotiations with Ishii. This request seems to have been generally complied with. O. G. Villard, *Fighting Years* (N.Y., 1939), p. 336.

Open Door and the integrity of China. With the issue squarely drawn, and with neither negotiator willing to compromise, there would have been no agreement if Lansing and Ishii had not taken refuge in ambiguous language. The understanding that was finally effected by an exchange of notes, November 2, 1917, recognized that "territorial propinquity creates special relations between countries," and that "Japan has special [not paramount] interests in China. . . ." This was followed by a solemn endorsement of the Open Door.[7]

Secretary Lansing was bitterly criticized for having given Japan a free hand in China by recognizing her "special interests" there, in return for a recognition of an Open Door that had already been recognized. In reply Lansing asserted that by "special interests" he meant economic interests. But the Japanese, who regarded the agreement as something of a diplomatic victory, did not, with considerable reason on their side,[8] interpret "special interests" so narrowly. Yet the recognition of these interests may have been the price paid for keeping Japan in the war. In his first conversation with Lansing, Ishii delicately stated that Germany had thrice sought to persuade Japan to forsake the Allies.[9] The hint was probably not lost on Lansing. In any case, the Japanese interpretation of the Lansing-Ishii agreement created deep distrust in the United States.

AMERICA—THWARTER OF JAPANESE ASPIRATIONS

The events of the Peace Conference increased rather than diminished tension between Japan and the United States. The Japanese, who resented America's discriminatory stand on immigration and landholding, fought bitterly for the inclusion of a racial equality declaration in the League Covenant. Wilson favored this proposal, but the British opposed it. Fearing the effect of such an innovation on their millions of restless colored subjects, they made it clear that they

[7] *Foreign Relations, 1917,* p. 264.

[8] See A. W. Griswold, *The Far Eastern Policy of the United States* (N.Y., 1938), pp. 218–219. The Japanese, however, gave up more than appeared on the surface. By a secret protocol it was agreed that "they [the two governments] will not take advantage of the present conditions to seek special rights or privileges in China which would abridge the rights of the subjects or citizens of other friendly states." *Foreign Relations, 1922,* II, 595. The Japanese presumably objected to putting the secret protocol in the published notes for fear that such a concession would cause unpleasant political reverberations at home. Not until 1938, after Lansing's *Memoirs* (published in 1935) told the story, did the Japanese government consent to the publication of the protocol. See R. S. Baker, *Woodrow Wilson* (Garden City, N.Y., 1939), VII, 329–330, 336.

[9] *War Memoirs of Robert Lansing* (Indianapolis, 1935), p. 293.

would arouse the yellow press in America against racial equality.[10] Partly, it appears, for this reason, Wilson used his influence to defeat the proposal when the final vote was taken. In any event, he received the blame; and the more outspoken Japanese newspapers bitterly attacked him as a "hypocrite" and a "transformed Kaiser."

Then came the Shantung question. The purposeful Japanese, having lost on the race equality issue, forced Wilson to yield to their demands and compromise with self-determination. The Hearst newspapers berated the "wily, tricky, fight-thirsty Japan"; and the usually conservative Boston *Transcript* decried this "insolent and Hun-like spoliation." The New York *Call* branded the affair as "one of the most shameless deeds in the record of imperialistic diplomacy." [11]

Relations between Japan and the United States had become further embroiled by an anomalous situation growing out of the Russian Revolution of 1917. The Allies had been anxious to rally the Russians against Germany and prevent great quantities of munitions from falling into German hands. So, with the ostensible purpose of rescuing a Czechoslovak force, the Allied command decided upon a joint expedition to Siberia. It was evident that Japan would send the largest army; and the Washington government, with the additional purpose of restraining them from permanently occupying strategic areas, reluctantly decided to participate. The total strength of the American contingent, commanded by General W. S. Graves, was 9000; that of the Japanese 72,000. Although no binding agreement had been made as to the relative size of the forces, the disproportionate strength of the Japanese caused widespread misgivings in the United States. There was constant friction between the Japanese commander and General Graves; and when, in 1920, the United States troops were withdrawn, the Japanese stayed.[12] The Hearst press indulged in a jingoistic outburst against Nipponese treachery, and the son of General Graves wrote for an American magazine:

[10] See Griswold, *The Far Eastern Policy of the United States*, pp. 247–252.

[11] During these months the American press was also disturbed by the Japanese suppression of a Korean uprising. For this incident and the Shantung affair see Tupper and McReynolds, *Japan in American Public Opinion*, pp. 125 ff.

[12] For a brief account of the Siberian expedition see Griswold, *Far Eastern Policy of the United States*, pp. 226 ff. On April 1, 1920, when the last American contingent sailed from Vladivostok, the Japanese band struck up "Hard Times Come Again No More." W. S. Graves, *America's Siberian Adventure, 1918–1920* (N.Y., 1931), p. 328. This is the interesting account of the American commander. For the less important participation of the United States in the Allied intervention in North Russia, see L. I. Strakhovsky, *The Origins of American Intervention in North Russia, 1918* (Princeton, 1937). Wilson was criticized for waging war in both these areas without Congressional sanction.

Is Japan preparing for a war with America, and was her Siberian expedition the first important step toward the realization of a Pan-Oriental plan calculated to make such a struggle possible and profitable? I am not a jingoist, but twenty months' intimate contact with the problem, as a staff officer of the American expedition, convinces me that such is the case.[13]

All these developments were interpreted by the Japanese—and in most cases properly—as an attempt on the part of the United States to thwart Nippon's aspirations in Asia. In November, 1917, Wilson made a further effort to halt Japanese economic penetration into China when he revived the four-Power consortium which he had killed shortly after coming to the presidency. The American bankers, after receiving assurances of support from the government, reluctantly consented to co-operate.[14] The Japanese, who were sorely displeased by the resurrection of a scheme that suggested the Knox neutralization proposal, finally fell into line, but only after reserving privileges in Manchuria and Mongolia. The four-Power consortium was formally signed on October 15, 1920.[15]

THE UNPACIFIC PACIFIC

As if all this were not enough, a controversy also developed with Japan over Yap, a strategically located Pacific island that had formerly belonged to Germany. This place was of considerable potential value as a cable station; and at Paris Wilson had expressed a desire, without coming to a definite understanding, that it should be internationalized.[16] But Yap was mandated to Japan, in accordance with the secret agreement with Britain by which the Japanese were to take over Germany's North Pacific islands. The Department of State thereupon made vigorous representations to Tokyo in support of America's claims. Many people in the United States, amused by the name of the island and its microscopic dimensions, refused to take the dispute seriously. Under the title "Yap for Yappers," an American humorist wrote a parody on a popular war song:

> Give us Yap! Give us Yap!
> The Yanks have put it,
> The Yanks have put it,

[13] *Current History*, XIV, 239 (May, 1921).
[14] Griswold, *The Far Eastern Policy of the United States*, p. 224.
[15] For text see *Foreign Relations, 1920*, I, 576–580.
[16] Griswold, *The Far Eastern Policy of the United States*, p. 265.

> The Yanks have put it,
> On the Map! [17]

But neither the State Department nor the Japanese Foreign Office laughed about Yap.

Far more ominous was the gigantic naval race in which Japan and the United States, as well as Great Britain, found themselves involved at the close of the war. Each had laid down ambitious programs and each was loath to stop while the other continued to build. Against whom was America constructing this enormous navy? Europe was prostrate, Britain was friendly. The obvious answer was Japan; and the Japanese knew it. War talk was alarmingly prevalent on both sides of the Pacific. In Japan, student mass meetings were arguing methods of fighting the United States; while in America there was much discussion of the "inevitable" war in the Pacific. Inflammatory books were being written and widely sold in the United States, among which may be mentioned Frederick McCormick's *The Menace of Japan*, Montaville Flowers' *The Japanese Conquest of American Opinion*, and Walter Pitkin's *Must We Fight Japan?* [18]

A basic element in the fevered condition of the postwar period was the Anglo-Japanese Alliance. It had originally been aimed at Russia and Germany, both of which had been temporarily removed from the international picture. "Big navy" advocates in America, vociferously backed by the Hearst press, were clamoring that the Alliance was now directed solely at the United States; and that in certain contingencies America would have to fight both Britain and Japan in the Far East.[19]

The Canadians, who saw eye to eye with America on the issue of Oriental immigration, were also apprehensive of the Anglo-Japanese Alliance. Canada had close commercial ties with the United States and she would undoubtedly be the battleground of a war between Britain and America. At the Imperial Conference in London, which opened in June, 1921, the Canadian Prime Minister, Arthur Meighen, almost single-handedly brought about acceptance of the idea that the Alliance

---

[17] New York *Nation*, CIX, 328 (Sept. 6, 1919).

[18] Tupper and McReynolds, *Japan in American Public Opinion*, p. 156.

[19] When, in December, 1920, the British made it known that they did not consider the Alliance binding in the event of war between Japan and the United States, the Hearst press, as well as other anti-British and other anti-Japanese elements in the United States, refused to believe the announcement. C. N. Spinks, "The Termination of the Anglo-Japanese Alliance," *Pacific Hist. Rev.*, VI (1937), 326. The strong opposition of American newspapers to the Alliance was an important factor in the calling of the Washington Conference.

should be terminated and that a new understanding should be effected at an international conference on Pacific affairs.[20]

THE RACE FOR DIPLOMATIC HONORS

The Republican party had blocked the League, through which Wilson had planned to bring about disarmament. The new Administration was therefore under a moral obligation to do something about the naval race and the tension that gave it momentum. On February 24, 1921, shortly before Harding's inauguration, Senator Borah had re-introduced a resolution looking toward the calling of a tri-Power disarmament conference. For various reasons, however, the new President did not favor this measure, and he secretly brought pressure to bear against it.[21] But the newspapers throughout the country responded cordially to the Borah proposal, and the people enthusiastically fell in line. Chambers of commerce and mass meetings passed resolutions of endorsement. A monster petition was drawn up in St. Louis and a great dial was erected in a public square; the hand moved forward with every thousand signatures; and with every ten thousand a special courier was sent to Washington. Before such a tidal wave of sentiment the Borah proposal passed the Senate on May 25, 1921, by a vote of 74 to 0, and the House, on June 29, by a vote of 332 to 4.

From then on the situation rapidly came to a head. On July 5, 1921, the British Foreign Secretary suggested to the American ambassador, George Harvey, that Harding invite the Powers to meet in a disarmament conference. Harvey cabled this information to Washington on July 8, and added that the British were about to make public the steps that they had taken toward calling the conference. He therefore urged that the President issue a statement to the press which would indicate that the United States had already taken the initiative. Otherwise, Harvey concluded, Harding would be robbed of his "rightful credit," and would appear in the unfortunate position of following the lead of Great Britain.[22]

[20] J. B. Brebner, "Canada, the Anglo-Japanese Alliance and the Washington Conference," *Pol. Sci. Quar.*, L (1935), 45.

[21] Harding apparently did not think the time ripe for a conference, and he resented Borah's attempt to usurp executive leadership. He therefore summoned two leading Republican Senators to the White House and urged them to fight the proposal. But the pressure of public opinion became so strong that the Administration Senators refused to continue their course unless Harding would come out in the open and support them. This he was unwilling to do, and the opposition collapsed. Interview with Senator Borah, April 21, 1937.

[22] *Foreign Relations, 1921*, I, 19–21.

Earlier on that same day, July 8, Secretary Hughes had cabled Ambassador Harvey to "ascertain informally" if the British government would agree to participate in a disarmament conference in Washington. The cablegram added that similar overtures had been sent to the French, Italian and Japanese governments. Upon receiving Harvey's dispatch, Hughes promptly prepared a statement for the press, and, in line with British desires, broadened his invitation of July 8 to include not only disarmament but also problems of the Pacific and the Far East. The British were quite content to permit the United States to lead the movement, for they did not want to stir up Anglophobe elements in the United States, and they did not wish to offend Japan by appearing to be too eager to forsake the Alliance.

Japan was the only one of the Powers to delay its response to Hughes' informal inquiry of July 8, 1921. A great many Japanese favored a continuance of the Alliance with Britain, and they feared that a review of their recent course in the Far East, especially by an Anglo-American tribunal, might result in substantial reverses. Japanese newspapers expressed the conviction that Japan was being tricked into something, and that an attempt was to be made to elbow her out of China.[23] The obvious reluctance on the part of Tokyo to participate caused an outcry in the American press. The Baltimore *News* was but one of a number of journals to be convinced that Japan was "too determined to pursue her own line of action to waste time discussing it."

Not until July 26, 1921, nearly two weeks after all the other acceptances had been received, did Japan agree to attend a conference, and she qualified her answer by adding that "problems such as are of sole concern to certain particular powers or such matters that may be regarded accomplished facts should be scrupulously avoided." [24] Despite this unmistakable reference to the Twenty-one Demands, Shantung, Siberia, and Yap, Secretary Hughes, taking a page from Hay's Open Door bluff, announced that the Powers had accepted the proposal.

CARDS-ON-THE-TABLE DIPLOMACY

On August 11, 1921, the United States sent formal invitations for a conference to meet in Washington. The five principal Powers which

[23] Yamato Ichihashi, *The Washington Conference and After* (Stanford University, 1928), pp. 17 ff.

[24] *Foreign Relations, 1921*, I, 45.

took part were the United States, Great Britain, France, Italy, and Japan, while the four minor Powers were Belgium, China, the Netherlands, and Portugal. These smaller nations did not figure in the disarmament program, but because of their stake in the Pacific were to participate in the discussions affecting that area. Vanquished Germany and Austria, as well as Bolshevist Russia, were not asked to come.

Each of the nine nations sent distinguished statesmen. President Harding, unlike Wilson in 1918, gave the Senate ample representation on the American delegation. In addition to Secretary Hughes, the group consisted of Elihu Root (a former Senator), Henry Cabot Lodge, chairman of the Senate Committee on Foreign Relations, and Oscar Underwood, leader of the Democratic minority in the Senate.

The first plenary session of the Washington Conference convened in the beautiful Memorial Continental Hall, November 12, 1921. The audience, packed with notables, sensed that history was being made. It was perhaps symptomatic of the shifting balance of power that the Conference—the most important of its kind yet to assemble —should be meeting in a capital of the New World.

President Harding delivered a somewhat effusive address of welcome, and the delegates settled back in their seats to listen to the customary opening-day banalities from Secretary Hughes, chairman and dominant figure of the Conference. Their repose was not disturbed by his long and conventional introduction. Then there came a somewhat sharper note: "We can no longer content ourselves with investigations, with statistics, with reports, with the circumlocution of inquiry. . . . The time has come, and this Conference has been called, not for general resolutions or mutual advice, but for action." [25] The audience applauded. Several of the delegates stirred uneasily.

Then the bomb exploded. With amazing candor Hughes asserted that the way to disarm was to disarm, and that the time to begin was at once, not in the distant future. He proposed a ten-year holiday in the construction of capital ships, and the scrapping of other battleships built or building, so that the navies of the three great Powers— the United States, Great Britain, and Japan—would ultimately be left at a ratio of 5–5–3 respectively in all categories. "Thus," he declared, "the number of capital ships to be scrapped by the United States, if this plan is accepted, is 30, with an aggregate tonnage (including that of ships in construction, if completed) of 845,740 tons." [26]

[25] *Conference on the Limitation of Armament, Washington, November 12, 1921– February 6, 1922* (Washington, 1922), p. 58.
[26] *Ibid.*, p. 62. Britain would scrap 19, Japan, 17.

This proposal was breath-taking. It combined idealism with what was perhaps the only practicable plan. Even if Hughes had then sat down his speech would be labeled as one of the most sensational utterances ever made by an American statesman.

But Hughes did not sit down. Not content with having sunk thirty American ships, he proceeded to tell the British and the Japanese delegates in a tomblike silence just what they should scrap. In less than fifteen minutes he destroyed sixty-six ships with a total tonnage of 1,878,043—more, as one British reporter put it, "than all the admirals of the world have sunk in a cycle of centuries." It was not only the greatest naval encounter on record, but probably the most dramatic moment in American diplomatic history.

The audience was stunned. Then Congressmen, Senators, and Supreme Court justices broke into wild applause like that of a political convention.[27] It seemed as if the millennium were being ushered in. The newspapers ran banner headlines. Enthusiasm throughout the United States mounted to a fever pitch. Sermons and prayers hailed Hughes as the savior of civilization, and besought divine guidance. The president of the American Civic Association caught the spirit when he proposed that the antiquated cannon encumbering the public parks be taken to the dump yards.

Was Hughes' supercandid diplomacy a mistake? It was well enough for the United States to scrap its own navy: the foreign nations would applaud. But to destroy the proud ships of other people was not only bold but dangerous. Colonel Repington, a British reporter, recorded:

It is an audacious and astonishing scheme, and took us off our feet. The few men to whom I spoke babbled incoherently. What will they say in London? To see a British First Lord of the Admiralty, and another late First Lord, sitting at a table with the American Secretary of State telling them how many ships they might keep and how many they should scrap, struck me as a delightfully fantastic idea.[28]

[27] After the Harding and Hughes speeches, the crowd called for Briand, head of the French delegation, in such strong Anglo-Saxon accents that some feared W. J. Bryan, who was among the reporters, might rise and speak. The spontaneous applause and other informal features of the gathering gave it an atmosphere that contrasted glaringly with the secrecy at Paris. The Conference was a great show; and its hippodrome features captivated the imagination of the American people. The resulting public interest and support were in large measure responsible for the achievements.

[28] Mark Sullivan, *The Great Adventure at Washington* (Garden City, N.Y., 1922), p. 27.

H. G. Wells, the well-known British author, wrote that "there was a feeling that we wanted to go away and think."

A more serious criticism is that Hughes flung his cards on the table face upward at the very beginning of the game. Britain had the largest navy in the world; but when the existing programs were completed —assuming that they would remain unchanged—the United States would be first. Hughes played his high trump of potential superiority at the very outset without using it to extort concessions. It was magnificent but it was not diplomacy—at least, not of the old school.

It is probable, however, that Hughes' audacious move gained more than it lost. It started the conference with tremendous momentum. It saved weeks of preliminary palaver and jockeying. It captured the imagination not only of the United States but of the world. One European dispatch declared that Hughes had become "a hero to all Europe's rank and file." And the dramatic proposal helped mobilize world opinion behind the Conference—a vital factor in the success of the negotiations.

DISARMAMENT BY EXAMPLE

The real work of the Conference was done in committee, as at Paris in 1919; and there was probably as much secrecy as there had been then.[29] The results were reported to the plenary sessions, which were in large measure window dressing. To be sure, reams of information were given to the press; but there was so much as to befuddle the average citizen and defeat the ends of publicity.

The three great naval Powers called upon to disarm were faced with different problems. The United States had potentially the most powerful navy. Having also the longest purse, it could theoretically continue the armament race beyond a point that would bankrupt war-burdened Britain and tiny Japan. But the trump of potential dominance was not so strong as it appeared. In the first place, the British and the Japanese might be forced to pool their forces in the face of a too powerful United States. In the second place, Secretary Hughes was bluntly informed by Senators Lodge and Underwood, who should

[29] H. O. Yardley, then in the employ of the State Department, writes that he and his associates decoded the cipher instructions to the foreign delegates at the Conference and made them available to the American representatives before their "morning coffee." "Stud poker," he adds, "is not a very difficult game after you see your opponent's hole card." Whatever the truth of his account, it is probable that representatives of all the Powers engaged in work of this kind. H. O. Yardley, *The American Black Chamber* (Indianapolis, 1931), p. 313.

have known, that Congress would not impose additional burdens upon the protesting taxpayer in order to attain the dubious and unnecessary honor of ruling the waves.[30]

Great Britain still had the largest navy; but, with the German fleet destroyed, supremacy was not so important as it had been. Besides, the nation's finances had been severely strained by the war, and the taxpayers would welcome a building holiday. Indeed, Secretary Hughes knew that Britain would support his 5–5–3 proposal because, in March, 1920, the London government had announced that it would be content with parity with the next greatest naval Power.[31]

The Japanese were in a different position, for Secretary Hughes was asking them to accept the small end of a 5–5–3 ratio. Ever sensitive to a suggestion of inferiority, they insisted that the proportions proposed did not represent either their defense requirements or their actual strength. In Japan, giant mass meetings and impassioned newspaper editorials supported the demands of the delegates for a larger ratio.

On December 15, 1921, the Tokyo government consented provisionally to the Hughes ratio, for the alternative to concession was a ruinous naval race. The Japanese, however, insisted upon and received important safeguards. America agreed not to fortify further her Pacific islands (except Hawaii), particularly the Philippines, Guam, Samoa, and the Aleutians. Without adequate bases on these outposts, the United States, even with the 5–3 ratio, could not hope to attack Japan successfully in Asiatic waters. The British consented to a similar prohibition with reference to their Pacific possessions. As far as the disarmament provisions were concerned, this was the crucial compromise. Japan accepted a smaller ratio, but obtained greater security; Great Britain and the United States consented to leave some of their possessions unprotected, but retained greater battleship tonnage.

The French Stumbling Block

Many people believed that the Conference would have clear sailing after the principal naval Powers—Britain, the United States and Japan—had accepted the 5–5–3 ratio. These three nations alone were

[30] P. C. Jessup, *Elihu Root* (N.Y., 1938), II, 449. The New York *Independent* noted that the country was "more afraid of the tax collector than of any more distant foe." CV, 117 (Jan. 29, 1921).

[31] R. L. Buell, *The Washington Conference* (N.Y., 1922), p. 142.

being asked to scrap ships. Italy and France, the only other considerable naval Powers, would keep essentially what they had, thus making the ratio 5–5–3–1.75–1.75.

But at this point the French, who were obsessed with the idea of
security against another German attack, threatened to wreck the Conference. They had consented to abandon their Rhineland demands
only when Britain and the United States had signed treaties agreeing
to come to their aid. The Senate, as we have seen, had spurned the
security treaty, thus invalidating the arrangement. The French therefore decided to rely on their own army, which they made the most
powerful in the world. They knew that the Conference hoped to bring
about disarmament on land as well as on sea; and since they realized
that their insistence upon keeping their armies would block progress in this direction, they were suffering from a curious defensive
complex.

This unfortunate situation caused a good deal of friction. The delegates of France were touchy about the translation of the speeches
orally into French; they were affronted when, on the opening day,
they found themselves seated just around the corner of the head table,
where sat the British and American delegates.[32] Moreover, Secretary
Hughes appears to have been a little too brusque in dealing with the
French. Before the war they had been a first-rank naval Power; but
in holding back Germany they had allowed their navy to fall behind.
They deeply resented the implication that they no longer counted,
and that they should not be allowed to regain their former position.

The French inferiority complex—and probably a horse-trading instinct as well—finally manifested itself in an astonishing demand for
350,000 tons of capital ships, twice as much as France was entitled
to on the basis of existing strength. The essence of the Hughes plan
was ratios based on *existing navies*. If defense needs had been made
the yardstick, as the French proposed, the Conference would almost
certainly have broken up in fruitless wrangling.

The disproportionate demands of the French alarmed the delegates, and in particular angered the British and the Americans.
Through one of the "calculated indiscretions" of Lord Riddell, British newspaper representative, the extravagant claims of the French
leaked out and aroused a storm of criticism all over the world. A

[32] This situation was corrected by some reshuffling. When the French refused to
sign the treaties unless the word "French" was placed before "English" in the clause
stating that both texts were authentic, the ordinarily unruffled Root lost his temper
and cried, "To hell with them! Let the whole business go to pot—I wouldn't care."
Hughes conceded the point in the interests of harmony. Jessup, *Elihu Root*, II, 465.

cartoon in the New York *World* showed France trying on a Prussian helmet. The Conference balanced on the brink of failure.

The situation was so critical that Secretary Hughes decided upon extraordinary measures. On December 16, 1921, he cabled an urgent appeal to the French Premier, Aristide Briand, who had just returned home from the Conference.[33] Hughes was so strongly supported by world opinion that France reluctantly consented to accept the 1.75 ratio. But, ominously, she would not permit any limitation on the number of cruisers, destroyers, or submarines. Italy accepted the same ratio, and the Five-Power Naval Treaty was drawn up.

An Entanglement by a Different Name

But in the background there still lay the skeleton of the Conference —the Anglo-Japanese Alliance. As long as it existed, no satisfying naval ratio could be worked out. Many Americans believed that in certain contingencies British and Japanese naval strength might conceivably be massed against the United States in the ratio of 8–5. If, on the other hand, the Alliance should be abrogated, the British and American navies could theoretically unite against Japan in the ratio of 10–3.

The problem of finding some substitute for the Alliance was discussed at great length in private conferences, and finally resulted in the Four-Power Treaty. At the fourth plenary session, December 10, 1921, Senator Lodge arose and with poetical embroidery presented this remarkable document to an astonished audience. It provided that Great Britain, France, Japan, and the United States agreed to respect one another's rights in the Pacific and to refer future disputes in that area to a joint conference. It further stipulated that if the rights of the four signatories were threatened by another Power they "shall communicate with one another fully and frankly in order to arrive at an understanding as to the most efficient measures to be taken, jointly or separately, to meet the exigencies of the particular situation." [34] Although this article was purposely vague, it certainly hinted at co-operative armed effort. It was indeed a strange document for Senator Lodge, foe of foreign entanglements, to be sponsoring.

Most important of all, the Four-Power Treaty specifically abrogated the Anglo-Japanese Alliance. It was the vehicle by which the British were able gracefully, yet rather obviously, to withdraw from their embarrassing commitments. Naturally, the Japanese were not

---

[33] *Foreign Relations, 1922*, I, 130–133.
[34] *Ibid.*, p. 35. (The treaty was signed on Dec. 13, 1921.)

altogether happy over the somewhat abrupt severance of their relationship with Great Britain. "We have discarded whiskey and accepted water," said one Japanese diplomat. But the substitute had much to commend it. The four great Powers bound themselves mutually to respect one another's insular possessions and dominions in the Pacific.[35] In a sense the Four-Power Treaty, though committing the signatories to talk rather than fight, was an enlargement of the old Anglo-Japanese Alliance to include the United States and France. In consenting to the treaty, America paid a cheap price for a termination of the Alliance and a guarantee of the Philippines.[36]

REHINGING THE OPEN DOOR

The thunderous applause at the plenary sessions, as well as the headlines in the press, indicated that the tax-conscious American people were far more concerned with disarmament than with any of the other problems confronting the Conference. Yet it was evident to even a superficial observer that any arrangement which left out of consideration the tense situation in the Far East would be illusory. Some of the Senators were threatening a revolt against the treaties unless the Conference did something for China, particularly in the matter of Shantung.

The delegates were weary and about to disband; but, under the driving leadership of Hughes, they concentrated their attention on China—"the Sick Man of the Far East." The most important result was the Nine-Power Treaty, concluded February 6, 1922, by which the signatories bound themselves to respect the "sovereignty, the independence, and the territorial and administrative integrity of China," and to uphold the principle of the Open Door.

The outline of this remarkable pact was proposed by the British. Having surrendered their naval superiority, they naturally sought some substitute to protect their Far Eastern holdings.[37] But, as in the case of the Monroe Doctrine, the Open Door notes, and the calling of the Washington Conference, the United States took the initiative

[35] Did this include Japan proper, which was entirely insular, or not? The American delegation announced that it did; Harding declared that it did not. One wag remarked that at Paris Wilson had not taken the American delegates into his confidence, while at Washington the delegates had not taken the President into their confidence. A supplementary agreement with Japan (signed Feb. 6, 1922) specifically excluded the homeland of Japan from the Four-Power Treaty. *Foreign Relations, 1922,* I, 46–47.

[36] Griswold, *Far Eastern Policy of the United States,* pp. 312–313.

[37] *Foreign Relations, 1922,* I, 271–272.

in carrying the proposal through. The self-denying pledge embodied in the Nine-Power Treaty would naturally limit the territorial aspirations of the Japanese in the Far East, and it was only after great pressure had been exerted by the United States and Great Britain that Japan consented to sign.[38]

The Nine-Power Treaty was the most specific and sweeping affirmation of the Open Door to which the Powers had yet agreed. America's traditional policy in the Far East was thus given, so it seemed, a broad, nine-Power base—as strong a foundation as paper and ink could give it. The American delegation expressed the belief (or was it a hope?) that the "Open Door in China has at last been made a fact." But the pact was purely self-denying; none of the signatories bound itself to defend the Open Door by force. Its validity rested primarily on the good faith of the contracting Powers.

In due course the Senate approved the sheaf of treaties growing out of the Conference, the most important of which were the Five-Power Naval Treaty, the Four-Power Treaty, and the Nine-Power Treaty. In general they were enthusiastically supported by the American press, with the notable exception of the anti-Japanese and anti-British Hearst chain. This determined manifestation of public opinion probably saved the pacts from being made the football of politics. The most serious opposition in the Senate was directed against the Four-Power Treaty, which was approved by the help of Democrats with only four votes to spare.[39] Henry Cabot Lodge reversed his position on the League and fought for the pact. When Senator Borah, who vigorously opposed the Four-Power Treaty, taxed Lodge with inconsistency, the Massachusetts Senator replied with a characteristic wave of his hands, "What are you going to do? It is an Administration measure." [40] Nevertheless, on March 24, 1922, the Senators tacked on the inevitable reservation. It declared that "there is no commitment to armed force, no alliance, no obligation to join in any defense."

This, however, is not the whole story. Other Far Eastern adjustments, though not the concern of the Conference as a whole, were by-products of the healthier atmosphere created in Washington. On February 4, 1922, Japan and China settled their Shantung controversy. The Japanese also withdrew the most objectionable of their Twenty-one Demands; agreed to evacuate Siberia; conceded to the

---

[38] Griswold, *Far Eastern Policy of the United States*, p. 324.

[39] For a convenient summary of the debates in the Senate see Fleming, *The United States and World Organization*, pp. 86 ff.

[40] Interview with Senator Borah, April 21, 1937.

United States (through the treaty of February 11, 1922) special cable rights on the island of Yap; and, on April 14, 1923, consented to an annulment of the Lansing-Ishii agreement. In short, Japan was either forced or induced to retreat all along the line—to the great dissatisfaction of her more vocal newspapers.[41]

BALANCING THE SCALES

The Washington Conference is best remembered in the United States for its achievements in limiting armaments. Yet these arrangements, though capturing the public imagination, were largely illusory. Although provision was made for a naval holiday in the construction of capital ships and aircraft carriers, the armament race merely shifted to smaller craft, which were not limited in number.

The not altogether satisfactory results of "disarmament by example" have given rise to the criticism that Uncle Sam was the honest greenhorn at the poker table; that he "junked" splendid new battleships, completed or nearly completed, so that Britain might scrap some of her obsolete craft and still maintain superiority in cruisers; and that he deliberately gave up naval supremacy to Great Britain and cheerfully accepted paper parity. The *Irish World* (New York) branded the Conference as "an ominous triumph for British diplomacy."

No less pointed were the charges directed against the Far Eastern agreements. If Japan chose to disregard her written promises and close the Open Door, the United States could not stop her, for the Japanese fleet was left without a rival in the Far East. Admiral Sims, *enfant terrible* of the American navy, remarked disgustedly, "Anybody can spit on the Philippines and you can't stop them."

But with the passage of time it becomes increasingly evident that the Washington Conference was not a triumph for anybody. In general, it recognized existing realities and attempted to freeze the *status quo*.[42] Like all compromises, it was not completely satisfactory to anyone. The United States, to be sure, surrendered *potential* naval supremacy, and *potential* fortifications on her Pacific islands. But the American delegation, knowing the mood of the taxpayers and recognizing that public opinion would not permit a war in behalf of the

---

[41] F. R. Dulles, *Forty Years of American-Japanese Relations* (N.Y., 1937), p. 177 The terms of the secret protocol of the Lansing-Ishii agreement were incorporated in the Nine-Power Treaty, Article I, clause 4.

[42] Griswold, *Far Eastern Policy of the United States*, p. 331.

Open Door, regarded these potentialities as liabilities rather than assets.

When both sides are balanced it is clear that the Conference was a landmark in history. It actually did bring about a temporary cessation of frantic naval building, with a consequent improvement of international feeling. In the Far East, where the achievements of the Conference were less dramatic but more important, the Anglo-Japanese Alliance was terminated; the Open Door was given a new lease of life; and the navies of the great Powers in the Pacific were so scaled down that none could hope to attack the other with reasonable prospect of success. This general air-clearing dispelled the fetid international atmosphere, and made possible a more satisfactory recuperation from the World War than would otherwise have been possible.

BIBLIOGRAPHICAL NOTE

The best brief account of the Washington Conference and its problems is A. W. Griswold, *The Far Eastern Policy of the United States* (N.Y., 1938), pp. 176–332. This treatment utilizes the recently published official documents. Two older books are still useful: R. L. Buell, *The Washington Conference* (N.Y., 1922), a contemporary account by an American scholar; and Yamato Ichihashi, *The Washington Conference and After* (Stanford University, 1928), a later treatment, somewhat broader in scope. Professor Ichihashi was secretary to Viscount Kato, senior delegate of Japan at the Conference. There is some valuable material on Root's contributions in P. C. Jessup, *Elihu Root* (N.Y., 1938), II, Ch. XLVII. Vivid journalistic impressions appear in Mark Sullivan, *The Great Adventure at Washington* (N.Y., 1922). Public opinion is treated rather fully in E. Tupper and G. E. McReynolds, *Japan in American Public Opinion* (N.Y., 1937); more sketchily in F. R. Dulles, *Forty Years of American-Japanese Relations* (N.Y., 1937). The debates on the Conference treaties are analyzed, with useful background material, in D. F. Fleming, *The United States and World Organization, 1920–1933* (N.Y., 1938), Chs. I–V. Important articles are: J. B. Brebner, "Canada, the Anglo-Japanese Alliance and the Washington Conference," *Pol. Sci. Quar.*, L (1935), 45–58; and C. N. Spinks, "The Termination of the Anglo-Japanese Alliance," *Pacific Hist. Rev.*, VI (1937), 321–340. Further references: see footnotes of this chapter.

RECENT REFERENCES. By far the best treatment of the naval aspects of the Washington Conference is Harold and Margaret Sprout, *Toward a New Order of Sea Power* (Princeton, 1940), which embraces a general study of American naval policy and world affairs from 1918 to 1922. Among other things, the authors reveal that Hughes, Assistant Secretary of the Navy Theodore Roosevelt, Jr., and two naval officers were the authors of the Hughes disarmament plan (p. 143). C. L. Hoag, *Preface to Preparedness* (Washington, D.C., 1941), is a careful study of public opinion in relation to the Washington Conference.

NEW REFERENCES; 4TH ED. REFS. See Bibliographical Appendix, p. 944.

CHAPTER XLII

Coolidge and the Diplomacy of Prosperity, 1923–1929

"The business of America is business."

President Coolidge, 1925.

UNCLE SAM BECOMES UNCLE SHYLOCK

WHEN Harding unexpectedly died, August 2, 1923, the frugal, taciturn, and conservative Vermonter, Calvin Coolidge, came to the White House.[1] The country was enjoying booming prosperity, and economic problems loomed large in the diplomacy of the United States. The new President entertained great respect for private property, legitimate investments, and just debts; and it was expected that as titular head of the big-business Republican party he would vigorously support American interests abroad. Nor did he disappoint these expectations.

In 1914 the United States was still a debtor nation, for its citizens owed foreign investors the net sum of approximately three billion dollars. But the World War changed the three billion dollar deficit to a sixteen billion dollar credit,[2] and for the first time in her history America became a creditor nation. In addition, during 1917 and 1918 the government in Washington lent the Allies slightly more than $7,000,000,000; after the Armistice it advanced an additional $3,000,000,000 in cash and supplies for reconstruction purposes. The total of official loans was thus raised to $10,350,000,000. Moreover, during the decade after the war private American investors, with a surplus of capital resulting from a favorable balance of trade, poured billions of dollars into foreign lands—much of it into Europe.

The guns had scarcely grown cold when the debtor nations began

---

[1] Coolidge's father reminisced: "It always seemed to me that Calvin could get more sap out of a maple tree than any of the other boys around here." E. E. Whiting, *President Coolidge* (Boston, 1923), p. 11.

[2] The latter figure is as of 1922. G. N. Peek, "Letter to the President on International Credits for Foreign Trade and other Purposes, 1896–1933" (Washington, 1934), p. 2.

WAR AND POSTWAR FOREIGN LOANS OF U.S. GOVERNMENT

	Pre-Armistice [cash]	Post-Armistice [Cash & Supplies]	Total Indebtedness
To Allies:			
Great Britain	$3,696,000,000	$ 581,000,000.00	$4,277,000,000.00
France	1,970,000,000	1,434,818,945.01	3,404,818,945.01
Italy	1,031,000,000	617,034,050.90	1,648,034,050.90
Belgium	171,780,000	207,307,200.43	379,087,200.43
Russia	187,729,750	4,871,547.37	192,601,297.37
Rumania		37,911,152.92	37,911,152.92
Greece		27,167,000.00	27,167,000.00
Cuba	10,000,000		10,000,000.00
Nicaragua		431,849.14	431,849.14
Liberia		26,000.00	26,000.00
To Countries Formed out of Allied Territory:			
Estonia		13,999,145.60	13,999,145.60
Finland		8,281,926.17	8,281,926.17
Latvia		5,132,287.14	5,132,287.14
Lithuania		4,981,628.03	4,981,628.03
To Areas or Countries Formed Partially or Wholly Out of Enemy Territory:			
Poland		159,666,972.39	159,666,972.39
Czechoslovakia		91,879,671.03	91,879,671.03
Yugoslavia	10,605,000	41,153,486.55	51,758,486.55
Austria		24,055,708.92	24,055,708.92
Armenia		11,959,917.49	11,959,917.49
Hungary		1,685,835.61	1,685,835.61
	$7,077,114,750	$3,273,364,324.70	$10,350,479,074.70

a vigorous campaign for the cancellation of their obligations to the Washington government. They argued that the money advanced by the United States was its contribution to the general cause. Supported by dollars, the Allies had held back the common enemy while America was raising and drilling her army. The European debtors also pointed out that most of the money in question had never left the United States. It had been used to buy war material for the Allies, and had made possible a period of amazing business activity. In a sense, therefore, the American people had already paid themselves back in war profits.

The debtor nations also asserted that they could not pay in gold, because there was not enough gold in Europe, and because they needed what they had to support their own currencies. If true, this meant that they could liquidate their obligations only through goods and services.

But they could not send goods in sufficient quantities because of the high American tariff walls. And the United States steadfastly refused to lower these economic barriers because it feared that its own factories would be closed and the unemployment problem would be aggravated. Then why not, asked the European debtors, wipe the books clean and end the feeling of financial uncertainty from which the entire world was suffering?

But the Americans insisted that a debt was a debt and that it should be honorably paid, or faith in international borrowing would be destroyed. Certainly no one could fail to see that if the debtor nations did not pay what they owed, the taxpayer in the United States would have to assume the burden himself. The Americans also asserted that at Paris the United States had received nothing but ingratitude, while the Allies secured rich territories, colonies, and reparations.[3] Nor could anyone deny that about one third of the sum involved was not an Allied war debt at all, but a post-Armistice loan.

At the Paris Conference, and later, the Allies made several determined attempts to persuade the United States that the repayment of the debts should be contingent upon obtaining reparations from Germany. But President Wilson flatly denied that any such legal connection existed, and he thus outlined the policy that was consistently followed by his successors.[4]

Palms Across the Sea

The loans by the United States government to the Allies had originally been made with the understanding that they would bear interest at five per cent, and that arrangements would later be worked out for repayment over a period of years. In February, 1922, Congress took the initiative when it empowered the World War Foreign Debt Commission to conclude terms with the nations concerned, subject to Congressional approval. This was the machinery used to make settlements with the principal debtors.

Early in 1923 the British Chancellor of the Exchequer, Stanley Baldwin, came to the United States as the head of a commission to discuss the debt problem. After involved negotiations it was agreed that the obligation should be repaid over a period of sixty-two years, and that the interest rate should be reduced from five per cent to an

[3] The Asheville *Times* remarked, "About all America got out of Europe was its Army." *Literary Digest*, XC, 15 (Sept. 4, 1926).

[4] See H. G. Moulton and L. Pasvolsky, *War Debts and World Prosperity* (N.Y., 1932), p. 69.

average of 3.3 per cent. Although the principal was to remain the same, this reduction in interest was in effect a cancellation amounting to 30.1 per cent of the entire debt. On the whole, American public opinion was pleased with the rather hard bargain driven with the largest debtor, and with Britain's recognition of her obligation.[5]

President Coolidge continued Harding's policy of noncancellation. "They hired the money, didn't they?" was his classic remark. But the principal remaining debtors, France, Italy, and Belgium, were reluctant to follow Britain's example. They were in large measure influenced by Germany's failure to meet the reparations payments, which had been fixed in 1921 at the astronomical figure of $33,000,000,000. In January, 1923, the French attempted to collect at the point of bayonet when they occupied the Ruhr Valley, the industrial nerve center of Germany. The tension finally became so great that the Reparations Commission appointed a committee, headed by an American acting in an unofficial capacity, General Charles Gates Dawes, whose underslung pipe and picturesque profanity attracted wide attention. The so-called Dawes plan, which was finally accepted by the Powers in August, 1924, provided for reparations payments more nearly commensurate with Germany's ability to pay.[6]

In an effort to force the recalcitrant debtors to meet their obligations, the Department of State adopted the policy of frowning upon private loans to countries in default. Some of the European nations were so desperately in need of funds that this proved to be a very effective club. On November 14, 1925, Italy came to terms and, on the basis of presumed capacity to pay, succeeded in having her interest rate reduced to 0.4 per cent, which amounted to a cancellation of 80.2 per cent of the amount owed. The liberal terms granted to Italy met with strong opposition in Congress, where Premier Mussolini was bitterly criticized.

France, though possessing a large gold reserve, was still reluctant to pay her debt. But the American loan policy acted as a powerful persuader, and the French resentfully came to terms in April, 1926. The interest rate was reduced to 1.6 per cent, which amounted to a

---

[5] See *Literary Digest*, LXXVI, 10 (Feb. 17, 1923).

[6] The United States government had no official connection with the Dawes plan, which was looked upon as a purely European problem, although Secretary Hughes played an important part in bringing about the appointment of the committee. See D. F. Fleming, *The United States and World Organization, 1920–1933* (N.Y., 1938), pp. 142–144. In 1929, another prominent American, Owen D. Young, serving like Dawes in a purely private capacity, headed a committee which drew up the Young plan. It further reduced the burden of reparations payments.

wiping out of 60.3 per cent of the entire indebtedness. Nevertheless, the settlement proved to be highly unpopular in France. Caustic press comments, a parade of war veterans, and discrimination against American goods were among the various evidences of dissatisfaction.[7]

It is clear that no development during the postwar period did more

OUR COLLECTIONS FROM FRANCE

(From the New York *World*.)

to embitter feelings on both sides of the Atlantic than the mutual recriminations over debts. Americans generally regarded Europeans as dishonest ingrates; the Europeans regarded Americans as grasping Shylocks. Isolationists in the United States were further confirmed in their conviction that the country would be well advised to stay out of Europe. Boards of education, American Legionnaires, and others began to demand a rewriting of textbooks so that the former Allies would not appear in so favorable a light. These were but manifestations of a growing spirit of extreme nationalism that was to become so important during the 1930's.

JAPAN AND THE IMMIGRATION ACT OF 1924

Relations with Japan, quite in contrast with Europe, were unusually amicable following the cloud-dispelling Washington Conference. In the background, however, lurked the problem of immigration. Although the Gentlemen's Agreement of 1908 had worked reasonably well, "picture brides" and a relatively high birth rate had brought about a substantial increase in the number of Japanese on the Pacific Coast, particularly in California, where Orientals made up about two per cent of the population. Japanophobe agitators, backed by the American Federation of Labor, the American Legion, and some of the newspapers, were stridently demanding a more effective method of exclusion.[8]

[7] See B. H. Williams, *Economic Foreign Policy of the United States* (N.Y., 1929), p. 91. Certain liberals in the United States, notably economists at Columbia and Princeton Universities, protested against the ungenerous terms of these settlements. See the Princeton "manifesto" in the New York *Times*, March 11, 1927, 1:3.

[8] See E. Tupper and G. E. McReynolds, *Japan in American Public Opinion* (N.Y., 1937), p. 182.

The existing immigration legislation was about to expire, and Congress was faced with the necessity of raising the bars against the destitute hordes of Europe. The proposed act of 1924 provided that foreign nations might send annually to the United States a maximum of two per cent of the nationals they had there in 1890. Secretary of State Hughes estimated that the Japanese would be entitled to 250 a year —certainly not an alarming number. But the bill as reported stipulated that "aliens ineligible to citizenship" were to be completely barred. Although this restriction technically applied to all Orientals, it would have the practical effect of not only discriminating against the Japanese but summarily abrogating the Gentlemen's Agreement.

This development alarmed Secretary Hughes. Noting that the discussions in Congress revealed much confusion of thought about the Gentlemen's Agreement, he urged Ambassador Hanihara, the Japanese representative in Washington, to draw up a statement of Japan's conception of the understanding. Hughes planned to send the note to Congress in the hope that this clarification would prevent the proposed discrimination against Japan.

The Japanese note was prepared in collaboration with the Department of State, and was finally presented to Secretary Hughes on April 10, 1924. The concluding paragraph, which came as a complete surprise, truthfully but most ill-advisedly referred to the "grave consequences" which complete exclusion would have upon the relations between the two countries. Secretary Hughes regretted the use of this phrase, which is one of the strongest in diplomacy, but he considered the note an admirable summation of the Gentlemen's Agreement. Time was pressing; so he sent it to Congress at once.[9]

The note had precisely the opposite effect from that which Secretary Hughes had hoped for. The anti-Japanese press in America was deeply offended, or professed to be, by this "veiled threat" of war. The Seattle *Times* declared it "the most insolent message this Government has ever received," while the Cincinnati *Enquirer* believed that "entrance of foreigners into this country is a privilege to be granted, not a right to be demanded." Congress was already annoyed because its constitutional prerogative of regulating immigration had

[9] This information was obtained during an interview in Washington, D.C., May, 1937, by Charles Evans Hughes, who at that time was Chief Justice of the Supreme Court. Hanihara may have been unaware of the implications of the phrase "grave consequences." It is interesting to note that this expression was used by the Japanese Minister for Foreign Affairs and by Baron Sakatani in the House of Peers (January 23, 1924) during a debate on the immigration bill then before Congress. Tokyo *Nichi Nichi*, Jan. 24, 1924 (Translation in Department of State files).

been taken over by the President in the Gentlemen's Agreement; and both houses quickly approved Japanese exclusion by overwhelming majorities. The vote in the Senate, April 16, 1924, was 71 to 4. Although it is probable that the measure would have passed anyway,[10] and although Congress may have seized upon the Hanihara note as a pretext for its action,[11] these developments were most unfortunate. President Coolidge reluctantly signed the general immigration bill (of which Japanese exclusion was a part) in lieu of something better.

Although a great body of intelligent Americans deplored this summary exclusion of Orientals,[12] the people of Japan regarded the Immigration Act of 1924 as a deliberate insult. Their press teemed with denunciations of the "outrageous enactment." [13] The Stars and Stripes were desecrated; a movement to boycott American goods was begun; an obscure Japanese disemboweled himself near the United States embassy in Tokyo. The date on which the law became effective was declared a day of national humiliation. Millions of Japanese could never forget.

THE GENEVA DISARMAMENT CONFERENCE

The growing tension between Japan and the United States after 1924 focused attention once more on the armament problem. The Washington Conference had applied the 5–5–3 ratio to larger ships only, that is, battleships and aircraft carriers. But a new and ominous naval race soon started in the construction of cruisers, submarines, and other smaller vessels. America failed to keep pace with the other Powers in building up her navy in all categories, for she was preoccupied at home, interested in economy, and hopeful of disarmament. She even failed to maintain the battleship strength to which she was entitled under the Washington Treaty.

President Coolidge hoped to emulate the success of Harding's Washington Conference. On February 10, 1927, therefore, he rather suddenly issued a call for a disarmament conference at Geneva.[14]

[10] Rodman Paul, *The Abrogation of the Gentlemen's Agreement* (Cambridge, Mass., 1936), p. 85.

[11] This is the opinion of the official already referred to.

[12] It seems reasonably clear that public opinion throughout the country (especially in the East) was opposed to this method of excluding the Japanese. Prior to 1924 the responsibility for discriminating against the Japanese rested upon the states; after 1924, upon the federal government.

[13] See Yamato Ichihashi, *Japanese in the United States* (Stanford University, 1932), p. 315.

[14] The invitations were issued with such haste that the proper diplomatic preparations could not be made. David Bryn-Jones, *Frank B. Kellogg* (N.Y., 1937), p. 209.

Japan and Great Britain accepted the invitation; but Italy and France, alleging prior obligations to the League's disarmament program, declined to take part. Despite these unfavorable auguries, the Conference convened in Geneva, on June 20, 1927. The American delegates sought to have the 5–5–3 ratio extended to smaller vessels, and to bring about a reduction in existing cruiser strength. But since no two of the participating Powers thought they had the same defense requirements, it was impossible to arrive at any agreement regarding large and small cruisers. Compromise was made all the more difficult by the presence of naval experts among the delegates—a violation of Lord Cecil's formula that "experts should always be on tap, but never on top." After holding sessions from June 20 to August 4, 1927, the Conference broke up in complete failure.[15]

The results were bitter feelings, a setback for the reduction of arms, and a keen disappointment to the American taxpayers. Many of them reluctantly came to the conclusion that the only way to bring about disarmament was to build up such a large navy that the other nations, in self-defense, would be forced to accept limitation.[16]

Outlawing War

One important by-product of the futile Geneva Conference was the increasing belief in the United States that the way to insure peace was not to limit arms but to abolish war completely.[17] During the previous decade a small but influential group had been urging that instead of having laws recognizing war as a legal condition, there should be laws against war. One of the leaders of this agitation was Professor James T. Shotwell, of Columbia University, who, while visiting France in the spring of 1927, presented his ideas to Foreign Minister Briand. The upshot was that on April 6, 1927, the tenth anniversary of America's entry into the war, Briand issued an address to the American people, through the Associated Press, in which he announced that France was prepared to enter into an agreement with the United States for the mutual outlawry of war.[18]

[15] Two years later, in August, 1929, it was revealed that American armament manufacturers had employed a lobbyist, William B. Shearer, to do what he could to sabotage the Geneva Conference. Much public indignation was aroused by this revelation, and a widely publicized investigation by the Senate resulted. See B. H. Williams, *The United States and Disarmament* (N.Y., 1931), pp. 175–176, 183–184.

[16] *Literary Digest*, XCIV, 9 (Aug. 20, 1927).

[17] Bryn-Jones, *Kellogg*, pp. 210–211.

[18] J. T. Shotwell, *War as an Instrument of National Policy* (N.Y., 1929), pp. 41–42.

Strangely enough, this extraordinary appeal passed virtually unnoticed by the American press for nearly three weeks. Then, on April 25, 1927, President Nicholas Murray Butler of Columbia University published a remarkable letter in the New York *Times*, in which he urged the United States to respond to Briand's invitation.[19] Butler's communication aroused dormant American opinion; the press seized upon the idea; and the phrase "outlawry of war" caught the popular fancy. But Secretary of State Kellogg, foreseeing some of the practical difficulties in the way of a two-Power pact with France, showed no enthusiasm for the proposal.[20]

Undaunted by the coldness of the State Department, the advocates of outlawry kept up their campaign. Senator Borah persuaded the National Grange (with a membership of 800,000) to endorse a resolution which he had prepared.[21] Petitions bearing two million signatures reached Washington. The pressure of public opinion for action finally became so strong that it could not be ignored. On December 28, 1927, nearly nine months after the original Briand overture, Secretary Kellogg presented a note to France in which he proposed, as Borah and others had been suggesting, that the contemplated Franco-American pact to outlaw war be expanded to include the other Powers.

Briand was not altogether pleased with the American offer, for France's obligation to the League and to her allies envisaged defensive war. After considerable diplomatic jockeying, the proposed treaty was so interpreted as to permit defensive wars but to outlaw war as "an instrument of national policy." Meanwhile Secretary Kellogg, who was now moving energetically, had been able to mobilize world opinion behind the pact by giving wide publicity to the negotiations and thus answering in advance many of the objections that would have been raised later.[22] On August 27, 1928, the Pact of Paris (the official name of the Kellogg-Briand agreement) was signed at Paris by representatives of the United States and fourteen other Powers. It was couched in the simplest possible terms, and bound the signatories to renounce war as an instrument of national policy. The treaty

[19] *Ibid.*, pp. 43–44.

[20] For Kellogg's own explanation of his delay see Bryn-Jones, *Kellogg*, p. 231.

[21] C. O. Johnson, *Borah of Idaho* (N.Y., 1936), p. 400.

[22] Kellogg later wrote: "I do not think the treaty could ever have been negotiated if we had pursued the old policy of secret communications . . . because nothing but the power of the public opinion of the world made possible the consummation of this treaty." Bryn-Jones, *Kellogg*, p. 233. See also the somewhat unreliable Drew Pearson and Constantine Brown, *The American Diplomatic Game* (Garden City, N.Y., 1935), p. 36.

was eventually approved by almost all nations, though in the case of Britain with a reservation as to defending her overseas empire.

There can be no doubt that American public opinion was overwhelmingly favorable to the pact.[23] The Boston *Herald,* for example, announced that "It is a thing to rejoice over, it is superb, it is magnificent. We should sing the *Te Deum Laudamus.* . . ."[24] On the other hand, hardheaded cynics declared that this was a long step toward the League; that the pact meant nothing because it permitted defensive war; that all nations always fight defensively; and that the treaty had no teeth. Kellogg himself declared that "the only enforcement behind the pact is the public opinion of the people."

The members of the Senate had few illusions about the treaty. Senator Reed of Missouri sneered at this "international kiss," while others scoffed at its efficacy. Although no formal reservations were attached to the pact, the Senate Committee on Foreign Relations did present an interpretation designed to reserve the right of self-defense, with specific reference to the Monroe Doctrine. The Senate voted its approval on January 15, 1929, by a count of 85 to 1.

Secretary Kellogg supplemented this new peace machinery by negotiating, from 1928 to 1931, a series of bilateral arbitration treaties with eighteen non-American nations. They provided for the submission of justiciable disputes to the Permanent Court of Arbitration at The Hague, or to some other competent tribunal. Although the Senate reserved the right to pass upon the nature and scope of each proposed arbitration, more questions were arbitrable under the new pacts than under the old Root treaties.

BACKDOOR CO-OPERATION

Despite these steps toward peace and international co-operation, America of the prosperous 1920's was hostile to the League of Nations, indifferent to Europe. "A change of Ministers in France," asserted the Los Angeles *Times,* "is of less importance to the residents of Los Angeles than a change of grade on an important thoroughfare."[25] President Harding, who was well aware of the temper of the country, shunned all official connection with the League. But he

---

[23] Kellogg estimated that the press was ninety per cent favorable. About January 1, 1928, the State Department was receiving some 500 letters a day, virtually all of them approbative. Bryn-Jones, *Kellogg,* p. 237.

[24] *Literary Digest,* XCVIII, 6 (Sept. 8, 1928).

[25] Quoted in *Time,* IX, 28 (Feb. 14, 1927).

did go so far as to espouse, with reservations, American adherence to the Permanent Court of International Justice (the World Court)—the autonomous judicial arm of the League.[26]

President Coolidge followed Harding's policy of aloofness toward the League of Nations, and energetically continued his campaign for adherence to the World Court. By the summer of 1924 public sentiment had so crystallized that the platforms of both major parties included declarations in favor of joining the tribunal. And on March 3, 1925, the House of Representatives, by a vote of 303 to 28, passed a resolution favoring adherence to the World Court.

But the staid Senate was not to be stampeded by pressure from numerous bodies representing the "better elements." The thinning phalanx of "irreconcilables" (Borah and Johnson were still present) rallied to oppose what they regarded as a backdoor entrance into the League. William Randolph Hearst, together with other isolationists, re-aroused the emotions of the League fight, and branded the World Court a "League Court." After a bitter debate and a threatened filibuster, the Senate approved adherence to the Court, January 27, 1926, by a vote of 76 to 17.

Yet the foes of the World Court did force five reservations into the resolution of acceptance—statements designed to safeguard what were assumed to be the interests of the United States.[27] The members of the World Court were able to accept all the reservations except the last part of the fifth, which related to advisory opinions. During the next few years attempts were made to work out a formula that would be acceptable to both the Senate and the League.

While the fight for adherence to the World Court was being carried on, the United States began to take increasing if cautious cognizance of the League of Nations. At first unofficial American "observers" sat with the League committees in a "consultative" or "advisory" capacity for the purpose of discussing strictly nonpolitical matters, such as

---

[26] The World Court is not to be confused with the Permanent Court of Arbitration (the Hague Court), which was organized in 1901. The World Court is a permanent body; the Hague Court is not, strictly speaking, a court but a panel from which tribunals may be formed as the occasion arises. M. O. Hudson, *The World Court, 1921–1938* (5th ed., Boston, 1938), pp. 1–2.

[27] They provided: (1) The United States was in no way committed to the Treaty of Versailles or the League; (2) the United States should exercise equality with the League states in filling vacancies on the Court; (3) the United States should pay its share of the expenses of the Court; (4) the United States might withdraw its adherence at any time; and the statute establishing the Court should not be amended without American consent; (5) certain restrictions were placed upon the rendering of advisory opinions. *Ibid.*, pp. 248–249.

health regulations and white slavery control. In 1924 American delegates were officially named to represent the United States at the Second Opium Conference of the League. Though they left the gathering after a stormy debate, the ice was broken, and by 1930 the United
States had taken part in more than forty League conferences, all presumably nonpolitical.[28] By 1931 the United States had five permanent
officials stationed at Geneva, the seat of the League, to represent American interests there. One of the most striking anomalies of the postwar
Republican regime is that the United States, though paying lip service
to isolation, moved from a position of hostility to the League to one
of active co-operation. There was a measure of truth in the isolationist
charge that the United States was becoming a member of the League
in all but name.

PEACE BY INTERVENTION IN NICARAGUA

While the Coolidge administration was taking these hesitant steps
toward the League, it was moving with vigor to protect American investments and national interests in the Caribbean area.[29] By 1924 the
financial policies of approximately half of the twenty Latin American
states were in some measure being directed by the United States. In
several of these republics marines had landed and were taking a hand
in preserving order.

The storm center was Nicaragua, where a vital interest in the
Panama life line and in the alternate canal route aroused a lively
concern. Although the marines were withdrawn for a short time in
1925, new revolutionary outbursts brought them back the next year.
In the hope of insuring stability, Secretary Kellogg rather hastily and
ill-advisedly recognized the Díaz government; [30] while Mexico recognized and supported the rival Sacasa regime. The Coolidge administration went so far as to place an embargo on arms to Sacasa, although
allowing them to go freely to Díaz, who paid for them with money
advanced by American bankers. Early in 1927 Coolidge had over

---

[28] Walter Lippmann, *The United States in World Affairs, 1931* (N.Y., 1932),
p. 228. By 1931 two hundred and twelve persons had been officially appointed to
represent the United States in League conferences. Fleming, *The United States and
World Organization*, p. 313.

[29] The treaty of 1924 with the Dominican Republic ended the military dictatorship
and resulted in the withdrawal of the marines. Before this was done adequate guarantees were secured to safeguard American financial interests. C. E. Chapman, *Republican Hispanic America* (N.Y., 1937), p. 164.

[30] Bryn-Jones, *Kellogg*, pp. 193–194. For the Nicaraguan situation see G. H.
Stuart, *Latin America and the United States* (3rd ed., N.Y., 1938), pp. 366 ff.

5000 troops in Nicaragua waging what his critics called a "private war."

These large-scale operations, which were undertaken without Congressional sanction, aroused a storm of condemnation in the United States, chiefly among anti-imperialists and members of the Democratic opposition. In Congress, one Democrat cried, "Oh, Monroe doctrine, how many crimes have been committed in thy name?"—to the accompaniment of applause from the members of his party.[31] President Coolidge, smarting under this barrage of criticism, sent a special message to Congress, January 10, 1927, in which he vigorously defended his policy. He stressed particularly the safeguarding of American lives and property, and the prevention of foreign influence in the Isthmus. Three months later he amplified his position: "Toward the governments of countries which we have recognized this side of Panama we feel a moral responsibility that does not attach to other nations." He also insisted that "We are not making war on Nicaragua any more than a policeman on the street is making war on passersby."[32]

Meanwhile the President had arranged to send Colonel Henry L. Stimson as his personal representative to Nicaragua. Arriving in April, 1927, the American mediator succeeded in working out an agreement between the rebels and the government by the terms of which an election was to be held the following year under American supervision. The results of the balloting were so satisfactory that both political parties united in requesting similar co-operation from the United States in the election four years later. One of the rebel leaders, General Sandino, refused to be pacified, and his "bandit" following made life miserable for the United States marines and delayed their withdrawal. On the whole, however, relations with Nicaragua were apparently improved by Stimson's good offices.[33]

A New Day in Latin American Relations

Intimately associated with the Nicaragua imbroglio, and to some extent growing out of it, were serious difficulties with Mexico. Article

---

[31] *Cong. Record*, 69 Cong., 2 sess., p. 1428 (Jan. 11, 1927).

[32] New York *Times*, April 26, 1927, 10: 6–7.

[33] H. L. Stimson, *American Policy in Nicaragua* (N.Y., 1927), pp. 87–89. In one of the American-supervised elections the fingers of those who had voted were stained with mercurochrome, thus preventing "repeating." Chapman, *Republican Hispanic America*, p. 270.

27 of the Constitution of 1917 vested in the Mexican nation the owner-ship of all mineral and oil resources, and American investors feared that this clause might be made retroactive. The unwillingness of the Mexican authorities to give satisfying assurances prompted the Wilson administration to refuse recognition to President Obregón, who, after a brief interval, had succeeded Carranza in 1920. Finally, in 1923, Mexico agreed to validate American subsoil and mineral rights ac-quired prior to 1917, and the United States resumed diplomatic relations.

President Calles, who succeeded Obregón in 1924, favored a retro-active interpretation of the Constitution of 1917, and supported an agrarian and anticlerical program that was highly offensive to investors and Catholics in the United States. At the height of the Nicaragua difficulty, Kellogg sent a note to the Senate, on January 12, 1927, charging that Russian interests in Mexico were encouraging Nicaragua to resist the United States. This unfortunate resurrection of the Bol-shevik bogey, together with other developments, served to whip up a first-class war scare, and the press seriously discussed the prospect of hostilities with Mexico. Democrats vehemently charged that the Re-publicans were "deliberately and consciously driving toward war in Mexico to protect American business interests." [34] But the evidence now available indicates that the Coolidge administration at no time seriously considered war, and was determined to avoid it at all hazards.[35]

Relations with Mexico were almost hopelessly embroiled when President Coolidge, in September, 1927, appointed a former Amherst College classmate, Dwight Morrow, as United States ambassador to Mexico. Though Morrow was criticized for being a partner in the House of Morgan, his sympathetic approach, combined with intel-ligence and tact, brought about a remarkable change of feeling among the Mexicans toward the United States.[36] He was even greeted on his travels with enthusiastic cries of approval from the masses. To give dramatic point to the new cordiality, Morrow arranged to have Charles A. Lindbergh, solo conqueror of the Atlantic, fly to Mexico City, in December, 1927. The aviator's reception was so over-

[34] *Literary Digest*, XCII, 5 (Jan. 22, 1927). The leading article of this issue of the *Literary Digest* was devoted to the agitation for or against war with Mexico.

[35] Bryn-Jones, *Kellogg*, pp. 183–184.

[36] Before leaving the United States, Morrow remarked, "I know what I can do for the Mexicans. I can *like* them." Harold Nicolson, *Dwight Morrow* (N.Y., 1935), p. 299.

whelming as to cause the Philadelphia *Evening Ledger* to suggest that the conduct of all foreign affairs be turned over to the air service.[37]

It is not surprising that Morrow's work was remarkably successful. Using informal diplomatic methods, and aided by a fortunate decision of the Mexican Supreme Court, he finally worked out a compromise by which American oil rights secured prior to the Constitution of 1917 could be retained. He also made some progress in the solution of other problems.

With the Mexican clouds clearing away, the Sixth International Conference of American States met at Havana, January 16, 1928. President Coolidge opened the sessions in person; and Charles Evans Hughes headed a strong American delegation. The United States was embarrassed by the presence of the marines in Nicaragua, and only with difficulty was Hughes able to block a resolution declaring that "no state has the right to intervene in the internal affairs of another." But on the whole the Conference seems to have been productive of good.[38]

President Coolidge, who had been re-elected "in his own right" in 1924, did not "choose to run" for a second elective term. The Republicans nominated the Secretary of Commerce, Herbert Hoover, and carried him to victory in November, 1928. Shortly after the balloting, the President-elect embarked upon a good will tour of eleven of the principal Latin American countries. The southern republics, flattered by this evidence of interest, gave Hoover a reasonably enthusiastic welcome. The Coolidge administration closed with Latin American relations in a gratifying state, and with "the retreat from imperialism," so important in the 1930's, definitely foreshadowed.

BIBLIOGRAPHICAL NOTE

For general accounts of the diplomacy of the Coolidge administration consult C. C. Hyde, "Charles Evans Hughes," in S. F. Bemis, ed., *The American Secretaries of State and their Diplomacy* (N.Y., 1929), X, 221–401. See also David Bryn-Jones, *Frank B. Kellogg* (N.Y., 1937), which contains valuable memoranda by Kellogg. For a more detailed study of important problems arising during the period consult C. P. Howland, *Survey of American Foreign Relations, 1928* (New Haven, 1928). F. H. Simonds, *American Foreign Policy in the Post-War Years* (Baltimore, 1935) is a challenging interpretation by a well-known journalist. For a brief study of the debts consult B. H. Williams, *Economic Foreign Policy of the United States* (N.Y., 1929), Ch. XII. Much more exhaustive are H. G. Moulton and Leo Pasvolsky, *World War Debt Settlements* (N.Y., 1926),

---

[37] *Literary Digest*, XCVI, 5 (Jan. 21, 1928).
[38] See Stuart, *Latin America and the United States*, pp. 23–27.

and the same authors' *War Debts and World Prosperity* (N.Y., 1932), particularly the latter. On the Immigration Act of 1924 R. W. Paul, *The Abrogation of the Gentlemen's Agreement* (Cambridge, Mass., 1936) is the most complete. See also Yamato Ichihashi, *Japanese in the United States* (Stanford University, 1932), Ch. XIX; A. W. Griswold, *The Far Eastern Policy of the United States* (N.Y., 1938), Ch. IX; and E. Tupper and G. E. McReynolds, *Japan in American Public Opinion* (N.Y., 1937). On the Kellogg-Briand pact see Bryn-Jones, *Kellogg* and J. T. Shotwell, *War as an Instrument of National Policy* (N.Y., 1929), the latter a valuable account by a leading participant. D. H. Miller, *The Peace Pact of Paris* (N.Y., 1928) is a detailed analysis by an expert. On the United States and the League see J. S. Bassett, *The League of Nations* (N.Y., 1928); on the World Court consult M. O. Hudson, *The World Court, 1921–1938* (5th ed., Boston, 1938). J. M. Callahan, *American Foreign Policy in Mexican Relations* (N.Y., 1932), Ch. XV, has a survey of the Mexican problem. Further references: see footnotes of this chapter.

RECENT REFERENCES. N. M. Butler, *Across the Busy Years* (N.Y., 1940), II, 202–212, tells of his part in inducing Briand to propose the Pact of Paris; in persuading Kellogg to accept it; and in arousing public support in behalf of it. C. M. Fuess, *Calvin Coolidge* (Boston, 1940), is an "official" biography devoted primarily to politics, though there are some pages (406–423) on foreign affairs. Coolidge was admittedly not a real student of foreign policy, and he was content to allow Hughes and Kellogg to carry the burden. *Foreign Relations, 1924*, II, 333–411, contains revealing documents on Japan and the Immigration Act of 1924. This material supports the view expressed in the present book that the famous Hanihara note was written at the suggestion of and in collaboration with the Department of State (p. 338). Coolidge stated that he would have vetoed the exclusion provision had it stood alone (p. 396). C. G. Dawes, *A Journal of Reparations* (London, 1939), describes in detail the making of the Dawes plan.

NEW REFERENCES. J. E. Stoner, *S. O. Levinson and the Pact of Paris: A Study in the Techniques of Influence* (Chicago, 1942), deals with a remarkable Jewish lawyer from Chicago who inaugurated a one-man crusade for the outlawry of war, although he had opposed the League and an unamended World Court. He used his own funds widely, and enlisted the support of men like Borah. He was clearly the mainspring of the outlawry movement, which eventuated in the Pact of Paris. S. F. Bemis, *The Latin American Policy of the United States* (N.Y., 1943), uses hitherto unexploited manuscripts in a discussion of the Havana Conference of 1928. Although the United States made its last defense of the Caribbean interventions, the Havana Conference took long steps toward the codification of international law with distinctively American features (p. 252). Argentina almost wrecked the conference when, in her efforts to take the lead against the United States, she raised the issue of intervention (p. 264). D. F. Fleming, *The United States and the World Court* (Garden City, N.Y., 1945), though sketchy, one-sided, and impassioned, is a useful survey of the effort to enter the Court.

4TH ED. REFS. Merze Tate, *The United States and Armaments* (Cambridge, 1948), discusses the Geneva Conference. Dorothy Borg, *American Policy and the Chinese Revolution, 1925–1928* (N.Y., 1947), reveals that a relinquishing of privileges, though opposed by some commercial groups, was favored by the Administration, some missionary boards, Congress, and the public.

CHAPTER XLIII

Hoover and the Diplomacy of Depression, 1929–1933

"I covet for this administration a record of having further con-
tributed to advance the cause of peace."
Herbert Hoover, Inaugural Address, 1929.

TOWARD WORLD CO-OPERATION

PRESIDENT Herbert Hoover, who took the oath of office on March 4, 1929, seemed unusually well qualified to direct the nation's foreign affairs. While engaged in his profession of engineering he had lived for many years in Australia, Mexico, China, India, Russia, Italy, South Africa, and other foreign lands.[1] His background and breadth of view were as cosmopolitan as those of Coolidge and Harding had been provincial. As the head of vast relief projects in Europe, both during and after the World War, Hoover had discharged with conspicuous ability the quasi-diplomatic tasks of administering an enormously complicated mechanism. As Secretary of Commerce under Harding and Coolidge, he had raised the Department to a new importance, and had familiarized himself with those international economic problems that overshadowed all others during the postwar years.

There can be little doubt that peace was the keynote of Hoover's foreign policy. As an engineer, he hated the waste of war; as a Quaker and humanitarian, he detested the bloodshed and suffering that it entailed. In his speech accepting the presidential nomination he declared:

I think I may say that I have witnessed as much of the horror and suffering of war as any other American. From it I have derived a deep passion for peace. Our foreign policy has one primary object, and that is

---

[1] Hoover and his family were besieged in Tientsin, China, during the Boxer disorders of 1900, and he later told how the beleaguered Americans rejoiced when they heard the band of the rescuing force playing "the precious strains of 'There'll Be a Hot Time in the Old Town To-night.'" W. S. Myers, ed., *The State Papers and other Public Writings of Herbert Hoover* (N.Y., 1934), I, 269.

peace. We have no hates; we wish no further possessions; we harbor no military threats.[2]

Hoover announced in his inaugural address that the United States would not join the League of Nations. This declaration was consistent with Republican policy, and appeared to be in conformity with the will of the people. Nevertheless the Administration continued the course pursued by its predecessor, and co-operated with the League in disarmament and numerous other nonpolitical activities.

Like Wilson, Harding and Coolidge, President Hoover strongly urged American adherence to the World Court. The issue had been in abeyance since 1926, when the members of that tribunal had found the Senate reservation regarding advisory opinions unacceptable. Elihu Root finally devised a formula for reconciling existing differences; and in December, 1930, Hoover submitted the necessary protocols to the Senate with a strong recommendation for acceptance. Many signs indicated that American public opinion was favorable to the World Court.[3] But the Hearst press, aided by other newspapers, cried that the tribunal was a "tool of the League of Nations"—a "den of international robbers." The "irreconcilable" Senators mustered great obstructive strength, and the issue was postponed to the Roosevelt administration.

Early in 1935 the pressure of public opinion, especially that of the "best people," became so great that the Senate was forced to move. Preliminary polls indicated that enough votes were assured to secure adherence to the World Court, though by a very narrow margin. But at the eleventh hour the isolationists summoned all their reserves. William Randolph Hearst and Father Coughlin (an influential "radio priest") addressed impassioned appeals to their large followings. An outpouring of telegrams, estimated at 200,000 and representing more than a million citizens, descended upon the Senate. The final vote, taken on January 29, 1935, was 52 yeas to 36 nays, seven short of the necessary two thirds. The isolationists naturally—and correctly—hailed their victory as the death of the Court issue.

[2] *The New Day: Campaign Speeches of Herbert Hoover, 1928* (Stanford University, 1928), p. 38 (August 11, 1928).

[3] An analysis of 1622 American newspapers, the results of which are deposited in the Hoover Library, Stanford University, reveals that press opinion favored the World Court in the ratio of nearly three to one.

The London Naval Conference and Disarmament

President Hoover viewed with dismay the costly rivalry in cruisers and other lighter craft that had gained momentum since the Washington Conference. But naval disarmament could not be achieved until Great Britain and the United States had ironed out the differences that had flared up at the ill-starred Geneva Conference. Prime Minister Ramsay MacDonald and the United States ambassador in London, Charles G. Dawes, began protracted negotiations which started with the assumption that both nations were to have equality in all categories of ships. After several months of discussion it was announced that all differences had been reduced to the type of gun for three large cruisers.

The next step was taken when President Hoover invited Mac-Donald to come to the United States for the purpose of considering Anglo-American problems and further preparing for the proposed naval conference. During his twelve-day visit, October 4 to 16, 1929, the distinguished Briton spoke in New York and before the United States Senate. Everywhere he went he made a splendid impression.

Friendly discussions between Hoover and MacDonald took place in Washington, and at the President's summer fishing camp at Rapidan, Virginia, where the press pictured the two statesmen sitting on a log and settling the affairs of the world. In this spirit of cordiality the conversations proceeded satisfactorily. The climax came on October 7, 1929, when Great Britain issued formal invitations for a disarmament conference at London. The other four great naval Powers accepted without undue delay. President Hoover selected a delegation of seven men, headed by Secretary of State Stimson, and including a leading Republican and a leading Democratic Senator.

The five-Power naval conference began its sessions on January 21, 1930, and speedily became bogged down in technical discussions. The French, who were still obsessed with a passion for security, demanded assurances of military support as the price of co-operation in arms limitation. Several members of the American delegation were rather favorable to the idea, but President Hoover flatly rejected any such commitment as leading to serious involvements.[4] After prolonged and somewhat acrimonious arguments, the naval treaty was formally completed, April 22, 1930. Though the representatives of each of the five great naval Powers signed the document, France and Italy subscribed to only relatively unimportant clauses.

[4] R. L. Wilbur and A. M. Hyde, *The Hoover Policies* (N.Y., 1937), p. 592.

Illusory though these results seemed to be, the outcome was a partial victory for disarmament. An upper limit was fixed in all categories of vessels, thus correcting the great weakness of the Washington naval treaty. Moreover, the British and the Americans were granted parity in all types of vessels. The Japanese, who retained the 10–10–6 ratio in capital ships, were forced to accept a compromise. Though granted parity in submarines, they had to content themselves with the small end of a 10–10–6 ratio in heavy cruisers, and a 10–10–7 ratio in light cruisers and other auxiliary craft. In this way competitive building among the great Powers was to be halted. Yet the so-called escalator clause provided that if one or more nations not bound by the treaty should begin building in such a way as to jeopardize a signatory power, the ratios thus established would no longer be considered obligatory.

The American taxpayer, who had expected extravagant accomplishments at London, read of the results with misgivings. The United States, to be sure, had won paper parity but would have to spend about a billion dollars in order to build up to it.[5] The New York *Journal of Commerce* declared that the Conference had "failed lamentably," while other newspapers referred to "only crumbs, rather poor crumbs, too." [6]

Like the press, Hoover could not have been altogether pleased with the treaty; but, accepting the half loaf, he strongly urged the Senate to consent to ratification. When that august body ignored his pleas and adjourned without taking action, the President called a special session, which opened July 7, 1930. The Hearst press cried that the British and Japanese had "put something over" on the United States; and the Senate, professing to fear some kind of secret commitment, requested Hoover to submit the confidential papers in his possession. The President declined to do so, however, on the grounds that such a betrayal of confidence would interfere with American negotiations in the future; but he did offer to show his private files to individual Senators.[7] After a stormy debate, the Senate approved the treaty, July 21, 1930, by a vote of 58 to 9. At the same time it passed a resolution

---

[5] Hoover issued a statement to the effect that as compared with the standards discussed at the Geneva Conference in 1927, the United States would save about a billion dollars in six years. *Hoover State Papers*, I, 233.

[6] See *Literary Digest*, CV, 9 (April 26, 1930).

[7] Hoover's advocacy of naval disarmament incurred the strong opposition of the Navy League and American shipbuilders. These interests allegedly contributed their money to defeat Hoover in 1932 and secure the election of Franklin D. Roosevelt, who was regarded as more "ship-minded." See C. A. and M. R. Beard, *America in Mid-passage* (N.Y., 1939), pp. 390–392.

which declared that the United States was not bound by any secret understandings.

The Administration, not content to rest on such laurels as it had won at the London Conference, co-operated wholeheartedly in the work of the World Disarmament Conference, which met in Geneva, February 2, 1932. President Hoover, acting through the American delegation, strongly urged the abolition of all offensive weapons. When the Conference failed to respond, he revitalized it by making the sensational proposal, on June 22, 1932, that all existing armaments be reduced approximately one third. Although the plan was enthusiastically received both in the United States [8] and at Geneva, it was finally buried beneath an impressive offering of "oratorical flowers." Among the factors contributing to the result were the unwillingness of France to disarm in advance of guarantees of security, the impracticability of treating disarmament as a simple problem in arithmetic, and the Japanese attack on Shanghai while the Conference was in session.[9] The world seemed to be inexorably headed toward extreme nationalism and crushing armament burdens.

THE HOOVER MORATORIUM

No less complicated than the disarmament problem was that of the intergovernmental debts. President Hoover, like Wilson, Harding, and Coolidge, was strongly opposed to cancellation in any form. Like his predecessors, he held that "reparations are necessarily wholly a European problem with which we have no relation." [10] These views were also those of a great majority of the American people.

The paralyzing stock market crash in the United States of October, 1929, prepared the way for a reconsideration of the debt problem. Financial stringency at home sharply reduced the amount of money Americans had to lend abroad. The Germans, who had been paying their reparations from American private loans, found it increasingly difficult to meet their obligations; and America's debtors, who in large part had been making their payments from reparations, were in turn severely pinched.

The crisis came in the spring of 1931, when financial panic developed in Austria and spread to Germany. It was evident that complete chaos

[8] The press analyses in the Hoover Library indicate that the proposal was favored by a majority of four to one.

[9] See D. F. Fleming, *The United States and World Organization, 1920–1933* (N.Y., 1938), pp. 378–380.

[10] *Hoover State Papers*, I, 593 (press statement of June 20, 1931).

would not only end the payment of governmental debts to the United States, but would also wipe out the hundreds of millions of dollars that American citizens had invested in Central Europe in the years following the war.

President Hoover decided that the situation called for drastic measures. In a statement to the press, on June 20, 1931, he dramatically proposed an all-around moratorium for one year on intergovernmental debts and reparations. Since this innovation would have to be passed upon by Congress, Hoover gave out the names of leaders in both the House and the Senate who had approved the plan, thus guaranteeing Congressional support. But he also made it clear that he was still opposed to cancellation and to the linking of debts and reparations.[11]

The next step was to win the approval of those nations that were entitled to reparations payments from Germany. France proved to be the big stumbling block. She had not been consulted in advance; and her traditionally sensitive pride was hurt. As the nation that had suffered most severely from the German invasion, she wanted assurances that the existing reparations arrangements would be continued at the end of the proposed holiday. Not until such assurances were forthcoming, some of them by transatlantic telephone,[12] did the government in Paris consent to the moratorium, July 6, 1931. Unfortunately, the two-week delay caused by these French negotiations brought about further financial disaster.

The effects of the "Hoover holiday" were both immediate and salutary, and a wave of optimism carried prices up with a rush on practically all the stock and commodity markets of the world. Public opinion in the United States, especially in the financial centers, was strongly favorable.[13] On the other hand, William Randolph Hearst declared himself as "uncompromisingly opposed to further reduction of the war debt"; and newspapers like the Wichita *Eagle* feared that when the year had ended "Europe may want to place the accent on that 'more' in moratorium."

On December 10, 1931, Hoover submitted the moratorium to Congress for approval. At the same time, he recommended that the World War Foreign Debt Commission be re-created for the purpose of re-

[11] *Ibid.*, I, 591–593. There was disagreement among the members of Congress and the Cabinet as to the length of the moratorium, some advocating two or three years.

[12] Hoover later said: ". . . For the first time in the history of the world, I made personal, hourly use of the newly installed trans-Atlantic telephone and talked with our Ambassadors in the presence of the leaders of the nations." *Ibid.*, II, 448.

[13] The press analyses in the Hoover Library indicate that American opinion favored the moratorium in the ratio of ten to one.

examining the war debts in the light of the existing emergency. Congress refused to heed the latter recommendation but approved the moratorium, on December 22, 1931, by ample majorities. Significantly, that body added an emphatic declaration to the effect that none of the foreign indebtedness to the United States was to be canceled or reduced.

THE BEGINNINGS OF DEBT DEFAULT

In September, 1931, several months before Congress approved the moratorium, Great Britain went off the gold standard, leaving France and the United States the only two great nations maintaining that standard. The depression was still acute; and since both countries were more or less in the same economic situation, Premier Laval of France was invited to come to America for a discussion of recovery policies.

The swarthy, black-mustached "peasant premier" arrived in the United States on October 22, 1931. After three days of discussion through the medium of interpreters, Hoover and Laval issued a guarded statement indicating that they had considered the war debts, reparations, and the gold standard. This rather vague announcement seemed to suggest an agreement that Germany should have relief from the reparations burden, but that the initiative should be taken by Germany through the Young plan, which fixed the existing obligation.

There was a tendency in Europe, particularly in France, to interpret the Laval understanding as meaning that if the former Allies scaled down their reparations demands, the United States would reduce its debts proportionately. Encouraged by these hopes, the interested Powers met at Lausanne, in June, 1932, and lowered German reparations to $714,000,000, which, when compared with the $33,000,000,000 originally assessed, amounted to cancellation. But the arrangement was made contingent upon a satisfactory readjustment of war debts with the United States.

This alleged trick to cancel debts aroused a furore in the United States. Mr. Hearst immediately mobilized his army of cartoonists and writers; and the members of Congress, so newspaper polls revealed, expressed strong resentment against the concerted action of the "league of debtors." Senator Borah, who wished to know if the Administration were a party to the Lausanne agreement, addressed an inquiry to President Hoover. The latter replied, on July 14, 1932, that reparations were a "strictly European problem," and that the

United States was "not a party to, nor in any way committed to any such agreements." [14] The press of the United States loudly applauded this emphatic declaration, for there can be no doubt that public opinion was strongly opposed to cancellation in any form. [15] The former Allies were highly displeased, and one Parisian daily, *La Liberté*, declared that "Americans are the only race which passed directly from barbarism to decadence without knowing civilization."

The debtor nations wisely forbore to push their pleas during the presidential campaign of 1932, in which problems arising from the depression overshadowed interest in foreign affairs. But in November of that year, after Hoover had been defeated by the Democratic candidate, Franklin D. Roosevelt, the debtors renewed their requests for a review of the question, and asked for an extension of the moratorium pending such a study. President Hoover realized that the problem needed immediate attention, but he was unwilling to commit the incoming Administration to policies which it might not approve. So at two White House conferences, and in other ways, he sought to secure the co-operation of the President-elect. But the two men were unable to come to an agreement, apparently because Roosevelt did not care to tie his hands in advance, and because he felt that the problem of economic recovery should be attacked on a wide front at home rather than through the international situation. [16] The President-elect was alleged to have remarked, whether correctly or not, that the war debt question was "not my baby."

Late in 1932 the State Department evinced a willingness to discuss debt revision after the payments that were due on December 15 had been received—the first since the moratorium. But it was now too late. On December 15, 1932, six of the debtors defaulted outright, most conspicuous among which were France and Belgium. The baby that Roosevelt had been loath to recognize lay on his doorstep when he took office.

THE MANCHURIAN CRISIS OF 1931

Important though the questions of disarmament and debts were, it was in the Far East that the Hoover administration encountered its most critical diplomatic problems. In the latter part of 1929 the ex-

[14] *Hoover State Papers*, II, 235.

[15] The press analyses in the Hoover Library indicate that the Hoover letter to Borah was approved by a ratio of about seven to one.

[16] *The Public Papers and Addresses of Franklin D. Roosevelt* (N.Y., 1938), I, 877–884; *Hoover State Papers*, II, 554–559.

plosive situation in the Orient was unpleasantly brought to the attention of the world when friction between China and Russia over the Chinese Eastern Railway led to an undeclared war.[17] Both Powers were signatories of the Kellogg-Briand pact, and the dispute in the Far East put the treaty to its first real test. As an outstanding sponsor of this agreement, the United States government took a leading part in bringing diplomatic pressure to bear upon the belligerents, and in mobilizing the support of the other Powers. In spite of the solemn pledge not to use war as an instrument of national policy, a Russian army crushed Chinese resistance in Manchuria, and the authorities there accepted provisional terms of peace on November 26, 1929. Although the incident did not result in a full-fledged war, Secretary Stimson's intervention had no demonstrable bearing on the outcome, and he was stingingly rebuked by Moscow for having presumed to give advice to a government which the United States refused to recognize.[18] The clash in the Far East revealed the danger of one Power taking the lead in trying to halt an aggressor, for the Kellogg-Briand pact clothed no nation with such a responsibility. The affair also showed the ineffectiveness of world opinion as a means of stopping war.

Far more serious complications resulted from strained relations between China and Japan over the latter's special interests in Manchuria. Following an explosion on the Japanese-controlled South Manchuria Railroad, on the night of September 18, 1931, the Japanese armies overran South Manchuria within forty-eight hours, completely overwhelming Chinese opposition. The rapidity and precision of the movement were interpreted by the State Department, as elsewhere, as evidence of an elaborately preconceived plan.[19]

Secretary Stimson promptly and vigorously reminded Japan of her treaty obligations; yet the military machine continued to roll relentlessly on. The League of Nations also undertook, without success, to end the undeclared war in the Far East. Hoping to secure needed American support, the League formally invited the United States, on October 16, 1931, to appoint a representative to sit with the Council in its consideration of the Manchurian crisis.

Hitherto America had spurned the advances of the League. To consent to co-operate at this time would certainly appear to the Japa-

[17] S. C. Y. Pan, *American Diplomacy concerning Manchuria* (Providence, R.I., 1938), pp. 190 ff.
[18] A. W. Griswold, *The Far Eastern Policy of the United States* (N.Y., 1938), p. 398.
[19] H. L. Stimson, *The Far Eastern Crisis* (N.Y., 1936), p. 32.

nese as an unfriendly act. Nevertheless, the Administration accepted the invitation, and authorized Prentiss B. Gilbert, who was then consul at Geneva, to attend the sessions of the League Council. He was carefully instructed to participate in the discussions only insofar as they related to America's obligations under the Kellogg-Briand pact. Otherwise he was to act solely in the capacity of "observer and auditor." [20]

On October 20, 1931, the League Council voted to invoke the Kellogg-Briand pact; yet the Japanese continued their drive into Manchuria. With the approval of the United States, the League appointed a neutral commission of five, headed by Lord Lytton, to study the situation in the Far East. One of the members of the Lytton commission was a United States army officer, Major General Frank R. McCoy, who was released from active duty for this purpose.

These indirect and half-hearted efforts at co-operation with the League elicited a loud outcry from the isolationist press of the United States. The New York *Daily News* warned, "Let's shinny on our side of the street," while an editorial in Hearst's New York *American* bore the caption, "Stimson's Folly." In fact, it is doubtful whether a strong majority of public opinion supported the Administration's course. [21] President Hoover, in his annual message of December, 1931, felt called upon to assure the country that the government had maintained complete freedom of action. [22]

STIMSON BEARDS JAPAN ALONE

By early January, 1932, the Japanese had crushed the last effective Chinese resistance in Manchuria. On January 7 Secretary Stimson, prevented by American opinion from acting with the League, addressed an identic note to Japan and China in which he set forth a significant doctrine. Proclaiming that Washington could not acquiesce in any arrangement involving Manchuria that hurt American rights, he concluded:

. . . It [the United States] does not intend to recognize any situation, treaty, or agreement which may be brought about by means contrary to the covenants and obligations of the Pact of Paris of August 27, 1928 [Kellogg-Briand pact], to which treaty both China and Japan, as well as the United States, are parties. [23]

[20] *Ibid.*, pp. 64–66.
[21] *Literary Digest*, CXI, 6 (Oct. 24, 1931). See also the press analyses in the Hoover Library and Fleming, *The United States and World Organization,* pp. 458 ff.
[22] *Hoover State Papers*, II, 76 (Dec. 10, 1931).
[23] Department of State, *Press Releases*, Jan. 9, 1932, p. 42.

This policy of nonrecognition, which has come to be known as the "Stimson" or the "Hoover-Stimson" doctrine,[24] was, in its basic principles, not new. It went back at least as far as Secretary Bryan's note of May 11, 1915.[25] But the Hoover-Stimson interpretation broadened the base of the nonrecognition doctrine by invoking the Kellogg-Briand pact, which had been endorsed by virtually all the nations of the world. Thus the Administration, while avoiding warlike measures, hoped to establish a strong moral sanction against aggression.

Stimson hoped that Britain and France, whose stake in the Far East was more vital than that of America, would vigorously endorse the new doctrine. Instead, London published a statement, on January 11, 1932, in which it professed to have faith in Tokyo's assurances regarding the Open Door.[26] The Japanese were not deterred by Stimson's bold note, for they recognized that the isolationist and pacifistic United States, acting alone and mired down by the depression, was in no position to stop them by force. Moral sanctions could therefore be laughed aside by the militarists of Japan.

Public opinion in the United States strongly supported the Hoover-Stimson doctrine,[27] yet there was a bitter undercurrent of criticism from those who held that the American note was as useless as it was dangerous. The Philadelphia *Record* entitled an editorial, "Don Quixote Stimson and the Japanese Windmill," while the Chicago *Tribune* hoped that the State Department would be content to rest and "cease sticking pins into Japan."

SHANGHAI—1932 VERSION

Although Japan was not without numerous and influential apologists in the United States, the American people generally sympathized with the Chinese underdog.[28] But this does not mean that public opinion became dangerously inflamed. The Far East was far away; and the depression was close at home. "The American people," asserted the Philadelphia *Record*, "don't give a hoot in a rain barrel who controls North China." Moreover, the Department of State did not at once publish the more inflammatory diplomatic interchanges, and it

[24] Apparently President Hoover had a large hand in framing the doctrine. Wilbur and Hyde, *The Hoover Policies*, p. 603.

[25] *Foreign Relations, 1915*, p. 146.

[26] Stimson later wrote that the British reply was "such as to be taken by most readers, including—what was most important—the Japanese government, as a rebuff to the United States." Stimson, *Far Eastern Crisis*, p. 101.

[27] The press digests in the Hoover Library show this.

[28] E. Tupper and G. H. McReynolds, *Japan in American Public Opinion*, pp. 294 ff.

earnestly admonished the newspaper correspondents not to give a sensational turn to happenings in the Far East.[29]

But the lid blew off on January 28, 1932. Smarting under a destructive boycott, Japanese troops clashed with Chinese forces at Shanghai; and during the ensuing fighting uncounted thousands of men, women, and children were bombed or burned to death. A wave of revulsion against these methods swept the United States. Editorial pages teemed with such expressions as "insane imperialism," "running amuck," and "beyond the pale of civilized warfare." Secretary Stimson, writing several years later, remembered that there came to his mind "the memories of the similar feeling which had been excited . . . at the outbreak of the World War by the news of the violation of the neutrality of Belgium. . . ."[30]

A few hotheads in the United States urged a declaration of war against Japan. A great many more, including prominent figures like President Lowell of Harvard University, agitated for an economic boycott. By February 26, 1932, the New York *Times* could announce that some five thousand civic leaders had signed petitions urging such a course. But a strong body of American opinion—probably a majority —opposed economic sanctions as too dangerous.[31] Although the Department of State was not unfavorable to co-operating with the League in the imposition of a boycott, Hoover strongly opposed such a departure, for he regarded economic coercion as the road to war.[32] Washington therefore contented itself with formal protests to Tokyo whenever American interests were injured at Shanghai. After the Japanese had finally driven out the defending army, they responded to joint pressure by the United States and the other Powers and withdrew, May 31, 1932. It was a belated victory for co-operation.

STIMSON'S SHIRT-SLEEVE DIPLOMACY

Before the termination of the hostilities at Shanghai, Secretary Stimson took another important step. Heretofore the representations

[29] Stimson, *Far Eastern Crisis*, p. 72.

[30] *Ibid.*, p. 156. The Massie rape-lynching scandal in Honolulu, which aroused bitter race feeling in the United States, did much to divert public excitement from the events in the Far East. It succeeded in keeping the Hoover-Stimson doctrine off the feature page of the *Literary Digest*.

[31] The Hoover Library press digests indicate that opinion was strongly against a boycott.

[32] Wilbur and Hyde, *The Hoover Policies*, p. 603. Secretary Stimson believed that the situation was kept under control in part because the United States fleet was then in Hawaiian waters, presumably ready to move on to the Far East. Stimson, *The Far Eastern Crisis*, p. 138.

of the Powers had been based on the Covenant of the League and the Kellogg-Briand pact. Stimson conceived the idea of making a strong protest to Japan on the basis of the Nine-Power Treaty of 1922, by which the signatories had guaranteed the territorial integrity of China. He had reason to expect that the other great Powers would co-operate in a joint appeal. Although Great Britain had been rather indifferent to the Manchuria invasion, Shanghai, the nerve center of vast British interests in China, was a different matter. Secretary Stimson held several transatlantic telephone conversations with Sir John Simon, British Foreign Secretary, and cabled him a draft of a proposed joint statement. But in the end the British government responded so coldly that Stimson was forced to abandon all plans for co-operative action.[33]

Stimson feared that if he again took the initiative in confronting Japan alone, he would suffer another humiliating rebuff and further antagonize the Japanese. So he worked out the scheme of presenting his views in a letter to Senator Borah, chairman of the Senate Committee on Foreign Relations. The statement would then be published, and it would receive just as much publicity as a formal note—probably a good deal more. Beyond question it would be carefully read by what Stimson later referred to as the "five unnamed addressees"—Japan, Britain, China, the League, and the American public.[34]

This interesting bit of shirt-sleeve diplomacy was carried through. The letter was prepared in collaboration with Senator Borah and President Hoover, and given to the press under date of February 23, 1932. It referred to the Nine-Power Pact and the circumstances of its making, and further declared that the United States would stand upon its treaty rights in the Far East. Stimson then directed attention to the nonrecognition doctrine, and invited the nations of the world to follow America's example.

The letter to Borah was quite favorably received by the American press.[35] Scores of newspapers in all parts of the country agreed with the *Christian Science Monitor* that it "ranks with the most important State papers in American history." It is impossible to say, however, what influence the letter had in securing support for the nonrecogni-

[33] *Ibid.*, p. 164. There are many who think that Britain made a major diplomatic blunder when she failed to join hands with the United States at one of the few times in history when the Washington government seemed willing to join hands. It appears, however, that Sir John Simon, rebuffed by Washington in 1931, preferred to work with the League system, rather than with a nation not a member of it. Griswold, *The Far Eastern Policy of the United States*, p. 431.

[34] H. L. Stimson and M. Bundy, *On Active Service* (N.Y., 1947), p. 249.

[35] The press digests in the Hoover Library show that the Stimson letter and co-operation with the other Powers met with general approval.

tion idea abroad. Certainly, it was something of a triumph for American policy when, on March 11, 1932, the League of Nations Assembly unanimously adopted a resolution which incorporated almost verbatim the Hoover-Stimson doctrine.[36]

Less than a week before the publication of Stimson's letter to Borah, the area previously known as Manchuria declared itself independent, and within a month a Japanese-controlled regent took office. Six months later, September 15, 1932, Tokyo formally recognized the new state of Manchukuo. The report of the Lytton Commission, which was published two weeks afterward, generally condemned Japan's action; and the Assembly of the League of Nations endorsed the findings of the investigators. Significantly, the State Department informed the League that it was in "substantial accord" with the conclusions of the Lytton Commission.

In dealing with the Sino-Japanese crisis of 1931–1932, the United States showed an extraordinary willingness to depart from its traditional policy of co-operation in the Far East and "go it alone." But this was because neither President Hoover nor American opinion would support joint-Power action looking toward economic or military sanctions. The British and French were fully aware of America's determination to avoid risk of war at all costs, and this knowledge helped restrain them from effective measures, thus leaving Japan with a free rein on the path of aggression. The inability of the Powers to act in concert showed that the Kellogg-Briand pact was an empty pretense, and that the League could be defied with impunity. These object lessons were not lost on Mussolini and Hitler in the years to come. In a very real sense World War II began in Manchuria.

BEGINNINGS OF THE GOOD NEIGHBOR

Even while involved in a theater so distant as the Far East, the Administration was deeply interested in cultivating friendly relations with neighboring peoples, north and south.[37] Hoover's good will trip to Latin America, as President-elect, facilitated in many ways a more amicable feeling. It was while in South America that Hoover proposed the formula by which the half-century-old Tacna-Arica dispute between Chile and Peru was finally adjusted. In his inaugural address

[36] The representatives of China and Japan did not vote.

[37] Except for minor friction over liquor smuggling into the United States, relations with Canada were amicable. The case of the *I'm Alone*, a Canadian rumrunner sunk by United States authorities well outside the three-mile limit in March, 1929, caused some momentary bad feeling; but the controversy was settled by arbitration in 1935.

the President confidently announced that "we have no desire for territorial expansion, for economic or other domination of other peoples." Secretary of State Stimson, who was widely known for his handling of the Nicaragua problem under Coolidge, further reassured the Latin American republics when he showed a willingness to accept the narrow interpretation given to the Monroe Doctrine by Undersecretary of State Clark.[38]

These promising assurances were given a severe test when an epidemic of revolutions, largely a by-product of the world-wide depression, broke out in Latin America. In March, 1929, an uprising occurred in the Mexican republic, with which relations had been unusually good since the Morrow settlement. The Washington government, pursuant to a joint resolution passed by Congress in 1922, embargoed arms for the rebels, while permitting war materials to be sold to the regularly constituted authorities. The disorders were promptly crushed. In October, 1930, when a revolution flared up in Brazil, the same policy was followed. Two days after the Hoover administration had declared an arms embargo against the rebels, the latter gained control, thus placing the United States in an embarrassing position. But recognition was accorded the next month. It is noteworthy that here we find the United States definitely abandoning the Wilson policy, and returning to the less troublesome principle of recognizing de facto governments, however questionable their antecedents.

The depression also contributed to a less aggressive attitude by the Washington government toward the smaller nations south of the Rio Grande. People in the great northern republic had less money; much of that which they had invested in foreign lands, particularly South America, had been lost; and citizens of the United States were bringing less pressure upon their government to intervene. In 1932 a treaty was signed with Haiti which provided for the withdrawal of American marines, and for a reduction of financial supervision. In Nicaragua, order was restored, despite the resistance of the "bandit" Sandino; and the last marines left in January, 1933. Altogether, relations with Latin America at the close of the Hoover administration were better than they had been at any time during the previous three decades.

---

[38] In 1930 the government published a 236-page *Memorandum on the Monroe Doctrine*, which had been completed by J. Reuben Clark in December, 1928. It gave a narrow interpretation to the Monroe Doctrine, and in particular repudiated the Theodore Roosevelt corollary. "The Doctrine," said Clark, "states a case of the United States *vs.* Europe, and not of the United States *vs.* Latin America." *Ibid.*, xxiv.

BIBLIOGRAPHICAL NOTE

A summary account of Hoover's foreign policy is R. L. Wilbur and A. M. Hyde, *The Hoover Policies* (N.Y., 1937), pp. 577–613. The authors were members of the Hoover Cabinet, and they supplement the documentary excerpts with valuable comments. For a stimulating journalistic interpretation see F. H. Simonds, *American Foreign Policy in the Post-War Years* (Baltimore, 1935). Detailed discussions appear in the volumes, *Survey of American Foreign Relations*, issued annually by the Council on Foreign Relations, and edited during 1929, 1930 by C. P. Howland, and published by the Yale University Press. These are followed by the volumes entitled *The United States in World Affairs*, issued for the years 1931, 1932, 1933, 1934–1935, 1936, 1937, 1938, and published in New York by the Council on Foreign Relations. A useful account of the League, disarmament, and the Manchuria crisis appears in D. F. Fleming, *The United States and World Organization, 1920–1933* (N.Y., 1938). There is material on the moratorium in W. S. Myers and W. H. Newton, *The Hoover Administration* (N.Y., 1936). For a summary treatment of the Geneva Conference see B. H. Williams, *The United States and Disarmament* (N.Y., 1931). Colorful but not very reliable accounts of the moratorium and the London Conference appear in Drew Pearson and Constantine Brown, *The American Diplomatic Game* (N.Y., 1935). A brief treatment of the Far Eastern crisis is A. W. Griswold, *The Far Eastern Policy of the United States* (N.Y., 1938), Ch. X. Secretary H. L. Stimson's revealing recollections are entitled *The Far Eastern Crisis* (N.Y., 1936). See also W. W. Willoughby, *The Sino-Japanese Controversy and the League of Nations* (Baltimore, 1935); H. S. Quigley and G. H. Blakeslee, *The Far East* (Boston, 1938); and E. Tupper and G. E. McReynolds, *Japan in American Public Opinion* (N.Y., 1937). On the Good Neighbor policy consult G. H. Stuart, *Latin America and the United States* (3rd ed., N.Y., 1938). Further references: see footnotes of this chapter.

RECENT REFERENCES. The best summary account is W. S. Myers, *The Foreign Policies of Herbert Hoover, 1929–1933* (N.Y., 1940). Though superficial and laudatory, it does reproduce some of Hoover's private papers. The story is confirmed that Hoover induced MacDonald to agree to build no more military or naval bases in the Western Hemisphere, but the Admiralty interposed a veto (pp. 64–65). Two letters written some months after the event by two of the Cabinet members give Hoover credit for originating the nonrecognition policy (pp. 164–168). The author denies that there was a secret understanding with Laval regarding debts. Of much greater value to the historian is C. G. Dawes, *Journal as Ambassador to Great Britain* (N.Y., 1939), which describes the negotiations leading up to the London Naval Conference and during it. The author has a strong admiration for Hoover, whose intimate knowledge of the intricate naval problems enabled him to detect an attempt by his Naval Board to interpret their own "yardstick" in such a way as to give them eight cruisers when they were entitled to only four and one half (p. 96). P. J. Treat, "Shanghai, January 28, 1932," *Pacific Hist. Rev.*, IX (1940), 337–343, points out that the initial clash came as a result of a misunderstanding as to the Japanese defense assignment in the city.

NEW REFERENCES; 4TH ED. REFS. See Bibliographical Appendix, p. 945.

CHAPTER XLIV

Franklin D. Roosevelt and New Deal Diplomacy

"In the field of world policy I would dedicate this Nation to the policy of the good neighbor. . . ."
Franklin D. Roosevelt, Inaugural Address, March 4, 1933.

THE LONDON ECONOMIC CONFERENCE

FRANKLIN D. ROOSEVELT, who took the presidential oath on March 4, 1933, was not new to Washington or to national affairs. He had served as Assistant Secretary of the Navy under Woodrow Wilson for seven years, and during the tempestuous World War days had fallen under the spell of Wilsonian idealism. Born to wealth, and given the opportunity to travel in Europe and learn foreign languages, Roosevelt came to the presidency with an unusual cultural background and with a more cosmopolitan outlook than most of his post-Jackson predecessors. Although he had shown a reluctance to co-operate with Hoover in advance of taking office, and although his was the first Democratic administration in twelve years, he generally followed the course plotted by the Republicans with respect to debts, disarmament, relations with Latin America and the Far East, and closer contacts with the League of Nations.[1]

With the depression still in an acute stage, Roosevelt was much interested in the International Economic Conference which convened in London, on June 12, 1933, and at which the United States was represented. The work of the Conference was proceeding rather favorably when the gold-bloc nations made a determined effort to commit America to a currency stabilization program. The fall of the dollar was beginning to bring about a faint blush of prosperity in the United States; and many Americans feared that stabilization would erase

[1] On May 22, 1933, Norman H. Davis, head of the American delegation at the Geneva Disarmament Conference, announced that the United States would be willing to co-operate in imposing sanctions upon aggressor nations. Department of State, *Press Releases*, May 27, 1933, p. 390. But since this offer was contingent upon thoroughgoing disarmament and Congressional support, nothing came of it. The United States joined the International Labor Office of the League of Nations in August, 1934.

these slight gains. Roosevelt apparently concluded that recovery begins at home, and on July 2, 1933, he sent a hastily drafted radio message in which he sharply rebuked the delegates for concentrating on currency stabilization to the exclusion of the whole broad program. "The Conference," he bluntly asserted, "was called to better and perhaps to cure fundamental economic ills. It must not be diverted from that effort." [2]

This stirring ultimatum was published on the Fourth of July; and the country applauded the President, for rumors of currency stabilization had already produced a sudden fall in prices. Some newspapers went so far as to hail the message as a "new Declaration of Independence." [3] But in London the delegates were angered both by the tone of the pronouncement and by the unwillingness of the United States to consider stabilization after having apparently agreed to do so in advance. Secretary of State Cordell Hull, who headed the American delegation, labored manfully to prevent the immediate breakup of the Conference; and although it lingered on impotently for several more weeks, nothing fundamental was accomplished. The United States was bitterly condemned for the disappointing results, but there is some doubt as to whether anything substantial would have been achieved even if Roosevelt had not intervened.[4] In any event, this disheartening failure dealt a heavy blow to international co-operation, and markedly accelerated the drift toward isolation, big-navyism, and extreme nationalism.

THE DEBTORS DEFAULT

The European Powers insisted that international economic stability could not be achieved without some adjustment of the debts they owed the United States; and they attempted to bring the problem before the London Conference. But Roosevelt, although willing to discuss the question with individual nations, steadfastly refused, like his predecessors, to couple debts with the general European situation.[5] When the next payments fell due, on June 15, 1933, Italy and Great Britain, rather than default outright as France and several others had done,

[2] *The Public Papers and Addresses of Franklin D. Roosevelt* (N.Y., 1938), II, 265.

[3] *Literary Digest*, CXVI, 6 (July 15, 1933).

[4] C. A. and M. R. Beard, *America in Midpassage* (N.Y., 1939), p. 467. Roosevelt's own defense appears in *Roosevelt Public Papers*, II, 266, 392.

[5] For the President's views see F. D. Roosevelt, *Looking Forward* (N.Y., 1933), p. 249.

made a "token payment"—that is, a relatively small sum acknowledging the existence of the debt "pending a final settlement."

American public opinion was dissatisfied with this evasion; so Congress took a hand. The Johnson Act, approved April 13, 1934, provided that no person or corporation under American jurisdiction could lend money to a government that was in default to the United States. Since the debtor countries either needed financial support then, or would need it in the event of another general war, this was interpreted as an attempt to club them into line.

The next question was: Did a token payment constitute a default? The United States Attorney General ruled that in the future foreign governments would have to meet their obligations completely if they were not to be considered as defaulters under the Johnson Act. Since the debtors could not or would not pay in full, and since they would get no credit for part payment, they all, except "brave little Finland," defaulted outright on June 15, 1934.

As long as American opinion would not permit cancellation or substantial reduction, and as long as European opinion would not permit payment, the debts were dead. The people of the United States were disillusioned and resentful as the obligations, principal and back interest, rapidly mounted from the original ten billion to over thirteen billions of dollars. The default of the debtors convinced Americans of the undesirability of having traffic with "faithless foreigners," and hastened the tendency toward isolation of the depression years.

THE RECOGNITION OF RUSSIA

The economic dislocations caused by the depression also brought about a changed relationship with Russia. Every administration since that of Wilson had consistently refused to recognize the Moscow regime on four counts: (1) Russia refused to assume the financial obligations incurred by the former governments; (2) she declined to recognize claims of American citizens for losses arising from official confiscations and revolutionary disturbances; (3) she attempted through subversive propaganda to overthrow the capitalistic system in other countries of the world.

For more than a decade after the close of the war the policy of nonrecognition was stanchly supported in the United States by conservatives and denounced by liberals. This was the general picture when the withering depression brought about a change of sentiment. American trade with Russia was falling off, and the optimistic thought that recognition might open up a great market. The Moscow government, responding to an invitation from President Roosevelt, sent Maxim Litvinoff, Commissar for Foreign Affairs, to Washington, and negotiations were opened in November, 1933. Although no agreement could be reached as to claims and debts, Litvinoff did give formal assurances that Russia would refrain from Communist propaganda in America.[6] On November 16, 1933, Washington formally extended recognition to the Moscow regime.

Russian recognition, baited as it was with the hope of foreign trade, seems to have been generally favored by the American press, though conservatives protested loudly. But the anticipated commerce with Russia failed to materialize; nor was the pledge of discontinuing propaganda kept to the satisfaction of Washington. In any event, the United States could no longer be criticized for refusing to have dealings with the established government of 160,000,000 people.

ECONOMIC DISARMAMENT

Other efforts of the Roosevelt administration were also directed toward opening up markets for foreign trade. The Smoot-Hawley Act of the Hoover administration had raised the tariff so high as to cause more than a score of nations to retaliate against American goods. The resulting ill will and trade dislocation were important factors in retarding world-wide economic recovery. The advent of Roosevelt presaged a change, for the Democratic party was traditionally the foe of high tariff walls, and Secretary Hull was a strong advocate of lowered economic barriers.

The Trade Agreements Act, approved June 12, 1934, provided that the President should have authority to raise or lower the existing tariff rates by as much as fifty per cent for those nations that were willing to make reciprocal concessions. Secretary Hull pushed his trade agreements program with zeal, and in a little more than four years concluded eighteen treaties. On November 17, 1938, he signed a renewal with Canada, and a sweeping trade pact with Great Britain. The latter was widely regarded as an attempt to bring the two nations closer together in the face of aggression by the dictator Powers of Europe. On April 1, 1939, the twenty-first trade agreement was concluded with Turkey. All these pacts together extended to areas that

[6] For the exchange of notes see *Roosevelt Public Papers*, II, 415–417, 465, 471–487. Recognition seems to have been motivated also by a desire on the part of the administration to strengthen Russia against Japan and Germany.

involved approximately three fifths of both American exports and imports. During the following months the State Department continued its negotiations for additional treaties.

The trade agreements operated to bring about a substantial, though piecemeal, whittling down of the tariff. The high-protectionist Republicans bitterly condemned this procedure, but were unable to prevail against the heavy Democratic majorities. Although it is difficult to determine with exactitude the economic consequences of the trade agreements policy, it has unquestionably done much to improve international good will, especially with the Latin American countries.

America Frees Herself from the Philippines

The depression not only contributed to a sharp reversal of America's tariff policy, but also brought about an epochal change in relations with the Philippines. Every President since McKinley had held out the hope of ultimate independence to the Filipinos. Yet thirty years after annexation—although the commercial potentialities envisaged by McKinley had not been realized—the Philippines seemed as far as ever from their goal.

Then came the depression. Unemployed laborers in the United States resented the presence of so many Filipinos on the Pacific Coast. Hard-pressed American sugar producers, to say nothing of the dairy, cordage, cottonseed oil and other interests, protested bitterly against the competition of duty-free Philippine products. Japan's imperialistic drive in the Far East made it clearer than ever before that the islands, upon which America had spent millions of dollars, were indefensible. Both economics and past promises called for a prompt divorce.

The independence movement gained great momentum late in the Hoover administration. American investors, imperialists, and big-navyites favored retaining the islands. But in the struggle between economic imperialism and economic nationalism the domestic agriculture-labor lobby proved too strong. One independence bill, repassed over President Hoover's veto, was rejected by the Filipinos. Another, the Tydings-McDuffie Act, was approved by Roosevelt on March 24, 1934, and unanimously accepted by the Philippine legislature on May 1, 1934, thirty-six years to a day after Dewey's memorable victory. This measure provided for complete independence after a ten-year intermediate period, at the end of which the United States would withdraw all military bases. Naval establishments were left for future discussion. The Filipinos were not altogether happy, for their economic life had become so dependent upon tariff-free American markets that economic prostration appeared to be the price of independence.[7]

The decision to abandon the Philippines was of high significance, even though doubts remained as to whether the United States would ultimately redeem its promises.[8] The action was regarded as a withdrawal from a dangerous commitment for which the American taxpayer had never been willing to provide adequate defense. Yet this backward step in the face of Nippon's aggression cost America "face" and did nothing to discourage the Japanese war lords.

THE GOOD NEIGHBOR POLICY

The depression left its mark upon American foreign policy not only in regard to the Philippines but also in regard to neighboring nations. The United States of the Hoover and Roosevelt years was not in an expansive or aggressive mood, and the Good Neighbor ideal that had been foreshadowed by Coolidge and urged by Hoover was given great impetus by Roosevelt.

The Seventh International Conference of American States, which met in Montevideo late in 1933, gave the Administration an opportunity to breathe greater reality into its Good Neighbor policy.[9] When the ghost of intervention again rose, Secretary Hull, who headed the American delegation, cordially supported a pact which declared in part that "No state has the right to intervene in the internal or external affairs of another." This agreement was unanimously adopted, and two days later, December 28, 1933, Roosevelt announced in a notable public address that "the definite policy of the United States from now on is one opposed to armed intervention." [10] The Montevideo conference adjourned with greater cordiality toward the United States than had been evidenced at any of the six previous gatherings.

The fine words of nonintervention were soon matched by deeds.

[7] The President appointed the Joint Preparatory Commission on Philippine affairs on April 14, 1937. It was charged with recommending a program for adjusting Philippine national economy to the changed status. After a careful investigation, the Commission recommended, among other things, that the 75 per cent of preferences existing on July 4, 1946 (independence date) be gradually eliminated by December 31, 1960. This was to be accomplished by treaty. See *Joint Preparatory Committee on Philippine Affairs: Report of May 20, 1938* (3 vols., Washington, D.C., 1938).

[8] See A. W. Griswold, *The Far Eastern Policy of the United States* (N.Y., 1938), p. 454.

[9] See G. H. Stuart, *Latin America and the United States* (3rd ed., N.Y., 1938), pp. 28–32.

[10] *Roosevelt Public Papers*, II, 545.

Grave disorders in Cuba, arising in part from the depression and from the mailed fist of dictator Machado, sorely tried the new policy. But troops were not landed, though warships were sent to Cuban waters. Of great importance was the signing of a treaty with Cuba, on May

THE UNITED STATES
IN THE CARIBBEAN, 1934

29, 1934, by the terms of which the island was released from the intervention trammels of the Platt Amendment. In August, 1934, the last marines were withdrawn from Haiti; and in March, 1936, a pact was signed with Panama by which some of the inequities of the Hay-Bunau-Varilla Treaty were removed.[11]

Early in 1936 Roosevelt suggested to the President of Argentina that a special Inter-American Conference for Peace be held at Buenos Aires. The Argentine government responded favorably; and after it had formally invited the other republics and had secured their acceptances, Roosevelt journeyed the seven thousand miles to Buenos

[11] The Senate did not approve the treaty until July 25, 1939. The three-year delay was caused in part by opposition from the United States Army and Navy.

Aires as "a traveling salesman for peace." Following an enthusiastic reception, he opened the conference with a dramatic speech, December 1, 1936, in which he declared that non-American states seeking "to commit acts of aggression against us will find a Hemisphere wholly prepared to consult together for our mutual safety and our mutual good." [12] This was properly interpreted as a sweeping invitation to make the Monroe Doctrine multilateral; but because of conflicting jealousies and because of obligations to the League of Nations, nothing noteworthy came of the proposal. Instead, the Conference adopted a consultative pact for further co-ordinating the existing peace machinery, [13] and reaffirmed the principle of nonintervention in a protocol which was unanimously approved by the United States Senate.

Difficulties with Mexico gave the Good Neighbor policy a severe test. In March, 1938, the Mexican government expropriated outright all foreign oil holdings, valued at about $400,000,000. This action was legal, provided proper pecuniary compensation was made; but the Washington government, having grave doubts on this score and responding to pressure from outraged American investors, made vigorous representations. [14] Although the assurances of the Mexican government were not satisfactory, it is noteworthy that the Roosevelt administration did not resort to drastic measures.

CANADA AND THE GOOD NEIGHBOR

Relations with Canada continued to be conspicuously friendly. The most important issue was the St. Lawrence Waterway Treaty, which had been signed on July 18, 1932, after painstaking negotiations under President Hoover. The pact provided for the deepening of the St. Lawrence-Great Lakes waterway so as to transform the lake ports into seaports, and for the development of electric power.

Strong opposition arose in the Senate from those who did not want

[12] *Roosevelt Public Papers*, V, 606.

[13] The peace machinery was the Treaty to Avoid and Prevent Conflicts between the American States, signed at Santiago, May 3, 1923 (known as the Gondra Treaty); the Treaty for the Renunciation of War, signed at Paris, August 27, 1928; the General Convention of Inter-American Conciliation, signed at Washington, January 5, 1929; the General Treaty of Inter-American Arbitration, signed at Washington, January 5, 1929; the Treaty of Non-Aggression and Conciliation, signed at Rio de Janeiro, October 10, 1933. Department of State, *Press Releases*, Dec. 26, 1936, pp. 536-537.

[14] On November 12, 1938, the State Department announced that Mexico had consented to an agreement to pay for expropriated agricultural (not oil) lands. New York *Times*, Nov. 13, 1938, 1:5.

to see the government in the power business, and from those who feared that traffic would be diverted from the railroads. A number of the states felt that their interests, economic and otherwise, would be adversely affected by the project. On March 14, 1934, the measure failed of the two-thirds vote by 46 yeas to 42 nays. President Roosevelt was not greatly disturbed by the result, for he announced that the scheme would ultimately be adopted "just as sure as God made little apples." [15] During subsequent months he reaffirmed his faith in the project.

The growing strength of the dictator states in Europe, and the possibility that they might attack the Americas, served to draw Canada and the United States closer together. On August 18, 1938, Roosevelt spectacularly announced in a speech at Kingston, Canada: "I give to you assurance that the people of the United States will not stand idly by if domination of Canadian soil is threatened by any other empire." This declaration was widely applauded in the Dominion, and generally interpreted as an extension of the Monroe Doctrine to America's northern neighbor.[16]

NEUTRALITY BY LEGISLATION

The most serious diplomatic problems confronting Roosevelt grew out of the troubled international situation. The failure of the League to halt Japan's drive into Manchuria encouraged the other "have-not" nations, Italy and Germany, to increase existing armaments in the hope of effectively asserting their claims. By the time of Roosevelt's inauguration many informed observers were speaking of the inevitable world war.

American interest in maintaining neutrality was tremendously stimulated by a number of sensational exposés of the international arms traffic that appeared in books and magazines in 1934. In response to a strong public sentiment, a Senate committee, headed by Gerald P. Nye of North Dakota, began public hearings on the munitions industry. The enormous profits which American armament manufacturers and bankers were shown to have made from 1914 to 1917 led a great many unthinking persons to conclude that these profiteers had

---

[15] *Roosevelt Public Papers*, III, 148.

[16] This seems to have been the first official explicit statement including Canada within the scope of the Monroe Doctrine. Roosevelt afterwards denied that his statement was an extension, for he did not interpret the Monroe Doctrine as excluding Canada. C. G. Fenwick, "Canada and the Monroe Doctrine," *Amer. Jour. of Internat. Law*, XXXII (1938), 782.

been primarily responsible for forcing the United States into the war. A swelling demand arose from the people that this sort of thing should not be permitted to happen again.

For a while it seemed as if neutrality legislation would be shelved as Congress became involved in domestic problems growing out of the depression. But the Italo-Ethiopian crisis of May, 1935, which threatened to precipitate a world conflict, focused attention on international affairs. Congress hurriedly passed a neutrality act, signed August 31, 1935, which provided that when the Chief Executive should proclaim the existence of war, it would be unlawful to sell or transport munitions to the belligerents. If the President considered it advisable to prohibit travel on ships of the warring nations, he could proclaim that fact; thereafter American citizens could take passage on them only at their own risk. The State Department much preferred an act which would enable it to discriminate against the aggressor nation in restrictions upon arms shipments; but Congress decided otherwise.[17] This remarkable change of policy indicated that henceforth the United States would not fight to uphold the full letter of its rights on the high seas, as it had done in 1917.

Following the passage of the act of 1935, interest in the maintenance of neutrality continued. In 1936 Congress widened the scope of the original measure by prohibiting loans to belligerents. The outbreak of civil war in Spain, in July of that year, revealed that the act of 1935 had envisaged only war between nations. On January 6, 1937, therefore, Congress passed a joint resolution forbidding the export of munitions "for the use of either of the opposing forces in Spain." This measure was widely criticized in the United States, for it worked to the disadvantage of the Loyalist government in Madrid, which was believed to be upholding the cause of democracy.[18]

The acts of 1935 and 1936 were of a temporary and makeshift character, and strong public pressure was exerted in the spring of 1937 to bring about "permanent neutrality." After considerable debate, Congress passed a new law, approved May 1, 1937. It retained re-

[17] Various polls taken during this period show that the people had more confidence in the ability of Congress than in that of the President to keep them out of war, and even more in themselves.

[18] See C. A. Beard and M. R. Beard, *America in Midpassage*, pp. 477–479. Although several thousand Americans served in the Loyalist army, there was much indifference in the United States. The American Institute of Public Opinion (Gallup Poll) found that 22 per cent of the people favored the Loyalists; 12 per cent the rebels; 26 per cent were neutral; and 40 per cent had no opinion. *San José* (Calif.) *Mercury Herald*, Feb. 14, 1937, 21:1–2. A poll by *Fortune* yielded almost identical results. XV, 204 (April, 1937).

strictions on munitions and loans, and made travel on belligerent vessels unlawful, rather than at the citizen's own risk. The measure applied to "civil strife" as well as to international war, and gave the President considerably larger discretionary powers in the administration of the act. Profit-conscious America was unwilling to embargo shipments of raw materials to the belligerents, but as a compromise the law stipulated that such commodities as the President should list would have to be paid for upon delivery, and taken away from the ports of the United States by the buyer—the so-called "cash and carry" plan. This provision was limited to two years.

The Neutrality Act of 1937 was strongly criticized in certain quarters because it did not permit the President to discriminate against the aggressor nation. Opponents also charged that the measure was not a neutrality act at all, because it favored the nations that held control of the sea and were able to take advantage of the "cash and carry" provision. Although there were few discerning persons who believed that such an inflexible measure was a perfect guarantee against America's involvement in a foreign war, it was felt that the safeguards erected would eliminate some of the dangers that the United States had encountered from 1914 to 1917.

The Breakdown of Naval Disarmament

Despite the unhealthy atmosphere produced by the aggressive policy of the "have-not" nations, the Roosevelt administration cherished the hope of substantial reduction in armaments. But finding that the other great Powers were constructing their quota of ships, while the United States lagged behind, Congress passed the Vinson Bill, in March, 1934. It authorized, but did not appropriate money for, the building of the navy up to treaty strength.

The London Naval Treaty of 1930 had made provision for another conference in 1935. During the preliminary conversations it became evident that the Japanese, on the grounds of prestige and security, would no longer accept the short end of any ratio. As Ambassador Hirosi Saito pithily put it, 5–5–3 sounded "to Japanese ears like Rolls-Royce—Rolls-Royce—Ford." On December 29, 1934, Japan formally denounced the Washington Naval Treaty of 1922, as she was privileged to do, by giving the necessary two years' notice.

The prospects were not at all favorable when the second London Naval Conference met late in 1935. The United States, with two long coastlines and with overseas possessions, was unwilling to concede parity to the Japanese, who thereupon withdrew from the discussions. A treaty providing for mild qualitative limitations and containing many "escape clauses" was finally signed, on March 25, 1936, by Great Britain, the United States, and France. But the agreement was virtually useless because of the nonadherence of Italy and Japan.

The fine dreams of the Washington Disarmament Conference were now completely shattered. President Roosevelt concluded that it was unwise for the United States to fall farther behind in a madly rearming world, and in January, 1938, he asked Congress for a billion dollar naval appropriation. In support of his program American experts emphasized the necessity of having a two-ocean navy, big enough to meet the combined fleets of the three "have-not" Powers. With Japan invading China and Germany absorbing Austria, the voices of the pacifists were drowned out, and in May, 1938, the billion dollar navy bill was passed. The United States, belated as usual, now had both feet in the greatest naval race in history.

THE NEW ORDER IN EAST ASIA

A potent factor contributing to the American rearmament program was apprehension aroused by Japan's aggressive course in the Far East. Secretary Hull continued the Hoover-Stimson policy when he refused to extend recognition to Manchukuo, and he also took a strong stand against what were believed to be Japan's efforts to close the Open Door.[19]

An ominous turn was given to the situation when, on July 7, 1937, fighting broke out between Japanese and Chinese troops in the vicinity of Peiping. Reinforcements from Japan began to pour into North China with great dispatch. The next month, while the Spanish crisis was effectively tying the hands of Europe, heavy fighting occurred at Shanghai, during which there was frightful loss of life among the civilian population of that teeming city. As in 1932, American public opinion was generally, though not overwhelmingly, sympathetic with the Chinese underdog, and appalled by the great loss among non-

[19] On April 17, 1934, a spokesman for the Tokyo Foreign Office, Eiji Amau, gave definiteness to what had for some time been referred to as the Japanese Monroe Doctrine when he bluntly warned foreign Powers to refrain from activity in China prejudicial to Japanese interests. The United States protested against Japan's stand on April 29, 1934. See Tupper and McReynolds, *Japan in American Public Opinion*, pp. 386–390. The State Department also registered strong opposition to measures detrimental to American oil interests in Manchukuo. S. C. Y. Pan, *American Diplomacy concerning Manchuria* (Providence, R.I., 1938), pp. 283 ff.

combatants.[20] After several Americans were incidentally killed or injured on American ships, a strong public demand developed that the United States withdraw as far as possible from the danger zones. The President, however, declined to invoke the Neutrality Act of 1937, ostensibly because no war had been declared, but presumably because the measure would operate more to the disadvantage of China than of Japan.[21]

Roosevelt did, however, take a strong stand in a sensational speech in Chicago, on October 5, 1937. He deplored the recent outburst of "international lawlessness," asserted that the United States would not be unaffected if another general war should occur, and suggested that the nations contributing to "international anarchy" should be quarantined. He further declared:

The peace, the freedom, and the security of 90 percent of the population of the world is being jeopardized by the remaining 10 percent, who are threatening a breakdown of all international order and law. Surely the 90 percent who want to live in peace under law and in accordance with moral standards that have received almost universal acceptance through the centuries, can and must find some way to make their will prevail. . . . There must be positive endeavors to preserve peace.[22]

Roosevelt's "quarantine" speech, with its reference to "positive endeavors," was hailed by advocates of collective security, both at home and abroad, as pledging the active co-operation of the United States in halting Japan in the Far East. On the other hand, the President was condemned by isolationists for attempting to draw the nation into involvements with which it had no direct concern. Whatever may have been in Roosevelt's mind, it soon became evident that public opinion would not support him in any course of armed action. Nevertheless, a number of private boycotts against Japanese goods were instituted.[23]

Meanwhile, at the instance of the British government, Belgium had issued an invitation for a conference at Brussels. The United States and eighteen other interested Powers accepted full membership; but

[20] A poll by the American Institute of Public Opinion showed that 55 per cent of the people took no sides, 43 per cent favored China, and 2 per cent Japan. San José (Calif.) *Mercury Herald*, Sept. 12, 1937, 21:8. More than a year and a half later public opinion was much more pro-Chinese, 74 per cent favoring China, 2 per cent Japan, and 24 per cent taking no sides. *Ibid.*, June 18, 1939, 13:4.

[21] See W. H. Shepardson, *The United States in World Affairs, 1937* (N.Y., 1938), pp. 199–200, 203. On the whole, the course of the Administration seems to have received public acquiescence.

[22] Department of State, *Press Releases*, Oct. 9, 1937, pp. 278–279.

[23] Shepardson, *The United States in World Affairs, 1937*, p. 224.

Germany and Japan declined to participate. Even before the Conference convened it was evident that Japan's invasion of China could be stopped only by force, and that neither Great Britain nor the United States, the two greatest naval Powers, was prepared to use force. After holding sessions from November 3 to November 24, 1937, the conference broke up in complete failure.

The climax of disagreeable incidents in Chinese waters came on December 12, 1937, when Japanese aviators repeatedly bombed a United States river gunboat, the *Panay*, which was displaying American colors. The vessel sank with a loss of two killed and some thirty wounded, ten seriously. On the same afternoon Japanese aircraft also destroyed three American Standard Oil Company tankers. Fearing that these attacks would create a genuine crisis, Foreign Minister Hirota promptly called on the United States ambassador in Tokyo, expressed the most profound apologies, and stated that the Japanese commander had accepted full responsibility for the unfortunate mistake.

American public opinion was deeply disturbed by what appeared to be a wanton attack on the American flag. Cartoonists represented the Japanese ambassador as saying, "So sorry—excuse please," while the bodies of mangled American sailors lay about. On December 14, 1937, the United States government presented a formal note of protest that called for apologies, reparation, and adequate precautions against the repetition of such incidents. On the same day the Japanese government transmitted a formal note of apology which included such assurances as had been requested. But the State Department was in no haste to accept Japan's explanations, for the reports that it received indicated that, contrary to the Japanese contention, the identity of the *Panay* could not have been mistaken. On December 25, 1937, Secretary Hull finally informed the Japanese government that the United States, though relying on the reports of its own officials, "observed with satisfaction" the promptness of Japan in admitting responsibility, expressing regret, and making amends.[24]

Though some American newspapers pointed out that the attack on the *Panay* was a more serious incident than the destruction of the *Maine*, public opinion in the United States viewed the incident with unusual calm.[25] The Far East was on the other side of the world; Americans had already been killed there; the country was being

---

[24] Department of State, *Press Releases*, Dec. 25, 1937, p. 499. The Japanese promptly paid damages in the sum of $2,214,007.36.
[25] See *Literary Digest*, CXXIV, 11 (Dec. 25, 1937).

plunged back into the depression; and a strong feeling was developing that the United States should not be inveigled into fighting China's battles.[26]

Disagreeable incidents of a less serious nature continued to arise between Japan and the United States during the following months.[27] On October 6, 1938, Ambassador Grew, in Tokyo, lodged a sharp protest, in which he complained of restrictions on Americans in China, and of violations of the Open Door. "In the opinion of my Government," he added, "equality of opportunity or the Open Door has virtually ceased to exist in Manchuria notwithstanding the assurances of the Japanese Government that it would be maintained in that area." [28]

The Japanese note of November 18, 1938, replied to the American charges at length, and concluded with these highly significant words:

It is the firm conviction of the Japanese Government that in the face of the new situation, fast developing in East Asia, any attempt to apply to the conditions of today and tomorrow inapplicable ideas and principles of the past [Open Door?] neither would contribute toward the establishment of a real peace in East Asia nor solve the immediate issues.

The Japanese declaration continued:

However, as long as these points are understood, Japan has not the slightest inclination to oppose the participation of the United States and other powers in the great work of reconstructing East Asia along all lines of industry and trade. . . .[29]

[26] The strength of the peace sentiment in the country was revealed when the issue of the Ludlow amendment to the constitution (requiring a nation-wide referendum on a declaration of war, except cases of actual invasion) was brought before the House of Representatives two days after the *Panay* bombing. Roosevelt, fearing that this measure would weaken his hand during the existing crisis, brought great pressure on Congress to reject the amendment. It was shelved by a vote of 209 to 188, although 218 members had signed the petition bringing it before the House. A poll conducted by *Fortune* asked: "In view of the recent Japanese attacks upon Americans in China do you think that we should withdraw entirely from China or that we should take steps to make them respect our rights?" 53.9 per cent believed that the United States should withdraw entirely; 29.9 per cent thought that steps should be taken to force respect for American rights; 5.1 per cent held that the government should do neither; and 11.1 per cent had no opinion. XVII, 109 (April, 1938).

[27] The third secretary of the American embassy at Nanking was slapped by a Japanese soldier on January 26, 1938. There was also much ill feeling in the Pacific Northwest because Japanese fishermen threatened the salmon of Bristol Bay, Alaska, with extermination. For legal aspects of the problem see J. W. Bingham, *Report on the International Law of Pacific Coastal Fisheries* (Stanford University, Calif., 1938).

[28] Department of State, *Press Releases*, Oct. 29, 1938, p. 283.

[29] *Ibid.*, Nov. 19, 1938, p. 353.

In brief, the Open Door and the treaties that supported it were dead; but if the United States would recognize this changed situation, it might hope for a share of East Asiatic trade.

In its reply of December 31, 1938, the State Department emphatically refused to recognize the existence of a "new order" and suggested that Japan, if dissatisfied with the existing treaties, could take steps to negotiate new ones. "Meanwhile," the note concluded, "this Government reserves all rights of the United States as they exist and does not give assent to any impairment of any of those rights." [30]

During the next six months the Far Eastern front was relatively quiet. But when, in June, 1939, the Japanese took strong action in an attempt to weaken Western influence in China (particularly in their blockade of the British concession at Tientsin), Secretary Hull again made it clear that he would not recognize a "new order" in China based upon unilateral action by Japan. When such representations proved unavailing, the Department of State suddenly, on July 26, 1939, gave the Tokyo government the formal six months' notice for abrogating the commercial treaty of 1911. This was obviously an attempt to bring pressure on Japan by clearing the way for an embargo on munitions shipments. The Japanese were stunned by this unexpected evidence of American determination, and sobered by the prospect of having to prosecute a major war without the invaluable munitions and raw materials from the United States. Following this action by the Washington government and the signing of the Russo-German non-aggression pact of August, 1939, which gave Russia a free hand to deal with Japan in the Far East, the Tokyo Foreign Office evidenced a more conciliatory attitude in its relations with the United States.

MUNICH AND AFTER

Relations with Germany, as well as with Japan, grew increasingly tense during these years. When Adolf Hitler rose to power, early in 1933, a period of Jewish persecutions began. Public opinion in the United States, particularly that of the influential Jewish element, expressed strong indignation and urged the State Department to intervene. Anger against the Hitler regime vented itself in other ways, and a series of disagreeable incidents continued to vex German-

[30] *Ibid.*, Dec. 31, 1938, pp. 490–493. On December 15, 1938, the government-financed Export-Import Bank, presumably with the encouragement of the State Department, advanced a credit of $25,000,000 to the Chinese, presumably to stiffen their resistance to Japan.

American relations.[31] In addition, President Roosevelt and prominent members of his Administration openly expressed their displeasure with the aggressions of Germany and the other dictator nations. The government-controlled German press replied to these strictures in vehement terms, and tension between the two nations grew ominously.

Late in September, 1938, the most dangerous crisis yet to menace postwar Europe came to a head. The main issue was Chancellor Hitler's demand for the German-populated Sudetenland of Czechoslovakia. Compromise broke down; armies were on the march; and it seemed inevitable that a general war would break out between the dictator nations, Germany and Italy, and the democracies, France, Great Britain, and Czechoslovakia.

On September 26, 1938, Roosevelt cabled a message to Hitler urging a peaceful settlement of the dispute. When this proved unavailing, the President sent a desperate, last-minute appeal on September 27th to Benito Mussolini, the Italian dictator, and another later that same day to the German Chancellor. Mussolini called Hitler on the telephone, and the latter consented to an international conference at Munich. It is impossible to tell what influence, if any, the three messages of Roosevelt had on this decision.[32] It seems clear, however, that the Administration considered a general war so inimical to American interests as to warrant an abandonment of the traditional policy of not meddling in the affairs of Europe.

The crucial conference at Munich met during September 29 and 30, 1938. France and Great Britain yielded to Hitler's demands for the Sudetenland. This concession, which was hailed as a victory for the dictator nations and as a reverse for the democracies, was in large measure made possible by the presumed preponderance of the German air force. The object lesson in preparedness was not lost on the other nations of the world, including the United States.

The American people were still profoundly disturbed by the success of sheer power diplomacy at Munich when unprecedentedly severe attacks on the German Jews broke out on November 9, 1938. The

[31] Notably the tearing down of the swastika emblem from the German liner *Bremen*, in New York (July 26, 1935); and Mayor La Guardia's speech in New York (March 3, 1937) in which he referred to Hitler as "that brown-shirted fanatic."

[32] Mussolini called Hitler between ten o'clock and noon of September 28. Roosevelt's appeal was not formally delivered until four o'clock in the afternoon; but its contents were known in Rome by ten o'clock. At approximately the same time the British government also appealed to Mussolini. See radio address of Undersecretary of State Welles, delivered Oct. 3, 1938. Department of State, *Press Releases*, Oct. 8, 1938, p. 238.

civilized world was horrified. In an extraordinary public statement President Roosevelt declared, "I myself could scarcely believe that such things could occur in a twentieth-century civilization." [33] On November 14, Hugh Wilson, the United States ambassador to Germany, was recalled to Washington, ostensibly to give first-hand information regarding the situation, but presumably as a protest against the German persecutions. Four days later the German ambassador was called home to report on the "singular attitude" of the United States toward "domestic affairs in Germany." Embassies in both countries were kept open; but relations could hardly have been worse short of an actual break.[34]

Meanwhile, preparations had been under way for the Eighth International Conference of American States, which convened at Lima, Peru, on December 10, 1938. The United States, fearing the rising power of the European dictator states and the penetration of their commerce and propaganda into Latin America, sought to align the twenty-one republics of the New World into a solid front against the "aggressor nations." Owing to the opposition of Argentina, Secretary Hull, who headed the delegation from the United States, found it impossible to secure as binding an agreement as he desired; and in the end the rather innocuous Declaration of Lima was unanimously adopted, December 24, 1938. It reaffirmed faith in international law and promised consultation and a common front should any American nation be menaced by outside aggression.[35]

During the months following the Lima Conference the Washington government sought in various ways to combat German and Italian propaganda in South America. It also increased its own influence by lending financial support to several of the Latin American states, notably Brazil, with which arrangements were made in March, 1939.

[33] New York *Times*, Nov. 16, 1938, 1:8.

[34] The German government attempted to present a protest against Secretary of the Interior Ickes' condemnation of Hitler as a "brutal dictator," but the State Department (Dec. 22, 1938) bluntly refused to receive it on the grounds that Ickes had represented the views of the American people. On the same day, Senator Pittman of Nevada, chairman of the Senate Committee on Foreign Relations, issued an extraordinary public statement in which he said that "The people of the United States do not like the Government of Germany." *Ibid.*, Dec. 23, 1938, 1:8.

[35] Department of State, *Press Releases*, Dec. 24, 1938, pp. 474–475. A total of 110 resolutions, declarations, and recommendations, ranging from such subjects as copyright to wild life preservation, were finally adopted. In addition to solidarity, declarations regarding peace and a reduction of tariff barriers were important. See W. H. Shepardson, *The United States in World Affairs, 1938* (N.Y., 1939), pp. 298–299.

DEMOCRACY AGAIN ON THE DEFENSIVE

As the year 1939 wore on it became increasingly clear that the Roosevelt administration was determined to throw its influence into the balance on the side of the democracies against the dictators. In his message to Congress on the state of the nation, January 4, 1939, Roosevelt emphatically declared that "Words may be futile, but war is not the only means of commanding a decent respect for the opinions of mankind. There are many methods short of war [boycotts?], but stronger and more effective than mere words, of bringing home to aggressor governments the aggregate sentiments of our own people." [36] Then, on January 12, 1939, as if to give point to his stand, the President asked for $552,000,000 additional for the national defense, most of the sum for aircraft.

Late in January, 1939, a dramatic incident precipitated what was perhaps the most violent debate over foreign policy since the League of Nations fight. A bombing plane, designed for the United States army, crashed in Southern California, and a French officer was dragged from the flaming wreckage. It was then learned that a French air mission was visiting the United States and that the President, allegedly over the protests of the War Department, had approved the sale of American planes to France. Roosevelt was apparently attempting to prevent a general war, in which the United States might be involved, by helping make the European democracies so strong that the dictators would not dare to attack them. [37] A cry immediately went up from isolationists and other critics of the Administration that the Chief Executive was effecting a secret military alliance that would involve the nation in hostilities.

Disturbed by this outburst, Roosevelt summoned the Senate Committee on Military Affairs to the White House, and, after pledging the members to secrecy, spoke at length on the policy of the United States. Immediately the report spread like wildfire that the President had declared, "The frontier of the United States is in France." Isolationists and Republicans redoubled their attacks upon the Chief Executive, while the press of the European dictator countries joined

---

[36] *Cong. Record,* 76 Cong., 1 sess., p. 77.

[37] A poll taken by the American Institute of Public Opinion showed that sentiment in the United States favored supporting the European democracies against the dictators by every means short of war. The vote was 69 per cent for, 31 per cent against. San José *Mercury Herald,* Feb. 26, 1939, 13:7. These figures indicated that the issues were already more clearly drawn than in 1914, and that the United States would encounter even greater difficulty in staying out of a general war.

An isolationist cartoon of the thirties. (From *The Saturday Evening Post* of May 20, 1939, in which it was reprinted by request from the issue of January 8, 1938. Reproduced by special permission of *The Saturday Evening Post*, copyright 1938, by The Curtis Publishing Company.)

in the outcry. On February 3, 1939, Roosevelt sprang to his own defense when he vigorously declared that some "boob" had invented this "deliberate lie." To quiet the opposition and spike rumors of entanglement he announced that his policy had not changed and "is not going to change." [38]

The next month, March, 1939, Hitler jarred an already distraught Europe by flouting his Munich pledge and forcibly absorbing what was left of the republic of Czechoslovakia. Acting Secretary of State Welles publicly condemned this act "of wanton lawlessness and arbitrary force," and appealed for support of "a program of order based upon law. . . ." [39] The world had not recovered from the shock of this aggression when, three weeks later, Mussolini seized Albania. Again America was profoundly disturbed, and Secretary Hull gave to the press a statement deploring this "additional threat to the peace of the world." [40]

With Europe seemingly on the brink of disaster again, President Roosevelt, on April 14, 1939, addressed a sensational appeal to both Hitler and Mussolini. He asked them for pledges that they would not attack any one of thirty specified states within a period of ten years, and he suggested an international conference at which problems of disarmament and international trade would be discussed. [41] Favorable responses poured in from the other nations of the world, and American public opinion reacted enthusiastically. But the dictators, after delaying their replies, flatly declined Roosevelt's proposals. One important result was to brand Italy and Germany more definitely than before as aggressor nations, and to cause American sympathies to turn even more strongly to Great Britain and France.

During the spring of 1939 a leading issue before the American people was revision of the Neutrality Act so as to permit greater assistance to Great Britain and France in the event of war. [42] On May 27 Secretary Hull outlined for Congress an Administration program. Among other things, it would permit belligerents to buy munitions in America, provided they acquired title before taking them away, and

---

[38] For Roosevelt's summary statement of his policy on this occasion see Department of State, *Press Releases*, Feb. 11, 1939, p. 99.

[39] Statement of March 17, in *ibid.*, March 18, 1939, pp. 199–200. The State Department followed this with a formal protest; and the Treasury Department announced countervailing duties on imports from Germany.

[40] Statement of April 8, in *ibid.*, April 8, 1939, p. 261.

[41] *Ibid.*, April 15, 1939, pp. 291–293.

[42] A Gallup poll during May, 1939, revealed that keeping out of war was the most important issue before the American people, outranking the unemployment problem. San José *Mercury Herald*, May 14, 1939, 13:7.

provided American ships kept out of the combat areas.[43] This, in effect, would place the arms factories of the United States at the disposal of the European democracies, for it was presumed that Great Britain and France would control the seas during a general war. The debate in Congress over neutrality was held in abeyance during the successful visit of the King and Queen of England, in June, 1939— a visit which increased Anglo-American cordiality. The discussion of neutrality was then resumed, but in July, 1939, all attempts at revision were thwarted by a determined isolationist bloc in the Senate. So the Neutrality Act of 1937 remained on the books, without the "cash and carry" clause, which had expired on May 1, 1939. When Congress adjourned without heeding the Administration's recommendations, the President expressed the belief that the failure to open America's munitions factories to the democracies would encourage the aggressive designs of the dictators, and he promised to call Congress in special session to revise the Neutrality Act if war should break out before the next regular meeting.

During the fateful month of August, 1939, events moved with breath-taking rapidity. Hitler became increasingly insistent in his demands upon Poland for the Polish Corridor and Danzig, both of which had been shorn from Germany at Versailles. The Poles, vigorously backed by their western allies, France and Britain, resisted the German demands and insisted upon peaceful negotiation. The position of these three Powers was strong, for it was believed that Russia was about to conclude a military alliance with them against Germany. But on August 23, 1939, the Berlin government astounded the outside world by signing a nonaggression pact with Russia, thus isolating the Poles. Hitler, doubtless thinking that Poland and her two allies would now have to yield, pushed his demands with renewed vigor.

With capitulation or war the only alternatives, Roosevelt, on August 24, 1939, cabled an urgent appeal to Chancellor Hitler, to the President of Poland, and to the King of Italy, urging arbitration, conciliation, or direct negotiation. The peace of Europe lay in Hitler's hands— and Hitler insisted upon his terms or war. On September 1, 1939, impatient of further parley, he issued the necessary orders, and the mechanized German hosts began to smash their way into Poland. The long-prophesied war had at length come.

On September 3, 1939, after Hitler had spurned ultimata to withdraw from Poland, Great Britain and France declared war on Germany. Two days later President Roosevelt issued the routine proclamations

[43] Department of State, *Press Releases*, June 3, 1939, p. 477.

of neutrality and invoked the Neutrality Act against the belligerents. Shortly before doing this he told the American people in a nation-wide radio address:

> I hope the United States will keep out of this war. I believe that it will. And I give you assurances that every effort of your government will be directed toward that end.

> As long as it remains within my power to prevent it, there will be no blackout of peace in the United States.[44]

BIBLIOGRAPHICAL NOTE

It is too early to expect a considerable number of substantial historical works on the events of the Roosevelt administrations. An excellent brief account, with emphasis on economic factors, is C. A. and M. R. Beard, *America in Midpassage* (N.Y., 1939), Chs. IX, X. Yearly surveys of importance are *The United States in World Affairs, 1933, 1934–35, 1936, 1937, 1938*, published in New York for the Council on Foreign Relations and prepared by W. H. Shepardson, W. O. Scroggs, Walter Lippmann and others. Indispensable are *The Public Papers and Addresses of Franklin D. Roosevelt* (5 vols., N.Y., 1938), which also contain many explanatory notes by the President himself. G. H. Stuart, *Latin America and the United States* (3rd ed., N.Y., 1938), develops the Good Neighbor policy. A critical account of the early neutrality legislation appears in Edwin Borchard and W. P. Lage, *Neutrality for the United States* (New Haven, 1937). On the Far East, see A. W. Griswold, *The Far Eastern Policy of the United States* (N.Y., 1938); H. S. Quigley and G. H. Blakeslee, *The Far East* (Boston, 1938); and E. Tupper and G. E. McReynolds, *Japan in American Public Opinion* (N.Y., 1937). Further references: see footnotes of this chapter.

RECENT REFERENCES. Two able surveys of the Good Neighbor policy from somewhat different points of view are Dexter Perkins, *Hands Off: A History of the Monroe Doctrine* (Boston, 1941), Ch. IX; and J. F. Rippy, *The Caribbean Danger Zone* (N.Y., 1940), Ch. XII. W. C. Johnstone, *The United States and Japan's New Order* (N.Y., 1941), is a careful analysis of the conflict with Japan over American rights and interests in China. W. E. Dodd, Jr., and Martha Dodd, eds., *Ambassador Dodd's Diary, 1933–38* (N.Y., 1941), while contributing little that is new, gives a picture of American diplomacy in Germany during this period. Raymond Moley, *After Seven Years* (N.Y., 1939), consists of the indiscreet revelations of a disgruntled "ex-Brain Truster" who was once close to the President. There are some important eyewitness observations on Roosevelt's unwillingness to co-operate with Hoover following the election of 1932, and particularly on the London Economic Conference, which the author thinks the President wrecked (p. 267). Moley must not be overlooked; but he must be used with great caution. Meno Lovenstein, *American Opinion of Soviet Russia* (Washington, 1941), is a useful analysis of various newspapers, magazines, books, and other media of opinion from 1917 to 1939.

NEW REFERENCES; 4TH ED. REFS. See Bibliographical Appendix, pp. 946–947.

[44] New York *Times*, Sept. 4, 1939, 6:4.

The War Comes to America: First Phase

"We must be the great arsenal of democracy."
Franklin D. Roosevelt, December 29, 1940.

INTERNATIONAL GANGSTERISM

THE war that came in 1939 invites comparisons with the war that came in 1914.

In 1914, the American people were surprised and smug. They could hardly believe that a world war had come; they were confident they could stay out of it.

In 1939, the American people were prepared for the worst. Only a year before they, together with the rest of the world, had been left trembling on the precipice of Munich. They wanted, by an overwhelming margin, to stay out; but they expected—or close to a majority of them expected—to be drawn in.[1]

In 1914, public opinion was uncertain and confused. Many were completely indifferent; many were pro-Ally; considerably fewer were pro-German. But the significant thing is that millions of Americans were convinced that Germany had the better case—and they argued their views with great vigor.

In 1939, public opinion was neither uncertain nor confused. About ninety per cent of the American people distrusted Hitler and favored the democracies.[2] There was no pro-German faction worthy of the name. Unlike Wilson in 1914, Roosevelt did not call upon his coun-

[1] A *Fortune* poll (Oct., 1939) found that only 3.3 per cent favored entering the war at once on the side of the Allies. *Pub. Opin. Quar.*, IV, 109. According to a Gallup poll (Oct. 24, 1939), 46 per cent expected the United States to go in, while 54 per cent expected to stay out. *Ibid.*, IV, 102. In August, 1939, the 46 per cent had been 76 per cent; by February, 1940, during the lull in Europe, it dropped to 32 per cent. By November, 1941, 85 per cent expected to go in. *Ibid.*, III, 598; IV, 356; VI, 149. Generalizations regarding public opinion in this chapter are based on an examination of all the relevant *Fortune* and Gallup polls. They may be conveniently found in each issue of the *Public Opinion Quarterly*.

[2] A Gallup poll (Oct. 22, 1939) revealed that 84 per cent wanted the Allies to win; 2 per cent wanted Germany to win; while 14 per cent had no opinion. *Ibid.*, IV, 102.

trymen to be neutral in thought. As he declared in his fireside chat of September 3, 1939: "This nation will remain a neutral nation, but I cannot ask that every American remain neutral in thought as well. Even a neutral has a right to take account of facts. Even a neutral cannot be asked to close his mind or his conscience." [3]

In 1914, both groups of belligerents attempted to woo American public opinion by extensive propaganda campaigns.

In 1939, and the months following, the Germans made some effort to appeal for American sympathy, but their seeds fell on barren ground. The Allies, generally speaking, refrained from large-scale propaganda activity: one does not waste energy and money in assaulting a fortress already won. As in 1914, the most effective work was done by volunteer agencies in America, notably the interventionist Committee to Defend America by Aiding the Allies.[4]

In 1914, the world was horrified when the Germans burst into Belgium; when, in following months, German Zeppelins dropped some bombs on England; when "Big Bertha" shelled Paris; when the *Lusitania* was sunk without warning.

By 1939, the world was calloused to an all-out war. The Shanghai shambles of 1932 and 1937, the Ethiopian massacres in 1936, the Barcelonian butcheries of 1938 had all conditioned public opinion. The wiping out of civilian centers had come to be recognized as a new development in the art of "civilized" warfare. Otherwise, the American people, shocked into a defense of outraged humanity, might have entered the war much sooner than they did.

In 1914, there was such a thing as international law; such a thing as the sanctity of treaties; such a thing as the plighted word of a nation. There were a few notable deviations, such as the Belgian "scrap of paper"; but in general both sets of belligerents found it to their interests to work within the framework of treaty guarantees and international law.

[3] S. S. Jones and D. P. Myers, eds., *Documents on American Foreign Relations* (Boston, 1940), II, 5.

[4] This powerful organization (founded May, 1940) was headed, and later partially repudiated, by the journalist W. A. White. Following the fall of France it bombarded the President and members of Congress with letters and telegrams, and used other techniques of the pressure group. Its strongest adversary was the isolationist America First Committee, which used similar techniques but which was handicapped by attracting to itself Bundists and other Nazi elements that wanted to keep America out, presumably for different reasons. J. W. Masland, "Pressure Groups and American Foreign Policy," *Pub. Opin. Quar.*, VI (1942), 115–122, concludes that these organizations made few converts but did succeed in "crystallizing existing attitudes." It was the rising menace of Hitler rather than propaganda which was decisive in changing American attitudes.

By 1939—certainly by 1940—Nazi Germany and her fellow "aggressors" had effected a revolution in international relationships. Treaties had become whole wastebaskets full of paper; nonaggression pacts were made to lull the prospective victim into a false sense of security; unoffending neighbors were attacked with devastating suddenness. International law—one-way international law—was of use to the "aggressor" Powers primarily as a means of cynically justifying prior violations of international law, and of preventing weak nations from acting effectively in their own defense.

In 1914, there was such a thing as "a decent respect to the opinions of mankind." Both world opinion and public opinion within the belligerent countries themselves—including Imperial Germany—operated as powerful brakes on completely ruthless action.

By 1939, the Hitler regime, with complete control of all domestic propaganda agencies, had little concern for home opinion. With the most terrifying striking power yet amassed, it cared scarcely more for world opinion. Apparently the only language the Nazis really respected was the language of superior force.

These facts are fundamental to any proper understanding of America's course from 1939 to 1941. The truth is that by the autumn of 1939, certainly by the late spring of 1940, Hitler had abolished neutral rights and unofficially declared war on all the democracies—including the United States.[5] The American people were reluctant to recognize this change—and this challenge. Many disillusioned persons thought it had been a mistake to enter the last war "to make the world safe for democracy"; many refused to be gulled again by the munitioneer and the profiteer; some regarded this as just another European war of imperialism.[6] Five years of neutrality debate and legislation had not

[5] Even if one dismisses Hitler's fulminations against the democracies as mere talk and denies that the National Socialist movement was a world revolution which had among its aims the destruction of democratic governments, one cannot ignore the rape of the Sudetenland in 1938, the wiping out of democratic Czechoslovakia in 1939, and the invasions of Norway, Denmark, Holland, Belgium, and Luxemburg in the spring of 1940, to mention only some of the more obvious indictments on the long list.

[6] A Gallup poll of April 5, 1941, showed that only 39 per cent then regarded it as a mistake to have entered the war in 1917, as contrasted with 64 per cent in April, 1937. This is interesting evidence as to how views change in wartime. A Gallup poll published on November 7, 1939, gave the following as the three principal causes for entrance into the War of 1917–1918:

1. America was the victim of propaganda and selfish interests—34 per cent
2. America had a just and unselfish cause   —26 per cent
3. America entered the war for her own safety   —18 per cent.

This is a striking indication of such influences as the Nye Committee. *Pub. Opin. Quar.*, IV, 102; V, 477.

only developed a neutrality-at-any-price complex, but had implanted a conviction that the nation could legislate itself away from the broils of the rest of the world.

BUSINESS AS USUAL

From the standpoint of America's formal participation, the war divides itself into two parts: the period before the fall of France, and the period after.

When the lid blew off in September, 1939, it was generally assumed in the Allied countries and in the United States that this war would follow the familiar pattern of 1914–1918. The supposedly impregnable Maginot Line would hold the Germans on the Western Front; the strangling noose of the British blockade would choke Germany to the point of starvation; and Berlin would sue for peace, just as in 1918.

But surprises were quickly forthcoming. Within the incredibly short time of three weeks the German panzer divisions overran Poland, and the Poles suffered their fourth modern partition—Russia coming in for her share of the spoils. Yet the Polish preview meant little to the "Maginot minds" in the Allied countries. They went ahead with their business-as-usual plans for prosecuting the war, while a long lull settled down on the Western Front and the bored journalists wrote disgustedly of the "phony war," the "Bluffkrieg," and the "Sitzkrieg." [7]

The journalists received an unexpected boon during this long winter when Joseph Stalin, evidently not trusting his dictator-friend Adolf Hitler, sought to secure from Finland certain strategic areas that would enable him to bolster the Leningrad defenses. "Brave little Finland" resolutely refused the proffered exchange. On November 30, 1939, Russia spurned Washington's offer of good offices and attacked her tiny neighbor, heavily bombing civilian centers in defiance of an appeal from Roosevelt.

The sympathies of the American people were overwhelmingly on the side of democratic Finland, who paid her debts and who seemingly was fighting in self-defense against a bullying and Communistic aggressor.[8] President Roosevelt promptly denounced the Russian invasion as "wanton disregard for law," and called for a moral embargo on

[7] In a move reminiscent of the House missions, Roosevelt sent Under Secretary of State Welles to the principal belligerent countries, in February and March, 1940, solely, it was announced, for purposes of seeking information.

[8] A Gallup poll (Dec. 31, 1939) showed that 88 per cent were pro-Finnish, 1 per cent pro-Russian, and 11 per cent neutral or without opinion. *Pub. Opin. Quar.*, IV, 102.

American shipments of planes and other war materials to Russia.[9] In February, 1940, the House of Representatives actually came within three votes of severing diplomatic relations with Russia by denying money for the upkeep of the Moscow embassy.

White-clad Finns on skis performed prodigies of valor, administering stinging defeats to the overconfident Muscovites, and kindling the enthusiasm of the American people for Finnish relief. Roosevelt asked the Treasury Department to set aside Finland's semi-annual debt installment, with the thought of eventual repayment; and Congress later voted a moratorium. Congress also granted Finland a loan of $10,000,000 for "agricultural and other civilian supplies"; and after prolonged debate passed a bill making it possible for the Export-Import Bank to lend $20,000,000 for nonmilitary purposes. The Finns needed airplanes and tanks, not plows and harvesters; but so determined was public opinion not to become involved in the war that no more could be done.[10] When Finland was finally flattened by the Russian steamroller in March, 1940, the American people could take some comfort from the thought that even if they had sent over arms with reasonable promptitude, these weapons probably would not have arrived in time or in sufficient quantity to have any real effect. The whole affair embittered Russian-American relations, and again showed the democracies in the role of coming forward with "too little" and that "too late."

Storm-Cellar Neutrality

We have already noted that the American people were virtually unanimous in agreeing upon two things: first, they wanted to keep out of war, and second, they wanted the democracies to win. The neutrality legislation then on the books—thanks to the unwillingness of Congress to respond to Administration warnings in the summer of 1939—was a handicap to the attainment of both these goals. The democracies, though perilously backward in their own armament programs and assaulted by a Germany armed to the teeth, could not legally buy a single cartridge in the United States. The cash-and-carry clause of the Neutrality Act of 1937 had expired in May, 1939, so American merchantmen, laden with copper, oil, steel, and other raw materials of war no less important than guns and tanks, were at liberty to steam

[9] See Jones and Myers, *Documents*, II, 725–728.

[10] A Gallup poll (Feb. 6, 1940) revealed that 58 per cent of those with opinions favored lending money for nonmilitary supplies, while 42 per cent were opposed. Of the 58 per cent who were favorable, only 39 per cent approved lending money for arms, while 61 per cent were opposed. *Pub. Opin. Quar.*, IV, 358–359.

through the European combat zones. Should this dangerous situation continue, it seemed inevitable that incidents similar to those which had brought America into war in 1917 would again occur.[11]

Fully cognizant of the trammels and loopholes in the Neutrality Act, President Roosevelt issued a call for a special session of Congress less than two weeks after the invasion of Poland. On September 21, 1939, he appeared before that body with a message urging a repeal of the arms embargo and "a return to international law." He took the position that America's "traditional" policy of neutrality had served her well, and that the one "disastrous" departure from this policy—the embargo and nonintercourse legislation of Jefferson and Madison—had been a "major cause" of the War of 1812, which in turn had resulted in "the burning in 1814 of part of this Capitol in which we are assembled." [12] In the interests of helping the democracies resist aggression, Roosevelt recommended a repeal of the arms embargo; in the interests of insulating the United States from the conflict, he asked for authority to prohibit American ships from sailing into the danger zones.

The ensuing debate—in Congress, in the press, over the radio—was one of the most heated and momentous in American history. Noninterventionists [13] insisted that the repeal of the arms embargo was unneutral, because it would mean changing the rules after the game had begun in order to help one side against the other; [14] they held that the arms embargo had nothing to do with a "departure" from international law, because the Neutrality Act was purely domestic legislation; and finally, they argued that the United States, after again developing a huge vested interest in selling merchandise of death to the Allies, would again be drawn into the conflict. But the noninterventionists heartily applauded one of Roosevelt's recommendations; namely, the establishment of prohibited danger zones.

The interventionists, on the other hand, argued that the existing

[11] Pending the passage of the Neutrality Act of 1939, Washington advised American shippers voluntarily to keep out of the danger zones. *Department of State Bulletin*, I, 343 (Oct. 7, 1939).

[12] Jones and Myers, *Documents*, II, 9. It will be noted that President Roosevelt's views regarding the embargo disagree with those expressed in this book, pp. 123, 138.

[13] In general, there were two types of noninterventionists: the isolationists, who believed that America could insulate herself from outside broils, and the others, who, while not going this far, wanted to keep out as a matter of policy. Interventionists could be classified as the extremist minority, who wanted to get into the war, and the others, who wanted to render aid short of war.

[14] In October, 1939, the New York *Herald-Tribune* polled thirteen distinguished international lawyers, three of whom thought that repeal would be a violation of America's "neutral obligations"; ten thought not. *Amer. Jour. of Internat. Law*, XXXIV (1940), 99 n.

strait-jacket policy was unneutral, because it was merely serving to throw American influence on the side of the "aggressors." They held that Hitler would never have attacked if he had not been assured that his victims could secure no arms in the United States.[15] Some of the repealists were candid enough to waive legalistic contentions about neutrality and international law, and place the issue squarely on the grounds of self-interest: it simply was to the advantage of America to have the democracies win. But the danger zone encountered strong opposition from the interventionists. They felt that it would leave the small neutrals completely at the mercy of Hitler, and that it would be an abdication of freedom of the seas.[16]

After six interminable weeks, the debate finally ended on November 3, 1939, when the Senate approved the conference report 55 to 24, and the House, 243 to 172. These figures roughly reflected public opinion.[17] The arms embargo was lifted and danger zones were authorized. But the purchasers of munitions would have to operate on a "come-and-get-it" and "cash-on-the-barrelhead" basis. (Even these halfway measures elicited violent condemnation from Nazi mouthpieces in Berlin.) In essence, the final act was a compromise in which the isolationists yielded the arms embargo for the danger zone, and the interventionists traded a danger zone for the arms embargo repeal.[18] Thus Congress made a final attempt at "storm-cellar neutrality."

THE ABOLITION OF NEUTRAL RIGHTS

Ominously, the war that broke out in 1939 began where the previous World War had ended. The *Lusitania*—the first of a list of passenger ships to be sunk without warning—was not torpedoed until the earlier

[15] This allegation, frequently made, is difficult to prove. In view of Hitler's reliance on the quick knockout, and in view of the current small output of America's arms factories, it may be doubted whether the Neutrality Act was a major factor in Hitler's thinking when he attacked Poland.

[16] It was pointed out at the time that if the repeal of the arms embargo was a return to America's historic policy, the establishment of forbidden zones was an even greater step in the opposite direction.

[17] Various Gallup polls showed that 50 per cent favored the arms embargo repeal in September, 60 per cent in October, and 56 per cent in November. The danger zone was much more popular, being favored in September by 84 per cent. *Pub. Opin. Quar.*, IV, 105–111.

[18] The act retained certain restrictions of the existing legislation, notably those regarding loans and travel on belligerent ships. The preamble specifically stated that the United States was waiving none of its "rights or privileges" "under international law," and that it reserved the right to repeal or change the measure at any time. Jones and Myers, *Documents*, II, 656–669.

conflict was nine months old. In 1939, on the very first day of the war, the British passenger ship *Athenia* was destroyed by a German submarine, without warning and with heavy loss of life. Other weapons and devices employed by the belligerents from 1914 to 1917 were adopted at the outset of hostilities, or very speedily.

With the object of erecting safeguards around evanescent neutral rights, the First Meeting of Foreign Ministers of the American Republics, authorized by the Buenos Aires and Lima Conferences, gathered in Panama, in September, 1939. Acting with surprising unanimity and dispatch, the delegates adopted a number of resolutions, the most noteworthy being the Declaration of Panama of October 3, 1939. This pact established a "safety belt" around the Americas south of Canada, ranging from approximately 300 to 1000 miles in width, and warned the belligerents to refrain from naval action within that area. The Declaration is of importance as a spectacular example of collective Pan-American action, as a step in the further "multilateralization" of the Monroe Doctrine, and as an attempt to restrict belligerent action on the high seas in the interests of regional security.[19] But as a practical matter the "safety belt" fell short of expectations, primarily because the American republics were unwilling to use force to uphold their position. The British, French, and German governments, alleging that their enemies might use the new zone to subserve their own interests, flatly rejected this innovation and boldly continued to sink each other's ships within the proscribed area.[20]

Meanwhile traditional neutral rights had been rapidly melting away before the hot blast of belligerent orders and edicts, just as in 1914–1917—only much faster. On September 8, 1939, five days after their declaration of war, the Allies announced a long-range blockade in retaliation for Germany's ruthless submarine attacks. In retaliation for the Allied blockade, Berlin promptly proclaimed a counterblockade, on September 11, 1939. During November, 1939, the Germans launched a destructive attack on Allied shipping with floating magnetic mines; the Allies retaliated by extending their blockade to exports as well as imports—even to those goods that were exported through the neutrals.

As in 1914–1917, the United States did not submit to these and other restrictions lying down. Washington formally reserved its rights under

---

[19] The Declaration is vigorously defended on legal grounds by P. M. Brown, "Protective Jurisdiction," *Amer. Jour. of Internat. Law*, XXXIV (1940), 112–116.

[20] The American republics took steps to deny their port facilities to belligerents disregarding the zone. Jones and Myers, *Documents*, II, 138. Whether as a result of this or of a decreasing number of German ships in American waters, warlike activity declined.

the exports embargo; protested against forcing American ships into British control stations; and made repeated representations against the wholesale and prolonged detentions of United States merchantmen in

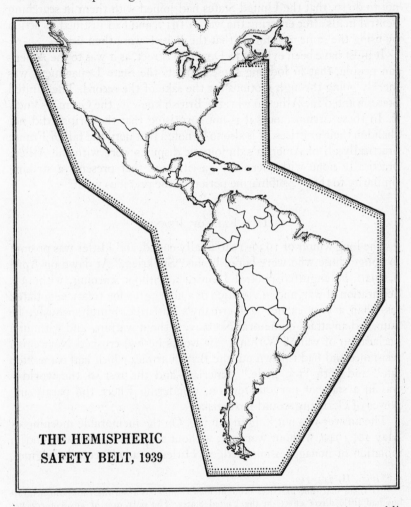

**THE HEMISPHERIC
SAFETY BELT, 1939**

British ports while undergoing search.[21] As in 1916, American public opinion became aroused over the searching of mails, particularly over the dramatic story that pouches had been removed from the Atlantic Clipper in Bermuda at the point of British bayonets. Washington lodged a formal protest against British searching of American mails,

[21] On these cases see *ibid.*, II, 705 *ff.*

using almost the same language it had employed in 1916; the London officials rejected the protest, using almost the same language they had employed in 1916.[22] They might have added, but were tactful enough not to do so, that the United States had joined with them in searching neutral mails after entering the war in 1917, and had justified its action by using the same arguments that the British were then using.

It must have been evident to Downing Street, as it was to the American people, that in lodging these protests the State Department was merely going through motions for the sake of the record. The United States wanted the Allies to win: the British knew it; the Germans knew it. In these circumstances it is not surprising that the British did not abandon their practices. It is also to be noted that until the fall of France practically all of America's diplomatic disputes were with the Allies; practically none with Germany—a situation that presents a striking similarity to the pre-submarine period of the previous war.[23]

The Fall of France

The long winter of 1939–1940 finally ended, and Hitler was prompt to oblige those who were bored by his "Sitzkrieg." At dawn on April 9, 1940, he engulfed neutral Denmark, without warning, without a declaration of war, and in violation of a nonaggression treaty negotiated less than a year earlier at Germany's initiative. Simultaneously, he launched an attack on neutral Norway, without warning and without a declaration of war.[24] Within a few weeks he had crushed Norwegian resistance and had thrown out the British armies which had come "too late" and with "too little." America—and the rest of the world—was in a state of nervous tension, wondering where the paralyzing power of Germany would next strike.

The answer was not long in coming. On the memorable morning of May 10, 1940, without warning, without a declaration of war, and in violation of nonaggression pledges, Hitler invaded neutral Belgium,

---

[22] *Ibid.*, II, 713–719.

[23] German maritime practices brought loud complaints from the European neutrals but had little direct effect on the United States. The only case of any consequence affecting German-American relations was that of the *City of Flint*, which was captured by the Germans in October, 1939, taken to a Russian port, and subsequently released by Norway. The main issue was not the seizure of the ship but whether it could be taken to a neutral port. *Ibid.*, II, 700–705. The dangers to America exemplified by this case hastened the passing of the Neutrality Act of 1939.

[24] On April 10, 1940, Roosevelt extended the maritime danger zone under the Neutrality Act to take in the new theater of operations. Other extensions were made as the war widened. See map on p. 787.

Holland, and Luxemburg. Within five days Holland had capitulated; within eighteen days Belgium had surrendered; within twenty days the British armies had been driven out of France, and but for the "miracle of Dunkirk" would have been annihilated.

On June 10, 1940, Mussolini, hoping for a jackal's share of France's carcass, pounced upon his neighbor from the rear. Desperately, Premier Reynaud of France appealed to Roosevelt, reminding him of his "quarantine" speech of 1937 against the "aggressors," and pleading for a public pledge that America would give the "Allies aid and material support by all means 'short of an expeditionary force.'" Four days later, on June 14, 1940, Roosevelt sent his "utmost sympathy," assurances that the United States would refuse to recognize forcible infringements upon the territory of France, and a promise that America would dispatch all the arms she could spare. He was careful to add that "these statements carry with them no implication of military commitments. Only the Congress can make such commitments." [25] This, of course, was the only position that Roosevelt could take under the Constitution, but it fell far short of a satisfactory reply to Reynaud's second appeal, broadcast to America only the day before, for "clouds of planes." A week later, on June 22, 1940, prostrate France was forced to sign an armistice, which was theatrically staged by her German conqueror in the same railway car on the same spot in the forest of Compiègne where the Armistice of 1918 had been concluded.

The six weeks that shook the world shook American "Maginot minds" out of their complacency. Britain, the last bastion of democracy in Europe, might momentarily go under, leaving a woefully unprepared United States to defend all of the Americas against a ruthless dictator who would have the economic and military power of Europe at his back—and, it was feared, the British navy as well. A large number of the American people were convinced that Hitler would come if he could; and for the first time they fully understood the relationship of the British fleet to the Monroe Doctrine. Not since the days of the Holy Alliance had the American people been faced with the prospect of fighting at such heavy odds.

A question that called for an immediate answer was what to do with the orphaned colonies of Denmark, Holland, and France, especially the Dutch and French West Indies and French Guiana. Their possible occupancy by the Nazis would create an intolerable threat to the Caribbean life line, to say nothing of the mainland of the United States. On June 17, 1940, the Senate passed a resolution, 76 to 20, opposing the

---

[25] For this interchange, see Jones and Myers, *Documents*, II, 424–426.

transfer of territory in "this hemisphere from one non-American power to another non-American power"; and the House followed suit the next day by a vote of 380 to 8. When Berlin was officially informed of this move, the Foreign Office replied that America's interpretation of the Monroe Doctrine gave to certain Powers the right to hold territory

(Berryman in the Washington *Evening Star*.)

in the Western Hemisphere, while denying that right to others. This view Germany found "untenable." The Foreign Office added that the nonintervention principle could be "legally valid only on condition that the American nations for their part do not interfere in the affairs of the European Continent." [26] In short, Germany flatly refused to recognize the no-transfer principle of the Monroe Doctrine, and thus further stimulated fears that she had designs on the Americas.

On June 19, 1940, three days before the signing of the French armistice, Washington announced the calling of the Second Meeting of Foreign Ministers of the American Republics at Havana. The delib-

[26] These documents relating to the Monroe Doctrine appear in *ibid.*, II, 86–93. The quoted passages are from a paraphrase of the German note issued by the Department of State.

erations opened on July 21; and responding to Secretary Hull's appeal for the establishment of a "collective trusteeship," the delegates disregarded Nazi threats and unanimously approved the Act of Havana on July 30. By its terms, territory of European Powers in danger of falling into unfriendly hands might be taken over and administered jointly by the American republics, pending a final disposition of the areas in question.[27] This was not only a defensive measure of the highest importance, but it was an outstanding milestone on the road to Pan-American co-operation. It was also the most significant step yet taken toward "multilateralizing" the Monroe Doctrine, for the United States would thereafter permit its Latin American neighbors to share in the application of that historic policy, insofar as it involved the no-transfer principle.

From the standpoint of defending the hemisphere, Canada was no less important than Latin America, perhaps more immediately important. On August 18, 1940, less than a month after the Act of Havana, President Roosevelt and Prime Minister Mackenzie King, meeting at Ogdensburg, New York, agreed upon a procedure for setting up the Permanent Joint Board of Defense, which would study defense problems relating directly to "the north half of the Western Hemisphere."[28] This was a strange pact indeed for a technical neutral to make with an actual belligerent; but the American people clearly recognized that the defense of Canada was also the defense of the United States.[29]

AID SHORT OF WAR

When Hitler loosed his bombers upon the Low Countries, Congress was parsimoniously paring down the comparatively modest budget

[27] The Act of Havana was not to become fully effective until two thirds of the twenty-one republics had ratified; nevertheless provision was made for action by individual countries (e.g., the United States) in case the emergency was so great that delay was intolerable. Such action, however, was subject to later review. This concession is important as a formal recognition by Latin America of Washington's right unilaterally to apply the Monroe Doctrine. Ibid., II, 93–95; III, 85–97. The United States Senate, on September 27, 1940, unanimously approved the pact. A number of the Latin American republics promptly followed suit. See Department of State Bulletin, V, 303 (Oct. 18, 1941).

[28] In November, 1940, the two governments agreed to modify the Rush-Bagot agreement so as to permit ship construction and other naval activity on the Great Lakes. Jones and Myers, Documents, III, 169–178.

[29] Gallup polls (June 19 and 23, 1940) showed that if Canada should be invaded the American people were willing to render aid with their Army and Navy. Of those with opinions, 87 per cent were favorable; 13 per cent opposed. Pub. Opin. Quar., IV, 553.

estimates that the President had submitted for the Army and Navy. The speedy collapse of the Dutch defenses caused a wave of near-hysteria to sweep over the country, especially on the Eastern seaboard, where Mayor La Guardia of New York declared that the United States could not even defend Coney Island. On May 16, 1940, Roosevelt appeared before Congress, and after sensationally outlining a bomber timetable from West Africa to Omaha, called for 50,000 airplanes and an immediate appropriation of $896,000,000. In subsequent weeks, he made additional and more sweeping requests for "total defense," and by October 8, 1940, Congress had voted $17,692,000,000, or nearly as much as was spent in the previous war. But voting money was much simpler than drafting manpower. It was not until September, 1940, and only after heated opposition from the isolationists, that Congress passed a conscription law—significantly the first peacetime measure of its kind in United States history.[30]

More immediately pressing were certain moves in the diplomatic theater. Prior to the spring of 1940 the Washington government, on the whole, had been impeccably neutral as regards the strict letter of the law. But the collapse of England would be the crowning catastrophe; and to give her the aid that she wanted as soon as she needed it would involve the United States in flagrantly unneutral acts. Confronted with this distressing dilemma, the Administration sharply reversed its previous policy. In the interests of "defending America by aiding the Allies," it resorted to as rapid and complete an abandonment of pre-1939 neutrality as public opinion, shot through with a strong isolationist minority, would permit. In order to quiet this minority and give the color of legality to its course, the United States government cited international law to justify departures from an international law which was now largely dead.

On April 10, 1940, the day after the Danish and Norwegian attacks, Washington froze the American credits of these two countries so that they would not be available to Germany. This was the first of a long series of "freezings" designed to deprive the Axis of potential loot in every country that it overran. Every important aggressive move by the dictators brought forth strong condemnatory statements from official Washington, as well as expressions of sympathy and in several cases promises of help for the victims. Speaking at Charlottesville, Virginia, the day Italy entered the war, Roosevelt made an unprecedented

[30] Indicative of the seriousness of the crisis is the fact that in 1917 conscription was not passed until six weeks *after* the formal declaration of war; in 1940 it was passed fourteen months *before* the declaration.

allusion to a fellow ruler when he deliberately and dramatically declared: "On this tenth day of June, 1940, the hand that held the dagger has struck it into the back of its neighbor." [31]

But these were mere words; action soon followed. In June, 1940, the Administration worked out a trade-in scheme, under an almost forgotten law of 1917, whereby the government would turn over to the airplane manufacturer a number of planes already completed, to be replaced by more recent models being built. The private manufacturer would then transfer the older craft to the Allies. In the same month, fifty to one hundred attack planes and eighty bombers, as a beginning, were thus made available. Under the same act of 1917 and a ruling of the Acting Attorney General, the government sold to private concerns a vast amount of 1917–1918 equipment, with the understanding that it would be resold to the British. This arrangement involved about 600,-000 Lee-Enfield rifles, 800 French and British 75's, and large stocks of machine guns, mortars, and ammunition, all of which was a godsend to the semi-defenseless British. In their final stages these transactions did not involve the United States government, which, under international law, consequently had a technical defense.[32]

During June, 1940, and subsequent months, Washington ruled that American planes could be flown directly to Canada without having to stop at the border to be pulled or pushed across; allowed thousands of British pilots to train in Florida, where flying conditions were better than in Canada; sent 105 obsolete tanks from an Illinois arsenal to Canada for training purposes; and permitted damaged British warships to undergo extensive repairs in American shipyards. This, of course, was not neutrality; but neither was this an ordinary war.

THE DESTROYER DEAL

Previous acts of favoritism to the Allies were as nothing when compared with the spectacular and momentous destroyer deal, announced on September 3, 1940. After several weeks of preliminary negotiation,

---

[31] Jones and Myers, *Documents*, II, 81. The President was evidently profoundly distressed by the failure of his efforts, described in detail in this speech, to dissuade Mussolini from entering the war.

[32] An Administration plan for transferring to Britain ten torpedo boats and ten subchasers had to be abandoned because of an irreconcilable conflict with existing legislation. A list of the June transactions appears in *ibid.*, II, 788–789. L. H. Woolsey, a distinguished international lawyer and Solicitor of the State Department under President Wilson, felt that the trade-in subterfuge raised serious questions of governmental neutrality. *Amer. Jour. of Internat. Law*, XXXIV (1940), 502–503.

the United States government agreed to turn over to the British—not through private media but directly—fifty overage but still serviceable destroyers, which were desperately needed to combat the submarine peril. The British, on their part, made the United States outright gifts, "freely and without consideration," of sites for bases on Newfoundland and Bermuda for ninety-nine years, while granting ninety-nine year, rent-free leases for sites at six places ranging from the Bahamas to British Guiana.[33]

Few Americans questioned the value of these potential bases. With Hitler on the loose, and with air power growing in destructiveness, it seemed highly desirable to station a "protective girdle of steel" far out in the Atlantic. Not only would America find these sites useful for defense but, if left undefended, they might be seized and used by the dictators for attack. "This," Roosevelt informed Congress, "is the most important action in the reinforcement of our national defense that has been taken since the Louisiana Purchase."[34]

But many Americans questioned the way in which the transaction was carried through—by an executive agreement pure and simple, without the advice and consent of the Senate. Britain was in such critical need of the destroyers that presumably the President thought it imperative to avoid the delay which deliberate Congressional action would have entailed. Although public opinion undoubtedly regarded the bargain as a good one,[35] the Republicans in particular felt that the President should never have committed the country to such an overt act of unneutrality without consulting Congress. The Republican presidential candidate, Wendell Willkie, though not opposing the deal as such, castigated it as "the most dictatorial action ever taken by any President." There were also many reputable students of international law who felt that the transaction, despite Attorney General Jackson's lengthy ruling, much of which hinged on the placement of a comma in the relevant statute, was a violation of both domestic and international law.[36]

---

[33] On September 2, 1940, Downing Street gave a formal pledge never to sink or surrender the British fleet. This was not a part of the destroyer deal but, as Roosevelt testified in a press conference, came purely "fortuitously." *The Public Papers and Addresses of Franklin D. Roosevelt: 1938 Volume* (N.Y., 1941), p. 382.

[34] Jones and Myers, *Documents*, III, 206. The materials relating to the transaction appear in *ibid.*, pp. 203-228.

[35] A Gallup poll (Aug. 17, 1940) revealed that some two weeks before the deal was consummated, 62 per cent of those with opinions favored selling fifty destroyers to Britain, while 38 per cent opposed. This question did not involve the island bases, which doubtless made the deal even more popular. *Pub. Opin. Quar.*, IV, 713.

[36] The *American Journal of International Law* for October, 1940 (vol. XXXIV)

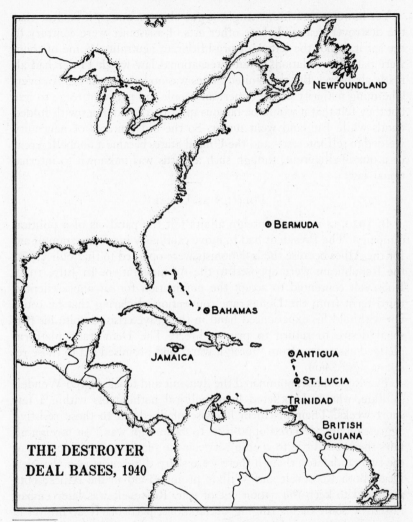

NEWFOUNDLAND

⊙ BERMUDA

⊙ BAHAMAS

JAMAICA

⊙ ANTIGUA

⊙ ST. LUCIA

TRINIDAD

BRITISH
GUIANA

THE DESTROYER
DEAL BASES, 1940

contained three able discussions of the destroyer deal by leading international lawyers. Professor H. W. Briggs concluded (p. 587) that "The supplying of these
vessels by the United States Government to a belligerent is a violation of our neutral
status, a violation of our national law, and a violation of international law." Professor Edwin Borchard similarly concluded (p. 697) that "there is no possibility
of reconciling the destroyer deal with neutrality, with United States statutes, or
with international law." Professor Quincy Wright, a leading interventionist, defended the transaction (pp. 688–689) on the grounds that Germany by her violations of the Kellogg-Briand pact and other transgressions was "not a lawful
belligerent, and parties to these instruments are not obliged under international law
to observe toward Germany and her allies the duties of a neutral." The United States,
he said, "is no longer a neutral from the point of view of international law."

Yet however much one might argue about commas, it is clear that the destroyer deal and these other acts of assistance were contrary to the spirit, if not the letter, of pre-Hitlerian neutrality. Some of them were patently violations of an international law which Hitler had already abolished. But the United States was no longer neutral. An overwhelming majority of the American people did not want to go to war but they felt that it would be fatuous to sit on the sidelines with folded hands while England went under. So the old concepts of neutrality yielded to self-interest—and the United States became a nonbelligerent or a quasi-belligerent, though such a status was unknown to international law.

POLITICS AS USUAL

In 1940, as in 1916, foreign affairs felt the paralysis of a political campaign. The President had to move cautiously in his program of aid for the Allies because the isolationists were opposed to that policy, and the Republicans were opposed to the Administration. In July, 1940, Roosevelt consented to accept the nomination for an unprecedented third term from the Democratic convention, declaring that he could not withhold his experienced hand in the grave crisis, despite his personal desire to return to private life.[37] The Democratic platform pledged abstention from "foreign wars" and promised aid to those resisting aggression.

The Republicans nominated the dynamic and tousle-haired Wendell Willkie, who had rocketed from political nothingness within a few short weeks. Their platform likewise pledged aid to those resisting aggression and declared opposition to "a foreign war." In foreign affairs there was little to choose between the platforms and speeches of the two candidates, though there were sharp differences over the New Deal. Both Roosevelt and Willkie promised aid to the Allies; both promised to keep the nation out of war. Roosevelt was later embarrassed by some of his ringing declarations, particularly at Boston in the closing days of the campaign, when he solemnly stated: "Your boys are not going to be sent into any foreign wars." [38]

In ordinary times the Republicans might have been able to defeat

---

[37] Roosevelt's critics in both parties hotly charged that he really wanted to continue in office and that he had arranged to have himself "drafted."

[38] *Roosevelt Papers, 1940,* p. 517 (Oct. 30, 1940). The war that finally came could, of course, be regarded as a struggle for defense rather than a "foreign war." Somewhat more emphatic was the pledge at Buffalo (Nov. 2): "Your President says this country is not going to war." *Ibid.,* p. 543.

Roosevelt by their charge that his attempt to shatter the third-term tradition was the entering wedge for a dictatorship. But these were not ordinary times. One of the most telling arguments used by the Democrats was that Hitler hoped for the defeat of the President, who had been openly hostile to the "aggressors" since his "quarantine" speech. Many of the voters felt that Roosevelt's experience was needed in the crisis; that he would prove more effective than Willkie in strengthening the country's defenses; that he would be more inspiring as a war leader should the United States become involved; and that one should not swap horses in the middle of the stream.[39] In November, 1940, the nation marched to the polls and Roosevelt won by a landslide in the electoral college, though his opponent polled an impressive popular vote. There was no rejoicing in Berlin or Rome or Tokyo.

THE LEND-LEASE ACT

His hands freed by the election, Roosevelt could next turn to the problem of rendering large-scale aid to bomb-battered Britain. The cost of the war was so colossal that the British were rapidly reaching the end of their financial tether—at least so their ambassador hinted in November, 1940. But to lend billions of dollars would be a slow and indirect process which would cause economic dislocation and inevitable postwar friction over repayment. "Now, what I am trying to do," Roosevelt told a press conference, "is to eliminate the dollar sign." To him the proper solution was to lend arms directly to those resisting aggression, and expect the return of those arms or replacements for them when the war was over.[40] This was the lend-lease scheme which Roosevelt outlined in December, 1940.

The historic lend-lease bill—entitled "An Act Further to Promote the Defense of the United States"—was introduced into Congress in January, 1941. The ensuing debate was comparable in bitterness and volume with that over the repeal of the arms embargo. The Aid the Allies group warmly espoused lend-lease as a "defense" measure which would keep the war away from America; the America First group denounced it as the "blank-check bill" and a sure guarantee of war. Republican Senator Taft of Ohio scoffed that "Lending war equipment is a good deal like lending chewing gum. You don't want it back."

[39] See the various polls in *Pub. Opin. Quar.*, V, 135, 137.
[40] See *Roosevelt Papers, 1940*, pp. 604 ff.

Isolationist Senator Wheeler of Montana branded lend-lease as the "New Deal's 'triple A' foreign policy—to plow under every fourth American boy." [41] But despite such bitter opposition, American public opinion, which favored lend-lease, was not to be denied.[42] The final vote was 60 yeas and 31 nays in the Senate; 317 yeas and 71 nays in the House. A half hour after the action of Congress Roosevelt signed the measure, March 11, 1941. Five minutes later he approved a list of articles for immediate shipment. The next day he asked Congress for an initial appropriation of $7,000,000,000 to implement the act, which was granted on March 27. Thus the United States pledged itself to the limit of its industrial and financial resources to lend "defense articles" to those governments "whose defense the President deems vital to the defense of the United States." [43]

The lend-lease act must take a high place among the most momentous laws ever passed by Congress. It was more than an abandonment of neutrality, for neutrality had already been abandoned; it was an unofficial declaration of war on the Axis—or rather a belated recognition of the fact that the Axis had officially or unofficially declared war on all the democracies.[44] Unlike the destroyer deal, it was not merely an executive agreement. It was a measure debated "over every cracker barrel in the land," supported by a strong majority of the population, and passed by comfortable margins in Congress. The American people, through their regularly elected representatives, had spoken. They still hoped to be able to stay out of a "shooting war"; but they were willing

[41] San Francisco *Chronicle*, Jan. 13, 1941, 4:8. Stung by Wheeler's remark, Roosevelt told his press conference two days later: "That really is the rottenest thing that has been said in public life in my generation." *Roosevelt Papers, 1940,* p. 712.

[42] By March 8, 1941, the count of the Gallup poll was 56 per cent favorable; 27 per cent opposed; 8 per cent qualified; and 9 per cent without opinion. *Pub. Opin. Quar.,* V, 325.

[43] Jones and Myers, *Documents,* III, 711–736. On the first passage the House vote was 260 yeas to 165 nays. Lend-lease to Canada was implemented by the Hyde Park Declaration of Roosevelt and Mackenzie King, on April 20, 1941, which was designed to dovetail the economies of the two countries so that each would provide the other with what it most needed. With joint defense also in view, Roosevelt revived the St. Lawrence waterway and power project, and submitted it to Congress on June 6, 1941. The proposal was sidetracked by more pressing problems.

[44] Professor Quincy Wright justified American unneutrality on the grounds that since Germany had "outlawed" herself by violating international law, the United States was justified under international law in resisting "basic attacks" on that law. This "new principle of permissive sanctions" was used by the Senate and House committees in support of the lend-lease bill, and was endorsed by the Attorney General in March, 1941. *Amer. Jour. of Internat. Law,* XXXVI (1942), 20–21. These advanced views did not, however, command the unanimous support of students of international law.

"The Lesser Evil." (Shoemaker in the Chicago *Daily News*.)

to stake the democracies to victory even at the risk of involvement themselves.[45]

BIBLIOGRAPHICAL NOTE

The most satisfactory surveys of American foreign policy continue to be W. H. Shepardson (in collaboration with W. O. Scroggs), *The United States in World Affairs, 1939* (N.Y., 1940), and the succeeding volume for 1940 (N.Y., 1941). An invaluable documentary collection is S. S. Jones and D. P. Myers, eds., *Documents on American Foreign Relations* (Boston, 1939–), three volumes of which have appeared covering the period from January, 1938, to June, 1941. These contain not only the texts of United States documents, but those pertaining to other countries as well, and are prefaced by excellent introductory statements. The *Department of State Bulletin* is less comprehensive in scope but contains many items of minor importance which have been omitted from Jones and Myers. *The Public Papers of Franklin D. Roosevelt: 1939 Volume* (N.Y., 1941); *1940 Volume* (N.Y., 1941), contain not only the speeches and other papers of the President but also unique after-the-event commentaries. On legal aspects of the various diplomatic controversies, the current numbers of the *American Journal of International Law* are extremely useful. This publication also contains in its Supplements the most important documents. Among the many secondary accounts, the following may be noted. D. E. Lee, *Ten Years* (Boston, 1942), devotes some attention to the place of the United States in the international scene, 1930–1940. F. L. Schuman, *Design for Power* (N.Y., 1942), covers essentially the same ground, with a racy style and strong interventionist predilections. Joseph Alsop and Robert Kintner, *American White Paper* (N.Y., 1940), is a sketchy journalistic description of the crises of 1938 and 1939 in Europe. Harold Lavine and James Wechsler, *War Propaganda and the United States* (New Haven, 1940), is the best account to date on the efforts of the belligerents during 1939 and 1940. C. G. Fenwick, *American Neutrality: Trial and Failure* (N.Y., 1940), is critical of "storm-cellar neutrality." H. B. Hinton, *Cordell Hull: A Biography* (N.Y., 1942), is an undocumented biography, the first of the Secretary of State. The periodic studies by the Foreign Policy Association are highly useful. Of magazine articles, the following by Dexter Perkins are noteworthy: "Bringing the Monroe Doctrine up to Date," *For. Affairs*, XX (1942), 253–265; and "The Monroe Doctrine To-Day," *Yale Review*, XXX (1941), 686–702. Further references: see footnotes of this chapter and the footnotes and bibliographies of the next.

NEW REFERENCES; 4TH ED. REFS. See Bibliographical Appendix, p. 948.

[45] In May, 1940, only 36 per cent favored aid at the risk of war. In January, 1941, this figure rose to 68 per cent; in April, dropped to 67 per cent; in May, dropped to 61 per cent. Gallup polls in *Pub. Opin. Quar.*, V, 481.

CHAPTER XLVI

The War Comes to America: Final Phase

"The delivery of needed supplies to Britain is imperative. This can be done; it must be done; it will be done."

Franklin D. Roosevelt, May 27, 1941.

TAKING THE DIPLOMATIC OFFENSIVE

WHILE the battle for lend-lease was being waged on the floor of Congress, no less portentous battles were being waged on the fighting front. In September and October, 1940, when the Roosevelt-Willkie campaign was approaching its climax, the gasconading Mussolini launched attacks upon the British forces in Egypt and upon tiny Greece, only to suffer humiliating reverses. The heroic resistance of the Greeks, like that of the Finns, captured the imagination of the American people, and enthusiasm for the doughty sons of Hellas reached a point in many ways reminiscent of the "Greek fever" of the 1820's.

But Greek triumphs in Albania and British victories in Libya were only spectacular flashes in the pan. With the spring of 1941 came the awakening. After herding Rumania, Bulgaria, and Hungary into the Axis fold, Hitler first overwhelmed Jugoslavia and then Greece. Effective resistance was completely crushed under the German jackboot before the aid which Roosevelt had pledged could possibly have arrived; and the isolationists loudly accused the Administration of encouraging these small nations to resist on the basis of false promises.

As the Nazi panzer divisions were pouring down the Balkan funnel, relations between Berlin and Washington rapidly worsened. On March 30, 1941, the United States government seized sixty-five Axis or Axis-controlled ships in American ports, and jailed nearly a thousand of the seamen, under an act of 1917, for attempted sabotage. Angry official protests from Berlin and Rome were to no avail. About a week later, on April 10, 1941, Roosevelt took cognizance of the Italian collapse on the northeastern coast of Africa when he proclaimed that the mouth of the Red Sea was no longer a combat area—thus permitting American ships to carry supplies to the hard-pressed British. Berlin insisted that the Red Sea was still a danger zone, and made it clear that American shipping would be subject to attack. Roosevelt belligerently replied in a press conference that the United States had already fought two undeclared wars in defense of freedom of the seas—the implication being that it might have to fight another.[1]

A long stride in the direction of an undeclared war was taken during the same month of April, 1941. Washington was deeply disturbed by reports of Nazi reconnaissance patrols in Denmark's motherless colony of Greenland. A German lodgment in this area would constitute an intolerable threat both to the mainland of the United States and to the lend-lease life line to Britain. The State Department entered upon negotiations with the Danish minister in Washington, Henrik Kauffmann, and he, though entirely without instruction and solely on his own responsibility, signed an agreement on April 9, 1941, permitting the United States to occupy Greenland for defensive purposes and without detriment to Denmark's sovereignty until the emergency was over. The Nazi-dominated Copenhagen government promptly disavowed this act and recalled Kauffmann. Secretary Hull, in a striking statement, declined to recognize the recall, and continued to regard Kauffmann as the regularly accredited minister.[2] This, of course, was entirely without precedent in American diplomatic history, and could not be supported on the basis of international law as of 1914.[3] But this was not 1914. The United States was dealing with an unprincipled adversary; and in the interests of the Monroe Doctrine and hemispheric defense the Administration was prepared to fight the devil with fire.

This evident determination of Washington to take the offensive was strikingly demonstrated when Roosevelt, finding that he was failing to prevent collaboration between France and her Nazi conquerors, made an unprecedented appeal directly to the French people, on May 15, 1941, urging them not to support their government.[4] Five days later

---

[1] Press conference statement of May 16, 1941. New York *Times*, May 17, 1941, 1 : 8. To bolster Britain in her Battle of the Atlantic, Washington, in the spring of 1941, transferred ten armed corvettes and twenty mosquito boats to the British flag, and, as a beginning, allocated fifty tankers for use in American waters.

[2] For the agreement and the papers relating to it, see S. S. Jones and D. P. Myers, eds., *Documents on American Foreign Relations* (Boston, 1941), III, 228–239.

[3] Professor H. W. Briggs, in a penetrating commentary, finds the agreement legally indefensible. *Amer. Jour. of Internat. Law*, XXXV (1941), 506–513.

[4] The appeal of the Washington government to the French people suggests Genêt's earlier attempt to appeal over the heads of the Washington government to the American people. The United States continued its policy of putting pressure on France. See particularly Secretary Hull's warning against fighting Germany's battles in Syria. *Department of State Bulletin*, IV, 715 (June 14, 1941).

it was announced by Berlin that the Egyptian steamer *Zam Zam*, with over one hundred American passengers on board, had been shelled and sunk in the South Atlantic, with injuries to American citizens. This brutal destruction of a neutral merchantman, without regard for the safety of those traveling under its flag, deeply stirred opinion in America. In part as a reply to Nazi ruthlessness, Congress passed a bill (signed June 6, 1941) designed to take over and use all foreign merchant ships immobilized in United States ports. Significantly, both houses rejected amendments to the effect that none of the vessels so seized be turned over to the British.[5] The country was obviously in a mood to take more than halfway measures.

THE SINKINGS START

While German glider-borne troops were overrunning the island of Crete, President Roosevelt, on May 27, 1941, went on the air. Solemnly declaring that the Nazi tide was rising, that the sinkings of Allied tonnage were twice the replacement capacity of British and American shipyards combined, and that Portugal's Cape Verde Islands were only seven hours from Brazil by bomber, he announced: "We insist upon the vital importance of keeping Hitlerism away from any point of attack in the world which could be used and would be used as a base of attack against the Americas." [6] He concluded his speech with a startling proclamation of an unlimited national emergency, and with an invocation of the spirit of those patriots who had signed the Declaration of Independence.

Even while the President was speaking, a gallant little band of survivors was slowly making its way to shore from the American merchantman *Robin Moor*, which had been torpedoed and shelled in the South Atlantic, on May 21, 1941, by what was assumed to be a German submarine. This was the first United States ship of any kind to be deliberately sunk by German hands, either in or out of the war zones.[7] Although no lives were lost, public opinion was profoundly shocked and angered. Senator Carter Glass expressed the sentiments of countless fellow interventionists when he said: "I think we ought to go over there and shoot hell out of every U-boat."

---

[5] The Axis ships seized on March 30, 1941, had been taken into "protective custody" to prevent further sabotage.

[6] Jones and Myers, *Documents*, III, 55.

[7] British ships, like the *Athenia*, had been sunk earlier with loss of American life. The United States merchantman, *City of Rayville*, had gone down in Australian

Washington promptly took steps that were interpreted as reprisals for the *Robin Moor* sinking. On June 14, 1941, five days after the news reached America, Roosevelt froze all German and Italian assets in the United States, as well as the assets of all other Axis-controlled countries not previously frozen. Italy and Germany promptly retaliated in kind. On June 16, 1941, the State Department requested the closing of all German consulates in the United States, on the ground that they were hotbeds of subversive activity. Germany and Italy speedily took similar action against all American consulates in their countries. And on June 20, 1941, Washington asked Italy to close all her consulates in the United States.[8] America and the Axis were fast drifting toward an open break.

Nazi spokesmen defiantly justified the sinking of the *Robin Moor* on the ground that it was carrying contraband to South Africa. Even granting the validity of this argument, it is clear that the Germans, in forcing the passengers and crew into small boats hundreds of miles from land, had not made provision for their safety in accordance with international law and with the Protocol of London, to which Berlin had voluntarily subscribed in 1936. On June 20, 1941, Roosevelt submitted a message to Congress in which he roundly condemned this act of "piracy" as a violation of freedom of the seas, and announced that full reparation would be expected. A copy of the message was sent to the German *chargé* in Washington, who, presumably objecting to the strong language, refused to transmit it to his government. Subsequent claims for damages were rejected by Berlin.[9]

The *Robin Moor* affair marks a turning point in German-American relations. Up to that time the Hitler regime, remembering the decisive effect of America's intervention in the last war, had avoided all attacks on United States ships. Up to that time Washington had little to complain of as far as America's specific rights were concerned—although there was much to complain of regarding Germany's ruthless attacks on the community of nations, of which the United States was a member. On legal grounds, Berlin had much better cause for protest against America's unneutral aid to the Allies than America had against

---

waters on November 8, 1940, presumably the victim of a mine, but clearly not of a deliberate attack.

[8] On March 6, 1941, Secretary Hull had asked the Italian government to restrict the movements of its consular officials in America, and to close the consulates in the manufacturing cities of Detroit and Newark.

[9] On September 19, 1941, Washington presented a bill for $2,967,092.00, which the German *chargé* rejected. *Department of State Bulletin*, V, 363–364 (Nov. 8, 1941).

Germany's infractions of American rights. The lend-lease act widened the breach irreparably. Henceforth, as the American people themselves admitted,[10] the United States was a cobelligerent of the Allies; and German commerce destroyers consequently regarded American ships as legitimate prey, despite Washington's invocation of freedom of the seas.

Strange Bedfellows Again

On June 22, 1941, while the *Robin Moor* case was still under discussion, Hitler astounded the world by launching a terrific, all-out attack on his associate in the nonaggression pact of 1939, Joseph Stalin. Except for the fall of France, no other development prior to Pearl Harbor so completely changed the complexion of the war.

Up to this point, the American people had felt little sympathy for the Soviet government. It had given Hitler the green light for his assault on Poland and had come in for its share of the spoils; it had absorbed the independent states of Lithuania, Latvia, Esthonia; it had taken Bessarabia and northern Bukovina away from Rumania; and it had attacked Finland—all of which areas (except Bukovina) had formerly been under the Czar's flag.[11] Moreover, Moscow had violated its solemn pledges by continuing Communist propaganda in the United States.[12] Condemnations and countercondemnations had echoed and re-echoed from the Dnieper to the Potomac.

Hitler's fateful attack on "the Mongol halfwits" of Russia effected an overnight revolution in American public opinion. On June 21, 1941, Stalin was a cynical, self-seeking, ruthless aggressor; on June 22 he was an ally—a very welcome ally—of those who were seeking to halt Hitlerism. Roosevelt promptly unfroze certain credits that had been frozen to keep them out of Soviet hands; he declined to invoke the Neutrality Act so that American ships could carry supplies to Soviet ports; he not only sent sweeping promises of aid to Stalin but made loans immediately available; and on November 6, 1941, having found the defense of Russia essential to the defense of the United States, he announced a pledge of one billion dollars in lend-lease aid. These were but the beginnings of a vast amount of material assistance to the Soviets.

---

[10] A *Fortune* poll asked (June, 1941) whether America was not already in the war for all practical purposes. The answers were 79.5 per cent affirmative, 10.9 per cent negative, and 9.6 per cent without opinion. *Pub. Opin. Quar.*, V, 477.

[11] All these post-Poland seizures came shortly after the fall of France, and presumably for the purpose of erecting buffers against Hitler.

[12] See Secretary Hull's letter to Senator Pittman, January 30, 1940. Jones and Myers, *Documents*, II, 496.

No less astonishing was the complete reversal of opinion regarding "brave little Finland." Alleging prior attacks, Russia reopened war on her, and the Finns fought back with Hitler's help. The same Americans who had applauded Finnish defeats of the Russians in the winter of 1939–1940 were now hoping for the success of Russian attacks on the Finns. Washington brought pressure to bear on Finland to withdraw from the war, while a number of Americans, including Herbert Hoover, condemned the Administration's reversal. The Berlin press screamed "criminal intervention" and "Jewish impudence," while the Finnish government politely declined America's invitation to stop fighting.

The American people, especially diehard conservatives, were not particularly happy over their new ally.[13] If Russia won, they asked, would not Europe go Bolshevik? Would Stalin prove to be a tractable associate at the peace table? Catholics and other religious denominations were deeply disturbed by the low state of the church in Russia.[14] "I have no more confidence in Stalin," declared Archbishop Curley of Baltimore, "than I have in Hitler." The isolationists saw in the Russo-German war additional evidence that the United States should stay out and let the Europeans slit each other's throats. The interventionists, on the other hand, saw in the heavy Russian reversals additional evidence that Hitler would soon have all Europe in his grasp. To them, and to the majority of the American people, the immediate, overwhelming menace was Naziism. Any recruit who would man the water buckets was welcome—and Russia was the lustiest possible recruit. Perhaps Communism was a latent danger, but there would be time enough to think about that when Hitler was charred in the ruins of Berlin.

THE ATLANTIC CHARTER

Several noteworthy events in the summer of 1941 highlighted the growing collaboration between belligerent Britain and nonbelligerent America. On July 7, 1941, Roosevelt announced to Congress that he had made arrangements with the Icelandic government whereby United States troops were gradually to take over the defense of the

---

[13] *Fortune* (Oct., 1941) revealed that 39.7 per cent of the American people thought the Russian government worse than or as bad as the German; 32.0 per cent regarded the Russian government as "slightly better"; 8.5 voted "far better"; 19.8, "don't know." *Pub. Opin. Quar.*, VI, 152.

[14] See Roosevelt's press-conference statement regarding freedom of worship as guaranteed by the Soviet constitution. *Department of State Bulletin*, V, 246 (Oct. 4, 1941).

island from Britain for the duration of the emergency, without detriment to the sovereignty of Iceland.[15] Like the destroyer and Greenland deals, this was an executive agreement designed to assist Britain in the Battle of the Atlantic and protect America against possible Nazi attacks. Further evidence of collaboration with London came on July 17, 1941, when Washington announced a blacklist of some 1800 Axis-connected firms in Latin America with which citizens of the United States were not to do business. If further proof were needed of the fact that America was already in an undeclared war, it should be noted that the Wilson administration had not published such a blacklist until eight months *after* entering the conflict in 1917.

Early in August, 1941, wild rumors began to circulate that Roosevelt and Prime Minister Churchill, both absent from their respective capitals, were meeting secretly at some unknown point. The rumors were sensationally confirmed when it was announced to the press, on August 14, that the two statesmen had met "at sea" [off the Newfoundland coast on a British and an American warship], that they had discussed lend-lease and other problems of common defense, and that they had agreed upon an eight-point declaration known as the Atlantic Charter. This statement set forth the "common principles" upon which they "base their hopes for a better future for the world"—in short, a peace program. In paraphrased form the points were: [16]

1. No territorial or other aggrandizement for either Power.
2. No territorial changes contrary to the wishes of the people concerned (*i.e.*, self-determination, one of the later Fourteen Points; in part also Points V and XII of the Fourteen).
3. The right of people to choose their own forms of government; restorations of governments to those deprived of them (*cf.*, territorial restoration, Points VI, VII, VIII, XI of the Fourteen).
4. Access by all nations, victor and vanquished, to the trade and raw materials of the world (*i.e.*, Point III of the Fourteen).
5. International collaboration for improved labor standards, economic advancement, and social security. (A combination of later objectives of the League of Nations and of the New Deal.)
6. A peace of security with freedom from fear and want (*i.e.*, two of Roosevelt's Four Freedoms).[17]

---

[15] *Ibid.*, V, 15 (July 12, 1941). A Gallup poll (July 24, 1941) showed that 61 per cent of the people favored the Iceland occupation; 17 per cent disapproved; 22 per cent had no opinion. *Pub. Opin. Quar.*, V, 686.

[16] Text in *Department of State Bulletin*, V, 125 (Aug. 16, 1941).

[17] Roosevelt had listed the Four Freedoms (January 6, 1941) as freedom of speech

7. A peace that "should enable all men to traverse the high seas and oceans without hindrance" (*i.e.*, freedom of the seas, Point II of the Fourteen.)
8. Abandonment of force; disarmament of the aggressor nations pending establishment of a "permanent system of general security" (League of Nations [?], Point XIV of the Fourteen); lightening of armament burdens (*i.e.*, Point IV of the Fourteen).

After all this hush-hush expectancy, public opinion in both America and Britain was definitely disappointed. The mountain had labored and brought forth a mixture of the New Deal and the old Fourteen Points. The Roosevelt-Churchill declaration was clearly designed to establish an Anglo-Saxon peace, and it could hardly be used to disarm Germany as the Fourteen Points had been—in fact, the "aggressor nations" were to be disarmed by force. The Eight Points, like the Fourteen, were heartening to those liberals who hoped for a better world order, and encouraging to conquered and underprivileged peoples everywhere. But fundamentally, from the standpoint of the United States, the Atlantic Charter was a tacit if not explicit acceptance of full responsibility for the defeat of Hitler and the establishment of a democratic peace. The isolationists denounced the agreement as one more move toward open collaboration with Britain, and the Chicago *Tribune*, a leading isolationist newspaper, wanted to know specifically what business Roosevelt had to discuss these matters with the head of a state already at war. Evidently the *Tribune* was unprepared to concede that the United States was at war also.

THE SHOOTING BEGINS

More immediately pressing than the Atlantic Charter was the problem of getting lend-lease goods to Britain through the wolfpacks of German submarines. From the point of view of pure logic it seemed foolish to start these shipments over and then make no adequate provision to get them to their destination. It would be much simpler, argued the interventionists, to dump the goods into the water from the Atlantic docks. This problem had to some extent been foreseen during the debates on lend-lease, at which time the question had been raised of clothing the President with authority to convoy. But the

---

and worship, and freedom from want and fear. The first two were omitted from the Atlantic Charter, allegedly out of deference to Stalin. For contrary evidence see R. E. Sherwood, *Roosevelt and Hopkins* (N.Y., 1948), pp. 361, 449.

troublesome issue of convoying was repeatedly shunted aside. From the standpoint of the interventionists it was better strategy to commit the nation to irrevocable courses one step at a time rather than defeat lend-lease by trying to look too far ahead.

Roosevelt first used naval patrols, from April, 1941, to warn the British of hostile U-boats. But when these proved ineffective, he quietly issued instructions, by virtue of his authority as commander-in-chief of the Navy, to convoy (July 11, 1941).[18] This momentous step was taken only four days after Roosevelt, in a message to Congress, had announced that he had given orders to the Navy "that all necessary steps be taken to insure the safety of communications in the approaches between Iceland and the United States. . . ." [19] This meant that destroyers would be used to shepherd lend-lease goods as far as Iceland. Four days later Secretary of the Navy Knox indicated to a Senate committee that American warships were dropping depth charges in self-defense against Axis submarines. The inevitable incident came on September 4, 1941, when Washington reported that a German submarine in Icelandic waters had fired two torpedoes at the United States destroyer *Greer*, without effect. The American vessel defended itself by dropping numerous depth charges. (More than a month later, the Navy Department revealed that the *Greer* had been trailing the U-boat for three and one-half hours and broadcasting the latter's position when the submarine turned and attacked.) [20]

Smarting from the *Greer* affair, and from the sinking of two American-owned merchantmen,[21] Roosevelt went on the air, Septem-

[18] C. A. Beard, *President Roosevelt and the Coming of the War, 1941* (New Haven), p. 115. As early as April 25, 1941, Roosevelt told a press conference that he was extending the naval patrol as far as American interests went. New York *Times*, April 26, 1941, 1:5.

[19] *Department of State Bulletin*, V, 15–16 (July 12, 1941). Public opinion seems to have been rather evenly divided on the convoy issue. According to Gallup polls, the figure rose from 41 per cent favorable in April, 1941, to 55 per cent favorable in June, 1941. After the occupation of Iceland, but just before the *Greer* affair, the figures were 52 per cent favorable; 39 per cent opposed; 9 per cent without opinion. *Pub. Opin. Quar.*, V, 485, 680.

[20] Statement of Admiral Harold R. Stark, Chief of Naval Operations. A British plane informed the Americans of the presence of the submarine, and before departing dropped four bombs in its vicinity. New York *Times*, Oct. 15, 1941, 6:1.

[21] The *Sessa*, a ship taken over from Denmark and registered in Panama, though American owned, was sunk on August 17, 1941, in the North Atlantic; the *Steel Seafarer*, flying the American flag, was destroyed by aerial bombs in the Red Sea, on September 5, 1941, an area proclaimed by Berlin a danger zone. During these months American shippers used the colors of Panama as a means of circumventing the Neutrality Act of 1939 and sending cargoes into the combat areas. The *Robin Moor* (May 21, 1941), the *Steel Seafarer*, and the *Lehigh* (October 19, 1941)

ber 11, 1941, and after reciting the list of recent German acts of "piracy," declared that henceforth United States patrols would defend freedom of the seas by striking first at all Axis raiders ("rattlesnakes of the Atlantic") operating within American defensive areas. Up to this time such action had evidently been limited to repelling attacks. The isolationists, who loudly proclaimed that under the Constitution only Congress could declare war, denounced the issuance of orders that would lead inexorably to shooting.

The President followed up his shoot-at-sight speech with a vigorous message to Congress, on October 9, 1941, urging repeal of the "crippling provisions" of the Neutrality Act of 1939 so that the nation could better uphold freedom of the seas. In particular, he asked for authority to place guns at once on American merchantmen for defensive purposes against "modern pirates," and he sought a repeal of the combat areas so that American ships could carry lend-lease aid directly to those countries fighting aggression. Senator Glass eloquently expressed interventionist approval when he declared that "we should repeal the whole damn thing." But the isolationists in Congress rallied for a bitter fight against what they regarded as one more step in the direction of open war. The country as a whole favored the change.[22]

Then, on October 17, 1941, came the news that the American destroyer *Kearny*, operating southwest of Iceland, had been seriously damaged but not sunk by a torpedo while engaging, it was later revealed, in a full-fledged battle with a German submarine or submarines.[23] On the same day, the House of Representatives, aroused by the loss of eleven American sailors on the *Kearny*, passed the ship-arming bill by a vote of 259 to 138. German spokesmen promptly denied the attack, and declared that it had been invented by Roosevelt to "bamboozle" Congress into approving the measure. Secretary Hull, when asked if he had made formal representations regarding the

---

seem to have been the only merchantmen flying the American flag whose sinkings were announced before Pearl Harbor, although about a dozen American-owned vessels of Panamanian registry were destroyed.

[22] According to Gallup (Oct. 2, 1941), 62 per cent approved "shoot-at-sight"; 28 per cent disapproved; while 10 per cent had no opinion. In April, 1941, the people had been two to one against permitting American vessels to enter the war zones. In October, Gallup showed that 54 per cent were favorable to sending ships to Britain; 37 per cent were opposed; 9 per cent had no opinion. *Pub. Opin. Quar.*, VI, 162, 163.

[23] Secretary Knox's report, New York *Times*, Oct. 30, 1941, 1:2. On October 29, the United States naval tanker *Salinas* was damaged by a torpedo southwest of Iceland. No lives were lost.

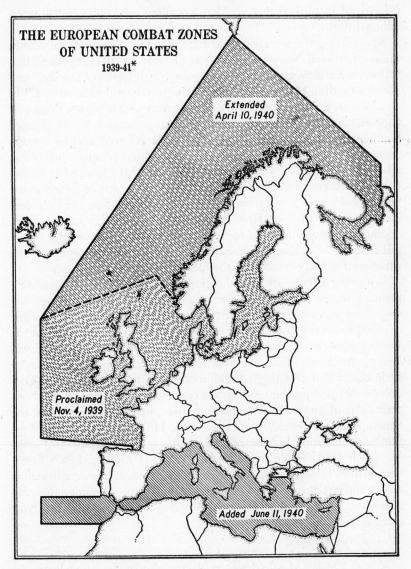

THE EUROPEAN COMBAT ZONES
OF UNITED STATES
1939-41*

Extended
April 10, 1940

Proclaimed
Nov. 4, 1939

Added June 11, 1940

*Zones barred to American citizens and ships by Presidential proclamations under the Neutrality Act of 1939. The extension of June 11, 1940, also included the mouth of the Red Sea. Another zone barred entrance to Canadian Atlantic ports. The national boundaries shown are pre-Hitler.

Kearny affair, replied that one does not often send notes to "an international highwayman." [24]

Recognizing the increasingly critical situation, President Roosevelt, in his sensational Navy Day speech of October 27, 1941, declared that "America has been attacked" by German "rattlesnakes of the sea," and notwithstanding her desire to avoid war, "the shooting has started." In a revelation that suggested the Zimmermann note of 1917, Roosevelt announced that he had a Nazi map in his possession which divided South America into "five vassal states." He referred also to a secret document which indicated that the German regime planned "to abolish all existing religions." The Nazi press branded that "Jewish liar Roosevelt" as a "faker" and a "forger," and damned the whole speech as the "ravings of a lunatic or a criminal." On the same day that the President spoke Secretary Hull declared frankly that the United States was abandoning international law as regards neutrality in favor of "the law of self-defense." [25] This, of course, was but candid official recognition of a situation that had existed since the fall of France in June, 1940.

With the echoes of the shooting-has-started speech resounding throughout the country, the American destroyer *Reuben James* was torpedoed and sunk off western Iceland, on October 30, 1941, while engaged in convoy duty. This was the first armed national vessel of the United States to be destroyed by Germany, and the loss of life was heavy, numbering about one hundred officers and men. There can be little doubt that this tragic event accelerated the movement in Congress for removing the most seriously restrictive sections of the Neutrality Act of 1939. On November 7, 1941, below tense galleries, the Senate voted for repeal, 50 to 37. But the House was in revolt against the Administration because of Roosevelt's failure to press anti-strike legislation, and the slogan of many was: "Get John L. Lewis first—then Hitler." Following a letter from the President urging affirmative action and promising effective intervention in the current labor disputes, the House voted for repeal, on November 13, by the narrow margin of 212 to 194. [26]

[24] *Ibid.*, Oct. 21, 1941, 1:7.

[25] *Ibid.*, Oct. 28, 1941, 4:1. Although the abandonment of conventional neutrality in favor of "the law of self-defense" had begun following the fall of France, the President apparently was reluctant to shock public opinion by openly announcing such a bold step, choosing rather to win over the noninterventionists by repeated appeals to the historic policy of freedom of the seas. Isolationists were quick to point out that this historic policy never embraced the convoying of lend-lease goods through German-proclaimed war zones to enemies of Germany.

[26] The closeness of this vote is misleading. According to Gallup (Oct. 8, 1941), 27 per cent thought the President had gone "too far" in helping Britain; 57 per

Thus "storm-cellar neutrality" was officially abandoned. The Act of 1939, far from being a failure, as the interventionists charged, was too successful. No American merchantman was ever sunk in the combat areas proclaimed by the President because none could legally go there. Such a prohibition in 1917 might have kept the United States out of the war. But this was 1941, and the American people did not wish to stay out of the danger zones, because they desired to bring the maximum amount of help to England. While remaining technically neutral, they wanted to engage in belligerent deeds, and when they found that the Neutrality Act tied their hands, they got rid of those portions that most seriously hampered them.[27] But by this time the nation was really at war; all that lacked was a formal declaration.

SOUTHWARD THE PATH OF EMPIRE

The official blowup came in the Far East, where the American public was least expecting it.[28] Following the invasion of Poland, and particularly following the fall of France, tension between Tokyo and Washington had grown increasingly ominous. The preoccupation of the democracies with the menace of Hitler left the sons of the shoguns free to take giant strides toward what they called the "New Order in East Asia" and the "co-prosperity sphere in Greater East Asia." Europe's distresses cleared the way for Japan's successes.

Throughout these war years, the United States continued to refuse recognition of territorial changes brought about by force; sent assistance to the Chinese, who were resisting Japan's aggression; insisted upon the inviolability of the Open Door; condemned indiscriminate and deliberate bombings of civilians; protested against widespread damage to American property and "strip-and-slap" indignities to American citizens.[29] The Japanese, on the other hand, took the position that

cent voted "about right"; 16 per cent "not far enough." Gallup revealed (Oct. 17, 1941) that 76 per cent of those with opinions approved Roosevelt's foreign policy; 24 per cent disapproved. *Pub. Opin. Quar.*, VI, 161, 163.

[27] Only three sections (2, 3 and 6) of the twenty in the Neutrality Act were repealed, but these were the ones that forbade trade with the belligerents, established combat areas, and prevented the arming of merchantmen. Other provisions, such as those which prohibited loans to belligerents and travel on belligerent ships, were retained.

[28] A Gallup poll, published December 23, 1941, following Pearl Harbor, showed that 64 per cent believed Germany the greater threat; 15 per cent believed Japan the greater threat; 15 per cent believed they were equal threats; 6 per cent were undecided. *Ibid.*, VI, 151–152.

[29] A lengthy list of cases involving damages and indignities was submitted by Roosevelt to Congress as an annex to his message of December 15, 1941. It is con-

as soon as "third Powers" stopped their interference and active support, the "China incident" would be liquidated and peace would come to the Far East. Tokyo also gave assurances that "third Powers" which co-operated with the New Order might expect a legitimate share of trade and investment—a share that would increase under the new era of peace and order established by Nippon.

China was regarded by America as the principal dike against Japanese aggression, and Washington went to extraordinary lengths to render her assistance. This took the form principally of a series of large loans, and the refusal of Roosevelt to invoke the Neutrality Act, thus making possible the shipment of munitions over the famed Burma Road. But the noninvocation of the Neutrality Act was not an unmixed blessing from the Chinese point of view, for America also sold the Japanese vast quantities of scrap iron, gasoline, and other war essentials— to the acute dissatisfaction of the friends of China in the United States and elsewhere.

By January, 1940, when America's denunciation of the commercial treaty of 1911 became effective, Washington was free to impose embargoes on shipments to Japan; but it then declined to do so, as Roosevelt later explained, for fear that the Japanese would be driven into the defenseless Dutch East Indies.[30] Evidently the policy of the Administration was to avoid provoking the militarists in Japan by drastic measures, to take gradual steps so as to impress the conservative elements there with the seriousness of America's position, and to postpone the evil day of a showdown until the ABCD Powers (Americans, British, Chinese, Dutch) were better prepared to combat Nippon. Although the great majority of the American people were unfavorable to an "appeasement" policy, Washington was able to pursue its own plan, in part because the Far East was far away and public sentiment was somewhat lacking in intensity.[31]

---

veniently published in the *Amer. Jour. of Internat. Law*, XXXVI (1942), 95–150 (Official Documents Supplement).

[30] Statement of Roosevelt. New York *Times*, July 25, 1941, 1:8.

[31] In June, 1939, Gallup showed that America was 2 per cent pro-Japanese; 74 per cent pro-Chinese; and 24 per cent neutral. *Pub. Opin. Quar.*, III, 599. In October, 1940, sentiment for an embargo on war materials to Japan was 90 per cent favorable; 10 per cent unfavorable. (These figures were worked out from a poll in which 8 per cent were without opinion.) *Ibid.*, V, 148. The affirmative vote had risen from 37 per cent in October, 1937, 66 per cent in June, 1939, and 82 per cent in August, 1939. *Ibid.*, III, 599; IV, 114. For an illuminating account of how missionary interests in China helped turn American public opinion against the Japanese, see J. W. Masland, "Missionary Influence upon American Far Eastern Policy," *Pacific Hist. Rev.*, X (1941), 279–296.

The fall of France, the desperate plight of Britain, and the semi-defenseless state of orphaned French Indo-China and the Dutch East Indies presented the Japanese, who were bogged down in China and rapidly losing face, with the opportunity of a millennium.[32] On April 15, 1940, Foreign Minister Arita revealed that Japan was eyeing the oil and rubber of the Indies when he declared that Tokyo would be "deeply concerned" over any development that might affect the *status quo* of these rich islands. Two days later Secretary Hull countered by saying that the United States was also concerned lest there be a change by other than peaceful means, and he specifically reminded Japan of her obligations under the Root-Takahira Agreement of 1908 and the Four Power Treaty of 1921. Roosevelt backed up this position, on July 25, 1940, when he issued a proclamation banning the export of oil and scrap metal without license; and five days later decreed that the sale of aviation gasoline was to be restricted to the Western Hemisphere. These, it will be noted, were the initial steps toward the long-talked-of embargo against Japan. The new regulations were nondiscriminatory; yet the Japanese, whose war machinery was heavily dependent upon American aviation gasoline, lodged strong but unavailing protests in Washington.

The restraining hand of Uncle Sam doubtless had much to do with holding back Japan from the coveted riches of the Indies in the spring of 1940. But the situation took a more ominous turn in July, when the Konoye cabinet came into power, with the militant Matsuoka in charge of foreign affairs. Two months later, in September, Tokyo put the screws on the hapless French government and extorted strategic bases in northern Indo-China. Secretary Hull roundly condemned this southward push and, presumably as a countermove, Washington agreed to lend the Chinese government an additional $25,000,000.

On September 27, 1940, a world already steeled against surprises was jolted by the sensational news that Japan had signed a treaty with Germany and Italy, under the terms of which the signatories agreed to attack jointly any Power not then a belligerent which should make war on one of their number. Since Russia, the only other important nonbelligerent, was specifically exempted, no one could doubt that the pact was designed to discourage America from going to war with either the Axis or Japan, lest she have a two-ocean war on her hands.

[32] Indicative of American ignorance of the Far Eastern situation was a Gallup poll of February 23, 1941, which found that while 60 per cent thought that American interests would be threatened by a Japanese occupation of Singapore and the Dutch East Indies, and 20 per cent thought not, an additional 20 per cent were undecided. *Pub. Opin. Quar.*, V, 333.

Washington had known for some time that something of this nature was brewing, and, presumably as a last-minute move to head it off, proclaimed on the previous day an embargo on all scrap iron and steel, save to the Western Hemisphere and Great Britain.

Although Senator Pepper of Florida described the new Triple Alliance as an "international squeeze play," Secretary Hull dismissed it as something which did not "substantially alter a situation which has existed for several years." Many Americans, despite repeated Japanese protestations to the contrary, regarded the whole business as a bluff. None of the three signatories had established an enviable reputation for honoring unpalatable treaty obligations, and it seemed clear that each would act according to its own interests when the crisis came. But it is significant that within two weeks the State Department warned Americans to leave the Far East.[33]

On November 29, 1940, two months after the signing of the Triple Alliance, Tokyo concluded a treaty with its puppet Chinese government at Nanking. Probably as a countermove, Roosevelt announced the next day that the United States was contemplating a credit of $100,-000,000 to China, $50,000,000 of which had already been decided upon. Two days later the Treasury advanced $50,000,000 for the stabilization of Chinese currency. During the ensuing weeks Japanese spokesmen bluntly advised the United States to mind its own business; stoutly reaffirmed Japan's adherence to the new Triple Alliance; offered mediation in the European war; and called upon the white race to cede Oceania to the Asiatics. More portentous than these mere words was the announcement that Matsuoka had signed a Russo-Japanese neutrality pact in Moscow, on April 13, 1941, which ostensibly gave Japan a freer hand to continue her fateful southward surge.

JAPAN SCORES THE FIRST TOUCHDOWN

Affairs drifted along without serious change in the existing tension until July, 1941, when the Konoye cabinet collapsed and was reorganized along more aggressive lines. With Russia reeling under the Nazi sledgehammer, Tokyo promptly made new demands on the helpless French government for the cession of bases in southern Indo-

---

[33] On October 23, 1940, Tokyo denounced the North Pacific Sealing Convention of 1911, effective one year later. Japan explained that she was prepared to negotiate a new pact—in fact, had tried to do so in 1925—because the protection of the seals did not also afford proper safeguards to her vital fishing industry. Jones and Myers, *Documents*, III, 281–282.

China, in addition to those already extorted in the north. When France was forced to yield, on July 23, 1941, the State Department strongly condemned this new act of aggression. Two days later Roosevelt took severe retaliatory action when he issued an order freezing all Japanese assets in the United States. Not to lose face, Tokyo promptly froze American assets in Japan. This drastic move, coupled with the increasingly rigid embargo restrictions of the United States, virtually paralyzed economic intercourse and brought the two nations close to the brink of war.

In August and September, 1941, Japanese-American relations apparently took a slight turn for the better. But on October 16 the Konoye cabinet again collapsed, presumably in large part because of its failure to win Washington's acquiescence, and a militarist group headed by the truculent General Tojo took over. Early the next month Tokyo announced that a special envoy, Saburo Kurusu, was flying to Washington to assist Ambassador Nomura with Japan's "last proposals." When the smiling Kurusu arrived in San Francisco he indicated that he had no more than a fighting chance to succeed, but he hoped to "go through the line for a touchdown."

Given the existing situation, there was indeed little hope for peace. The brutal fact is that the United States was already waging an economic war with Japan, and a shooting (though undeclared) war with Japan's ally, Germany.[34] Eight months before Kurusu arrived in Washington, Congress had passed lend-lease; two months before, the *Greer* had been attacked and Roosevelt had issued shoot-at-sight orders; one month before, the *Kearny* had been torpedoed; and two weeks before, the *Reuben James* had been sunk. If the three-Power Axis alliance had any vitality, Japan could hardly be expected to stay out much longer.

Under the shadow of these incidents Kurusu and Nomura opened negotiations with the State Department. The United States laid down as its basic principles:

1. Respect for the territorial integrity and the sovereignty of each and all nations.

[34] Indicative of the tacit alliance between Britain and America was the public warning of Churchill, on November 10, 1941, that the British would declare war on Japan "within the hour," should the United States become involved in war with Japan. The Congressional investigation of 1945 revealed that at the Atlantic Charter conference Churchill and Roosevelt worked out a protest against Japanese aggression which the Washington government presented to Japan in watered-down form, on August 17, 1941, immediately upon Roosevelt's return. A similar Churchill proposal

2. Support of the principle of non-interference in the internal affairs of other countries.

3. Support of the principle of equality, including equality of commercial opportunity.

4. Non-disturbance of the *status quo* in the Pacific except as the *status quo* may be altered by peaceful means.[35]

The Japanese, on the other hand, argued that they were only seeking peace for Eastern Asia, and that they were being thwarted in this objective by American aid to China and by American embargoes. On November 20, 1941, Tokyo made a show of concession when it offered to move Japanese troops from southern Indo-China to northern Indo-China, provided the United States would co-operate in securing goods for Japan from the Netherlands East Indies, restore commercial relations to the pre-freezing basis, supply Japan with a required quantity of oil, and refrain from "such measures and actions as will be prejudicial to the endeavors for the restoration of general peace between Japan and China." The Tokyo government was willing to remove all Japanese troops from Indo-China upon the restoration of peace in East Asia, and agree not to make any armed advances into Southeastern Asia and the South Pacific.[36]

The high point—and breaking point—of the negotiations came when the State Department, on November 26, 1941, presented its comprehensive note. Japan was to withdraw all her armed forces from China and Indo-China, and lend her support to the Chinese nationalist government at Chungking. As a pledge of future good behavior, Tokyo was to enter into a multilateral nonaggression pact designed to guarantee the stability and territorial inviolability of East Asia. Partially to sweeten the bitter pill, the United States would grant Japan a favorable trade agreement; unfreeze Japanese assets; co-operate in the stabilization of the dollar-yen rate; and work for the abolition of extraterritoriality in China.[37]

Five days later, on December 1, 1941, the Japanese Foreign Minister publicly rejected the principles underlying America's demands as

of November 30, 1941, seems not to have been acted on. New York *Times*, Nov. 25, 1945, 1:8.

[35] *Department of State Bulletin*, V, 538 (Dec. 20, 1941).

[36] *Ibid.*, V, 540 (Dec. 20, 1941).

[37] For text of note see *ibid.*, V, 461–464 (Dec. 13, 1941). Critics of the State Department later called the note of November 26 an ultimatum to Japan; Hull's reply was that the note of November 20 was an ultimatum from Japan.

"fantastic"; [38] but privately Tokyo requested that the discussions con tinue. Yet the time for compromise and concession had evidently passed: the positions of the two nations were in head-on conflict. The United States government, with its various commitments to China, was determined to accept no less than a complete Japanese withdrawal from that country. Japan, after four and one-half years of bloody losses, could not about-face and abandon her vital interests in China. As Tokyo insisted in its formal reply of December 7, "the proposal in question ignores Japan's sacrifices in the four years of the China Affair, menaces the Empire's existence itself and disparages its honor and prestige." [39]

In the midst of the futile conversations in Washington it was learned that the Japanese were massing troops in Indo-China for an invasion of Thailand. Roosevelt cut short his vacation at Warm Springs and rushed back to the capital. On December 2, 1941, he asked Tokyo for explanations; and this proving unavailing, he sent an extraordinary personal message to Emperor Hirohito, on December 6, appealing for peace through a withdrawal of Japanese armed forces in Indo-China.

Subsequent investigations revealed that the United States had "cracked" the Japanese secret code more than a year before Pearl Har- bor; that the high authorities in Washington knew perfectly well that Japan was preparing to attack, especially after the breakdown of negoti- ations on November 26; [40] and that warnings were issued to command- ers in the field, including Hawaii. The official view was that if hostilities were inevitable it was best for American public opinion that Japan should strike the first blow. But the irruption was expected in the Far East, not in Hawaii; and this fact, coupled with faulty liaison between the State Department, the Army, and the Navy, does much to explain the complete surprise. The armed forces had protested that they were not ready to fight Japan, and in response to their urgent pleas for time the State Department had seriously considered a plan to "stall" the Japanese with minor concessions. But the war-ravaged Chinese, who objected to being "sold down the river," reacted so violently as to

---

[38] New York *Times*, Dec. 1, 1941, 1: 6.

[39] *Department of State Bulletin*, V, 469 (Dec. 13, 1941).

[40] The Japanese naval force, though trained earlier for the purpose, did not leave its rendezvous in Japan for Hawaii until November 25, 7 P. M. (Washington time), the day before the November 26 diplomatic impasse. But it could have been recalled by radio a short time before the actual attack. "Investigation of the Pearl Harbor Attack," *Sen. Doc.*, no. 244, 79 Cong., 2 sess., pp. 57, 195 (Committee report of July 20, 1946).

arouse fears that they would withdraw from the conflict. When asked to choose between fighting when unprepared, on the one hand, and losing a valuable ally, on the other, the Roosevelt Administration preferred to risk war. The result was the uncompromising note of November 26; and the Japanese war lords, rather than ultimately be strangled by the American economic blockade, launched their furious hara-kiri attack.

"Remember Pearl Harbor!"

The astounding assault at Pearl Harbor and elsewhere came without a declaration of war, contrary to "the principles of honor and good faith demanded by international law." [41] December 7, 1941—so Roosevelt solemnly told Congress—was "a date which will live in infamy," for on that day the Japanese launched their "unprovoked and dastardly" attack while peaceful conversations were continuing in Washington, "at the solicitation of Japan." [42] The Japanese had clearly been using the continued negotiations as a blind; in fact, many Americans believed that the Kurusu mission had been a blind from the beginning.

The historian may now record that the ghastly gamble of the Japanese was a blunder of the first magnitude. The damage at Pearl Harbor was heavy but not irreparable; and even if there had not been such losses, it is reasonably clear, as Roosevelt later stated, that American naval strength in the Pacific was not sufficient to prevent the fall of Malaya, the Dutch East Indies, and the Philippines.[43] If the Japanese had continued their Hitlerian tactics of piecemeal penetration, if they had moved step by step into Thailand, Malaya, and the Dutch East Indies, the problem of declaring war would have been put squarely before an America which had a large and very vocal isolationist bloc.[44] It is probable that a vote for war might not have been mustered; or if

[41] Lester H. Woolsey, in *Amer. Jour. of Internat. Law*, XXXVI (1942), 78. Mr. Woolsey has here an able discussion of the legal aspects of attack without warning. The Roberts Commission reported that Japan—ostensibly to clear herself of the ignominy of attacking without a declaration—planned to announce a severance of relations in Washington at 1 P.M., Eastern Standard Time, and simultaneously begin the attack, which actually took place twenty-five minutes later. New York *Times*, Jan. 25, 1942, 30: 2. Because of delays in decoding instructions, the Japanese representatives did not see Secretary Hull until one hour after the attack, and their formal reply to the American note of November 26, 1941, at least as published, contained no inkling that relations had been severed. *Ibid.*, Dec. 8, 1941, 11: 1.

[42] *Department of State Bulletin*, V, 474 (Dec. 13, 1941).

[43] Speech of February 23, 1942. *Ibid.*, VI, 185 (Feb. 28, 1942).

[44] A Gallup poll (Aug. 2, 1941) asked whether or not America should take steps to keep Japan from becoming more powerful, even at the risk of war. A total of 51 per cent was favorable; 31 per cent unfavorable; and 18 per cent undecided. By

"Just What They Accomplished by the Attack on Pearl Harbor." (Bishop in the St. Louis *Star-Times*.)

mustered, not until after many months had passed, and then only after embittered debate, injured feelings, partisanship as usual, strikes as usual, growing disunity, and a protracted postponement of the all-out war effort. The torpedoes that sank the American battleships in Pearl Harbor also sank "America Firstism." "The only thing now to do," said isolationist Senator Wheeler, "is to lick hell out of them."

The decision to begin an all-out war, for the first time in the experience of the United States since 1783, was not made by Congress. That body, in the war resolution placed before it, was merely asked to recognize a "state of war" which "has thus been thrust upon the United States" by Japan. On December 8, 1941, the day after Pearl Harbor, the Senate approved the resolution 82 to 0; the House, 388 to 1.[45] On December 11, four days after Pearl Harbor, Germany and Italy announced that they regarded themselves as in a state of war with the United States. Again American opinion was spared the confusion of a debate over fighting the European Axis, for the decision was taken out of the hands of Congress, which formally acted that same day. This time the vote in the Senate was 88 to 0 for war with Germany; in the House, 393 to 0. On the resolution to recognize a state of war with Italy the count was 90 to 0 in the Senate; 399 to 0 in the House. This unprecedented unanimity was in part a recognition of the fact that war had already come; [46] in part, an answer to Pearl Harbor.

FRUITS OF THE GOOD NEIGHBOR POLICY

The United States, though less unprepared than usual, suddenly found itself plunged into a desperate, multi-ocean war, the outcome of which might well depend upon the co-operation of its southern neighbors. Fortunately for it, the Good Neighbor policy had salved many of the wounds of yesteryear; [47] fortunately also for it, the excesses of Naziism had stimulated hemispheric solidarity, particularly

September, the 51 per cent had become 70 per cent; by November, 64 per cent. *Pub. Opin. Quar.*, V, 687; *ibid.*, VI, 163.

[45] The lone dissentient was Representative Jeannette Rankin of Montana, who had also voted "nay" on the war resolution against Germany in 1917. She refrained from voting on the resolutions involving Germany and Italy.

[46] On November 21, 1941, sixteen days before Pearl Harbor but following the loss of the *Reuben James*, Gallup announced that 26 per cent favored a war resolution against Germany; 63 per cent were unfavorable; and 11 per cent were undecided. San José *Mercury Herald*, Nov. 22, 1941, 2:6.

[47] The United States liquidated an embarrassing hang-over from the pre-Good Neighbor period when it officially ended the Dominican customs receivership, on April 2, 1941, pursuant to an agreement signed September 24, 1940.

as evidenced in the "safety belt" devised at Panama, and in the no-transfer resolution adopted at Havana. But much else remained to be done if Pan-Americanism was to be completely changed from a phrase to a fact.

Throughout the war years the Division of Cultural Relations of the Department of State engaged in an intense if somewhat belated and inadequate effort to combat widespread Nazi propaganda in Latin America, particularly in Argentina and Brazil, where there were large and well-organized German populations. A steady stream of good-will missions flowed south from the United States, consisting of pro-fessors, journalists, actors (such as Douglas Fairbanks, Jr.), and other unofficial envoys; while to a lesser extent similar groups traveled north from Latin America. There was some little resentment among the republics to the south against this obvious, eleventh-hour courtship—"good-will slumming" it was cynically called. But on the whole these efforts appear to have been productive of better understanding.

In the interests of co-ordinating hemispheric defense, a half dozen or so military, naval, and economic missions were sent to Latin America or received in the United States. To an increasing degree Washington opened its capacious coffers to the southern republics, notably when it advanced $50,000,000 to Argentina in December, 1940, and when it announced, in October, 1941, that it was prepared to lend $70,000,000 a month to Latin America. On their part, these nations recognized their growing community of interest with the United States, particularly when several of them requisitioned Axis shipping following similar action by Washington, and when some half dozen of them, either formally or informally, made available their defense facilities to their great northern neighbor.[48]

Perhaps most significant of all was the partial *rapprochement* with Argentina. This influential South American country had been reluc-tant to fall behind Washington's leadership, in part because Yankee tariff barriers against Argentine grain, as well as quarantines on meat, had caused a vast amount of bitterness. In January, 1940, the State Department was regretfully forced to announce that negotiations for a trade agreement with both Argentina and Uruguay had completely broken down; and by September the situation had so far deteriorated that Buenos Aires actually proclaimed a temporary embargo on all United States imports. But in the face of the growing Nazi menace

---

[48] When, on November 23, 1941, United States troops took over Dutch Guiana as a protective measure, pursuant to an agreement with the Netherlands government in exile, Brazil gave her formal consent to this action.

these differences were composed and in October, 1941, an important trade agreement was signed.[49]

No less significant was the growing friendliness between Mexico and the United States. When war began in 1939 there was still considerable bitterness on both sides of the border, especially over the unsettled oil-expropriation problem. In May, 1940, Mexico City flatly rejected a proposal from Washington for arbitrating the dispute. But the invasion of the Low Countries acted as a tonic to closer co-operation. The Mexican government, among other things, agreed to collaborate in important defense matters, and refused to protest against the United States blacklist of Axis-connected firms in Mexico, despite pressure from Berlin that it do so. Finally, on November 19, 1941, the two republics were able to announce a pact that was epochal in Mexican-American relations. The United States agreed to help stabilize the peso, purchase Mexican silver, lend money for roads, and begin negotiations for a trade agreement. On her part, Mexico bound herself to make substantial payments on general American claims, and consented to a procedure for settling the oil-expropriation dispute.[50]

The violent attack of the Japanese on a sister republic brought forth many manifestations of hemispheric solidarity from the Latin American countries, and this response was highly gratifying to Washington.[51] The situation contrasted most favorably with 1917 and 1918, when Mexico was downright hostile and other states more or less openly flirted with Germany. It is true that the danger to the Western Hemisphere seemed more acute in 1941 than in 1917; but it is also true that the Good Neighbor policy had laid substantial foundations for a common understanding.

WHY THE WAR CAME TO AMERICA

Someone has said that the writing of history is the process by which a complex truth becomes a simple lie. Complicated though the period from 1939 to 1941 is, several fundamental facts emerge with clarity.

Prior to the fall of France, the American people, by overwhelming majorities, did not want to get into the war. They hoped, by similarly

---

[49] The Trade Agreements Act had been renewed for three years in April, 1940, but only after a close contest in the Senate, where the measure carried by five votes. Gallup (Feb. 4, 1940) found that only 10 per cent of those interviewed understood the term "reciprocal trade treaties." Of those who did, 71 per cent were favorable, while 29 per cent disapproved. *Pub. Opin. Quar.*, IV, 363.

[50] See H. W. Briggs, "The Settlement of Mexican Claims Act of 1942," *Amer. Jour. of Internat. Law*, XXXVII (1943), 222–232.

[51] See *Department of State Bulletin*, V, 545–551 (Dec. 20, 1941).

overwhelming majorities, that the Allied cause would triumph. But they were confident that this victory could be won even though the United States should send only cash-and-carry assistance.

The collapse of France left America writhing on the horns of a cruel dilemma. The great majority of the people still—and to the very end [52]—did not want to enter the fray; the great majority still hoped the Allies would win; a strong minority feared that Hitler would win.[53] But would he be content to stay in Europe? Three fourths of the American people believed that as soon as possible he would seek a lodgment in Latin America, and from there attack the United States.[54] Should he succeed, he would bring his brown shirts, his Jewish pogroms, his Gestapo, his junior Fuehrers. And this would spell the end of American liberties—of "the American way of life."

Hitler scoffed at American fears. "As far as I am concerned," he said in November, 1941, "South America is as far away as the moon." But in 1938 he had also said that he had no more territorial claims in Europe; that he did not "want any Czechs." Charles A. Lindbergh and his America First following insisted that Hitler did not wish to come; that the United States could prevent his coming; and that Americans could "do business with Hitler" when the war was over.

We shall never know whether this was true or not. The American people—faced with Hitler's record of broken promises, pledges, and pacts—were simply unwilling to take a chance.[55] If they guessed wrong, the cost would be catastrophic—the loss of their liberties. The alternative to this kind of guessing was to bolster up Britain, even at the risk of war. The monetary cost of lend-lease would be high, but that would be cheaper than open hostilities. Germany, of course, might

[52] A Gallup poll as late as July 19, 1941, showed that while 21 per cent of those with opinions wanted to go in, 79 per cent still wanted to stay out. *Pub. Opin. Quar.*, V, 680. The figures were exactly the same for October 4, 1941. *Ibid.*, VI, 164.

[53] A Gallup poll (Sept. 17, 1939) revealed that 82 per cent thought the Allies would win; 7 per cent thought Germany would win; while 11 per cent had qualified opinions or none at all. *Ibid.*, IV, 101. After the collapse of the Low Countries, *Fortune* (July, 1940) reported that 40.1 per cent believed Germany would win; 30.3 per cent thought the Allies would win; 29.6 per cent had no positive opinions. *Ibid.*, V, 712. When Hitler failed to invade Britain, a majority gradually began to feel that the Allies might win.

[54] A *Fortune* poll (Aug., 1941) showed that 72.2 per cent believed that Hitler would not be satisfied until he had conquered everything, including the Americas; 14.5 per cent thought that he would engage only in trade penetration; 6.6 per cent thought that he was not interested in America; and 6.7 per cent had no opinion. *Ibid.*, V, 677.

[55] According to a Gallup poll (Nov. 8, 1941), 68 per cent thought it more important that Germany be defeated than that America stay out. In the early months of the war, two out of three had believed the opposite. *Ibid.*, VI, 150–151.

accept the challenge, but that was a risk which the American people were prepared to face. The great majority of them were convinced that it was better to render all-out assistance while Britain was still afloat than to wait until Britain went under, and then prepare alone—and in the face of great odds—for the fight to the finish with Hitler. So America sent aid to Britain, and war came.[56]

The American people were not dragged into the conflict by the munitioneers, the profiteers, or the sloganeers. They were not seduced by Allied propaganda. They did not go in primarily to fight for Britain. They entered upon what they regarded as a war of self-defense because they felt, overwhelmingly, that their most precious traditions and institutions were menaced by international gangsters.[57]

The people of the United States believed that the world cannot endure half Fascist and half free.

BIBLIOGRAPHICAL NOTE

See the detailed references for the previous chapter, all of which are relevant. J. E. Davies, *Mission to Moscow* (N.Y., 1941), is a favorable appraisal of the Soviet regime by the United States ambassador in Moscow. Of the various secondary accounts the following may be noted: W. C. Johnstone, *The United States and Japan's New Order* (N.Y., 1941), which is an able analysis based primarily on published documents; C. A. Buss, *War and Diplomacy in Eastern Asia* (N.Y., 1941), a readable work more general in scope; and W. W. Willoughby, *Japan's Case Examined* (Baltimore, 1940), an unfavorable summation by an adviser of the Chinese Embassy in Washington. H. S. Quigley, *Far Eastern War, 1937–1941* (Boston, 1942), treats the United States in the larger setting. Charles Wertenbaker, *A New Doctrine for the Americas* (N.Y., 1941), is an interesting journalistic sketch of United States relations with Latin America, particularly in recent years. C. H. Haring, *Argentina and the United States* (Boston, 1941), is a brief but well-balanced account, with particular attention to current problems. W. S. Holt, "The United States and the Defense of the Western Hemisphere, 1815–1940," *Pacific Hist. Rev.*, X (1941), 28–38, outlines the problem of Pan-American co-operation for defense from the beginning, with emphasis on the abor-

[56] From polls and other sources it is reasonably clear what the people wanted—much clearer than in 1917. In general, also, public opinion was ahead of Congressional action. But whether that opinion was well founded; what influences were at work shaping it, including the Administration; and whether Roosevelt's leadership was wise—all these are questions that cannot be finally answered without proper perspective, the complete official documents, and the essential private papers.

[57] President Roosevelt wrote in a preface to his published papers (July 17, 1941): "Our policy is not based primarily on a desire to preserve democracy for the rest of the world. It is based primarily on a desire to protect the United States and the Western Hemisphere from the effects of a Nazi victory upon ourselves and upon our children." *The Public Papers of Franklin D. Roosevelt: 1940 Volume* (N.Y., 1941), p. xxx.

tive move by Wilson in 1914. Further references: see footnotes of this chapter and the references at the end of the preceding chapter.

NEW REFERENCES. Sumner Welles, *The Time for Decision* (N.Y., 1944), has considerable material on the Atlantic Charter and the final negotiations with Japan. Roosevelt wanted the Atlantic Charter so as to avoid Wilson's mistake of not agreeing on war aims in advance (p. 174). F. Davis and E. K. Lindley, *How War Came: An American White Paper; From the Fall of France to Pearl Harbor* (N.Y., 1942), is high-class journalism, in part officially inspired and hence favorable to the Roosevelt administration; there is much useful though undocumented material. One of the same authors, Forrest Davis, wrote *The Atlantic System: The Story of Anglo-American Control of the Seas* (N.Y., 1941), which is less revealing. Frederick Moore, *With Japan's Leaders* (N.Y., 1942), is by an official counsellor who saw a good deal of the Japanese embassy in Washington at close range just before Pearl Harbor. T. A. Bisson, *America's Far Eastern Policy* (N.Y., 1945), is a sound survey; G. E. Taylor, *America in the New Pacific* (N.Y., 1942), is broadly interpretative; and E. A. Falk, *From Perry to Pearl Harbor* (Garden City, N.Y., 1943), is a journalistic sketch with emphasis on naval development. E. M. Earle, *Against This Torrent* (Princeton, 1941), is a cogent plea for intervention to protect fundamental freedoms. J. W. Masland, "Commercial Influence upon American Far Eastern Policy, 1937–1941," *Pacific Hist. Rev.*, XI (1942), 281–299, shows that American business interests had little influence on Washington's policy; they were subordinated to American security.

4TH ED. REFS. *The Memoirs of Cordell Hull* (2 vols., N.Y., 1948) are valuable; the author insists that not he but the Japanese presented an ultimatum. Norman Hill, "Was There an Ultimatum before Pearl Harbor?" *Amer. Jour. of Internat. Law*, XLII (1948), 355–367, concludes that neither side presented a bona fide ultimatum. H. L. Stimson and M. Bundy, *On Active Service in Peace and War* (N.Y., 1947), reveals that Stimson disapproved strongly of Roosevelt's uncandid methods of dealing with the convoy-submarine issue (pp. 368–376). Consult R. E. Sherwood, *Roosevelt and Hopkins* (N.Y., 1948), especially on aid to Russia. See also S. E. Morison, *The Battle of the Atlantic* (Boston, 1947), which reveals that a U.S. destroyer dropped depth charges near a U-boat as early as April 10, 1941 (p. 57). The same author's *The Rising Sun in the Pacific, 1931–April, 1942* (Boston, 1948), notes that Japan would have rejected the *modus vivendi* (p. 75), and concludes that the oil embargo and assets freezing made war inevitable (p. 63). The best-balanced single-volume account of the events leading to Pearl Harbor is Walter Millis, *This is Pearl!* (N.Y., 1947). Light is thrown on the situation in Hawaii by S. D. Porteus, *And Blow Not the Trumpet* (Palo Alto, Calif., 1947). George Morgenstern, *Pearl Harbor: The Story of the Secret War* (N.Y., 1947), grossly misuses evidence in an attempt to prove that Roosevelt conspired to get the country into war. C. A. Beard, *President Roosevelt and the Coming of the War, 1941* (New Haven, 1948), does essentially the same thing more subtly. While presenting many unpalatable truths, he has written a prosecutor's brief rather than a sound historical treatise. The report of the Congressional committee on Pearl Harbor (July 20, 1946) is in *Sen. Doc.*, no. 244, 79 Cong., 2 sess. Dividing generally along partisan lines, the majority report absolves Roosevelt and his associates of inciting the Japanese; the minority report finds them guilty.

CHAPTER XLVII

The Diplomacy of Co-ordination

"We shall have to take the responsibility for world collaboration, or we shall have to bear the responsibility for another world conflict." Franklin D. Roosevelt, reporting to Congress on the Yalta Conference, March 1, 1945.

TIMES THAT TRIED MEN'S SOULS

THE sneak attack at Pearl Harbor plunged the United States into war with the most devastating naval defeat in its history. The ensuing year was an almost unbroken nightmare, and the United Nations, in order to keep afloat, were forced at times to throw principle to the sharks of expediency.[1] Even so, the government in Washington made a determined effort to adhere to the basic principles of the Atlantic Charter.

On the day of Pearl Harbor the Russians were desperately defending their capital, having lost invaluable agricultural and industrial areas; the Chinese were being kept alive by the scanty and uncertain nourishment motored over the backdoor Burma Road. The bomb-shattered British were in deadly peril: their Mediterranean lifeline had been cut by Italy, and their naval ascendancy was jeopardized by the danger that Hitler might at any moment wring the French fleet from the Vichy government of unoccupied France. The German U-boat campaign was shifted to American waters shortly after Pearl Harbor, and for many terrible months sinkings exceeded launchings. The submarine blockade of the American coast and of the British Isles became so critical that the United States, already hanging on by its finger tips in the Pacific, was forced to transfer powerful naval units to the Atlantic.

The Philippines were speedily engulfed, and the riches of the East Indies fell like overripe fruit to the sons of the Rising Sun. The "impregnable" fortress of Singapore, with its gigantic guns pointing

[1] President Roosevelt on one occasion revived an ancient Balkan proverb: "In times of great peril, my son, you may walk with the Devil until you have crossed the bridge." Quoted in the *New Republic*, Sept. 10, 1945, p. 307.

proudly out to sea, was taken from the rear by infiltrating jungle fighters, and the United States was deprived of vital supplies of rubber and tin. The little yellow men were now on the road to Mandalay; Burma was an easy conquest, and with it went the lifeline to China. The Japanese next seized islands in the Bay of Bengal, and destiny seemingly beckoned to India, where the scantily clad Gandhi and his followers were in a state of near rebellion.

Australia was placed in jeopardy when the Mikado's minions easily secured bases to the north on New Britain, New Guinea, and the Solomons. Brilliant operations by American naval and aerial forces in the Coral Sea, at Midway, and near the Solomons repelled Japanese thrusts, though not until the enemy had seized Attu and Kiska in the fog-girt Aleutians, uncomfortably close to the North American mainland. Within a few weeks Japan had won a staggeringly rich empire; and if given time to consolidate her gains, she would control the destinies of half the world's population. Henceforth the Pacific war was largely a race between Japanese exploitation and American production.

The dreary days of 1942—days of defeat and retreat—held still more disagreeable surprises. The Nazis aimed a knockout punch at the oil of the Caucasus, synchronizing the northern arm of their pincers with that of the "Desert Fox" Marshal Rommel, whose armored Afrika Korps raced across the sands of North Africa and was halted almost within sight of Alexandria and the Suez Canal. Had he broken through and effected a junction with the Japanese in India, the war might well have been lost. But he failed, and the other arm of the pincers, having thrust deep into the Caucasus, was amputated at heroic Stalingrad.

By the end of that dismal 1942—"nineteen fortitude" it was called —the crisis had passed, and the initiative was wrested from the enemy. The Russians were about to launch their gigantic winter offensive —a forward movement which was never seriously reversed. Marshal Rommel, crushed at El Alamein, was scurrying across North Africa with the British in hot pursuit. The "end of the beginning" definitely came when, in November, 1942, a tidal wave of American boys hit the coast of French North Africa and, joined by their Allies, assailed Rommel from the rear. On the far side of the world the United States marines had won their toehold in the steaming jungles of Guadalcanal, and the Japanese were in retreat across the mountains of New Guinea, having failed in their thrust toward Australia.

With America's mighty productive power gradually being thrown upon the scales, it seemed to be no longer a question of victory, but how long victory would take. Italy surrendered in September, 1943. Long-awaited "D-Day" came when American and Allied troops splashed ashore on the beaches of French Normandy, June 6, 1944. Nutcrackered between the advancing Allies in the west and the Russians in the east, the Germans formally surrendered on May 8, 1945. The final step was to transfer Allied forces to the Far East and blast Japan into submission.

The point to remember is that the war could have been lost in 1942, and almost was lost. Time was of the essence. The conventional diplomatic dallying seemed like criminal folly in the face of the danger that a few months or even weeks of extra time might enable Hitler to perfect a secret weapon, and thus make impossible an invasion of Fortress Europe.

THE NATIONS UNITED

The hodgepodge of nations that had been forced into war against the Axis constituted an overwhelming proportion of the population and resources of the globe. If they could be given time and opportunity to overcome their unpreparedness and co-ordinate their vast strength, they were certain to win. The great secret weapon of Nazi Germany was not a man-made meteor but propaganda—especially anti-Soviet propaganda—designed to split the Allies. Unity was a crying need.

Two weeks after Pearl Harbor, Prime Minister Churchill and his advisers arrived in Washington and entered upon extended discussions with President Roosevelt and the representatives of other co-belligerents. The upshot was the memorable Declaration of the United Nations, dated January 1, 1942, and signed by the representatives of twenty-six countries at war with the Axis. This solemn pronouncement bound the signatories to the principles of the Atlantic Charter; assured the full employment of resources against the common enemy; and pledged no separate armistice or peace.[2] Nations not yet at war with the Axis were privileged to sign later.

The Declaration of the United Nations is of epochal significance in American diplomatic history. It not only insured unity for war but provided the nucleus of a new world organization for peace. It was in effect a binding military alliance, and as such a significant departure from America's centuries-old nonentanglement tradition. It was not a treaty formally approved by the Senate, but an executive

[2] Text and other data in L. M. Goodrich, ed., *Documents on American Foreign Relations* (Boston, 1942), IV, 203–209.

agreement signed by the President. It was immediately and widely applauded in the United States—a reaction which revealed both the desperate need for Allied unity and the growing maturity of the American people in international affairs.

But unity among the Allies was easier to achieve on paper than in practice. The problem was complicated by great confusion in the United States over war aims. Most Americans knew what they were fighting *against* rather than what they were fighting *for:* America had been attacked and her aggressors had to be punished and shackled. A year after Pearl Harbor nearly four out of ten persons could confess that they had no clear idea of why they were waging war. Many people felt that the nation should fight first and think about peace afterwards; others believed that in time of war one should prepare for peace. There was heated dispute as to whether Hitler or Hirohito was Public Enemy Number One. There was even a strong reluctance to recognize that by the time of Pearl Harbor the global war had become America's war; *as late as 1945 eight out of ten persons believed that in December, 1941, Roosevelt should have been trying to keep the country out of the conflict.*[3] One can only surmise what the disunity would have been if the perpetrators of Pearl Harbor had not electrified the nation.

The American and British peoples, wedded by a common foe, enjoyed unusually close relations during the war years, particularly through joint boards and other agencies. Canadian industry was further meshed with that of the United States, and although President Roosevelt was rebuffed by the Senate for a third time when he tried to revive the St. Lawrence waterway project,[4] other joint enterprises were pursued with harmony, notably the great "Alcan" highway to Alaska and the Canol oil project. The presence of considerable American forces in other British outposts, such as India and Australia, combined with the operations of lend-lease,[5] established new relationships and further

---

[3] National Opinion Research Center, *Opinion News,* April 3, 1945, p. 1. Compare this 80% of 1945 with the 79% of 1941 who had declared that the United States should not enter the war *now.* Gallup poll (Oct. 4, 1941), *Pub. Opin. Quar.,* VI, 164.

[4] The Senate vote (December 12, 1944) was 56 to 25, despite a last-minute plea from Roosevelt. In 1942 the two governments made temporary provision for the seals, following Japan's denunciation of the 1911 convention. L. M. Goodrich and M. J. Carroll, eds., *Documents on American Foreign Relations* (Boston, 1945), VI, 586–597. A *Fortune* poll (June, 1942) indicated that only 24% of the American people would welcome the annexation of Canada; a Gallup poll in Canada (June 22, 1943) found as many as 21% favorable. *Pub. Opin. Quar.,* VI, 493; VII, 504.

[5] Virtually identical Master Lend-Lease Agreements with the principal Allies, beginning with Britain on February 23, 1942, provided that the beneficiaries would furnish United States forces with reverse lend-lease goods, and in this way lessen the

widened horizons. Australia and England both provided an unexpected and unofficial type of reverse lend-lease in the persons of thousands of war brides.

The British Isles, which received enormous shipments of lend-lease supplies and which were used as advanced bases for training American troops, took on a new importance. Although the British resented the intrusion of the United States into their perennial Indian problem, and although the two countries differed sharply on policy toward groups in the occupied or liberated countries (France, Italy, Greece), these were but minor ripples on the surface of a new cordiality. By early 1945 Anglophobia and isolation had so far disappeared that six out of ten Americans could favor a permanent military alliance with Great Britain.[6]

MORAL TONIC FOR CHINA

At the time of Pearl Harbor, China was in a desperate plight, ravaged and exhausted by more than four years of fighting. She was vastly enheartened by the Japanese attack, for with America and Britain on her side the hour of deliverance had surely come. The hour of disillusionment came instead. The myth of white supremacy was dealt a shattering blow when the Americans and British were hurled out of the Far East. The United States and Great Britain, unable to conduct a full-fledged war on both sides of the world, wisely decided to concentrate first on Hitler, while leaving China to the tender mercies of Nippon. There was grave danger that disheartened China, potential springboard for an invasion of Japan, would be forced to come to terms with her foe.

The American public, ignorant of strategic necessities, brought considerable pressure on Washington to make Hirohito instead of Hitler the number one priority, and demanded that in any event there be less verbal and more material assistance for China.[7] A half-billion dollar loan was authorized in February, 1942, and two months later

---

total bill. Vague provision was also made for a postwar settlement of accounts. E. R. Stettinius, Jr., *Lend-Lease: Weapon for Victory* (N.Y., 1944), pp. 163–164, 340–347.

[6] *Pub. Opin. Quar.*, IX, 47.

[7] Senator A. B. ("Happy") Chandler of Kentucky, soon to be made "baseball czar," was a leader in 1943 of the get-Hirohito-first group. Acclaimed by former isolationists, he declared that America's European allies would forsake her when Germany was crushed, and that Japan should not be given time to dig in. The New York *Herald Tribune* prayed to be "spared the braying of this long-eared legislator. . . ." *Current Biography, 1943,* p. 120.

an aerial Burma Road ("over the hump") was established from India to China, enabling American flyers to scrape over the world's loftiest mountains with a growing driblet of supplies. The aid-for-China campaign was highlighted by a visit to the United States of the American-educated Madame Chiang Kai-shek, charming wife of the Generalissimo, whose personal appeal to the House of Representatives, in February, 1943, was tumultuously applauded.

Yet vastly more than handclapping was needed to bolster China's sagging morale, and to offset Japanese propaganda charging that the Occident was determined to continue its exploitation and discrimination in the Orient. The State Department therefore announced in the autumn of 1942 that the United States was prepared to sign a treaty renouncing its extraterritorial and other special privileges in China, some of them nearly a hundred years old. This dramatic announcement, following Wendell L. Willkie's globe-girdling stop in Chungking, aroused jubilation among the Chinese. The ensuing negotiations moved rapidly, paralleling similar steps by the British, and on January 11, 1943, the treaty was formally signed.[8] It was in effect a juridical declaration of independence for China, and did much to remove from her the stigma of semi-colonial status and put her on an equal footing with the other United Nations.

Yet Chinese immigrants, like other Orientals, were still completely excluded from the United States by the Act of 1924. President Roosevelt, responding to popular agitation, sent a message to Congress (October 11, 1943) recommending that the Chinese be put on the quota basis like Europeans and be granted naturalization privileges as well. He urged that this be done to "correct a historic mistake and silence the distorted Japanese propaganda." Congress was already considering such legislation, and it moved all the more willingly because China was an ally and Japan was a foe. The act that was passed (signed December 17, 1943) made thousands of Chinese aliens in America eligible for citizenship, and permitted 105 immigrants to enter annually from China. This memorable law, though a move in the direction of nondiscrimination, served to underscore the remaining discrimination against other Asiatic nationalities. Many liberal Americans thought it strange that in a war against Hitler, high priest of the master-race

[8] The treaty was unanimously approved by the Senate, February 11, 1943. Similar negotiations were near success in 1931 when the Japanese invaded Manchuria. See T. A. Bisson, *America's Far Eastern Policy* (New York, 1945), pp. 28, 137–140. For treaty text and other data, consult L. M. Goodrich and M. J. Carroll, eds., *Documents on American Foreign Relations* (Boston, 1944), V, 485–501.

cult, the United States should continue its laws against "inferior" peoples.[9]

Chinese-American relations suffered a sharp setback in succeeding months when reports of totalitarian control and other antidemocratic practices leaked out of China, together with alleged evidence that the Nationalist government of Chiang Kai-shek was more intent on using lend-lease supplies to fight the Chinese Communists than the Japanese. The United States and Britain were nevertheless committed to bolstering up China as the Asiatic counterpoise against a resurgent Japan. China was to be mistress in her own house, and under no compulsion to grant special privileges to outsiders. The multi-Power Open Door was presumably dead, for it had been a valid concept only when the Chinese were too weak to protect themselves against extortion or aggression. Henceforth, if things worked out as planned, a fully sovereign China would be the guardian of her own door—a unilateral open door.

"A RIDDLE WRAPPED IN A MYSTERY" [10]

The weakest link in the unity of the United Nations was Russia. She was the key to the winning of the war, for her stout warriors "clawed the guts" out of the German army (in the phrase of Churchill) and saved the Western Allies. She was the key to the peace, for she was potentially the greatest Power, and could become, if she refused to co-operate for peace, the world's greatest menace.[11]

The naked truth is that Russia was deeply suspicious of her allies, and not without reason. They had in 1918–1920 opposed the "foul baboonery of Bolshevism" (Churchill's phrase) with considerable vigor, utilizing both money and armed intervention, and they had been slow to accord official recognition to Moscow. The United States had been the slowest of the major Powers. The Russian people traditionally have been suspicious of foreigners, but American policy since 1917 had done little to quiet their fears.

[9] Some Congressmen opposed the law because they feared that it would be the entering wedge for an Oriental deluge; even the 105 would have a bad effect on unemployment! Others felt that the law did not go far enough, for the Chinese still did not have all the privileges of Europeans. A number of other nations followed the example of the United States and removed discrimination against Chinese. See Bisson, *op. cit.*, pp. 140–143; Goodrich and Carroll, *Documents*, VI, 607–617.

[10] Churchill referred to Russia (October 1, 1939) as "a riddle wrapped in a mystery inside an enigma. . . ."

[11] See Sumner Welles, *The Time for Decision* (N.Y., 1944), pp. 334–335. Welles was Under Secretary of State, 1937–1943.

The Western Powers had rebuffed Russia's proposals for disarmament in the 1930's, whether made sincerely or not, and had left her out in the cold at the time of Munich. Reactionary groups in France and England had wanted to egg Hitler onto Stalin so that the two menaces would kill each other off; instead, Stalin turned the tables in his fateful nonaggression pact of 1939. When the Soviets reoccupied former Russian territory in Poland and in the Baltic states, the United States not only refused to recognize these territorial changes, but together with Britain extended recognition to the increasingly anti-Russian Polish government-in-exile at London.[12] And when Russia in 1939–1940 sought the acquisition of territory in Finland so as to protect Leningrad, the Western Powers—Britain, France and the United States—took steps that verged on war.

After Pearl Harbor, Stalin had other grievances. He was offended by America's willingness, even though in the name of military expediency, to traffic with Fascist elements in France and Italy. He was annoyed by Washington's reluctance to break relations with Finland, long after that tiny nation had entered the war against him and was attacking Leningrad. He was dissatisfied with the trickle of lend-lease supplies which America, colossus of production, was able during 1942 to send him over circuitous and hazardous routes.

More vexatious to Moscow was the refusal of Britain and the United States to open a real second front in Western Europe until their preparations were complete. The suspicion grew in the Kremlin that the Allies, fearful of a potent postwar Russia, wanted her "bled white" before they moved into the fray. When Drew Pearson, the well-known columnist, charged that this was the official policy of the State Department, Secretary Hull ringingly replied that such statements were "monstrous and diabolical falsehoods." [13] Even after the North African and Italian campaigns were opened, these operations engaged so few of the common enemy that Stalin stubbornly refused to recognize them as a real second front.

To cap it all, irresponsible agitators in America, unconsciously paralleling the German propaganda line, were openly twisting the bear's tail by predicting that the next great war would have to be with the engulfing Communist menace. Such fears multiplied as the

[12] The United States continued to recognize the Washington envoys of Latvia, Lithuania, and Estonia throughout the entire war. Sumner Welles excused Soviet conduct on the ground that Stalin was trying to establish regional security by setting up friendly governments on his borders, much as the United States has done in Latin America. *Ibid.*, pp. 332–333.

[13] *Department of State Bulletin*, IX, 154.

Soviet armies neared Berlin. The Russian army newspaper, *Red Star*, complained bitterly of such a headline in Hearst's New York *Journal-American* as "RED WAVE THREATENS TO DROWN CHRISTIAN CIVILIZATION," and of a headline in the Chicago *Tribune*, "SOVIET UNION IS ONLY AGGRESSOR IN THE WORLD." [14]

THE SHADOW OF THE HAMMER AND SICKLE

American suspicions of Russia, on the other hand, were far from unjustified. In the 1920's and 1930's Moscow had undeniably sponsored a vigorous propaganda for world revolution through the Communist International (Comintern). Even before the outbreak of World War II the Russian regime had become more practical and realistic, but most Americans were ignorant of this change. As one versifier put it:

> When to sleep I lay my head
> Upon my bed,
> I'm sure a Russian's underneath,
> Armed to the teeth,
> Or, if not that,
> At least a British diplomat.[15]

Some of this distrust was removed when, on May 22, 1943, Moscow announced the dissolution of the Comintern, and a year later the Communist party in the United States declared itself dissolved.

Bloody Soviet purges, restrictions on personal liberty, control of the press, and especially attacks on religion—Karl Marx's "opiate of the masses"—had aroused deep distrust in the United States, particularly among Catholics. Before Pearl Harbor the Soviets had taken some steps to restore the Church, but in America these facts were not known or were disbelieved. Ignorance rather than religious faith was the real barrier in the path of better relations.[16]

[14] Quoted in San Francisco *Chronicle*, Jan. 6, 1945. A *Fortune* survey (Sept., 1945, p. 234) revealed that 73% of the American people could think of nothing the United States had done since World War I to cause Russia to doubt America's friendship. W. L. White's highly critical *Report on the Russians* (N.Y., 1945), a best-seller based on a six-week tour and widely publicized by the *Reader's Digest*, caused bitterness in Russia reminiscent of America's early reaction to British travel books.

[15] *New York Times Magazine*, July 15, 1945, p. 18. In contrast with the overwhelming sentiment for military alliance with Britain, wartime polls found opinion rather evenly divided on a similar pact with Russia. *Pub. Opin. Quar.*, IX, 49–50, 254.

[16] Special surveys during the war revealed that only one American in ten was even reasonably well informed about the Soviet economic and political organization. One in three distrusted Russia. Wealthy and conservative Americans (hence better edu-

Stalin may have had compelling reasons for freeing Hitler in 1939 to attack the Western Powers, for assaulting Finland, and for absorbing former Russian territory, but to the outside world this all spelled aggression. These suspicions were inflamed, after Pearl Harbor, by the unwillingness of the Soviets to share military secrets with their allies, and by their practice of unilaterally recognizing or establishing governments in reconstructed Europe that were pleasing or subservient to Moscow.

Most serious of all to many Americans was the failure of Stalin to attack Japan, or at least to offer Siberian bases so that the Pacific war might be shortened. Such persons seem not to have realized that Russia had to exert every ounce of her strength to beat back Germany, that if she had attacked Japan she might have fallen prey to both foes, and that if this had happened her Siberian bases would have been useless to herself or to her allies.

If Russians were annoyed by American news-

"He Won't Talk" (Manning in *Phoenix Republic and Gazette* Syndicate)

papers, Americans were no less annoyed by theirs. Communist journals like *Pravda* and *Izvestia* repeatedly launched inexplicable attacks, even upon such a staunch friend of Russia as Wendell L. Willkie. Although it could not be proved that these tirades were inspired by the Kremlin,

cated and informed) showed considerable confidence in Russia, while the poorer groups, to whom Communism was supposed to appeal, revealed the most distrust. *Fortune,* Sept., 1945, pp. 233–243; Nat. Opin. Research Center, *Opinion News,* July 10, 1945, pp. 1–4; Nov. 13, 1945, pp. 3–6; *Pub. Opin. Quar.,* VIII, 426, 455, 513–522, 588–589; IX, 225, 254.

it seemed clear that they could have been suppressed if the government had so desired. A long and rocky road would clearly have to be traveled before Soviet-American relations could even begin to approach cordiality.

GLOBAL DIPLOMACY

The prevalence of disunity among the Allies pointed to the necessity of conferences for a closer co-ordination of the war effort. Some two weeks after Pearl Harbor, on December 22, 1941, Prime Minister Churchill, with cigar embedded in cherubic features, dropped out of the skies for extended discussions in Washington with President Roosevelt. He signed the United Nations pact, and addressed a joint session of Congress, truthfully promising "many disappointments and unpleasant surprises," but urging the two peoples to "walk together in majesty, in justice and in peace." A new day had indeed dawned when the first wartime British prime minister to visit the United States could receive an ovation from a Congress whose original hall had been burned by British troops in 1814.

Six months later (June 18–27, 1942) Churchill and his aides came again for extended strategy conferences, in which the Washington representatives of China and Russia participated. The headlines were proclaiming disaster to Allied arms in Libya, yet the conferees issued optimistic statements and promised an attack that would relieve the German pressure on Russia.

The sensational Allied landings in North Africa redeemed the promise made at Washington but created problems which necessitated another conference (January 14–24, 1943), this time in recently captured Casablanca, French Morocco, under conditions of danger and secrecy. Roosevelt flew the Atlantic for the first time, inspected American troops in a jeep, lunched from a regular mess kit, and engaged in protracted conversations with Churchill and other Allied leaders.[17] Stalin, though cordially invited, was busy directing the giant Soviet offensive, but both he and Chiang Kai-shek were kept fully informed of developments. Roosevelt requested that this meeting be called the "Unconditional Surrender Conference" because the conferees solemnly agreed that the war would be waged until the enemy surrendered unconditionally. American opinion generally applauded the idea of unconditional surrender, though isolationist Sen-

[17] For relevant documents, see Goodrich and Carroll, *Documents*, V, 251–255. Roosevelt was the first President to leave the United States in wartime; the first since Lincoln to visit a fighting zone.

ator Wheeler of Montana later branded it as a "brutal" and "asinine" policy.[18]

Some four months later the pudgy British prime minister again came to Washington (May 11–27, 1943) and, with the North African campaign ending, laid plans for further military blows. Again addressing a joint session of Congress, Churchill received an ovation when he vigorously replied to Senator A. B. ("Happy") Chandler of Kentucky, who had claimed that as soon as the European phase of the war ended, Britain would leave the United States in the lurch. Churchill returned to America for conferences at high-cliffed Quebec (August 17–24, 1943), to which both he and Roosevelt journeyed after preliminary meetings at the President's Hyde Park estate in New York. A Chinese representative was present at Quebec, though Stalin was not, presumably because the discussions chiefly concerned the war with Japan.

Anglo-American-Chinese co-ordination was clearly proceeding satisfactorily, but that with Russia was not. Stalin was plainly aggrieved over the Allied failure to open a real second front. Even while the Quebec conference was in session the Soviet army paper *Red Star* complained that the Allied Mediterranean operations had "failed to divert a single German division" from Russia. Russo-American relations were dangerously tense by the late summer of 1943.

At this critical juncture Cordell Hull stepped into the breach. The seventy-two year old Secretary, suffering from poor health and plagued by heavy criticism of his Department, boarded an airplane for the first time, and undertook the wearisome round trip to Moscow, where he conferred with British Foreign Secretary Eden and Soviet Foreign Commissar Molotov (October 19–31, 1943). Discussions proceeded with unexpected cordiality, and on the last night Stalin played host to the Allied delegates at a dinner in the Kremlin. A series of declarations was forthcoming from the conference, the most memorable of which pledged the four Powers (including China) to the establishment of a new organization for peace.[19]

The Moscow Conference—a personal triumph for Secretary Hull —was one of the great Allied victories of the war. It broke the log jam of non-co-ordination, for henceforth Russia was actively represented in international conferences dealing with non-Far Eastern sub-

---

[18] One survey found opinion 81% favorable, though 12% did not know what the phrase "unconditional surrender" meant. Nat. Opin. Research Center, *Opinion News*, March 20, 1945, p. 2.

[19] Goodrich and Carroll, *Documents*, VI, 226–232. The Chinese ambassador in Moscow signed the declaration for an international organization.

jects, and later even with Far Eastern subjects. The conference also pledged the Powers to establish a new world organization, and set the machinery in motion for the tentative Dumbarton Oaks draft and the final San Francisco Charter. Hull returned a conquering hero, received the warm greetings of President Roosevelt at the Washington airport, and responded to an unprecedented invitation from Congress to present a personal report on his trip.[20]

THE ROAD TO YALTA

The Pacific theater, where the tide had turned, was now claiming increased attention. With American marines driving on to the Gilbert Islands ("Bloody Tarawa"), Roosevelt secretly journeyed to Cairo, Egypt, where, near the shadow of the Pyramids, he took part in a memorable conference on the Far East (November 22-26, 1943). Stalin was not present, though a Russian delegate discussed non-Japanese subjects, but Chiang Kai-shek was there, with his cultured wife as interpreter. The meeting was a milestone in Allied collaboration, for it was the first time that the head of the Chinese state had taken part in a conference with Roosevelt and Churchill.

The ensuing declaration of Cairo, while disavowing any aggressive territorial designs, pledged that Japan would be shorn of all the Pacific islands which she had occupied or seized since 1914, and that China would be given back Manchuria, Formosa, and the Pescadores.[21] Japanese-dominated Korea was promised her independence "in due course"—a vague phrase that alarmed Korean nationalists. The Cairo declaration was a public pledge to force the Japanese genie back into the pre-Perry bottle, and while it may have steeled the slant-eyed sons of Nippon to more fanatical resistance, it bolstered the morale of the Chinese and other exploited peoples of the Far East.

From Cairo, Roosevelt and Churchill secretly flew to the Iranian capital, Teheran, where they met with Marshal Stalin in the compound of the Russian embassy. The four-day discussion (November 28-December 1, 1943) was primarily military, and designed specifically to co-ordinate the Soviet attack on Germany with the forthcoming Anglo-American second front in France. This decision evidently pleased Stalin and cleared the air, for the Russians could no longer complain of being treated as step-brothers in arms. Although the three

---

[20] November 18, 1943. *Ibid.*, pp. 11–16.

[21] *Ibid.*, pp. 232–233. Precautions had to be taken at Cairo to guard the Allied statesmen against Axis plots. One expense item read, "six fezzes for the FBI." New York *Times*, Dec. 5, 1943, IV, 1: 6.

leaders pledged themselves to make an enduring peace, the most important diplomatic result was that for the first time the Sphinx of the Kremlin had consented to meet as one of the Big Three.[22]

The German lines were everywhere buckling when, some fourteen months later (February 4–11, 1945), the Big Three met again behind a veil of secrecy at Yalta, a beautiful but Nazi-ravaged health resort on the warm southern shore of the Crimean peninsula.[23] Plighting their faith with vodka, the conferees crowned their labors with a document known as the Crimean Charter. It announced that plans had been worked out for the final sledgehammering of Germany, and for the occupation, punishment, and control of the beaten foe. Poland was promised a more representative government, based on free elections and designed to supplant both the Russian-sponsored Lublin regime and the Allied-sponsored London regime. The new Poland was to have its Russian inhabited areas cut off in the east by (roughly) the Curzon line, but was to be compensated by German territory in the west. It was further announced that a formula had been worked out for big-Power voting in the forthcoming world organization, and that a conference would meet at San Francisco in April, 1945, for the purpose of whipping the new world charter into final form.

The Yalta conference—the last of the series attended by Roosevelt —was in some ways the most important of all. As a further step in Allied co-operation with Russia, it foreshadowed some of the peace terms and took a giant stride toward the long-awaited world charter. Upon returning from his 14,000-mile trip, Roosevelt made a personal report to Congress (March 1, 1945), and urged that body to rise to its high responsibilities in peacemaking. Although remarking with a smile that the Roosevelts (including his peripatetic wife) throve on travel,[24] he significantly sat down for the first time in making such an address; the ten-pound steel braces on his legs admittedly bothered him. It was his last appearance before Congress.

The Crimean Charter was immediately subjected to a barrage of

[22] A second Cairo conference took place, December 4–6, 1943, when Roosevelt and Churchill, returning from Teheran, conferred with the President of Turkey. *Department of State Bulletin*, IX, 412. Following the Allied invasion of France, Roosevelt and Churchill met again in Quebec (September 11–16, 1944) for a discussion of war strategy involving Germany and particularly Japan, against which Russia had not yet declared war.

[23] For the Crimean Charter, see *ibid.*, XII, 213–216.

[24] Franklin D. Roosevelt, by far the most-traveled President, altogether covered some 300,000 miles, a substantial part of them in the "Flying White House." As an indication of the nation's increased maturity, it is interesting to recall the storm of criticism when Wilson announced his trip to Paris in 1918.

criticism. The decision as to the Curzon line, which by returning pre-1919 Russians to Russia lopped off about one third of pre-1939 Poland, aroused bitter denunciation among powerful Polish and Catholic groups, both at home and abroad. Congressman O'Konski of Wisconsin, supported by Congressman Lesinski of Michigan, assailed the "crime of Crimea" as a "stab in the back" for Poland and as a "second Munich." From Moscow the Communist journal *Pravda* thundered back at the "political buffoonery" of this Polish spokesman, and regretted that his remarks should have been applauded in the House of Representatives.[25] Senator Butler of Nebraska (Republican) assailed the secrecy at Crimea, while Senator Wheeler of Montana (Democrat) condemned "the cynical partition of Poland." Yet the American public, while recognizing that these arrangements involved compromise, generally approved the published results.[26] The secret results leaked out later. (pp. 845, 863)

THE FIGHTING FRENCH

Co-operation with France, no less than with Russia, presented the Western Allies with many delicate problems. The large northern and western part of France occupied by Hitler in 1940 was clearly enemy territory; the technically neutral remainder, including an important overseas empire, was left under a quasi-independent government set up at Vichy under the head of Marshal Pétain, an eighty-four year old hero of World War I. Conspicuous among those struggling for power behind this bemedaled throne was the swarthy Pierre Laval, who openly consorted with Nazis. Outside France, a determined band of French patriots, led by the zealous but austere General Charles de Gaulle, maintained headquarters in London, defied the so-called collaborationist policy of the aged Pétain, and feebly kept aloft the tarnished banner of the republic.

Vichy was the only legal government of France, and as such the State Department continued official diplomatic relations with it, though openly deploring the growing influence of Hitler. Grim-faced Secretary Hull was subjected to savage criticism for nearly a year because he would not break off relations with Pétain and Laval, and because his policy smelled suspiciously like "appeasement."

[25] San Francisco *Chronicle*, Feb. 19, 1945.
[26] Gallup (March 10, 1945) found 61% favorable, 9% unfavorable, and 30% undecided. *Pub. Opin. Quar.*, IX, 95. The voting power of Polish groups in the United States was feared by politicians.

Yet an official severance of relations would have meant the with-drawal of all American diplomatic and consular agents from France and her colonies, particularly French North Africa, where the under-cover work of American representatives was of indispensable im-portance in preparing the path for invasion.[27] Admiral William D. Leahy, United States Ambassador at Vichy, who won the confidence of Pétain, exercised strong influence to counteract German propa-ganda, to resist Nazi slave-labor and anti-Jewish decrees, to save count-less refugees, to keep the fleet out of German clutches, and to prevent French colonies from falling further under Axis control. The need for official American ears, eyes, and voices in France was underscored by the fact that the French had broken completely with London in 1940, when the British, fearing that the French fleet would go over to Hitler, had attacked important units in Algeria.

The task of maintaining relations with Vichy was complicated by the necessity of encouraging the Free French (later Fighting French) under General de Gaulle.[28] Washington extended lend-lease aid to his London National Committee, and recognized his control over certain French outposts in the Pacific and Africa. All of these steps evoked protests from Vichy, which naturally felt that its authority was being compromised.

The Allied surprise assault on French North Africa, November 7, 1942, enabled the United States to tear off the mask and reveal that its trafficking with Vichy had been primarily for military purposes. Pétain promptly countered by severing diplomatic relations with Washington. Hitler forthwith seized unoccupied France, and French officers scuttled the bulk of their navy at Toulon to keep it out of Nazi hands (November 27). At one stroke the menace of the French fleet disappeared, and an invasion was launched which proved to be an important foundation stone in the victory arch.

The Vichy episode is a classic example of the difficulties growing out of public pressure in a democracy, particularly when the State Depart-ment is not free to reveal its ultimate purposes.

[27] For the work of American agents, particularly Mr. Robert Murphy and Ad-miral Leahy, see Welles, *Time for Decision*, pp. 160–161. Admiral Robert, in charge of the French West Indies, remained obdurately loyal to Vichy and was suspected of succoring German submarines. He was finally forced out, in July, 1943, by a United States food embargo. See *Department of State Bulletin*, IX, 32.

[28] Washington was strongly criticized when it objected to the seizure by the Free French of two small French islands in the Gulf of St. Lawrence (December 24, 1941). The State Department feared that its delicate negotiations with Vichy would be jeopardized. Goodrich, *Documents*, IV, 465–466.

THE DIPLOMACY OF EXPEDIENCY

As the zero hour for the invasion of North Africa neared, it was evident that General de Gaulle, who was erroneously alleged to be a puppet of Britain, did not command enough support among French troops there to be entrusted with the responsibility of persuading them to cease fire. Much to the distress of De Gaulle's supporters in America and elsewhere, the Allies selected for this purpose General

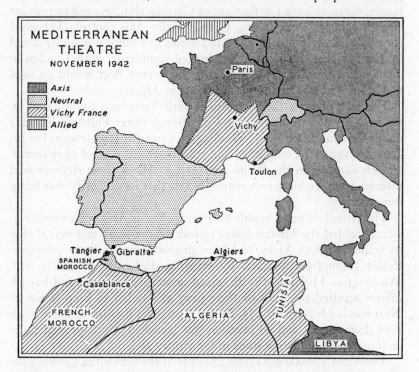

MEDITERRANEAN THEATRE

NOVEMBER 1942

- Axis
- Neutral
- Vichy France
- Allied

Henri Giraud, a gallant French officer who had attained some notoriety during both wars by daring escapes from German prisons. He was peculiarly acceptable because he was a conservative and, unlike De Gaulle, so naïve politically that he could be used for Allied ends. Smuggled into North Africa by submarine, he gave the orders to end resistance, but they were not obeyed. The success of the invasion teetered in the balance.

At this perilous juncture Admiral Darlan, vice premier of Vichy France, was in North Africa for the ostensible purpose of visiting his sick son. Although distrusted and hated by the Allies as a leading collaborationist, Darlan evidently perceived that Hitler might now be beaten, and he revealed a willingness, as chief of the French forces, to issue the command to cease fire. General Eisenhower, the Allied commander who had to make this difficult decision, agreed to accept Darlan's co-operation, and the landings were accomplished with relative speed and with remarkably few casualties.

Darlan's assistance was of undeniable military value. More important perhaps than the saving of lives, both Allied and French, was the saving of time. Prolonged French resistance would have enabled the Germans to entrench themselves more effectively in French North Africa, and Hitler might have been tempted to make a lightning thrust through Spain, thus placing the whole Allied enterprise in peril. Darlan also turned over remaining naval units to the Allies, persuaded the French Governor General at Dakar (across from Brazil) to surrender his important outpost, and made available several hundred thousand potential French troops for Allied use. Hitler, master of the double-cross, was himself royally double-crossed.

But the deal with Darlan was understandably nauseous to De Gaullists, to many British, to Communists, and to American liberals. It looked as though the United States were grooming this distrusted Vichyite as Fascist dictator of postwar France, to the discouragement of democrats in France and oppressed liberals everywhere. President Roosevelt made haste to explain that France alone would determine her postwar government, and that the dealing with Darlan was only "temporary expediency." But Wendell L. Willkie, the voice of outraged American liberals, cried: "The United States has lost moral force . . . and by it we may lose the peace. . . . With all my soul I hate this false finagling with expediency." [29]

An assassin's bullet removed Darlan, on Christmas Eve, 1942, but affairs did not go smoothly under his successor, General Giraud, whose political appeal did not match his gallantry. Notorious Vichyites cropped up in the new administration, perhaps inevitably, and anti-Jewish decrees and other Fascist proscriptions remained on the books. Professional liberals in America and elsewhere demanded that General de Gaulle be installed and propped up, if necessary, by Allied bayonets. But the local political situation was extremely complicated, with leftists and reactionaries struggling for control, and the American military authorities deemed it best to fight the war first and let the French decide upon their government later.

This decision, though open to valid criticism, had much to com-

[29] *American Yearbook*, 1942, p. 18.

mend it. To have mixed in local politics might well have delayed military operations; and with fearsome secret weapons in the making, delay was dangerous. The Atlantic Charter promised postwar self-

BRIGHT SWORD BUT A TATTERED BANNER

(Fitzpatrick in *St. Louis Post-Dispatch*)

determination for France; and there was then no way of accurately determining popular support for General de Gaulle in Nazi-dominated France. To have backed De Gaulle under these circumstances would have run counter to the policy of nonintervention which had been strikingly reaffirmed under the Roosevelt administrations.[30]

The American North African policy sacrificed much moral ground, and probably saved many lives—possibly victory. Whether the price was unnecessarily high may be debated endlessly.

FRANCE FREE AND UNITED

General de Gaulle's perseverance finally gained him a substantial victory when, in June, 1943, a Committee of National Liberation was established in French Algiers under the joint presidency of De Gaulle and Giraud. The latter was to have charge of military affairs but was gradually eased out. Late in August, 1943, following the Quebec Conference, the Big Three extended a limited recognition to General de Gaulle. But he was determined that his organization should be given a more dignified status, and on June 2, 1944, the French Committee of National Liberation declared itself the Provisional Government of the French Republic.

The Roosevelt Administration was meanwhile being subjected to strong public pressure to reverse itself and recognize De Gaulle.[31] In spite of the general's personal unpopularity in Washington, and in spite of doubts as to his possible Napoleonic ambitions, there could be no question by this time that his patriotism and radio eloquence had won for him a wide following in France. It was plain that Roosevelt had bet on the wrong horse when he backed Giraud, and it was evident that unless De Gaulle was recognized before the D-Day invasion of Fortress Europe, a serious conflict of authority might arise in France, as in fact it did.

Roosevelt to some extent made amends when, in July, 1944, he invited the French leader to Washington for conferences, and several months later (October 23) the Big Three recognized De Gaulle's committee as the provisional government of the French Republic. France finally became a full-fledged member of the United Nations on January 1, 1945, after having traveled a long and humiliating road since the dismal days of 1940.

Thus it came about that before the end of the war the principal

[30] As the State Department pointed out, the forcible setting up of regimes favorable to one's ideology was precisely what the Nazis were doing. See Goodrich and Carroll, *Documents*, VI, 691–698.

[31] A Gallup poll (June 27, 1944) showed that 66% of Americans favored recognizing the De Gaulle Committee as the provisional government of France, while 34% did not. *Pub. Opin. Quar.*, VIII, 452. De Gaulle was irked because France was not invited to the Yalta Conference, and refused to be bound by its decisions. He also declined to see Roosevelt in Algeria during the latter's return trip from Yalta.

Allies, including France and Russia, had achieved a more satisfactory degree of co-operation than had earlier seemed possible.

BIBLIOGRAPHICAL NOTE

Authoritative books on these recent years are scarce; for documentary material consult footnotes of this chapter. Two major participants have given us personal accounts: E. R. Stettinius, Jr., *Lend-Lease: Weapon for Victory* (N.Y., 1944); and Sumner Welles, *The Time for Decision* (N.Y., 1944), which is highly revealing. W. L. Willkie's best-selling blast against isolationism, *One World* (N.Y., 1943), was both a book and an event. T. A. Bisson, *America's Far Eastern Policy* (N.Y., 1945), has useful chapters on China. F. R. Dulles, *The Road to Teheran* (Princeton, 1944), is a sketchy but helpful summation of Russo-American relations from the beginning. Senator E. D. Thomas, *The Four Fears* (Chicago, 1944), discusses fear of Russia. On the North African affair two eye-witness accounts may be used with caution: Renée Pierre-Gosset, *Conspiracy in Algiers, 1942–1943* (N.Y., 1945); and Kenneth Pendar, *Adventure in Diplomacy* (N.Y., 1945). Material of a more general nature may be found in: J. T. Shotwell, *The Great Decision* (N.Y., 1944); Walter Lippmann, *U.S. War Aims* (Boston, 1944); and L. W. Holborn, ed., *War and Peace Aims of the United Nations* (Boston, 1943). See also references at end of next chapter.

4TH ED. REFS. *The Memoirs of Cordell Hull* (2 vols., N.Y., 1948), though self-justifying, contain much information. At Moscow Stalin, without asking concessions, promised Hull to come into the Far Eastern war (p. 1309). Also indispensable are R. E. Sherwood, *Roosevelt and Hopkins* (N.Y., 1948), and H. L. Stimson and M. Bundy, *On Active Service* (N.Y., 1947). Elliott Roosevelt, *As He Saw It* (N.Y., 1946), is an untrustworthy account of the major conferences by the President's son; the latter harbors an anti-British bias and reports conversations that he could not have remembered exactly. J. G. Winant, *Letter from Grosvenor Square* (Boston, 1947), is a charming and sympathetic account of the American ambassador's wartime years in London. D. D. Eisenhower, *Crusade in Europe* (Garden City, N.Y., 1948), throws some light on the African venture. Werner Levi, *American-Australian Relations* (Minneapolis, 1947), is a full length study, pointed toward the period of World War II. Herbert Feis, *Seen From E.A.* (N.Y., 1947), discusses the struggle behind the scenes for rubber and oil. A major contribution is W. L. Langer, *Our Vichy Gamble* (N.Y., 1947). The author, an historian who during the war was in government service, including the State Department, had unlimited access to the official records. He defends Washington's policy with ability, though conceding that by the spring and summer of 1942 the Administration might have changed its support to de Gaulle (p. 394). For sharply dissenting views see Louis Gottschalk, "Our Vichy Fumble," *Jour. of Mod. Hist.*, XX (1948), 47–56; and Ellen Hammer, "Hindsight on Vichy," *Pol. Sci. Quar.*, LXI (1946), 175–188. As things turned out, certain mistakes were made, but at the time Washington had to come to decisions on the basis of what it then regarded as valid assumptions.

CHAPTER XLVIII

Toward a New World Order

"If we do not want to die together in war, we must learn to live together in peace." President Harry S. Truman, April 25, 1945, opening San Francisco Conference.

TURNCOAT ENEMIES

THE principal United Nations were not the only countries to harass Washington with delicate diplomatic problems. There were in addition the enemy states, the neutrals, and the Latin American republics.

The enemy nations presented a confusing picture, for all of Hitler's satellites—Italy, Hungary, Bulgaria, Rumania, and Finland—not only dropped out of the war but turned against the master gangster and became virtual or actual co-belligerents of the United States.[1] The Department of State had no direct diplomatic contacts with Germany; such business as the exchange of nationals and protests against war crimes was carried on through a neutral intermediary. The same in general was true of Japan, to which many protestations were made against the atrocious treatment of American prisoners.

The Italian people, who had been dragged into the war by the bullying Mussolini, did not have their hearts in the fight. After the Allied invasion of Sicily, in July, 1943, Italian resistance wilted rapidly, Mussolini was deposed, and a new government under Marshal Badoglio, the Fascist-tainted conqueror of Ethiopia, came to terms with the Allies. Those liberal elements in America who had decried the Darlan deal were distressed by continued traffic with Marshal Badoglio and the servile King Victor Emmanuel III, but the Germans had to be driven out of Italy and, as in North Africa, the Allied military leaders deemed it best to get on with the fighting and worry about local politics later. The King partially abdicated in June, 1944, and after Italy had declared war on Hitler she was accepted as a co-belligerent, though not by Mussolini-raped Ethiopia.

[1] Congress unanimously declared war on Bulgaria, Hungary, and Rumania on June 4, 1942 (approved June 5), six months after these countries had all declared war on the United States in December, 1941.

Finland was even more of a diplomatic curiosity. On the day of Pearl Harbor the Finns, having won back their lost territory, were attacking Russian lines before Leningrad in uneasy partnership with Hitler. So ingrained was American admiration for debt-paying Finland that Congress could not bring itself to follow Britain's example and declare war on her, even though Moscow complained bitterly. For two years and a half the State Department labored to induce Finland to terminate what Roosevelt called a "hateful partnership," but to no avail. Three weeks after D-Day, and probably under Russian pressure, Washington finally broke off relations (June 30, 1944); and some three months later the beaten Finns signed an armistice with the Soviet Union. The United States informally resumed relations in January, 1945, and "brave little" Finland was then permitted to pay further installments on her debt.[2]

NEUTRAL ANACHRONISMS

Unlike ill-fated Finland, six European nations preserved a precarious neutrality throughout all or virtually all of the conflict, either because they were on the outskirts of the war or because the fighting swirled around their mountain barriers. They were Eire, Sweden, Turkey (which came in at the very end), Spain, Portugal, and Switzerland.[3] Upon all of them the United States exerted pressure, acting alone or with its allies, to induce them to limit their assistance to the Axis; and in pursuing this policy America's "economic warriors" revived and strengthened such potent persuaders as the blacklist, export control, and the rationing agreement.

The Irish Free State, nursing a centuries-old hatred of England and grieving over the retention by the British of Northern Ireland, determined upon a rigid official neutrality. Eire was unwilling that Britain should use former anti-submarine bases (even though they were desperately needed); it protested against the landing of American troops in Northern Ireland; it refused to remove Axis espionage agents; it declined to give assurances regarding asylum for Nazi refugees; it protested to the United States against attacking Rome (the head of its church); and it offered formal condolences upon the

---

[2] Formal relations were resumed August 31, 1945.

[3] Switzerland was useful to the Allies as the source of smuggled parts for precision instruments. The accidental bombing of Schaffhausen by American aviators, with tragic loss of life and property, brought an apology and pecuniary reparation from the United States. *Department of State Bulletin*, X, 314.

announcement of Hitler's death. Although Eire unofficially conferred many benefits on the Allies, and although thousands of Irishmen volunteered for service in the British Army, the anomaly is that the Irish, whose love for a fight is proverbial, officially shunned the greatest conflict in history.[4]

The most important of the northern neutrals was Sweden, which shipped vital ball bearings and enormous quantities of high-grade iron ore to the Nazi war machine. The democratic and freedom-loving Swedes were unsympathetic toward Hitler's brutalitarianism, but in the war's early stages they were so weak that they had to knuckle under. When Germany was thrown on the defensive by the Russian steam-roller, the Swedes could safely yield to joint American-British pressure, and in the autumn of 1944 they severely curtailed or completely stopped their shipments of war materials to the hard-pressed Reich.

Turkey was also neutral, though technically allied with Britain; and while the high tide of Nazi conquest was licking toward the Caucasus and Egypt, she dared not enter the fray. During these anxious days the United States bolstered her up with lend-lease goods. When the Nazi tide receded, the Turks were reluctant to abandon the profits of neutrality, including trade with Germany in steel-hardening chrome. Washington expressed its displeasure by canceling lend-lease shipments and by joining with Britain to force a break in economic and diplomatic relations with Germany (August 2, 1944). Turkey finally declared war on the disintegrating Reich, in February, 1945, and joined the United Nations just in time to secure a seat at the San Francisco Conference.

American public opinion was highly critical of Turkish and especially of Swedish assistance to the Nazi warlords. The ordinary citizen forgot that neutrality was a time-honored American policy, that America had maintained a protracted neutrality during both World War I and World War II, and that she had refused to admit that these were her wars until she had actually got into them. The truth is that during most of the conflict neither Turkey nor Sweden was in a position to resist the demands of Hitler, and that both served the Allied cause best by avoiding Nazi conquest.

[4] Gallup found (Feb. 22, 1942) that on the question of Ireland's declaring war on the Axis, 71% of Americans were favorable, 16% unfavorable, and 13% undecided. Among Irish-Americans the vote was 56% yes, 32% no, and 12% undecided. *Pub. Opin. Quar.*, VI, 311.

FOR WHOM THE BELL TOLLS

Portugal and Spain, both under the rule of dictators, were of immense economic and strategic importance. The Portuguese, who had maintained friendly treaty relations with Britain for nearly six hundred years, were much less troublesome than Spain. With Hitler in the unbreakable embrace of the Russian bear and hence unable to punish Portugal, the British invoked the ancient treaty of 1373, antedating Columbus, and temporarily secured for themselves and for the United States strategic antisubmarine bases in the Portuguese-owned Azores. Appropriately enough, the announcement was made on Columbus Day (October 12), 1943—nearly 451 years after the Great Navigator had sailed past the "gray Azores." The British and the Americans, exerting pressure jointly, later induced the Portuguese, in June, 1944, to cut off completely from Germany valuable shipments of steel-hardening wolfram.

Spain was a different problem. The dictator Franco, who had ridden into power with the openly secret help of Hitler and Mussolini, repaid his debt with noisy sympathy for the Axis, even to the extent of permitting the volunteer Spanish Blue Division to serve with the German army against "Communist" Russia. If Franco had been driven into the arms of his brother dictators, the western Mediterranean would have been cut off, the African coast and outlying islands would have become Axis bases, the North African invasion would have been impossible, and the war might well have been lost by the Allies or prolonged interminably.[5]

Spanish neutrality was of particular importance to the British, who secured nearly half their iron ore from Spain. The Germans were likewise beneficiaries, for their steel mills obtained most of their wolfram from the Iberian peninsula. In the noiseless battle of the checkbooks ("preclusive buying"), American and British agents were able to outbid their Nazi competitors, and to force prices up to such a figure as to bring veritable gold rush days to Spain.[6]

The projected invasion of French North Africa made it imperative that the United States keep Franco in line. A distinguished Catholic

---

[5] Franco had already caused some concern when, in June, 1940, and contrary to solemn treaty engagements, he had occupied the international city of Tangier, across from Gibraltar.

[6] Allied purchases of Spanish woolens caused the death of many Nazis in frozen Russia. The much-criticized oil shipments to Spain were essential to the financing of a preclusive purchase campaign. See David Gordon, "How We Blockaded Germany," *Harper's Magazine*, CXC, 14–22 (Dec., 1944).

layman, the historian Dr. Carlton J. H. Hayes of Columbia University, was drafted as ambassador to Spain, in March, 1942, to carry out this difficult and thankless assignment. His efforts met with considerable success, despite the embarrassment of loud criticism from certain liberal and leftist elements in the United States who at times seemed more eager to make war on Franco than to win the war against Hitler.[7]

When the invasion of North Africa started, Roosevelt immediately conveyed assurances to Madrid that the United States had no designs on Spanish territory. Yet it was necessary to detach a large American force to guard against a possible flank attack by Franco's army of an estimated 150,000 men in Spanish Morocco. This precarious situation explains why the United States sought to convince the Spaniards of the blessings of neutrality by permitting them to receive cargoes of urgently needed supplies, especially petroleum.

With the victorious conclusion of the North African campaign, the United States and Britain were free to deal more firmly with Franco. Early in 1944 oil shipments were suspended, and before they were renewed Spain was forced to make important concessions to the Allies, principally in a limiting of wolfram shipments which amounted to a drying up of exports to Germany.[8] As the fortunes of the United Nations improved, Franco veered around from pro-Axis non-belligerency, to neutrality, and finally to a neutrality that was benevolent to the Allies.

The Discovery of Latin America

The devastating assault at Pearl Harbor aroused the Latin American nations, for, in the words of the Havana declaration of 1940, an attack upon one was an attack upon all. Most of the republics promptly severed relations with the Axis, or declared war, and even such laggards as Chile and Argentina extended unneutral privileges to their belligerent sisters. Significantly, those nations which acted most vigorously were in or near the Caribbean area, where the influ-

---

[7] Franco was more anti-Russian than pro-Axis; there was in fact considerable pro-American and pro-British sentiment in Spain. The nation was still suffering from the recent civil war, and had no real desire to fight again. C. J. H. Hayes, *Wartime Mission in Spain, 1942–1945* (N.Y., 1945), pp. 44–45, 50, 74. Ex-ambassador Hayes' account abounds in examples of how ignorant public opinion at home hampered the larger strategical purposes of the government. See especially pp. 146–148, 306–307, 309.

[8] L. M. Goodrich and M. J. Carroll, *Documents on American Foreign Relations* (Boston, 1945), VI, 690.

ence of the United States was strong and where its Navy could most easily provide defense.

AMERICAN REPUBLICS AND THE WAR, 1941–1945 *

NAME	DECLARED WAR ON AXIS: GERMANY (G.); ITALY (I.); JAPAN (J.)	BROKE RELATIONS WITH AXIS	SIGNED UNITED NATIONS DEC- LARATION
United States	Dec. 8, 1941 (J.) (Dec. 11, 1941, G.I.)		Jan. 1, 1942
Costa Rica	Dec. 8, 1941 (J.) (Dec. 11, 1941, G.I.)		Jan. 1, 1942
El Salvador	Dec. 8, 1941 (J.) (Dec. 12, 1941, G.I.)		Jan. 1, 1942
Guatemala	Dec. 8, 1941 (J.) (Dec. 11, 1941, G.I.)		Jan. 1, 1942
Haiti	Dec. 8, 1941 (J.) (Dec. 12, 1941, G.I.)		Jan. 1, 1942
Honduras	Dec. 8, 1941 (J.) (Dec. 13, 1941, G.I.)		Jan. 1, 1942
Nicaragua	Dec. 8, 1941 (J.) (Dec. 11, 1941, G.I.)		Jan. 1, 1942
Cuba	Dec. 9, 1941 (J.) (Dec. 11, 1941, G.I.)		Jan. 1, 1942
Panama	Dec. 10, 1941 (J.) (Dec. 12, 1941, G.I.)		Jan. 1, 1942
Dominican R.	Dec. 11, 1941 (G.I.)		Jan. 1, 1942
Mexico	May 22, 1942 (G.I.J.)	Dec. 8, 1941 (J.) (Dec. 11, 1941, G.I.)	June 14, 1942
Brazil	Aug. 22, 1942 (G.I.) (June 6, 1945, J.)	Jan. 28, 1942 (G.I.J.)	Feb. 6, 1943
Bolivia	Apr. 7, 1943 (G.I.J.)	Jan. 28, 1942 (G.I.J.)	Apr. 7, 1943
Colombia	Nov. 27, 1943 (G.I.)	Dec. 8, 1941 (J.) (Dec. 19, 1941, G.I.)	Jan. 17, 1944
Ecuador	Feb. 2, 1945 (J.)	Jan. 29, 1942 (G.I.J.)	Feb. 14, 1945
Paraguay	Feb. 7, 1945 (G.J.)	Jan. 28, 1942 (G.I.J.)	Feb. 14, 1945
Peru	Feb. 11, 1945 (G.J.)	Jan. 24, 1942 (G.I.J.)	Feb. 14, 1945
Chile	Feb. 12, 1945 (G. J.)	Jan. 20, 1943 (G.I.J.)	Feb. 14, 1945
Venezuela	Feb. 14, 1945 (G.I.J.)	Dec. 31, 1941 (G.I.J.)	Feb. 20, 1945
Uruguay	Feb. 22, 1945 (G.I.J.)	Jan. 25, 1942 (G.I.J.)	Feb. 24, 1945
Argentina	Mar. 27, 1945 (G.J.)	Jan. 26, 1944 (G.J.)	

* Declarations of war and declarations of a state of belligerency are here regarded as the same. For complete data on alternate dates, see *Bulletin of the Pan American Union*, Sept., 1945, p. 528.

The Pan-American machinery that had been laboriously constructed since 1936 was quickly thrown into gear, and in the darkest days of 1942 the Third Meeting of Ministers of Foreign Affairs assembled in the hospitable atmosphere of the Brazilian metropolis, Rio de Janeiro (January 15–28). The chief objective of the United States and its co-belligerents was to secure unanimous agreement to a resolution pledging all the American republics to sever relations with the Axis as a consequence of the attack on one of them. But Argentina and Chile, which were the farthest removed from the protective naval

(Bishop in St. Louis *Star-Times*)

arm of Uncle Sam, led a successful fight to make the declaration recommendatory rather than mandatory. Even in its watered-down version the unanimously adopted compromise preserved the Pan-American front, and struck a blow at the Axis propagandists, who had counted on disunity—all of which was no mean achievement when one considers the then desperate plight of the Allies.[9] Within a day after the conference adjourned, all the Latin American republics that had not yet done so severed relations with the Axis, except Argentina and Chile.[10]

The ensuing war years constituted something of a honeymoon period. One wag observed that in 1492 Columbus discovered America; in 1942 the United States discovered Latin America. The Great Neighbor of the North extended vast loans for building up war industries, provided extensive lend-lease supplies, purchased enormous quantities of raw materials, arranged for numerous military and naval missions, and expanded the educational program of the Co-ordinator of Inter-American Affairs.[11]

The Good Neighborism of the 1930's paid exceptionally rich dividends in contiguous Mexico, whose attitude, in striking contrast with 1917–1918, was conspicuously friendly. The lending of many thousands of Mexican laborers, the final financial adjustment of the oil imbroglio, and an exchange of visits by Presidents Roosevelt and Camacho were happy incidents.[12] A promising example of international co-operation was the boundary waters treaty of 1944, which was chiefly concerned with a fair division, for irrigation and other purposes, of the waters of the Rio Grande and the Tijuana and Colorado rivers.[13]

Brazil, in 1942 as in 1917, was the first South American republic to declare war, though not until U-boats had attacked her shipping.

[9] The final act at Rio comprises a series of declarations and resolutions, of which severance of relations was the most important. See L. M. Goodrich, ed., *Documents on American Foreign Relations* (Boston, 1942), IV, 279–329.

[10] Elongated Chile was vulnerable to German submarine attacks, and this fact, together with a confused political situation and other considerations, caused the government to delay a break in relations with the Axis until January 20, 1943. The rupture followed a sensational public accusation by Under Secretary Welles that Nazi agents were using Chile and Argentina as bases from which to direct U-boat attacks. *Department of State Bulletin*, VII, 810. Although the charge was substantiated, both Chile and Argentina formally protested, and the Chilean president canceled a projected visit to the United States.

[11] The wooing of Latin America was fraught with dangers. Walter E. Disney's film, "Saludos Amigos," was generally well received, though Chile thought her share overbrief, and those nations which had no place at all were doubtless hurt. A. P. Whitaker, ed., *Inter-American Affairs, 1942* (N.Y., 1943), p. 97.

[12] The oil companies were to receive $29,137,700.84, or about seven cents on the dollar of what was doubtless an inflated valuation. *Department of State Bulletin*, IX, 230–231. The presidents of the two countries had not met since the days of Taft (1909).

[13] Treaty signed February 3, 1944; approved by the Senate April 18, 1945, 76 to 10, after strong opposition from California.

Traditionally the most friendly toward the United States of all the major Latin American countries, she gravitated even closer toward the Colossus of the North. The two republics were by far the largest in the Americas; they were the most important non-Spanish nations in the Pan-American concert; and their products, as was conspicuously not true of Argentina, were largely complementary. (Brazil was the coffee bag of the United States.) Washington shipped large quantities of lend-lease arms to Brazil, took active steps to revive rubber production, and granted huge loans for steel and other industries, even at the risk of future competition. Brazil for her part raised a considerable expeditionary force (the only Latin American country to do so), and provided air bases which were of great value in ferrying reinforcements across the "Atlantic narrows" to North Africa.

Bolivia played a crucially important role, for with Malaya cut off she was the most important remaining source of tin. Ecuador granted the United States temporary naval facilities, including a base on her long-coveted Galápagos Islands. Panama permitted the acquisition of new areas for the further protection of the Canal. Other republics sold products as the needs of the Allies dictated, though there was considerable preclusive purchasing to keep supplies out of Axis hands. Latin America was quite content to make hay, while the sun of Fascism shone, at the expense of rich Uncle Sam.

The costliness of this war program aroused the suspicion of Senator Butler (Republican, Nebraska), who after a hasty trip through Latin America reported his findings to the Senate. His chief complaint was that "good neighborism" had become "rich uncleism," that the Treasury was lavishly buying good will, and that the cost of this hemispheric "boondoggling" had in three years amounted to $6,000,000,000. For good measure, he pilloried the educational, social, democratic, and governmental shortcomings of the Latin Americans.

The befuddled senator, whether through ignorance or malice or both, included in his calculations not only legitimate war and defense costs but also repayable lend-lease. Senator McKellar (Democrat, Tennessee), in a devastating reply, demonstrated that the $6,000,-000,000 had been inflated by 95%.[14] Yet Senator Butler's ill-founded charges, which were widely distributed by the *Reader's Digest* under the title "Our Deep Dark Secrets in Latin America," caused violent reactions both north and south of the border. The sensitive good

[14] For Butler's report (Nov. 26, 1943) and McKellar's speech in reply (Dec. 18, 1943), see *Sen. Doc.*, No. 132, 78 Cong., 1 sess.

neighbors, aside from being scolded for their shortcomings, did not like to be told that their friendship was purchasable, that the Good Neighbor policy was but a marriage of convenience, and that a divorce suit would probably be filed when the shadow of Hitler had passed.[15]

THE ARGENTINE PROBLEM CHILD

Argentina stood alone, throughout 1943, as the only American republic to dishonor its vote at Rio and refuse to break relations with the Axis. The explanation is complicated.

As the wealthiest and most progressive of the Latin American states for about half a century, Argentina regarded herself as the natural leader of her sister republics, and resented the overshadowing dominance of the United States. If she could not lead, she would not follow. Her civilization was Latin, and she looked to Latin Europe for cultural inspiration, while scorning the crudities of Yankeeland. The antipathy of the would-be Colossus of the South for the so-called Colossus of the North explains in part why proud Argentine statesmen for several decades had consistently sought to checkmate Uncle Sam at international conferences.[16]

Back of this inferiority complex lay economic rivalry. Argentina's twin kings—meat and wheat—were unwelcomed competitors in the United States, and Uncle Sam's tariff barriers and meat-quarantine restrictions (hoof-and-mouth disease) were regarded as blows below the trade belt. The great Argentine export market was Europe; and Argentina, with bursting granaries, did not want to antagonize potential postwar customers, Fascist or otherwise. She was not prepared to gamble on an Allied victory, particularly in the uncertain days of 1942, when the United States could not even protect its own coasts, let alone those of Argentina. The policy of both Argentina and Chile, at least in the early stages, seems to have been not so much

[15] The Butler report largely undid the good work of Vice President Wallace, who, knowing how to speak Spanish, had made a widely publicized speaking tour of Latin America in the spring of 1943. But he was shelved the next year; and this fact, together with the resignation of Under Secretary Welles in September, 1943 (Welles was generally regarded as the "chief architect" of the Good Neighbor policy), was disquieting to Latin America, even though both changes were made for personal or political reasons. See A. P. Whitaker, ed., *Inter-American Affairs, 1943* (N.Y., 1944), pp. 40–41.

[16] Until January 1, 1943, Argentina had ratified only six of ninety Pan-American conventions signed since 1890. This, says Dr. S. F. Bemis, "makes Argentina easily the greatest non-ratifier of all time." *The Latin American Policy of the United States* (N.Y., 1943), p. 261 n.

pro-Axis as pro-"playing it safe"—a course which was also commercially profitable.[17]

Argentina not only had a strong isolationist group (like the pre-Pearl Harbor United States) but she was subjected to a barrage of Axis propaganda. She had moreover a dictator tradition, despite nineteenth century democratic gains, dating back to the redoubtable Gaucho Rosas. Native military-Fascist elements looked with admiration upon Franco of Spain, and worked hand in glove with the numerous German and Italian immigrant population, as well as with the more recent German "tourists." Argentina also eyed with distrust the huge loans and lend-lease supplies with which Uncle Sam was strengthening the military power of her most-feared rival, Brazil, which was now supplanting her as the foremost Power of Latin America.[18]

An uprising of the "Colonel's Clique" in Buenos Aires, June, 1943, installed General Ramírez, whose government had the effrontery to ask lend-lease support from the United States. Secretary Hull administered a resounding rebuff.[19] In succeeding months the Argentine militarists not only followed the Hitlerian formula of clamping down on labor unions, on Communists, on political parties, and on Jewish newspapers, but even went so far as to support a Fascist *coup* in tin-rich Bolivia. Probably fearing reprisals from the Allies, Buenos Aires belatedly broke relations with Japan and Germany on January 26, 1944—two years after the joint Rio recommendation.

The extreme militarists were so angered by this nominal rupture of relations that they unhorsed General Ramírez, in March, 1944, and elevated the Vice President, General Farrell. In June, Washington recalled its ambassador "for consultation," a month later Buenos Aires did likewise, and the State Department publicly denounced Argentina for "deserting the Allied cause." A protesting crowd of Argentines gathered before the United States Embassy in Buenos Aires, distributing leaflets warning, "YANKEES SHOULD BE

[17] Reprisals from a victorious Hitler were certain; highly unlikely from the Allies. Neutrality immunized Argentine shipping from U-boat attacks, and enabled the La Plata Republic to send immense quantities of its products to the Allies, with benefits to both. Yet some of these exports reached Germany by way of Spain; and the Axis Powers were able to use their diplomatic missions in Buenos Aires as headquarters for their espionage in America. Argentina, in common with the rest of (Catholic) Latin America was reluctant to fight on the same side as Soviet Russia. See Whitaker, *Inter-American Affairs, 1942*, pp. 20–21, 35.

[18] This distrust was a factor in the military-Fascist coup in Argentina, in June, 1943. *Ibid., 1943*, p. 23.

[19] For the extraordinary Argentine note of August 5, 1943, and Secretary Hull's reply, see *Department of State Bulletin*, IX, 159–166.

MADE TO UNDERSTAND," and carrying a banner proclaiming, "ARGENTINA WEARS LONG PANTS." [20] The Roosevelt administration, resorting to the distinction between the people and their government, was now falling back on Wilsonian nonrecognition, moral castigation, and diplomatic quarantine in an effort to bring about a regime more to its liking.[21] To many Latin Americans it began to look as though a difference between Argentina and all her sisters had degenerated into a quarrel between Argentina and the United States.

All for One (Except One)

The policy of Argentina was probably now more pro-Fascist than pro-Axis, but the net result was to give both material and moral aid to Germany and Japan. Public anger in the United States rose rapidly and manifested itself in demands for a rigid economic boycott.[22] Such a drastic type of intervention, which no doubt would have aroused the Argentine masses to a more vigorous support of their government, was opposed by the British, who would have lost their vital beef supply —a deficiency which the already-rationed United States would have had to make good.[23] Yet in August and September, 1944, Washington froze Argentine gold stocks, and, in addition to the existing blacklist and export restrictions, forbade United States ships to pick up Argentine cargoes. These measures fell far short of a complete embargo. Buenos Aires, as a countermove, sought to bring about a meeting of foreign ministers to review the situation, but the United States and its Latin American co-belligerents were able to sidetrack this maneuver.

With affairs thus deadlocked, and with the conflict in Europe roaring to its end, an Inter-American Conference on Problems of War and Peace met from February 21 to March 8, 1945, in historic Cha-

[20] New York *Times*, July 27, 1944, 10:1. For Hull's statement of July 26, see *Department of State Bulletin*, XI, 107–111.

[21] For a criticism of this policy, see Sumner Welles, *The Time for Decision* (N.Y., 1944), pp. 237 ff. It is significant that Washington, while condemning Argentina, permitted critically important manufactured goods to go to her. It may also be noted that the United States did not object to dictators, like Vargas of Brazil, so long as they were tractable.

[22] One poll (Aug. 8, 1944) showed that the people of the United States strongly approved Hull's nonrecognition policy, and that they overwhelmingly (80%) favored trade stoppage with Argentina, even at the cost of sacrifices at home. *Pub. Opin. Quar.*, VIII, 450.

[23] The liberal British *Manchester Guardian* observed: "We like the Argentine brand of Fascism as little as does Mr. Cordell Hull, but we also prefer Argentine beef to American pork." Quoted in A. P. Whitaker, ed., *Inter-American Affairs, 1944* (N.Y., 1945), p. 19.

pultepec Castle, Mexico City—the same castle that General Winfield Scott had stormed in 1847. Its major purposes were to strengthen Pan-American solidarity, to intensify the war effort, and to lay the foundations for postwar stability. The most significant resolution adopted was the Act of Chapultepec, which in effect made all the American republics co-guardians of the Monroe Doctrine, *even against an American aggressor*. Thus the multilateralizing of the Doctrine, highlighted at Havana in 1940, was expanded into a kind of Pan-American defense doctrine. Much embarrassment was caused by the "absent sister" Argentina, the only republic unrepresented; and after protracted debate it was made clear by formal resolution that if she would subscribe to the principles of Chapultepec and enter the war, she would be eligible for admission to the United Nations.[24]

Hitler's Reich was rapidly crumbling when, as an act of deathbed conversion, Argentina unenthusiastically declared war on Japan and Germany (March 27, 1945), and adhered to the Act of Chapultepec. Washington and the other American governments to the south, accepting these steps as made in good faith, lifted economic restrictions and, on April 9, 1945, resumed full diplomatic relations. Argentina made some show of changing her Fascist stripes, as when she permitted the exhibition of hitherto banned movies, such as "For Whom the Bell Tolls," "Mission to Moscow," "The Hitler Gang," and "Confessions of a Nazi Spy." Yet these gestures deceived few. Genuine democratic elements existed in Argentina, but they were stifled. The United Nations had fought to make the world safe against Fascism, but World War II came to a victorious end with the most important center of Fascism, with the possible exception of Franco's Spain, defiantly entrenched in the Western Hemisphere.

PRE-POSTWAR PLANNING

As the prospect of a new peace conference assumed greater reality, public sentiment in the United States began to insist that steps be taken to avoid repeating the ghastly failure of 1919–1920.[25] The

[24] For the Act of Chapultepec and the resolution concerning Argentina, see *Department of State Bulletin*, XII, 339–340, 450–451. The Monroe Doctrine, as usual, was not formally mentioned by name; it conjured up too many unpleasant memories.

[25] According to Gallup (July 1, 1944), 53% thought that America should have joined the League of Nations in 1919; in August, 1941, the figure had been 37%. In 1937 only 26% had approved joining a new League of Nations; by July, 1944, the figure had risen to 72%. *Pub. Opin. Quar.*, VIII, 454. On the eve of the San Francisco Conference (April 9, 1945), Gallup found that 81% favored a world organization *with police power*. *Ibid.*, IX, 253.

memory of that tragedy was so poignant that the Allies, in making plans for the future, were chained down to the uncertain minimum of what the Senate might accept. It was evident that advance assurances of co-operation from this unpredictable body would make possible the drawing up of a more binding world settlement.

In March, 1943, a bi-partisan group of senators—Ball, Burton, Hatch and Hill—introduced a resolution, popularly known as the

The Weakest Link (Crawford in *Newark Evening News*)

B₂H₂ resolution after the initials of its sponsors, committing the United States in broad terms to a future organization for peace. Although Senator Wheeler insisted that he would oppose such a platitudinous pronouncement "with all the fight I have in me," teams of Congressmen toured the country whipping up popular support for it. A similar resolution was introduced in the House, during June, 1943, by Representative (later Senator) Fulbright of Arkansas, and it passed 360 to 29.[26] Representative Hamilton Fish of New York, the violently isolationist grandson of the former Secretary of State,

[26] September 21, 1943. The vote squares with a Gallup poll (July 9, 1943) revealing 78% favorable, 9% unfavorable, and 13% undecided. *Ibid.*, VII, 499–500.

branded this "pious declaration" as a "mirage." "Let's win the war," he allegedly sneered, "and then fight it out with our allies." [27]

Then came Secretary Hull's memorable trip to Moscow, with the resulting clearing of the air and the foundation-stone declaration for world organization. Senator Connally thereupon sidetracked the B_2H_2 resolution for a substitute designed to dovetail with the new developments. Although Senator Johnson of California, the once rabid anti-Leaguer, spoke quaveringly against it, the proposal carried, on November 5, 1943, by the lopsided vote of 85 to 5. The Senate thus substantially advanced the cause of peace by proclaiming to the world that it would support any reasonable plan for a postwar organization.

Another move forward was taken when, following informal discussions and at the invitation of Secretary Hull, a bi-partisan committee of eight was created in the Senate, during April, 1944, to consult with the State Department and the President on matters of foreign policy. Numerous conferences were held, and this intimate co-operation, quite unlike Wilson's in 1919, did much to smooth the path for favorable Senate action.

The disquieting fear still remained, despite these favorable signs, that the Senate might again fail to muster a two-thirds vote. This led to widespread agitation for a constitutional amendment that would permit approval of treaties by a simple majority of both houses.[28] The House of Representatives, which would naturally appreciate such a share in treaty-making, overwhelmingly passed a resolution to that effect.[29] But the amending process is so difficult, the Senate is so jealous of its prerogatives, the public is so apathetic or ignorant, and the alternatives are so vulnerable to criticism, that the proposal was quietly buried.

[27] Quoted in *New Republic*, Oct. 11, 1943, p. 490.

[28] A Gallup poll (June 16, 1945) showed that 58% of the people favored ratification by the President and a simple majority of Congress to any other method, while only 21% supported the existing two-thirds rule. *Pub. Opin. Quar.*, IX, 248.

[29] The vote was 288 to 88, on May 9, 1945. One survey in 1944 disclosed that 68% of the people did not know that the Senate has to approve treaties by a two-thirds vote, that only 40% had ever heard or read about the Atlantic Charter, and that only 44% knew that the United States had never joined the League of Nations. *New York Times Magazine*, May 14, 1944, p. 9. Gallup (April 12, 1942) revealed that only 50% could name the Congressman from their district, and 65% did not know his pre-Pearl Harbor stand on interventionism. Another poll (March 5, 1944) showed that only 31% could name both their United States senators. *Pub. Opin. Quar.*, VI, 476; VIII, 281.

KEEPING THE SAME QUARTERBACK

In the midst of a desperate, global war it was necessary to take time out for the presidential election of 1944. Roosevelt, though obviously ageing under the strain, was the inevitable choice of the Democrats for a fourth nomination. There was no other rival; the two-term tradition had already been shattered; and with a war and a peace yet to be won he seemed more than ever an "indispensable man." Vice President Wallace, whose boat-rocking ideas were distasteful to conservative Democrats, was shelved for the more steady Senator Harry S. Truman, a quiet Missourian who had won some repute as head of the Senate War Investigating Committee.

The Republicans likewise snubbed their 1940 standard bearer, the liberal internationalist Wendell L. Willkie, and, seeking a candidate with the greatest vote-appeal, turned to the dynamic young prosecutor-governor of New York, Thomas E. Dewey. Conservative Republicans were not overjoyed by Dewey's recent advocacy of world collaboration, and they chose as his running mate Governor John W. Bricker of Ohio, a handsome near-isolationist who vaguely preached "co-operation without commitments," and who was damned by William Allen White as an "honest Harding." The greater enthusiasm of the convention for the vice presidential nominee led to the quip, "The delegates loved Bricker but married Dewey." [30]

Dewey could doubtless have disrupted the nation and delighted the German propagandists by arousing bitter controversy over the Administration's conduct of the war and its plans for world collaboration. Yet he commendably put patriotism above party, and substantially endorsed Roosevelt's program for international organization. This meant that foreign affairs would to an unusual degree be kept out of the dusty arena of politics.[31] Certain other Republicans were less scrupulous, notably Congresswoman Clare Booth Luce ("the Blonde Bombshell"), who violently charged Roosevelt with having "lied us into a war because he did not have the political courage to lead us into it." [32]

With foreign policy soft-pedaled, and with the voters more concerned about unemployment than peace,[33] the Republicans concen-

---

[30] *American Year Book, 1944,* p. 32.

[31] In an effort to subordinate partisanship, John Foster Dulles, Dewey's adviser on foreign affairs, had a three-day conference with Secretary Hull, ending August 25, 1944. Dewey sought to win the Scandinavian and Polish votes by capitalizing on the European situation, while Roosevelt made his bow to the Italians and Irish.

[32] New York *Times,* Oct. 14, 1944, 9:2.

[33] See polls in *Pub. Opin. Quar.,* VIII, 281, 337, 595. As late as April 2, 1945, Gallup found that the people listed the most important public issues (aside from

trated their fire on the alleged domestic shortcomings of the New Deal. The rich baritone voice of Dewey tirelessly hammered home the slogan, "That's why it's time for a change!" In foreign affairs the chief question was: Which party could be trusted to win the war and negotiate the peace?

The arguments for Roosevelt—the constitutional "commander-in-chief"—were strong. He was winning the war, and one should not change commanders any more than quarterbacks when one's side is winning a close decision. A shift might delay or imperil victory, and keep the boys overseas longer. Roosevelt was on intimate terms with Churchill and Stalin; he had laid the groundwork for peace; and (so his followers claimed) he should be permitted to finish the job.

Dewey on the other hand was young and inexperienced, and while he favored international co-operation, a powerful and noisy bloc of his supporters, including the Chicago *Tribune*, very definitely did not. The Republicans in 1920 had similarly promised to collaborate in world organization, but after the election their isolationist wing had taken control and betrayed these promises—a fact which the Democrats did not fail to stress.[34] The Allies were quietly praying for Roosevelt, as he was a known quality; while the Nazis were hoping for Dewey. German gunners bombarded American lines with insulting leaflets:

> Jews govern, suckers fight;
> Vote for Roosevelt's Hebrew might.[35]

Roosevelt, though attracting less support than usual, won with his customary landslide, and with the votes of many who opposed his domestic policies but regarded peacemaking as more important.[36] The campaign was a great tribute to the maturity of the American people,

---

winning the war) in this order: unemployment, economic problems, permanent peace. *Ibid.*, IX, 228.

[34] The polls consistently showed that the Democrats were somewhat more co-operationist than the Republicans. One political advertisement for Roosevelt read:
> Dewey, Tom,
> On matters foreign,
> Sounds a lot like
> Harding, Warren.

Stanford (University) *Daily*, Nov. 3, 1944.

[35] San Francisco *Chronicle*, Nov. 9, 1944.

[36] One poll showed that 63% preferred Roosevelt at the peace table to 26% for Dewey. *Pub. Opin. Quar.*, VIII, 335. Senator Ball (Rep., Minn.) spectacularly bolted his party for Roosevelt, largely because Dewey would not speak concretely on empowering an American delegate on a security council to use American troops. *American Year Book, 1944*, p. 24.

because foreign affairs, which in the nature of things should be non-partisan, were kept on a relatively high plane. The winds of public opinion were setting in strongly for world co-operation, and there was a great dropping of overripe isolationists, including Representative Hamilton Fish and Senator Nye. In an unprecedented declaration, sixteen newly elected senators of both parties pledged their support to the President; and Senator Vandenberg, a Michigan Republican hitherto regarded as strongly isolationist, dramatically spoke in favor of world alliance.[37] Politicians could not profitably ignore the tremendous pressure of co-operationist sentiment.

FOUNDATION STONES OF PEACE

The Atlantic Charter and the Moscow Declaration had laid the groundwork for international co-operation in the political field, but thus far little had been done in the economic field.[38] Yet the world had come to recognize that economic wars beget shooting wars; or, as Roosevelt put it, "economic diseases are highly communicable." With the object of insuring greater financial stability, the United Nations Monetary and Financial Conference met at the fashionable Bretton Woods resort, in New Hampshire, amid the majestic White Mountains. The representatives of forty-four nations—some 1300 experts altogether—engaged in protracted discussions (July 1–22, 1944), and after compromising their widely divergent views drafted a two-pronged plan.

First, an international loan fund of $8,800,000,000 ($2,750,000,000 from the United States) would help stabilize national currencies in terms of gold and facilitate payments across international boundaries. Second, a world bank capitalized at $9,100,000,000 ($3,175,000,000 from the United States) would provide loans to needy nations, primarily for reconstruction and economic development.[39] Strong op-

---

[37] See New York *Times*, Jan. 11, 1945, 1:1.

[38] The United Nations Conference on Food and Agriculture had met at Hot Springs, Virginia, May 18–June 3, 1943. It arranged for the creation of the Food and Agriculture Organization of the United Nations, with long-range powers to improve world conditions relating to nutrition, food, and agriculture. Goodrich and Carroll, *Documents*, V, 297–337; VI, 415–442. A temporary organization, the United Nations Relief and Rehabilitation Administration (UNRRA), came into being on November 9, 1943, when representatives of forty-four nations signed an agreement at the White House designed to assist liberated peoples in Europe and the Far East. Ex-Governor Herbert H. Lehman of New York was elected Director General, and the original budget of some $1,862,000,000 was provided by the principal signatories on the basis of one per cent of their 1943 national incomes.

[39] Text in *International Conciliation*, Sept., 1945, No. 413, Sec. 2, pp. 563–639.

position to these arrangements was immediately voiced by American banking interests, who feared government competition with their profitable business, and the indications were that the Bretton Woods agreement would meet with a stormy reception in Congress.

The political counterpart of the Bretton Woods conference was held from August 21 to October 7, 1944, at Dumbarton Oaks, a strikingly beautiful colonial residence, now the property of Harvard University, in the Georgetown outskirts of Washington.[40] Representatives of the Big Four (the United States, Britain, Russia, China) labored earnestly on a tentative draft of a new world charter which, unlike the defunct League of Nations Covenant, would provide an international police force to discipline disturbers. Russia, fearing the anti-Communist prejudices of other nations, was not willing to deny herself a veto voice in disputes concerning herself, nor for that matter was the United States. So the voting problem, as well as the perfecting of the Dumbarton Oaks draft, was postponed for later decision.[41]

At Yalta, President Roosevelt succeeded in working out a voting compromise with Stalin, and the call was then issued for a United Nations conference at San Francisco. Roosevelt promptly chose a representative American delegation. Cordell Hull, who had been forced to end his unprecedentedly long career as Secretary of State because of declining health, was made a member and senior adviser, though unable to go to San Francisco.[42] The titular head of the American delegation was the handsome, prematurely white-haired new Secretary of State, Edward R. Stettinius, Jr., a newcomer in the field of foreign affairs, who was presumably asked to head the State Department because the President planned to be his own Secretary and wanted a man who would carry out orders.

In addition to Hull and Stettinius (both Democrats), the President

[40] The Americans, British and Russians met from August 21 to September 29. The Russians then retired and discussions were concluded with the Chinese. Text of Dumbarton Oaks draft in *Department of State Bulletin*, XI, 368–374.

[41] The Russians also aroused some distrust by their refusal to attend the International Civil Aviation Conference, held in Chicago, November 1 to December 7, 1944, on the ground that certain pro-Fascist nations had been invited. The conference evolved a compromise which called for a central authority with limited powers. *American Year Book, 1944*, p. 99.

[42] Hull resigned on November 27, 1944. Stettinius, a former high official of the U. S. Steel Corporation and later Lend-Lease Administrator, had served for a year as Under Secretary of State, in this capacity heading both a mission to London and the Dumbarton Oaks delegation. When *Fortune* asked (Nov., 1942) white high school pupils to name "really great" living Americans, Hull ran sixth, just behind "Babe" Ruth, who had retired from playing baseball seven years earlier. The Negroes, who voted strongly for Roosevelt and pugilist Joe Louis, did not name Hull among the first ten. *Pub. Opin. Quar.*, VII, 167–168.

chose Commander Harold E. Stassen, a prominent liberal Republican and ex-governor of Minnesota; two leading members of the Senate Foreign Relations Committee, Senator Connally of Texas (a Democrat) and Senator Vandenberg of Michigan (a Republican); two members of the House Foreign Affairs Committee, Representative Sol Bloom (a Democrat) and Representative Charles A. Eaton (a Republican); and Dean Virginia C. Gildersleeve (independent Democrat), a well-known educator of Barnard College whose appointment was regarded as a recognition of the growing influence of women in national and international affairs.[43]

Roosevelt had evidently been at pains to avoid some of Wilson's mistakes. The Senate was adequately represented (two members), and the House as well (two members). Politics were pushed into the background: no violent partisan was appointed and both parties were honored (four Democrats, three Republicans, one independent Democrat). The San Francisco conference was not a peace conference designed to perfect terms of peace; its sole task was to hammer the Dumbarton Oaks draft into a new covenant for a world organization. This meant that the delegates would not get bogged down, as Wilson did at Paris, in such technicalities as boundaries and reparations. The Dumbarton Oaks plan had been published well in advance, unlike the League of Nations Covenant, and ample opportunity was given for microscopic examination and needed amendment. The public was accorded unusual recognition when forty-two national organizations, such as the National League of Women Voters, were invited to send consultants to San Francisco. Finally, the new charter was to stand on its own feet and, unlike the League Covenant, was not to be riveted into a new Treaty of Versailles, good or bad.

REUNION IN SAN FRANCISCO

Germany was collapsing in a vast Wagnerian Götterdämmerung, and the omens for success at San Francisco seemed favorable, when, on April 12, 1945, less than two weeks before opening day, President Roosevelt suddenly died. At a time of all times when leadership of a high order was needed, the leader's hand was taken away. The nation was stunned.

The inexperienced new President, Harry S. Truman, partially revived confidence when, in the face of rumors to the contrary, he promptly and vigorously announced that the conference would be

[43] The San Francisco Conference was unusual for the sprinkling of women delegates and advisers.

held on schedule. The death of Roosevelt seems indeed to have shocked men into a deeper sense of their responsibilities. Forty Republican senators promptly volunteered an unprecedented pledge of loyalty, quite in contrast with the Round Robin of 1919; and Marshal Stalin, who had hitherto betrayed some lack of confidence by naming minor delegates to the conference, responded to an earlier appeal from Washington by agreeing to send Foreign Commissar Molotov.[44] This concession strengthened the growing cordiality that had followed Russia's action, only nine days earlier (April 5, 1945), in denouncing the nonaggression pact with Japan preparatory to the long-awaited declaration of war.

With flags flapping at half-staff in a drizzling rain, delegates from the forty-six United Nations—later fifty [45]—gathered in the classic-styled War Memorial Opera House, in San Francisco, on April 25, 1945. Among the some 200 representatives of every race and clime, including the begowned Saudi Arabians, were such distinguished figures as Britain's Foreign Secretary Eden, Russia's Foreign Commissar Molotov, China's Foreign Minister Soong, and South Africa's Marshal Smuts, a white-goateed veteran of the Paris Peace Conference. Seated before a brilliantly lighted operatic stage on which were clustered the flags of the participating nations, the assemblage listened to several addresses of welcome, including one by the new President of the United States (broadcast from Washington), and one by the hardly less new Secretary of State. Then the delegates solemnly filed out, deeply conscious that civilization must not fumble its second chance.

The United Nations Conference on International Organization got off to a discouraging start when the Russian delegation seized the initiative and threw the inexperienced Americans off balance. Custom and courtesy both decreed that the chairmanship of the conference go to the host nation (the United States), but Molotov demanded and finally secured a Big Four rotating chairmanship. The Russians, by invoking a secret agreement at Yalta, next brought about an expansion of their representation to three, thus including the quasi-independent Ukraine and White Russia.[46] The aggressive Russians

[44] New York *Times*, April 15, 1945, 1:6.

[45] The Ukraine, White Russia, Argentina, and Denmark were admitted before the conference adjourned. The announcement that only a declaration of war on the Axis and membership in the United Nations would entitle a country to representation, brought a flurry of last minute declarations from states ranging from Syria and Turkey to Chile and Venezuela.

[46] At Yalta, it was secretly agreed that Russia and the United States might seek three votes in the Assembly of the new world league to offset the six of the British Empire. When this news came out, March 29, 1945, there was a great uproar in the

then insisted that the Soviet-sponsored Lublin regime in Poland also be given representation. But Britain and the United States, arguing that the Lublin faction did not measure up to the democratic formula adopted at Yalta, continued their recognition of the London group in exile. It was ironical indeed that ravaged Poland, which had been the first to stand up against Hitler's fury, should thus be excluded from the conference, although a place was left for her signature.[47]

The Latin American bloc, loyal to the pledges of Chapultepec, and allergic to intervention in any form, fought for the admittance of Argentina to the conference. The United States, while not approving the Argentine regime, reluctantly sponsored the move, in part because Buenos Aires had nominally carried out its end of the bargain by declaring war. Molotov, unable to understand why Fascist Argentina should be admitted while anti-Nazi Poland was excluded, carried his fight to the press and to the floor, but his dramatic plea against inviting the Latin American republic was defeated 31 to 4.[48] The Argentine delegation thereupon made haste for San Francisco.

The Big Four (Eden, Molotov, Soong, Stettinius) had meanwhile been meeting privately in Stettinius' penthouse apartment atop the Fairmont Hotel, and so successfully did their discussions proceed that on May 5, 1945, they could announce agreement upon twenty-two of the scores of proposed amendments to the Dumbarton Oaks draft.[49] With this ground gained, and with the problems of peace pressing in Europe, Molotov, Eden, and other leading figures took plane for home, leaving the drudgery of committee work to competent if less distinguished hands.

THE SECOND CHANCE

The most continuously obstructive element in the conference consisted of the small Powers, ably led by Herbert V. Evatt of Australia.

United States over secret diplomacy, and Washington renounced the three votes for the United States. *Ibid.*, March 30, 1945, 1 : 2; April 4, 1945, 1 : 3. It will be noted that the Assembly was much less powerful than the Security Council, on which each member nation would have only one vote each.

[47] On July 5, 1945, Britain and the United States finally recognized the newly reconstituted Polish regime, and thus adjusted their differences with Russia. *Ibid.*, July 6, 1945, 1 : 8.

[48] April 30, 1945. The Argentine decision aroused widespread condemnation in the United States; many people criticized the conference not so much for admitting Argentina as for denying Russia a brief delay. Two months after the conference had adjourned, Assistant Secretary of State Nelson A. Rockefeller publicly condemned the Argentine government for faithlessness to its Chapultepec pledges. *Ibid.*, Aug. 25, 1945, 1 : 3.

[49] *Ibid.*, May 6, 1945, I, 29 : 1.

Seeking a larger voice in the new organization, they proposed numerous amendments and doggedly fought big-Power domination.[50] The Russian delegates, representing at once a big Power and a Communist outcast, both agreed and disagreed with their Big Four colleagues. But the press, seeking sensational copy, overplayed Soviet obstruction while underplaying that of the small Powers.

The first major crisis to develop—crises invariably develop at important international conferences—concerned the fate of backward or dependent peoples. The Russians, without overseas colonies, favored a liberal policy; the British, French, and Americans (who wanted to retain strategic Pacific islands so dearly bought with American blood) were hesitant.[51] A compromise finally emerged in the form of a Trusteeship Council and a rather vague promise of ultimate independence for subject peoples. The United States was thus left free to secure strategic bases in the Pacific.

A second and more serious crisis arose over regionalism. The Russians professed to fear that regional security arrangements, such as had recently been perfected at Chapultepec, would hamstring the over-all security organization. But the Latin Americans were unwilling to scrap their hard-won Pan-American front, and some of them began to complain that with Roosevelt hardly cold in his grave the Good Neighbor policy was being sacrificed to appease Stalin. After discouraging days of deadlock, a formula was finally devised by which regional groupings could still work usefully for peace within the new organization, particularly in the settlement of local disputes.

The third and most serious crisis developed over the proposed big-Power veto in the Security Council. The Russians, relying upon alleged assurances at Yalta, insisted that any one of the Big Five be privileged to veto any decision of substance in the Council—even a motion to permit debate. The small Powers, ever sensitive to big-Power domination, bitterly resented this attempt at "gag rule" by the nondemocratic Russians.

The deadlock became so ominous that President Truman instructed Harry L. Hopkins, who had recently flown to Moscow as presidential negotiator, to approach the Kremlin. The ailing Hopkins scored what appears to have been a major diplomatic triumph when he induced

[50] So sensitive were the small Powers to slights that it was necessary to make a daily change in the position of the United Nations flags in the Civic Center. *Ibid.*, May 20, 1945, IV, 2:5.

[51] Polls taken from 1942 to 1945 showed that the American people favored retaining naval bases, while emphatically rejecting territorial imperialism. See Nat. Opin. Research Center, *Opinion News*, Sept. 4, 1945, p. 1.

Stalin to give way. The welcome news, announced in San Francisco by Stettinius on June 7, 1945, elicited a spontaneous cheer. The great Powers would still retain their veto on matters of substance, but they would permit the small Powers to bring vexatious issues before them for discussion and thus to appeal to world opinion.

The final crisis, which was perhaps second in importance only to that over the veto, came when the small Powers demanded a larger hand and greater flexibility in the amending process. After heated discussion, an acceptable compromise was finally worked out.

With the last log jams broken, the conference moved under great pressure toward the final drafting of the charter. President Truman flew out to close the conference, and in an impressive scene in the Opera House the delegates unanimously approved their handiwork, June 25, 1945, two months after the opening session.[52] The formal signing of the blue, leather-bound charter took place the next day, with the Chinese delegation, whose country had suffered the longest in the war, first brushing its signatures. After President Truman had formally closed the conference, the charter was flown to Washington, where the hospitalized Hull affixed his name to a document that was peculiarly his own.[53]

The United Nations charter was probably as satisfactory a document as could have been framed in the pre-atomic age. While it is true that the powerful Security Council (dominated by the Big Five), the Assembly (dominated by the small Powers), and the new International Court of Justice (World Court) all suggested the old League of Nations, there were many changes for the better over the Dumbarton Oaks draft. The new Economic and Social Council, with large investigatory authority, highlighted the emphasis on "the dignity and worth of the human person," as did the provisions for trusteeship. Above all, machinery was set up for continuous consultation, and for an international police force made up of national complements and under the direction of the Security Council.

All this did not mean that the charter was perfect, or that it was a self-executing guarantee of peace. But the machinery had been blueprinted for an organization which, if supported by men of good will and amended to meet changing conditions, held promise of mitigating the age-old curse of war. Both the statesmen and the people of 1945 were far more realistic than those of 1919.[54] They were not seeking

[52] Text in *Department of State Bulletin*, XII, 1119–1143.

[53] New York *Times*, June 30, 1945, 11:2.

[54] From 1943 to August, 1945 (and even after the atomic bomb) there was strong sentiment for peacetime conscription. On the eve of the San Francisco Conference (Gallup, March 16, 1945), 54% believed that the United States would have

to make the world safe for democracy; the most that they could hope for was to make the world safe.

THE SENATE MAKES AMENDS

President Truman personally presented the United Nations charter to the Senate on July 2, 1945, and unlike Wilson on a similar occasion twenty-six years earlier, was given a heart-warming reception. As he sailed for Europe, five days later, to consult with the Allied leaders and plan the final blows against Japan, he could take cheer from the multiplying evidence that a tidal wave of nonpartisan opinion would not this time tolerate frustration.[55]

The Senate Foreign Relations Committee, as in 1919, arranged for public hearings, and a number of distinguished witnesses appeared, including ex-Secretary Stettinius, who had recently been supplanted by Secretary James F. Byrnes.[56] A few cranks were also permitted to testify, but Chairman Connally, unlike Lodge in 1919, sternly held his watch over them. Certain bizarre characters branded the charter "a Communist plot" and a "godless and unconstitutional" document framed by a lot of "foreigners out at San Francisco who ate up our scarce food." But these silly denunciations served only to betray the weakness and disorganization of the opposition.

The more serious objections to the charter were aimed at the absolute veto of the Big Five, at the commitment to send American boys overseas, and at the wisdom of authorizing the United States delegate on the Security Council to employ American forces. But after only five days of hearings, the Committee agreed, on July 13, 1945, to report the charter without a single reservation or amendment, in striking contrast with Lodge's forty-nine in 1919. The committee vote was 20 to 1, with the aged and ailing irreconcilable, Johnson of California, sending in the sole dissent from his sick room.

to fight another war in 50 years. *Pub. Opin. Quar.*, IX, 100. Another Gallup poll (July 25, 1945) asked whether the San Francisco Charter would prevent future wars. The results were 15% unqualifiedly yes; 27% yes, *provided* the nations stuck together; 36% no; and 22% undecided. Nat. Opin. Research Center, *Opinion News*, Aug. 7, 1945, p. 6.

[55] On the San Francisco Charter, Gallup (July 25, 1945) found opinion 66% favorable, 3% unfavorable, and 31% undecided. *Ibid.*

[56] Stettinius, who had never been elected to a public office and who had close connections with the monied interests, would have become President in the event of Truman's death. He was gracefully kicked upstairs to the post of United States representative on the Security Council in order to make room for the inexperienced but politically potent Byrnes, who was nominated on June 30, 1945. During 1944 and 1945, the much-criticized Department of State underwent extensive reorganization and undertook to bring itself into closer touch with the people.

By this time, if not before, ratification was a foregone conclusion. Even the anticipated opposition to other measures for international economic collaboration had melted away under the hot breath of public opinion. Some three weeks before the Senate committee had reported the charter favorably, the Senate, on June 20, 1945, approved a House renewal (and expansion) of the Trade Agreements Act for three years, in full conformity with the President's recommendation.[57] On July 19 the Senate took final action on the Bretton Woods bill. Significantly, this measure exempted member nations from the restrictions placed on defaulting debtors by the Johnson Act of 1934. An outburst of opposition was led by Senator Taft of Ohio, who denied that modern wars have economic roots and who feared that Uncle Sam would become a sort of international Santa Claus. The Senate nevertheless approved the measure, with only minor amendments, by the one-sided vote of 61 to 16.[58] The United States was the first nation to ratify.

In this favorable atmosphere, formal debate on the San Francisco charter was opened, on July 23, 1945, by the stentorian-voiced Senator Connally. Referring dramatically to the killing of the Covenant in 1919–1920, he cried, "Can you not still see the blood on the floor?" Election-conscious isolationist senators were not impervious to the tremendous public pressure for action. The only major speech in opposition was a three-hour effort by Senator Wheeler, who branded the charter "a declaration of pious intentions," but who concluded that he would vote for it anyhow. After only six days of debate, and in marked contrast with the futile eight months of 1919–1920, the charter was approved, on July 28, 1945, by the almost unanimous vote of 89 to 2. (Senator Johnson sent word from his death bed that if present he would have voted nay.) A few days later President Truman returned from his European conferences to sign the document and complete formal ratification, on August 8, 1945. In comparison with the complete negation of 1919, the United States was the first Power, great or small, to take final action.

[57] This renewal, the fourth since 1934, authorized the President to go beyond the previous 50% and slash tariffs under the existing Smoot-Hawley tariff of 1930 to a maximum of 75%. The vote in the House was 239 to 153 (May 26, 1945); in the Senate, 54 to 21. Various polls revealed wide ignorance of the Trade Agreements Act, and a much stronger disposition to co-operate with other nations politically than economically.

[58] The House vote, on June 7, 1945, had been 345 to 18. The Senate on July 20 unanimously expanded the foreign lending powers of the Export-Import Bank by $2,800,000,000, and on July 21 overwhelmingly approved membership in the Food and Agriculture Organization of the United Nations

Yet the victory had been deceptively easy. The isolationists realized that they could not obstruct, so they were content to lie low, wait for popular enthusiasm to wane, and bore from within. The issue was no longer isolationism versus internationalism, but weak internationalism versus strong internationalism.

ATOMIC PEACE

The titanic world conflict had meanwhile been rushing toward its breathlessly dramatic close in the Far East. President Truman, following his submission of the charter to the Senate, sailed for Europe with his aides on the historic cruiser *Augusta*. In a Potsdam palace near Berlin he met with Stalin and Churchill (later Attlee) around a circular table.[59] The seventeen-day conference (July 17 to August 2, 1945) proceeded in an atmosphere of cordiality, for the San Francisco conference had been successful, and the Senate was taking favorable action on the charter.

Two momentous documents emerged from the Potsdam conferences. The first was a surrender ultimatum addressed to Japan on July 26, 1945, and designed to weaken Japanese resistance by assurances of non-enslavement. Japan was to be disarmed, shorn of her fifty-year conquests, and deprived of her economic war potential; yet permitted access to raw materials and allowed an opportunity for democratic self-development. If she did not surrender, she would be destroyed.[60]

The second Potsdam document, issued August 2, 1945, was a blueprint for the control of Germany and for the settlement of numerous European problems, including some provisional territorial adjustments in Germany and Poland. Germany was not only to be de-Nazified and disarmed (including control of war industries), but her leaders were to be punished as war criminals and her resources were to be used to repair damages inflicted on her neighbors. The Potsdam declarations foreshadowed ultimate peace treaties.

Then came the eight days that shook the world. Japan—though battered, broken and beleaguered—had failed to respond to the Potsdam surrender ultimatum, and on August 6, 1945, an American plane

---

[59] Yalta was the last meeting of the original Big Three. Truman was new at Potsdam, and the British elections brought in Attlee before the meetings ended. Stalin got along well with Truman, who on one occasion entertained him with a piano rendition of Beethoven's Minuet in G. San Francisco *Chronicle*, July 21, 1945.

[60] Text in *Department of State Bulletin*, XIII, 137–138. Stalin, not yet at war with Japan, did not sign; the Chinese government concurred in the ultimatum.

(Carmack in *Christian Science Monitor*)

dropped a single atomic bomb on Hiroshima which virtually wiped out the city.[61] The scientists of Germany and Japan had also been working on the atom, but in the Battle of the Laboratories the United Nations won. The flash that flattened Hiroshima was the dawning light of a new age—military, diplomatic, industrial.

The Russians declared war on Japan two days later (August 8, 1945), and began a lightning advance into Manchuria and Korea. The six-day Soviet war on Nippon was probably hastened by the imminence of Tokyo's surrender, but Stalin had agreed at Yalta, even before informed of the atomic bomb, to come in for the kill.[62] His delay had presumably been due primarily to the difficulty of transferring troops across Russia and Siberia. Stalin not only entered the war but further confounded his critics, at least temporarily, by signing an air-clearing treaty with Nationalist China renouncing presumed Russian designs on Manchuria and China.[63]

A stunned Nippon still failed to make overtures; and on August 9, 1945, the Americans dropped a second atomic bomb, this time on Nagasaki. The next day Tokyo sued for peace, though attempting to salvage the 2000 year-old throne of the god-emperor Hirohito. The Japanese saved some face but lost an empire when it was agreed, on August 14, that the Emperor might be retained but that he would be subject to the orders of the Allied supreme commander. It was now all over but some desultory shooting.

On September 2, 1945, nineteen days after Japan had agreed to capitulate, the final terms of surrender were signed in Tokyo Bay, on board the United States superdreadnaught *Missouri*. The flag of Commodore Perry had been flown across from Washington for the ceremony. How painfully different this signing was from the one which had taken place ninety-one years earlier, and only a short distance away, on the sacred soil of Nippon!

Thus the stupendous holocaust known as World War II came to a formal close. Men cherished hope for the new United Nations, but grave misgivings gnawed at their hearts. The prospects of a lasting peace were far from reassuring. A disconcerting parallel could be found in the closing months of 1945 for almost every development that had

[61] *Ibid.*, 153–161.

[62] See Truman's report, New York *Times*, Aug. 10, 1945, 12: 3; see also *ibid.*, Feb. 12, 1946, 1: 2, when the details of the agreement were made public.

[63] Announced August 14, 1945. Russia agreed to aid the Nationalist rather than the Communist regime; to refrain from meddling in China's internal affairs; and to recognize Chinese sovereignty in Manchuria, though provision was made for joint use of the railways and of the naval base at Port Arthur, wrested from Russia by Japan in 1905. Text in *ibid.*, Aug. 27, 1945, 4: 1.

cursed international relations in the period of 1919–1920. Then America had been the great nonparticipator. Would her place be taken by Soviet Russia?

One thing seemed crystal clear. The nations of the world would have to work together or atomize their civilization off the face of the planet. Perhaps they would be unable to do so. But the alternatives were plain: co-operation or chaos.

BIBLIOGRAPHICAL NOTE

Consult the footnotes of this chapter and the Bibliographical Notes of the last. C. J. H. Hayes, *Wartime Mission in Spain, 1942–1945* (N.Y., 1945), is an important contribution by a major participant. It may be supplemented by the official documents in E. K. Lindley and E. Weintal, "How We Dealt with Spain," *Harper's Magazine*, CXC, 23–33 (Dec., 1944). On Latin America, see A. P. Whitaker, *Inter-American Affairs, 1942* (N.Y., 1943), and the succeeding annual volumes. These are of indispensable value. See also F. O. Wilcox, "The Monroe Doctrine and World War II," *Amer. Pol. Sci. Rev.*, XXXVI (1942), 433–453. An able survey of present and prospective problems is Crane Brinton, *The United States and Britain* (Cambridge, 1945). Two books on public opinion may be noted: W. A. Lydgate, *What America Thinks* (N.Y., 1944), which is a summation of polls; and Archibald MacLeish, *American Opinion and the War* (N.Y., 1942). Prospective treaty ratification lent interest to the following: K. W. Colegrove, *The American Senate and World Peace* (N.Y., 1944); E. S. Corwin, *The Constitution and World Organization* (Princeton, 1944); and J. B. Whitton, ed., *The Second Chance: America and the Peace* (Princeton, 1944). Robert Bendiner, *The Riddle of the State Department* (N.Y., 1942), is a one-sided criticism. See also J. M. Jones, *A Modern Foreign Policy for the United States* (N.Y., 1944). J. P. Warburg, *Foreign Policy Begins at Home* (N.Y., 1944), stresses the interrelationship of domestic and foreign affairs, with emphasis on the period of Hitler. See also A. H. Hansen, *America's Role in the World Economy* (N.Y., 1945). Among "peace books" of varying merit one may single out Norman Cousins, *Modern Man is Obsolete* (N.Y., 1945); W. T. R. Fox, *The Super-Powers* (N.Y., 1944); Herbert Hoover and Hugh Gibson, *The Problems of Lasting Peace* (Garden City, N.Y., 1942); R. J. S. Hoffman, *Durable Peace: A Study in American National Policy* (N.Y., 1944); Owen Lattimore, *Solution in Asia* (Boston, 1945); L. L. Lorwin, *Postwar Plans of the United Nations* (N.Y., 1943); Nathaniel Peffer, *America's Place in the World* (N.Y., 1945); Emery Reves, *The Anatomy of Peace* (N.Y., 1945); and H. M. Wriston, *Strategy of Peace* (Boston, 1944).

4TH ED. REFS. *The Memoirs of Cordell Hull* (2 vols., N.Y., 1948) have especially useful materials on the Argentine problem and on planning for world organization. R. E. Sherwood, *Roosevelt and Hopkins* (N.Y., 1948) is most revealing. At Teheran, Stalin voluntarily agreed to enter the war against Japan (p. 800), and on May 28, 1945, told Hopkins that the Soviet army would be properly deployed by August 8 (p. 902). That was the day on which Moscow finally declared war, following the dropping of the first atomic bomb. Elliott Roosevelt, *As He Saw It* (N.Y., 1946) is useful but untrustworthy. H. L. Stimson and M. Bundy, *On Ac-*

tive Service in Peace and War (N.Y., 1947), is indispensable on inter-Allied co-operation and the decision to use the atomic bomb. J. F. Byrnes, *Speaking Frankly* (N.Y., 1947), has firsthand reports on Yalta and Potsdam. J. R. Deane, *The Strange Alliance* (N.Y., 1946), is a participant's account of the efforts of the American military mission in Russia to co-operate effectively, in the face of almost pathological suspicion. H. A. Wallace, *Soviet Asia Mission* (N.Y., 1946), is an account of the wartime mission to Siberia by the then Vice President. Herbert Feis, *The Spanish Story* (N.Y., 1948), throws more light on wartime dealings with Franco. J. T. Flynn, *The Roosevelt Myth* (N.Y., 1948), while containing much truth, has a venomously unfair attack on Roosevelt's foreign policy. A. C. Millspaugh, *Americans in Persia* (Washington, 1946), is a participant's account of the interaction of Russian, British, and American foreign policy. An important defense of Yalta by one of the participants is E. R. Stettinius, Jr., *Roosevelt and the Russians: The Yalta Conference* (Garden City, N.Y., 1949). A few impressions on foreign policy are recorded in Eleanor Roosevelt, *This I Remember* (N.Y., 1949).

CHAPTER XLIX

The Rift Between East and West

"We may well ask, 'Why have they [the Soviets] deliberately acted for three long years so as to unite the free world against them?'" Winston Churchill, speech at Boston, March 31, 1949.

TWO WORLDS

WHEN THE war jarred to a close in 1945, the people of the United States still retained a vast reservoir of good will toward their valiant Russian ally. They were confidently counting on Soviet co-operation to create a warless world through the United Nations, and many of them were in favor of lending Russia the money and technical assistance with which to repair the ravages of the Nazi invader.

But the men in the Kremlin spurned the outstretched American hand, presumably because co-operation with the capitalistic west would retard the Communist revolution. The ideal of One World thus collided solidly with the actuality of the Communist world. This was the most overshadowingly significant and frightening development of the postwar years.

Numerous public opinion polls showed that before the summer of 1946, and even earlier in some cases, the American people by substantial or overwhelming majorities had reached the following disquieting conclusions. Soviet Russia could not be trusted to co-operate with the United Nations; her dominance over her satellite neighbors was prompted by aggressive rather than defensive designs; she was not a peace-loving nation; she was bent on dominating the entire globe; another world war was probable within twenty-five years; and the Russians were most likely to start it.[1]

Thus within a few short months the aggressive tactics of Moscow had wrought a psychological Pearl Harbor which awakened the great body of Americans to the nature of the Communist menace. The United

---

[1] This summary is based on scores of polls. The high point in American good will toward Russia came in April, 1945, on the eve of the San Francisco Conference, at which time about half of those polled favored a military alliance with Moscow. *Pub. Opin. Quar.*, IX, 254.

States, forewarned and alerted, drastically reoriented its foreign policies and bolstered its defenses in a determined effort not to be caught napping again.

"I'm Here to Stay, Too." (Herblock in Washington *Post*)

Apologists for the U.S.S.R. have insisted that the Soviets turned against America because America first turned against them, and that if Franklin D. Roosevelt had not come to an untimely end, he would have been able to co-operate with the Kremlin. The truth is that by mid-March, 1945—one month before the President's death—the Soviets were clearly taking over Poland and Rumania in violation of their published pledges at Yalta.[2] Roosevelt died knowing—or strongly suspecting—that he had failed in his efforts to wean Communist Russia from its dangerous ideas by kindness and lend-lease largesse.

The leaders of Soviet Russia, though soft-pedaling their ideal of world revolution during the desperate years of World War II, had evidently never abandoned it. The man on Main Street overlooked this fundamental fact during that era of wishful thinking, but the men of Moscow did not. Little wonder they were so suspicious of America— their capitalistic ally but ideological foe—during the struggle against Hitler.

Soviet distrust of the western world was deepened by the temporary monopoly of the atomic bomb by the United States. A tiny but vocal minority of Americans, including ex-Governor Earle of Pennsylvania, were demanding a "preventive war" against the U.S.S.R. while the United States had this horrendous new weapon, and the Russians did not. The "rattling of the atomic bomb" took on greater reality as American forces retained bomber bases within striking distance of the Soviet Union, and undertook impressive naval demonstrations in the eastern Mediterranean.[3] Soviet suspicions were further increased as Washington delayed or halted lend-lease shipments, and as the American public grew increasingly cold toward a proposed loan of $6,000,000,000.[4]

PEACE BY DEADLOCK

The ominous split between Soviet Russia and the western democracies was brought more nakedly into the open by repeated but futile

[2] J. F. Byrnes, *Speaking Frankly* (N.Y., 1947), pp. 54–55; R. E. Sherwood, *Roosevelt and Hopkins* (N.Y., 1948), pp. 875–876. The Soviets assumed that before Yalta and through the Anglo-Russian agreement of 1944 they had been granted the Balkans, north of Greece, as a sphere of influence. *The Memoirs of Cordell Hull* (N.Y., 1948), II, 1458. For numerous alleged violations of the Potsdam agreement by the Russians in Germany, Austria, Poland, Hungary, Bulgaria, Rumania, Korea, and Manchuria, see *Sen. Report*, No. 1440, 80 Cong., 2 sess.

[3] A power vacuum was created in western Europe when the splendid American army was hastily demobilized, in response to a "I wanna go home" agitation vigorously supported by anxious parents. Winston Churchill expressed the opinion in 1949 that only the existence of the atomic bomb held back the Soviets. New York *Times*, April 1, 1949, 10: 7.

[4] In October, 1945, Gallup found only 27% favorable to the loan, with 60% unfavorable, and 13% without opinion. *Pub. Opin. Quar.*, IX, 533.

attempts at peacemaking. The foreign ministers of the victorious Powers met in London in September, 1945, primarily to begin work on the Italian treaty. Unable to agree even on procedural matters, they adjourned after three weeks of fruitless wrangling, with the Soviet representative, V. M. Molotov, the chief wrangler and Secretary of State Byrnes his principal opponent. A current quip was, "Molotov fiddles while Jimmy Byrnes."

The Big Four Powers tried again in snow-mantled Moscow during December, 1945, and although the results were disappointing, the conferees did manage to agree on a peace conference at Paris to draft treaties with Italy and four of Hitler's smaller satellites—Finland, Rumania, Bulgaria, and Hungary.

The foreign ministers had to meet twice in Paris—from April to July, 1946—before they could perfect final arrangements for the projected conference. The chief stumbling block was the noisy demand of Communist Yugoslavia, backed no less noisily by Communist Russia, for Italy's Adriatic port of Trieste. This particular log jam was not broken until the delegates finally agreed upon the internationalizing of Trieste under the United Nations.

The Paris peace conference, with twenty-one nations represented, met from July 29 to October 15, 1946, more than a year after the shooting had stopped. Amid angry charges by Molotov that the democratic bloc was trying to railroad decisions through by a simple majority vote, the five treaties were at length drafted. They were whipped into final form by another Big Four meeting of foreign ministers in New York, November–December, 1946, during which Molotov made unexpected concessions.[5]

The United States was not a party to the Finnish treaty, not having declared war on Finland, but the other four treaties in which it participated—those with Hungary, Bulgaria, Rumania, and Italy—were not popular with the American public. Among other things the arrangements for reparations gave the Soviet Union an objectionable amount of continuing control. But the United States Senate—operating on the principle that the pacts with Hungary, Bulgaria, and Rumania were the best that could be had—approved them without enthusiasm by a voice vote.

The treaty with Italy, which provided heavy reparations for the Soviet Union, was assailed in the United States by powerful Italian-American groups. It was criticized more generally by non-hyphenated Americans on the ground that the occupying Powers, including the

[5] Byrnes, *op. cit.*, p. 154.

United States, would have to withdraw their troops, and then the militant Communist party would be free to take over. But the Senate finally approved the pact, 79 to 10, after hearing arguments that the United Nations would help defend Italian democracy when foreign forces had departed. The treaty was also denounced in Italy, where a former prime minister publicly regretted that Columbus had ever discovered America.

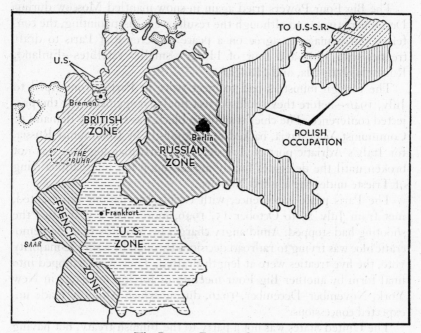

The Postwar Zones of Germany

QUADRIPARTITE CHAOS IN GERMANY

The German Reich, pursuant to agreements concluded at Yalta in 1945, was sliced into four administrative zones: the American, the British, the French, and the Soviet. The rubble heap known as Berlin, deep in the Russian zone, was cut into four sectors, on a similar basis.

The United States at the outset was committed to the Morgenthau plan, a vindictive scheme devised by Secretary of the Treasury Morgenthau, in opposition to the saner views of the State Department, and rather hastily accepted by Roosevelt and Churchill in 1944.[6] Its pur-

[6] H. L. Stimson and M. Bundy, *On Active Service in Peace and War* (N.Y., 1947), pp. 576–578; Hull, *Memoirs*, II, 1602 *ff.*

pose was to remove Germany forever as a menace by de-industrializing her and turning her into what was popularly called a "potato patch."

The embarrassing truth was that an agrarian economy simply could not begin to support the teeming millions of Germany.[7] Even before the war ended, the policy makers in Washington became belatedly aware that a re-industrialized German Reich was the key to the economic recovery of Europe, and a crucially important dike against the westward surge of Russian Communism. The United States therefore swung over in support of a rehabilitated but shackled Germany—de-cartelized, demilitarized, de-Nazified, and democratized. Although the new policy still showed strong traces of the Morgenthau mentality, the British generally supported it.

The French, whose soil had thrice been polluted since 1870 by the German boot, were vehemently opposed to a revitalized Germany, and during the malleable six months or so after victory were even less co-operative than the Russians. In 1946 Secretary Byrnes, departing sharply from the no-alliance tradition, offered the other members of the Big Four a twenty-five year treaty designed to keep Germany demilitarized—an offer which both he and his successor later raised to forty years. But the Russians objected that such guarantees did not go far enough.[8]

Reparations also proved to be a meaty bone of contention. The Russians insisted that they had been promised $10,000,000,000 at Yalta, and began to seize goods from current German production. The Americans replied that the figure had merely been accepted as a *basis for discussion,*[9] and that while the Russians might remove factories, they were violating the Potsdam agreement and discouraging incentive when they carted away the output of those factories.

The Soviets were also eager to turn Germany into a satellite state. They set up a puppet party in their own zone, and through it (and in violation of the Potsdam agreement) drenched the other three zones with Communist propaganda. They retained hundreds of thousands of German prisoners of war, contrary to agreement, and presumably for purposes of Communist indoctrination.

The Russians did co-operate more satisfactorily with the three western allies in bringing the leading Nazi war "criminals" before the bar of justice at Nuremberg, Germany. These trials were designed to establish an international law governing war crimes, and thus to discourage

---

[7] Morgenthau favored shipping the 30,000,000 or so surplus Germans to North Africa, as well as flooding the mines of the industrialized Ruhr.

[8] Byrnes, *op. cit.,* pp. 125, 171, 174, 176.

[9] *Ibid.,* pp. 28–29. The total figure had been $20,000,000,000, with half for Russia.

future aggressors by guaranteeing a noose instead of a halo. The proceedings were criticized to some extent in the United States as "judicial lynchings" in violation of the *ex post facto* principle: that is, a man should not be tried for an offense that was not a crime when the deed was committed.[10] Finally, on October 1, 1946, nineteen leading Nazis were found guilty. Twelve were sentenced to death, but the demedalled Hermann Goering dramatically cheated the gallows by swallowing poison in his cell. Trials of lesser Nazis for varying crimes went forward for many months.

The Postwar Zones of Austria. (Adapted from New York *Times*, June 26, 1949)

The problem of Austria, which likewise was carved into four zones, proved hardly less vexatious than that of Germany. The United States regarded the Austrians as a liberated people, on the principle that they had been raped by Hitler in 1938; the U.S.S.R. regarded them as a conquered people, on the principle that they had been willingly seduced. Friction was generated between Moscow and the western Powers over such problems as reparations, the Soviet seizure of Austro-German assets, and Russian support for Yugoslavia's claim to a chunk of Austria (Carinthia).

[10] For a dissenting view, see Stimson and Bundy, *op. cit.*, pp. 588–591.

The four-way tangle in Germany finally called for bold action. The Potsdam agreement had stipulated that Germany should be treated as an economic unit. Yet the Soviets flatly refused to send food from their predominantly agricultural zone to the industrialized western zones.[11] The British and Americans, burdened with heavy occupation costs and seeking to make their own zones self-sufficient, arranged for a bi-zonal economic merger late in 1946, to the accompaniment of cries from the Soviets that the Potsdam Pact had been broken. The French were ultimately persuaded to join the other two western zones, and Trizonia became the basis for the new German federal republic under a constitution drawn up by the Germans at Bonn in 1949. Trouble loomed ahead, with two Germanys and two Berlins, each caught in the middle of an east-west tug of war, and each seeking to draw the other to itself.

The Chinese Puzzle

At Yalta, when Stalin had agreed to attack Japan, the inducements offered him had been kept secret, for fear of provoking the Japanese into premature attack. The terms were not officially published until exactly one year later, by which time the most disturbing concessions had gradually leaked out.[12]

The Kurile Islands, strung out like a pearl necklace northeast of Japan, were to be handed over to the Soviet Union. This decision was greeted with vigorous criticism in America, largely because Soviet bombers could be brought that much closer to the United States. Southern Sakhalin, ceded to the Japanese in 1905, was to be returned to the Russians. In Manchuria the harbor of Dairen was to be internationalized, the lease of Port Arthur as a naval base (lost to Japan in 1905) was to be restored; and the Manchurian railroads were to be operated jointly by Chinese and Russians—all of which arrangements foreshadowed ultimate Soviet domination of a key economic and strategic area. The position of Russia in Manchuria was now more favorable than it had been in 1899, when John Hay had tried to jockey her out.

At the time of Yalta the American public, faced with the prospect of staggering casualties in the invasion of Japan, was anxious to have the Soviets share the losses. But when the Japanese surrendered only six days after Moscow's declaration of war, it became painfully apparent

[11] The American General L. D. Clay remarked that in the division of Germany the Russians got the agriculture, the British the industry (Ruhr), and the Americans the scenery. Moscow vainly sought a hand in the control of the Ruhr.

[12] *Department of State Bulletin*, XIV, 282 (Feb. 24, 1946).

that the United States had not needed the Soviet "victory parade" after all. Moreover, when the news finally leaked out that Roosevelt had given the Russians a heavy bribe to lure them into a war which they were determined to enter anyhow, the legend took quick root that the sickly Roosevelt, advised by the sickly Harry Hopkins, had been sold a gold brick by the crafty Joseph Stalin. This judgment was less than fair to the American negotiators, who could not part the veil of the future.[12a]

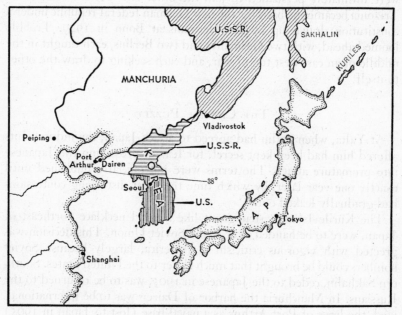

The Postwar Far East

When the victorious Red Army finally left Manchuria in 1946, it systematically wrecked or removed most of the factory machinery from this industrial heart of China, presumably to keep it from the anti-Communist Nationalists of Chiang Kai-shek. The Soviets also delayed their departure so as to permit the Chinese Communists to secure a foothold, which they rapidly expanded with captured Japanese arms conveniently "abandoned" by the Russians. All this aroused grave misgivings among Americans, many of whom perceived with growing

[12a] For a full defense of the Yalta arrangements by one of the American participants, see E. R. Stettinius, Jr., *Roosevelt and the Russians* (Garden City, N.Y., 1949).
The author concludes (p. 303) that the real trouble lay not in the Yalta agreements
but in the failure of the Russians to live up to them.

clarity that the Chinese Communists were not mere "agricultural reformers" but ideological cousins if not bedfellows of Moscow.

General George C. Marshall, fresh from his wartime laurels as United States Chief of Staff, was sent to China late in 1945 in a final effort to end the decades-old civil clash between Communists and Nationalists. After negotiating for a year, and after attempting to reconcile the irreconcilable with various kinds of pressures and persuasions, he was forced to confess failure.[13] Returning home early in 1947, he was sworn in as Secretary of State to succeed James F. Byrnes, who had resigned because of ill-health. The unprecedented appointment of a high ranking general to perhaps the highest civilian post, coupled with the employment of generals elsewhere in the diplomatic service, aroused genuine fears of a drift toward military dictatorship. But the glint of brass, which proved temporary, indicated that the war was not actually over and that the most pressing problems were those of power politics.

Washington rather haphazardly continued to send financial and military aid to the corrupt and inefficient government of Nationalist China, which was rapidly forfeiting the confidence of its own people. The Chinese Communists, looking upon the United States as their chief enemy, condemned this intervention, which amounted since mid-1945 to about two billion dollars in money alone, to say nothing of military supplies and other assistance. The dam began to break late in 1948, when the Communists overran Manchuria and pushed southward into the heart of China. In desperation the glamorous Madame Chiang Kai-shek undertook another trans-Pacific flight to Washington, in November, 1948, vainly seeking large-scale support for her faltering husband. Chiang was forced to bow out as president of China in January, 1949, although still retaining much behind-the-scenes control.

The collapse of Nationalist China was undeniably a resounding victory for the Communists in their world-wide struggle against the western democracies. Critics of the Truman Administration, chiefly Republicans spearheaded by such men as the well-known ex-diplomat, Patrick J. Hurley, charged that the catastrophe had been engineered by Communists in the American diplomatic service who had thwarted the prompt sending of adequate aid. In relation to China the bi-partisan foreign policy was most severely strained, largely because, so the Republicans claimed, they had not been consulted in its formulation. Many of them continued to demand further financial aid for National-

[13] For Marshall's report, see J. K. Fairbank, *The United States and China* (Cambridge, 1948), pp. 343–349.

ist China, even at the expense of grants for the recovery of Europe.

The Department of State, hoping to head off what it regarded as further expensive injections into a dead horse, issued a sensational White Paper on August 5, 1949.[14] Absolving the United States of all responsibility for the debacle, it put the blame squarely on the Nationalist regime—a regime which it represented as so inept, selfish, purblind, and faithless as to be lost beyond hope of resurrection. But the Truman Administration promised to assist such elements in China as would rally in the future against Communist ("foreign") domination.

This scorching denunciation of a presumably friendly government, though criticized by many Republicans, was generally upheld by public opinion.[15] Most Americans were apparently willing to accept Washington's policy, not wishing further to antagonize the victorious Communists (with whom American merchants would have to do business), and hoping that 450,000,000 hungry and war-ravaged Chinese would prove a lethal millstone around the neck of the Communist cause. The Open Door at all events seemed to be a mirage from a bygone era.

DEMOCRACY IN EASTERN ASIA

The United States came into direct contact with the Soviets in Korea, which was divided into American and Russian zones of occupation by the 38th parallel. In their northern zone the Soviets set up a puppet Communist clique and trained a Communist army, all the while fighting strenuously in the United Nations against a South Korean government.

In the southern zone the United States—bedeviled by internal dissension, Communist agitation, and economic prostration—attempted to foster a democratic order. The Soviets in their zone had only to make a minority Communist; the Americans had to make a majority democratic and keep them that way—at great expense to the taxpayers at home. Whenever the United States troops were withdrawn, the Communist armies would presumably swarm down and take control.

The situation in Japan was considerably more favorable to American aims in the early postwar years. The United States, as the principal conqueror, was chiefly responsible for the Allied occupation, with General Douglas MacArthur in the driver's seat, and with the multi-Power Far Eastern Commission in Washington providing directives. The able

---

[14] *United States Relations with China* (Washington, 1949).

[15] As early as May 27, 1949, Gallup (News Release) found that only 22% favored help to China, as compared with 55% a year before (April 28, 1948). See *Pub. Opin. Quar.*, XII, 548.

but rather high-handed MacArthur evoked bitter but futile protests from the Russians, who did not relish being dosed with their own authoritarian medicine. Unable to make satisfactory headway in communizing Japan, the Soviets blocked all progress toward a peace treaty with Tokyo, except on their terms. They also continued to retain hundreds of thousands of Japanese prisoners of war, contrary to agreement, but clearly for purposes of Communist indoctrination.

The leading Japanese war lords, including Tojo, were given a protracted trial and executed in December, 1948, after the pattern of the German war crimes trials. Under the stern but paternal hand of General MacArthur the proposed democratization of Japan went forward, in an effort to eliminate Fascist features, and in 1947 a new constitution was established. Whether democracy under these auspices would "take" was an open question, but there was no doubt that after the Communist victories in China the Japanese archipelago became more valuable to the United States as an offshore anti-Communist bastion. The MacArthur regime in 1948 completed great bombing bases within reach of Soviet Russia's industrial vitals.[16]

Farther south in Asiatic waters significant changes were taking place. The Philippine Islands were formally given their long-promised independence in colorful ceremonies at Manila on the Fourth of July, 1946. The United States agreed, among other things, to pay the infant republic $620,000,000 for damages sustained in fighting the Japanese, and to grant tariff preferences for a period of years. But in return American citizens were to have equality with Philippine citizens in exploiting the rich resources of the archipelago. The United States also retained, as ninety-nine-year leaseholds, twenty-three military and naval bases, which seemed even more desirable as the tides of political uncertainty, including the Communists, swirled into southeastern Asia.

THE NEW PARLIAMENT OF MAN

The world forum known as the United Nations was organized in London early in 1946, when the Assembly and the Security Council came into being. After voting to establish a permanent home in the United States, the organization found temporary quarters in the New York City area, pending the construction of permanent buildings on a Manhattan site donated by John D. Rockefeller, Jr.

[16] Curiously invoking freedom of the seas, the Soviets twice protested in 1948 against low-flying American planes circling their merchantmen in Far Eastern waters. New York *Times*, Feb. 2, 1948, 1 : 1; March 5, 1948, 1 : 2.

The judicial arm of the United Nations—the International Court of Justice—was adhered to by the United States Senate, on August 2, 1946, by a vote of 60 to 2. But this adherence was weakened when the Senators, in line with traditional practice, voted to exempt from "compulsory jurisdiction" all disputes involving domestic affairs, such as tariffs and immigration, with the United States being the sole judge of what was "domestic."

Washington was eager to retain the small but strategically important Japanese mandated islands in the Pacific as a trusteeship from the United Nations. These hard-won outposts were the only territorial gains that the man in the street desired from the war. After President Truman had bluntly announced that the islands would be kept anyhow, the Security Council, on April 2, 1947, awarded them to the United States. The Soviets rather surprisingly acquiesced in this decision, but not until Secretary Byrnes had delicately hinted that Washington might not support their title to the Kuriles and Sakhalin when the final peace terms were drafted.[17]

The Soviets from the outset openly used the United Nations as an agency to promote communism and combat anti-Communist forces. Although criticizing the amended version as too weak, they had a large hand in pushing an anti-Fascist resolution through the United Nations General Assembly recommending a withdrawal of ambassadors from the capital of Franco's Spain. (This the United States and other nations did.) The Russians used their veto to block an American-backed investigation of Communist support for the Greek guerrillas, and to blackball the admission of new states with allegedly "Fascist" coloration, such as Ireland and Portugal—states that would join the "capitalistic" camp. The Soviet Union also declined to participate in many of the functions of the United Nations.[18]

Most alarming of all was Soviet opposition to American plans for international control of atomic energy. The Washington government, with what it regarded as unique generosity, offered to share its terrible "secret," provided adequate safeguards were erected. The chief obstacle to any such restrictions was the natural unwillingness of the secretive Soviets to permit international inspectors to prowl around their country. The Russians further demanded that the bomb first be outlawed, and that the United States destroy its stockpiles, preparatory to world-wide arms reduction—something that the American people,

---

[17] Byrnes, *op. cit.*, p. 221.

[18] The Soviets also refused to join the two financial organizations set up at Bretton Woods: the International Bank for Reconstruction and Development and the International Monetary Fund.

already dismayed by Soviet behavior, were unwilling to do.[19] Finally in 1948, after all western schemes for atomic control had been deadlocked by the Russians, the United Nations had to suspend its efforts in this direction. The terrifying race in new weapons of mass destruction was sharply accelerated after President Truman, in a startling statement released September 23, 1949, announced that the Russians had recently exploded an atomic bomb.

The Veto Issue

The abuse of the veto in the Security Council by the Soviet Union brought congenital paralysis to the United Nations. The original intent of the western democracies had been that this weapon would be rarely used, and never to obstruct procedure or choke off discussion. But the Soviets, perceiving that they were heavily outnumbered by the capitalistic powers, proceeded to exercise the veto in a routine and ruthless fashion.

The case of Iran (Persia) early spotlighted the widening chasm between Soviet Russia and the democracies. The oil of Iran was coveted by both the Soviet Union and the non-Communist world, while the soil of Iran could be used by the democracies as bomber bases within easy reach of Soviet centers. The deadline came early in 1946 for the evacuation of Iran by Red Army troops, but they remained. The Iranians, over the wrathful objections of the Soviets, brought their case before the Security Council. The Soviet delegate stalked out, and continued to absent himself whenever the issue was discussed. Pressure from both world opinion and the United Nations finally induced the Russians to withdraw, but the basic issue was postponed rather than settled.

To the workaday American, who had earnestly prayed for a sure guarantee against future war, the United Nations was a cruel disappointment. There was a tendency to belittle its solid achievements in helping to bring peace to such places as Indonesia and Palestine, and to overlook entirely its substantial but unspectacular progress in the fields of social and economic welfare. The suspicion grew in America that Soviet Russia had joined the new world organization merely to snarl it up and use it as a global sounding board for Communist propaganda— a suspicion that deepened when in 1947 the Soviet delegate began to let fly with violent charges of "warmongering."

The United Nations Charter made provision for an international

---

[19] Gallup found (Dec. 15, 1946) that 72% were opposed to destroying the bombs made and discontinuing the manufacture of others. *Pub. Opin. Quar.*, XI, 139.

police force to keep the peace, but largely because of Soviet objections such a contingent was not organized. A popular drive began to develop in America to strengthen the United Nations by equipping its toothless gums with adequate dentures. The United World Federalists, envisioning world government, were most conspicuous in their demands for a more powerful organization, and they received considerable backing from a number of state legislatures and from Congress.[20] In 1948 sixteen United States Senators of both parties demanded a revision of the United Nations, with or without Russia.

But Soviet Russia could veto all changes in the charter, as well as any effective move to expel her from the United Nations. If she continued her obstinacy, the western Powers would either have to learn to live with her or draw apart into an organization of their own, leaving her and her satellites to bury the corpse that they had strangled in the cradle.

BEHIND THE IRON CURTAIN

The distrustful and invasion-conscious Soviets, for understandable reasons, were determined to have subservient satellites on their flanks, and this largely accounts for their numerous violations or alleged violations of solemn agreements. The descent of the "iron curtain" [21] over the neighbors of Russia did perhaps more than anything else to arouse the citizenry of the United States against the Communist peril.

Soviet darkness gradually enshrouded Rumania, Bulgaria, Albania, and Hungary, as Moscow-manipulated marionettes took command. Washington made repeated protests to the Kremlin against coercion and intimidation, assertedly in violation of the Yalta pledges. It also made forceful but no less futile representations to the satellites themselves concerning such offenses as infractions of treaties, the execution of political prisoners, and the persecution of religious leaders.

Night likewise spread over Poland when a Soviet-dominated regime was set up in 1945, also in defiance of Yalta. With Moscow's backing, the Polish government proclaimed that its western boundary, vaguely defined at Yalta, was permanent, although the western Powers regarded it as tentative pending a peace settlement. After exasperating delays, the farcical "free and unfettered" election, promised at Yalta,

[20] Gallup found (Aug. 18, 1946) a world government, in control of all armed forces, favored by 54%, while opposed by 24%. *Ibid.*, X, 618.

[21] The phrase was used by Winston Churchill in his speech at Fulton, Missouri, March 5, 1946.

was finally held early in 1947. The Communists polled about a 90 per cent vote, although the American ambassador reported that in an honest election the opposition party would have won 60 per cent of the votes.[22] Washington's protests against what it regarded as the flouting of Yalta were wasted paper and ink.

Yugoslavia, a presumed Communist satellite under the iron hand of Marshal Tito, reacted rancorously against American opposition to its proposed grab of Trieste. The internationalization of the city created

"A QUESTION OF GEOGRAPHY"

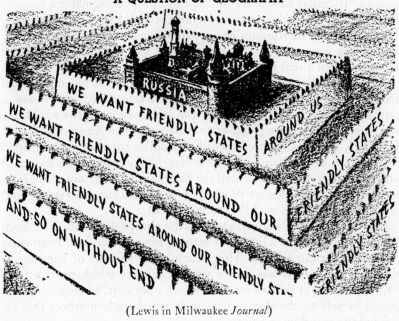

(Lewis in Milwaukee *Journal*)

an explosive situation that brought numerous minor clashes between United States and British troops on the one hand, and the Yugoslavs on the other.

In August, 1946, an American army transport, allegedly flying over Yugoslavian soil in the face of protests against this practice, was deliberately shot down with a loss of five lives. Even assuming that the Americans had violated Yugoslavian sovereignty, the punishment did not fit the crime. The State Department, backed by an irate public, presented an ultimatum. Tito was forced to apologize, and shortly thereafter paid an indemnity of $150,000. But the feeling was general in

[22] A. B. Lane, *I Saw Poland Betrayed* (Indianapolis, 1948), p. 287.

America that he would not have been guilty of such an outrage if he had not had at least the silent backing of Stalin.[23]

BOLSTERING BRITAIN

The westward sweep of Communism served as a reminder that Britain, in 1945 as in 1940, was the only dependable major bulwark of democracy left in Europe. Ex-Prime Minister Winston Churchill, in a reverberating speech at Fulton, Missouri, on March 5, 1946, proposed a "fraternal association" of the English-speaking nations to check the U.S.S.R. This scheme was generally received with disfavor in the United States. The Russians had apparently not yet turned completely against the west; the no-alliance tradition was still deep-seated; and there was then a real though diminishing faith in the United Nations.

Once-proud Britain, whose foreign trade was her life blood, emerged from six years of war with ships sunk, markets closed, and overseas capital bleeding away. Like most of the other nations of the world, she was forced to buy more goods from Americans than Americans bought from her, as a consequence of which her dollar balances in the United States were disappearing. This "dollar hemorrhage" afflicted most other countries, and underscored the fact that the American giant, even more so than at the close of World War I, was the last great stronghold of capitalism and the world's creditor to boot.

The British, who were shocked by the abrupt termination of lend-lease in 1945, sought a gift or at least an interest-free loan from their opulent American cousins. After nearly three months of haggling, a fifty-year agreement was drawn up late in 1945 which provided for $3,750,000,000 at the low interest rate of 2 per cent. In return, Britain bound herself to abandon certain preferential trade practices that restricted the free flow of goods.

The agreement was promptly approved by Parliament, although not without sneers at the tight-fisted Uncle Sam. The debate in Congress, despite the need for haste, was heated and long-winded, lasting about seven months. Britain was attacked as a poor risk (Senator Taft of Ohio favored $1,250,000,000 as an outright gift); she had defaulted on her war debt of World War I; the United States had given her enough already; the American citizens needed the money themselves; and the taxpayers were already groaning. The recent turn of Britain toward socialism also inspired biting criticism, including that of Rep-

---

[23] American opinion of Tito improved when in 1948 he split with Moscow. Various kinds of American aid were then made available to him.

resentative Knutson of Minnesota, who complained, "We are being called upon to finance the socialization of the British Empire." Representative Celler of New York, a prominent legislator of Jewish faith who shared the bitterness of his co-religionists against Britain's anti-Jewish policy in Palestine, was quoted as saying that the loan would "promote too damned much socialism at home and too damned much imperialism abroad."

The Truman Administration realistically urged that the loan be approved on the basis of American self-interest. Britain's recovery was essential for world recovery, without which America's prosperity would presumably wither away. Non-Administration spokesmen also urged the necessity of bolstering the British against communism, and of not driving them into the arms of Russia. The obstreperous behavior of the Soviets at the peace conference then being held in Paris gave emphasis to this argument, which may well have been the decisive one.

The loan was never popular in the United States, and it may never have commanded majority support.[24] Yet many people, not deaf to the call of humanity, argued that rich and unscathed America owed poor and battered Britain an enormous debt for having halted the Nazis in 1940. The final vote in Congress, in July, 1946, was favorable but close: 46 to 34 in the Senate, and 219 to 155 in the House.[25] Neither Americans nor Britons were happy over the outcome. The debate in Congress had dragged on so long, and the prices of American goods had skyrocketed so sharply, that the purchasing power of the loan had shrunk materially since the British had committed themselves to its terms.

THE WANDERING JEW COMES HOME

The Palestine problem came to a boil at the time of the debates over the British loan, and introduced new complications. The Jews had long dreamed of securing a national home in their ancestral lands, and with tens of thousands uprooted by the war, and additional millions butchered by the Nazis, they were determined to get it. But the Arabs, who outnumbered the Jews about two to one in Palestine, had established

[24] Gallup reported (Oct. 29, 1945) that only 27% were favorable to a British loan. Pub. Opin. Quar., IX, 533. Another poll found that when the purposes of the grant were explained a plurality approved; otherwise a plurality disapproved. Nat. Opin. Research Center, Opinion News, March 5, 1946, p. 1.

[25] Signed by President Truman, July 15, 1946. Text in U.S. Code, 1946 ed., II, 2286–2288. The two per cent annual interest would be waived under specified adverse circumstances. In the same agreement Britain's lend-lease obligations were scaled down to a nominal $650,000,000.

rights through centuries of residence, and they could not be elbowed aside without grave injustices. The British, who still held a League of Nations mandate over Palestine, had obligations to the Arabs, whom for reasons of imperial defense they were loath to antagonize. In a series of heart-rending scenes, British patrols turned back a number of steamers laden with Jewish refugees within sight of the Promised Land.

The United States, which needed oil and bases for a possible struggle with Soviet Russia, was also reluctant to alienate the Arabs. Yet if the Arabs had the oil, which was far away, the American Jews had the vote, which was near at hand, and the latter might, especially in New York, turn the forthcoming presidential election against Harry S. Truman. With an obvious play for votes, but much to the annoyance of the British, both President Truman and his prospective opponent, Governor Thomas E. Dewey of New York, urged Britain in 1946 to admit a minimum of 100,000 Jews to Palestine.

The financially exhausted British, weary of the Palestine encumbrance, finally dumped it on the doorstep of the United Nations, in April, 1947. A scheme for partitioning Palestine between Arabs and Jews was devised,[26] but it was strenuously opposed by Arab members of the United Nations, whose population numbered many millions, as contrasted with fewer than 600,000 Jews in Palestine. The Truman Administration, with what was criticized at home as more regard for Jewish votes than for American strategic interests, used the enormous influence of the United States to force partition through the United Nations.[27]

When it became clear that the Arabs would not accept partition, the Truman Administration proposed a temporary United Nations trusteeship over Palestine to keep the peace. This seeming reversal was assailed, both at home and abroad, as an effort to sacrifice the Jews on the altar of oil-imperialism. The Jews nevertheless went ahead with their plans, and on May 14, 1948, announced the formation of the new

[26] The experts in the State Department opposed partition. These same experts believed that the Soviets supported it because they hoped to create a danger spot favorable to Communist machinations.

[27] American opinion, though showing much indifference, rather strongly favored the partition of Palestine, with the admittance of large numbers of Jewish refugees. There was heavy opposition to sending American troops to defend them, or to admitting large numbers of Jews to the United States. *Pub. Opin. Quar.*, X, 418: XII, 161, 162. American opinion did not respond with conspicuous humanitarianism to the plight of the hundreds of thousands of Displaced Persons (DP's) in Europe. In June, 1948, after prolonged delay, Congress voted to admit 205,000, under restrictions which were criticized as prejudicial to Catholics and Jews.

state of Israel. Eight hours and five minutes later President Truman, presumably still thinking of the next election, stole a march on London and Moscow by hastily extending *de facto* recognition.

Invading columns from the hostile Arab states penetrated Israel, but were hurled back by numerically inferior but better trained Jewish forces, who were aided in both money and man power by their co-religionists in the United States. Mediation by the United Nations, with the distinguished American Negro, Dr. Ralph J. Bunche, winning many of the plaudits, finally brought the fighting to a halt. A new state was born, under circumstances as fantastic as the Arabian nights, which seemed destined to take the place of Ireland as the leading object of American hyphenate concern.

BIBLIOGRAPHICAL NOTE

The best general surveys of the postwar years are J. C. Campbell, *et al.*, *The United States in World Affairs, 1945–1947* (N.Y., 1947), and the same authors' *The United States in World Affairs, 1947–1948* (N.Y., 1948). Critical and journalistic but not without merit is E. A. Mowrer, *The Nightmare of American Foreign Policy* (N.Y., 1948). See also Sumner Welles, *Where Are We Heading?* (N.Y., 1946); W. B. Willcox and R. B. Hall, *The United States in the Postwar World* (Ann Arbor, Mich., 1947). A specialized study is L. S. Cottrell, Jr. and Sylvia Eberhart, *American Opinion on World Affairs in the Atomic Age* (Princeton, 1948). Extremely valuable first-hand observations appear in J. F. Byrnes, *Speaking Frankly* (N.Y., 1947), and important excerpts from the Hopkins papers in R. E. Sherwood, *Roosevelt and Hopkins* (N.Y., 1948). Former Ambassador A. B. Lane presents the inside story in *I Saw Poland Betrayed* (Indianapolis, 1948). An indispensable documentary collection is continued by L. M. Goodrich and M. J. Carroll, *Documents on American Foreign Relations, July 1944–June 1945* (vol. VII, Princeton, 1947), and R. Dennett and R. K. Turner, *Documents on American Foreign Relations, July 1, 1945–December 31, 1946* (vol. VIII, Princeton, 1948). On Russia, Vera M. Dean, *The United States and Russia* (Cambridge, 1948), is sympathetic and concerned primarily with recent developments. H. H. Fisher, *America and Russia in the World Community* (Claremont, Calif., 1946), is also sympathetic but broader in its historical approach. Apprehensive of Russia is W. H. Chamberlin, *The European Cockpit* (N.Y., 1947), and violently so is W. C. Bullitt, *The Great Globe Itself* (N.Y., 1946). Of the numerous books on Britain, some of them ephemeral, the following may be singled out: W. H. Chamberlin, *America: Partner in World Rule* (N.Y., 1945); P. E. Corbett, *Britain: Partner for Peace* (N.Y., 1946); Keith Hutchinson, *Rival Partners: America and Britain in the Postwar World* (N.Y., 1946); and George Soule, *America's Stake in Britain's Future* (N.Y., 1945). See also F. L. Benns, "The Two Paris Peace Conferences of the Twentieth Century," in D. E. Lee and G. E. McReynolds, eds., *Essays in History and International Relations in Honor of George Hubbard Blakeslee* (Worcester, Mass., 1949), pp. 153–170; Harold Nicolson, "Peacemaking at Paris: Success, Failure or Farce?" *Foreign Affairs*,

XXV (Jan. 1947), 190–203; and B. U. Ratchford and W. D. Ross, *Berlin Reparations Assignment* (Chapel Hill, N.C., 1947). On the Far East, consult K. S. Latourette, *The United States Moves Across the Pacific* (N.Y., 1946), and J. K. Fairbank, *The United States and China* (Cambridge, 1948).

CHAPTER L

The Cold War

"Let us not be deceived—we are today in the midst of a cold war."
Bernard Baruch, April 16, 1947.

THE TRUMAN DOCTRINE

THE FEAR-INSPIRING gains of Russian communism had by early 1947 swung American opinion around in favor of a "get tough" policy toward the U.S.S.R. The Truman Administration, aware of imminent Communist inroads and confident of strong public backing, prepared to take drastic action.

The explosion was touched off in February, 1947, when the overburdened British shocked Washington by announcing that they could no longer provide full-scale economic support for the "rightist" government of Greece. When they curtailed or withdrew their assistance, the Communist guerrillas, who were thought to be receiving help from their Communist neighbors, would probably seize control. Greece would then gravitate within the Soviet orbit, the position of Turkey would become untenable, and the strategically vital eastern Mediterranean would fall into Communist hands—with momentous consequences for the western world.

After hurried conferences with military and Congressional leaders, President Truman appeared before Congress, on March 12, 1947, to make a truly epochal pronouncement. In unimpassioned but solemn tones, he described the plight of war-racked Greece, and then declared:

> One of the primary objectives of the foreign policy of the United States is the creation of conditions in which we and other nations will be able to work out a way of life free from coercion. . . . We shall not realize our objectives, however, unless we are willing to help free peoples to maintain their free institutions and their national integrity against aggressive movements that seek to impose upon them totalitarian regimes. [Applause.] This is no more than a frank recognition that totalitarian regimes imposed on free peoples, by direct or indirect aggression, undermine the foundations of international peace and hence the security of the United States.[1]

[1] *Cong. Record*, 80 Cong., 1 sess., p. 1981 (March 12, 1947).

Truman thereupon concluded that "it must be the policy of the United States to support free peoples who are resisting attempted subjugation by armed minorities or by outside pressures." With such a goal in view he specifically requested an appropriation of $400,000,000 for the economic and military succor of both Greece and Turkey. This, he conceded, was a "serious course," but the alternative of drifting was "much more serious. [Applause.]" The United States had invested the colossal sum of $341,000,000,000 in the recent war to guarantee its freedom; the proposed appropriation—only "one tenth of 1 per cent" of that amount—was to insure the huge investment, which otherwise might be lost. The implication was clear that Congress had better expend a modest amount of the taxpayers' money rather than expend the taxpayer himself.

The nation, though now willing to halt Soviet advances by risky measures, was momentarily stunned by the President's bombshell. But the feeling was general that while the "Truman Doctrine" was fraught with peril, a course of dangerous do-nothingism was even more hazardous. The only two major groups that expressed strong hostility were the Henry A. Wallace "liberals" and the old-line isolationists, of whom the Chicago *Tribune* was a leading spokesman.[2]

Among the most telling arguments against the Truman Doctrine were the following: The scheme would cost too much; the initial appropriation would be a mere drop in the bucket. A bad precedent would be established, and rich though America was she would bankrupt herself by bolstering bankrupts all over the world. Communism could not be fought with dollars. In Greece particularly, the United States would be betraying its sacred traditions by fostering "Fascist" reaction against "democratic forces." Americans would be poking their noses into the internal affairs of foreign governments, and would thus unite the world against them. Although Truman had been careful not to mention Soviet Russia by name, there could be no doubt that he was aiming his doctrine at her, with imminent danger of goading her into war.

Weighty also was the charge that Truman had cavalierly by-passed the United Nations, thereby weakening it at a time when it was getting off to a wobbly start. The President had admittedly taken unilateral

---

[2] J. C. Campbell, *et al.*, *The United States in World Affairs, 1947–1948* (N.Y., 1948), p. 34. Gallup found (March 28, 1947) that 56% favored the loan to Greece; 49% the loan to Turkey. 54% opposed sending American military advisers to Greece; 44% to Turkey. 56% opposed by-passing the United Nations completely. 54% did not believe that the aid program was likely to involve America in war. Nat. Opin. Research Center, *Opinion News*, April 15, 1947. The Truman-aid program became more popular with the passage of time.

action, presumably because of a sure Soviet veto in the Security Council. Yet he had gone out so far on the end of a limb that he could not be repudiated without weakening the position of the United States at a critical hour. Senator Vandenberg, who with a majority of his Republi-

"Where to?" (Seibel in Richmond *Times-Dispatch*)

can colleagues continued to support a bi-partisan foreign policy, helped carry through Congress a face-saving amendment which stipulated that whenever the United Nations was prepared to take over the burden the United States would lay it down.[3]

[3] *U.S. Statutes at Large*, vol. LXI, pt. I, pp. 103–105.

After a wordy debate of about two months, Congress finally approved the initial Truman Doctrine appropriations of $400,000,000, on May 15, 1947. The vote, which reflected widespread public support, was 67 to 23 in the Senate and 287 to 107 in the House.

The Truman Doctrine was of incalculable significance. Through it the United States seized the tactical offensive in the "cold war" to contain communism. Although limited for the present to Greece and Turkey, the new policy was general in scope and led by direct steps to the vastly more important Marshall Plan and Atlantic Pact. It was a kind of lend-lease, this time against communism rather than fascism; and as was true of the original lend-lease, the United States preferred the evils of chance-taking to those of side-line sitting. The Truman Doctrine reversed the nonintervention principle of the original Monroe Doctrine, but like the Monroe Doctrine it aimed at long-range defense.[4] As historic champions of democracy, the American masses were embarrassed to be supporting reaction in Greece, but the world crisis was such in 1947 that they were prepared to put security above democracy, in the hope that democracy would come later.

THE MARSHALL PLAN

Once the people of the United States had accepted the principle of helping independent governments resist the creeping paralysis of communism, they gradually perceived that aid for only Greece and Turkey —aid of a military or stopgap relief nature—was quite inadequate. War-blasted Western Europe, further scourged by the winter of 1946–1947, was not making the necessary economic recovery. Local Communists, in various countries, were deliberately sabotaging progress by strikes and other incendiary tactics. If the chaos that was so favorable to communism should develop, the Communists would probably seize control of Italy and France. All Western Europe would then fall into their grip, and Moscow's influence would sweep to the English Channel.

Into the breach stepped Secretary Marshall, who in an address at Harvard University (June 5, 1947) announced a policy which eclipsed the Truman Doctrine in importance. He said in essence that if the nations of Europe would get together (this was later interpreted to include Britain and Russia), devise far-visioned plans for economic re-

---

[4] Monroe promised to stay out of Greece; Truman urged that America go into Greece. In 1823 America's defense line was the Gulf of Mexico; in 1947 the Gulf of Corinth.

covery, concentrate on self-help and mutual assistance, and present to Washington a specific statement of their needs, the United States would support them with financial help "so far as it may be practical. . . ."

This was not a clear-cut promise, and it put the burden of initiative squarely on Europe's shoulders. As a consequence the speech did not at once make a great splash in the United States.[5] But gradually the American people perceived that the Marshall scheme was no unilateral

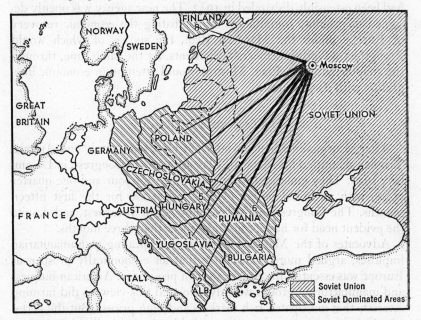

The Tide of Communism. (Adapted from New York *Times*, April 18, 1948)
Figures indicate order of Soviet domination.

Truman Doctrine aimed at military aid or temporary relief but an inclusive plan looking toward long-range rehabilitation.

The foreign ministers of France and Britain, recognizing the breathtaking implications of Marshall's overture, arranged a meeting at Paris, to which the Soviet foreign minister was invited. After a short but controversial stay, Molotov walked out, spurning the opportunity to tie up the Marshall Plan with obstructionism.

The British and French thereupon issued invitations to twenty-two countries (all Europe west of Russia except Spain) to attend a Paris

[5] Gallup found (July 23, 1947) that of the 49% who had heard of Marshall's proposal, 57% were favorable, and 21% opposed. *Pub. Opin. Quar.*, XI, 495.

conference for the discussion of specific needs. The eight nations under the shadow of the hammer and sickle declined, or were forced by Moscow to decline.[6] The sixteen-power Paris conference, meeting from July to September, 1947, finally hammered individual "shopping lists" of desired items into an integrated program.

One answer of the Soviet Union to the Marshall Plan was the nine-nation Communist Information Bureau (Cominform), announced October 5, 1947. It was in effect a revival of the old Comintern, which had been ostensibly disbanded in 1943. The new agency was openly designed to promote communism by combating the economic recovery of Europe under the Marshall Plan, the success of which would strengthen wavering democratic elements. At the same time, through the counter Molotov Plan, Moscow would attempt an economic integration with its satellites.

DOLLARS TO THE RESCUE

After securing emergency winter aid for France, Italy and Austria, Truman submitted his Marshall Plan estimates to Congress, in December, 1947. They embraced $17,000,000,000 for four and one quarter years, with an initial outlay of $6,800,000,000 for the first fifteen months. The Congressional debate now began in earnest, and despite the evident need for haste, consumed more than three months.

Advocates of the Marshall Plan, while appealing to humanitarian impulses, argued more realistically that an economically prosperous Europe was essential for America's own prosperity. American business and manufacturing groups warmly seconded this view, as did farming interests that anticipated rich markets and high prices.[7] But the necessity of halting communism was probably the compelling argument. The Marshall Plan was admittedly a calculated risk. It might not work, but it was cheaper than war, and if successful in redressing the European balance, it might head off a war that would be infinitely costly and destructive. A Committee for the Marshall Plan, reminiscent of the aid-the-Allies groups of World War II, harped persistently on this theme.

Critics of Marshall aid charged that it was just another "Operation Rathole." "Uncle Santa Claus" had already poured too much into the

[6] The eight were Albania, Bulgaria, Czechoslovakia, Finland, Hungary, Poland, Rumania, and Yugoslavia. The sixteen Marshall Plan countries were: Austria, Belgium, Britain, Denmark, Eire, France, Greece, Iceland, Italy, Luxembourg, the Netherlands, Norway, Portugal, Sweden, Switzerland, and Turkey.

[7] Campbell, *op. cit.*, p. 487.

pockets of ungrateful Europeans—about $12,000,000,000 in various loans and grants since mid-1945. The whole scheme was a costly gamble —a "share-the-American-wealth plan." America had better make herself strong at home, conserve her resources, and help her own needy people. By shipping her scarce goods abroad, she would further inflate prices, and perhaps bring back wartime economic controls. She would offend the Russians (who were already offended), divide Europe (which was already divided), and lay herself open to the charge (which had already been made) of interference through "dollar imperialism." The whole device, cried Henry A. Wallace, was a "Martial Plan."

The officials in the Kremlin unwittingly did much to spur the languishing Marshall Plan appropriation through Congress. The Communist coup in Czechoslovakia, in February, 1948, followed by the suicide of Foreign Minister Masaryk under circumstances that suggested foul play, had a profound effect, as did the forcing of "Brave Little" Finland into a distasteful alliance with the Soviets. At the same time Communist tactics also sped through Congress an unprecedented peacetime conscription law and an appropriation for a mighty air force, bringing the total military budget to staggeringly high levels.

Senator Vandenberg, again heading the Republican bi-partisan bloc in the Senate, did yeoman work for the Marshall Plan, while the nationalist Republican Senators—such as Taft of Ohio and Wherry of Nebraska—registered stiff opposition or insisted on cutting down the proposed funds by meat-axe methods. The members of Congress were unwilling on principle to bind future Congresses by a long-term appropriation, so the bill in its final form provided $6,098,000,000 for various purposes during the first twelve months, with a tacit understanding that similar sums would be forthcoming throughout the following three years, and with a proviso, forced upon the Administration by the pro-Chiang Republican bloc, of $463,000,000 for Nationalist China. In a more remarkable maneuver, the House included Fascist Spain among the beneficiaries—a change that dumfounded European liberals and caused Communists abroad and at home to upbraid the hypocrisy of Uncle Sam. This surprise move merely underscored the fact that the appropriation bill was largely anti-Communist in nature, and that the hitherto disreputable Franco was coming to be regarded as an increasingly reputable bulwark against communism. But partly out of deference to world opinion, Spain was finally dropped. The Marshall Plan appropriation passed the House 329 to 74 and the Senate 69 to 17, and was signed by Truman on April 3, 1948.

The Marshall Plan—officially known as the European Relief Program (ERP)—was approved just in time to influence the Italian election.[8] The militant Communist party, crying "Death to Truman," was threatening to gain control and undermine disastrously the position of

Look Who's Talking! (Brodie in San Francisco *Chronicle*)

the democracies in Europe. The United States had been courting Italian favor by a lenient policy on reparations and other issues, and on the

[8] Paul G. Hoffman, president of the Studebaker Corporation, was selected by Truman to head the European Recovery Program as Economic Cooperation Administrator of the Economic Cooperation Administration (ECA).

eve of the balloting proposed that Trieste be returned to Italy. The Italians were also bombarded with thousands of letters from relatives and friends in the United States urging them to repudiate both Marx and Moscow. Confronted with a choice between the concrete aid of the Marshall Plan and the abstract benefits of communism, the Italian people returned a smashing verdict against the Communists. This was the first great victory of the west over communism in the postwar years, and it may have marked the turn of the tide in the cold war.

The Marshall Plan pledged the economic resources of the United States to halt communism, just as lend-lease had pledged the economic resources of the United States to fight fascism. It was intervention of a sort—or rather counterintervention against the previous intervention of communism—but intervention designed to create economic and political conditions in which free men could make a free choice of government.

The Cold War Grows Hotter

In the weeks following the voting of Marshall aid, relations between Moscow and the west deteriorated with ominous speed. The Soviets were angered by the success of the democracies in unifying their three German zones and in establishing currency reform. On June 24, 1948, the Russian authorities shut off non-Russian traffic to Berlin, except by air, evidently reasoning that the western Powers, unable to supply the garrisons and the populace in their sectors, would abandon the city, leaving it in Soviet hands as a rallying point for the unification of a Communist Germany.

The Americans and British responded to this challenge by inaugurating the Berlin airlift, through which they undertook the herculean task of supplying their garrisons and the civilian needs of some 2,500,000 people as well.[9] The amazing success of "Operation Vittles," combined with a counterblockade of the Russian zone of Germany, testified to the determination and resourcefulness of the democracies. The west gained much popularity with the Germans, while the Soviets lost ground correspondingly.

With the democratic world on edge, not knowing when Russian fighter planes or anti-aircraft fire would turn the cold war into a shooting one, the brutality of Soviet methods was brought home to the American people. In August, 1948, Mrs. Oksana S. Kasenkina, a Rus-

---

[9] One national poll (Sept. 15, 1948) showed that 85% were for staying in Berlin, 7% for leaving, and 8% undecided. *Pub. Opin. Quar.*, XII, 764.

sian school teacher, leaped to the pavement from the third floor of the Russian consulate in New York City, rather than suffer further detention. The American authorities refused to surrender the hospitalized victim, and demanded the recall of the Soviet consul general in New York for improper activity. Moscow retaliated by withdrawing consular privileges from the United States at Vladivostok and Leningrad.

Mrs. Kasenkina's disconcerting dive gave further prominence to the anti-Communist probe of the House Committee on Un-American Activities, which was accused by its foes of being "headline happy." The inquisition had been going on for many months, with smaller culprits being uncovered, when the nation was startled by the revelations of a former Moscow-connected Communist, Whittaker Chambers, who alleged that in 1937–1938 Alger Hiss, then an official in the State Department, had turned over to him secret official documents. Whether true or not, the charges burst into the headlines and gave further prominence to well-recognized Soviet espionage techniques.[10]

All these developments induced the United States, at first much opposed to such methods, to match Soviet weapons on the propaganda front. When the war came to a close an economy-minded Congress gave niggardly and uncertain support to an informational and cultural program, popularly known as the "Voice of America," and designed to instruct other peoples in the American way of life and thus to combat communism. But when it became evident that the Soviets were ruthlessly propagandizing abroad, and that the only way to bring the truth to their own people and to their satellites was by short-wave radio, effective opposition melted away, and early in 1948 Congress unanimously put the "Voice of America" program on a more permanent basis with reasonably adequate funds.[11]

Spectacular ammunition came to the "Voice of America" on January 21, 1948, when Washington, in its war of words with the Soviet Union, released captured German documents. These caused Russia to appear in a less favorable light by proving that Hitler and Stalin, in a secret protocol at the time of the nonaggression pact of 1939, had divided Poland and other booty *in advance* of Hitler's assault. The exposé also revealed that Hitler later negotiated with Molotov for sharing much

---

[10] A sensational and best-selling exposé of the U.S.S.R., though probably in some degree fictionized, was earlier published by a renegade Soviet official, V. A. Kravchenko, under the title, *I Chose Freedom* (N.Y., 1946). Mrs. Kasenkina's own story appears in her *Leap to Freedom* (Phila., 1949).

[11] Gallup found that in June, 1947 a plurality of 46% was opposed to short-wave broadcasts to Russia, but by December, 1948, 58% were favorable to spending as much in Europe for propaganda as Russia was. *Ibid.*, XI, 493; XIII, 171. Soviet "jamming" of American broadcasts reduced their effectiveness.

of the world, including the British Empire, but gagged on Russian demands for dominance in the Balkans, and then clandestinely prepared to attack his ally. The chief result of these disclosures in America was to deepen distrust of Soviet motives.[12]

A Victory for Bi-Partisanism

Harry S. Truman was nominated for the presidency in 1948 by the Democratic party, the southern wing of which—the "Dixiecrats"—bolted over his program of civil rights for Negroes. The overconfident Republicans renominated their unsuccessful standard bearer of 1944, the dapper Governor Dewey of New York.

Truman and Dewey, concentrating their fire on domestic problems, succeeded fairly well in keeping foreign policy on the new bi-partisan level. Dewey criticized the Administration for its "wobbling and fumbling" tactics rather than for its over-all policy and objectives. While favoring a "firm" stand toward Moscow, he urged going further in aiding China than the Administration desired. "Harassed Harry" Truman, undaunted by the seeming odds against him, toured the country in a "whistle stop" campaign, during which he sniped at the costly and cheese-paring Republican isolationism since 1920.

The already confused campaign was further complicated by the antics of Henry A. Wallace. An idealist and visionary who hated war, Wallace had been forced out of Truman's cabinet as Secretary of Commerce when in a New York speech (September 12, 1946) he had advocated a go-easy-on-Russia policy, while Secretary of State Byrnes, then negotiating at the Paris conference, was upholding a get-tough-with-Russia policy. Republican Senator Vandenberg cuttingly remarked, "We can only co-operate with one Secretary of State at a time."

Wallace thereafter was indefatigable, both at home and abroad, in excoriating the bi-partisan anti-Soviet policy of Washington, and in May, 1948, touched off what his followers called a "peace scare" by addressing an open letter to Stalin, to which the latter replied with seeming cordiality.[13] But the State Department spurned these highly irregu-

[12] R. J. Sontag and J. S. Beddie, eds., *Nazi-Soviet Relations, 1939–1941* (Washington, 1948), pp. 78, 226–254. The Soviets countered with documents of their own, charging among other things that the United States had financed the Nazis. See New York *Times*, Feb. 10, 1948, 1:8.

[13] This letter may well have been a violation of the Logan Act of 1799, which as revised forbids unauthorized negotiations with foreign governments regarding matters in dispute with the United States. *U.S. Code*, 1946 ed., II, 1842. But the Administration apparently did not want to make a martyr of Wallace and add to his votes. Less assailable on legal grounds but nevertheless extraordinary, was the speaking tour that Wallace made in western Europe in 1947, during which he denounced American foreign policy as Wall Street dominated and imperialistic.

lar overtures. It reasoned that nothing could be accomplished by a bilateral negotiation of problems which involved many countries; that Washington had repeatedly proposed a discussion of these problems with Russia and had been consistently rebuffed; and that the United Nations existed to iron out current misunderstandings—a United Nations which the Soviet Union had repeatedly paralyzed with the veto virus.

Unable to force the Truman Administration to soften its Soviet policy, Wallace made good his threat to head a third party when he further split the Democrats by accepting the Progressive nomination in July, 1948. His platform denounced the Truman policies as inspired by Wall Street and professional militarists, condemned the recent peacetime draft, and demanded an end to the stalemate in Soviet-American relations. These views attracted many "liberals" and various disaffected elements, who naturally received clamorous support from American Communists. Wallace, dripping rotten eggs in some Southern cities, grew even more intemperate in his assaults on Truman's attitude toward Russia. His efforts undoubtedly weakened the position of the United States abroad, and by promising even greater disunity, may have encouraged the Kremlin to continue its stiff-necked course, especially in regard to the Berlin blockade. Not since the days of the Federalists had an important political group so openly espoused the foreign policy of another government.

President Truman was elected in an incredible upset, partly because of his own vigor and largely because of Dewey's vagueness. Wallace polled only 1,157,100 votes out of the 48,680,416 cast.[14] This evidence that the nation was behind Washington's "firm" Soviet policy may have had a sobering effect on the Kremlin, which began to adopt a somewhat more conciliatory tone.[15]

Enheartened by the triumphant election in "his own right," Truman keynoted his inaugural address by urging, under Point Four, a "Bold New Program" designed to build up prosperous customers in that half of the world in which the masses lived in misery or near-misery. In contrast with the Marshall Plan, American technicians and private investors were to be encouraged to carry the burden, in a manner sugges-

---

[14] Wallace lost considerable strength through an inability to get his name on the ballot in some states.

[15] The ailing and weary Secretary Marshall resigned after the election, on January 8, 1949, to be succeeded by former Undersecretary of State Dean Acheson, whose nomination was confirmed only after the Senate had assured itself of his "toughness" regarding Russia. This appointment, like that of Stettinius and Marshall, continued the recent trend toward non-political secretaries of state.

tive of President Taft's dollar diplomacy. The basic thought was that prosperous customers would increase American trade while combating Russian communism. But the rank-and-file taxpayers, who were somewhat weary of global well doing, responded with scant enthusiasm.

THE LATIN AMERICAN HONEYMOON ENDS

The Bold New Program could obviously be applied with greatest profit to the vast, undeveloped areas south of the Rio Grande. It would further bolster the Latin American policy of the United States, which since the end of the recent conflict, and as a phase of the cold war, had sought to create a solid front in the Americas against communism. The Great Republic of the North was fearful lest the smaller republics to the south, especially those near the Panama lifeline, fall into the clutches of Communists, whose rallying cry was "Abajo Imperialismo Yanqui!" [16] In May, 1946, President Truman urged Congress to provide friendly Latin American states with arms, thus lessening their dependence on European military missions, strengthening them against Communist aggressors, and drawing them further under the wings of the United States. But Congress for various reasons failed to respond.

Argentina continued to be the most formidable obstacle to an all-American front. The dynamic Colonel Perón succeeded in consolidating his dictatorship late in 1945, despite strong protests from United States Ambassador Braden. In the midst of the controversy Braden was brought home to be made an Assistant Secretary of State. On February 12, 1946, the Department of State, in what appeared to be an attempt to defeat Perón in the impending presidential election, published a dynamite-laden Blue Book. It consisted of captured German documents which exposed Nazi influences in Argentina and implicated Perón himself in a conspiracy with the Nazis to undermine the governments of neighboring republics, notably Bolivia. The Peronistas, denouncing the action of Washington as intervention contrary to the Good Neighbor Policy, raised the cry, "Perón or Braden!" Interference by Washington probably swung many votes to Perón, who won by a comfortable margin.

This triumph for dictatorship called for a shift of policy, because the people of the United States were not willing to forsake good neighbor-

[16] Meaning, "Down with Yankee Imperialism!" The United States abandoned most of its wartime bases in Latin America, but negotiated an agreement with Panama for retaining important outposts necessary for the defense of the canal. Mounting nationalist opposition, some of it Communist-inspired, caused the Panama Assembly to reject the pact unanimously on December 23, 1947. New York *Times*, December 24, 1947, 1:8.

ism and undertake strong-arm methods on a large scale. Secretary Byrnes announced in April, 1946, that Washington would welcome Argentina into the fold if she would fulfill her Chapultepec pledges and stamp out Nazi infection. The Argentine regime was more tender with the Nazis than the United States liked, but in June, 1947, President Truman proclaimed that Buenos Aires had carried out its commitments. Henceforth Washington managed to get along with Perón, who, like Franco, was anti-Communist and who, like Franco, grew in respectability as the Soviet shadow lengthened.

The Act of Chapultepec (1945), while aligning the American republics against the Axis assailants, was in its defense aspects primarily a wartime measure. The new danger of Stalinism emphasized the necessity, referred to in the Act itself, of a permanent pact that would set up effective safeguards against aggressors. With this object in view a special conference of American states was finally scheduled for Rio de Janeiro, in August, 1947. Attesting to its importance, the President of the United States journeyed south to close the meetings, amid shouts of "Viva Truman!" The most memorable achievement of the conference was the Treaty of Rio de Janeiro. It provided for action by all the contracting nations against an armed attack on any American nation, from whatever quarter, pending measures by the Security Council of the United Nations. This pact, which the United States Senate approved 72 to 1, further strengthened the multilateralization of the Monroe Doctrine and constituted the most significant inter-American agreement to date.[17] It was also an important regional defense pact, as envisioned by the United Nations, and as such served as both a model and precedent for the North Atlantic Treaty of 1949.

The next regular International Conference of American Republics—the ninth since 1889—met at Bogotá, Colombia, in March and April of 1948. The Latin Americans, experiencing a postwar slump and eyeing the Marshall Plan plums with envy, were hopeful of generous aid through a "little Marshall Plan." The suggestion of President Truman that a mere half-billion dollars might be made available through the Export-Import Bank in Washington left them cold. But Secretary Marshall himself, who headed the American delegation at Bogotá, regarded the most pressing business as the fashioning of an anti-Communist pact. As if to give point to his pleas, a horrible local revolt, in which local Communists clearly had a large hand, wrecked the city and took some 1500 lives. The conference was forced to interrupt its labors for several days, by which time it was prepared to take construc-

17 Text in *Department of State Bulletin*, XVII, 565–567 (Sept. 21, 1947).

tive steps to unite the Americas against the Red peril. These included the adoption of an anti-Communist resolution, the establishment of a defense council, and the formation of the Charter of the Organization of American States.[18]

The Soviet threat had thus caused the Latin American republics by 1948 to draw together with the United States more closely than ever before. In this sense Pan-Americanism was at an all-time peacetime high. But there was acute and understandable dissatisfaction in Latin America growing out of the economic dislocations of the postwar period, and the reluctance of the United States to continue the deluge of dollars. The Latin Americans did not perceive with complete clarity that the European nations were on the firing line of communism, and that since the financial resources of even rich Uncle Sam were limited, Washington had to work on the principle of the first things first. But the "Bold New Program" of President Truman held promise of substantial help.

THE NORTH ATLANTIC ALLIANCE

What America regarded as the menace of Moscow continued to bring extraordinary developments. On March 17, 1948, five nations of western Europe—Britain, France, Belgium, the Netherlands, and Luxembourg—signed at Brussels a fifty-year defensive pact, by which they agreed to aid one another should an aggressor attack. The United States, as their chief economic underwriter and as the leader of the drive to stem communism, was irresistibly drawn toward the new alliance.

Nearly three months later, on June 11, 1948, the United States Senate, by a lopsided vote of 64 to 4, passed the Vandenberg resolution, which affirmed American support for such regional security pacts as that adopted at Brussels. With this go-ahead signal plainly posted, the State Department pressed negotiations to include the United States in the union. Moscow stridently proclaimed that Washington was weakening the United Nations (which the Soviets had already hamstrung), and was forming an aggressive bloc (which the Soviets had already formed by a network of treaties with their satellites). Regional security pacts were within both the letter and spirit of the United Nations, and the purpose of the proposed Atlantic alliance was clearly defensive rather than aggressive.

With appropriate white-tie pageantry, the representatives of twelve

[18] Text in *ibid.*, XVIII, 666–673 (May 23, 1948).

western nations finally met in Washington, on April 4, 1949, to sign the North Atlantic Treaty.[19] They were the United States, Canada, Britain, France, Italy, Belgium, the Netherlands, Luxembourg, Norway, Denmark, Iceland, and Portugal. After paying their respects to the United Nations, the signatory Powers stipulated that an attack by an aggressor on one was an attack on all, and that each of the other nations, individually or in concert, would take "such action as it deems necessary," including "armed force." This did not flatly commit the United States to war, or remove from Congress the war-declaring power, but it seemed to be a moral commitment to aid the victims of aggression.

The North Atlantic Pact was unquestionably a treaty of alliance, the first the United States had ever concluded in peacetime. Yet despite this drastic departure from tradition, the pact met with widespread public favor, which in itself attests to the growing fear of Soviet Russia.[20] There was a general feeling that if another world war broke out America would be sucked in from the beginning, and since this was so, she might be able to avert it, as she did not in 1914 and 1939, by serving notice on potential aggressors that they would have to reckon with her at the outset. The loudest opposition to the alliance came from last-ditch isolationists, Wallaceites, and Communists, whose leading organ, the New York *Daily Worker*, branded the pact as "International Murder, Inc."

Three weeks after the signing of the alliance, the Soviets, in what may have been an attempt to head off American ratification, agreed to lift the Berlin blockade, with the proviso that the western allies consent to another meeting of the Big Four foreign ministers at Paris. The conference met for a month (May 23–June 20, 1949), and although nothing substantial was done about the larger problem of Germany, the Soviets formally agreed to end the Berlin blockade and to permit the drafting of a peace treaty with Austria. The Russians seemed less bumptious and less sure of themselves, perhaps because of the success of the Marshall Plan, the Berlin airlift, and the Atlantic Treaty.

The historic North Atlantic Pact was approved by the Senate on July 21, 1949, by a vote of 82 to 13, and with surprisingly little opposition. Isolationists of the Taft stripe feared entanglements in Europe's broils, a loss of the war-declaring power of Congress, and commitments to heavy and dangerous expenditures. They made a deter-

[19] Text in *ibid.*, XX, 339–342 (March 20, 1949).
[20] Gallup found that 67% favored ratification (with 12% opposed) and 65% favored the granting of arms (with 16% opposed). Gallup Release, May 18, 1949.

mined effort to relieve the United States of any obligation to rearm western Europe, but all proposed reservations were beaten down by wide margins.

Much more serious opposition developed in the country and in Congress against a request by President Truman for $1,450,000,000 with which to arm the new western allies. Such a scheme was branded as unprecedented, expensive, prodigal, provocative, and dangerous. After the House had cut the proposed sum nearly in half, the Senate substantially restored it on September 22, 1949, by a vote of 55 to 24, and six days later the House concurred by a vote of 223 to 109. The most persuasive argument for the appropriation was that the United States, having gone this far, must help tide over the western democracies while they were regaining their strength.

Thus the militancy of Russian communism within a few short years had brought about a major revolution in American foreign policy. The United States had reversed the Monroe Doctrine with reference to Greece, it had forsaken nonintervention by enacting the Marshall Plan, and it had tossed overboard the tradition of no entangling alliances. It had adopted peacetime conscription and a wartime military budget. It had embarked upon such departures with extreme reluctance but basically in response to the instinct of self-preservation. From the point of view of the Communist world, the Soviets were justified in much that they did; from the point of view of the democratic world, they were not. But the fact remains that the new American policies, defensive in their purpose, were authored more by the men in the Kremlin than by the men in Washington.

BIBLIOGRAPHICAL NOTE

Highly useful is the continuing survey, J. C. Campbell, *et al.*, *The United States in World Affairs, 1948–1949* (N.Y., 1949). Also helpful are the studies published by the Brookings Institution of Washington, D.C., entitled *Major Problems of United States Foreign Policy*, of which one has appeared for 1947, and another for 1948–1949. A series of newspaper articles on relations with Russia were published by Walter Lippmann in *The Cold War* (N.Y., 1947). See also L. S. Stavrianos, "The United States and Greece: The Truman Doctrine in Historical Perspective," in D. E. Lee and G. E. McReynolds, *Essays in History and International Relations in Honor of George Hubbard Blakeslee* (Worcester, Mass., 1949), pp. 36–59. Broad but valuable surveys are Dexter Perkins, *The United States and the Caribbean* (Cambridge, 1947); and A. P. Whitaker, *The United States and South America: The Northern Republics* (Cambridge, 1948). Carlos Davila, *We of the Americas* (Chicago, 1949), calls upon the United States not to ignore Latin America in its concern with Europe and Asia. See also Bibliographical Note at end of preceding chapter.

CHAPTER LI

Retrospect and Prospect

"We are participants, whether we would or not, in the life of the world. The interests of all nations are our own also. We are partners with the rest. What affects mankind is inevitably our affair as well as the affair of Europe and of Asia."

Woodrow Wilson, May 27, 1916.

FORCES AND FACTORS

LOOKING back over the panorama of American diplomatic history, we note that a number of influences have shaped the nation's foreign policy. Among the more important the following may be listed.

1. *Geographical position.* Physical separation from Europe and Asia by two wide oceans permitted the United States to pursue, notably in the nineteenth century, a policy of isolation. This was of vital importance during the years when the republic was too weak to risk involvement in outside affairs, and when it was forced to adopt the strategy of playing for time until it became strong. Yet in recent decades the advantage of geography has largely been eliminated by modern mechanical miracles.

2. *Room to expand.* The presence close at hand of great virgin areas, virtually uninhabited, made it possible for the United States to expand without long and exhausting wars, and to acquire natural resources of incalculable value.

3. *Weak neighbors.* The United States, during most of its national history, did not have to fear attack from its neighbors. The dangers of a French empire in Louisiana and Mexico, of a strong Texas, and of a powerful Southern confederacy were in turn removed. The witty Jules Jusserand, French ambassador in Washington, once said that America was fortunate among the nations. On the north she has a weak neighbor; on the south another weak neighbor; on the east, fish; on the west, fish. This favorable situation enabled the United States to dispense with large standing armies, and to avoid being used as a makeweight in an American balance of power manipulated by European imperialists.

4. *A nation of hyphenates.* The United States has drawn its population from all the other countries of the world. So strong are racial ties that upheavals in foreign lands have inevitably produced serious disturbances in America. But as the melting pot bubbles behind immigration barriers, and as emigrants from the "old country" are carried to the grave, this influence is becoming less and less potent.

5. *A democracy.* The devotion of the United States to the democratic ideal has colored the psychology of the people, and has caused them to adopt an unfriendly attitude towards monarchs and dictators. This same state of mind has also led to general sympathy with democratic or liberal movements all over the world.

6. *The power of public opinion.* The American people, exercising their democratic privileges and enjoying freedom of speech and press, have shaped their own basic foreign policies. Although the Department of State has given direction to these policies, it has never dared to deviate far from the wishes of the nation in major decisions.[1] In demanding the Spanish-American War, the Washington Conference of 1921–1922, and the Kellogg-Briand pact—to take only three examples—the people literally forced the executive branch to act against its will.

7. *The primacy of domestic affairs.* The American people, except for occasional brief periods, have never been so much concerned with foreign as with domestic problems. An isolated position, together with the enormous and absorbing task of conquering and exploiting a continent, has made this possible. If, for example, the nation had not been involved in the slavery controversy at the time of the Ostend Manifesto, the results probably would have been different. The secondary place of foreign relations in the life of the people accounts in part for the slow development of a professionalized diplomatic service. Where a nation is not vitally concerned with diplomacy, mistakes are less costly, and highly trained diplomats are not so urgently needed. Yet it would be folly to carry this happy state of indifference into the shrunken world of the atomic age. Domestic affairs have become foreign affairs, and foreign affairs domestic affairs.

[1] Stanley K. Hornbeck, Adviser on Political Relations, Department of State, declared in a radio address on August 1, 1938: "The attitude of the Nation gives direction to policy and establishes limitations for and of action. An administration may lead or may follow public opinion, but it cannot in any major matter proceed successfully without regard to or in disregard of the attitude and inclination of the Nation as a whole." Department of State, *Press Releases*, Aug. 6, 1938, p. 89. Secretary of State Cordell Hull declared at Buenos Aires on December 5, 1936: "Since the time when Thomas Jefferson insisted upon a 'decent respect to the opinions of mankind,' public opinion has controlled foreign policy in all democracies." New York *Times*, Dec. 6, 1936, 47: 2. Yet the government can and does take steps to shape public opinion.

8. *A mercantile and industrial people.* The United States, with its incomparable natural advantages, has from the earliest days been a mercantile nation, vitally concerned with freedom of the seas. Later it also became a great industrial Power, with enormous manufactured as well as agricultural surpluses to export. Still later, it became the world's creditor. Commercial, industrial, and financial enterprises have inextricably involved the American people in the affairs of the world.

9. *Europe's distresses.* The presence of great hostile camps in Europe, to say nothing of domestic disturbances within those nations, has consistently operated to the advantage of America, and enabled her, while weak, to consolidate her position. "Sir," said the Swedish ambassador in London to John Adams in 1784, "I take it for granted, that you will have sense enough to see us in Europe cut each other's throats with a philosophical tranquillity." [2] The United States generally pursued such a course in the nineteenth century, and profited enormously by it. But in the twentieth century Europe's distresses and Asia's distresses increasingly became America's distresses.

FUNDAMENTAL POLICIES

The foreign policies of the United States have evolved from long and painful experience. They are based on self-interest, as are those of all other nations. The American people, though inclined to be idealists, must look out for themselves first; and their government, which is their trustee, would be censurable if it did otherwise. In international relations, as George Washington suggested in 1796, one cannot expect something for nothing. There are, however, numerous instances in which the government, by conferring advantages on others, has reaped even greater advantages for itself, notably in remitting the Boxer indemnity to China.

Leaving aside such general aims as peace, security, justice, and freedom, we may consider the following specific foreign policies of the United States: [3]

1. *Isolation, nonintervention, and nonentanglement.* This means that the American people have wished to wrap their two oceans around

---

[2] C. F. Adams, ed., *The Works of John Adams* (Boston, 1853), VIII, 178 (Adams to President of Congress, Feb. 10, 1784).

[3] Such policies as expatriation, nonrecognition, territorial expansion, reciprocity, Dollar Diplomacy, imperialism, the Good Neighbor, disarmament, and protestations against the persecution of minorities have not been included because they have been less fundamental than those listed above, or because they have been pursued during limited periods. It may be noted that nonrecognition is beginning to establish itself as a fundamental policy.

them, and work out their own destiny without becoming embroiled in the conflicts of the outside world. Keeping one's nose out of other people's business is generally praiseworthy, but not even the United States was able to pursue such a policy with complete success. The nation deliberately forsook isolation in order to secure the advantages of the French alliance in 1778, entered great global conflicts in 1917 and 1941, and approved the Atlantic Pact in 1949. The ancient ideal of isolation now seems but a nostalgic dream.

2. *The Monroe Doctrine.* If isolation meant that the United States would stay out of Europe, the Monroe Doctrine meant that Europe (and Asia) must stay out of America. European forms of government and European military establishments have long been regarded as inimical to the interests of the American people. Though most Americans have only a vague idea of its meaning, the Doctrine has a powerful hold on the public imagination.[4] It should be noted that since 1940 the Monroe Doctrine has undergone a fundamental change; no longer the sole property of the United States, it is shared by all twenty-one republics of the Americas.

3. *Freedom of the Seas.* The United States, as a mercantile nation, has consistently contended for the right to do business in time of war with a minimum of interference from the belligerents, and that within the framework of international law. This principle figured prominently as a cause for hostilities in 1812, 1917, and 1941. The neutrality legislation of the 1930's was a partial and temporary abandonment of America's historic position, but even then the nation insisted upon its fundamental rights, and specifically reserved them in the Act of 1939.

4. *The Open Door.* In general, the Open Door means the right of American citizens to engage in trade and industry abroad on an equal basis with other foreigners. This doctrine is usually applied to China. American trade with that great Asiatic country has never been more than three or four per cent of American foreign commerce, normally one or two per cent. Investments in China constitute an even smaller percentage of the holdings of United States citizens abroad. Partially if not primarily for these reasons, the Open Door has never commanded the vigorous popular support accorded to isolation and the Monroe Doctrine. The American people have never been willing to fight for equal commercial opportunity in China, and this perhaps explains why the policy has been pursued with such indifferent success.

---

[4] Mrs. Mary Baker Eddy, the founder of Christian Science, once said: "I believe strictly in the Monroe doctrine, in our Constitution, and in the laws of God." J. W. Garner, *American Foreign Policies* (N.Y., 1928), p. 131 n.

The Open Door, in so far as China is concerned, has been tossed aside by the flood of revolutionary change. With an antipathetic, Moscow-connected Communist regime in power, the United States can hardly hope for the equal opportunity of John Hay's ideal.

5. *The pacific settlement of disputes.* Although the United States has occasionally been involved in war, it has in general favored the settlement of international differences by pacific means. It has been a pioneer and a leader in disarmament and arbitration.

6. *Pan-Americanism.* The objective of Pan-Americanism has been the closer association of the American republics for the achievement of common aspirations, especially peace and security. This ideal embraces commercial and political as well as cultural relations. The United States has favored Pan-Americanism as a means of decreasing European influence in the New World and further strengthening the Monroe Doctrine. The Good Neighbor policy and Pan-Americanism are intimately related.

7. *Opportunism.* Much of American diplomacy—perhaps most of it—has been the adjustment of minor difficulties wherever they have arisen.[5] This has frequently been done on an opportunistic or *ad hoc* basis, without reference to any of the fundamental principles.

The student of American diplomacy must constantly bear in mind that some of the republic's basic foreign policies have been applied to certain areas and not to others. The United States generally pursued a policy of nonintervention, nonentanglement, and nonco-operation toward Europe in the nineteenth century. (A later exception was World War I, but when it was over the American people tried to crawl back into their shell.)

In Latin America, the picture was completely different. Until the Good Neighbor era, the United States followed a policy of entanglement and armed intervention. This was particularly true of the Caribbean area, where the United States still feels anxiety for its Panama life line.

The Open Door was likewise a regional doctrine, applicable to the Far East. Throughout the nineteenth century the United States, quite in contrast with its general policy of isolation, freely co-operated with the other Powers in keeping the door open. Both Secretaries Knox and Stimson forsook co-operation for singlehanded action, and both were conspicuously unsuccessful. The naval historian Mahan aptly sum-

---

[5] While Secretary of State, Elihu Root wrote that "to keep the country out of trouble . . . in the right way, is the main object of diplomacy." P. C. Jessup, *Elihu Root* (N.Y., 1938), II, 4 (Root to St. Loe Strachey, Sept. 9, 1905).

marized American regionalism before 1914 as follows: in the Caribbean, predominance; in Europe, abstention; in the Far East, co-operation.

CANADA LOOKS AT THE UNITED STATES

How has America been regarded by other nations in her dealings with them? The ordinary American—busy, self-contained, and self-assured—seldom takes time to look at himself, much less to see himself as others see him.

The United States, in its relations with its northern neighbor, has not always appeared to good advantage. Twice, in 1775 and again in 1812, American armies invaded Canada with intent to absorb it. Nor should we forget the constant bickering over fisheries; assistance to the Canadian rebels in 1837; and the infuriating remarks about Canadian subservience to the British monarchial yoke.[6]

The Maine and Oregon settlements left the Canadians resentful; the somewhat spiteful abrogation of the Reciprocity Treaty in 1866 caused further hard feelings; the Fenian forays following the close of the Civil War aroused much hostility, as did the braggadocio of the Americans about taking over all Canada. The curious agitation for annexation in British Columbia during the sixties, and that in Canada during the eighties, though probably foredoomed to failure, were repelled by the clumsy advances of the United States. Theodore Roosevelt's strong-arm methods of settling the Alaska boundary dispute, and the loud Yankee talk at the time of the reciprocity agitation of 1911, also left rankling wounds.

It is not surprising that, until recent years, the Canadian has been uneasy about the proximity of his powerful and aggressive neighbor.[7] The American, on the other hand, has revealed the psychology of the strong toward the weak, and has been indifferent to the sensitiveness of Canada, brusque, outspoken, little realizing how easy it is to give offense. But with the disappearance of annexation agitation, with the increased maturity of Canada, and with the drawing together of these two democracies in the face of outside peril, relations have become extraordinarily friendly. It is true that in the past there has been much friction, primarily because there have been numerous points of fric-

---

[6] As late as 1920 Senator Reed of Missouri declared: ". . . I refuse to consider the Canadian people, as a whole, the equals of the people of the United States. If they loved liberty as we do . . . they would not stay under the British flag." *Cong. Record*, 66 Cong., 2 sess., p. 4018 (March 8, 1920).

[7] For manifestations of this feeling see H. F. Angus, ed., *Canada and Her Great Neighbor* (New Haven, 1938).

tion. Yet in spite of their previous differences, the two nations have presented to the world for over a century an unarmed land and water boundary thousands of miles in length.

LATIN AMERICA LOOKS AT THE UNITED STATES

In dealing with Latin America the people of the United States have also revealed the psychology of the strong toward the weak, and they have long entertained numerous misconceptions based upon ignorance and indifference.[8] Many citizens of the great Northern Republic still regard Latin Americans as illiterate mongrels ("veneered Indians"), whose chief characteristics are corruption, farcical elections, and revolutions.

The Latin Americans hasten to point out that some of their nations, notably Argentina and Chile, have a larger percentage of white population than the Colossus of the North; that corruption is the exception rather than the rule (the United States, with its great urban political machines, is in no position to cast stones); that democracy has not worked with complete success because the people of Latin America (unlike the Yankees) were plunged into self-government without adequate preparation; that revolutions are frequently the only way to overthrow a dictator; that such outbreaks are usually not long or bloody (unlike the American Revolution or the terrible American Civil War); and that political assassinations also take place in the United States. Besides, geography has been unfavorable to harmonious relations between the Northern Republic and Latin America. The most backward and revolution-torn nations are located nearest the United States and its vital Isthmian canal, while the most stable countries, where revolutions have less frequently occurred, are the farthest away.

From the Wars of Independence until 1846 relations between the United States and Latin America were relatively satisfactory. The inhabitants of the newly born republics appreciated the sympathy of the Yankee during their struggle for liberty. Although some of them recognized that the Monroe Doctrine, enunciated in 1823, was designed primarily to safeguard the United States, they were not ungrateful for this protecting shield. Intelligent Latin Americans have never violently opposed Monroe's principles *in their original form*.

Then came the annexation of Texas and the shearing away of one

---

[8] A Haitian came to the United States thinking that the entire nation was bent on devouring his country. "Why," he said upon his return, "they don't even know where Haiti is!" C. L. Jones, H. K. Norton, and P. T. Moon, *The United States and the Caribbean* (Chicago, 1929), pp. 135–136.

half of Mexico, followed by the Gadsden Purchase and Walker's filibustering expeditions. The Latin Americans became profoundly distrustful of *El Imperialismo Yanqui*. Blaine's diplomacy, and particularly Harrison's handling of the *Baltimore* affair, caused a wound
that was not healed by Cleveland's heroic course during the Venezuelan boundary controversy. Then, at the turn of the century, came the
Platt Amendment, the rape of Panama, the Roosevelt corollary, the
bombardment of Vera Cruz, and various landings of the marines in
pursuance of Dollar (life line) Diplomacy. Professor W. R. Shepherd, writing in 1927, thus summarized the situation:

In about thirty years we have created two new republics—Cuba and
Panama; converted both of them and three other Latin-American countries—the Dominican Republic, Nicaragua and Haiti—into virtual protectorates; intervened by force at least thirty times in the internal affairs
of nine supposedly sovereign and independent nations; made the period of
intervention last anywhere from a few days to a dozen years; enlarged
our investments from a paltry two or three hundred millions of dollars
to the tidy sum of upwards of three billions, and installed in four states
our own collectors of customs to insure payment. Incidentally, we have
annexed Porto Rico and the Virgin Islands, built a canal, secured an option to construct another and gathered in several naval stations.[9]

The Latin Americans have bitterly resented the paternalistic attitude of the United States under the Monroe Doctrine, which they have
regarded as a cloak behind which the Colossus of the North was attempting to strangle them. They are willing to grant that there was
once a Holy Alliance, and that they were then weak and defenseless.
But continued paternalism seemed out of place when there was no Holy
Alliance, and when the Latin American republics had considerable
armies and navies of their own. As one Chilean remarked in 1908,
"We don't want any papa." [10] The fear and detestation of the United
States aroused by the Roosevelt corollary to the Monroe Doctrine,
particularly during the two decades after 1905, seem scarcely credible
to a citizen of the United States at the present time.[11]

The temporary adjustment of the Mexican difficulty in 1914 and

[9] *New Republic*, XLIX, 266 (Jan. 26, 1927).

[10] Garner, *American Foreign Policies*, p. 130 n.

[11] F. García Calderón, a prominent Latin American publicist, wrote in 1913: "To
save themselves from Yankee imperialism the American democracies would almost
accept a German alliance, or the aid of Japanese arms; everywhere the Americans of
the North are feared." *Latin America: Its Rise and Progress* (London, 1913), p. 298.
A Chilean poet declared, "Two things unite all Spanish America: a common lan-

the outbreak of the World War in that same year brought about a turning point in relations with the United States. The preoccupation of Great Britain and Germany with their conflict enabled the Yankees to win temporary primacy in the foreign trade of Latin America. The great Northern Republic, under Wilson's inspiring leadership, upheld the cause of democracy, which was popular south of the Rio Grande. When the United States entered the war, eight of the Latin American nations followed suit and five others broke off diplomatic relations with Germany.[12] This action was widely regarded as evidence of growing Pan-American solidarity. But the United States lost much of its new prestige when it abdicated leadership and, unlike most of Latin America, refused to join the League of Nations.

Late in the Coolidge administration, following the adjustment of the Mexican difficulty by Dwight Morrow, a new era in Latin American relations was ushered in. President Hoover showed a willingness to narrow the Monroe Doctrine; adopted a more satisfactory recognition policy; and withdrew the marines from Nicaragua. President Roosevelt stressed the Good Neighbor policy; worked for closer economic relations with the Latin American republics; withdrew the marines from Haiti; freed Cuba from the trammels of the Platt Amendment; liquidated the Dominican intervention; and adjusted the oil difficulty with Mexico. Such developments, combined with the menace of Hitlerism, brought about a degree of co-operation, especially after Pearl Harbor, that did much to efface a century of Yankee-phobia. The threat of Stalinism has had a similarly cohesive effect. But much latent resentment remains.

The Far East Looks at the United States

The Orientals, like the Latin Americans, have been puzzled by a number of inconsistencies in American foreign policy. The Chinese have thought it strange that the Washington government should insist upon extraterritorial jurisdiction, while scores of their countrymen were being openly murdered in America. Yet China has never demanded Chinese consular courts in San Francisco, nor gunboats on

guage and a common hatred of the United States." G. H. Blakeslee, *The Recent Foreign Policy of the United States* (N.Y., 1925), pp. 163–164. Before the Good Neighbor policy, public opinion in Ecuador would not permit sanitary engineers from the United States to clean up the pesthole of Guayaquil. Hiram Bingham, *The Monroe Doctrine: an Obsolete Shibboleth* (New Haven, 1913), pp. 82–83.

[12] This subject is treated at length in P. A. Martin, *Latin America and the War* (Baltimore, 1925).

the Mississippi. And the United States, though posing as the champion of the Open Door and of equal opportunity, has erected high tariff barriers against the cheap goods of Eastern Asia.

In 1898 the Americans seized the Philippines and Guam, islands strategically located in the very back yard of Japan. Yet by the Lodge corollary to the Monroe Doctrine the United States would not permit Japan to establish a naval base in American waters and would not even allow Japanese private companies to secure leases in Mexico for legitimate business enterprises.

The Japanese have particularly resented the immigration policy of the United States. They do not deny the right of the American republic to exclude immigrants, but they bitterly resent the discriminatory act of 1924, a measure that played into the hands of the military faction in Japan and silenced friends of the United States. The discrimination against China was not removed until 1943.

When the Japanese turned to the mainland of Asia for expansion, the Washington government took extraordinary and seemingly unfriendly steps to stop them. Then, when Tokyo recognized the so-called "puppet state" of Manchukuo, the United States expressed strong official displeasure, though Theodore Roosevelt had acted much more precipitately in recognizing the "puppet state" of Panama.[13]

After more than one hundred years of expectation, the United States has not as yet developed the "illimitable markets" of China. American producers actually sell vastly more goods to some 13,000,000 Canadians than to some 450,000,000 Chinese. During prewar years Japan was by far America's best customer in the Far East. Would it not have been better, assert the Japanese, if the United States had played along with its best customer, and indirectly shared in the exploitation of China?

The American is quick to reply that his Far Eastern policy is more concerned with international law and order than with dollars and cents. He also adds that the Open Door has nothing to do with the immigration and tariff policies of the United States; that control of immigration is a purely domestic matter which the nation may handle as it sees fit; that the republic became involved in the Philippines accidentally and temporarily; and that the Panama and Manchukuo affairs are not parallel.

[13] It was contemporaneously reported in the press that when a prominent Japanese was asked how soon Tokyo planned to recognize Manchukuo, he replied that Japan was in no hurry; she did not plan to construct a canal there!

EUROPE LOOKS AT THE UNITED STATES

The European, as well as the Canadian, the Latin American, and the Oriental, has found occasion to complain of the United States and its foreign policy. To those living in the Old World the Yankee, particularly during the nineteenth century, was crude, boastful, and belligerent. The American replies that his was a crude, frontier civilization, and that much of his so-called bluster was a "defense mech-- anism" against foreign criticisms of democracy. And as the nation has come of age, much of this offensiveness has disappeared.

In European eyes the Yankee has frequently been aggressive, bellicose, and rapacious. He provoked foreign wars; he invaded his neighbors' territory; he acquired two thirds of his domain by force. Now that he is rich and has all the land he needs, he joins the church and says that war is immoral. The American answers that most of the territory he seized was virtually uninhabited, and that he has put it to the uses of civilization. Besides, on a number of occasions he has avoided war under great provocation.

To the Europeans the American has been meddlesome and incon- sistent. He has openly supported democratic uprisings all over the world, while bitterly resenting sympathy for his own Civil War rebels. He cannot make his own democracy work well, yet he wants to foist it on other peoples. He cannot solve his own Negro problem, yet he criticizes Europe for not solving its minority problems. He cannot satisfactorily manage some 2,000,000 Puerto Ricans, but he knew how Britain should deal with some 400,000,000 inhabitants of India. He preaches disarmament for other nations, and, though the United States is the most isolated of the great Powers, insists upon a navy "second to none." In reply, the American declares that the Washington government has in general been neutral during revolutionary uprisings, but that it has been impossible to control strong public sympathy. Freedom of speech is an American ideal, and the government cannot stop ill-advised criticism of foreigners. And although the United States has been a pioneer and leader in disarmament, it cannot, with long coastlines and overseas possessions, disarm faster than other nations.

The Yankee, says the European, demands arbitration for other people, yet refuses to arbitrate vital issues, as in the cases of the Oregon boundary and the canal tolls. The American answers that he has long been a leading advocate of the pacific settlement of disputes. Occasionally, however, it has been necessary to decline arbitration when the vital interests and the honor of the nation have been involved.

From the point of view of Europe the Americans have gone to ridiculous lengths in paying obeisance to the advice of Washington. They forced the League of Nations upon the other countries of the world, and then refused to join it themselves. The result was the complete breakdown of collective security. In answer, the American says that the League would have failed anyhow, just as soon as a nation with the power and determination challenged it. Besides, the Washington government cannot co-operate abroad more fully than public opinion at home will permit.

In the eyes of Europeans the Yankee has been a grasping creditor, a veritable Shylock. He advanced money when he had no men ready to hold back the enemy in 1917–1918; then he wanted it all repaid—with interest. The American answered that the money was an honest obligation; that cancellation would weaken faith in international dealings; and that if the debtors did not pay it back, the American taxpayer would have to raise the money himself. And even though lend-lease was contributed to a common cause from 1941 to 1945, the United States will have to foot that part of the bill which is unpaid.

The European has often concluded that politics control American diplomacy.[14] Congress thinks nothing of affronting friendly nations; foreign offices must expect stump speeches in the guise of diplomatic notes, as well as reversals of policy when one administration succeeds another. The American admits that this charge, though exaggerated, contains much truth. Politics will be involved in foreign affairs as long as America is a democracy. Yet few foreign nations have followed several basic policies more consistently than the United States.

Europeans and other foreigners have at times found America's diplomatic service a disgrace. Her representatives have been ill-trained, ill-housed, ill-paid. Able men cannot live in the principal embassies on their salaries, so the vaunted American democracy often sends wealthy politicians instead. Until recent years the United States was spending more to build a single battleship than it paid for the support of its entire diplomatic service, which may avert war. The

---

[14] Referring to Secretary Bryan and his intense desire to negotiate the "cooling off" treaties, the British ambassador in Washington (Spring-Rice) wrote: "Remember that in this country all things are personal, and that Christ, if he had been an American, would have run for the governorship of Judea with the Sermon on the Mount for his platform." Stephen Gwynn, ed., *The Letters and Friendships of Sir Cecil Spring-Rice* (Boston, 1929), II, 201 (to Tyrrell, Jan. 27, 1914).

American concedes that unfortunately many of these charges are true, but he points out that much improvement has been made in recent years.[15] Even so, he adds, the haphazard system of the United States has on the whole worked well. Where among Americans can one find a group who committed blunders comparable with those of "Copenhagen" Jackson, Dupuy de Lôme, Lionel Sackville-West, or Constantin Dumba? And how many better men than Benjamin Franklin, Charles Francis Adams, Townsend Harris, Anson Burlingame, or Dwight Morrow have the systems of Europe produced? And how many foreign ministers have had a surer touch than John Quincy Adams, Daniel Webster, Hamilton Fish, and John Hay?

One final point. Despite the accusing finger of critics, the foreign policy of the United States, with relatively few exceptions, has over the years been conducted on an unusually high plane of honesty, decency, and candor. Other great nations may well be challenged to produce as good a record.

TOWARD THE FUTURE

A thousand years were telescoped into that fraction of a second when the first atomic bomb exploded at Hiroshima. Many old concepts of diplomacy and international order, of military and naval strategy, of economic and political organization, were blown up in a billowing cloud. In the light of these revolutionary new conditions it would be folly not to subject traditional American foreign policy to a rigorous re-examination. We must constantly bear in mind that policies are made for nations, not nations for policies; and that it would be stupid to cling to outmoded ideals simply because some great name is attached to them.

Few clear-headed persons will assert that isolation has not been given a fair trial. Nine world wars—nine involvements. One hundred per cent failure. And the atomic bomb is but the primitive prototype of the push-button weapons of a potential World War III. It is no longer One World but One Room. We must dispose of the maniacs, and learn to live with the rest of our fellow men.

The tragedy of modern man is that while he is clever enough to blow up the world, he has thus far not been clever enough to live in peace with his neighbors. The physical sciences have developed with frightening speed, while the social sciences in some respects are back

[15] The best book on this general subject is G. H. Stuart, *American Diplomatic and Consular Practice* (N.Y., 1936).

in the days of Noah's Ark. If this gap is not substantially closed, we are in danger of writing finish to everything.

The statesmen in charge of American foreign policy, as well as the better-informed citizens, know that isolation is not only dead but dangerous; that we must learn to see the other nation's problems as they appear to its eyes; that we must cultivate tolerance and understanding; that we must sublimate suspicion and ill will; that we must yield pride and prestige; that we must meet the other fellow half way, sometimes more than half way; and that we must invest some of our precious sovereignty in effective world organization—perhaps some kind of world government.

But the average citizen—indifferent, ignorant, or misled by ill-informed and sometimes unscrupulous editors, columnists, radio commentators, and politicians—does not see all these things. Yet, as we have repeatedly observed throughout this book, American public opinion in the long run determines basic foreign policies. If the American people, through their Congress, insist upon isolation, non-co-operation, ruinous tariff barriers, and other impediments to world recovery, they will have their way—with consequent disaster.

Water can rise no higher than its source, and the level of American foreign policy cannot rise substantially higher than the people will let it. Recent polls have shown that as one goes lower in the educational scale, one finds more provincialism; more isolationism (the horrors of war are soon forgotten); more militarism; more jingoism; more indifference to foreign affairs and more preoccupation with domestic trivia; more race prejudice; more distrust of foreigners (especially Russians and British); more desire for nationalistic textbooks; more demand for high tariff barriers and other instruments of economic non-co-operation; more insistence on harsh terms for international debtors; more reluctance to pay public servants adequate salaries; more short-sightedness in foreign affairs (a demand for the present short-range gain rather than the larger long-run gain); more attachment to the concept of sovereignty; and more opposition to even an embryonic world government.

A tremendous job in public education needs to be done, for narrowness, intolerance, bigotry, and demagoguery fatten on ignorance. Our educational institutions must be better supported by the taxpayer, for the proper kind of education is a relatively cheap form of international life insurance. Our schools and colleges must offer more and better work in foreign languages, history, geography, foreign affairs, comparative government, international economics, international law, and international organization. Our press, our radio, our public forums, and other agencies must rise to their responsibility to present sound and impartial information.

Upon every citizen in our democracy rests a solemn obligation to inform himself, so that he may shape American foreign policy—*his foreign policy*—along constructive and far-sighted lines.

BIBLIOGRAPHICAL NOTE

Of the numerous books that comment on American foreign policy in general terms the following may be mentioned. J. F. Rippy, *America and the Strife of Europe* (Chicago, 1938), an excellent interpretation; J. W. Garner, *American Foreign Policies* (N.Y., 1928), a provocative commentary; G. H. Blakeslee, *The Recent Foreign Policy of the United States* (N.Y., 1925); and Quincy Wright, ed., *Interpretations of American Foreign Policy* (Chicago, 1930). F. H. Simonds, *American Foreign Policy in the Post-War Years* (Baltimore, 1935), is a critical journalistic interpretation. Economic factors are stressed in C. A. Beard, *The Idea of National Interest* (N.Y., 1934); and the same author's *The Open Door at Home* (N.Y., 1934). S. F. Bemis, "A Clarifying Foreign Policy," *Yale Review*, XXV (1935), 221–240, stresses the mistakes of American diplomacy. On Canadian-American relations in general consult H. L. Keenleyside, *Canada and the United States* (N.Y., 1929); R. A. Falconer, *The United States as a Neighbour from a Canadian Point of View* (Cambridge, Eng., 1925). On Latin American relations see G. H. Stuart, *Latin America and the United States* (3rd ed., N.Y., 1938); W. S. Robertson, *Hispanic-American Relations with the United States* (N.Y., 1923); C. H. Haring, *South America Looks at the United States* (N.Y., 1928); C. L. Jones, *The Caribbean since 1900* (N.Y., 1936). The best book on the Far East is A. W. Griswold, *The Far Eastern Policy of the United States* (N.Y., 1938). Further references: see footnotes in this chapter and Bemis and Griffin, *Guide*, pp. 708–716.

RECENT REFERENCES. T. C. Smith, *The United States as a Factor in World History* (N.Y., 1941), is sketchy but useful. C. A. Beard, *A Foreign Policy for America* (N.Y., 1940), argues vigorously for a noninterventionist policy, while R. L. Buell, *Isolated America* (N.Y., 1940), contends for an abandonment of narrow isolationism. N. J. Spykman, *America's Strategy in World Politics* (N.Y., 1942), is a useful study of geography, raw materials, and other factors as they affect the nation's position in international affairs. J. W. Gantenbein, *Financial Questions in United States Foreign Policy* (N.Y., 1939), stresses more recent problems. Dexter Perkins, *Hands Off: A History of the Monroe Doctrine* (Boston, 1941), is brilliantly written and penetrating, by far the best single volume on the subject. J. F. Rippy, *South America and Hemisphere Defense* (Baton Rouge, 1941), is a series of four lectures by an outstanding authority, chiefly concerned with politico-economic relationships. W. H. C. Laves, ed., *Inter-American Solidarity* (Chicago, 1941), is a group of seven lectures by experts who deal with strategy, trade, raw materials, and similar subjects. J. B. Lockey, *Essays in Pan-Americanism* (Berkeley, Calif., 1939), brings together in convenient form a number of articles published elsewhere and bearing on subjects of less recent interest. John Mac-

Cormac, *Canada: America's Problem* (N.Y., 1940), is an able journalistic account which emphasizes the importance of Canada in United States foreign policy and defense preparations.

NEW REFERENCES. The most substantial new surveys are: S. F. Bemis, *A Diplomatic History of the United States* (Rev. Ed., N.Y., 1942); and R. W. Van Alstyne, *American Diplomacy in Action: A Series of Case Studies* (Stanford University, 1944). Albert Shaw, *International Bearings of American Policy* (Baltimore, 1943), is less revealing than this distinguished editor's participation in the events would lead one to hope. Walter Lippmann, *U.S. Foreign Policy: Shield of the Republic* (Boston, 1943), though containing some stimulating observations, is unreliable as history. Brief but stimulating interpretations are Allan Nevins, *America in World Affairs* (N.Y., 1942); and Senator E. D. Thomas, *The Four Fears* (Chicago, 1944). Hugh Gibson, *The Road to Foreign Policy* (Garden City, N.Y., 1944), is an able criticism by a veteran diplomat. Heinrich Hauser, *The German Talks Back* (N.Y., 1945), is an intemperate criticism of America by a disgruntled German. On the Far East, see G. E. Taylor, *America in the New Pacific* (N.Y., 1942); and S. K. Hornbeck, *The United States and the Far East* (Boston, 1942), the latter by a high State Department official. A general historical survey of Russo-American relations is F. R. Dulles, *The Road to Teheran* (Princeton, 1944). The optimism of sociologist P. A. Sorokin, in *Russia and the United States* (N.Y., 1944), as to future Russo-American amity is realistically challenged by D. J. Dallin's *The Big Three: The United States, Britain, Russia* (New Haven, 1945). For Latin American views, see Luis Quintanilla, *A Latin American Speaks* (N.Y., 1943); and Carleton Beals, *et al.*, *What the South Americans Think of Us* (N.Y., 1945). See also C. H. Haring, *Argentina and the United States* (Boston, 1941); Hubert Herring, *America and the Amercas; an Appraisal and a Forecast* (Claremont, Calif., 1944); and M. M. Ball, *The Problem of Inter-American Organization* (Stanford University, 1944). General treatments are S. F. Bemis, *The Latin American Policy of the United States* (N.Y., 1943); and the fourth edition of G. H. Stuart, *Latin America and the United States* (N.Y., 1943). Earlier surveys on Canada have to a considerable extent been superseded by E. W. McInnis, *The Unguarded Frontier* (Garden City, N.Y., 1942); and particularly by the broad approach of J. B. Brebner, *North Atlantic Triangle: The Interplay of Canada, the United States and Great Britain* (New Haven, 1945).

4TH ED. REFS. T. A. Bailey, *The Man in the Street: The Impact of American Public Opinion on Foreign Policy* (N.Y., 1948), discusses the problem in its historical setting. More concerned with current developments is Lester Markel *et al.*, *Public Opinion and Foreign Policy* (N.Y., 1949). An indispensable documentary collection in R. J. Bartlett, ed., *The Record of American Diplomacy* (N.Y., 1947). Readings relating to recent developments are L. H. Chamberlain and R. C. Snyder, eds., *American Foreign Policy* (N.Y., 1948), and Harold and Margaret Sprout, eds., *Foundations of National Power* (Princeton, 1946). An excellent brief survey is Dexter Perkins, *The Evolution of American Foreign Policy* (N.Y., 1948). See also Emil Lengyel, *America's Role in World Affairs* (N.Y., 1946); M. W. Graham, *American Diplomacy in the International Community* (Baltimore, 1948); Quincy Wright, ed., *A Foreign Policy for the United States* (Chicago, 1947); A. H. Hansen, *America's Role in the World Economy* (N.Y., 1945); S. E. Harris, ed., *Foreign Economic Policy for the United States* (Cambridge,

1948); William Reitzel, *The Mediterranean: Its Role in America's Foreign Policy* (N.Y., 1948); E. A. Speiser, *The United States and the Near East* (Cambridge, 1947). The viewpoints of foreigners are set forth in H. S. Commager, ed., *America in Perspective: The United States through Foreign Eyes* (N.Y., 1947); André Visson, *As Others See Us* (Garden City, N.Y., 1948); and Carlos Davila, *We of the Americas* (Chicago, 1949), which is an arresting presentation of the Latin American view. The standard treatment of the subject is now G. H. Stuart, *The Department of State* (N.Y., 1949).

Appendix A

GLOSSARY OF DIPLOMATIC TERMS *

[ABBREVIATIONS: cf. (*compare*); e.g. (*for example*); Fr. (*French*); Lat. (*Latin*).
The page references are to examples in this book.]

abrogate. Formally to annul, as of agreements
ad hoc (Lat.). Pertaining to this case alone, as an *ad hoc* committee
ad interim (Lat.). Temporary, as an ad interim agreement
admiralty court. A court having jurisdiction of maritime questions
aide-mémoire (Fr.). Written outline or summary of a document
ambassador. A diplomatic agent of the highest rank
Anglophile. A great admirer of England or things English. Cf. Francophile, etc.
Anglophobe. One strongly averse to England. Cf. Japanophobe, etc.
armistice. A suspension of military operations by mutual agreement
asylum. Extension of protection to political refugees by a foreign government or
its representatives
attaché (Fr.). An official attached to a diplomatic staff, as a military attaché
autarchy. A state of economic self-sufficiency
autonomy. The power or right of self-government
balance of power. Such an equilibrium in the power of neighboring states to wage
war on one another as to deter or preclude hostilities
belligerency, recognition of. Recognition (as by a proclamation of neutrality) that
a state of war exists between two or more governments. P. 413
belligerent. A nation engaged in waging war
benevolent neutrality. Technical neutrality that favors one belligerent
bilateral. Affecting reciprocally two parties, as a bilateral treaty
blacklist. In wartime a list of enemy-connected firms, at home or in a neutral country, with which a belligerent forbids its nationals to trade. P. 637
blockade. The interdiction of communication by armed force; traditionally the
patrolling of an enemy's ports so closely by warships as to make ingress or
egress hazardous. Pp. 347, 617
broken voyage. See continuous voyage
buffer state. A small independent state between two larger rival states
capital ship. Defined in 1922 as a warship (not an aircraft carrier) of more than
10,000 tons, or carrying larger than 8 inch guns
capitulation. A surrender on stipulated terms; an agreement (usually in Near East)
granting extraterritorial rights. *See* extraterritoriality
career diplomat (or man). Professional diplomat, in contrast to political appointee
cartel. An agreement between contending belligerents regulating their intercourse;
a combination of trusts to promote monopolistic practices
casus belli (Lat.). An alleged justification for war
casus foederis (Lat.). A case within the provisions of a treaty
chancellery. The office of an embassy or legation
chargé d'affaires (Fr.). Commonly *chargé.* A temporary substitute for the regular
diplomatic representative; a regular diplomat of inferior grade

* The working definitions that follow are confined largely to U.S. experience and
are necessarily reduced to brief compass. Consult unabridged dictionaries for fuller
definitions. Omitted are familiar or obvious terms, some terms defined in the text, and
highly technical terms.

closed incident. A settled diplomatic question

collective security. Maintenance of world peace by concerted action of the Powers, or an organization of the Powers, against an aggressor or potential aggressor

Colossus of the North. Opprobrious synonym for U.S.A. in Latin America

Cominform. Communist Information Bureau, established 1947. P. 882

Comintern. Communist International, established in Moscow, 1919. P. 812

comity of nations. The consideration and good understanding among nations that lead each to respect the laws and institutions of the other. Hence an act of comity

communiqué (Fr.). A piece of information given out officially

condominium. A joint administration by several Powers. P. 464

consortium. An international business or banking combination. Pp. 595, 686

consul general; consul; vice-consul; consular agent. Officials, usually ranked in the order given, appointed by a foreign country to serve the commercial interests of that country abroad; also to protect seamen

consulate. Office of a consul

consulate general. Office of a consul general

continuous voyage. A voyage which, in view of its obvious purposes, is regarded as continuous, even though interrupted. Pp. 109, 348

contraband of war. That which may be seized by a belligerent when being sent to its enemy. Before "total war" made such distinctions illusory, exports to a belligerent were classified as absolute contraband (e.g., explosives); conditional contraband (depending on their use for warlike or peaceful purposes, e.g., horses); and noncontraband (e.g., soap)

convention. A treaty; often multi-Power and specific in nature, such as one relating to postage or copyright

convoy. To protect merchantmen with armed escort; a group of ships so convoyed

counselor. A high career officer assigned to an embassy or legation

coup d'état (Fr.). Sudden forcible overthrow of a government

credentials. Documents issued by a government to its diplomatic agent showing that he is entitled to exercise the official power of representation

dean; doyen. Senior member in service of a given group of diplomats

de facto (Lat.). A *de facto* government is one actually functioning, usually after armed upheaval, but not permanently established or recognized

de jure (Lat.). A *de jure* government is one deemed lawful, though it may or may not be *de facto*

démarche (Fr.). A diplomatic step or representation

denounce. To give formal notice of termination of treaty or agreement

dispatch. A written report, commonly sent to home office by agent in field

diplomatic agent. A diplomatic representative of a state. In order of conventional rank: ambassador; minister (full title: envoy extraordinary and minister plenipotentiary); minister resident; *chargé d'affaires*

diplomatic immunity. See immunity, diplomatic

dollar diplomacy. Governmental use of private investors to promote foreign policy (p. 578); conducting foreign policy to help private investors

Downing Street. Location in London of British Foreign Office (No. 10) and other offices; hence synonym for Foreign Office or British government

doyen. See dean

embassy. The ambassador and his suite; his residence or office *entente* (Fr.). An understanding or agreement between two or more nations

envoy. General term for an official on a diplomatic mission

envoy extraordinary and minister plenipotentiary. Full title of diplomatic agent ranking between an ambassador and a minister resident

executive agent. Personal envoy of President, not subject to Senate approval. Several hundred have been used in U.S. history; e.g., Colonel House (p. 620)

executive agreement. One made by or on behalf of the President, and not subject to Senate approval. P. 770

exequatur. Written recognition of his authority given to a consular officer by the government to which he is accredited

expatriation, right of. Right of a person to change his citizenship. P. 408 n.

expropriation. Confiscation of property by a national government

extradition. The surrender of a person charged with crime by one nation to another

extraterritoriality. Exemption from the jurisdiction of local laws, as in China, where foreigners were long tried in their own special courts. P. 326

face. Dignity; prestige, as in the Oriental term, "lose face"

fait accompli (Fr.). Something accomplished and presumably irrevocable

faux pas (Fr.). A false step; a mistake

filibuster. To lead an unauthorized armed force against a friendly nation. Participants in filibusterism are filibusters or filibusterers. P. 294

free ships, free goods. Immunity of noncontraband enemy goods from capture while being carried on neutral ships. P. 18 n.

freedom of the seas. Right of merchantmen to traverse high seas. P. 897

freezing. Impounding assets of a foreign nation or foreign nationals. P. 780

full powers. Written authority given a diplomatic agent or other representative by his government

genocide. Mass extermination of whole groups of people; e.g., Jews

gentlemen's agreement. Agreement based on honor of parties to it. P. 571

good offices. Services of a third party in bringing disputing parties together. Usually a prelude to mediation. *See* mediation

hegemony. The preponderant authority of a government or state

hyphenated Americans; hyphenates. Immigrants attached to "Old Country." P. 895

identic. Identical, as an "identic" note

imbroglio. Complicated or embarrassing state of affairs; embroilment

immunity, diplomatic. Immunity of foreign envoys from local jurisdiction

impasse (Fr.). A predicament permitting no escape

imperialism. Policy of seeking to extend the domain or control of a nation in or over foreign territory

indefeasible allegiance. Citizenship which a nation asserts is incapable of being changed

instructions. Directions or orders by home foreign office to envoy in the field

insurgency. State of revolt short of an organized revolutionary government, not recognized as amounting to belligerency. P. 413

intern. To hold or detain persons or ships in wartime, whether enemy or neutral

international law; law of nations. Body of principles which civilized nations regard as binding on them in their dealings with one another

jingo. A supporter of a bellicose policy in foreign affairs; a chauvinist

justiciable. Recognized as being suitable for adjudication. P. 590

Kremlin. Seat of Soviet government; hence synonym for that government

legation. Official residence of a diplomatic minister

letter of marque and reprisal. Written authorization from a government permitting the recipient to engage in privateering. *See* privateer

Logan Act. U.S. statute forbidding unauthorized private negotiations. P. 887 n.

mandate. Territory administered by a mandatory nation under a commission granted, for example, by the League of Nations. P. 658

mediation. Intercession of a third party in a dispute on the initiative or with the consent of the disputants. *See* good offices

minister. See envoy extraordinary and minister plenipotentiary

mission. An envoy or body of special envoys; permanent foreign embassy or legation

modus vivendi (Lat.). Temporary arrangement of affairs pending a final settlement

most-favored-nation clause. Treaty clause by which one nation grants to another nation such privileges as it may grant to third nations. P. 324

multilateral. Participated in by more than two nations, as an agreement. P. 767

note. A formal communication from one government to another

nuncio. Representative of the Pope at a foreign capital

open door. Equal opportunity for commercial intercourse. P. 897

order in council. In British government, an executive act by the sovereign and privy council which in the nineteenth century was in fact an executive order by the cabinet alone. P. 115 n.

Pan-Americanism. Policy of co-operation among the American Republics. P. 898

paper blockade. A blockade not effectively enforced; hence no penalties should be attached to ignoring it. *See* blockade

persona grata (Lat.). A person acceptable as an envoy; opposite of *persona non grata*

plebicite. Vote of the people in a given region, usually on sovereignty

plenary. Full; entire, as a plenary session

plenipotentiary. Diplomatic agent with full power to negotiate as instructed

Porte. Government of the former Turkish Empire; also known as Sublime Porte

pourparler (Fr.). Informal conference to discuss a diplomatic issue

power politics. International politics by which a nation advances its interests by superior coercive power

precedence. Right of diplomats to go before others at public functions

privateer. An armed private ship authorized by its government to prey on enemy shipping, subject to restrictions. Practice abolished by European Powers at Paris in 1856 (p. 350 n.); not used by U.S. since 1815

prize court. A court authorized to judge upon captures at sea in wartime

protectorate. Dependent nation over which another nation assumes protection

protocol. Preliminary memorandum of discussions; rules of diplomatic etiquette

Quai d'Orsay. French foreign office or government (from its location)

quid pro quo (Lat.). Something in return; an equivalent

rapprochement (Fr.). An establishment of cordial relations between Powers

ratify. To make valid. In U.S. the Senate does not *ratify* treaties; it *approves* a treaty by a 2/3 vote. The President then *ratifies* the treaty, and ratifications are normally exchanged with the other government

reciprocity. Granting commercial privileges to another nation (usually lowering of tariff rates) in exchange for reciprocal concessions

recognition. Recognizing a new government as exercising the powers of a state by entering into formal relations with it; often a recognition of independence. Also of insurgency or belligerency

reparations. Payments in money or goods by a Power for damage inflicted

reprisal. Retaliatory action by one nation against another. P. 780

reservation. Limiting conditions attached to treaty or other instrument

right of visit and search. Right of a belligerent to search merchantmen on high seas to determine nationality or cargo

St. James's (Court). The British court (after St. James's Palace)

sanctions. Penalties (economic, military, etc.) established for breach of an international obligation. P. 727

self-determination. Asserted right of a people (usually homogeneous) in a territorial unit to determine their political status. P. 650

shirt-sleeve diplomacy. Direct, informal, unconventional diplomacy

sine qua non (Lat.). An indispensable thing or condition. P. 147

sovereignty. Supremacy in rule or power; sovereign power

sphere of interest. Also sphere of action, sphere of interest, zone of influence. An area in which one Power is permitted by others to exercise more or less exclusive influence. P. 526

state. In diplomacy, a sovereign nation or Power

status quo (Lat.). State of affairs now existing

status quo ante bellum (Lat.). State of affairs existing before the war. P. 152

suzerain. A state exercising political control (sovereignty) over another state

territorial waters. Marginal belt included within a state's boundaries.

three-mile limit. Extent to which a nation's marginal belt has traditionally (though not invariably) extended over adjacent seas

trusteeship. Area granted to a trustee nation by United Nations. P. 868

two-thirds rule. Constitutional provision by which Senate approval of treaties requires a two-thirds vote of those senators present

ultimate destination. Final destination of goods, especially contraband, under doctrine of continuous voyage. *See* continuous voyage

ultimatum. Final terms. Their rejection usually ends negotiations

unilateral. One sided; said of single-handed action by one member of a group

Vatican. The papal government (after Pope's palace)

visa. Endorsement made on passport permitting bearer to proceed

visit and search. See right of visit and search

Whitehall. British government (after thoroughfare of that name)

Wilhelmstrasse. Imperial German Foreign Office (after street on which located)

Appendix B

TERRITORIAL ACQUISITIONS OF THE UNITED STATES

DATE (if treaty, date of signing)	ACQUISITION	AREA (sq. mi.)	HOW ACQUIRED	PRICE
1783	Original Territory	892,135	Treaty—Gt. Br.	
1803	Louisiana	827,987	Purchase from France	$15,000,000 in cash and assumed claims
1819	Floridas	72,101	Treaty with Spain	$5,000,000 in assumed claims and relinquishment of Texas claim
1845	Texas	389,166	Independent Republic Annexed	
1846	Oregon	286,541	Treaty with Gt. Br.	
1848	Mexican Cession	529,189	Conquest from Mexico	$15,000,000 plus maximum claims of $3,250,000
1853	Gadsden Purchase	29,670	Purchase from Mexico	$10,000,000
1867	Alaska	586,400	Purchase from Russia	$7,200,000
1867	Midway Islands	1½	Occupation	
1898	Hawaiian Islands	6,407	Independent Republic Annexed	
1898	Philippine Islands	114,400	Conquest from Spain	$20,000,000
1898	Puerto Rico	3,435	Conquest from Spain	
1898	Guam	206	Conquest from Spain	
1899	Wake Island	3	Occupation	
1899	American Samoa	76	Division with Germany and Gt. Br.	
1903	Panama Canal Zone (perpetual lease)	549	Treaty with Panama	$10,000,000; annual payment of $250,000 beginning 9 years after ratification
1916	Virgin Islands	133	Purchase from Denmark	$25,000,000

916

Appendix C

PREVIOUS DIPLOMATIC EXPERIENCE OF PRESIDENTS

PRESIDENT	DATE	PARTY		DIPLOMATIC EXPERIENCE
George Washington	Apr. 30, 1789– Mar. 4, 1797	Fed.		
John Adams	Mar. 4, 1797– Mar. 4, 1801	Fed.	1778 1780 1779–83 1785–87	France Netherlands Peace Commissioner Great Britain
Thomas Jefferson	Mar. 4, 1801– Mar. 4, 1809	Rep.[1]	1785–89 1790–93	France Secretary of State
James Madison	Mar. 4, 1809– Mar. 4, 1817	Rep.	1801–09	Secretary of State
James Monroe	Mar. 4, 1817– Mar. 4, 1825	Rep.	1794–96 1803–04 1803–06 1805 1811–14	France France Great Britain Spain Secretary of State
John Quincy Adams	Mar. 4, 1825– Mar. 4, 1829	Rep.	1794–97 1797–01 1809–14 1814 1815–17 1817–25	Netherlands Prussia Russia Peace Commissioner Great Britain Secretary of State
Andrew Jackson	Mar. 4, 1829– Mar. 4, 1837	Dem.		
Martin Van Buren	Mar. 4, 1837– Mar. 4, 1841	Dem.	1829–31 1831–32	Secretary of State Great Britain (un-confirmed)
William Henry Harrison	Mar. 4, 1841– Apr. 4, 1841	Whig	1828–29	Colombia
John Tyler	Apr. 6, 1841– Mar. 4, 1845	Whig		
James Knox Polk	Mar. 4, 1845– Mar. 4, 1849	Dem.		
Zachary Taylor	Mar. 5, 1849– July 9, 1850	Whig		
Millard Fillmore	July 10, 1850– Mar. 4, 1853	Whig		
Franklin Pierce	Mar. 4, 1853– Mar. 4, 1857	Dem.		

[1] The Republican party of Jefferson's time is not to be confused with the present Republican party, which was organized in 1854.

PRESIDENT	DATE	PARTY	DIPLOMATIC EXPERIENCE	
James Buchanan	Mar. 4, 1857–	Dem.	1832–33	Russia
	Mar. 4, 1861		1845–49	Secretary of State
			1853–56	Great Britain
Abraham Lincoln	Mar. 4, 1861–	Rep.		
	Apr. 15, 1865			
Andrew Johnson	Apr. 15, 1865–	Rep.		
	Mar. 4, 1869			
Ulysses Simpson Grant	Mar. 4, 1869–	Rep.		
	Mar. 4, 1877			
Rutherford Birchard Hayes	Mar. 5, 1877–	Rep.		
	Mar. 4, 1881			
James Abram Garfield	Mar. 4, 1881–	Rep.		
	Sept. 19, 1881			
Chester Alan Arthur	Sept. 20, 1881–	Rep.		
	Mar. 4, 1885			
Grover Cleveland	Mar. 4, 1885–	Dem.		
	Mar. 4, 1889			
Benjamin Harrison	Mar. 4, 1889–	Rep.		
	Mar. 4, 1893			
Grover Cleveland	Mar. 4, 1893–	Dem.		
	Mar. 4, 1897			
William McKinley	Mar. 4, 1897–	Rep.		
	Sept. 14, 1901			
Theodore Roosevelt	Sept. 14, 1901–	Rep.		
	Mar. 4, 1909			
William Howard Taft	Mar. 4, 1909–	Rep.	1902	Special envoy to Pope
	Mar. 4, 1913			
Woodrow Wilson	Mar. 4, 1913–	Dem.		
	Mar. 4, 1921			
Warren Gamaliel Harding	Mar. 4, 1921–	Rep.		
	Aug. 2, 1923			
Calvin Coolidge	Aug. 3, 1923–	Rep.		
	Mar. 4, 1929			
Herbert Clark Hoover	Mar. 4, 1929–	Rep.		
	Mar. 4, 1933			
Franklin Delano Roosevelt	Mar. 4, 1933–	Dem.		
	Apr. 12, 1945			
Harry S. Truman	Apr. 12, 1945–	Dem.		

Appendix D

PREVIOUS DIPLOMATIC EXPERIENCE OF SECRETARIES OF STATE

PRESIDENT	PARTY	SECRETARY OF STATE	DATES OF SERVICE	DIPLOMATIC EXPERIENCE	
Washington	Fed.	Thomas Jefferson	Mar. 22, 1790– Dec. 31, 1793	1785–89	France
		Edmund Randolph	Jan. 2, 1794– Aug. 20, 1795		
		Timothy Pickering	Dec. 10, 1795–		
Adams	Fed.	Timothy Pickering	May 12, 1800		
		John Marshall	June 6, 1800– Feb. 4, 1801	1797–98	France
Jefferson	Rep.[1]	James Madison	May 2, 1801– Mar. 3, 1809		
Madison	Rep.	Robert Smith	Mar. 6, 1809– Apr. 1, 1811		
		James Monroe	Apr. 6, 1811– Sept. 30, 1814	1794–96 1803–04 1803–06 1805	France France Great Britain Spain
Monroe	Rep.	John Quincy Adams	Sept. 22, 1817– Mar. 3, 1825	1794–97 1797–01 1809–14 1814 1815–17	Netherlands Prussia Russia Peace Commissioner Great Britain
Adams	Rep.	Henry Clay	Mar. 7, 1825– Mar. 3, 1829	1814	Peace Commissioner
Jackson	Dem.	Martin Van Buren	Mar. 28, 1829– May 23, 1831	1831–32	Great Britain (not confirmed by Senate)
		Edward Livingston	May 24, 1831– May 29, 1833		
		Louis McLane	May 29, 1833– June 30, 1834	1829–31	Great Britain
		John Forsyth	July 1, 1834–	1819–22	Spain
Van Buren	Dem.	John Forsyth	Mar. 3, 1841		
Harrison	Whig	Daniel Webster	Mar. 6, 1841–		
Tyler	Whig	Daniel Webster	May 8, 1843		
		Abel P. Upshur	July 24, 1843– Feb. 28, 1844		
		John C. Calhoun	Apr. 1, 1844– Mar. 10, 1845		

[1] The Republican party of Jefferson's time is not to be confused with the present Republican party, which was organized in 1854.

PRESIDENT	PARTY	SECRETARY OF STATE	DATES OF SERVICE	DIPLOMATIC EXPERIENCE
Polk	Dem.	James Buchanan	Mar. 10, 1845– Mar. 7, 1849	1832–33 Russia
Taylor	Whig	John M. Clayton	Mar. 8, 1849– July 22, 1850	
Fillmore	Whig	Daniel Webster	July 23, 1850– Oct. 24, 1852	
		Edward Everett	Nov. 6, 1852– Mar. 3, 1853	1841–45 Great Britain
Pierce	Dem.	William L. Marcy	Mar. 8, 1853– Mar. 6, 1857	
Buchanan	Dem.	Lewis Cass	Mar. 6, 1857– Dec. 14, 1860	1836–42 France
		Jeremiah S. Black	Dec. 17, 1860– Mar. 5, 1861	
Lincoln	Rep.	William H. Seward	Mar. 6, 1861–	
Johnson	Rep.	William H. Seward	Mar. 4, 1869	
Grant	Rep.	Elihu B. Washburne	Mar. 5, 1869– Mar. 16, 1869	
		Hamilton Fish	Mar. 17, 1869– Mar. 12, 1877	
Hayes	Rep.	William M. Evarts	Mar. 12, 1877– Mar. 7, 1881	
Garfield	Rep.	James G. Blaine	Mar. 7, 1881–	
Arthur	Rep.	James G. Blaine	Dec. 19, 1881	
		Frederick T. Fre- linghuysen	Dec. 19, 1881– Mar. 6, 1885	
Cleveland	Dem.	Thomas F. Bayard	Mar. 7, 1885– Mar. 6, 1889	
Harrison	Rep.	James G. Blaine	Mar. 7, 1889– June 4, 1892	
		John W. Foster	June 29, 1892– Feb. 23, 1893	1873–80 Mexico 1880–81 Russia 1883– Spain 1889– Special Mission to Spain
Cleveland	Dem.	Walter Q. Gresham	Mar. 7, 1893– May 28, 1895	
		Richard Olney	June 10, 1895– Mar. 5, 1897	
McKinley	Rep.	John Sherman	Mar. 6, 1897– Apr. 27, 1898	
		William R. Day	Apr. 28, 1898– Sept. 16, 1898	1897–98 Asst. Sec. of State

PRESIDENT	PARTY	SECRETARY OF STATE	DATES OF SERVICE	DIPLOMATIC EXPERIENCE	
McKinley (*cont.*)		John Hay	Sept. 30, 1898–	1865	Sec. of Leg., Paris
Roosevelt	Rep.	John Hay	July 1, 1905	1869	Sec. of Leg., Madrid
				1867	Sec. of Leg., Vienna & chargé d'affaires
				1879–81	First Asst. S. of S.
				1897–98	Great Britain
		Elihu Root	July 19, 1905– Jan. 27, 1909		
		Robert Bacon	Jan. 27, 1909– Mar. 5, 1909		
Taft	Rep.	Philander C. Knox	Mar. 6, 1909– Mar. 5, 1913		
Wilson	Dem.	William Jennings Bryan	Mar. 5, 1913– June 9, 1915		
Wilson	Dem.	Robert Lansing	June 24, 1915– Feb. 13, 1920		
		Bainbridge Colby	Mar. 23, 1920– Mar. 4, 1921		
Harding	Rep.	Charles E. Hughes	Mar. 5, 1921–		
Coolidge	Rep.	Charles E. Hughes	Mar. 4, 1925		
		Frank B. Kellogg	Mar. 5, 1925– Mar. 28, 1929	1924–25	Great Britain
Hoover	Rep.	Henry L. Stimson	Mar. 28, 1929– Mar. 4, 1933	1927	Special representative to Nicaragua
Roosevelt	Dem.	Cordell Hull	Mar. 4, 1933– Nov. 27, 1944		
		Edward R. Stettinius, Jr.	Dec. 1, 1944	1943–44	Under Sec. of State
Truman	Dem.	Edward R. Stettinius, Jr.	June 27, 1945		
		James F. Byrnes	July 3, 1945– Jan. 20, 1947	1945	At Yalta
		George C. Marshall	Jan. 21, 1947– Jan. 20, 1949	1945–47	China mission
		Dean G. Acheson	Jan. 21, 1949–	1941–45	Asst. S. of S.
				1945–47	Under S. of S.

Appendix E

BIBLIOGRAPHICAL APPENDIX

These notes are in general recent references for which there was not room at the ends of the chapters in the text. Sometimes they represent an overflow. In each case first consult *Recent References, New References,* and *4th Ed. Refs.* under the Bibliographical Note at the end of the relevant chapter.

GENERAL

International Law. See the second revised edition of C. C. Hyde, *International Law, Chiefly as Interpreted and Applied by the United States* (3 vols., Boston, 1945). G. H. Hackworth, *Digest of International Law* (8 vols., Washington, 1940–1944), has been completed.

Diplomatic Machinery. See E. E. Dennison, *The Senate Foreign Relations Committee* (Stanford University, 1942); and A. C. F. Westphal, *The House Committee on Foreign Affairs* (N.Y., 1942); J. R. Childs, *American Foreign Service* (N.Y., 1948). The standard work on the subject is now G. H. Stuart, *The Department of State* (N.Y., 1949).

Unofficial Documents. W. R. Manning, *Diplomatic Correspondence of the United States: Canadian Relations, 1784–1860* (Washington, 1940–) has in the fourth volume come through 1860. *The Collected Papers of John Bassett Moore* (7 vols., New Haven, 1944), are a monument to a distinguished international lawyer and diplomatist.

Government Documents. The official *Papers Relating to the Foreign Relations of the United States* have now come down through the year 1932. Hunter Miller, ed., *Treaties and other International Acts of the United States of America* (Washington, D.C., 1948), vol. VIII, continues the monumental series.

CHAPTER IV. FOREIGN AFFAIRS UNDER THE ARTICLES OF CONFEDERATION

RECENT REFERENCES. A. L. Burt, *The United States, Great Britain, and British North America* (New Haven, 1940), Ch. VI, strongly disagrees with Bemis' *Jay's Treaty* when he contends that the primary motive of the British in retaining the posts was not a desire to keep the fur trade but rather to pacify their Indian allies, who had been deserted in the Treaty of 1783. By holding the forts, the British could liquidate the problem gradually, prevent a bloody outbreak on the frontier, and keep the Indians under their influence as a buffer against the advancing Americans. There is much force in these arguments; but in building up his case for the Indian-pacification motive, Burt gives the impression that the fur-trade motive was negligible, which is hardly correct. The truth is that both motives were important and intertwined; and the author renders a useful service when he directs attention to an aspect of the problem which hitherto had been only inadequately presented.

N. V. Russell, *The British Régime in Michigan and the Old Northwest, 1760–1796* (Northfield, Minn., 1939), briefly develops the Indian-pacification motive, which is also discussed by A. L. Burt in an earlier book, *The Old Province of Quebec* (Minneapolis, Minn., 1933).

A useful survey of Confederation diplomacy may be found in Chapter V of A. B. Darling, *Our Rising Empire, 1763–1803* (New Haven, 1940).

E. W. Lyon, *The Man Who Sold Louisiana: The Career of François Barbé-Marbois* (Norman, Okla., 1942), is a scholarly and readable biography, the first full-length life of this remarkable Frenchman, who, from 1779 to 1785, lived in America as secretary to the French minister and then as *chargé d'affaires*. The book throws considerable light on chaotic conditions in America under the Confederation, and particularly on problems of extradition arising from an attack on Barbé-Marbois by a disgruntled compatriot (pp. 36–43).

4TH ED. REFS. Valuable documents are published in Lawrence Kinnaird, ed., *Spain in the Mississippi Valley, 1765–1794*, vols. II, III, Amer. Hist. Assn., *Annual Report, 1945* (Washington, D.C., 1949).

CHAPTER IX. DRIFTING INTO WAR WITH GREAT BRITAIN, 1809–1812

RECENT REFERENCES. A. L. Burt, *The United States, Great Britain, and British North America* (New Haven, 1940), Chs. XI–XIII, has a challenging discussion of the causes of the War of 1812 which cannot be overlooked by any serious student of the problem. He restresses the impressment and neutral rights issues, and takes strong issue with Pratt on the Indian-menace theory, advancing instead the hypothesis that the West wanted Canada as a hostage to extort compensation from the British in other quarters (p. 310). Burt also suggests (p. 306) that the vote of the maritime East against war may have in part reflected the vulnerability of that area to blockade, bombardment, and invasion. In support of this point it may be noted that large areas on the New York and Vermont frontier, which were vulnerable to invasion from Canada, voted against war. Burt makes much of the point that the Louisiana purchase was a fundamental cause of the conflict, because British and American policy, which had become closer in the face of the French threat, tended to diverge sharply after 1803 (p. 225), precisely as Napoleon had hoped it would when he sold the territory. Although Burt argues most of his points with great cogency, the present writer feels that he tends to underestimate Western influence.

W. H. Goodman, "The Origins of the War of 1812: a Survey of Changing Interpretations," *Miss. Valley Hist. Rev.*, XXVIII (1941), 171–186, is an arresting historiographical study. The author's principal findings follow: (1) The causes of the war were more complex than is generally believed, and we need a careful synthesis of *all aspects* of the problem based upon a re-examination of the sources. Writers like Pratt and Taylor, in dealing with only "one set of causes," have unwittingly brought about a distortion. (2) The influence of the West, though decisive, has been overemphasized. The declaration of war could not have been passed without a considerable supporting vote from the Eastern states. Maps giving a heavy shading to the areas that voted for war seriously exaggerate the role of the West, for the states in this region were but scantily populated. (3) The idea of conquering Canada was not solely a product of the West; it was clearly advanced by Southern newspapers as early as 1807. (4) Taylor's thesis as to Western concern over loss of markets through Britain's maritime practices must be given much weight. (5) The pendulum has swung from maritime grievances in the nineteenth century, to Western aspirations in the twentieth; now it is swinging back in the general direction of maritime grievances.

J. H. Parks, *Felix Grundy* (University, La., 1940), is the biography of a War Hawk, whom Federalists grouped with James Madison and "the Devil" as a precipitator of the war.

CHAPTER XI. THE UNITED STATES AND THE FLORIDAS, 1803–1821

NEW REFERENCES. S. F. Bemis, *The Latin American Policy of the United States* (N.Y., 1943), Chs. II, III, surveys the Florida negotiations against the background of unneutral assistance to the Latin American rebels. The no-transfer resolution, passed by Congress in 1811 partly because of British opposition to the acquisition of West Florida, is stressed as one of the foundation stones of the Monroe Doctrine (p. 30).

Harry Bernstein, *Origins of Inter-American Interest, 1700–1812* (Phila., 1945), is a detailed treatment of the early economic, cultural, and ideological ties between Latin America and the United States.

J. H. Powell, *Richard Rush, Republican Diplomat, 1780–1859* (Phila., 1942), Ch. V, emphasizes the dangerous atmosphere created in England by Jackson's Florida adventure. Spanish propagandists were allegedly active in London, and Rush thought that war with Britain could not have been averted had not the Convention of 1818 already done much to clear the air (p. 126). The friendly Castlereagh, far from trying to block ratification of the Spanish-American treaty, as alleged, actually advised Madrid to consummate the transaction (p. 144). It also seems evident that France and Russia, rumor to the contrary, made no attempt to interfere.

J. J. Johnson, "Early Relations of the United States with Chile," *Pacific Hist. Rev.*, XIII (1944), 260–270, outlines the influence of United States traders and propagandists in implanting revolutionary ideas (the Declaration of Independence and the Constitution were circulated), and describes the assistance given the revolutionists.

CHAPTER XII. EUROPE, AMERICA, AND THE MONROE DOCTRINE, 1815–1825

RECENT REFERENCES. A. P. Whitaker, *The United States and the Independence of Latin America, 1800–1830* (Baltimore, 1941), points out that the United States did not really reject Canning's memorable proposal, because the impatient Foreign Secretary turned aside to France while the Administration was still considering it (pp. 445–447). Canning's real purpose was to keep the United States out of Cuba (p. 500). Monroe told the representative of Buenos Aires in Washington that he was primarily concerned with stopping France (p. 502), though it is doubtful whether France would have taken aggressive action, even if Canning had not intervened to secure the Polignac pledge. Whitaker believes (contrary to Perkins) that Adams was more alarmed over the Holy Alliance than he appeared to be (p. 480). Moreover, at the time the message was proclaimed there was no real assurance that Canning's policy was such that the British fleet would be used to guarantee America's position (pp. 494–495), though Monroe's failure to prepare for war with the Holy Alliance indicates that British support was expected. Chapter XVI is a penetrating discussion of the authorship question. This account, on the whole, gives Monroe considerably more credit than he has received in recent years. Whitaker also stresses the fact that Adams was loyally subordinate to his chief (pp. 425–426), and that while Adams undoubtedly was the principal author of the noncolonization clause, he had much less to do with other aspects (p. 491). Whitaker strongly argues that an important new principle was introduced by Monroe; namely, that the United States, if necessary, would fight for the independence of its sister republics, a position that had been consistently avoided up to this point (pp. 518, 520).

NEW REFERENCES. S. F. Bemis, *The Latin American Policy of the United States* (N.Y., 1943), denies any real Hispanic origin of the Monroe Doctrine (p. 49), and shows that Canning wanted to use the United States in the scale of world politics to balance the setbacks to British diplomacy in Europe (p. 62). The Washington government rejected several appeals for assistance from the Latin American republics (p. 68), who clearly wanted to involve the United States in war with Spain. Dr. Bemis thinks that the great immediate contribution of the Monroe Doctrine was "in galvanizing the preponderant *republican character* of the new states at the outset" (p. 71). This meant a carrying out of the ideals of both the American Revolution and the French Revolution, all of which were anathema to the Holy Alliance and to Tory England.

J. H. Powell, *Richard Rush, Republican Diplomat, 1780–1859* (Phila., 1942), Ch. VI, concludes that if Minister Rush had not been distrustful of British illiberalism and particularly of Canning, he might have accepted the latter's proposal without referring it home. This would have changed the whole nature of the Doctrine and of American relations with Britain (p. 165). When the news of Monroe's message reached England, the value of Spanish-American stocks rose on the exchanges; the safety of the new republics was no longer considered doubtful (p. 167).

Laura Bornholdt, "The Abbé de Pradt and the Monroe Doctrine," *Hispanic Amer. Hist. Rev.*, XXIV (1944), 201–221, contradicts Schellenberg and belittles the influence of De Pradt, French cleric and publicist, on Jefferson's thinking regarding the Monroe Doctrine.

T. B. Davis, Jr., "Carlos De Alvear and James Monroe: New Light on the Origin of the Monroe Doctrine," *ibid.*, XXIII (1943), 632–649. Alvear, an Argentine diplomat, interviewed Monroe nearly a year after the latter's message, and found that the President had most feared French intervention. Monroe uncandidly added that his declaration was an unequivocal promise to protect Latin America, although neither he nor his associates so regarded it (p. 637). Monroe also misled De Alvear into thinking that the United States was making vigorous military preparations to back up the Doctrine (p. 639).

A. G. Mazour, "The Russian-American and Anglo-Russian Conventions, 1824–1825: An Interpretation," *Pacific Hist. Rev.*, XIV (1945), 303–310, shows that the two treaties were unexpectedly generous because Russia wanted to free her hands in Europe so as to be able to push for the straits outlet. The treaty of 1824, by admitting American traders to Alaska, spelled the ruin of the Russian-American Company and thus resulted in the sale of Alaska. Russia declined to press the ukase of 1821 or to challenge the Monroe Doctrine, largely because she did not

want embroilments in America to injure her chances for the straits. [Once again
Europe's distresses worked to the advantage of the United States.]

S. R. Tompkins, "Drawing the Alaska Boundary," *Canadian Hist. Rev.*, XXVI
(1945), 1–24, considers the negotiations leading up to the treaty of 1824 against
the larger international background.

CHAPTER XIII. SIGNS AND PORTENTS, 1825–1840

RECENT REFERENCES. A. P. Whitaker, *The United States and the Independence of Latin America, 1800–1830* (Baltimore, 1941), has an excellent chapter
(XIX) on the Panama Congress. The author notes that fear of economic competition
from Latin America worked against United States participation, and concludes that,
all things considered, the Congress was well attended (p. 581).

R. A. McLemore, *Franco-American Diplomatic Relations: 1816–1836* (University, La., 1941), has the most thorough study of the French claims controversy.
He is particularly strong on backgrounds and on public opinion in America, France,
and England. The author concludes that the United States came off well, in spite
of unpreparedness and partisan division, because slowness of communication permitted passions to cool, because Jackson had conservative advisers, and because other
international complications were powerful preservers of peace (p. 211). The
Russian menace was of particular concern to both France and Britain (pp. 178 ff.).

A. B. Corey, *The Crisis of 1830–1842 in Canadian-American Relations* (New
Haven, 1941), is an able study, especially complete on public opinion in both
America and Canada. Other contributions of this book are considered in the Biblio-
graphical Appendix of the next chapter.

W. B. Hatcher, *Edward Livingston* (University, La., 1940), considers the re-
lations of the United States minister in Paris to the claims controversy. The
author stresses the political situation in France, particularly the weakness of the
King; the effect of Whig attacks against Jackson on French intransigence; and
Livingston's part in inducing Jackson to submit and later soften his messages to
Congress.

C. P. Stacey, ed., "A Private Report of General Winfield Scott on the Border
Situation in 1839," *Canadian Hist. Rev.*, XXI (1940), 407–414, brings out the
difficulties arising from the sympathy of United States enforcement officers with
the rebels.

CHAPTER XIV. ANGLO-AMERICAN RELATIONS AND THE
WEBSTER-ASHBURTON TREATY

RECENT REFERENCES. A. B. Corey, *The Crisis of 1830–1842 in Canadian-
American Relations* (New Haven, 1941), Chs. IX to XI, discusses the McLeod
case and the Webster-Ashburton treaty. He points out that the McLeod affair
was but an incident; the real grievance of the United States was the failure of the
British to make proper reparation for the *Caroline* (p. 179). The trial of McLeod,
from the American point of view, was an anticlimax; the honor of the United
States was sustained when it was understood that New York might go ahead with
the trial (pp. 136–137). Corey concludes that America came out of the Webster-
Ashburton negotiations very well. Ashburton readily agreed to a compromise line
between the Great Lakes and the Lake of the Woods which gave the United

States invaluable iron ore deposits, even though that region was known to be rich in ore. The Canadians received the Maine overland route, but paradoxically this route was menaced by Rouses Point. The author believes that the loss of territory by Maine was more than compensated for by the granting of navigational rights on the St. John River, by the cession of Rouses Point, and by other concessions (pp. 168–169).

O. P. Chitwood, *John Tyler: Champion of the Old South* (N.Y., 1939), Ch. XX, emphasizes the large and generally disregarded part that the tactful President Tyler played in co-operating with Webster and in conciliating Ashburton. Perhaps his most important contribution was suggesting to Webster that the various parts of the settlement be put into one treaty rather than into several (p. 315); otherwise, some of the matters agreed upon might not have run the senatorial gauntlet.

NEW REFERENCES. Background accounts are E. W. McInnis, *The Unguarded Frontier* (Garden City, N.Y., 1942), Chs. VII, VIII; and J. B. Bretner, *North Atlantic Triangle* (New Haven, 1945), Ch. VIII.

The fullest treatment for the years indicated is Max Berger, *The British Traveller in America, 1836–1860* (N.Y., 1943), which may be used in connection with the older accounts already cited, as well as with J. G. Brooks, *As Others See Us* (N.Y., 1908), and Jane Mesick, *The English Traveller in America, 1785–1835* (N.Y., 1922).

G. S. Gordon, *Anglo-American Literary Relations* (Oxford, 1942), contains a series of charming lectures on British travelers, transatlantic friendships, and particularly the absence of an international copyright (Lecture V), which under the pretense of free trade not only robbed British authors but stifled American talent.

4TH ED. REFS. R. N. Current, "Webster's Propaganda and the Ashburton Treaty," *Miss. Valley Hist. Rev.*, XXXIV (1947), 187–200, portrays Webster as a skilled propagandist who secured a favorable reaction by manipulating the press in Maine and coloring the news sources in Washington. Thomas Le Duc, "The Maine Frontier and the Northeastern Boundary Controversy," *Amer. Hist. Rev.*, LIII (1947), 30–41, reveals how the situation was complicated by Maine politics and the determination of the British to guard their overland lifeline against the advancing Maine frontier. See also M. M. Kampelman, "The United States and International Copyright," *Amer. Jour. of Internat. Law*, XLI (1947), 406–429; and Allan Nevins, *America through British Eyes* (N.Y., 1948), a revision of an older work.

CHAPTER XVI. THE ANNEXATION OF TEXAS, 1821–1845

NEW REFERENCES. A. W. Williams and E. C. Barker, eds., *The Writings of Sam Houston, 1813–1863* (8 vols., Austin, Tex., 1938–1943), in completed form brings the story to July, 1863.

H. G. Warren, *The Sword Was Their Passport: A History of American Filibustering in the Mexican Revolution* (Baton Rouge, La., 1943), shows that public opinion in the United States largely negatived the nominal neutrality of the Washington government, whose official correctness was partly due to a desire to acquire Florida—and possibly Texas—by peaceful means (p. 255). [It is interesting to note that while the Mexicans were quite willing to take advantage of American unneutrality during their own revolution, they did not have the same attitude toward the Texan revolution.]

J. D. Hill, *The Texas Navy* (Chicago, 1937), reveals that command of the Gulf by the tiny Texan flotilla paved the way for victory at San Jacinto. Mexico gained the ascendancy in 1837–1838, but her fleet was destroyed in the Pastry War with France. Texas then entered into a *de facto* alliance with Yucatan, and as late as 1843 was fighting on the sea with Mexico. The Texan fleet, by diverting Mexican energies and attention elsewhere, was an important factor in preventing reinvasion.

W. S. Robertson, "French Intervention in Mexico in 1838," *Hispanic Amer. Hist. Rev.*, XXIV (1944), 222–252, notes that the Pastry War which France waged with Mexico for the collection of debts caused the passage by the United States House of Representatives, in 1839, of a nonintervention resolution that foreshadowed the nonintervention doctrine of Calvo.

CHAPTER XVIII. THE FITFUL FIFTIES

RECENT REFERENCES. W. H. Gray, "American Diplomacy in Venezuela, 1835–1865," *Hispanic Amer. Hist. Rev.*, XX (1940), 551–574, shows, among other things, that beginning in 1850 the United States failed on five different occasions to support Venezuela under the Monroe Doctrine in the latter's collisions with European Powers.

G. A. Nuermberger, "The Continental Treaties of 1856: An American Union 'Exclusive of the United States,' " *ibid.*, XX (1940), 32–55, describes an abortive attempt at Latin American union (Chile, Ecuador, and Peru) which was motivated largely by fear of Walker's forays.

NEW REFERENCES. Gerstle Mack, *The Land Divided* (N.Y., 1944), examines the various proposals for transisthmian transit that were under discussion in the 1850's and later. Note particularly the plans for an ingenious ship-railroad across Tehuantepec (Ch. XIX).

Hunter Miller, ed., *Treaties and other International Acts of the United States of America* (Washington, 1942), VI, 111–167, 667–742, has much data on the British claims convention of 1853 and the Reciprocity Treaty of 1854.

A. J. May, *Contemporary American Opinion of the Mid-Century Revolutions in Central Europe* (Phila., 1927), especially pp. 126–128, shows that Kossuth failed because of the nonintervention tradition; the unwillingness of the anti-abolitionist South to support foreign intervention; and the conservatism of the Catholic church. The most important result in the field of foreign affairs was the reaffirmation and strengthening of the noninterventionist tradition.

CHAPTER XX. THE DAWN OF ASIATIC INTERESTS

4TH ED. REFS. The only full-length survey of the subject is F. R. Dulles' readable, *China and America: The Story of Their Relations since 1784* (Princeton, 1946). See also J. W. Pratt, ed., "Our First 'War' in China: The Diary of William Henry Powell, 1856," *Amer. Hist. Rev.*, LIII (1948), 776–786. The most complete and best-rounded account is Arthur Walworth, *Black Ships Off Japan: The Story of Commodore Perry's Expedition* (N.Y., 1946). It may be supplemented by A. B. Cole, ed., *A Scientist with Perry in Japan: The Journal of Dr. James Morrow* (Chapel Hill, N.C., 1947). See also S. W. Livermore, "Early Commercial and Consular Relations with the East Indies," *Pacific Hist. Rev.*, XV (1946), 31–58; Gordon Greenwood, *Early American-Australian Relations from the Arrival of the Spaniards in America to the Close of 1930* (Melbourne, 1944).

CHAPTER XXII. CIVIL WAR DIPLOMACY, 1862–1865

4TH ED. REFS. Margaret Clapp, *Forgotten First Citizen: John Bigelow* (Boston, 1947), shows that the consular and diplomatic services of Bigelow in France (1861–1866) were hardly less important than those of Adams in London. Through clever propaganda he caused the French and Continental press to become much more friendly to the North (p. 181), and through skilful diplomacy he prevented blockade breaking ships and commerce destroyers from sailing from France against the Union (p. 232). M. B. Hamer, "Luring Canadian Soldiers into Union Lines during the War between the States," *Canadian Hist. Rev.*, XXVII (1946), 150–162, discusses friction growing out of this practice.

CHAPTER XXIII. FRANCE AND MAXIMILIAN'S MEXICAN EMPIRE, 1861–1867

RECENT REFERENCES. N. L. Ferris, "The Relations of the United States with South America during the American Civil War," *Hispanic Amer. Hist. Rev.*, XXI (1941), 51–78, reveals that the prestige of the United States reached a new high point at this time. Only Brazil recognized the belligerency of the Confederacy, and not out of a spirit of unfriendliness. Northern propagandists advertized the idea that success for the Union would result in the abolition of slavery, in the preservation of democratic principles, and in protection against foreign intervention. This last point had much appeal, as the Maximilian venture and other aggressive European designs demonstrated the desirability of having an undivided United States. Moreover, if the South had won her independence, the Latin American countries could have expected further filibustering forays. When the war came to an end, the influence of the United States rapidly declined, in part because of Washington's failure to support Chile and Peru in their quarrel with Spain in 1866.

4TH ED. REFS. Margaret Clapp, *Forgotten First Citizen: John Bigelow* (Boston, 1947), describes Bigelow's efforts to warn Napoleon of his folly and Washington to go slowly. H. W. Casper, *American Attitudes toward the Rise of Napoleon III* (Washington, D.C., 1947) further reveals American hostility to the monarchical principle. C. C. Hauch, "Attitudes of Foreign Governments towards the Spanish Reoccupation of the Dominican Republic," *Hispanic Amer. Hist. Rev.*, XXVII (1947), 247–268, points out that the resistance of the natives, plus yellow fever, did more than the threatened power of the United States. R. W. Frazer, "Trade between California and the Belligerent Powers during the French Intervention in Mexico," *Pacific Hist. Rev.*, XV (1946), 390–399, describes the unfavorable reaction of the Mexican government to the shipping of supplies to Maximilian. R. W. Frazer, "Latin-American Projects to Aid Mexico during the French Intervention," *Hispanic Amer. Hist. Rev.*, XXVIII (1948), 377–388, demonstrates that such efforts failed partly because of the refusal of the United States to participate. Two general works of merit are: H. M. Hyde, *Mexican Empire: The History of Maximilian and Carlota of Mexico* (London, 1946), and Ralph Roeder, *Juarez and His Mexico* (2 vols., N.Y., 1947).

CHAPTER XXIV. POSTWAR EXPANSION, 1865–1867

4TH ED. REFS. S. R. Tompkins, *Alaska: Promyshlennik and Sourdough* (Norman, Okla., 1945), has a convenient summation of the purchase story. W. E. Nagengast, "The Visit of the Russian Fleet to the United States: Were Americans Deceived?" *Russian Rev.*, VIII (1949), 46–55, attempts to prove that the American public was fully aware of the real reasons for the demonstration. Yet the evidence is handpicked, chiefly from a few New York newspapers, without regard for abundant contrary evidence. About all the author proves is that more editors *guessed* correctly than formerly had been suspected. The conclusions also conflict with A. P. Coleman and M. M. Coleman, *The Polish Insurrection of 1863 in the Light of New York Editorial Opinion* (Williamsport, Pa., 1934).

CHAPTER XXVI. THE NADIR OF DIPLOMACY, 1877–1889

RECENT REFERENCES. E. C. Sandmeyer, *The Anti-Chinese Movement in California* (Urbana, Ill., 1939), does not supplant the earlier work by Coolidge, but adds some useful details, particularly on local legislation and its conflict with federal jurisdiction.

An American Democrat: The Recollections of Perry Belmont (2nd ed., N.Y., 1941), contains two interesting chapters on Blaine by a Democratic member of the House who was prominent in investigating the Secretary's South American entanglements. There are also discussions of the fisheries, the Belgian Congo, and the Isthmian Canal question.

J. F. Rippy, "Justo Rufino Barrios and the Nicaraguan Canal," *Hispanic Amer. Hist. Rev.*, XX (1940), 190–197, shows how the machinations of the Guatemalan dictator in connection with control over the canal route had much to do with causing Nicaragua to conclude the abortive Frelinghuysen-Zavala treaty with the United States.

L. F. Sensabaugh, "The Attitude of the United States toward the Colombia-Costa Rica Arbitral Proceedings," *ibid.*, XIX (1939), 16–30, treats the opposition of Blaine, and the even stronger opposition of Frelinghuysen, to the Costa Rica-Colombia treaty of 1880. The author believes that the United States has not been hostile to European arbitration as such, but in this case the State Department's position was based on the belief that "treaty rights and obligations might be affected."

NEW REFERENCES. Gerstle Mack, *The Land Divided* (N.Y., 1944), is full of the French venture in Panama, which came nearer to success than is commonly supposed; the basic error was De Lesseps' insistence on a sea level canal rather than a lock canal, to which a change was made when too late (p. 371). Although De Lesseps was personally honest, his American propaganda organization spent a huge sum (p. 308).

G. T. Davis, *A Navy Second to None* (N.Y., 1940), is an able survey which may be used together with that of Harold and Margaret Sprout, previously cited.

C. C. Tansill, *Canadian-American Relations, 1875–1911* (New Haven, 1943), Chs. I–III, deals in great detail with the fisheries dispute, and exposes Republican partisanship.

G. R. Dulebohn, *Principles of Foreign Policy under the Cleveland Administration* (Phila., 1941), discusses the fisheries and the seals; and concludes (Ch. V) that Cleveland's general policy was (1) to preserve national security; (2) to avoid participation in power politics; and (3) to adjust international disputes by peaceful means. His keynote was conservatism, that is, no departure from nonentanglement and other policies.

Paul Knaplund and C. M. Clewes, eds., "Private Letters from the British Embassy in Washington to the Foreign Secretary, Lord Granville, 1880–1885," Amer. Hist. Assn., *Annual Report, 1941* (Washington, 1942), I, 73–183, throws new light on Irish disorders, which were aggravated by the famine in Ireland and by the visit of C. S. Parnell to the United States (81–82); on the fisheries, notably the Fortune Bay affair (p. 80, *passim*); on the refusal of the British minister to attend the Yorktown celebration (p. 80, *passim*); on the alleged construction of a torpedo boat for the Fenians in New York [an *Alabama* case in reverse!] (pp. 144–146); and on Sackville-West, who emerges an abler diplomat than generally regarded. His scandalous background is treated authoritatively (pp. 157–158). The Gladstone government was currently under fire for allegedly betraying British interests in Africa and Asia; hence it could not yield to Blaine on the Clayton-Bulwer issue (p. 81).

J. F. Rippy, "Relations of the United States and Guatemala during the Epoch of Justo Rufino Barrios," *Hispanic Amer. Hist. Rev.*, XXII (1942), 595–605, discusses relations in the late 1870's and early 1880's with the dictator Barrios, who admired the United States and encouraged United States mining, railroad, and other activity. This account is to be read in connection with Dr. Rippy's earlier article on Barrios, listed above.

4TH ED. REFS. Herbert Millington, *American Diplomacy and the War of the Pacific* (N.Y., 1948), retells the story, principally from government documents. Opinion in the United States was rather indifferent to the conflict but warmed up after Blaine entered the arena with his "pugilistic" diplomacy (pp. 30, 82). See also J. A. Karlin, "Anti-Chinese Outbreaks in Seattle, 1885–1886," *Pacific Northwest Quar.*, XXXIX (1948), 103–130.

CHAPTER XXVII. BLAINE AND SPIRITED DIPLOMACY, 1889–1893

RECENT REFERENCES. A. T. Volwiler has edited *The Correspondence between Benjamin Harrison and James G. Blaine, 1882–1893* (Phila., 1940), which is primarily political. Much more revealing for our purposes is Volwiler's "Harrison, Blaine, and American Foreign Policy, 1889–1893," Amer. Philosophical Soc. *Procs.*, LXXIX (1938), 637–648. The author feels that war with Chile was imminent, and adduces further evidence to support the conclusion that Harrison was far more bellicose than Blaine. In fact, the President had a direct hand in drafting a number of the important papers. Harrison, a Civil War soldier, was particularly concerned about the insult to the American uniform. At a Cabinet meeting he leaned forward and said to Blaine (who had never served in the armed forces): "Mr. Secretary, that insult was to the uniform of the United States sailors (p. 640)." Evidence that Peru and Argentina were willing actively to co-operate with the United States in a war with Chile may have had a restraining effect on the latter.

J. A. Karlin, "The Italo-American Incident of 1891 and the Road to Reunion," *Jour. of Southern Hist.*, VIII (1942), 242–246, sees in the outburst of patriotic fervor, both North and South, an important factor in helping close the bloody chasm.

L. L. Montague, *Haiti and the United States, 1714–1938* (Durham, N.C., 1940), Ch. IX, has a critical account of the unsuccessful efforts of Blaine to lease a coaling station (Môle St. Nicholas) in Haiti. A browbeating naval demonstration aroused Haitian resentment and backfired on Washington.

The part played in this episode by the United States minister, a distinguished colored man, is set forth in interesting detail in L. M. Sears, "Frederick Douglass and the Mission to Haiti, 1889–1891," *Hispanic Amer. Hist. Rev.*, XXI (1941), 222–238.

NEW REFERENCES. C. C. Tansill, *Canadian-American Relations, 1875–1911* (New Haven, 1943), Chs. X–XI, has a detailed and authoritative treatment of Blaine and the seal problem.

Sister M. O. Kolbeck, *American Opinion on the Kulturkampf, 1871–1882* (Washington, 1942), gives reactions to Bismarck's struggle with the Catholic church, and provides some background material for the pork controversy.

L. L. Snyder, "The American-German Pork Dispute, 1879–1891," *Jour. of Mod. Hist.*, XVII (1945), 16–28, shows that Bismarck was more concerned about the economic health of the important land-owning class than with the physical health of the German people. Proposed retaliatory action against German sugar, authorized by the McKinley tariff of 1890, helped bring about a final settlement (p. 28). Other nations, notably Italy, Hungary, and France, preceded Germany in embargoing American pork, which, however, was probably the best prepared in the world.

J. A. Karlin, "The Indemnification of Aliens Injured by Mob Violence," *Southwestern Soc. Sci. Quar.*, XXV (1945), 235–246, describes how Harrison, wishing to avoid delay and inflammatory discussion in Congress, paid the $25,000 indemnity to Italy from the State Department emergency fund. Congress was angered at being by-passed, and so bitter was its reaction that this sort of thing was not done again.

William Williams, "Reminiscences of the Bering Sea Arbitration," *Amer. Jour. of Internat. Law*, XXXVII (1943), 562–584, an account by one who, with Robert Lansing, was appointed American junior counsel, gives many interesting details and contends that the United States (Blaine) had a much stronger case than popularly supposed. Allowance must be made for the author's natural bias.

S. W. Livermore, "American Strategy Diplomacy in the South Pacific, 1890–1914," *Pacific Hist. Rev.*, XII (1943), 33–51, deals with efforts to secure a naval base at Chimbote, Peru. An excellent opportunity passed in 1892 when Blaine, tired and ill, counseled delay (p. 36). Theodore Roosevelt became interested in Chimbote, as a means of protecting the Canal against Chile, but Peruvian opinion was unfavorable, and Chile became so aroused that there was almost another *Baltimore* incident at Valparaiso in 1905 (p. 43). Peru seems to have deliberately involved the United States so that Uncle Sam would pull her chestnuts out of the Chilean fire (p. 42).

CHAPTER XXVIII. SAMOA AND HAWAII: IMPERIALISTIC BEGINNINGS

NEW REFERENCES. G. R. Dulebohn, *Principles of Foreign Policy under the Cleveland Administrations* (Phila., 1941), Ch. III, shows that the President was more determined to pursue a policy of anti-imperialism in Hawaii than in Samoa, where the international situation was more unsettled.

H. W. Bradley, *The American Frontier in Hawaii: The Pioneers, 1789–1843* (Stanford University, 1942), is an outstanding monograph which treats in greater detail some of the ground previously covered by Kuykendall. Chapter VIII deals with growing American influence, subsequent friction with the British, and the Hawaiian mission to the United States, Great Britain, and France to bring about a guarantee of independence. The British officer Paulet did not come to seize the islands, but after he had made a show of force, the Hawaiian government threw itself on his mercy (pp. 431–432). He was disavowed by his superior officer, who sailed in later; but Aberdeen in England was slow to repudiate the transfer, presumably because he wanted to use the incident as a means of clubbing France into a joint guarantee of Hawaiian independence (p. 462). The author thinks that Tyler's message of December 30, 1842, was really an extension of the Monroe Doctrine to Hawaii (pp. 444–445).

H. W. Bradley further considers Hawaii as the oldest and wealthiest part of the American frontier in "Hawaii and the American Penetration of the Northeastern Pacific, 1800–1845," *Pacific Hist. Rev.*, XII (1943), 277–286. By 1842, Hawaii, though independent, was "economically and spiritually a part of the American frontier (p. 286)."

D. M. Dozer, "The Opposition to Hawaiian Reciprocity, 1876–1888," *ibid.*, XIV (1945), 157–183, notes that the reciprocity treaty, the longest-lived of its kind in United States history, conferred one-sided benefits on Hawaii and was bitterly attacked by American sugar and rice interests. But Cleveland regarded economic considerations as subordinate to the necessity of offsetting British and possible German penetration. The anti-imperialist wing of the Democratic party opposed the Pearl Harbor amendment.

W. A. Russ, Jr., "The Role of Sugar in Hawaiian Annexation," *ibid.*, XII (1943), 339–350, concludes that while the sugar barons in general opposed annexation (which would make contract labor illegal), leadership of the revolution fell into the hands of middle class whites who were more concerned about the prospective Oriental inundation. The author feels that sugar affected annexation principally through its bearing on the race issue.

W. A. Russ, Jr., "Hawaiian Labor and Immigration Problems before Annexation," *Jour. of Mod. Hist.*, XV (1943), 207–222, describes how Oriental immigration (Japanese in 1898) complicated the annexation problem.

4TH ED. REFS. S. K. Stevens, *American Expansion in Hawaii, 1842–1898* (Harrisburg, Pa., 1945), is the most useful full-length story of annexation to date. Helpful background materials are in Theodore Morgan, *Hawaii: A Century of Economic Change, 1778–1876* (Cambridge, 1948). R. D. Weigle, "Sugar and the Hawaiian Revolution," *Pacific Hist. Rev.*, XVI (1947), 41–58, demonstrates that the "sugar barons" opposed annexation, because of contract labor, but that the "outlanders," chiefly Americans, though hurt by the loss of the sugar bounty, were moved primarily by larger concepts of security.

Chapter XXIX. Cleveland and the Venezuela Crisis with Great Britain

New References. G. R. Dulebohn, *Principles of Foreign Policy under the Cleveland Administrations* (Phila., 1941), notes that the Nicaragua affair, involving Britain, was in principle more menacing to the Monroe Doctrine than the Venezuela dispute (p. 31). The Brazilian revolution of 1893, with its danger of foreign intervention, threatened to involve the Monroe Doctrine (pp. 35–37). Cleveland was an arch foe of imperialism, and the author does not think it fair to say that he touched off the imperialistic upsurge (p. 90). [This conclusion ignores the fact that some of his actions unwittingly contributed to that end.]

G. S. Gordon, *Anglo-American Literary Relations* (Oxford, 1942), has some interesting observations on the Anglo-American literary *rapprochement* near the end of the century.

G. B. Young, "Intervention under the Monroe Doctrine: the Olney Corollary," *Pol. Sci. Quar.*, LVII (1942), 247–280, concludes that Olney backed neither Venezuela nor England, but pursued a rigorously independent course to secure vindication of the Monroe Doctrine (p. 251). The brusque Secretary revealed skill as a negotiator in securing the treaty settlement of 1897, an achievement overshadowed by his earlier and more spectacular course (p. 274). He dealt highhandedly with Venezuela in coercing her into signing, and succeeded in arousing a popular outburst in Venezuela against the settlement (pp. 276–277). The absence of naval activity in the United States during the height of the crisis is contributory proof that Cleveland was bluffing and had no intention of resorting to war (p. 259). The Olney corollary, *i.e.*, intervention to force a settlement of a dispute involving the Monroe Doctrine, was as definitely an addition to the original dictum as the more famous Roosevelt corollary (p. 279).

N. M. Blake, "The Olney-Pauncefote Treaty of 1897," *Amer. Hist. Rev.*, L (1945), 228–243, stresses the opposition of the "silverites" and particularly the Irish. The lobbyists present on the day of the vote included one of the most prominent Irish members of the British Parliament (p. 238). Among other things, the treaty would have been regarded abroad as the forerunner of a treaty of alliance, and a consequent discouragement to England's foes (p. 241). Although the public was educated, America's leadership for arbitration was lost (p. 242).

Chapter XXX. The Coming of the War with Spain, 1895–1898

Recent References. A substantial contribution to our understanding of public opinion is G. W. Auxier, "Middle Western Newspapers and the Spanish-American War, 1895–1898," *Miss. Valley Hist. Rev.*, XXVI (1940), 523–534. The author finds that the press of this section was less influenced than is generally thought by the yellow journals, but was concerned about the "basic interests of the United States in the Caribbean" and Spain's threat to them, rather than about the sensational de Lôme and *Maine* incidents.

The same author deals with an important but hitherto neglected subject, "The Propaganda Activities of the Cuban *Junta* in Precipitating the Spanish-American War, 1895–1898," *Hispanic Amer. Hist. Rev.*, XIX (1939), 286–305. The *Junta*, with headquarters in New York and a branch in Washington ("Cuban Legation"), and composed chiefly of naturalized American citizens, sent out filibustering expeditions, raised money in various ways ("Sympathy Meetings"), and distributed great quantities of propaganda. The results of its work were seen in liberal interpretations of United States neutrality laws, sentiment in Congress favoring a recognition of Cuban belligerency, and finally, armed intervention. The *Junta* openly opposed McKinley's attempt to secure relief for the Cuban civilian population, lest such action remove the chief grounds for insisting on intervention (p. 303). The *Junta* also claimed credit for the Teller Amendment, though the United States beet-sugar interests were also strongly behind it.

NEW REFERENCES. The work of Auxier on Cuban propaganda may be complemented by *Correspondencia diplomática de la delegación cubana en Nueva York durante la guerra de independencia de 1895 a 1898* (Habana, 1943), of which the first volume has been published.

G. R. Dulebohn, *Principles of Foreign Policy under the Cleveland Administrations* (Phila., 1941), has a brief discussion of Cleveland's Cuban policy.

W. H. Callcott, *The Caribbean Policy of the United States, 1890–1920* (Baltimore, 1942), Chs. I, II, traces the background of the Cuban problem from secondary works.

4TH ED. REFS. J. E. McLean, *William Rufus Day* (Baltimore, 1946), is the first full-length study, though primarily legalistic, of the secretary of state. Nathan Sargent, comp., *Admiral Dewey and the Manila Campaign* (Washington, D.C., 1947), is essentially Dewey's "official" version. J. T. Farrell, "Archbishop Ireland and Manifest Destiny," *Catholic Hist. Rev.*, XXXIII (1947), 269–301, describes the efforts of Ireland, serving as an emissary of the Pope, to avert war by negotiations in Washington, and his subsequent enthusiasm for the new "Manifest Destiny."

CHAPTER XXXI. THE UNITED STATES AS A WORLD POWER, 1898–1900

4TH ED. REFS. The new accord is freshly discussed in N. M. Blake, "England and the United States, 1897–1899," in D. E. Lee and G. E. McReynolds, eds., *Essays in History and International Relations in Honor of George Hubbard Blakeslee* (Worcester, Mass., 1949), pp. 257–283. E. H. Zabriskie, *American-Russian Rivalry in the Far East, 1895–1914* (Phila., 1946), is a solid monographic study. W. M. Gibson, "Mark Twain and Howells: Anti-Imperialists," *New England Quar.*, XX (1947), 435–470, shows that Twain was fiery; Howells more placid; both were effective.

CHAPTER XXXII. ACQUIRING THE PANAMA CANAL ZONE, 1900–1903

NEW REFERENCES. W. H. Callcott, *The Caribbean Policy of the United States, 1890–1920* (Baltimore, 1942), Ch. III, tells the conventional story of the Panama affair.

Gerstle Mack, *The Land Divided* (N.Y., 1944), presents the problem in its broadest setting. The author concludes that a Nicaragua canal would have served about as well (p. 436), and that a little more cash and tact would have brought Colombia around (p. 454). The $40,000,000 paid to the French company was by no means completely thrown away; a good deal was obtained in machinery and other things. The United States controlled the sea, so the Colombian army became bogged down in the jungles when it undertook an overland invasion of Panama (1903–1904) [p. 468].

N. J. Padelford, *The Panama Canal in Peace and War* (N.Y., 1942), is concerned primarily with the legal aspects of administration by the United States.

John Patterson, "Latin-American Reactions to the Panama Revolution of 1903," *Hispanic Amer. Hist. Rev.*, XXIV (1944), 342–351, refutes the traditional belief that Latin America arose as one man against Roosevelt's tactics. There was at first considerable division of opinion, and some disposition to condone the United States. The appeal of Colombia to her sister republics met with a discouraging response, and most of them promptly recognized Panama, whose grievances were widely regarded as well founded. Brazil, traditionally friendly, defended the United States, while Chile and Peru, both of which particularly wanted the canal built, did not waste too much sympathy on Colombia. The weakness of this article, which breaks important new ground, is that it is based solely on the contemporary observations of United States diplomats in Latin America, some of whom were ill-informed and ill-equipped to gauge opinion; and the investigation goes only a few weeks into the period following the revolt. It appears that after some time had passed, and after Roosevelt's role became clearer, much more opposition developed.

CHAPTER XXXIII. THEODORE ROOSEVELT AND BIG STICK DIPLOMACY, 1901–1906

NEW REFERENCES. The present writer has been privileged to read the unpublished manuscript of Dr. Fritz-Konrad Kruger, of Springfield, Ohio, "The Venezuela Affair of 1902–1903: A Study in Diplomacy and International Law." It does not materially alter the main outlines of the story herein given.

E. A. Powell, *Yonder Lies Adventure!* (N.Y., 1932), contains a memorandum of a four-hour interview with Roosevelt, March 28, 1909, which, if authentic, further demonstrates that the President's dramatic story regarding Venezuela was well established in his mind before he left the Presidency. There are also observations on the Japanese question and on other foreign problems of the period. See particularly pp. 311 *ff.*

C. C. Tansill, *Canadian-American Relations, 1875–1911* (New Haven, 1943), Chs. V–IX, has the most detailed account of the Alaska boundary squabble. The author thinks that Turner and Lodge showed up rather well, but not Root, who followed Lodge's lead. Alverstone pursued a questionable course (p. 261). It appears that the British went through with the so-called arbitration partly because they wanted to make amends for their Venezuela blunder of 1902–1903 (p. 215).

F. W. Howay, W. N. Sage, and H. F. Angus, *British Columbia and the United States* (Toronto, 1942), Ch. XV, refers to the Alaskan boundary settlement as the last territorial gain of the United States in North America, and concludes that Canada lost nothing of great value. In an earlier draft Alverstone awarded all four islands to the Canadians; when the award was made he had changed his views (p. 373).

W. H. Callcott, *The Caribbean Policy of the United States, 1890–1920* (Baltimore, 1942), Chs. IV, V, concludes that America's Caribbean policy makes sense only if related to defending the approaches to the Panama Canal. The Caribbean defense doctrine was really a new concept, paralleling the Monroe Doctrine, but the American people are so precedent loving that it had to be sanctified by attachment to an old name (p. 210). Root is credited with getting the Santo Domingo treaty through the Senate (p. 228).

S. F. Bemis, *The Latin American Policy of the United States* (N.Y., 1943), thinks that it was a mistake to identify the Monroe Doctrine with intervention, for instead of saying "hands off" to Europe the Doctrine now seemed to say "hands on" to the United States (p. 157). Yet something needed to be done, since the decision of the Hague Tribunal (Permanent Court of Arbitration) [February 22, 1904] gave priority to the claims of those Powers that had intervened by force, thus placing a premium on armed intervention (p. 151).

C. Adler and A. M. Margalith, *American Intercession on Behalf of Jews in the Diplomatic Correspondence of the United States, 1840–1938* (N.Y., 1943), is full of persecutions during the Roosevelt period, and shows how Jewish groups helped force Congress in 1911 to abrogate the treaty of 1832 with Russia, owing to the latter's refusal to honor passports issued to American Jews.

L. J. Hall, "A Partnership in Peacemaking: Theodore Roosevelt and Wilhelm II," *Pacific Hist. Rev.*, XIII (1944), 390–411, indicates how Roosevelt ranged himself with Anglo-Japanese-French interests in both the Far East and Morocco.

D. M. Dozer, "Secretary of State Elihu Root and Consular Reorganization," *Miss. Valley Hist. Rev.*, XXIX (1942), 339–350, reveals how Root, by using tact with the Senate, secured a much-needed reform of the consular service. Congress was reluctant to let patronage plums slip out of its hands.

See also the Livermore article in this Bibliographical Appendix, listed under New References, Ch. XXVII.

CHAPTER XXXIV. THEODORE ROOSEVELT AND JAPANESE AMERICAN RELATIONS

4TH ED. REFS. W. B. Thorson, "American Public Opinion and the Portsmouth Peace Conference," *Amer. Hist. Rev.*, LIII (1948), 439–464, demolishes the myth that Russian propaganda "overnight" turned American sympathies from Japan to Russia. Count Witte had some success with a few journals, but even at the end of the conference the bulk of the American press was still pro-Japanese. The real shift against Japan was to come later. O. J. Clinard, *Japan's Influence on American Naval Power, 1897–1917* (Berkeley, Calif., 1947), is a substantial monograph that bears indirectly on diplomacy. E. H. Zabriskie, *American-Russian Rivalry in the Far East* (Phila., 1946), brings the most recent scholarship to bear on these problems. See also J. A. Miller, "The United States and Chinese Territorial Integrity, 1908," in D. E. Lee and G. E. McReynolds, eds., *Essays in History and International Relations in Honor of George Hubbard Blakeslee* (Worcester, Mass., 1949), pp. 233–256.

CHAPTER XXXV. TAFT AND DOLLAR DIPLOMACY

RECENT REFERENCES. J. F. Rippy's *The Caribbean Danger Zone* (N.Y., 1940), pp. 134–240, has some useful material on Dollar Diplomacy, which the author contends is but a more recent name for age-old economic motivation. He also believes that manifestations of this phenomenon were discernible in the United States even before the Civil War, and that Roosevelt and Root were as persistent dollar diplomats as Taft and Knox (p. 148). Rippy also has some interesting pages on unsuccessful attempts at Dollar Diplomacy in Guatemala and Honduras under Taft (pp. 206–223), and he concludes that pure Dollar Diplomacy, divested of strategic and other considerations, reached a high point under Harding and Coolidge (p. 139).

Dexter Perkins, *Hands Off: A History of the Monroe Doctrine* (Boston, 1941), Ch. VII, has some useful material on Dollar Diplomacy in Central America under Taft and Knox.

NEW REFERENCES. F. M. Huntington Wilson, *Memoirs of an Ex-Diplomat* (Boston, 1945), has some personal observations on the Canal tolls, Dollar Diplomacy, Knox, Root, the administrative reorganization of the State Department, and especially the bankers' consortium in China. Further evidence is presented to show the reluctance of the bankers and the necessity of appealing to them on patriotic grounds (p. 215).

W. F. Sands and J. M. Lalley, *Our Jungle Diplomacy* (Chapel Hill, N.C., 1944), contains some reminiscent material by a former diplomat on the workings of Dollar Diplomacy, particularly in Latin America.

W. H. Callcott, *The Caribbean Policy of the United States, 1890–1920* (Baltimore, 1942), deals with Dollar Diplomacy in conventional terms. Taft believed that Huerta's sins fell under "criminal" rather than "international" law, and he was willing to support recognition if Huerta would agree to a claims settlement. Huerta hesitated, and the opportunity passed (p. 302).

S. F. Bemis, *The Latin American Policy of the United States* (N.Y., 1943), especially pp. 165–167, regards Dollar Diplomacy as an unfortunate misnomer; the bankers had to be urged to invest abroad, because they could make more money from investments in the United States. The Caribbean interventions were primarily strategic, an honest attempt to forestall foreign intervention by introducing stability. Nicaragua, the Dominican Republic, Panama, and Haiti were among the nations of the world in which the United States had the least money invested. Latin America has probably profited more from United States investments than the investors themselves; where American capital has gone there has been a lessened danger of intervention.

C. C. Tansill, *Canadian-American Relations, 1875–1911* (New Haven, 1943), thinks that the Canadians drove a hard bargain on the seals, and it was suspected that Taft made concessions in order to get commercial reciprocity (p. 371). The rejection of reciprocity by Canada was due, among other things, to earlier rebuffs by the United States and to the Alaska boundary unpleasantness. But the storm blew itself out, and made for perhaps a friendlier co-operation during World War I (see pp. 465–466).

S. W. Livermore, "Battleship Diplomacy in South America: 1905–1925," *Jour. of Mod. Hist.*, XVI (1944), 31–48, shows that the most successful phase of the Knox-Taft Dollar Diplomacy was the use of diplomatic pressure to sell American-constructed battleships in South America, particularly to Argentina, even at the risk of revealing Navy secrets. The Navy wanted to keep an armament manufacturing backlog in the United States, and it favored strengthening the "Monroe Doctrine countries." The policy of the Washington government led to some curious excesses, and probably stimulated competitive armaments.

S. W. Livermore, "American Strategy Diplomacy in the South Pacific, 1890–

1914," *Pacific Hist. Rev.*, XII (1943), 33–51, notes the interest under Taft in a naval base at Chimbote, Peru. The negotiations collapsed, but Chile was incensed by Washington's appearing to be an ally of Peru (p. 49).

4TH ED. REFS. E. H. Zabriskie, *American-Russian Rivalry in the Far East, 1895–1914* (Phila., 1946), discusses the failure of Taft's dollar diplomacy in the Far East. W. C. Askew and J. F. Rippy, "The United States and Europe's Strife, 1908–1913," *Jour. of Politics*, IV (1942), 68–79, show that the Taft Administration was little concerned over the Morocco crisis of 1911.

CHAPTER XXXVI. WILSON AND THE NEW DIPLOMACY, 1913–1917

RECENT REFERENCES. Dexter Perkins, *Hands Off: A History of the Monroe Doctrine* (Boston, 1941), Ch. VII, discusses aspects of the American interventions in Nicaragua, Haiti, and Santo Domingo. The landings of German and French armed forces in Haiti gave some basis for concern in the United States over the Monroe Doctrine. Among other things the author points out that Bryan and Wilson invoked the Monroe Doctrine to discourage France from seeking partnership with the United States in political-financial control over Haiti (p. 265).

Selig Adler, "Bryan and Wilsonian Caribbean Penetration," *Hispanic Amer. Hist. Rev.*, XX (1940), 198–226, describes at length Bryan's metamorphosis from a devout anti-imperialist to an apostle of Dollar Diplomacy. The writer concludes that the Secretary was influenced by economic forces beyond his control, by realistic advice from members of the State Department about political conditions in Latin America, by concern for the Monroe Doctrine, and by a desire to "carry the gospel of Wilsonian Democracy southward . . . (p. 226)."

L. L. Montague, *Haiti and the United States, 1714–1938* (Durham, N.C., 1940), Chs. XII to XVI, is a detailed consideration of American occupation and control.

NEW REFERENCES. F. M. Huntington Wilson, *Memoirs of an Ex-Diplomat* (Boston, 1945), makes unsympathetic observations on President Wilson's policy, and explains the strange circumstances attending the author's resignation from the State Department (pp. 244 ff.).

Josephus Daniels, *The Wilson Era: Years of Peace, 1910–1917* (Chapel Hill, N.C., 1944), though viewing Wilson with rose-tinted spectacles, has some helpful observations. He describes his success (and Wilson's) in curbing high-placed war mongers in America at the time of the 1913 crisis with Japan (pp. 163, 166). He thinks that Admiral Mayo went too far in his ultimatum to Mexico, and though backing him up, issued orders to prevent a repetition of such an incident (p. 191). The futility of the Vera Cruz landing is underscored by the fact that the German ship laden with arms finally got through (p. 201).

S. F. Bemis, *The Latin American Policy of the United States* (N.Y., 1943), Chs. X, XI, is highly critical of the basic morality and results of Wilson's nonrecognition policy in Mexico (see pp. 183–184). There was little difference between the Nicaragua policy of Wilson and that of his predecessors (p. 187). Yet the Latin Americans on the whole trusted Wilson, and enabled him to lay the foundations of the later Good Neighbor policy (p. 199). Symptomatic of Wilson's thinking was his draft in 1914 of the Pan-American liberty pact, which was blocked by Chile but which emerged later in modified form as Article X of the League of Nations Covenant (pp. 196–197).

W. H. Callcott, *The Caribbean Policy of the United States, 1890–1920* (Baltimore, 1942), Chs. VII–VIII, deals with the usual topics, and stresses the inconsistency between the idealism and practicality of both Bryan and Wilson.

Elton Atwater, *American Regulation of Arms Exports* (Washington, 1941), treats the fluctuations and inconsistencies in the American arms embargo policy toward Mexico, the most complicated in United States history (p. 103). Partiality in employing such embargoes led to reprisals (p. 100).

Gerstle Mack, *The Land Divided* (N.Y., 1944), discusses the tolls controversy and notes that the repeal was an act of expediency, for the legislation affirmed the right to re-enact a similar exemption at a future time. Repeated attempts have been made to revive the issue (p. 555).

H. C. F. Bell, *Woodrow Wilson and the People* (Garden City, N.Y., 1945), is a biographical treatment with some attention to foreign affairs.

4TH ED. REFS. On the Japanese problem see O. J. Clinard, *Japan's Influence on American Naval Power, 1897–1917* (Berkeley, Calif., 1947). L. F. Sensabaugh, "The Coffee-Trust Question in United States—Brazilian Relations: 1912–1913," *Hispanic Amer. Hist. Rev.*, XXVI (1946), 480–496, shows that the Wilson administration dropped trust-busting action against the alleged distributional monopoly on assurances from Brazil that no monopoly was involved. See also R. R. Hill, "The Nicaraguan Canal Idea to 1913," *ibid.*, XXVIII (1948), 197–211.

CHAPTER XXXVII. WORLD WAR NEUTRALITY: FIRST PHASE, 1914–1915

NEW REFERENCES. A brief but masterly analysis of the larger aspects of America's pre-World War I diplomacy is Dexter Perkins, *America and Two Wars* (Boston, 1944), Chs. I, II.

Josephus Daniels, *The Wilson Era: Years of Peace—1910–1917* (Chapel Hill, N.C., 1944), Pt. VII, has some interesting sidelights on the preparedness and neutrality issues. These revelations are less important than one would expect from the then Secretary of the Navy. Of perhaps greatest interest is the author's account of Wilson's "Sunrise Conference" (p. 580).

H. C. F. Bell, *Woodrow Wilson and the People* (Garden City, N.Y., 1945), sketches the neutrality problems against a biographical background.

Elton Atwater, *American Regulation of Arms Exports* (Washington, 1941), deals with aspects of the huge armaments trade with the Allies.

R. G. Albion and J. B. Pope, *Sea Lanes in Wartime: The American Experience, 1775–1942* (N.Y., 1942), has interesting chapters on the shipping and submarine problems.

Senator G. W. Norris, *Fighting Liberal* (N.Y., 1945), tells of his early reactions to the war, describes his part in the armed ship filibuster, and reveals that some members of Congress were with him on this issue and in opposing a declaration of war, although they did not have the courage to vote their convictions (pp. 178–179, 191, 198). Chapter XXI on the League fight is not very revealing.

A localized study is Cedric Cummins, *Indiana Public Opinion and the World War, 1914–1917* (Indianapolis, 1945).

R. A. Billington, "The Origins of Middle Western Isolationism," *Pol. Sci. Quar.*, LX (1945), 44–64, though surveying the problem broadly to recent times, is particularly useful on the 1914–1917 period. The author stresses the growing economic self-sufficiency of the Middle West; the rise to political power of immigrants (who feared that Old World participation would threaten peace); and the evangelical sects, notably the Lutherans, who preached freedom from the greedy imperialistic wars of Europe (p. 53). Middle Western public opinion opposed preparedness, and Middle Western Senators favored keeping American citizens off Allied merchantmen (pp. 54–55). One Milwaukee and one St. Louis newspaper defended the sinking of the *Lusitania*.

4TH ED. REFS. On the dilemma that faced America in 1914–1917, see E. M. Earle, "A Half-Century of American Foreign Policy: Our Stake in Europe, 1898–1914," *Pol. Sci. Quar.*, LXIV (1949), 168–188. Edwin Costrell, *How Maine Viewed the War, 1914–1917* (Orono, Maine, 1940), concludes that following the German announcement of unrestricted warfare in 1917, "Maine wanted war fervently. . . ." (p. 91). J. C. Crighton, *Missouri and the World War, 1914–1917: A Study in Public Opinion* (Columbia, Mo., 1947), reveals that the state, despite a large German population, was stirred to fight after the submarine announcement and the Zimmermann revelation by a desire to safeguard American rights and a world balance of power favorable to the United States. The isolationism of the Middle West has "perhaps been overestimated" (p. 187).

CHAPTER XXXIX. THE PEACE OF VERSAILLES, 1918–1919

RECENT REFERENCES. Paul Birdsall, in addition to his *Versailles Twenty Years After*, has published an excellent bibliographical article, "The Second Decade of Peace Conference History," *Jour. of Mod. Hist.*, XI (1939), 362–378, which supplements R. C. Binkley's earlier work. In this study, House, with his tendency to compromise, further shrinks in stature.

P. M. Burnett, *Reparation at the Paris Peace Conference from the Standpoint of the American Delegation* (2 vols., N.Y., 1940), is a contribution of the first importance. It is primarily a collection of documents with an extended introduction. The author makes it clear that the American experts believed that the inclusion of pensions was a violation of the pre-Armistice note of November 5, 1918, but they were partially reconciled to this breach of faith because they expected that in the end Germany's inability to pay would lead to a more equitable solution (p. 64).

W. E. Stephens, *Revisions of the Treaty of Versailles* (N.Y., 1939), is principally concerned with European problems, with some consideration of the United States, particularly in regard to reparations payments.

Herbert Hoover, *America's First Crusade* (N.Y., 1942), is a portion of Hoover's personal reminiscences of the Conference, written in 1934–35, and published in magazine form late in 1941 with the obvious purpose of warning America against involvement in European difficulties. The author of this tiny volume particularly stresses the confusion resulting from committees acting independently of one another, and describes at length the breakdown of the Fourteen Points.

René Albrecht-Carrié has followed up his monograph, *Italy at the Paris Peace Conference* (N.Y., 1938), with a series of articles, most of which have little direct relevance to American diplomacy. The central difficulty stressed by these studies is that the Big Three, who were primarily concerned with Germany, turned late in the negotiations, after tempers were badly frayed, to Italy, which was primarily concerned with Austria-Hungary. On the whole the British and French agreed with Wilson's position but were quite content to let him incur Italian resentment (*ibid.*, pp. 113, 150). The two articles by Albrecht-Carrié which bear most directly on Wilsonian diplomacy are: "New Light on Italian Problems in 1919," *Jour. of Mod. Hist.*, XIII (1941), 493–516; "Italy and her Allies, June, 1919," *Amer. Hist. Rev.*, XLVI (1941), 837–843. The author has an excellent discussion of how the settlement actually worked out in "Versailles Twenty Years After," *Pol. Sci. Quar.*, LV (1940), 1–24. He concludes that if on the one hand the treaty caused "certain grievances, on the other it redressed greater ones; this is especially true of the territorial settlement." The real failure, he adds, was in the "application" of the various articles; and their success was vitiated by a lack of confidence which was the "inevitable aftermath of war (p. 23)."

Ingram Bander, "Sidney Edward Mezes and 'The Inquiry,'" *Jour. of Mod. Hist.*, XI (1939), 199–202, describes some of the difficulties involved in organizing this group of experts.

Harold and Margaret Sprout, *Toward a New Order of Sea Power* (Princeton, 1940), pp. 59–69, have a highly revealing account of the "Naval Battle of Paris." The British, who were disturbed by America's growing naval power, worked out an agreement with Wilson to the effect that they would support the League of Nations in return for a suspension of the naval program then before Congress.

T. A. Bailey, *The Policy of the United States toward the Neutrals, 1917–1918* (Baltimore, 1942), is the most complete study of the subject. It concludes that the Washington government took few liberties with the strict letter of international law in dealing with these weaker nations.

NEW REFERENCES. Dexter Perkins, *America and Two Wars* (Boston, 1944), Chs. III–IV, is a perspicacious analysis of diplomacy during the war and the making of the peace.

H. C. F. Bell, *Woodrow Wilson and the People* (Garden City, N.Y., 1945), deals sympathetically and briefly with the problems of the peace.

Roger Burlingame and Alden Stevens, *Victory without Peace* (N.Y., 1944), and Alan Cranston, *The Killing of the Peace* (N.Y., 1945) are both racily written, superficial, and one-sided journalistic accounts, unworthy of the attention of the serious student.

Karl Schriftgiesser, *The Gentleman from Massachusetts: Henry Cabot Lodge* (Boston, 1944), although by a journalist, is more soberly written. Based upon the more obvious printed materials, and continuing the conventional attack on Lodge, it oversimplifies the problem and adds little to what was already known.

H. R. Rudin, *Armistice, 1918* (New Haven, 1944), is a solid and well-documented study which, though largely devoted to the European scene, sheds some light on Wilson's problem.

F. S. Marston, *The Peace Conference of 1919, Organization and Procedure* (London, 1944), is primarily concerned with machinery.

R. J. Bartlett, *The League to Enforce Peace* (Chapel Hill, N.C., 1944), is an important study of a pressure group, headed by Taft, which had a good deal to do with arousing popular support for the League. While much useful new material is presented, the author is unwilling to recognize that Wilson was to some extent responsible for the impasse that developed, and that there was something to be said for Taft's willingness to compromise when there seemed to be no other way of securing the League.

Stephen Bonsal, *Unfinished Business* (Garden City, N.Y., 1944), which adds detail rather than important new material on the Conference, is a diary kept by a journalist who served Wilson as an interpreter.

R. S. Baker, *American Chronicle* (N.Y., 1945), contains reminiscences of the Conference which add some detail to the author's previously published work, especially regarding publicity.

Josephus Daniels, *The Wilson Era: Years of War and After, 1917–1921* (Chapel Hill, N.C., 1946), has considerable color and detail recorded by an octogenarian eyewitness of some of the events.

W. H. Callcott, *The Caribbean Policy of the United States, 1890–1920* (Baltimore, 1942), Ch. IX, shows how diplomacy in the Caribbean during the war years had a vital impact on general American foreign policy.

J. R. Mock, "The Creel Committee in Latin America," *Hispanic Amer. Hist. Rev.*, XXII (1942), 262–279, describes the efforts that were made to publicize the war effort and the peace aims of the United States.

An indispensable documentary collection is *Papers Relating to the Foreign Relations of the United States, 1919; The Paris Peace Conference* (13 vols., Washington, 1942–1947).

4TH ED. REFS. T. A. Bailey, *Wilson and the Peacemakers* (N.Y., 1947) brings together in one volume *Woodrow Wilson and the Lost Peace* and *Woodrow Wilson and the Great Betrayal*, both previously cited. Ruth Cranston, *The Story of Woodrow Wilson* (N.Y., 1945), is eulogistic. George Creel, *Rebel at Large* (N.Y., 1947), reviews propaganda service during World War I, and offers some pro-Wilson sidelights on the Paris Conference and the League. *The Autobiography of William Allen White* (N.Y., 1946) contains a journalist's impressions of the Conference. R. W. Logan, *The Senate and the Versailles Mandate System* (Washington, D.C., 1945), stresses race prejudice in the treaty debates growing out of the mandates issue. S. W. Livermore, "The Sectional Issue in the 1918 Congressional Elections," *Miss. Valley Hist. Rev.*, XXXV (1948), 29–60, concludes that Wilson's failure to put a price ceiling on the cotton of the Democratic South so angered the price-controlled grain growers of the North as to cause the blunder of the October appeal by comparison to be a "minor matter" (p. 58). S. W. Livermore, "The Azores in American Strategy-Diplomacy, 1917–1919," *Jour. of Mod. Hist.*, XX (1948), 197–211, describes how the U.S. Navy rather highhandedly moved in on its Portuguese ally. See also R. H. Fifield, "Disposal of the Carolines, Marshalls, and Marianas at the Paris Peace Conference," *Amer. Hist. Rev.*, LI (1946), 472–479; Werner Levi, "American Attitudes toward Pacific Islands, 1914–1919," *Pacific Hist. Rev.*, XVII (1948), 55–64; E. S. Pomeroy, "American Policy Respecting the Marshalls, Carolines, and Marianas, 1898–1941," *ibid.*, 43–55.

CHAPTER XL. THE FIGHT FOR THE TREATY IN AMERICA, 1919–1920

NEW REFERENCES. T. A. Bailey, *Woodrow Wilson and the Great Betrayal* (N.Y., 1945), analyzes the fight over the League in its larger aspects, concludes that the United States would have entered the League if Wilson had consented to the Lodge reservations, discusses rather fully the League as an issue in the campaign of 1920, and points to some of the broader consequences of the Great Betrayal, *i.e.*, America's refusal to honor her commitments to Europe. Important new manuscript materials have been utilized, and the approach is considerably more critical than that of the earlier work by Fleming.

Most of the books cited above under New References in connection with the previous chapter are relevant to this aspect of the problem, particularly those by Bartlett, Bonsal, and Baker. Bonsal presents material that causes Lodge to appear in a more favorable light than customary (pp. 272–280). Baker's *American Chronicle* contains some observations by an eyewitness close to Wilson. The President told Baker in the winter of 1919–1920, "It would probably have been better if I had died last fall (p. 469)." The author describes his vain efforts to induce Wilson to adopt a more compromising spirit on reservations (pp. 471–473). But Wilson feared that if he accepted the Senate reservations, Lodge would merely screw on more (p. 474). There is reason to believe that such a fear was not well founded. See Bailey, *Woodrow Wilson and the Great Betrayal*, p. 199.

4TH ED. REFS. See 4th Ed. Refs. of previous chapter. J. M. Cox, *Journey Through My Years* (N.Y., 1946), is an autobiographical account in which Cox insists that he was determined to make the League the paramount issue even before he visited Wilson (p. 243).

CHAPTER XLI. HARDING AND THE WASHINGTON CONFERENCE

NEW REFERENCES. F. R. Dulles, *The Road to Teheran* (Princeton, 1944), has helpful survey chapters on American intervention in Russia and the postwar "Red scare."

L. I. Strakhovsky, *Intervention at Archangel: The Story of Allied Intervention and Russian Counter-Revolution in North Russia, 1918–1920* (Princeton, 1944), a sequel to the author's *The Origins of American Intervention in North Russia, 1918* (Princeton, 1937), describes how 5,000 American troops co-operating for legitimate military objectives (p. 105), ended by becoming involved in the Allied attempts to support the White Russians against the Bolsheviks. The whole enterprise collapsed following the withdrawal of the Allied force.

G. W. Pepper, *Philadelphia Lawyer: An Autobiography* (Phila., 1944), is by a man who became Senator in 1922, and who opposed the League and even the World Court in unamended form. There are some sidelights on the 1920 fight for the League.

Allan Nevins and L. M. Hacker, eds., *The United States and Its Place in World Affairs, 1918–1943* (Boston, 1943), may profitably be used in connection with all important aspects of the period since 1918. The chapters are written by a number of specialists who approach the problem broadly.

H. E. Davis, ed., *Pioneers in World Order: An American Appraisal of the League of Nations* (N.Y., 1944), has chapters on disarmament, the World Court, the International Labor Organization, etc.

4TH ED. REFS. A sketchy account of the Washington Conference appears in F. L. Paxson, *Postwar Years: Normalcy, 1918–1923* (Berkeley, Calif., 1948); a fuller account in Merze Tate, *The United States and Armaments* (Cambridge, 1948). W. B. Thorson, "Pacific Northwest Opinion on the Washington Conference of 1921–1922," *Pacific Northwest Quar.*, XXXVII (1946), 109–127, shows that except for the Hearst press the newspapers generally supported the proceedings and hailed the results with tempered enthusiasm.

CHAPTER XLIII. HOOVER AND THE DIPLOMACY OF DEPRESSION, 1929–1933

NEW REFERENCES. Sumner Welles, *The Time for Decision* (N.Y., 1944), Ch. V, is a discussion of the Good Neighbor policy by one of its architects, who discounts the work of Coolidge and Hoover. Hoover's efforts, particularly in Haiti and in the abandonment of Wilson's nonrecognition policy, were offset in Latin American eyes by his association with the Republican cabinets and by the reactionary economic policy of his party, notably the Smoot-Hawley tariff (pp. 190–191).

S. F. Bemis, *The Latin American Policy of the United States* (N.Y., 1943), Ch. XII, indicates that the liquidation of so-called imperialism in Latin America began with the Republican restoration in 1921 (pp. 202–203). Hoover's record was impressive (p. 222).

D. F. Fleming, *The United States and the World Court* (Garden City, N.Y., 1945), Ch. VIII, shows that the final defeat was in part due to the lukewarmness of the Roosevelt Administration (which did not want to hurt its domestic program), and to the ineptness of the Court's friends in the Senate.

B. J. Wallace, under the ironical title "How the United States 'Led the League' in 1931," *Amer. Pol. Sci. Rev.*, XXXIX (1945), 101–116, shows that the United States did not lead but deliberately chose to follow.

Documents on the Manchuria and subsequent crises appear in *Peace and War: United States Foreign Policy, 1931–1941* (Washington, 1943), and in *Papers Relating to the Foreign Relations of the United States: Japan, 1931–1941* (2 vols., Washington, 1943).

4TH ED. REFS. On the London Conference of 1930 see Merze Tate, *The United States and Armaments* (Cambridge, 1948), and H. L. Stimson and M. Bundy, *On Active Service in Peace and War* (N.Y., 1947), which is a distinguished autobiography by the former Secretary of State. New light is thrown on the Manchurian crisis by this book and by a number of other studies, some of which have grown out of *Foreign Relations, 1931*. See Sara R. Smith, *The Manchurian Crisis, 1931–1932* (N.Y., 1948); Robert Langer, *Seizure of Territory: The Stimson Doctrine and Related Principles in Legal Theory and Diplomatic Practice* (Princeton, 1947); P. H. Clyde, "The Diplomacy of 'Playing No Favorites': Secretary Stimson and Manchuria, 1931," *Miss. Valley Hist. Rev.*, XXXV (1948), 187–202; E. R. Perkins, "The Nonapplication of Sanctions against Japan, 1931–1932," in D. E. Lee and G. E. McReynolds, *Essays in History and International Relations in Honor of George Hubbard Blakeslee* (Worcester, Mass., 1949), pp. 215–232. The record now proves, legend to the contrary, that in 1931 the United States at no time proposed anti-Japanese sanctions which the British and French rejected. The League took the initiative in sounding out Washington on sanctions, which Stimson rebuffed, though indicating that the United States Navy would "probably" not interfere with an embargo (*For. Rels., 1931*, III, 496). The United States, far from supporting the League four-square, co-operated in a most gingerly manner (Clyde, *loc. cit.*, pp. 192, 198, 199). China was eager to drag the United States into a general war (*For. Rels., 1931*, III, 496–497). Stimson, though opposing sanctions in November, 1931, because of the possibility of war (Stimson and Bundy, p. 233), became more aggressive in 1932, but was restrained by Hoover. The latter, in line with American tradition, American opinion, and his Quaker background, would go no further than moral sanctions (*ibid.*, pp. 243, 244, 258). Stimson therefore could use only his nonrecognition policy and the force of world opinion. Although in 1932 the British rebuffed Stimson in connection with his nonrecognition policy and the Borah letter, they may have been motivated in part by Stimson's rebuff of League sanctions in 1931.

The Stimson book also throws considerable light on the London Naval Conference, disarmament, and debts. It is clear that the isolationist Hoover and the internationalist Stimson were at odds on many fundamental issues, especially on the debts, though Stimson respected Hoover. As late as 1932, Hoover thought that the debts should and could be paid; Stimson held that the "damn debts" should not and could not be paid (*ibid.*, 211–219).

Chapter XLIV. Franklin D. Roosevelt and New Deal Diplomacy

NEW REFERENCES. Sumner Welles, *The Time for Decision* (N.Y., 1944), Ch. V., deals with the Good Neighbor policy, in the shaping of which the author had much to do. Roosevelt is praised, particularly in regard to Cuba, which was the acid test of the policy in its early days (p. 200). At the personal insistence of the President, the Mexican oil difficulty was handled with velvet gloves (p. 203). Roosevelt had the foresight to prepare against the aggressors by planning the Buenos Aires Conference, which was intrinsically the most important held, in that it laid the foundations for Lima and subsequent gatherings (p. 206). The Lima Conference, although almost disrupted by Argentina, was significant in that it made provision for the emergency meetings of foreign ministers (p. 209). The author thinks that there was "no more cardinal error" in American foreign policy than the neutrality legislation regarding the Spanish Civil War, and hints that if Roosevelt had not been at Buenos Aires, he might have been able to block the measure (p. 61). Even though the Quarantine Speech was too far ahead of public opinion, Roosevelt was finally dissuaded from following it up with an appeal for reduced armaments only by the vehement protests of his advisers and the temporary lukewarmness of the British. Welles thinks that abandonment of the plan was a grave mistake (pp. 64–69).

S. F. Bemis, *The Latin American Policy of the United States* (N.Y., 1943), Chs. XIII–XVI, has many challenging observations. The United States deserves much credit for codifying American international public law by abolishing intervention (pp. 226–227). Argentina has made an abominable record in international co-operation. Chapter XIX ("Dollar Diplomacy in Reverse") shows how Latin America has exploited United States investors by defaulting on bonds, especially in the 1930's. The Washington government has never resorted to force to collect these debts (p. 334). Chapter XX ("The Myth of Economic Imperialism") contends that the United States, far from exploiting Latin America, has been exploited by Latin America (p. 350). The Washington government was lenient at the time of the Mexican oil expropriation because Roosevelt coveted the American labor vote, and because he wanted Mexico to line up against the aggressors (pp. 345–347). The "New Dollar Diplomacy" consists of lending enormous sums to Latin American countries to strengthen them against outside aggression (pp. 352–353), just as the old Dollar Diplomacy was designed to keep foreign powers away from the Caribbean danger zone.

W. C. Gordon, *The Expropriation of Foreign-Owned Property in Mexico* (Washington, 1941), is primarily economic with some attention to international aspects.

Elton Atwater, *American Regulation of Arms Exports* (Washington, 1941), deals ably with aspects of the neutrality legislation.

Carl Kreider, *The Anglo-American Trade Agreement: A Study of British and American Commercial Policies, 1934–1939* (Princeton, 1943), is primarily economic.

First-hand observations by the former United States ambassador in Tokyo are J. C. Grew, *Ten Years in Japan* (N.Y., 1944); and *Report from Tokyo: A Message to the American People* (N.Y., 1942).

A useful compilation is *Roosevelt's Foreign Policy, 1933–1941: Franklin D. Roosevelt's Unedited Speeches and Messages* (N.Y., 1942).

For the Far East, see the documentary collections listed above under the New References of the preceding chapter.

4TH ED. REFS. Indispensable and monumental are *The Memoirs of Cordell Hull* (2 vols., N.Y., 1948). This work fills in and adds details rather than changes the broad outlines of the story. Especially valuable are the chapters on the trade agreements, Latin America, Japan, neutrality, the Nye Committee, the Ethiopian crisis, the London Economic Conference, and Russian recognition. On the last-named subject Hull should be read in connection with the earlier accounts by G. S. Moyer, *Attitude of the United States towards the Recognition of Soviet Russia* (Phila., 1926), and F. L. Schuman, *American Policy toward Russia Since 1917* (N.Y., 1928). J. M. Cox, *Journey Through My Years* (N.Y., 1946), adds personal observations on the London Economic Conference, and concludes that the great mistake was not to have held it earlier in the days of Coolidge or Hoover (p. 352). On the oil problem during the Ethiopian crisis consult Herbert Feis, *Seen From E.A.* (N.Y., 1947). H. L. Stimson and M. Bundy, *On Active Service* (N.Y., 1947), present the views of the former Secretary of State as an outsider; Frances Perkins, *The Roosevelt I Knew* (N.Y., 1946), gives the reactions of an insider, with little attention to foreign affairs. Josephus Daniels, *Shirt-Sleeve Diplomat* (Chapel Hill, N.C., 1947), is concerned primarily with Daniels' mission to Mexico, where, despite his earlier connection with the Vera Cruz incident (which Roosevelt had forgotten, p. 4), he enjoyed considerable success. C. A. Beard, *American Foreign Policy in the Making, 1932–1940* (New Haven, 1946) is an unfair, one-sided, isolationist attack unworthy of so distinguished a scholar. W. S. Churchill, *The Gathering Storm* (Boston, 1948), reveals that Roosevelt daringly braved isolationist displeasure when early in 1938 he proposed a multi-Power conference in Washington to consider the current crisis, but he was rebuffed by Prime Minister Chamberlain (pp. 251–255). John Norman, "Influence of Pro-Fascist Propaganda on American Neutrality, 1935–1936," in D. E. Lee and G. E. McReynolds, eds., *Essays in History and International Relations in Honor of George Hubbard Blakeslee* (Worcester, Mass., 1949), pp. 193–214, is concerned with the Italians. W. G. Carleton, "Isolationism and the Middle West," in *Miss. Valley Hist. Rev.*, XXXIII (1946), 377–390, discusses the role of his section in the neutrality legislation of the 1930's.

CHAPTER XLV. THE WAR COMES TO AMERICA: FIRST PHASE

NEW REFERENCES. Sumner Welles, *The Time for Decision* (N.Y., 1944), describes the author's mission to Europe in 1940. There is also interesting material on the destroyer deal (p. 173).

Walter Johnson, *The Battle Against Isolation* (Chicago, 1944), is a revealing account of William Allen White and his Committee to Defend America by Aiding the Allies. White and many of his followers looked upon the organization as a genuine means of keeping America out of the war by bolstering Britain; he said that the motto of the Committee should be "The Yanks Are Not Coming" (p. 182). But many others were using the committee to promote active intervention, and when White found that this group was running away from him he resigned the headship, though weariness and his wife's ill health were contributing factors (p. 197).

Dexter Perkins, *America and Two Wars* (Boston, 1944), is a masterly brief analysis of the period.

See also the New References of the preceding chapter (above), particularly the books by Bemis, Atwater, and Grew; and the documentary collections published by the State Department on the Far East.

4TH ED. REFS. *The Memoirs of Cordell Hull* (2 vols., N.Y., 1948) provide a great deal of the behind-the-scenes detail. R. E. Sherwood, *Roosevelt and Hopkins* (N.Y., 1948), gives much material on the work of the President's executive agent. W. S. Churchill, *Their Finest Hour* (Boston, 1949), presents his own version of the destroyer-deal negotiations. H. L. Stimson and M. Bundy, *On Active Service* (N.Y., 1947), records the observations of Roosevelt's new Secretary of War. C. A. Beard, *American Foreign Policy in the Making, 1932–1940* (New Haven, 1946), is a biased indictment of the Administration. Some light on White as a pro-Ally propagandist is found in Walter Johnson, *William Allen White's America* (N.Y., 1947), and Walter Johnson, ed., *Selected Letters of William Allen White, 1899–1943* (N.Y., 1947).

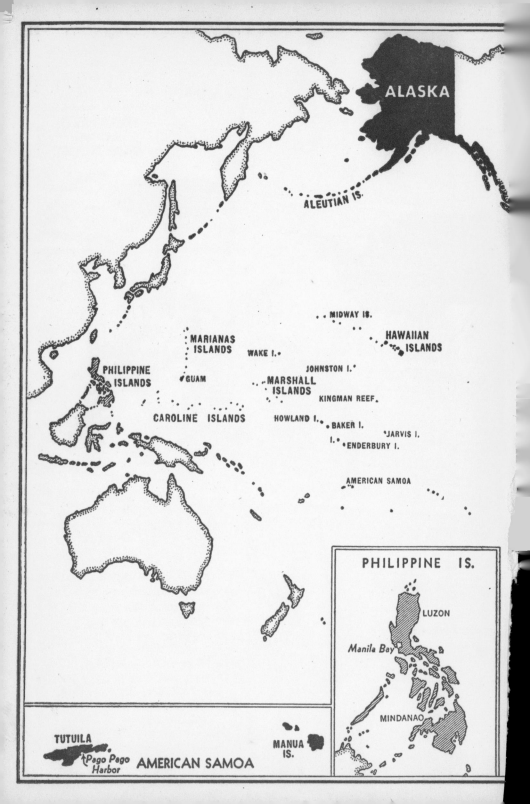